Kenya

THE ROUGH GUIDE

There are more than eighty Rough Guide titles covering
destinations from Amsterdam to Zimbabwe

Forthcoming titles include
China • Corfu • Jamaica • New Zealand • South Africa
Southwest USA • Vienna • Washington DC

Rough Guide Reference Series
Classical Music • The Internet • Jazz • Rock • World Music

Rough Guide Phrasebooks
Czech • French • German • Greek • Italian • Mexican Spanish
Polish • Portuguese • Spanish • Thai • Turkish • Vietnamese

Rough Guide credits

Editor:	Paul Gray
Series editor:	Mark Ellingham
Editorial:	Martin Dunford, Jonathan Buckley, Samantha Cook, Jo Mead, Alison Cowan, Amanda Tomlin, Annie Shaw, Catherine McHale, Vivienne Heller
Online editors:	Alan Spicer (UK), Andrew Rosenberg (US)
Production:	Susanne Hillen, Andy Hilliard, Judy Pang, Link Hall, Nicola Williamson, Helen Ostick
Cartography:	Melissa Flack, David Callier
Marketing & Publicity:	Richard Trillo, Simon Carloss (UK), Jean-Marie Kelly, Jeff Kaye (US)
Finance:	John Fisher, Celia Crowley, Catherine Gillespie
Administration:	Tania Hummel, Margo Daly

Thanks a million to everyone at Rough Guides. I especially want to thank my editor, Paul Gray, who gave the book his patient and skilful attention for longer than he ever expected, and Henry Iles who artfully designed and produced the colour section. Many thanks also to Kate Berens and Sarah McAlister for assisting in the editing, Helen Ostick for diligent typesetting, Mick Bohoslawec for beautiful new maps, and Simon Carloss for support and unflappability.

On this edition, I owe a huge debt of gratitude to the meticulous enthusiasm of writer-researchers Emma Gregg and Jens Finke, who took the bumps up-country and delivered the goods brilliantly. Many thanks also to Doug Paterson for playing musical chairs, Tony Stones for his swiftly delivered contributions on birds, Michelle Cox for wonderful letters and first-rate fixing, Narrell Leffman and Ann Muchnick for Oz and US Basics research, and for company and assistance to Abdul Rahman, Nigel Watson, Marcel Jouve, Lisa Salvato, David Anderson and Jangilly Juma. On previous editions, for aid, ideas and encouragement in diverse forms, my continuing indebtedness to Jeremy Torr for his now historic bike, Marc Dubin, David Else, Jackie Switzer, Rosie Mercer, Robert Gordon and family, and the Khan family in Kisii. Lastly and mostly, to my family, especially Teresa for another spell of endurance and Alex, who is already showing dangerous signs of interest ("is that place really a hotel?"), all my love.

Emma would like to thank Azim Nanji, Nicholas, Flora and Suzy of Kakamega Forest, Mark Wilkinson, Ben Meyer, everyone at Keekorok, Peter Millard, Abi Patton, and, for endlessly loyal support, Piers Northam and James McCormick.

Jens would like to thank Professor Ojwang and Patrick Sana of Nairobi for howling, scowling rhythms and scattish blues, Mark Kariuki at La Belle Inn, Francis Ndungu Njau of Karagita for the chai (!), and Justina Hart, hard-bitten drinker and demonic rally driver.

Grateful acknowledgements to the people who gave support on the ground and the readers whose letters were sifted for this edition appear overleaf.

This fifth edition published October 1996 by Rough Guides Ltd, 1 Mercer St, London WC2H 9QJ.
Distributed by the Penguin Group:

Penguin Books Ltd, 27 Wrights Lane, London W8 5TZ
Penguin Books USA Inc., 375 Hudson Street, New York 10014, USA
Penguin Books Australia Ltd, 487 Maroondah Highway, PO Box 257, Ringwood, Victoria 3134, Australia
Penguin Books Canada Ltd, 10 Alcorn Avenue, Toronto, Ontario, Canada M4V 1E4
Penguin Books (NZ) Ltd, 182–190 Wairau Road, Auckland 10, New Zealand

Typeset in Linotron Univers and Century Old Style to an original design by Andrew Oliver.
Printed by The Bath Press.
Illustrations in Part One and Part Three by Edward Briant.
Illustrations on p.1 by Jane Smith and p.459 by Henry Iles.

A catalogue record for this book is available from the British Library.
ISBN 1-85828-192-X.

Kenya

THE ROUGH GUIDE

Written and researched by
Richard Trillo

With additional contributions by
Jens Finke, Emma Gregg, Doug Paterson and Tony Stones

THE ROUGH GUIDES

THANKS FOR YOUR HELP

This fifth edition owes a massive debt to the readers and users of previous editions of the Rough Guide to Kenya and the German Traveller Handbuch translation published by Stefan Loose Verlag in Berlin. Special thanks to:

Michael Adams, Marc Aertsens, Pat Anderson, Dave Armstrong, Simon Atkins, Felicity Barnett, Scott Bartle, Michael Bate, Thomas Baumgaertel, David Beadle, John Bennett, Mark Bennett and Marina Gerova, Anne Bergenström, Joe Bivona, John Blarney, Tansy Bliss, John Blissett, Dorothy Brewer, Anita Burgess, Julia Burrell, L Burt, Nick Burton, Lisa Byfield-Green, Patty Caldwell, David Carson, Anthony Clarke, Simon Cole, Mary Coombs, Arnold Critchley, Alastair and Monica Darroch, Angie and Ken Dunkin, Petra Eisbach, Sarah Fraser, Peter Gately, Albert J Gopin, Neil Grant, Chris Green, Richard Gurney, Ure Birgit Hagner, David Harris, David and Elizabeth Harris, the Hartley family, Derek Hawksworth, Niek Heering, Tim Hill, Gernot Hoffman, Martin Horn, John Humphries, Nick Hynes, Colyn Jaffe, Angela Jones, Helen Jones, J R Jones, Hugh Kelly, Mark Kendall, David Kiddell, Marko Kuhn, Tony Lane, Chris Lang, Adrian Legge, Juliet MacRae, David I Marks, Jane Martin, Marilyn and Terry Mason, Hans-Georg Mayer, Oscar J Merne, John Mills, Jon Mills, Hans Moder, Claire Morgan, Wilmar Müller, Bernadette Murphy, Chris Naylor, Abdi Noor, Michaela Oes, Peter Oliver, Bernd Ostrowski, Mark Ottaway, Carolyn Payne, Janet Petersen, Mrs P Pierers, Dawn Pollock, Paolo Possa, John and Frances Potter, Hannah Roberts, Katja Röken and Johannes Dingler, Bernadette Roskrow, Gabriele Roth, Andrew Rowlands, Joachim Schulz, Angella Shiundu, Ian Sinclair, Paula Slack, Elizabeth Stinson, Charles Szlapak, Arne Thurich, Simon Towers, Mary Versteck, Michi Vojta, Harriet Watford, Jo Watson, Nigel Watson, Paul Weeks, Sabine Felicitas Wehinger, Andy Williams and Sally Coates, David Williams, Sue Willows-Raznikov, and Alison Yager.

Many thanks also to the following people who helped so generously on this edition, either on the ground or by replying to enquiries. Keep us posted!

In particular, we should like to extend a warm thank you to: Stuart Britton of Somak Holidays, Bruce Buckland of the Driftwood Club, Alan Dixon and Breda Wood of Let's Go Travel, Anjali Gautama of Sarova Hotels, Steven Kamuyu of African Tours & Hotels, Jake Grieves-Cook of Tropical Places, Prem Gupta of Gupta's Tours and Travel, Raymond Matiba of Alliance Hotels, Tinu Mhajan of the Oakwood Hotel, Jonathan Mutua of Nyali Beach Hotel, Liz Nicholas of Lonrho, Najma Poona of Habib's Tours and Travel, Javed Rasul of Rasul's Cars, and Roger Sylvester and Fatma Muses of Block Hotels. Others, whose interest and support is gratefully acknowledged, include: David Chianda of Gametrackers, Meriel Destro of Camel Trek, Francis K Ethuron of Kalokol Lodge, Jenny Fondo of Fondo Wehu Guesthouse, Glynn Davies of Club Salima, Hans van Lorsch of Mwazaro Beach, Jane Moser of Border Camp, and Noorudin Tejpar of Farways Safaricentre.

HELP US UPDATE THIS EDITION

We've gone to great lengths to ensure that this fifth edition of *The Rough Guide to Kenya* is as complete and up-to-date as possible. Kenya changes fast, however, and if you feel there are places we've under-rated or over-praised, or find we've missed something good or covered something which has now gone, then please write. The latest on your favourite hotel, restaurant or club is as useful as details of obscure routes through the bush. Please locate places as accurately as possible (sketch maps are a help). All letters are answered and we'll acknowledge you in the next edition. A free copy of that, or any other Rough Guide if you prefer, will be sent for the most useful (and legible!) letters.

Please mark letters "Kenya 5 Update" and send to:
Rough Guides, 1 Mercer St, London WC2H 9QJ,
or Rough Guides, 375 Hudson St, 9th floor, New York NY 10014.
Or send E-mail to: kenya@roughtravl.co.uk

Online updates about this book can be found on Rough Guides' homesite at
http://www.roughguides.com/

THE AUTHOR

Richard Trillo was conceived in Canada in 1956 and born in England. He spent most of his youth dreaming about travelling and plotting his big escape. There were several attempts, and then a hitchhiking trip to Timbuktu with a friend and $100 cash between them. They had to be helped home. Since then he has travelled extensively in Africa, writing and co-writing the Rough Guides to Kenya and West Africa along the way. He is married, with three young children, who recently made their first trips to Africa.

LIST OF MAPS

MAP SYMBOLS

═══ Major road		✈	Airport
══ Minor road		⌂	Lodge
── Very minor road		Λ	Campsite
▬▬ Railway		♦	Ruin or other monument
── Ferry route		★	Bus stop
▬▬▬ International border		ⓘ	Information office
▒▒▒ District border		Ⓒ	Telephone
─── Chapter division boundary		⊠	Post office
⌒⌒ Mountain range		ⓜ	Monastery
▲ Mountain peak		✡	Synagogue
⪡ Escarpment		☾	Mosque
〒〒 Cliff		✝	Church
⌓ Cave		■	Building
⌇ Waterfall		⊹	Cemetery
ⵋ Lighthouse		▨	National Park
ⱅ Marshland		▦	Park
ⵣⵏ Viewpoint		▒	Beach

CONTENTS

Introduction xii

• CHAPTER 6: THE COAST 340-448

• CHAPTER 7: THE NORTH 449-498

PART THREE CONTEXTS 499

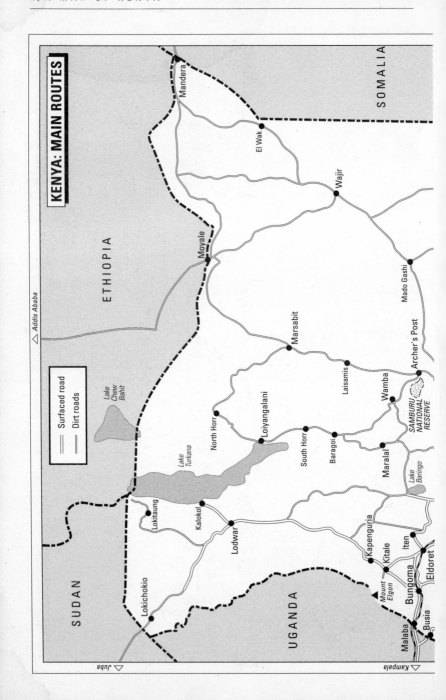

KENYA: MAIN ROUTES

— Surfaced road
— Dirt roads

SUDAN

ETHIOPIA

SOMALIA

UGANDA

△ Addis Ababa

△ Juba

△ Kampala

Mandera

El Wak

Wajir

Moyale

Marsabit

Mado Gashi

Laisamis

Wamba

Archer's Post

SAMBURU NATIONAL RESERVE

North Horr

Loiyangalani

South Horr

Baragoi

Maralal

Lake Chew Bahit

Lake Turkana

Lake Baringo

Lokitaung

Kalokol

Lodwar

Kapenguria

Iten

Lokichokio

Kitale

Mount Elgon

Bungoma

Eldoret

Malaba

Busia

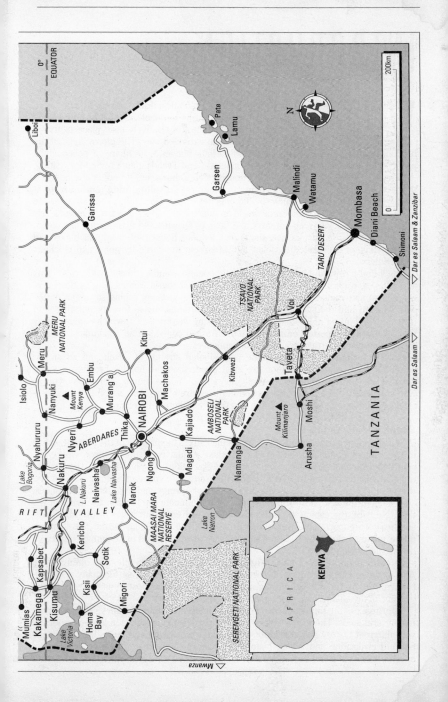

INTRODUCTION

W ith its long, **tropical beaches** and dramatic **wildlife parks, Kenya** has an exotic tourist image. Justifiably, for this is one of the most beautiful lands in Africa and a satisfyingly exciting and relatively easy place to travel, whether on a short holiday or an extended stay. The glossy hype of the brochures ignores the country's less salubrious images – its share of post-colonial poverty and political tension – but is true in its way and a valid enough reason for visiting.

Treating Kenya as a succession of tourist sights, however, is neither the best nor the most enjoyable way of experiencing the country. **Travelling independently**, or at least with eyes open (something this book is designed to facilitate), you can enter the more genuine and very different world inhabited by most Kenyans: a ceaselessly active, contrasting landscape of farm and field, of streams and bush paths, of wooden and corrugated-iron shacks, tea shops and lodging houses, of crammed buses and pick-up vans, of overloaded bicycles, and of streets wandered by goats and chickens and toddlers.

You'll find a rewarding degree of warmth, openness and curiosity in Kenya's towns and villages, especially off the more heavily trodden tourist routes. Out in the wilds, there is an abundance of authentic scenic glamour – vistas of rolling savannah dotted with **Maasai** and their herds, high **Kikuyu** moorlands, dense **forests** bursting with bird song and insect noise, and stony, shimmering **desert** – all of which comes crisply into focus when experienced in the intense African context of an economically belea-guered country three decades after Independence.

On the **Indian Ocean coast**, the palm-shaded strands of beach and an almost continuous, reef-protected lagoon are even better than the holiday brochures would have you imagine – no photo can really do justice. And, of course, everywhere you go Kenya's **wildlife** (see the colour section in the centre of this book and the complemen-tary piece in *Contexts*) adds a startling and rapidly addictive dimension.

Shape and divisions

Physically, Kenya consists mostly of broad plateaux. The majority of the population live in the rugged highland areas in the **southwest** quarter of the country, where the ridges are a sea of *shamba* smallholdings and plantations. Ripping through the heart of these highlands sprawls the **Great Rift Valley**, an archetypal east African scene of dry, thorntree savannah, splashed with lakes and hot springs and studded by volcanoes. The walls of the Rift, and **Mount Kenya** itself, dominate the horizon for much of the time. **Nairobi**, the capital, feels like the centre of Kenya, but it lies at the highlands' southeastern edge, only a three-hour drive from the Tanzanian border. The famous **game parks**, watered by seasonal streams, are mostly located in savannah country on the highland fringes.

Further west, towards **Lake Victoria**, lies gentler countryside, less often visited. And in the **north** the land is **desert** or semi-desert – a surprise for many visitors – broken only by the natural highlight of **Lake Turkana**, almost unnaturally blue and gigantic in the wilderness.

Southeast of the highlands, separating the interior from the Indian Ocean, there are further arid lands. There, the barrier of the **Taru Desert** accounts in large part for the very different history and culture of **the coast**: a surprising and quite distinct Islamic **Swahili** civilization and a long historical record in its mosques, tombs, and ruins of ancient towns cut from the jungle.

Where to go

Where to travel clearly depends on your personal interests, and the time you have available. **Nairobi** (Ch. 1) is usually only used as a gateway. **The coast** (Ch. 6) and major **game parks** (Ch. 5) are the most obvious targets; and if you come to Kenya on an inclusive tour you're likely to have your time divided between these two attractions. If you like the idea of walking or climbing, there's the hot, dry **Rift Valley** (Ch. 3) and the high forests and moors of the **Central Highlands** – Mount Kenya itself is a major target and feasible for most people (Ch. 2). For the best immersion in Kenyan life and culture, the **western** region (Ch. 4) stands out as accessible and untouristy. For serious adventure, **the north** (Ch. 7) is one of the most spectacular and memorable of all African regions.

More detailed rundowns on the specific character and appeal of each region are given in the **chapter introductions**. There too, and at times within the main text, you will find brief backgrounds on the various **Kenyan peoples**. The ten main language groups can no longer be wholly identified with the regions (and moves towards the cities and intermarriage are blurring distinctions), but some understanding of cultural differences is worth achieving. See also "Kenya's People, Languages and Religions", in *Basics*.

When to go

As far as **climate** is concerned, Kenya has complicated and unpredictable shifts. Broadly, the pattern is that January and February are hot and dry, while from March to May it is hot and wet – this period is known as the "long rains". From June until October the weather is warm and dry, and then come the "short rains", making November and December warm and wet.

Temperatures, though, are determined largely by altitude. Nairobi's are surprisingly moderate compared with, say, London's (see box, overleaf). You can reckon on a drop of 6°C (or 11°F) in temperature for every 1000m you climb from sea level. The low-lying coast and the north remain hot all year round, while the highlands (which range to over 4000m and peak above 5000m) are generally warm or mild during the day but much cooler at night. Nairobi, higher than the Cairngorms or the Appalachians, can drop to 5°C (41°F).

At the highest altitudes, it may **rain** at almost any time. Western Kenya has a scattered rainfall pattern influenced by Lake Victoria. Temperatures tend to climb towards the end of the dry seasons, particularly in late February and early March, when it can become very humid before the rains break. It's worth noting that Kenya's climate has been drying out in recent years – the charts overleaf paint a slightly rainier picture than you'll find in the country now.

The main **tourist seasons** tie in with the rainfall patterns: the biggest influxes are in December and January and, to a lesser extent, July and August. **Dry season** travel does have a number of advantages, not least a greater visibility of wildlife as animals are concentrated along the diminishing watercourses. July and August are probably the **best months**, overall, for game-viewing. October to January are the months with the clearest seas for **snorkelling** and **diving** – especially November. In the "long rains", the mountain parks are sometimes closed, as tracks are no longer drivable. But the **rainy seasons** shouldn't deter travel unduly: the rains usually come only in short afternoon or evening cloudbursts, and the landscape is strikingly green and fresh even if the skies may be cloudy. There are bonuses, too, in the lack of tourists: hotel and often car rental prices are reduced and people generally have more time for you.

If you're concerned about being part of a horde of tourist arrivals, don't let it bother you too much. Kenya's million-odd annual visitors seem few compared with the tens of millions that descend on many Mediterranean countries. There is nothing to prevent you escaping the predictable bottlenecks and tourist "oases" for a completely separate experience and, even on an organized tour, you should not feel constrained to follow the prescribed plan.

KENYA'S CLIMATE

	JAN	FEB	MAR	APR	MAY	JUN	JUL	AUG	SEP	OCT	NOV	DEC
NAIROBI (Alt 1661m)												
Av day temp (°C)	25	26	25	24	22	21	21	21	24	24	23	23
Av night temp (°C)	12	13	14	14	13	12	11	11	11	13	13	13
Days with rainfall	5	6	11	16	17	9	6	7	6	8	15	11
Rainfall (mm)	38	64	125	211	158	46	15	23	31	53	109	86
MOMBASA (sea level)												
Av day temp (°C)	31	31	31	30	28	28	27	27	28	29	29	30
Av night temp (°C)	24	24	25	24	24	23	22	22	22	23	24	24
Days with rainfall	6	3	7	15	20	15	14	16	14	10	10	9
Rainfall (mm)	25	18	64	196	320	119	89	66	63	86	97	61
KISUMU (Alt 1135m)												
Av day temp (°C)	29	29	28	28	27	27	27	27	28	29	29	29
Av night temp (°C)	18	19	19	18	18	17	17	17	17	18	18	18
Days with rainfall	6	8	12	14	14	9	8	10	8	7	9	8
Rainfall (mm)	48	81	140	191	155	84	58	76	64	56	86	102

LONDON'S CLIMATE

	JAN	FEB	MAR	APR	MAY	JUN	JUL	AUG	SEP	OCT	NOV	DEC
LONDON (Sea level)												
Av day temp (°C)	6	7	10	13	17	20	22	21	19	14	10	7
Av night temp (°C)	2	2	3	6	8	12	14	13	11	8	5	4
Days with rainfall	15	13	11	12	12	11	12	11	13	13	15	15
Rainfall (mm)	54	40	37	37	46	45	57	59	49	57	64	48

PART ONE

THE
BASICS

GETTING THERE FROM BRITAIN AND IRELAND

Flying to Kenya is invariably the cheapest way of getting there from the British Isles, and London the best departure point. Alternatively, buying an inclusive package holiday can make a lot of sense as some, based around charter flights to Mombasa and mid-range coast hotels, are very cheap. If you choose carefully, you shouldn't feel too packaged. Some of the tour brochures contain quite interesting safari itineraries and a number of independent companies specialize in adventure packages. Another option, of course, is to make your way to Kenya overland. If you're considering taking a bicycle to Kenya, see p.11 and p.42.

FLIGHTS

Many British travel agents offer tickets for scheduled flights at substantially **discounted rates** – well below the official fares agreed by *IATA*, the association to which most airlines belong (see "Airlines' Own Fares" on p.6). In the past, airlines prepared to sell off their tickets through these agents were generally the less reputable carriers left with the most unsold seats. But more and more major carriers are cashing in – though some admittedly are doing so as part of a "restricted eligibility" arrangement where the passenger has to be a student, for example, or under a certain age. There are also a number of short-stay, "flight only" package deals on **charter flights** to Mombasa from London or Manchester. For full details of airline schedules from London to

Nairobi, see the "Airlines" box on p.7; for details of charter flight operators see the "UK Package Tour Operators" box on p.9.

There are no direct flights to Kenya from Ireland. From **Belfast**, the only good connections are on *British Airways* (daily, via London Gatwick, overnight). Other airlines will get you there, but you'll have to change planes twice: possibilities include *Air France* via London Heathrow and Paris; *Olympic* via Heathrow and Athens. From **Dublin**, the picture is slightly better, with convenient through-connections on *British Airways* (daily, via London Gatwick, overnight); *Sabena* via Brussels (Mon, Wed and Fri, overnight); *KLM* via Amsterdam (Mon, Wed and Fri); and *Air Inter/Air France* via Paris Charles de Gaulle (Mon, Thurs, Fri, Sat and Sun, overnight).

It's worth knowing the approximate **flight routing**. From Europe, most flights head southeast over the eastern Mediterranean from Greece to Cairo, follow the Nile to Khartoum, then fly over western Ethiopia, crossing into Kenyan airspace to the west of Lake Turkana. On overnight flights, Turkana is often reached at dawn and can be seen quite clearly on the left, 8km below. The normal route thereafter is to Nairobi (with the pimple of Mount Kenya on the left); then, if it's a charter flight to Mombasa, a slight left turn towards the coast, with Kilimanjaro the snow-capped bulge on the right. **Flight times** are: London–Nairobi non-stop from 8hr 30min to 9hr; London–Mombasa, including a one-hour refuelling stop, 10hr 30min. Remember Kenya is two hours ahead of Britain in summer and three hours ahead in winter. Because of the small time difference you won't experience any jet lag.

BOOKING SEATS AND BUYING TICKETS

The so-called **bucket shops** are, almost without exception, respectable travel agents, even if first impressions sometimes indicate otherwise. If you phone around, you'll quickly get an idea of the set-up by throwing a few destinations at them.

When **booking**, note whether the agent reserves seats to Nairobi directly with the airline by telephone or on a computer system, or has to go through another agent. Fraud isn't a problem but confusion and delays are common enough. Don't expect to see your ticket until you've paid in full; while many agents have ticketing agreements with certain airlines and can write tickets on the premises, they may have to order some tickets from the nominated **consolidator** of the airline concerned, which usually means another agent.

Always ask what **refund** you'll get if anything goes wrong and find out how easy it will be to **change your reservation dates** once you've got your ticket. You can sometimes leave a return ticket "open-dated" on its return portion, but in that case you'll have to make a seat reservation yourself with the airline in Kenya. It's just as easy, and more prudent, to have a confirmed seat and change the date if necessary (and if seats are available). Note that if you book through a discount agency, you cannot deal direct with the airline on your booking until you have your ticket, though you can always quote them the details and ask them to check the reservation is held under your name. If it's not, don't panic: it will probably be held under the agent's block seat allocation.

Airline **seasons** for Kenya vary a little but generally departures in July, August and December will be the most expensive. Most airlines have low-season rates from February to June, and often again from October to early December. This also ties in with student and youth fares which are always more in summer and Christmas holiday periods.

Book as far in advance as you can. Six months isn't too long. Some airlines are full to capacity at peak periods, especially Christmas, and discounted seat availability is often snapped up quickly. On the other hand, if you find early on that flights seem to be "full", check the same outlets again nearer your departure date – assuming you haven't got something by then – for reservations not taken up and released allocations.

TYPES OF TICKET

Return tickets are generally of three types – short excursions (usually one month), three-month excursions and one year (never more). A **one-way** fare (valid one year) is normally half the relevant "yearly" fare. You may be able to fly out to Nairobi and back from somewhere else (an "open jaw"), depending on the airline and the agent's contract.

In rare cases, you may also be able to purchase **tickets *back* from East Africa** before you leave – useful if you're travelling out overland. *Egyptair* tickets can be bought like this,

though the ticket is collected from their office in the city in question. Such arrangements, known as *PTAs*, are surprisingly reliable.

If you want to travel onwards from Kenya and only need a one-way flight, check the cancellation charge for cashing in the unused half of a return ticket. While it doesn't apply much to the land borders, passing through immigration at the airport is always smoother if you have a flight out again.

STUDENT AND YOUTH FARES

If you're a **student, academic or under 32**, ask if the agent has special fares – some of the better airlines (including *British Airways*, the only airline flying London–Nairobi non-stop) grant various **restricted eligibility fares** to certain, selected agents which are not available in theory to the general public. Note that the advantage of some of these discretionary fares may lie more in the length of stay they offer and an easing of booking regulations than purely in their price. They are not automatically cheaper than anything else, but they may, all considered, be much better value.

DISCOUNTED AGENTS' FARES

As regards **discount prices**, you can pay anything from under £250 (approx. US$375) to over £700 ($1050) for a discounted London–Nairobi return (round-trip) ticket. One-ways will always be over £200 ($300). The **airlines to watch** for the cheapest fares are *Aeroflot*, *Sudan Airways* and *Balkan Bulgarian*.

Aeroflot tickets are always valid for a full year and, on a one-way, these are generally the cheapest. Fortnightly flights connect through Moscow, with a current stop-over of about eight hours (or a basic hotel at their expense). Some agents won't deal with *Aeroflot* because they're slow to make refunds.

Sudan Airways fares are excellent value at between £245 and £465 for a London–Nairobi return. **Balkan Bulgarian** seats can be had for as little as £350, but, again, some agents will not deal with them, in this case because of recurrent problems with schedules and reservations. At the time of writing they were running a summer service only (no flights between September and March).

Other good deals can be obtained on, surprisingly enough, **British Airways**, **Air France** and **Kenya Airways**. Low-season, limited-availability discounts offered by these airlines have been

DISCOUNT AGENTS IN BRITAIN AND IRELAND

Africa Travel Shop, 4 Medway Court, Leigh St, London WC1H 9QX (☎0171/387-1211, fax 0171/383-7512). *Helpful and resourceful.*

Apex Travel, 59 Dame St, Dublin 2 (☎01/671 5933). *Long-haul flights, including Africa.*

Bridge the World, 47 Chalk Farm Road, Camden Town, London NW1 8AN (☎0171/911-0900, fax 0171/813-3350). *Competitive independent travel firm, for one-off flights or tailor-made round-the-world itineraries.*

Brightways Travel, 94 The Green, Southall, Middlesex UB2 4BG (☎0181/574-2622, fax 0181/574-8273). *Good fares to Nairobi via Paris.*

Campus Travel
Student/youth specialists. Thirty branches nation-wide including:
Main office: 52 Grosvenor Gardens, London SW1W 0AG (☎0171/730-8111);
541 Bristol Rd, Selly Oak, Birmingham B29 6AU (☎0121/414-1848);
61 Ditchling Rd, Brighton BN1 4SD (☎01273/570226);
39 Queen's Rd, Clifton, Bristol BS8 1QE (☎0117/929-2494);
5 Emmanuel St, Cambridge CB1 1NE (☎01223/324283);
53 Forrest Rd, Edinburgh EH1 2QP (☎0131/668-3303);
The Academy, University of Manchester, Oxford Rd, Manchester M13 9PQ (☎0161/274-3105);
13 High St, Oxford OX1 4DB (☎01865/242067).

Council Travel, 28a Poland St, London W1V 3DB (☎0171/437-7767). *Student discount agent.*

Inflight Travel, 92–94 York Rd, Belfast 15 (☎01232/740187). *Long-haul specialists.*

Joe Walsh Tours, 8–11 Baggot St, Dublin (☎01/676 3053). *General budget fares agent.*

North South Travel, Moulsham Mill Centre, Parkway, Chelmsford, Essex CM2 7PX (☎01245/492882). *Friendly, competitive travel agency, offering discounted fares worldwide – profits are used to support projects in the developing world, especially the promotion of sustainable tourism.*

Quest Worldwide Travel, 29 Castle St, Kingston, Surrey KT1 1ST (☎0181/547-3322). *Small, personal agent. Recommended.*

Sam Travel, 14 Broadwick St, London W1V 1FH (☎0171/434-9561); and 805–807 Romford Rd, London E12 5AN (☎0181/478-8911). *General discount agent.*

Soliman Travel, 113 Earl's Court Rd, London SW5 9RL (☎0171/244-6855). *Particularly good on Egyptair flights via Cairo.*

Somak Travel, 545 High Rd, Wembley, Middlesex, HA0 2DJ (☎0181/903-8526). *Good deals on BA, Kenya Airways and Caledonian.*

STA Travel
Large range of fares and airlines for Kenya, from 24 offices in the UK and over 100 worldwide. Special fares for students and young people as well as a specialist Africa Desk.
Main office: 86 Old Brompton Rd, London SW7 (☎0171/361-6262).
Africa Desk: 117 Euston Rd, London NW1 (☎0171/465-0486, fax 0171/388-0944).
25 Queens Rd, Bristol BS8 1QE (☎0117/929-4399).
38 Sidney St, Cambridge CB2 3HX (☎01223/366966).
88 Vicar Lane, Leeds LS1 7JH (☎0113/244-9212).
75 Deansgate, Manchester M3 21BW (☎0161/834-0668).
36 George St, Oxford, OX1 4AH (☎01865/792800).

Tradewings, 5th Floor, 320 Regent St, London W1R 5AG (☎0171/631-1840). *Good deals on Sudan Airways flights via Khartoum, Balkan Bulgarian flights via Sofia, and other offers.*

Trailfinders, 42–48 Earl's Court Rd, London W8 6EJ (☎0171/938-3366); and 58 Deansgate, Manchester M3 2FF (☎0161/839-6969). *Respected discount flights agency with a convenient range of other services. Some reasonable fares, but not especially geared up for Africa.*

Travel Cuts, 295 Regent St, London W1 (☎0171/255-2082). *Student and youth travel specialists.*

Twohigs, 8 Burgh Quay, Dublin 2 (☎01/677 2666); 13 Duke St, Dublin 2 (☎01/670 9750). *Long-haul flights including Africa.*

Unique Tours & Travel, 2nd Floor, 169 Piccadilly, London W1 (☎0171/495-4848). *Specializes in Aeroflot flights via Moscow.*

USIT
Student and youth specialists.
Fountain Centre, Belfast BT1 6ET (☎01232/324073).
Patrick St, Cork (☎021/270900).
33 Ferryquay St, Derry (☎01504/371888);.
Aston Quay, Dublin 2 (☎01/679 8833).
Eyre Square, Galway (☎091/565177).
O'Connell St, Limerick (☎061/415064).
36–37 Georges St, Waterford (☎051/72601).

Wexas, 45 Brompton Rd, London SW3 1DE (☎0171/589-3315). *If you're unable to visit others, this membership-only organization handles everything competently by post. Detailed brochures and fare and airline information.*

World Travel Centre, 35 Pearse St, Dublin 2 (☎01/671 7155). *Long-haul flights including Africa.*

RESERVATIONS GLOSSARY

Apex Advance purchase excursion fare. Usually the cheapest return deal an airline will offer to you direct.

Charter A flight chartered from an airline by a tour operator.

Classes Every seat has its class. The common ones are F (first), J (business), C (club) and Y (economy). Any other class is likely to be an economy seat with a special price.

Confirmed (OK) What your reservation has to be to get a seat (written as "OK" on the ticket); a guarantee in Europe, not always in Africa.

Direct flight A flight that takes you from departure point to destination without your having to leave the plane (not necessarily a non-stop flight).

Flight number Every scheduled flight has one, made up of the two-letter airline code and three digits. It's unique to the airline, the route and the day of the week, but not specific to the date.

MCO Miscellaneous Charges Order. A refundable receipt for funds held in your name by an airline, no longer of any use in immigration situations where you need an onward ticket.

Pax Passengers.

PTA Passenger ticket advice. Prepayment for a ticket back home to be collected in the city of departure.

Reconfirm What airlines like you to do direct with them before departure. It's vital to do this in Africa 72 hours before departure or you may find your seat bumped. Note that, on scheduled flights, your ticket nearly always remains a valid travel voucher even if you miss your confirmed reservation or lose your seat.

Requested (RQ) A booking which has this status isn't even on the waiting list.

Scheduled A flight operated by the airline to a regular timetable regardless of demand. In Africa these are sometimes cancelled, diverted or simply unknown.

Stop-over A voluntary stay in a city/country en route to your destination where you would otherwise stay in the plane or make a simple connection.

Waitlisted (WL) On a waiting list for cancellations in a particular class, or for empty seats from other agents' expired allocations.

known to bring the price of a return flight down to under £250. With **Alitalia** (via Rome), **Olympic** (via Athens) **Emirates** (via Dubai) or **Sabena** (via Brussels), it's usually possible to fly for under £450 return (low season) or £525 (high season).

Egyptair excursion fares (three-month maximum) can be found from around £455. They give you the chance of a stop-over in Cairo for as long as you like at no extra cost. One-ways, though, are relatively expensive. There are daily flights to Cairo, with Thursday and Sunday overnight connections non-stop on to Nairobi.

Lastly, you might ask about **Saudia** and **Ethiopian Airlines**, both of which are reputable carriers with good fares, but often forgotten by agents. *Ethiopian* now offers one-week stopovers in Addis on the return leg. *Saudia* sometimes has seats at Christmas when everything else is full.

AIRLINES' OWN FARES

In principle, the **airlines' own fares** should all be about the same (see the "Airlines" box opposite for addresses). Current **British Airways** return fares from London Gatwick to Nairobi (valid for a 14–45 day stay) start at £489 (departure in April & May), £539 (Sept–Nov, Feb & March), £635 (June–Sept) or £770 (Dec & Jan). A book-anytime, non-seasonal one-way fare is £449.

If you want to make stop-overs en route (for example, on *BA* flights, in Cairo, Entebbe or anywhere on the *BA* network), you can do so – but for bigger fares. If you want to do some detective work, ask the airline to give you details of their consolidators. Some are only too happy; others refuse.

"FLIGHT-ONLY" CHARTER PACKAGES

If you're happy to fly into Mombasa, there are several **charter operators** with whom you can get seats from as little as £350 ($525). The three main charter operations to Kenya are *Monarch*, *Caledonian Airways* and *Britannia* (*Thomson's* charter airline). All three have a weekly service from Gatwick, overnight on Sunday, and *Monarch* and *Britannia* also fly from Manchester. *Somak* is one of the few agents to offer flight-only charter deals on a regular basis, but you may also find a seat through the *Africa Travel Shop*. *Hayes and Jarvis*, *Tropical Places*, *Inspirations* and *Cosmos*

AIRLINES FROM LONDON TO NAIROBI

The following airlines currently fly London Heathrow to Nairobi (except *British Airways*, which flies from Gatwick). Mombasa is served only by *Kenya Airways* connections and by direct charter flights. Departures are given as overnight (meaning arrival the next morning) or by day (meaning arrival same evening). Try to avoid a flight which arrives at night – definitely not the best time for a first encounter with Nairobi. If that isn't possible, don't be alarmed: it's worth seeing how much a pre-booked hotel room would cost (*STA* and *Trailfinders* can be helpful here, or call one of the hotel reservation numbers on pp.48–50).

Aeroflot (SU) 70 Piccadilly, London W1 (☎0171/355-2233, fax 0171/493-1892); reservations in Dublin ☎01/679 1453, Shannon ☎061/472299. Fortnightly; out overnight Wed; back overnight Thurs; change in Moscow (8-hr stop-over).

Air France (AF) Colet Court, Hammersmith Road, London W6 (☎0181/742-6600 or linkline ☎0345/581393); 29–30 Dawson St, Dublin 2 (☎01/677 8899). Out overnight daily except Tues, Wed; back overnight daily except Mon, Wed; change in Paris.

Alitalia (AZ) 205 Holland Park Ave, London W11 (☎0171/602-7111 or linkline ☎0345/212121); 63 Dawson St, Dublin 2 (☎01/677 5171). Out by day Wed or overnight Fri; back overnight Thurs, Sun; change in Rome.

Austrian Airlines (OS) 10 Wardour St, London W1V 4BJ (☎0171/434-7300, fax 0171/734-7219). Out overnight Mon, Wed, Sat; back by day Tues, Thurs, Sat; change in Zurich.

Balkan Bulgarian (LZ) 322 Regent St, London W1 (☎0171/637-7637, fax 0171/637-2481). Out overnight Mon, Wed; back overnight Wed, Fri; change in Sofia (long flight; summer only).

British Airways (BA) 156 Regent St, London W1 (☎0181/897-4000 or linkline ☎0345/222111); 9 Fountain Centre, College St, Belfast BT1 6ET (☎0345/222111); Dublin reservations (☎1800/626747). Out from Gatwick daily overnight, plus a daytime flight on Sat; back daily overnight; all non-stop.

Egyptair (MS) 29–31 Piccadilly, London W1V 0PT (☎0171/437-6426, fax 0171/287-1728). Out overnight Thurs, Sun; back by day Mon, Fri; change in Cairo.

El Al (LY) 185 Regent St, London W1 (☎0171/437-9255). Out overnight Mon but no same-day connection from London; back overnight Mon (dep. 4.20am Tues); change in Tel Aviv.

Emirates (EK) Gloucester Park, 95 Cromwell Road, London SW7 (☎0181/808-0808, fax 0181/808-0080). Out overnight Thurs, Sun; back overnight Mon, Fri; change in Dubai.

Ethiopian Airlines (ET) 166 Piccadilly, London W1 (☎0171/491-2125, fax 0171/491-1892). Out overnight Fri, Sat; back by day Mon, Sun; change in Addis Ababa.

Gulf Air (GF) 10 Albemarle St, London W1 (☎0171/408-1717). Out overnight Fri, Sun; back overnight Sat, Mon; change in Muscat or Abu Dhabi (long flight).

Kenya Airways (KQ) 16 Conduit St, London W1 (fares ☎0171/409-0185, reservations ☎0171/409-0277, fax 0171/499-2973). Out daily overnight (direct on Tues, Thurs, Fri, Sun; other days via Frankfurt, Paris, Rome or Zurich); back daily overnight. No plane change.

KLM Royal Dutch Airlines (KL) 8 Hanover St, off Regent St, London W1 (☎0181/750-9000, fax 0180/750-9090). Out by day Mon, Wed, Thurs, Sat; back overnight Tues, Thurs, Fri, Sat; change in Amsterdam.

Lufthansa (LH) 10 Old Bond St, London W1X 4EN (linkline ☎0345/737747, fax 0181/750-3460); Dublin reservations ☎01/844 5544. Out by day Tues, Thurs, Fri, Sat; back overnight Tues, Thurs, Fri, Sat; change in Frankfurt.

Olympic Airways (OA) 11 Conduit St, London W1 (☎0171/409-3400, fax 0171/493-0563); 45 Dawson St, Dublin 2 (☎01/677 4555). Out overnight Tues, Thurs, Sun; back by day Tues, Thurs, Sat; change in Athens.

Sabena (SN) 1 Swiss Court, Swiss Centre, Leicester Square, London W1 (☎081/780-1444). Out by day Mon, Wed, Fri; back overnight Mon, Wed, Fri; change in Brussels.

Saudia (SV) 171 Regent St, London W1 (☎0181/995-7777, fax 0181/995-8444). Out overnight Fri, Sun; back overnight Mon or by day Sat (very early start); change in Jeddah.

Sudan Airways (SD) 12 Grosvenor St, London W1 (☎0171/499-8101, fax 0171/499-0976). Out overnight Fri; back by day Sun; change in Khartoum.

Swissair (SR) Swiss Centre, 10 Wardour St, London W1 (☎0171/434-7300); 54 Dawson St, Dublin 2 (☎01/677 8173). Out overnight Mon, Wed, Sat; back by day Tues, Thurs, Sun; change in Zurich.

don't sell seats on charter flights except as part of a package, but they occasionally have flight-plus-accommodation offers that work out at less than the cost of a scheduled flight.

It's important to realize that these are strictly **holiday flights**, not scheduled services. There's usually a maximum stay of four or six weeks, with the price depending on the number of days you stay, and you won't be able to change your dates. Also of more than passing interest, these are not comfortable flights. Mombasa, their destination, is further than Nairobi and, while *Monarch* and *Britannia* fly direct, *Caledonian* makes a one-hour refuelling stop, effectively adding a couple of hours to the journey time. You'll fly by Airbus A300, DC-10 or 767, and the seating is tight: people of above-average dimensions are likely to find it a trial. The experience is particularly tedious with small children (under-2s don't get their own seats and on some charter flights baby bassinets are not available). Families might seriously consider spending the extra for greater comfort, and a better start to the holiday, on a scheduled flight to Nairobi.

PACKAGE HOLIDAYS

Using charter flights, **packages** of flight and two weeks' dinner, bed and breakfast (half-board) in a beach hotel have crashed in cost to as little as £499 ($750) or even less. If you take on board the drawbacks of the flight described above, it does make sense to consider this option for a short holiday. You don't have to stick with the crowd all the time – or even stay at the hotel – and you could do several short independent trips around the country if you wanted.

Coast hotels vary greatly in price, atmosphere and amenities. Find out as much as possible about the establishment (look it up in the *Rough Guide*) and beware of spending hundreds of pounds more on a place that isn't actually a lot nicer than the one next door. The tropical beach environment is so impressive in itself that much of what you're paying extra for (staff in smarter uniforms, pricier furniture, carpets) is likely to be almost irrelevant to your enjoyment. While there are a few quite dismal hotels, some of the nicest places are also the most reasonable.

It's important to realize, too, that a **safari** component in a package tour always knocks the bill up a lot: a week on the beach may look cheap, but add a week's safari and £750 will be the absolute minimum cost, inclusive of flight – and that's in May or June (*Tropical Places*).

TYPES OF SAFARI

Before arranging the details, think about whether you want comfort or a more authentic experience. Internal flights (an **"air safari"**) will add enormously to the cost and comfort of your trip and give you spectacular views but a much less intimate feel of Africa. On the other hand, **long bumpy drives** to meet the demands of an itinerary can be completely exhausting while hours of your time may be eaten away in a cloud of dust. Note that the **"balloon safaris"** you see advertised are short balloon flights, not complete tours. They take place at dawn and last a couple of hours at most. They can be done in several parks, most popularly in the Maasai Mara, and the bill is a big one – about £240 (sometimes slightly cheaper if pre-booked with a package from the UK). There are more details on p.331.

Many safaris take you from one game park hotel (known as **lodges**) to another, using **minibuses** with lift-up roofs for picture-taking. Make sure you have a window seat and ask about the number of passengers and whether the vehicle is shared by several operators or is for your group only. More details about the food and accommodation you can expect from a package are covered in relevant sections further on.

The alternative to a standard lodge safari is a **camping safari**, where the crew – or you, if it's a budget trip – put up your tents at the end of the day and you spend all your time in the open air. With this kind of trip you have to be prepared for a degree of discomfort along with the self-sufficiency: insects can occasionally be a menace, you may not get a shower every night, the food won't be so lavish and the beer not so cold.

The minibus safaris fitted into most of the inexpensive charter packages venture no further afield than the three national parks easily accessible from the coast – Tsavo East, Tsavo West and Amboseli (trips up to Samburu or west to Maasai Mara are more expensive). On some of the cheaper itineraries (especially if you're camping), your experience is effectively portion-controlled, with the distances driven and the fuel consumed all carefully logged by the driver. There are more details on what to expect and how to improve it on p.63.

On the best camping safaris, you travel in a fairly **rugged vehicle** – a four-wheel-drive land

UK PACKAGE TOUR OPERATORS

Below are listed both mainstream operators whose brochures are likely to be found in every high street travel agent, and several more unusual companies. If you're considering a package, look also at the companies in the "Overland and Adventure Tour Operators" box. Where no address is given, bookings are by phone only or through travel agents.

Abercrombie and Kent, Sloane Square House, Holbein Place, London SW1 (☎0171/730-9600, fax 0171/730-9376). Very upmarket long-haul specialists, with unusual offerings, a dedicated and very flexible manner and a wide knowledge of Kenya, where the company originated. Busy Nairobi operation.

Art of Travel, 21 The Bakehouse, Bakery Place, 119 Altenburg Gardens, London SW11 1JQ (☎0171/738-2038, fax 0171/738-1893). Innovative travel stylists with a personal approach, specializing in tailor-made trips. Tempting combinations of game driving, walking, horse riding and beach lounging, with accommodation in luxury lodges or off-the-beaten track farmhouses (from around £2200 for 2 weeks).

British Airways Holidays, Astral Towers, Betts Way, London Rd, Crawley, West Sussex RH10 2XA (☎01293/723181, fax 01293/722650). Impressive range of safari and beach combinations; some keen prices but you'll find certain hotel packages offered for less elsewhere.

Cosmos (☎0161/480-5799). Not a firm that springs immediately to mind for Kenya, but good value if you choose the right hotel. Two weeks, including a Tsavo/Amboseli/Mara safari, from £929.

Elite Vacations, 90–100 Bessborough Rd, Harrow, Middlesex HA1 3DT (☎0181/864-4431, fax 0181/426-9178). Numerous holiday options including the combination of a classic Kenyan safari with 4-7 nights spent on Mauritius or the Seychelles.

Hayes and Jarvis, Hayes House, 152 King St, London W6 0QU (☎0181/748-5050, fax 0181/741-0299). Long-established, experienced operator, originally from Kenya, whose wide-ranging options stretch from budget self-catering and no-frills safaris to luxury escorted tours.

The Imaginative Traveller, 14 Barley Mow Passage, Chiswick, London W4 4PH (☎0181/742-8612, fax 0181/742-3045). Inspired range of hotel/lodge-based and camping safaris, with the option of adding on a mountain trek, a spell on the coast, or an escape to the Seychelles.

Inspirations, Saxley Court, Horley, Surrey RH6 7AS (☎01293/822244, fax 01293/821732). A plentiful choice of reasonably priced beach holidays with safari options.

Kuoni (☎01306/743000, fax 01306/744222). Reputable long-haul holiday operator, with a flexible approach and lots of experience. Good choice of safaris and coastal destinations.

Somak Holidays, Somak House, Harrovian Village, Bessborough Road, Harrow on the Hill, Middlesex (☎0181/423-3000, fax 0181/423-7700). Long-established Kenyan company with busy offices in Nairobi (PO Box 48495, ☎02/224481, 211112 or 335725) and Mombasa (PO Box 90738, ☎011/315837, 315304 or 313871). Wide selection of safaris, detailed hotel descriptions and this-is-what-you-get prices. Good value *Caledonian, BA* and *Kenya Airways* flights. Recommended.

Thomson, Greater London House, Hampstead Rd, London NW1 7SD (☎0990/502399 or 0171/707-9000; late availability offers on Teletext p.289). The big one as far as British visitors are concerned. Lots of choice, spread over two comprehensive brochures (*Faraway Shores* and *Worldwide*). fourteen-day safari and beach from £795; fourteen-day beach only from £625. Some strikingly good-value holidays.

Tropical Places, Freshfield House, Lewes Rd, Forest Row, East Sussex RH18 5ES (☎01342/825123, fax 01342/822364; information and special offers on ITV Teletext p.259 & p.269). Good-value coast packages using a choice of scheduled or charter flights from London Gatwick or Manchester to Mombasa (from £499 for 2 weeks by *Caledonian*, or £649 by *British Airways*), plus inexpensive short safaris.

Wildlife Discovery, The Old Bakery, South Rd, Reigate, Surrey, RH2 7LB (☎01737/223903). Individual operator with a firm emphasis on high-quality safaris using good accommodation. Tailor-made arrangements, or fixed-itinerary safari including *BA* flight and professional guides. Excellent value. Office in Nairobi.

Worldwide Journeys and Expeditions, 8 Comeragh Rd, London W14 9HP (☎0171/381-8638, fax 0171/381-0836). Well-designed trips with unusual emphases, including "homestead" safaris, staying on private estates as the guests of experienced guides and wildlife experts (from £2765 inclusive), and a Naivasha/Mara/Lake Victoria safari (from £2175 inclusive).

cruiser or even an open-sided lorry – giving more flexibility about where you go and how long you stay. The more expensive camping safaris come very expensive indeed and tend to model their style on images culled from *Out of Africa*; they can easily cost over £200 ($300) a day. At the other end of the scale, you can pre-book a week-long camping safari from the UK for hardly any more than this – without flights. Decide where and how you want to go, and find a tour to fit. You can do this in advance or when you get there (see the listings of operators in the Nairobi section).

Most high-street travel agents can fix you up with brochures for the more **mainstream tour operators** whose packages generally (though not always) fall into the lodge and minibus category. For more **off-beat adventure trips**, or a better selection of camping safaris, you should contact the

operator directly. Note that the **single-person supplement** tends to be high on conventional beach and safari packages and somewhat less (or you can share) on the more adventure-spirited trips.

And a last vital tip: **leave the coast until the end of your holiday**.

WORK CAMPS

The **Kenya Voluntary Development Association** is a locally inspired organization, founded in 1962, with international friendship and grass roots development its twin goals. It exists to bring Kenyans and foreigners together for a few weeks or a few months on work camps – digging irrigation trenches, making roads, building schools, or just making as many mud bricks as possible. An international work camp is no holiday, as the literature implies: "Our camps are serious". And condi-

UK OVERLAND AND ADVENTURE TOUR OPERATORS

The **"overland tour"** catch-all covers most of the organized holidays that don't feel like packages. Not many of them are *overland* the entire way. The option of flying out, touring around by truck, and flying back is an increasingly popular one. Note that operators sometimes run trips "in association" with each other and the number of long, ex-UK trips offered each year is actually quite small. Most run occasional evening slide and video sessions, when you can decide if a packaged adventure is for you. A number of other, smaller operators also advertise regularly in *BBC Wildlife* magazine. As well as the operators listed here, check the "Package Tour Operators" and "Discount Agents" boxes. Many of the latter are agents for companies below.

Absolute Africa, 41 Swanscombe Rd, Chiswick, London W4 2HL (☎0181/742-0226, fax 0181/995-6155). A keenly priced 22-week London–Nairobi trip and a limited number of 4- to 12-week East and southern Africa trips based out of Kenya.

Acacia Expeditions, 27D Stable Way, Latimer Rd, London W10 6QX (☎0181/960-5747, fax 0181/960-1414). A very wide variety of East and southern Africa overland trips from 6 days to 12 weeks.

African Trails, 126B Chiswick High Rd, London W4 1PU (☎0181/742-7724, fax 0181/742-8621). Very cheap East, southern and trans-Africa trips.

Africa Travel Shop, 4 Medway Court, Leigh St, London WC1H 9QX (☎0171/387-1211, fax 0171/383-7512). An interesting selection of inexpensive trips in and around Kenya, bookable in advance – eg a 7-day Rift Valley/Mara safari for £430 including park fees; 14-day game park/gorilla safari in Kenya, Zaire and Uganda for £295; 6 weeks in northern Kenya and Ethiopia for £550 (all, of course, excluding flight). Office in Nairobi.

Bukima Africa, 55 Huddlestone Rd, Willesden Green, London NW2 5DL (☎0181/451-2446, fax

0181/830-1889). A small agent which runs trans-Africa journeys and uses Nairobi as the launch pad for shorter trips to visit East African highlights.

Dragoman, 96 Camp Green, Kenton Rd, Debenham, Suffolk IP14 9LA (☎01728/861133, fax 01728/861127). Personal and creative operators with notably good trucks and competitive prices. Regular East, southern and trans-African departures, many of which start or finish in Kenya.

Encounter Overland, 267 Old Brompton Rd, London SW5 9JA (☎0171/370-6951, fax 0171/244-9737). A well-respected overland operator with a number of trips (2–9 weeks) through East and southern Africa, including an unusual Kenya–Ethiopia trip. Straightforward no-extras pricing.

Exodus Expeditions, 9 Weir Rd, London SW12 0LT (☎0181/675-5550, fax 0181/673-0779). Several trips a year between Nairobi and Southern Africa (from £650 for 21 days, excluding flights and provisions). Also a round trip exploring the Kenyan, Tanzanian and Ugandan Rift Valley from Nairobi (22 days, from £980 excluding flights and provisions), walking tours of Mount Kenya and the

tions are usually primitive, with volunteers sharing the local water supply problems, eating very basic food and organizing their own sanitary, washing and cooking facilities. But they seem to be a lot of fun, too, and are undoubtedly worthwhile. There is no upper age limit but volunteers older than 25 are unusual; the minimum age is 18. A typical camp, building a school near Migori, consisted mostly of students – 6 Britons, 12 Germans, 8 Dutch, 6 Danes, 2 Spanish and 5 Kenyans.

The registration fee is $200 or, if you're very energetic, $300 for two consecutive work camps (they last about three or four weeks). Write to KVDA, PO Box 48902 Nairobi, Kenya (☎02/225379).

CYCLING HOLIDAYS

If nothing as sedentary as a work camp interests you, you might like to try an organized **bicycle**

tour of Kenya. *Leisure Activity Safaris*, 19 Bishops Court, Bishopsteignton, Devon, TQ14 9RS, England (☎01626/775070, fax 01626/777903), offer various long and short bike safaris. Or contact *Bicycle Africa*, 4887 Columbia Drive South, Seattle, WA 98108–1919, who offer mountain-bike trips with a pioneering spirit and a wide variety of accommodation.

You can fix up similar arrangements in Kenya through a number of agents and operators (addresses on p.118) and book short jaunts to Hell's Gate and Lakes Naivasha, Nakuru, Baringo and Bogoria.

Cycling Kenya by Kathleen Bennett (ISBN 0933201427) is a worthwhile supplementary guide that won't weigh down your bar bag. Also see the section on cycling independently in Kenya, on pp. 42–43.

Aberdares, or Mount Kenya and Kilimanjaro (17 days, from £1730 including flight), and a camping tour of western Kenya (15 days, from £1570 including flight).

Explore Worldwide, 1 Frederick St, Aldershot, Hampshire, GU11 1LQ (☎01252/319448, fax 01252/343170). Highly respected small groups operator which runs an interesting Rift Valley tour through Kenya, Uganda and Tanzania (23 days, around £1500 excluding flights), and a Samburu–Baringo–Nakuru–Mara safari with the fine bonus of walking in the Loita Hills (16 days from about £1100, excluding flights).

Footloose Adventure Travel, 105 Leeds Rd, Ilkley, West Yorkshire LS29 8EG (☎01943/604030, fax 01943/604070). Small, enthusiastic independent outfit offering a classic Mount Kenya–Kilimanjaro trek for mountain enthusiasts; they'll tailor-make a safari to fit your budget and interests, offer advice on overland travel options, and track down good-value flights.

Guerba Expeditions, Wessex House, 40 Station Rd, Westbury, Wiltshire BA13 3JN (☎01373/826611, fax 01373/858351). The acknowledged African experts, running a string of Kenya trips, including a 9-day camping safari for under £500 and a 7-day lodge safari for under £800 (excluding flights), plus longer East African trips. Offices in Nairobi.

Kumuka Expeditions, 40 Earls Court Rd, London W8 6EJ (☎0171/937-8855, fax 0171/937-6664). Three different overland trips from Nairobi to Harare or vice versa, all of them taking in the Rift

Valley and the Maasai Mara (5–10 weeks, £845–1495 excluding flights and provisions), and short adventure tours in Kenya and Tanzania, including climbing tours of Mount Kenya and Kilimanjaro (from £425 for 5 days).

Phoenix Expeditions, College Farm, Far St, Wymeswold, Leicestershire LE12 6TZ (☎01509/881818, fax 01509/881822). Well-equipped outfit offering a 14-week overland trip from Istanbul to Nairobi via Cairo (from £1200, excluding flights and provisions), plus 4- to 10- week trips through East and southern Africa.

Sherpa Expeditions, 131a Heston Rd, Hounslow, Middlesex TW5 0RD (☎0181/577-2717; 24hr ☎0181/577-7187). Trekking specialists, with a combined 17-day Mount Kenya–Kili trip to satisfy the most masochistic (from about £2000, flight included).

Tracks Africa, 12 Abingdon Rd, London W8 6AF (☎0171/937-3028, fax 0171/937-3176). London–Nairobi overland (or vice versa), and a choice of short, well-priced safaris in Kenya, or Kenya plus Tanzania or Uganda (eg 8-day highlights from £460, 15-day safari from £680, both excluding flight and provisions).

Truck Africa, 37 Ranelagh Gardens Mansions, London SW6 3UQ (☎0171/731-6142, fax 0171/371-7445). Personal but professional and enthused over by past clients. A big trans-Africa expedition from London to Kenya/Zimbabwe, and East Africa trips based out of Nairobi. From around £700 for 4 weeks (excluding flights).

OVERLAND TO KENYA

Opportunities to **travel overland** to Kenya from Europe are liable to change as Africa's borders open and close in the wake of political and military conflicts. But there is no shortage of expedition operators promising the journey of a lifetime. Some practical information and background about Kenya's neighbouring states is given on pp.70–73.

OVERLAND VIA EGYPT AND SUDAN

Heading south from the Mediterranean, it has in the past been possible to cross from Egypt into Sudan, and thence overland via Eritrea and Ethiopia into Kenya, with the option of diverting south via the Red Sea. At the time of writing – and since 1984 – the **Nile route through Sudan** is impassable, with most of the countryside in the south controlled by the various factions of the anti-government Sudanese People's Liberation Army. Sudan is shaky at present, and visas not issued routinely. Unless you find something discounted, the necessary flight from Khartoum to Nairobi will cost over £260 ($390). If the route is reopened, Nile steamers ply upriver as far as Juba in the rainy season (April–Oct) from where a road, one day to be surfaced, connects with Lodwar in Kenya.

OVERLAND VIA NORTH AND WEST AFRICA

The journey **across the Sahara and via west Africa** is a long one, and currently the Sahara traverse is all but closed while Algerian fundamentalists wage a murderous guerrilla war against secular society and any foreigners rash enough to visit the country. As a viable alternative, it's possible for convoys and overland groups to travel down the coast **from Morocco to Mauritania**.

Once in west Africa the main route is through Nigeria, thence south through Cameroon, east across the Central African Republic, southeast through Zaire (again a flight may be necessary depending on Zaire's state of turmoil), east over the highlands and through Uganda to Kenya. The West African portion of this trip is covered in the encyclopedic and invaluable *Rough Guide to West Africa*.

OVERLAND EXPEDITIONS

For a number of years, **operators of overland expeditions** have been following the west Africa route as far as Zaire and then cutting south around Lake Victoria and through Tanzania, taking in some of the rich scenic and faunal variety of that country's northwest region. Since the convulsions in Rwanda and Burundi began in 1994, the variety of routes has increased, as each company seeks the most practicable way through the region. Most organized trips finish in Nairobi.

If you're interested in one of the more **inexpensive expedition companies** – sometimes regrettably one-off outfits – that advertise in the classified columns, it's worth paying them a visit. It seems unfair to throw blanket disapproval over them, but even more unfair on you if things go disastrously wrong. Scrutinizing their blurb gives a good indication of their probable preparedness and real know-how. And if the blurb looks cheap or hasty you should forget it.

GOING UNDER YOUR OWN STEAM

The other option – **driving yourself**, or entering into partnership with others (sometimes located through classified ads) to fix up a vehicle and head off to Africa – is obviously peppered with potential pitfalls. Depending on the situation in various countries (follow the news through the journals listed on p.36) it's perfectly feasible – thousands do it every year – as is setting off alone, or with a companion, using **public transport**, hitching lifts and walking. This latter, more economical option in fact has a higher chance of success, bearing in mind the possible breakdowns that can befall a vehicle. Don't go into an independent overland trip via North and west Africa if you have less than six months: the adventure, otherwise, becomes a race.

BY SHIP TO KENYA

It is still possible to get to East Africa **by ship**, a romantic idea, but you can expect to pay considerably more for a berth for the four-week passage than you would for an air ticket (in fact you pay roughly the same as the first-class air fare). The *Strand Cruise & Travel Centre*, Charing Cross Shopping Concourse, The Strand, London WC2N 4HZ (☎0171/836-6363, fax 0171/497-0078), is the main agent in Britain for **passenger-carrying cargo ship voyages**. It can fix you up on one of the *Mediterranean Shipping Company*'s monthly sailings from Felixstowe, through the Med via Livorno and

FLIGHTS FROM AFRICAN CITIES

Within Africa, direct (and sometimes non-stop) flights to Nairobi are available from Abidjan, Accra, Addis Ababa, Brazzaville, Bujumbura, Cairo, Dar es Salaam, Entebbe/Kampala, Gaborone, Harare, Johannesburg (see "Getting There from South Africa", p.19), Khartoum, Kigali, Kinshasa, Lagos, Lomé, Lusaka, the Seychelles and Zanzibar.

Flights from other capitals connect through these cities, often with long delays.

Fares, which are rarely discounted, can seem a little high – around £420 ($630) one-way Accra–

Nairobi for example, and around £600 ($900) for a one-month excursion. If you're planning on taking Nairobi in as part of broader air travel in Africa, you may well find some saving in making separate trips out of London. The main transcontinental carriers operating to and from Kenya are *Ethiopian Airlines* (for central and west Africa) and *Kenya Airways* (for southern and East Africa). There are also twice-weekly flights on *Cameroon Airlines* between Douala and Nairobi.

Naples and the Suez Canal to Port Sudan, Djibouti, Dar-es-Salaam and Tanga and back north to Mombasa. The voyage lasts 28 days and costs from £2080 one-way through to Mombasa.

Also approximately monthly, the German *Ahrenkiel Shipping Line* operates Felixstowe, Hamburg, Antwerp, Fos-sur-Mer, Suez, Port Sudan, Djibouti, Dar-es-Salaam and Mombasa, a voyage of about 28 days from £1980 one-way.

GETTING THERE FROM THE USA AND CANADA

There are currently no direct flights from the USA or Canada to East Africa: you are going to have to change planes and quite possibly airlines. The fastest routes to Nairobi are from New York via Paris on *Air France* or via London on *British Airways*. These are daytime flights, arriving the following morning. For such convenience, you're not likely to get much discount, if any, below the airlines' own fares. Unless time is a big consideration you are likely to make an overall saving by flying to London – usually

the cheapest departure point in Europe – stopping over for a day or two and picking up a discounted flight there. For more details on buying discount flights – and complete information on the airlines that fly into Nairobi – turn back to the pages covering "Getting to Kenya from Britain and Ireland".

Other locations for cheap flights to Nairobi – useful if you plan to tie in your trip to Africa with further travels – include **Athens**, **Cairo** and **Tel Aviv**. These cities are accessible by direct flights from New York, and the national carriers, *Olympic*, *Egyptair* and *El Al*, all fly to Nairobi.

Buying an **all-inclusive vacation** can, however, make a lot of sense if time rather than money is a limiting factor: spending half a week travelling in each direction takes a lot out of a three-week trip. And even if time is not a problem, a "package holiday" out of the UK can be an economical way of visiting Kenya. Prices have plummetted in recent years with charter flights operating direct from London to Mombasa. Note, however, that this tends to be travel at the level of bargain vacations to Hawaii or Mexico – distinctly unglamorous in all aspects, from the packed planes to the minibus safaris. Choose carefully.

GENERAL DISCOUNT AGENTS IN THE USA

Around the World, 2241 Polk St, San Francisco, CA 94109 (☎415/673-9950).

Flytime, 45 W 34th St, Suite 305, New York, NY 10001 (☎212/760-3737).

Hariworld, 25 W 45th St, New York, NY 10036 (☎212/997-3300).

Interworld, 800 Douglas Rd, Coral Gables, FL 33134 (☎305/443-4929).

Magical Holidays, 501 Madison Ave, New York, NY 10022 (☎212/486-9600 or 1-800/228-2208).

Pan Express Travel, 25 W 39th St, New York, NY 10022 (☎212/719-9292 or 1-800/518-7726); 209 Post St, Suite 921, San Francisco, CA 94108 (☎415/989-8282).

Swan Travel, 400 Madison Ave, New York, NY 10017 (☎212/421-1010).

Travel International, Ives Building, 114 Forrest Ave, Suite 205, Narbeth, PA 19072 (☎1-800/221-8139).

UniTravel, Box 12485, 1177 N Warson Rd, St Louis, MO 63132 (☎1-800/325-2222 or 314/569-2501).

COUNCIL TRAVEL OFFICES IN THE USA

Head office: 205 E 42nd St, New York, NY 10017 (☎212/822-2700 or 1-800/226-8624).

Other main offices at:

530 Bush St, Suite 700, San Francisco, CA 94108 (☎415/421-3473);

14515 Ventura Blvd, Suite 250, Sherman Oaks, CA 91403 (☎818/905-5777);

1138 13th St, Boulder, CO 80302 (☎303/447-8101);

3300 M St NW, 2nd Floor, Washington, DC 20007 (☎202/337-6464);

1153 N Dearborn St, Chicago, IL 60610 (☎312/951-0585);

273 Newbury St, Boston, MA 02116 (☎617/266-1926);

1501 University Ave SE, Room 300, Minneapolis, MN 55414 (☎612/379-2323);

2000 Guadalupe St, Suite 6, Austin, TX 78705 (☎512/472-4931);

1314 NE 43rd St, Suite 210, Seattle, WA 98105 (☎206/632-2448).

STA TRAVEL OFFICES IN THE USA

☎1-800/777-0112 (nationwide information number).

Main offices at:

10 Downing St, New York, NY 10014 (telesales ☎212/627-3111);

6560 N Scottsdale Rd, Suite F-100, Scottsdale, AZ 85253 (☎1-800/777-0112);

ASUC Travel Center, MLK Jr Bldg, 2nd Floor, UC, Telegraph at Bancroft Way, Berkeley, CA 94720 (☎510/642-3000);

7202 Melrose Ave, Los Angeles, CA 90046 (tele-sales ☎213/934-8722);

166 Geary St, Suite 702, San Francisco, CA 94108 (☎415/391-8407);

J Wayne Reitz Union, Suite C3, Museum Rd, University of Florida, Gainsville, FL 32611 (☎352/338-0068);

297 Newbury St, Boston, MA 02116 (☎617/266-6014);

3730 Walnut St, Philadelphia, PA 19104 (☎215/382-2928).

TRAVEL CUTS OFFICES IN CANADA

Head Office: 187 College St, Toronto, ON M5T 1P7 (☎416/979-2406).

Other main offices at:

MacEwan Hall Student Centre, University of Calgary, Calgary, AB T2N 1N4 (☎403/282-7687);

12304 Jasper Ave, Edmonton, AB T5N 3K5 (☎403/488-8487);

Student Union Building, Dalhousie University, Halifax, NS B3H 4J2 (☎902/494-2054);

1613 rue St Denis, Montréal, PQ H2X 3K3 (☎514/843-8511);

1 Stewart St, Ottawa, ON K1N 6H7 (☎613/238-8222);

2383 Ch Ste Foy, Suite 103, Ste Foy, Quebec, PQ G1V 1T1 (☎418/654-0224);

Place Riel Campus Centre, University of Saskatchewan, Saskatoon, SA S7N 0W0 (☎306/975-3722);

710-802 W Hastings, Vancouver, BC V6B 1P2 (☎604/681-9136);

University Centre, University of Manitoba, Winnipeg, MA R3T 2N2 (☎204/269-9530).

The last option, if you have all the time in the world, is to get to Europe, then **travel overland** to Kenya (more details on p.10).

FLIGHTS FROM THE USA

Any flight from Europe to Nairobi can be tacked on to a transatlantic routing. But the flights usually advertised, with reasonable connections, all hub through New York and then connect with a flight to Nairobi in one or other of the following European capitals – Amsterdam, Brussels, Geneva, London, Paris, Rome or Zurich.

Purchasing direct from the airline, current one-month **Apex** fares are only for the fuller budget, the price out of New York extending upwards from $2608 and out of Los Angeles from $3090. *Kenya Airways*, although they don't operate transatlantic flights, have a New York office at 342 Madison Ave, NY 10017 (☎212/681-1200 or 1-800/343-2506), but can't offer any special deals with transatlantic partners and insist you'll do better with consolidators (ticket discounters) – as indeed you will.

For those intending to build a trip to Kenya into an extensive travel plan, **round-the-world fares** from discount agents start at roughly $2600 for economy and around $5000 for first-class. As a general rule you must decide your itinerary and stopover cities in advance, travelling in a single direction, either eastbound or westbound with no backtracking. You set a date for the first outbound flight in advance, and then reserve the others as you go, completing the entire journey within either six months or a year.

FLIGHT DEALS FROM THE EASTERN USA

Especially if you're a student, youth (under 26) or teacher, check out *Council Travel*, with cheap New York–London round-trips, and New York–Nairobi from $1370 (students/under-26s, on *Air France*) or $1565 (non-students, on *Gulf Air*). *STA Travel*, who have a large international network of offices, offer round-trip fares to Nairobi from $1003 (on *Air France*), on the basis of restricted eligibility and depending on season.

Classified advertisers in the Sunday travel section of *The New York Times* offer various **discounted seat fares** open to all on good airlines (*Virgin* or *BA*, and *Kenya Airways*, for example), though the cheapest "bucket shops" will find you something at a lower price using one of the less convenient European airlines. Good one-way deals are very rare.

USEFUL AIRLINES FOR KENYA FROM THE USA AND CANADA

Air Canada (in BC, ☎1-800/663-3721; in Alberta, Saskatchewan and Manitoba, ☎1-800/542-8940; in eastern Canada, ☎1-800/268-7240; in US, ☎1-800/776-3000).

Air France (☎1-800/237-2747; in Canada, ☎1-800/667-2747).

Alitalia (☎1-800/223-5730; in New York, ☎1-800/442-5860; in Canada, ☎1-800/361-8336).

Austrian Airlines (☎1-800/843-0002).

Balkan Airlines (☎212/371-2047).

British Airways (in US, ☎1-800/247-9297; in Canada, ☎1-800/668-1059).

Canadian Airlines (in Canada, ☎1-800/665-1177; in US, ☎1-800/426-7000).

Continental Airlines (domestic, ☎1-800/525-0280; international, ☎1-800/231-0856).

Delta Airlines (domestic, ☎1-800/221-1212; international, ☎1-800/241-4141; in Canada, call directory inquiries, ☎1-800/555-1212, for local toll-free number).

EgyptAir (☎1-800/334-6787).

El Al (☎1-800/223-6700).

Gulf Air (☎1-800/553-2824).

KLM (in US, ☎1-800/374-7747; in Canada, ☎1-800/361-5073).

Lufthansa (in US, ☎1-800/645-3880; in Canada, ☎1-800/563-5954).

Northwest Airlines (domestic, ☎1-800/225-2525; international, ☎1-800/447-4747).

Olympic Airways (☎1-800/223-1226).

Sabena (☎1-800/955-2000).

Swissair (in US, ☎1-800/221-4750; in Canada, ☎1-800/267-9477).

TWA (domestic, ☎1-800/221-2000; international, ☎1-800/892-4141).

United Airlines (domestic, ☎1-800/241-6522; international, ☎1-800/538-2929).

US Air (domestic, ☎1-800/428-4322; international, ☎1-800/622-1015).

Virgin Atlantic Airways (☎1-800/862-8621).

AFRICA AND ADVENTURE TRAVEL SPECIALISTS

Most agents are representatives not only for North American companies but also for many of the adventure travel operators whose head offices are in Britain (see pp.10–11), and can offer flight deals.

US AGENTS AND TOUR OPERATORS

Abercrombie & Kent,1520 Kensington Rd, Oak Brook, IL 60521 (☎1-800/323-7308 or 708/954-2944). *Leading upscale operator with over 30 years of experience organizing African safaris. Comprehensive and professional programme in Kenya; offices in Nairobi. Tour options include The Adventurer Safari (classic Kenya safari, 14 days from $2670 land only), The Kenya Family Safari (15 days from $3860 adults, $2500 under-12s, land only), Pearls of Africa (18-day safari escorted by Lynne Leakey or Wendy Corroyer, $7400), plus deluxe air safaris and Kenya–Tanzania or Kenya–Egypt combinations.*

Adventure Center, 1311 63rd St, Suite 200, Emoryville, CA 94608 (☎1-800/227-8747 or 510/654-1879). *Wide range of affordable adventure tours and safaris.*

African Adventure Company, 1600 S Federal Highway, Pompano Beach, FL 33062 (☎1-800/882-WILD or 954/781-3933). *One of the best agencies in the business, offering over 100 programmes to Africa and thousands of safari options, from $1850 land only.*

Africa Travel Centre, 197 Wall St, West Long Branch, NJ 07764 (☎908/870-0223, fax 908/870-0278). *Sister company of London-based Africa Travel Shop offering a broad range of packages from no-frills camping to extensive land expeditions.*

Geo Expeditions, 67 Linoberg St, Sonora, CA 95370 (☎1-800/351-5041).

Global Safaris, 5250 West Century Blvd, #311, Los Angeles, CA 90045 (☎714/738-7979 or 1-800/757-6625). *A wide range of safaris staring at $1995.*

Holbrook Travel, 3540 NW 13th St, Gainesville, FL 32609 (☎904/377-7111). *Top-quality natural history tours and safaris led by experts, from $3500 including flight.*

Horizon Holidays, 61 Broadway, Suite 2825, New York, NY 10006 (☎1-800/248-5608). *Affordable 11-day Kenya safari, from $2350 including round-trip air fare from NY.*

Journeys, 1536 NW 23rd Ave, Portland, OR 97210 (☎503/226-7200); and at *Powell's Travel Store*, Pioneer Courthouse Sq, Portland (☎503/226-4849). *Tailor-made trips for individuals and groups, plus flights through consolidators.*

Luxury Adventure Safaris, 4635 Via Vistosa, Santa Barbara, CA 93101 (☎805/967-1712). *No expense spared here: escorted wildlife safaris and first-class accommodation; $3000–6000, land only.*

Mountain Travel Sobek, 6420 Fairmount Ave, El Cerrito, CA 94530 (☎1-800/227-2384 or 510/527-8100). *Mountaineering, hiking, white-water rafting and other activity tours, from $2900.*

Nature Expeditions International, PO Box 11496, Eugene, OR 97440 (☎503/484-6529 or 1-800/869-0639). *Education and adventure in travel, offering wildlife, natural history and cultural expeditions. 18- or 23-day East Africa Wildlife Safari led by expert naturalist, from $4300 land only.*

Safari Center, 3201 N Sepulveda Blvd, Manhattan Beach, CA 90266 (☎1-800/223-6046 or 310/546-4411). *Deluxe, economy or adventure safari options, as well as off-the-beaten track safaris; $800–4000.*

Spector Travel, 31 St James Ave, Boston, MA 02116 (☎617/338-0111 or 1-800/TRY AFRICA). *African specialist with a good record.*

Tamsin & Cooke, PO Box 8, Franklin Lakes, NJ 07417 (☎201/337-6151, fax 201/337-0212). *Customized itineraries based on 30 years' residence in Africa, with emphasis on luxury, away-from-it-all accommodation and safaris on foot, horseback and by camel.*

Wilderness Travel, 801 Allston Way, Berkeley, CA 94710 (☎510/548-0420 or 1-800/369-2794). *Small-group expeditions to the great game parks of Kenya, led by an experienced guide (13 days, lodge and camping, $2800), a 20-day East African Wildlife Safari ($4000), and Perspectives on East Africa, a symposium and safari programme with Jane Goodall and other experts ($595/person plus flight and accommodation).*

CANADIAN AGENTS AND OPERATORS

Blyth & Co, 13 Hazelton Ave, Toronto, ON M5R 2E1 (☎416/964-2569 or 1-800/387-1387). *Custom tours to Kenya.*

Western Treks, 8412 109th St, Edmonton T6G 1E2 (☎403/439-9118 or 1-800/227-8747, fax 403/439-5494).

Worldwide Adventures, 36 Finch Ave West, Toronto, ON M2N 2G9 (☎416/221-3000 or 1-800/387-1483). *Natural history safaris, from $3395 (17 days, land only).*

FLIGHT DEALS FROM THE WESTERN USA

Give *Council* and *STA Travel* a call first – *STA*'s LA–Nairobi fares start at around $1200 for students (on *Air France*) and sometimes they have deals open to all. Then check out the agents listed opposite or make a search of the Sunday travel pages of the *Los Angeles Times* or the *San Francisco Examiner/Chronicle* for discounted round-trip fares.

FLIGHTS FROM CANADA

The airlines' Toronto–Nairobi Apex fares *start* at around CDN$3200 – most travel agents get their customers to Britain first. *Travel Cuts* offers a few deals to Nairobi, some of which, using trans-atlantic charters, are open to all: from Toronto, fares are around CDN$1385–1920 round-trip depending on season. Currently the lowest fares are offered by *El Al* and *Alitalia*.

INCLUSIVE TOURS

A large number of tour operators offer **inclusive vacation and safari packages** to Kenya. When checking with them, remember that most of the quotes you'll be given are for the land arrange-ments only, with flight extra (which may be purchased from the travel operator or from another source). Prices, not including flights, start at around $1000 per week, with most of the tour spent on safari. Hotel-based beach extensions work out somewhat cheaper and are more subject to seasonal variation.

WARNING: BAGGAGE LIMITS

North American passengers who expect to use **transatlantic baggage quotas** – two unweighed pieces of hold luggage – may have problems flying on to Kenya from Europe where a **20kg weight limit** (44lb) applies. The 20kg rule is most likely to be enforced if you have broken your journey in Europe: you won't have any difficulty if you are connecting through. Coming back from Kenya, however, you are, to some extent, subject to the whim of the handler you deal with.

GETTING THERE FROM AUSTRALASIA

There are no direct flights from Australia or New Zealand – all require a stop-over either in Asia or in the carrier's home city. The most direct flights are via either Harare or Mauritius. Another option is to take a round-the-world flight via Harare, including Nairobi as a side trip.

From Australia, the best deals are on *Gulf Air* via Singapore and Bahrain (from A$1900), and *Egyptair* via Bangkok and Cairo (from A$1880 out of Sydney or Melbourne; A$2015 out of Brisbane; A$2080 out of Adelaide or Hobart). More expen-sive is *Ansett-Air Mauritius* via Mauritius (from A$2320 out of Brisbane or Melbourne; A$1920 out of Perth). Both *Qantas* and *Air Zimbabwe* fly via Harare twice weekly from eastern cities (from A$2696) and Perth (from A$2296). In the high season (mid-Nov to mid-Jan), expect to pay an extra $300 or so. As an alternative to taking the Harare–Nairobi flight connection, you could take

AFRICA AND INDEPENDENT TRAVEL SPECIALISTS

Many of these agents are representatives not only for Australian companies but also for adventure travel operators whose head offices are in Britain (see p.10).

AUSTRALIA

Abercrombie & Kent, 90 Bridport St, Albert Park, Melbourne, VIC 3206 (☎03/9699-9766). *Long-established, up-market operator selling its own exclusive holidays.*

Adventure World, 73 Walker St, North Sydney (☎02/956-7766, toll-free 1800/221-931); 8 Victoria Ave, Perth (☎09/221-2300). *Accommodation, car rental, discounted air fares and a varied selection of tours from city mini-stays in Nairobi and Mombasa to camping and overland safaris.*

Africa Travel Centre, Level 12, 456 Kent St, Sydney, NSW 2000 (☎02/9267-3048). *Sister company of the London-based Africa Travel Shop: accommodation, self-drive, Nairobi and Mombasa stop-overs and a comprehensive range of safaris.*

Africa Wildlife Safaris, 1st Floor, 259 Coventry St, South Melbourne, VIC 3205 (☎03/9696-2899).

Specialists in upmarket camping and lodge-based safaris.

Exodus Expeditions, Suite 5, Level 5, 1 York St, Sydney (☎02/9521-5430, toll-free 1800/800-724). *Wholesaler, offering a 17-day Aberdares/Mount Kenya game-viewing trek (A$3000).*

Flight Centres, Circular Quay, Sydney (☎02/9241-2422); Bourke St, Melbourne (☎03/650-2899); plus other branches nationwide.

Peregrine, 258 Lonsdale St, Melbourne (☎03/9663-8611). *Beach stays, overland trips and all-inclusive game safaris; offices in Brisbane, Sydney, Adelaide, Perth and Hobart.*

STA Travel, 732 Harris St, Ultimo, Sydney (☎02/9212-1255, toll-free 1800/637-444); 256 Flinders St, Melbourne (☎03/9347 4711); other offices in Townsville, state capitals and major universities.

NEW ZEALAND

Abercrombie & Kent, Floor 14, Brandon Brookfield House, 17 Victoria St, Auckland (☎09/358-4200).

Adventure Travel Shop, 50 High St, Auckland (☎09/303-1805).

Adventure World, 101 Great South Rd, Remuera, PO Box 74008, Auckland (☎09/524-5118). *Agents for Exodus Expeditions and Peregrine, Australia.*

Africa Travel Centre, 21 Remuera Rd, PO Box 9365, Newmarket, Auckland (☎09/520-2000). *From the same stable as the Australian company.*

Flight Centres, National Bank Towers, 205–225 Queen St, Auckland (☎09/309 6171); Shop 1M, National Mutual Arcade, 152 Hereford St, Christchurch (☎09/379 7145); 50–52 Willis St, Wellington (☎04/472 8101); other branches countrywide.

STA Travel, Travellers' Centre, 10 High St, Auckland (☎09/366 6673); 233 Cuba St, Wellington (☎04/385 0561); 223 High St, Christchurch (☎03/379 9098); other offices in Dunedin, Palmerston North, Hamilton and major universities.

---

the train through Zambia and Tanzania; go overland by local transport; or hook up with any number of foreign-operated overland trips from Harare to Nairobi, most of which are very good value for money and take a month or so for the trip.

From New Zealand, *Ansett-Air Mauritius* fly twice weekly to Nairobi via Melbourne and Mauritius (from NZ$2700). Alternatively it's possible to pick up a cheap combination ticket via Singapore or Bangkok, or to fly to Harare and then on to Nairobi. There are twice-weekly flights

via Sydney and Harare on *Air New Zealand–Air Zimbabwe* (from NZ$2505) and *Qantas* (from NZ$2600).

A **round-the-world** fare that could include Nairobi as a side trip is *Qantas–BA*'s "Global Explorer", which allows six free stop-overs worldwide and additional stop-overs for A/NZ$100 each (from A$2499 or NZ$2799).

Among recommended agents for deals via Harare and other routes, *STA* is probably the most reliable. They have offices all across Australia and New Zealand (for the main ones, see box above).

AIRLINES IN AUSTRALIA AND NEW ZEALAND

Air New Zealand, 5 Elizabeth St, Sydney (☎02/9223-4666); Quay St, Auckland (☎09/357-3000).

Ansett Australia, 501 Swanson St, Melbourne (local-call rate ☎13 1300); branches throughout Australia.

Ansett New Zealand, 75 Queen St, Auckland (☎09/307-6950); branches throughout New Zealand.

British Airways, 64 Castlereagh St, Sydney (☎02/9258-3300); 154 Queen St, Auckland (☎09/356-8690).

Egypt Air, 630 George St, Sydney (☎02/9267-6979); no NZ office.

Gulf Air, 403 George St, Sydney (☎02/9321-9199); no NZ office.

Qantas, Chifley Square, Hunter/Phillip St, Sydney (☎02/957-0111); Qantas House, 154 Queen St, Auckland (☎09/357-8900).

GETTING THERE FROM SOUTH AFRICA

Direct **flights from Johannesburg** (the only departure point) to Nairobi are operated by *South African Airways* (Tues, Fri, Sat; ☎011/356 1111) and *Kenya Airways* (Mon, Thurs, Sat; ☎011/337 8620–4, fax 011/337 3670). Booking direct with the airlines, fares start at R2200 for a one-month trip on an Apex ticket; open yearly returns cost R3520.

Useful **tour operators and travel agents** include:

Abahamba Overland Safaris, PO Box 389, Buhrmannsdrif 2867 (☎01213/45290). *Budget overland trips.*

Adventures, 9 Sunbird Place, Swallow Drive, Fourways, Johannesburg (☎011/465 1288, fax 011/465 9320).

African Outposts, PO Box 4593, Rivonia 2128 (☎011/884 6848, fax 011/883 8690). Specialists in "environmental education through tourism".

African Routes, PO Box 1835, Tourist Junction corner of Pine St and Gardener, Durban 4000 (☎031/304 6358, fax 031/304 6340). Overland operator and agent.

Africa Travel Centre, corner of Military Rd and New Church St, Cape Town 8001 (☎021/235 555, fax 021/230 065). Local branch of the London-based Africa overland specialist.

Drifters, PO Box 48434, Roosevelt Park 2129 (☎011/888 1160, fax 011/888 1020). Fortnightly overland departures to Nairobi.

Kebatla Africa, PO Box 3714, Cresta 2118 (☎011/888 6364, fax 011/782 7557; E-mail adventure@icon.co.za; Web site: http://www.icon.co.za/). Wide range of options at many budgets.

Let's Go Travel/Wild Frontiers, PO Box 844, Halfway House, Johannesburg 1685 (☎011/315 4838, fax 011/315 4850). Wide range of mid-priced tours.

Student Travel Centre, The Arcade, off Mutual Gardens, corner of Oxford Rd and Tyrwhitt Ave, Rosebank 2196, Johannesburg (☎011/447 5551, fax 011/447 5775). Good fares for students and non-students.

Wilderness Safaris, PO Box 651171, Benmore 2010 (☎011/884 1458, fax 011/883 6255). Up-market specialists.

TAKING CHILDREN

Kenya is a terrific country for families. If you're considering taking young children, however, you should ask yourself if you can really be bothered with all the hassle. It's a good start if your children are already enchanted with the idea of Africa and its wildlife. But pre-school children have few notions about such things and derive little thrill from experiencing them for themselves.

The following is aimed principally at families with babies and under-fives. For the under-fives, Kenya is a mixture of fun – in the pool, on the beach, with other kids – and tedium – in the car or plane, on a game drive, in a restaurant. And for their parents it's a toss-up whether they really have a better time on holiday than — assuming it can be arranged — being farmed out at home.

HEALTH

Health issues figure most prominently in most people's minds: with the exception of malaria, however, you can discount fears about your children getting tropical diseases in Kenya. Remember how many healthy second-generation expatriate children have been brought up there. (The biggest health problem for Kenyan children is poverty.)

It can, however, be very difficult to persuade small children to take **malaria** pills, under any guise: chloroquine is available as a syrup, but is really not much use in Kenya, while Paludrine is only in tablet form. Breast-feeding babies will be as protected as their mother. With toddlers you may have to choose between ramming pills down their throats — inducing hysterical tears — or giving in and risking it. In the latter case, up-country Kenya is much safer territory than the coast, but you should be extremely careful to cover them with Deet repellent early each evening and be sure they sleep under secure nets. Take a small net for babies, or try to get something like Fisher-Price's "Pop-Up Baby Cabana", a fully enclosed miniature mosquito net tent, discontinued, but previously available in the USA; about $80. For more on malaria see p27.

As for sanitation, if you use disposable nappies, bring your own supply for a short stay. Any longer and you'd want to buy them in Kenya (from modern supermarkets), but they are expensive at around Ksh1000 for 36. Baby foods are also available in large supermarkets, but here you'll have few problems if you're staying in hotels as there's usually a good variety of fresh food and staff who are happy to prepare it for infantile tastes given some warning.

Unless your time is to be spent exclusively on the coast, bring some **warm clothing** for up-country mornings and evenings. Temperatures in some parts drop low and hotels are not heated.

Probably the most important health concern is the **sun**. On the equator, even when the altitude keeps temperatures down, the effect of half an hour's ultra-violet on delicate skin can be severe. Keep them thoroughly smothered in factor 40 (seriously) and insist they wear hats. Children should also wear T-shirts when swimming, and especially if snorkelling. Sunglasses, too, are a good idea, even for babies, to reduce the intense glare: you can always find little novelty ones that will fit.

And of course, make sure they drink plenty of water.

TRAVEL WITH CHILDREN

Air travel with under-twos (who get no seat for their 10 percent fares) can be a nightmare. Make every possible effort to get — and retain — bulk-head seats and a bassinet (hanging cradle) for the baby. These requests should be a priority in your plans. When you reconfirm 48 hours before flying, double-check you still have them. If you have lively children who won't easily settle, consider the simple drugging method: trimepra-zine (one brand is called Vallergan) can be obtained on prescription and they'll sleep right through the flight and wake up disgustingly refreshed.

For a young family, going on a group **safari** (whether organized from home as part of a package or booked in Kenya) is probably not on. **Hiring a car** is quite feasible, however, and gives you the flexibility and privacy you need for changing nappies, toilet stops and shouting at each other. For babies and children too small for seat belts, you'll need a **car seat** which, if you have the right model, also works as an all-purpose carrier, pool-side recliner and picnic throne.

If you have a light, easily collapsible **buggy**, bring it. Many hotels and lodges have long paths from the central public areas to the rooms or cottages. A **child-carrier** backpack is another very useful accessory: the Tomy Snugli is a good one, and is also free-standing.

For flying with all this baggage, remember you have a full luggage allowance for each passenger with a seat.

SAFARIS AND HOTELS

On safari with young children in tow, your driving time is more likely to be spent in getting from one lodge to the next than in purposeful game drives, but if the children are old enough to enjoy spotting the animals, make sure they have their own **binoculars**.

Small children find it frustrating trying to pick out animals at great distances. And **long drives** are always a big turn-off. For these reasons, some parks are more child-friendly than others. **Nairobi National Park** is great (if you can divert their attention from the planes landing at the airport) and **Lake Nakuru** is a hit as well, as distances are small and the animals close. Equally, **Amboseli**'s small size and the presence of large numbers of elephants make it popular with younger children.

Most **hotels, lodges and tented camps** do not specifically exclude children of any age (indeed, if you yourself book you'll find the vast majority give huge **reductions**), but a number of organized tours have a **minimum age** of 7, while several of the more exclusive tented camps and all four of the "tree hotels" have minimum ages (7, 8 or even 10). *Treetops* and *The Ark* occasionally have "children's nights".

The **coast hotels** are on sandy beaches facing a warm sea, safely protected by the reef. Particularly suitable family hotels are mentioned in the text.

PROBLEMS AND REWARDS

In hotels, the biggest recurring problem is **meal times**. Some have children's menus and early sittings but it's not something you can count on and it doesn't solve the problem of when the parents eat: it's always a good idea to stick to your established routines if possible. If you're eating as a family, young children will often need something to amuse them (take a good stock of puzzle and colouring books, and as many of their favourite toys as possible).

In the evenings, you'll need a **babysitter**. Very few hotels make permanent provision for this.

The management will usually find a local woman to come in, given a few hours' notice, but they tend to leave the question of payment up to you. To avoid inflating the economy, Ksh200 would normally be fine if the arrangement is informal, but Ksh500 for a full evening is the most you should ever pay. Alternatively, if the children are asleep, speak to the restaurant manager and arrange for an *askari* (night watch) to sit outside.

Swimming pools, focus of attention for most children, are only sure to be warm on the coast. In the higher, up-country regions, including Nairobi, unheated pools are always chilly, which can be a big disappointment for keen splashers.

If your child only thrives with **friends** the same age, being stuck with you in a beautiful hotel for a day or two can be numbingly boring. It's obviously not difficult to track down other, child-infested guests and suggest the kiddies amuse themselves together, but if this doesn't work you may want to look for children in the neighbourhood – not as far-fetched as it sounds in, for example, Naivasha or the suburbs of Nairobi.

Wherever you go, the reaction of **local people** to families and their children is warm and exceptionally welcoming. Waiters and other hotel staff invariably have kids of their own (usually living far away) and greet and talk to children unselfconsciously. Mothers will find their status breaks the ice with local women (if any needed breaking) and visits with your children to Maasai *enkangs* and similar "ethnic tourism" will always be more rewarding than going on your own.

TRAVELLERS WITH DISABILITIES

Although by no means easy, Kenya does not pose insurmountable problems for people with disabilities. While there is little government involvement in improving access, tourist industry staff – not to mention passers-by – are usually prepared to help whenever necessary. Considering, principally, wheelchair-users, many hotels have ground-floor rooms; a number on the coast have ramped access walks to public areas; and larger hotels in Nairobi have elevators. Safari vehicles can usually manage wheelchair-users.

GETTING THERE

British Airways and *Kenya Airways* offer the only **non-stop flights** from London to Kenya (note that *Kenya Airways* "direct" flights to Mombasa do require a plane change to a domestic *Kenya Airways* flight in Nairobi). These airlines, together with *Air France*, *KLM*, *Lufthansa* and *Swissair* are the best airlines for disabled passengers. They're sometimes more costly, but less physically demanding than the cheapies. You may need the extra energy for Nairobi airport, where accessibility means how well you cope in a scrum. If you're flying by **charter**, you'll arrive at Mombasa, which has very basic facilities, but no steps or long distances to negotiate – just the steps down from the plane, where you will have to be carried.

From **North America**, *Virgin* and *Air Canada* come out top in terms of disability awareness (and seating arrangements) and may be worth contacting first for any information they can provide.

If you're looking for an all-in tour, contact the upmarket Kenya specialists *Abercrombie & Kent* (addresses in the "Getting There" sections above) who have some experience in carrying disabled passengers on their regular itineraries.

IN KENYA

Attitudes to disabled people are generally good – there are always willing hands to help you over any obstacle. All the international-class **hotels** in Nairobi have elevators, as do several of the cheaper places (details in the text). **Getting around** the city, however, to do some of its limited sightseeing or to book safaris, is difficult in a wheelchair. While distances are short, there is little ramping of pedestrian areas and drivers are not used to wheelchairs crossing the road. The capacious London taxi cabs, however, are a boon.

Safari vehicles have superb springing, but taking a pressure cushion is a wise precaution.

CONTACTS FOR TRAVELLERS WITH DISABILITIES

BRITAIN AND IRELAND

Disability Action Group, 2 Annadale Ave, Belfast BT7 3JH (☎01232/91011). *Information about access for disabled travellers abroad.*

Holiday Care Service, 2nd Floor, Imperial Buildings, Victoria Rd, Horley, Surrey RH6 7PZ (☎01293/774535). *Information on all aspects of travel for people with special needs.*

Irish Wheelchair Association, Blackheath Drive, Clontarf, Dublin 3 (☎01/833 8241). *A national voluntary organization, with related services for holidaymakers with disabilities.*

RADAR (Royal Association for Disability and Rehabilitation), Unit 12, City Forum, 250 City Rd, London EC1V 8AF (☎0171/250-3222; Minicom ☎0171/250-4119). *Good source of information on all aspects of travel.*

TRIPSCOPE, The Courtyard, Evelyn Rd, London W4 5JL (☎0181/994-9294). *Phone-in travel information and advice service for the elderly and disabled.*

US AND CANADA

Directions Unlimited, 720 N Bedford Rd, Bedford Hills, NY 10507 (☎1-800/533-5343). *Tour operator specializing in custom tours for people with disabilities.*

Jewish Rehabilitation Hospital, 3205 Place Alton Goldbloom, Montréal, PQ H7V 1R2 (☎514/688-9550). *Guidebooks and travel information.*

Mobility International USA, PO Box 10767, Eugene, OR 97440 (Voice and TDD: ☎503/343-1284). *Information and referral services, access guides, tours and exchange programs. Annual membership $20 (includes quarterly newsletter).*

Society for the Advancement of Travel for the Handicapped (SATH), 347 Fifth Ave, New York, NY 10016 (☎212/447-7284). *Non-profit travel-*

industry referral service that passes queries on to its members as appropriate; allow plenty of time for a response.

Travel Information Service, Moss Rehabilitation Hospital, 1200 W Tabor Rd, Philadelphia, PA 19141 (☎215/456-9600). *Telephone information and referral service.*

Twin Peaks Press, Box 129, Vancouver, WA 98666 (☎206/694-2462 or 1-800/637-2256). *Publisher of the Directory of Travel Agencies for the Disabled ($19.95), listing more than 370 agencies worldwide; Travel for the Disabled ($19.95); the Directory of Accessible Van Rentals ($9.95) and Wheelchair Vagabond ($14.95), loaded with personal tips.*

AUSTRALIA AND NEW ZEALAND

ACROD (Australian Council for Rehabilitation of the Disabled), PO Box 60, Curtin, ACT 2605 (☎06/682-4333); 55 Charles St, Ryde (☎02/9809-4488).

Disabled Persons Assembly, PO Box 10, 138 The Terrace, Wellington (☎04/472-2626).

Even then, off-road trips can be very arduous. It's perhaps better to use Nairobi as a base, and go on one of the many one-day excursions, to Nakuru, Naivasha or *The Outspan* near Mount Kenya for example. If you are determined, however, any of the luxury lodges and tented camps should be accessible, with help, making a proper safari quite feasible, especially if you fly. One or two places even have baths (as well as showers). Only on the most adventurous trips, with temporary camps set up in the bush, and long-drop toilets, would wheelchair-users really have problems.

The all-night **Nairobi–Mombasa sleeper train** to Mombasa sounds improbable but, again, is possible. On this, though, you would have to be carried – with some difficulty – from your cabin to the toilets and dining car, as the corridors are very narrow. Your wheelchair would go in the luggage van, too, so expect a delay in retrieving it on arrival. With the exception of the "luxury" coaches plying between Nairobi and Mombasa, other public transport in Kenya is not at all wheelchair-friendly.

For more **information** on all this, see *Nothing Ventured: Disabled People Travel the World*, a *Rough Guide* special (distributed by Penguin), which contains first-hand accounts by disabled travellers to Kenya; and contact the organizations in the box opposite.

RED TAPE AND VISAS

Obvious, but still worth stating, check that your passport is current. And check that it will remain valid for at least six months beyond the end of your projected stay in Kenya. If you're travelling further afield in Africa, you'll need to allow for this, and ensure your passport has plenty of spare pages for stamps. British citizens need no visa to enter Kenya. Nor do other Commonwealth citizens – with the exceptions of Indians, Pakistanis, Australians, New Zealanders, Sri Lankans and Nigerians – or passport holders from Ireland, Germany, Denmark, Finland, Ethiopia, Sweden, Spain, and Turkey, all of whom can enter Kenya freely, with just a visitor's pass, issued routinely on arrival. South Africans do not require a visa unless they intend to stay for more than a month.

VISAS AND VISITORS' PASSES

Visas can be obtained in advance from any Kenyan embassy, consulate or high commission, or from a British embassy in countries where Kenya has no diplomatic representation. Visas normally take 24–48 hours to process, require two passport-size photos and usually an **air ticket** out of the region (not just to Uganda or Tanzania). This requirement is usually waived if the embassy is satisfied of your alternative arrangements or financial responsibility. Standard fees are £30, US$45 or A$70 for New Zealanders; £25 or US$40 (or equivalent) for French and Canadians; and £18, US$30 or A$40 for Americans, Australians and other nationalities. Remember that Kenyan diplomatic missions are **closed on Kenyan public holidays** (see p.58 for a list of holidays).

Visas are normally valid for entry within three months of the date of issue. It's possible to get a **visa on arrival** at the airport but this may cause delays, and cost slightly more than the standard fee. If you're arriving at night it's best avoided. Transit visas (valid for seven days) can be bought on arrival for around $15.

On arrival in Kenya you will be issued with a visitor's pass limiting the **length of stay** actually granted to you (whether or not you require a visa to enter). Various factors may determine the length of time granted, including your appear

KENYAN EMBASSIES, CONSULATES AND HIGH COMMISSIONS

AUSTRALIA: 33 Ainslie Ave, PO Box 1990, GPO Canberra (☎06/247-4748); also serves **New Zealand**.

AUSTRIA: Rotenturmstrasse 22, 1010 Vienna (☎01/63 32 42).

BELGIUM: Av Joyeuse Entrée 1–5, Brussels (☎02/230 30 65).

CANADA: 415 Laurier Ave East, Ottawa, Ontario K1N 6R4 (☎613/563-1773).

EGYPT: 20 Boulos Hanna St, PO Box 362, Dokki, Cairo (☎02/704455).

ETHIOPIA: Hiher 16, Kebelle 01, Fikre Mariam Rd, PO Box 3301, Addis Ababa (☎1/18 00 33).

FRANCE: 3 rue Cimarosa, 75116 Paris (☎1/45.53.35.00).

GERMANY: Villichgasse 17, 5300 Bonn 2 (☎0228/35 60 41).

INDIA: 66 Vasant Marg, Vasant Vihar, New Delhi (☎11/672280).

ITALY: CP 10755, 00144 Rome (☎6/808 2718).

JAPAN: 24-20 Nishi-Azabu 3-Chome, Minato-Ku, Tokyo (☎03/479 4006).

NETHERLANDS: Konninginnegracht 102, The Hague (☎70/350 42 15).

NIGERIA: PO Box 6464, 53 Queen's Drive, Ikoyi, Lagos (☎01/682768).

RUSSIA: Bolshaya Ordinka, Dom 70, Moscow (☎095/237 4702).

RWANDA: Blvd de Nyabugogo, PO Box 1215, Kigale (☎772774).

SAUDI ARABIA: PO Box 95458, Riyadh 11693 (☎01/488-2484).

SUDAN: Street 3, Amarat, PO Box 8242 Khartoum (☎11/40386 or 43758).

SWEDEN: Birger Jarlsgatan 37, 2st 11145 Stockholm (☎08/21 83 00).

TANZANIA: 4th Floor, NIC Investment House, Samora Ave, PO Box 5231, Dar-es-Salaam (☎51/31502).

UGANDA: 60 Kira Rd, PO Box 5220 Kampala (☎41/231861).

UNITED ARAB EMIRATES: PO Box 3854 Abu Dhabi (☎02/366300).

UNITED KINGDOM: 45 Portland Place, London W1N 4AS (☎0171/636-2371).

USA: *Embassy*, 2249 R St NW, Washington, DC 20008 (☎202/387-6101); *Consulate*, 424 Madison Ave, New York, NY 10017 (☎212/486-1300); 9150 Wilshire Blvd, Suite 160, Beverly Hills, CA 90212 (☎310/274-6635).

ZAIRE: Plot 5002, ave de l'Ouganda, BP 9667, Zone Gombe, Kinshasa (☎12/30117).

ZAMBIA: 5207 United Nations Ave, PO Box 50298, Lusaka (☎01/212531).

ZIMBABWE: 95 Park Lane, PO Box 4069, Harare (☎04/792901).

ance, how much money you have and (fortunately) how long you actually want to stay. They normally give visitors' passes of up to three months.

If you're planning on visiting Uganda or Tanzania out of Kenya, you can cross the border freely within the validity of your Kenya visa (assuming of course you have a visa for Uganda or Tanzania if you need one), but for other trips outside Kenya, you will need to reapply for a visa to re-enter.

EXTENDING YOUR STAY

It's important to know just how long a stay you've been granted in Kenya, particularly, perhaps, if you don't require a visa. There have recently been a number of cases of travellers **overstaying** the limits of their visitors' passes by a few days and finding themselves invited to spend the night behind bars while a suitable fine was discussed – anything up to the equivalent of £100 (US$150). The problem can arise if, for example, you can't decipher KVP5W/H ("Kenya Visitors' Pass 5-Week Holiday"). Ask what's been stamped when you arrive and renew well in advance. You will certainly have to renew after three months.

Extensions to visitors' passes and **visa renewals** can be done at the immigration offices in Nairobi, Mombasa or Kisumu. If you're in Kisumu, that is easily the most straightforward place to do it; otherwise it's most easily done at Nyayo House in Nairobi (Mon–Fri 8.30am–12.30pm & 2–3.30pm).

If your passport requires a visa and you have stayed a total of **six months** in the country and don't have resident's status, you will have to leave not only Kenya, but East Africa, in order to obtain a new visa to allow you to return.

For **neighbouring countries' embassies** in Nairobi see "Nairobi Listings".

CUSTOMS

At the **customs** benches, you will normally be asked if you have any photographic equipment, video camcorders, cassette players and so on. Unless you're some kind of professional, with mountains of specialist gear, there shouldn't be any question of paying duty on personal equipment, though some customs officers like to make notes of it all in your passport to ensure it is re-exported. If you have friends in Kenya, however, and are taking presents for them, you are likely to have to pay duty if you declare the items.

MONEY AND COSTS

Kenya's currency, the Kenyan shilling (Ksh), is a colonial legacy based on the old British currency. It's now worth less than a quarter of its original 5 pence sterling (one shilling) equivalent. People occasionally talk in "pounds", meaning Ksh20, and often in "bob", meaning shillings. You'll also hear "quids" for pounds. There are Ksh1000, 500, 200, 100, 50, 20 and 10 notes and coins of Ksh5, 1, 50 cents (half a shilling), 20 cents, 10 cents and 5 cents, though in practice you will rarely come across coins of less than Ksh1. Until recently Kenyan shillings had no value outside the country and their import or export was illegal; now it is possible to export up to Ksh100,000 and some foreign banks stock shillings should you wish to buy some before you arrive in Kenya.

At the beginning of 1993, Kenya successively devalued its currency, dropped IMF and World Bank free market policies, floated the currency and then returned to the donors' fold once more, sending the Kenyan shilling all over the place. Now, at last, some kind of stability has been attained.

At the time of writing (mid-1996), the **rates of exchange** are around Ksh90: £1 or Ksh60: $1. There's no longer a black market for foreign currency – don't change money on the street.

MONEY

You can **exchange** hard currencies in cash or travellers' cheques at banks all over the country, and at most large hotels for a marginally poorer rate. US dollars and British pounds sterling are always the most acceptable and will cause the least delay where the rates aren't immediately to hand; always ask first what commission and charges will be deducted. *Barclays* or *The Commercial Bank of Africa* are normally fastest. **Banks** are usually open Mon–Fri 9am–3pm and Sat 9–11am.

HAVING MONEY SENT TO KENYA

Try to avoid **sending home for money**. It's expensive and even telexed draft orders can take weeks to reach you at the counter even though the normal delay should be four or five working days. *Western Union* does not send money to Kenya: their nearest agent is in Kampala, Uganda

CARRYING IT AND KEEPING IT

Travellers' cheques are the obvious way to carry your funds. There's really little advantage to **cash** and it can't be replaced if lost or stolen. It's definitely worth **shopping around** for the cheapest travellers' cheques, as some banks levy large charges.

It's wise to carry valuable hard currency (as opposed to Kenyan shillings) in a very **safe place**, ideally in a leather pouch under your waistband, looped to your belt. You may not have a waistband, but ingenuity counts. Pouches hanging around your neck aren't too great and ordinary wallets are a disaster. As for Kenyan shillings, you'll be carrying around large quantities of coins and paper money. Be aware that, except in the towns, Ksh1000 bills can be hard to change (few people have that sort of money) – so make sure you have a safe purse or secure zip pocket to stuff all the small denominations in. Ksh1 coins can be stored neatly in empty film containers.

CREDIT CARDS

As for **plastic**, *VISA*, *American Express* and *Diners' Card* are widely accepted for tourist services such as upmarket hotels and restaurants, flights, safaris, car rental; *Mastercard/ Access* is more limited. There's usually a two- to five-percent mark-up on top of the price but, as establishments are charged a fixed percentage of their transactions, this is obviously negotiable. A credit card can be very useful for leaving a deposit for car rental (frequently thousands of shillings). *Barclays Bank* will give you **cash advances** in US dollars on *VISA* cards – a useful service, but expensive.

Abuse of credit cards is not uncommon in Kenya. If you're paying a sum in shillings by credit card, make sure that the voucher specifies the currency before you sign. If it doesn't, it's all too easy for the vendor to fill in a dollar sign in front of the total after you've left.

COSTS

Most **prices** in this guide are given in Kenyan shillings, now a relatively stable currency. However, we've given prices in US$ for those establishments, especially tourist services such as safaris and car rental, which still quote their rates in the "hard" dollar. You will still usually be able to pay at these establishments in Ksh, although often at an inferior rate of exchange.

BARGAINING

You'll need to get into **bargaining** quickly (see p.57), but be cautious, at first, over your purchases, until you've established the value of

things. Once you start, it's surprising how little is sold at a strictly fixed price: it's nearly always worth making an offer. In places that see tourists and travellers, prices sometimes vary considerably through the year. This "seasonal factor" seems to be increasing in importance, too.

TRAVELLING CHEAPLY

Kenya can clearly be expensive if you want to hire a car or go on organized safaris. But it doesn't need to be. By staying in the more economical hotels, eating in local places and using public transport, you can get by easily enough on **£10–15 ($15–22)** a day, or less if you camp and buy your own food (many Kenyans who survive on the fringes of the money economy manage on less than Ksh300 a week). On a daily average budget of **£20 or a little more (say $35)**, you would be living very well most of the time, even staying in the occasional more luxurious tourist hotel.

Staying put for a while you'll find it much easier to live cheaply: a week or so in Lamu on the coast or Lake Naivasha in the Rift Valley need not cost you much more than **£8 ($12)** a day.

Travel costs

For people on low budgets, **travel** is probably still the biggest expense. Getting around by **bus and pick-up van** (*matatu*) is cheap, but the crucial disadvantage is that they can't drive you around the game parks. In order to do that, **renting a vehicle** – and paying for fuel – will add at least £50 ($75) a day to your costs, though shared between two or more this isn't cripplingly expensive for a week or so. Petrol costs only about 33p per litre (50¢), which is about $2 per US gallon.

You can also find all-inclusive camping safaris from around £40 ($60) a day, sometimes less – though if you throw in your luck with one of the flighty safari outfits who claim they'll do everything for about £26 ($40) a day, beware (read the "Camping Safaris" section – p.62 – carefully).

Lodgings

Rooms in local "Boarding and Lodgings" start at less than £1.50 ($2.25) for a single, or perhaps £2 ($3) for a twin or double. They rarely go much above £5 ($7.50) for a twin room. Prices depend largely on whether the room has self-contained (s/c) facilities, with a shower and toilet, or whether the guests share a toilet and shower room. Simple up-country hotels generally charge around £5.50–11 ($8–17) for a twin or double, with breakfast. Tourist hotels, lodges and tented camps are very much more expensive. See "Accommodation" (p.45).

Food costs

As for **food**, many basic commodities – including soft drinks, cigarettes, bread, cornmeal (*ugali*), sugar, milk and tea – had low, fixed prices for many years. With the recent advent of market liberalization, their prices, like that of **beer**, which also used to be price-controlled, are climbing rapidly, bringing widespread hardship. To Kenyans, for whom a "pound" is still a substantial sum of money (you don't get many of those in a day's wages), bread at Ksh20, milk at Ksh16 and a daily paper at Ksh15 is a disaster. Not to currency-rich tourists, though. In international terms, Kenya is still pretty cheap, and, if you're determined to eke out your savings on a shoe-string budget this is the right country. All the basics are a good deal cheaper than in Europe, North America or Australasia.

Eating out is not a Kenyan tradition and few Kenyans would consider it cheap. Still, in the most basic local restaurant, decent **meals** can be had for less than £2 ($3) and sometimes for half that. For fancier meals in touristy places, expect to pay up to £10 ($15) – rarely more – for a large meal of international-style dishes.

HEALTH

For arrivals by air from Europe, Australia, or North America, Kenya has no required inoculations. Entering overland, though, you may well be required to show both yellow fever and cholera International Vaccination Certificates. If you fly on an airline that stops en route in Africa, you should have the yellow fever shot before you leave and get a form that looks like a cholera vaccination certificate but doesn't mean you've had the jab (in Britain, most GPs will give you this – the cholera shot is widely considered completely ineffective). You may otherwise be subjected to them at the airport. Plan ahead and start organizing your jabs at least six weeks before departure. Remember that a yellow fever certificate only becomes valid ten days after you've had the jab. You should also start taking malaria tablets before departure and don't forget to continue taking them for the prescribed time after you return.

OTHER JABS

You should have **tetanus** and **polio** boosters and doctors usually recommend **typhoid** jabs (beware

that these tend to render you *hors de combat* for a couple of days). Opinion is divided about gamma-globulin (or immunoglobulin) shots against **hepatitis A**. The disease itself is debilitating, taking up to a year to clear up, but the injection is only effective for a few months, sometimes it seems not at all. The alternative, if you have time and are prepared to spend a little more, is a course of two or three Havrix injections – two jabs (the second 2–4 weeks after the first) for one year's protection, and, for protection lasting about five years, a third jab six months later.

To reduce the risk of contracting hepatitis, be extra careful about cleanliness and in particular about contamination of water – a problem wherever a single cistern holds the whole water supply in a cockroach-infested toilet/bathroom, as often happens in Lamu.

MALARIA

Protection against **malaria** is absolutely essential. The disease – caused by a parasite carried in the saliva of some mosquitoes – is endemic in tropical Africa; many people carry it in their bloodstream and get occasional bouts of fever. It has a variable **incubation period of a few days to**

IMMUNIZATIONS AND ADVICE

In **Britain** your first source of advice and probable supplier of jabs and prescriptions is your general practitioner. Family doctors are often well informed and are likely to charge you a (relatively low) flat fee for routine injections. For yellow fever and other exotic shots you'll normally have to visit a specialist clinic, often in a county town health authority headquarters.

In London, advice and low-cost **inoculations** are available from the Hospital for Tropical Diseases, 4 St Pancras Way, London NW1 0PE (☎0171/387-4411). The Travel Clinic (open Mon–Fri 9am–5pm) produces a series of useful fact sheets, and you can make an appointment for a consultation and/or a course of jabs. With a referral from your GP, the Hospital for Tropical Diseases will also give you a complete **check-up** on your return if you think it may be worth it.

Also in London, the *British Airways Travel Clinic*, 156 Regent St, London W1 (☎0171/439-9584), is open Monday to Friday 9.30am–5.15pm, and Saturday 10am–4pm (no appointment required). They can provide you with a wide variety of unusual shots like plague, anthrax and rabies as well as the usual ones, anti-malarial tablets and various hardware. There are more than thirty similar *BA Travel Clinics* around England, plus one in Cardiff (☎01222/811425) and one each in Edinburgh (☎0131/336-3038) and Aberdeen (☎01224/624669). Phone ☎01276/685040 for the address of your nearest one.

The travel agency *Trailfinders* has its own travel clinic (see *Discount Agents* box, p.5). You might also visit the *Nomad Traveller's Medical Centre*, 3–4 Wellington Terrace, Turnpike Lane, London N8 0PX (☎0181/889-7014), for jabs, prescriptions, and medical kits (pharmacist on site Wed & Thurs 2–5.30pm, Sat 9am–5.30pm). It's attached to the excellent *Nomad* equipment shop, which has a free travel reference centre, with a selection of books, brochures, and accommodation details.

If you don't live near a clinic, or you're passing through the UK, you may want to check out the services of MASTA (Medical Advisory Services for Travellers Abroad, Bureau of Hygiene and Tropical Diseases, Keppel St, London WC1E 7HT; ☎0171/631-4408) who provide very detailed, personalized "Health Briefs" for whichever country you're visiting. They advise on which inoculations you need and when to get them, give rundowns on all the diseases you may fall victim to and include up-to-date health news from the countries concerned. The "Concise Brief" seems pretty complete but the "Comprehensive" one is amazingly so and a

delight for hypochondriacs (students half-price). *MASTA* also sell Neat Deet insect repellent, various mosquito nets and Sterile Emergency Kits – basically sterile needles and drip.

Other major tropical disease centres in the UK are:

Liverpool School of Tropical Medicine, Pembroke Place, Liverpool L3 5QA (☎0151/708-9393).

Communicable Diseases Unit, Ruchill Hospital, Glasgow G20 9NB (☎0141/946-7120).

Telephone helplines (24hr recorded information):

Hospital for Tropical Diseases Healthline ☎0839/337733 – user-friendly service offering comprehensive advice over the phone or fax.

MASTA Healthline ☎0891/224100 – Health Brief ordering system (written information sent by post if you leave details of your itinerary) followed by general advice.

London School of Hygiene and Tropical Medicine Malaria Helpline ☎0891/600350 – advice on malaria prevention.

In **Ireland**, *Travel Medicine Services*, PO Box 254, 16 College St, Belfast 1 (☎01232/315220), and the *Tropical Medical Bureau*, Grafton St Medical Centre, Dublin 2 (☎01/671 9200), offer medical advice before a trip and medical help afterwards in the event of a tropical disease.

In the **USA and Canada**, all travellers heading for Kenya should call the *Center for Disease Control* (☎404/639-3311) and ask for "Health Information for International Travel" – a very informative booklet giving details on jabs and bugs and general advice. Their 24-hour Voice Information System (☎404/332-4555) gives recorded information on general health concerns for travellers. The *Travelers Medical Center*, 31 Washington Square, New York, NY 10011 (☎212/982-1600), offers a consultation service on immunizations and treatment of diseases. *Travel Medicine*, 351 Pleasant St, Suite 312, Northampton, MA 01060 (☎1-800/872-8633), sells first-aid kits, mosquito netting, water filters and other health-related travel products.

In **Australia**, vaccination clinics include the *Travellers' Medical and Vaccination Centre*, 428 George St, Sydney (☎02/9221-7133); 393 Little Bourke St, Melbourne (☎03/9602-5788); 29 Gilbert Place, Adelaide (☎08/8267-3544); 247 Adelaide St, Brisbane (☎07/3221-9066); and 1 Mill St, Perth (☎09/321 1977). In **New Zealand**, there's the *Auckland Hospital*, Park Rd, Grafton (☎09/797 440).

several weeks so you can get it long after being bitten (but you can't get it soon after arrival). If you get malaria, you'll probably know: the fever, shivering and headaches are something like severe flu and come in waves. If a child gets malaria, however, you might not know: take any fever very seriously indeed. Malaria is not infectious but it can be very dangerous and sometimes even fatal if not treated quickly. The destruction of red blood cells by the *falciparum* type of malaria parasite can lead to **cerebral malaria** (blocking of the brain capillaries) and is the cause of a nasty complication called **blackwater fever** in which the urine is stained by excreted blood cells.

PREVENTION

It is essential therefore to do everything possible to avoid being bitten, and it's normally considered vital to take anti-malaria tablets (the oft-promised vaccine has yet to materialize).

In the UK, **anti-malarials** are only available on private prescription. Your doctor or clinic will advise as to which to take: currently the preferred option is **mefloquine** (trade name Lariam). Much has been made in the media of the side effects associated with this drug; although the manufacturers claim that the risks are minimal compared to the dangers of contracting malaria (it is estimated that 22 percent of patients taking Lariam are likely to suffer mild bouts of nausea or dizziness and around one in ten thousand may experience neuro-psychiatric problems such as depression and sleep disturbances), this prophylactic is not recommended for periods of over six months, and is not suitable for pregnant women, people with liver or kidney problems, epileptics, or infants under 3 years. The dose is one tablet per week, for a minimum of six weeks, starting two weeks before entry into a malarial zone and continuing for at least two weeks after leaving.

For those for whom Lariam is counter-indicated – or if you're simply not convinced by the manufacturers' claims about its minimal risks – it's worth taking an alternative regime of anti-malarials. Proguanil (trade name Paludrine; taken daily) and chloroquine (trade name Avlochlor; taken weekly) still provide a high enough level of protection to make them worth persevering with. Again keep a careful routine and cover the period before and after your trip with doses. These too may leave you feeling nauseous; the dose is best taken at the end of the day, and never on an empty stomach.

Once in Kenya, chloroquine-based tablets (eg Nivaquin, Aralen and Resochin), as well as Paludrine and Daraprim, can be bought everywhere, but the newer drugs to which *falciparum* malaria is less resistant – Lariam, Halfan and Fansidar – are only available in big towns. Fansidar is not recommended as a prophylactic. The chloroquine-based drug Malaraquin is widely marketed and cheap in Kenya but it's practically useless. Some pills give people mouth ulcers – you may want to be prepared with suitable remedies.

There is a growing interest in **homeopathic** anti-malarial treatments among travellers who are unable or unwilling to risk the side effects of standard prophylactics, but the claims of homeopathy are still hypothetical, and protection cannot be guaranteed.

It can't be overstressed that the best way to avoid getting malaria is to **avoid getting bitten**. Sleep under a **mosquito net** when possible – they're not expensive – and burn **mosquito coils** (readily available in Kenya) for a peaceful night. Don't use Cock Brand or Lion, which are said to contain DDT and are banned in many countries. If you're carrying your own mosquito net, it's worth impregnating it with pyrethrum or Deet (see below).

Female *Anopheles* mosquitoes – the aggressors – prefer to bite in the evening. They can be distinguished from other mosquitoes by their rather eager, head-down position. After dark, always cover your exposed parts with something strong. Deet (the insecticide diethyltoluamide) works well – look for a product with at least 50 percent concentration, such as *Nomad Neet Deet*. The idea of soaking wrist and ankle "sweat bands" (bought from a sports shop) with Deet seems a good one, but it's fiddly in practice; the stuff gets everywhere and corrodes most artificial materials. If you don't like all this synthetic protection, there are now some good, natural alternatives: a particularly effective, pyrethrum-based formulation, not tested on animals, is X-Gnat skin gel (X-Gnat Laboratories, Cumbernauld, Scotland). Strangely, the most effective mosquito repellent of all is said to be Avon "Skin-so-soft" bath oil – not that they market it as such. Some people swear by the effects of vitamin B tablets in deterring mosquitoes.

In Nairobi and the highlands the malaria risk is low, but you should under no circumstances break your course of pills as it's vital to keep your para-

GOING DOWN WITH MALARIA

If you go down with malaria, you'll need to take a cure. Don't compare yourself with local people who may have considerable immunity. The priority, if you think you might be getting a fever, is **treatment**. Delay is very risky.

First, confirm your diagnosis by getting to a doctor and having a **blood test** to identify the strain. If this isn't possible, and you're not on the coast, **quinine tablets** are recommended as the best treatment – 600mg twice a day for five days, and then three Fansidar tablets. If you notice no improvement after the first dose of quinine, it's a safe bet that your malaria is chloroquine-resistant –

take three Fansidar tablets straight away. If you're on the coast and can't get to a doctor, any malarial symptoms should be treated as chloroquine-resistant *falciparum*, so take three Fansidar tablets straight away. Fansidar is effective but is not sold in the West due to its very rare but dangerous side-effects. Lariam (mefloquine) can also be taken as a cure: take three tablets, then two more after six hours, then one more 24 hours after the first dose.

While giving the cure time to work you should dose up on painkillers to help ease the worst of the discomfort, take plenty of fluids, and keep eating (but avoid milk-based products).

site-fighting level as high as possible. On the coast, the malaria situation is still quite serious and chloroquine is reckoned to be quite ineffective.

OTHER DISEASES

Bilharzia is a dangerous disease. The usual recommendation is never to swim in, wash with, or even touch, lake water that can't be vouched

for. In fact, while various lakes and rivers harbour the disease – in places – the only inland water you would probably want to swim in is Lake Turkana or Lake Naivasha, both of which are bilharzia-free.

Bilharzia, the medical name of which is **schistosomiasis**, comes from tiny flukes (the schistosomes) that live in freshwater snails and which,

MEDICINE BAG

There's no need to take a mass of drugs and remedies you'll probably never use – and best not to plan to dispense pharmaceutical relief by giving away a lot of miscellaneous pills. Various items, however, are immensely useful, especially on a long trip, and well worth buying in advance.

On a local level, if you're interested in herbal and other natural remedies, you'll find a wealth of examples in markets. Intuition, common sense and persistent enquiries are all you need to judge whether they're worth trying.

Paracetamol Safer than aspirin for pain and fever relief.

Iodine tincture (with dropper) or water purifying (chlorine) tablets Taste horrid but do the trick. Shop around – they vary greatly in price.

Anti-malaria tablets Enough for prophylactic use plus several courses of Fansidar and/or quinine tablets in case of attack.

Codeine phosphate This is the preferable emergency anti-diarrhoeal pill but is on prescription only. Some GPs may oblige. Lomotil is second best.

Antibiotics Ciproxin or Bactrim are good in a lower bowel crisis. Amoxil (amoxycillin) is a broad spectrum antibacterial drug useful against many infections. Flagyl (metronizadole) is the recommended treatment for giardia and amoebic dysentery. None should be used unless you cannot see a doctor.

Antihistamine cream To treat insect bites.

Zinc oxide powder Useful anti-fungal powder for sweaty crevices.

Antiseptic cream Cicatrin is good but creams invariably squeeze out sooner or later so avoid metal tubes. Bright red or purple mercurochrome liquid dries wounds.

Alcohol swabs Medi-swabs are invaluable for cleaning wounds, insect bites and infections.

Sticking plaster, steri-strip wound closures, sterile gauze dressing, micropore tape You don't need much of this stuff. If you use it up, supplies can be replenished in Nairobi.

Lip-salve/chapstick Invaluable for dry lips.

Thermometer Very useful. Ideally you'll be 37°C. A Feverscan forehead thermometer is unbreakable and gives a ready reckoning (from pharmacists).

Lens solution If you wear contact lenses you'll need a good supply of solution.

Many people get occasional **heat rashes**, especially at first on the coast. A warm shower, to open the pores, and cotton clothes should help. And, on the subject of heat, it's important not to overdose on **sunshine** in the first week or two. The powerful heat and bright light can mess up your system. A hat and sunglasses are strongly recommended.

Some people **sweat** heavily and lose a lot of salt. If this applies to you, sprinkle extra salt on your food. Salt tablets are a waste of money but you do need to keep a healthy salt balance.

Papaya – if you like it – can be eaten as a kind of tonic. The fruit contains excellent supplies of invigorating minerals and vitamins, and is reckoned to help the healing process and to aid digestion. Papaya seeds, which taste like watercress, are good for you, too. If you're not wild about lowland papayas, try the smaller and much more fragrant **mountain** variety.

If you're going to be on the road for a long time, it may be worth considering taking some **vitamin tablets** with you.

as part of their life cycle, leave their hosts and burrow into animal (or human) skin to multiply in the bloodstream. The snails only favour stagnant water and the chances of picking up bilharzia are small. Of course, if you feel major fatigue and pass blood – the first symptoms – see a doctor: it's curable.

The only other real likelihood of your encountering a serious disease is if it's **sexually transmitted**. Venereal diseases are widespread, particularly in the larger towns, and the **HIV virus** which can cause AIDS is alarmingly prevalent and spreading all the time (see p.68). It's very easily passed between people suffering relatively minor, but ulcerous, sexually transmitted diseases, and the very high prevalence of these is thought to account for the high incidence of heterosexually transmitted HIV.

WATER AND BUGS

Until a few years ago, most visitors to Kenya drank **tap water**, or, in doubtful cases, boiled water. Then someone hit on the idea of bottling spring water and making it the most expensive soft drink in the country. In most places, the tap water can be drunk and is considered pure (it is, in any case, the same water that is used to make bottled drinks). But since bad water is the most likely cause of **diarrhoea**, you should be fairly cautious about drinking rain- or well water if you can't get clean tap water. Endless cups of superheated *chai* are the obvious solution, if your teeth can stand it. It can't do any harm, except to your purse, to drink bottled water only – it costs around Ksh40–50 per litre – but it can mean you don't drink enough, especially on long, hot journeys.

In truth, serious **stomach upsets** don't afflict a large proportion of travellers. If you're only staying a short time, it makes sense to be very scrupulous: purifying your drinking water with tablets or, better, iodine (six drops per litre of water), or boiling it for half an hour (or both) kills most things. For longer stays, think of **re-educating your stomach** rather than fortifying it; it's virtually impossible to travel around the country without exposing yourself to strange bugs from time to time. Take it easy at first, don't overdo the fruit (and wash it in clean water), don't keep food too long, and be very wary of salads served in cheap restaurants.

Should you have a **serious attack**, 24 hours of sweet, black tea and nothing else may rinse it out. The important thing is to replace your lost fluids. If you feel the need, you can make up a **rehydration mix** with four heaped teaspoons of sugar or honey and half a teaspoon of salt in a litre of water. Flat Coca Cola is quite a good tonic; avoid coffee, strong fruit juice, and alcohol. If it seems to be getting worse – or, horrifically, you have to travel a long distance – any chemist should have name brand anti-diarrhoea remedies. These – Lomotil, Codeine phosphate, etc – shouldn't be overused. Stay right away from the popular Kaomycin and Imodium, neither of which is safe to use and can even encourage diarrhoea. And avoid jumping for antibiotics at the first sign of trouble: they annihilate what's nicely known as your "gut flora" (most of which you want to keep) and will not work on viruses. Most upsets resolve

"TRAVELLER'S HEALTH"

Edited and regularly updated by Richard Dawood, *Traveller's Health* (OUP/Viking Penguin) is a sane, detailed and well-written guide, with something for just about every imaginable symptom.

HOSPITALS

If you need serious treatment in Kenya, you'll discover a frightening lack of well-equipped **hospitals**. The Consolata Sisters' hospitals – the Nazareth Hospital on Riara Ridge, outside Nairobi (☎02/335684), and another in Nyeri (☎0171/72032) – are reassuring exceptions. Nairobi itself is fairly well provided: the Nairobi Hospital in Argwings Kodhek Rd is reasonably good (☎02/722160).

themselves. If you continue to feel bad, you should seek a doctor.

INJURIES AND ATTACKS

Take more care than usual over minor **cuts and scrapes**. In the tropics, the most trivial scratch can quickly become a throbbing infection if you ignore it. Take a small tube of antiseptic with you – Bacitracin is recommended.

Otherwise, there are all sorts of potential bites, stings and rashes which rarely, if ever, materialize. **Dogs** are usually sad and skulking, posing little threat. **Scorpions and spiders** abound but are hardly ever seen unless you deliberately turn over rocks or logs: scorpion stings are painful but almost never fatal, while spiders are mostly quite harmless. **Snakes** are common but, again, the vast majority are harmless. To see one at all, you'd need to search stealthily; walk heavily and they obligingly disappear.

TEETH

Get a thorough **dental check-up** before leaving home and take extra care of your teeth while in Kenya. Stringy meat, acid fruit and sugary tea are some of the hazards. You might start using a freshly cut "toothbrush twig" (*msuake*), as local people do. Some varieties contain a plaque-destroying enzyme; you can buy them at markets.

If you lose a filling and aren't inclined to see a dentist in Kenya, try and get hold of some *gutta-percha* – a natural, rubbery substance – available from some pharmacists, or from your dentist. You heat it and then pack it in the hole as a temporary filling. Using chewing gum is a bad idea.

INSURANCE

Insurance, in the light of all these medical possibilities, is too important to ignore. Before you purchase special travel insurance, whether for medical or property mishaps, check to see that you won't duplicate the coverage of any existing plans which you may have or be covered by. Travel facilities paid for with credit cards are routinely insured, but this won't help you if your camera is stolen or your jeep is rammed by a rhino.

Home insurance may cover theft or loss of documents, money and valuables while overseas, though exact conditions and maximum amounts vary from company to company. Students may even be covered by their parents' policies. Travel insurance policies usually offer only limited cover for the loss of valuables such as cameras, jewellery and watches (typically £250–£350 in total, with a maximum of £150–£250 per item; a camera, including lenses, counts as one item).

You should, however, be most interested and concerned about insuring your **health** and being certain that if you have to spend time in hospital, or even have to be repatriated, you'll be covered.

BRITAIN AND IRELAND

Premiums among **British** insurers vary widely – from the very reasonable ones, offered primarily through student and youth travel agencies (though available to anyone), to ones so expensive that the cost for anything more than two months of coverage will probably equal the cost of the worst possible combination of disasters. You should note also that few – if any – insurers will arrange on-the-spot payments in the event of a major expense or loss; you will usually be reimbursed only after going home.

ISIS travel insurance, available through branches of *STA Travel* or *Endsleigh* (in London, 71 Old Brompton Rd, SW7 3JS, ☎0171/589-6783; or 97–107 Southampton Row, WC1, ☎0171/436-4451) is one of the cheapest and best available in Britain. £42–50 per month will cover you against all sorts of calamities as well as lost baggage, flight cancellations and hospital charges. You might also contact *Suretravel*, The Pavilion, Kiln Park Business Centre, Kiln Lane, Epsom, Surrey KT17 1JG (☎01372/749191). Their insurance cover (sold direct or through travel agents) covers risks like watersports that many other insurers don't as a rule. If you plan to take several trips over the course of a year it would make sense to consider an annual or multi-trip policy: you could try *Worldwide Travel Insurance Services*, PO Box 99, Elm Lane Offices, Elm Lane, Tonbridge, Kent TN10 3XS (☎01732-773366), who, again, cover you for watersports.

If you need to claim, you *must* have a police report in the case of theft or loss, and supporting evidence in the case of hospital and medication bills. Keep photocopies of it all and don't allow months to elapse before informing the insurer.

In **Ireland**, travel insurance is best obtained through a travel specialist such as *USIT* (see box on p.5), with policies costing from £43 for a month. Discounts are offered to students of any age and anyone under 26.

US AND CANADA

American and Canadian holders of **ISIC** cards (which cost $18 with valid youth/student ID) are entitled to $3000 worth of basic sickness and accident coverage and sixty days ($100 per diem) of hospital in-patient benefits for the period during which the card is valid. University **students** will also often find that their student health coverage extends for one term beyond the date of last enrolment. Bank and charge **accounts** (particularly *American Express*) will also often have certain levels of medical or other insurance included.

Canadians are usually covered for medical expenses by their provincial health plans (but may only be reimbursed after the fact).

Only after exhausting these possibilities might you want to contact a specialist travel insurance firm; your travel agent can usually recommend one. Companies you might consider include: *ISIS*, sold by *STA Travel* (☎1-800/777-0112), with policies for $80–105 for a month (depending on level of coverage); *Travel Guard*, 1145 Clark St, Stevens Point, WI 54481 (☎1-800/826-1300 or 715/345-0505), who offer cover for a premium of $69 on a $1000 trip or $109 on a $2000 trip; and *Access America*, 600 Third Ave, New York, NY 10163 (☎1-800/284-8300 or 212/949-5960), who provide a deluxe plan at similar prices with a daily rate of $2.50 per day for trips of over 31 days.

A most important thing to keep in mind – and a major disappointment to would-be claimants – is that nearly all of the currently available policies do not insure against **theft**. North American travel policies apply only to items **lost** from, or **damaged** in, the custody of an identifiable, responsible third party, such as a hotel porter, airline, luggage consignment, etc. Even in these cases you still have to contact the local police to have a complete **report** made out for your insurer to process the claim.

AUSTRALIA AND NEW ZEALAND

In **Australia and New Zealand**, travel insurance is put together by the airlines and travel agent groups in conjunction with insurance companies. They are all comparable in premium (around A$180/NZ$210 for one month, A$260/NZ$300 for two months and A$330/NZ$380 for three months) and coverage (most adventure sports are covered). Companies worth contacting include: *UTAG*, 347 Kent St, Sydney (☎02/9819-6855; toll-free 1800/809-462); *AFTA*, 144 Pacific Hwy, North Sydney (☎02/956-4800); *Cover More*, Level 9, 32 Walker St, North Sydney (☎02/9202-8000; toll-free 1800/251-881); and *Ready Plan*, 141–147 Walker St, Dandenong, Victoria (toll-free ☎1800/337 462), and 10th Floor, 63 Albert St, Auckland (☎09/379 3208).

FLYING DOCTORS

Kenya's flying doctor **Air Ambulance** service (which also operates in Tanzania) offers free evacuation by air to a medical centre – very reassuring if you'll be spending time out in the wilds. It costs around £17 ($25) for a month or £50 ($75) for a year. The income goes back into the service and the African Medical Research Foundation

behind it. You can contact them in advance (PO Box 30125, Nairobi; ☎02/336886, emergency line ☎02/501280) or buy their insurance on arrival: they have an office at Wilson Airport, whence most of their rescue missions set out.

MAPS AND ADVANCE INFORMATION

Kenya Tourist Offices abroad tend to be thin on useful maps and information (the Ministry of Tourism relies on the private sector to promote Kenya), but they are always worth visiting if you're nearby – the one in Stockholm is said to be excellent. Try to buy maps in advance – with the exception of the inexpensive Kenya Survey maps they're usually cheaper.

If you're going to Kenya for some time, there's a growing list of **libraries, resource centres and journals** which can give you some insight into the country before you touch down.

In Nairobi, there's a good selection of maps at the **Public Map Office** (see "Nairobi Listings" for details on how to obtain the Survey maps, which you might want to do months in advance) and it's really worth getting hold of the Survey of Kenya park maps (three of which have now been superseded by Macmillan's publications for Tsavo, Amboseli and Maasai Mara) before taking off for the wilds: with the aid of the numbered junctions, you can actually find your way around. At the park gates they're usually either out of stock or twice the price.

UK MAP AND TRAVEL BOOK SUPPLIERS

Africa Bookcentre, 38 King St, London WC2E 8JT (☎0171/240-6649). Located in the Africa Centre, Mon–Wed & Fri–Sat 10am–5.30pm, Thurs 10am–6.30pm. A very wide selection of books from and about the continent, with an emphasis on African writers and academic works.
Daunt Books for Travellers, 83 Marylebone High St, W1M 4AL (☎0171/224-2295). Huge selection of guides and maps, plus history and novels.
Nomad Books, 791 Fulham Rd, London SW6 5DH (☎0171/736-4000). Small, friendly travel book specialist.
John Smith and Sons, 57–61 St Vincent St, Glasgow G2 5TB (☎0141/221 7472).
Stanford's, 12–14 Long Acre, Covent Garden, London WC2E 9LP (☎0171/836-1321; also mail order); 52 Grosvenor Gardens, London SW1W 0AG; 156 Regent St, London W1R 5TA. One of the world's best map and guidebook suppliers.
The Travel Bookshop, 13 Blenheim Crescent, London W11 2EE (0171/229-5260). The oldest travel bookshop in London, with a good selection of second-hand classics and old travelogues.

LIBRARIES AND RESOURCE CENTRES IN LONDON

Africa Centre, 38 King St, London WC2E 8JT (☎0171/836-1973). Office and reading room open Mon–Fri 9.30am–5.30pm. Britain's best independent charity institute for African affairs, open to all: reading room with magazines and newspapers; exhibitions; music; theatre; cinema; language teaching (good Swahili classes); bar and restaurant open all week. A good place to meet people.
Commonwealth Institute, Kensington High St, London W8 6NQ (☎0171/603-4535). Large centre offering library and resource services, shop, exhibitions, workshops. Performance venue.

KENYA TOURIST OFFICES ABROAD

CANADA: 415 Laurier Ave East, Ottawa, Ontario K1N 6RY (☎613/563-1773).

FRANCE: 5 rue Volney, Paris 75002 (☎1/42.60.66.88, fax 1/42.61.18.84).

GERMANY: Neue Mainzer Strasse 22, 60311 Frankfurt (☎69/23 20 17, fax 69/23 92 39).

HONG KONG: 1309 Liu Chong Hing Bak Building, 24 Des Voeux Rd, Central GPO Box 5280, Hong Kong (☎523 6053).

JAPAN: RM 216 Yurakucho Building, 1-10 Yurakucho, 1-Chome, Chiyoda-Ku, Tokyo (☎3/214 4595).

SWEDEN: Birger Jarsgatan 37 2TR, 11145 Stockholm (☎8/24 04 45, fax 8/50 92 61).

SWITZERLAND: Bleicherweg 30, CH-8039 Zurich (☎1/202 22 44, fax 1/202 22 56).

UNITED KINGDOM: 25 Brooks Mews, London, W1Y 1LF (☎0171/355-3144, fax 0171/495-8656).

USA: 424 Madison Ave, New York, NY 10017 (☎212/486-1300, fax 212/688-0911); 9150 Wilshire Blvd, Suite 160, Beverly Hills, Los Angeles CA, 90212 (☎310/274-6635, fax 310/859-7010).

SOUTH AFRICA: 302 Brooks St, Menlo Park 0081, Pretoria D102 (☎012/342-5066, fax 012/342-5069).

Royal Geographical Society, 1 Kensington Gore, London SW7 2AR (☎0171/581-2057). Helpful Expedition Advisory Service provides a wealth of information, including maps and technical guides.

School of Oriental and African Studies Library, Thornhaugh St, Russell Square, London WC1H 0XG (☎0171/637-2388). A vast collection of books, journals and maps in a modern building. Day visits are allowed but membership to borrow is expensive and requires a reference.

US MAP AND TRAVEL BOOK SUPPLIERS

The Complete Traveler Bookstore, 199 Madison Ave, New York, NY 10016 (☎212/685-9007); 3207 Filmore St, San Francisco, CA 92123 (☎415/923-1511).

Forsyth Travel Library, 9154 W 57th St, Shawnee Mission, KS 66201 (☎1-800/367-7984).

Latitudes Map & Travel Store, 4811 Excelsior Blvd, St Louis Park, Minneapolis, MN 55416 (☎612/927-9061).

Map Link, 25 E Mason St, Santa Barbara, CA 93101 (☎805/965-4402).

Oceanie Afrique-Noire Books (OAN), 15 W 39th St, New York, NY 10018 (☎212/840-8844). Bookshop specializing in African art and culture.

Phileas Fogg's Books & Maps, #87 Stanford Shopping Center, Palo Alto, CA 94304 (☎1-800/233-FOGG in California; ☎1-800/533-FOGG elsewhere in US).

Rand McNally, 444 N Michigan Ave, Chicago, IL 60611 (☎312/321-1751); 150 E 52nd St, New York, NY 10022 (☎212/758-7488); 595 Market St,

San Francisco, CA 94105 (☎415/777-3131); 1201 Connecticut Ave NW, Washington, DC 20003 (☎202/223-6751). For other locations, or for maps by mail order, call ☎1-800/333-0136 (ext 2111).

The Savvy Traveller, 310 S Michigan St, Chicago, IL 60602 (312/913-9800).

Sierra Club Bookstore, 730 Polk St, San Francisco, CA 94109 (☎415/923-5500).

Travel Books & Language Center, 4931 Cordell Ave, Bethesda, MD 20814 (☎1-800/220-2665).

Traveler's Bookstore, 22 W 52nd St, New York, NY 10019 (☎212/664-0995).

CANADIAN MAP AND TRAVEL BOOK SUPPLIERS

Open Air Books & Maps, 25 Toronto St, Toronto, M5C 2R1 (☎416/363-0719).

Ulysses Travel Bookshop, 4176 St-Denis, Montréal (☎514/289-0993).

World Wide Books and Maps, 1247 Granville St, Vancouver, BC V6Z 1E4 (☎604/687-3320).

MAP AND TRAVEL BOOK SUPPLIERS IN AUSTRALIA AND NEW ZEALAND

Bowyangs, 372 Little Burke St, Melbourne (☎03/9670-4383).

The Map Shop, 16a Peel St, Adelaide (☎08/8231-2033).

Perth Map Centre, 891 Hay St, Perth (☎09/322-5733).

Specialty Maps, 58 Albert St, Auckland (☎09/307-2217).

Travel Bookshop, 20 Bridge St, Sydney (☎02/9241-3554).

MAPS

You'd do well to buy a good, large-scale **map of Kenya** before leaving. Other, locally useful maps are mentioned in passing through the guide.

Bartholomew This offering makes all the roads look the same so can't be recommended as a travelling companion.

Macmillan Clear and fairly tough, but it could be more detailed (and is irritatingly devoid of distances) though it has Nairobi and Mombasa plans on the reverse. Macmillan also does park maps for Amboseli, Tsavo and Maasai Mara.

Nelles Verlag German, but published in English, and detailed (though poor on minor road numbers and missing various highways built in the last ten years). Includes a good chunk of Northern

Tanzania and some inserts, together with mostly accurate annotations.

New Holland Globetrotter Travel Map Very clear, and detailed enough for most purposes but not for off-the-beaten-track adventuring; also published in atlas form with large-scale maps of tourist areas.

If you're doing more in Africa than visiting Kenya alone, you probably want one or more of the **Michelin** series, nos. 953, 954 or 955, still the best all-purpose travel maps for Africa. Kenya comes out small at this scale but with surprising detail.

MAGAZINES AND PERIODICALS

Worthwhile Africa-centred magazines, worth checking through for news before you go, and not likely to be available once you're there, include the following:

Africa Confidential, Miramoor Publications, 73 Farringdon Rd, London EC1M 3JB (☎0171/831-3511). Fortnightly eight-page newsletter with solid inside info. Subscription only.

African Business, IC Publications, 7 Coldbath Sq, London EC1R 4LQ (☎0171/713-7711). Good general coverage.

BBC Focus on Africa, Bush House, PO Box 76, Strand, London WC2B 4PH (☎0171/379-0519 or 257-2906). News, general-interest features, and information from the *BBC World Service*.

New African, IC Publications, 7 Coldbath Square, London EC1R 4LQ (☎0171/713-7711). Another in the IC stable, this is a news and lifestyle magazine after the style of the French *Jeune Afrique*, with quarterly special supplements.

Safara, Goldcity Communications, suite F11, Shakespeare Business Centre, 245A Coldharbour Lane, London SW9 8RR (☎0171/737-5933). Quarterly round-up of news aimed at those with business interests in Africa.

KENYA ON LINE

Early 1996 saw three major launches of full Internet services in Kenya – Africa Online, Formnet and KenStream – and a number of businesses in the travel industry are already using E-mail. There is also now an Internet café in Nairobi. As for what you can learn about Kenya from surfing the Worldwide Web, the picture is not a very

exciting one. Many sites lead to each other, rather than to new sites, and this is particularly true where much of the site consists of links. Nevertheless, if you have Internet access, it's well worth clicking away at the Web sites listed below. Also look at two news groups, **rec.travel.africa** and **soc.culture.kenya**, which are genuinely useful information forums and good sources for new Web sites.

http://www.robin.no/~erte/ken-links.htm
Lots of links.

http://www.lawrence.edu/~bradleyc/ kenya.html
Dozens of links from this site, called "Buibui".

http://www.fco.gov.uk/reference/ travel_advice/kenya.txt
British Foreign Office latest advice. Never to be ignored, but always inadequate.

http://www.stolaf.edu/network/travel- advisories.html
US State Department's travel advice. Cautious and long-winded, but you feel you're getting nanny's full concern.

http://www.africaonline.co.ke/AfricaOnline/ index.html
Nicely packaged in the USA, but with a slightly official feel ("Kenya is a stable and peaceful country . . ."). Excellent music info.

http://www.rcbowen.com/kenya/
Tends to be a bit out of date, but has useful information.

http://www.spidergraphics.com/khr/ khrld.html

Follow the case of prisoner of conscience Koigi wa Wamwere. A quick course in the current condition of human rights in Kenya.

http://www.africaonline.co.ke/AfricaOnline/music.html

Excellent introduction to Kenyan pop music and some of the current clubs and bands.

http://members.gnn.com/dpaterson/eamusic.htm
Another good site for Kenya music fans.

GETTING AROUND

A quick reference round-up of regional travel details is given at the end of each chapter. Details refer both to routes within the chapter and to routes from towns covered in the chapter to places in other chapters. Hence, for example, details of getting to the coast are covered in the Nairobi chapter. Bus and train telephone booking numbers are also given.

BUSES, MATATUS AND TAXIS

There's a whole range of vehicles on Kenya's roads. Alongside the flashy **"video coaches"** tearing up one or two of the main highways, you'll find smaller **"country bus"** companies operating a single battered Leyland. In towns of any size, a whole crowd of **minibuses**, **pick-up vans** and **Peugeot taxis** hustle for business constantly. The transport scene is a screaming hive of confusion, but somehow you'll always arrive.

Fares vary a great deal according to the competition and the condition of the road. There is also great variation on fares between the speed and comfort of a Peugeot 504 station wagon and the grinding progress of a clapped-out country bus. But fares in the latter type of vehicle can still be less than Ksh2 per kilometre and shouldn't be above Ksh3 per kilometre in a Peugeot except on short routes. This means that most journeys of up to a day in length will cost under £8 ($12) and quite often half this. Rarely will anyone attempt to charge you more than the going rate. **Baggage charges** are usually supplementary, however, and have to be bargained over. Never pay more than half your fare for luggage – it should be a lot less – and always talk to other passengers to find out how much they paid.

It is worth considering your general **direction** through the trip and which side will be shadier. This is especially important on dirt roads when the combination of a slow, bumpy ride, dust and fierce sun through closed windows can be horrible.

URBAN TRANSPORT

Nairobi and Mombasa have the municipally run **Kenya Bus Services** (*KBS*) and city **taxis**. The taxis are about the only means of getting around late at night, but always settle on a fare before getting in because the meters hardly ever work.

BUSES
Ordinary **buses** cover the whole country, getting you close to almost anywhere. Some, on the main runs between Nairobi and Mombasa, and to a lesser extent the west, are fast, comfortable and keep to schedules: you generally need to **reserve** seats on these **a day in advance**. The large companies – in particular *Akamba Public Road Services* – have ticket offices near the bus stations in most towns, where they list their routes and prices. But their parking bays are

rarely marked and there are no published time-tables. The easiest procedure is to mention your destination to a few people at the bus park and then check out the torrent of offers. Keep asking – it's virtually impossible to get on the wrong bus. Once you've acquired a seat, the wait can be almost a pleasure if you're in no hurry; as you watch the throng outside and field a continuous stream of vendors proffering wares through the window. (If you want something, ask one of them to get it for you; there'll be a tiny mark-up.)

MATATUS

Public vehicles at the smaller end of the spectrum have a gruesome safety record and their drivers, on the whole, a breathtaking lack of road sense; this is especially true of **matatus** – usually pick-up vans fitted with wooden benches and a canvas roof (for some comments on accident statistics see "Driving in Kenya", p.41). But *matatus* are often the most convenient and sometimes the only means of transport to smaller places off the main roads. If there's any choice, take a larger vehicle – Nissans are the best – even if this means a longer wait for places to fill. Be warned, however, that *matatu* minibuses tend to have low windows, so you don't get much of a view. Best are the small, **25-seater coaches** which are fairly roomy and have good visibility.

Some of the *matatus* are clearly falling apart: they break down often and travel terrifyingly fast when they're able to. But on occasions they can be an enjoyable way of getting about, giving you close contact (literally) with local people, and some hilarious encounters. The best places in a *matatu* are right at the back by the door or up near the cab, but it's a good idea to wear sunglasses if your face is near a front window – they sometimes shatter.

Some *matatu* **terminology**: "stage" or "stand" – the *matatu* yard; *manamba* or "turn-boy" – the one whose job it is to tout for business, take the fares and hang on dramatically to the back; "dropping" – what you do when you're getting off, as in "I am dropping here".

TAXIS

Peugeot taxis – faster, more comfortable, business-like and expensive – usually drive directly from one point to another with a full complement of passengers. This should consist of one passenger in the front (who sometimes pays a supple-ment), three in the middle and three in the back. Any more and they're overloaded and will be stopped by the police all along the route, paying in bribes any extra fares they may have collected.

Always choose a vehicle that's full and about to leave or you'll have to wait inside until they are ready to go – sometimes for hours. Beware of being used as bait by the driver to encourage passengers to choose his car. Competition is intense and people will lie unashamedly to persuade you the vehicle is going "just now".

In particular, don't hand over any money before you set off; or, if the taxi does get going, wait until you've left town. This isn't a question of being ripped off (though discreetly noting the licence plate of the vehicle is never a bad idea), but too often the first departure is just a cruise around town rounding up passengers and buying petrol (with your money) and then back to square one.

If your destination doesn't lie on a standard shared taxi route, or if you don't want to wait for a car to fill up (or, indeed, if you just want to travel in style), drivers will happily negotiate a price for the rental of their whole car. This will normally be the same as the sum total of the fares they would receive from a full complement of paying passengers over an equivalent distance.

TRAINS

Although the **railways** aren't used a great deal by travellers, an extremely popular exception is the **Nairobi–Mombasa run**. This is a travelling experience in its own right and one of the world's great railway journeys.

The trains run once a day in each direction, leaving with perfect punctuality at 7pm, and arriving anytime between 8am and 10am the following morning. Frustrating though the (almost routine) delays can be, they at least mean you're likely to have at least a couple of hours of morning light to watch the passing scene: approaching Nairobi, the animals on the Athi Plains; approaching Mombasa, the sultry crawl down from the Taru Desert to the ocean.

There are some other **branch lines**, including two lines to the west, to Malaba on the Uganda border and Kisumu on Lake Victoria, the latter now reconnected to the Uganda line to Kampala. Thanks to lack of investment the Kisumu line is notoriously unreliable, but it's relatively cheap, and some of the views are remarkable. The line

NAIROBI–MOMBASA TRAIN RESERVATIONS

It's important to **make reservations** for the trains, especially if you want a first-class compartment. While it may be fine to leave this until a couple of hours before departure during the low season, it's advisable to reserve well in advance if you plan to travel during the busy Christmas and New Year period when trains are often full. Ticket offices at the stations in Mombasa (☎011/312221) and Nairobi (☎02/221211) are open mornings and afternoons, and will take reservations weeks ahead. **Travel agents** will usually do the work for you, sometimes for a fairly hefty supplement. A number of overseas agents will handle first-class train reservations, too, though you can expect to pay a little more. To travel first-class, you have to take a private two-berth compartment. Second-class compartments are shared by four people and are single-sex, though, with the consent of the occupants, this can sometimes be disregarded. The third-class carriages have seats rather than bunks.

Fares are Ksh2750 first-class, Ksh1930 second-class and Ksh330 third-class (all one-way). The first- and second-class fares include pre-paid dinner, breakfast and bedding vouchers. An attendant will make up your bed while you are in the dining car for dinner, and will clear the bedding away during breakfast. Both dinner and breakfast are hearty cooked meals, and eating in the dining car is an experience in itself, but don't expect *haute cuisine*. Wine, beer and sodas cost extra. If you buy from *Kenya Railways* direct you can elect to pay just for your berth.

Note that you can't normally reserve Mombasa–Nairobi berths in Nairobi (and vice versa).

Couples thinking of travelling first-class should note a couple of other things: that first-class compartments have rather small windows, compared with second class; and secondly that it's quite possible to book a whole second-class compartment for two adults and two children (a popular trick, as the children only pay half-fare), but if the children are not present when the ticket inspector makes his rounds, be prepared for the mother of all arguments.

---

cuts through the Nairobi slums, a memorable sight in themselves. Taking the train to Nakuru over the fantastic escarpment route is worthwhile too, since it leaves Nairobi at 3pm and the food is rated better than on the Mombasa line. There are also two small branch lines with infrequent services in the south: one down to Lake Magadi from Konza (mostly freight), the other from Voi to Taveta on the Tanzanian border (now reconnected to Moshi). Some maps mark **misleading branch lines**: Kitale, Thika and Nyahururu no longer have passenger services.

PLANES

Kenya has a number of reasonably priced **internal air services** and it's well worth seeing the country from the eagle's point of view at least once. There are details of schedules and fares at the end of each chapter. Daily flights on *Kenya Airways* from Jomo Kenyatta Airport connect **Nairobi** to Kisumu, Mombasa and Malindi. There are several flights daily from Wilson Airport to the Maasai Mara lodges, Malindi, Lamu and Kiwaiyu, among other destinations. Occasionally,

you can pick up non-scheduled flights at Wilson by being rightly placed and timed – to towns in the northern deserts, for example – and you might even hitch a ride if you're persuasive.

Along the **coast**, *Eagle Aviation* and *Air Kenya Aviation* are the recommended carriers, with daily scheduled flights between Mombasa, Malindi and Lamu (details in Chapter 6) and between Nairobi and the coast and the main national parks. The flight from Lamu to Malindi/ Mombasa is an exotic and exhilarating one over reefs and jungle. Airlines' details are given in the appropriate town "listings".

Baggage allowances on internal flights, apart from *Kenya Airways*, are usually under 20kg and may be as little as 10kg. Fortunately the excess baggage charges are nominal. There is an airport tax of Ksh100 on all domestic flights.

Lastly, note that ordinary **connecting times** shouldn't be relied on if you're flying to catch an international departure. Many of the cheaper flight tickets to Europe cannot be endorsed to another airline if you miss your flight and domestic services are often delayed.

FERRIES

Travel **by boat**, in a country with few large rivers, is rarely a functional way of getting around. On the coast, the only regular ferries of any importance are those connecting the islands of the Lamu archipelago and sporadic services between Mombasa and Zanzibar. On Lake Victoria, which used to have a network of steamer routes, the only regular local services are the small ferries, operated by *Kenya Railways*, which churn around the Winam Gulf and out to a couple of the islands. After an eighteen-year suspension, the international passenger steamer service between Mwanza (Tanzania), Kisumu (Kenya) and Port Bell (Uganda) was resumed in early 1996. Some commercial vessels will also take passengers across the lake.

HITCHING

This is how the majority of rural people get around – by **waving down a vehicle** – but they invariably pay, whether it's a bus, a *matatu*, a lorry or a private vehicle with a spare place. Private vehicles, except on the main Kisumu–Nairobi–Mombasa artery and one or two through routes, are comparatively rare and usually full. Because of the cheapness of buses, travellers don't try it much, but hitching can be a good change of pace, enabling you to cover distances fast and usually in safety. Along the coast, where there are relatively fewer *matatus* and more private cars, it's often easy. More calculatingly, if you're on a low budget, hitching rides with private cars can throw you in with Asians and Europeans, often resulting in opportunities to visit national parks and reserves.

Hitching **techniques** need to be fairly exuberant; a modest thumb is more likely to be interpreted as a friendly, or even rude, gesture than a request for a lift. Beckon the driver to stop with your palm. And if you can't afford to pay, say so right away; generosity will often provide you a lift anyway.

CAR RENTAL AND DRIVING

Renting a car has advantages over any other means of transport which make it seriously worth considering for a week or two. All the parks and reserves are open to private and rented vehicles (as well as organized tours), and there's a lot to be said for the freedom of choice that having your own wheels gives you. Unless there are more than two of you, though, it won't save you money over one of the cheaper camping safaris. You're also required to leave a hefty deposit, roughly equivalent to the anticipated bill. Credit cards are useful for this.

CHOOSING A VEHICLE

Four-wheel-drive (4WD) **Suzuki Jeeps** are the most widely available vehicles and they make ideal safari transport: light, rugged and capable of amazing feats of negotiation. Don't expect them to top more than their legal limit of 80kph (50mph), however, and beware their notorious tendency to fall over on bends or on the dangerously sloping gravel hard shoulders that line many Kenyan roads. Long-wheel-base Suzukis, with luggage space behind the rear seats, three doors and enough room for four, or five at a pinch, are more stable and easier to drive. It would be wise to avoid driving a Mitsubishi Pajero at present: they are much in demand in Somalia and there's a risk of hijack.

Petrol (gasoline) costs about Ksh30 per litre. You should get between 12km per litre and 15km per litre out of a Suzuki fuel tank (which holds about 38 litres, or about 8.5 US gallons). That's around 33mpg (US) or 38mpg (imperial). It's not difficult to run out of petrol, so keep topping up. All towns and villages (except the very smallest) have petrol for sale but if you're intending to do a lot of driving in a remote area you should definitely carry spare fuel in cans.

Renting a car is often cheaper by the week if you do enough kilometres, and many firms are prepared to negotiate a little as well, especially off season. Reckon on driving an average of 1000 kilometres per week (around 600–700 miles).

There are one or two car-rental places in the smaller towns and along the coast but the only real choice is in Nairobi and Mombasa. The minimum age is usually 23. Foreign driving licences are OK for up to three months; you're supposed to have them validated at a provincial headquarters, but few people seem to bother. Check the insurance details and always pay the daily **collision damage waiver** premium: even a small bump could be very costly otherwise.

Don't automatically assume the vehicle is roadworthy: have a good look at the engine and tyres, and don't set off without checking the spare (preferably two) and making sure you have a few vital tools. Ideally, always carry a tow rope, *panga* (a multi-purpose small machete), spare water and fuel.

Four-wheel drive (4WD) is always useful but, except in mountainous areas and on some of the marginal dirt roads during periods of heavy rain, not essential. However, few, if any agencies will hire out non-4WD vehicles for use in the parks, and most park rangers will turn away such cars at the gate, regardless of season. This does depend on the park: Maasai Mara and the mountain parks (Mount Elgon, Mount Kenya and the Aberdares) are the most safety-minded.

DRIVING IN KENYA

A **useful book** for driving around Kenya, which has some good routes and lots of useful detail, is *On Safari* by Phillippe Oberlé (widely available in Kenya, about Ksh700).

When **driving**, beware of unexpected rocks and ditches – and animals and people – on the road; it's accepted practice to honk your horn stridently to warn pedestrians. Kenya drives on the left, though in reality vehicles often keep to the best part of the road until they have to pass each other.

Driving-test examiners aren't incorruptible and Kenya's **accident statistics** are horrifying. Counting the casualties is a national obsession: there was recently a campaign – miserably failed – to keep the annual death toll below 2000. Police records currently suggest that an average of eight to nine people die on Kenya's roads every day. To put some perspective on this, there are 48,000 road deaths per year in the USA, but also ten times as many people (and only a small fraction of Kenya's population regularly use vehicles or go near busy roads).

Beware of "**speed bumps**". Occasionally you'll see a sign like "Rumble strips ahead", but more usually the first you'll know of them is when your head hits the roof. They are found both in rural areas, wherever a busy road has been built through a village, and on the roads in and out of nearly every large town. Since they cause such destruction and render vehicles unsafe, it seems likely they are responsible for more lives lost than saved.

On the question of **driving etiquette**, it's common practice to flash oncoming vehicles, and to signal right to indicate your width and deter drivers behind you from overtaking. You may find both practices disconcerting at first. Left-hand signals are used to say "Please overtake" but you shouldn't assume the driver in front can really see. In fact, never assume anything about other drivers.

Driving at night is to be avoided, especially in a Suzuki, as its lights are hopeless (though remember if you've been off the road and you can't seem to see ten metres in front, your head-lamps may be caked in mud). Be especially careful when passing heavy vehicles, and even more so when passing lorries groaning uphill: sometimes a line of them churning out diesel fumes

---

BOOKING CAR RENTAL IN ADVANCE

It's quite easy to book a vehicle before you even set foot in Kenya, pay for it at home, then pick it up when you arrive. It costs very much more to do this than tracking down a good deal locally – and prices are extremely variable – but if time is short (or money no object) you may find it preferable.

UK
Avis ☎0181/848-8733.
Europcar ☎0345/222525.
Hertz ☎0181/679-1799.

IRELAND
Avis ☎01232/240404.
Europcar ☎01232/450904 or 423444.
Hertz ☎01/660-2255.

US AND CANADA
Avis ☎1-800/331-1084.
Hertz in US ☎1-800/654-3001; in Canada ☎1-800/263-0600.
National ☎1-800/CAR-RENT.

AUSTRALIA
Avis, Level 2, 15 Bourke Rd, Mascot, NSW (toll-free ☎1800/225533).
Hertz, 10 Dorcas St, South Melbourne (local-call rate ☎13 19 18).

NEW ZEALAND
Avis, Building 4, 666 Great South Rd, Penrose, Auckland (☎09/525-1982).
Hertz, 154 Victoria St West, Auckland (☎09/309-0989).

can cut off your visibility without warning – extremely dangerous on a narrow mountain road.

On most of the main paved highways you can make good time, but as soon as you leave them, **journey times** are very unpredictable. We've tried to give some idea of road conditions in various places throughout the book, but they can change radically in half a year. The north and highland regions are the worst, particularly during periods of heavy rain when districts may become virtually cut off. In 1993 a study funded by the World Bank concluded that the increase in vehicle operation costs (due to wear on vehicles, wasted petrol on tortuous routes, etc) resulting from the disrepair of many of Kenya's roads totalled three times Kenya's shortfall in road maintenance expenditure.

Signposting in Kenya, while generally useful, is haphazard – especially on dirt roads. If a junction appears to lack a sign, it's assumed you'll keep to the busiest track.

Should you have the misfortune to have a **breakdown** on the road, or an **accident**, the first thing to do is pile **bundles of sticks or foliage** fifty metres or so behind and in front of the car. These are the universally recognized "red warning triangles" of Africa, and their placing is always scrupulously observed (as is the wedging of a stone behind at least one wheel). When you have a puncture, as you will, get it mended straight away – it costs very little (Ksh50–60) and can be done almost anywhere there are vehicles. Local mechanics are usually very good and can apply creative ingenuity to the most disastrous situations. But spare parts, tools and proper equipment are rare off the main routes. Always settle on a price before the work begins. And beware of scams and con-artists: the "oil leak" under your parked car still catches many people out (see p.202).

Parking in towns, you should obviously never leave your vehicle with anything of value in it. That said, finding somewhere to park is rarely a problem, even in Nairobi or Mombasa. There are parking metres in both cities: if you get a ticket (fines are nominal), it's reasonable to take it, and the money, back to the car-rental company and they will settle it.

Being **stopped by the police** – even when they can see you're likely to be a tourist – is becoming increasingly common: one or two regular checkpoints are mentioned in the text. Checkpoints are generally marked by low strips of spikes across the road with just enough room to slalom round. You should always stop if signalled. The usual reason given is that you were speeding (and they do indeed have one or two radar traps), but that is not why they stop cars. Don't reach into your purse: apologize; agree that it's a pity you will have to go to court; and wait to be sent on your way with a caution (court appearances are just work for all concerned). It's worth knowing that you may be asked to produce evidence that your rented car has a **PSV licence** as a "passenger service vehicle". You should have a windscreen sticker for this and you're strongly advised to check it out with the company before you leave.

BUYING A CAR SECOND-HAND

Lastly, if you're going to be in Kenya for some time, or you're planning to travel more widely, **buying** a second-hand vehicle in Nairobi, though prices are inflated, is a realistic possibility if you're confident about engines. Rental companies sometimes have vehicles to dispose of, and the *Nation* and *Standard* carry lots of ads. The *Sarit Centre* in Nairobi has a weekly used-car sale, on Sunday mornings, and you can sell back fairly easily in Nairobi.

CYCLING

Kenya's climate and varied terrain make it challenging **bicycling** country. If it appeals to you – whether you're a lycra-laminated pro or just use a bike once in a while – it's one of the best ways of getting around. With a bike, given time and average determination, you can get to parts of the country that would be hard to visit by any other means except perhaps on foot. And what would take several days to hike can be cycled in a matter of hours. It's also one way you will get to see wildlife outside the confines of the game parks. For details about inclusive cycling tours see p.11.

BUYING LOCALLY

These days it's quite easy to buy a half-decent **mountain bike** in Nairobi, as well as the traditional old-fashioned 28-inch **roadsters** from India. If you buy one of these three-speed heavyweights in Nairobi (see p.118) you can then sell it at the end of your trip. There's a ready market for second-hand ones, which doesn't exist to anything like the same extent for fancy machines.

BIKES BY AIR

Bringing your own bicycle by air is easier than it might at first appear. As long as it's a lightweight machine and you keep your baggage weight down, you needn't go much above 20kg – and it's remarkable how much weight you can get in a small bag as cabin luggage. Airlines are unpredictable about bicycles, sometimes making an exception of them, other times scrupulously charging one percent of the first-class fare for every kilo overweight. It's worth asking them – though they'll usually just give you the rule book – and checking if there are any packing requirements for your bike.

Few airlines will insist your bike be boxed or bagged. But it's best to turn the handlebars into the frame and tie them down, invert the pedals and deflate the tyres. Probably the most helpful airline for bikes (so long as you don't take them for granted) is *KLM*.

You should do everything to facilitate your transit from check-in desk to plane: write in advance to the ground operations manager of the airline and arrive several hours before the flight to get to know the check-in staff. It's rare that you'll be obliged to pay.

It's much harder, as a rule, to avoid excess fees on charter flights. Let them know in advance and plead your case. The 20kg weight allowance, which your bike and luggage is likely to exceed, is a notional figure, with no bearing on air safety, used to extract more profit from the passengers.

PRACTICAL CONSIDERATIONS

Whatever you take – and a mountain bike is certainly best – it will need low gears and strongly built wheels and you should have some essential **spare parts**.

If you're taking a bike with you, then you'll probably want to carry your gear in **panniers**. These are fiendishly inconvenient when not attached to the bike, however, and you might consider sacrificing ideal load-bearing and streamlining technology for a backpack you can lash down on the rear carrier. An arrangement like this is probably what you'll have to do if you buy a bike in Kenya. With light wood, or the kind of cane used to make cane furniture, plus lashings of inner tube rubber strips you can create your own highly unaerodynamic **carrier**, with room for a box of food and a gallon of water underneath.

With a bike from home, take a battery **lighting system** (dynamo lighting is a pain) – it's surprising how often you'll need it. The front light doubles as a torch and getting the large-sized U2 batteries is no problem.

Also take a **U-bolt cycle lock**. In situations where you have to lock the bike, you'll always find something to lock it to. Out in the bush it's less important. Local bikes can be locked with a padlock and chain in a length of hosepipe which you can buy and fix up in any market.

If you have a sympathetic local bike shop, you might consider leaving a deposit with them so they could send you spare parts if and when necessary. A combination of fax and courier service could get them to you in a couple of days.

Cycling won't restrict your travel options. Buses and *matatus* with roof-racks will always **carry** bicycles for about half-fare – even if flagged down at the roadside – and trucks will often give a lift. The trains take bikes, too, at a low fixed rate.

You need to consider the **seasons** however; you won't make much progress on dirt roads during the rains when chain sets and brakes become totally jammed with sticky mud.

Obviously, you also need to be cautious when **cycling on main roads**. A mirror is essential and, if the pavement is broken at the edge, give yourself plenty of space and be ready to leave the road if necessary. That said, cycle tourists are still a novelty in Kenya: drivers often slow down to look and you'll rarely be run off the road.

OUTDOOR ACTIVITIES

Kenya is a country with huge untapped potential for outdoor activities. Safaris are covered in a separate section further on. The following brief notes suggest the possibilities for walking, riding, fishing, diving, climbing, caving and rafting. Cycling is covered in the previous section and under "Getting there from Britain and Ireland".

WALKING

Walking, if you have plenty of time and the relevant Survey of Kenya maps, is highly recommended and gives you unparalleled contact with local people. In isolated parts, it's often preferable to waiting for a lift, while in the Aberdares, Mau and Cherangani ranges, and on Mounts Kenya and Elgon, it's the only practical way of moving away from the main tracks. You will sometimes come across animals out in the bush, but buffalo and elephant, unless solitary or with young, usually move off. Don't ignore the dangers, however, and stay alert. *Mountain Walking in Kenya*, by David Else (McCarta, UK; ISBN 1853052059) is a useful book. For walking you will need to carry several litres of water much of the time (which means several *kilos*), especially in lower, drier regions.

Before plunging off into the bush, though, you might prefer to go on an organized walking safari, at least as a starter. Walking safaris are offered by a number of safari companies in Nairobi (see p.118).

RIDING

There are good **riding opportunities** in the Central Highlands and an active equestrian community in Nairobi. *Safaris Unlimited* (address on p.120) offer riding safaris near the Maasai Mara National Reserve.

Camel safaris are popular too, though the best operators to contact tend to change from year to year. Contact any of the addresses under "Special Activity Safaris" on p.119.

FISHING

Many of the highlands' streams are well stocked with **trout**, which were imported early this century by the settlers. A few local fishing associations are still active and the usual rules about seasons and licences apply. *Naro Moru River Lodge* and the *Izaac Walton Inn* in Embu offer rods for hire. The Fisheries Department headquarters, next to the National Museum in Nairobi, can supply details. For **lake fishing**, it's possible to rent rods and boats at Lakes Baringo, Naivasha and Turkana, and there are luxury fishing lodges on Rusinga, Mfangano and Takawiri islands on Lake Victoria. The **Indian Ocean** offers excellent sport fishing opportunities: enthusiasts have the chance to land an impressive tally of species including sailfish, marlin, swordfish, barracuda and shark. Kenya's superb stretch of off-shore coral reef, with its deepwater drop-offs and predictable northerly currents, is ideal for near-shore angling. Watamu, Malindi and the resorts around Mombasa are the most popular centres for ocean fishing.

DIVING

Kenya's coastal waters are warm all year round so it's possible to **dive** without a wetsuit. Most of the diving bases are located at Malindi, Watamu or on the coast south of Mombasa; Diani Beach is probably the most popular area. There are centres here which will provide training to PADI leader level (for details see Chapter 6). For underwater photographers, in particular, the immense coral reef is a major draw – the landscape is spectacularly varied, with shallow coral gardens and blue-water drop-offs sinking as deep as 200m, and, as there are few rivers to bring down sediment, visibility is generally excellent.

CLIMBING

Apart from **Mount Kenya**, there are climbing opportunities at all grades in the **Aberdares**, **Cheranganis**, **Mathews Range**, **Hell's Gate** and **Rift Valley volcanoes** – including Longonot and Suswa. If you have time to get acquainted with it, the Mountain Club of Kenya (PO Box 45741 Nairobi; club house at Wilson Airport; club nights Tues 8pm; ☎02/501747) is a good source of advice and **contacts**, not just for climbing, but for outdoor pursuits in general. If you intend to do any serious climbing in the country, you should make early contact in writing. Don't expect them to answer detailed route questions, however;

leave that until you arrive. If you want to go climbing with a guide, safari companies in Nairobi offer everything from a simple hike to technical ascents of Batian and Nelion (see p.119).

CAVING

Caving, which has a large following – and a tremendous amount of material – in Kenya, is organized around the Cave Exploration Group of East Africa, whose address is *Kenya Caverns and Lodges*, PO Box 47363 Nairobi, Kenya). Avid cavers arriving in Nairobi can also contact its "Caving Equipment Officer" on ☎02/582257.

RAFTING

Both the **Tana and Athi rivers** have sections which can be rafted when they're in spate. Approximate dates are November 1 to March 15 and April 15 to August 31. *Savage Wilderness Safaris* is the main operator (p.120) and most trips are for one day only.

ACCOMMODATION

Accommodation in Kenya exhibits a fine diversity, ranging from campsites and local lodging houses for a pound or two a night to genuinely excellent, luxury hotels costing fifty or a hundred times as much. Beds can also be found in "tented camps" and "tree hotels" at the expensive end of the spectrum and *bandas* and a clutch of youth hostels at the budget end.

BOARDING AND LODGINGS

In any town, down to the very smallest, you'll always find **Boarding & Lodgings** (for which we've coined the abbreviation "B&Ls"). These can vary from a mud shack with water from the well, to a little multi-storey building of self-contained rooms ("s/c") with washing facilities, a bar and restaurant. B&Ls tend to be noisy; they're sometimes rather airless and often double unofficially as brothels, but the better ones are clean and comfortable.

Prices of rooms aren't always a good indication of the standard. Always try to bargain for a good price. It's worth checking several places, testing the hot water (if any), and asking to see the toilets; you won't cause offence by saying no thanks. Some places actually seal the doors of rooms as a supposed guarantee of freshness: if they won't let you look because they'd have to reseal, we suggest you move on. And if the place seems noisy in the afternoon, it will probably become cacophonous during the night, so ask for a room away from the source of the din.

Boarding & Lodgings are covered in some detail through the regional chapters; there's nearly always at least one good example in every town. As yet, there isn't an official body to represent them or to set standards and prices.

If you're driving, some lodgings have lock-up yards where you can park – an important consideration unless you bring all your equipment into the room.

HOTELS

More **expensive hotels** are a variable commodity. At the top end of the range are the big tourist establishments, many in one of the country's four or five chains. In the game parks, they are known as **lodges**. Some establishments are extremely good value: a night in a good hotel can be tremendously fortifying if you're usually roughing it. Others are shabby and overpriced, so check carefully before splurging. If possible you should try to reserve the more popular establishments in advance (see box below), especially for the busiest season from December to February. As a rule expect to pay anything from Ksh1000 to Ksh 8000

ACCOMMODATION PRICE CODES

Most accommodation rates in this guide have been price-coded according to the categories below. The prices indicated are non-resident rates for standard **double or twin rooms**. For dormitory accommodation and hostels (which charge per person), exact prices have been given where possible.

Where there are **seasonal differences**, as in some park lodges and in all tourist- or luxury-class accommodation on the coast, the high- and low-season price codes are given. All Nairobi hotels, most up-country hotels and most places in the ①–④ categories have non-seasonal tariffs.

Cheap hotels quote their rates in **Kenya shillings**, while hotels in categories ⑤ and above still tend to quote their rates in **dollars**. You should still be able to pay at these establishments in Ksh, although often at an inferior rate of exchange.

Special rates for **Kenya residents** (typically discounts of 15–30 percent) are offered at some establishments in category ④ and above.

Facilities in each category are as follows, unless otherwise specified in the guide's reviews. The rates of exchange used in the following conversions are approximately Ksh90 to £1 and Ksh60 to $1.

① Under Ksh300 (under approx. £3.30/$5): very basic B&L with shared facilities (ie non-s/c)

② Ksh300–500 (£3.30/$5–£5.50/$8): B&L with elementary comforts, non-s/c

③ Ksh500–1000 (£5.50/$8–£11/$17): B&L or cheap hotel with some s/c rooms; B&B basis

④ Ksh1000–2000 (£11/$17–£22/$33): adequate hotel with s/c rooms; B&B

⑤ Ksh2000–4000 (£22/$33–£44/$67): mid-range local hotel or modest tourist-class hotel; B&B

⑥ Ksh4000–6000 (£44/$67–£67/$100): tourist-class hotel; FB

⑦ Ksh6000–8000 (£67/$100–£89/$133): luxury hotels and lodges; FB

⑧ Ksh8000–10,000 (£89/$133–£111/$167): luxury hotels and lodges with special facilities; FB

⑨ Over Ksh10,000 (over £111/$167): as preceding category

for a double or twin, and not much less for a single occupancy (except in the low season). Out of the towns, lodges in the top price brackets are normally quoted on a full-board basis, and prices can go right into orbit. Most of these hotels cut their prices in the low season, April–June (see "Seasons" box, p.26), and many have much lower rates for Kenyan residents (sometimes citizens) which you might get if you're convincing. Look in

the newspapers, especially *The Standard*, for some excellent deals advertised from time to time.

Between the hotels featured in the glossy brochures and the cheap lodging houses come all the **medium-priced**, middle-class places. Some of them were once slightly grand, others are old settlers' haunts that don't fit modern Kenya, and some newer ones are catering for the black

ACCOMMODATION TERMS AND ABBREVIATIONS

AC – air-conditioned, usually only on the coast.

banda – basically a thatched cottage or chalet, sometimes round and dubbed "rondavel", generally cheap, occasionally furnished into upmarket "bush" accommodation for tourists.

B&B – bed and breakfast.

B&L – a Boarding and Lodging house.

cube – sometimes used to refer to a small room in a B&L.

FB – full board, meaning all meals included.

HB – half board, meaning dinner, bed & breakfast.

hoteli – a cheap restaurant or greasy spoon rarely a hotel.

lodge – designer hotel or country house, usually in the game parks.

long-drop – self-explanatory; the kind of non-flushing toilet found in some B&Ls, and in most *bandas* and campsites.

s/c – "self-contained", with private shower and toilet.

tented camp – hotel in the bush, or in a game park, using large tents and *bandas*, often with all the usual hotel facilities plumbed into a solid bathroom at the back.

tree hotel – an animal-viewing hotel in the trees, or on stilts, after the style of *Treetops*.

middle class. A few are fine – delightfully decrepit or bristlingly smart and efficient. Most are boozy and uninteresting; it adds more colour to your travels to mix the cheapest lodgings with the occasional night of luxury.

COTTAGES, VILLAS AND HOMESTAYS

Increasingly, it's possible to book **self-catering apartments, villas or cottages**, especially on the coast. *Kenya Villas*, Westminster House, Kenyatta Ave, Nairobi (PO Box 57046; ☎02/338041, fax 02/338072), and *Holiday Homes Ltd*, ABC Place, Waiyaki Way, Westlands (PO Box 10723; ☎02/444052, fax 02/444053), are agents for a wide range of holiday homes. Try writing, but they may need a phone call. Another style of accommodation on the increase is **homestays** – inclusive accommodation in a (usually Anglo-Kenyan) household in the countryside. Meals and drinks are generally part of the package, and excursions and safaris with generous helpings of local insight, or occasionally prejudice, are optional. *Let's Go Travel* (address p.122) have details of some.

YOUTH HOSTELS

Disappointingly, Kenya's **youth hostels** are few indeed. Nairobi's youth hostel is the only one that really rates in international terms. It's affiliated to the International Youth Hostel Association (IYHA), and is well run and very popular. Non-members normally have to join the association first. This hostel, and the one at Mount Kenya, can be booked from outside Kenya through the IYHA (in the UK, call ☎01727/855215 for information; in Canada ☎613/237-7884 or 1-800/663-5777, in the US ☎202/783-6161, in Australia ☎02/565 1325, in New Zealand ☎03/379 9970). The "YMCA" at Lake Naivasha is perennially popular and always a nice place to stay, and there's a "youth hostel" at *Fisherman's Camp*, also by the lake. There are **YMCAs** and **YWCAs** in Kisumu, Nairobi and Mombasa, and church-run hostels and dormitories in a number of small towns including Kikambala, Makindu, Maralal and Nanyuki. In these, the atmosphere can be a cloying contrast to the sleazier lodging houses.

CAMPING

While a **tent** is dead weight whenever you sleep in a hotel, Kenya has enough campsites to make it worthwhile carrying one, and camping rough is

very often a viable option, too. Bring the lightest tent you can afford or consider **making your own**. A few weekends with a sewing machine, rip-stop nylon and some netting should see the job done: make a scale model in paper first, and test the tent under wet conditions before taking it to Kenya. Camping in the rain doesn't make much sense (whatever the protection, you're likely to get wet); the main point of a tent is to keep insects out, but it's still good to be protected against unexpected showers. Nylon netting with a sewn-in groundsheet is the basic tent. A rip-stop nylon fly sheet adds privacy. Outside poles back and front can be used for guys and tension, but you'll probably resort to trees if there are any.

If you'd rather **buy a tent**, the best are made by The North Face (Scotland) Ltd, PO Box 16, Industrial Estate, Port Glasgow, PA14 5XL (☎0475/741344). Their US address is 2013 Farallon Drive, San Leandro, CA 94577 (☎510/618-3500). They manufacture a range of craftily designed lightweight tents making extensive use of "no-see-um" mosquito netting, providing excellent ventilation, total insect protection and all-round visibility when the fly sheet is off.

CAMPSITES AND CAMPING ROUGH

Campsites, wherever they exist, are mentioned in the main body of the guide and listed in the index. Those in the parks are usually very cheap and equally basic. The mysterious "special campsites" in a number of parks, are, in reality, simply restricted sites which you can reserve on an exclusive basis for private use – and they cost a lot more. Some of them are especially attractive – so they draw film crews and the like – but they are all quite devoid of facilities. To book them, either write to the warden enclosing a cheque or visit/write to Special Campsite Reservations, Kenya Wildlife Service, Langata Rd, PO Box 40241 Nairobi (☎02/501081): this office is one of those right by Nairobi National Park main gate. On top of the flat advance booking fee of Ksh5000, you have to pay daily camping charges at the prevailing rates (see box on p.61).

A handful of privately owned sites have more in the way of facilities. In rural areas, hotels are often amenable if you ask to camp discreetly in their grounds.

Camping rough depends on whether you can find a suitable space. In the more heavily populated and farmed highland districts, you should

HOTEL RESERVATIONS

Local addresses and telephone numbers for most hotels are included in the guide. Many are part of chains or management groups; rooms can be reserved by phoning or writing to the head offices. Some chains don't have overseas offices, but travel agents will often make the reservations.

AFRICAN TOURS AND HOTELS (AT&H)

Partly state-owned chain, middling to high quality.
Kenya: Utalii House, Uhuru Highway, PO Box 30471 Nairobi (☎02/336858, fax 02/218109 or 218396); counter bookings also in the ex-Tourist Information Office, Watalii St, opposite the *Hilton* (☎02/221855).

Lodges

Buffalo Springs Tented Lodge, Buffalo Springs
Kilaguni Lodge, Tsavo West National Park
Lake Bogoria Hotel, Lake Bogoria
Mountain Lodge, Mount Kenya
Ngulia Safari Lodge, Tsavo West National Park
Olkurruk Mara Lodge, Maasai Mara National Reserve
Voi Safari Lodge, Tsavo East National Park

Town hotels

Kabarnet Hotel, Kabarnet, near Lake Baringo
Milimani Hotel, Nairobi
Sunset Hotel, Kisumu

Coast

Golden Beach Hotel, Diani Beach
Mombasa Beach Hotel, North Coast
Trade Winds, Diani Beach

ALLIANCE HOTELS

Small, highly rated group with very pleasant hotels, noted for their good food and experienced management.
Kenya: College House, University Way, PO Box 49839 Nairobi (☎02/337501 or 337508, fax 02/219212).

Lodges

Naro Moru River Lodge, Naro Moru, Mount Kenya

Coast

Africana Sea Lodge, Diani Beach
Jadini Beach Hotel, Diani Beach
Safari Beach Hotel, Diani Beach

BLOCK HOTELS

Consistently good, state-of-the-art, package-tour establishments, which are popular with Kenya residents, too.
Kenya: Block House, Lusaka Rd, off Uhuru Highway, PO Box 40075 Nairobi (☎02/540780, fax 02/540821).

UK: Block Hotels Europe, Travel House, Spring Villa Park, Spring Villa Road, Edgeware, Middlesex HA8 7EB (☎0181/905-7383, fax 0181/905-6947).

Lodges and tented camps

Keekorok Lodge, Maasai Mara National Reserve
Lake Baringo Club, Lake Baringo
Lake Naivasha Country Club, Lake Naivasha
Larsens Tented Camp, Samburu National Reserve
Ol Tukai Lodge, Amboseli National Park
Outspan Hotel, Nyeri
Samburu Lodge, Samburu National Reserve
Shimba Hills Lodge, Shimba Hills National Park
Treetops, Aberdares National Park

Nairobi

Jacaranda Hotel, Westlands

Coast

Indian Ocean Beach Club, Diani Beach
Nyali Beach Hotel, Mombasa

CONSERVATION CORPORATION OF EAST AFRICA

Small, exclusive group.
Kenya: c/o *Mayfair Court Hotel*, Msapo Close, off Parklands Rd, PO Box 74957 Nairobi (☎02/748258, 750298 or 750780, fax 02/746826).
UK: c/o *Unique Hotels*, The Old Warehouse, Old Market, Nailsworth, Gloucestershire GL6 0DU (☎01453/835801, fax 01453/835525).
USA: c/o *Abercrombie & Kent*, 1420 Kensington Rd, Oak Brook, IL 60521 (☎1-800/323-7308 or 708/954-2944).
Australia: c/o *Abercrombie & Kent*, 90 Bridport St, Albert Park, Melbourne 3206 (☎03/699-9766).

Lodges and tented camps

Kichwa Tembo, Maasai Mara National Reserve
Siana Springs Tented Camp, Maasai Mara National Reserve

Nairobi

Mayfair Court Hotel

GOVERNORS' CAMPS

Kenya: *Musiara Ltd*, 3rd Floor, International House, Mama Ngina St, PO Box 48217 Nairobi (☎02/331871, 336169 or 337344, fax 02/726427).

Lodges and tented camps
Governors' Camp, Maasai Mara National Reserve
Governors' Paradise Camp, Maasai Mara National Reserve
Governors' Private Camp, Maasai Mara National Reserve
Little Governors' Camp, Maasai Mara National Reserve
Loldia, Lake Naivasha
Mfangano Island Camp, Lake Victoria

HILTON HOTELS
Kenya: *Hilton*, Mama Ngina St, PO Box 30624 Nairobi (☎02/334000, fax 02/339462).
UK: Reservations dept, Maple Court, Central Park, Reeds Crescent, Watford WD1 1HZ (☎0345/581595).
US & Canada: ☎1-800/445-8667.
Australia: ☎1800/222255.
South Africa: ☎11/880 3108.

Nairobi
Hilton International
Lodges
Taita Hills Lodge, Salt Lick Lodge and *Safari Hilton Camp*, Taita Hills Wildlife Sanctuary

INTERCONTINENTAL HOTELS
Kenya: *Intercontinental*, City Hall Way, PO Box 30353 Nairobi (☎02/240224, fax 02/210675).
UK: Reservations dept, The Thameside Centre, Kew Bridge Rd, Brentford, Middlesex TW8 0EB (☎0181/847-2277, fax 0181/968-9555).
US & Canada: ☎1-800/327-0200.
Australia: ☎008/221335.
New Zealand: ☎0800/442215.
South Africa: ☎0800/121377.
Germany: ☎0130/853955.

Nairobi
Nairobi Intercontinental
Coast
Mombasa Intercontinental

KILIMANJARO SAFARI CLUB
Kenya: Stanbic Bank Building, Kimathi St, PO Box 30139 Nairobi (☎02/227136, fax 02/219982).

Lodges
Amboseli Lodge, Amboseli National Park
Kilimanjaro Buffalo Lodge, near Amboseli National Park

Kilimanjaro Safari Lodge, Amboseli National Park
Kimana Lodge, between Amboseli and Tsavo West
Tsavo Inn, Mtito Andei, Mombasa Highway
Tsavo Safari Camp, Tsavo East National Park

LONRHO HOTELS
Very up-market, and highly recommended if money is no object.
Kenya: c/o *Norfolk Hotel*, Harry Thuku Rd, PO Box 58581 Nairobi (☎02/216940, fax 02/216796 or 216896).
UK: c/o *London Metropole Hotel*, 225 Edgware Rd, London W2 1JU (☎0171/262-3409, fax 0171/262-7792).
USA: 620 Longview, Longboat Key, Florida 34228 (☎813/387-0301, fax 813/387-0028).

Lodges and tented camps
Aberdare Country Club, Mweiga, north of Nyeri
The Ark, Aberdares National Park
Mara Safari Club, Maasai Mara National Reserve
Mount Kenya Safari Club, Nanyuki/Mount Kenya
Sweetwaters, Laikipia, near Nanyuki
Nairobi
Norfolk Hotel

MSAFIRI INNS
A group formed to look after some of the *Kenya Tourist Development Corporation*'s less successful hotels. Standards vary, but the lodges, at least, are in fine locations.
Kenya: 11th floor, Utalii House, Uhuru Highway, PO Box 42013 Nairobi (☎02/330820, 229751 or 222661, fax 02/227815).

Lodges
Marsabit Lodge, Marsabit
Meru Mulika Lodge, Meru National Park
Mount Elgon Lodge, Mount Elgon
Town hotels
Golf Hotel, Kakamega
Homa Bay Hotel, Homa Bay, Lake Victoria
Izaac Walton Inn, Embu, Mount Kenya
Tea Hotel, Kericho

PRESTIGE HOTELS
Kenya: Warren House, Loita St, PO Box 74888 Nairobi (☎02/338084 or 335208, fax 02/213387).
Europe: c/o *International Marketing Concepts*, rue Bermont 4, 1204 Geneva, Switzerland (☎22/312 4611, fax 22/312 4620).

Continued overleaf...

ask someone before pitching in an empty spot. Out in the wilds, hard or thorny ground is likely to be the only obstacle (a foam sleeping mat is a good idea if you don't mind the bulk). During the dry seasons, you'll rarely have trouble finding wood for a fire so a stove is optional, but don't burn more fuel than you need. You're not allowed to collect firewood in the mountain parks. Camping gas cartridges and packaged, dried food is available in variety in Nairobi, but the easiest and cheapest camping food is *ugali* (see "Eating and Drinking" opposite), flavoured with curry powder or sauce mixes if you like.

SAFETY
Camping out is generally pretty safe. A fire may worry local people and delegations armed with *pangas* sometimes turn up to see who you are, and might want to stay and chat. But in most places there is undoubtedly less chance of being attacked or robbed than if you were to camp rough in Europe or North America. Camping right by the road, in dried-out river beds, or on trails used by animals going to water, however, are all unwise.

On the subject of **animals**, if you're way out in the bush, lions and hyenas are very occasionally curious of fires, but will never attack you unless provoked.

An important exception to the safety of rough camping is the Indian Ocean coast. Almost anywhere between Malindi and the Tanzanian border, **sleeping out on the beaches** should be counted as an invitation to robbery. North of Malindi, there are fewer tourists and the risks are correspondingly less.

EATING AND DRINKING

Not surprisingly, perhaps, Kenya has no great national dishes: the living standards of the majority of people don't allow for frills and food is generally plain and filling. For culinary culture, only the coast's long association with Indian Ocean trade has produced distinctive regional cooking, where rice and fish, flavoured with coconut, tamarind and exotic spices, are the dominant ingredients. The modern tourist industry has resulted in good, international-style restaurants in many places.

HOME-STYLE COOKING

If meals are unlikely to be a lasting memory, at least you'll never go hungry. In any *hoteli* (a small restaurant, not a hotel), there's always a number of predictable dishes intended to fill you up at the least cost. Potatoes, rice and especially *ugali* (a stiff, cornmeal porridge) are the national staples, eaten with chicken, goat, beef, or vegetable stew, various kinds of spinach, beans or sometimes fish. Portions are usually gigantic: half-portions (ask for *nusu*) aren't much smaller. But even in small towns, more and more **cafés** are appearing where most of the menu is fried – eggs, sausages, chips, fish, chicken and burgers.

Snacks, which can easily become meals, include samosas, chapatis, miniature kebabs, roasted corn cobs, *mandaazi* and "egg-bread". *Mandaazi* – sweet, puffy, deep-fried dough cakes – are made before breakfast and served until evening time, when they've become cold and solid. Egg-bread (misleadingly translated from the Swahili *mkate mayai*) is a light wheat-flour

"pancake" wrapped around fried eggs and minced meat, usually cooked on a huge griddle. While you won't find it everywhere, it's a delicious Kenyan response to the creeping burger menace.

The standard blow-out feast for most Kenyans is a huge pile of **nyama choma** (roast meat). *Nyama choma* is usually eaten at a purpose-built *nyama choma* bar, with beer and music (live or on a jukebox) the standard accompaniment and *ugali* and spinach optional. You go to the kitchen and order by weight (half a kilo is plenty) direct from the butcher's hook or out of the fridge. There's usually a choice of beef or mutton. After roasting, the meat is brought to your table on a wooden platter and chopped to bite-size with a sharp knife.

BREAKFAST

The first meal of the day varies widely. Stock **hoteli fare** consists of a cup of sweet *chai* and a doorstep of white bread, thickly spread with margarine (on both sides *and* the edges). At the other extreme, if you're staying in a **luxury hotel** or lodge, breakfast is usually a lavish acreage of hot and cold buffets that you can't possibly do justice to. In the average **mid-priced hotel**, you'll get "full breakfast", like something from an English B&B – greasy sausage, bacon, eggs and baked beans, with instant coffee (in a pot) and soggy toast.

RESTAURANT MEALS

Indian restaurants in the larger towns – notably Nairobi and Mombasa – are generally excellent (locally, there's often a strong Indian influence in *hoteli* food as well), with *dahl* lunches a good stand-by and much fancier regional dishes widely available too.

When you splurge, apart from eating Indian, it will usually be in hotel restaurants, with food often very similar to what you might be served in a restaurant at home. It will rarely cost more than Ksh900 a head, though there's a handful of classy establishments in Nairobi, Mombasa and Diani Beach which take delight in charging, for Kenya, outrageous prices for lavish meals – up to Ksh2500 – generally with some justification.

Kenya's **seafood** and **meat** are renowned and they are the basis of most serious meals. Game meat is a bit of a Kenyan speciality, farmed on ranches. It's somewhat unpredictable. Giraffe, zebra, impala, crocodile and ostrich all regularly appear at various restaurants, and often on a weekly basis in hotel buffets. Zebra is good, not the horse meat you might imagine.

The lodges usually have buffet lunches at about Ksh500–1200, which can be great value if you're really hungry, with table-loads of salads and cold meat. Among Kenya's exotic cuisines, you'll find Italian restaurants and pizzerias, various Chinese cuisines, and French, Japanese, Korean, and even Thai food.

VEGETARIANS AND FRUIT

If you're a **vegetarian** staying in tourist-class hotels, you should have no problems, as there are always mountains of fruit and salads with every meal. Vegetarians on a strict budget don't have an easy time because meat is the conventional focus of any kind of special meal – in other words, any meal not eaten at home – and *hotelis* seldom have much else to accompany the starch. Even vegetable stew is normally cooked in meat gravy. Nor are salads and green vegetables served much in the cheaper *hotelis*. Eggs, at least, can be had almost anywhere, and fresh milk is distributed widely in wax paper tetra-packs. With bread and tinned margarine, two more staples available everywhere, you won't starve. Look out for **Indian vegetarian restaurants** where you can often eat remarkably well at a very low cost.

Fruit, of course, is the main delight, whether you eat meat or not. Bananas, avocados, papayas

MENU AND FOOD TERMS

The lists below should be adequate for translating most Swahili menus and explaining what you want. Spelling may vary: see "Language" in *Contexts*.

Basics

Food	*Chakula*	Spoon	*Kijiko*	Pepper	*Piripiri*	Egg/Eggs	*Yai/Mayai*
Water,	*Maji*	Knife	*Kisu*	Bread	*Mkate*	Fish	*Samaki*
juice		Fork	*Uma*	Butter,	*Siagi*	Meat	*Nyama*
Ice	*Barafu*	Bottle	*Chupa*	margarine		Vegetables	*Mboga*
Table	*Meza*	Bill	*Hesabu*	Sugar	*Sukari*	Sauce	*Mchuzi*
Plate	*Sahani*	Salt	*Chumvi*	Milk	*Maziwa*	Fruit	*Matunda*

Snacks

Chapati	Unleavened, flat wheat bread, baked on a hot plate or in an oven (*tandoor*)	*Maziwalala*	Yogurt
		Mkate Mayai	"Egg-bread": soft thin dough wrapped around fried egg and minced meat
Keki	Cake		
Kitumbuo	Deep-fried rice bread	*Samosa*	Deep-fried triangular case of chopped meat and vegetables
Mandaazi	Deep-fried sweet dough, sometimes flavoured with spices, known as *mahamri* on the coast	*Tosti/Slice*	Slice of bread
		Halwa	Sweetmeat; Turkish delight

Dishes

Irio/Kienyeji	Potato, cabbage and beans mashed together (Mount Kenya region)	*Sukuma wiki*	Green leaves boiled, usually a kind of spinach
Kima	Mince	*Ugali/Sima*	Cornmeal boiled to a solid porridge with water, occasionally milk; yellow *ugali* is considered inferior to white but is more nutritious
Matoke	Mashed plantain		
Mboga	Vegetables: usually potatoes, carrots and onions in meaty gravy		
Mchele	Plain white rice	*Uji*	Porridge or gruel made of millet; good for chilly mornings
Michicha	Spinach cooked with onions and tomatoes	*Wali*	Rice with added fat and spices; almost *pilau*
Pilau	Rice with spices and meat		

and pineapples are in the markets all year, mangoes and citrus fruits more seasonally. Look out for passion fruit, cape gooseberries, custard apples and guavas – all highly distinctive and delicious. On the coast, roasted cashew **nuts** are cheap, especially at Kilifi where they're grown and processed (never buy any with dark marks on them), while coconuts are filling and nutritious, going through several satisfying changes of condition (all edible) before becoming the familiar hard brown nuts.

DRINK

The national beverage is **chai** – tea. Universally drunk at breakfast and as a pick-me-up at any time, it's a weird variant on the classic British brew: milk, water, lots of sugar and tea leaves,

brought to the boil in a kettle and served scalding hot. It must eventually do diabolical dental damage but it's curiously addictive and very reviving. Instant **coffee** – fresh is rare – is normally available in *hotelis* as well, but it's expensive (ironically, in Kenya), so not as popular as tea.

Soft drinks ("sodas") are usually very cheap and crates of Coke, Fanta and Sprite find their way to the wildest corners of the country where, uncooled, they're pretty disgusting. Krest, a bitter lemon, is a lot more pleasant. Krest also make a ginger ale but it's watery and insipid; instead go for Stoney's which has more of a punch. Sometimes you can get Vimto, which is supposed to do you some good, and occasionally plain soda water, which can't do you any harm. There are fresh **fruit juices** available in the towns, especially on the coast. Passionfruit, the cheapest, is

Meat

Kuku	Chicken	Ngombe	Beef
Mushkaki	Kebab–small pieces of grilled, marinated meat on or off the skewer	Nguruwe	Pork
		Steki	Steak, grilled meat
		Mbuzi	Mutton, goat meat

Terms

Choma	Roast (*nyama choma* – roast meat – is the food for parties and celebrations)	Chemka	Boiled	Baridi	Cold
		Kaanga	Fried	Nusu	Half
		Moto	Hot	Ingine	More, another

Fruit

Limau	Lime	Matopetope	Custard apples	Papai	Papaya/ Pawpaw
Machungwa	Oranges	Nanasi	Pineapple		
Madafu	Green coconuts	Nazi	Coconuts	Parachichi	Avocado
Maembe	Mangoes	Ndimu	Lemon	Pera	Guava
Mastafeli	Soursops	Ndizi	Bananas	Sandara	Mandarins

Vegetables

Maharagwe	Red kidney beans, often cooked with coconut	Muhogo	Cassava
Mahindi	Corn	Ndizi	Bananas or plantains (often served with meat dishes)
Mbaazi	Pigeon peas, small beans	Nyanya	Tomatoes (also means grandmother)
Mtama	Millet (made into a gruel for breakfast)	Viazi	Potatoes
		Vitunguu	Onions

Drinks

Chai, chai kavu, chai strungi	Tea, black tea, strongly spiced tea	Kahawa	Coffee
Maziwalala	Fermented milk/almost-yogurt (literally "sleeping milk")	Bia	Beer
		Pombe	Home-brewed "beer"
		Soda	What else?
		Tembo	Coconut palm wine

excellent. Some places serve a variety: you'll sometimes find carrot juice and even tiger milk – from tiger (chufa) nuts.

Ordinary bottled **mineral or spring water** is expensive and only available in large towns or major hotels. Mains water (see "Water and Bugs", p.31) is usually quite drinkable, but it's best to take heed if your hotel or lodge advises against it.

BEER

Kenyan **lager beer** is generally good, though sadly no longer sold at fixed prices according to the grade of the bar. But it can still cost as little as Ksh40 a bottle and is never more than Ksh140. Tusker, White Cap and Pilsner are the main brands, sold in half-litre bottles (or the first two in "export" one-third-litre sizes, commonly the only size available at fancier establishments and hotel bars). White Cap seems to be the old colonials' brew and Tusker is certainly the biggest seller. Everyone adopts a brand but you may eventually realize you can't reliably tell the difference between any of them. Premium, however, in a small bottle, is noticeably stronger.

There are two points of **beer etiquette** worth remembering. Firstly, never take your bottle out of the bar (bottles carry deposits and this is considered theft – surprisingly ugly misunderstandings can ensue). Secondly, in small places out of the cities (especially in western Kenya), men buy each other beers and accumulate them on the table in a display of mutual generosity. When he's drunk enough, each customer takes his unopened presents back to the bar and stores them for the next day.

OTHER ALCOHOLIC DRINKS

Kenya Cane (white rum) and **Kenya Gold** (a gooey, coffee-flavoured liqueur) deserve a try perhaps, but they are expensive and nothing special.

More interesting is **papaya wine**, Kenya's desperate solution to its shortage of vineyards. This – ostensibly in medium or dry, white and rosé – is certainly an acquired taste, but it's one you might acquire quickly: the stuff is potent and much cheaper than imported wine. A whole range of fruity wines has recently appeared, including passion and mango. But there are now several quite drinkable **white wines** made from Kenyan grapes – notably the products of *Naivasha Wineries* – and reasonably priced South African wine is widely available.

You won't often find **cocktails** except in more expensive hotels and restaurants. One Kenyan mix to try, cautiously, is a *dawa* ("medicine") – vodka, white rum, honey and lime juice.

There's a battery of laws against **home brewing and distilling** – perhaps because of the loss of revenue in taxes on legal booze – but these are central aspects of Kenyan culture and they go on. You can sample **pombe** (beer) under many different names all over the country. It is as varied in taste and colour as its ingredients: basically fermented sugar and millet or banana, with herbs and roots for flavouring. The results are frothy and deceptively strong, and can cause you to change your plans for the rest of the day.

On the coast, where the coconuts grow, merely lopping off the growing shoot produces a naturally fermented **palm wine** (*tembo),* which is indisputably Kenya's finest contribution to the art of self-intoxication. Though there's usually a furtive discretion about *pombe* or *tembo* sessions, nobody ever seems to get busted.

Not so with spirits. Think twice before accepting a mug of **chang'aa**. It's treacherous firewater, and is also frequently contaminated, regularly killing drinking parties en masse, and filling a niche in the Kenyan press currently taken by crack cocaine in the West. Sentences for distilling and possessing *chang'aa* are harsh, and police raids common.

THE MEDIA

Kenya's main languages are English and Swahili, a simplified version of the older coastal Kiswahili. English tends to predominate; higher education and Parliament get by almost exclusively on it, and the media use it heavily.

You'll always find English-speakers in the towns. Out in the country, local languages come to the fore, with Swahili used as a lingua franca where strangers have to communicate – on the road, at markets, in official business. While it's helpful, and not difficult, to speak some Swahili (see *Contexts*), you'll rarely have problems without it — just more demonstrative conversations.

RADIO AND TV

KBC radio has three services, broadcasting in English, Swahili and vernacular languages, as well as a new FM station, Metropolitan FM, competing with the recently launched independent Capital FM. Kenyan **television**, much of it imported, is in English and Swahili. There are two main channels, the stuffy and hesitant KBC and the upbeat, CNN-dominated KTN, which also carries a lot of MTV. KBC also operates a pay channel, KBC2, which is run in conjunction with South Africa's M-NET.

With a short-wave set, you can also pick up the BBC World Service and Voice of America.

THE PRESS

Kenya, like Britain, is a nation absorbed in its press. Nevertheless, the established **newspapers** are limited. The *East African Standard* — Lonrho-owned and the settlers' rag — is dull, lightweight and eclipsed now by the *Daily* and *Sunday Nation*, owned by the Aga Khan, which has meatier news coverage, a more daring editorial line, and a letters page full of insights into Kenyan life. The Nation Group also publishes *The East African* on Mondays, a relatively weighty, conservatively styled round-up of the week's news in Kenya, Uganda and Tanzania. The *Kenya Times* is a stodgy KANU organ partly owned by Britain's Mirror Group Newspapers. All are available just about anywhere.

Other papers, *Taifa Leo* and *Kenya Leo*, are in Swahili. The *Weekly Review* is always worth picking up (as are *Society*, *Law* and *Finance* — if you can find any copies that haven't been confiscated by the authorities for one crime of the pen or another). Despite continued suppression, the Kenyan press has enjoyed a renaissance since the unbanning of the opposition and there are many magazines and occasional papers, all of which carry interesting articles from time to time and often surprise their readers with their outspokenness. *Drum* and *Presence* (a women's magazine) are two lifestyle mags that are usually available.

Of the **foreign press**, the *Daily Telegraph* gets to all sorts of settler-ish bastions. British Sunday and daily papers (such as the *Times*, *Express* and *Mail* and more occasionally *The Guardian*) and the *International Herald Tribune* can usually be found in Nairobi or, a few days old, at one or two stores around the country. They tend, however, to be unavailable when Kenya's internal affairs make international news.

Time and *Newsweek* are hawked widely and, together with old *National Geographics* and copies of *The Economist*, filter through many hands before reaching the second-hand booksellers.

POST AND TELEPHONES

Keeping in touch by mail and telephone is generally easy. Mail takes a few days to Europe and perhaps ten days to North America, Australia and New Zealand; times from these places to Kenya are slightly longer. Kenya's telephone system is improving, though lines are often busy.

RECEIVING AND SENDING MAIL

Poste restante is free, and fairly reliable in Nairobi, Mombasa, Malindi and Lamu. Have your family name marked clearly but look under any combination of initials and be ready to show your passport. Smaller post offices will also hold mail but your correspondent should mark the letter "To Be Collected". Parcels can be received, too, but expect to haggle over import-duty payment when they're opened. Ask the sender to mark packages "Contents To Be Re-exported From Kenya".

When posting things home, out of Kenya, airmail packages are expensive but **surface mail** (up to a maximum of 20kg) is good value, reliable and worth considering if you've accumulated things on your travels. Parcels must be no more than 105cm long and the sum of the three sides less than 200cm, and must be wrapped in brown paper and tied with string. They are usually examined in advance, so everything has to be checked, in the post office, before you wrap it.

Stamps can be bought only at post offices and large hotels. There are main post offices in all the towns and, except in the far north, sub-post offices throughout the rural areas. Prepaid **"aerograms"** are the cheapest way of writing home, but they tend to sell out quickly. If you want speedy delivery, pay a little extra for express. The internal service, like the international one, is pretty efficient.

ADDRESSES IN KENYA

All addresses in Kenya have a post office box number except out in the sticks, where some are just given as "Private Bag", or "PO", followed by the location of the post office. There's no home delivery service. In large towns, business and office addresses are usually identified by the "House" or "Building" in which they're situated.

TELEPHONES

The local **telephone service** is generally dependable and inexpensive, though outside the big towns, you can spend a long time waiting for a connection or passing the time of day with the operator.

To make **local telephone calls** from a call box you need a good handful of shillings; you can also try using Ksh5 coins which are supposed to fit, but they often jam. When you pick up any pay phone you'll hear a sustained tone and, in the background, a series of beeps. After five beeps you dial (you can dial before that, but you might lose your money). Use the area code or dial 900 for the operator. You line the shillings up at the top and put the one that's to go into the machine at an angle – it drops in when the call is answered. The engaged tone is more rapid than the ringing tone.

The easiest and most economical way to make an **international** call is to dial direct from a **cardphone** (found outside *Extelcoms* in Nairobi and outside post offices in most large towns). The prepaid, credit-card-sized plastic phonecards used in them can in theory be bought at newsstands as well as at post offices. Cardphones are also useful for using a **charge card** from your own telephone company (they don't take ordinary credit cards). You dial ☎0800/44 for the UK or ☎0800/10 for the USA or Canada and get through to an international operator in your country. The operator should be able to tell you how much the call – debited to your account – will cost; the Kenyan telecom people have no idea.

In the absence of a cardphone it's possible to make operator-assisted international calls from a main post office. **Charges** are about £3 ($4.50) per minute to Europe and North America for standard-rate station-to-station calls. When you ask for a station-to-station connection, you pre-pay for a specified number of minutes (minimum of three, costing around £9/$13.50), and you get your money back if you fail to get through, but not if the conversation ends up taking less time than you expected, for example if you get through to an answerphone. If you want more minutes you

---

INTERNATIONAL DIRECT DIALLING CODES

Kenya's international dialling code is 254. Then dial the number omitting the first 0 from the area code. If you have to be connected by the operator, call your own international operator and quote the exchange and number.

Calling out of Kenya, dial 001 then:

Australia 61	**Germany 37**	**Netherlands 31**	**UK 44**
Canada 1	**Ireland 353**	**New Zealand 64**	**USA 1**

For international operator service and directory enquiries call 0196.
Kenya is **3hr ahead of GMT** (2hr ahead of British Summer Time).
4am New York=9 or 10am London=noon Kenya=7pm Sydney=9pm New Zealand.

have to specify how many – all very user-unfriendly. For person-to-person calls, where you specify a name, there's a supplementary charge equivalent to two minutes and a small charge if the person isn't there.

Reverse-charge (collect) calls can also be made, but not from call boxes. Three minutes' worth costs about £13 ($20). It works out cheaper overall if you call your correspondent briefly and ask them to call you back.

Larger post offices have **fax** machines – the international rate is around £6 ($9) per page – or you can use a private fax bureau, where the rate will sometimes be cheaper. Charges for receiving faxes, however, are nominal.

Post office opening hours are usually 8am–5pm on weekdays; larger ones are open on Saturday mornings. Otherwise, you can usually phone from large hotels, but you'll pay up to twice the price for this facility.

OPENING HOURS AND SHOPPING

Standard opening hours, where there are any, follow familiar patterns: in larger towns, the major stores and tourist services will be open from 8am to 5 or 6pm, offices and museums at similar times, though offices will often break for lunch. Banks and post offices are generally open Monday to Friday and sometimes Saturday mornings. In rural areas and out in the bush, small shops can be open at almost any hour, and may double as *hotelis* or *chai* kiosks.

SHOPPING

What constitutes something worth buying is really up to you. Sculptures and carvings in **wood** and **soapstone** (*kisii-stone*) are cheap and ubiquitous. The most striking carvings are in the dramatically vertical and delicate **makonde** style from Tanzania, ostensibly carved in ebony, but in Kenya usually made of blackened rosewood or something similar. Which shouldn't deter you: it saves on ebony forests' stocks and looks just as wonderful on your mantlepiece.

The familiar **sisal baskets** (*chondo*, or *vyondo* in the plural) come in a huge variety of patterns and can be made from cheap nylon string as well as sisal and, much more rarely, baobab bark twine, with beads woven in. They're all light, and functional.

Beadwork (*ushanga*, *mkufu*) and **tribal regalia** – weapons, shields, drums (*ngoma*), musical instruments, stools, headrests and metal jewellery – are common as well, but much more expensive when authentically used rather than made for the tourist industry.

Masks are mostly imported from west and central Africa (they're not a feature of traditional Kenyan art) and by no means sure to be old or "authentic".

Textiles, notably a profusion of printed women's wraps in cotton – **kanga** – and heavier-weave men's loincloths – **kikoi/vikoi** – are really good buys on the coast, and older ones represent collectable items worth seeking out. *Kangas* are always sold in pairs and are printed with intriguing Swahili proverbs. They're usually found to have been manufactured in the Far East.

Whether or not you have children or are buying presents for kids, the **toys** you can come across from time to time are highly recommended souvenirs. Most worthwhile are the beautifully fashioned, and sometimes large and intricate, wire buses, cars and lorries, fitted with stick-up steering wheel, that lucky boys in rural areas get given by older brothers and uncles. These are rarely for sale, but you might commission one, if you have time. More widely available are various push-along bikes, birds and monkeys, and pottery *matatus*, these latter for the tourist market.

Other local specialities are mentioned through the guide. In the end, what you take home is going to depend partly on how much you can carry. It's easy, with attractive items and low prices, to get quite carried away, but carvings (especially ebony *makonde*) and soapstone are extremely heavy.

Ivory, incidentally, carved or otherwise, and in any quantity, is strictly illegal. Most countries have banned all ivory imports. It will be seized and, in many countries, the carrier is subject to a heavy fine.

BARGAINING

Bargaining is an important skill to get into. Every time you pay an unreasonable price for goods or services, you contribute to local inflation. You're expected to knock most negotiable prices down by at least half: souvenirs are sometimes offered at first prices ten times what the vendor is prepared to accept. You can avoid the silly first prices by having a chat first and establishing your streetwise credentials. The bluffing on both sides is part of the fun; don't be shy of making a big scene. Where prices are marked, they are generally fixed – which you'll quickly discover if you walk out and aren't called back. Once you get into it, you'll rarely end up paying more than the going rate for food, transport or accommodation and, ironically, hospitality and pride will quite often see you getting a better deal than local people.

FESTIVALS AND HOLIDAYS

Both Christian and Muslim holidays are observed, as well as secular national holidays. Local seasonal and cyclical events, peculiar to particular ethnic groups, are less well advertised.

THE RALLY

The only regular national event that gets much international attention is the Easter **Safari Rally**. From the beginning of the year, the Kenyan papers wax eloquent about this "toughest motor rally in the world", the teams and drivers who will be entering, and the cost of their preparations. Asian and European entrants predominate; while the whole country seems gripped with rally fever, the costs are prohibitive for most Kenyans and no African driver has yet won.

The rally usually takes place from Good Friday to Easter Monday and the route seems to circle Kenya about three times, most of it on appalling roads, often in heavy rain. Stone-throwing and road-sabotaging take place every year – usually, it seems, the actions of frustrated onlookers; there have been many fatal accidents, of course.

Be warned: drivers tend to do practise legs all over the country in March – an additional and unexpected road hazard if you're driving around

at that time. Don't forget the rally takes place on ordinary roads, among the traffic. If you'd like to be in the right place at the right time, information can be had from the Automobile Association at their Hurlingham headquarters in Nairobi (PO Box 40087; ☎02/720382).

AGRICULTURAL SHOWS

The annual **agricultural shows** put on by the Agricultural Society of Kenya (ASK) are lively, revealing occasions, borrowing a lot from the British farming show tradition, but infused with Kenyan style. As well as stock and produce competitions, and the usual beer and snack tents, there are often some less expected booths: women's groups, family planning, beekeeping, soil conservation, herbalism. Large towns have an ASK fairground (sometimes reasonable places to camp, incidentally) and the shows happen at roughly the same time each year. Many smaller towns have annual district shows as well.

PUBLIC HOLIDAYS

Public holidays, when all official doors are closed, are: Christmas Day and Boxing Day (December 26), New Year's Day, Good Friday and Easter Monday, May 1 (Labour Day), June 1 (Madaraka Day, celebrating the granting of self-government in 1960), October 10 (Moi Day), October 20 (Kenyatta Day, the anniversary of his imprisonment) and December 12 (Jamhuri Day, or Independence Day).

ASK SHOWS

Eldoret	Late Feb
Nanyuki	First week in May
Meru	Early June
Nakuru	Early July
Kisii	Mid-July
Garissa	Third week in July
Kisumu	First week in Aug
Embu	Second week in Aug
Mombasa	Last week in Aug
Nyeri	Early Sept
Nairobi	First week in Oct
Kitale	First week in Nov
Kakamega	Last week in Nov

THE ISLAMIC CALENDAR

On the coast, throughout the northeast, and in Muslim communities everywhere, the lunar **Islamic calendar** is followed, parallel to the Gregorian one. The Muslim year has 354 days, with 355 days eleven times every thirty years, so dates recede against the Western calendar by an average of eleven days each year. Only the month of fasting called **Ramadan**, and Id ul Fitr — the feast of relief at the end of it which begins on the first sighting of the new moon — will have much effect on your travels. During Ramadan, most stores and *hotelis* are closed through the daylight hours in smaller towns in Islamic districts. Public transport and official business continue as usual. **Maulidi**, the celebration of the prophet's birthday, is worth catching if you're on the coast at the right time, especially if you'll be in Lamu.

ISLAMIC FESTIVALS: APPROXIMATE DATES

	1997	1998	1999
Beginning of Ramadan (1st Ramadan)	11 Jan	1 Jan	21 Dec (1998)
Id ul Fitr/Id al-Saghir (1st Shawwal)	9 Feb	30 Jan	19 Jan
Tabaski/Id al-Kabir (10th Dhu'l Hijja)	19 April	9 April	29 Mar
New Year's Day (1st Moharem)	9 May	28 April	17 Apr
Ashoura (10th Moharem)	18 May	7 May	26 Apr
Maulidi/Mouloud (12th Rabia I)	18 July	8 July	27 June

DANCE, MUSIC, THEATRE AND SPORTS

Kenya's espousal of Western values has belittled much traditional culture, so only in remote areas are you likely to come across traditional dancing and drumming which doesn't somehow involve you as a paying audience. If you're patient and reasonably adventurous in your travels, however, you'll be able to witness something more authentic sooner or later – though most likely only by accident or if you stay somewhere off the beaten track long enough to make friends.
Kenyan popular music and spectator sports are more accessible.

DANCE

Best known are **Maasai and Samburu dancing**: hypnotic swaying and military displays of effortless leaping. Similar dance forms occur widely among other non-agricultural peoples. Foremost among exponents of drumming are the Akamba and the Mijikenda. **Mijikenda** dance troupes (notably from the Giriama people) perform up and down the coast at tourist venues. As with the Maasai dancing, it's better to ignore any purist misgivings you might have about the authenticity of such performances and enjoy them as distinctive and exuberant entertainments in their own right.

MUSIC

As for **popular music**, apart from what your ears pick up on the street and in buses (often amazingly loud), the live spectacle is limited to Nairobi, coastal entertainment spots, and a fair scattering of up-country discos and "country clubs". The indigenous music scene seems overshadowed by foreign influences: British and American soul and jazz-funk, reggae (especially in the sacred image of Bob Marley) and a vigorous contribution from Zaire predominating on KBC radio and in record shops. Zairean music has had a pervasive influence on local sounds, too. The guide to the **Nairobi club and music scene** (p.113) includes a detailed rundown on where to hear the home-grown product. The article in *Contexts* at the end of the book gives a condensed history of music in Kenya and a current discography.

If you're lucky enough to be invited to a coastal Swahili wedding with all the trimmings, a **tarabu** band may be playing. *Tarabu* music is hauntingly beautiful, an effervescent blend of African, Arabic and Indian musical influences. Steady drumbeat, tambourines, accordions, an instrument called the *udi* – like a lute – and plaintive Swahili lyrics are the traditional components, while electric guitars, fiddles and microphones are modern additions.

THEATRE AND FILM

Cinema in Kenya revolves almost entirely around imports. The big towns have cinemas and a few drive-ins, while smaller towns may have one cinema with the occasional screening. American and Indian box-office hits are the staple fodder.

Theatrical performances are effectively limited to one or two semi-professional clubs in Nairobi and Mombasa and one or two up-country amateur dramatic groups. African actors and scripts tend to be rare but things are improving, at least in Nairobi, where there are a number of groups performing in English.

Indigenous theatre was dealt a severe blow in 1978 when the innovative Kamiriithu Community Education and Cultural Centre in Limuru put on a Kikuyu language play by Ngugi wa Thiongo and Ngugi wa Mirii (*I Will Marry When I Want*), which, after seven weeks of playing to packed houses, was banned. The authorities mistrusted the play's power to mobilize people and question the status quo in Kikuyu rather than English; Ngugi wa Thiongo was detained without trial for a year as a result. In such a climate – which doesn't appear to have altered much – the notion of popular, issue-raising theatre gets automatically labelled as subversive and hasn't much hope of emerging again. Kamiriithu's brief but spectacular success only shows the potential.

SPORTS

Sports received encouragement from Kenya's much-vaunted – if financially disastrous – hosting of the 1987 All Africa Games. The country's Olympic successes are indisputable, with a regular clutch of gold and silver in the track events. Kenya's athletes are the continent's leaders and the country's long-distance runners the best in the world, with Moses Kiptanui, from Kapcherop in the Cherangani Hills, the most dazzling recent record-breaker.

Kenya has possibly the most successful athletics training school in the world in St. Patrick's High School, Iten, in the Rift Valley. You'll also find evidence of keen amateur involvement – joggers, martial arts tourneys and road cyclists in training.

Soccer is wildly popular. Kenya was to have hosted the Nations Cup finals in early 1996 and it was a major disappointment when they had to pull out due to insufficient funds. The national team, Harambee Stars, win the East and Central Africa Challenge Cup frequently and, in Division One, Nairobi's AFC Leopards and Gor Mahia rank with the best clubs on the continent. Crowds are pretty well behaved, perhaps because forking out for the modest gate fee precludes getting drunk as well.

NATIONAL PARKS AND RESERVES

The national parks are administered by the Parks Authority in Nairobi as total sanctuaries where human habitation (apart from the tourist lodges, of course) is prohibited. National reserves, run by local councils, tend to be less strict on the question of human encroachment. Parks and reserves are not fenced in (except Nakuru National Park and the north side of Nairobi National Park), and the animals are free to come and go, but they tend to stay within the boundaries, especially in the dry seasons when cattle outside compete for water.

NATIONAL PARKS DAILY FEES

Park entry fees are charged per person per day, payable in advance (though in practice it's possible to pay for extra days on leaving if you've stayed longer than you originally intended). If you arrive in the evening, intending to stay for just one night, you may well be charged for two days, so it's worth making sure that your time of arrival is noted in the gate record book.

The Kenya Wildlife Service has recently been clamping down on foreign visitors trying to claim resident status (claims which some rangers used to find plausible enough, especially if a tip was added). If you qualify as a resident, you must have ID to prove this; if you don't, it is strongly recommended that you pay the proper fee and get the right receipt. The Kenya Wildlife Service, and thus the future of Kenya's national parks, depends heavily on this gate money: if you defraud the KWS, you're conspiring in the destruction of Kenya's wildlife. High as they are compared to residents' rates, the fees are a small price to pay. The current daily fees were set on March 1, 1996. Note that Maasai Mara and Samburu/Buffalo Springs are national reserves, with their own fee structures.

ENTRY FEES	Non-residents (US$)	Residents (Ksh)
Category A: Aberdares, Amboseli, Lake Nakuru		
Adults	27	250
Children, students, organized groups	10	50
Category B: Tsavo East, Tsavo West		
Adults	23	200
Children	8	50
Students, organized groups	10	50
Category C: Nairobi, Shimba Hills, Meru		
Adults	20	150
Children	5	50
Students, organized groups	10	50
Mountaineering		
Adults	10	100
Children	5	50
Students, organized groups	5	100
Nairobi Animal Orphanage		
Adults	5	50
Children, students, organized groups	2	10
Marine parks		
Adults	5	100
Children	2	50
Students, organized groups	2	10
Category D: all other parks		
Adults	15	100
Children, students, organized groups	5	50
BANDAS		
Adults	10	250
Children, students, organized groups	5	50
CAMPING		
Adults, public campsites	8	150
Adults, special campsites*	10–15	200
Children, students, organized groups	2	50
*(The booking fee for special campsites, per week is Ksh5000).		

OTHER FEES
Vehicles of less than 6 seats are charged at Ksh200 per day, 6–12 seats Ksh500, 13–24 seats Ksh1000.
Guide service costs, per person per guide, Ksh500 for a day, Ksh300 for half a day (4hr).

The parks and reserves are all open to private visits (though it's worth noting that foreign-registered commercial overland vehicles are not allowed in). A few parks have been heavily developed for tourism with graded tracks, signposts, lodges and the rest, but none has any kind of bus service at the gate for people without their own transport. The largest and most frequently visited are covered in depth in Chapter 5. An introduction to the main game parks, giving you some idea of what to expect from them and the best times to visit, is given on p.299. Details about smaller and lesser-known parks and reserves, some of which can be visited on foot, are included in the rest of the guide.

The system of **entrance fees** has recently been revised to take account of environmental considerations, volume of visitors, and development opportunities: popular parks with fragile ecosystems have higher entrance fees, while fees for entry to the lesser-known parks are lower in order to encourage more visitors. Kenyan citizens and resident expatriates are eligible for reduced rates. With a **student card** (ISIC), you can get fifty-percent reductions. Additionally, unless you have booking vouchers for a lodge, you will usually have to pay **camping fees** at the gate if you're staying until the next day.

For residents, there's a special one-year **"National Parks Pass"** (Ksh6000 per adult or Ksh10,000 per couple; Ksh1000 per child under 16). The pass allows you and your vehicle unlimited access to KWS national parks and reserves, excluding the Maasai Mara and the Samburu complex. You can get the pass in person from the licensing section at the Parks headquarters at Nairobi National Park main gate (Mon–Fri 8.30am–noon & 2–3.30pm), or you can write to them enclosing all the details, including passport photos of the adults (PO Box 40241 Nairobi; ☎02/501081).

CAMPING SAFARIS

Once in Kenya, choosing a safari company to spend your money on can be fairly hit or miss. Unless you have the luxury of a long stay, your choice will probably be limited by the time available. Remember, though, that you may be able to use this to your advantage; if you ask, many companies are willing to discount a trip in order to fill unsold seats if you're buying at the last minute. Some outfits will also give student discounts if you ask. In fact, any angle you can use to get a good deal, you should use.

This is not to recommend the very cheapest outfits: as the competition in Nairobi becomes more cut-throat, some budget camping operators, not all of them licensed (and none of them included in our listings on p.119), are pushing safaris at the very bottom of the market in a **price war** which completely undercuts the legitimate firms. Any safari which is offered at much less than £40 ($60) per day is likely to be cutting corners. The easiest way for disreputable operators to cut costs is to avoid paying park entry fees. Give these fly-by-night companies a miss.

A number of **recommended operators** are given in the Nairobi account on p.119 but it's notoriously difficult to find a company that's absolutely consistent (if they're a member of KATO – see below – that's a good sign). Group relations among the passengers can assume surprising significance in a very short time and other **unpredictables** such as weather, illness and visibility of animals all contribute to the degree of success of the trip. More **controllable factors**, like breakdowns, food, camping equipment and competence of the drivers and tour leaders, really determine reputations. The companies we've listed all have pretty good records and get regularly mentioned in readers' letters, but even they turn up the occasional duff trip. Give them a try unless an alternative sounds especially good. The Nairobi grapevine is probably your most reliable guide on this.

If anything goes wrong, reputable companies will do their best to compensate on the spot (an extra day if you broke down, a night in a lodge if you didn't make it to a campsite, partial refunds without demur). But, these days, there's a great deal of competition and corners do get cut. If your grievance is unresolved, you might want to contact the Kenya Association of Tour Operators (KATO), PO Box 48461, 5th Floor, Jubilee Insurance Exchange Building, Mama Ngina St, Nairobi (☎02/225570, fax 02/218402), who can certainly intercede with their members. If this fails, try *Tourist's Kenya* (PO Box 40025; ☎02/337169), who publish the fortnightly pamphlet of the same name. They might be able to help if the company concerned advertises with them.

In going on a camping safari (or any safari for that matter), it's important not to take a passive attitude to the trip. Although some of the itinerary may be fixed, it's not all cast in stone, and similarly, daily routines may be altered to suit the clients easily enough if you ask. It's common on camping safaris, for example, to spend the hot part of the day at the campsite. While some are shady and pleasant, that's not always the case, and, where there are lodges with swimming pools, cold beer and the rest, there's no reason not to spend a few hours in comfort. Similarly, if you want to go on an early game drive, don't be afraid to suggest you skip breakfast, or take sandwiches. In too many companies, interpretations of what customers want are passed from management to drivers and cooks and rarely questioned.

As long as they know there will be reasonable **tips at the end of the trip**, most staff will go out of their way to help. Tipping on budget trips, however, can often cause days of argument and misunderstanding between the clients, who are usually expected to organize themselves to give collective gratuities on the last day. Good companies make suggestions in their briefing packs. Something like Ksh100–200 per employee per day from each client seems to be the norm. Ask when you book.

PHOTOGRAPHY

Kenya is immensely photogenic and with any kind of camera you'll get beautiful pictures. If you take photography seriously, you will probably want a single-lens reflex (SLR) camera and two or three lenses; but remember, these are heavy, relatively fragile and eminently stealable. Except in the game parks (where some kind of telephoto is essential if you want pictures of animals rather than savannah), you don't really need cumbersome lenses. It's often easier and less intrusive to take a small compact and keep your money for extra film.

Whatever you decide to take, **insure it** (if ordinary travel insurance won't cover it, check the insurers who advertise in photo magazines) and make sure you have a dust-proof bag to keep it in, as film in the camera gets scratched otherwise. Take spare **batteries** – they can be outrageously expensive in Nairobi. **Film** is no longer especially expensive, but try to bring all you'll need just the same, particularly if you use colour transparency film or black and white. Try to keep it cool by stuffing it inside a sleeping bag. If you're away for some time, posting it home seems a good idea; packages rarely go astray if registered. Processing in Kenya tends to be hit or miss, but again is no longer particularly expensive: one or two places in Nairobi have a decent enough reputation (see p.127).

SUBJECTS

As for subjects, **animal photography** is a question of patience and not taking endless pictures of nothing happening: if you can't get close enough, don't waste your film. While taking photos, try keeping both eyes open, and, in a vehicle, always turn off the engine.

The question of **photographing people** is more prickly. Every two seconds, somebody in Kenya has their photo taken by a tourist – and they're getting pretty fed up with it. Considering the reality of the situation, in fact, most people are amazingly tolerant of the camera's harassment. The Maasai and Samburu – Kenya's most colourful and photographed people – are usually prepared to do a deal, and in some places you'll even find professional posers making a living at the roadside. If you're motivated to take a lot of pictures of people, you might seriously consider lugging along a Polaroid camera and as much film as you can muster – most people will be very pleased to have a snap. Or you could have a lot of photos of you and your family printed up with your address on the back, which should at least raise a few laughs when you try the exchange.

One thing is certain: if you won't accept that some kind of **interaction and exchange** are warranted, you won't get many pictures. Taking the subject's name and address and sending a print when you get home is an option that some people prefer, but it is decreasingly popular with subjects who look on the photo call as work and have fixed the rates they're prepared to accept. Blithely aiming at strangers is arrogant; it won't make you any friends and it may well get you into trouble.

On the subject of sensitivity, it's a bad idea to take pictures of anything that could be construed as strategic, including any military or police building, prisons, airports, harbours, bridges and His Excellency the President. It all depends on who sees you, of course – protesting your innocence won't appease small-minded officials.

TECHNICAL BUSINESS

Getting (slightly) **technical**, use skylight or UV filters to block haze and protect your lens and yellow filters for dramatic black and white shots. Take several speeds of film (don't let anyone tell you it's unnecessary to have fast film) in rolls of twenty, so you don't get stuck at the wrong speed too long. And if you feel it's worth taking a camera bag of lenses for your SLR, then it really makes no sense not to take two camera bodies as well – less lens changing, more film speeds available, and you could shoot the same subject in (say) fast black and white and slow, fine-grain colour.

Early morning and late afternoon are the **best times for photography**. At midday, with the sun almost directly overhead, the light is flat and everything is lost in a formless glare. In morning and evening, the contrast between light and shade can be huge, so be careful to expose for the subject and not the general scene. And remember, as you negotiate for your next Maasai masterpiece, that black skin usually needs a little more exposure (think of people as always back-lit); a half stop is normally enough. The **rainy seasons** are rewarding, especially when the first rains break: months of dust are settled, greenery sprouts in a few hours, the country has a lush, bold sheen, and the sky is magnificent.

TROUBLE

There are still places in Kenya where you can leave an unattended tent for the day and find it untouched when you return in the evening. And there are a few spots where walking alone after dark is almost guaranteed to get you mugged. As a general rule, though, **you have a far higher chance of being a victim in touristy areas**. It's only fair to point out that the number of "attack on tourist" stories that appear in the world press is not unconnected with the hundreds of thousands of tourists who pass through, and the hundreds of journalists based in Africa's most comfortable city – Nairobi. On an encouraging note, in all the trips to Kenya for research on this book the only first-hand experience was a snatched necklace (failure to follow our own advice).

AVOIDANCE

After arriving by air for the first time, an incredible number of people get ripped off during their **first day or two in Nairobi**, perhaps because, with pallid skin, and possibly new luggage and clean shoes, they stick out a mile.

You should at first be acutely conscious of your belongings: never leave anything unguarded even for fifteen seconds, never take out cameras or other valuables unless absolutely necessary, and be careful of where you walk, at least until you've got the pack off your back and you're settled in somewhere. If you want to conclusively avoid looking like a tourist, dress like a local – short-sleeved collar shirt or blouse, slacks or skirt, and sunglasses – and never carry a bag, particularly

TROUBLE FROM MISUNDERSTANDINGS

It's very easy to fall prey to misunderstandings in your relations with people (usually boys and young men) who offer their services as guides, helpers or "facilitators" of any kind. You should absolutely never assume anything is being done out of simple kindness. It may well be, but, if it isn't, you must expect to pay something. If you have any suspicion, it's invariably best to confront the matter head on at an early stage and either apologize for the offence caused by the suggestion, or agree a price. What you must never do, as when bargaining, is enter into an unspoken contract and then break it by refusing to pay for the service. If you're being bugged by someone whose help you don't need, just let them know you can't pay anything for their trouble. It may not make you a friend, but it always works and it's better than a row and recriminations.

not the little day-pack over your shoulder which will virtually identify you as a tourist.

The only substantial risks otherwise are down at the coast (where valuables often disappear from the beach or occasionally get grabbed), in the other big towns (Nakuru and, to a lesser extent, Kisumu), and in some of the game parks – Samburu and Maasai Mara have had a number of incidents in recent years.

If you're **driving**, it's never a good idea to leave even a locked car unguarded if it has anything of value in it. In towns, there's usually someone who will volunteer to guard it for you for a few shillings.

Doping scams seem to be on the rise at present, with operators on different public transport routes managing to drug tourists and relieve them of their belongings. Be very wary of accepting any food, drink or cigarettes on public transport.

All of this isn't meant to induce paranoia. But if you flaunt the trappings of wealth where there's urban poverty, somebody will want to remove them. There's always less risk in leaving your valuables in a locked hotel room or – judiciously – with the management, than in taking them with you. It should go without saying that you don't wear dangling earrings or any kind of chain or necklace. If you clearly have nothing on you, you're unlikely to feel, or be, threatened. In Nairobi, the rush hour at dusk is probably the worst time, but it's a good idea to be alert getting off a night bus early in the morning, too. It's also worth tuning into the monthly cycle of poverty and wealth among urban Kenyans; there are always more pickpockets about at the end of the month, when people are carrying the salaries they've just been paid.

When you have to **carry money**, put it in several places if possible. Avoid socks, though; it

seems thieves are on to that and people have had their footwear literally ripped off. Velcro pocket closures seem a good idea.

CONS AND SCAMS

Approaches in the street from "schoolboys" with sponsorship forms (only primary education is free, and even then, books, uniforms, even furniture have to be bought) and from "refugees" with long stories are not uncommon and probably best shrugged off. Some, unfortunately, may be genuine.

One scam, almost "traditional" by now and surprisingly successful to judge by the number of tourists who fall for it, relies entirely on people's belief in the paranoid republic. It involves an approach by a "student", followed by a request for a small sum of money. As you leave with a sigh of relief, a group of heavies surround you and claim to be police, interested in the discussion you've been having with that "subversive", or "Sudanese terrorist", or whoever, and the funds you provided him. A large fine is demanded. You can tell them to go to hell, or suggest you all go to the police station. Such aggressions are never the real thing.

A treat for Nairobi motorists is a small boy popping up and slapping you in the face as you get out after parking. As you make to go after him in outrage, his friends grab what they can from the car. Other car tricks are described in the "Car Rental and Driving" section on p.40 and in the sections on Nakuru and Isiolo – where they seem most popular.

Lastly, an old one that still catches people out: if you're grabbed by a man who has just picked up a wad of money in the street and seems oddly willing to share it with you in a convenient nearby alley, you'll know you're about to be robbed.

MUGGINGS

If you get mugged, the usual rule applies: don't resist; knives and guns are occasionally carried. It will be over in an instant and you're unlikely to be hurt. But the hassles, and worse, that gather when you try to do anything about it make it imperative not to let it happen in the first place. Thieves caught red-handed are usually mobbed – often killed – so when you shout "Thief!" ("*Mwizi!*" in Swahili), be ready to intercede once you've retrieved your belongings.

Usually you'll have no chance, or desire, to catch the thief, and the first reaction is to go to the **police**. Unless you've lost a lot of money (and cash is virtually irretrievable) or irreplaceable property, however, think twice about doing this. They rarely do something for nothing – even stamping an insurance form will probably cost you – and secondly you should consider the ramifications if you and they set off to try and catch the culprits. This kind of scenario, with you in the back of a police car expected to point out the thief in the crowds, is a complete waste of time. And, whatever you do, never agree to act as a decoy in the hope that the same thing will happen again in front of a police ambush. Police shootings take place all the time and you may prefer not to be the cause of a cold-blooded murder. As angry as you may feel about being robbed, the desperation that leads men and boys to risk their lives for your things gives a lot of support to the idea that capital punishment is no deterrent.

If you have to visit the police in Nairobi, go to the main police station (marked on the map), not any of the smaller posts and offices.

DEALING WITH THE POLICE

Kenyan police are probably no worse than most others. There are few possible generalizations, and stories do sometimes get recounted of extraordinary **kindness** at times of trouble and of occasional bursts of **efficiency** that would do credit to any police force. But, badly educated and poorly paid as the police mostly are, you would be wise to steer clear as far as possible. If you have **official business** with the police, then politeness, smiles and handshakes always help. If you're expected to give a bribe – as you usually are – wait for it to be hinted at and haggle over it as you would any payment; the equivalent of a dollar or so is often enough to oil small wheels.

In **unofficial dealings**, the police, especially in remote outposts, can go out of their way to help you with food, transport or accommodation. Try to reciprocate. Police salaries are low – no more than a few thousand shillings a month – and they rely on unofficial income to get by. Only a brand new police force and realistic salaries could alter a situation which is now entrenched.

IN TROUBLE WITH THE POLICE

Common ways of exciting police interest are infringements of currency laws and drug possession, either of which will land you a large fine and deportation at least – don't expect to buy yourself out of this kind of trouble. Driving offences are less serious, though being stopped at the fairly frequent road checkpoints is becoming increasingly common. It's worth knowing that some forces have speed-trap radar equipment which they set up outside towns: drive with caution as speed limits are often vague.

UNSEEMLY BEHAVIOUR

Be warned that failure to observe the following points of **Kenyan etiquette** can get you arrested or put you in a position where you may be obliged to pay a bribe. Stand in cinemas and on other occasions when the national anthem is playing. Stand still when the national flag is being raised or lowered in your field of view. Don't take photos of the flag or His Excellency the President (often seen on state occasions in Nairobi). Pull off the road completely when scores of motorcycle outriders appear, then get out and stand by your vehicle (for it is he). Never tear up a banknote, of any denomination. And don't urinate in public.

WOMEN'S KENYA

Machismo, in its fully fledged Latin varieties, is rare in Kenya and male egos are usually softened by reserves of humour. Women's groups flourish across the country, but are concerned more with improvement of incomes, education, health and nutrition than social or political emancipation.

SEXUAL HARASSMENT

Women, whether travelling alone or together, may come across occasional **persistent hasslers** but seldom much worse. Universal rules apply: if you suspect ulterior motives, turn down all offers and stonily refuse to converse, though you needn't fear expressing your anger if that's how you feel. You will, eventually, be left alone. Really obnoxious individuals are usually on their own, fortunately. These tactics are hardly necessary except on the coast, and then particularly in **Lamu**. Avoid walking alone down beach access roads north or south of Mombasa, however, as there's a danger of violent robbery for either sex.

Blonde women suffer more, though cutting your hair short or dyeing it seem drastic and rather prejudicial steps. There is already enough discouragement in the world to women wanting to travel without the company of men – and Kenya is probably easier in this respect than most countries.

For a book packed with anecdotes, information and encouragement, get the *Rough Guide* special, *More Women Travel.*

BROADER ISSUES

In 1985, when Nairobi hosted the International Women's Decade Conference, Kenya's **women's movement** was still embryonic. Ten years on, the fourth UN World Conference on Women, held in Beijing in 1995, gave fresh incentive to women's groups throughout Kenya to work together to improve women's status and conditions. Women are becoming increasingly vocal in their call for political representation at local and national levels. The Maendeleo ya Wanawake Organization (MYWO) is seen as the national network best equipped to implement issues tackled in Beijing. Having started to help women at a very basic level forty years ago, Maendeleo now encourages economic independence and, as annual membership costs only Ksh20, almost every woman in Kenya can belong. The umbrella group teaches basic literacy, family planning and nutrition and is working hard to abolish the practices of ritual female genital mutilation – known, in a classic bit of male anthropologese, as "female circumcision". Kenya, tragically, is still used as a contraceptive testing ground; Depoprovera, high-level oestrogen pills and the Dalkon shield have all been foisted on Kenyan women.

For more information and contacts, get in touch with Maendeleo (see Nairobi "Listings"). You might also try writing to the Pan-African Women's Trade Union, PO Box 61068 Nairobi, or contact the Forum for African Women's Education, which has a good library.

SEXUAL ATTITUDES

Sexual mores in Kenya are refreshingly hedonistic and uncluttered, nor is prostitution the rigid, secretive transaction of the West. Unfortunately, sexually transmitted diseases, including the HIV virus, are rife. Attitudes in Kenya are waking up to this reality, but you should be aware of the very real risks should you accept a proposition. Various surveys have revealed that anything from one in four to nine out of ten Nairobi prostitutes are HIV positive. It goes without saying that casual sex without a condom is a deadly gamble and you should assume any sexual contact to be HIV positive.

Despite this, female **prostitution** flourishes enthusiastically everywhere and a remarkable number of the cheaper hotels double as brothels, or at least willingly rent their rooms by the hour.

Gigolos and male prostitutes – far fewer – are limited mostly to Nairobi and the coast.

Among tourists, enough arrive expecting sexual adventures to make flirtatious pestering a fairly constant part of the scene, irritating or amusing as it strikes you. And if you're here looking for a holiday affair, Lamu seems to be the place.

As for attitudes to **gay life**, they're rather hard to pin down. While there is no gay scene as such, male homosexuality is an accepted undercurrent on the coast, where it finds most room for expression in Lamu, and to a small extent in Nairobi. The Lake Victoria region has a fairly relaxed attitude, too. *Msenge* is Swahili for gay man. Elsewhere, homosexuality *seems* scarce enough not to be an issue. On the statute books, however, it remains illegal.

KENYA'S PEOPLE, LANGUAGES AND RELIGION

Whether called peoples, ethnic groups or tribes, Kenyans have a multiplicity of racial and cultural origins. Distinctions would be simple (and dangerous) if similarities in physical appearance were shared by those who speak the same language and share a common culture: the term "tribe" tends to imply this kind of banal stereotype. But "tribes" have never been closed units, and

appearance, speech and culture have always overlapped. Families, for instance, often contained members of different tribes. In the last fifty years, tribal identities have broken down still further as broader class, political and national ones have emerged.

The most enduring ethnic distinction is language. A person's **"mother tongue"** is still important as an index of social identity and a tribe is best defined as people sharing a common first language. But, in the towns and among affluent families, even language is increasingly unimportant. Many people speak three languages (their own, Swahili and English) or even four if they have mixed parentage. And for a few, English has become a first language. The complex issues of tribal identity are becoming critical with the emergence of multi-party democracy and the simultaneous eruption of chauvinistic tribalism among some leaders who would prefer democracy to go away.

There are pieces throughout the book on aspects of the history and cultures of the main language groups in each region.

AFRICAN LANGUAGE GROUPS IN KENYA

This, broadly, is the breakdown of Kenya's language groups into separate ethnic identities. You'll find variations on these spellings, and inconsistencies in the use of prefixes (ie Kamba instead of Akamba, Agikuyu instead of Kikuyu, and so on).

BANTU-SPEAKING

Western Bantu: Luyia, Gusii, Kuria.

Central Bantu: Akamba, Kikuyu, Embu, Meru, Mbere, Tharaka.

Coastal Bantu: Swahili, Mijikenda, Segeju, Pokomo, Taita, Taveta.

NILOTIC-SPEAKING

Lake-River Nilotic: Luo.

Plains Nilotic: Maasai and Samburu (Maa-speakers), Turkana, Teso, Njemps, Elmolo.

Highland Nilotic: Kalenjin group including Nandi, Marakwet, Pokot, Tugen, Kipsigis, Elkony.

CUSHITIC-SPEAKING

Southern Cushitic: Boni.

Eastern Cushitic: Somali, Rendille, Orma, Boran, Gabbra ("Galla" is often used to describe all these language groups except the Somali).

NAMES AND GROUPS

Books continue to use various unwieldy terms: **Bantu** and **Nilotic** are language groups (like Indo-European or Semitic) and, restricted to a linguistic sense, fair enough. But Hamitic, which still pops up occasionally, is almost meaningless and hedged with racist overtones. "Hamitic influence" has been credited with many technological, social and political innovations in the past. The biblical origins of the word give it away: it reflects the early European presumption that lighter-skinned people with thinner lips and straighter noses were more intelligent than other Africans. The origins of these people in northeast Africa and their implied association with the wellsprings of Mediterranean civilization were further "evidence" of this. The term "Nilo-hamitic" (often used to refer to the Maasai and other pastoralists admired by the Europeans) just confuses the issue further; it implies the cross-cutting cultural, linguistic and racial overlays that most Kenyans have inherited, without abandoning the idea of racially superior influences from the north.

Biologically, of course, Negroid inheritance predominates among Africans, with Caucasoid elements clear enough in many regions. But physiology doesn't have much to do with language or culture. Travelling around Kenya, you become aware of just how far off the mark the old racist doctrines really were.

Apart from the African majority, who make up about 99 percent of the population, Kenya has a considerable and diverse **Asian** population – perhaps over 150,000 – most of whom live in Nairobi, Mombasa, Kisumu and Nakuru. Descendants in part of the labourers brought over to build the railway, they also number many whose parents and grandparents came in its wake, to trade and set up businesses. And some families, notably on the coast, have lived in Kenya for centuries. Predominantly Punjabi and Gujerati speakers from northwest India and Pakistan, they are overwhelmingly dominant in business. There's a dispersed Christian Goan community, too, who tend to have less formalized relations with other Kenyans. And a persistent, but diminishing **Arab**-speaking community remains on the coast.

Lastly, there are still an estimated ten thousand **European** residents – a surprisingly motley crew from British ex-servicemen to Italian aristocrats – scattered through the highlands and the rest of the country, some four thousand of whom hold Kenya citizenship. Some maintain a scaled-down version of the old planter's life, and a few still hold senior civil service positions. Increasingly, though, the community is turning to the tourist industry for a firmer future – and a life beyond Kenya if necessary.

RELIGION

In the matter of **religion**, broad-based, non-fundamentalist **Sunni Islam** dominates the coast and the northeast, and is in the ascendant throughout the country. Many towns have several mosques (or dozens on the coast), but one usually serves as the focal **Friday mosque** for the whole community. Shiite fundamentalism was previously almost unknown among African believers, but the Islamic Party of Kenya (IPK) has some vocal fundamentalist campaigners among its supporters. The Aga Khan's **Ismaili** sect is an influential Asian constituency with powerful business interests. **Hindu** and **Sikh** temples are found in most large towns, and there are adherents of **Jainism** and the **Bahai** faith, too. Varieties of **Catholicism** and **Protestantism** are present more in the highlands and westwards. In the far west, especially towards Lake Victoria, there are many minor **Christian sects** and churches, often based around the teaching of local prophets and preachers.

Indigenous religion (mostly based around the idea of a supreme god) continues to play a large part in many people's lives, however, with sacrifices and appropriate rituals performed from time to time; belief in Christianity or Islam is rarely watertight.

ETIQUETTE

Islamic moral strictures tend to be generously interpreted. On the coast, it's always best to **dress** in loose-fitting long sleeves and skirts or trousers in the towns, but shorts and T-shirts won't get you into trouble: people are far too polite to admonish strangers. Malindi, in particular, is very relaxed. Lamu calls more for *kikoi* and *kanga* wraps for both sexes and, because it's so small, more consideration for local feelings. Suitably dressed and hatted men, and often women, can enter **mosques**. Few are very grand, however, and you rarely miss much by staying outside.

KENYA'S NEIGHBOURING STATES

Many travellers start trans-African journeys in Kenya. And even if you don't intend to cross the continent, Kenya gives multiple options for onward travel. The following pieces are intended as brief, introductory notes. Embassy addresses in Nairobi can be found on p.124.

TANZANIA

Visas: Americans, British and most Commonwealth nationals need visas; Irish, Swedes and Norwegians exempted.
Exchange rate: about Tsh800–950:£1 (Tsh535–635:$1), with a black market offering slightly higher rates, but most costs are paid in hard currency.
Useful language: Swahili.
Health: yellow fever certificate.
Safaris: from about $60/day (Kilimanjaro climb from about $400 all in for five days).
Park fees: $20/day.
Transport: trains (to the capital, Dodoma, and to the Zambian border) and buses (rough roads, long journeys); the Mwanza to Moshi bus trip through Serengeti is recommended.

BACKGROUND AND ATTRACTIONS

Years of socialism under **Julius Nyerere** have given way to a fragile free market under **Ali Hassan Mwinyi**. The country's first multi-party elections were held in late 1995. Swahili is the national language and there are few tribal tensions. Grass-roots democracy and human rights

are (relatively) secure but the economic infrastructure is badly lacking, and services unreliable.

Arusha, the country's safari capital, and a day's bus journey from Nairobi, makes a good base for exploring the northern game parks: the **Serengeti**, a continuation of the Maasai Mara but a dozen times bigger; **Ngorongoro Crater**, where a complete ecosystem is contained inside an extinct volcano; **Lake Manyara**; and the twin-peaked massif of **Kilimanjaro**.

The coast is alluring – twice the length of Kenya's and strewn with the sizeable islands of Zanzibar, Pemba and Mafia. **Bagamoyo**, on the mainland, and **Kilwa**, far to the south, are pretty hideaways, too. **Zanzibar** shares Lamu's appeal, but is larger and more rural; the east coast has cheap beach houses. The bureaucracy of Zanzibar (which retains the trappings of a separate country, united with the mainland) can be a tedious introduction, but the human welcome is a wonderful palliative.

The rest of the country, mostly a vast dry plateau, is tough travelling. Worth the long journey and fairly high cost, though, is a visit to the chimpanzees at **Gombe Stream National Park** on the shore of **Lake Tanganyika**.

UGANDA

Visas: required by South Africans; British, American, Canadian, Australian, New Zealand and European nationals exempt.
Exchange rate: about Ush1500:£1 (Ush1000:$1); no black market.

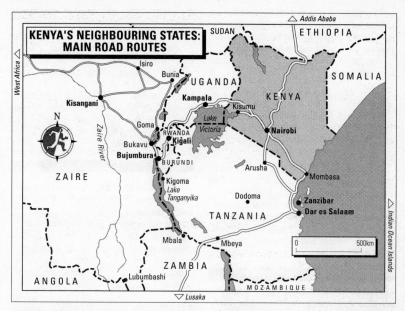

Useful language: English.
Health: yellow fever certificate.
Safaris: from about $100/day.
Park fees: variable.
Transport: trains from Kampala to Kasese (Zaire border) and Malaba (Kenyan border), and buses and *matatus* on a reasonable road system. Most of the northeast is closed.

BACKGROUND AND ATTRACTIONS

Exceptionally friendly people and polite treatment by officials are partly why Uganda is currently so popular. Uganda's reputation has suffered nearly as much as its people over the last thirty years, though with the support being given now to **President Museveni** (at least in the south and west), things seem to be improving at last. Travel in the north is less secure due to recent guerrilla activity around the Sudanese border and the guerrilla campaign being waged by a group called the "Lords Resistance Army" against the government and civilians.

The central region's plains splashed with rivers and swamps rise westwards to **Lakes Edward and Albert**, the **White Nile**, the snow-streaked **Ruwenzoris** (the Mountains of the Moon) and the high border with Zaire. This west-

ern part holds the country's major attractions, including the reopened and far from empty **Muchison Falls National Park**. In Lake Victoria, the relatively isolated **Ssese Islands** are becoming popular.

The **mountains** offer superb hiking and bush-walking amid equatorial mountain vegetation. In the southwest, a clutch of parks (some dense jungle) are opening up again. **Bwindi National Park** is a good area to track **mountain gorillas** but, though cheaper and less organized than the Zaire and Rwanda gorilla industries, it's also less certain you'll find them. It's advisable to make arrangements in Kampala first.

RWANDA AND BURUNDI

Visas: required by all except Germans (Rwanda).
Currency: Rwandan franc and Burundi franc; rates are subject to wide swings and the black market option.
Useful language: French.
Health: yellow fever certificates required.

BACKGROUND AND ATTRACTIONS

Small highland states, Rwanda and Burundi are mountainous, heavily cultivated, highly popu-lated, poor, francophone and expensive. Kigali and Bujumbura – their respective capitals – are difficult for low budgets. Before its civil war and the genocide waged against the Tutsis in 1994, Rwanda had established an embryonic tourist industry for transiting overlanders, and its **mountain gorillas** had become a magnetic draw in their own right. The country won't be receiving many visitors, however, until some sort of stability is achieved, and you are firmly advised not to visit as a tourist. Burundi, meanwhile, with no compelling attractions of its own, has been hovering on the verge of civil war and is equally to be avoided.

Rwanda and Burundi reflect the old feudal traditions of cattle-herding fiefdoms with rigid tribal distinctions. After the Belgians left – having further divided the peoples – both countries experienced waves of revolt and counter-revolt, pitching pastoral Tutsis, the traditional aristocrats, against Hutu cultivators, their traditional tenant farmers.

ZAIRE

Visas: required by all, and usually a letter of recommendation from your own embassy is needed.
Exchange rate: about 17,250 New Zaire: £1 (NZ11,500: $1), with runaway inflation.
Useful languages: Swahili (east) and French.
Health: yellow fever and cholera certificates.
Safaris: Virunga National Park gorilla-tracking costs about $120 for the day.
Transport: chronically bad with virtually no buses; use lorries, ferries, one or two train services and, above all, your legs. At present, venturing beyond the immediate eastern tourist zone is risky.

BACKGROUND AND ATTRACTIONS

Zaire is dissolving as a functioning country. The tyrant dictator **Mobutu** and his well-looked-after praetorian guard are in permanent conflict with the constitutionally appointed government and the bulk of the army – who survive by looting (and pose a threat to travellers).

Major attractions are the climbable volcanoes (one still active), and gorillas of the **Virunga National Park**.

Much of the **northern rainforest** region is enclosed by the trailing tributaries of the Zaire River. This is where most overlanding travellers pass and it has always been, essentially, anarchic. Society and economy are left to manage as best they can: teachers and civil servants are forgotten; roads and bridges collapse for weeks on end. Everything is expensive. Here you'll find torsos of roast monkey for sale in the markets, pygmy hunters melting into the forest, Greek and Portuguese plantation barons, narrow-gauge railways, steamboats teeming with passengers, and jungle in every direction. At the time of writing, the crossing point from Zaire to the Central African Republic at Bangui was closed.

SUDAN

Visas: required by all; can take weeks to issue.
Exchange rate: about S£1000: £1 (S£700: $1).
Useful language: English.
Health: yellow fever and cholera certificates.
Transport: train and truck, some buses. Nile steamers do not go upstream of Kosti and all overland routes to Kenya, Uganda and Zaire are closed. The Egyptian and Central African Republic borders are unsafe and sometimes closed.

BACKGROUND

The whole of southern Sudan bordering Uganda and Kenya is closed to tourists, making overland travel out of the question. At the time of writing, as the country writhes in the grip of a brutal dictatorship which allies itself with Saddam's Iraq, and comes down with an iron fist against the divided southern resistance movements, the prospects for travel anywhere in Sudan are bleak.

ETHIOPIA AND ERITREA

Visas: required by all; visas for Ethiopia are issued in Nairobi if you have an air ticket to Addis.
Exchange rate: about 10birr: £1 (7birr: $1).
Useful language: English.
Health: yellow fever and cholera certificates are mandatory.
Transport: improving, with a good bus network .

BACKGROUND AND ATTRACTIONS

One of Africa's most compelling countries, Ethiopia is an ancient mountain kingdom considerably expanded in the last two hundred years, but Christian at its Amharic heart since the fourth century. Colonialism affected it only briefly when the Italians usurped its independence from 1936 to 1941. Revolution in 1974 deposed Emperor **Haile Selassie** and plunged Ethiopia from feudal misery into military dictatorship. **Mengistu** was overthrown in 1991, and **Eritrea**, which had been fighting the Addis governments for decades, held a referendum and declared independence in 1993.

Restrictions on touring the country have been lifted and visits to its **seventeenth-century castles**, **rock-hewn churches**, the **Semyen Mountains**, the **Bale Mountains National Park** and a string of jewel-like **lakes** in the Ethiopian Rift Valley are fascinating and rewarding. Travelling through Eritrea just about makes possible an unusual and recommended overland route into (or out of) Africa through **Djibouti** and **Yemen** – though you'll have to fly into or out of Yemen's capital, **Sana'a**.

SOMALIA

Visas: required by all, but few if any Somalian embassies are open.
Currency: the Somali shilling, but US$ are required.
Useful languages: English, Italian.
Health: yellow fever and cholera certificates are mandatory.
Transport: infrastructure badly broken down; public transport patchy and insecure.

BACKGROUND

On no account should you aim or expect to travel here as a tourist. Somalia has disintegrated as a functioning nation state. The north is relatively peaceful and governed independently as "Somaliland", but this state does not have international recognition.

INDIAN OCEAN ISLANDS

Visas: Seychelles – not required; Comoros – on arrival; Mauritius – not required for most nationalities; Madagascar – required by all.
Exchange rates: 7.5 Seychelles rupees: £1 (5SR: $1); Comoros franc tied to French franc; 29 Mauritian rupees: £1 (20MR: $1); about 6000 Madagascar francs: £1 (4000MF: $1).
Useful languages: French (Seychelles and Comoros, Madagascar), English (Seychelles, Mauritius), Swahili (Comoros).
Transport: *Air Seychelles, Air Madagascar, Air Mauritius* (see p.123).

BACKGROUND AND ATTRACTIONS

Entry to the **Seychelles**, is simple – just arrive with your cholera certificate – and the archipelago is a delightful place for a holiday. You can help keep the costs down with guest houses (especially off season), hired bicycles and inter-island ferries (rather than flights).

The **Comoros islands** are equally amenable, and very little known, though one or two tourist developments have been established. Politically, however, they are highly unstable – check with the Foreign Office, State Department or other relevant government department for the latest advice.

Tourists flock to **Mauritius** of course – the majority of them South African – and the hilly, wooded interior and fabulous beaches are spectacular assets.

Madagascar is worth making an ultimate goal for your travels: for its diverse scenery, unique wildlife, the distinctive Malgache people and language, and unusual mixture of African and southeast Asian cultures. You may need persistence to get a seat on the plane from Nairobi, but it's worth any amount of hassle if you can afford the fare.

DIRECTORY

Beggars are fairly common in the touristy parts of Nairobi and Mombasa. Most are visibly destitute; many are cripples, lepers or homeless mothers with children. Some have regular pitches, others keep on the move. They are harassed by police and often rounded up. Kenyans often give to the same beggar on a regular basis and, of course, alms-giving is a requirement of Islam believed to benefit the donor.

The hundreds of glue-sniffing boys (most aged 8–14) is a sad development of recent years in Nairobi and Nakuru. They're responsible for much of the cities' petty crime – and often pay a swift, final price.

Books Less than fifty percent of Kenyans are literate but books and reading material have a high profile. Bookstores in Nairobi, Mombasa and in the tourist hotels have imported paperback selections. Second-hand book stalls are often worth looking over, too. Or ask other travellers: bring one book and keep exchanging. For suggestions on reading matter, see "Books" in *Contexts*.

Clothes Particularly if you're only coming for a short stay, it's important to bring what you need to be comfortable. Take cotton clothes and good-quality tennis or sports shoes, plus at least one really warm sweater or, better still, a soft-lined jacket with pockets. (See the "Mount Kenya" section for advice on what you need at high altitudes.) A cotton jersey tracksuit is ideal for early-morning game runs when you'll quite often set off before sunrise. And, even if you're

on a shoestring, take some nicer clothes to wear in lodges: access is often difficult for the ragged.

Contraceptives Condoms are available from town pharmacies. Family planning clinics in most main towns are helpful (see Nairobi and Mombasa "Listings") and will sometimes provide them and – with a prescription – oral contraceptives, free or for a small charge. If you use pills, though, it's far wiser to bring all you'll need.

Departure tax When leaving Kenya by air there's a departure tax equivalent to US$20, payable in foreign currency or Kenyan shillings (around Ksh1200 at the current rate of exchange). If you don't have the right money, change will be given only in Kenyan shillings. Some airlines (*BA* for example) will collect this payment in Nairobi on the day of departure if you prefer. If you're booked on a package, you are likely still to have to pay the tax yourself. Departure tax on domestic flights is Ksh100. Neither kind of departure tax is payable for infants.

Drugs Grass (*bhangi*) is widely cultivated and smoked and is remarkably cheap. Officially illegal, the authorities do make some effort to control it. Use and attitudes vary considerably but you should be very discreet if you're going to indulge. The ruling KANU party's "Youth Wingers" have broadened their operations from political thuggery to snooping on tourists – especially on the coast. Watch out who you get high with. Official busts result in a shakedown by the police, a heavy fine and deportation at the very least. Your embassy will not be sympathetic. Anything harder than marijuana is rarely sold and will get you in worse trouble if you're caught. Miraa, a mild herbal stimulant chewed with bubble gum, is legal and widely available, especially in Nairobi, Mombasa and in the north. It's the East African lorry driver's "upper" and something of an acquired taste.

Electricity Kenya's electricity supply is usually reliable and, like Britain's, uses square, three-pin plugs on 220–240V. Only fancier hotels have outlets or shaver points in the rooms.

Emergencies For Police, Fire and Ambulance dial ☎999. They usually take ages to arrive.

Gifts Ballpoint pens and postcards are about the only small items worth taking and can always be given to children. Off the beaten track, they'll be appreciated by many adults, too, though few people will have an exaggerated idea of their real value. If you'll be travelling or staying for some time and really want to prepare, get a large batch of photos of you and your family with your address on the back. You'll get lots of mail.

"Kenya" or "Keenya"? Although you'll hear "Kenya" most of the time, the second pronunciation is still used, and not exclusively by old colonials. It seems that the colonial pronunciation was closer to the original name of the mountain, Kirinyaga. This was early on shortened to Kinya and spelt "Kenya" (with affinity to English "key"). With the arrival of modern African orthography, this spelling came to be pronounced with a short "e", and when Kenyatta became president the coincidence of his name was exploited.

Laundry There are no launderettes/laundromats in Kenya and it's usually easiest to wash your own clothes: you can buy packets of Omo soap powder, and things dry fast. Beware of New Blue Omo – it's very strong and wrecks clothes if you use it for long. Otherwise, there's often someone wherever you're staying who will be prepared to negotiate a laundry charge. Don't spread clothes on the ground to dry: they might be infested by the tumbu fly, which lays its eggs in them for the larvae to hatch and burrow into your skin.

Place names Place names all over Africa (not just Kenya) are remarkably confusing to outsiders. In some parts every town or village seems to have a name starting with the same syllable. In the Kenya highlands, you'll find Kiambu, Kikuyu, Kiganjo, Kiserian, Kinangop etc. Further west you confront Kaptagat, Kapsabet, Kabarnet, Kapsowar . . . As soon as you detect a problem like this, just get into the habit of "de-stressing" the first syllable. A more practical problem all over rural Kenya is the vague use of names to denote a whole district and, at the same time, its nucleus, be it a small town, a village, or just a cluster of corrugated iron shops and bars. Sometimes there'll be two such focuses. They often move in a matter of a few years, so what looks like a junction town on the map turns out to be away from the road, or in a different place altogether. Ask for the "shopping centre" and you'll usually find the local hive of activity and the place with the name you were looking for.

Snorkelling If you plan to do a fair bit of goggling, try to bring your own mask and snorkel. They aren't highly expensive, or particularly heavy, and you'll benefit from having equipment that fits and works, and save money you'd otherwise spend renting it . Don't forget that although certain parts of the coast have exceptional stretches of reef, you can have a rewarding dip under the waves almost anywhere.

Student cards If you qualify, get hold of an International Student Identity Card (ISIC) from student unions or student/youth travel agents. In

---

THINGS TO TAKE

In no particular order, and not all essential:

● **Binoculars** (the small, fold-up ones) are invaluable for game watching. Without them you'll miss half the action. Take a pair for each person.

● **Sunglasses** are a health precaution worth bringing even if you're not used to them, and they're expensive to buy in Kenya.

● **Plastic bags** are invaluable: large bin-liner bags to keep dust off clothes, small resealable ones to protect cameras and film.

● Take a multipurpose **penknife**, a **torch**, an **alarm clock** (handy for pre-dawn starts) and a **padlock** – vital in lodgings where doors don't lock.

● **Camping gas stoves** are light and useful even if you're not camping. The cylinders can be bought in Nairobi (see "Listings", p.126) and in a number of other places.

● A tube of **ant-killer** comes in handy if you're camping, particularly on the coast.

● Down on the coast, too, **plastic sandals** are best for walking on the reef; you can buy them cheaply in Kenya.

● You might want to take your own **flip-flops/thongs** for cheap hotel bathrooms (though a pair is often provided).

● **Earplugs** are a help in some lodgings if you're a light sleeper.

● A **sheet sleeping bag** (sew up a sheet) is essential for low-budget travel.

● If you shave bring a supply of disposable **razors**.

● For driving around the parks and hiking, a **compass** is immensely useful.

Kenya, it's no passport to automatic cheap deals, but it can be worth showing for discounted park and museum entry fees (it rarely works in the popular parks, especially in the high season). Note that only American ISIC cards provide automatic basic insurance cover for their holders.

Tampons Available in town chemists but expensive, so bring supplies.

Time Kenya is three hours ahead of Greenwich Mean Time all year round, which means two hours ahead of Britain during the summer, eight hours ahead of Eastern Standard Time, and seven hours behind Sydney.

With slight variations east and west, it gets light at 6am and dark at 6pm. If you're learning Swahili, remember that "Swahili time" runs from dawn to dusk to dawn rather than midnight to midday to midnight. 7am and 7pm are both *saa moja* (one o'clock) while midnight and midday are *saa sita* (six o'clock). It's not as confusing as it first sounds – just add or subtract six hours to work out Swahili time (or read the opposite side of your watch).

People and things are usually late in Kenya. That said, if you try to anticipate, you're generally caught out. Trains nearly always leave right on time; buses often have punctual departures as well. In more remote areas though, if a driver tells you he's going somewhere "today", it doesn't necessarily mean he expects to arrive today . . .

Tipping If you're staying in tourist-class establishments, and travelling a lot, you will often have to tip staff. In expensive hotels, Ksh100 wouldn't be out of place for portering a lot of luggage, but coins are usually adequate, or small notes at the most. With the peculiar, upside-down logic of the world of service indus-

tries, in the very humblest establishments, tipping is not the custom. Note that on safaris, tips are considered almost part of the pay and you're expected to shell out at the end of the trip (see p.63).

Toilets Carry toilet paper – which you can buy in most places – as few cheap hotels provide it. Town public toilets (*Wanawake* = Women; *Wanaume* = Men) are invariably disgusting. Public buildings and hotels are unlikely to turn you away if you ask.

Weddings Many of the coastal hotels and a few game lodges will lay it on thick if that's what you really want – garlands of flowers, gospel choirs, "complimentary" cakes and tributes, tree-planting ceremonies ("If it dies, we shall plant another") and so on. The whole experience can feel rather conveyor-belt-driven (you may be just one of half a dozen happy couples getting hitched on the same day at your dream resort hotel), and you might find that being gawped at by holiday-makers in swimming togs as you say "I do" doesn't do much for the solemnity of the occasion. Choose your venue carefully.

Work Unless you've lined up a job or voluntary work before leaving for Kenya, you have little chance of getting employment. Wages are extremely low – for university lecturers, for example, they start at not much more than the equivalent of £150 ($225) per month – and there's serious unemployment in the towns. Particular skills are sometimes in demand – mechanics at game park lodges, for example – but the employer will need good connections to arrange the required papers. It's illegal to obtain income in Kenya while staying on a visitor's pass. You may be able to find work on a voluntary work camp, however: see pp.10–11.

THE IMPACT OF TOURISM

If you're at all concerned about the impact of tourism upon the social fabric and environment of Kenya, then you might be interested to find out more about the following organizations. **Tourism Concern** (Southlands College, Wimbledon Parkside, London SW19 5NN, UK) is an organization that campaigns for the rights of local people to be consulted in tourist developments

affecting their lives. They produce a quarterly magazine of news and articles. **CERT**, the Campaign for Environmentally Responsible Tourism (PO Box 4246, London SE21 7ZE), lobbies to educate tour operators and tourists in a sensitive approach to travel, focusing on immediate practical ways in which the environment can be protected.

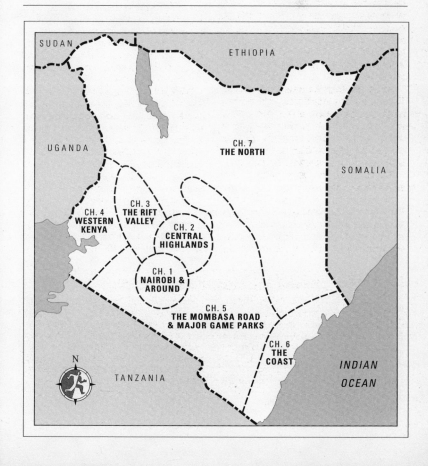

SUDAN

ETHIOPIA

UGANDA

CH. 7
THE NORTH

SOMALIA

CH. 3
THE RIFT
VALLEY

CH. 4
WESTERN
KENYA

CH. 2
CENTRAL
HIGHLANDS

CH. 1
NAIROBI &
AROUND

CH. 5
THE MOMBASA ROAD
& MAJOR GAME PARKS

CH. 6
THE
COAST

N

TANZANIA

INDIAN
OCEAN

CHAPTER ONE

NAIROBI AND AROUND

E asily the largest city in East Africa, **Nairobi** is also the youngest, the most modern, the fastest growing and, at 1700m, the highest. The superlatives could go on forever. "City in the sun", runs one tour brochure sobriquet, "City of flowers", another. Less enchanted visitors growl "Nairobbery". The city catches your attention at least. This is no tropical backwater.

Most roads, particularly paved ones, lead to Nairobi and, like it or not, you're bound to spend some time here. But walking down Kenyatta Avenue at rush hour, or up Tom Mboya Street after dark, when the security men cluster around their fires on the pavement, it's perhaps easy to forget how quickly you can leave the city and be in the bush. Apart from being the **safari** capital of the world, Nairobi is an excellent **base for travel**, just eight hours by road to the coast, or an overnight train journey, about the

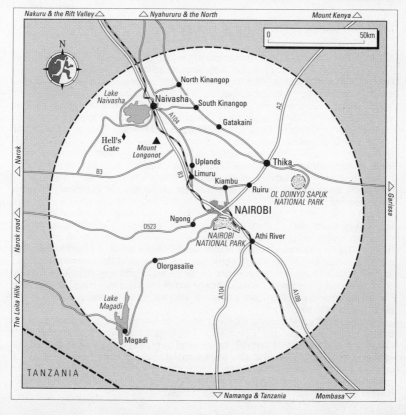

ACCOMMODATION PRICE CODES

Rates for a standard double or twin room. For a full explanation of these price codes, see p.46

① Under Ksh300   (under approx. £3.30/$5)
② Ksh300–500   (£3.30/$5–£5.50/£8)
③ Ksh500–1000   (£5.50/$8–£11/$17)
④ Ksh1000–2000   (£11/$17–£22/$33)
⑤ Ksh2000–4000   (£22/$33–£44/$67)
⑥ Ksh4000–6000   (£44/$67–£67/$100)
⑦ Ksh6000–8000   (£67/$100–£89/$133)
⑧ Ksh8000–10,000   (£89/$133–£111/$167)
⑨ Over Ksh10,000   (over £111/$167)

same time to the far west, and just a couple of hours west to the great trough of the Rift Valley or north to the slopes of Mount Kenya.

For **shorter trips**, worthwhile destinations, covered at the end of this chapter, lie all around, with the first and closest target **Nairobi National Park**, a wild attraction where you'd expect to find suburbs. **Lake Naivasha** to the west and **Lake Magadi**, south, are two utterly different Rift Valley lakes, each just a few hours away from the capital – a day trip by car, two or three days if hitching or taking the bus. The prehistoric site of **Olorgasailie** is on the way to Magadi. If you're looking for greener and cooler destinations, an interesting hiking (or biking) route runs from **North Kinangop to Thika**. For loftier heights turn north to the central highlands (Chapter Two).

NAIROBI

NAIROBI is one of Africa's major cities: the UN's fourth "World Centre", East Africa's commercial and aid hub, and a significant capital in its own right, with a population of well over a million. As a traveller, your first impressions are likely to depend on how – and where – you arrive. Coming here overland, from one of Kenya's suffering neighbour states, some time resting up among the fleshpots can seem a pleasant proposition. Newly arrived by air from Europe, though, you may wonder – amid the rash of signs for *California Cookies*, *Brunchburgers* and *Oriental Massage* – just how far you've travelled. Nairobi, less than a century old, has real claims to Western-Style sophistication but, as you'll soon find, it lacks a convincing heart. Apart from some lively musical attractions – some of East Africa's busiest **clubs** and best **bands** – there's little here of magnetic appeal, and most travellers stay long enough only to take stock, make some travel arrangements and maybe visit the **National Museum**, before moving on.

If you're interested in getting to know the real Kenya, though, Nairobi is as compelling a place as any and displays enormous vitality and buzz. The controlling ethos is commerce rather than community, and there's an almost wilful superficiality in the free-for-all of commuters, shoppers, police, hustlers and tourists. It's hard to imagine a city with a more fascinating variety of people, and almost all of them newcomers. Most are immigrants from rural areas, drawn to the presence and opportunities of money, and Nairobi, on the surface at least, seems to accept everyone with complete tolerance. On any downtown pavement you can see a complete cross-section of Kenyans, plus every variety of tourist.

Nairobi's rapid growth inevitably has a downside however (read any newspaper or talk to any resident and you'll hear some jaw-dropping stories of crime and police shootings), and you should certainly be aware of its reputation for **bag-snatching** and **robbery**, frequently directed at new tourist arrivals (see "Security" box overpage). If you plan to stay for any length of time, learn the art of survival; with the right attitude, you're unlikely to have problems. For the few days that most people spend in Nairobi – if initial misgivings can be overcome – it's a stimulating city.

Some history

Nairobi came into being in 1899, an artificial settlement created by Europeans at Mile 327 of the East African railway line, then being systematically forged from the coast into the interior. It was initially a supply depot, switching yard and campsite for the thousands of Indian labourers employed by the British. Its site, bleak and swampy, was simply the spot where operations came to a halt while the engineers figured out their next move, namely getting the line up the steep slopes that lay ahead. The name came from the local Maasai term for the valley, *Ewaso Nairobi*, "Stream of Cold Water", though the spot itself was originally called *Nakusontelon*, "Beginning of all Beauty".

Unexpectedly, the unplanned **settlement** took root. A few years later it was totally rebuilt after an outbreak of plague and the burning of the original town compound. By 1907, it was so firmly established that the colonists took it as the capital of the newly formed "British East Africa" (BEA). Europeans, encouraged by the authorities, settled in large numbers, while Africans were forced into employment by tax demands or onto specially created **reserves** – the Maasai to the Southern Reserve and the Kikuyu to their own reserve in the highlands.

The capital, lacking development from any established community, was somewhat characterless – and remains so. The **original centre** retains an Asian influence in its older buildings, but today it is shot through with glassy, high-rise blocks, indistinguishable from those in any western city. Surrounding the commercial hub are thousands of acres of **suburbs**: wealthiest in the west and north, increasingly poor to the south and especially the east, where they become, in part, out-and-out slums.

Names of these suburbs – Parklands, Lavington, Eastleigh, Shauri Moyo, among others – reflect the jumble of African, Asian and European elements in Nairobi's population, none of whom were local. The term "Nairobian" isn't in circulation because it would scarcely apply to anyone. Although it has a predominance of Kikuyu, the city is not the preserve of a single ethnic group, nor is it built on any distinctively tribal land. Standing as it does at the meeting point of Maasai, Kikuyu and Kamba territories, its choice as capital, accidental though it may have been (Kikuyu **Limuru** and Kamba **Machakos** were also considered), was a fortunate one for the future of the country.

Arrival

Getting into central Nairobi presents few problems, and once you're there, you'll have little trouble finding your way around. The city has widespread suburbs but its inner area is relatively small: a triangle of stores, offices and public buildings, with the railway station on the southern flank and the main bus stations on the east. Note that if you're arriving on a Sunday, it will all seem strangely quiet: most shops and many restaurants are closed.

Arriving by air

Arriving by air, you'll find yourself at **Jomo Kenyatta International Airport**, 15km out of town to the southeast on the Mombasa highway. Arrivals are normally straight-

---

DEPARTURES FROM KENYA – GETTING TO THE AIRPORT

Remember to **reconfirm** your flight reservations and also try to check that the plane is scheduled to arrive on time (telephone numbers on p.123). To get to the airport, either take the *KBS Stagecoach* #34 bus (from the *Ambassadeur*), or get the *Discount Airport Shuttle* from Barclays Plaza (see below for details), with hourly departures until 6pm. After 6pm you'll have to get a taxi; all hotels will arrange this.

forward. Check your **luggage** is intact as soon as you get if off the carousel. If anything appears to be missing go straight to the "Lost Luggage" desk before passing through customs. For customs advice, see p.24.

There's a **24-hour bank** (in theory), which you should try to get to as soon as possible, and an office of the **Flying Doctors** organization, where you can buy their special brand of life-saving insurance if you expect to be out in the wilds a lot. The *Simba Restaurant* at the top of the arrivals building is surprisingly good and reasonably priced.

Invariably, hordes of **taxi** drivers assail you once you are through customs. You need not be alarmed by this, but if you'd prefer to be met, try contacting *Save Taxi Service* (PO Box 10148; ☎02/222953 ext. 6, *Ambassadeur Hotel*) or *Let's Go Travel* (address on p.122). For the London-style cabs there's a fixed price to the city centre

SECURITY

Read the "Trouble" section in *Basics*, p.66.

An alarming number of new arrivals have to deal with a **robbery** in their first day or two in Nairobi, before they've adjusted to the city's pace and ways. Despite the fact that it usually carries armed police, a lot of people get ripped off within an hour of arriving on the **#34 bus** from the airport to the youth hostel. Victims get distracted in conversation or jostled, or have their hands grabbed and shaken by strangers. It's no joke and the best way to avoid losing wads of newly changed shillings is to secrete them all out of harm's way before you go anywhere near the bus; and likewise cameras or any other precious hand luggage you had on the plane. If anything starts to happen, make a lot of noise – it's no time to be shy. Sometimes it's enough just to clock the thieves – often young – and let them know you've seen them, which, surprisingly enough, usually stops them, and you can all have a (nervous) laugh.

Once in town, to avoid being victimized, you should take exaggerated care of your valuables, keep your hands out of reach and be – rationally – suspicious of everyone until you've caught your breath. It doesn't take long. Every rural Kenyan coming to the city for the first time goes through exactly the same process, and many are considerably less streetwise than you, having never been in a city before.

As suggested in *Basics*, dressing like a local expatriate and not carrying a bag will help you avoid ninety percent of unwanted approaches.

Beware of the fact that certain areas have acquired local notoriety and the carrying of knives, and indeed guns, is on the increase. In particular **Uhuru** and **Central parks** look peaceful enough, but walking through them after dark would be absolute lunacy. On the south side of Kenyatta Avenue, down to Haile Selassie, there is rarely a problem but **north of the avenue**, though relatively safe, is decidedly dodgier – be on your guard for con-merchants here rather than out-and-out thieves. The whole area **between the centre and Nairobi Hill**, where the youth hostel is located, is dangerous after dark – take a bus, *matatu* or taxi. Similarly, the area **near the Museum and Casino** is generally unsafe at night. The **post office building** on Kenyatta Avenue used to be the scene of phenomenal pickpocketing and bag-snatching. It's too early to say whether its new incarnation will have better security. The **main** *KBS* **bus depot** has a similar reputation.

These are all parts of the city where tourist pickings are fairly rich – and there are always a few who haven't read a guidebook. If you head out from the centre to poorer districts there seems to be less of a threat. However, the one major exception is **River Road district** which in practical terms means anything east of Moi Avenue (indeed, sometimes including the eastern side of the avenue). If you feel streetwise and have little to lose, then the area poses little threat. However, if you're even slightly anxious or have any valuables or bags with you, do *not* walk there – take a taxi or an *askari* (security guard), at least until you know your way around. And walking at night there is just asking for trouble.

and it should be about Ksh900. Other taxis to the city centre should be less than this – they don't have meters, so bargain firmly. Don't be afraid to ask several drivers their price. Given that even a good fare is a rip-off, tipping is not really necessary.

At present, there are two kinds of **buses** serving the airport. *Discount Airport Shuttle* (☎02/219156–7) runs an hourly service to and from the airport until 6pm, and can drop you at most hotels in town; it costs Ksh400 and terminates at Barclays Plaza near Uhuru Highway. *Kenya Bus Services* (*KBS*) *Stagecoach* bus #34 operates only until 6pm and costs just a few pennies. It enters the city through the eastern suburbs (rather than running straight up the proud artery of Uhuru Highway) and stops at the central *KBS* terminal before continuing to the youth hostel on Nairobi Hill. (See the warning opposite in the "Security" box about robbery on the #34 bus.) Lastly, it may be worth enquiring about the *Kenya Airways* bus which used to have eight departures daily but is currently suspended.

You will be obliged to take a taxi if your plane arrives **late at night** – *Alitalia*, *KLM*, and *Sabena* have such flights. You may well feel intimidated by a night-time first contact with central Nairobi and you'll find many of the cheapest hotels are already closed before midnight. An obvious alternative is simply to curl up in a corner of the arrivals hall until the first bus in the morning. Remember, though, this isn't a large airport: comforts and even basic facilities are very limited and dossing in a corner is barely tolerated.

Arriving by train

Arriving by train, either from Mombasa or western Kenya, you'll find yourself virtually in the city centre. From the **railway station** (watch out for taxi drivers and porters who, once again, will more or less kidnap your luggage if you let them), just walk straight out through the station concourse and follow Moi Avenue into town. The only real attention you'll attract is from **safari touts** (see "Safari Operators", p118) – they're persistent but friendly enough, and useful if you need an escort to one of the cheaper River Road addresses; a small tip would be appreciated.

Arriving by bus

Most **bus companies** have their booking offices or parking areas in the urban sprawl along the south banks of the Nairobi River (these days more of a ditch) and, again, this is just a short walk from the city centre. If you've been following the map and know where you are, however, you can generally ask to be dropped off anywhere along the bus route into town.

Orientation

The triangle of **central Nairobi** divides into three principal districts bisected by the main thoroughfares of **Kenyatta Avenue** and **Moi Avenue**.

The grandest and most formal part of town is the area around **City Square**, in the southwest. This square kilometre is Nairobi's heart: government buildings, banks and offices (most of them housed in commercial buildings with names like Jubilee Insurance Building and Lonrho House) merge to the north and east with upmarket shopping streets and luxury hotels. The area's big landmarks are the extraordinary **Kenyatta International Conference Centre**, with its huge cylindrical tower and artichoke-shaped conference centre, the blue-glass skyscraper of **Lonrho House**, and the bizarre zebra-striped "legs" of the **Nation Centre**, all visible from points miles outside the city.

North of Kenyatta Avenue, there's a shift to smaller scale and lesser finance. The **City Market** is here, surrounded by a denser district of shops, restaurants and hotels.

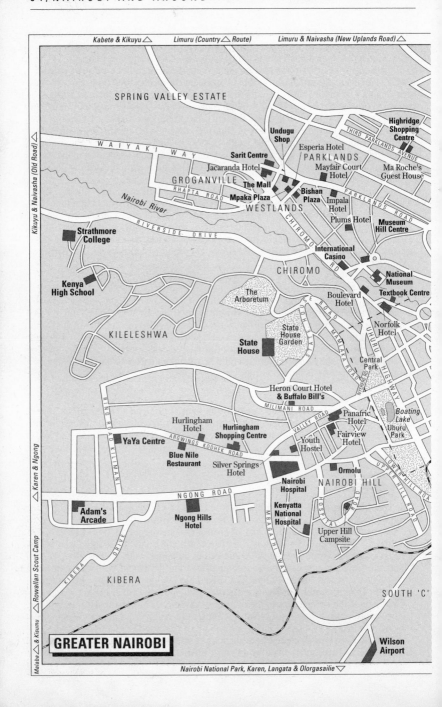

Kabete & Kikuyu △   Limuru (Country △ Route)   Limuru & Naivasha (New Uplands Road) △

Kikuyu & Naivasha (Old Road) △

SPRING VALLEY ESTATE

Highridge Shopping Centre

THIRD PARKLANDS AVENUE

Undugu Shop

W A I Y A K I   W A Y

Esperia Hotel

PARKLANDS

Sarit Centre

Mayfair Court Hotel

Ma Roche's Guest House

Jacaranda Hotel

GROGANVILLE

The Mall

PARKLANDS ROAD

RHAPTA ROAD

Mpaka Plaza

Bishan Plaza

Impala Hotel

Nairobi River

WESTLANDS

Plums Hotel

Museum Hill Centre

CHIROMO

RIVERSIDE   DRIVE

Strathmore College

International Casino

CHIROMO

National Museum

Kenya High School

The Arboretum

Boulevard Hotel

Textbook Centre

UHURU

Norfolk Hotel

KILELESHWA

State House Garden

State House

Central Park

HIGHWAY

Heron Court Hotel & Buffalo Bill's

MILIMANI   ROAD

Boating Lake

Uhuru Park

Hurlingham Hotel

Hurlingham Shopping Centre

Panafric Hotel

ARGWINGS KODHEK ROAD

Fairview Hotel

YaYa Centre

Youth Hostel

RING ROAD KILIMANI

Blue Nile Restaurant

Silver Springs Hotel

Ormolu

NAIROBI HILL

Nairobi Hospital

UPPER HILL ROAD

Adam's Arcade

NGONG   ROAD

Ngong Hills Hotel

Kenyatta National Hospital

KIBERA   DRIVE

Upper Hill Campsite

MBAGATHI   WAY

KIBERA

SOUTH 'C'

Karen & Ngong △

Rowallan Scout Camp △

Malaba △ & Kisumu △

GREATER NAIROBI

Wilson Airport

Nairobi National Park, Karen, Langata & Olorgasailie ▽

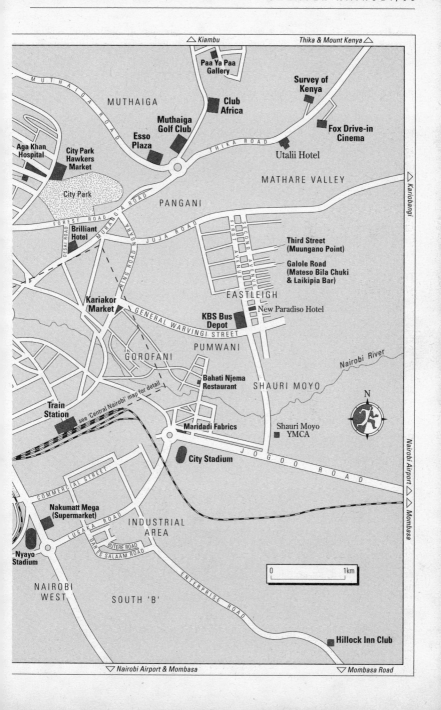

△ *Kiambu*   *Thika & Mount Kenya* △

Paa Ya Paa
Gallery

Survey of
Kenya

Club
Africa

MUTHAIGA

Muthaiga
Golf Club

Esso
Plaza

Fox Drive-in
Cinema

THIKA ROAD

Utalii Hotel

Aga Khan
Hospital

City Park
Hawkers
Market

MATHARE VALLEY

△ *Kariobangi*

City Park

FOREST ROAD

PANGANI

Brilliant
Hotel

JUJA ROAD

Third Street
(Muungano Point)

Galole Road
(Mateso Bila Chuki
& Laikipia Bar)

Kariakor
Market

EASTLEIGH

GENERAL WARINGI STREET

KBS Bus
Depot

New Paradiso Hotel

GOROFANI

PUMWANI

Nairobi River

Bahati Njema
Restaurant

SHAURI MOYO

N

Train
Station

see 'Central Nairobi' map for detail

Maridadi Fabrics

Shauri Moyo
YMCA

City Stadium

JOGOO   ROAD

△ *Nairobi Airport*

COMMERCIAL STREET

△ *Mombasa*

Nakumatt Mega
(Supermarket)

INDUSTRIAL
AREA

LUSAKA ROAD

BUTERE ROAD

Nyayo
Stadium

DAR ES SALAAM ROAD

0   1km

ENTERPRISE ROAD

NAIROBI
WEST

SOUTH 'B'

Hillock Inn Club

▽ *Nairobi Airport & Mombasa*   ▽ *Mombasa Road*

The **Jeevanjee Gardens** are a welcome patch of greenery (though avoid walking through after dark), and a little further north is Nairobi's oldest establishment, *The Norfolk*, contemporary with the original rebuilding of the city.

East of Moi Avenue, the character changes more radically. Here, and down towards the Nairobi River, is the relatively poor, inner-city district identified with **River Road**, its main thoroughfare. The River Road quarter is where most long-distance buses and *matatus* start and terminate, and it's where you'll find the capital's cheapest restaurants and hotels, as well as the highest concentration of African-owned businesses. It is also a somewhat notorious area, with a traditional concentration of sharks and pickpockets (see "Security" box). Some unwary *wazungu* (white people) consider themselves likely victims here; you can meet European residents who work five minutes' walk away and in all their years in Nairobi have never been to this part of town.

City transport

Getting around central Nairobi is straightforward. By day, most visitors **walk**; by night, they take a **taxi**. Unless you're only here for a day or two, though, it's certainly worth getting to know the city's **public transport** systems.

Taxis

While Nairobi's **taxis** are overpriced by Kenyan standards, at night, when certain parts of the city are definitely not recommended for pedestrians, you'll almost certainly want to make use of them. Grey, London-style taxi cabs (*Kenya Taxi Cabs Association*; ☎02/ 215352) crowd around key spots in the city – notably the *Hilton* area – and have pretty fixed prices, with the current bottom-line fare for any trip in the city centre well known by all (the cheapest ride isn't likely to be less than around Ksh200). It's really only possible to bargain with the private drivers. The *Save Taxi Service* (PO Box 10148; ☎02/222953 ext. 6, *Ambassadeur Hotel*) promises fixed fares to all destinations, at a shade over the lowest bargainable rates. They're good for early-morning airport runs and similar requirements. Another useful number is *Kenatco* (☎02/221561), who also have an office at Jomo Kenyatta Airport.

Buses and matatus

The **public transport** – buses or *matatus* – used by the ordinary people (the *wananchi*) of Nairobi will save you money on getting around, certainly for longer trips out of the city centre, but it takes some figuring out. The *KBS Stagecoach* **buses** roar around Nairobi all day, usually packed far beyond capacity. They're cheap and very unpredictable. Buses are numbered but bus stops aren't and routes change frequently. For points recommended in this chapter, appropriate buses (#34 and so on, and where to board them) have been indicated. **Matatus** can be slightly easier. They tend to take the same routes as buses and often display the same route numbers. They're generally faster, if more dangerous, though bad accidents rarely happen in the city. The confusion in Nairobi is occasionally exacerbated by clumsy police sweeps in which *matatu* and bus drivers are "netted" for overloading their vehicles, leaving their passengers stranded – usually at rush hour when they cause maximum chaos.

The main *KBS* city **bus terminus** for both Nairobi and national services is off the bottom end of River Road, behind the bizarre-looking Siri Guru Singh Sabha Temple on Uyoma Street. Other principal bus and *matatu* stops include the *Ambassadeur Hotel* on Moi Avenue (for east- and northbound services), the *Hilton* around the corner on City Hall Way (for west- and northbound services), Kimathi Street outside the *New Stanley Hotel*, and outside the unfinished GPO tower on Kenyatta Avenue.

Accommodation

Finding a place to stay in Nairobi isn't usually difficult. Hotels, with a few noted exceptions, are rarely full even during the peak season, and it's only during the occasional large international conferences that you may have problems finding a room. The main question is which area fits your needs: the city lacks a long-established focus, so travellers end up congregating at a number of different spots determined by budget and requirements. The following listings are arranged by approximate location: they are all keyed, or named, on the maps (key numbers refer to hotels marked on the "Nairobi: Commercial Centre" map). If you're arriving in town very early, beware that most places won't allow you to take a room before 10am. If you're travelling by rented car, and concerned about safe parking, don't panic: most hotels employ *askaris* (security guards), who can be persuaded to up their work load for a modest tip. Leave nothing in, or attached to, the vehicle. To help you aim straight for the best places, the hotels in the following short list meet with near-universal approval: *Iqbal* (low-budget); *Terminal* (basic comforts); *Hurlingham* (peaceful and old-fashioned); *Boulevard* (reliable mid-range safari base); *Serena* (justifiably very expensive).

East Nairobi

The very cheapest lodgings are around **River Road**, the main drag through the city's poorest quarter – although in recent years, a number of more expensive hotels have been built here. In several of those listed below you can expect to run into other travellers, but numerous other establishments, particularly towards the country bus station, may be as good as, or better than, these. If you're genuinely broke, try the welcoming **Sikh Temple** on Gaberone Road: overnights and meals are free, though you're expected to leave a donation.

For a total change of atmosphere, you might think about taking a bus out to **Eastleigh** (the main *KBS* bus depot is there, so an endless stream of buses goes there from the centre). The focus for Ethiopian and Somalian refugees in Nairobi, Eastleigh is low-rise, dusty and scruffy, with its parallel streets fading east into dry scrub and no man's land, and north to the slum wilderness of Mathare Valley.

River Road area: cheap lodgings

Abbey Hotel (1), Gaberone Rd (PO Box 75260; ☎02/331487). A noisy, boozy place, rather expensive nowadays, but the rooms are clean and fresh, with tiled bathrooms. ③.

Al Mansur B&L (2), Munyu Rd (PO Box 22020; ☎02/336336). Cheapest of the cheap, though if you're single you may have to share. Good food downstairs. ①.

Hotel Bujumbura (3), Dubois Rd (PO Box 28078; ☎02/221835). An inexpensive, very ordinary lodging, but utterly dependable. ①.

Cana Lodge Hotel (4), Duruma Rd (PO Box 41237; ☎02/217254). Simple, clean s/c rooms and good security. ③.

Dolat Hotel (5), Mfangano St (PO Box 45613; ☎02/222797). Clean, spacious and, though not fancy, excellent value, and it's friendly. One of the best of the cheapies (though breakfast not included). ③.

Evamay Lodge (6), River Rd at the junction with Duruma Rd (PO Box 16000; ☎02/216218). Very good value for the price with clean s/c rooms, all with phones and nets. Good security. ③.

Hotel Gloria (7), Duke House, Ronald Ngala St (PO Box 32087; ☎02/228916). A slightly better-than-basic B&L at the lower end of the price bracket, with breakfast (included) served in your room. Not noticeably welcoming, and it's on a noisy, hustly corner. ③.

Iqbal Hotel (8), Latema Rd (PO Box 11256; ☎02/220914). Number one in the budget travellers' popularity stakes for many years, often full and well worth booking in advance. Main advantage is the location, ideally situated between upmarket and downmarket Nairobi. Rooms are secure

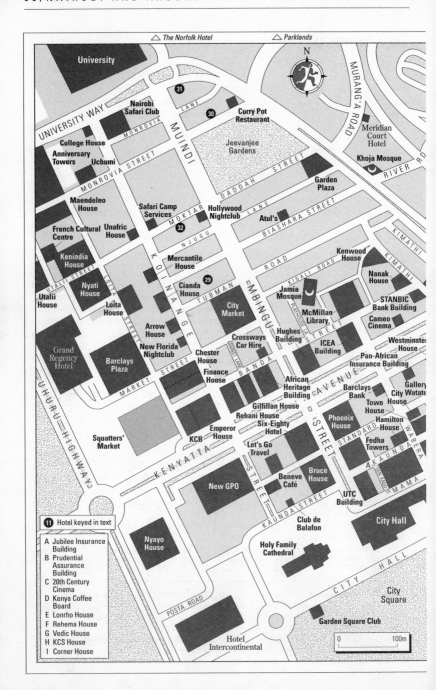

△ The Norfolk Hotel   △ Parklands

N

University

MURANG'A ROAD

UNIVERSITY WAY

31

Nairobi
Safari Club

MONROVIA STREET

30

Curry Pot
Restaurant

Jeevanjee
Gardens

RIVER RD

Meridian
Court
Hotel

College House

Anniversary
Towers   Uchumi

MONROVIA STREET

MUINDI

LANE

DADDAH   STREET

Khoja Mosque

Garden
Plaza

KIMATHI

Maendeleo
House

French Cultural
Centre

Unafric
House

Kenindia
House

Utalii
House

Nyati
House

Safari Camp
Services

32

Hollywood
Nightclub

MOKTAR

NJUGU

Mercantile
House

KONANGE

Cianda
House

29

Atul's

BIASHARA STREET

LANE

ROAD

KIGALI ROAD

Jamia
Mosque

TUBMAN

EMBINGU

City
Market

McMillan
Library

Kenwood
House

Nanak
House

STANBIC
Bank Building

Cameo
Cinema

Westminster
House

KIMATHI

Loita
House

UTALII STREET

LOITA STREET

Arrow
House

New Florida
Nightclub

Crossways
Car Hire

Hughes
Building

ICEA
Building

Pan-African
Insurance Building

PLAYHOUSE STREET

Grand
Regency
Hotel

UHURU HIGHWAY

Barclays
Plaza

MARKET

Chester
House

Finance
House

MARKET LANE

STREET

BANDA

African
Heritage
Building

AVENUE

Barclays
Bank

Gilfillan House

Town
House

Gallery
City Watatu
House

Phoenix
House

Hamilton
House

STANDARD

Squatters'
Market

KENYATTA

KCB

Rehani House
Emperor
House

Six-Eighty
Hotel

Let's Go
Travel

Fedha
Towers

AKAUNDA

STREET

WABERA

MAMA NGINA

New GPO

Beneve
Café

Bruce
House

KAUNDA STREET

UTC
Building

11 Hotel keyed in text

A Jubilee Insurance
    Building
B Prudential
    Assurance
    Building
C 20th Century
    Cinema
D Kenya Coffee
    Board
E Lonrho House
F Rehema House
G Vedic House
H KCS House
I Corner House

Nyayo
House

Club de
Balafon

Holy Family
Cathedral

City Hall

CITY

HALL

City
Square

POSTA ROAD

Hotel
Intercontinental

Garden Square Club

0   100m

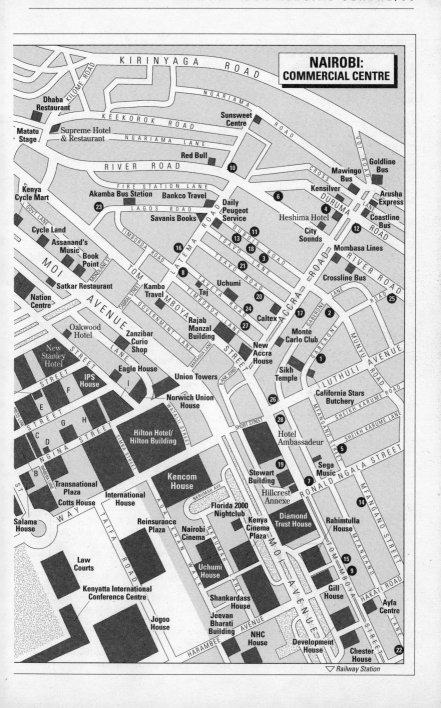

(though not s/c and those at the front are noisy) and it's cleaner than you might expect. Daily hot water; cheap laundry service; lock-up store; safari booking office; busy noticeboard. There's a café upstairs with a breezy terrace for residents. The *Iqbal* is a good rendezvous: go early and put your name on the waiting list for a day or so if necessary. ②.

Mercury Hotel (9), Tom Mboya St. Next door and similar to the *Princess Hotel* (see below), but cheaper and not as well furnished. ②.

New Kenya Lodge (10), River Rd (PO Box 43444; ☎02/222202). Like the *Iqbal*, a long-established backpackers' haunt with a popular communal area, though altogether earthier. Friendly, cheap and unhygienic, with uncertain security and little or no hot water. They also organize cheap safaris which, by all accounts, are perfectly reasonable. The "annexe" on Duruma Rd (☎02/338348) is even less tempting (though breakfast is thrown in). ②.

New Safe Life B&L (11), Dubois Rd (PO Box 10035; ☎02/221578). Lives modestly up to its name, with large rooms, a splash of hot water and average hygiene. ②.

New Swanga Lodge (12), Duruma Rd (PO Box 46387; ☎02/213777). The rooms here, though not large, are comfortable and secured behind spectacular, time-consuming, triple locks. A very friendly place in the heart of the bus and *matatu* area. Clean sheets daily. Good value, though hardly quiet. ③.

Nyandarua Lodge (13), Dubois Rd (PO Box 10027; no telephone). Dirt cheap, with water problems. But the rooms are large, and from the street-side ones at the top (28–31) there are views of Mount Kenya on exceptionally clear days. ①.

Paris Hotel (14), Mfangano St (PO Box 72632; ☎02/337483). Very decent, well-priced twin and single rooms with good showers and toilets. Excellent value. ③.

Princess Hotel (15), Tom Mboya St (☎02/214640). Very busy, local establishment with bars on all floors. It's something of a gay rendezvous, and much cheaper if you're a couple. Basic but adequate, and it fills up quickly. ③.

Sunrise Lodge (16), Latema Rd (PO Box 48224; ☎02/330362). Small, secure, well-kept lodging house, but lacks regular running water. Some rooms are exceptionally noisy due to its location next to the *Modern Green Bar*. Don't dawdle after dark in the alley between them. ②.

River Road area: pricier lodgings and mid-range hotels

Accra Hotel (17), Accra Rd (PO Box 75862; ☎02/338875). Astonishingly overpriced for a basic B&L, but perhaps worth it for a night's clubbing in the wild neighbourhood, and its own exuberantly noisy day and night club. ④.

Hotel Africana (18), Dubois Rd (PO Box 47827; ☎02/220654, fax 02/223031). Clean, with hot water. Recommended if you want to be near the Latema Road area but need a little more comfort, though not as smart as it was. ③.

Diplomat Hotel (19) Tom Mboya St (PO Box 30777; ☎02/245050, fax 02/220475). Fifty large, well-kept rooms with telephones. Good value in this range. ④.

Grand Holiday Hotel (20), Tsavo Rd (PO Box 69343; ☎02/241983). Rather spartan rooms but quite acceptable at this level. Tall people beware: the staircase lintels are low. Its bar is rather anodyne. ③.

Hotel Greton (21), Tsavo Rd (PO Box 55909; ☎02/331865 or 336648, fax 02/242892). Rather small rooms, but they have phones and it's friendly, with good security and attentive management. A clean, pleasant, value-for-money hotel. Recommended. ③.

Hotel Hermes (22), corner of Tom Mboya St and Haile Selassie Ave, close to the American Embassy and handy for the station (PO Box 62997; ☎02/340066, fax 02/443016). New, well located and good value for comforts (including AC), if a little noisy (rooms at the back are quieter). Good bar-restaurant with an economical buffet lunch most days. ④.

Marble Arch Hotel (23), Lagos Rd (PO Box 12224; ☎02/245720 or 245656, fax 02/245724). The newest and plushest of the area's hotels. The coffee shop, bar and restaurant are replete with polished marble, brass fixtures and tacky fountains. Rooms are of a similar standard: wall-to-wall carpet, direct-dial phone, bath, video, TV and "piped music". A second wing is planned with pool, sauna and jacuzzi. ⑥.

Oriental Palace Hotel (24), Taveta Rd (PO Box 72237; ☎02/217600, fax 02/212335). One of the best-appointed hotels in the district: all 108 rooms here have TV (with in-house video), direct-dial phones, and all you'd expect at these prices, including, fortunately, ceiling fans (the *Little India* restaurant on the ground floor generates a ubiquitous curry atmosphere). Elevators. ⑥.

Sagret Hotel (25), River Rd (PO Box 18324; ☎02/333395). Comfortable and efficiently managed, very clean and very secure, but very loud and too expensive. There's a sister hotel, the *Sagret Equatorial*, out of the centre on Milimani Rd. ④.

Hotel Salama (26), corner of Luthuli Ave and Tom Mboya St (PO Box 28675; ☎02/225898). The rooms here are not quite up to the standard you'd expect: you pay for the helpful staff and the location, a stone's throw from the *Hilton*. ④.

Samagat Hotel (27), Taveta Rd (PO Box 10027; ☎02/220604). A large place, with elevators. It used to be an apartment block, so rooms are spacious. Good value. ④.

Solace Hotel (28), Tom Mboya St (PO Box 48867; ☎02/227061, fax 02/220129). Somewhat overpriced, but the decent rooms here (above the hubbub of the street) have telephone and bath. ④.

Eastleigh

New Paradiso Hotel, corner of First Ave and Tenth St, very near the bus depot. The accommodation is in itself nothing special, but the owner is charming and the Ethiopian food in the restaurant delicious: many varieties of *wat* with *njera*, with great Amharic music in the background and no shortage of interesting conversation. ①.

Usalama Hotel and Bedsitters Ltd, Second Ave, Eastleigh (PO Box 11386; ☎02/332789). Worth considering if you find the *New Paradiso* full, or for that matter closed: a safe, friendly atmosphere with hot water available, where the staff toil under the encouraging motto "Service Without Bitterness". ②.

West of Moi Avenue

The following listings cover the more moneyed parts of the city, roughly north as far as the museum and west as far as Central Park. There are a number of **medium-priced places** on the west side of Moi Avenue up near Jeevanjee Gardens and City Market. For the faint-hearted, this may be a better prospect than the River Road area – quieter and possibly safer (at least more salubrious).

West of Moi Avenue: mid-range hotels

Hotel County, County Lane (PO Box 41924; ☎02/226190, fax 02/213889). A very reasonable, functional block and quieter than most: the first hotel from the airport, close to the station and Railway Museum, but relatively far from the main shopping streets. ④.

Hotel Embassy (29), Tubman Rd, right behind the City Market (PO Box 47247; ☎02/224087, fax 02/224534). Scruffy but clean and quite decent, with ancient telephones lovingly preserved in some rooms (they don't all work) and a nice restaurant. ④.

Parkside Hotel (30), Monrovia St (PO Box 53104; ☎02/214154–6). Facing Jeevanjee Gardens, large and pleasant with airy s/c rooms, hot water and telephones, but slightly overpriced. Its restaurant is nothing special. ④.

Plums Hotel, Ojijo Rd (PO Box 40747; ☎02/745222). Pleasant establishment near the museum, with good car security if you're driving. ③.

Suncourt Inn (31), University Way (PO Box 51454; ☎02/221413, fax 02/217500). Seems a touch expensive but it's not at all bad, right on top of the *Norfolk* and totally unpatronized by tourists – plus the phones work. Its quirky *Wisemen's Corner* is a businessmen's bar. The carpetless rooms offer the best value. ⑤.

Hotel Terminal (32), Moktar Daddah St (☎02/228817). A long-time favourite, with large, clean, well-kept rooms and extraordinarily helpful staff. All rooms have nets and hot water. Definitely good value, and highly recommended. ③.

West of Moi Avenue: upmarket and luxury hotels

Central Nairobi has over twenty **luxury places** and many more trailing close behind. They all take credit cards. Reservation addresses for those that are part of chains or management groups can be found on p.48.

Hotel Ambassadeur, Moi Ave (PO Box 30399; ☎02/336803, fax 02/211472; reservations through *Sarova*). A modern, adequate, international-style hotel, sensibly priced but surprisingly noisy: if possible get a double-glazed, top-floor room. Guests can use the *New Stanley*'s pool. ⑤.

Hotel Boulevard, Harry Thuku Rd, right by the museum (PO Box 42831; ☎02/227567–9, fax 02/334071). Perhaps the best mid-range address in the city – functional rather than extravagant, well cared for, in a pleasant setting and with a good pool (though unfortunately it's on the traffic side of the building). To overcome Uhuru Highway's noise, get a room at the back in the middle, overlooking the garden. ⑥.

Hilton Hotel, Mama Ngina St (PO Box 30624; ☎02/334000, fax 02/339462; reservations through *Hilton*). A very average example of the species, though for over 20 years one of the city's most outstanding tourist and business focuses. Rooms get better the higher you go; but the "rooftop pool" is down at 2nd-floor level and rather overshadowed. Very overpriced, and room only. ⑨.

Hotel Intercontinental, City Hall Way (PO Box 30353; ☎02/335550, fax 02/210675 or 214617; reservations through *Intercontinental*). Thirty years old, and not one of the group's best – but has some surprisingly secluded corners in the grounds. Many amenities, and if you're not a regular in such places, still fairly palatial. Room only. ⑨.

Meridian Court Hotel, Murang'a Rd, off the top of River Rd, on the way out to Parklands (PO Box 30278; ☎02/333916, fax 02/333658). Rooms with kitchenettes (though they have no cooking facilities); nice staff; underground parking; rooftop pool and sauna; special rates for Peace Corps volunteers. Room only. ⑥.

Nairobi Safari Club, University Way (PO Box 43564; ☎02/330621, fax 02/331201). A prestigious address but not as exclusive as you might imagine (they'll even discuss the rate). Small pool. Prices of suites (no standard rooms) increase with altitude. No children under 12. Room only. ⑨.

New Stanley Hotel, Kimathi St (PO Box 30680; ☎02/333233, fax 02/229388; reservations through *Saravoa*). Complete with its famous *Thorn Tree Café* rendezvous, an (originally) Edwardian hotel and a popular downtown base, especially for American package tours. Pleasant 5th-floor pool and health club. It is due for refurbishment, which will close parts of the hotel until 1998; prices are likely to rise once the refit is complete. Room only. ⑥.

Norfolk Hotel, Harry Thuku Rd (PO Box 40064; ☎02/335422 or 216798, fax 02/336742; reservations through *Lonrho*). Traditional haunt of celebrities visiting Nairobi and still recommended on the whole, though arguably much too expensive. However, a major refurbishment programme has been announced which should equip all rooms with air-conditioning and better bathrooms. A people-watching meal (reliably good food) or a drink on the hotel's street-side *Lord Delamere Terrace* is always fun. Room only. ⑨.

Oakwood Hotel, Kimathi St (PO Box 40683; ☎02/220592, fax 02/332170). A small, older hotel – all wood panelling and antiquated elevators – which used to be *the* place to stay, but needs serious repairs and refurbishment to justify the expense (when it rains, you may have a pool in your room). It has a pleasant bar, though, overlooking the more touristy *Thorn Tree Café*. ⑤.

Serena Hotel, Nyerere Rd (PO Box 46302; ☎02/725111, fax 02/725184; reservations through *Serena*). Highly polished and sumptuous, the *Serena* really pulls it off, even getting away with elaborate decor. By any standards, a fine place to stay, with impeccable rooms, first-class service, a calming atmosphere and exceptional food. There's even a rustle of wildlife to be seen around the verdant pool terrace that fronts onto Central Park. Unlikely to disappoint. Room only. ⑨.

Six-Eighty Hotel, corner of Kenyatta Ave and Muindi Mbingu St (PO Box 43436; ☎02/332680, fax 02/332908). A 340-room, recently renovated, 1970s tower, right in the heart of the city, and quite soulless. Safe underground parking and convenient for shopping. Guests can use the *Boulevard*'s pool. Room only. ⑥.

Accommodation out of central Nairobi

Two of the main focuses for budget travellers, the youth hostel and *Ma Roche's Guest House* (see "Greater Nairobi" map, p.84), are a short journey away from the city centre, in the suburbs, and both have their devotees. Some of the city's nicest hotels are also to be found on the outskirts of Nairobi.

Camping and budget lodgings

Ma Roche's Guest House, Third Parklands Ave, opposite the Aga Khan Hospital. A private home, in the predominantly Asian suburb of Parklands. Take a bed either in one of the cabins or in Mrs Roche's bungalow, or camp in the garden, or sleep on the verandah. The meditative, doggy ambience is popular with worn-out motorized overlanders and travellers who really loathe Nairobi. Fall into either category and you should love it. It is a good place to meet people and it's often possible to fix up shared arrangements to drive to the game parks or head on through Africa – use the notice board. There's also a laundry and a convenient lock-up store to leave surplus gear while you travel, but there's no *askari* – don't leave valuables in your tent. Take a *matatu* from Latema Rd, opposite the *Iqbal*, asking for "Aga Khan". Ksh 300 per person.

Nairobi Youth Hostel, Ralphe Bunche Rd (PO Box 48661; ☎02/723012). A gentle introduction to the city, recently totally rebuilt, and full most of the time. The rate's Ksh300 per person per night, plus you have to have IYHA membership (which is either a token daily payment, or Ksh360 for full membership) and put up with usual YH rules, including a ban on booze. The small compound can get claustrophobic, and it's a bad idea to walk into (or back from) town after dark. Still, it's a well-run place with lots of other hostellers to talk to, a good noticeboard and an informative journal of visitors' travel tips. Many buses and *matatus*, including #34 from the airport, pass by one end or the other of Ralphe Bunche Rd.

Rowallan Scout Camp, off Kibera Drive, south of Jamhuri Park (PO Box 41422; ☎02/568111). See "Nairobi Area" map, p.130. Deep in the Ngong Road forest, over 2km walk from the Ngong Road, the Kenya Scouts Association camp has basic facilities (pit latrines, firewood sold for the outdoor kitchen, cold showers, limited supplies from the *duka*), but does have electricity (a fridge for sodas), and a large, rather green, swimming pool. The huge site is patrolled by two police officers and its own two *askaris*. You could leave valuables with the helpful warden. The forest is traced through with narrow paths and it's a good area for birdwatching; there are even some caves here. An ideal place for overland groups to camp, but inconvenient for backpackers. Some crude *bandas* available. Very cheap.

Upper Hill Campsite, Menengai Rd, off Hospital Rd (☎02/720290, fax 02/723788). A new camp-site, already well discovered by the overland trucks, with beds in dorms (Ksh250 per person) and clean double rooms (③) also available. Hot showers, kitchen, a bar, restaurant and relaxed atmos-phere; cheap tent hire possible. Good security. Take a #8 bus from the railway station or #18, #20, #25 or #59 from Kenyatta Ave to the hospital.

Wildlife Clubs of Kenya Hostel, Langata Rd in Nairobi South "C", past the Animal Orphanage next to the Bomas of Kenya (☎02/891904). A new option for those who prefer Nairobi at arm's length, with dormitory-style rooms (Ksh300 per person) and decent facilities.

Out-of-centre hotels

With the exception of the *Central YMCA*, which is marked on the "Central Nairobi" map (see p.96), the following hotels can all be found either on the "Greater Nairobi" map (see p.84) or on the "Nairobi Area" map (see p.130).

Central YMCA, State House Rd, on the west side of Uhuru near the university (PO Box 63063; ☎02/724116). There are other *YMCA*s in Muhoho Ave, off Langata Rd in Nairobi South "C" (☎02/504896), and on Ambira Rd in Shauri Moyo (☎02/558383). You won't run into many other *wazungu* travellers at these latter two. The central hostel is the best equipped, not markedly different from a modest hotel with well-priced food and an excellent pool, and its guarded parking lot is ideal for drivers. South and Shauri Moyo hostels are more basic. Rates (for B&B at Central and South, FB only at Shauri Moyo, which is the cheapest) vary from ④ to ⑤, with only a small reduction for long stays (for extended stays check out the *YWCA* – see "Long Stays", below).

Esperia Hotel, Muthithi Rd, Westlands (PO Box 14642; ☎02/742818). In an old colonial-era, wood-panelled, administration building, with adequate rooms and safe parking. ④.

Fairview Hotel, Bishops Rd (PO Box 40842; ☎02/723211 or 711321, fax 02/721320). A peaceful, rambling country-style place with an excellent reputation for its pleasant grounds and wide variety of accommodation (some rooms share bathrooms). Very popular with families, so reserve ahead. Guests can use the pool at the *Panafric*. No credit cards. ⑤–⑥.

Hurlingham Hotel, Argwings Kodhek Rd (PO Box 43158; ☎02/721920, fax 02/726691). An inex-pressible pre-war feeling lingers here and people enjoy it, too, for the excellent cooking, with touches like wholemeal bread. While some of the 17 rooms could do with a revamp, and some beds with replacing, it's still highly recommended and well worth making a reservation. Close to the YaYa Centre shopping mall. B&B. ④.

Impala Hotel, Parklands Rd (PO Box 14144; ☎02/742346–7). Not at all touristy, with reasonably priced rooms, good parking facilities and a shaded, leafy bar. ④.

Landmark Hotel, Westlands (PO Box 14287; ☎02/448713, fax 02/448977; reservations through *Block*, see p.48). After a bad decline in recent years, the former *Jacaranda* hotel reopened in May 1996 after a $2.5 million refit. 121 rooms, each with satellite TV. It remains to be seen whether the expedition-type package tours will continue to frequent it. ⑦.

Mayfair Court Hotel, Parklands Rd (PO Box 74957; ☎02/746708). New hotel on a par with the *Norfolk* (the original structure was a 1930s hotel), and its bar now attracts the weekend *wazungu* crowds who used to frequent the *Norfolk* until its beer prices went up. Hourly courtesy bus to the city centre. ⑧.

Panafric Hotel, Kenyatta Ave, Nairobi Hill (PO Box 30486; ☎02/720822, fax 02/726356; reservations through *Sarova*, see p.50).Potentially a good uptown option, but currently very inadequate – a major overhaul is planned. B&B. ⑥.

Safari Park Hotel, Thika Rd, 14km from town (PO Box 45038; ☎02/802493, fax 02/802477; reservations at Kimathi House, Kimathi St, Nairobi, ☎02/216070, fax 02/217677). Although far out of town, this Korean-owned hotel is an attractive base for an upmarket stay, with 64 acres of landscaped gardens, wonderful swimming pools, four-poster beds in all rooms, six restaurants (remarkably affordable), discotheque, piano bar, and faultless service. Everything you could wish for, and certainly should expect at this price. Room only. ⑨.

Silver Springs Hotel, Valley Rd/Argwings Kodhek Rd (PO Box 61362; ☎02/722451–7, fax 02/720545). A large and rather grey establishment overlooking the hospital, with comfortable rooms, pool, health club and massage, but lacking the class of its competitors. ⑤.

Utalii Hotel, Thika Rd, 6km from town (PO Box 31067; ☎02/802540–7, fax 02/803094). This offers something different, with unbeatable standards. It's run by the Utalii College, Kenya's college of tourism, so you get impeccable, if slightly hesitant, service. Pool, tennis courts, and an astonishingly good restaurant. Facing it, across the banana tops, sprawls one of Nairobi's worst slums, Mathare Valley. Free bus service to the city centre. B&B. ⑥.

Windsor Golf & Country Club, Kigwa Rd, 15km north of the city (PO Box 45587; ☎02/862300, fax 02/802322). More than anything else, this new resort complex is worthwhile for its brilliant location in 200 acres of indigenous forest; unless, of course you're a golfer, in which case the impressive facilities – 18-hole course and resident pro – are the big draw. An outdoor heated pool, fishing and riding are among many other facilities. Good value compared with its competitors. Room only (cottages also available). ⑨.

Long stays

For long stays in Nairobi, cheap **flats, rooms and studios** are advertised in the classified columns of the *Nation* and the *Standard*. Otherwise contact an apartment agency (Westlands is probably the most promising area), or there's a very useful noticeboard at the supermarket in Karen. Remember, if the place has no *askari* (security guard), the danger of burglary is very real. If your stay is more temporary, the YWCA is your best bet, and much cheaper, on a monthly basis, than the YMCAs.

Heron Court Apartment Hotel, Milimani Rd (PO Box 41848; ☎02/720740–3, fax 02/721698). Much used by volunteers and their kin, and fine, especially if self-catering appeals. Reasonable rooms or studio apartments. There's a pool and the dubious benefit of *Buffalo Bill's*, a seedy pick-up bar, which can be rather noisy at night but is kept separate from the hotel itself. Monthly rates Ksh22,500 (per night ③–④).

New Fairview (same management and phone number as *Fairview Hotel*, see above, p.93). three-room flats available for three-month stays or longer at Ksh69,000 per flat per month.

YWCA, Mamlaka Rd, off Nyerere Ave (PO Box 40710; ☎02/724699). Best value for men as well as women (and couples can share). Rates for room only are in the order of Ksh6000 per month for a double room with wash basin, or about Ksh4000 per month for a single. There are flatlets for about Ksh8000. Write to reserve well in advance.

Around central Nairobi

Kenyatta Avenue is the obvious place to start looking around Central Nairobi. A good initial overview of it – and lots else besides – can be had from the vertigo-inducing, glass-walled lifts in the **ICEA building**, on the northwest corner of Wabera Street. If the guards at the bottom need an excuse, tell them you're visiting the Japanese Embassy on the 15th floor; they may even be persuaded to escort you onto the roof.

Kenyatta Avenue

Kenyatta Avenue was originally designed to allow a twelve-oxen team to make a full turn. Broad, multi-laned and planted with flowering trees and shrubs, it remains (along with the Kenyatta Conference Centre) the capital's favourite tourist image. The avenue is smartest – and most touristy – on its south side, with would-be moneychangers and itinerant souvenir hawkers assailing you from every direction, and shoeshiners inspecting each passing pair of feet from their stands. The focus of the avenue's eastern end is the *New Stanley Hotel's* **Thorn Tree Café**, opposite *Nakumatt* on the corner of Kimathi Street. The *Thorn Tree* is Nairobi's one proper pavement café and, despite irritatingly slow service ("we are stocktaking"), an enduring meeting place. Around the imposing thorn tree in question is a message board intended for personal notes but always worth scanning for vehicle-sharing deals, things for sale, and so on.

Proceeding to the other end of Kenyatta Avenue, you come to the **General Post Office** (GPO) and, just before it, **Koinange Street**, named after the Kikuyu Senior Chief Koinange of the colonial era. The peculiar **Galton-Fenzi Memorial**, just here on the left, is a monument to the man who founded, of all things, the Nairobi branch of the Automobile Association. Fenzi was also the first motorist to drive from Nairobi to Mombasa, back in 1926.

City Square and Parliament

Head down Koinange Street and on to Kaunda Street, passing the *Intercontinental* on your right and, crossing City Hall Way, you enter **City Square**. This is Nairobi's front room. Jomo Kenyatta's statue sits benevolently, mace in hand, on the far side of the wide, flagstoned court; his mausoleum, with flickering eternal flames, is on the right as you approach the Parliament building. When the flags are out for a conference it all looks very bright and confident.

Kenya's **Parliament** is open to the public. Talk to the guards at the gate, who will tell you when the next session is taking place (usually at 2.30pm on Wed and Thurs) or, when it's not in session, how to get a tour of the building. If you're assigned a guide make sure both parties are clear about how much you'll pay. To sit in the public gallery you must first register at the gatehouse on the corner of Parliament Road and Harambee Avenue, leaving all your belongings with the attendant outside. Once seated, be on your best behaviour. The gallery tends to be full of very well-behaved schoolchildren – which of course is more than can be said of the members of parliament. Although with the admission of opposition members in 1993 proceedings have been livelier than for decades, don't expect any startling revelations: the tone of debate is aptly suggested by the legend over the main doors, "For a Just Society and the Fair Government of Men". But try to get hold of a copy of the Orders of the Day; there may be a juicy question or two worth anticipating.

Kenyatta Conference Centre

From Parliament, walking down Harambee Avenue along the shady pavement, you come to Nairobi's pride and joy – the **Kenyatta International Conference Centre** (KICC) and its tall brother, "KANU tower", the ruling party headquarters (all enquiries ☎02/332383). This, the tallest building in Kenya, is capped by a mile-high, revolving restaurant (a mile above sea level that is). Confusion has always arisen on the ground floor about whether anyone was allowed up to the 28th. The restaurant has closed, but it's worth making an effort to get as high as possible; if you talk to the security staff in the foyer, assent is usually given for ascent partly because it has become accepted prac-

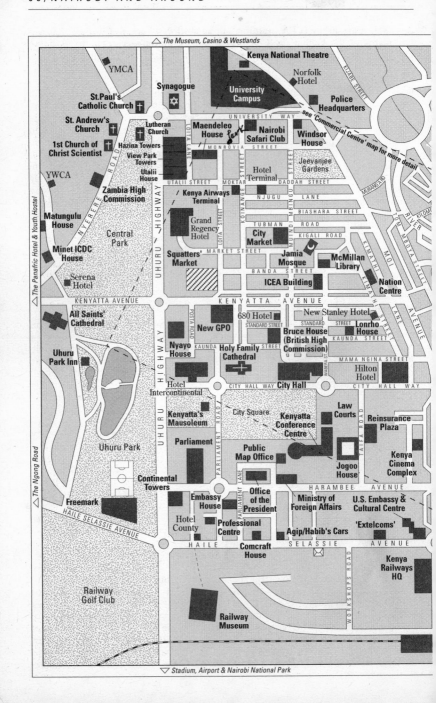

△ The Museum, Casino & Westlands

Kenya National Theatre

YMCA

Synagogue

St.Paul's Catholic Church

St. Andrew's Church

1st Church of Christ Scientist

YWCA

Matungulu House

Minet ICDC House

Zambia High Commission

Lutheran Church

Hazina Towers

View Park Towers

Utalii House

Serena Hotel

Norfolk Hotel

University Campus

Police Headquarters

UNIVERSITY WAY

Maendeleo House

Nairobi Safari Club

Windsor House

see 'Commercial Centre' map for more detail

MONROVIA STREET

Kenya Airways Terminal

UTALII STREET

MOKTAR

Hotel Terminal

Jeevanjee Gardens

DADDAH STREET

NJUGU LANE

Grand Regency Hotel

TUBMAN ROAD

City Market

BIASHARA STREET

KIGALI ROAD

Squatters' Market

MARKET STREET

Jamia Mosque

McMillan Library

BANDA STREET

ICEA Building

Nation Centre

KENYATTA AVENUE

KENYATTA AVENUE

All Saints' Cathedral

POSTA ROAD

New GPO

680 Hotel

STANDARD STREET

New Stanley Hotel

STANDARD STREET

Lonrho House

Uhuru Park Inn

Nyayo House

KAUNDA STREET

Holy Family Cathedral

Bruce House (British High Commission)

KAUNDA STREET

MAMA NGINA STREET

Hilton Hotel

Hotel Intercontinental

CITY HALL WAY

City Hall

CITY HALL WAY

Kenyatta's Mausoleum

City Square

Kenyatta Conference Centre

Law Courts

Reinsurance Plaza

Parliament

Public Map Office

Jogoo House

Kenya Cinema Complex

Uhuru Park

HARAMBEE AVENUE

Continental Towers

Freemark

Embassy House

PARLIAMENT LANE

Office of the President

Ministry of Foreign Affairs

U.S. Embassy & Cultural Centre

'Extelcoms'

HAILE SELASSIE AVENUE

Hotel County

Professional Centre

Agip/Habib's Cars

HAILE SELASSIE AVENUE

Comcraft House

WORKSHOPS ROAD

Kenya Railways HQ

Railway Golf Club

Railway Museum

△ The Ngong Road

▽ Stadium, Airport & Nairobi National Park

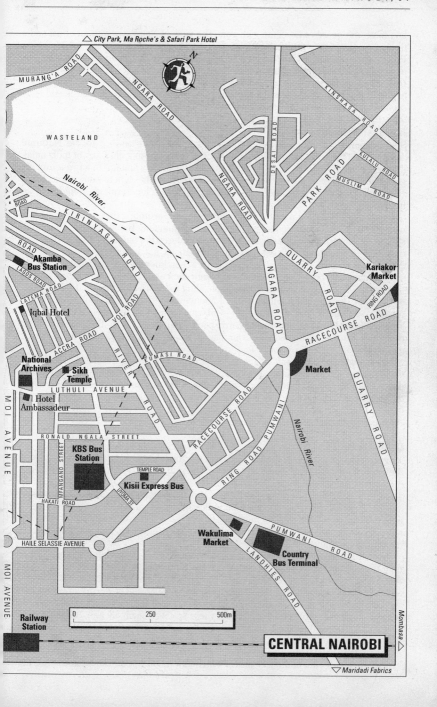

△ City Park, Ma Roche's & Safari Park Hotel

MURANG'A ROAD

NGARA ROAD

WASTELAND

Nairobi River

KIRINYAGA ROAD

ROAD

LAGOS ROAD

TATEMA ROAD

VOI ROAD

RIVER ROAD

ACCRA ROAD

PUMASI ROAD

NGARA ROAD

DESAI ROAD

KINSHASA ROAD

PARK ROAD

KUIALI ROAD

MUSLIM ROAD

QUARRY ROAD

QUARRY ROAD

RACECOURSE ROAD

RING ROAD

Akamba Bus Station

■ **Iqbal Hotel**

National Archives

■ **Sikh Temple**

LUTHULI AVENUE

■ **Hotel Ambassadeur**

RONALD NGALA STREET

MFANGANO STREET

KBS Bus Station

TEMPLE ROAD

Kisii Express Bus

UYOMA ST

HAKATI ROAD

RACECOURSE ROAD

RING ROAD PUMWANI

Market

Kariakor Market

Wakulima Market

Country Bus Terminal

PUMWANI ROAD

LANDHIES ROAD

Nairobi River

MOI AVENUE

HAILE SELASSIE AVENUE

MOI AVENUE

Railway Station

0   250   500m

CENTRAL NAIROBI

◁ Mombasa

▽ Maridadi Fabrics

tice to tip the guards who come with you. The view of Nairobi is without equal and a firm reminder of the vastness of Africa. Just 4km to the south, you see the Mombasa Road leave the suburbs behind and take off across the yellow plains. Northwards, hills of coffee – and, at higher altitudes, tea – roll into the distance. If you pick a good day in December or January you really can see Mount Kenya in one direction and Kilimanjaro in the other. Immediately below, the traffic swarms – and Jogoo House is suddenly seen to be built remarkably like a Roman villa.

National Archives

Straight down Harambee Avenue, cut across Moi Avenue and up to the **National Archives** (PO Box 49210; ☎02/228959). Housed in the striking old Bank of India building on the bend of Moi Avenue across from the *Hilton*, they amount to a **museum/art gallery** in the heart of the city, which few visitors to Nairobi seem to know about; entry (Mon–Fri 8.30am–4.30pm, Sat 8am–1pm) is free and a look around should take an hour or so.

The ground floor is a public gallery with Joseph Murumbi's (briefly vice-president under Kenyatta) oddball collection of paintings dominating the walls. The collection, sold to the government in 1966, ranges from uninteresting dabbles to some beautiful drawings and striking collages, but in a city that's not exactly cluttered with art collections, it does deserve a look. There's scant information available about the artists, many of whom were students, although the curator seems well aware of this: there are notices pinned up on the walls pleading for more information. In the centre of the floor there's also a fair amount of anonymous ethnographia – musical instruments, weapons, domestic artefacts – all catalogued but unlabelled. The actual archives (mainly books, papers and correspondence) are closed to the general public, though if you're interested you can pay a small fee (just Ksh50) for a year's membership.

More rewarding, and immediate, is the second-floor collection of black-and-white press **photos**, highly revealing as a record of the early part of Daniel Arap Moi's presidency, with foreign tours figuring prominently. There's also a number of fascinating portraits of tribal elders, mostly from the colonial era. Lastly, there are weekly screenings (Sat mornings at 10am) of often fascinating, sometimes obscure, films relating to culture, politics or wildlife. Admission is free.

Cultural venues

To get an idea of the image the United States would like to project to Kenyans, call in at the **American Cultural Centre** (PO Box 30143; ☎02/337877; back along Harambee, then turn right up Aga Khan Walk), on the main floor of the National Bank building. There are daily film shows of ABC news and documentaries: a schedule is posted outside. A well-stocked library and a periodicals room are available for the purpose of letting "ideas contest in an open marketplace", as the leaflet prosaically puts it. Perhaps more palatable are the two or three feature films shown every month (details in monthly programmes). It's all free.

Apart from occasional exhibitions, the only art galleries deserving the name (other than the National Archives) are **Gallery Watatu** on Standard Street (PO Box 41855; ☎02/228737), which was reshaped in 1990 as part of Lonrho House and is now the equal, in terms of facilities, space and lighting, of any Stateside or European equivalent; and the **Paa Ya Paa Art Gallery** on Ridgeways Road, Ridgeways (☎02/512257; see "Greater Nairobi" map). The work at both these spaces, usually by East African artists, is often a lot better than the popular elephants-in-a-dustbowl school of painting. *Gallery Watatu* is also the venue for occasional "alternative" events.

With a few exceptions, things to do north of Kenyatta Avenue have a commercial bent. Two slightly out-of-the-way places which you might not otherwise notice are the

French Cultural Centre in the Maison Française (PO Box 49415; ☎02/336263), and the **Goethe Institut** in Maendeleo House (PO Box 49468; ☎02/224640), both of which pursue their activities rather less chauvinistically than the United States. Both places are at the top of Loita Street near Uhuru Highway. The Goethe Institut puts on art exhibitions, both German and Kenyan, and has a monthly programme of subtitled German films. The French Cultural Centre operates a more dynamic and better-financed programme, offering a space for Kenyan dance and theatre as well as staging events and activities derived from France. Long the most active cultural and intellectual focus in Nairobi, it's well worth checking out during your stay.

The Jamia Mosque
The **Jamia Mosque** stands near the City Market. The ornate green and white exterior contrasts strikingly with the simple interior, where the large central dome appears far larger from beneath than it did from the courtyard outside. Although most Kenyan towns now have at least one mosque, often financed by Saudi Arabia, few are as large or as beautiful as the Jamia. In recent years, non-Muslims have often been refused entry, which is by no means something prescribed by Islam. Polite requests and the usual modesty of attire (limbs covered, feet unshod) should help, but there's no guarantee. So for an alternative, bird's-eye view of the mosque, the top of the ICEA building is (again) a good vantage point.

The museums and parks

Covered here are the handful of parks and museums in Nairobi itself. Nairobi National Park gets separate coverage in the "Nairobi Province" section later in this chapter (see p.129), as do the Bomas of Kenya, the Karen Blixen Museum and the Langata Giraffe Centre. Unless you have your own wheels you may be better off joining a tour for them. The following sites, however, are all easily walkable.

The National Museum

Daily 9.30am–6pm; Ksh200; guides (free) available on request; ☎02/742161.

The **National Museum** is probably the city's prime sightseeing attraction but surprisingly few travellers make the small effort to get to it. You should: it's the best possible prelude to any tour around the country, and it's only about a half-hour walk from Kenyatta Avenue – and only a few minutes by taxi or bus (#119 from Moi Avenue or #21 or 23 from the *Hilton*). Allow yourself a morning or afternoon to look around. Having said this, however, the exhibits are something of a jumble at present and a thorough revamp would certainly not go amiss. If museum fatigue hits you, the pleasant *Café Bustani* is open daily until 6pm.

Natural history and geology
The museum's most extensive collections are **ornithological**, with most of Kenya's thousand-plus species of birds represented. Kenya's birdlife usually makes a strong impression, even on non-birders. Look out for the various species of hornbills, turacos and rollers, and for the extraordinary standard-wing nightjar, which frequently has people doing a double-take the first time they see it fluttering low over a swimming pool at dusk in its hunt for insects. There's also a multitude of stuffed game heads, dioramas of Kenyan mammals in the large mammal room, casts of fish, even a whale skeleton, as well as the skeleton and a fibreglass replica of the famous elephant from Marsabit, "Ahmed". The African Rainforest exhibition is as elusive as a rainforest's wildlife: it's worth asking if it has reopened.

Especially useful if you're going anywhere near the Rift Valley, the **Geology Gallery** is a mine of information on plate tectonics and the life-cycle of volcanoes, with a good collection of rocks and minerals which you may see on your travels.

Gallery of Contemporary East African Art

On the second floor, next to the birds, the **Gallery of Contemporary East African Art** is an exhibition space and **showroom** for principally Kenyan, Tanzanian and Ugandan artists to display their work and wares. Everything is for sale and the gallery, although non-profit-making, takes a commission from what's sold and ploughs this back in to running the place, and in to acquiring work for the museum's own, planned Modern Art Gallery.

Human prehistory

The special interest of Nairobi's museum lies in the cultural, human and quasi-human exhibits. The **Prehistory Gallery**, where the palaeontology exhibits are housed, has walls disguised with stunning reproductions of a series of Tanzanian rock paintings. Ahead, on the floor, is a cast of wide-splayed, human-looking footprints – the small pair following in the prints of the larger one – which were discovered at Laetoli in Tanzania. They belong, almost certainly, to *Homo erectus*, believed to be the direct ancestor of our own species. They were squeezed into the mud about 1,500,000 years ago. Down the hall, eerily life-sized reconstructions of a family of *Homo erectus* (rather like a scene from "Planet of the Apes") wolfing down an antelope carcass, as well as other dioramas of the more primitive (and ultimately unsuccessful) australopithecines, bring the story of human evolution vividly to life.

There's a separate display telling the story of the Lake Turkana **Koobi Fora excavations** – "The Origins of Man in Kenya" – on the ground floor to the right of the Prehistory Gallery entrance.

Ethnography and history

In contrast, the rather dry second-floor cases of **ethnographic** exhibits aren't awfully illuminating. However, they contain some fascinating odds and ends – don't miss the "divining sandals" made of elephant hide tanned in dung and urine. If you're planning on travelling through any of the areas inhabited by pastoral peoples (especially Samburu, Maasai or Turkana), then seeing some old and authentic handicrafts beforehand is a good idea. This will also be a big help when you find yourself faced with, for example, an urgent vendor offering you a dozen different carved headrests – not an uncommon experience. The collections indicate the tremendous diversity of Kenya's cultures, a quality impressively evoked by Joy Adamson's series of ethnic portraits mounted on the walls. (Her beautiful **botanical paintings** are displayed downstairs by the main entrance.)

The **photographic exhibition** of the **struggle for independence** is compelling – not just for its content but because this is almost the only public place (apart from the National Archives on Moi Avenue) where Kenyans can be reminded of the period in their history euphemistically called "The Emergency".

Finally, in the **Lamu Gallery** on the main floor, the once excellent exhibition "The Kenya Coast 9th–19th Century", is now sadly depleted and looks to all appearances as though it has been ransacked.

The Snake Park and Aquarium

Same prices and times as the museum.

Opposite the museum and going downhill (in both senses of the word) is the **Snake Park**. It's only fair to say that you'd have to be very enthusiastic about reptiles to find this interesting, and very insensitive to find it enjoyable. Exhibits take in East African and American snakes, a crocodile or two, some murky terrapins, emaciated monitor lizards and boring fish tanks. There are much better (and cheaper) snake parks on the coast. An emphatic miss.

The Railway Museum

Daily 8.30am–5pm; Ksh200, residents Ksh100.

Now privately run, Nairobi's **Railway Museum** is a natural draw for rail fans and of more than passing interest to anyone else. It's signposted, ten minutes' walk from the station. You should be aware, however, that there have been several grab-and-run robberies down here: it might be best, if you're walking, to go to the end of Haile Selassie Avenue, and turn left immediately after the *Shell* station opposite Ukulima Co-operative House, for a hundred-metre walk across the waste ground.

The main hall contains a mass of memorabilia: photos of early stations, of the line being built, and the engineering feats involved in getting the carriages up and down the escarpment; drawings of the plans; and strange pieces of hardware, such as the game-viewing seat mounted at the front of the train. Passengers who risked this perch were reminded that "The High Commissioner will not be liable for personal injury (fatal or otherwise)". In the museum annexe, the motorized bicycle inspection trolley is quite a sight but, as the write-up explains, the experiment in the 1950s "was not really successful", as the wheels kept slipping off the rail.

The engines

Outside, rustingly exposed to the elements, is the museum's collection of old **locomotives**, most of them built in England. You can clamber inside any of the cabs to play with the massive levers and switches. The restriction of forward visibility on some of the engines seems incredible: the driver of the Karamoja Express couldn't have had any idea what was in front of him while steaming down a straight line. If it all fills you with nostalgic delight, you should also note that Nairobi and Mombasa stations both have locomotive graveyards which, with enthusiastic persistence, you should be able to look around.

Lions figure prominently in the early history of the Uganda Railway: look in the shed for first-class coach no. 12 to learn the story of Superintendent C. H. Ryall. During the hunt for the "Maneaters of Tsavo" in 1898, Ryall had readied his gun one evening, settled down in the carriage and offered himself as bait. Somehow he nodded off . . . He was dragged from this carriage and devoured while colleagues sat frozen in horror. The coach, together with the repainted loco no. 301, took part in the filming of *Out of Africa* at Kajiado.

The city's parks

A colour map of Nairobi suggests a multitude of cool green spaces around the city. The parks aren't always very inviting, but several are pleasant places to retreat to for a while. Biggest and best is **City Park** in the north, a half-hour stroll from the National Museum down Forest Road and Limuru Road, or by bus #19 from the *Iqbal*. City Park has a wealth of tropical trees and birdlife, several troops of Vervet Monkeys, a small stream with wooden bridges, gravel paths, shady lawns, and, on weekends, families everywhere. During the week it's delightful, though not for women alone. And as usual, hang onto your possessions.

The Arboretum is less frequented and in a predominantly European, as opposed to Asian, district. Somewhat overgrown, almost jungly in parts, it is still a lovely place to wander or picnic, and, of course, a must if you're botanically inclined. You may be reassured – or unnerved – by the officious plain clothes policemen who stalk the glades (it backs onto State House).

Uhuru and Central parks, on the western side of Uhuru Highway, have the city's worst reputation for muggings, particularly after dark. They're unfenced and never closed but to walk across either park after 6pm is, to put it mildly, asking for trouble. It's probably safe to take a rowing boat out on the lake in Uhuru Park on a Sunday afternoon.

In a more reputable part of the city (though a night walk even here would be foolish), try **Jeevanjee Gardens**, especially during a weekday lunchtime when you can picnic on a bench and chat with the office workers who aren't thronging the nearby restaurants. You can listen, too, to the preachers who have made Jeevanjee their church and the bemused picnickers their congregation. The park contains a curiously small statue, just about recognizable, of Queen Victoria, presented to Nairobi by nineteenth-century business tycoon A. M. Jeevanjee, founder of the *Standard* newspaper.

Markets and shopping

It doesn't take long to realize that commerce is Nairobi's *raison d'être*. Disappointingly perhaps, the form which trade takes here is not always very exotic. But Nairobi is the best place in East Africa to buy **handicrafts**, with the widest (if not the cheapest) selection and the best facilities for posting the stuff home. The city also has some lavish **produce markets**, enjoyable even if you only want to browse.

Bargaining is expected at all Nairobi's markets and most shops, with the exception of supermarkets and stores selling imported goods. Be aware, however, that the "last price" will vary seasonally and can sky-rocket when a major conference hits town.

Produce markets and food

It doesn't offer the city's lowest prices, but for a colourful and high-quality range of fruits and vegetables the **City Market** is the obvious target. If you're buying, the best-value stalls are in the outside aisle flanking the main hall on the right. Fish and meat are on either side of the main building, and the supermarket at the entrance has a good variety of Kenyan cheeses. The other large produce markets are the **Wakulima** (farmers) market, a cavernous and dank hall at the bottom of River Road, just before the country bus station (fruit and vegetables are pretty cheap here), and a good, open-air one at the end of Racecourse Road, just across the Nairobi River.

There are usually dozens of children and young women selling a few oranges, mangoes, whatever, on street corners. Blink, and they may be gone, tipped off that city *askaris* are about to "swoop". So buy from them while you have the chance.

There are **supermarkets and groceries** all over the city. Branches of *Uchumi* and *Nakumatt* (both usually 8.30am–8.30pm) are always very cheap, and a good bet for bottled water. Also good, with a fast turnover, is *K&A* on Koinange Street, across from the GPO. *Samaki & Tilley*, on Kaunda Street, are first-class **butchers** and **fishmongers**; there's a good **cheese shop** in the *YaYa Centre* in Hurlingham, and a number of excellent delicatessens in *Lenana Forest Centre* on Ngong Road (see "Shopping malls" below). For a good, and cheap, selection of Kenyan and South African **wines**, try *Joles Ltd* at Hamilton House on Kaunda Street. An excellent **bakery**, with daily supplies of fresh rye and wholemeal bread, is *Oscarsson's* in 20th Century Cinema Plaza, Mama Ngina Street.

Crafts

For the exhausting business of buying **crafts and curios**, it's advisable to decide what you want before stepping into a shop or looking at a stall. At some of the more pretentious places you can browse for ages undisturbed, but at the cheaper outlets dilly-dallying is not encouraged and the pressure may be on to part with your "quids". To browse and to establish comparative values, pay a visit to *African Heritage* on the north side of Kenyatta Avenue (PO Box 17871; ☎02/333157), which has some beautiful things, mostly at absurdly inflated prices. It's the largest curio shop in Kenya, with eager suppliers in many parts of Africa. If you can't get out to the *Kazuri Beads Centre* in Karen (see overleaf), try their showroom here.

Curio shops and hawkers

Elsewhere, there are dozens, maybe hundreds, of **curio shops** and, depending on any number of factors, you might get a good deal at almost any of them. The more upmarket ones are clustered on Standard, Kaunda and Mama Ngina streets. The *Zanzibar Curio Shop* on Moi Avenue always has a wide range and not unreasonable prices. There's also the good *Arki Ethiopian Curio Centre* in Barclays Plaza, just the place for those Coptic crosses you always wanted (they also have guidebooks). Clearly, however, the cheaper prices will usually be at places where they don't have to pay a shop rent – **street stands** and **market booths**. Once again the booths at the City Market are an obvious choice, especially for soapstone, batiks and, to the back, off Koinange Street, basketwork; but the whole area is something of a tourist trap, and while you'll probably find what you're looking for, you're unlikely to knock it down to a good price. Better deals are found at a handful of stands in the square between the City Market and Jamia Mosque, and in the side streets to the east of the mosque. If you have any skill at bargaining, you should get a good deal at all these stands. The **traditional masks** you'll see everywhere are imported from elsewhere. Only a handful of Kenyan tribes make masks, the Kikuyu being the best known, and these are still very much in use and resolutely *not* for sale. *Mount Kenya Sundries*, Vedic House, Mama Ngina Street, have one of the best selections from West and Central Africa, albeit mostly reproductions, and are knowledgeable about their varied significance and use in ritual.

Buying curios from **strolling vendors** is generally unwise. You're not going to get a good deal from a cruising hawker, whose wares are almost bound to be low quality. Furthermore, while you're being distracted on one side, you may be being ripped off on the other. If you're not interested, say *Sitaki biashara* – "I don't want to do business". The **elephant-hair bracelets**, incidentally, often are just that – collected, they say, not poached. When lit, the strands should smell of burnt hair; some smell of burnt grass, which is what they are. Said one bracelet salesmen: "We follow the animal softly and when it goes to sleep we sneak up quietly and cut off the tail hair with scissors." Another, hardly more plausible, vouchsafed: "We follow the animal until it goes to sleep, then all the hairs fall out and we collect them in the morning when it has gone away." Suggestions that they shot the elephants between the eyes with an elephant gun were met with convincingly reproachful tongue-clicking. In actual fact they're from Tanzania, where protection orders are less widely enforced.

Community craft centres

Nairobi has a number of craft shops with charitable status, or based on development or self-help projects. Although sometimes a little expensive – and you can't bargain – they are worthy of support, and often have unusual and well-made stock (some of which finds its way into the Christmas charity catalogues overseas). Some are a little way out of town, but well worth making special journeys to visit – good tonics if you're suffering from curio shop fatigue.

Kazuri Bead Centre, Mbagathi Ridge, Karen, close to the Blixen Museum (☎02/882362; Mon–Sat 8.30am–4.30pm, Sun shop only, 11am–4.30pm). *Kazuri*, which means "small and beautiful", employs nearly a hundred women (mostly unsupported or destitute) to make an extraordinary variety of handmade jewellery and beads, principally ceramic, and there's also a pottery showroom. You can watch the whole process from shaping and colouring to firing. They also have an outlet at *African Heritage* in Nairobi, on the north side of Kenyatta Ave.

Kenya Artisans Craft Show, Bishan Plaza, Mpaka Rd, Westlands. An open-slot space with ten stalls, changed every six months. Distinctly un-touristy, with well-made and unusual work: bead-work, batiks, soapstone and clothes, many from tribal womens' groups from around the country. Recommended.

Maridadi Fabrics, City Stadium roundabout, Jogoo Rd, 1km past the main entrance to the Country Bus Station (☎02/554288; Mon–Fri 8am–5pm; buses #21, 34, 36 from *Ambassadeur*). Church-based, like *Undugu* (see below), *Maridadi* was created in 1966 as an income-generating community project for women in one of Nairobi's oldest slum areas – Pumwani and Shauri Moyo. The main workshop is a delight if you're into making your own clothes. A large screen-printing workshop (on view from the visitors' gallery) produces the wide range of prints for sale in the shop; the bark cloth prints are especially appealing. Bark cloth, a natural weave obtained from beneath the outer bark of certain trees, is soaked, stretched, hammered before use, and was used for cloth-ing by many East African peoples until the end of the last century. In the district around the *Maridadi* workshop, there's a huge diversity of enterprises, with two distinctive market areas – Gikomba (clothes) and Landhies Mawe (scrap metal processing) – both recommended. The latter is deafeningly unmistakable, the place to go to get that handmade tin suitcase.

Ormolu, Chyulu Rd, off Haile Selassie Ave, where it joins Ngong Rd (☎02/727484). An outlet for naturally dyed sisal baskets and mats woven by rural women.

Ostrich Park Arts & Crafts Village, off Langata Rd, past the National Park Main Gate (☎02/891021; daily 9am–5.30pm). A curious combination with a small entry fee. On the one hand an ostrich farm; on the other a community of craft workers manufacturing a wide range of items from their dark huts – everything from soapstone carvings to fishing flies: an excellent selection but high prices. Good for picnics (miles better than the filthy picnic site at the National Park Main Gate) and ideal for kids, who can feed the ostriches and play in the play area. There are also tortoises and a small herb garden.

The Spinner's Web, Longonot Place, Kijabe St, behind the *Norfolk Hotel* (☎02/228647). A large shop, with a Germanic influence, selling a lot of good stuff – crafts, textiles, woollen goods and jewellery, much of it made by self-help groups, including *Meru's Makena Textile Workshop*.

Undugu, Woodvale Grove, Westlands, behind the main shopping centre (☎02/443525; Mon–Fri 8.30am–5pm). This is the *Undugu* (brotherhood) society's retail outlet, helping raise funds for an expanding list of development and community self-help programmes, notably for the homeless and jobless, young men in particular. With its roots in the church, *Undugu* is the most vigorous society of its kind in the country and, by promoting cooperation, goes some way to patching up the worst effects of the struggle for existence in Nairobi. The shop sells a good selection of well-priced, high-quality crafts with some unusual items as well, such as Ethiopian jewellery and basketwork. A free booklet about the *Undugu* society is available and you may be able to have a look around the workshops.

Utamaduni Crafts Centre, Bugani East Rd, between the Ostrich Park and Giraffe Sanctuary, Langata (☎02/890464; daily 10am–6pm). Eighteen individual craft shops in one large house, opened by Richard Leakey in 1991 (a portion of the profits go to the Kenya Wildlife Service). It has every-thing you might want, much of it made on site or from street-kid projects, but prices are very high.

The Maasai Market

If you're after Maasai traditional and tourist gear, the **Maasai Market** every Tuesday from 9am to 3pm is a hot recommendation. Anything from twenty to fifty Maasai women display their wares on the waste ground beside the roundabout connecting Murang'a Road and Kijabe Street (past the *Meridian Court Hotel*). Assuming that they don't get evicted (as they were from their previous site), you'll find prices here well below those in any tourist mart, or even in the Narok/Mara area, with especially good deals on the simpler designs of beaded jewellery, and also on baskets and gourds. You can bargain to as little as ten percent of the sort of prices marked in fancy curio stores. And the beauty of it all is the absence of hassle.

Kariakor Market

A real artisans' market is **Kariakor Market**, between Racecourse Road and Ring Road (buses #6, 7, 14, 30, 32, 46). This is without question *the* place in Nairobi to buy **sisal baskets** (*vyondo*). Inside and outside the market there are thousands of baskets available, and since many are made here, you can buy just the basket without the leather pieces or straps which raise the price. Long sisal straps can be bought separately for a few shillings. *Vyondo* come in sisal, coloured with natural or artificial dyes, in garish plastic, or in cord manufactured from the bark of the baobab tree. Some of these last baskets are truly exquisite, occasionally quite old, with tiny beads included in the tight weave.

Kariakor (named after the wartime "Carrier Corps") is closer to an oriental bazaar than most markets in Kenya, with permanent booths for the traders. Inside, there's as much manufacture and finishing going on as selling – sisal weavers, leather workers, makers of tyre-rubber sandals ("5000-mile shoes", about Ksh60 a pair and surprisingly comfortable), carpenters, toy-makers, tailors, hairdressers, and a row of good, very cheap, amazingly clean eateries, popular at lunchtime with local workers. A number of booths sell vaguely pharmaceutical oddities – snuff, remedies, charms, amulets and so on – where you can pick up anything from feathers to snakeskin. Outside, you can find the odd African literary gem from the second-hand bookstalls.

General merchandise, clothes, shoes and toys

For everyday **general merchandise stores**, the eastern part of the City Market district is the most worthwhile area. **Biashara Street** (*biashara* means commerce) is the street for fabrics and the best place to buy a mosquito net, though check prices carefully; *Atul's* is the place for camping and backpack gear (see "Listings" on p.126). For cheap and not-so-cheap imports, the hangar-like *Freemark Pavillion* in south **Uhuru Park** has hundreds of stalls. **Tubman Road** and **Kigali Road** have a lot of open-fronted (and tight-fisted) groceries with dry food in sacks; as it happens, this part of the city has retained its early character fairly well. The upper part of Moi Avenue is Nairobi's busiest ordinary shopping street, all colonnaded shop-fronts and antiquated name boards, fun to wander past. Clothes shops you'll find all over, with high-fashion outlets on Standard and Kaunda streets, and more down-to-earth gear on Kenyatta Avenue, Moi Avenue and Kimathi Street (on the latter, try *Colpro* for **safari gear**, where Michael Palin was fitted up for the BBC's *Pole to Pole*). Good value **footwear** is available from the *African Boot Co*, on Moi Avenue opposite *Bookpoint*, and even cheaper footwear at *Miniprice Footwear Supermarket* on River Road, by the *Bull Café*. If you're buying **toys**, the best items are locally made wire and fabric confections – cars, bicycles, flapping birds – which are sometimes beautiful works of art. Scouring the out-of-centre markets will find you some, but the best are usually made at home for sons and nephews and not for sale. The best general toy shop, full of standard imports, is *Hobby Centre* on Kaunda Street in the Jubilee Insurance Building.

Shopping malls

Nairobi now has the dubious distinction of having more **shopping malls** than any other African city, barring those in South Africa – over twenty of them, providing a hassle-free environment for getting on with ordinary shopping and office business. They cater to the expatriate and more affluent Kenyan markets and many include banks, travel agents and an assortment of cafés and restaurants. If you have a young family, they're very useful. The following is a selection:

Esso Plaza, Muthaiga Rd, Muthaiga. One of the newest, boasting a good health-food shop, a bagel bakery and the tacky *Celebrities Nightclub*.

Lenana Forest Centre, half a kilometre before the racecourse on Ngong Rd. Notable for a number of great delicatessens and French-style *charcuteries*.

The Mall, Westlands (buses #21, 25, 29, 30 and many others). Shops and offices include branches of *Textbook Centre* and *Let's Go Travel*, a sports shop, a French bakery, ice-cream parlour, a *7/11*-style convenience store and numerous fashion and clothing stores.

Museum Hill Centre, Museum Rd. Not exactly a "mall" as such, but has a good French bakery and an excellent (and cheap) Kenya Wildlife Service shop with loads of well-made trinkets.

Sarit Centre, Westlands (buses as for *The Mall*). A big, established complex, with over 60 shops and offices, including a dry cleaners, a health-food shop, a watch repairers and a post office.

YaYa Centre, Hurlingham (bus #46). Escalators, fountains and all. There's a good cheese shop here, a useful newsagents on the 2nd floor with a wide selection of mainly British magazines, a health-food shop, French bakery and a useful "for sale" notice board.

Eating and drinking

Nairobi has no shortage of **eating places**. Their diversity is one of the city's best points and eating out, in default of much else in the way of entertainment (but see the following sections "Film and theatre" and "Nightlife and music"), is an evening pastime which never dulls. Admittedly, African food is generally not highlighted in the more expensive hotels and restaurants. What stands out in these places, gastronomically speaking, is a range of Asian and European food, and spectacular quantities of meat.

This bias isn't really a problem. You can save money *and* eat African and Asian food in hundreds of unpretentious places, though to catch the cheap eats you'll have to go out early: by 8pm most of the cheaper restaurants have finished the day's food. And if you must have a burger or a pizza or a huge steak or totally vegetarian salad, it's all available.

With few exceptions, the following listings are restricted to the city centre; but Nairobi, including the suburbs, has hundreds of restaurants with new ones opening every month. **Westlands**, in particular, is a culinary growth area. As for locating them, most of those which are not marked on the maps can be found in relation to street intersections or other buildings.

Cheap eateries and snacks

The **River Road area** has all the very cheap places with one *hoteli* (cheap restaurant) after another on most streets. A few others – either special, or especially useful because of their locations – are listed too. At any of the following you should be able to eat hugely for around Ksh100 or less.

BREAKFASTS

Get up for breakfast. It's the only time of the day to really enjoy *mandaazi* and *chai*. You can get fried eggs and bread in many cheap places, too (look for Swahili menus saying something like *Mayai kukaanga* or sometimes "Eggs fly"). None of it is healthy, or aims to do anything but inject you with hot calories, but it tastes good on a chilly Nairobi morning.

You can get an excellent **continental breakfast** at the *Goldstar Restaurant*, on Koinange Street near the *Terminal Hotel* (Mon–Sat 7am–10pm, Sun 7am–3pm). A good place for something more hearty is the *Y-Not* on Tom Mboya Street, near the small post office (Mon–Fri 7am–7pm, Sat 7am–5pm) – stacks of well-prepared eggs, sausages, beans and toast. The big hotels do lavish breakfast **buffets**, and, if you wake up in a certain frame of mind, you might go down to the *Hilton* for theirs: it's pretty highly rated. Alternatively, the *Ambassadeur*'s is also good, and a sum cheaper. For something simpler, all the cafés and snack bars listed cater for early-birds, as does *Pasara* (see "Salads") on Kaunda Street. *Calypso Bar*, on Standard Street, does pancakes and waffles.

STREET FOOD

Strictly speaking, **street food** is limited to **roasted corn cobs** (which are so tough and take so long to eat you'll feel you've had a whole meal) and **fruit**. But places like the shacks near the country bus station can fill you up with tea and *mandaazi* for next to nothing. On Haile Selassie Avenue by the *Agip Garage*, women cook up *githeri* which you eat squatting down on the pavement. The best place, though, is the **hawkers' market** at the western end of Kenyatta Avenue, on a site earmarked for a new National Theatre. Here, dozens of *chai*, *ugali* and *nyama choma* joints vie for business, the meat and fish all totally fresh and sizzling outside on charcoal grills, as reggae music blares: prime rump steak, brains or sweetmeats, it's all there, and if you're thirsty, several dodgy bars oblige. It's a great little place; **Kariakor Market** has a similar enclosure.

River Road area

Afro-Arab Restaurant, Ronald Ngala Rd. Good cheap *mushkaki* with reggae accompaniment.

Baba's, Kijabe St. Totally vegetarian place, with an off-putting interior, wonderful crispy pizzas and splendid service.

Benrose, Gaberone Rd. Busy, bustling and *fast* food. Gorgeous *chai* and samosas.

Bull Café, Ngariama Rd, off River Rd, right by the *New Kenya Lodge*. Huge meals and small bills.

City Fry's, Murang'a Rd. Excellent stand 'n' eat fish 'n' chip shop.

Ismailia's, River Rd. Very inexpensive, welcoming and comfortable, with a good vegetarian selection.

Malindi Dishes, Gaberone Rd. Mainly snacks; less intimate than *Benrose*, more like a cafeteria but still welcoming.

New Flora (and the more refined *Zaiqa New Flora* on the 1st floor), Tsavo Rd. Used to be extremely popular among locals and travellers alike for very good budget meals with tandoori bread; but the sometimes terrible service is a drawback. Open for lunch and early dinner.

Prestige, Tsavo Lane. Delicious fish, several vegetarian dishes, and outstandingly friendly waiters.

Reata Fish & Chips, corner of Taveta and Accra Rd. A renowned purveyor.

Sarodena Hotel, Duruma Rd, below *New Swanga Hotel*. Excellent fry-ups, busy and cheerful.

Sunrise Lodge, Latema Rd, across from the *Iqbal Hotel*. Standard *hoteli* fare in a reasonably bright, workaday atmosphere. Take a table at the front and watch street life on Latema Road.

Sun Sweet Centre, Ngariama Rd. Vegetarian Indian place, bright and appetizing, with tempting sweets and – for once – open till late.

Super Hotel, River Rd (closes 7pm). Good, all-you-can-eat vegetarian meals – basically curries with excellent chapatis and *lassi*.

Further afield

Bahati Njema, Shauri Moyo district (see "Greater Nairobi" map, p.84), about ten minutes' walk up from *Maridadi Fabrics* on the corner of Lamu Rd and Digo Rd near the Nairobi River. A great little place (the name means "Good Luck") for very cheap Swahili food.

Booggy café, Aga Khan Hospital grounds, Third Parklands Ave. Usually a popular place for those staying at *Ma Roche's*.

Everest Bar, Third Parklands Ave, near *Ma Roche's*. Cheap cold beers and tasty evening curries.

Stop & Eat, Third Parklands Ave. A roadside shack, also useful for *Ma Roche's* guests, for filling breakfasts and good *githeri*, with or without meat.

Cafés, snack bars and ice-cream parlours

Cafés and snack bars are mostly situated in the upmarket business district **north of City Hall Square**. Most are closed on Sundays after lunch. Passion juice is widely advertised these days, but check whether it's fresh or factory-pressed or, worse, just syrup and water.

Al-Momin Coffee House, Banda St. Excellent samosas and other Indian snacks.

Beneve Coffee House, Koinange St. Across from the new post office site, a clean and cheap self-service joint, popular with office workers.

Express Bakery, Standard St, next to *Let's Go Travel*. Always crowded at lunchtime but otherwise a good place to sit and recoup your energy.

K&A Coffee House, corner of Standard St and Koinange St. Next door to *K&A* supermarket, a simple little cafeteria with good brioches and coffee.

Kahawa Coffee House, Fedha Towers, Kaunda St. Crowded, notably upmarket, and great for breakfast – fried eggs, milkshakes, samosas and iced tea.

Kencake Coffee Shop, 9 Kaunda St. Good for ice cream.

Kenya Coffee Board, Mama Ngina St (closed Sat pm and Sun). The KCB's *Coffee House* does the best cup in town. Faded murals on the walls hark back to a not-so-distant era of African coffee estate labourers, white overseers and continental café loungers. You can also buy the house blends by the kilo for something like a quarter of what you'd pay at home (call in before flying home).

Sno-Cream, corner of Koinange St and Monrovia St (daily until 9.30pm). Best parlour in town, with amusing retro decor depicting various ice cream fantasies – all of them presumably available.

Swiss Cake Shop, corner of Moi Ave and Nkrumah Rd. Fresh juices and very sweet cakes.

Restaurants

The following listings are mostly of more upmarket eating houses, at some of which it's a good idea to reserve a table (many are closed one day a week, often Sunday or Tuesday, and most are closed between 2.30pm and 6.30pm). Prices, without drinks, should normally work out at under Ksh400 a head, though you can certainly eat more cheaply at several of the curry houses. In the more international league, specializing mainly in meat, prices are higher (say Ksh400–700 a head) and you'll pay up to Ksh1200 at fancy establishments. The city has famously good beef and other fleshy delights so, if you enjoy it, indulge while you're here, as the rest of the country is much less well endowed.

"African", Ethiopian and Swahili

Many hotel restaurants offer an "African night" once a week, or in some cases lunchtime African buffets. Regular African nights include Tuesday at the *Fairview*, the *Utalii Hotel* and the *Nairobi Safari Club*; and Wednesday at the *New Stanley Hotel*. The *Suncourt Inn* and the *Solace Hotel* both do weekday lunchtime buffets. For a different Ethiopian experience, Elias Dinguja and his family (☎02/223604) offer an authentic dinner and coffee ceremony at their Eastleigh home (daily, phone to book), with advice on travel in that country thrown in.

African Heritage, Banda St (☎02/337507; daily). Quite expensive, but worth it, is the Ethiopian buffet on Friday evenings – phone ahead to check – at the eating half of the swanky gallery-cum-crafts shop, with accompaniment from the band of the same name (though, for culinary and budgetary balance, compare it with the *New Paradiso* in Eastleigh – see p91).

Blue Nile Ethiopian Restaurant, Argwings Kodhek Rd (no telephone; daily). Very pleasant, laid-back place, with a good range and a helpful "mix dish" where you can try everything out for just Ksh200. The wines are excellent but their *tej* (a mead-like Ethiopian beer) is no longer "officially" brewed.

Daas Ethiopia Restaurant, Kirichwa Rd, off Ngong Rd (bus #3, 4, 102 to Adam's Arcade; ☎02/727353; daily). A bit of a revelation if you thought you'd eaten traditional African food. The basic staple *njera* "bread" does take some getting used to, but the spicy overall effect of *doro wat* (chicken in a spicy sauce) or *anye* (spinach, cheese and spices), washed down with copious quantities of the mead-like *tej*, is a fine culinary experience. Food is cooked on your own table's *jiko* (stove). A little costly, but recommended.

Chinese, Thai and Mongolian

Bangkok Restaurant, Rank Xerox House, Westlands (☎02/751311). Kenya's only exclusively Thai restaurant; fine as long as you don't expect it to taste like real Thai.

Great Chung Wah, Kenyatta Ave and Standard St (☎02/212945; daily). A new place, filling and cheap rather than exquisite, with good lunchtime offers.

Hong Kong, Koinange St (☎02/228612; daily). Excellent Cantonese, related to the *Hong Kong* in Mombasa, though not particularly friendly.

The Manchurian, Brick Court, Mpaka Rd, Westlands (☎02/444263; daily). A great Mongolian place, suitably expensive, where you serve yourself with raw meats, vegetables and sauces and the chefs then stir-fry it for you.

Meridian Mandarin, 5th floor, *Meridian Court Hotel* (☎02/333916). Usual high quality with a very affordable "business lunch" for Ksh270.

Pagoda, First Floor, Shankardass House, Moi Ave (☎02/338205; daily). Highly recommended Szechuan cooking, but pricy.

Rickshaw Chinese Restaurant, 1st floor, Fedha Towers, Kaunda St (☎02/223604; daily). A pleasant Cantonese restaurant with impressive service and not unduly expensive. Beef with orange, and unshelled prawns dowsed in chillis, are both recommended.

Silver Sun, Loita Street, opposite Kenindia House (☎02/330858). Good Szechuan and a reasonable selection of Thai dishes. Expensive in the evenings but a bargain at lunchtime.

Winners Pavillion, Safari Park Hotel (☎02/802493–7). One of six equally excellent restaurants in the vast Thika Road complex, with surprisingly affordable Szechuan cuisine.

French

Alan Bobbe's Bistro, Cianda House, Koinange St (☎02/224945; Sat dinner only, Sun closed). Any first impression of pretentiousness is soon belied by the genuine interest in seriously good food. One of the oldest restaurants in the city (since 1962); still devoutly French and devotedly patronized. Very expensive (Ksh1000 a head is normal), but you'd pay five times more in a European equivalent. Highly recommended.

Zephyr, 1st floor, Rank Xerox House, Parklands Rd (☎02/750055). A shade cheaper and still cordon bleu, with a Japanese chef.

Indian

Curry Pot, Monrovia St (☎02/251403; daily). Cheap and always busy, majoring on chicken and tandoori.

Dhaba, Kilome St (☎02/222799; daily). A Punjabi restaurant, with wonderful *Taka-tak Jeera* chicken. They have a *nyama choma* place upstairs, with a sort of verandah.

Mayur at the *Supreme Hotel*, corner of Kilome Rd and Keekorok Rd at the top of River Rd (☎02/225241; daily 7–9.30pm). In a class of its own, this presents a real challenge to any prospective restaurateur in Nairobi. The food is South Indian vegetarian (this is the only *certified* vegetarian restaurant in the city centre), but so delicious and so well presented that to miss eating at the *Mayur* would be a shame. The buffet upstairs (lunch and dinner, at Ksh200 an absolute bargain, even with a large tip expected) is worth starving all day for – in fact it's advisable – and the waiters are too polite to say anything if they notice you dropping sweetmeats into a napkin. Downstairs, in the cheaper *Supreme* itself (open daily), there's a less lavish choice, and you have to put up with maddeningly chirpy *muzak*, but they have substantially the same dishes, and also a good selection of sweets by the kilo. Takeaway also available.

Minar, Stanbic Bank House, Banda St (☎02/330168; daily). Slick, Mughlai restaurant with a first-class reputation. Alcohol available. There are branches in the YaYa Centre, Hurlingham (☎02/561676) and Sarit Centre, Westlands (☎02/748340), with occasional Bhangra nights.

New Three Bells, Utalii House (mezzanine floor), Loita St, near the French Cultural Centre (☎02/220628; daily). Quite classy and very good value.

Safeer, at the *Hotel Ambassadeur*, Moi Ave (☎02/336803; daily). An excellent Mughlai restaurant with a rich and spicy menu, including vegetarian dishes (though there's talk of it moving to the *Panafric Hotel*). Alcohol available.

Satkar, Dodo Lane, off Moi Ave (☎02/337197; daily). South Indian vegetarian, very popular and exceptionally good value.

Slush's Happy Eater, Tubman Rd, off Kimathi St (☎02/220745; daily). Indian vegetarian, with a good variety of snacks and takeaways.

Swagath Hotel, Diamond Plaza, Highridge, Parklands (☎02/750148; daily). Superb vegetarian restaurant with an extensive menu, including tasty *bajia* (potatoes fried with spices).

Taj, Taveta Rd (no telephone; daily). Very cheap and filling; good birianis.

Italian

Bon Appetit, Hamilton House, Kaunda St (☎02/217851) and *Bon Apetit Annexe*, in the City Hall garden courtyard at the corner of Mama Ngina St and Wabera St (☎02/229076; both branches Mon–Sat 7am–10pm, Sun 7am–3pm). By no means exclusively Italian, and not the greatest cuisine, but wholesome, plentiful and – in the annexe – pleasantly relaxing.

Giardino, 1st floor, View Park Towers, Uhuru Highway (☎02/330169; on Sun, dinner only). Rather cold and impersonal but well priced and some excellent and unusual specialities. Lamb and *pesce en cartoccio* (oven-baked tilapia fillet seasoned in herbs and white wine) are outstanding.

La Cucina, 2nd floor, YaYa Centre, Hurlingham (☎02/562871; Mon–Sat). Popular, well-priced, excellent pizzas.

La Scala Pizzeria, Phoenix House Arcade, Standard St (☎02/332130; daily until midnight). One of the cheapest, with quite decent food but agonizingly slow service. Its lunchtime specials are a bargain.

Marino's, NHC House, Aga Khan Walk, behind the American Embassy (☎02/557404; closed Sun). An excellent Italian restaurant, better, quieter and naturally more expensive than the *Trattoria* (see below). Delightful service.

Toona Tree, Chiromo Rd, and also accessible from the Casino (☎02/742600; closed Mon). Very pleasant above-ground, open-air place, set among the boughs of the eponymous tree, and majoring on seafood. Regular live music.

Trattoria, Town House, corner of Wabera St and Kaunda St (☎02/340855; daily until midnight). Usually gets enthusiastic notices from low-budget travellers having a splurge, though it's sometimes too busy for its own good (at lunchtime, full meals only). The pasta dishes and pizzas are the real thing and the cakes and ice cream – when they come – magnificent.

Japanese

Akasaka, Standard St (☎02/220299). Without doubt one of Nairobi's best restaurants, with impeccable service and food. Its "lunchboxes" at Ksh400 are good value. Highly recommended.

Shogun, Argwings Kodhek Rd (☎02/716080; closed Sun; reservations advisable for traditional Japanese "rooms" – no shoes). Similarly excellent, slightly less formal than *Akasaka* and also much cheaper, though dreadful Muzak does rather spoil the atmosphere. Their *sashimi* (raw fish) is excellent. A huge range of dishes. Highly recommended.

Mainly meat

Angus Steak House, Uchumi House, Aga Khan Walk (☎02/224306). Excellent steaks, salad bar and beer for around Ksh300.

Carnivore, Langata Rd towards the National Park entrance (☎02/501775; daily). Grossly named and yes, there is a connection – the all-you-can-eat menu (lunch Ksh885, dinner Ksh985) includes charcoal-grilled game meat – impala, giraffe, zebra, ostrich, crocodile (the selection varies). A meal here has become part of every package itinerary and it's often tacked onto the tour outfits' excursions to Nairobi National Park. It's touristy – with discos at the end of the week and at weekends in the adjoining *Simba Saloon* – but very few people seem to dislike it. There is a vegetarian buffet, too, and on Saturday afternoons you can get rid of the kids at their *Funland*: games, magic shows, face-painting – enough to keep them happy for a few hours. See also the *Carnivore*'s listing under "Live Music Venues". There are buses past the entrance road (#31, 34, 125, 126) from where you should get a lift, but otherwise it's still 1km to walk – overall much easier by taxi.

Meateater's Den, Imenti House, Moi Ave (☎02/331189). Endless supplies of the fauna you thought was carefully protected, served as you like it. The game meat comes largely from private farms. Shares premises with the *Lobster Pot*, a seafood restaurant.

Porterhouse, KCS House, Mama Ngina St (☎02/221829). Great steaks.

Professional Centre Restaurant, Parliament Rd (☎02/220014; closed Sun). Wide choice of well-prepared steaks, as well as a number of decent vegetarian dishes. In the same building as *Phoenix Players* (see "Film & Theatre").

Red Bull, 1st floor, Transnational Plaza, Mama Ngina St (☎02/228045; on Sat & Sun, dinner only). A very 1970s German/Swiss "theme" restaurant, now aiming more upmarket. Wonderful steaks, game meat, seafood and vegetarian selection.

Steak House Limited, 3rd floor, Chester House, Koinange St (☎02/339715; on Sun, dinner only). Their 1.2-kilo T-bone is very large indeed, though quality is sometimes variable.

Mainly fish

Stavrose, Mezzanine Floor, Postbank House, Market Lane, behind *African Heritage* (☎02/335107). A little-known fish restaurant, famed among those in the know for its tilapia fish, cooked any way you want it. They also do good salads.

Salads

Calypso, Bruce House, entry from Standard St or Kaunda St (☎02/501519; Mon–Sat 8am–5pm). Full of smart young business types. Fresh salad buffet.

Pasara, 2nd Mezzanine Floor, Lonrho House, Standard St (☎02/338247; Mon–Fri). Delicious lunches, including sandwiches, muffins and pancakes.

Zanzebar, 5th Floor, Kenya Cinema Plaza, Moi Ave (☎02/222568; daily). Quiet, lunchtime getaway with an economical salad buffet and KTN television and soft rock in the background. Famous for its "12-inch hot dogs". Lively bar in the evening and sometimes live bands.

Bars

Sooner or later, a **drink** at the *Norfolk Hotel* is a must, though it's no longer the bargain entertainment in people-watching that it was when beer prices were fixed; at times, too, it can feel uncomfortably close to a pub in the City of London. The Friday night *wazungu* crowd have voted with their feet and now frequent both the *Mayfair Court Hotel* on Parklands Road and the popular and cliquey *Gipsy Bar* (aka *Tropicanna*; ☎02/440964) on Woodvale Grove, near the *Jacaranda Hotel*. Both serve tapas and are open until the early hours. The *Thorn Tree Café* at the *New Stanley Hotel* (see p.92), is hard to avoid, as it's in the thick of the worst zone for tourist hustling, so a welcome refuge. The *Hurlingham Hotel* hosts an international working crowd and has darts, but closes at 10pm, while the *Hilton*'s effort, *The Jockey Club* on City Hall Way next to *Egyptair*, has a more traditional pubby feel. If you're staying up on Nairobi Hill on the other side of Uhuru Highway, you might also pay a visit to the remarkably seedy *Buffalo Bill's* at the *Heron Court Hotel* in Milimani Road – a cowboy theme bar with a waiting woman in every "covered wagon" drinking booth. Noisy and high-spirited at night (the bar closes at 11.30pm), the tone is much gentler by day, with occasional live jazz on Saturday and Sunday afternoons.

Otherwise, unless you go to unmemorable hotel bars, central Nairobi is a bit of a dead loss after office hours. It's more fun to venture out, suitably stripped down (the clothes on your back and a little cash), to the land of **"Day & Night Clubs"**. The River Road district vibrates from dawn to dusk and back to dawn again with the sound of beery mayhem and jukeboxes (see the "Nightlife and music" section below) – if you like the sound of it, you might consider taking a room nearby to avoid the hassle of getting back.

Film and theatre

Nairobi has twelve **cinemas**, including two drive-ins, but the quality of the movies on offer is in sad decline. **Theatre** in the city is gradually improving, with a number of active stage venues and a dedicated local acting community.

Screen

The twin-screen *20th Century* on Mama Ngina Street (☎02/338070), the *Nairobi*, in Uchumi House, Nkrumah Lane just off Harambee Avenue (☎02/226603), and the *Kenya* on Moi Avenue (☎02/226982) screen fairly recent mainstream releases – usually blockbusters or award winners – when they can get them. Other movie theatres tend to show Kung Fu, vintage James Bond, old Westerns and, of course, Hindi movies which you don't need to understand to enjoy – the *Fox Drive-In* on the Thika Road (☎02/802293) has gone over pretty well exclusively to the genre. The *Embassy* (☎02/225385) and the *Odeon* (☎02/222030), both on Latema Road near the *Iqbal Hotel*, and the *Cameo* on Kenyatta Avenue (☎02/226843) are popular for weekend matinees. Seats cost Ksh60 or less and daily programmes can be found in the *Nation* and the *Standard* newspapers (the *Nation*'s two-line resumés are often more entertaining than the movie in question).

Stage

The small theatre at the **Professional Centre**, at the end of Parliament Road (box office and enquiries ☎02/225506, Mon–Fri 10am–5pm), has now assumed the old *Donovan Maule Theatre*'s mantle as Nairobi's leading playhouse. Its energetic repertory company, the **Phoenix Players** (formed in 1948), stage contemporary works by Kenyan or foreign playwrights, or sometimes perform classics adapted for Kenya. Their productions, especially in the less self-censuring climate of the 1990s, are always worth catching and sometimes excellent: they have some fine actors and superb singing voices, and the centre is a pleasant, intimate venue.

Under the dynamic directorship of Agatha Ndambuki, the **Kenya National Theatre** in Harry Thuku Road, opposite the *Norfolk* (☎02/220536), gives considerable emphasis to Kenyan drama and African theatre in general – though with a less hectic schedule than the Phoenix Players.

You should also see what's going on at the University (they often have festivals of African and Caribbean theatre performed in the Education Department Lecture Theatre). Otherwise, see if the **Serekasi Players** are doing anything in the basement of the Kenyatta Conference Centre; check out the productions of the **Miujiza Players**, often at *Rahimtulla Trust Library Theatre* in Mfangano Street (☎02/210363); and enquire about the **Tamduni Players**, a long-established group run by a Gambian woman, Janet Young, who do occasional productions.

If you're interested in the state of the theatre in Kenya, the French Cultural Centre, the Goethe Institut, or even Gallery Watatu, may be able to tell you more, and the first two sometimes host productions. The *Standard*'s Thursday edition and the *Sunday Nation* carry theatre pages.

BIRDWATCHING IN NAIROBI

Birdwatching need not be exclusively a bush pursuit. For any visitor staying in central Nairobi, an impressive sight during the early morning and late evening is that of groups of **black kites** circling over the city as they move between feeding and roosting sites; amongst these are **pied crows**, readily identified black and white birds. **Marabou storks**, **sacred ibises** and **silvery-cheeked hornbills** can sometimes be seen flying over the city, while flocks of **red-winged starlings** call noisily from office buildings.

The leafier areas of the city are likely to produce even more birds, although care should be taken when visiting certain parks and gardens in the city (see "Security", p.82). The gardens adjacent to the National Museum are an interesting and relatively safe area to start birdwatching. Here, keen birdwatchers may encounter the **little bee-eater**, a common, small, green bee-eater of open areas with scattered bushes. The plants and flowering shrubs outside the front steps of the museum provide excellent opportunities to observe **sunbirds**: several species, including variable and Hunter's sunbirds can be seen here. Another bird of the gardens is the **African paradise monarch**, a species of flycatcher. In breeding plumage, the silvery-white males have long tail streamers, which trail behind them like ribbons, as they flit from tree to tree.

Nightlife and music

With the limited range of cultural activities available, it's not surprising that **drinking and dancing** are what a night out in Nairobi is usually about. Entrance fees are low by international standards and prices for drinks are much the same as you'll pay everywhere in the country. Be warned, however, that, male or female, if you're not accompanied by a partner of the opposite sex, you will soon be.

One place that draws fair numbers of tourists is the **International Casino**, close to the *Hotel Boulevard* and museum. The complex consists of the main gaming room itself (main entrance off Chiromo Road; open from 9pm weekdays, 4pm weekends; smart casual dress code; nominal entrance fee), a couple of restaurants (see *Toona Tree* on p.110), a slot machine hall, the *Lucky Strike* – a bit of a dive but the view is good – and two clubs, *Galileo's* and *Bubbles* (basically just a disco), both of which are covered in the following listings. Beware that the whole area around the casino is dodgy – and extremely unsafe after dark – with clusters of prostitutes and drug-hawkers to waylay you and live opportunities for being mugged with your winnings. If you really have more money than sense, the two newcomers to the casino market are *Florida Casino* on Loita Lane (tables 6pm–6am daily; slot machines, restaurant and 24-hour cafeteria) and the *Safari Park Hotel* on Thika Road, sumptuous in every respect (and it stays open, obligingly, until the last bankruptcy), but rather too far to walk back from.

Live-music venues

Given the volatile nature of the music business in Kenya, **venues and bands** change at a moment's notice. Although there are a few downtown music places, much of Nairobi's live music action takes place on the perimeter of the city. The following listings include all the places that have been around for some time, plus the latest information on new ones. In addition, you might check out Friday's *Daily Nation* for announcements of one-off gigs.

City centre venues

African Heritage, Kenyatta Ave (☎02/333157; Sat 2.30–5pm). Easy-going, informal, Saturday afternoon mix of reggae, soukous and more traditional music – though closed for renovation at the time of writing.

Arturo Restaurant, Tumaini House, Moi Ave (☎02/226940). Not exactly a restaurant (though the food's OK) and not really Italian, but its first-floor verandah has live music (could be anything: Zairean, Kikuyu, Luo) on Wed, Fri and Sat nights. Very danceable, very local and entrance is free.

Foresta Magnetica, Corner House, Kimathi St (☎02/218953; closed Sun). This restaurant – and sometime piano bar – generally features a mix of the sort of pop, reggae, soukous, and "chakacha beat" often found in the coastal tourist hotels. Currently closed for "renovations" and there are rumours of it being taken over by the late, tacky and unmissed *Visions Nightclub*.

Freemark Capital Centre, Uhuru Park. An odd, hangar-like venue, where the quality of live shows can be erratic, though recent acts have included Bora Bora and Princess Faridah, "the queen of chakacha".

STARTING TIMES

Starting times vary considerably for all the clubs. On weekdays, 7.30 or 8pm wouldn't be too early, while weekend warm-ups usually begin around 9–10pm, and some may not get really rolling until midnight. But don't judge any band by their first hour. Many run through some pretty dreadful warm-up material to begin with. Remember, too, that many clubs have Sunday afternoon matinées that can be just as lively as the evening shows – convenient if you don't want to be taxiing around the city late at night.

Galileo's Private Members' Club (☎02/742600; Tues–Sun) at the International Casino. Flashpoint Band play nightly.

Garden Square Restaurant, City Hall Way (☎02/226474; daily 7am–midnight or later; safe parking; about Ksh60 on band nights). Not frantically raunchy, but relaxed and a good place to bop, this is less intimidating than most spots if you're not part of a couple and don't wish to be. At lunchtime, and some evenings, the African buffet is pretty good value, and it's not a bad place to hang out with a beer at any time, though on weekdays all you'll get musically is background sounds. Fridays and Saturdays (and sometimes Wed) are traditionally band nights; the music starts at 9.30pm and runs into the early hours. Sunday is all-day reggae, kicking off at noon with records and warming up to the band at about 8pm. Although they haven't had much live music of late *Garden Square* is definitely worth checking out.

Hard Rock Café, Mezzanine 2, Barclays Plaza (☎02/220802; daily 9am–2am; free admission). Overpriced food with silly names, outrageously daft cocktails, old Chevrolets lunging in through the ceiling – wallow in the glory nostalgia of the American Dream. The Pressmen have a residency on Wed, Fri and Sat (see box on "Nairobi Bands").

The Jazz Bar, 2nd floor, YaYa Centre, Hurlingham (☎02/711473; daily 10am till late). A sadly pretentious (and expensive) piano bar rather than the jumpin' jazz joint that Nairobi really needs. Still, it hosts smooth US jazz artists from time to time – check press for details.

Mang' Hotel, Haile Selassie Ave (☎02/340692). An exuberant local venue where soukous reigns. Mpingo Band play Wed and Fri from 6pm; there's a disco on other nights and more live soukous after midnight.

Sirona Hotel, Keiyo Rd, off Forest Rd, Parklands (☎02/742730). Within easy striking distance if you're staying at *Ma Roche's*. Sunday afternoons have featured the reggae sounds of Mpendo Moja.

Suburban and out of town

Bombax Club, Ngong Rd, across from the Kenya Science Teachers College at Dagoretti Corner in the southwest of the city (☎02/561421; see "Nairobi Area" map; Ksh80 Fri & Sat). A small, friendly bar with tasty, though not lightning fast, food and wonderful music Thurs–Sun from Tanzanian transplants Les Wanyika – ecstatic stuff, with John Ngereza on lead guitar and Professor Omari on rhythm. The crowd here is always happy and relaxed, and they're usually a more mature gathering than the usual clubbers. Take bus #1, 2, 3, 4 or any bus that passes Dagoretti Corner from the GPO on Kenyatta Ave (but plan on taking a taxi back to town).

Calabash Bezique, 20km down Thika Rd at Kahawa Sukari, opposite Kenyatta University (☎02/811084). A large, new, 24-hour *nyama choma* place with rather studenty discos Thurs–Sat and occasional live bands – phone in advance for details. Get there on a *matatu* from Koinange St, or #137 bus from the KBS depot (last bus 10pm).

Cantina Club, Wilson Airport entrance, Langata Rd (☎02/506085; open 24hr every day; some nights free, otherwise Ksh100). No tourist panderings here – this is an old African club with *nyama choma*, a great record archive and a big following of devoted locals. Like the *Bombax*, although it's much bigger, the *Cantina* attracts a slightly older crowd that keeps the atmosphere both boisterous and mellow at the same time – and it's pleasantly spacious and airy.

Carnivore Simba Saloon, off the Langata Rd on the way to Nairobi National Park (☎02/501779; no music Mon & Tues; otherwise Ksh100–150). A successful meld of live music and disco in a pleasant, outdoor environment (see p.110 for the restaurant write-up). Wednesday nights are rock, till 2am, with free entry and a happy hour before the music begins (at 9pm). Thursday is jazz night, 6pm–midnight, with free entry before 9pm; the American Rahn Burton is resident but rather bland. Friday is Simba Groove night (soul, funk, samba, from 8pm until early; Ksh50 for women, Ksh100 for men); Saturday Simba Disco, with a more African sound selection (6pm until dawn; Ksh100 for all); and Sunday is Simba Soul (6pm until 2am; free until 9pm, then Ksh50). Visiting groups sometimes take the Sunday afternoon slot. Buses #31, 34, 125 or 126 will drop you at the *Carnivore*'s entrance road, where someone is bound to give you a lift. Taxis have fixed rates here – not a lot in a group.

Gringos, Limuru Rd, Ruaka, 1km past Runda Estates, on the road towards Limuru and Naivasha on our "Greater Nairobi" map (☎02/521231). A Tex-Mex restaurant that's been known to have some pretty good Zairean soukous on Fri and Sat – and a nice spot to go on a Sun afternoon – if you've got transport. Its food, though, is not always fresh.

Hillock Inn, Enterprise Rd near the Ngong River bridge (☎02/358685). This is a place to go when their house band is *not* playing. Give them a call to see if anything special is coming up – they often host some of the top Kikuyu names on their guest nights, which are always well worth hitting.

NAIROBI BANDS

The big names to watch out for are the Tanzanian group **Les Wanyika** (*Bombax Club*) and their "cousins" the **Mavalo Kings** (currently at the *Garden Hotel*, Machakos); the **Maroon Commandos** (*Little Villa*), **Super Mazembe** (currently at *Wayside Hotel* in Nakuru), **Juma Toto & Toddy Nationale**, **Prince Bwami Fan Fan & Les Matata Five** (*Motherland* in Kariobangi), **Tshackatumba** (a mix of Zairean and Kenyan musicians), the **Seiko System Band** (playing a fusion of *benga* and rumba), rumba from **Bilenge Musica d'Afrique** (*Legacy Africa* in Parklands), **Bora Bora** featuring fantastic sax players Twahir Mohamed and Rama Athumani (*Makuti Park*), *benga* man **Aziz Abdi** (*Sportsview Hotel*) and the one-off *benga*/soukous blender **Ochieng Kabaselleh**.

Possibly less interesting sounds come from the voices and instruments of a clutch of tourist and international-style pop and rock bands – **Them Mushrooms** (*Splash!*), the **Pressmen** (*Hard Rock Café*), **Tangerine Fusion** and **Hakuna Wafungwa**.

Since 1994 there's been a huge **gospel** trend in Nairobi. You're bound to hear of some of the following artists: **Mary Atino, Augustus Baraza, Wilson Majale, Joseph Mwaura** and **Kimani Thomas**. The best-known name is that of **Joseph Kamaru** who renounced raunchy Kikuyu folk-pop for the word of the Lord and depressed millions of fans. *Benga* superstar **Daniel Owino (DO) Misiani** is rumoured to be following the same path.

RECORDS AND CASSETTES

Pirated cassettes may seem a good deal at about Ksh60 but quality and durability are so bad they're practically worthless. Identify them by plastic wrapper and absence of labels on the cassette itself. For LPs and tapes, try *Assanand's*, Moi Avenue, *Nakumatt* on Kenyatta Avenue or, better still, any of a host of shops and stalls on and around River Road. For the best selection of 45s, especially for vernacular music, check out *City Sounds* in River Road (they often have second-hand singles they're virtually giving away).

JKA Resorts Club, Mombasa Rd, just beyond the JKA airport turn-off from Nairobi (☎02/822066). Although some way out of town and a little difficult to get to unless you have your own vehicle, *JKA Resorts* usually features a regular band on Fri and Sat nights and Sun afternoons into the evening. Watch the papers, too, for announcements of special *JKA* entertainment events often coinciding with holidays. The club area has a pleasant, garden setting and, at cooler times of the year, they light fires in hearths on either side of the dance floor. Buses to Athi River from Tusker House bus terminal can get you there, but only about once an hour. And, while it's easy enough to hitch back in daylight, after about 9pm (when the last bus returns) a taxi is your only option. Given taxi fares these days, an overnight at the *JKA Hotel* attached to the club, while not very cheap, might be worth considering.

Little Villa Club, Kiambu Rd. Recently started live music on Sat afternoons and evenings; the opening night was fronted by the Maroon Commandos, who may become residents.

Makuti Park Club, Nairobi South "B" Shopping Centre (☎02/545957); *matatus* from Haile Selassie/Moi Ave. Live music at least from Fri to Sun, currently featuring the group Bora Bora with a pair of dynamite sax players from Tanzania; Bora Bora play Wed 8pm–midnight, Fri & Sat 9pm–3am, & Sundays at 4pm.

Ngong Hills Hotel, Ngong Rd (☎02/566677). Currently one of the best venues, very popular, and few *wazungu*, this hotel has recently been hosting a group called the Orchestra Malembe Stars. The atmosphere is not at all intimidating and the bands (Kenya's coolest, Tanzania's hottest and some Lingala) uniformly excellent (Wed, Fri & Sat). Sunday afternoons host a very laid-back jam session, complete with dancers, acrobats, tight-rope walkers and *nyama choma* by the pool. Ideal for bringing kids. Ample parking.

Peacock Inn, Nairobi South "B" Shopping Centre; *matatus* from Haile Selassie/Moi Ave. On Fridays this is well worth checking out for occasional visits by Tanzanian bands, including Arusha's Ngamiani Band.

Splash!, 300m from *Carnivore* (see above; ☎02/603777; Ksh150). Live music Fri nights, and you can still go swimming. Them Mushrooms (see "Nairobi Bands" box above) are the resident band.

Sportsview Hotel, Thika Rd, near the Moi Sports Complex at Kasarani (☎02/803890). Another outsize *nyama choma* joint which occasionally books some interesting groups. Currently resident is Aziz Abdi's *benga* orchestra, which plays upbeat Swahili dance music. Call ahead to see if there's live music at the weekend. You can get there on buses #45 and 145 from Tusker House – last run at 8pm – but you'd be better off sharing a taxi for the evening in a group.

Discos

Reggae is the popular staple sound of the **cheap discos**, often not much more than "Day & Night Clubs". The government's anti-rasta drive of a few years back fizzled out and reggae music is back on the airwaves and in the street. Nairobi also has a scattering of **disco palaces** complete with flashy interiors and the latest dance hits from Europe and America. If this style appeals, try one of the established places below (or the *Carnivore* or *Galileo's* from the "Live Music" listings). In the glitzy places, men usually pay more than women, around Ksh200–300 as against Ksh100. In the rootsier discos, entrance is free or very cheap.

Reggae discos
Brilliant Hotel, Forest Rd at Desai Rd, on the south side of City Park (☎02/762200). The main nights are Wed, Fri and Sun, but phone for details of special nights. *KBS Stagecoach* bus #44 and 108 will drop you here, or *matatus* #25 and 30, or it's 20 minutes' walk from *Ma Roche's*.
Hollywood, Moktar Daddah St (☎02/27949; Wed–Sun). This is mostly a drinking club, with dancing something its regulars do to keep from falling asleep. Jah'mbo Soul have their residency here, though the action closes early. Live reggae on Sun.
Monte Carlo Club, Accra Rd (☎02/223181). A cavernous place, open daily till dawn; reggae disco Wed from 8pm, Sat from 4pm, Sun from 2pm; admission Ksh100. "No weapons or *miraa*".
New Congoni Day & Night Club, River Rd, off Lithuli Ave (☎02/331789). Reggae discos on Sun afternoons. Unpredictable live music, predictably smelly toilets.

Disco palaces – in and out of town
The big discos all put on floor shows for those who stay late enough – gyrating trios, limbo dancing and all.
Bubbles, International Casino, Museum Hill (☎02/742600). Sometimes has live music – currently the Pressmen.
Club Africa at *Rib Shack*, Kiambu Rd, Muthaiga north (☎02/512439). An upmarket *nyama choma* joint with jazz-funk Wed, pure and disco-trash Fri to Sun morning. Last Fri of the month is "Africa Nite". Cheaper than *Carnivore*.
Club de Balafon, Kaunda St (daily). Slushy, saccharine "snack bar and dancing"; oddly enough, still popular.
Dolce Club, Cianda House, Koinange St (☎02/218298). Slick and smooth soukous and soul for a glitzy crowd; deafening sound system.
Florida 2000, Commerce House, Moi Ave near the *Kenya Cinema* (☎02/217269). The *New Florida's* sister establishment attracts similar clients and offers equally unambiguous entertainment.
New Florida, Koinange St (☎02/334870). Irresistible for its tackiness, this big orange mushroom of a building is always full of hookers and rather desperate-looking business types, but the atmosphere is merely steamy, not heavy. Reggae on Wed.
Sahara City/Dreams, at the *Bedouin Complex*, Mombasa Highway (☎02/822933). Nairobi's top disco with the best sound system – an excellent place for dance freaks, with the best DJ working Wed–Sun. Few *wazungu*, no tourists and plenty of young affluent Asians dancing *mujurrah*.
Zanzebar, Kenya Cinema Plaza, Moi Ave (☎02/222568; Tues–Thurs Ksh70, Fri Ksh150, Sat & Sun Ksh100). Very swish pine, chrome and neon club full of trendy types fretting over whether your unwashed garb is simply dirty or the latest style in swinging London or Milan. Tues and Thurs is Karaoke; Wed soul (of the diva sort); Fri and Sat Lingala, funk and soul; Sun has live afternoon jazz.

Local dives – city centre

On **Latema Road**, people contort themselves just to get into the *Modern Green Day and Night Club*. Here, entrance is free, cold beer is not the fashion – though you can get it, from the barman in his security cage – and the floor show is you and the rest of the customers. Just why the place is so popular is hard to say. For the girls it's partly because of the steady trickle of potential customers from the *Iqbal* and other lodgings nearby – it's amazing how many *wazungu* are still prepared to play with HIV. For some of the men it's a place to chew *miraa* all night for the price of a soda. From the outside, with the usual arguments and hustle going on in the doorway, it might appear a place to avoid, but squeeze inside, drink a beer or two, and soak up the elevated atmosphere. People make friends quickly here, though having a conversation over the racket of the throng and the din of the jukebox is exhausting.

If you can't take the pace, try the *New Congoni Day and Night Club* on River Road, off Lithuli Avenue (see "Reggae Discos" above), or dozens of similar places in Nairobi. There's nothing to keep you from checking out others – plenty of people do. Try, for example, the local *pombe* at the *Mlachahe Bar & Restaurant* opposite *Malindi Dishes* in Gaberone Road. Or give the *Habari Day & Night Club* and *Lizzie's Bar* a try, both on Luthuli Avenue – and both raucous and cheap like the *Modern Green* but minus the hustling young women. Also worth a mention is the *California Stars Butchery* on Gaberone Road, actually a bar and *nyama choma* joint, with tables out on the street opposite the Sikh Temple.

Local dives – Eastleigh

Aside from the city centre clubs and the fairly touristy places which draw their custom from a wide area, there are plenty of other nightspots catering for a more local clientele in the outlying communities. One of the livelier of such communities, musically or otherwise, is **Eastleigh**. Although only a ten-minute bus ride from town, it has a completely different look and feel from the modern centre.

Quite a number of bars in Eastleigh feature **live music** (another reason to think of staying out there), if not necessarily on a regular weekly schedule. Check out *Mateso Bila Chuki* and *Laikipia Bar* along Galole Road (between Fifth and Fourth streets, a short walk from the big *KBS* bus depot), both interesting nightspots that sometimes feature bands. For more adventurous music-seekers, there's the *New Kibigori Day and Night Club* on Juja Road (buses #28, 32 and 42 from *Ambassadeur*) which occasionally hosts big names.

Catching Luo, Kikuyu and Kamba bands

"**Vernacular music**" – as opposed to songs in Swahili or Lingala – is performed in and around Nairobi, sometimes quite frequently, but the gigs are most often one-night stands. Doyens of this catch-all non-genre are Daniel Owino (DO) Misiani and his **Shirati Jazz**, the Luo-speaking, "Benga beat" stars whose international tours have been resoundingly successful. They used to play most weekends at *River Yala Club* in Kariobangi shopping centre. Kariobangi isn't the greatest place to wander at night so go first on a Sunday afternoon. Also well worth checking out in Kariobangi is *Motherland Bar & Restaurant*. Buses #28, 31 and 40 among others go to Kariobangi from *Ambassadeur*. Once on Kamunde Road – the one that encircles Kariobangi – get off at the first stop, then backtrack to the first cross street and follow it to the shopping centre.

For a taste of traditional Luo music, the charming **Professor Ojwang** plays the *nyatiti* at the *Thorn Tree* on Thursday to Saturday, early evenings. The instrument has both drum heads played by the feet, and bass strings played by hand. You may also catch him at the Bomas of Kenya (see p.133) on Friday to Sunday (7–11pm), or ask whether he'll be playing elsewhere. Otherwise, if you'd like to catch a Kamba or Kikuyu group, your best bet is to look around the River Road area for **posters** announcing forthcoming appearances.

Nairobi travel and safari plans

Nairobi is the travel hub of Africa with a mass of opportunities for **safaris** around Kenya, and good facilities for making **travel arrangements** across the continent – and more or less anywhere else in the world. There are literally hundreds of safari operators, car rental outlets and travel agents. The following summaries aim to make sense of the whole business and pick out some recommended firms. Public transport details are given in the "travel details" section at the end of the chapter. If you want to make simple hotel and lodge reservations, either do it through a travel agent, or contact the hotel reservation services in person (addresses and hotel lists on p.48). Most of the commercial buildings which house the offices in the following listings are marked on our "Nairobi: Commercial Centre" map.

Cycling

Before making any bookings, one option you might not have considered is **cycling** (see p.42). Although the big game parks will still be out of your reach, several of the smaller parks will let you in (Hell's Gate at Naivasha, Lake Bogoria Reserve, Kakamega Forest) and much wonderful cycling country is explorable. The cheapest Chinese and Indian three-speed machines are widely available, as well as large numbers of cheap mountain bikes (from around Ksh5500) and a few lightweight models with good specification – even front fork suspension. These can be good value, but you'll have trouble reselling. There is unfortunately no bicycle rental available yet: see if *Gitonga Cycle Dealers* can help.

Cycle Land, Moi Ave (☎02/223955). Good range in stock, including some quality mountain bike imports.

Gitonga Cycle Dealers, Landhies Rd (☎02/253022). Beyond the Country Bus Station.

Kenya Cycle Mart, Moi Ave (☎02/223417). A traditional cycle store.

Sardar Singh Vohra Ltd, River Rd, next to Evamay Lodge (☎02/222715). One of the cheaper outlets with reasonable 18-speed mountain bikes for Ksh12,000. Spares for all specs.

Westlands Cycle Mart, Old Uchumi Building, opposite The Mall (☎02/448055). The best place to resell your bike (or try the Sun morning second-hand vehicle market along Parklands Road).

Safari operators

You can pick up plenty of leaflets about safaris from touts, or at any travel agent or ticket-booking company. Armed to the teeth with brochures and anxious to take you to operators' offices, **touts** are by no means a bad thing, as they often work for several companies and their commission is never added to the price you pay. Indeed, some are very knowledgeable and will be able to advise you relatively truthfully about which companies are currently good for what. The best of the **travel agents** are reputable (see under "Travel agents and airline bookings", p.122), but it's always a good idea to meet the company you're travelling with in advance and to try to ensure that it is that company (the operator) and not you (the punter) who is paying the agent their commission. The following listings are classified broadly – several operators could be put into more than one bracket. Note that if you're a student, you should get a reduction on park entry fees.

Camping safaris

First, read the section on "Camping Safaris" in *Basics* (p.62). Every other shop seems to belong to a safari outfit and it's obviously impossible to mention more than a few. With so much to go wrong, spotless reputations are hard to maintain but the following, who run most of their **camping trips by truck or minibus**, are good value and only rarely come in for criticism.

Gametrackers, 1st Floor, Kenya Cinema Plaza, Moi Ave (PO Box 62042; ☎02/338927, fax 02/330903). Popular and consistently good operator with some 20 tours, including – apart from game safaris – cycling, camel treks, Aberdares walking and Mount Kenya climbs, as well as trips further afield (they have branches in Tanzania and Uganda). Around $60–80 per day and up. They run an excellent eight-day Turkana safari via the Chalbi Desert, which is highly recommended ($480).

Kenia Tours and Safaris, 4th Floor, Jubilee Insurance Building, corner of Kaunda St and Wabera St (PO Box 19730; ☎02/223699, out of hours ☎02/444572, fax 02/217671). Proficient general Kenya camping safaris specialist. A keenly priced and conscientious operation. $45–55 per day.

Let's Go Travel, Caxton House, Standard St (PO Box 60342; ☎02/340331, fax 02/336890). Apart from acting as agents, *Let's Go* also run their own well-organized budget camping safaris. $60–75 per day.

Rhino Safaris, Hilton Building, Mama Ngina St (PO Box 48023; ☎02/228102). Veteran safari firm, the parent company of UK long-haul specialists *Hayes & Jarvis* and operators of their safaris. Budget camping and lodge trips, with good drivers and cooks. From around $70 per day; $150 per day for lodge safaris.

Safari Camp Services, lower ground floor, Barclays Plaza (PO Box 44801; ☎02/228936 or after hours ☎02/891348, fax 02/212160). For years the reputable operators of the original "Turkana Bus" and also of a "Wildlife Bus" trip emulated by many others. Their limited number of tried and tested safaris keeps standards up and prices fairly well down; the combined 13-day Turkana Bus and Camel Trek in the Mathew's Range and Lake Turkana should be brilliant ($800). No-frills safaris $60–70 per day; more comfortable, less streamlined, small-group camping safaris, around $150 per day; luxury get-away, up to $600 per day.

Safari Seekers, 5th floor, Jubilee Insurance Building, Kaunda St (PO Box 32834; ☎02/211396). General operator, offering mountain bike safaris in cooperation with an American company, *Paradise Bicycle Tours*. From $70–80 per day.

Savuka Tours & Safaris, 4th Floor, Pan-Africa Insurance Building, Kenyatta Ave (PO Box 20433; ☎02/225108, fax 02/215016). Recommended by many for, more than anything else, their customer relations. From about $65 per day.

Scenic Safaris, Biashara St (PO Box 49188; ☎02/229092). Wide range of shorter trips and reasonably priced lodge safaris. Camping from around $60 per day; lodges from $150 per day.

Special Camping Safaris, 1st Floor, Gilfillan House, Kenyatta Ave (PO Box 51512; ☎02/338325, fax 02/211828). Noted for their long Turkana trip but they offer a range of interesting, quite unconventional, options. From $65 per day.

Tour Africa Safaris, Corner House, Kimathi St/Mama Ngina St (PO Box 34187; ☎02/336767, fax 02/338271). A Swedish-run outfit with a very competent travel agency, famed for its half-day "Big Simba" safari to Nairobi National Park ($50). "Big Simba Two" is another converted Fiat army truck which covers Nakuru and Maasai Mara ($100 per day). Also half-board holidays in Tanzania ($100 per day, including flights).

Twiga Tours, 4th floor, Victor House, Kimathi St (PO Box 14365; ☎02/332364, fax 02/337330). A relative newcomer with tailor-made tours for as few as two people from $90–$100 per person per day.

Venture Africa, 3rd floor, Rehema House, Standard St (PO Box 8696; ☎02/219888, fax 02/219263). Upstart, middle-range operator with no bad reports. From $60 per day.

Special activity safaris

The following are recommended because they offer unusual, if normally much more expensive, trips – notably **foot safaris**, **bicycle safaris** and safaris using **pack animals**. Those that don't have walk-in addresses are usually small companies: enquire and book with a large agent like *Let's Go Travel* (see above). For information on balloon "safaris", see p.8.

Bateleur Safaris, Mezzanine Floor, Hilton Building, Mama Ngina St (PO Box 42562; ☎02/227048, fax ☎02/891007). Specialists in walking safaris for ornithologists.

Bike Treks, no walk-in office (PO Box 14237; ☎02/446371, fax 02/442439; or book through *Let's Go Travel*). Truly adventurous trips, with vehicle back-up, led by a veteran mountain bike enthusiast; the trans-Mara ride during the migration is quite something. Around $120 per day.

Bushbuck Adventures, 3rd Floor, Gilfillan House, Kenyatta Ave (PO Box 67449; ☎02/212975, fax 02/218735). Very professional long-established outfit with unusual trips featuring private campsites and walking itineraries in the Mara, western Kenya, Meru, the Aberdares and the north, with a bumper 18-day "Northern Frontier Expedition" that goes all over. From $80 per day.

Camel Trek, no walk-in office (PO Box 15076; ☎02/891079, fax 02/891716). An established company offering upmarket camel safaris around Isiolo district (3 or 5 nights). Closed March to July and mid-Oct to mid-Dec (rains). $250 per day.

Classic Aerial Safaris, no walk-in office (PO Box 76362; ☎02/712114). Fancy yourself as Biggles, in flying goggles, silk scarf and bomber jacket? Reach for the sky and plunge into your wallet for the only operational bi-plane trips in East Africa. From $200 for 20 minutes, to $900 (for 2) for flying and trout fishing around Mount Kenya. All flights from *Mount Kenya Safari Club*, Nanyuki.

Hiking & Cycling Kenya, 2nd Floor, Arrow House, Koinange St (PO Box 39439; ☎02/218336, fax 02/224212). Half a dozen tours concentrating on walking, with a ten-day, vehicle-assisted Ngong–Mara–Bogoria cycle trip at about $700.

Naturetrek Adventure Safaris, no walk-in office (PO Box 70933; ☎02/220491, fax 02/219638). Specialists in walking safaris, notable for a seven-day walk in the Rift Valley and Loita Hills on the Tanzanian border, and a 13-day jaunt in Tanzania itself encompassing Mount Meru, lakes Manyara and Natron, and Ngorongoro. From $200 per day.

Safaris Unlimited Ltd, Langata Rd (PO Box 24181; ☎02/891168, fax 02/891113). Riding in Maasailand from $230 per day.

Savage Wilderness Safaris, no walk-in office (PO Box 44827; ☎02/521590, fax 02/501754). Excellent programme of technical climbing and walking trips on Mount Kenya; "white-water" rafting on the Athi River; walking safaris in the Chyulu and Loita Hills; and sea kayaking in the Lamu archipelago and Tana delta. One-day rafting from $70. Other trips $100 per day and up depending on numbers.

Tropical Ice, Suite 8, Muthaiga Shopping Centre, Muthaiga Rd (PO Box 57341; ☎02/740811). Walking safaris along the Galana river for $160 per day.

Yare Safaris (PO Box 63006; ☎02/213445). One of the leaders in North Kenyan safaris, they offer various off-beat tours and camel treks in the Samburu district from their base in Maralal.

Upmarket safaris

If you can afford it, the **expensive safari outfits** are mostly operated to very high standards. They often depend heavily on reputations passed by word of mouth among clients and overseas operators. The following firms will give good return for your money if you are in the $300–1000 per day league and want something special. At this level, what you do is "tailor-made" – in other words, it's largely up to you. Transport is usually by land cruiser; accommodation is in luxury lodges or pre-set private campsites; and leader/tour guides tend to be white hunter types who know the ground well and their clients' requirements even better.

Abercrombie & Kent, Bruce House, Standard St (PO Box 59749; ☎02/334955, fax 02/228700).

Bonham Safaris, Nandi Rd, Karen (PO Box 24133; ☎02/882521).

Cheli & Peacock, Triad House (PO Box 39806; ☎02/749064).

Cottar's Safari Service, Westminster House, Kenyatta Ave (PO Box 44191; ☎02/212372, fax 02/228875).

Kerr & Downey Safaris, corner of Busia Rd and Enterprise Rd, Industrial Area (PO Box 41822; ☎02/556466, fax 02/552378).

Tor Allan Safaris, (PO Box 41959; ☎02/891190).

Other contact addresses

Kuoni, *Panafric Hotel*, Kenyatta Ave (PO Box 30486; ☎02/710637).

Pollman's Tours & Safaris, Pollman's House, Mombasa Rd (PO Box 45895; ☎02/544346, fax 02/337171).

Somak Travel, 8th floor, Corner House, Mama Ngina St (PO Box 48495; ☎02/337333, fax 02/218954).

Thomas Cook, 12th Floor, International House, Mama Ngina St (PO Box 49387; ☎02/336536, fax 02/218889).

United Touring Co (UTC), Fedha Towers, Muindi Mbingu St (PO Box 42196; ☎02/331960, fax 02/331422).

Universal Safari Tours (UST), Ground floor, Cotts House, Wabera St (PO Box 49312; ☎02/221446).

Wildlife Safari, 13th Floor, International House, Mama Ngina St (PO Box 56803; ☎02/340319, fax ☎02/338972).

Cars and rental

First read the section on "Car rental and driving" in *Basics* (see p.40). The minimum age is usually 23 and, remember, you'll need to pay a deposit plus extra for insurance; expect to pay between $50 and $75 per day all in for a short-wheelbase 4WD Suzuki jeep, the most popular vehicle. Prices can be variable, with some quoted in Kenya shillings, though most in dollars. Shop around for the best deals (making sure you're quoted the inclusive price) and try to negotiate as you might with any purchase, bearing in mind the season and how long you're renting: this is easier with independent companies than the big-name franchises. However, bear in mind also that the big names are much better insured for damage and collision while some of the independent companies may leave you liable for up to $1000 in the event of an accident.

Do not assume your vehicle is roadworthy; the best companies sometimes send out vehicles in a terrible state. Check it as carefully as you can. You are, of course, responsible for any ongoing **repair and maintenance work** that needs doing while you're renting the vehicle (see the next section). The commonest requirement is for a new tyre. Try to get a list of recommended service stations from the rental company: to avoid bogus repairs some of them will insist you use certain garages. Always bargain hard before work begins.

For **motorbike rental**, try *Kijana Bikes* at *Blair Lodge*, Riara Road, near Dagoretti Corner, where you should be able to negotiate a good deal.

Car rental companies

Avis, College House, University Way (PO Box 49795; ☎02/334317; *Hilton* branch ☎02/229576, fax 02/215421; Airport ☎02/822186).

Budget Rent-A-Car, Ground Floor, Jubilee Insurance Building, Wabera St (PO Box 59767; ☎02/223304).

The Car Hire Company/Galu Safaris, New Stanley Hotel, Standard St (PO Box 56707; ☎02/225255, fax 02/216553).

Car Hire Services, 3rd Floor, Unga House, Muthithi Rd, Westlands (PO Box 25108; ☎02/743270).

Central Rent-A-Car, Fedha Towers, Standard St (PO Box 49439; ☎02/222888, fax 02/339666).

The Chequered Flag Ltd, Ring Rd, Westlands (PO Box 14483; ☎02/441171).

Concorde Car Hire, *Agip Garage*, Waiyaki Way, Westlands (PO Box 25053; ☎02/448953).

Crossways, Banda St (PO Box 10228; ☎02/223949, fax 02/214372).

Europcar, Bruce House, Standard St (PO Box 40433; ☎02/334722; Airport ☎02/822348).

Habib's Cars, Agip House, Haile Selassie Ave (PO Box 48095; ☎02/220463, fax 02/220985).

Hertz/UTC, Fedha Towers, Muindi Mbingu St (PO Box 42196; ☎02/214456, fax 02/216871; booking office on the corner of Kaunda St and Muindi Mbingu St, ☎02/217259; Airport ☎02/822339).

Intasun, 3rd Floor, Kenwood House, Kimathi St (PO Box 42977; ☎02/224037).

Let's Go Travel, Caxton House, Standard St (PO Box 60342; ☎02/340331).

Payless, Hilton Building, Simba St (PO Box 49713; ☎02/223581, fax 339779; Airport ☎02/822370, 24hr).

Polay's Car Hire, 1st floor, NCM House, Tom Mboya St (PO Box 31532; ☎02/334207).

Rasul's, Butere Rd, Industrial Area (taxi to Mater Misericordiae Hospital; PO Box 18172; ☎02/558234, fax 02/540341).

Buying cars and repairs

If you're looking to buy a vehicle in Kenya, scan the classified ads in the papers or visit the Sarit Centre, Westlands, on a Sunday morning, when there is a regular second-hand vehicle sale all along Parklands Road.

You're only likely to need work done in Nairobi itself if you're travelling in Africa in your own vehicle. For repairs, the *Undugu Society* workshop, near *Maridadi Fabrics* by the city stadium roundabout (☎02/755631), is reliable. The following also come highly recommended for serious repair work.

Aquva Fabricators, Baricho Rd, off Bunyala Rd, Industrial Area (PO Box 48641; ☎02/557360).

Dash Engineering Works, corner of Munyu Rd and Luthuli Ave (PO Box 10798; ☎02/227050).

Travel agents and airline bookings

Reputable general travel agents include:

Africa Travel Shop, 1st Floor, Union Towers, Moi Ave (PO Box 63006; ☎02/214099, fax 02/213445). Kenyan branch of the London-based Africa travel specialist.

Bunson Travel Service, Pan African Insurance Building, Standard St (PO Box 45456; ☎02/337712, fax 02/214120).

Flamingo Tours Ltd, 3rd floor, Langata House, Wilson Airport (PO Box 44899; ☎02/600900).

Guerba Kenya, 1st floor, International House, Mama Ngina St (PO Box 43935; ☎02/218783, fax 02/216972). The Kenyan arm of the respected Africa overland specialists, primarily dealing with their overseas clients but also offering safaris to walk-in customers, usually on a small commission.

Just the Ticket, Unga House, Muthithi Rd, Westlands (PO Box 14845; ☎02/741755, fax 02/740087).

Karen Connection, behind *The Horseman* restaurant at Karen (☎02/884091, fax 02/882160). A useful agent, which also handles *Leisure Activity Safaris* bicycle tours.

Let's Go Travel, Caxton House, Standard St (PO Box 60342; ☎02/340331, fax 02/336890); branches in Karen shopping centre and The Mall, Westlands. Kenya's most useful independent agent/operator, *Let's Go* are outstanding, providing complete lists of hotel tariffs and helpful, not pushy, advice on just about everything, including international flights. They are the sole agents for a number of *banda* sites, including *El Karama*, Laikipia; *Ngulia* and *Kitani* safari camps in Tsavo West; *Island Camp*, Lake Baringo; *Meru Mt Kenya Lodge*; and a number of ranches and homestays around Lake Naivasha. They also offer some specially negotiated deals on some of the more expensive hotels, and their own excellent camping safaris.

Chartering a plane

Details of domestic flights out of Nairobi are given at the end of the chapter; see also *Classic Aerial Safaris* on p.120. If you're in the market to **charter** a light aircraft, a couple of dozen small operators, mostly based at Wilson Airport (☎02/501941–3), will oblige. It's not as outrageously expensive as you might assume and the opportunities for photography and just seeing the country are without equal. The current standard rate for a Cessna 182 (three passengers) is $1.35 per mile (1.6km) – the minimum mileage is usually 500 miles (or 3 hours' flying) for $675 – though that takes you a very long way. You shouldn't be charged for *démarrage* (the plane parked on the ground) if you're coming back the same day. Try first:

Boskovic Air Charters Ltd, Wilson Airport (PO Box 45646; ☎02/501210, fax 02/505964).

East African Air Charters, Wilson Airport (PO Box 42730; ☎02/504731, fax 02/502358).

International flights

Flights to **African destinations** are rarely discounted; for these, visit *Ethiopian Airlines*, which has the best network, or the national carrier of your destination (see box). For **flights to Europe and Asia** (there are no direct flights to the Americas or

AIRLINE OFFICES

Most airline offices are open Mon–Fri 8am or 8.30am–1pm & 2–4.30pm or 5pm, and Sat 8.30am–1pm. The following operate flights:

Aeroflot, Corner House, Mama Ngina St (☎02/220746, fax 02/212213)

Aero Zambia, Ground floor, International House, Mama Ngina St (☎02/246519)

Air Botswana, *Hilton Hotel*, Mama Ngina St (☎02/331648, fax 02/212041)

Air France, 2nd floor, International House, Mama Ngina St (☎02/216954, fax 02/217517)

Air India, Jeevan Bharati Building, Harambee Ave (☎02/334788, fax 02/340582)

Air Kenya Aviation, Wilson Airport, Langata Rd (☎02/501421–3, fax 02/500845)

Air Madagascar, Hilton Building, Mama Ngina St (☎02/225286, fax 02/218393)

Air Malawi, Hilton Hotel Arcade, Mama Ngina St (☎02/333683, fax 02/340212)

Air Mauritius, International House, Mama Ngina St (☎02/229166, fax 02/221006)

Air Namibia, *Hilton Hotel*, Mama Ngina St (☎02/331648, fax 02/212041)

Air Seychelles, 6th floor, Lonrho House, Standard St (☎02/229359)

Air Tanzania, Chester House, Koinange St (☎02/336224)

Air Zaïre, 1st floor, Consolidated House, Koinange St (☎02/230143, fax 02/217412)

Air Zimbabwe, Chester House, Koinange St (☎02/339524, fax 02/331983)

Alitalia, *Hilton Hotel*, Mama Ngina St (☎02/224361, fax 02/337439)

Austrian Airlines, Stanbic Bank Building, Kimathi St (☎02/214465, fax 02/338969)

Balkan-Bulgarian Airlines, Royal Card Centre, Mpaka Rd, Westlands (☎02/445900)

British Airways, International House, Mama Ngina St (☎02/334362, fax 02/217437)

Cameroon Airlines, Rehani House, Kenyatta Ave (☎02/224827, fax 02/219677)

Eagle Aviation, Wilson Airport (☎02/606015–6, fax 02/606017)

Egyptair, Hilton Building, City Hall Way (☎02/226821, fax 02/213198)

El Al Israel Airlines, 9th floor, Charity Sweepstake (KCS) House, Mama Ngina St (☎02/228123, fax 02/212318)

Ethiopian Airlines, Bruce House, Muindi Mbingu St (☎02/330837, fax 02/211986)

Gulf Air, *Global Travel*, International House, Mama Ngina St (☎02/822934, fax 02/822399)

Kenya Airways, Barclays Plaza, Loita St (☎02/229291, fax 02/823488)

KLM, 12th Floor, Fedha Towers, corner of Muindi Mbingu and Standard St (☎02/332673–7, fax 02/332788)

Lufthansa, Ambank House, University Way (☎02/226271, fax 02/222161)

Olympic Airlines, *Hilton Hotel*, Mama Ngina St (☎02/338026, fax 02/338441)

Pakistan International Airlines, ICEA Building, Kenyatta Ave (☎02/333901, fax 02/218706)

Qantas, Rehema House, Kaunda St (☎02/213221, fax 02/216871)

Royal Swazi National Airways, 4th floor, KCS House, Mama Ngina St (☎02/210670)

Sabena, 3rd floor, International House, Mama Ngina St (☎02/222185, fax 02/215508)

Saudia, Anniversary Towers, University Way (☎02/334270, fax 02/337565)

South African Airways, Lonrho House, Kaunda St (☎02/229663, fax 02/227488)

Sudan Airways, UTC Building, General Kago St (☎02/225129)

Swissair, Mezzanine 2, Corner House, Kimathi St (☎02/250288, fax 02/331437)

Uganda Airlines, 1st floor, Uganda House, Kenyatta Ave (☎02/221354, fax 02/214744)

Airlines that maintain reservations and enquiries offices only:

Air Canada, 6th Floor, Lonrho House, Standard St (☎02/218776, fax 02/212871)

Air Rwanda, Room 230, JKI Airport (☎02/215216, fax 02/219154)

American Airlines, 20th Century Plaza, Mama Ngina St (☎02/242557, fax 02/212871)

Cathay Pacific Airways, Lonrho House, Standard St (☎02/230235, fax 02/212871)

Iberia, *Hilton Hotel*, Mama Ngina St (☎02/331648, fax 02/212041)

Japan Airlines, International House, Mama Ngina St (☎02/220591, fax 02/333277)

Nigeria Airways, *Hilton Hotel*, Mama Ngina St (☎02/822026)

Transworld Airlines, Rehema House, Standard ST (☎02/224036, fax 02/216226)

VARIG Brazilian Airlines, Lonrho House, Standard St (☎02/220961, fax 02/338916)

EMBASSIES, HIGH COMMISSIONS AND CONSULATES

In addition to the following, Nairobi has a number of other Latin American and Asian embassises.

Algeria, 4th floor, Comcraft House, Haile Selassie Avenue (PO Box 53902; ☎02/337283)

Australia, Icipe House, Riverside Drive off Chiromo Rd (PO Box 47718; ☎02/445034)

Austria, 2nd Floor, City House, corner of Standard and Wabera St (PO Box 30560; ☎02/228281)

Belgium, Parklands (PO Box 30461; ☎02/741567)

Burundi, 14th Floor, Development House, Moi Ave (PO Box 44439; ☎02/218458)

Canada, 6th Floor, Comcraft House, Haile Selassie Ave (PO Box 30481; ☎02/214804)

China, Woodlands Rd, off State House Rd (PO Box 30508; ☎02/722559)

Cyprus, 5th Floor, Eagle House, Kimathi St (PO Box 30739; ☎02/220881)

Czech Republic, Embassy House, Harambee Ave (PO Box 30204; ☎02/210494)

Denmark, 11th Floor, Hughes Building, Kenyatta Ave (PO Box 40412; ☎02/331088)

Egypt, 7th Floor, Harambee Plaza, corner of Uhuru Highway and Haile Selassie Ave (PO Box 30285; ☎02/211560)

Eritrea, 2nd floor, New Rehema House, Raphta Rd (☎02/443163)

Ethiopia, State House Ave, Nairobi Hill (PO Box 45198; ☎02/723027)

Finland, 2nd Floor, International House, Mama Ngina St (PO Box 30379; ☎02/334777)

France, 9th floor, Barclays Plaza (PO Box 41784; ☎02/339978)

Germany, Williamson House, Fourth Ngong Ave (PO Box 30180; ☎02/712527)

Greece, 13th floor, Nation Centre, Kimathi St (PO Box 30543; ☎02/340722)

Hungary, Ole Odume Rd (PO Box 61146; ☎02/560060)

Iceland, 7th Floor, Norwich Union House, Mama Ngina St (☎02/521487)

India, 2nd Floor, Jeevan Bharati Building, Harambee Ave (PO Box 30074; ☎02/225104)

Ireland, 4th Floor, Maendeleo House, Monrovia St (☎02/226771)

Israel, Bishops Rd (PO Box 30354; ☎02/724021)

Italy, 9th Floor, International House, Mama Ngina St (PO Box 30107; ☎02/337777)

Ivory Coast, Standard St (☎02/220179)

Japan, 15th Floor, ICEA Building, Kenyatta Ave (PO Box 60202; ☎02/332955)

Lebanon, 9th floor, Maendeleo House, Monrovia St (☎02/223708)

Lesotho, 4th floor, International House, Mama Ngina St (PO Box 44096; ☎02/224876)

Liberia, 9th floor, Maendeleo House, Monrovia St (☎02/334878)

Luxembourg, 8th Floor, International House, Mama Ngina St (☎02/224318)

Australasia), you might visit the general travel agents listed above first (for seats on European airlines their prices are not much higher than those of the "bucket shops").

At the lower end of the market, there has been a proliferation of discounted ticket agencies in recent years (some are listed below) and you'll only find the cheapest seat by checking them out one by one. You can expect prices broadly in line with European discount fares. Seats are purchased by the shops (or subsequently from each other) at the airline's unofficially discounted rate, so variations entirely depend on the shops' mark-ups. Fares tend to be lowest if you book in a group. You may be able to pay for tickets in Kenya shillings at the Central Bank of Kenya rate, but government policy on this varies from time to time. As ever, the cheapest seats to Europe are with *Aeroflot*, *Egyptair* and *Sudan Airways*, with *Balkan Bulgarian*, *Gulf Air* and *Olympic* also competitive.

For days of flights and routings see p.154. For **flight arrivals and departures information** call Jomo Kenyatta Airport on ☎02/822111 or 822206.

Bankco Tours & Travel, Mulji Jetha Mansions, Latema Rd (PO Box 11536; ☎02/336144, fax 02/331874). Best deals on *Sudan Airways*.

Madagascar, 1st Floor, *Hilton Hotel*, Mama Ngina St (PO Box 41723; ☎02/226494)
Malawi, Waiyaki Way, between Mvuli Rd and Church Rd (☎02/440569)
Mauritius, 1st Floor, Union Towers, Moi Ave (☎02/330215)
Morocco, 3rd Floor, Diamond Trust House, Moi Ave (PO Box 55847; ☎02/222264)
Netherlands, 6th Floor, Uchumi House, Nkrumah Ave (PO Box 41537; ☎02/581125)
New Zealand, 3rd floor, Minet/ICDC House, Mamlaka Rd (PO Box 47383; ☎02/722467)
Nigeria, Lenana Road, Hurlingham (PO Box 30516; ☎02/564116)
Norway, 9th Floor, Hughes Building, Kenyatta Ave (PO Box 46363; ☎02/337121)
Pakistan, Church Rd, Westlands (PO Box 30045; ☎02/443911)
Poland, Kabarnet Rd, off Ngong Rd (PO Box 30086;☎02/566288)
Portugal, 10th floor, Reinsurance Plaza, Taifa Rd (PO Box 34020; ☎02/338990)
Russia, Lenana Rd (PO Box 30049; ☎02/728700)
Rwanda, 12th Floor, International House, Mama Ngina St (PO Box 48579; ☎02/240563)
Saudia Arabia, Muthaiga Rd (PO Box 58297; ☎02/762781)
Seychelles, 7th floor, Agip House, Waiyaki Way (PO Box 20400; ☎02/445599)
Somalia, 5th Floor, International House, Mama Ngina St (PO Box 30769; ☎02/224301)
South Africa, Lonrho House, Standard St (PO Box 42441; ☎02/215616)
Spain, 5th Floor, Bruce House, Standard St (PO Box 45503; ☎02/335711)
Sudan, 7th Floor, Minet ICDC House, Mamlaka Rd (PO Box 74059; ☎02/720853)
Swaziland, 3rd Floor, Transnational Plaza, Mama Ngina St (PO Box 41887; ☎02/339231)
Sweden, 10th floor, International House, Mama Ngina St (PO Box 30600; ☎02/229042)
Switzerland, 7th Floor, International House, Mama Ngina St (PO Box 30752; ☎02/228735)
Tanzania, 5th Floor, Continental Towers, corner of Uhuru Highway and Harambee Ave (PO Box 47790; ☎02/331104)
Uganda, 5th floor, Uganda House, Kenyatta Ave (PO Box 60853; ☎02/330801)
United Kingdom, Lower Hill Rd, off Haile Selassie Ave (PO Box 30465; ☎02/335944, fax 02/333196). Consular section: 3rd floor, Bruce House, Standard St (PO Box 48543; ☎02/335944, fax 02/225094)
USA, Moi Ave (PO Box 30137; ☎02/334141)
Yemen, Ngong Rd, off Kabarnet Rd (PO Box 44642; ☎02/565417)
Zaïre, 12th Floor, Electricity House, Harambee Ave (PO Box 48106; ☎02/229771)
Zambia, Nyerere Rd (PO Box 48741; ☎02/724796)
Zimbabwe, 6th Floor, Minet ICDC House, Mamlaka Rd (PO Box 30806; ☎02/721049)

Crocodile Travel, Stewart Building, Tom Mboya St (PO Box 20380; ☎02/335250).
Haidery Tours & Travel, 1st Floor, Impala House, Tom Mboya St (PO Box 45728; ☎02/335256, fax 02/211949).
Hanzuwan El-Kindy Tours & Travel, 4th Floor, Rajab Manzil Building, Tom Mboya St (PO Box 49266; ☎02/213890).
Kambo Travel, Tom Mboya St opposite Latema Rd (PO Box 41819; ☎02/228131, fax 02/228734). Good deals to London and Frankfurt on *Balkan*.
Prince Safaris, Ground Floor, Kenyatta Conference Centre (PO Box 51096; ☎02/219499, fax 02/217692). Very competitive *Egyptair* deals.

Nairobi listings

American Express, *Express Kenya*, Bruce House, Standard St (PO Box 40433), is the main walk-in office (☎02/334722, fax 02/334825). All the usual services and they'll hold card-holders' mail.

Artists' materials *Sciencescope*, Victor House, by the Nation Centre, Kimathi St (☎02/229241), is the place for professional oils, acrylics, pastels, paper etc. They have a branch at the YaYa Centre, Hurlingham.

Automobile Association, Hurlingham Shopping Centre. (PO Box 40087; ☎02/720382) – buses #46 and 46A from GPO.

Banks There are branches of *Barclays* everywhere (Head Office: Bank House, PO Box 30120; ☎02/332230, fax 02/335219). Better rates are had at *CFC Bank*, Corner House, Kimathi St (☎02/340091; Mon–Fri 9am–4pm, Sat 9am–1pm) and at *Commercial Bank of Africa* in the *Hilton Hotel* (Mon–Sat till 11pm). There are no banks open on Sundays but the larger hotels may oblige with exchange facilities.

Barbers Very cheap, no-fuss cuts at *Boston's*, Uganda House Arcade, Kenyatta Ave/Standard St.

Blood tests See "Doctors".

Books The best bookshop in Nairobi is the uninspiringly named *Textbook Centre*, Kijabe St, with branches at the Sarit Centre and The Mall in Westlands. The main downtown bookshops are: the *Nation Bookshop*, corner of Kenyatta Ave and Kimathi St, and *Book Point*, Moi Ave. All these sell imports as well as Kenyan publications. For a good second-hand selection, try *Book Stop*, YaYa Centre, Hurlingham, or the curiously named *Toddler Bazaar*, on the corner of Market St and Koinange St, across from the City Market, who also exchange books. *East African Educational Publishers* have their sales office on Kijabe St (☎02/222144).

Camping gas Available at a number of places including *Nakumatt* for about Ksh60 a cartridge. It's twice the price anywhere else in Kenya so buy it while in town.

Camping equipment rental and repairs *Atul's*, Biashara St (PO Box 43202; ☎02/228064, open Mon–Fri 8.30am–12.30pm and 2–5.30pm, closes 4.30pm Sat), has a large range of outdoor equipment – especially useful if you're going to Mount Kenya – but also something of a monopoly, resulting in prices which can seem excessive to budget travellers. They are fully equipped for repair jobs. Tents can be bought or repaired at *Kenya Canvas Ltd*, India House, Muindi Mbingu St (PO Box 45688; ☎02/333509; same hours as *Atul's*).

Chemists *Kam Pharmacy*, Mpaka Rd, Westlands (☎02/443776) is open till 1.30pm on Sundays. There's also a late chemist in the *Hilton*.

Contraceptives Oral contraceptives are available from the Family Planning Clinic, 5th Floor, Phoenix House, Phoenix Arcade, Standard St (☎02/335775).

Doctors Recommended are: Dr R. Kaushal in Westlands (☎02/441176 or 582040) and Dr Sheth, 3rd floor, Bruce House, Standard St (☎02/221741); or ask your embassy for a list. For blood tests, *Nairobi Laboratories Ltd*, Pioneer House, Moi Ave (☎02/331954), are very good. A malaria check costs about Ksh400. If you prefer homeopathic treatment, consult Dr Kevin Collins, 1st floor, Waumini House, Chiroma Rd, Westlands (☎02/440529).

Flight information ☎02/822111 or 822206 at Jomo Kenyatta Airport.

Football (soccer) Moi Stadium (bus #28 from the *KBS* station). Seats are priced betwen Ksh60 and Ksh120. Highly recommended, whether you're a regular fan or not, but especially for international matches. Getting back to the town centre afterwards by public transport can be a problem.

Freight Air freight is cheaper than sea freight except for very large items. *Express Kenya*, Standard St (see under "American Express"), is helpful.

Gems For loose gems try *Treasures and Crafts Ltd*, Jubilee Insurance Building, Kaunda St.

Guides For almost anywhere in Kenya, guides can be arranged through Utalii College, Kenya's college for tourist-oriented trades, though it would be advisable to contact them well in advance (PO Box 31052; ☎02/802540–7).

Horse racing Frequent buses on race days (usually Sun) to Ngong Road Race Course from the *KBS* bus station.

Horse riding *Arifa Riding School*, Marula Lane, Karen (☎02/882937), offers lessons and hire. *Kitengela Polo Club*, Karen (☎02/882782), also has lessons, "game drives", picnic rides and, of course, polo.

Hospitals The Consolata Sisters' Nazareth Hospital (☎02/335684), on Riara Ridge Rd, near Limuru, about 25km from Nairobi (bus #117 from bus station), charges reasonable rates and is highly recommended if you need to be in for some time (and if you have any choice in the matter). The Nairobi Hospital (PO Box 30026; ☎02/722160) is reckoned to be the best one in the city, and the Aga Khan Hospital in Third Parklands Ave also has a good reputation (PO Box 30270; ☎02/740000); or ask your embassy. For emergencies, dial 999 (free calls).

Language schools *Trans Africa Language Services*, Joseph Kangethe Rd, Adam's Arcade, off Ngong Rd (PO Box 21394; ☎02/561160; buses #1, 2, 3, 4, 5 and 8 from *Hilton*), offer Kiswahili courses individually and in groups. Other languages are also available. A similar service is offered by *Makioki Language* Services, Kijabi St (☎02/242330). *Nairobi Cultural Institute*, Ngong Rd (☎02/569205) runs Kiswahili courses. For private teaching, check the notice board at *Gallery Watatu*.

Laundry There are no launderettes/laundromats in Nairobi but plenty of dry-cleaners. *Pearl* branches are everywhere and cheap, whilst the equally ubiquitous *White Rose* is more expensive but has an express service. Hotels and lodgings will always do washing for you at prices appropriate to the room charges. Some indeed will insist you don't wash your own.

Left luggage Bags can be left safely at the railway station left-luggage office for a small fee. It's open daily 8am–noon & 2–6.30pm. There is no left-luggage facility at the airport.

Libraries The British Council, ICEA Building, Kenyatta Ave (☎02/334855; Tues–Fri 10am–5pm, Sat 9am–noon), has British newspapers and magazines, in addition to videos for rent, and film/video screenings on Tues and Thurs at 5.30pm. McMillan Memorial Library, Banda St (Mon–Fri 9am–5pm, Sat 9.30am–1pm; Ksh50), has many books, plus the "Africana" reading room. The American Cultural Centre Library, National Bank Building, Harambee Ave (Mon, Tues, Thurs 9am–5pm, Wed 9am–noon, Fri 9am–4pm; Ksh50) is good on periodicals. For more serious research, the reading room in the National Archives, Moi Ave, is highly recommended (Ksh50 for annual membership); for more details, see p98.

Maps Game park maps (some of which are now terribly out of date), *City of Nairobi* and *Nairobi and Environs* are available from bookshops; so, too, are the city-wide A–Z of Nairobi (*Kenway Publications*) and general maps of Kenya. For Survey of Kenya maps the procedure is complicated to say the least: you first visit the Public Map Office, Harambee Ave (just west of the Conference Centre), to find out which of the sheets you want are available, and note their numbers (they sell all the game park maps, too). Then you go to the Survey of Kenya offices (PO Box 30046) out on the Thika road (see "Greater Nairobi map", p.84) where you make a formal written request stating which sheets you want, why ("I am a tourist wishing to visit. . ."), and leaving your address. They will, eventually, get back to you, with an authorization to buy the maps. You might want to do all this before even reaching Kenya, though in fact some of the supposedly "sensitive" maps are available to order through stockists in Europe and America. The British Ordnance Survey is one such agent.

Newspapers and magazines Foreign papers such as the *International Herald Tribune* are available from several news stands around Kenyatta Ave, as are *Newsweek* and *Time*, and most of the British dailies and Sundays. If you're really counting the pennies, you can sometimes rent a paper for a small charge.

Notice boards The obvious and best-known one is the Thorn Tree at the *New Stanley Hotel*, though buying and selling on it is frowned upon and such notices are usually removed. The *Iqbal's* notice board is probably the best in town for budget travellers. *Ma Roche's* also has a budget-oriented notice board, as does the Youth Hostel, which also maintains a "Hostellers' Comments Book" of lively and up-to-date news and revelations on travelling in East Africa. The *Fairview Hotel* has a slightly more upmarket notice board, used by travellers. *Gallery Watatu*, Standard St, has a board likely to be of more interest to long-stay visitors, as does the YaYa Centre in Hurlingham (vehicles for sale, houses for rent, etc).

Opticians All your needs, including contact lenses and solutions, at *Eye Masters Ltd*, Kenya Cinema Plaza, Moi Ave (☎02/222601; Mon–Fri 7.30am–6pm, Sat 9am–2pm).

Ornithology The Museum Ornithology Society organizes bird walks or bird drives around Nairobi. Enthusiastic non-members are welcome if they make a donation. Meet at the museum on Wed at 8.30am.

Pharmacists See "Chemists".

Photo booths There's a "Photo-Me" on Kenyatta Ave just west of Kimathi St, and one at Vedic House on Mama Ngina St.

Photocopying There are numerous places throughout Nairobi, the largest being *Mita Copier Centre* on Muindi Mbingu St/Kaunda St, and *UBIX* in the Peugeot Salesroom on Haile Selassie Ave/Harambee Ave.

Photography For camera repairs, try *Camera Clinic*, Biashara St (☎02/222492). For camera batteries, *Ebrahim Camera House*, corner of Kimathi and Standard streets, is cheap. Buying a camera is approximately twice as expensive as in Europe. Instead, check Nairobi notice boards (see under "Notice boards"). To rent cameras and binoculars, the main outlet is *Elite Camera House*, Kimathi

St, south of Kenyatta, but they are not recommended for repairs. *Expo Camera*, Esso House, Mama Ngina St (next to the *Kenya Coffee Board*), offer a fast, reliable service for prints and slides and also do good repairs. Any branch of *Colorama* is likely to be reliable, and there's an efficient 1-hour service from the lab across from *American Express* on Standard St.

Photo studios Five-minute passport photo service at *Studio One*, corner of Moi/Nkrumah avenues, and at *Custom Color*, Kaunda St.

Postal services Until the new GPO on Kenyatta Ave is opened, poste restante and everything else is at the parcels post office on Haile Selassie Ave by the pedestrian footbridge (Mon–Fri 8.30am–5pm, Sat 9am–noon). Letters normally take 3–6 days to arrive from Europe, although 3–4 weeks is not unheard of. The parcels office is upstairs (open for posting Mon–Fri 8am–5pm, Sat 9am–noon; open for collecting Mon–Fri 8am–1pm & 2–5pm). Parcels from home can be addressed to you at poste restante: you'll get a note from the Parcels Section. On the northeast side of town, there's a smaller post office on Tom Mboya St which gives quicker service if you just want to post mail. Alternatively, one of the larger hotels may oblige by selling you stamps.

Post and parcel couriers If you have valuable items to send home, *DHL* courier service has its main office at Longonot Place, Kijabe St (☎02/223063); *EMS Speedpost*, Posta Rd, is also useful.

Selling things Many of the safari companies are often on the lookout for good, used, camping equipment, especially two-person tents. *Atul's*, in Biashara St, will buy from you, too.

Swimming pools One of the best pools is at *Hotel Boulevard*, a nice setting with delightful water and better value than the *Norfolk*'s. Another welcoming pool is the one at the *YMCA* on the west side of Uhuru Highway, near the university. The pool at the *Panafric* is handy if you're staying at the youth hostel; the pool at *Silver Springs Hotel*, Valley Rd, behind the hostel, is even better. A day by an ordinary pool usually costs around Ksh100–200. If you're staying at *Ma Roche's*, you should certainly check out the modern sports complex behind the Aga Khan Hospital – fantastic pool, diving board, lounging area, snooker rooms, gym and team-sport pitches and courts all for about Ksh60 a day. More central are the pools at *New Stanley Hotel* (including jacuzzi and steam room), *Meridian Court Hotel*, and *Hotel Intercontinental* (use of the steam room, jacuzzi and sauna for a mean Ksh600, though you stay as long as you like). For the genuinely skint, *Heron Court Hotel* charges a mere Ksh40 for its pool. For real water-freaks, a trip to *Carnivore*'s new venture *Splash!* is a must – waterslides, fountains, ecstatic children and sometimes a disco at night (buses #31, 34, 125 or 126).

Telephone, fax, telex See the details in *Basics* on p.56. The 24-hour International Telecommunications (*Extelcoms*) centre on Haile Selassie Ave, situated next to the US Embassy, is the place you need. Phone calls are made from here through the operator, with forms to fill in and general confusion (not to mention noise). It's easier – if they have any cards – to use the IDD card phones outside, or to use a charge card from your own phone company. If all else fails, you can make calls from large hotels: you pay through the nose for this but at least you can talk in peace. The public telex is efficient and three minutes' worth (say 100 words) costs less than a phone call. You can receive telexes here, too. Faxes can also be sent and received at *Extelcoms* and at the GPO on Kenyatta Ave (when it finally opens); one page to North America or Europe costs around Ksh400. You can do the same at numerous, pricy, fax bureaux around the city centre and in Westlands. *American Express* (see above) will receive faxes for Ksh100, whether or not you use their cards.

Tourist information What used to be an information bureau outside the *Hilton* has basically become a *Kenya Airways* and *African Tours & Hotels* safari shop. Which means that Nairobi has no official tourist information service – a lamentable state of affairs. The free and widely circulated *Tourist's Kenya* and *What's On in Kenya*, the first fortnightly, the second monthly, are always worth a glance, though they often carry information literally years out of date. If you can't find a copy, ask at the Nation Centre, Kimathi St. *Tourist's Kenya*, 1st Floor, Union Towers, Moi Ave (PO Box 40025; ☎02/337169 or 331274), offers free practical and legal advice on tourist matters. The *Standard* and *Nation* newspapers are a useful source of current info and special offers.

Vaccinations Cholera, yellow fever, typhoid and hepatitis jabs can be obtained from City Hall, City Hall Way, or from Dr C. S. Sheth, 3rd floor, Bruce House, Standard St (☎02/221741), who can also advise about malaria.

Visitor's passes/visas Visitor's pass extensions can be obtained at Nyayo House, Posta Rd, behind the GPO (☎02/332110; Mon–Fri 8.30am–12.30pm & 2–3.30pm). This is usually done while you wait. Do not go there if you have overstayed your permit (see p.23).

Women's movement The Maendeleo ya Wanawake ("Women's Progress") organization has its main office in Maendeleo House on Monrovia St (PO Box 44412; ☎02/222095). Founded in 1952, the MYWO also has a shop on Muindi Mbingu St, selling crafts without the middle men. The

Forum for African Women Educationalists (FAWE), established in 1992, aims to improve girls' and women's education (PO Box 53168; ☎02/226590, fax 02/210709).

Worship As well as large numbers of mosques and temples, Nairobi has a number of churches, two cathedrals, and a synagogue (all on the "Central Nairobi" map). The synagogue has services at 6.30pm on Friday and 8am on Saturday and the rabbi is delighted to see visitors. The four main churches are located in the northwest of the city centre (near the synagogue) and the area is a lively focus for Christians on Sunday mornings. All Saint's Cathedral, a beautiful church behind Uhuru Park, has often been a gathering point for peaceful opposition protest to the government (Holy Communion Tues 1.15pm, Wed 7.10pm, Thurs 11am, Sun 7.15pm).

NAIROBI PROVINCE

Nairobi Province stretches way beyond the city suburbs, taking in an area of some 690 square kilometres (270 square miles) ranging from agricultural and ranching land to jungle and national park.

For visitors, most of the interest lies to the **south**, in the predominantly Maasai land that begins with **Nairobi National Park** and includes the watershed ridge of the **Ngong Hills**. It's a striking landscape, vividly described in Karen Blixen's *Out of Africa*.

North of the city, the land is also distinctive: narrow valleys twisting down from the Kinangop plateau, some still filled with jungle and, it's said, leopards. In spite of that, the steep slopes here are high-value real estate, in the process of development as exclusive suburbs, planted with shady gardens and festooned with security signs. To the **west**, the railway cuts through largely Kikuyu farmland, densely cultivated with corn, bananas and the cash crop insecticide plant, pyrethrum. **East**, beyond the shanty suburb of Dandora, are the wide Athi plains, which are mostly ranching country.

Nairobi National Park

Open daily dawn to dusk; $20; Warden PO Box 42076 (☎02/500622); Map – the most up-to-date is on Macmillan's "Kenya", 1cm: 480m.

If you don't think you'll be able to see any of the big Kenyan game reserves, try at least to spend a morning or afternoon in Nairobi's own **National Park**. Despite the hype, it really is remarkable that this 28,000-acre (113-square-kilometre) patch of plains and woodland should exist almost uncorrupted – complete with more than eighty species of large mammals – literally within earshot of the downtown traffic. The park has no elephants but this is a small deficiency among a surprisingly high concentration of animals. For all the low-flying planes, tourist buses and lines of minibuses, you have a greater chance of witnessing a kill here than in any of the other parks. Kenya residents use the park as a route from Karen and Langata to the airport – it does make a pleasant way of leaving the country if you can work it into your flight times.

Practical information

The park gates open each morning at 6.15am and the first hours of the day are always best for game-watching. Without your own transport, the cheapest and most adventurous **way in** is to **hitch a ride** at the main gate. This is probably easiest on a Saturday or Sunday morning, when Kenyans are most likely to visit. The weekends are also by far the busiest time; during the week you'll find it very quiet. Take bus #125 or 126 at 5.40am from Nairobi's main bus station to the main gate.

Alternatively, you should be able to swing a good deal on a **rental car** for a single day – you won't need anything more than a saloon car and kilometre charges won't amount to much. You could compare the cost with that of hiring a taxi for a few hours; if you do that, be dead sure of what you'll get for the agreed price – petrol will cost you.

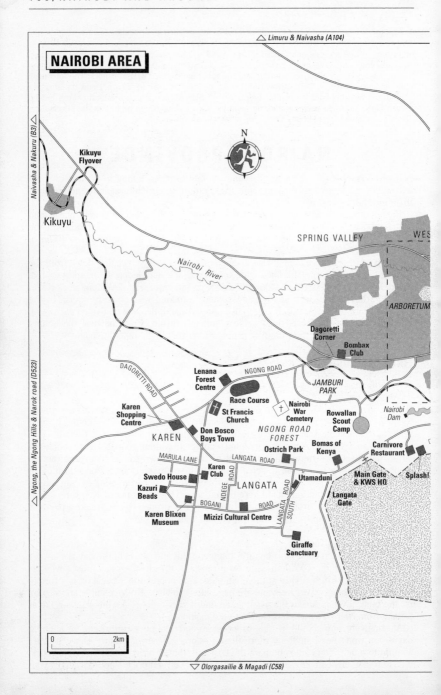

NAIROBI AREA

Limuru & Naivasha (A104)

Naivasha & Nakuru (B3)

N

Kikuyu Flyover

Kikuyu

SPRING VALLEY

WES

Nairobi River

ARBORETUM

Dagoretti Corner

Bombax Club

DAGORETTI ROAD

Ngong, the Ngong Hills & Narok road (D523)

NGONG ROAD

Lenana Forest Centre

JAMBURI PARK

Race Course

St Francis Church

Nairobi War Cemetery

Nairobi Dam

Karen Shopping Centre

Rowallan Scout Camp

Don Bosco Boys Town

NGONG ROAD FOREST

KAREN

Bomas of Kenya

Carnivore Restaurant

MARULA LANE

Ostrich Park

LANGATA ROAD

Karen Club

Splash!

Swedo House

NDEGE ROAD

LANGATA

Utamaduni

Main Gate & KWS HQ

Kazuri Beads

BOGANI ROAD

LANGATA ROAD SOUTH

Langata Gate

Karen Blixen Museum

Mizizi Cultural Centre

Giraffe Sanctuary

0   2km

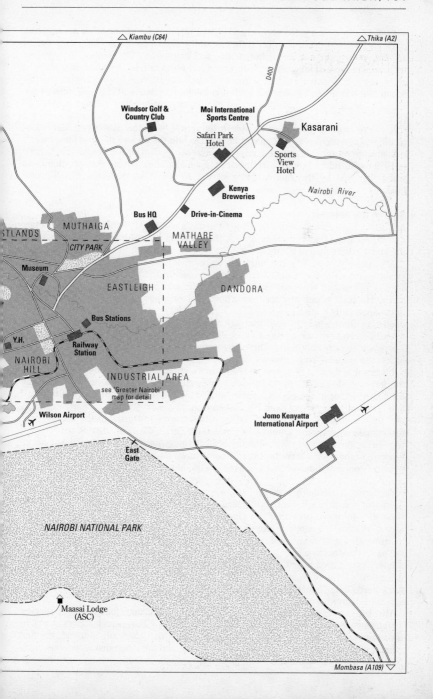

△ Kiambu (C64)   △ Thika (A2)

D400

Windsor Golf &
Country Club

Moi International
Sports Centre

Kasarani

Safari Park
Hotel

Sports
View
Hotel

Nairobi River

Kenya
Breweries

Bus HQ   Drive-in-Cinema

MUTHAIGA

STLANDS

CITY PARK

MATHARE
VALLEY

Museum

EASTLEIGH

DANDORA

Bus Stations

Y.H.

Railway
Station

NAIROBI
HILL

INDUSTRIAL AREA

see 'Greater Nairobi
map for detail

Wilson Airport

Jomo Kenyatta
International Airport

East
Gate

NAIROBI NATIONAL PARK

Maasai Lodge
(ASC)

Mombasa (A109) ▽

Lastly, most of the safari shops in town sell three- to four-hour **trips around the park** for Ksh2000–3000. They're rarely full, so if you turn up at the *Thorn Tree Café* at 1.15pm, you might well get a last-minute special rate on "Big Simba", a converted Italian army lorry. The problem with organized tours is that they normally leave at 10am and 2pm, which are not ideal times – though late afternoon is better than midday. A trip like this doesn't guarantee anything, but your chances of sighting most of the animals are high. Note that open-topped minibuses provide better vantage points than cars.

If you're looking for a spot to **picnic** on arrival, skip the disgusting Main Gate picnic site and go instead a couple of kilometres into the park to the first fork: there's a shady site on the left, beside a raised mound of elephant tusk ash, publicly burned in 1989 by President Moi to mark the start of a major offensive on ivory poaching and smuggling, led by the then director of the Kenya Wildlife Service, Dr Richard Leakey.

Seeing the animals

Ask any ranger on arrival and you'll get the day's results, "Number 13 for a cheetah; two rhinos at 6; lions at number 4 . . .", the numbers referring to the road junctions, marked on every map of the park.

Alternatively, just follow your nose. If you're driving around independently, go to the western end, near the main entrance, where most of the woodland is concentrated. This is where you are most likely to see giraffe and, just after dawn, if you're very lucky, a leopard – back perhaps from a nocturnal foray into Langata, hunting for guard dogs (apparently quite a problem). The highest point here, known as **Impala Hill**, is a good spot from which to scan the park with binoculars, but **lions**, usually found in more open country, are more easily located by checking with the rangers at the gate. There are literally only two or three **cheetahs** in the park at present. You have to be lucky, and seasonal long grass will make seeing them very difficult.

It's not that difficult to see some of the park's **rhinos**, however, most often found in the forest glades in the west. **Hippos** can usually be viewed at a pretty pool in the **Mbagathi River** in the east. The Mbagathi forms the southern boundary of the park and is the only permanent river. It's fringed with the yellow acacias that early explorers and settlers dubbed "fever trees" because they seemed to grow in the areas where fever (malaria) was most common. Several of the park's seasonal streams are dammed to regulate the water supply: in the dry season, these **dams** – all located on the northern side of the park where the streams come down off the Empakasi plain – draw the heaviest concentrations of animals. Many of the herds cross the Mbagathi every year and disperse across the Athi plains as the rains improve the pasture, returning to the park during the drought. Before 1946, when the park was opened, only the physical barrier of Nairobi itself diverted the northward migration. The erection of fences along the park's northern perimeter has changed that, but the occasional lion still finds its way up as far as the suburb of Karen.

Although the western end has the best cross-section of wildlife, there are two gates out onto the Mombasa road in the east, so you don't have to retrace your route. There's a lovely picnic area near the "Leopard Cliffs" here. This route gives you a chance to drive through the open savannah country favoured by **zebra** and **antelope**. There are large herds of introduced **buffalo** which you can see – they're hard to miss – out here and almost anywhere in the park.

Birdlife in the park is staggering – a count of more than four hundred species. Enthusiasts won't need priming, and will see rarities from European latitudes as well as the exotics. Even if you're fresh off the plane and ornithologically illiterate, the first glimpses of ostrich, secretary bird, crowned crane and the outlandishly hideous marabou stork never fail to impress.

The animal orphanage

If you don't go straight out onto the Mombasa road, return by an alternative route to the main gate and have a look in at the moderately interesting **Nairobi animal orphanage** (daily 4–6pm; Ksh300). Here, a motley and shifting collection of waifs and strays, protected from nature, have for some years been allowed to regain strength before being released. That anyway was the idea, though many of the inmates seem to be established residents and it appears doubtful whether "this orphanage is not a zoo", as the sign claims. At least it's a zoo with a difference: there are as many wild monkeys outside the cages as in them.

On a similar theme, note that the David Sheldrick Wildlife Trust elephant and rhino orphanage (☎02/890053), which opened to the public a few years ago, is closed and private once more. They were besieged by visitors – which hindered their delicate hand-rearing work – and have managed to establish better funding.

The Bomas of Kenya

Forest Edge Road, at the junction with Magadi Rd, 1km past National Park Main Gate; performances Mon–Fri 2.30–4pm, Sat & Sun 3.30–5pm; $5, students/children $2.50, residents' rates available (PO Box 40689; ☎02/891801).

The **Bomas of Kenya** were originally an attempt to create a living museum of indigenous Kenyan life, with a display of traditional homesteads (*bomas*) and an emphasis on regional dances. Unfortunately the place has always suffered from a lack of proper funding, though some recent revamping suggests improvements may be under way – at least it's not getting any worse. Its vitality is channelled mainly into souvenir-selling. The homesteads, representing the architectural styles of Kenya's people, are for the most part sadly unkempt. Even so, if you're looking to fill an afternoon, or you want a change from the national park, they can be enjoyable enough, particularly on weekends when they're crowded and a disco follows the dance show.

Surprisingly, perhaps, the dances (performances start, depending on demand, on weekdays at 2.30pm, and on weekends at 3.30pm) are not performed by the appropriate Kenyan nationalities – the **Harambee Dancers** doing fast costume changes between acts and presenting the nation's traditional repertoire as professionals rather than participants. If the sound system were good, the acoustics bearable and the whole place less of an amphitheatre, the impression would undoubtedly be better. As it is, most people find the spectacle somewhat degrading, and one hour quite enough of the two-hour show. At least you do get a very comprehensive taste of Kenyan dance styles, from the mesmeric jumps and sinuous movements of the Maa-speaking peoples to the wild acrobatics of some of the Mijikenda dances. But this is definitely a theme park, not a living museum.

Giraffe Manor

Gogo Falls Lane off Langata South Rd (follow signs); bus #24; open, in school term time, Mon–Fri 4–5.30pm, weekends 10am–5.30pm, and during holidays, daily 11am–5.30pm; feeding time 4.30pm (pellets supplied); adults $2, children $1 (PO Box 15004; ☎02/891658).

Although promoted as a children's outing, the **Langata Nature Education Centre**, run by the AFEW (African Fund for Endangered Wildlife), has serious intentions: it has successfully boosted the population of the rare Rothschild's giraffe and educates children about conservation. The original nucleus of giraffes here came from the wild herd near Soy. You'll get some great mug shots from the giraffe-level observation tower, where they push their huge heads through to be fed. Try to go in the morning or on a dull day as afternoon shots into the sun can be tricky. There are various other animals around, including a very large, and fearsomely tame, warthog.

Mizizi Cultural Centre

In Langata, halfway between the giraffe centre and the Karen Blixen Museum; take the #24 bus or matatu from outside the GPO on Kenyatta Ave; PO Box 10620; ☎02/890721; daily 9am– 5.30pm; Ksh300, children Ksh150, residents Ksh30.

Mizizi means "roots of culture". This is a new venture aimed at the preservation and propagation of traditional cultures as expressed through dance, music, handicrafts, foods and architecture, intended not so much for tourists (as the Bomas of Kenya plainly are) but for Kenyans themselves, particularly as a place where schoolchildren can learn about their nation's rich tribal heritage. It's a noble idea which deserves success, although it's too early to say how the centre will fare. Plans include a multi-tribal Kenyan restaurant and artisans working on site. The best thing about the centre is the hands-on approach it encourages (phone for details of its workshops), rather than set pieces such as the **Utamaduni Dancers** (Mon–Fri 2.30–4pm, Sat & Sun 3.30– 5pm) whose sheer professionalism detracts somewhat from the "authentic" aspect of traditional dances. It must be said, however, that the centre's director has in the past collaborated with the Royal Ballet and Cleo Parker, among others; and there's no short-age of imagination or enthusiasm, which means that if you want to learn to play the *nyatiti*, just ask – someone is sure to be happy to teach you.

Karen

Until recently, **KAREN** was the quintessential white suburb – five-acre plots spaciously set on eucalyptus-lined avenues amid fields grazed by ponies. And whilst African homes are few, their number is steadily increasing as the middle classes become more affluent and move out of Nairobi itself. Karen *dukas*, the shopping centre at the crossroads, includes the mock-Tudor *Horseman Restaurant*, a *Barclays Bank*, and an arty riding-tack and gift shop. Still separated from Nairobi by a dwindling patch of dense, bird-filled woodland – the Ngong Road Forest – Karen is a reminder of how completely the settlers visualized and created little Europes for themselves. In Karen you could almost be in the English shires – or, for that matter, northern California.

The *Horseman Restaurant* (☎02/882782; daily to 11pm) is certainly worth a visit, with several separate speciality kitchens (including Mongolian and fondue) and a wide choice of game meat. The food is fresh and imaginative: Zanzibari fish and coconut soup is well worth trying, as is "Beach and Bush" (crab claws, green bananas, *ugali* in coconut, and medallions of Thompson's gazelle).

On the way to Karen, if you're driving the more direct way from the city, along Ngong Road, you pass **Jamhuri Park** (the Agricultural Society of Kenya showground, see p.58), the **Nairobi War Cemetery** and the **Racecourse** (see p.126). The War Cemetery, for victims of 1939–45, is a peaceful and dignified burial ground, set far back from the busy road among shady trees, with pink stone and carefully tended lawns.

Buses to Karen include the #111 (fast) and the interminable #24 from the *KBS* bus station. *Matatus* also run the route.

Karen Blixen Museum and Swedo House

Bus #24 can drop you at the **Karen Blixen National Museum**, Karen Road (daily 9.30am–6pm; Ksh200), the house where much of the action of Karen Blixen's *Out of Africa* took place. The Danish government presented it to Kenya as an Uhuru gift along with the agricultural college built in the grounds. It's a beautiful, well-proportioned house with square, wood-panelled rooms; the restoration of its original appearance and furnishings has evidently been very thorough. A guided tour is included in the price but can be somewhat rushed, especially at weekends, and there's no guarantee that they'll let you wander around on your own, which is unfortunate.

On weekends, too, you may be suffocated by Mozart and tour groups complaining about how little Denys Finch Hatton resembles Robert Redford, but come during the week and it's more peaceful. The gardens, laid out as in former times, are delightful. If you're a true fan, you can come on an organized tour from town (around $35) – often including the *Giraffe Manor*.

The fake-1920s Nairobi that was built, not far away, for the shooting of *Out of Africa* would have been a more magnetic attraction than the Bogani house. Strangely, political dictates ensured its demolition once the film crews left. Just up the road towards Karen *dukas* is **Swedo House**, an old Swedish coffee plantation manager's residence, built in 1912, now open to the public as the "Karen Blixen Coffee Garden" (daily 10am–6pm) in much the same manner as the Blixen Museum. The house contains a shop full of souvenirs and chintzy memorabilia and its walls are a gallery of rather dubious "modern art" (all for sale). Next door there's a restaurant, *Charlie's* (☎02/882508; 10am–5.30pm, Tues–Sun); a full lunch or buffet won't cost more than Ksh500.

The Ngong Hills

Ngong village, the jumping-off point for the **Ngong Hills** ahead, is 8km past Karen *dukas* (bus #111 every 30min, every 20min at weekends; also bus #126). If you have the chance, stop on the way at **Bulbul** and take a look at the pretty mosque of this largely Muslim village. As often happened in Kenya, Islam spread through the settlement of discharged troops from other British-ruled territories – this time Sudanese Nubia. Ngong itself is basically just a small junction town with limited shops and services and the D523 road trailing out to the right towards the Maasai Mara.

The hills are revered by the Maasai, who have several traditional explanations of how they were formed. The best known says that a giant, stumbling north with his head in the clouds, tripped on Kilimanjaro. Thundering to the ground, his hand squeezed the earth into the Ngongs' familiar, knuckled outline. An even more momentous story explains the Ngongs as the bits of earth left under God's fingernails after he'd finished creating.

The walk along their sharp spine was once a popular day's hike and picnic outing. The views, of Nairobi on one side and the Rift Valley on the other, are magnificent, and the forested slopes are still inhabited by buffalo and antelope. Unfortunately, the number of attacks and robberies of unwary walkers has discouraged people, Kenyans included, and the north side is considered especially dangerous. The route up from the village is now patrolled by police most of the time. Check things out at Ngong police station, where they'll usually provide you with an escort. Women travelling without men are, as usual, at a disadvantage. All this is a great pity as the walk, even simply up to the radio relay station above Ngong village, is a fine one.

With a car (4WD if it's been raining), you can get to the summit, **Point Lamwia** (2459m), which offers 360 degrees of view. Down on the lower ridges, almost due east of the highest point, is the **Finch Memorial**, Karen Blixen's tribute to the man who took her flying. It's on privately owned land and there's a Ksh100 entrance fee.

SHORT TRIPS FROM NAIROBI

Once they decide to leave Nairobi, many travellers overlook the attractions of the surrounding area. **Naivasha**, a strange and lovely Rift Valley lake, is the most obvious example: a highly recommended first staging post, with birdlife and hikes enough to keep you busy for several days. On from here (a short bus ride) is the wilder and more spectacular country around **Kinangop** – again, rewarding for walkers.

To the south, **Lake Magadi**, a soda lake, is a harsh, fiercely hot place, virtually ignored by Nairobi. If you're driving, this is a possible day's excursion from the capital.

But it's best taken more slowly, allowing time to see the prehistoric site at **Olorgasailie** on the way. **Thika**, to the east, has little of the romance of its name, but **Fourteen Falls** and **Ol Doinyo Sapuk National Park** nearby are worth the short drive.

Lake Naivasha and around

Naivasha, like so many Kenyan place names, is a corruption of a local (Maasai) original: *E-na-iposha* (heaving waters), a pronunciation still used by Maa speakers you'll meet in the vicinity. The grassy shores of the lake were traditional Maasai grazing land for centuries, prior to its "discovery" by Joseph Thomson in 1884. Before the nineteenth century was out, however, the "glimmering many-isled expanse" had seen the arrival, with the railway, of the first European settlers. Soon after, the Maasai *laibon* Ole Gilisho, whom the British had appointed chief of the Naivasha Maasai, was persuaded to sign an agreement ceding his people's grazing rights all around the lake – and the country houses went up. Today the Maasai are back, though many of the properties here are still owned by Europeans: the hissing of lawn sprinklers is one of Naivasha's characteristic sounds.

The lake, a slightly forbidding but highly picturesque waterscape with its purple mountain backdrop and floating islands of papyrus and water hyacinth, has some curious physical characteristics. It is fresh water – Lake Baringo is the only other example in the Rift – and the water level has always been prone to mysterious fluctuations. It dropped massively in the 1980s (partly the unmysterious result of farmers to the north taking off some of the Thurusha River's inflow to irrigate their crops) though the shore has not receded enough to regain the areas that were cultivated in the 1950s when the lake was half its present size. The outer edge of the fringing band of papyrus marks the shoreline the settlers knew and you can still see fence posts sticking up.

Perhaps of more immediate and visible interest is the lake's **wildlife**, especially its protected **hippo** population. The dull earth tremors you sometimes feel if you're camping add considerably to the already exciting African night. Despite their bulk, hippos seem to be remarkably sensitive creatures, and they must be able to see in the dark, too, for nary a guy-line is twanged. By day, you can occasionally see **giraffes**, floating blithely through the trees, taking barbed wire and gates in their stride. Naivasha has extraordinary **birdlife** too: all kinds, from the grotesque marabou storks to pet shop lovebirds in pairs, doves cooing in the woods and splendid fish eagles, whose mournful cries fill the air like seagulls. These, and the area's climate, with a light breeze always drifting through the acacias, make Naivasha a hard place to beat as a first stop out from Nairobi.

Naivasha town

All told, **NAIVASHA** town has little to offer as a place to stay: unless you arrive late in the day, you may as well head straight on down to the lake once you've done the shopping.

The most enjoyable way to **arrive** is on the Friday or Saturday **train** from Nairobi to Malaba (leaving Nairobi at 3pm and arriving in Naivasha at about 7pm). Don't bother buying dinner (you'll arrive before it is served); instead, go for a pot of tea in the wood-panelled dining car. Alternatively, the Nairobi–Kisumu service arrives around 9am daily, or the Thursday through-train to Uganda arrives at 1pm. Coming from Nairobi on the **old, lower road** (see map, opposite) you could ask to be dropped off at the lake road turning. If you're hitching or in a private vehicle, you're likely to arrive on the faster **Uplands road** and might be dropped at the top junction, uphill behind the town. It's possible to catch a *matatu* or bus straight down to the lake, but if you plan to stay any time in the area, you should go into the town of Naivasha first to stock up on essentials. Most travellers tend to do their own cooking and there's a much wider choice of

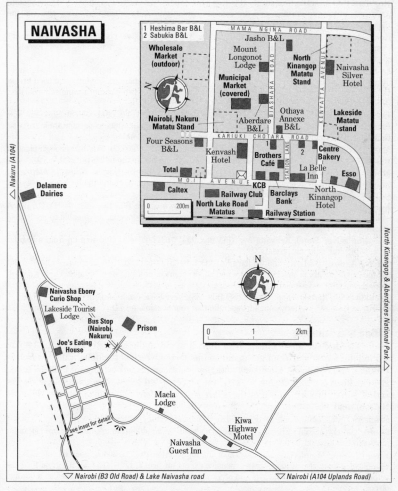

supplies in town than at the lake itself. For **food supplies**, the fruit stalls on the main road are good though there is more choice at the covered market. The oddly named *Naivasha Mattresses Supermarket*, at the upper end of Biashara Road, is cheaper and has more variety than the *Multiline Supermarket*. There is good lake fish opposite *La Belle Inn* and, if you're driving, super-fresh milk and yoghurts at *Delamere Dairies*, 3km north on the Nakuru road. There's a **post office** on Moi Avenue (Mon–Fri 8am–1pm & 2–5pm, Sat 9am–noon) and two **banks**, *Barclays* and *KCB*, both on Moi Avenue (both Mon–Fri 9am–3pm, Sat 9–11am).

Accommodation

If you do **stay in town**, there's one favourite old hotel, the *La Belle*, and numerous lodgings ranging from the quite decent to the unspeakable.

Heshima B&L, Kariuki Chotara Rd (PO Box 1141; ☎0311/20631). Not as cheap as it was, though the rooms at the top are nice and the café is popular with Zaire music fans. They also run the *Waboko Hotel* on Moi Ave. ③.

Kenvash Hotel, just up from Moi Ave (PO Box 211; ☎0311/30049, fax 0311/30084). Naivasha's biggest hotel (61 rooms), with impersonal but efficient service, and reasonably quiet. Excellent rooms, safe parking. ④.

La Belle Inn, Moi Ave (PO Box 532; ☎0311/21007). A popular old staging post on the main street through town, with a variety of rooms and a generally reliable restaurant, serving great fried breakfasts. All 22 rooms are to be s/c by 1998. They may have one or two cheaper rooms still available. ⑤.

Lakeside Tourist Lodge, Moi Ave (PO Box 894; ☎0311/30267, fax 0311/30268). Spacious new construction just off the Nairobi–Nakuru road. Good rooms, good food (especially their "African Buffet") and efficient service, but unfortunately no lakeside views. ④.

Maela Lodge, Kenyatta Ave, 1km from the town centre (☎0311/20023). Friendly enough place, if you want to stay out of town, but the *Naivasha Guest Inn*, higher up the hill, is preferable. ②.

Mount Longonot Lodge, Biashara St (PO Box 19; ☎0311/21026). Next to *Naivasha Mattresses*, with an indifferent front restaurant, though the 20 s/c double rooms round the back are a pleasant surprise. All rooms have nets and comfy wicker chairs. ③.

Naivasha Guest Inn, Kenyatta Ave, 2km from the town centre (PO Box 491; ☎0311/20712). A well-kept joint to collapse into if you've just been dropped at the junction. Reasonable rooms (all s/c) with a nice terrace-bar-restaurant. Secure parking. ②.

Naivasha Silver Hotel, Kenyatta Ave (PO Box 999; ☎0311/20640). One step up from a regular B&L, with some quite nice rooms. ③.

Othaya Annexe B&L, Kariuki Chotara Rd (PO Box 651; ☎0311/20770). Cheap and cheerful but not too clean; the s/c rooms have a large bed and a set price for a single or a couple. There's a good *hoteli* downstairs and a bakery on the premises. ①.

Sabukia B&L, Kariuki Chotara Road (PO Box 433). Very basic establishment in a yellow building, wearily welcoming or utterly squalid, depending on your sensibilities. ①.

Eating and drinking

There's a whole clutch of cheap, local **places to eat** at the western end of Moi Avenue around the *Caltex* and *Total* gas stations, the best of which is the delightful *Joe's Eating House*, with good *ugali*, meat stew and chapati, accompanied by singing in the kitchen and chickens pecking at your toes. Of the places listed below, don't miss *La Belle Inn* and, if you're driving, call in at the *Kiwa Highway Motel* above town on the Nakuru–Nairobi road.

Brothers Café, Station Lane. Long-established and good value – with music.

Centre Bakery, Kariuki Chotara Rd. Naivasha's main bread shop (though *La Belle Inn* caters for more esoteric tastes).

Kiwa Highway Motel, A104 Highway, near the top junction (☎0311/30406; open till midnight). A windblown *nyama choma* joint, fairly expensive except for beef at Ksh150 a kilo. It's great for kids, who love the goats, chickens, cows and other animals loose in the grounds. There's also a bar and disco.

La Belle Inn, Moi Ave (see "Accommodation" above). Recommended dishes include barbecued tilapia, curried Louisiana crayfish and Naivasha bisque (lakefish soup); they have a wide choice for vegetarians (easily the best in town) and a nice line in pizzas and real croissants. They also sell choice picnic supplies, honey and capers.

North Kinangop Hoteli, Moi Ave. Inexpensive fish and chips and amazingly filling *mandaazi*.

Nightlife

Music is inescapable in Naivasha, as almost all the B&Ls double as café-bars which bounce along on the infectious rhythms of Zairean and South African sounds. The *Salama Bar and Hotel* on Moi Avenue, opposite the station, is perhaps the liveliest; it also has cheap rooms, should the night's revelry prove too much. Among the established **clubs**, the *Railway Club* by the station (☎0311/20552) has live bands on

Thursday to Sunday (closing time 3am). Otherwise, the *Golf Club* (north up Moi Avenue) is an almost exclusively white meat market, its "members only" rule applied only to locals.

Lake Naivasha

The fast new lakeside road has brought thousands of migrant workers to the **farming estates**, where they grow string beans, mangetout and flowers, all exported by air to European supermarkets. Hundreds of acres of acacia scrub have been cleared since the late 1980s to make way for the expansion of the farms, and ugly lines of field-hand housing have sprouted in the dust between the plantations. Passing through this scene of ragged-clothed backs stooping between the rows – with rambling country houses in the background – it's difficult to ignore the images of American slavery that repeatedly spring to mind. There are always people looking for work, of course (there seems to be little disapproval of the development), and there's a fair scattering of Europeans of very modest means eking out a living between the landowners. But the scale of the distinction between rich and poor is brutally apparent all the same. Happily, there are still patches of relatively undisturbed bush and the lakeshore remains a magnet for savannah game – zebra, giraffe and waterbuck congregate in certain areas, such as Crescent Island.

To **get to the lake** from Naivasha town, there's easily hitchable traffic, a regular shuttle of *matatus*, and a bus every hour or so (with regular 8am and 1pm return departures from *Fisherman's Camp*; see below).

Lakeshore accommodation

There's a wide variety of accommodation along **Moi South Lake Road** – everything from frugal *bandas* or camping to stately hotels. For these places, the number of kilometres (in brackets) refers to the distance from the lake road junction with the main Nairobi road (which is 3km from Naivasha town itself). Places to stay off **Moi North Lake Road** are generally more difficult to get to – full directions are given in the listings where appropriate.

BUDGET ACCOMMODATION AND CAMPING

J C Burch Lakecrops (2.3km; PO Box 40; ☎0311/20154). There's a choice here of camping in the garden, or boats pulled ashore as accommodation. Hot showers are available and farm produce for sale, and you may be glad to rent a blanket for the night. Nice people, too, and they offer water-skiing. The place tends to be full of visitors from Nairobi at weekends, but is empty most of the week. ①.

Fisherman's Camp (19.3km; PO Box 79; ☎0311/30088; reservations through *Let's Go Travel*, address on p.122). The favourite budget hideaway, with rowing boats for hire, consists of three areas: deeply shaded by tall, beautiful fever trees, **Bottom Camp** (700m off the main road), a spacious camping site (Ksh450) with tents for hire, and four s/c, well-equipped *bandas*, quite close to the water's edge and good for families (④); a "**Youth Hostel**", with seven very basic dormitories, each with four narrow bunk beds, sometimes occupied by British soldiers on "Jungle Training" (Ksh500); and **Top Camp** (☎0311/30276; ③), with six further *bandas* and three simple chalets, overlooking the lake and high above the road. *Top Camp bandas* offer a fine view but basic shelter only (not as well equipped as *Bottom Camp*), with open cooking on gas fires outside and bedding available (extra). The three chalets are comfortable, fully equipped and good for small families. The locally run bar has limited food, as does nearby *Watalii Kiosk* (see "Shopping and services" below).

Yelo Green Hotel (0.8km; PO Box 561; ☎0311/30269). A *nyama choma* bar, but no more discos until 1997 – the hall burned down in November 1995. The owner remains cheerful but it's all rather sad. S/c rooms available and a camping site (Ksh150). ④.

YMCA (15.1km; PO Box 1006; ☎0311/30396). The idyllic, rural ambience the YMCA once had has been progressively nibbled away as the farms press in on all sides and the lake recedes – it's now a

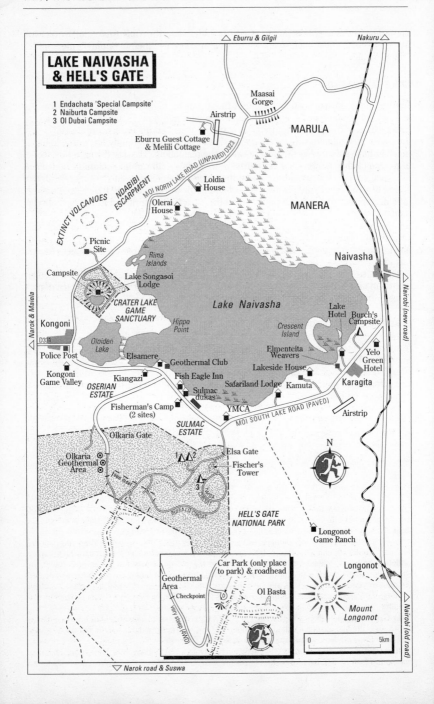

△ *Eburru & Gilgil*   *Nakuru* △

LAKE NAIVASHA & HELL'S GATE

1 Endachata 'Special Campsite'
2 Naiburta Campsite
3 Ol Dubai Campsite

Maasai Gorge

Airstrip

MARULA

Eburru Guest Cottage & Melili Cottage

MOI NORTH LAKE ROAD (UNPAVED) D323

Loldia House

NDABIBI ESCARPMENT

EXTINCT VOLCANOES

Olerai House

MANERA

Picnic Site

Rima Islands

Naivasha

Campsite

Lake Songasoi Lodge

CRATER LAKE GAME SANCTUARY

Lake Naivasha

Lake Hotel

Burch's Campsite

Kongoni

Hippo Point

Crescent Island

D331

Oloiden Lake

Police Post

Elsamere

Geothermal Club

Elmenteita Weavers

Yelo Green Hotel

Kongoni Game Valley

Kiangazi

Fish Eagle Inn

Lakeside House

Karagita

OSERIAN ESTATE

Sulmac dukas

Safariland Lodge

Kamuta

Fisherman's Camp (2 sites)

YMCA

Airstrip

Olkaria Gate

SULMAC ESTATE

MOI SOUTH LAKE ROAD (PAVED)

N

Olkaria Geothermal Area

1 △△ 2

Elsa Gate
Fischer's Tower

3

HELL'S GATE NATIONAL PARK

River road

BUFFALO CIRCUIT

Longonot Game Ranch

Longonot

Geothermal Area

Checkpoint

Car Park (only place to park) & roadhead

Ol Basta

Mount Longonot

Very steep (4WD)

N

0   5km

△ *Nairobi (new road)*

△ *Nairobi (old road)*

▽ *Narok road & Suswa*

Narok & Maiela

fifteen-minute walk away. The "Y" is still one of the lake's cheapest places to stay – either camping in what's left of the acacia grove or renting one of the spartan *bandas* – and certainly the easiest base if you're planning an early-morning hike into Hell's Gate National Park, as the Elsa Gate (hard to believe it's not a deliberate pun) is just up the road. Firewood, eggs, lake fish and milk, warm from the cow, are sporadically available, but the shop has almost nothing. Hot showers are dependent on your lighting and stoking the fire under the water tank. ②.

HOTELS AND LODGES

Fish Eagle Inn (19.3km; PO Box 1554; ☎0311/30306). This pricey restaurant and *banda* complex opened in 1993. Use of pool, sauna, steam room and gym are all extra, even for residents, and reductions for children are minimal; with the opening of the *Geothermal Club*, its restaurant is outclassed as well as overpriced. Still, the *bandas* are roomy and well appointed, if expensive. ⑤.

Lake Naivasha Country Club (3.8km; PO Box 15; ☎0311/20013; reservations through *Block Hotels*, address on p48). The best hotel on the lake (still usually known as the *Lake Hotel*), this makes an excellent alternative base to Nairobi, with magnificent gardens and bird-watching opportunities, good facilities (including a chilly swimming pool) and a lounge evocative of the old colonial days between 1937 and 1950, when flying-boats used to land on the lake en route between London and Cape Town, and the passengers stayed here. It's suitable for children (small adventure playground and huge lawns) and visitors with disabilities (all ground-floor rooms; a few steps up to the dining room), but the generally old-fashioned rooms vary considerably from adequate to luxurious, so don't be afraid to ask. For casual visitors, the entry fee (Ksh200) is redeemable against services – including the sumptuous garden lunch buffets. HB ⑥ low, ⑨ high.

Lake Naivasha Holiday Villas (3.5km; PO Box 685; ☎0311/20611 or 30298, fax 0311/21156; reservations in Nairobi at Arrow House, Koinange St; PO Box 70559; ☎02/226778). A new lodge in uncluttered, airy style with, at present, 12 double rooms, s/c and spotless, each with private verandah overlooking the enormous gardens. A golf course is under construction (2 holes already completed), and a pool is planned. The only drawback is that it's a good 10-minute walk to the lakeshore. Secure parking. Full or half board. ⑥.

Lake Songasoi Lodge (reservations through *Safaris Cordon Bleu*, PO Box 70560 Nairobi, or through *Let's Go Travel*, p.122). A luxury tented lodge currently being built beside the crater lake and game sanctuary (see "Green Crater Lake" below), replacing the *Crater Lake Camp*. Rates should be around Ksh4500 per person.

Safariland Club (10.3km; PO Box 72; ☎0311/20241, fax 0311/20521; reservations through 5th Floor, ICEA Building, Kenyatta Ave, PO Box 70462, Nairobi; ☎02/212910, fax 02/216872). The other large, lakeside hotel, and somewhat run-down these days, with rooms that don't appear to be occupied very often. Still, set amid glorious gardens, with horse riding, tennis, swimming pool, fishing and boat trips all on hand, it retains a very pleasant atmosphere. Rooms are way overpriced and the food, while good, is not in abundant variety. The lodge allows **camping**, for rather high fees (which include use of the pool and all facilities). There's a *duka* (opposite the hotel entrance) for basic supplies. HB ⑥ low, ⑧ high.

RANCHES, COTTAGES AND HOMESTAYS

For the ideal antidote to Nairobi, a number of extremely luxurious ranch and farmhouses lie dotted around the lake, as well as a couple of idyllically situated cottages, these being well within the reach of even the lowliest budget. Reservations are handled by *Let's Go Travel* in Nairobi (see p.122) unless otherwise stated.

Eburru Guest Cottage. Formerly known as *Mayers Soyet*, this is part of the as yet undeveloped "Green Park Development", in beautiful walking country (beware of buffalo). Two double bedrooms in a basic but fully s/c cottage with gorgeous views over the lake and Mount Longonot. Part of its charm is its inaccessibility – bring all your food (a kitchen-cum-lounge is at your disposal). Water is provided. *Matatus* run twice daily (once on Sundays) from Moi Ave in Naivasha, leaving you with a 2km walk from Green Park Development gate; taxis Ksh700–1000. Hitching a ride on a *shamba* vehicle is also possible: ask at *La Belle Inn*. If you're making your own way here, see *Melili Cottage* below. ④.

Elsamere (22.1km; PO Box 1497; ☎0311/21055, fax 0311/21074). Joy Adamson's former home, open to the public as a conservation centre (see, p.144), offers comfortable and very peaceful rooms (though they don't put up children under 8 years old). They don't like the house to be treated as a hotel – which it is not – and prefer a measure of enthusiasm for the lady and her works, or at least for natural history. Full board ⑥–⑦.

Kiangazi (25.5km; PO Box 719, Naivasha; ☎0311/21052, fax 0311/21059). A very personable home-stay as guests of the family in a separate guest house. Two artificial game pools (for buffalo, zebra and antelope) provide entertainment, and game drives are included in the price. ⑨.

Kongoni Game Valley (28.5km; PO Box 15026, Nairobi; ☎02/890184, fax 02/890096). The plush-est homestay in Naivasha, though not exactly the most tasteful: an enormous, overly modernized ranch house built by the Count and Countess de Perigny at the turn of the century. ⑨.

Lakeside House (Dan Shaw Safaris) (6.5km; PO Box 1262; ☎0311/20908, or Nairobi on ☎02/567424). Very personalized homestay, with Anglo-Kenyans who have lived by the lake for decades. Renowned for country-style cooking and a slightly white-hunterish atmosphere, the package includes all meals and drinks (except wine and spirits), and excursion options if you give notice. It's very expensive for overseas visitors – residents' rates are several times cheaper. They prefer a family, or two couples. ⑨.

Loldia House (Rick Hopcraft, PO Box 199, Naivasha; ☎0311/30024). Naivasha's oldest stone house, built in the 1940s by Italian POWs with predictably delightful period charm. Sweeping views of Mount Longonot over the grassy lawn, a grand piano in the lounge and a claw-foot bathtub in the master bedroom. There's a small guest cottage nearby. Horse riding can be arranged. ⑨.

Longonot Game Ranch (10.5km; PO Box 43341, Nairobi; ☎02/332132, fax 02/729508). A tradi-tional long ranch house (3 doubles) atop a hillock under the shadow of Mount Longonot, built by Martha Gellhorn, one-time wife of Ernest Hemingway. The attractions are manifold: stunning scen-ery, escorted game walks, stables and horse riding. To get there, turn off Moi South Lake Rd, opposite *Safariland Club*, and follow the track for a rough 8km. ⑨.

Melili Cottage. Next to *Eburru Guest Cottage* and similarly delightful. Ideal for families (sleeps 4) but bring your own food, sheets and towels. If you're driving to either cottage, turn left 13km north of Naivasha on to Moi North Lake Rd (unsurfaced and in places badly pitted). Turn right immedi-ately, then left 3km further on, and then follow the road up through "Maasai Gorge". Ignore the turn-off to Gilgil and take the next right. Pass the barrier, go over the airstrip and turn left at a reflective arrow, 100m past *Eburru Cottage*. ⑨.

Olerai House. Four kilometres past the "Green Park" turn-off is the former home of Iain and Oria Douglas-Hamilton, who were involved in the struggle to ban the ivory trade (they still live on the estate). Six s/c double beds; breakfast and lunch are served under fever trees from a long dug-out boat. Excursions, walks and boat rides are included in the price. ⑨.

Eating, drinking and shopping

The number of kilometres (in brackets) refers to the distance along South Lake Road from the lake road junction with the main Nairobi road (which is 3km from Naivasha town itself).

Karagita Village (4km). A little adobe and tin-plate village of workers, immigrants and victims of ethnic strife elsewhere in the Rift, but very friendly if you take a genuine interest in the people and their way of life. This is not a tourist attraction, despite the roadside souvenir stalls, and intrusive photography will not be welcome. The black and white *Punda Bar*, at the start of the village, is a friendly place to hang out.

Elmenteita Weavers (4.3km; PO Box 30725, Nairobi; ☎02/520641). Just down the road from the *Lake Hotel* (on the right) is the entrance to *Elmenteita Weavers*, 800m from the road (Mon–Sat 9am–5.30pm, Sun 9am–4pm): a quite expensive, but good-quality weaving shop, with looms behind the showroom. Carpets and rugs, sweaters (some superb), *kangas* and *kikois* compete with various other bought-in crafts. Very browsable.

"Sulmac" shops and hotelis (17.6km). *Sulmac* (near *Fisherman's Camp*) is one of the biggest flower plantations in the area, employing over 4000 people. Near the main entrance, there's a small shopping centre where you can eat for next to nothing. Newspapers are on sale in the morning by the farm gate and, 500m further west, you'll usually find a gathering of ladies selling the produce from their small vegetable plots. If there was any land free, this would undoubtedly evolve into a small town. It's the main south lake transport focus, though a bus goes on as far as *Fisherman's Camp* and then back to Naivasha town around 8am and 1pm every day.

Watalii Kiosk (19.4km; PO Box 785; ☎0311/21327). *Watalii Kiosk*, on the road to Hell's Gate, is run by an energetic local councillor. Here you can rent out bikes (Ksh420 a day, including a soft drink), stock up on supplies, or collapse in the speakeasy he set up for locals (pineapple wine Ksh10 a glass). The owner is a font of information and also organizes safaris, including speciality tours of tea, coffee, flower and barley (beer) cultivation processes. He also offers homestays

(Ksh500) and a laundry service. If he manages to buy a Land Rover, he may even pick you up from Nairobi airport.

Geothermal Club (21.8km). A gem of a place, recently taken over by *La Belle Inn* (see p.138), with some of the best views over the lake. Entrance is free, and a day's use of the pool costs Ksh100. Excellent English breakfasts and gastronomic African dishes for lunch and dinner. Very relaxed, and drinks are cheap. Highly recommended.

Getting around

It's possible to go **out in a boat** at most of the lakeshore establishments. *Burch's*, the *Lake Hotel*, *Safariland Club* and *Fisherman's Camp* all have various vessels. *Fisherman's Camp* has a fast motorboat at about Ksh1750/hour and a half-speed one for Ksh1000 (both take up to 8 passengers). You need an hour in the fast boat to get over to the main concentration of hippos and back. Their small rowing boats are Ksh200 an hour. Splashing along the papyrus-fringed shore just after the sun has come up, drifting among the pelicans and past other people's back gardens, is a rare pleasure – though large areas are now filled with a rank growth of weed and lilypads which makes it an exhausting one too. With luck (and a rod), you'll catch a tilapia.

Bicycles are a good way of exploring the lakeshore, and particularly for getting around Hell's Gate National Park: both *Fisherman's Camp* and *Watalii Kiosk* (see above) rent out bikes, and both have good photocopied sketch maps of the lake and Hell's Gate. Incidentally, by all means give lifts if you're cycling – the locals, understandably, find it hilarious that *wazungu* should shed sweat for them, and it's a great way of making friends on equal terms.

Circumnavigating the lake by road is difficult unless you have wheels. With a vehicle, you soon reach the 30km mark and hit the dust and potholes which were the notorious condition of the whole lake road until a few years back; there's 35km of this (between an hour and two hours' worth) before you reach the Naivasha–Nakuru highway at a point 9km north of Naivasha. If you're hitching or using public transport, you'll find very few vehicles have reason to go beyond Kongoni Village and it's not really worth trying to go the whole way.

Just over 6km from the lake road junction (with the same entrance as *Lakeside House*) is the base of *Air Naivasha* (Kamuta Ltd/Simpson Safaris, PO Box 411; ☎0311/30091), with a three-passenger *Cessna 182* that's available, usually at short notice, for **charter flights** anywhere in Kenya, at $150/hour (in which time it flies 200 straight kilometres). More realistically for most people, they do wonderful, highly recommended **short flights** around Lake Naivasha and over Hell's Gate ($25 each for 30min). They also do day trips to the Maasai Mara which, at around $200 each for three people, are much better value than 1-hour balloon rides down there. *Simpson Safaris* also run tailor-made **camping safaris** by land cruiser that start from about $90 per person per day.

Exploring on foot can also be very pleasant. From *Fisherman's Camp*, it's worth walking up to the superb viewpoint overlooking **Small Lake**, and visiting *Elsamere* (see below).

LAKE DANGERS

Beware, out on the lake. The possibility that underground springs may feed it, its location on the floor of the Rift Valley, and its shallowness all combine to produce notoriously fast changes of mood and weather: grey and placid one minute, suddenly green and choppy with whitecaps the next. Watch out, too, for hippos, which can overturn a small boat easily enough if frightened or harassed. Naivasha shouldn't be underestimated, as boating mishaps are all too common; but swimming, when the hippos are distant, is said to be safe enough and bilharzia is absent.

Elsamere and the Environmental Education Centre

Moi South Lake Rd, 22.1km; PO Box 1497; ☎0311/21055, fax 0311/21074; daily 3–6pm; Ksh200.

Elsamere, former home of the naturalist and painter Joy Adamson, is now a conservation centre, open to the public in the afternoons: there's a video (which you don't have to watch), followed by a copious and civilized afternoon tea on the lawn. When there are guests staying, you may also be able to get a very reasonably priced lunch here. If the house is somewhat shrine-like, the garden is a fine place to while away a couple of hours with a pair of binoculars: a troop of colobus monkeys (normally found only in moist forests) can be seen in the acacias around the grounds.

Elsamere, and the neighbouring **Environmental Education Centre**, is the focus for the Naivasha region's environmental issues, with regular seminars and the involvement of Leicester University in England and the Earthwatch organization. Not only are there continuing worries about the lake's fluctuating levels but the use of pesticides, especially by the big flower combines, is causing concern for the future well-being of the lake's eagles. Earthwatch recently called for the lake to be declared a protected wetlands area, a decision that, unsurprisingly, was stalled by the collusion of business and political interests.

Crescent Island Game Sanctuary

A very popular short trip is a visit to the **Crescent Island Game Sanctuary**. The "crescent" is the outer rim of a volcanic crater which forms a deep bay, the deepest part of the lake. The island is attached to the shore by a narrow causeway on the private land of *Sanctuary Farm* (about 6km from the lake road junction), but don't try to enter there; go instead to *Lake Naivasha Country Club* and ask at the reception desk about a **boat**. The fixed price is Ksh500 (plus Ksh200 entrance) and you have to state at which time you wish to be picked up – if you miss the boat, you'll be charged for the cost of a search party. The boatmen are most obliging, and will detour to show you the hippos and giant kingfisher. Once there, you're free to wander as you will. At first you may think there's nothing there, but the island, barely two square kilometres, is home to hundreds of species of birds as well as gazelle, giraffe, waterbuck (caution – they can be dangerous) and some startlingly large, though harmless, pythons. **Horse riding** is available at *Sanctuary Farm*, at about $6 per hour.

Green Crater Lake – Lake Songasoi

Now that people are visiting it, the once-mysterious (because rarely visited) **Green Crater Lake** is a straightforward target for a short trip – preferably with a vehicle, as it's 17km past *Fisherman's Camp* and 6km beyond the end of the tarmac and reliable transport. There is one *matatu* daily, leaving Crater Lake at 9am, returning towards 4pm (it leaves Naivasha at 3pm), which is really only of use if you're camping or staying at the *bandas* by the lake. A proper **game sanctuary** has been set up all round the crater, with entrance fees (currently just Ksh100, and Ksh50 extra if you bring a car), and there's an exclusive tented lodge in the crater itself (see p.141). In the sanctuary there are various tracks you can take, though the one to the crater rim is only for hikers or 4WD vehicles. You'll see a fair amount of plains game if you follow the perimeter fence: there are plenty of buffalo in the sanctuary, so exercise caution.

The brilliant, jade lake is quite breathtaking, in a small way: the Maasai consider its deep alkaline waters good for sick cattle, but it's also a favourite place for them, with sacred associations. From the main viewpoint on the west rim, it's possible to scramble up for ten minutes to the highest point. There are not many places where you can get down to the crater floor but the easiest are on the south side.

Hell's Gate National Park

Daily dawn to dusk; $15, students/children $5; $8 to camp, $10 at "special" campsites; the road to the park at Olkaria Gate, 21.5km from the lake road juntion, is tarred all the way (5km) through the geothermal area, but there's a very steep descent to the gorge and roadhead at the end.

The best expedition in the Naivasha area is the hike through the Njorowa gorge – **Hell's Gate**. This is a spectacular and exciting area, the gorge's red cliffs and undulating expanse of grassland providing one of the few remaining places in Kenya where you can walk among the **herds of plains game** without having to go a long way off the beaten track. Buffalo, zebra, eland, hartebeest, Thomson's gazelle and baboons are all usually seen; lions and leopards hardly ever, but you might just see a cheetah, and you'll certainly come across their pug marks if you scan the trail. There are servals, one of the most delicate cats, and, high on the cliffs, small numbers of klipspringer ("cliffjumper") antelope. Njorowa is a fairly small area and the quantity of wildlife varies seasonally. The gorge is occasionally rather empty of animals.

The main entrance road to Hell's Gate is just south of the YMCA, but the Elsa Gate is a further 1.5km along this track. If you're wheel-less you should ideally get there as early as possible in the day: it's about 25km to the roadhead and back and, while a fair number of vehicles visit at weekends, there are far fewer during the week, making your chances of a lift somewhat slim. The best time to arrive is dawn, when most animals are about. Try at any cost to avoid the midday hours, as the heat away from the cooling lake is intense. You'll need to carry plenty of water and some food (the only place to buy anything in the park is a simple staff kiosk in the Olkaria Geothermal Area).

There are also several **campsites** in the park if you want to stay overnight, with picnic benches and shower stands but no water or toilets (the rangers at Elsa Gate have a tap). The nicest camping is at the shady and superbly sited *Ol Dubai* campsite on the clifftop south of Fischer's Tower. *Nairburta* and *Endachata* campsites (the latter a more expensive "special campsite") are across the gorge on the northern cliffs (see map "Lake Naivasha & Hell's Gate", p.140).

The upper gorge

From Elsa Gate, take a look first at the rock known as **Fischer's Tower**, after the German explorer who arrived at Lake Naivasha via Hell's Gate. The rock is a volcanic plug – the hard lava remaining from an ancient volcano after the cone itself has been eroded away. It's now the home of a colony of very astute rock hyraxes ("dassies"), which look like large, shaggy guinea pigs and expect to be fed.

Continuing through the gorge along the main track, more and more animals are visible on the slopes leading up to the sheer cliffs. Ornithologists probably don't need reminding that at least one pair of rare **lammergeier eagles** used to nest on the cliffs. But they haven't been reliably seen since 1984 – report any sightings to a ranger. More obvious are the secretary birds: these you'll always see, mincing carefully through the grass at a safe distance.

If you're driving or on a mountain bike, you can take the longer Twiga and Buffalo Circuits. Twiga climbs up to the left from just inside Elsa Gate before you reach Fischer's Tower and then Buffalo Circuit ploughs through thick bush. These tracks are insanely dusty but, when the dust clears, the views out over Hell's Gate and across to the Aberdares range are magnificent.

Hell's Gate is somehow a very authentic-looking part of East Africa. Its colours and acoustics give it a distinct sense of place. It has been used several times as a film location, most recently for that stirring epic *Sheena – Queen of the Jungle* (a number of fibreglass rocks still litter the deep part of the gorge). Hell's Gate's more enduring significance is as the one-time outlet for the prehistoric freshwater lake that stretched from here to Nakuru and, it's believed, would have supported early human communities on its shores.

The lower gorge

At the southern end of the gorge (12km from the entrance), a second rock tower – **Ol Basta** – marks its transition into tangled ravine. Here, there's a car park where, if you're driving and want to get out, you'll have to continue on foot, as there's nowhere to park on the narrow, rocky track that follows the gorge to the south for a short distance. The nearby "Interpretation Centre" is now a **viewpoint**, a good place to picnic and to shelter from rain or sun. The best move you can make from this **roadhead** is to cross the gorge and follow the "Nature Trail" round the north side of Ol Basta. There's nothing nature trail about it but it's easy enough to follow as far as the rock tower where most people turn back.

If you want to **hike in the ravine**, from Ol Basta the trail becomes more indistinct and it's quite easy to lose your way until you turn down into the head of the ravine itself. Beware of suggestions that there's a path around the south side of Ol Basta, directly above the eastern branch of the ravine: there is not and trying to prove otherwise is dangerous. Equally dodgy is the very steep way down into the ravine just south of the gorge crossing, near the car park. You need tough walking shoes for this and shouldn't attempt it alone. Once down on the ravine floor, you've a one-hour walk or thereabouts southwards to the point where you can climb up to the road on the west side again. Watch out for unexpected slippery surfaces and seek advice if it's been raining as flash floods sometimes rip through the ravine. It's a tough, exhilarating and realistic hike that most people should be able to do quite easily.

If you've come equipped for a night out, you can press on, to emerge after a further (and difficult) 12km at the end of the canyon – still 15km short of the Narok road. For orientation, aim for **Mount Suswa** – itself an area of great exploring interest, only properly documented in the last few years.

Otherwise, either turn back and retrace your path to Elsa Gate, or else climb up towards the noise and steam of Olkaria geothermal station. Here on the cliff-top you can look out over the gorge and a Maasai *enkang* below, with your back to the first productive **geothermal installation** in Africa. The underground temperature of the super-heated, pressurized water is up to 304°C, one of the hottest sources in the world, and the station is eventually expected to supply half of Kenya's energy requirements. Surprisingly, although the whole complex is working at full tilt, the impact on the local environment appears to be small, and it certainly doesn't spoil the landscape until you're in the complex itself.

Heading for the main buildings through the scrub, and the maze of pipes and hissing steam jets, you meet a perfect new **tarmac road**: from here, you shouldn't have any problem getting a ride with plant workers down to the lake road at a point 2km past *Fisherman's Camp*. The road emerges near the Oserian farm where they produce carnations. If you hike it, allow about three hours to complete this section. There are fine views of Small and Green Crater Lakes.

Mount Longonot

Daily dawn to dusk; $10, students/children $5; $2 to camp.

Especially when the weather's right (most likely Jan–March and July–Oct), **Mount Longonot** is worth climbing for the fabulous views in every direction as you circle the rim. Don't try to make the ascent from the lake road or Hell's Gate, however – it's further and steeper than it looks, and is covered in dense bush on its north slopes, frequented by buffalo. Moreover it's a national park and you have to do things the right way. Head for Longonot village on the old Nairobi road.

If you're **driving**, there's a road that leads the six or seven kilometres from just southeast of the level crossing by the main road to the base of the mountain, and you can leave your car there safely and get a drink. There's only one straightforward route up to the crater rim, and you'll be escorted by *Kenya Wildlife Service* rangers. For **overnight stays** on the mountain, special permission may be needed from the warden and you need a tent; there are no official campsites. In the village, *Jogoo Bar B&L* is right by the train station – very cheap and basic, but friendly.

Up the mountain

Longonot's name comes from the Maasai *oloonong'ot*, "mountain of many spurs" or "steep ridges", and you soon find out why. The cone is composed of very soft volcanic deposits that have eroded into deep gulches and narrow ridges. The **hike to the rim** takes about an hour. At the top you can collapse (the last section is rather steep), and look back over the Rift Valley on one side and the enormous, silent crater on the other. Joseph Thomson, the first *mzungu* up here, was overcome:

> *The scene was of such an astounding character that I was completely fascinated, and felt under an almost irresistible impulse madly to plunge into the fearful chasm. So overpowering was this feeling that I had to withdraw myself from the side of the pit.*

If you feel the same urge, you can now walk, or scramble, down a steep **crater path**; you turn left from the gravelly landing on the rim and find the path after about ten minutes' walk. Exciting encounters with buffalo on the crater floor aren't uncommon: a 1937 guidebook observes that "any attempt to descend into the crater is accompanied by hazard".

The walk **around the crater rim** is what most climbers do. The anti-clockwise route is easier because the climb to the summit on the western side is quicker and steep sections more negotiable. It doesn't look far, but allow two to three hours. Much of the path is over crumbly volcanic tufa and has been worn, by a combination of walkers and rain, into a channel so deep and narrow that it's almost impossible to put one foot in front of the other.

Until recently, Longonot's crater was famous for its steam jets (the volcano is classed as "senile", not "extinct"). Although their vents, like pockmarks, are still visible in several places around the rim and on the crater walls, their emissions of steam have decreased since the Olkaria plant went on line, though the hot-air thermals are said to be still sufficient to deflect light aircraft. Another rumour is the existence of a tunnel running from the inside base of the crater on the south side and out onto the plain beyond.

From Kinangop to Thika

If you're serious about hiking, mountain biking, or fairly adventurous expeditionary driving, the route from **North Kinangop to Thika** is a dramatic and attractive one. It cuts up from the Rift Valley and right over the southern flank of the Nyandarua (Aberdare) range – still, in large part, virgin mountain rain forest.

The approach from Naivasha is quite straightforward, as frequent *matatus* make the journey up to North Kinangop. Routine though it may be, this part of the journey is still spectacular. The road climbs constantly towards the **Kinangop Plateau**, with the Rift Valley and Lake Naivasha way below. The land hereabouts is Kikuyu farming country, once widely settled by Europeans, who were lured by the wide open moors, rocky outcrops and gushing streams. Sheep and cattle graze everywhere. If you're doing this under your own steam, follow the route description for getting up to Aberdares National Park given on p.185, turning right or straight ahead rather than left when you reach the end of the fourteen-kilometre stretch of reasonably intact tarmac.

North Kinangop is nowadays a rather isolated rural community, a village of big rubber boots and raggy sweaters (it can freeze here at night), whose road becomes nearly impassable during the long rains. Transport onwards from here outside the rainy season, though, is usually little problem – at least as far as South Kinangop. Tractors will pick you up and there are a few old lorries, too, trundling around. **South Kinangop** (also known as **Njabini**) is livelier than its northern counterpart, a small trading centre with a paved road straight to Naivasha (look out for the quaint, red-tiled colonial buildings which are now a *Caltex* station). You can also get *matatus* direct to South Kinangop from Naivasha. If you get stuck in South Kinangop, give the *Gimwa Rest Lodge* a try at the Thika end of town – clean, very inexpensive s/c rooms and good hot showers.

Beyond here – heading towards Thika – you're pretty much down to walking. A murram road (the C67) does continue, but there's very little traffic as it switchbacks in descent, across a series of streams flowing south from the Aberdares to the Chania River. The road follows the river, with tremendous scenic variation, though almost always through forest – sometimes wild, sometimes conifer plantation. But after the turn-off (left) for **Kimakia forest station**, the occasional *shambas* and all signs of habitation stop completely: from here down, the forest is untouched mountain jungle, trees with huge dark green leaves, birds shrieking in alarm, the crashing of colobus monkeys, chameleons wobbling across the road. In the wrong season the road becomes an appalling quagmire, really just for tractors (though you don't see many), but on foot, or even by mountain bike, there's no danger of getting stuck.

You reach tarmac and human population again at **Gatakaini**, and, just before you do, there's the very pleasant *Kimakia Fishing Camp* (*bandas*, toilets and running water), unsupervised but a good place to spend the night with your own tent. The camp is run by the Fisheries Department (headquarters next to the National Museum in Nairobi). At Gatakaini you can also find *matatus* and buses to get you down to the relative metropolis of Thika. Irritatingly, towards evening public transport thins out and the country bus may leave you stranded at Gatura. If you have no luck hitching, give the excellent, but no longer appropriately named, *Tarmac End Inn* a try: a clean B&L with hot water, well inside the ① bracket.

South Kinangop to Gatakaini is a thirty-kilometre stretch, taking seven to eight hours on foot. It's also a great mountain bike trip. It proves, again, how many exhilarating areas there are close to Nairobi – and how many more there must be.

Thika and nearby

Despite the literary connections (Elspeth Huxley's *The Flame Trees of Thika*), **THIKA** is a dull little town – suitably humdrum if you've just arrived from the wilds of the Kinangop or Garissa – not even redeemed by the profusion of flame trees you might expect. These days it's essentially a satellite town of Nairobi.

Pineapples, introduced in 1905, are Thika's contemporary claim to fame. Thousands of acres flourish here, easily confused with the sisal that is also grown in the area. Until 1968, most of the valuable export crop was produced on *shambas*; since then Del Monte has held the lion's share of the plantations.

Thika is off the tourist route – or at least the main road to Mount Kenya – but it's noticeably cheaper than Nairobi and a laid-back, friendly sort of place. If you stay, the best-value **accommodation** is *New Fulila Hotel* (PO Box 1161; ☎0151/21840; ②)

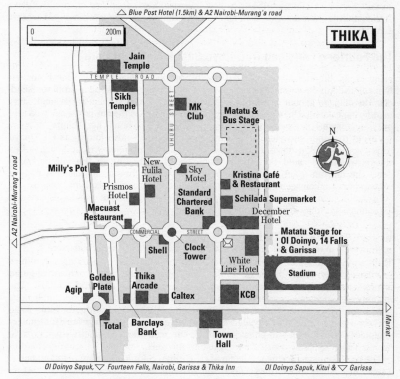

THIKA

0   200m

Jain Temple

TEMPLE ROAD

Sikh Temple

UHURU STREET

MK Club

Matatu & Bus Stage

N

A2 Nairobi-Murang'a road

Milly's Pot

New Fulila Hotel

Sky Motel

Kristina Café & Restaurant

Prismos Hotel

Standard Chartered Bank

Schilada Supermarket

Macuast Restaurant

December Hotel

COMMERCIAL STREET

Matatu Stage for Ol Doinyo, 14 Falls & Garissa

Shell

Clock Tower

White Line Hotel

Stadium

Golden Plate

Thika Arcade

Agip

Caltex

KCB

Market

Total

Barclays Bank

Town Hall

Ol Doinyo Sapuk, ▽ Fourteen Falls, Nairobi, Garissa & Thika Inn   Ol Doinyo Sapuk, Kitui & ▽ Garissa

which has clean self-contained rooms. Other, slightly more expensive, possibilities include *December Hotel* (PO Box 156; ☎0151/22140; ②), whose enormous rooms are clean and have telephones (ask for s/c), though hot water is erratic; and *White Line Hotel* (PO Box 290; ☎0151/22857; ②), which is fairly acceptable and has a lively bar, but only non-self-contained singles. The upmarket choice, out of town on the Nairobi–Muranga'a road, is *Blue Posts Hotel* (PO Box 42; 0151/22241; ④), which is older than the town itself, dating from 1908. Although you might expect a certain quaint shabbiness, the old place has been refurbished and rooms in the Chania Wing are excellent: en suite with balconies overlooking lush gardens, with glimpses of the Chania Falls. Its restaurant has a sweeping view of the falls, and tea with pastries costs only Ksh120.

Restaurants in town include the swish (and expensive) *Prismos Hotel*, the *New Fulila*'s bar-restaurant, which is a deal cheaper, *Macuast Restaurant* for fish and chips, and good local eats at *Golden Plate* and *Milly's Pot*. Being **coffee** land (the plantations around Thika are the nearest to Nairobi), there are several places that make an excellent cup: *December Hotel* has a great Parisian-style pavement café which was opened by Kenyatta himself in December 1970; *Kristina Café & Restaurant*, around the corner, is also good for lunch; or try *Special Services Hotel* on Uhuru Street.

Foot-tappers should try out *MK Club* on Uhuru Street, which plays **Lingala and reggae**, sometimes live (Wed & Fri–Sun). **Disco** freaks can head for the *Vybestar Club* on Wednesday, Friday and Saturday nights, with a Sunday jam session twice monthly; it's 3km south of town at *Thika Inn* (where 35 bedrooms are due to open shortly, for around Ksh700 a night; ☎0151/31590). Otherwise, *Cascades Disco* at the *Blue Posts* entertains Nairobi clubbers, whilst heavy-duty drinkers can fade away at *Sky Motel Day & Night Club*.

The Fourteen Falls and Ol Doinyo Sapuk National Park

From Thika, the trip out to tiny **Ol Doinyo Sapuk** National Park and the **Fourteen Falls** on the Athi River is a popular one with motorized travellers and Nairobi weekenders. The falls are genuinely impressive when heavy rains flood them into a single, red, thundering cataract. But a vague, obnoxious smell hangs in the air, presumably caused by effluent from Thika's emerging industries. There are no hotels hereabouts.

To get to either site, head for Kilima Mbogo village – also known as Ol Doinyo Sapuk – some 20km down the Garissa road. There are *matatus* from Thika to this village, which is located 4km off the main road. The **turning to the falls** is 2.5km down the murram road, on the left, before you reach the actual village. A rash of robberies at the Fourteen Falls car park, ten minutes' walk away, explains the presence of two policemen every day until 5pm. Morning is the best time to visit; locals consider afternoon visits to be inviting trouble.

Ol Doinyo Sapuk National Park

Daily dawn to dusk; $15, students/children $5; $8 to camp, $10 at "special" campsites.

The **national park gate** is reached by crossing the Athi river, then taking a right turn in Kilima Mbogo village. The gate is 3km from the village and you get an armed guard to protect you from animal and human dangers. You're not allowed in on foot. The quantity of buffalo is enough dissuasion but the usual population of thugs and bandits is said to pose a terrific threat as well (they must be immune to the buffalo). You'd probably catch a ride if you waited at the gate (especially on a weekend). Ordinary camping is possible at two sites, just inside the gate and a kilometre up the track; there's also a "special campsite", reservable by the week.

The park contains just the mountain of **Ol Doinyo Sapuk** (Maasai: "big mountain"), known to Kikuyu speakers as *Kilima Mbogo* (buffalo mountain). Visiting it consists basically of driving 8km up the steep dirt road to the top. Alternatively, you can hike up, accompanied by a ranger from the gate. At the 7km mark, you come to the grave of Sir William Northrop McMillan, the fattest of famous settlers, whose intended burial place on the summit had to be abandoned when the modified tractor-hearse's clutch burned out. He rests here with his wife, maid and dog. Views from here are tremendous and you're not likely to get further in a vehicle, even with four-wheel drive, because the final couple of kilometres of track is particularly bad. Between the McMillans' graves and just below the summit the track winds through dense forest cover. If you make it to the top, the 360-degree panorama over a huge oxbow in the Athi River, Thika's pineapple fields and Mounts Kenya and Kilimanjaro can be wonderful in December and January, when the air is really clear.

Olorgasailie and Lake Magadi

The journey to the prehistoric site at **Olorgasailie** and the dramatic salt lake of **Magadi** takes you instantly out of the commotion of Nairobi and down into a hot, sparsely inhabited part of the Rift Valley. There should be two **matatus** leaving in the early afternoon; alternatively, the *Akamba* **bus** (1pm & 3pm; 3hr) is cheap, and the Maasai, who invade the bus *en masse* at Kiserian, are lovely company.

KISERIAN is your chance to buy last-minute provisions, as further south there's almost no food available; if you decide to stay in Kiserian, *Kituo Bar* is a basic **B&L** at the eastern end of the market square, with good *nyama choma* and a first-floor balcony overlooking the wonderful commotion of the market. There is also a surprisingly good **restaurant** in the *Makena Village Inn*, a couple of kilometres back to Nairobi on the main road.

The scenery opens out dramatically as you skirt the southern flank of the Ngong Hills and descend steeply down the escarpment. Try to get a front seat, as giraffe and other animals are often seen. If you're travelling under your own steam, there's a pleasant picnic site at *Olepolos Country Club*, a dozen kilometres after Kiserian.

Olorgasailie

Daily dawn to dusk; Ksh200.

Olorgasailie Prehistoric Site (1.5km from the main road) is signposted 3km after **Oltepesi**. You need to bring all requirements apart from water (ie food and bedding). The **accommodation** and **museum** are just above the excavations on a ridge overlooking what was once a wide, shallow lake. There are double *bandas* (you can make reservations in advance through the Director's Office at the National Museum in Nairobi to be sure of beds, but it's rarely necessary; ②), or you can camp. Do-it-yourself showers and free firewood are also available. Olorgasailie is a peaceful place to stay, while the **guided tour** around the excavations (included in the entrance charge) is not to be missed. A group from the Los Angeles County Museum and Smithsonian Institute refurbished the displays in 1994, and the site itself is endowed with numerous pathways, catwalks and informative signs.

The hand axe site

Between 400,000 and 500,000 years ago the lakeshore was inhabited by "people", probably *Homo erectus*, of the **Acheulian culture** (after St. Acheul in France, where it was first discovered). They made a range of identifiable stone tools: cleavers for skinning animals; round balls for crushing bones, perhaps for hurling or possibly tied to vines to be used, à la gaucho, as *bolas*; and heavy hand axes, for which the culture is best known, but for which, as Richard Leakey writes, "embarrassingly, no-one can think of a good use". The guides tell you they were used for chopping meat and digging. This seems reasonable but some are very large, while hundreds of others, particularly at the so-called factory site, seem far too small. The story here is that they were made by children practising. . . At least it's almost plausible. The great thing about places like Olorgasailie is that the answers are not cut and dried. There's plenty of room for the imagination to construct scenarios of how it *might* have been.

Mary and Louis Leakey's team did most of the unearthing here in the 1940s. Thousands of the stone tools they found have been left undisturbed, *in situ*, under protective roofs. Maybe most impressive is the fossilized leg bone of a gigantic extinct elephant, dwarfing a similar bone from a modern elephant placed next to it. It was long hoped that human remains would also be uncovered at Olorgasailie, but despite extensive digging none have been found – more scope for speculation.

Staying on

Although you could conceivably look around the site before the next bus passes two hours later, and then ride down to Magadi, it's much better to give yourself a day and a night. Sitting in the shade of the open-sided picnic *bandas* with a pair of binoculars and looking out over what used to be the lake can yield some rewarding animal-watching, especially in the brief dusk. Go for a walk out past the excavations towards the gorge and you'll see more: gerenuk, duiker, giraffe, eland and baboons.

Contacts with Maasai are good here, too. If you'd like to take pictures, food is a more acceptable payment than money. There's usually also some jewellery for sale. And if you're enchanted with the peace and presence of Olorgasailie, and stay longer than you'd anticipated, you can cultivate further friendships – and collect some scant **provisions** – at the cluster of desolate *dukas* at Oltepesi, 3km back along the Nairobi road, where they also have warm beer and soft drinks.

Lake Magadi and west to the Nguruman escarpment

Heading south and descending, **LAKE MAGADI** is a vast shallow pool of soda, a sludge of alkaline water and crystal trona deposits lying in a Rift Valley depression a thousand metres below Nairobi. This is one of the hottest places in the country. On a barren spit of land jutting out across the multicoloured soda, the *Magadi Soda Company*, until 1991 an *ICI* interest, has built the very model of a company town. Everything you see, apart from the homes of a few Maasai on the shore and a few *dukas* and places to eat in town, is owned and run by the corporation. You pass a company police barrier and enter over a causeway, past surreal pink salt ponds. Now on company territory, a sign tells visitors "in their own interest" to report their arrival to the town police station. You should do so. Though the formalities are not taken seriously, there's a useful map of the area on the wall.

The atmosphere here, somewhat surprisingly because of the nature of the work and harshness of the environment, is relaxed and welcoming. By comparison with the rest of Kenya, the company pays high wages; people tend to get drunk a lot, and accommodation and services are free.

Practicalities

Having arrived, you might wonder how you'll fill the time until the bus leaves for Nairobi the next morning. Behind the police station, which stands on the highest point of the peninsula, the lake glows unnaturally in the afternoon sun. Looking the other way (to the west), the road to the left leads to the "European" end of town, where a dozen or so managers live and where there's a strange, barren golf course; to your right, the town slopes gently down to a crusty shore where most of the Kenyan employees live. There's a *Barclay's Bank* here with spectacularly unhelpful hours (11am–2pm, Wed only – and you can't even bank on that). There is also a thriving **daily market**, although choice is limited. *Oguts Hotel & Bakery* serves cheap and filling **meals**, and for a drink (you'll be refused entry at all three staff "clubs"), try the madhouse *Maasai Bar*, opposite the mosque.

The company has built blocks of apartments, a church, a mosque and schools and, with a touch of inspiration, a large, glittering **swimming pool**. The sign says "for residents only" but a beetroot face and rolling eyes should convince them otherwise. The poolside bar and *nyama choma* kiosk are popular in the evenings and, on weekends, there are even a few picnickers from Nairobi. Magadi has one **hotel** opposite the hospital, the *Lower Guesthouse* (PO Box 8; ☎0303/33000 ext. 278 or 0303/33278 out of hours; ②), and you can pitch a tent almost anywhere – the golf course would probably be a good place, though baking hot during the day and a favourite haunt for baboons – but it's likely you'll be invited home by employees anyway.

The lake

Many visitors come to Magadi specifically for its **birdlife**. There's a wealth of avifauna here including, usually, large numbers of flamingos at the southern end of the lake. At this end, there are also freshwater swamps which attract many species.

The **lake** itself is fascinating to walk across (on the causeways: in practice only the inlet between Magadi and the eastern shore). On the eastern side, where you first arrive, you can watch the sweepers in rubber boots shovelling the by-product, sodium chloride (common salt), into ridges on the technicolour "fields". Sodium chloride crystallizes on top of the sodium carbonate (the "soda") and is loaded on to tractor-drawn trailers and taken away to be purified for human and animal consumption.

But the company is primarily concerned with extracting the soda. Magadi is the second largest source of sodium carbonate in the world, after the Salton Sea in the USA, and the company's investment here is guaranteed – hot springs gush out of the earth's crust to provide an inexhaustible supply of briney water for evaporation. The dried soda is exported, first by rail to Mombasa via Kajiado and Konza, thence, much of it, to Japan. Magadi soda, used principally for glass-making, is Kenya's most valuable mineral resource after oil. But, despite the "high" wages, you wonder how anyone can be persuaded to work in this lurid inferno: the first rains here are usually "phantom rain", the ground so hot that the raindrops evaporate before hitting the surface. It's important to wear sunglasses and a hat while out in the sun.

Across from the town, on the eastern shore, Maasai will sell you *pombe* made from a base of roots and herbs, and fermented with honey. It's a lot cheaper than beer, and stronger, too. Asked if there was another name apart from the generic *pombe* they said, "We just call it Ups". Drinking it in the middle of the day is not advisable.

Onwards from Magadi

Returning to Nairobi from Magadi, the *matatu* leaves at 5am and the **buses** at 6am and 7am, or you could ask about hitching a ride on the **train** to Kajiado (on the main Kenya–Tanzania highway) or to Konza and Mombasa if you're headed that way. There's supposed to be a passenger service on Wednesday, usually leaving late afternoon – though you're advised to arrive early.

With your own vehicle (or Ksh500 to rent a company car if you meet a worker with a day to spare – it's the worker, not you, who can rent the car), you can drive on from the town, across the lake to the **hot springs** on the western side. Check the map in the police station first. From the hot springs, you can drive further, at least as far as the Ewaso Ngiro River at the foot of the **Nguruman Escarpment**. To climb the escarpment, cross the river and report to the game warden there. Carry on along the road to a track which branches off – the soda company's "Pipeline Road". This takes you to a small river which supplies Magadi with its water. Ford the river (4WD only) and continue on up the now rough track to the top. The view over the lake is superlative – but beware lions and leopards. To camp you simply drive along the river from the game warden's hut and pick your spot. The local Maasai and game rangers will keep you occupied and you're likely to encounter plenty of animals, including baboons, gazelle, ostriches and giraffes. The river is good for bathing and there's plenty of dry wood, but although there are one or two *dukas*, you should bring your food requirements – and of course lots of water. They get no visitors here – it's another good place to meet untouched Kenya. If you want to stay but don't have a tent, return to the main road and head west to the village of **Ngurumani** and its AMREF hospital – there's a single B&L behind the grocery and the butchers.

An even wilder option is to drive south, from either side of the lake, to Lake Magadi's Tanzanian relation, the spectacular **Lake Natron**.

travel details

Getting out of Nairobi by public transport is normally a fairly haphazard business. The following is intended to lend a degree of structure to a chaotic scene, but to make it comprehensive would be a never-ending task. If in doubt, ask. You'll always get where you want to, somehow.

By road the principal destinations, in order of frequency of service (ranging from almost continuous to no more than a few each day) are: Nakuru, Mombasa, Kisumu, Kericho, Nyeri, Kisii, Kakamega, Meru, Eldoret, Machakos, Isiolo, Embu, Kitale, Nyahururu. Most services will sell seats to towns on the way, when space permits. Seats should, if possible, be reserved in advance at the bus offices.

MATATUS

If you decide to take a *matatu* out of Nairobi, you'll find that vehicles for different destinations congregate in different areas of town, the most useful of which are listed here. Be warned, however, that their locations change fairly frequently – ask around. You can take your choice of ordinary pick-ups, battered Berlins, Hiaces, Toyotas and the rest, but remember, the reputation attached to *matatus* isn't entirely the result of paranoia. *Matatus* to Nakuru, Naivasha and Mombasa have a particularly bad reputation.

Nairobi and environs

To **north Nairobi** (Limuru district): River Rd on the square facing *Dhaba* and *Supreme* restaurants.

To **northwest Nairobi** (Kikuyu district): from the railway station end of Moi Ave.

To **south and west Nairobi** (including Ngong, Karen, Westlands, Rongai, Bomas of Kenya): at the railway station end of Moi Ave.

To southeast Nairobi: on Latema Rd outside *Sunrise Lodge*.

To Eastleigh and *KBS* bus depot: #6 or 9 from Accra Rd or Tom Mboya St.

To Naivasha: northbound sides of Tom Mboya Ave and Uhuru Highway.

To Thika: on Koinange St.

Further afield

To **Meru**, **Nanyuki** and **Embu** (Ch 2): on the central reservation of Accra Rd outside *Heshima Hotel*.

To **Karatina** and **Nyeri** (Ch 2): opposite *Crossline* office on Accra Rd or at the junction of River Rd and Accra Rd.

To **Machakos** (Ch 5): in the car park just north of Country Bus Station (aka "Machakos Airport").

To **Isiolo** (Ch 7): outside the *Heshima Hotel* on Accra Rd.

BUSES AND EXPRESS SHARE TAXIS

Slower, cheaper and infinitely safer than *matatus* are the bus services which cover almost all of Kenya bar the north and the northeast (Ch 7). The largest long-distance operator is the ever-reliable *Akamba Bus*, with a huge fleet comprising old buses for daytime services and sleek, fast liners for overnighters. Addresses and phone numbers for all bus and share-taxi companies mentioned are given below.

First, a couple of **warnings** about buses and bus stations: drugging of food, drink, cigarettes and chewing gum is rife – do not accept such gifts, even at the risk of giving offence, nor leave your own stuff unattended. Secondly, as the most useful services often leave at night, getting to the bus station can be a problem, especially in Nairobi (though the buses themselves are considered safe). Needless to say, walking unaccompanied with your luggage at night is the height of folly – take a taxi, hire an *askari* escort from your hotel, or else catch a daytime service.

Akamba Bus, Lagos Rd (PO Box 40322; ☎02/221779). Most services go from outside the office, with some from the Country Bus Station.

Arusha Express, Cross Rd (PO Box 28801; ☎02/212083 or 338322).

Coastline, Accra Rd (PO Box 16030; ☎02/217592).

Crossline Bus, Duruma/Accra Rd (PO Box 11074; ☎02/245358).

Davanu Shuttle, Windsor House, University Way (☎02/222002).

Daily Peugeot Service (DPS), Dubois Rd (☎02/242824). There are a number of other hole-in-the-wall, or office-less, Peugeot services around. Ask.

Eastern Express, Racecourse Rd, Eastleigh (PO Box 41683; ☎02/766962). Services from the Country Bus Station and Eastleigh *KBS* depot.

Garissa Express (Garex), Racecourse Rd, Eastleigh (☎02/764998), next to Kenya Bus Workshop.

Goldline, Cross Rd/Ngariama Rd (PO Box 10098; ☎02/221963).

Gusii Deluxe, Opposite OTC (behind the *KBS* bus station), Temple Rd (☎02/220059).

Kensilver Express, Kirinyaga Rd (☎02/221839).

Mawingo Bus, Accra/Cross Rd (PO Box 45352; ☎02/223069).

Meru Express, Kirinyaga Rd, near the Globe roundabout.

Mombasa Lines, Accra/River Rd (PO Box 60885; ☎02/241564).

Mutitu Coach, Eastleigh *KBS* depot.

Mwingi Coach, Eastleigh *KBS* depot (PO Box 16405; ☎02/765763).

Nyayo Bus, main depot at Ruaraka on Thika road (PO Box 47174; ☎02/860216).

Stagecoach (ex-*Kenya Bus Service*), General Waruingi St (PO Box 30563; ☎02/764606). Services from central *KBS* bus station (☎02/210227).

For bus journeys to places in this chapter: head for the mêlée of the **Country Bus Station** where many of the smaller bus companies operate. A continual stream of buses leaves for Thika and destinations in Kiambu district, with others to Machakos, Namanga, Narok and the Central Highlands. Many buses call at Naivasha en route for points west. For Olorgasailie, *Akamba* buses leave from Lagos Rd.

To the Mount Kenya region (Ch 2): apart from *Akamba*, the busiest service is provided by *Kensilver*, with its rather dodgy 25-seaters to Meru, and *Eastern Express*. *Arusha Express* have a service to Nanyuki and Nyeri. It may be worth enquiring about the increasing scope of *KBS Stagecoach* services: most other companies operate from the *KBS* depot anyway. *Meru Express* has a comfortable and reliable service to Chogoria up to 8 times daily.

To Nakuru and the Rift Valley (Ch 3): the majority of seats are found in souped-up *matatus*, minibuses and Peugeot 504 station wagons, with most operators hanging out in the Duruma/Accra roads area. Nakuru and Naivasha are covered by most westbound (Ch 4) services, but check before buying a ticket for Nakuru that the bus actually stops there – otherwise you may have a long walk into town.

To the West (Ch 4): *Akamba*, *Mawingo Bus*, *Eastern Express* and *Gusii Deluxe* are the main companies, with several daily and overnight departures to most locations. Faster and roughly twice as expensive is *Daily Peugeot Service (DPS)*, which covers most of the region: Kisumu, Siaya District, Busia, Bungoma, Webuye, Kakamega, Eldoret, Malaba.

To the Coast (Ch 6): Competition is fierce over the Kisumu–Nairobi–Mombasa route, with reputations tarnished all round. Safest of the lot are *Akamba*. *Coastline* and *Mombasa Liners* have newish coaches, but safer are the older (and slower) vehicles of *Arusha Express* and *Garissa Express*. *Crossline's* twice-daily minibus is suicidally fast, whilst *Goldline's* fleet is astonishingly rickety. Most companies run at least two day buses and one at night. It's hard to decide which is worse – arriving after dark or driving all night (note also that accidents generally occur in daylight, but the occasional hijackings and shootings usually happen at night).

To the North (Ch 7): *Mwingi Coach*, *Garissa Express* and *Mutitu Coach* run the route to Garissa (via Kitui) from the *KBS* depot in Eastleigh, travelling in convoy from Mwingi. There are no onward services from Garissa at present, although you may find connections to Wajir and Mpeketoni (for Lamu), should security improve. The rest of the North is equally ill served, with the northernmost limits of bus services being Isiolo (*Akamba* and *Eastern Express*, both daily), Maralal (*Goldline*) and Kitale. See "travel details" in Chapters 4, 6 and 7.

To Uganda: *Akamba*, *Mawingo* and *Eastern Express* run both day and night services to Kampala (via Busia), as do *Daily Peugeot Service*.

To Tanzania: Arusha is served by a number of operators, and prices vary greatly. Tickets are invariably cheaper if bought from an agent such as *Let's Go Travel* or *Savuka* (see p.119). Reputable operators include *Arusha Express*, *Davanu Shuttle* (twice daily from the *Norfolk* and *New Stanley* hotels) and *Arusha Shuttle*, run by *Discount Travel Services* (☎02/219156) and currently the cheapest option.

HITCHING

Here are some **jumping-off points** to get you started:

To Naivasha and beyond: take #102 or 103 from the central *KBS* bus station or *matatu* #115 from the train station as far as the "Kikuyu flyover".

To Thika and beyond: take bus #25 or 29 from the *KBS* bus station or Koinange St as far as *Kenya Breweries*.

TRAINS

See *Basics*, p.38. Reservations on ☎02/221211.

To Mombasa: Daily at 7pm, arriving at 8.17am (calling at Voi around 4.30am).

To Malaba (Ugandan Border): Fri & Sat at 3pm, via Naivasha (6.50pm), Nakuru (8pm) and Eldoret (3am).

To Kisumu: Daily at 6pm, arriving at 7.10am via Naivasha (9pm) and Nakuru (10.50pm).

To Kampala (Uganda): Tues at 10am, arriving at 8.55am (returning from Kampala on Wed at 4pm, arriving Thurs at 2.25pm). The train stops at Naivasha, Nakuru and Eldoret.

To Moshi (Tanzania): Fri, 7pm train to Mombasa connects at Voi for the 5.05am service to Moshi.

PLANES

Booking desk addresses are given in the "Airlines" box on p.123. Note that several internal operators have only a 10kg baggage allowance, although a blind eye is sometimes turned.

Kenya Airways flights from JKI airport

Mombasa: at least 6 daily, non-stop (1hr–1hr 15min depending on aircraft), with extra flights at weekends and in high season. First flight at 7am, last flight at 8–9pm.

Malindi: 2 daily, non-stop (1hr 10min).

Kisumu: 1 or 2 daily (1hr).

Zanzibar: 3 weekly (2hr).

Economy class fares: Mombasa $85; Malindi $85; Kisumu $47; Zanzibar $126 (plus $20 departure tax). Always check in with time to spare – overbookings are commonplace.

Air Kenya Aviation from Wilson Airport

Amboseli Lodges: daily at 7.30am by *Twin Otter* (roughly 45min depending on lodge).

Kiwaiyu: daily at 1.15pm by *Cessna* (1hr 45min).

Lamu: daily at 1.15pm by *Cessna* (1hr 45min).

Maasai Mara Lodges: daily at 10am and 3pm by *Douglas DC3* (roughly 45min depending on lodge).

Malindi: Fri via Mombasa, Sun non-stop by *Fokker Friendship* (1hr 15min–2hr 15min).

Mombasa: Mon, Fri and Sat non-stop, Sun via Malindi by *Fokker Friendship* (1hr 15min–2hr 15min).

Nanyuki and **Samburu**: daily at 9.15am by *Twin Otter* (45min and about 1hr 20min respectively).

Other flights from Wilson Airport

There are about a dozen commercial and NGO aviation companies who may also take passengers; all have offices at Wilson Airport. Some flights are advertised in *The Nation* and *The People*.

To the Coast (Mombasa, Malindi and Zanzibar, Lamu): *Eagle Aviation*.

To Tsavo West (Finch Hatton's): *East African Air Charters*.

To the Northwest (Lokichokio): *Trackmark*.

To the Northeast (Mandera, Wajir, Liboi, Dadaalo): *Blue Bird Aviation; FUF Aviation; MAF; Sarman Aviation; Suez Air*.

To Somalia (Mogadishu): *Blue Bird Aviation; Prestige Air; Red Cross*.

To Zaire: *Aim Air; Boskovic*.

CHAPTER TWO

THE CENTRAL HIGHLANDS

P olitical and economic heartland of the country, the **Central Highlands** stand at the focal point of Kenyan history. Mount Kenya, Africa's second highest peak, gave the colonial nation its name and the majority of British and European settlers carved their farms from the countryside around it. Later, and as a direct consequence, it was this region which saw the development of organized anti-colonial resistance culminating in *Mau Mau*.

Until Independence, the fertile highland soils ("A more charming region is not to be found in all Africa," thought Joseph Thomson, exploring in the 1880s) were reserved largely for Europeans and considered, in Governor Eliot's breathtaking phrase, "White Man's Country". The **Kikuyu peoples** (Kikuyu, Meru and Embu) were skilled farmers and herders who had held the land for centuries before the Europeans arrived. They were at first mystified to find themselves "squatters" on land whose ownership, in the sense of exclusive right, had never been an issue in traditional society. They were certainly not alone in losing land, but, by supplying most of the fighters for the Land and Freedom Army, they were placed squarely in the political limelight. In return, they have received a large proportion of what Kenyans call the "Fruits of Independence".

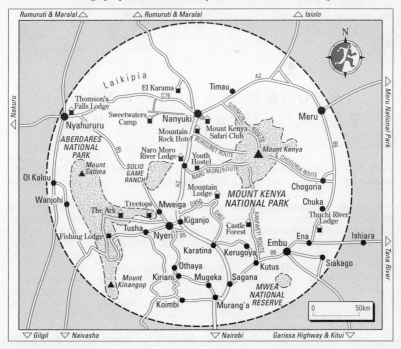

ACCOMMODATION PRICE CODES

Rates for a standard double or twin room. For a full explanation of these price codes, see p.46.

① Under Ksh300	(under approx. £3.30/$5)	⑤ Ksh2000–4000	(£22/$33–£44/$67)
② Ksh300–500	(£3.30/$5–£5.50/$8)	⑥ Ksh4000–6000	(£44/$67–£67/$100)
③ Ksh500–1000	(£5.50/$8–£11/$17)	⑦ Ksh6000–8000	(£67/$100–£89/$133)
④ Ksh1000–2000	(£11/$17–£22/$33)	⑧ Ksh8000–10,000	(£89/$133–£111/$167)
	⑨ Over Ksh10,000	(over £111/$167)	

Today most of the land is in African hands again, and it supports the country's highest rural population. There is intensive farming on almost all the lower slopes, as well as much of the higher ground, beneath the **National Parks** of **Mount Kenya** and **the Aberdares**.

There are considerable rewards in travel through the Highlands. Above all, if you're into hiking, there's the ascent of Mount Kenya. And, while hikes lower down and in the Aberdare range are easier, they are scarcely less dramatic, with the bonus of a chance to see some of the highland **wildlife**. If you like **fishing**, the mountain streams are full of the trout that were introduced early this century, and most tourist lodges will rent out fishing tackle even if you're not staying there. Nor is travel itself ever dull in the Highlands, where the range of scenery is a spectacular draw in its own right: primary-coloured **jungle** and **shambas**, pale, windswept **moors**, and dense **conifer plantations**, all with a mountain backdrop. People everywhere are friendly and quick to strike up a conversation. Towns are animated and markets colourfully chaotic.

Prospects for **hitching** are well above average, but **public transport** is good, too, and bus journeys invariably packed with interest and amusement. For **accommodation**, you'll find a handful of tourist hotels and lodges – including the famous *Treetops* – that will give fair return for your cash if you're in the mood to splurge. But there's also a wide range of reasonably priced lodgings. *Hotelis* are plentiful and serve gargantuan portions.

AROUND MOUNT KENYA: THE KIRINYAGA RING ROAD

After the main game-viewing areas and the coast, this natural **circuit** is one of the most travelled in Kenya. Not that it's overcrowded, or even really touristy (such places are few indeed up-country), but there are always a few safari minibuses to be seen somewhere on the road and there are other signs that the whole tourist industry up here is beginning to grow.

At present, the whole region is wonderfully untouched by anything much more than the steady encroachment of *shambas* up the ridges and the burgeoning of small towns into larger ones. Apart from the high forests, moors and peaks, little of this remains wild country, but you have to hand it to them: the Kikuyu, Meru and Embu are amazingly hard workers and they have created an extraordinary spectacle of cultivation on the steep slopes, gashed by the road to reveal brilliant red earth.

As you travel, you're also aware of the looming presence of **the mountain**. Its twin peaks are normally obscured by clouds, but early in the morning and just before sunset, the shroud can vanish suddenly, leaving them magically exposed for a few minutes. With a base 80km across, Mount Kenya is one of the largest free-standing volcanic cones in the world, and the peaks – when you can see them from the road – are always distant. To the east and south, the mountain slopes steeply away to the

THE KIKUYU PEOPLES: SOME BACKGROUND

The ancestors of the **Kikuyu** migrated to this region over successive generations between the sixteenth and eighteenth centuries, from somewhere northeast of Mount Kenya. Stories describe how they found various hunter-gatherer peoples already living in the region they now occupy: the **Gumba** on the plains and the **Athi** in the forests. A great deal of intermarriage, trade and adoption took place; the newcomers cleared the forests and planted crops, giving the hunters gifts of livestock, honey, or wives in return for using the land. As this Bantu-speaking, cultivating, livestock-keeping culture expanded and consolidated in the Highlands, the indigenous peoples gradually lost their old identities.

Between the Kikuyu and the **Maasai**, relations were less easy. They both placed (and still place) high value on the ownership of cattle, the Maasai depending entirely on livestock. During bad droughts, Maasai might raid their Kikuyu neighbours' herds, with retaliation at a later date being almost inevitable. But such **intertribal warfare** often had long-term benefits, as ancient debts were forever being renegotiated and paid off by both sides, thus sustaining the relationship. There was lively trade and **intermarriage** between the two peoples, and married Kikuyu women enjoyed a special immunity enabling them to organize trading expeditions deep into Maasai-land, often with the help of a *hinga*, a Kikuyu of Maasai descent, to oil the wheels.

As well as these economic and social relations, the Kikuyu had, in the past, close **cultural affinities** with the Maasai. Many visitors are surprised when they first see the evidence of this – for example, in traditional dress styles – in museums or old photos. Like the Maasai, the Kikuyu advanced in status as they grew older, through named age-sets, with appropriate rituals at each stage. And although age is figured more chronologically these days, it's still an important social index: a Kikuyu who discovers you're both the same age is likely to say "We're age mates then!"

Circumcision, of young men and women, still marks the important transition into adulthood for most Kikuyu, though "female circumcision" (clitoridectomy) is illegal and performed less and less. In the past, the operations were accompanied by changes in dress and ornament. Once circumcised, boys could grow their hair long and dye it with ochre in the style of Maasai warriors (in fact, the Maasai got their ochre from the Kikuyu, so it may really be the other way around). They also wore stacks of glass beads around their necks, metal rings on their legs and arms, and pulled their ear lobes out with heavy weights and ear plugs. Women wore a similar collection of ornaments and, between initiation and marriage, a headband of beads and discs, still worn today by most Maasai women.

Traditionally the Kikuyu had no centralized **authority**, no tribal or clan chiefs: "chiefs" were only installed by the colonial administration. When disputes had to be settled or far-reaching decisions made, the elders of a district would meet as a council, usually with a little persuasion in the form of meat or beer from the people summoning them, and the matter would be cleared up in public, with a party to follow. After their deaths, elders – as ancestors – continued to be respected and consulted.

Although Christianity has altered the picture in the last few decades, many church-goers still believe strongly in an **ancestor world** where the dead have powers for good and bad over their living descendants because of their closeness to *Ngai* (God). The Kikuyu traditionally believed that *Ngai*'s most likely abode, or at least his frequent resting place, was **Kirinyaga**, the "Place of Brightness", Mount Kenya. Accordingly, they tried to build their houses with the door always looking out towards the mountain; hence the title of Jomo Kenyatta's book, *Facing Mount Kenya*.

Today the Kikuyu remain in the forefront of Kenyan development. Despite entrenched nepotism and a growing poverty gap, they are accorded grudging respect as successful business people and formidable politicians – though their political power at national level has been much eroded in recent years and is only starting to return with the legalization of political opposition. There is considerable political rivalry between the **Kiambu Kikuyu** of the tea- and coffee-growing district north of Nairobi (Jomo Kenyatta's district and now a Democratic Party stronghold), and the **Nyeri Kikuyu**, who rely on a more mixed economy and where there is more support for the FORD Asili and FORD Kenya parties.

broad expanse of Ukambani (Akambaland) and the Tana River basin. Westward, it drops more gently to the rolling uplands of Laikipia, drier than the east and for the most part treeless.

Getting here is an easy trip from Nairobi up a busy road: if you're not driving, either buy a bus ticket from Nairobi direct to any of the towns in this section, or make **Thika** (p.148) or **Murang'a** a first destination before heading clockwise or anti-clockwise around the mountain. **Naro Moru**, the usual base for climbing Mount Kenya, lies on the west side some 25km south of **Nanyuki**, an alternative base for a climb from the north. On the eastern slopes, **Chogoria**, between **Meru** and **Embu**, offers arguably the finest route up the mountain.

Murang'a

Leaving Thika behind, **MURANG'A** is the first town of any size you come to. Established as the administrative outpost of **Fort Hall** in 1900, it has since come to be thought of as the "Kikuyu Homeland" because of its proximity to *Mukuruwe wa Gathanga*, the "Garden of Eden of the Kikuyu". Here, in Kikuyu mythology, God made husbands for the nine daughters of Gikuyu and Mumbi, spiritual ancestors of all the Kikuyu people. The husbands, who became the ancestors of the nine Kikuyu clans, were found by Gikuyu under a large fig tree. Take a *matatu* to **Mugeka** and walk from there if you'd like to see it; there used to be a museum at the site, though this, and apparently the original *mukuruwe* (fig tree), are no longer in evidence.

Fort Hall was never a settlers' town. The district was outside the zone earmarked for white colonization and most of it comprised the "Kikuyu reserve". Richard

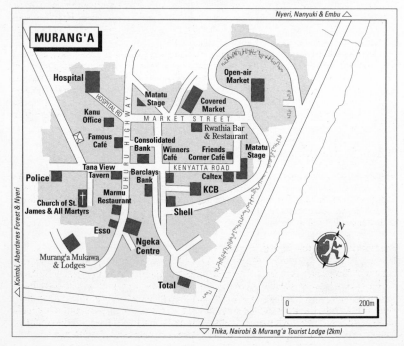

Meinertzhagen, an officer in the King's African Rifles posted here in 1902, found the time (when not shooting animals – or people) to write:

> *If white settlement really takes hold in this country it is bound to do so at the expense of the Kikuyu who own the best land, and I foresee much trouble.*
>
> Kenya Diary (Kenway Publications, Kenya 1989)

That said, Meinertzhagen helped put down some of this trouble, launching "punitive expeditions" from Fort Hall with his African troops.

Present-day Murang'a even has a bit of sightseeing. In the **CPK Cathedral** (formerly the Church of St James and All Martyrs) hangs an unusual *Life of Christ* mural sequence by the Tanzanian artist Elimo Njau. It depicts the Nativity, Baptism, Last Supper, Gethsemane and Crucifixion of an African Christ in an African landscape – curiously appropriate for the muddled history of black–white relations here. The murals were painted in 1955, the year the church was founded by the Archbishop of Canterbury, as a memorial to the thousands of Kikuyu victims of *Mau Mau* attacks.

Practicalities

At the beginning of this century, Fort Hall consisted of "two grass huts within a stone wall and a ditch". Present-day Murang'a, perched above the busy main road, remains small, but there are a number of decent, basic hotels on the steep hillside if you feel like staying – and it's a happy enough place, bustling energetically. Recommended **lodgings** are *Murang'a Mukawa & Lodges* on Uhuru Highway (PO Box 207, Maragua; ☎0156/22542; ③), large and clean with a somnolent bar-restaurant, but no nets in the bedrooms, and *Murang'a Tourist Lodge*, 2km down the Thika road (PO Box 52; ☎0156/22120; ②), similar to the *Mukawa* with airier rooms and nets, but breakfast costs extra. *Rwathia Bar* on Market Street (PO Box 243; ☎0156/22527) is very basic but clean with a pleasant courtyard, and is the best of three adjacent day and night club lodgings; the *Manguo* next door has good *kienyeji*.

There's no shortage of **hotelis** either. *Famous Café* has great samosas, *Marmu Restaurant* has a good range of snacks, and the *Tana View Tavern* is recommended not only for its fine balcony but for its lightly curried rabbit dishes (Ksh60 with chips), a strange delicacy introduced to a sceptical Murang'a (rabbit meat was previously seen as children's food) by the *Tavern*'s congenial proprietor. *Nankas Bakery* is in Ngeka Centre above the *Co-op Bank*, and spicy *chai* is served at the zebra-striped *Friends' Corner Café* by the *matatu* stage.

Onwards from Murang'a

There are three onward travel options from Murang'a: clockwise around Mount Kenya via Karatina and Naro Moru (see below); anti-clockwise around the mountain via Embu (see p.181); or up to Nyeri and the Aberdares (p.184). Nyeri, a few kilometres off the Mount Kenya circuit, is a recommended detour and one which most public transport on the ring road will include.

Routes west into the Aberdare range

If you want to get up into the **Aberdare forest**, take one of the two minor roads leading out of Murang'a to the west. They join at Kiriani and dip north to Nyeri via Othaya. If you have all day to dawdle, either of them would make a nice, circuitously backwoods route to Nyeri. *Matatu* availability may determine which you take. If you have your own wheels, the longer of the two, via Koimbi, takes you past the start of a rough, snaking, high-altitude track which climbs as far as Tusha, just 10km from the Aberdare National Park's Kiandongoro Gate, one of the two park entrances above Nyeri.

Towards Mount Kenya: Karatina and Mountain Lodge

If you pass through the feverish commercial centre of **KARATINA** on a Monday or Wednesday, stop to have a look around the market: it's one of East Africa's biggest cattle and produce sales. There are several **lodgings** in town, including the reasonable *Karatina Tourist Lodge* (Private Bag, Karatina; ☎0171/71522, fax 0171/72520; ③) which has safe parking. Cheaper options include the clean *New Mugi Motherland Hotel 1995*, the more lively *Three-in-One Hotel* (PO Box 768; ☎0171/72316), and *Ibis Hotel* (PO Box 240; ☎0171/72777) opposite *Agip*. **Camping** is possible at *Wa Jee Campsite* – turn off the main road 2km north of town. There's good filling **food** at *Samaria Hotel* at the north end, and at *Karatina Express Café* by the railway, with its shaded terrace and smooth service.

Karatina is also the base for **Mountain Lodge**, the most accessible of Kenya's three highland "tree hotels" (the other two being *Treetops* and *The Ark*) and the only one on the slopes of Mount Kenya. The signposted turning is just on the Nairobi side of town; the hotel (PO Box 123, Kiganjo; ☎0171/4248; reservations through *AT&H*, address p.48; ⑨) is set at an altitude of 2200m, about 30km from Karatina, mostly along good tarmac (the President's Sagana State Lodge is also up this way; be discreet with your camera).

Mountain Lodge has consistently good game-viewing over the floodlit water hole, and larger rooms than either of its competitors. The rooms have private bathrooms and balconies and there's good food. You can stay up all night, with continuous supplies of tea and coffee on hand. Or you can be choosy about your animal-watching, tick off what you're interested in being woken to see, and then slumber through the herds of buffalo and antelope. They wake you at 6am in any case.

Towards Mount Kenya: Castle Forest Lodge

From Murang'a, a different kind of Mount Kenya accommodation is easily accessible. **Castle Forest Lodge**, nestling in the forest on the southern slopes of the mountain, is a private home, reputedly built for British royalty before World War I. Large, comfortable rooms and several cottages in the grounds can be reserved in advance (PO Box 564, Kerugoya; reservations through 3rd floor, Arrow House, Koinange St, Nairobi, PO Box 70460, ☎02/212387, fax 02/214020, or via *Let's Go Travel*; ④ low, ⑤ high) but it's not normally necessary. Meals are available to order and, in between sleeping and eating, you can walk in the woods, sit by the waterfalls of the Karute stream, or fish in it for trout. The only problem, if you don't have transport, is access. *Castle Forest* is about 50km from Murang'a, via Sagana and Kutus on the B6. From Kutus, head east on the B6 for just 400m, then turn left on the tarmac D458 and, after 2.5km, at Rukenya, turn left again onto a *murram* track. Fifteen kilometres up here you reach the Mount Kenya forest boundary (gate and *Thiba Fishing Camp*), and 5km further, the house.

If you're keen to try an unusual approach to the summit of Mount Kenya, the seldom-used **Kamweti route** begins at the roadhead, eight steep kilometres north of *Castle Forest*. The managers at the house should be able to advise on guides and porters, though you'd most likely have to arrive fully equipped.

North to Naro Moru

Continuing up the A2 from Karatina, passing the turning to Nyeri (see p.188), and then going through Kiganjo (a second road turns left to Nyeri here and then one to the right to *Mountain Lodge*) you emerge from the folded, shambolic landscape of Kikuyu cultivation onto a high, windswept plain. Here, you're crossing one of the great animal migration routes, severed by human population pressure over the last eighty years. Until 1948, when the two mountain parks were created, every few years used to see the mass migration of **elephants** from one side to the other. In 1903, a herd estimated at seven hundred animals was seen wending across the open country from Mount Kenya to the Aberdares. When the parks were opened, it was decided to keep the elephants away from the crowded farmlands in between, so an eight-kilometre ditch was dug across their route.

Naro Moru

The road climbs gently and steadily (on its appalling surface) to **NARO MORU**, which stands on the watershed between the Tana and the Ewaso Nyiro river basins. The most straightforward **base for climbing Mount Kenya**, or simply exploring the mountain forests lower down, Naro Moru is nondescript, built around its now disused railway station. There's a post office (Mon–Fri 8am–1pm & 2–5pm) but no bank and not a lot in the food department, either, though things are improving. If you plan to spend several days on the mountain, buy any special food you want in Nairobi. Naro Moru's offerings are strictly in the bread and milk, *karanga na chapati*, line.

There are several **accommodation** options in the ② category should you need a room at the end of the day. Besides the ominous-sounding *Silent Lodge*, and the fresh and reasonable *Naro Moru Hotel '86*, complete with *Kirinyaga*-viewing balcony, there's the much improved and recommended *'82 Lodge*, with s/c rooms, and *Mountain View Hotel* (☎0176/62088) also with a balcony.

Out of town, there's a clutch of alternatives. Cheapest and closest is the rather exposed **campsite** (Ksh200 per person), with its freezing showers and pretty expensive firewood, which is to be found at *Naro Moru River Lodge* (about 2km north of town and signposted). With the B&Ls in town, there's not really much point in paying over the odds for a hard bunk in one of the bunkhouses. **Naro Moru River Lodge** itself (PO Box 18, Naro Moru; ☎0176/62212, fax 0176/62211; reservations through *Alliance*, address p.48; half-board ⑤ low, ⑥ high; self-catering cottages ⑤ low, ⑥ high) is the only place where you can indulge yourself if you're feeling in need of creature comforts. It has a welcoming log-fire atmosphere, pretty gardens, a trout stream and good bird-watching. It tends to be full of upmarket mountain-climbing package clients and has an expensive but well-stocked equipment-rental shop.

The **Youth Hostel** (PO Box 27, Naro Moru; ☎0176/62412, fax 0176 62211; Ksh400 per person) used to be a wonderful old converted farmhouse with log fires, but sadly, it burned to the ground in 1988 when a camping cooker exploded. It has, however, since been rebuilt and is once again a popular travellers' place. The dorms are basic and comfortable, the kitchen well equipped, and camping is welcomed in the grounds. They also have a limited amount of equipment for rent (most of it was lost in the fire), at prices a good deal cheaper than the *Naro Moru River Lodge*.

If you're alone, and on a budget, the youth hostel is probably the best place to **team up with others for the ascent** (campers with their own vehicles tend to use the more expensive set-up at *Naro Moru River Lodge*). The youth hostel site lies about 9km up the well-signposted track to Mount Kenya. You may get a lift up from the main road; otherwise break your walk with a *chai* at the *Kariaku Restaurant*. Three little *dukas* up the track, a kilometre or so beyond the youth hostel, sell one or two vital commodities, but they're very basic indeed.

Mount Kenya National Park

$10 per person daily, $5 students/children; $2 per night. Entry allowed on foot; minimum group two people (Warden: PO Box 69 Naro Moru; ☎0171/21575).

An extinct volcano, some three and a half million years old, with jagged peaks rising to 5200m, **Mount Kenya** is Africa's second highest mountain. Its heart is actually the remains of a gigantic volcanic plug, from which most of the outpourings of lava and ash have eroded away to create the distinctive silhouette. These peaks are permanently iced with snow and glaciers, while on the upper slopes the combination of altitude and a position astride the equator results in forms of **vegetation** that only exist here and at a few other lofty points in East Africa. Seemingly designed by some 1950s science fiction writer, it's hard to believe the "water-holding cabbage", "ostrich plume plant" or "giant groundsel" when you first see them. Mount Kenya is unexpectedly different and, unless your time is very limited, too good to miss.

Europe first heard about the mountain when the missionary Krapf saw it in 1849, but his stories of snow on the equator were not taken seriously. It was only in 1883 that the young Scottish traveller, Joseph Thomson, confirmed its existence. The Kikuyu, Maasai and other peoples living in the vicinity had venerated the mountain for centuries: park rangers still occasionally report finding elderly Kikuyu high up on the moorlands, drawn by the presence of *Ngai*, whose dwelling place this is. It's not known, however, whether anyone had actually scaled the peaks before Sir Halford Mackinder reached the highest, Batian, in 1899. Another thirty years passed before Nelion (10m lower but a tougher climb) was conquered. Both are named after nineteenth-century Maasai *laibon* or ritual leaders.

Climbing Mount Kenya: the practicalities

There are **four main routes**. The **Naro Moru trail** provides the shortest and steepest way to the top. The **Burguret** and **Sirimon trails** from the northwest are less well trodden: Sirimon has a reputation for lots of wildlife, while Burguret passes through a long stretch of dense forest. The fourth, the **Chogoria trail**, is a beautiful but much longer ascent up the eastern flank of the mountain.

Batian (5199m) and Nelion (5188m) are accessible only to experienced, fully equipped mountaineers – they look almost vertical – and the easiest route is Grade IV, making them a lot more testing than most of the routes up the Matterhorn. If you want to climb these peaks, you should join the Mountain Club of Kenya (PO Box 45741, Nairobi; ☎02/501747; their clubhouse is at Wilson Airport, bus #34). They will not only put you in touch with the right people but also give you reductions on hut fees.

On the question of **cost**, even with the halving of park fees in 1996, climbing Mount Kenya is an extremely expensive business. A four-day trek for two people, excluding guides or porters, costs anything between Ksh6000 and Ksh11,000 (park fees, overnights, food, and transport to the roadhead, not including any additional equipment and tent rental). The cost of one porter/guide for this period would add anything between Ksh2000–4500 to the tally, whilst an organized trek easily costs over $100 a day. The park itself operates a sign-in/sign-out system, and you pay fees on entry for your anticipated stay. It's a bad idea to try to evade the exit gate on departure: they will go looking for you and eventually organize an air search if you don't show up. Stories circulate of people being pursued to Nairobi and beyond for non-payment of huge rescue service bills.

If you need to change money, do so in Nairobi or in the big ring-road towns – Chogoria has no exchange facilities (Chuka town is the nearest), neither has Naro Moru, and a trip to Nanyuki would be time wasted.

Location and climate

Anyone who is reasonably fit can have a crack at **Point Lenana** (4986m), but this climb has somehow acquired the reputation of being fairly easy, and lots of people set off up the mountain quite unprepared for high-altitude living – indeed, some 25 percent of attempts fail for this reason. If you try it, forget you're on the equator. Over about 4000m, the mountain is **freezing cold and windy** – wickedly so after dark; the air is thin, and it rains or snows, at least briefly, almost daily, though most precipitation comes at night. Mount Kenya's **weather** is notoriously unpredictable. Even during the rainy seasons, there are days when it's fairly clear, but driving up the muddy roads to the park gates may be nearly impossible, and if it's really bad, you probably won't be allowed in anyway. The **most reliable months** are February and August, although January and most of July can be fine, too.

Preparations

Above all, it's essential to have a **really warm sleeping bag**, four-season at the very least, ideally with an additional liner and/or Goretex bivouac bag. One **thick sweater** at the very least (better still, several thinner ones), and either a **windproof jacket** or a down- or fibre-filled one are absolutely necessary. A **change of footwear** is pretty much essential, too, as you're bound to have wet feet by the end of each day. **Gloves** and a **balaclava or woolly hat** will seem vital to some, but are probably not to hand in your backpack. A light cagoule or anorak is good to have, as is a set or two of thermal underwear for the often shivering nights: judge the season and weather for yourself. Out of season (that is, most of the year), an **emergency foil blanket** is advisable and weighs and packs down to next to nothing. Another prerequisite is a **stove**, as you'll be miserable without regular hot fluids: firewood is not available and cannot be collected once you enter the park. For **food**, dehydrated soup and chocolate are perhaps the most useful. Remember, excess baggage can be left for about Ksh60 a day at *Naro Moru River Lodge*, so take only what you'll need. Here you can also purchase a packaged mountain climb, all inclusive (PO Box 18, Naro Moru; ☎0176/62212).

The *River Lodge* has a **rental** shop where you can get just about anything, at prices that may make you wish you'd simply bought it in Nairobi (see under "Camping equipment rental" in the Nairobi Listings); the youth hostel has a limited range of items for rent. Be cautious of anyone who approaches you offering to rent out gear.

If you are travelling alone and don't meet a suitable companion (you're not allowed to make the climb alone), it's possible to hire a **guide/porter** at the *Naro Moru River Lodge*, at the *Transit Motel* in Chogoria, or at the youth hostel (the latter is a good place to find someone much more cheaply). Expect to pay up to Ksh750 per day plus all his park fees, but insist on a written agreement showing the wages, the number of days, who's providing the food – everything. You shouldn't pay the full fee until the trip is finished; nor should you entirely *rely* on your guide to make every necessary preparation. Note that you're not likely to find a guide up at the park gates.

For a quick **taste of the mountain**, you can fix up a day's hike to *Mackinder's*, inclusive of lifts up to the gate and back down again, for around $35 (plus park fees), through one of the caretakers of the youth hostel.

Mountain health

While good physical fitness certainly won't hinder your climb, the ascent itself is mostly just a steep hike, if rough underfoot in parts. It is the altitude rather than the climb itself that may prevent you from reaching the top. Much more germane than the training programmes that some people embark on is giving yourself enough time to acclimatize, so your body has a chance to produce extra oxygen-carrying red blood cells. Above 4000m, you are likely to notice the **effects of altitude** and it's how fast you climb that is critical. Physical symptoms are unpredictable; they vary between individuals, and appear to be unrelated to how fit you are – indeed, fit young males often suffer the most acute symptoms. Breathlessness, nausea, disorientation and even slurred speech are all possible, and headaches are fairly normal at first, especially at night. All this can be largely avoided by taking your time over the trek, as minor symptoms gradually disappear. You may consider bringing a tent for this reason, to avoid the sometimes rapid climbs between huts. Do not attempt to climb from the base of the

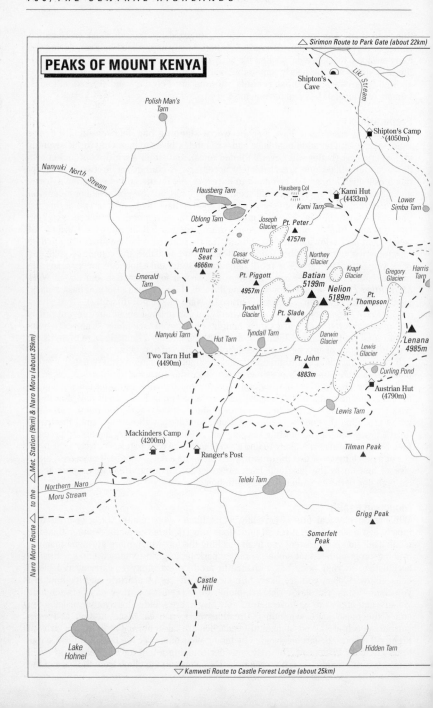

PEAKS OF MOUNT KENYA

△ Sirimon Route to Park Gate (about 22km)

Liki Stream

Shipton's Cave

Shipton's Camp (4050m)

Polish Man's Tarn

Nanyuki North Stream

Hausberg Tarn

Hausberg Col

Kami Hut (4433m)

Kami Tarn

Lower Simba Tarn

Oblong Tarn

Joseph Glacier

Pt. Peter 4757m

Arthur's Seat 4666m

Cesar Glacier

Northey Glacier

Krapf Glacier

Gregory Glacier

Harris Tarn

Emerald Tarn

Pt. Piggott 4957m

Batian 5199m

Nelion 5189m

Pt. Thompson

Tyndall Glacier

Pt. Slade

Darwin Glacier

Lenana 4985m

Nanyuki Tarn

Tyndall Tarn

Lewis Glacier

Hut Tarn

Two Tarn Hut (4490m)

Pt. John 4883m

Curling Pond

Austrian Hut (4790m)

Lewis Tarn

Mackinders Camp (4200m)

Ranger's Post

Tilman Peak

△ to the Met. Station (9km) & Naro Moru (about 35km)

Northern Naro Moru Stream

Teleki Tarn

Grigg Peak

Naro Moru Route ▽

Somerfelt Peak

Castle Hill

Lake Hohnel

Hidden Tarn

▽ Kamweti Route to Castle Forest Lodge (about 25km)

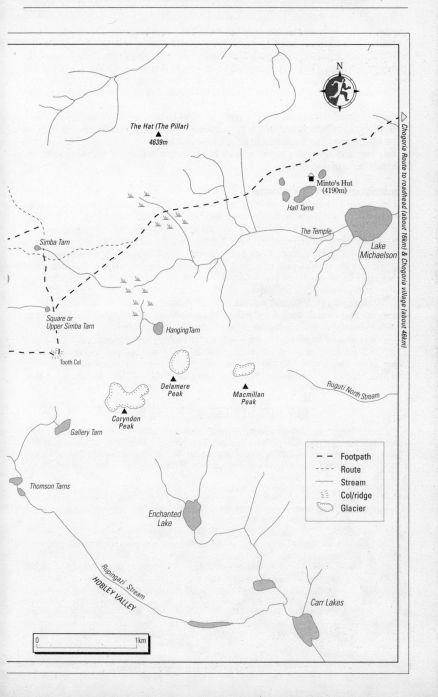

mountain (that is, from the ring road) to Point Lenana in less than 72 hours; if you've just arrived in Kenya, allow five days for the ascent. Giving yourself a week for the whole trip is a good idea. Keeping your fluid intake as high as possible will also help (three to five litres a day is recommended) and it's best to avoid alcohol. If someone in your group shows signs of being seriously tired and weak, stay at that altitude. Should the symptoms develop into unsteadiness on the feet and drowsiness, **descend imme-diately**, whatever the circumstances. The effects of altitude are remarkable – especially on bodies tuned only to sea level – and can quickly become very dangerous. Every year, dozens of climbers are struck by pulmonary oedema (in which water collects in the lungs), accounting for almost half the cases worldwide.

You may find Ibuprofen works against headaches and Diamox helpful against the general effects of altitude.

Accommodation on the mountain

Taking a **tent** is, outside the months of February or August, almost essential because the only other **accommodation on the mountain** is a handful of very basic cabins and mountain huts, which can become so cold at night as to threaten hypothermia and rob you of a night's much needed sleep. For the Naro Moru route, these are supposed to be reserved at *Naro Moru River Lodge*. In practice, this is rarely necessary unless you want to be sure of getting a bunk at the *Meteorological Station* or *Mackinder's Camp* (also known as *Teleki Valley Lodge*). If you have a tent, you can **camp** anywhere in the park, the only practical advantage of the campsites at the *Met Station* (3050m) and *Mackinder's* (4175m), and various other designated campsites on the mountain, being water pipes and "long drop" toilets. Most water on the mountain is reckoned to be safe to drink (exceptions are noted) and you're never far from it.

The *Met Station bandas* ($16) are good, but often burgled by monkeys. *Mackinder's Camp* ($22 for a bed in a concrete cell) has an informal, and perhaps less certain, alter-native in the shape of the *Rangers' Cabin* nearby, with negotiable rates usually costing you about half the *Mackinder's Camp* price. Camping is allowed here and it's altogether

---

GUIDEBOOKS AND MAPS

The topographical map, *Mount Kenya 1:50,000 Map and Guide* by Andrew Wielochowski and Mark Savage (available from Executive Wilderness Programmes, 32 Seamill Park Crescent, Worthing, BN11 2PN, UK; also available in Kenya) covers just the mountain itself at 1cm:500m and includes a detailed rundown on the huts and technical information for scalers of Nelion and Batian.

If you're a **climbing** enthusiast, you'll want to get hold of the Mountain Club of Kenya's *Guide Book to Mount Kenya and Kilimanjaro* or the *East Africa International Mountain Guide* by Andrew Wielochowski (West Col Productions, 1 Meadow Close, Goring, Reading, Berks, RG8 9AA, UK; also available in Kenya), which is adequate on the technical ascents.

Trekking in East Africa by David Else (Lonely Planet) is a usefully detailed, general companion.

As for **maps**, don't expect to find any in the Naro Moru area or at any of the park gates. The recent *Tourist Map of Mount Kenya National Park and Environs* (Ordnance Survey, through regular stockists) is an updated version of an excellent Survey of Kenya map. At 1cm:1.25km, it provides a very useful – and visually pleasing – overview of the whole district, showing all the routes, the region around the base and most of the ring road. It's frankly not much use for the final ascent, however.

There's also a quite user-friendly, small Survey of Kenya topographical **map of the peak area** at 1cm:250m that's worth getting hold of in Nairobi if you're intending to walk around the peaks.

a friendlier place to huddle than *Mackinder's*, with a fire burning most nights. Porters around *Mackinder's* will cook up a huge meal (given sufficient notice) for $3–4.

On the Chogoria and Sirimon routes there are several other basic **bunkhouses and cabins**, some permanently staffed (details follow under each route). The best accommodation on the mountain is the *Meru Mount Kenya Lodge* self-service *bandas* on the Chogoria route.

Also available are the small, bare **huts** built by the Mountain Club of Kenya, which normally have four walls, a roof, bunks, and nothing else (free; the wardens at the gates used to collect fees but recently washed their hands of the affair given the deplorable state of the huts – details are given under the relevant routes). These are located near the peaks, thus making it possible to spend a day or two around the high tarns and glaciers before returning to the base of *Mackinder's Camp* (warmer and more oxygen). *Top Hut*, next to *Austrian Hut*, is reserved for MCK members. The huts have no facilities or staff – you must be entirely self-sufficient. Their foam mattresses disappeared long ago (presumably burned to warm the frost-bitten nights), and a closed-cell bedroll is essential.

The Naro Moru route

From the main A2 road to the *Meteorological Station*, where the drivable earth road ends, is a 26-kilometre haul; even from the youth hostel it's at least a five-hour walk. *Naro Moru River Lodge* will taxi you up here – for an extortionate price – or you may be lucky and get a lift, but a completely free ride would be a miracle.

Some 9km from the youth hostel, you come to the airstrip, the **park gate and HQ**, and usually three or four gigantic buffalo chewing the cud on the lawn. Entry is the usual $10 National Parks fee if you're going in for the day. Porters pay the residents' rate, and student card holders pay half-price. Don't overestimate; there are no refunds. From the gate, you leave the conifer plantations and occasional *shambas* behind as the road twists and climbs through shaggy forest into a zone of colossal **bamboo**. Look out for elephant and particularly **buffalo** if you walk this stretch, though you'll more often see their droppings and footprints. If you find buffalo on the path, you're supposed to lob stones at them – and they're supposed to move out of the way. But exercise caution if they're about.

The final 3km to the *Met Station* is a series of steep hairpins usually drivable only in 4WD. You start to get some magnificent views out over the plains from up here, while right under your nose you may find a three-horned **chameleon**, stalking cautiously through the foliage like a miniature dinosaur. The high forest is its favourite habitat. **Black panthers** – the melanistic form of the leopard found at high altitudes – can also be seen in this habitat, and the latest local denizen was a lion, who walked into a tent at the *Met Station* recently and made off with a duvet jacket.

With an early start, it's quite possible to reach *Mackinder's* (4175m) in one day, but unless you're already acclimatized, you'll probably feel well below par by the time you get there. It is far better to take it easy and get used to the *Met Station's* 3050-metre altitude; perhaps stroll a little higher or, if you have a tent, climb an hour or so up to the tree line and camp there. Ready-erected tents can be hired at the *Met Station* if you can't afford the *bandas* (though, after the lion incident there was no camping for some months). The mountain's weather is another good reason to stop here: after midday, it often gets foul, and the infamous vertical bog is no fun at all in heavy drizzle and twenty-metre visibility.

Up the Teleki Valley

An early start from the *Met Station* the next morning should see you to *Mackinder's* by lunchtime, before the clouds start to thicken up. In fair weather, the **vertical bog** is not

MOUNT KENYA'S HIGH ALTITUDE FLORA

The mountain's **vegetation** is zoned by altitude. Above about 2000m *shambas* and coniferous plantations cease and the original, dense cloud forest takes over, with the best and broadest stands on the mountain's southern and eastern, rain-facing slopes.

As you gain altitude (2400m), forest gives way to giant bamboo, with clumps up to 20m high. The bamboo, a member of the grass family, appears impenetrable, but dark-walled passages are kept open by elephants and buffalo. Again, the best bamboo areas are to the south, while on the dry, northern slopes, there's very little of it.

Above the bamboo (2800m) you come into more open country of scattered, twisted *Hagena* and St John's Wort trees (*Hypericum*), and then the tree line (3000m) and the start of the peculiar, afro-alpine moorlands. Above about 3300m you reach the land of the giants – giant heather, giant groundsel, giant lobelia. Identities are confusing: the cabbages on stumps and the larger candelabra-like "trees" are the same species – giant groundsel or tree senecio – an intermediate stage of which has a sheaf of yellow flowers. They are slow growers and, for such weedy-looking vegetables, they may be extraordinarily old – up to two hundred years. The tall, fluffy, less abundant plants are a species of giant lobelia discovered by the explorer Teleki and found only on Mount Kenya. The name plaque below one of these (there's a little nature trail along the ridge above the Naro Moru stream) calls it an "Ostrich plume plant" (botanical name: *Lobelia telekii*), and it is the only plant that could fairly be described as cuddly. The furriness which gives it such an animal quality acts as insulation for the delicate flowers.

as daunting as it sounds: you keep to the left of the red and white marker posts where it isn't as wet. In wet conditions, however, it can be ghastly, as the rosette plants hold just enough freezing water to be able to reach certain parts in a bracing manner whenever you slip. As you reach the bog, you enter another vegetation zone, that of **giant heather**. Beyond and above the bog, the path follows a ridge high above the **Teleki Valley** with the peaks straight ahead, rising brilliantly over a landscape that seems to have nothing in common with the hazy plains below.

For **Mackinder's Camp**, you follow the contours across the valley side and jump, or cross by stepping stones, over the snowmelt Northern Naro Moru stream. The camp, virtually at the head of Teleki Valley, is a long stone and concrete bunkhouse with dishevelled tents tacked into the icy ground around it. Certainly no hotel, it does at least provide some warmth and the company of others: climbers, Kikuyu guides and porters. **Batian** and **Nelion** tower magnificently over the valley, with a third pinnacle, **Point John**, even closer. There's usually a fresh icing of snow every morning but early sunlight melts most of it by midday.

Point Lenana

If you want to climb **straight to Point Lenana**, you're likely to find at least one group leaving early the following morning (say around 3am) with a guide, though it's not that difficult to find your own way up, especially if there's a moon. Leaving this early allows you to get to the top by dawn for a fabulous view (sometimes) from northern Kenya on one side to Kilimanjaro on the other. It's not advisable to rush into this final ascent, however. For most people, day three is better spent getting acclimatized in the Teleki Valley, making the climb to Point Lenana the next morning. And note: spending your third night on the mountain at *Austrian Hut*, just below Point Lenana, is a bad idea. Not only is *Austrian* in a disgusting state, but sleeping unacclimatized at high altitude is literally a nightmare.

Trekking around the peaks

Though most people head straight up to Point Lenana, **trekking round the peaks** is really a far more exhilarating experience, with the added chance to explore some of the tarns and glacial valleys on the north side. It's supposed to be easier to do this anti-clockwise in two or three days. If you want to do it in one, however, set off clockwise from *Mackinder's* via *Two Tarn Hut* by **Hut tarn**, set in a glorious and eerily silent col beneath the glaciers and scree. The walk from here round to Point Lenana is very much a switchback affair but, as long as the mists stay away, the scenery is fairy-tale. If you're fairly fit and acclimatized, it should take eight to ten hours. *Kami Hut*, on the north side of the peaks, and *Austrian Hut* (as well as *Two Tarn*), are suitable night stops, though, again, you may not get much sleep, particularly at *Austrian Hut*, which is the highest.

Incidentally, your nights up in the mountain huts will normally be shared with large numbers of persistent **rodents** which you won't see until it's too late. Remember to isolate your food from them by suspending it from the roof. The familiar diurnal scavengers that you'll see are **rock hyraxes**, which are especially tame at *Mackinder's Camp*: the welfare service provided to them by tourists preserves elderly specimens long past their natural life span. Hyraxes are not rodents: the anatomy of their feet indicates they share a distant ancestry with elephants. You're likely to come across **other animals** at quite high altitudes, too, notably the duiker antelope on the moorlands.

When you're ready to come down, it doesn't take long. You can do so in one day, right to Naro Moru or further, assuming you've left your vehicle at the *Met Station*, or else manage to find a lift. Rather than retrace your steps to Naro Moru, a more exhilarating and less frequently used alternative is to descend by one of the other routes: the Chogoria trail, for example. This would mean taking all your gear up with you, as well as extra food.

The Chogoria route

The **Chogoria trail** is scenically far superior to any of the others, and it's become more popular now that the road around the east side of the mountain has been paved. It is also the longest route, requiring good shoes and probably a plentiful supply of blister pads. A tent is preferable for the trek beyond the park gate. From the eastern side, the hike to the top can be done in three days, but it's easier to allow four or five if you're setting out from Nairobi.

Up to the park entrance

The strangely unfriendly village of **CHOGORIA** is your first target (*Akamba* buses leave Nairobi at 10am and 9pm, *Nyayo Bus* at midday; the journey takes 4–6hr). The *Transit Motel*, 3km south of Chogoria centre (PO Box 190, Chogoria; ☎0166/22096; ③) is the best of several **lodgings**, with reasonable self-contained rooms, most with a balcony but no nets, and a very slow restaurant. *Chogoria Guest House* and *Chogoria Cool Inn* (both ②) are in the village and considerably cheaper. The *Motherland Hotel* still serves **food** from its burned-out shell; for an antiseptic contrast, *Lenana Restaurant*, in the Presbyterian Mission Hospital, has cheap snacks in a linoleum-lined hall.

There are a number of porter/guide associations in Chogoria, the most reliable of which (but also the most expensive) is *Mount Kenya Chogoria Guides & Porters* (PO Box 114), based at the *Transit Motel*. Their official (bargainable) rates are Ksh400 a day for a porter, Ksh460 a day for a guide, and Ksh750 a day for a porter-guide (remember, if you're alone you must have one to be allowed to stay in the park overnight, and he needs to possess an offical KWS guiding permit). From the hamlet of Mutindwa, 4km up the the mountain, it's about 26km to the park gate. On weekends, you may stand a better than average chance of getting a lift.

Otherwise, you could **rent transport** at the *Transit Motel* or elsewhere in Chogoria. There are a number of options: halfway to the park gate (15km drive, 15km walk: up to Ksh500); two-thirds (20km drive to Bairunyi Clearing, 10km walk: up to Ksh2000); to the park gate (30km: Ksh3000–4000); or to the roadhead, some 7km further (Ksh4000). It's a good idea not to pay (at least not everything) until reaching the destination – a feat that for most of the year is by no means guaranteed because of the weather. You may prefer to walk up, in any case, because it gives you a chance to acclimatize. If you get a lift up early in the day, do avoid climbing any higher before stopping for the night.

Walking up from **Mutindwa**, there's a good campsite after just a couple of kilometres at the **Chogoria Forest station**, with firewood available. Exciting, dense rain forest follows, where you're likely to see colobus monkeys, spotted hyena, buffalo and numerous elephant droppings. Before, during and after the rains, though, you will probably be more occupied with fending off swarms of hungry tsetse fly, which isn't much fun and runs the (slight) risk of sleeping sickness. The next available camping site is the only clearing in the forest, at a place called **Bairunyi Clearing**, 14km further up the track (no water). The National Park's **Chogoria Gate** is 8km further up the increasingly steep and rough track (4WD vital, and not always enough), flanked by giant, creaking bamboo forest. If you arrive late in the day and are not going beyond the roadhead (7km on – the actual boundary of the national park), the rangers may waive park fees for that day, but be sure to keep receipts for the fees you pay to satisfy the rangers at whichever gate you exit from.

Park entrance and roadhead

The best **place to stay** is the very good and wonderfully sited *Meru Mount Kenya Lodge*, a group of self-service *bandas* just before the gate (no park fees payable), run by the district council (it may be worth booking in advance, through *Let's Go Travel*, PO Box 60342 Nairobi; ☎02/340331, fax 02/336890; ④). They have a spartan shop that sells beer, and blissful wood fires in each *banda*. They're often visited by buffaloes, and you can sometimes see elephants at the nearby water holes, visible from the ridge of the hill behind the *bandas*.

Assuming you're not staying in the *bandas*, but it's time to stop for the day, you might as well stay put by the gate with your tent (if you have a tent), or go on to *Parklands Campsite*, twenty minutes' walk away with toilets and, usually, water (stay on the main track for 500m then fork left: keep a look out, the turning is easily missed). Alternatively, follow the main track up from the park gate and you'll come to a "special campsite" with running water and toilet. This is a beautiful place to camp, but has special fees (reservable through the warden; $10 per person).

The nearest **mountain hut** is reached by branching left off the main track (it's well signposted) and continuing past *Parklands Campsite*: the uninviting *Urumandi Hut* is an hour's walk up the track. It's long overdue for a refit, only retains three unbroken beds and, like all the *MCK* huts, has lost its complement of mattresses. There's water from the ravine nearby. The neighbouring *Urumandi Campsite* is equally unprepossessing – little more than an overgrown swamp and a derelict shed.

Both the main track and the side branch eventually meet up at the **roadhead**, 6km further. The side branch, via Urumandi, is the more interesting walk, but tougher on vehicles. The roadhead, with a small parking area, is on the north side of the Nithi stream and there's a very pleasant **campsite** here, with good stream water.

There are good walks round about, useful for acclimatizing to this three-thousand-plus-metres altitude. Short scrambles from the roadhead take you to the four sets of **Nithi Falls**, while longer walks (3–6hr round trip) take you north to **Mugi Hill**, **Lake Ellis** and the flat-topped peak Kilingo – the **Giant's Billiard Table**.

On the mountain

From the roadhead, all wheels are abandoned as you slog on foot up to *Minto's Hut*, a six-hour (9hr from *Meru Mount Kenya Lodge*) stint away in the high moorlands. The route tracks along the axis of an ascending ridge, then flattens onto the rim of the spectacular **Gorges Valley**, carved deep by glaciation. There are unobstructed and encouraging views up to the peaks as you hug the contours of the valley wall.

Minto's Hut, like *Mackinder's* on the west side of the mountain, is three to five hours from Point Lenana. Situated by the four small "Hall Tarns", it's perched above the larger Lake Michaelson at the head of the valley below – a very beautiful place, inspiringly set off by giant groundsel, lobelia plants and weird volcanic formations inhabited by rock hyraxes. **"The Temple"**, a short walk away, is right above Lake Michaelson. Unfortunately, the hut itself is one of the worst: slummy, freezing cold at night and wet in the morning; the available tarn water is not pure. Beware: boiling it at this altitude will not kill the bugs so you should use purifying tablets or iodine.

In the morning you have two options. The first is to head up to the ridge west of *Minto's* and follow it, through pretty scenery, to **Simba Tarn**, below Simba Col. From there, head due south around the peaks and past little **Square Tarn** before turning right to follow the contours for a tough kilometre to the so-called **Curling Pond** (matches have been held on the ice here: at present there's a great ice cave cut into the glacier) and *Austrian Hut*. Note, if you're thinking of a short cut straight up to Square Tarn, it's very steep.

Alternatively, from *Minto's* make for the base of the ridge extending east from Point Lenana, then tackle the cruel scree slope to the south for a ninety-minute scramble up to a saddle followed by a straight drop to the head of the **Hobley Valley** with its two tarns. From here, it's just an hour across to the base of Lenana Ridge, behind which, again, is *Austrian Hut*. Mercifully, whichever route you choose, this day's hike is a short one and at this altitude (over 4000m), you'll be glad to spend the rest of the day at one of the huts, recuperating for the final ascent. Considering the altitude, a safer and probably more comfortable option would be to spend a second night, acclimatizing, at the base of Simba Tarn (tent only), followed by a pre-dawn assault on Point Lenana.

After the climb to Lenana, you have a ninety-minute **descent** from *Austrian Hut* along the edge of Lewis Glacier, tracking back and forth over miserable scree, to the Teleki tarn at the head of the Naro Moru stream. *Mackinder's*, and the scent of civilization, is just an hour away down the valley. But if you can resist that lure, and it is still early in the day, *and* if you have enough food and water, you can continue around the west side of the peaks to Hut Tarn, then up and down over the ridges to *Kami Hut*, at the head of the Sirimon route on the north side.

If you want to do it, and you feel acclimatized, there's no problem making it from *Minto's* to Point Lenana and on down to the *Met Station* in one day.

The Sirimon and Burguret routes

A good alternative to Naro Moru as a convenient base on the west side is **Mountain Rock Hotel**, the former *Bantu Lodge* (PO Box 333 Nanyuki; ☎0176/62625, fax 0176/62051), about 8km north of Naro Moru. The entrance can't be missed, as it's marked by two enormous Kikuyu figures carved out of tree trunks and flamboyantly painted. They have decent and fairly reasonably priced **rooms** (⑤) with log fires, and a good restaurant and bar (hearty meals with plenty of fresh veg for around Ksh300). You can **camp** in the grounds ($5, or $15 using their tents). There's even a small water hole in the back garden that attracts elephants once in a while, and a resident accordion player who serenades each new guest with Kikuyu tunes. There's **horse riding** at about Ksh300 per hour (reduced rates for longer periods). The limited tack needs careful checking, and ask about fodder and water before galloping off. You can also do inexpensive escorted walks through the forest in the vicinity of the lodge.

The Sirimon route

The **Sirimon route** leads up from the Mount Kenya ring road some 14km east of Nanyuki. It has certain advantages: it's relatively drier throughout the year than the others, the scenery is more open and it is renowned for its wildlife. *Mountain Rock* specializes in inclusive three- or four-day **guided tours** up to Point Lenana using this route. Prices are from around $200 per person (3 days) in a group of four, including transport to and from the base of the trail, all food and equipment, and a last night at *Mountain Rock*. It's a good deal if you're unequipped or wary, especially compared with *Naro Moru River Lodge's* tour prices, but it's considerably more expensive for singles or couples. Park fees are an additional expense.

Unpackaged walking on this route is fine if you're in a small group, but you're much less likely to find company up here than on the Chogoria or very busy Naro Moru routes as there isn't any real "base town" to start from. The route climbs over the northern moorlands, giving superb views on the way of the main peaks as well as the twin "lesser" peaks of Terere and Sendeyo (4714m and 4704m), which have small glaciers of their own.

Mountain accommodation on the way consists of the recently refurbished *Old Moses Camp* (3300m, at the roadhead; Ksh900) and *Shipton's Camp* **bunkhouses** (4200m; Ksh1100), bed space at both of which is bookable at *Mountain Rock Hotel* or at their Nairobi office (Room 232, Jubilee Insurance House, Wabera St; ☎02/228178–9, fax 02/333448).

The Burguret route

Mountain Rock Hotel's preferred route used to follow the **Burguret River** through thick bamboo forest and moorland. It begins at the hotel. A four-wheel-drive vehicle can drive up to 3000m on this route and it terminates at *Two Tarn Hut* behind Teleki Valley. En route, it passes a clutch of caves described as a "*Mau Mau* conference centre". *Mountain Rock* is no longer offering walking trips along this route, which is mostly overgrown and hard to follow.

Other routes

The four trails described here represent only the most obvious of the mountain's hiking possibilities. All ground above 3200m is within the boundaries of the national park, and if you had time and sufficient food, you could hike the forests and moors for weeks. The southern flanks of the mountain seem to have largely escaped the notice of hikers, but there are several forest stations in the vicinity of Embu and plenty of scope for exploration – the Kamweti route is a possibility (see p.162). Most of the southern slopes were a designated "Kikuyu reserve" during the colonial period, so few European climbers created routes up here.

Over the equator: Nanyuki and around

From Naro Moru, the road rolls on over yellow and grey downs, scattered with stands of tall gum trees, roamed by cattle and overflown by brilliant blue roller birds. Then it drops to the equator and Nanyuki. You might be forgiven for expecting something momentous to take place at **the equator**, but there's no "crossing of the line ceremony" here. Still, if you have any control over your transport, you'd have to be pretty cool just to breeze by.

There's a splendid yellow sign, or even two ("This sign is on the Equator"), and, in case there was any doubt, a veritable bazaar of souvenir stalls with salesmen who will go to absurd lengths to entice you ("Hey guy! Want cocaine?"). What they actually offer is all the usual beadwork, carvings, soapstone and bangles at the sorts of prices you'd expect.

The town centre is just 1.5km down the road, so you could reasonably ask to be dropped at the equator and then walk in.

Nanyuki

NANYUKI has the dual distinction of being Kenya's air force town (a base which has had a lot of attention lavished on it in recent years) as well as playing host to the British Army's training and operations centre. Nevertheless it remains in atmosphere very much a country town. A wide, tree-lined main street and the mild climate lent by its altitude of 2000m lend an unfamiliar, cool spaciousness that seems to reinforce its oddly colonial character. Shops lining the main road include the *Settlers Store* (since 1938), the *Modern Sanitary Store* (which sells camping gas), and *United Stores* with its pile of *Daily Telegraphs*.

The first party of settlers arrived in the district in 1907 to find "several old Maasai *manyattas*, a great deal of game and nothing else"; Nanyuki is still something of a settlers' town and European locals are always around. The animals, sadly, are not. Although you may see a few grazers on the plains, the vast herds of zebra that once roamed the banks of the *Ngare Nanyuki* (Maasai – Red River) were decimated by hunters seeking hides, by others seeking meat (particularly during World War II, when 80,000 Italian prisoners of war were fed a pound each day), but most of all by ranchers protecting their pastures. As the zebra herds dwindled, so the lions became a greater threat to livestock; they retreated – under fire – to the mountain forests and moors. And the rhinos have just disappeared.

Practicalities

If you're passing through Nanyuki, wholesome **food** is available at the *Maridadi Café* and the very nice *Mid Pines Café*, behind the petrol station. Good snacks and occasion-

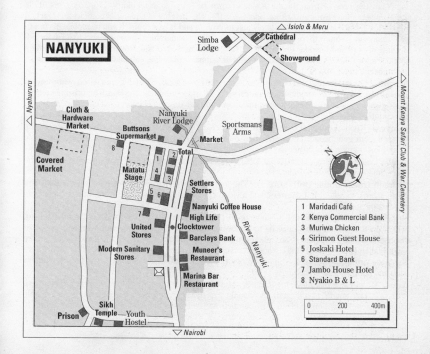

NANYUKI

△ Isiolo & Meru

Simba Lodge

Cathedral

Showground

◁ Nyahururu

▷ Mount Kenya Safari Club & War Cemetery

Cloth & Hardware Market

Nanyuki River Lodge

Sportsmans Arms

Buttsons Supermarket

Market

Covered Market

Matatu Stage

Total

Settlers Stores

Nanyuki Coffee House

High Life

United Stores

Clocktower

Barclays Bank

Modern Sanitary Stores

Muneer's Restaurant

Marina Bar Restaurant

River Nanyuki

1 Maridadi Café
2 Kenya Commercial Bank
3 Muriwa Chicken
4 Sirimon Guest House
5 Joskaki Hotel
6 Standard Bank
7 Jambo House Hotel
8 Nyakio B & L

0   200   400m

Sikh Temple — Youth

Prison

Hostel

▽ Nairobi

ally great curries are had at *Muneera's Restaurant*; *Mother's Choice Café*, next door, has sweet cakes and sausages. For a lively **drink**, try the *Marina Bar* opposite the post office, a popular hangout for tourists and soldiers (unfortunately you may meet with some verbal abuse while in Nanyuki, presumably on account of the British base and most likely if you are – or might be mistaken for – an off-duty serviceman). Next door is *High Life Day and Night Club* which, not surprisingly, attracts all the low life. For **money-changing** in town, the best bet is the *KCB* (bureau de change open Mon–Fri 9am–3pm, Sat 9–11am).

If you have time before leaving, pay a visit to the **Nanyuki Spinners and Weavers** workshop, located about 1km out of town on the Nyahururu road, opposite the District Hospital. This women's group provides the *Spin 'n' Weave Shop* in Nairobi with rugs and other articles woven on hand looms, which you can buy here at reduced prices. There's also astonishingly ambrosial **wild honey** from the *dukas* a kilometre or so east of the last police barrier, on the road to Meru.

For **overnight stays**, you have a number of options, including **camping** at the *Sportsman's Arms*. Or try one of the following:

ACCOMMODATION

High Life "Self-contained Rooms". Basic but tolerable and very economical. ①.

Jambo House Hotel. Reasonably comfortable, and central, with a lively bar. ①.

Joskaki Hotel (PO Box 228; ☎0176/22820). Recommended for its generally excellent food and good rooftop views of the town and Mount Kenya. Unfortunately it's a vast, corridor-riddled warren and can be indescribably noisy when the bar is open all night, or there's a disco. A copy of the *Rough Guide* may get you a discount. ③.

Mount Kenya Safari Club, about 8km southeast of Nanyuki, accessible either from just north of the *New Silverbeck*, or from the north side of town (PO Box 35, Nanyuki; ☎0176/22960, fax 0176/22754; reservations through *Lonrho*, address p.48). The heights of equatorial comfort are reached here – not a place at which you're likely just to drop in and take a room. If you're mobile it's fun to call in anyway, though there's a fairly expensive daily membership for non-guests (Ksh350 including use of pool and bowling green). A big range of activities in and around the hotel – including tennis, riding, fishing, gyms, heated pool and an animal orphanage – all fill the day very pleasantly. Magnificent meals. ⑨.

Nanyuki Guest House (PO Box 211, Meru; ☎0176/22822). Useful if you're on your way to Nyahururu, because it is about ten minutes' walk out of town in that direction. The prison-like exterior belies a good atmosphere, helpful manager and probably the cheapest self-contained rooms in the country. ①.

Nanyuki River Lodge (PO Box 101; ☎0176/32523). Reasonable rooms, hustly touts at the entrance, but good value. They have their own porters' association for Mt Kenya with reasonable rates (porter-guide Ksh600 per day) for tackling the Sirimon Route. ③.

Simba Lodge (PO Box 211; ☎0176/22556). A peaceful place and actually quite pleasant despite the barrack-like rooms. Safe parking. ③.

Sirimon Guest House (☎0176/32344). The tour drivers' favourite digs – sleazy but amiable, with clean rooms, excellent hot showers, and a video cinema (admission Ksh10). Slightly cheaper than the *Joskaki* and *Jambo*. ①.

Sportsman's Arms (PO Box 3 Nanyuki; ☎0176/32348, fax 0176/22895). An old establishment, which used to be the base for visits to the *Secret Valley* (a *Treetops*-type establishment) until that burned down in 1981. Letters and photos smother the walls, reminders of the good old days. The slightly dilapidated sprawl of s/c wooden cottages gives you a wide choice and you'll probably have the place virtually to yourself. The new wings (built 1994) are better equipped, and there's a fitness club and pool. Rooms ④; cottages ⑤–⑥.

Youth Hostel at *Emmanuel Parish Centre*, Market Rd, near the post office (PO Box 279 Nanyuki; ☎0176/22112; not IYHA-affiliated). A friendly place, with very cheap beds in single and double rooms. Accommodation is clean but cramped and very spartan, and makes no concessions to privacy – unless you're the only guest, of course, in which case it's not a problem. The toilets are a hazard. ②.

NANYUKI: ACCOMMODATION/177

Moving on to Nyahururu – and ranch stays

If you're **heading to Nyahururu**, beware of the unpaved C76 road. It's become fiend-ish of late, even in the dry season; and in periods of heavy rain vehicles get stuck along it for days on end. Despite the setbacks, it's a good road for wildlife-spotting: you've every chance of seeing giraffes, gazelles and even elephants if you set off early. And it seems nowadays that even the **black rhinos** may make a comeback if the intro-ductions at Laikipia Ranch north of Nanyuki prove successful. Here, a herd of rhinos are part of an experiment in integrated ranching. As browsers, they don't interfere with cattle pasture, and do well in the same environment as long as the bush isn't cleared.

There are several other **game ranches** in the wide country that stretches out north and west of Nanyuki towards the desert. **El Karama**, one of the better known, is open to the public and recommended if you have a way to get to it: it's 42km northwest of Nanyuki off the track to Maralal and on the banks of the Ewaso Nyiro. You're welcome to pitch your tent, and they provide a small amount of cheap farmhouse and *banda* accommodation and game rides on horseback (PO Box 172, Nanyuki; reservations through *Let's Go Travel*, PO Box 60342, Nairobi; ☎02/340331, fax 02/336890; ④).

Alternatively, if you're up to a more expensive stay, the private **Ol Pejeta Game Reserve**, on the south side of the road, some 40-odd kilometres towards Nyahururu, is another excellent chance to see some of the Laikipia region's biggest concentrations of wildlife, again including black rhinos. Ol Pejeta covers some 400 square kilometres, nearly a quarter of which is given over to a rhino sanctuary, one inmate of which – "Morani" – is tame enough to be approached very closely.

There's one accommodation option, upmarket but good value when compared with similar set-ups in the national parks and reserves. *Sweetwaters Camp*, which specializes in night game drives, is a well laid-out tented camp (popular with Kenya residents, especially families), with high-quality food and service (PO Box 763, Nanyuki; ☎0176/55620, fax 0176/23414; ⑨ high, ⑦ low, not including activities). The lower tents are probably preferable to the ones set on stilts. Reservations are through *Lonrho* (address on p.48) – and look out for special offers in the press.

Also worth a mention, if only for its being possibly Kenya's costliest option, is *Borana Lodge*, also in Laikipia district (Tandala Ltd, PO Box 24397, Nairobi; ☎02/568804, fax 02/564945) which has six rooms and offers trips to the nearby **Ngare Sergoit Rhino Reserve**, for a princely $580 per person per day. Booking via *Let's Go Travel* in Nairobi (see p.122) may be cheaper.

Moving on: east to Meru

Leaving Nanyuki eastwards, the ring road skirts closer to the mountain than at any other point in its circumference. If you'd like a barbecued trout lunch on the way, call at *Kentrout*, 14km from Nanyuki, just before Timau (☎14 Timau; delicious, *al fresco* meals about $5). There's camping, with colobus monkeys in the nearby trees, and good walking and bird-watching in the *Kentrout* forest.

From here on the scenery acquires a real grandeur, changing completely yet again before you reach Meru. The 70km from **Nanyuki to Meru** couldn't illustrate better the amazing variety of climate and landscape in Kenya. The road climbs steeply to almost 3000m, passing alternative routes to the peaks and giving unparalleled views of them in the early morning. But a spectacle you might not have guessed at (until now) is the panorama that spreads out to the north as the road drops once again: on a really clear day, after rain has settled the dust, this is devastatingly beautiful. Even on an aver-age day, you can see as far as the dramatic mesa of **Ol Olokwe**, nearly 100km north in the desert. Isiolo (p.475) lies out there, too, first stop on the way to the northern wilderness.

Meru

For Meru, the road lies straight ahead, suddenly plunging through verdant **jungle**, with glimpses through the trees of the **Nyambeni Hills** and the volcanic pimples dotting the plain. **Meru oak** is the commercial prize of this forested eastern side of the mountain, though judging by the number of active sawmills at the upper end of the town, supplies won't last much longer. The forest still comes almost to the town's edge, however, and paths lead off to cleared *shambas* where, for a year or two, just about anything will grow. The moist, jungly atmosphere around Meru, with wood smoke curling up against a background of dark forest, is very reminiscent of parts of West Africa – a total change of mood after the dryish grasslands on the northwest side of the mountain.

Meru is, of course, the base for visits to **Meru National Park** (p.335). Hitching there can be a frustrating experience. It's better to get to the end of the tarmac before you start trying: take a *matatu* to Maua but hop out 3km before, at the national park turning.

Meru town

MERU town is strung out over two or three kilometres, the main road in from Nanyuki dropping steeply across the hillside to the town centre. It's an unusual place in an interesting location – there are great views from the upper (**Kinoru**) half of town over the densely settled slopes – and well worth a stay.

Meru's municipal **market** is a large one and sells a wide range of goods – baskets, clothes, domestic utensils – as well as the agricultural produce of the district. This is cheap and excellent: they grow the best **custard apples** in Kenya here, and if you like *miraa*, you won't find bigger or better bunches anywhere. Also known as *qat* or *gatty*, **miraa** is a small tree whose bark contains a mild stimulant and appetite suppressant. The freshly plucked twigs and leaves are chewed with bubble gum and, though frequently denounced, it's legal in Kenya. Meru district, where it grows wild but is also now cultivated, is the main source; northeastern Kenya is the biggest home market, and uncounted tons are exported to Somalia, Yemen and Djibouti. There's a trading corner devoted to *miraa* in the town centre, which also has lip-smacking roast yams and sugar cane by the yard. The outdoor market in Kinoru seems reserved largely for small traders offering more, wonderful, cheap *shamba* produce.

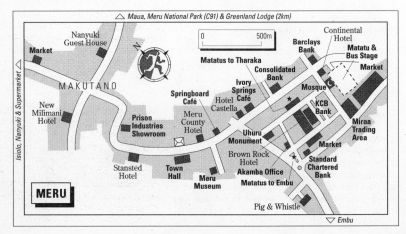

The tiny but fascinating **Meru museum** (PO Box 592; ☎0164/20482) is also a treat. It occupies the oldest stone building in town, a former District Commissioner's office, where you're likely to be the only visitor (entrance Ksh200), shown around by a guide/ticket-seller who turns the lights on as you proceed, and off again behind you. Emphasis is on the traditional culture of the Meru people: small ethnographic exhibits, pick-up-and-feel blocks of local stone and timber, stone tools from the Lewa Downs, prehistoric site and some woefully stuffed animals.

Outside there's a particularly good **herbal pharmacopoeia** – a collection of traditional medicinal plants growing in the garden, where you can see what a *miraa* bush looks like, among others. Nearby, several psychotically aggressive monkeys try to get at you through their cage bars. The **Meru homestead** is well presented and feels authentic – you get the impression someone actually lives here on the museum grounds, a feeling accentuated by the escape route in the perimeter fence for fleeing from invaders, which seems to have the well-worn look of years of use.

If you're interested, you might like to ask the guide about the **Njuri Njeke**, the traditional Meru courthouse, recently donated to the museum.

Practicalities

Meru is a hub for transport south, west and east. Numerous **bus** companies have their offices between the mosque and *miraa* trading area, and special (inflated) rates apply for its transport. Recommended are *Stagecoach Express* (☎0164/30186) and *Arusha Express*, which runs two daily services to Malindi. As for **matatus**, most destinations are served from the main stage, with the exception of Embu (at the western end of Moi Avenue) and Tharaka, a little-visited district dominated by a series of dammed reservoirs on the Tana River.

For **eating**, Meru will treat you well, at little expense. *Ivory Springs Café* is the friendliest place and has excellent samosas and passion juice (it may also have rooms in future); the *Springboard Café*, opposite the *KCB*, does good snacks; and opposite the cavernous *Continental Hotel* (a real drinkers' bar even for breakfast) is *African Restaurant*, a butchery and *nyama choma* joint; also recommended for *nyama choma* is the *Standview* on Moi Avenue, with its first-floor balcony. There's a fresh milk bar next to the *KCB* bank, and a supermarket – the *Self-Choice* – 2km up the Nanyuki road at the upper end of town.

In keeping with its market-town functions, Meru has no shortage of **accommodation**. If you have transport, there are a few places to consider even before you arrive.

LODGINGS ON THE NANYUKI/MAUA ROADS

Greenland Lodge, 3km from town on the Maua road (PO Box 2065; ☎0164/20409). A "country club" venture with flimsy and overpriced cabins, but the swimming pool is worth dropping in for. They'll make good (tourist-priced) meals if you're passing through, and allow you to use the showers. Unfortunately, "No Picnics" probably also means no camping, though you could ask. ③.

Moran Hotel Meru, 7km out of town on the Nanyuki road (PO Box 1200; ☎0164/244387). Another "country club" which has clearly seen better times – there's a haunted feel about the empty smoke-filled dining rooms. The pool's pump is currently broken, and it's rather damp, and overpriced. ④.

Nanyuki Guest House, some way out of town on the Maua road (PO Box 211; ☎0164/20677). Cheap, clean and very acceptable B&L. ①.

Rocky Hill Inn, some 8km out of town on the Nanyuki road. An ornate construction with chalets among pseudo-Japanese gardens; it has no proper water supply and is perhaps more a weekend *nyama choma* bar than anything else, but for all that it's endearingly weird (beware the "soup trees") and astonishingly cheap. ①.

LODGINGS IN TOWN

Brown Rock Hotel, overlooking Makutano stage and its market (PO Box 247; ☎0164/20247). A large, new establishment with cool rooms, though some are a little dark; the rooms up front or higher up are best. Hot water on request. ②.

Hotel Castella (PO Box 78; ☎0164/20873). Basic B&L. ①.

Continental Hotel & Bar (PO Box 133; ☎0164/30755). Just a little more inviting than the *Castella*, rowdy and very local. ①.

Meru County Hotel (PO Box 1386; ☎0164/20427). Fairly upmarket and metropolitan place. Bright rooms with balconies, a video lounge and good snack bar. ④.

New Milimani Hotel. A long haul back up the hill, but better than the *Stansted*. Rooms here are decent and the menu long (specialities are curries and *kinyeji*, the Meru version of *irio*). It's also the cheapest place with safe parking in town. Lively at weekends, when there are discos – but dead during the week, when it's deserted. ③.

Pig and Whistle (PO Box 1809; ☎0164/20433). Without doubt the best place in town and well worth the price. Well-appointed individual cottages (concrete or wood), all with telephones and baths, set in pleasant, shaded grounds. The hotel lounges and bar are wooden, with creaking floor-boards, and there's an inescapable atmosphere of colonial langour. Affordable menu, and *nyama choma* joint in gardens. ③.

Stansted Hotel, just over 1km up the hill from the main *matatu* stage (PO Box 1337; ☎0164/20360). Some decent enough rooms, some not; some hot water, but generally overpriced and not particularly friendly. ③.

Embu and district

From Meru to Embu the new (and regrettably fast) road swoops around the eastern slopes of Mount Kenya through brilliant, vibrant scenery. Five kilometres south of Meru you cross the **equator** once again. Hundreds of streams – run-off from luxuriant rainfall blown in by the southeast monsoon – cut deeply into the volcanic soil of this eastern flank. As a result, this side of the mountain has a much broader covering of jungle, which extends, *shambas* permitting, down to the level of the road and beyond. You plunge from one green and tan gorge to the next, and whether you enjoy the magnificent landscape or not depends on whether you dare take your eyes off the road. If you take the early-morning bus (slow, and considered safe), you can relax and admire. Sit on the right side for glimpses of snow-capped peaks, normally visible at this time of day.

Most public transport stops at **Chogoria**, a base for the eastern Mount Kenya ascent (see p.171), although if you're staying overnight you might consider continuing to the livelier (and friendlier) market town of **CHUKA**, which has a bank with exchange facili-

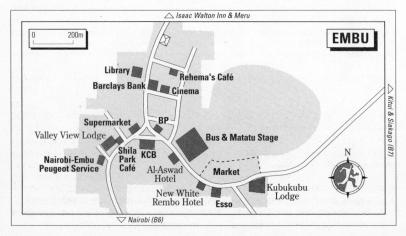

ties and the *Farmer's Lodge Hotel* (PO Box 394; ☎302885; ③). In order to climb Mount Kenya from Embu, you'll need to get yourself over to *Castle Forest Lodge* and the Kamweti route (see p.162).

Thuchi River Lodge

If you have independent transport, or don't mind walking the 3km from the main road, there's an interesting **accommodation** option to investigate on this side of the mountain in the shape of *Thuchi River Lodge*, an establishment left over from the road-building exploits of the French company *Kier*, who constructed the road from Kangonde to Embu and built their own accommodation (PO Box 4, Runyenjes; ☎0161/62101; ③). It has a pool (currently undergoing repairs), squash courts and nice bathrooms. Located a few hundred metres above the Thuchi river, it's exactly 27km south of Chogoria (29km north of Embu), then 3km south of the main road along the E652 track to nowhere.

Embu town

EMBU, like Meru, is situated at the bottom of a hill: at any rate, the town begins high and descends, with your expectations, to the centre. There's very little to get excited about here, though there's talk of a museum – one day. It's not obvious why it was chosen as the capital of Eastern Province. Certainly, without the apparatus of a provincial headquarters, Embu would amount to little.

There is **accommodation**, however, should you need or want to spend the night here. The *Izaac Walton Inn*, at the top end of town on the way in from Meru (PO Box 1, Embu; ☎0161/20128–9; ⑤ room only), is pleasant, if a little overpriced. You can get a very satisfying buffet breakfast here for about Ksh120. In the centre, the cheaper *Valley View Lodge* (PO Box 563; ☎0161/30369; ③) is the best in town: rooms are fresh, with nets, there's hot water daily and it's the only hotel with safe parking. *Kubu Kubu*, on the Kitui road, has small, clean and comfortable rooms, and a lively bar playing blues and funk and serving cool fried chicken (PO Box 180; ☎0161/20191; ②). The *New Rembo* is a cheap, though slightly run-down, B&L for singles only (PO Box 934; ☎0161/20647; ①); the *Al-Aswad* (PO Box 664; ☎0161/20679; ①) is preferable thanks to its popular restaurant, but it's not especially clean, and it's best to demand a room with a lock.

Rehema's café, a little way up the hill, is a busy **eatery**, well known for excellent spicy samosas; and the spotlessly clean, Somali-run *Zamzam Hotel* serves sweetly spiced pilau and *mataha* (rice, maize, beans, vegetables and potatoes all mashed together and eaten with beef). At weekends, *Owood Annexe* on the B6 Nairobi road, 3km out of town, has local **live music**.

Onwards from Embu

An alternative to the two-hour trip straight **back to Nairobi** (the *Kensilver* bus is fast and safe; *Akamba's* twice-daily run is slower and safer still) is to head on – past the huge Tana reservoirs, the Mwea National Reserve and the Mwea rice scheme (a major resettlement area for landless farmers, supported in part by Japanese NGOs and companies). The **Mwea National Reserve** is accessible, in theory, all year round from Mavuria via the Kamburu Dam, but the bridge over the Thiba River on this route is often down. The other way to the reserve, from Kaewa via Masinga Dam, is strictly a dry-season route only, and liable to be impassable at any time. There's a **lodge** at the dam, overlooking the reservoir and Mount Kenifdear (④). Whichever way you get there, the Mwea Reserve can be well worth the effort. You need a tent and, once you've paid fairly nominal entry fees, you can camp either by the main gate, which is not brilliant, or near the shore of the dam lake itself, which usually is. It's a beautiful, peaceful area with a wealth of ornithological interest and crocs and elephants often in evidence.

Bypassing Mwea, on the newly surfaced B7 road between Embu and Kangonde (the latter a small centre on the Garissa highway where you'll swiftly get transport back to Thika or Nairobi) you'll have to rely on fairly infrequent *matatus*. If you cross the highway, however, and continue southwards, traffic onwards to Kitui (p.290) and then back to Machakos (p.288) is heavier. Continue south from Kitui on the same B7 and you eventually reach Kibwezi, half-way down the Mombasa highway.

There's also an intriguing alternative travel option out of Embu – the **Kiangombe Hills**, described next.

Siakago and the Kiangombe Hills

The main centre of the **Kiangombe Hills**, Siakago, can be reached from Embu by *matatu* five or six times daily, in all conditions except the worst rains. The relatively modest altitudes of the Kiangombes (Kiangombe peak is 1804m) aren't enough to lure climbers – even those willing to go off the beaten track. But the hills, upstaged by Mount Kenya, and ignored by tourists and travellers, are emphatically worth a visit if you retain a romantic view of the world. Recent reports suggest you are required to take a guide, organized by writing ahead to the Embu Forest Office, PO Box 2, Embu.

The hills are the home of the **Mbere**, related to the Kikuyu, Embu and Meru. The Mbere have a reputation in Kenya as possessors of magical powers. Some villages have elderly sages, **Arogi**, credited with terrifying abilities; though others – the **Ago** – have more beneficent gifts like the ability to foretell the future or find missing goats.

Information is hard to come by; local people either laugh or look blank when directly questioned about such "unprogressive" activities. Numerous cups of tea and endless slices of bread and *Blueband* elicited the story from one local man that a village called Uba-Riri was a place where the *Ago* were active; but he couldn't quite remember where it was, and if he had pointed the way, he explained, legend had it he would have lost the finger he pointed with.

Yet the *Ago* do make their existence known at critical times, as in 1987 when their bush fires are said to have brought on the delayed rains. And the forest rangers on the hills threaten poachers and illegal firewood-cutters with *Arogi* medicine to make their teeth fall out – witchcraft comes to the aid of conservation!

The identity of these "witches" – at best a hazy and mysterious one which people aren't in any hurry to talk about – is further confused by the supposed existence in the hills of a race of **"little red men"** whose small size (estimated at 1.2m) and fleeting appearance and disappearance in the bush have led the odd, dreaming scientist to suppose that they might be australopithecines – ape-men hanging on into the twentieth century in their remote forest tracts. They, and the *Ago-Arogi*, may be just part of the "old people" mytho-history of central Kenya, which is at least partially based on the real, ancient and probably Cushitic-speaking peoples of two thousand or more years ago.

Such, anyway, are the stories that might draw you from Embu. If you've ever entertained thoughts of seeing a Bigfoot, or a Yeti, or the Loch Ness Monster – and if you kept an eye open for Nandi bears near Eldoret (see p.260) – it's an interesting trip.

Siakago

A bumpy thirty kilometres from Embu, **SIAKAGO** is a one-street town with a few *dukas*, one B&L, a market (main days Thursday and Friday), a *matatu* terminus and a large Catholic mission set amid the huts and *shambas* on the outskirts. Siakago isn't a ki-Mbere word and its derivation is uncertain. It may well have derived from "Chicago", along with a group of American anthropologists who based themselves here in the 1930s and started the ape-men stories.

The anthropologists were appalled at the **poverty** of the district, whose soil barely supports the population with corn and sorghum and sustains only the scrappiest *shambas* of cotton and tobacco as cash crops: their plan was to relocate the Mbere to better land, a recommendation fortunately never acted upon. The Mbere are still living a tenuous existence, but after the horrific famines and cholera outbreaks of the early 1980s, when the district's proximity to well-off Embu meant that they were largely overlooked, conditions have begun to improve.

In **practical terms**, the very cheap *Check Inn* provides the best accommodation and is a good base if you're going hiking. They have water and electricity thanks to the dam 25km back along the wires. *New Stanley's Hotel* has to be visited for its name and imaginative murals, if not for the rather limited menu.

The Kiangombe Hills

The Kiangombes rise behind Siakago town and look deceptively easy to **climb**. In fact, it's a stiff hike to the top. The main route approaches the summit area from the huts of the **forest rangers' station** beyond the village of Kune, 10km north of Siakago. You should pick up a guide at the forestry station, which usually has to be arranged the day before. Escorted, you can make it up to the peaks and down again in five or six hours, but it's better as a two-day trip, with a self-contained overnight camp in the hills. Out of Siakago, *dukas* are few and poorly stocked and there's no commercial accommodation.

MOUNT KENYA TO LAMU: THE CROSS-COUNTRY ROUTE

From the Mount Kenya region the obvious route to the coast is back to Nairobi, then down via Mombasa. It may be feasible, however, to strike out **east from the Mount Kenya ring road** and, using a combination of available public transport and foot-slogging, make for Mwingi, Garissa and Lamu. Beware, however, of getting yourself into unsafe territory: northeastern Kenya is full of people displaced by the Somali civil war. At the time of writing, Garissa and environs, and the Garissa–Lamu route were out of bounds. Read Chapter 7, "The North", and seek local advice.

The easiest departure point on the ring road is the small centre of Ena, 16km northeast of Embu. Ena is at the junction of the new highway with the old "Mate road" (after Bernard Mate, a member of the Kenya's pre-Independence Legislative Council), the circuitous C92 that used to be the route around the eastern side of the mountain until the tarred highway was completed.

Buses and *matatus* run fairly frequently east along the C92 from Ena to Ishiara, which has a few B&Ls. On Mondays or Tuesdays there's a bus from Ishiara to Katse. Otherwise, from Ishiara, it's a three-hour walk to the new concrete bridge over the **Tana River**, where there's a *hoteli* and a tailor and not a lot else.

Another three hours' hike downstream on the right bank brings you to Konyu, where you shouldn't have trouble finding somewhere to put up for the night. The primary school may oblige: there are stunning views from here when the air is clear.

You can now proceed by earth road, but on foot, around the **hills east of Konyu** (first head north, then turn back south) to Katse (at least two days); or else try to find companions in Konyu to walk with you on a more direct (six-hour) **short-cut route** to Katse along a watercourse over the baobab-tufted hills (highest peak Mt Mumoni, 1747m).

Katse has a pretty **lodging house** and a bus departure at 7am every morning down to Mwingi, on the A3 Nairobi–Garissa highway – only a sixty kilometre run but it takes hours. You should be able to get to Garissa the same evening and Lamu the next evening.

This is an interesting route to take, virtually unheard of, full of rewarding encounters and unexplored districts and wilderness. If you plan on walking much of the first part of the route, allow a week for the whole trip. Again, see Chapter 7 first.

There's no transport between Siakago and Kune, so you'll probably have to find your way on foot (unless you're driving), asking as you go. The walk should take about three hours. Once at the forestry station (thirty minutes' hike beyond Kune), ignore the vehicle track which winds into the hills; it's no longer used and soon becomes difficult to follow. Instead, use the **footpath** leading straight up from behind the huts. At any time but the end of the dry season much of your way is likely to be impeded by thick vegetation. If you're alert to every photographic possibility, you'll find that concentrating on following the overgrown trail is tiresome – especially without a *panga* to trail-blaze with. As you climb, human population quickly thins out; this is red-people territory and traditionally feared by the Mbere.

About four hours' hiking from the forest station you reach the peaks area. From the **mountain meadows** just below the forested peaks you can look back over the lower hills and down to the hut- and *shamba*-specked plains beyond. With luck, Mount Kenya and the Aberdares can be seen poking through their respective cloudy wreaths. But you may need help from an *Ago*, as well as luck, to see one of the little red people.

AROUND THE ABERDARES

The **Aberdare Range**, which peaks at 4000m, is less well known than Mount Kenya. The lower, eastern slopes have long been farmed by the Kikuyu (more recently by European tea and coffee planters), and the dense mountain forests covering the middle reaches are the habitat of leopard, bongo, buffalo and some six thousand elephant. Above about 3500m, lions and other open-country animals roam the cloudy moorlands. Melanistic forms – especially of leopard, but also of serval cat and even bushbuck – are also present.

The Kikuyu called these mountains *Nyandarua* ("drying hide", for their silhouette) long before Thomson in 1884 named them after Lord Aberdare, president of the Royal Geographical Society. In their bamboo thickets and tangled forests, **Kikuyu guerrillas** hid out for months and years in the 1950s, living off the jungle and surviving thanks to techniques learned under British officers during the Burma campaign in World War II, in which many of them had fought. Despite the manhunts through the forests and the bombing of hideouts, little damage was done to the natural habitat and Aberdares National Park remains one of Kenya's most pristine forest reserves.

On the western side, the range drops away steeply to the Rift. It was here, in the high **Wanjohi Valley**, that a concentration of settlers in the 1920s and 1930s created the myth of **Happy Valley** out of their obsessive – and unsettled – lives. There's not much to see (or hear) these days. The old wheat and pyrethrum farms were subdivided after Independence and the valley's new settlers are more concerned with making their market gardens pay. The memories live on only among veteran *wazungu*.

The Kinangop plateau (p.147) was settled by Europeans, too, but the high forest and moorland here was declared **Aberdares National Park** in 1950. The park, which stretches 60km along the length of the peaks, with the "Treetops Salient" on the lower slopes reaching out east, includes, like Mount Kenya National Park, the worst of the weather. Rainfall up here is high, often closing the Aberdares to vehicles in the wet season, although the "tree-hotel" game lodges – *The Ark* and *Treetops* – stay open all year. Somewhat inaccessible, the park is nevertheless close enough to Nairobi to be well worth the effort of getting to **Naivasha** or **Nyeri**, the usual bases. You'll find less transport **travelling** in the lower Aberdares than around Mount Kenya, but it's still relatively easy to get around, with regular bus and *matatu* services between the villages. Heading over the mountains and **through the park**, however, **hitching** is the sole, very uncertain, option if you don't have a vehicle. Determination can pay dividends; but in this case, you could wait for days. If you're going to try, it's suggested you stop at the *Outspan Hotel* in Nyeri and try to arrange a lift. If you tire of this, *matatu*-hop your way towards **Ruhuruini Gate**, deep in the forest, and try waiting at the gate itself. This, like **Matubio Gate** on the Naivasha side (which you could also probably reach in a half-day of lifts and walking) is friendly and helpful and would certainly allow you to camp.

Nyahururu, the other important town in the region, has **Thomson's Falls** as a postcard attraction, and is also the setting-off point for a wild cross-country journey to Lake Bogoria in the Rift Valley, 1500m below (Chapter 3). From here, too, begins one of the four routes into the northern deserts (Chapter 7), in this case to Maralal and Loiyangalani on the eastern shore of Lake Turkana.

Aberdares National Park

Daily fees $27 per person, $10 students/children; $8 to camp, $15 in "special" campsites. Entry on foot with permission of the warden: PO Box 22, Nyeri; ☎0171/55024 or Mweiga ☎24.

If you're **driving into the park** (which is the only really practicable way to do it, other than taking a trip by safari van), you need four-wheel drive – it can rain at any time and the route across the mountains is sometimes closed during heavy rains. It's also a very sensible idea to have two spare wheels.

Once you're in, it's a beautiful drive, with waterfalls and sensational views more than compensating for comparatively scarce **wildlife**: buffalo, elephants (and colobus monkeys lower down) are most often seen. For animals in quantity, and for any real chance of seeing rhinos, giant forest hog, or the Aberdares' prize inhabitant, the bongo antelope, you really have to spend a night at one of the two **game-viewing lodges**, *The Ark* or *Treetops* – expensive perhaps, but not an experience you're likely to forget.

The only **accommodation** in the high park is the self-help *Kiandongoro Fishing Lodge*, located on open moors above the Magura River. There are two stone-built, tin-roofed cottages, each with three separate bedrooms of two, four and six beds. You book as much space as you need through the warden (or take a chance and pay at the park gate), and share the central open-fire cooking and eating area with other guests. You need to take everything with you except water – food, warm sleeping bags, firewood. Wood-fired boiler tanks outside will produce hot water. Sadly, rumours abound of its imminent closure – check at the park gates or with the authorities in Mweiga (PO Box 24). Near the *Fishing Lodge*, the basic *Reedbuck Campsite* is the only public site in the park; there are a number of "special campsites", but these are very expensive (Ksh5000 reservation fee, plus $15 per person per night), are equally bereft of facilities and were, in any case, closed until recently and may close again in future. Your last camping option is to be accompanied by an armed ranger.

The high moorlands have some exceptional **walking** and the three peaks – Satima (the highest) in the north, Kinangop in the south, and Kipipiri, an isolated cone outside the park above the Wanjohi Valley, in the west – can be climbed relatively easily, given good weather conditions: ask the *Mountain Club of Kenya* in Nairobi for details. Hiking in the park is allowed only with the approval of the warden, so apply in good time. You may be offered, or required to take, a guide (whom you'll have to pay). If you drive, it's usually permissible to wander a short distance from your car. The situation changes from time to time: over the years there have been a number of near-misses with several, apparently human-hungry, lions.

Road conditions vary considerably from one period of heavy rain to the next. Early in 1993, the northen route from Chania Falls to Wanderis Gate was impassable, while the southen circuit, including the Ruhuruini track, was in excellent shape. Surfaces are mostly red murram, though there are a few, very steep, rocky sections.

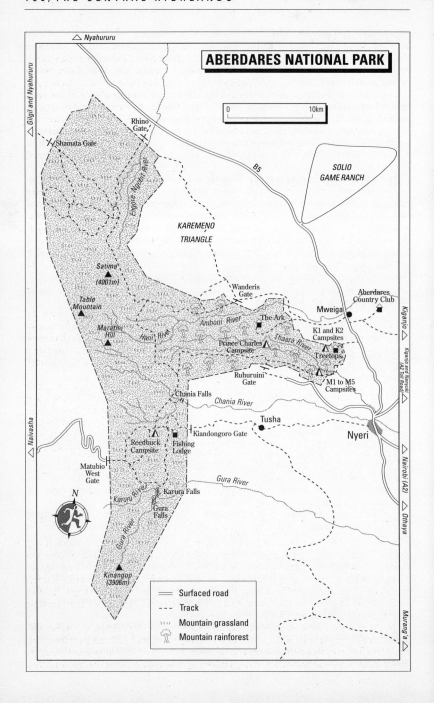

△ Nyahururu

ABERDARES NATIONAL PARK

0   10km

Rhino
Gate

Shamata Gate

Engore Napoti River

B5

SOLIO
GAME RANCH

KAREMENO
TRIANGLE

Satima
(4001m)

Table
Mountain

Maratni
Hill

Hani River

Amboni River

Wanderis
Gate

The Ark

Prince Charles
Campsite

Thaara River

Aberdares
Country Club

Mweiga

K1 and K2
Campsites

Treetops

Ruhuruini
Gate

M1 to M5
Campsites

Chania Falls

Chania River

Tusha

Kiandongoro Gate

Nyeri

Reedbuck
Campsite

Fishing
Lodge

Matubio
West Gate

Gura River

Karuru River

Karura Falls

Gura
Falls

Gura River

N

Kinangop
(3906m)

△ Gilgil and Nyahururu

Naivasha

Kiganjo

Kiganjo and Nanyuki (A2 Toll Road) ▷

Nairobi (A2) ▷

Othaya ▷

Murang'a ▷

Surfaced road
Track
Mountain grassland
Mountain rainforest

Through the park

The park splits into two different environments – the **high moorland and peaks** which form the park's main body, and the lower **Salient** to the east where the vegetation is dense rain forest and there is considerably more wildlife. The Salient slopes (location of *Treetops* and *The Ark*) are closed to casual visitors; all the earth access roads have locked barriers. You can get keys to these, in theory, from the warden in Mweiga, or possibly from the rangers at the eastern gates (but not from Matubio Gate in the west).

The government recently pledged to establish a wholly enclosed **rhino sanctuary** in this area, and to this end the rangers are currently busy clearing a path on which to erect some 270km of electrified fence. More information on the project can be obtained from *Rhino Ark* (PO Box 32879, Nairobi; ☎02/749655).

Unless you're planning several days of walking, fishing or camping, the most straightforward visit to the moorlands is to take a day driving through from one side to the other between the main gates. There are two other eastern gates further from Nyeri (Wanderis and Kiandongoro) and two at the remote north end of the park (Shamata, accessible from Nyahururu; and Rhino Gate, from the B5 Nyeri–Nyahururu road), but there's no reliable route through the park from south to north, and the small circuit of tracks in the north is very rough. Driving via the park from Naivasha to Nyeri (or vice versa) is easy enough in good weather. If conditions are less than ideal, however, and you get stuck, you could be in for a long day – or a rather miserable night.

Naivasha to Matubio Gate

From Naivasha, follow the signs for the park via the Uplands road as if going to Nairobi, as far as the junction for Kinangop on the north side of town. From here, you climb about 14km, on reasonably intact tarmac, to another junction where the bad road begins. Go easy if you're driving: the cambered, rock-built surface is perfect for punctures. After another 5km or so you reach Kipipiri junction and, seasonally, a strange egret nesting colony in eleven conifers along the roadside.

At **Ndunyu Njeru** centre you pass the last chance of a puncture repair or petrol (fuel isn't always available) and the final stop of *matatus* up from Naivasha, before a few more kilometres of very bad surface. Finally the road runs out of reasons to continue except to the national park itself – becoming a narrow, quite acceptable, tarmac switchback that is apparently forty years old – and climbs through the vegetation zones, with increasing evidence of elephants (dung everywhere), to pitch out finally through the highest extent of the forest to Matubio Gate, right on the threshold of the moorland. Along the last seven kilometres there are some excellent views back over the climb and down to Lake Naivasha. Allow two to three hours to get this far.

Matubio Gate to Ruhuruini Gate

Allowing four hours from Matubio Gate to Ruhuruini Gate gives time enough, in good weather, for visits to the Chania Falls and the Karuru Giant Falls.

Proper access to the top of the **Karuru Falls** (there's no way down to the bottom) was only built in 1992, by the British Army's Royal Engineers, and they've created two superb, dizzy, timber viewpoints, one on each side, from which you can look across through dripping, afro-alpine vegetation, to the babbling, four-metre-wide Karuru stream as it plunges over the abyss, dropping nearly 300m in three stages. To the south, the distant veil of the **Gura Falls**, a kilometre or two across the yawning canyon, seems to make for a surfeit of dramatic beauty.

The much lower, sheer drop of the **Chania Falls** has old, rickety access walks and platforms (be very careful if they have not been replaced) and you can gaze from the top, or the bottom, and even contemplate a swim in the pool. It was in this vicinity in 1984 that an American tourist was badly mauled by a lion, an incident that so unnerved the park's authorities that they have only recently relaxed the rules on unaccompanied walking. This followed a controlled lion cull, aimed as much at public relations as at giving various herbivores (such as giant forest hog and bongo) a chance to rebuild their endangered populations. A cautionary sign by the path still warns about "wild animals", though there seems no reason to believe they favour this spot over any other.

Turning east, the fifteen kilometres to **Ruhuruini Gate** descends in a breathtaking helter skelter through the cloud forest, with stunning views across the jungle-cloaked valleys. Once out of the gate, the road down to Nyeri is in good condition and you soon reach tarmac.

Nyeri and around

Self-styled capital of Kikuyuland – a title the Kikuyu of Kiambu might dispute – **NYERI** is, more prosaically, the administrative headquarters of Central Province and one of the liveliest highland towns. Another former military camp, it emerged as a market town for European coffee growers in the hills and for settlers on the ranching and wheat farms further north. Located beneath the Aberdares, it was on the front line – as much as there was one – during the war for Independence. Of more specialist interest, Nyeri was also the last home of Robert Lord **Baden-Powell**, founder of the worldwide scouting movement, whose cryptically named *Paxtu* cottage, now a small museum (Ksh50), stands in the grounds of the *Outspan Hotel* and whose grave and memorial are to be found on the north side of town.

An active, and attractive, trading centre, Nyeri nestles in the green hills where the broad vale between Mount Kenya and the Aberdares drops towards Nairobi. Tumultuous markets, dozens of *dukas*, and even a few street entertainers playing on soda bottles and bottle tops, lend it an air of irrepressible commercialism.

The Outspan

Nyeri's role as rural business centre and major transport crossroads means there are plenty of **places to stay**. Foremost is the *Outspan Hotel* (PO Box 24; ☎0171/2424; reservations through *Block*, see p.48), twenty minutes' walk, or a short taxi ride, from the town centre. *The Outspan*, set in beautiful gardens, with Mount Kenya rising like a backdrop behind, is the stately base for all visits to *Treetops*. If you're booked to spend a night at "the hotel in the trees", you check in here for lunch and are driven up in the afternoon. *The Outspan* has huge rooms with wonderful old baths (rooms 11, 12, 14, 24, 26, 31, 33 and 35 are apparently the ones to target; B&B ⑤ low, ⑦ high). If you don't stay, you'll be very welcome in any case for a meal there, or for tea on the lawn and a swim in the pool (Ksh100). Breakfast and buffet lunch are expensive – worth every shilling and highly recommended, especially if you've just walked down Mount Kenya. There are some good walks along the Chania River bank down on the fringes of the lovely gardens, though you have to go with a guard from the hotel (Ksh150, or Ksh300 for a bird walk). The hotel's *Kirinyaga Bar* has good fish and chips, and is pleasant enough for a beer in the evening in civilized surroundings, but it's not a hugely stimulating night out. With the right approach, though, you might find yourself a lift over the Aberdares – but ask early in the day, when people would be setting off, rather than later.

Lodgings and restaurants in town

Plenty of **accommodation** can be found, more sparingly than at the *Outspan*, in the town centre, and there are some interesting alternatives for **eating**, too. Note that Nyeri also has a **cheese** factory: lots of its produce is available locally.

Bahati Restaurant & Lodging, Kimathi Way (PO Box 148; ☎0171/2312). A good B&L, well known for its chicken. ②.

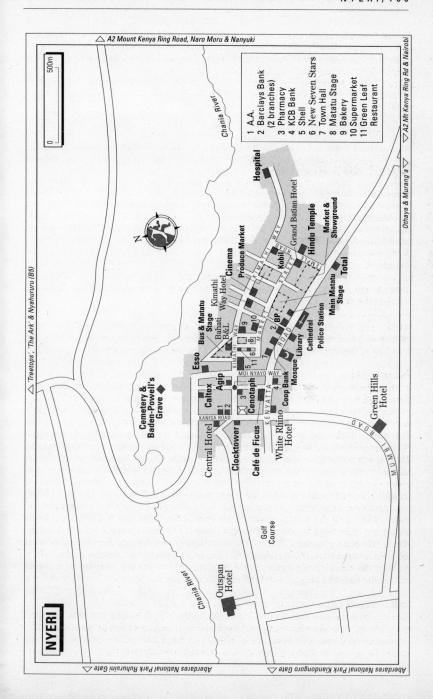

NYERI

△ A2 Mount Kenya Ring Road, Naro Moru & Nanyuki

◁ 'Treetops', 'The Ark' & Nyahururu (B5)

▷ A2 Mt Kenya Ring Rd & Nairobi

▽ Othaya & Murang'a ▷

▽ Aberdares National Park Kiandongoro Gate

▽ Aberdares National Park Ruhuruini Gate

500m

0

1 A.A.
2 Barclays Bank
  (2 branches)
3 Pharmacy
4 KCB Bank
5 Shell
6 New Seven Stars
7 Town Hall
8 Matatu Stage
9 Bakery
10 Supermarket
11 Green Leaf
   Restaurant

Chania River

Chania River

Cemetery &
Baden-Powell's
Grave

Outspan
Hotel

Golf
Course

Central Hotel

Clocktower

Café de Ficus

White Rhino
Hotel

KANISA ROAD

Caltex

Agip

Cenotaph

Coop Bank

Mosque

Esso

Bus & Matatu
Stage

Bahati
B&L

Kimathi
Way Hotel

Cinema

Produce Market

Hospital

MOI NYAYO WAY

KENYATTA

MARKET ROAD

KIMATHI ROAD

KIMATHI WAY

Library

Police Station

Cathedral

BP

Kobil

Grand Batian Hotel

Hindu Temple

Market &
Showground

Main Matatu
Stage

Total

TEMPLE ROAD

MUMBI ROAD

Green Hills
Hotel

Batian Grand Hotel (PO Box 12465; ☎0171/4494). An excellent new place with a good bar and safe parking, but expensive. ⑤.
Central Hotel, Kanisa Rd (PO Box 446; ☎0171/4233). Clean, pleasant and good value, with a restaurant. ③.
Green Hills Hotel, Mumbi Rd (PO Box 313; ☎0171/30709). The biggest hotel with the best facilities in town (*Outspan* excepted) and discos on Wed, Fri and Sat. ④.
Greenleaf Restaurant (PO Box 2169; ☎0171/2126). Fairly decent s/c rooms with hot water. The bar has great views over the street corner, and the restaurant has great trout and *nyama choma*. ②.
Kimathi Way Motel (PO Box 2188; ☎0171/2799). A cheap lodging, with filling meals, but noisy (especially at weekends) and not terribly clean. ②.
Msafiri Hotel. A decent, budget *hoteli*. Try a "half dinner" – an enormous plateful for next to nothing.
New Seven Stars Lodgings, off Kimathi Way (PO Box 316; ☎0171/2817). Very cheap, and with hot water, but get there early to be sure of a room. ②.
Nyeri Cinema. Beer garden and restaurant, *nyama choma banda*, and an ice cream parlour, now taken over by the *Batian Grand Hotel*.
Nyeri Coffee House. Run by the Coffee Board of Kenya and serving a good brew.
Seremai Hotel. The place to fuel up on *mandaazi*.
White Rhino Hotel, Kenyatta Rd (PO Box 30; ☎0171/30934). A laid-back atmosphere and *the* place for conscientious boozing. Reasonable rooms, nice gardens. ④.

Treetops

Reservations for Treetops through Block Hotels (see p.48). Minimum age 10 years (no child rates but enquire about occasional "children's nights"); HB ⑨. Aberdares National Park entry fees are extra ($27 each).

Having invested heavily for a night in **Treetops**, and the opportunity to breathe the same air as the rich and/or famous, you might, in retrospect, wish you'd spent your money on a night at the *Outspan Hotel* instead. After the hype from the Nairobi tourism machine, *Treetops* is at first a disappointment. The lodge is no longer *in* the forest. The original tree house was looted and burned down in 1955: the present, much larger building is built on stilts among the trees. Down by the **water hole**, a large area is now virtually bare – red dust and dead wood – the result of foliage destruction by elephants. One patch has even been fenced in, presumably to protect new plant growth.

The problem, as always, is balancing tourist receipts with the needs of wildlife – which already conflict with those of farmers on the slopes nearby. Many of the animals that come to *Treetops* are lured by the **salt** which is spread beneath the viewing platform every afternoon before the visitors arrive. This draws large herds of elephant and buffalo, but in the long term seems to ensure the ruination of the environment around the lodge and certainly discourages those animals that need plenty of forest cover.

Inevitably rather contrived, the lodge itself is tremendous fun, with growing branches of cape chestnut twisting through the public rooms. But the bedrooms are tiny, and with shared bathrooms. What you pay for is the experience of *Treetops*. Photographs and letters framed on the varnished walls hark back to the 1930s, 40s and 50s, and various Royal and State visits. Famously, Princess Elizabeth became Queen Elizabeth II, on the death of her father King George VI, while she was staying in the original *Treetops* on the other side of the water hole. All this does instill a sense of elitism in some visitors.

With the creaking atmosphere of a wooden ship, and a dining room with trestle tables and polished benches – intentionally like an officers' mess – this million-dollar-a-year industry is the closest you'll get on a package tour to the exclusive way of "living bush". The fact that it's always booked solid, and not just by safari-suited tour groups, affirms its attraction, though this has to do partly with the other fact that you can't check it out beforehand; even if you could find the track up to the park gate, only the accompanied group with bookings is allowed in. Once there, the sense of illusion is never far below the surface. Through the forest, Kikuyu *shambas* and homesteads are visible in every direction; the main Nyeri road passes by just 3km away.

RECENT HISTORY

The extraordinary density of **cultivation** in the tightly spaced *shambas* around Nyeri (maize, beans, potatoes, cassava, bananas, sugar cane, millet, squash and melons, tomatoes, citrus fruit, cabbages and carrots, as well as tea, coffee and macadamia nuts) is partly a hangover of white settlerdom, when a rapidly growing population was deprived of huge tracts of land and forced to cultivate intensively. Partly, too, it's the result of land consolidation: the "rationalization" of fragmented land holdings into unitary *shambas* that took place in the 1950s and turned people who had held traditional rights into deed-holding property owners. And partly it's the simple consequence of an excellent climate and soil plus a birth rate reckoned (like Kisii's, p.253) to be one of the highest in the world.

There's no doubt that the **changes** which have taken place in Nyeri district have been some of the most profound and rapid anywhere in the country. Even the villages of Kikuyuland are nearly all innovations of the last forty years, the irreversible effects of The Emergency. Until then, the Kikuyu had mostly lived in scattered homesteads among their crops and herds. British security forces, unable to contain open revolt in the countryside, began the systematic internment of the whole Kikuyu population into fenced and guarded villages, forcing the guerrillas into the high forests. And the villages of today have mostly grown from such places.

On Nyeri's main street, Kimathi Way, is a cenotaph, unusual in the frankness of its inscription: *To the Memory of the Members of the Kikuyu Tribe who Died in the fight for Freedom 1951–1957.*

When the sun goes down and the floodlights come on, this can be forgotten; the wildlife below takes over and the cameras start clicking in earnest. Herds of heavy-weights can be taken for granted; **rhinos** are fairly common visitors and the curious **giant forest hog** sometimes turns up as well. But **leopards** are rarely seen and the large **bongo**, that "shy and elusive forest antelope", hasn't put in an appearance for many years – understandably.

The Ark and Aberdares Country Club

Reservations for The Ark through Lonrho (see p.49); minimum age 7 years (no child rates but enquire about occasional "children's nights"); ⑦ low, ⑨ high. Aberdares National Park entry fees are extra ($27 each).

For better game viewing, **The Ark**, *Treetops'* upstart competitor, is set at a higher altitude, actually in the mountain forest. Here, they do on occasion see leopard and bongo, though game viewing is only at night by a floodlit pool (you're woken by buzzers announcing the arrival of one of the "big five"). The accommodation has recently been comprehensively upgraded, though the rooms are disappointingly gloomy and cramped. *The Ark*'s base is the luxuriously rural *Aberdare Country Club* (PO Box 449, Nyeri; ☎0171/55620, fax 0171/55224; ⑦ low, ⑧ high) near **Mweiga**, on the road between Nyeri and Nyahururu. It's an exceptionally nice, atmospheric place, dating from 1938, with rooms in stone cottages (room numbers 28 to 31 have the best views). The temporary membership fee (Mon–Thurs Ksh200, Fri–Sun Ksh400) includes use of the pool and a visit to their game sanctuary with its comical warthogs. They also organize game drives.

Routes out of Nyeri – and Solio Game Ranch

A signposted route leads **west**, past the *Outspan*, up into the Aberdares and the park's Kiandongoro gate in the high moorland. In the other direction, the road splits out of town, forking **south** to Murang'a via Othaya, or continuing **east** to the A2 Mount Kenya ring road and the quickest return route to Nairobi.

A fourth route takes you in a northwest direction heading out of town, splitting in two after 2km. Keep straight on if you want the Mount Kenya ring road, northbound for Naro Moru and Nanyuki via Kiganjo. This, the A2, is a super new highway with a toll staion before Nanyuki.

Fork left and the road sweeps past the track for the Ruhurini Gate in the forest of the Treetops Salient, then the unmarked tracks for *Treetops* and *The Ark* – with the turning for the *Aberdares Country Club* between them, just before the hilltop centre of **Mweiga**. The highway continues, in excellent condition, across lonely, forested ridges and wide savannahs to Nyahururu (Thomson's Falls), on the northern fringes of the Highlands.

The private **Solio Game Ranch** (PO Box 30595, Nairobi; ☎02/763638 or locally ☎0171/55271) lies off this road to the north of Mweiga. Solio used to be one of the best places to see rhinos: many of the relocated rhinos at Nakuru National Park's Rhino Sanctuary were bred here. If you're independently mobile you could stop in and ask, but you will usually be referred to the *Aberdare Country Club* (see above) who handle bookings. Visits are then made in the estate's own vehicles. For a less conventional visit, the *Gliding Club of Kenya* operates from a field 2km south of Mweiga (☎0156/22467), with two-seater aircraft and instructors available to introduce you to the sport.

Nyahururu (Thomson's Falls)

Like Nanyuki, **NYAHURURU** is almost on the equator, and it shares much of Nanyuki's character. It is high (at 2360m, Kenya's highest town), cool (or very cold on January and February mornings), and set on open savannah lands with patches of indigenous forest and plenty of coniferous plantation. Since the fast, B5 road to Nyeri was completed, Nyahururu has been less cut off, but still there's an air of slightly wild isolation about it. It's something of a frontier town for routes heading north to Lake Turkana and the desert: a tarred road goes out as far as Rumuruti and then the fun begins (see p.460). Other roads join Nyahururu with Nanyuki (the C76; a dastardly bad road, but good for game viewing), Gilgil (p.198), and Nakuru and the remainder of the Northern Rift Valley (p.216).

Joseph Thomson gave the town its original name when he named the nearby waterfall after his father in 1883. Many still call it "T Falls" – and not just the old settlers you might expect. Thomson's Falls was one of the last settler towns to be established. The first sign of urbanization was a hut built by the Narok Angling Club in the early 1920s to allow its members to fish for the newly introduced trout in the Ewaso Narok, Pesi and Equator Rivers. In 1929, when the railway branch line arrived, the town began to take shape. The line has closed now, but the hotel built in 1931, *Thomson's Falls Lodge,* is still going strong, and Nyahururu remains an important market town – and not, in any sense, a tourist centre. Local people can react rather oddly to the presence of travellers in Nyahururu's lodging houses. If you're staying in town, be sensitive to the fact that some think you should stay in the lodge by the falls.

Thomson's Falls Lodge

For **accommodation**, most people do head out to the lodge (PO Box 38; ☎0365/22006, fax 0365/32170; reservations in Nairobi on ☎02/221855; B&B ⑤), which – so long as you're content with nothing fancy – is good value, with its solid, highlands-farmhouse atmosphere, log fires in the rooms and big old-fashioned baths. The dining room offers decent meals, a little over the odds, and a cheap snack menu. Nor does it feel remote from the life of the town itself, as it doesn't fill its rooms with mainstream package tourists. (It's a good place to spend Christmas, but book ahead.) Alternatively, you can **camp** in the grounds, still within earshot of the falls. The campsite (Ksh600), popular with budget safari groups, has *hot* showers (remind them at reception to turn on the heater) and ample firewood included in the price.

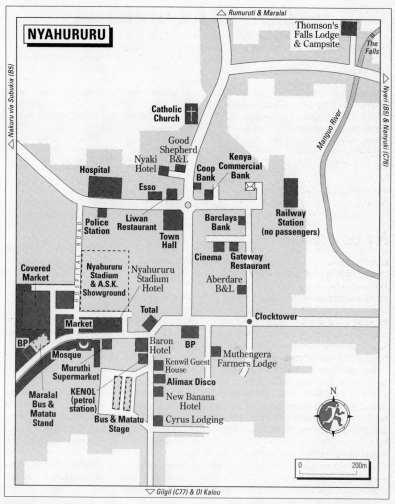

△ *Rumuruti & Maralal*

NYAHURURU

Thomson's Falls Lodge & Campsite

The Falls

△ *Nakuru via Subukia (B5)*

▷ *Nyeri (B5) & Nanyuki (C76)*

Manguo River

Catholic Church

Good Shepherd B&L

Nyaki Hotel

Kenya Commercial Bank

Coop Bank

Hospital

Esso

HOSPITAL ROAD

Police Station

Liwan Restaurant

Town Hall

Barclays Bank

Railway Station (no passengers)

Covered Market

Nyahururu Stadium & A.S.K. Showground

Nyahururu Stadium Hotel

Cinema

Gateway Restaurant

Aberdare B&L

Total

Clocktower

Market

BP

Mosque

Muruthi Supermarket

Baron Hotel

BP

Kenwil Guest House

Muthengera Farmers Lodge

Alimax Disco

Maralal Bus & Matatu Stand

KENOL (petrol station)

New Banana Hotel

Cyrus Lodging

Bus & Matatu Stage

N

0   200m

▽ *Gilgil (C77) & Ol Kalou*

Lodgings in town

If the rooms at the lodge are out of your price range and you don't have a tent, the next place down is something of a drop: the *Baron Hotel*, a "tourist-class" establishment on the Ol Kalou road (PO Box 423; 0365/32056; ④), suffers greatly from the *Alimax Disco* over the road and the *matatu* stand next door, the former jumping till 4am, the latter honking from 6am. Similarly overpriced is the *Nyaki Hotel* (PO Box 214; ☎0365/22313; ④), a newish apartment block with rather pokey self-contained rooms and safe parking; singles are much cheaper at Ksh200. A much better option is the friendly and clean *Nyahururu Stadium Hotel* (formerly *Manguo Lodge*; PO Box 152; ☎0365/22608; ②) by the *ASK* showground, above the *Karabui Gospel Music Store*; it also has good security. *The Good Shepherd*, in a traditional compound by the *Nyaki Hotel*, has singles only

THE MUSIC OF THE PREACHERMAN

Ever since Independence and the lifting of restrictions on religious groups, Kenya has become something of a free-for-all for the enterprising evangelical: Christian denominations in Kenya alone are said to number over a thousand. Nowhere is this fervid upsurge better evidenced than in Nyahururu, with its dozens of churches and gospel halls (some no more than someone's front room), religious bookshops, and hundreds of sermons, Biblical extracts and gospel choirs recorded on cassette and available on almost every street corner.

The choirs convene most days, whilst Sunday mornings resound to uplifting choruses from all parts of the town. Sunday also witnesses the descent of the itinerant preachermen, either at the stadium or at the *Total* garage roundabout, with their gesticulating sidekicks and rickety PA rigs. Their fiery sermonizing is full of vivid exhortations and threats of dire consequences, leavened with snippets of traditional dance music, which rouses the otherwise solemn crowd to leap and whirl in time with the rhythms. The posters announcing the coming of these zealots are cluttered with promises of redemption, miracles, even the cure of AIDS.

The more cynical say that it is only the music which attracts the crowds, so forget your cynicism, if only for a day, and follow your ears: you will be made more than welcome.

(Ksh140). Of the dozen or so other very basic B&Ls in town, the least squalid are the cheery yellow *Aberdare B&L*, *New Banana Hotel*, which has s/c singles only, and the noisy *Kenwil Guest House* and *Cyrus Lodging*.

For **meals**, *Liwan Restaurant & Café* (☎0365/32613; closed Sun) is the best: clean, quiet and cheap, with a patio shaded by white bottle-brush trees. For fried tilapia, try *Gateway Restaurant* by the cinema, whilst *Muthengera Farmers' Lodge* is recommended for chicken, a poultry replacement for its now sadly moribund bar. There's more meat at the *Nyaki Hotel*'s rooftop *nyama choma* joint and bar (order in advance); vegetarians should head for the *Cyrus*'s own restaurant, *Arafa*.

Whether eating out or not, the **market** is well worth a browse, especially on Saturdays. Find it anywhere west of the stadium – it sprawls out over most of the district, an indication of the town's rapid growth over the last decade or so.

For action **after dark**, check out *Alimax Disco*, the cause of insomnia at the *Baron Hotel*, with reggae and soukous (sometimes live) to midnight, and soul divas on tape thereafter. For more action in the dark, the **cinema** screens box office flops twice every evening, with an extra matinée on Sundays for those escaping church.

Thomson's Falls – and walks in the area

The Falls themselves are pretty rather than spectacular – though they can be pretty spectacular after heavy rain. They're a popular stop-off for tourists travelling between Samburu and Maasai Mara game reserves (14 minibuses at one time is nothing), and the lawns above the falls get crowded with picnickers from town at weekends. At such times, the souvenir sellers on the cliff edge can be a pain. When the crowds leave, they're good company, if you want it. The town council has long been trying to evict them, though apparently not for any aesthetic reason, but in order to make room for the planned tourist pavilion of a local political heavy.

The path leading down to the bottom of the 75-metre falls is somewhat dangerous, especially when wet. But certainly don't attempt to climb up again by any other route because the cliffs are extremely unstable. With several hours to spare, you can search for a longer **walk** down into the forested valley, following the Ewaso Narok River. If you want to try this, cross the bridge first, then look for a way downstream. The spray-laden trees are shaken periodically by troops of colobus monkeys and, as on Mount Kenya, three-horned chameleons are always around if you look hard for five minutes. This area is also fruitful for ornithologists – recent sightings include a crowned eagle with a colobus monkey in its claws.

A much shorter stroll also takes you over the bridge and past the electricity substation, beyond which the first trail you come to leads to the top of a hill with a communications tower and a skeletal lookout post. Excellent views from here stretch south towards Ol Kalou and the marshy trough of Lake Ol Bolossat.

Another nearby stroll takes you in quest of the highest **hippos** in Kenya. Incredible as it seems, several hippos do live in the swampy area a kilometre or two back upriver above the falls. Directions: 1km from the turning off to the *Lodge* on the Nyeri road you come to a small cluster of *dukas* on the right. Walk down towards the houses closest to town and, about 300m from the road, you emerge by a large lake. Immediately by the access path the area is thick with reeds, but walk round the lake to the clump of trees and you can shin up one of these and select a natural observation platform. Sit and watch and you may see as many as six hippos.

Onwards from Nyahururu

There are several buses and *matatus* each day down to Nyeri, or you could hitch from outside the *Lodge*. The road was built, for most of its length, along a new route, so villages are few; for the most part it either bucks up and down across forested valleys or soars across immense plains of swaying grass. It's a fast road, not much used by heavy transport and still in good condition.

Nyahururu's other transport connections are mentioned below in "travel details". Remember the unsurfaced road to Nanyuki can be treacherous in wet weather. For a **spectacular change of scene**, take the road down the scarp to Nakuru, via the Subukia valley, following the route to Lake Bogoria described in Chapter Three.

travel details

BUSES AND MATATUS

Around Mount Kenya

Unless you have a specific destination in mind, simply **getting to the next town** on the circuit is always easy. Apart from the big lines, the country bus services act as shuttles between neighbouring towns. **Nyeri** is something of a break in this "chain" and you may need to rely on *matatus*. **Nanyuki–Nyahururu** and **Nanyuki–Isiolo** also have limited bus services. **Between Meru and Nairobi**, both *Akamba* and *Kensilver* are recommended.

Around the Aberdares

From **Nyahururu to Nyeri** and vice versa, take the daily service between Nakuru and Nairobi, via the *east* side of the Aberdares.

To Rumuruti and Maralal (see Chapter Seven): two daily buses, but the last through bus leaves at 11am (5–6hr).

To Gilgil: frequent country bus and *matatu* runs; some go on to Nairobi.

To the coast: **Mombasa** is the only feasible destination, given the insecurity along the old route to **Lamu**. *Arusha Express* run daily from **Meru**, bypassing Nairobi. Other services invariably call at the capital.

TRAINS

There is no longer a passenger service to any town in this chapter.

PLANES

Daily flights on *Air Kenya* from **Nyeri** (departs 9.55am) to **Nanyuki** (10min) and **Samburu Lodges** (30min more), returning same day. Return flight departs Nanyuki 11.30am for Nyeri and **Nairobi** (arrives 12.20pm). Daily flights on *Air Kenya* direct from **Nanyuki to Mara Lodges** at 10am (1hr 30min).

Forget about flying **Nyeri–Nanyuki** no matter what the circumstances: the airstrips are so close together and so far from the towns they serve that you could drive the 60-kilometre journey faster.

CHAPTER THREE

THE RIFT VALLEY

K enya's **Great Rift Valley** is only part of a continental fault system that runs six thousand kilometres clean across Africa from Jordan to Mozambique. Perhaps Kenya's most important topographical feature, it is certainly one of the country's great distinguishing marks, a human and natural divide. As such, it has come to be seen as a monumental valley of teeming game and Maasai herders, a trough of grasslands older than mankind. This image is not entirely borne out by reality. The valley certainly is spectacular, a literal rift across the country, with all the stunning panoramas and gaunt escarpment backdrops you could wish for, and the plains animals are still abundant in places (such sights as a cheetah with cubs crossing the main highway near Nakuru are possible); nevertheless, much of the game has been dispersed by human population pressure onto the higher plateaus to the southwest, and most of the Maasai nowadays live further south.

At least the Rift Valley's **historical influence** cannot be diluted. People have trekked down it, generation after generation, over perhaps the last two or three thousand years, from the wetlands of southern Sudan and the Ethiopian highlands. Some of these immigrants were the forefathers of the **Maasai**, who dominated much of the valley and its surroundings for several centuries before the Europeans arrived. Until the beginning of this century, they lived on both sides, and the northern **Ilaikipiak** group were a constant threat to caravans coming up from the coast. With European settlement, they were forced from their former grazing grounds in the valley's turbulent bottleneck and confined to the "Southern Reserve" for much of the colonial era. Although many have now returned to the valley, and many towns retain their ancient Maa names, the Maasai are at their most conservative and traditional in southern Kenya; hence more background is included in Chapter Five.

In **practical terms**, the part of the Rift Valley covered in this chapter offers several exceptional **lakes**, a couple of excellent fast roads, lots of spectacular twisting tracks, and some of the wildest country in central Kenya. (The southern regions of the Rift are covered in chapters One and Five; the north – Turkana – in Chapter Seven.) If you're at all interested in wildlife, especially birds, you'll find it a source of endless fascination, with wonderful **nature reserves** at **Lakes Nakuru** and **Bogoria**, and a freshwater ecosystem at **Baringo**.

Apart from **Nakuru** itself and the string of towns up the western escarpment (**Njoro**, **Elburgon**, **Molo**), the area covered in this chapter contains few places larger than a

ACCOMMODATION PRICE CODES			
Rates for a standard double or twin room. For a full explanation of these price codes, see p.46.			
① Under Ksh300	(under approx. £3.30/$5)	⑤ Ksh2000–4000	(£22/$33–£44/$67)
② Ksh300–500	(£3.30/$5–£5.50/$8)	⑥ Ksh4000–6000	(£44/$67–£67/$100)
③ Ksh500–1000	(£5.50/$8–£11/$17)	⑦ Ksh6000–8000	(£67/$100–£89/$133)
④ Ksh1000–2000	(£11/$17–£22/$33)	⑧ Ksh8000–10,000	(£89/$133–£111/$167)
	⑨ Over Ksh10,000	(over £111/$167)	

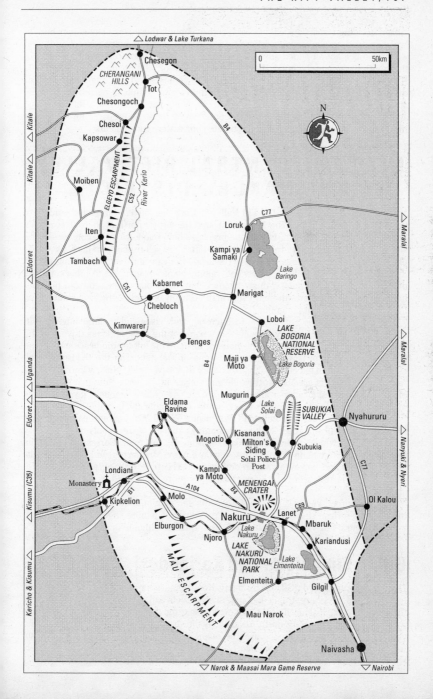

village: **lodgings**, strictly speaking, are scarce. Though there is usually somewhere to lay your head, this is a region where a **tent** will be worth its extra weight, and good walking shoes are an added advantage. **Transport** in the higher, agricultural parts of the south is generally good, but northwards, or off the main Nakuru–Baringo–Kabarnet axis, you can expect long waits, next to no buses and infrequent *matatus*. For **drivers**, the roads are steadily improving in this region, thanks in part to presidential favours earned: the B4 up to Baringo is superb. Note that the northern Rift is lower – and consequently hotter – than most up-country regions, so be prepared for some very **high temperatures** and don't underestimate your **water** requirements.

INTO THE CENTRAL RIFT VALLEY: THE NAKURU DISTRICT

Many travellers' first view of the Rift Valley is from the souvenir-draped shoulders of the **A104 Uplands road**. This barrels through the forests north of Nairobi, crosses a broad, bleak plateau, then flirts with the precipice before following the contours of the slopes above Naivasha and dropping into the Rift. They sell rhubarb up here, as well as plums, carrots and potatoes. In the wet season, you can find yourself driving over a thick, white carpet of hailstones between gloomy conifer plantations. All this contrasts dramatically with the endless, dusty plains below. With binoculars, you can pick out herds of gazelle, Maasai with their cattle and, bizarrely, a satellite-tracking station near the grey cone of Mount Longonot.

The Uplands road is a good one to hitch on, and buses and *matatus* often use it, although the latter, especially Nissans, have some of the most reckless drivers in the country, which is quite something; remember to sit on the left for the best views. If you have a car of your own, you can stop at some of the stands on the roadside: small sheepskins are often excellent value, but check they have been properly cured; the big woven grass baskets are also worthwhile and surprisingly cheap. Note that the last set of stands in the best location is also the most expensive. More seriously, if you are driving, treat this road as a continuous **black spot** – overtaking can be lethal.

The "**old road**", built by Italian POWs during World War II, runs parallel to and lower than the Uplands road; it's insanely bumpy and narrow and is only used by heavy goods vehicles which in theory are banned from the top road. Corresponding to its lower altitude, vegetation down here takes on a more Mediterranean aspect, candelabra euphorbia and spikey agave predominating. The little **chapel**, also Italian-built, seems fitting in this scene. Sadly neglected, it's more often used as a pit-stop picnic site.

Whichever road you use, you pass Naivasha and continue, on Kenya's contribution to the Trans-African Highway (a projected paved ribbon joining Lagos with Mombasa), into the Central Rift Valley – and the area around Lakes Elmenteita and Nakuru.

Gilgil, Elmenteita and Kariandusi

GILGIL – pronounced "Girgir" by many Kenyans – is as dull a town as you could expect to find anywhere: fragile-looking, dusty streets and shops and, on the outskirts, the serried, pastel-coloured ranks of new housing for the town's telecommunications workers. If you're heading north towards Nyahururu and Maralal, you may well find yourself hitching or changing buses or *matatus* here. The pretty rooms and clean, threadbare beds at the cheap *Salama Lodge* (PO Box 721; ☎03671/2102) can be safely recommended as probably the best in town, which in Gilgil is not saying much. Water

THE KALENJIN

In this part of the Rift Valley, the **Kalenjin** form the majority of the population. Their name, actually a recent adoption by a number of peoples speaking closely related languages, means "I tell you" in all of them. The principal Kalenjin are the Nandi, Terik, Tugen, Elgeyo, Elkony, Sabaot, Pokot, Marakwet and Kipsigis. They are some of the earliest inhabitants of Kenya and probably absorbed the early bushmen or pygmy peoples who were here for hundreds of thousands of years before.

Primarily **farmers**, the Kalenjin have often adapted their economies to local circumstances. It is supposed that the first Kalenjin were herdsmen whose lifestyle has changed over the centuries. The pastoral **Pokot** group, who still spurn all kinds of cultivation and despise peoples who rely on anything but livestock, call the **Marakwet**, living against the western Rift escarpment, *Cheblong* (the Poor), for their lack of cattle.

The **Okiek** are another interesting clue to the past: these hunter-gatherers are a Kalenjin-speaking people, living in scattered groups in the forests of the high slopes flanking the Rift. Unlike most hunter-gatherers, they do very little gathering. Meat, and honey from their hives, are the traditional staples. They consider wild fruits and vegetables barely palatable, though cornmeal and gardening have been introduced; and they now keep some domestic animals, too. They may be the descendants of Kalenjin forebears who lost (or ate) their herds: there are other groups in Kenya who live mostly by hunting – Ndorobo or Wanderoo – for whom such a background is very likely.

Many of the mainstream Kalenjin played key roles in the founding of the Kenya African Democratic Union (KADU – now disbanded), but the most famous of their number in recent years has been President Moi, a **Tugen** from Baringo district. Coming from a small ethnic group, his presidency for years avoided the accusations of tribalism levelled so bitterly against Kenyatta, and he still devotes time to touring the country, holding *Harambee* meetings and spurring development. In the run-up to the 1992 elections, however, what had long been muttered about became increasingly obvious: the country was not being run for the benefit of all. The president's firm grip on the reins of power was being exercised through the Kalenjin-dominated civil service rather than the more ethnically mixed cabinet. This fact, coupled with the "ethnic cleansing" in the Rift Valley of non-Kalenjin by groups of surprisingly well-organized young men (widespread evictions from Rift Valley villages, the burning of compounds and several hundred people killed) fulfilled the president's own prophecy that multi-partyism would do nothing to harmonize tribal relations in the country.

supplies seem problematic, but in Gilgil maybe you should just count your blessings. The town has a post office (Mon–Fri 8am–1pm & 2–5pm) and bank but not much of anything else.

Gilgil War Cemetery

En route to Nyahururu – "T Falls" if it slips off the tongue more easily – you'll pass **Gilgil Commonwealth War Cemetery**. If you've a couple of hours to spare, walk the two or three kilometres out of town into the quiet, breezy savannah and have a look: it's a good place to stop for a picnic and some moments of contemplation before flagging down a vehicle.

There are about two hundred graves here from the East African campaign of World War II and from the War for Independence – "the Emergency" – in the 1950s. Whether by accident (which doesn't seem credible) or design, the African graves are all at the bottom of the slope. They record no personal details apart from name and rank. The graves of British soldiers are higher up and the stones inscribed with family messages. Most are from World War II, but there are also poignant reminders of lives lost between 1959 and 1962, after the British government's futile attempt to prevent the inevitable (see p.508). The fact that not a single freedom fighter is buried here demonstrates the ambivalent attitude of Kenyans to their struggle for *Uhuru*. The Gilgil cemetery, one of over forty in Kenya tended by the Commonwealth War Graves Commission, is lovingly maintained, one of the most meticulously kept in the country.

The road climbs past *Gilgil Country Club* on through moorland and conifer plantations around the resettlement zone of Ol Kalou, where some of the most violent *Mau Mau* attacks took place, and over the equator to Nyahururu (p.177), Kenya's highest town.

Lake Elmenteita

Beyond the turn for Gilgil, the fast road sweeps the eastern wall of the Rift Valley and pushes up high above **Lake Elmenteita.** This soda lake, which shrivelled to a huge white salt pond as recently as 1985, is a good site for flamingoes, but rather expensive for a casual visit ($10 per person), since most of it is on private land and is part of the Delamere Estate's *Soysambu* property. The lake once had a herd of hippos, but the droughts have pushed them out. You can get a good view from the big "parking lane"

RIFT VALLEY SIDE TRACKS

Between Gilgil and Nakuru, if you're hiking – or driving or cycling with a few hours to spare – give the fast (but by no means smooth and occasionally unnerving) main A104 a miss and follow the tarmac **former route** which mostly runs parallel to the new road a few hundred metres off to one side. The old road, lightly potholed in parts, but quite negotiable, is almost unused by vehicles and serves as a rural footpath for people carrying firewood or cycling to the next hamlet.

You can join the old road at Gilgil by turning off the main highway, either at the police checkpoint or at the main junction. Go right through the quiet businesses and petrol stations of Gilgil and you arrive, 4km to the north of the town, at a fine viewpoint over Lake Elmenteita. Shortly after, on the right, you pass the obscure little **Church of Goodwill** – a settler's sentimental folly, by all appearances abandoned, though still locked and tended – in whose small graveyard rest the remains of a few old colonials and military men.

Shortly after the church, you pass Kariandusi prehistoric site and, rounding a bend, the diatomite mine (both left). Between the two, by the crash barriers to the right, a pale-coloured, rocky, 4WD track leads, in 3km, up over the railway line to a stream. Here you can leave your vehicle and climb (guided by the usual retinue of boys) to a crystal-clear, **warm water source** in the woods – known, blandly enough, as *maji moto*. You can swim in the natural swimming pool – there are usually people about, washing clothes or bathing. Beyond the Kariandusi junction, the old road dries up and you have to rejoin the highway. You can get onto the quiet road again at the turning to "Mbaruk", 3km further on, then follow the railway to Lanet, a suburb of Nakuru.

If you want to take further time out and see a remote part of the Central Province highlands, take a right turn off the old road, 4km after the "Mbaruk" turning and follow the steep dirt road under the railway bridge and steeply up to the **Mbaruk valley**. This is a beautiful road, rugged in parts (again, you're best off with 4WD) but with splendid compensation in the lush, forested cliffs across its far side. There's even a little **waterfall** 3km along the way, though it's easy to miss unless it's in spate. At the Ngorika crossroads (tasty *chapatis* at the *hoteli* on the corner) turn left and you hit the tarmac C69 after 6km, where, turning left again, you start to make a fine, looping descent to the Rift Valley floor, with distinctive flat-topped acacias between the sloping *shambas* and the glint of Lake Nakuru down in the distance.

To follow this route in the other direction, Nairobi-bound, take the left turning for the C69 immediately before the Lanet *Esso* petrol station, before you reach the railway bridge bend.

viewpoint – if you survive the rather desperate assaults from the curio sellers. And from this lay-by it's supposed to be possible to follow a track down to the lake. Clear it with anyone you come across down there. There are two newish establishments offering **accommodation** on the lakeshore: *Delamere Camp*, a luxury tented camp within the private **Soysambu Wildlife Sanctuary**, which is highly recommended for enthusiastic amateur naturalists (reservations thorugh *Delamere Camps Ltd*, Fedha Towers 2nd Floor, Standard St, PO Box 48019 Nairobi; ☎02/335935, fax 02/331191; ⑦ low, ⑨ high); and *Lake Elementeita Lodge* (PO Box 561 Nakuru; reservations through Arrow House, 2nd Floor, Koinange St, Nairobi; ☎02/224998; ⑦ low, ⑧ high), a slightly more affordable ranch-style place, built around the 1930s brick homestead of the cattle farmer Lord Cole, with spacious grounds overlooking the lake and its swathes of pink flamingoes. In its short life, the lodge's **restaurant** has already acquired a good reputation.

Around the once-lush shores are a number of prehistoric sites. **Gambles cave**, 10km southwest of Elmenteita village, is the most famous; if you're an enthusiast, you can visit it by making arrangements ahead of time – ask first at the National Museum in Nairobi.

Digs and mines: Kariandusi

For an easier shot of prehistory, try a no-fuss visit to **Kariandusi**, with a surprising sideshow in the shape of a neighbouring diatomite mine. Kariandusi (signposted 1.5km right, 20 minutes' walk from the highway; daily 8am–6pm; Ksh200) is an **Acheulian site** characterized, like Olorgasailie (p.151), by heavy hand-axes and cleavers. The site is very small, consisting of just two excavated areas cleared by Louis Leakey in 1928, each displaying a scattered assortment of stone tools, many of them made of the black glassy volcanic rock, obsidian.

Neither Kariandusi nor Olorgasailie have any signs of permanent habitation and it's been suggested that they were simply **butcheries**, places where the kill was habitually portioned off and consumed, the tools made on the spot and left for the next occasion. But the tools are far from left untouched since they were carefully exposed by Leakey; the obligatory guide will casually pass you various stone tools to hold. Nothing much is known about the tool-makers – apart from the fact that they obviously had a formidable grip – but a likely candidate is **Homo erectus**, a primitive early hominid whose remains have been found at Olduvai Gorge in Tanzania alongside Acheulian artefacts.

The diatomite industry

Even if you look around the tiny museum, half an hour is plenty of time at Kariandusi. However, right next door, just 800m from the highway, is a **diatomite mine** (Diatomite Industries, PO Box 32 Gilgil; ☎03671/2097), which is a fascinating complement – in fact, as a spectacle, it easily eclipses the prehistoric site. Diatomite is a light, white, crumbly rock composed of the compressed silica skeletons of microscopic sea organisms (diatoms). The Kikuyu used it as body paint (*karia andus*), but it also makes an excellent filter and it absorbs water like silica gel. Brewers use it for filtration and it makes an effective insecticide in grain silos by dehydrating the weevils without poisoning the grain.

The manager will gladly tell you more about diatomite, but the real excitement comes when you walk down into the mine itself: they're happy to receive visitors. A track spirals down the inside of a giant bowl, scooped out of the ground by pick and shovel over the last fifty years. Before digging stopped, they reached a level, about fifty metres down, where a high-grade, brilliant white diatomite is found. Here, a dozen or more **tunnels** dive into the cliffs to form a maze of ghostly subterranean passages, almost architectural in design and home to thousands of fluttering **bats**. The tunnels are wonderfully cool and vents keep the air circulating. You'll be assured that the structure of diatomite makes rock falls extremely unlikely, but a number of shored-up passageways may leave you unconvinced and glad to have along an accounts clerk – or some other conscripted employee – to guide you. You need a torch even though the light goes in a surprisingly long way, but you can't really get lost.

Foreign competition, principally from open-cast pits in California, has forced the closure of this particular mine and they now quarry the diatomite from an open-cast pit near Lake Elmenteita. Up on the surface, however, an ancient, rusting kiln is periodically fired up to dry the diatomite for packing. The whole place has a somewhat archaic air about it – which must have disappointed the group of Ceausescu-era Romanians once found taking unnecessarily furtive photographs from the main road.

Nakuru and nearby sites

As you approach **NAKURU** along the main highway from Nairobi, you pass an optimistic "Trans-African Highway" sign ("Kampala 496km; Lagos 5749km"). The *shamba-* and conifer-cloaked mound directly ahead is the southern flank of Menengai crater, while to the left are the scrub-covered eastern heights of Nakuru National Park.

Were it not for the fact that Nakuru is a major transport hub and has its own national park even closer to its town centre than Nairobi's, there would be no special reason to visit. A noisy, dusty town, Nakuru is Kenya's fourth largest city (though it projects a noticeably busier and more energetic image than Kisumu, the third); it is also capital of the enormous, sprawling Rift Valley Province that stretches from the Sudanese border to the slopes of Kilimanjaro.

Nakuru came into existence on the thrust of the Uganda railway and owed its early growth, at least in part, to **Lord Delamere**, the colony's most famous figure. In 1903, he acquired four hundred square kilometres of land on the lower slopes of the Mau escarpment, followed by two hundred more at Soysambu, on the other side of the lake. Eager to share the empty vistas with compatriots – though preferably with other Cheshire or Lancashire men – he promoted in England the mile-square plots being offered free by the Foreign Office. Eventually, some two hundred new settler families arrived and *Nakuru* – a name which as usual could mean various things, including "Place of the Waterbuck" (Swahili) and "Swirling Dust" or "Little Soda Lake" (Maasai) – became their country capital. It lies on the unprepossessing steppe between the lake and the flanks of Menengai crater. This desolate shelf has a nickname: "the place where the cows won't eat grass" (the pasture was found to be iron-deficient). Farmers near the town turned to the better prospects of pyrethrum, the plant used to make insecticide, as a cash crop.

Nakuru town

Still largely a workaday farmers' town, with unadorned old seed shops and veterinary paraphernalia much in evidence on the main street, Nakuru is a little Nairobi without

---

ROADSIDE RIP-OFFS

Warning: if you're driving, beware of anyone around Nakuru telling you there's anything wrong with your car: this is the con-mechanic capital of Kenya. **Tricksters** hang around along the roadside either between Lanet and the town centre or between the town centre and the national park main gate. They work in teams, pointing one after another at your wheels as you drive past, or, if you stop anywhere, "discovering" oil dripping from your engine – anything to get you into their garage for a bogus repair job. Be especially wary if the police roadblocks aren't in operation, when the gangs become particularly brazen.

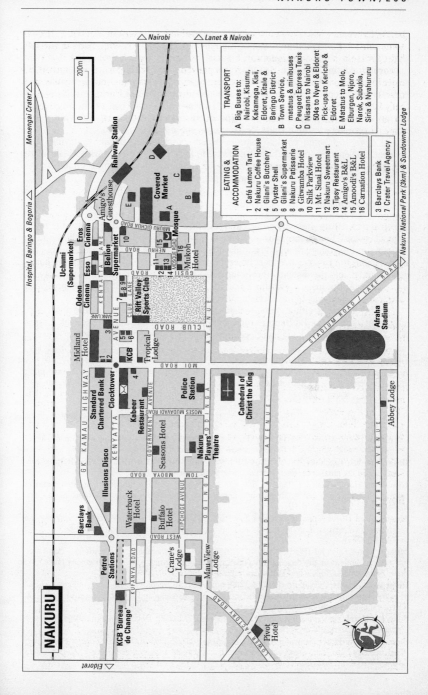

NAKURU

△ Nairobi   △ Lanet & Nairobi

△ Menengai Crater

◁ Hospital, Baringo, Baringo & Bogoria

▷ Nakuru National Park (3km) & Sundowner Lodge

◁ Eldoret

0   200m

Railway Station

Amigo's Guesthouse

Covered Market

Eros Cinema

Uchumi (Supermarket)

Odeon Cinema

Esso

Belion Supermarket

Mosque

Mukoh Hotel

Rift Valley Sports Club

Midland Hotel

Tropical Lodge

KCB

Standard Chartered Bank

Clocktower

Kabeer Restaurant

Police Station

Illusions Disco

Cathedral of Christ the King

Seasons Hotel

Nakuru Players' Theatre

Barclays Bank

Waterbuck Hotel

Buffalo Hotel

Afraha Stadium

Petrol Stations

Crane's Lodge

Mau View Lodge

Abbey Lodge

KCB 'Bureau de Change'

Pivot Hotel

GK KAMAU HIGHWAY

KENYATTA   AVENUE

BANK LANE

KENYATTA LANE

TABITHA LANE

MERU ROAD

GICHUA ROAD

MOSQUE ROAD

GUSII ROAD

NEHRU ROAD

CLUB ROAD

MOI ROAD

CLUB ROAD

GOVERNMENT AVENUE

MOSES MUDAVADI ROAD

ODINGA AVENUE

RONALD NGALA AVENUE

KARIBA AVENUE

STADIUM ROAD / LAKE ROAD

MBOYA ROAD

TOM MBOYA ROAD

OGINGA ODINGA

KIPCHOGE AVENUE

WEST ROAD

KUFANYA ROAD

LOWER ASTORY ROAD

N

EATING & ACCOMMODATION

1 Café Lemon Tart
2 Nakuru Coffee House
4 Gilani's Butchery
5 Oyster Shell
6 Gilani's Supermarket
8 Nakuru Patisserie
9 Gitwamba Hotel
10 Shik Parkview
11 Mt. Sinai Hotel
12 Nakuru Sweetmart
13 Tipsy Restaurant
14 Amigo's B&L
15 Amoodi's B&L
16 Carnation Hotel

3 Barclays Bank
7 Crater Travel Agency

TRANSPORT

A Big Buses to:
   Nairobi, Kisumu,
   Kakamega, Kisii,
   Eldoret, Kitale &
   Baringo District
B Town Service,
   matatus & minibuses
C Peugeot Express Taxis
D Nissans to Nairobi
   504s to Nyeri & Eldoret
   Pick-ups to Kericho &
   Eldoret
E Matatus to Molo,
   Elburgon, Njoro,
   Narok, Subukia,
   Siria & Nyahururu

A B C D E

the flashy veneer, its streets frequently undergoing ear-shattering repairs. Recent ethnic tension has meant an influx of Kikuyu refugees from outlying parts of the Rift Valley: it is, in many ways, more of a social barometer than Nairobi. The town can appear intimidating at first, especially if you arrive in the evening, and the beggars and street kids, many sniffing poppers and other solvents, are amongst the most pitiful you will ever see. Since it's a stone's throw from **Nakuru National Park**, equally close to the prehistoric settlement site at **Hyrax Hill** and the vast bowl of the **Menengai crater**, and the jumping-off point for **trips down into the northern Rift Valley**, you may find yourself passing through Nakuru more often than you'd like.

The town has some positive aspects, worth emphasizing if you're staying. The **market**, certainly, is animated and a pleasure to look around, though with its fair share of hassle. And there's a glimmer of charm still remaining in its colonnaded old streets and the **jacaranda**-brushed avenues at the edge of town.

Accommodation

The **train and bus stations** are packed together at the east end of town with **lodgings** all around. For **cheap rooms**, plenty of other places apart from the following can be found in the centre, though few of them shine. A number of **mid-range hotels** are dotted about the western avenues; however, the sewers there can turn even the hardiest stomachs, and the distantly throbbing noise from the *Buffalo Hotel* nightclub is also a nuisance. At the **luxury** end there's nothing at all in Nakuru: most of the thousands of tourists on their way to the park stay in one of the two lodges there.

If you're **camping**, either go to the national park (see p.209) or try out the new campsite about 7km up the B4 Baringo road – great views of the town and the pink-fringed lake. It's well signposted and has clean long-drops and showers with hot water to order.

Cheap and mid-range lodgings

Amigo's B&L, Gusii Rd (PO Box 1461; ☎037/210170). Not to be confused with the day and night club of the same name off Kenyatta Ave, this is one of the most popular cheapies, recently extended – a very basic secure lodging with a nice welcome, though rather dirty. The water, when there is any, is hot. ②.

Amoodi's B&L, Nehru Rd (PO Box 1731; ☎037/41939). A no-frills B&L with excellent security, plenty of hot water and the cheapest twin beds in town. Strictly run. ①.

Carnation Hotel, Mosque Rd, 1st floor (PO Box 1620; ☎037/43522). A large but well-run and attentive establishment – the best in the town centre and very good value. ④.

Cranes Lodge, Kipchoge Ave (PO Box 7011; ☎037/213304). Built in 1992 but already run-down; rooms are on the small side. Recommended only for its safe parking. ③.

Gitwamba Hotel, Gusii Rd (PO Box 586; ☎037/40754). One of the best joints in this quarter of town, with light, clean and roomy s/c and non-s/c accommodation, though it's raucous on disco nights – Wed & Fri–Sun. ①–②.

Mount Sinai Hotel, Gusii Rd (PO Box 238; ☎037/21779). Nakuru's newest cheapie, opposite the coffin-makers. Great staff, good security and cool, functional rooms; restaurant down below. A tad overpriced. ③.

Mukoh Hotel, Gusii Rd (PO Box 238; ☎037/213516). Rather shambling place with 56 s/c and non-s/c rooms, those over the courtyard baptized daily by the Christco Fellowship gospel choir next door. Beds spotless, toilets less so. Overpriced. ③.

Pivot Hotel, Lower Factory Rd (PO Box 1369; ☎037/42473). Despite resembling a military hospital in every aspect, this is recommended: the rooms are shiny clean and have new mosquito nets. Go for rooms 1–15 to avoid the deafening disco din on some weekend nights. ③.

Seasons Hotel, Government Ave (PO Box 3163; ☎037/45218). Decent enough rooms – all self-contained – but dark and overpriced. ③.

Shik Parkview Hotel, Kenyatta Ave (PO Box 614; ☎037/212345 or 212346). Seventy-two rooms, clean and airy but on the small side. Separate bar and restaraunt. Nakuru Chess Club is resident upstairs Wed & Fri 5pm, Sun 2pm. ②.

Tropical Lodge, Moi Rd (PO Box 4193; ☎037/42608). A presentable, if rather gloomy, option with rooms big enough to swing several cats in and hot water morning and evening. A bargain, though. ①.

More expensive hotels

Kunste Hotel, on the Nairobi road, 2.5km from the town centre (PO Box 1369; ☎037/212140). A good new hotel with sensibly priced rooms. ⑤.

Midland Hotel, GK Kamau Highway (PO Box 908; ☎037/212125, fax 037/44517). Long-established, but very average – basically a huge pub with rooms, all of which are s/c and comfy, if a tad gloomy. The old wing, normally more pleasant, is currently being refurbished. Two bars, both open until midnight. Good disabled access. ⑤.

Stem Hotel, Nairobi road, close to the Nakuru National Park Lanet Gate, 8km from the town centre (PO Box 1076; ☎037/85391). Pleasant (in a functional, motel manner) and good value, it's also convenient for an early-morning park visit. And they do excellent Indian food. ⑤.

Sundowners Lodge, 1km down Kanu St off Lake Rd, in Langa Langa suburb (PO Box 561; ☎037/214216, fax 037/211204). Reasonable little place, run by the management of *Lake Nakuru Lodge*, but overpriced. ⑦.

Waterbuck Hotel, West Rd (PO Box 3327; ☎037/215672, fax 037/214163). As the town centre's most prominent hotel this seems to be the current "upmarket" choice, although it looks like an army barracks. It does a respectable and very reasonably priced buffet lunch, and the breakfasts are huge, but the accommodation is over-rated. It also has a new but rather dusty *nyama choma* joint round the back. ⑤.

Eating, drinking and entertainment

Finding good **meals** is getting easier in Nakuru: as a guide, older, more down-at-heel establishments are bunched towards the east end of town near the railway station, while the west end, especially along Kenyatta Avenue, tends to be more upmarket.

Restaurants

Kabeer Restaurant, Government Ave. Very relaxing place for a serious feed, at about Ksh240; lunch curries Ksh200.

Nakuru Sweet Mart, Gusii Rd. A long-established Indian eatery which does an excellent and massive vegetarian *thali*, and a good range of breads. Very cheap.

Oyster Shell Restaurant, Club Rd/Kenyatta Ave, 1st floor. Magnificent dinners for under Ksh500, breakfast around Ksh200. Great service and atmosphere – real flowers and similar touches – although the dinner ambience can be marred by the *XTC Discotheque* upstairs.

Railway Station Restaurant. An utterly time-warped retreat where you can have silver-service cornflakes and toast for breakfast – and equally immaculately served (though no less gastronomically uncreative) colonial repasts at lunch and dinner. Around Ksh200.

Tipsy Restaurant, Gusii Rd. Next door and similar to, but cheaper than, *Nakuru Sweet Mart*, and for the less hungry.

Snacks and bars

Buffalo Hotel, Government Ave. Quite a pleasant beer garden and *nyama choma* joint – not a hotel – with thatched huts, wicker chairs and a wicked sound system.

Café Lemon Tart, Moi Rd. For snacks or breakfast this would be hard to beat.

Nakuru Coffee House, Moi Rd. A reliable venue for real coffee and a bite to eat.

Waterbuck Hotel, West Rd. A good snack menu all day, and a lively bar on Saturday nights.

Food shopping

If you're passing through in your own car, check the *Sita Supermarket* for **food supplies**, at the *Sita* shopping centre a few kilometres east of the town centre on the Nairobi road – the *Have More Restaurant* here is a good snack bar – or else the shopping centre 4km west of town on the Kisumu road. The best supermarket in town is the main *Uchumi* on Kenyatta Lane, just off GK Kamau Highway (also open Sun, 9.30am–

2pm). A smaller grocery is *Gilani's* on Club Road, while *Gilani's Butchery* on Moi Road has a good **cheese** counter where you can count on getting the cheap and excellent McLellan's Farmhouse brie-style rounds. *Nakuru Patisserie* on Club Lane has a wholesome selection of **bread** and baked bites. The main **produce market**, near the transport parks and railway station, has the full display of fruit and vegetables.

Entertainment and nightlife

Nakuru has little to offer in the fields of culture and entertainment. The **nightspot** of the moment is *Illusions* on Kenyatta Avenue, where the line-up varies but tends towards the rootsier end of the scale (Wed–Sun; Ksh50 cover). Slightly less steamy are the famous weekend discos at the *Pivot Hotel* – and their music is not at all bad – and the glitzy *XTC Discotheque*, above the *Oyster Shell Restaurant*. For down-at-heel local drinking, *Amigo's Day and Night Club*, Mburu Gichua Road is an experience – watch yourself as they watch you. If you're in town for more than a day you may get the chance to see the Nakuru Players in action at their dour-looking **theatre** (☎037/40805) on Kipchoge Avenue. Of the two main **cinemas**, both on GK Kamau Highway, the smaller *Eros* (screenings at 6pm and 9pm, and Saturday matinées at 3pm; very cheap, even in the circle) is the more inviting.

Listings

Banks Scattered all over the town; there's a *KCB* with a "Bureau de Change" flagged on the western outskirts. All Mon–Fri 9am–3pm & Sat 9–11am; *Standard Chartered*, Moi Rd, has a Moneylink terminal.

Books *Ereto Bookshop*, Kenyatta Lane, has a good range of African writers.

Car repairs If you really do have a problem, try and find out exactly what it is before approaching the myriad workshops at the western ends of Government and Kipchoge avenues. Get quotes from several places before bringing your vehicle down.

Chemist/pharmacy A proficient one is *Medika Chemists*, 1st floor Equator House, Kenyatta Lane, next door to *Uchimi* (☎037/214847).

Hair-braiding For that ethnic *mzungu* look, *Penny Classic*, next door to *Eros Cinema on* GK Kamau Highway (Mon–Sat 9am–6pm; ☎037/45985), is happy to oblige.

Medical clinic *Nakuru Medical Clinics*, by *Barclays* on Kenyatta Ave (☎037/214655), have a range of specialists.

Music There seems little chance of your stumbling into a live performance, but if you want to beef up your cassette collection, Nehru Rd is the street to aim for, and *Pop Hit Music Sounds* (on the right going down) the pick of the bunch.

Parking This can be something of a problem, with a high chance of break-ins, dripping-oil scams and the like. Whether you're staying the night or not, the best plan is to park in a guarded hotel parking area – absolutely essential if all your luggage is inside.

Post office Moi Rd/Kenyatta Ave (Mon–Fri 8am–5.30pm & Sat 9am–noon), with good telephone and fax facilities.

Travel agents *Crater Travel*, Inder Singh Building, just off Kenyatta Ave (PO Box 2631; ☎037/214896, fax 037/215019), offers a full service for air ticketing, plus the usual range of (expensive) tour deals. For general local arrangements, especially Nakuru National Park visits and other safaris, *Blackbird Tours* at the *Carnation Hotel* (PO Box 4162; ☎037/45383, fax 037/210350) are friendly and competent: park tours, picked up from your hotel, from around $60 for a half-day or $75 a full day (2 people), plus park fees.

Nakuru travel details

Travel options **from Nakuru** are wide open. You're less than two hours from Nairobi – a journey as easy to hitch as any in the country. The train is inconsiderate of sightseeing and leaves at night, so the climb up the escarpment isn't an attraction.

Heading the other way, the **bus** lines all run regular services to Eldoret, Kisumu, Kisii and points west. Alternatively, you can take the quieter road west, through the highlands towns of Njoro, Elburgon and Molo, a route covered in this chapter on p.214. Southwards, you can get to Narok by a smoking **matatu** up the fantastic Mau escarpment (not a great distance but allow the day to arrive). The most obvious destinations – in this chapter – are further north in the Rift Valley, around Lakes Baringo and Bogoria especially, with at least two buses daily to Kampi ya Samaki at Lake Baringo and *matatus* making the run to Kabarnet in the hills to the west. There's also a lavishly scenic route to Nyahururu through the Subukia valley, an ascent of the Rift that, for sheer grandeur, comes close to the Naivasha escarpment (daily bus and *matatu* runs). A useful tip when entering Nakuru **bus station** from the railway station side is to go in via "Exit" to avoid the bevy of enthusiastic touts who hang around at "Entrance".

Menengai crater

Containing an enormous caldera, 12km across and nearly 500m deep in places, the extinct volcanic giant **Menengai** rises directly behind Nakuru. Its sloping mass is somehow not especially noticeable from the town. To reach it, head up Menengai Drive and take the fourth left turn (Crater Climb) through the modestly affluent suburbs above the town. Some 4.5km up the hill you come to a sign referring to a *Campsite and Picnic Area*, but no evidence of either. You could presumably camp by the trees here and get water from nearby houses, but you'd be ill advised to leave your tent unattended and you should bring food. Half a kilometre away is a telecommunications tower: head for this then turn right, following the path through a fragrant forest of gum trees for twenty minutes, to a fire lookout tower on the bare cliff. From the top of this, the massive crater spreads out beneath you, a spectacular sea of bush-covered lava, its black waves frozen solid.

The crater was the site of a battle in which the Ilpurko Maasai defeated the Ilaikipiak, whom they considered upstarts disrespectful to Mbatian, the *laibon* of the time. At intervals throughout the nineteenth century, these **Maasai civil wars** flared up over the issue of true Maasai identity: in this case, it was not simply a matter of honour but also of grazing rights in the Rift Valley, especially around Lake Naivasha and on the scarp slopes. The Ilpurko were herders, while the Ilaikipiak from the north grew crops as well. Both had been preparing for battle for some time and it is said that hundreds of Ilaikipiak *morans* were hurled over the crater rim to their deaths. The place retains a sinister reputation and local people prefer not to go near the edge.

A century later, on the highest point of this windy, doom-laden crest, the Rotary Club erected one of their familiar hyperbolic signposts, laden with multiple pointers. Apart from informing you that Nairobi is 140km away and Rome 5997km in the opposite direction, it also points out that the crater wall is 2272m above sea level and its area some 90 square kilometres – the whole dramatic extent of which you can see. You'll get fantastic views over Lake Nakuru if you walk down the dirt road along the south side of the gum-tree plantation.

From Nakuru town centre it's about an eight-kilometre (three-hour) hike to the crater rim; on weekends, you might be lucky and get a lift, but there's no public transport. Taxis will take you of course. If you walk, you're best advised to go up in company.

Hyrax Hill

Daily 9.30am–6pm; small fee.

HYRAX HILL is an easy target, 3.5km out of town, just to the left of the Nairobi road. *Matatus* bound for Lanet and Gilgil will drop you at the turn, then it's a one-kilometre walk to the small museum where you pay your fee. If you're driving, don't be misled by the sign next to the *Kunste Hotel* which appears to indicate a left turn here (the Subukia road): it's about a kilometre further to the entrance track. The hill, named for the hyraxes which once scampered over it, has been a settlement site for a least three thousand years and finds here date from the Neolithic period. It was discovered by Louis Leakey in 1926, excavated by Mary Leakey in 1937–38 and by others in 1965, 1973 and 1987. There's an excellent guide booklet (1983) on sale in the museum and a reprint of the paper in the journal *Azania* describing the most recent excavations. You can normally **camp** here, free or for a small fee (staff facilities only).

The Northeast Village

The path leading out to the right of the museum winds its way around the north side of the hill to an excavated pit dwelling, or at any rate a "sunken enclosure", with baulks left in place to show the depth of material that was removed during the digging. There are thirteen similar depressions in this "**Northeast Village**" (curiously named, as it is in the north*west*) but it's uncertain exactly how they were used. They have yielded a tremendous quantity of pottery shards, tools made from flakes of obsidian and animal-bone fragments, but the absence of post-holes normally needed to support a roof suggests they may have been shelters for livestock rather than humans. Just as plausibly, a roof might have been added whenever needed, leaving no trace, and animals and people may have shared the shelters. The floor of the pit has been left exposed and is littered with stones and obsidian chips. It's easy to convince yourself you've discovered a little knife or part of an arrowhead. Several reconstructed examples of the site's characteristic late Iron Age pottery (the Iron Age in Kenya essentially continued until the twentieth century) are displayed in the museum.

Recent excavations at Hollow F have discovered the floors of three oblong **houses**, facing onto the main pit, with rather frail foundations, suggesting a kind of lean-to or bender. This research, which included radiocarbon dating showing occupation of different hollows from something like 1100 to 1500 AD, led to the conjecture that the "village" had not all been occupied at the same time, but that pits and attached houses would be used for a number of seasons until uninhabitable, then abandoned for a newly built area nearby. Far from being a community, this could have been the home base of a single family, or even just an occasional encampment in the seasonal cycle.

It is believed the inhabitants would have been semi-nomadic Sirikwa- or Kalenjin-speaking herders. Today, Kalenjin-speakers mostly live further west, but they're associated with so-called pit-dwellings elsewhere (see "In Search of the Sirikwa Holes", p.228) and, in the case of Hyrax Hill, they may have been forced to flee by an expanding Maasai population from the north.

The fort and burial sites

Following the path towards the top of the hill, you come to an exposed **"fort"** facing out towards Nakuru. It consists of a circle of hefty boulders enclosing a flattened area. Said to have been an Iron Age lookout post, there's no way of being certain what this actually was, nor even how old it might be, since no artefacts have been found. From the fort, you can scramble over the volcanic boulders – the whole hill is a tongue of Menengai's lava – to the summit, where you get a good view of the southern part of the site and the lake. Now several kilometres away, the lake once extended, probably as fresh water, right to the base of the hill and across much of the Rift Valley, turning Hyrax Hill into a peninsula or even an island.

A hundred metres down the hillside you come to more Iron Age pits and a **trench**. An extraordinary collection of bits and pieces was dug up here in 1974, including some eight thousand stone tools and six **Indian coins** between sixty and five hundred years old. Whether the oldest of these really implies the very early penetration of overseas foreigners into the interior or whether the coins were simply buried or smothered is another ponderable question. Most likely they'd been handed down for generations and were either lost or hidden for safekeeping.

Nearby, in a fenced-in shelter, the massive stone slab which sealed a **Neolithic burial mound** has been removed to display part of a skull and some limb bones. The remains of a further nineteen Neolithic skeletons were discovered north of this, beneath a more recent Iron Age occupation area marked by the two stone circles (which were hut foundations). Nineteen Iron Age skeletons were also discovered, over-lying the Neolithic graves, mostly of young men apparently buried unceremoniously or in a hurry, their skulls and limbs in tangled heaps; possibly the mutilated remains of slain warriors.

These enigmatic graves have further, cultural implications: nine of the Neolithic skeletons are thought to be female and, unlike the male remains, they were found with accompanying **grave goods** in the form of domestic implements – dishes, pestles and flat mortars. The finds pose unanswerable questions. Certainly, many Kenyan peoples remember oral traditions of times when women were more socially and politically powerful than today: the female burials with grave goods might be evidence of this past. But the burials themselves are curious. The coincidence of nineteen skeletons at each level may be just that – coincidence. But did the Iron Age survivors who buried their young men know about the ancient Neolithic graves beneath?

Neolithic recreation

For a less dramatic, but more accessible, impression of life at Hyrax Hill, the **Bau game**, cut into the rock just before you get back to the museum, is a delightfully fresh record. *Bau* is the Bantu name for a game of skill and – depending on the set of rules used – amazing complexity that has been played all over Africa for a very long time. Two people play, moving pieces (cowries, seeds or pebbles) from one hole to another to win. There are a number of these "boards" around the hill; the one near the museum is a particularly good example. In many ways they are the most fascinating relics on the site.

Lake Nakuru National Park

Daily fees: $27, $10 students/children; $8 to camp, $15 in a "special" campsite. No entry on foot. Warden: PO Box 539, Nakuru; ☎037/41605. Maps: Survey of Kenya "Aberdares & Lake Nakuru" at 1cm:1.5km (1982); Rowanya Enterprises "Lake Nakuru National Park" at 1cm: 500m (1990).

Though not large – some 10km by 25km – **LAKE NAKURU** is a beautiful park, the terra firma mostly under light **acacia forest**, well provided with tracks to a variety of hides and lookouts. It's also one of the easiest parks to visit, with or without a vehicle of your own. Towards the end of the dry season in March, the lake is often much smaller than the maps suggest; consequently, water birds are a greater distance from the park roads. The **northern side** of the park is commonly fairly busy with tour vehicles, but the **southern parts** are usually empty. A pleasure to drive around (about three hours if you keep going), its easy-to-follow topography means you really can't get lost or go far without arriving somewhere. And the contrast and apparent dislocation between the shallow soda lake with its primeval birds and the animated woodlands all around give it a very distinctive appeal.

The mystery of the vanishing flamingoes

Lake Nakuru has always been considered a flamingo lake *par excellence*; at one time, it was believed that up to two million **lesser flamingoes** (perhaps one third of the world's population) were massing in the warm alkaline water to feed on the abundant algae cultivated by their own droppings. Then, in the late 1970s, a combination of increased rainfall and decreased evaporation (there's no outlet) lowered the lake's

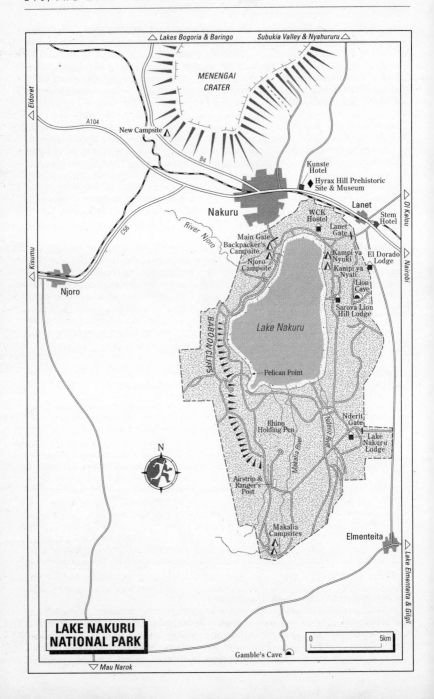

△ Lakes Bogoria & Baringo   Subukia Valley & Nyahururu △

MENENGAI CRATER

△ Eldoret

A104

New Campsite △

B4

C56

C56

△ Kisumu

River Njoro

Njoro

Kunste Hotel

◆ Hyrax Hill Prehistoric Site & Museum

Nakuru

Lanet

△ Ol Kalou

WCK Hostel

Stem Hotel

Main Gate
Backpacker's Campsite

Lanet Gate

Njoro Campsite

Kampi ya Nyuki

El Dorado Lodge

Kampi ya Nyati

△ Nairobi

Lion Cave

Sarova Lion Hill Lodge

Lake Nakuru

BABOON CLIFFS

Pelican Point

Rhino Holding Pen

Makalia River

Nderit River

Nderit Gate

Lake Nakuru Lodge

N

Airstrip & Ranger's Post

Makalia Campsites

Elmenteita

△ Lake Elmenteita & Gilgil

LAKE NAKURU NATIONAL PARK

0   5km

Gamble's Cave

▽ Mau Narok

salinity and raised the water level. The flamingoes began to disperse, some to Lakes Elmenteita, Magadi and Natron (the latter in Tanzania), some up to Turkana, but the majority to Lake Bogoria.

Since then, flamingoes have been sporadically seen again in the surreal pink swarms that have become a photographic cliché. The situation, however, has become increasingly unpredictable, with the flamingoes returning for two or three years then disappearing again. At the time of writing, the lake is almost totally dry and the flamingoes have fled once more. There are hopes, however, that heavy rains might now lure them back, while a great debate rages in the press about the causes of their disappearance and its detrimental effect on the tourist trade. Pollution from Nakuru town's sewer effluent is believed to be a factor (Kenya Wildlife Service and the World Wide Fund for Nature have just completed nine new "refuse chambers" for the town), as are water diversion and even sand-harvesting along the Njoro River. The introduction of a species of tilapia fish – partly to control mosquitoes – has encouraged large flocks of **white pelicans** in recent years and it's likely that their presence is another disruptive element (on Elmenteita a breeding colony of greater flamingoes was forced off by the pelicans). The Nakuru Wildlife Trust has been studying the ecology of Rift Valley lakes since 1971 in an effort to find some of the answers.

Greater flamingoes can also be seen at Nakuru, though in much smaller numbers than their lesser relations. They're as tall as a small person and have less hooked beaks, with which they sift for small crustaceans and plankton, their heads underwater.

Lake Nakuru's other wildlife

Fortunately, in view of the flamingoes' here-today-gone-tomorrow caprice (they have been absent since autumn 1995), there is a lot more to the lake's spectacle than the pink flocks. Its multifaceted shores and the surrounding woodlands are home to some four hundred other species of **birds** including, during the northern winter, many migratory European species.

There's a good number of **mammals** here as well. The lake isn't too briny for **hippos**: a herd of a dozen or more snort and splash by day and graze by night at the northern end. Nakuru has also become a popular venue for introduced species: there are **Rothschild's giraffe** from the wild herd near Kitale, and **lion** and secretive **leopard** from wherever they're causing a nuisance.

More recently, a number of **black rhinos** have been relocated from less safe parts of Kenya (present population 34); ten **white rhinos** were donated by South Africa in 1994, bringing their number to eighteen. Electric fencing has been installed around the entire perimeter of the park – the only park in the country to be so enclosed – with the intention of maintaining a viable number of rhinos in one well-protected zone, secure from poachers. A huge investment, substantially from the World Wide Fund for Nature, has been expended on this major effort to save the rhino from extinction at a cost per beast – adding up to some £4000 per year – that is perhaps ten times the average income of the people on the other side of the fence.

You soon understand how Nakuru got its Swahili name: the park is **waterbuck** heaven. With only a handful of lions and small numbers of leopards to check their population, the shaggy, red-deer-sized beasts number several thousand and the herds (either bachelor groups or a buck and his harem) are large and exceptionally tame. **Impala**, too, are very numerous, though their lack of fear means you rarely witness the graceful flight of a herd vaulting through the bush.

The two other most often-seen mammals are **buffalo** – which you'll repeatedly mistake for rhinos until you get a look through binoculars – and **warthog**, scuttling nervously in singles and family parties everywhere you look.

Elephants are absent but you're likely to see **zebra, dikdik, ostrich** and **jackals** and, in the southern part of the park, **eland** and **Thomson's and Grant's gazelles**.

More rarely you can encounter the odd **striped hyena** loping along the road in the eastern euphorbia forest at dawn, **reedbuck** down by the shore and **bushbuck** dashing briskly through the herbage. Along the eastern road, near *Lake Nakuru Lodge*, are several over-tame **baboon troops** to be wary of.

The park is also renowned for its very large **pythons** – the patches of dense **woodland** in the southwest, between the lakeshore and the steep cliffs, are a favourite habitat. One of these huge snakes dammed up the Makalia stream a few years back, when it died of internal injuries after swallowing a gazelle.

Lastly, if you tire of the living spectacle, go looking for the **Lion Cave**, beneath Lion Hill ridge in the northeast: it's an excavated prehistoric rock shelter and rarely contains lions.

Access and other practicalities

The park has three gates. **Main Gate**, at the edge of Nakuru town is also the park headquarters and has the main campsites nearby, plus a good, hand-painted map showing the most recent circuits, most of which are in fair condition.

Entering through **Lanet Gate** gives the most direct access to the park's two **lodges** from Naivasha or Nairobi and avoids the congestion of Nakuru town. It's not properly signposted, however. Before you reach the edge of town, the 1.5-kilometre track to the gate starts opposite the *Stem Hotel*; if you've crossed the railway bridge you've overshot.

Nderit Gate, down in the southeast corner, is only useful if you're coming cross-country from Lake Naivasha or over the Mau escarpment from Narok.

Low-budget visits

The most straightforward way to see the park if you don't have a vehicle is **by taxi**, especially as some of the taxi drivers around Nakuru town know the park well. The *Midland Hotel* is as good a place as any to track one down. This naturally works out cheaper for a group, but you'll probably want to reach an agreement with the driver *before* you're all present. Reckon on some stiff bargaining, then three hours at about $15 an hour, with park fees on top. Alternatively, contact *Blackbird Tours* at Caleb's Arcade in the *Carnation Hotel* (see Nakuru "Listings").

An alternative – though admittedly not always a very practical one – is to **hitch at the Main Gate**, about an hour's walk from the town centre. The rangers are usually sympathetic to low-budget travellers: they may help by asking drivers on your behalf, you'll have no park fees to pay unless you get a lift, and if you don't you can camp at the backpackers' campsite. You should expect to spend the night in the park once you get a ride, so be prepared for this.

If you're on foot and don't have a tent either, things look more difficult, but you could always stay the night at the cheap and cheerful *Florida Day & Night Club B&L* right on the boundary between park and town. This won't give you a restful night, but you'll want to be up bright and early waiting for a lift in any case; there's the added bonus that you're bound to meet park staff here.

Apart from camping, the only reasonably priced accommodation is at the somewhat run-down **Wildlife Clubs of Kenya Hostel** on the northern side of the park (book through PO Box 33 Nakuru, or just turn up). The dorm beds (Ksh600 per person) and do-it-yourself catering arrangements seem just about adequate – the kitchen is well-equipped. You can also camp in the enclosed compound (same charge). Popular with Nairobi weekenders is the pricier *Eldorado Lodge* (bookings through *Let's Go Travel* in Nairobi; ⑤), on the eastern side past the turning to Lanet Gate. It's actually more of a *nyama choma* joint: its breeze-block chalets aren't overly attractive but it's a good place to fix up a lift into the park.

For **accommodation under canvas**, there's a specific "**backpackers' campsite**" (cold showers, high-level toilets, communal tap) on a pleasant grassy site under fine old yellow acacias (beware the audacious vervet monkeys). There are two other regular campsites in the park: **Njoro campsite**, a couple of kilometres down the west shore road and set back in the woods, and the somewhat elusive **Makalia campsites** in a wonderful location at the southern tip of the park, on either side of the stream of the same name and close to the waterfall. Very few organized tours come down this way; but should you feel isolated, you may be reassured to know there's a ranger station fairly close by.

There are also a couple of "**special campsites**" in the northeast part of the park – **Kampi ya Nyati** (Buffalo Camp) and **Kampi ya Nyuki** (Bee Camp). They are both located in clearings among the trees between the road and the open shore but the lighter and grassier *Nyuki* is the nicer of the two. Both have splendid "private" access to quiet vantage points on the shore through drivable tunnels of undergrowth. Bookings, as usual for special campsites, are supposed to be made in advance with the warden or through the National Parks headquarters at Nairobi National Park (see p.129).

Self-drive – and more luxury

The best option has you **driving around in your own vehicle** and stopping where you choose: the park has a number of areas where you can walk and, of course, this gives you the option of staying, or eating, at the stylish **lodges** in the bush.

Sarova Lion Hill Lodge, 12km from the city centre (☎2129 Radiocall Nairobi; reservations through *Sarova*, address p.50). Converted a few years back from a tented camp, this is extremely comfortable, with a low-key atmosphere, helped along by friendly staff. There are good views from the very pleasant, chalet-style rooms stacked high above the main parts of the lodge; and the excellent meals are slightly cheaper than at *Lake Nakuru Lodge*; pool and sauna ($3 for visitors); $90/hr for game vehicle (carries up to 9 people). ⑨ high, ⑦ low.

Lake Nakuru Lodge (PO Box 561 Nakuru, ☎037/85446; reservations in Nairobi at Arrow House 2nd floor, Koinange St, PO Box 70559, ☎02/226778). Established lodge based around an old Delamere Estate house in shady gardens, with a pool ($5 for visitors) and uninterrupted views of the lake, though several kilometres from it. The *banda*-style rooms are on the small side and rather dark, though the new and much more expensive chalet suites, down a viewing platform-cum-walkway, are first-class. The food is nothing special. ⑧.

Around the park

The **northern shores** of the lake are the most opened-up, with a busy route between the Main Gate and *Sarova Lion Hill Lodge*. The vegetation here is mostly lightly wooded acacia forest and, close to Nakuru town and its noise and pollution, this is the least interesting area for wildlife.

Heading clockwise, the main track runs through the woods, past the lodge and into an exotic-looking forest of candelabra **euphorbia** – great cactus-like trees up to 15m high. At the southern end of this zone you come into a spell of more open country, past the turning (left) up to *Lake Nakuru Lodge*, and one or two side tracks down to the mud and the lakeshore (right), and then the road turns west into the southern park's dense acacia jungle. This is where you may see a **leopard** and, if they overcome their shyness, one of the park's thirty-odd **black rhino**. Several kilometres further, the road opens again onto wider horizons with plenty of buffalo, waterbuck, impala and eland all around. This is also the most likely area for seeing the park's introduced **Rothschild's giraffe** herd, which numbers some sixty or seventy, in several groups.

Down in this **southern part of the park**, take a northerly side track and you can circle around the southern savannah; opt for a southerly side track and you plunge into deep scrub and thicket – perfect rhino country. Eventually, heading south, you reach the electric boundary fence and the perimeter patrol track, which you can follow, east or west, back to the main circuit route.

The **west shore**, especially "pelican corner", has the best opportunities for seeing the **flamingoes** in their dense, rose-coloured photogeneity. In places the road runs on what is virtually a causeway, past the lake's edge, with high cliffs rearing up behind. Photo conditions obviously depend on the time of day and the weather, but late afternoon usually produces the best results on this side of the lake: be careful not to over-expose – the most effective shots tend to be on the dark side.

Still heading clockwise, the main route leaves the shore and ploughs north, through **thick forest** with many high trees and dense undergrowth, back to the Main Gate.

Good **vantage points** around the lake include the northern **mud flats** (follow established tracks across the dry surface); the dead tree **watchtower** (northeast); *Kampi ya Nyuki* and *Kampi ya Nyati* campsites; *Lake Nakuru Lodge*, for a general view across unobstructed savannah; and the high **"baboon cliffs"** in the west.

West of Nakuru: out of the Rift Valley

West of Nakuru, the A104 is a fast, busy, single-lane road, hair-raising if you're driving yourself and equally wearing on the nerves if you're travelling by *matatu*. Long-distance lorries and buses thunder by at top speed. The surface varies but it's generally good, the worst stretch running from Timboroa, some 90km west of Nakuru, for about twenty hilly, winding kilometres to Nabkoi. Beyond there it's mostly excellent.

If you're heading into western Kenya, there's a scenic and much quieter alternative to the main highway. This, the C56, climbs gently up to Njoro, Elburgon and Molo – in ascending order of altitude and size – before rejoining the Kisumu-bound fork of the main road (the B1).

Njoro

The turn-off (left) to **NJORO** and the Mau escarpment is 5km west of Nakuru, usually marked by the presence of a police roadblock. Njoro is the home town of **Egerton University** (main campus 5km out of town on the main road to Narok), whose other, equally remote, outpost is up the escarpment near Kinangop, north of Naivasha.

The jacaranda-fringed main road runs straight past the "centre" of town – a great acreage of mud (or, at best, dust), backed by a humble row of *dukas* and *hotelis*. The only feature of note is the white and green mosque on the right, which broadcasts sermons and a noisy accompaniment from its congregation on Friday mornings – strange in this bleak highlands town. There are one or two very basic B&Ls, but nothing notable.

Beyond the Narok junction there's another and more soulful Njoro of wooden colonnaded, tin-roofed, one-storey *dukas*. On this side of town are the post office and telephones (coin boxes only), a branch of the *KCB* bank and the *Njoro Farmer's Petrol Station*, a *Shell* garage. You emerge on the other side of town, past timber yards, into flat cereal country, with herds of dairy cattle and race horses between the lines of gum trees and copses of acacia.

Elburgon and Turi

ELBURGON is a good deal bigger than Njoro, and higher up. You're into seriously muddy, conifer country up here, the buildings, characteristically chalet-style, built of dark, weathered planks. In the centre, the town's second street branches off in a sea of mud (or dust) to the railway tracks and open-air market place. Down this street you'll find the post office, a branch of *Barclays* and several dirt-cheap B&Ls.

Elburgon is first and foremost a timber town, with logs and logging everywhere evident. Notice the little eating house near the tracks called *Wood Money Hotel*. It's wood money that gives Elburgon a degree of commercial prosperity and can be the only reason for the massive investment in the *Hotel Eel* (PO Box 36 Elburgon; ☎0363/31271 or 31471, fax 0363/31477; ④). This oddly named **hotel** ("Eel" is an acronym) beats anything in Nakuru, although if you don't qualify as a Kenyan resident the rates are far higher than you'd expect in an up-country town. On offer are clean, comfortable rooms and cottages, secure parking, a disco and an adventure playground set in well-landscaped grounds. The **restaurant** serves good breakfasts and an imaginative choice of main meals (excellent steak with bacon and red wine). During the week the place has all the atmosphere of an out-of-season holiday camp, but things liven up at weekends and holidays, when discos, video shows and traditional dancing are laid on.

En route to Molo, **St Andrew's School** at **Turi** has a locally renowned **teachers' club** on Thursday nights and sometimes at weekends. You can have a meal and a few drinks and pass an evening in as wide a range of company as you're likely to find anywhere.

Molo and the Mau forest

West of Elburgon, the road winds and dips through the thick Mau forest for several kilometres, with glimpses of railway viaducts across the valleys, until it emerges, still higher up, among the cereals and pyrethrum fields at **MOLO**.

Molo straggles for several kilometres down into a broad valley across the rail tracks and up the other side, where you find post office, banks and several petrol stations with carefully tended floral forecourts. *Green Garden Lodge* is further on, on the left, a plain but pleasant old place, decently kept up for no particular reason (there seem to be few, if any, guests). Stay here and you tend to rattle about. They offer 24-hour hot water and a cheap, tasty menu; sometimes they even have an old guitarist singing songs in the bar. Normally, though, you can do better at the *Molo Highlands Inn* (PO Box 142 Molo), which is tremendous value for its huge, wood-floored rooms with log fires. If only it wasn't so dead it would be a place to target: the moist, misty gardens are pleasant, and they have riding stables, but the bar and dining room only wake up a little in the evenings as various long-term guests return from a day's work on local civil engineering projects.

South of Molo, up into the **Mau forest**, a newly graded road runs to **Keringet** (where the huge old estate, once owned by Italians, and exhibiting all the most ostentatious trappings of colonial wealth, is gradually crumbling) and on to **Olenguerone**. From here, the road tunnels eerily through a forest of huge gum trees, traipsed by elephant and even rhino, to Bomet (see p.321). There are several daily *matatu* runs along this route from Molo.

The Kenya Wildlife Service has been trying to obtain funds to open up the mountain forest, like the Aberdares Park. There is some resistance however, not least from the forest's indigenous Okiek (Dorobo) hunter-gatherers. There's more background on this area, and details of the Mau route to the Maasai Mara, on p.320.

Londiani and Kipkelion Monastery

West of Molo, there are two possible places to stay in the highlands, neither of them exactly routine receivers of visitors. The first, the *Kenya Forestry College Guest House*, is near **Londiani**, a small town off the B1 highway, 12km west of the straggling row of huts and *dukas* that marks the railway's highest (2650m) point – **Mau Summit**. Londiani is about 3km from the main road, with the odd *matatu* running there. For the *Guest House* you need to take the right turn a kilometre or so before the centre, sing-posted to "Ministry of Environment and Natural Resources . . .", and follow this narrower track, Forest Road, for 2km. Anyone around the new buildings should be able to direct you to the simply furnished bungalow guest house on the north side of the little campus: if in doubt ask to see the director. Although it's intended for the use of visiting academics and reseachers, it is occasionally used by birdwatchers and passing hikers and is a peaceful, country retreat. The *Guest House* manager (reservations: PO Box 8 Londiani) is welcoming and flexible – you can self-cater or she can prepare meals. Camping, allowed until recently, is no longer permitted.

The Cistercian monastery

The second unusual target in the district is **Our Lady of Victoria Abbey**, a Cistercian Monastery between Londiani and **Kipkelion**. The area was formerly known by the Maasai as "Lumbwa", but Kipkelion ("Kif*kel*ion") is the original and much preferred Kipsigis name. Founded in 1956, this is the only Cistercian monastery in Africa and, deep in this rural hill country, the tall cement-block church is a remarkable sight – focal point of a small but impressive community of Danish, Dutch, Kenyan, Ugandan, Tanzanian, English and Irish monks. They make a living from their dairy herd and chickens and run the only hospital in the area and an important school. Our Lady of Victoria (named after the lake rather than the queen) began as a Trappist monastery, with the silence and strict rules the reformist order stipulates, but later reverted to the rather less stringent code of the older Cistercian order. The brothers still talk only when necessary, but they are happy to receive people (men and women) on retreat and ordinary lay vistors in their guest rooms and dining room. One of the brothers is reponsible for visitors and you're likely to receive a very warm, and surprisingly loquacious, welcome: it's hardly necessary to say there's no phone, but if you like the idea of silence and contemplation in a harmonious rural setting, write to let them know you're coming (PO Box 40 Kipkelion). You should obviously leave appropriate donations.

The monastery is sited rather remotely north of the C35 backroad that leads beyond Londiani towards Kisumu. A few **matatus** service this road, but to get up to the monastery without your own vehicle you need luck in scoring a lift or several hours to walk it. The monastery is 11km up a rough track – signposted "Monastery Hospital" – from the small centre of **Baisheli** on the C35 (which is 15km west of Londiani), and the track is rough, narrow and steep in parts, winding through intensively cultivated Kipsigis *shambas*. If you're approaching from the west, the easiest route to the monastery is via **Kipkelion station**, signposted off the main B1 highway, 25km east of Kericho. The road to Kipkelion station, 10km of good tarmac, gives out at the valley-floor station itself: to continue to the monastery you have a rocky, three-kilometre climb, then, turning right onto the C35, 6km to the track (left) up to the abbey. There's a "short cut" up to the monastery which is signposted ("Trappist", overwritten with "*Cistercian* Monastery 6km") just after you get onto the C35 – this track is often impassable. Note that none of the available maps of Kenya are any real guidance in this district: distances are significantly longer than they look.

THE NORTHERN RIFT

North of Nakuru, the Rift Valley drops away gently and, as the road descends, so temperatures rise, the landscape dries and human population becomes sparser. Not far from Nakuru or Nairobi, and no longer, necessarily, a difficult journey, this region has a bright, harsh beauty, quite different from the central Rift: its lakes both make alluring targets, but freshwater **Baringo** scores over **Bogoria** simply because access is easy and you don't need to be self-sufficient to stay there.

It's worth remembering also that this region offers three possible routes up to Lake Turkana (Chapter Seven), two of them joining with the Kitale–Lodwar road west of the lake, the third curving up to Maralal for the east side. Although public transport is virtually nonexistent and the roads pretty rough, the **Kerio valley** route (see p.225) deserves a special recommendation if you're visiting the west side of Turkana.

Lake Bogoria National Reserve and around

See the map on p.222. National Park fees apply (category D), see p.61; access usually permitted on foot or bicycle; Warden: PO Box 64 Marigat or PO Box 53 Kabarnet; ☎0328/22068.

One of the least-visited lakes in the Rift Valley, **LAKE BOGORIA** is a sliver of saline water – unbelievably foul-tasting – entrenched beneath towering hills 60km north of Nakuru. Recently adopted feeding ground of tens of thousands of **lesser flamingoes**, the lake and its shores are a national reserve, and one of the few places where **greater kudu** antelope can easily be seen. But the reserve is worth visiting as much for its physical spectacle as for the wildlife. It's largely a barren, baking wilderness of scrub and rocks, from which a series of furious **hot springs** erupts on the western shore and the bleak walls of the Siracho range rise sheer from the east. Even in the far north of the country there are few places so unremittingly severe. Fortunately the rigour of the landscape is relieved by three superb, shady **campsites**, one of which is nearly perfect. There's also a decent new **hotel** just outside the main gate of the reserve. The **warden** at Bogoria is quite an authority on **birds** and, if he's free, will happily take you around, or accompany you in your vehicle (it's a good idea to try to arrange this in advance).

Main approaches and gates

The excellent B4 road running north from Nakuru to Baringo slices through a thinly populated region and carries little traffic – tortoises in the road present the greatest hazard to motorists speeding along the fast new tarmac. The road skirts to the west of Lake Bogoria by a margin of 20km or more and the lake can seem effectively off limits without your own vehicle. **Access to the reserve from the north** is the most straightforward, whether you're driving or on foot. You turn off the B4, a few kilometres south of Marigat, at the junction signposted "E461 Loboi", and from here a tarmac road takes you straight to the **Loboi Gate**. There are infrequent *matatus* from Marigat to the Loboi Gate, or you could simply wait for a lift at the junction – it's a safe bet something suitable will pass within the hour.

Sixteen kilometres from the junction, 3km before the Loboi Gate, *Lake Bogoria Hotel*'s best feature is a sanitized **thermal pool** (though it also has an ordinary, chlorinated "cold pool"). A large stuffed lion dominates the lobby but even this does little to alleviate the blandness: it's really a town hotel in the bush and quite out of keeping with the area. Rooms and cottages are functional and taste-free (PO Box 208 Menengai West; ☎037/42696, fax 037/40896; reservations through *AT&H*, address on p.48; ⑧). A new alternative is the *Papyrus Inn* (PO Box 186 Marigat, ☎ Loboi 1; ③; sister hotel to the *Papyrus Annex*, which overlooks Lake Baringo). Situated very near the Loboi Gate, this inn is particularly geared up for group visits, with a large garden bar and restaurant, and an area set aside for camping (Ksh150 per person). There's also the option of camping at the Loboi Gate, just outside the reserve – there's usually water here but you'll need your own stove or firewood and supplies.

Driving in from the south is shorter on the map, but takes much longer on the rough roads and most vehicles visiting Bogoria are coming from Lake Baringo rather than directly from Nakuru. Using the main southern approach, the reserve is signposted (right) off the B4, 36km north of Nakuru at **Mogotio**. Some 23km from this junction, shortly afer **Mugurin**, you fork left for the western **Maji ya Moto Gate** (about 17km further, bringing you to the hot springs and tarmacked lakeshore road), or right/straight ahead for the southern Emsos Gate (a further 13km, which brings you to the woooded part of the reserve). There is virtually no public transport.

If you have a 4WD vehicle or are into hiking or mountain biking, you might like to consider the **cross-country approach** to Bogoria's Emsos Gate, described next.

Subukia and the cross-country route to Lake Bogoria

An adventurous alternative to taking the main road north to Bogoria from Nakuru is to approach the lake from the southeast, initially using the B5 tarmac route that ascends from the Rift Valley floor at Nakuru to the brim of the eastern escarpment at Nyahururu. Along the way, there are several turnings, northwest, towards the lake. The tarmac portions of this trip can be made by country bus or *matatu* (there are several daily runs between Nyahururu and Nakuru via Subukia), but you should be prepared to **hike** the rest of the way down to Bogoria if necessary – a good two days.

Aside from the pleasure of tackling roads used by very few tourists, this route gives you a special feel for the Rift Valley's striking topography as it drops from one monumental block of land to another, with dramatic changes of climate and scenery. When you reach the plain at the bottom you've an indelible impression of the way the earth has split apart and sunk to form the Rift over the last twenty million years.

From Nakuru, it's a short trip, 14km, past Menengai crater (left) to the unsignposted fork for the police post at Solai (left, 14km, on rough dirt) and Nyahururu (right). The Nakuru–Nyahururu road is busy with *matatus* and buses; a fertile, rural backwater has been opened up since the route was hard-surfaced in the late 1980s. Beyond the fork you enter a steep, hilly landscape of Kikuyu *shambas*, increasingly interspersed with plots of tea bushes and pyrethrum.

From Nyahururu, the target is also the Solai police post, though the early part of the route there is particularly stimulating as it falls in a series of breathtaking steps over the fault lines until it reaches a high scarp above Subukia, where it hairpins its way steeply down to the valley. From the cool highlands around Nyahururu, you start to feel the heat building up: fields of sugar cane and bananas seem to grow before your eyes in the hothouse atmosphere and the earth takes on a rich, redolent smell.

The Subukia Valley and Lake Solai

The **Subukia Valley** was the Maasai's "Beautiful Place", *Ol Momoi Sidai*, and its lush pastures their insurance against the failure of the grass up on the Laikipia plateau. But they were evicted in 1911 to the "Maasai Reserve" and the way was clear for the settler families. It's easy to see why they chose this high valley because, despite its isolation (even greater in the 1920s), it has a soft, arcadian beauty far removed from the windy plateaus above or the austere furnace of the Rift Valley floor below.

The village of **SUBUKIA** has a scattering of *hotelis* and *dukas*, and a *Total* filling station. Buses and *matatus* stop at this T-junction: there are one or two *matatu* to Solai police post (see "Down to Bogoria", below).

If you have transport of your own and two or three hours to spare, or a couple of days to walk it, you can take a major **diversion up the Subukia valley**, then turn west and cut back south again, past small Lake Solai. To get started on this route, from the grubby junction at Subukia village where the main road passes head north about 700m to an old T-junction signposted "Nakuru" (left) and "Lower Subukia" (right). Take the latter. The track, consisting of rough dirt and rocks, is easy to follow, but will clock up some 45km. Sources of food along the way are negligible, so you must be self-sufficient, and, although the road is being "improved" (made broader and more boneshaking), there are few if any *matatus* along the way.

Lake Solai is a curiously isolated soda lake with a reedy shoreline grazed by cattle and a scattering of sisal plots. For many years it was a seasonal lake only, but it has been a permanent feature since the early 1980s. South of Lake Solai, the road climbs through scattered euphorbia and acacias to the junction (hard right) at **Solai police post** with its road sign ("Lake Hannington") ancient but useful, and pretty mauve smudges of jacarandas. Lines of jacaranda streak the scenery at intervals all over this district; they border old driveways, evidence of the erstwhile community of **settlers**, nearly all of whom have left.

Down to Bogoria

The most **direct route from Subukia village to Bogoria** begins by climbing 4km out of the valley on the tarmac to Nakuru. A signposted right turn (or left if you've just come from Nakuru) goes over the hill past the curious apparition of **St Peter's** – a quaint Anglican church that looks as if it just flew in from England – and then 15km down to the Solai police post.

From here, the fifty kilometres to Bogoria is rough in many places, though normally quite negotiable in a 4WD vehicle (allow 3hr). Hitching, however, varies from slow to impossible from this point on and there is no public transport. If you're on foot or bicycle and still want to do it, check your emergency water and food supplies, tighten your bootlaces, check your brakes and set off west.

The road descends steeply to the Solai Valley with its disused railway line, which you cross at a place called **Milton's Siding**. When you reach the tracks, follow the road, parallel, to the right which runs for a kilometre and then turn sharp left to cross them. The road descends in a series of steps to a broad, flat valley with a sharp, right-hand bend up the hill on the far side, which it crosses to reach **Kisanana** – life-saving *chai* and a place to stop for the night if necessary, though there's no formal accommodation.

From Kisanana, you turn left at the old signpost and follow decent murram tracks for some 5km to a fork around some buildings. Here you head left and are soon pitching up a diabolical slope – rarely used by motor vehicles and by all appearances dynamited out of solid bedrock – which winds up and over a scrub-covered **hog's back ridge** for some 7km, eventually twisting north and dropping to better red murram, interspersed, strata-wise, with white, rocky stretches. You come to a crossroads (turn left), then after a few hundred metres a T-junction at a place of a few huts called **Mugurin** (turn right), where you may find a solitary *hoteli* open with good tea and chapatis. From here, you're within the compass of the lake, some 25km away. The road descends steadily now as you travel north – there's only the odd signpost but no danger of taking a wrong turn: if in doubt head right.

Emsos Gate: practicalities

Hidden in its deep bowl, **Lake Bogoria** – when it is approached from Mugurin – is only visible when you're almost on top of it. The final stretch of the track leading down to the Emsos Gate is steep, rocky as well as being savagely beautiful, the landscape transformed into a strident dazzle of red and blue and splashes of green. The lake itself, a glistening pool of soapy blue and white, has a mirage of pink flamingoes tinting its shores. During the middle hours of the day, the heat is relentless but the unparalleled **Fig Tree Campsite** is the incentive to make the trip: it's only forty minutes' walk from Emsos Gate and an absolute delight. Except, perhaps, if your visit coincides with a fresh covering of vegetation after the rains. Although this makes for an unusually verdant and picturesque scene, you'll also be welcomed by squads of determined tsetse flies. Be prepared to do battle. Note, if you're driving, that the road around the southern shore is very rocky and slow-going, and that access to *Fig Tree Campsite* is difficult for trucks and large vehicles as certain stretches are narrow and rock-bound.

You should normally be allowed into the reserve without a vehicle to stay, at *Fig Tree*, but before heading down to the thickly wooded shore at the south end, ask the rangers at Emsos about **food**; a few basics are usually available nearby to eke out your rations. **Water** is not a problem: a permanent, miniature brook, clear and sweet, runs right through the campsite and provides a natural jacuzzi. Less delightfully, the magnificent glade of giant fig trees which bathe the site in shade is a favourite haunt of baboons who gorge themselves day and night. In the fruiting season (Dec–Feb) you should be wary of camping directly beneath any concentrations of figs, for reasons which need no elaboration. Buffalo also graze near here and are not to be trifled with.

Getting around

Since a huge rock fall blocked it several years ago, the **east shore road** has been quite impassable so there is no circuit round the lake. The WWF (World Wide Fund for Nature) is currently exploring the feasibility of reopening the road but, in the meantime, *Fig Tree Campsite* is a dead end and if you're down here and don't have your own vehicle, you may be in for a long wait before someone turns up to give you a lift out again. Your only option is to walk the 15km around to the hot springs on the western shore, passing *Riverside* and *Acacia Tree* campsites. If you're driving up this southern stretch, there's a river bed to negotiate before you reach the tarmac, for which four-wheel drive is essential. There are picnic sites near the hot springs, and, although notices prohibit it, there seems little to prevent you from camping in the vicinity. The Bogoria Reserve **paved road** between the hot springs and the Loboi Gate is mostly in fair condition: by the hot springs is the junction for the dirt road out to the western, Maji ya Moto, gate.

The hot springs

However you enter the reserve, you're bound to want to see the **hot springs**: a series of boiling water spouts on the shore. They burst up from huge natural cauldrons of super-heated water not far below the surface and drain into steaming rivulets that cut through the crusty ground, continuously collapsing and reforming their courses down to the lake. Even at midday, when the sun glares like a furnace, clouds of steam drift across this infernal scene: tufts of grass tempt you to sit down and reward you with vicious spines, while, closer to the lakeshore, the macabre bleached skeletons of flamingoes lie strewn in the sand (visions of them landing in the wrong pool), and, in the background, the dull thundering of the springs fills the air. It's like some water garden in Hell. It is also **dangerous** and the sinister fascination too merciless for familiarity. Picnickers sometimes think it's fun to boil eggs and heat tins of food in the pools, but the consequences of a slip can be messy and even fatal: over the years a number of people have slipped and died as a result. An *askari* has now been posted to watch out for visitors but if you scald yourself, help might still be a long time coming.

None of which should keep you from going. Although they hardly touch Yellowstone or Rotorua standards, "hot springs" is a tame appellation for this very impressive, terrifying and brilliantly photogenic phenomenon. And the **flamingoes**, for some curious reason – possibly chemical – tend to flock in their greatest numbers to the shallows opposite the hot streams' debouchment. The Bogoria **fish eagles**, incidentally, have made a gruesome adjustment to their fierce, fishless environment: they prey on flamingoes.

The mild and nervous **kudu** formerly lived predominantly in the northeastern part of the reserve, but they have spread and multiplied significantly in recent years and they are now frequently seen in the more exposed western parts of the reserve. The greater kudu is a splendidly unmistakable, striped antelope; the bulls have long, spiral horns, shaggy dewlaps and enormous, spoon-like ears. Once widespread, the great rinderpest epidemics of the last century which took such a toll on cattle wiped out much of the kudu population too, leaving pockets only in the least favourable cattle country. Today, Bogoria is the most southerly part of their range in Kenya.

Lake Baringo

At one time a barely accessible retreat favoured by just a few weekenders, **LAKE BARINGO** now has a fine road from Nakuru. At present, it remains a peaceful oasis in the dry-thorn country, rich in birdlife and with a captivating character entirely its own.

The lake is freshwater (Naivasha is the only other Rift Valley lake that's not saline), so its fish support **birds** less often seen – fish eagles, pelicans, cormorants and herons, for example – as well as a scattering of flamingoes, nibbling along the shoreline, and quite a sizeable **crocodile** population. **Hippos** are common, too. Though you rarely see much more than ears and snout by day, they come ashore after dark, and on a moonlit night their presence can be unnervingly obvious; even in pitch darkness, they're too noisy to be ignored. The crocodiles are reckoned to be quite safe, too small to be dangerous, and rarely provoked by hunters as their skins are undersized – but if you're swimming, you might like to know that a supposed man-eater was shot in 1981.

The **Njemps** people of the lakeshore villages live by an unusual mixture of fishing and livestock herding, breaking the taboo on the eating of fish which is the norm among pastoralists. Speaking a dialect of Maa – the Maasai language – these *Ilchumps* fishermen paddle out in half-submerged dinghies made from saplings of the fibrous *ambatch* tree that grows in profusion at the southern end of the lake.

The lake itself is heavily silted with the red topsoil of the region, and it runs through a whole range of colours every day from yellow to coral to purple, according to the sun's position and the state of the sky. Years of drought had reduced it so that a broad swathe of grass and reeds grew between the water's edge and the lakeshore properties. In recent years there have been some heavy rains and lakeside acreage has been cut back once again by the advancing waters.

Baringo transport – and Marigat

Buses from Nakuru **to Kampi ya Samaki** run twice daily, but Nakuru *matatus* come up only as far as **Marigat**. From Marigat you can hitch or get a local *matatu* to the lake. Kampi ya Samaki is 2km from the main road. Boats to **Ol Kokwe Island** leave on request from the jetty on the north side of Kampi ya Samaki.

Marigat
MARIGAT, by virtue of its location, ought to become the hub of the Baringo–Bogoria tourist circuit, but for now, at least, it's a bland, dust-blown little place where visitors are greeted with indifference. Urban development here follows what seems to be an unusual course, as among the tin shacks stands an impressive bright green and white mosque. With two tiers of large windows and a capacity that obviously exceeds the area's Muslim population, it dwarfs its humble wooden predecessor to the rear. Muslim Nubians from Eldama Ravine, working on the irrigation project south of Marigat, are supposed to explain the building of this mosque, but it seems impossible that the funds could have been local. If you need **to stay** in Marigat, there are a couple of B&Ls on the main road near the junction with the B4, but they're nothing special, so you might as well follow the sign at the junction to *Marigat Inn*, 1500m (②). It's just off the main road on the eastern side of town, a place with character which has clean, s/c rooms with hot showers, looked after by helpful staff. There's a small jungly garden, a shop selling essentials, and a friendly restaurant where the food, while not exactly cordon bleu, is more than edible.

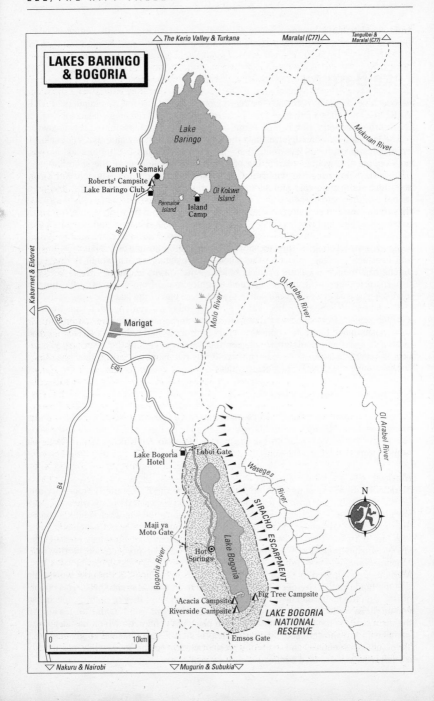

LAKES BARINGO & BOGORIA

Back to Nakuru

Returning to Nakuru, the first bus leaves Kampi ya Samaki at 6.30am but Marigat is an easier departure point. You should find a local vehicle going there. If you have your own vehicle you might stop south of Marigat to investigate a pool to the east of the road, just before the "Nakuru 84" kilometre sign, which was recently home to a pair of quite large crocodiles. How they got to the pool – and what they subsist on, assuming they're still there – are unfathomable mysteries.

Beyond Baringo

Travelling north of Baringo is a hit-or-miss affair without your own wheels, so try to arrange something with mobile tourists. Otherwise you'll have to hitch: there's little transport either to Maralal or to Tot and Lodwar from here.

If you're **driving**, there's the highly recommended and not too rough C77 D road from Lake Baringo towards Maralal (one day) or Samburu National Reserve (best done over two). This route swings up from the lakeshore, leaving tarmac and tourism behind, and takes you into the rugged country of the Lerochi plateau, dotted with Tugen and Pokot settlements. With the right conditions, there are stunning views back over Baringo. You join the terrible Rumuruti–Maralal road as far as Kisima, where you choose between a short journey to Maralal or some inspiring but wheel-shattering driving to Samburu (see p.295). There's **fuel** at Marigat, sometimes at Kampi ya Samaki (and normally at *Lake Baringo Club*), but none after that until Maralal or Archer's Post.

Lakeside accommodation

Inexpensive accommodation at Lake Baringo is headed by the *Roberts' Campsite* in a large, acacia-shaded garden with lots of space, showers and firewood bought from the *askari*. But it's scarcely cheap camping: Ksh200 per person, plus Ksh50 per bundle of firewood. There are good *bandas*, with electricity and bedding, though they are often booked up for months on end (PO Box 1051 Nakuru; ☎ Kampi ya Samaki 3; ④). If you want to cook, or for some reason prefer to shower separately from the campers, there's an adjacent, private kitchen/shower block that can be rented for about Ksh400 per night. The Roberts have their own shop too, which sells frozen meat, canned food, toiletries, cold drinks, stamps and various other bits and pieces (open daily 7am–8pm); there's also a bar of sorts.

If you'd prefer less of an outdoor atmosphere, there's a good choice of basic B&Ls in **Kampi ya Samaki**, the lake's only, and very small, town. Best of them is the *Papyrus Annex* (PO Box 16; ☎ Kampi ya Samaki 35; ②), which has clean new rooms with mosquito nets, and decent washing facilities in a separate block. It's a popular place; locals gather to watch television in the restaurant and there are stunning lake views from the verandah bar. The owners (who also run the *Papyrus Inn* at Lake Bogoria) can arrange boat trips from the jetty below the house. There are cheaper places in the village: *Hippo Lodge*, off to the left as you arrive, has reasonable rooms with mosquito nets (①); don't expect a quiet night here, though, as it's a tour drivers' hangout. So is the *Bahari Lodge*, near the post office, which is cleaner and better, with a welcoming bar-restaurant (ask for an upstairs room; ①). The *Lake View Lodge* offers little to justify the extra few shillings; it's quiet, but the view, such as it is, is only dimly seen through the mosquito screens (①). The *Ushirika Lodge* is very cheap and worth a try as a last resort (①).

Lake Baringo Club and Island Camp

In a totally **different league** you're faced with a difficult choice from two very attractive places to stay. *Island Camp* is the more expensive, but they both offer substantial off-season and residents' reductions. And if this is not your sort of budget, it is still worth splashing out for cold drinks and a swim on a casual visit.

Lake Baringo Club (☎ Kampi ya Samaki 1 or 2, or 2259 Radiocall Nairobi; reservations through *Block*, address p.48). A sumptuous and unpretentious hotel, this is a regular stop on ornithologial tours of Kenya; the lakeshore gardens are bursting with birds. Nurturing an interest in the natural environment is top of the agenda, with regular wildlife films and nightly audio-visuals to introduce guests to the local bird species. Children are made very welcome and will be round-eyed at the experience of encountering lake hippos at close range when they come to graze the well-watered lawns after dark (guards keep a careful watch). Reasonable **entry fees** are charged to casual visitors, but these are set against your bill if you eat – and the meals are generally excellent. There's an extra charge to use the small but irresistible swimming pool. ⑥ low, ⑧ high.

Island Camp (managed by *Hennessy Hotels*, PO Box 24434 Nairobi; reservations through *Let's Go Travel*, 1st Floor, Caxton House, Standard St, PO Box 60342, Nairobi, ☎ 02/340331 or 213033, fax 214713 or 336890). A no-comfort-ignored tented camp on Ol Kokwe Island in the middle of the lake. *Island Camp* charges day visitors more than *Lake Baringo Club*, with landing fees and a swimming pool fee, on top of the short but expensive motorboat crossing from their jetty on the north side of Kampi ya Samaki. It's a good day out, though: the scenic little island is dense with birdlife. ⑨.

Exploring the lake

Most **activities** tend to centre around *Lake Baringo Club* or *Island Camp*: boat trips around the shores (from about $6/hr), water-skiing ($60/hr) and wind-surfing ($12/hr), camel rides (the *Club* has two resident "riding camels" very much in evidence, about $5 per half-hour), morning tours of Lake Bogoria (about $55), and visits to a nearby Njemps *enkang* (about $5). The headman here, Lenjanoi Lekiseku, is paid a retainer by the *Club* and in return allows visitors to look around his compound and freely photograph his wives and children. The visit isn't a particularly comfortable one – you may feel obliged to buy some of the decorated gourds inscribed with planes and ostriches (among other motifs) which the women lay out – but your presence isn't resented. Here's a chance at least to come to terms with your camera's rarely welcome eye.

There are, of course, private, cheaper ways of arranging excursions in the vicinity of the lake. You'll receive plenty of offers of boat trips. The local boatmen may not all be trained wildlife experts but most of them are practised at luring fish eagles by tossing them fresh fish; take your camera for spectacular close-ups as the birds swoop down for the bait. For the equivalent of $15 or $20, you can get a boat trip to Ol Kokwe in the morning and a drive to the small hot springs on the lake's northeast shore in the afternoon. Share this between two or more and it becomes excellent value, but you'll probably need to spend a night or two in Kampi ya Samaki to make the arrangements.

Birdwatching

Baringo's 448 species of **birds** are one of its biggest draws, and even if you wouldn't know a superb starling from an ordinary one, the enthusiasm of others tends to be infectious. The bird population rises and falls with the seasons (the dry season is the leanest time for twitching; many birds return with the rains) but the lakeshore resounds with birdsong at most times of year (try responding to some of the calls). It's surprisingly easy to get within close range of the birds – some species, such as the starlings and the white-bellied go-away bird, are positively brazen – so you will find rapt amateur photographers lurking behind practically every bush.

Lake Baringo Club offers short, informal, morning or late-afternoon lecture **tours** with its resident ornithologist for around $6. The 5pm walk goes along the lake's reedy margin, while the 7am trip takes you out near the main road under some striking red cliffs, an utterly different habitat where, apart from hyraxes and baboons, you can see several species of hornbill, sometimes the massive nest of a hammerkop (wonderful-looking birds in flight, resembling miniature pterodactyls with their strange crests) and, with luck, the rare Verraux's eagle, a pair of which nest in the vicinity. You'll have a few dozen species pointed out to you in an hour. The world record "bird watch" for 24 hours is 342 species – held by former Baringo ornithologist, Terry Stevenson.

Of course you can do your own birdwatching. There's some interesting bush just beyond the *Club* to the south (accessible by walking back along the road), where you should see some unusual species such as the white phase of the paradise flycatcher, grey-headed bush shrike, violet wood hoopoe and various kingfishers. Hippos commonly graze here, too, even in daylight hours.

Kabarnet and the Kerio Valley

Many people make this trip in reverse order from Eldoret but, in either direction, it mirrors the journey down the eastern side of the Rift from Nyahururu, covered in the "Lake Bogoria" section. If you're setting out from Marigat, frequent *matatus* climb the first stage to Kabarnet.

Kabarnet

KABARNET, for all its piny preamble and the zippy new road cutting up the escarpment, is a major letdown. Its setting is superb, perched on the **Kamasia massif** – the slab of rift country, also known as the Tugen Hills, that remained upstanding on the brink of the Kerio Valley when the rest of the rift sank. But the town itself could hardly be more dull. Consisting of a small nucleus of *dukas* on the hillside, it has been considerably expanded in every direction in accordance with its designated function as capital of Baringo District. The result is a motley scattering of offices and civil servants' housing interspersed with wasteland; the planners must hope this will rapidly fill with enterprising businesses and workshops. President Moi's home town, Kabarnet is clearly earmarked for development, but is expanding in area faster than it's growing in significance. The **post office**, **supermarket** and covered **market** are about all that could interest you, and even then the market's selection is very limited.

Standing above it all, the faintly pompous *Kabarnet Hotel* (PO Box 109 Kabarnet; ☎0328/22094; reservations through *AT&H*, address p.48; ⑤); seems to be jumping the gun: it sometimes suffers from water shortages but it's worth a visit for its mountain views and above-average food. There's even a swimming pool – though at this altitude it's not an overwhelmingly tempting prospect. The best alternative in town is the *Sinkoro*, off the main road near the cinema (PO Box 256; ☎0328/2245; ③).

Into the Kerio Valley

The excitement of this route builds only after you leave Kabarnet and plunge **into the Kerio Valley**, a drop of 1000m in not much more than the same distance. With the completion of the paved **Tambach escarpment road**, you'll find pretty constant *matatu* traffic across the valley; the road has magnificent views as it rolls through **Chebloch**, with its old bridge over the Kerio River, then turns sharply up to **Iten**, a tiny grass-verged market town, and thence to Eldoret. If you want to explore the valley off this now somewhat beaten track, you'll notice a serious dearth of any kind of public transport on the other trans-valley routes. As usual, having your own four-wheel-drive vehicle is insurance against detours or setbacks on the rough tracks. Except during the heavy rains which usually fall in April–May (if local people are lucky), high clearance for rocky roads is more important than good traction.

Making your way **on foot and by available transport** off the main road, you'll usually get through, though your precise choice of route may be constrained by the direction in which vehicles are moving. The main alternative to the Tambach–Iten

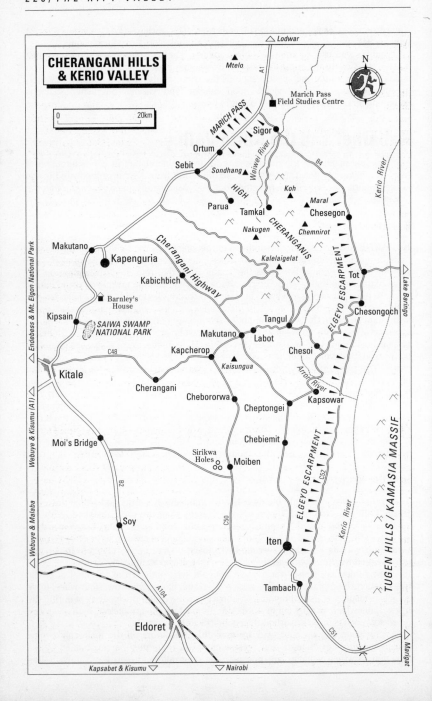

CHERANGANI HILLS & KERIO VALLEY

0   20km

route heads through **Tenges** and Kimwarer. To Tenges, a surfaced road twists spectacularly south from Kabarnet along the spine of the Tugen Hills, with lovely views across
the valley. You'll find some public transport to Tenges from Kabarnet, but very little
when you turn right (west) for Kimwarer down in the valley.

Along the valley
Kimwarer is the largest community in the Kerio Valley, a company town for the **fluorspar mine** at the head of the Kerio River. With nothing but bush, Kalenjin herders and
the occasional party of honey-hunters round about, Kimwarer's tidy managerial villas
and staff quarters come as a surprise, and "Fluorspar Primary School" looks positively
progressive with its brilliant paint job and playground trees all neatly labelled with their
Latin names.

The town has grown rapidly in the last few years as plans for the production of a
thousand tonnes a day of fluorspar have been realized. Fluorspar (calcium fluoride) is
used in the manufacture of steel, aluminum, cement – and CFCs. If you're interested,
arrangements can be made to visit the "rock crusher". For the route from Eldoret to
Kimwarer, see p.264.

It's possible to **hitch** the length of the Kerio Valley from here, leaving it at Tot and
picking up transport on the Lodwar–Kitale road. Most of the time, however, you'll probably be "footing" or waiting by the side of the road: no matter (as long as you have
several days), for this road, following one of the country's most beautiful valleys, is
worth a few blisters. Climatic conditions are best in the few months of vivid greenery
after the long rains – and fiercest in February and March, just before they break.
Densely wooded and not much cultivated in the south, for most of the year the valley
resonates with dry heat and the rattle of cicadas and crickets. A new nature reserve,
the **Kammarok/Kerio Valley National Reserve**, has been established around the
Kerio gorge, but for the time being you can hike everywhere and there are villages at
reasonably frequent intervals along the road.

The Tambach escarpment road provides a quick exit from the southern end of the
valley, up the route that used to cause a lot of problems for rally drivers each Easter.
The **Torok Falls**, near Tambach, are said to be worth a visit.

The Elgeyo Escarpment and Cherangani Hills

The Rift Valley is not short of astonishing vistas, but even here few roads match the
track up the **Elgeyo Escarpment** south of Tot for precipitousness and sheer daring. A
thousand, two thousand, metres below, spreading like a grey-green carpet into the haze,
are the scrubby, bush-covered plains of Pokot and south Turkana. Dozens of tiny wisps
of smoke from charcoal burners combine to smudge out the distant peaks of Mount
Kenya to the southeast. Places where trees grow thicker mark the passage of tempera-
mental seasonal streams which flood and dry up with the rains: Pokot gold-panners still
find enough gold in them to trade with anyone passing through. To add to this distinctive sense of place, the escarpment itself is the location of an ancient **irrigation system**,
feeding water from the hills down to the lush cultivation at the foot of the scarp.

Practicalities
Most easily approached on the returning leg of a trip to Turkana, the Elgeyo
Escarpment road is diabolical: too rocky for any kind of ordinary car and too steep for
any but the most steel-nerved of drivers. It's a thrilling, gut-wrenching trip in a Land
Rover – someone else's preferably – but think twice before driving up here yourself: it
is very, *very* steep. As a walk, getting to the top in one day from Tot is perfectly feasible.
You may be lucky and find a ride, if you want it.

IN SEARCH OF THE SIRIKWA HOLES

To seek out the **Sirikwa Holes** near Moiben purely for their own sake would require a certain degree of scholarly dedication, but if you're approaching the Cherangani Hills from the Iten to Eldoret road, or following the route out of the northern Kerio Valley, a visit does make an interesting diversion. Perhaps needless to say, it's a lot easier with your own wheels. *Matatus* run daily from Eldoret or Iten to Moiben (continuing on to Chebororwa on the edge of the Cheranganis); you might have to change at the junction where the murram road to Moiben leaves the new paved road. Occasional farm vehicles pass this way, but you could be in for a long wait.

The Sirikwa Holes are some 6km west of Moiben. From the crossroads by the upper primary school and chief's office, follow the dirt track past another school on the left and out into farmland. You may need to ask directions, first for Rany Moi Farm and then for the holes themselves – known locally as "Maasai holes" or "Maasai homes". Don't ask for "Sirikwa Holes", as Moiben is the main location of Sirikwa District and you'd probably be directed to the district offices.

The holes are a collection of depressions, some circular, about ten metres across and a few metres deep, others a longer oval shape, all ringed by large stones. Some holes are alone, others are joined by passages dug a metre or so into the ground. They closely resemble the pit dwellings at Hyrax Hill near Nakuru. So far, the site is relatively undisturbed, except for gaps in the stone rings where the odd stone has been removed for building. But as the pressure from local farms increases, it seems likely that these enigmatic remains will eventually be demolished and ploughed over.

Tot, apart from being something of a route focus and a delightfully isolated, peaceful village, offers nothing special, but it's the sort of place where you might happily spend a week doing just that. Camping would probably be okay, but you may also be offered accommodation at the civil servants' quarters on the east side of the road or at one of the small *hotelis*. Leaving again, you'll probably find a lift from Tot to **Chesegon** on Sundays and Wednesdays when Chesegon has its market – quite a spectacle as people come from the bush from miles around. From there you'll get a *matatu* on to Sigor and the Marich Pass (see Chapter 4, p.269), where you'll soon find transport down to Kapenguria and Kitale.

Tot to Chesoi – the Marakwet water channels

From Tot, you can walk or hitch (but don't count on seeing a vehicle, much less on its having space) the 25 breathtaking kilometres up to **Chesoi**, turning right halfway at **Chesongoch** for the main ascent. The rocky, almost perpendicular slopes are dotted with **Marakwet** homesteads, the huts unusual in being built of stone (there's a limitless supply up here), which gives them an ancient-looking permanence rarely seen in Kenyan rural architecture.

The irrigation system

The Marakwet may have arrived on these slopes as far back as a thousand years ago. Part of the broadly related Kalenjin group of peoples, they claim to have taken over the **irrigation system** on the escarpment from its previous users. They say the channels were there long before their own forefathers arrived, and it is possible the original irrigators were a mysterious group called the **Sirikwa**. These people have disappeared, or more likely been absorbed, and the only reminders of them are their name and a lot of curious **holes**, earthworks and cairns (see box above) noticed by archeologists around the Kerio Valley and in other parts of western Kenya.

Marakwet elders still remember stories of a small people called the **Terngeng**, who may have lived in pits in the ground something like those at Hyrax Hill and Moiben. Other stories refer to tall, long-haired, bearded men who roamed the Rift Valley. Either or both of these groups might have been responsible for the building of the irrigation system, but neither sounds very agricultural; perhaps the Marakwet's claim to have inherited the system but not built it is just a way of saying how old it really is.

The Marakwet canals and Chesoi

Whatever the truth about their origins, **the waterworks** are undeniably impressive in scope, if not especially in appearance, stretching north–south for over 40km to divert water from the Cherangani Hills' gushing streams into a branching layout of furrows and aqueducts. Instead of plummeting straight into the Kerio River, the water gets neatly distributed along the escarpment, with complex, unwritten laws to ensure that each Marakwet sub-clan is fairly provided for. It's a system without parallel anywhere else in the country and the results, as you'll see along the base of the scarp, are spectacular. Indeed, for a considerable distance up the Kerio Valley, there's a band of intensive, luxuriant gardening: tiny *shambas* slotted back-to-back between the spurs and down towards the main river. Magnificent, richly flavoured bananas are on sale everywhere. Many of the irrigation channels now pass under the road, but a few still flow over it and a great deal of ongoing repair work is obviously needed to keep the streams flowing in the right direction.

The best place to see a good furrow is up near **Chesoi** over the crest of the scarp. The land here buckles like a patchwork quilt, with the Cherangani Hills stretching west. "Chesoi canal" is a major water supply a couple of kilometres behind Chesoi centre, a metre-wide channel clinging to the hillside (ask someone to show you). In other places, the irrigation system has become almost a piped water supply, with hollow logs used as aqueducts, but this channel has been built with cement (which sells out everywhere as fast as it becomes available). Unfortunately, the water round about, diverted from the Arror River, tastes disgusting, even when boiled: it's a problem you encounter often in the Cheranganis.

There's nothing in Chesoi village itself – no water, no *hotelis* and certainly nowhere to stay – so stop down at the junction if you plan to overnight here. At least the people up here at the edge of the Cheranganis are delighted to meet strangers: as a start, go to the *Kosutany hoteli* (a small *chai* shop), and ask if you can sleep on the floor. You could also camp easily, just about anywhere, if you can find a flat space – ask the landowner.

Onwards from Chesoi: walking in the Cheranganis

If you have the time and inclination, **walking in the Cheranganis** is exhilarating. The thickly forested hills are wild, hardly explored, and still home to bongo antelope. Higher up (Kamelogon peak on Mount Chemnirot is 3517m), they give onto mountain moorland and giant Afro-alpine vegetation: some superb hiking country where you're very unlikely to meet any others doing the same. A couple of days will see you over the southern ridges to Kapcherop on the so-called "Cherangani Highway", where you'll have no difficulty picking up transport west to Kitale or southeast into the Rift Valley.

For this route, you first climb through Chesoi village and past the mission for about ninety minutes through *shambas*; then there's an hour's walk through forest, mostly flat; ninety minutes of climbing through bamboo forest; and a further two hours though hilly pasturelands and woods before you reach **Tangul**. Tangul is a crossroads centre, a suitable stop for the night with a few *hotelis* and a morning and/or evening *matatu* run. From Tangul, routes lead: northwest to Kalelaigelat summit (motorable to the base in a couple of hours, but with no *matatus* and no water); north to the main

Cherangani peaks (again motorable in 2–3hr or a day's walk); and south on a little-used road for two to three hours to **Labot** and – 5km further – **Makutano** (*not* the Makutano near Kapenguria). Labot has some *hotelis*; Makutano has none, but is on another significant crossroads. South of Makutano, a quiet motor road leads down through grassland, then forest to **Kapcherop** (home of Kenya's international athletics champion Moses Kiptanui) – about a three-hour walk. Note if you're driving that the Tangul–Chesoi part of this route is non-motorable and you can only drive to Tangul from the south or west.

If your hiking plans are more ambitious, get hold of the relevant *Survey of Kenya* 1:50m-scale maps (see application details on p.127) and set off, suitably equipped, over the high central districts of the massif. There are several, relatively easily scaled peaks up here. *Mountain Walking in Kenya* by David Else (Robertson McCarta, UK) provides detailed guidance on certain routes.

Chesoi–Kapsowar–Eldoret

Altogether more straightforward as a continuation from Chesoi is the murram road **towards Eldoret**. To be sure of a *matatu* from Chesoi, you'll need to be up and ready by 6am; one or two other vehicles may come through later in the day but this transport can't be relied on. Alternatively, it's a fine and easy twenty-kilometre walk (mostly downhill) around the **highland spurs** to **Kapsowar**. Much of the time you'll seem to be doubling back on yourself – Kapsowar and Chesoi are only 8km apart as the crow flies. Kapsowar's hospital makes it a local magnet and there's no problem finding onward transport from here.

Beyond Kapsowar, the road changes its mind less often and, after climbing again out of Kapsowar's valley through patches of **forest**, it emerges onto the Uasin Gishu plateau. Then it's all rolling ranch lands, wheat fields and stands of conifers and gum trees as far as Eldoret (p.260).

travel details

Nakuru is the whole region's travel hub. More local details are given in the appropriate sections.

Trains

Reservations can be made through *Kenya Railways* in Nakuru on ☎037/40211.
From **Nakuru** to:
Kisumu daily at 12.30am (all stations).
Nairobi daily at 2.25am.
Eldoret, **Malaba** Tues at 3pm, Fri & Sat at 12.45am.

Buses

From **Nakuru** to:
Kisumu 7 daily; 4hr 30min.
Nairobi 16 daily; 3hr.
Eldoret 3 daily; 4hr.
Nyahururu 8am & 9pm daily.
Many other lines operate out of Nakuru, eg to **Kampi ya Samaki** (2 daily; 3hr).

Peugeot taxis

From **Nakuru** to:
Nairobi a constant stream; 90min.

Matatus

From **Nakuru** to: **Mau escarpment towns**, **Nairobi**, **Subukia**, **Nyahururu**, **Narok**, **Marigat**, **Kabarnet** and all over western Kenya.

Hitching

From **Nakuru** to:
Nairobi Stand on the road out of town just past the railway bridge. Walking further isn't very helpful.
Westwards Difficult, so take a *matatu* to get out of town and onto the right road, the A104.
Northwards OK as far as Kampi ya Samaki (Lake Baringo). The paved road stops at the end of the lake.

CHAPTER FOUR

WESTERN KENYA

L
ike the tiers of a great amphitheatre, **western Kenya** slopes down to face the stage of Lake Victoria, away from Nairobi, the major game parks and the coast. Cut off by the high Rift wall of the **Mau and Elgeyo escarpments**, the western region of dense agriculture, rolling green valleys and pockets of thick jungle is one of the least-known parts of the country to travellers. Although more accessible than the far north, or even some of the big parks, it has been neglected by the safari operators – and that's all to the good. You can travel for days through lush landscapes from one busy market town to the next and rarely, if ever, meet other tourists or travellers.

It's not easy to see why it has been so ignored. Granted, the disastrous history of Uganda up until the late 1980s discouraged the through traffic that might otherwise have thrived. But there's a great deal more of intrinsic interest than the tourist literature's sparse coverage would suggest. What the west undeniably lacks are teeming herds of antelope and zebra, lions at the side of the road and narcissistic warriors in full regalia. What it does offer is a series of delightfully low-key, easily visited attractions. There are **national parks** at **Kakamega Forest**, a magnificent tract of equatorial rain forest bursting with species found nowhere else in Kenya; **Saiwa Swamp**, where pedestrians, for once, have the upper hand; and **Mount Elgon**, a volcano to rival Mount Kenya in everything but crowds. **Lake Victoria**, with the region's major town, **Kisumu**, on its shores, is a draw in its own right, dotted with out-of-the-way islands.

Travel is generally easy: the region has a high population and many well-paved roads, so you'll rarely have long to wait for a bus or *matatu*, and driving is often a pleasure. If you're inclined to plan ahead, there *is* a vague circuit that begins in Kisumu (as this chapter does) and runs through **Kisii** (of Kisii-stone fame), Kericho, Eldoret, Kitale and Kakamega. You could easily do this in a couple of weeks – or a couple of months. But it's often more rewarding to let events dictate your next move: this area will repay your interest repeatedly if you take time to look around. Much of it, even areas of intensive farming, is ravishingly beautiful: densely animated jungle near **Kakamega** and **Kitale**, regimented landscapes of tea bushes at **Kericho**, highland pastures and forests in the **Cherangani Hills**, dank swamp and grasslands alive with birds by the lake.

There's almost no tourist infrastructure – the west has only a handful of hotels that could by any stretch of the imagination be described as luxurious – but there's no lack of good, modest **lodgings**. **Food** is as cheap as anywhere and generally excellent; most

---

ACCOMMODATION PRICE CODES

Rates for a standard double or twin room. For a full explanation of these price codes, see p.46.

① Under Ksh300   (under approx. £3.30/$5)
② Ksh300–500   (£3.30/$5–£5.50/$8)
③ Ksh500–1000   (£5.50/$8–£11/$17)
④ Ksh1000–2000 (£11/$17–£22/$33)
⑤ Ksh2000–4000   (£22/$33–£44/$67)
⑥ Ksh4000–6000   (£44/$67–£67/$100)
⑦ Ksh6000–8000   (£67/$100–£89/$133)
⑧ Ksh8000–10,000 (£89/$133–£111/$167)
⑨ Over Ksh10,000   (over £111/$167)

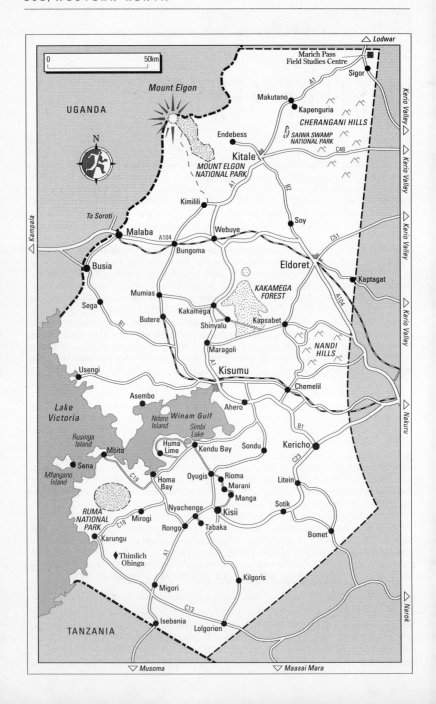

0   50km

Mount Elgon

UGANDA

N

To Soroti

Kampala

Malaba   A104
                        Bungoma
Busia

Sega

Mumias

Butere

Kimilili   Webuye   Soy

Endebess

Kitale

*MOUNT ELGON
NATIONAL PARK*

Makutano

Kapenguria

CHERANGANI HILLS

*SAIWA SWAMP
NATIONAL PARK*

Marich Pass
Field Studies Centre

Sigor

A1

Lodwar

Kerio Valley

Kerio Valley

Kerio Valley

Kerio Valley

Kerio Valley

C48

B2

Eldoret   Kaptagat

*KAKAMEGA
FOREST*

Kakamega

Shinyalu   Kapsabet

Maragoli

Kisumu

Chemelil

Ahero

*NANDI
HILLS*

A104

C51

Nakuru

A1

*Lake
Victoria*

Asembo

*Ndere
Island*

Winam Gulf

*Simbi
Lake*

*Rusinga
Island*

Mbita

Sena

*Mfangano
Island*

*RUMA
NATIONAL
PARK*

Karungu

Huma
Lime

Kendu Bay

Homa
Bay

C19

Mirogi

C18

Rongo

Oyugis

Nyachenge

Rioma

Marani

Manga

Kisii

Tabaka

Sondu

Kericho

C23

Litein

Sotik

Bomet

B1

Usengi

◆Thimlich
Ohinga

A1

Migori

Kilgoris

Isebania   Lolgorien

C13

TANZANIA

△ *Musoma*   ▽ *Maasai Mara*   *Narok*

of Kenya's tea and sugar comes from the west, and agricultural concerns are paramount.

Ethnically, the region is dominated by the **Luo** on the lakeshore lowlands, but other important groups speak Kalenjin languages (principally the **Nandi** around Eldoret and the **Kipsigis** in the Kericho district) and there are Bantu-speaking **Luyia** in the sugar lands north of Kisumu and **Gusii** in the formidably fertile Kisii Hills.

AROUND LAKE VICTORIA: LUOLAND

Lake Victoria is the obvious place to make for in the west, but frustratingly few main roads get close to its shores. In the still, sultry atmosphere of **Kisumu**, the regional capital, the distinctive smell of the lake – not unpleasant – blows in on a vague breeze from central Africa, but the layout of the town offers only incidental lake vistas. Turning its back on the lake, Kisumu focuses instead on its commercial centre and its land links to the rest of Kenya. The town went through a period of disintegration when the decline of lake traffic destroyed its status as a major port, but nevertheless it retains a great deal of character and tattered charm. As a town with a sense of dignity as well as a sense of purpose, it has much more in common with Mombasa than with the hassle and grime of Nairobi or Nakuru.

In order to get a good look at the lake itself, take the short trip out of town to **Hippo Point** and the fishing village of **Dunga**, or take advantage of the ferry services and visit one or two islands. Kisumu's ancient motor vessels carry passengers and cargo along the shores of the Winam Gulf to **Mbita** (for **Rusinga Island**) and, twice a week, out to **Mfangano Island**. The other ports around Victoria's eastern shores are something of a disappointment except as staging posts: you could disembark at **Kendu Bay** or **Homa Bay** for the short journey inland to Kisii. **Kuwur Bay** is the port for Huma Lime, a village with nearby hot springs at the base of Mount Homa. See the ferry timetables on p.241.

Kisumu

Kenya's third largest town, **KISUMU**, has always been decidedly distinguished. Expensive cars cruise the broad, colonnaded commercial streets and, in the well-to-do residential district, well-guarded mansions are discreetly spaced along quiet, fragrant avenues. But Kisumu's fortunes were founded on the lucrative lake shipping business, funnelling goods between Kenya, Uganda and Tanzania, and the town suffered badly as a result of the East African Community's break-up. During the 1980s and early 1990s, the port was practically dormant, with little or no merchandise passing through and signs of dereliction everywhere – empty warehouses, broken windows, deserted dock-workers' houses. The shipping services to Tanzania and Uganda have now resumed on a modest scale and the port sporadically buzzes with activity, but it will take a long stretch of sustained growth to restore Kisumu to its former affluence.

Some history

The **railway line** from Mombasa had been stretched out as far as the lake by 1901 (pleasing and reassuring the British public who, after so many years, were beginning to have serious doubts about the project ever reaching completion), but the first train only chugged into **Port Florence** station in 1903 when the Mau Escarpment viaducts were completed. By that time, European transport had already arrived at the lake in the

LAKE VICTORIA

The westward view from Kisumu gives you little sense of the vastness of **Victoria Nyanza (Lake Victoria)**. The shores of the relatively narrow Winam Gulf curve gently to left and right, and it's difficult to grasp the fact that there's another 300km of water between the horizon and the opposite (Ugandan) shore, and an even greater distance south to Mwanza, the main Tanzanian port. Victoria, the second largest freshwater lake in the world (after Lake Superior), covers a total **area** of close on 70,000 square kilometres – more than twice the size of Wales – of which only a fraction belongs to Kenya.

Our knowledge of **Victoria Nyanza (Lake Victoria)** is relatively recent. It was barely five centuries ago that the **Luo** first settled beside the vast equatorial lake they called **Ukerewe**, and the lake remained uncharted and virtually unknown outside Africa until well into the second half of the nineteenth century. Then, in the midst of the scramble to pinpoint the **source of the Nile**, the lake suddenly became a focus of attention.

To the nineteenth-century explorers, the search for the source of Africa's longest river was something of a crusade, and none was more obsessed with the pursuit of this geographical Holy Grail than the English adventurer **John Hanning Speke**. As soon as Speke set eyes upon Ukerewe in 1858, he was convinced that the long search was over, and he promptly renamed the lake in tribute to his sovereign, Queen Victoria. He returned to explore the area more comprehensively in 1860, and, in 1862, became the first European to sail the length of the Nile from Lake Victoria all the way to Cairo, famously confirming his discovery by cabling the Royal Geographical Society in London with the words "The Nile is settled". However, sceptics continued to counter that Lake Tanganyika was the true source, and it took a daring circumnavigation of Victoria, led by Stanley in 1875, to prove Speke right. Sadly, Speke didn't live to glory in the vindication – he was killed in a shooting accident in 1874.

Lake Victoria was of great strategic significance to the explorers but it was no paradise. **Bilharzia-carrying snails** flourished in the reeds around the lake's fringes, and the steamy shore was a fertile breeding ground for **malarial mosquitoes**. These hazards persist today. The Luo wash, swim and sail their vividly painted, dhow-like, mahogany canoes in and on Victoria Nyanza, but the danger of bilharzia is all too real. Instances of the disease are rare after brief contact with infected water, but for the visitor it's not worth the risk: take care if you're going fishing or boating on the lake, and don't even think about going swimming. Newer health scares surface from time to time: recently, scientists have speculated that the islands off the Ugandan shore may have served as hatcheries for HIV, the AIDS virus.

LAKE ECOLOGY

Lake Victoria is not part of the rift system. Unlike the Rift Valley lakes it is shallow – no more than 80m deep. Interestingly, it contains nearly 200 different species of brilliantly

form of a steamship brought up from Mombasa piece by portered piece, having steamed out from Scotland in 1895 (there's an obscure subplot to this story of European incursion: many of the ship's parts were evidently seized en route from the coast and recycled into Nandi ornamentation and weaponry: it was five years before a complete vessel could be assembled and launched on its maiden voyage across the lake to Port Bell in Uganda).

Kisumu was, by all accounts, a pretty disagreeable place in the early years. Apart from the endemic sleeping sickness, bilharzia, malaria and the nasty malarial complication known as "blackwater fever", the climate was sweltering and municipal hygiene primitive. But it quickly grew into an important administrative and military base; and with the consolidation of the colonies in the 1930s and 1940s, it became a leading East African entrepôt and transport hub, attracting Asian investment on top of the businesses that had been set up at the railway terminus when the Indian labourers

coloured tropical **fish**, known as haplochromines or **cichlids** – all of them unique to the lake. Scientists, puzzling over how such a dazzling variety of species came to evolve in this largely uniform environment in the space of no more than a million years, have suggested that, at some stage in its history, the lake must have dried into a series of small lakes in which the fish evolved separately. Lake Victoria's cichlids are popular aquarium fish, and one of the commonest larger species, the tilapia, is a regional speciality, grilled or fried and eaten whole.

When, over the last couple of decades, the cichlid population seemed to be dwindling, accusing fingers were pointed at the new-fish-on-the-block, the **Nile perch**. Native to the Nile, but not to Lake Victoria, these carnivorous fish were introduced in the late 1950s, and established themselves extremely quickly. For the lake peoples they were a boon: they can grow to weigh as much as 250kg, and are both consumed locally and sold for export (in France Nile perch steaks are sold as *capitaine*). But the voraciousness of these fish began to send shock waves through the lake ecosystem, and ecologists were thrown into a panic by the prospect of the perch eating their way through the entire cichlid population and ultimately starving to death themselves. The expert verdict was that the murderous perch should be fished to extinction in order to save the other species, but the perch received a stay of execution when it was suggested that over-fishing using fine-meshed nets was even more of a threat to the cichlids than predation. Despite a boom in the fish trade, fishing restrictions are now in place.

Over-fishing is in fact just one of a series of factors responsible for the **deterioration** of Lake Victoria and its shoreline. Oxygen levels in the lake appear to be falling, with the result that algae are proliferating and the fish population is under threat. The link to human population growth is a direct one – recent studies have estimated that over three million litres of human waste is drained into the lake every day, while sand harvesting, over-grazing and clearance of lakeshore vegetation for cultivation have all disturbed the fine ecological balance of the shore area. The building of the causeway from Mbita to Rusinga Island turned the Winam Gulf into a pond with only one outlet, inhibiting air circulation, with serious consequences for the local lake environment. A more sinister threat comes from the insidious **water hyacinth**. This floating weed grows quickly around the lakeshore, blocking out the light and slowly choking the lake to death. In Uganda, troops have been mobilized to collect any plants they come across and treat any new areas of growth with weed-killing chemicals; Tanzania has been experimenting with weed-eating weevils; but Kenya has yet to take any decisive action beyond investigating the possibility of importing beetles from Benin to eat the plants. Boatmen have been asked to collect any water hyacinth they see and, rather than throwing it away, take it back to shore and burn it. The weed is already encroaching round the pier area at Kendu Bay.

were laid off. Since the community's collapse in 1977, however, Kisumu's star has waned so low that even the huge molasses refinery, which would have given a much needed boost to the region's economy (still heavily reliant on sugar cane), has never been finished, and there's no immediate prospect of any progess. The lamentable catalogue of stalled initiatives also includes the Rice Mill, Omino Plaza and Lake Basin Development Authority headquarters construction projects. As the crisis has deepened, employment has become scarcer and scarcer; skilled manpower has migrated to other towns, and the population has dropped to under 250,000. Kisumu is a United States Peace Corps and British VSO centre, and the volunteers maintain a fairly high profile – at least in relation to the air of stagnation all around.

But the picture isn't entirely bleak. Kisumu does have considerable charm, and it's no small advantage to be one of the few up-country towns with real character (though the slightly time-warped atmosphere of a place that's been treading water for most of two

THE LUO

The **Luo** are the third largest ethnic group and one of the most cohesive "tribes" in Kenya. Their language, Jaluo, is distinctive and closely resembles the Nuer and Dinka languages of southern Sudan, from where their ancestors migrated south at the end of the fifteenth century. They found the shore and hinterland of Lake Victoria only sparsely populated by hunter-gatherers, scattered with occasional clearings where Bantu-speaking farmers had settled over the previous centuries. Otherwise, the region was wild: untouched grasslands and tropical forest, dense with heavy concentrations of wildlife.

The Luo were swift invaders, driving their herds before them, always on the move, restless and acquisitive. They raided other groups' cattle incessantly, and within a few decades had forced the Bantu-speakers away from the lakeshore. Nevertheless, over the generations, **intermarriage** (essentially, the buying of wives) was common and the pastoral nomads were greatly influenced by their Bantu-speaking in-laws and neighbours, ancestors of the present-day Luyia and Gusii.

The Luo today are best known as fishermen but they also cultivate widely and still keep livestock. Culturally, they have remained surprisingly independent. They are one of the few Kenyan peoples who don't practise circumcision. Traditionally, children had six teeth knocked out from the lower jaw to mark their initiation into adulthood, but the operation is rarely carried out these days.

Early in the **colonial period**, the Luo benefited from some inspired, if dictatorial, leadership. They had inherited the institution of the *ruoth* (king or chief) from the original immigrants from Sudan. The *ruoth* of Gem, a location northwest of Kisumu, was Odera Akang'o, an ambitious and perceptive young man with an almost puritanical attitude to his duties. He had a private police force to inspect farms and report any idleness to him, and he regularly had his subjects beaten or fined for "unprogressive" behaviour. He introduced new crops and, under British protection, made himself quite a sizeable fortune. He was widely feared.

In 1915, the colonial government sent him, with two other chiefs, to Kampala; he returned full of admiration for the European education and health standards there, and ashamed of Gem and Luoland in general. Fired with enthusiasm, he applied his style of schooling and hygiene, bullying his subjects into sending their children to classes and keeping their shirts clean, while the British turned a blind eye. The results were rapid educational advances in Gem, which is still considered a progressive district today. Odera, unfortunately for him, was employed by the British to use his methods on the Teso people in Uganda, where they singularly failed. He was accused of corruption and sent into internal exile, where he died.

decades may not be much comfort to its inhabitants). To anyone who's ever travelled in central Africa, Kisumu seems to have more in common with that region than with the rest of Kenya. It's a distinctly tranquil, easy-going town, the *manambas* in the bus station are unusually laid-back, and any anticipation of claustrophobia is quickly soothed by the spacious, shady layout. On Sunday evenings it seems the entire Asian community takes a constitutional along Oginga Odinga Avenue. The contrast with Nakuru is striking.

Arrival and accommodation

Kisumu is a natural base, excellently located for exploring western Kenya: half a day's travelling should get you to any of the centres detailed in this chapter. The **bus and train stations** are on opposite sides of town: the first is sited by the big junction of the Nairobi and Kakamega roads, the second down the hill in the port area. It is a good idea to install yourself soon after arriving, before starting any energetic wanderings, as it gets tremendously hot here. Try not to arrive on a Sunday: more than most towns, on the "day of rest" just about everything in Kisumu shuts down – even restaurants.

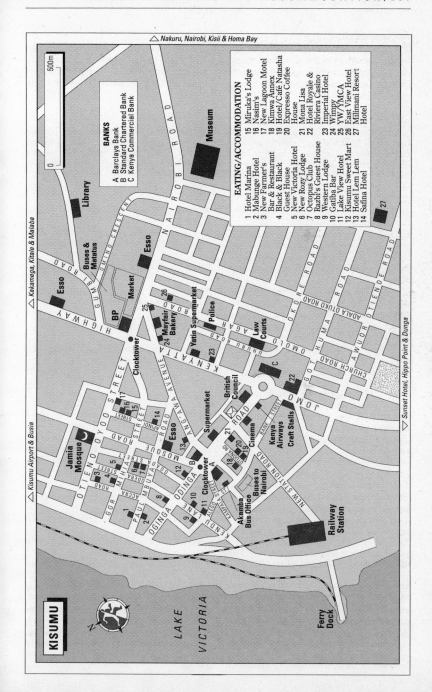

Accommodation

There's a wide choice of **places to stay**, with a good number of modest, mid-range hotels, though prices tend to be somewhat higher than usual. Temperature, humidity and mosquitoes will conspire to give you an uncomfortable night if you don't have a net or a fan (and preferably both), so it's worth paying a little more for the few nights you may be in town.

CAMPING

Dunga Refreshments, Hippo Point (PO Box 96; ☎035/42529). Cheap, but shadeless, lakeside camping on grass with good security and showers. A wooden building ("Resting Room – Campers Only") serves as a day lounge, complete with mosquito screens and couches, but may be used, at a pinch, by tent-less overnighters. The place is famous for its meals (see "Eating, drinking and night-life"). Camping Ksh100 per person, Ksh300 to stay inside.

BOARDING & LODGINGS

Hotel Beograda, Omino Crescent (PO Box 920; ☎035/3424). Close by the bus station, this has had many thumbs down of late. ②.

Catherine Guest House, Dunga, on the road to Hippo Point (PO Box 1364; ☎035/21302). Guest rooms with hot water and mosquito nets in a welcoming and secure compound with a bar and restaurant. ③.

Mabunge Hotel, Paul Mbuya Rd (PO Box 1607). Not spotless but light and airy; restaurant down-stairs.③.

Miruka's Lodge, Apindi St. Basic, cheap, grubby rooms. ①.

Mona Lisa, Oginga Odinga Rd. Seedy s/c rooms behind the long-established restaurant. ②.

Nasim's, Apindi St. Another no-frills option for the hard up. ①.

New Lagoon Motel, Otieno Oyoo St (PO Box 1400; ☎035/42118). Very run-down, but at least the rooms (some s/c) are a decent size. ①.

New Rozy Lodge, Ogada St, next to the *Octopus Club* (PO Box 548; ☎035/41990). Dingy, unfriendly and overpriced. ②.

Razbi's Guest House, Oginga Odinga St (PO Box 1418; ☎035/41312). A well thought-of stand-by – basic, but good value, clean and secure, and a popular volunteers' hangout at weekends. One of the rooms has a lake view of sorts. ①.

Safari Hotel, Omino Crescent, next to the *Beograda*, but better and cheaper. ①.

Safina Hotel, Apindi St. A favourite divey hotel – cheap enough, but ask for a room away from where the cars pull up at night. Women travelling alone might find the atmosphere a little threatening. ①.

YW/YMCA, off Ang'awa Ave. Offers rather bland good value but it's friendly and cheap, if errati-cally supplied with water. There's a canteen and it's also possible to camp here, though few people do. Triple rooms Ksh150 per person.

CHEAP HOTELS

Black & Black Guest House, Gor Mahia Rd. Not quite as badly overpriced as the *New Victoria*, just up the hill, but don't expect your room to have mosquito nets or private facilities. ③.

East View Hotel, Omolo Agar Rd. Tranquil and spotlessly clean, this place is handy if you've just crawled off the bus. And, if you're driving, good for its safe parking. ③.

Lake View Hotel, Alego St (PO Box 45055). No exceptional views, though with its corner position, it does offer some breeze. Fairly comfortable but overpriced. ③.

Hotel Marina, Paul Mbuya Rd (☎035/23485). Very comfortable, well-furnished rooms and a quiet restaurant/bar that aims upmarket. A good choice. ③.

Hotel Natasha, Otuona Rd. Decent s/c rooms with hot water but there are better deals to be had elsewhere. ③.

New Victoria Hotel, Gor Mahia Rd (PO Box 276; ☎035/21067). Quite adequate but out of the budget bracket. Room 209 is the best. ③.

Western Lodge, Kendu Lane (PO Box 1519; ☎035/42586). Clean, secure (with a large locking cupboard in every room), inexpensive and friendly, this is an excellent little place. Half the rooms have lake views. Unfortunately there's no food, and, when the nearby goods yard and port road are busy and the bar opposite turns the music up, it's noisy. ②.

MID-RANGE HOTELS

Imperial Hotel, Jomo Kenyatta Highway (PO Box 1866; ☎035/41485). The first choice of wealthy Kenyans, this seems determined to eclipse the opposition in terms of prices and flashiness. B&B; ⑥.

Milimani Resort Hotel, off Got Huma Rd (PO Box 2652; ☎035/23245, fax 035/23242). A brand new hotel in a secure compound in Kisumu's quiet residential district, with comfortable rooms and self-catering apartments. The staff are friendly and gracious and there are good views from the upper floors. Downstairs is a restaurant and lounge (no alcohol served); planned additions include cottages and a pool. For now it's good value. ④.

Hotel Royale, Jomo Kenyatta Highway (PO Box 1690; ☎035/44240). Formerly a good place to meet people and highly rated for its Thursday evening Indian barbecue, the rooms still aren't up to much considering the alternatives. The frontage is dominated by the *Riviera* slot machine casino and a raffish terrace bar. ④.

Sunset Hotel, Aput Lane, slightly out of town to the south (PO Box 215; ☎035/41100, fax 035/42534; reservations most recently through *AT&H*, see p.48, but the hotel is due to change hands). These days rather middle-of-the-road, though there are views of beautiful sunsets from every room, for which privilege you pay the second highest rates in town. If you retain a sense of proportion and prefer Kisumu's more soulful places, you can still drop in for a whiff of plasticky high-life – and the sunsets. First-class swimming pool in verdant, well-tended gardens complete with monkeys and parrots. ⑤.

The Town

The **market** by the bus station is the biggest and best in western Kenya, crammed with fruit and vegetables (including some oddities like breadfruit), and all the usual household paraphernalia – pots and plates, reed brushes, wooden spoons. It's an absorbing place to wander. The market is such a success that it has mushroomed out into the adjacent municipal park, much to the consternation of the local authorities. Three new market buildings were built in 1984 with a multi-million-shilling World Bank loan, but, convinced that high rents on the new buildings coupled with unequal competition from squatters would slash their profits, the traders have steadfastly refused to move, and the buildings are still empty, concrete white elephants for which nobody can think of a use. For more on shopping in Kisumu, see "Souvenirs and artefacts" in the "Kisumu Listings" on p.242.

The prayer calls from Kisumu's pastel green and white **Jamia mosque**, not far away down Otieno Oyoo Street, sound odd in this town, but Islam is well established here, and Mumias (see p.283) an important regional influence dating from well into the last century. The orthodox Shafi'ite mosque was built in 1919, though the women's section on the right was only finished in 1984. It currently has two imams, a Tanzanian and a Pakistani. Inside, the beautiful long mats are from Saudi Arabia.

Kisumu Museum

Daily 8.30am–6pm; Ksh200; curator PO Box 1779; ☎035/40804.

Foremost among the town's sights is **Kisumu Museum**. Engaging and ambitious, it is highly recommended, just a short walk east from the market. The single-roomed main gallery stands in a large garden with carefully labelled trees. Apart from the usual row of game heads around the walls, there are cases of "Mammals", "Primates", "Birds" (including two stray bats), "Amphibians and Reptiles", "Fish and Crustaceans from the Sea" and "Insects", all displayed with considerable flair and imagination. One of the prize exhibits is a 189kg Nile perch, caught near Siaya in 1978, its gruesomely embalmed body now marooned on sturdy plywood supports. Heavier perch have been landed since, but at the time this mighty fish was a record-breaker. Particularly good use has been made of old and moth-eaten exhibits from Nairobi's National Museum. A free-swinging vulture, for example, spins like a model aircraft over your head while, best of all, centre stage, a lion is caught in full, savage pounce, leaping onto the back of a hysterical wildebeest in the most action-packed piece of taxidermy you're ever likely to see (unless, oddly enough, you're ever in Abidjan, where you'll see an identical stuffed attack in the window of *Cath Voyages*).

The **ethnographic** exhibits are uncommonly illuminating, too. The Maasai aren't the only people who take blood from their cattle for food: Kalenjin peoples like the Nandi and the Kipsigis once did the same, and even the Luo lived mostly on cow's blood with milk before they arrived at Lake Victoria and began to cultivate and fish. There's a good selection of **musical instruments**, including a fine *nyatiti* (a Luo lyre, the East African equivalent of the kora); it is the kind of thing crudely reproduced in a hundred curio shops and now occasionally heard at African concerts abroad. And look out for the disembodied hands pumping the bellows in the metal-working display.

Railway enthusiasts may be interested in the small display of early twentieth-century photographs of the opening of the Port Florence terminus of the so-called Lunatic Line. The museum's other photographic display shows excavation work in progress at the remarkable Zimbabwe-like walled enclosures of the Thimlich Ohinga archeological site in South Nyanza (see p.244).

In separate halls from the main gallery are a disappointing **aquarium**, where you can see what your curried tilapia looked like before it left the lake, and a **snake house** with a fairly comprehensive collection of Kenyan species. Among them are venomous snakes from the Kakamega Forest and some unnervingly lethal-looking black mambas and forest cobras from the Kisumu area. Outside, a tortoise pen, a snake pit – one of the pythons was rescued from a hole beneath the tea counter at the bus station – and a croc pond are rather pointless extras. The crocodiles are fed on Mondays.

In the **"Traditional Luo Homestead"** you may come across the Kisumu Museum drama group rehearsing. An old Luo man used to live in the "First Wife's house", and would tell you in slow Swahili that this is how all the Luo used to live, and indeed how he himself was brought up. He seems to have gone to the ancestors, but the museum is good on guides and enthusiastic members of staff are often willing to show you around.

Walks around town: Dunga

For a pleasant walk out of town, you could head for Hippo Point and the Luo fishing village of **DUNGA**. From the vicinity of the *Sunset Hotel* you follow the main road – or the shoreline – south: close by is the small **Impala Wildlife Sanctuary** (inhabited by a herd of impala; daily 6am–6pm) and an adjoining Wildlife Service **orphanage**, which you might care to visit (the cages are distressingly small).

The Kisumu Yacht Club along the lakeshore has seen far better days – to judge by the number of boats moored – but it remains strictly members-only: the *askaris* will let you in and kindly turn you straight out again (though they can arrange boat trips; see "Listings", p.242). Five hundred metres further on you come to **Hippo Point**, where you can watch often riotous sunsets from the rock-strewn shore. Hippos are still seen here, and boatmen will offer to take you out to see them, but cold beers and curries from *Dunga Refreshments*, 500m beyond the point, are a more certain attraction, making this an outing popular with Kisumu's large Asian community. There's a strong, warm breeze at dusk, and it's a curiously stifling sensation to sit by this giant body of water without a whiff of ozone in the air. Around the lake, Luo fishermen cast their lines from the shallows. If you take kids, heed the playground warning – "Children Playing at Their Own Risk" – in front of the various indescribable pieces of machinery. And if you fetch up in town and can't face the walk, try giving *Dunga Refreshments* a call (☎035/42529) and see if someone could come to collect you.

Dunga village itself is some 2km further, on the headland, a picturesque settlement with Dunga Fishermen's Co-operative Society the main feature on the shore. If you'd like to spend a night with the **fishermen** on their boats, the co-op is the first place to ask, though you should expect some good-natured negotiations first.

THE LAKESHORE AND FERRY TRIPS

Enjoyable as much for the change of pace as anything else, the *Kenya Railways* motor **ferries**, which ply between Kisumu and several lakeshore towns and villages, are a reliable alternative to *matatus* and buses. The timetable given here is as up to date as possible: it's been much the same for years and is rigidly adhered to when conditions are favourable, but strong westerly winds at the end of the year can delay the outward legs.

Fares are low. You need to be at the ticket office on the Kisumu wharf by 8am and get on board as soon as you can. The ferries are usually full, but few people bother to buy anything more than a third-class ticket as classes tend to be ignored (second-class has softer seats). There's good *chai* and often a few snacks on the boats. You will be welcome enough on the bridge for a chat with the captain if the idea appeals.

TIMETABLES

MV Tilapia			MV Alestes			
Tues, Fri & Sun:			Tues	d.	**Kisumu**	10am
d.	**Kisumu**	9am		a.	Kuwur Bay	3.40pm
a.	Kendu Bay	11am		a.	Homa Bay	5.05pm
a./d.	Kuwur Bay	1.10pm	Wed	d.	Homa Bay	7am
a.	Homa Bay	2pm		a.	Mbita	10.30am
d.	Homa Bay	2.30pm		a.	Mfangano	2.50pm
a.	Asembo Bay	5pm	Thurs	d.	Mfangano	10am
				a.	Mbita	2.05pm
Following day (Wed, Sat & Mon):				a.	Homa Bay	5.20pm
d.	Asembo Bay	8am	Fri	d.	Homa Bay	7am
a.	Kuwur Bay	9.50am		a.	Mbita	10.30am
a.	Homa Bay	10.40am		a.	Mfangano	2.50pm
d.	Homa Bay	11.10am	Sat	d.	Mfangano	10am
a.	Kuwur Bay	11.50am		a.	Mbita	2pm
a.	Kendu Bay	2pm		a.	Homa Bay	5.20pm
d.	Kendu Bay	2.45pm		d.	Homa Bay	11pm
a.	**Kisumu**	4pm	Sun	a.	**Kisumu**	5.30am

Eating, drinking and nightlife

Kisumu has a number of reasonable **places to eat** – except on Sundays, when chips are about all that's on offer, and most places are closed anyway. Fish is the commonest dish, but there are some tasty curries around, too. A number of places only come to life in the evenings and are essentially clubs. If you're looking for some action after dark, you might try to catch some local music at the *Town Hotel*, 100m from the *Beograda* near the bus station. They sometimes have **live music** in the evening, the group playing "until they get sick of it or sacked". Sounds just right for a long, hot night.

Dunga Refreshments, Hippo Point (☎035/42529). The much touted weekend curry buffet lunches are reasonably priced (around Ksh300), but it doesn't do to arrive late. Otherwise, there's quite a long and varied evening menu, with vegetarian options. Drinkers and diners can enjoy gazing out over the water from the lakeside terrace – spectacular at sunset, mellow after dark. Closed Mon.

Expresso Coffee House, Otuona Rd. A recommended volunteers' hangout with a long menu of fry-ups, juices and milk shakes, all of it actually available.

Gatiba Bar, Kendu Lane. Loud music, thin crowds.

Imperial Hotel. As well as a restaurant proper there's a barbecue terrace with good *nyama choma* for under Ksh160.

Kimwa Annex, Otuona Rd (☎035/21412). A bright, clattery, new canteen/bar with a reliable menu, popular with families and volunteers. Good for cheap, filling plates of *kima* (mince) with rice or *githeri* (lentil stew).

Kisumu Sweet Mart, Oginga Odinga Rd. Reliable for really cold sodas, bhajias and other snacks.

Hotel Lem Lem, Ang'Awa Ave (☎035/22021). A lively bar-restaurant serving good stews, and drawing large crowds of beer-drinking locals.

Hotel Marina. The upstairs restaurant deserves to be more popular – the decor may be bland but the food (whole grilled tilapia and chips and other standards) is well prepared and good value.

Mona Lisa, Oginga Odinga Rd. Highly rated for breakfast, but otherwise variable. Closes 6pm.

Café Natasha, Otuona Rd. A bistro-style place with a young, relatively upmarket following; good for big plates of chicken or steak and chips.

New Farmers' Bar & Restaurant. A pleasant little den.

Octopus Bottoms Up Night Club, Ogada St (☎035/40835). A pick-up joint of the first order – but for an enjoyable night out, this is relaxed enough if you just want to mingle over a beer or two. The restaurant is often empty, but the **disco** is always lively and the *Pirate's Den* roof terrace (with barbecue and dartboard) is a popular, breezy rendezvous point.

Sunset Hotel. The Sunday buffet lunch, at about Ksh600, is a real blow-out but expensive compared with *Dunga Refreshments*.

Wimpy, Ang'Awa Ave, corner of Jomo Kenyatta Highway. A burger bar with pretensions to exclusivity, complete with manicured lawn.

Listings

Banks *Standard*, *Barclays* and *Kenya Commercial Bank*; all Mon–Fri 9am–3pm, Sat 9–11am. *Barclays* is OK.

Boat trips People at the Kisumu Yacht Club can arrange boat trips on the lake.

British Council, Oginga Odinga Rd (PO Box 454; ☎035/45004). The library is open Tues–Fri 10am–6pm, Sat 9.30am–1pm. British papers and magazines, occasional BBC news videos and films, and useful Survey of Kenya maps, showing Kisumu district, on the wall.

DHL agent *Kisumu Travels Ltd*, Oginga Odinga Rd, near *Barclays*.

Ferries For domestic services, see the timetable on p.241. International connections, on the MV *Bukoba*, were resumed in early 1996 after an eighteen-year interval – see "Travel details" at the end of the chapter. Cargo ships are sometimes prepared to take passengers across the lake – ask at the docks.

Golf One day's membership fee, equipment rental and caddy at the Golf club on the Mumias road will set you back around $6. Be alert to the rules relating to local difficulties like hippos and pythons in the rough.

Immigration The Immigration Department (PO Box 1178; ☎035/45015), in a building behind Alpha House on Oginga Odinga St, opposite the British Council, is exceptionally helpful, stamping visa and visitor's pass extensions on the spot without objection. If you need a photo, there's a booth inside the entrance to the market.

Kakamega Forest Buses and *matatus* run from Kisumu's main transport park to Kakamega town, from where it's possible to find transport to the forest (for details see p.279).

Kenya Airways Oginga Odinga Rd (PO Box 1427); reservations ☎035/44055 or 44056, fax 43339, airport ☎035/40125 ext. 6.

Kisumu Show Held in the first week of August.

Library Mon–Thurs 9.30am–6.30pm, Fri 9.30am–4.30pm, Sat 9am–1pm.

Post office Mon–Fri 8am–5.30pm, Sat 9am–1pm. Poste restante available. If you want to make an international call through the operator, be prepared to wait. You're far better off buying a phonecard and queuing up to use the cardphone outside. Telex and fax services are also available.

Souvenirs and artefacts The row of craft stalls opposite the *Hotel Royale* is one of the region's best hunting grounds for souvenirs. The things to buy here (if you have space) are the heavy, three-legged Luo stools. The best are intricately inlaid with beads, and dark brown from repeated oiling. Also on offer are bangles, wooden carvings, and row upon row of soapstone knick-knacks. Soapstone (or Kisii-stone) is more expensive to buy in Kisumu than at source (Tabaka, near Kisii), but it's cheaper than in most places, and the craftsmen will carve designs to order. *Pendeza Weavers* (PO Box 1786) is a worthwhile visit, about 3km out of town past the museum on the Nairobi road, past the chief's camp (on the right in the large field) and indicated by a small white sign on the right. Handwoven *kikois* here are as cheap as you'll find; they turn up later at *Spinner's Web* in Nairobi.

Swimming pools A swim at the *Sunset Hotel* is always a pleasure – non-residents pay Ksh100. You might also take a dip in the *Royale*'s pool. The *Imperial* has a less enticing, semi-indoor pool, surrounded by a very plain concrete terrace.

Siaya district and the road to Uganda

Heading northwest out of Kisumu, down a broad avenue of flame trees, you pass the Sunni Muslim, Ismailia and Hindu cemeteries, the last smoking gently, then pass the golf club and emerge into the wide plains of **Siaya district**. Transport to the border town of Busia is fairly constant. The region is pleasantly rural but unremarkable; the one place on the road where you might want to stop for the night is the *Jera Inn* (PO Box 14 Sega; Sega ☎66; ③), well signposted near **Sega**. This "country club" set-up has rooms, food, discos (Wed, Fri, Sat & Sun) and a generally happy ambience that have brought it widespread fame in the district. The **rooms** – in fact very smart *bandas* – are self-contained and really good value.

USENGI, a short bus ride from Kisumu, is something of a diversion if you're en route to Uganda, but it's a useful target if you're planning an exploration of the district, and a town of precolonial historical significance in its own right. The nearby hill, Got Ramogi, is by tradition the site where the first Luo arrived at the lake from further north. It's not a hard climb to the top for a satisfying view over the island-dotted lake, the lagoon below (Lake Saru), and the land which the Luo fought for and eventually won from the Bantu-speakers at the end of the fifteenth century. Usengi itself is a pretty town with a causeway over the lake that connects with the Uganda road. Lodgings there are cheap.

Busia

BUSIA, on the Uganda border, is a surprisingly nice little town and a preferable place to cross than Malaba, the busier frontier post on the railway line further north. The formalities are straightforward enough. Busia consists of a line of shacks and bars on the Kenya side, with a similar line in Uganda. If you're staying the night, the optimistically named *Silent Lodge* is as cheap as they come, and sometimes even has warm water.

Whether you have a visa for Uganda or not (and British passport holders now need one), you're normally allowed to **cross the border** to look around on the Ugandan side. Unless you're desperate for a bottle of cheap whisky however, there's little point. For further, and more encouraging, information about **Uganda**, see "Kenya's Neighbouring States" in *Basics*, p.70.

From Kisumu to Kisii

If you want it to be, the ride **from Kisumu to Kisii** can be a rapid transition along the main A1 highway from dusty or flooded plain (depending on the season) up into the ample, fecund hills of the Gusii. But there are various ornithological diversions along the way, if you're independently mobile or enthusiastic enough to make the effort with public transport and your own feet.

There's also a fine **alternative route** from Kisumu to Kisii, using the first-class paved **lakeshore road** from Katito (south of Ahero) to Kendu Bay (see p.252), and then taking the road to Oyugis back on the A1, just a short journey from Kisii. Except when the latter road is in very bad condition after heavy rain, the route takes barely longer than the direct approach.

Kisumu bird sanctuary

The swampland beyond Kisumu to the southeast is very rich in birdlife and the first place worth investigating off the main A1 road is the **heronry** (Kisumu Bird Sanctuary) on the way to **Ahero**. From April to May, especially, this is the nesting site of hundreds of pairs of not just herons, but ibises, cormorants, egrets and storks, the dark and curiously scruffy open-bill stork included. Ornithologically world-famous, the sanctuary is a must if you're interested in birds.

To get there, take a right turn (south, towards the lake) around 7–8km from Kisumu (about 16km west of Ahero), to the school at **Orongo**, and from there branch left and follow the track for another 2 or 3km. Ask local people's advice, as the best sites and the easiest access to the colony move each year. The site is usually a good place to camp. This low-lying region between Kisumu and the western highlands is known as the **Kano plains** – disablingly hot, humid flatlands, swaying with sugar cane and rice fields, fertilized by occasional disastrous flooding.

There are a number of other breeding sites for herons and ibises beyond the sanctuary, some 20km from Kisumu, again to the right of the road in the marshy district southwest of Ahero.

Oyugis and the pelicanry

Climbing into Kisii district's round, picture-book hills, you arrive at the crossroads town of **OYUGIS**; like a number of other places, it was originally named *Oyugi's* after a local culture-hero. Apart from the sprawling *matatu* stage, whose speeding vehicles presumably account for the battered state of the main street, and a few reasonable B&Ls – *Nyadendi's Palace* (PO Box 30; ③), *Oyugis Safe Lodge* (PO Box 98; ③) and, on the main road out towards Kisii, *Hotel Ragama* (②) – Oyugis offers little but its pelican-breeding site.

The **pelicanry** is reached by leaving the main road (left, southeast) before the *Caltex* station and continuing (past *Safe Lodge*) up the murram in a three-kilometre arc, until you reach two huge fig trees, in a narrow stream bed 200m from the road on the left. From August to March, you'll see the parents wheeling in the air from some distance, and when you get closer there's the distinctive smell of pelican guano to guide you. With binoculars you can watch the shaggy **chicks** in their treetop nests ramming their heads down the parents' throats for fish; then, yakking desperately for more, attempting the same manoeuvre on each other.

To Kisii

If you arrive at Oyugis early in the day and are feeling very fit, you can continue on the track past the pelicanry all the way to Kisii, along a route that becomes more and more beautiful as you climb up through dense *shambas* and forests, out onto **Manga ridge** above the town (see p.256). You might be lucky and get a lift some of the way – but don't count on it. If you have your own car, it's a pleasant half-hour drive.

South Nyanza

The territory south of Kisumu is interesting to explore – it's fairly easy to get around, if you're willing to go by *matatu*, and includes a number of small towns, the Lake Victoria islands, a national park and even an archeological site. This section covers the unlovely main town of **Homa Bay**, **Ruma National Park**, the newly uncovered site of **Thimlich Ohinga**, the islands of **Rusinga and Mfangano** (perch fishing for the rich;

walking and hanging out for the poor), the agreeable little town of **Kendu Bay** and, down near the Tanzanian border, the rougher town of **Migori**.

The **lakeshore** west of Migori is remote and, in parts, beautiful, with **Karungu Bay** a rewarding side trip. In the other direction, **Kihancha**, on the south bank of the Migori River, on another back-country route to Maasai Mara, is reputedly a pretty area.

South Nyanza is largely Luo country, but there are also scattered, rural communities of **Kuria** people down here. The Kuria have an interesting, quasi-matriarchal system found in various parts of Africa, which essentially allows women means to "marry" younger women in order to have children without the need to live with a man. In practice, it's often a married woman who can't have children who invites a younger woman into her home. The young "bride", in turn, chooses a male partner, often in secret, to father (biologically speaking) her children, who are brought up by the two women without the involvement of the father or the older woman's husband. The older woman is sometimes a widow, sometimes simply a single woman. In any case, she lives like a male elder – attending to light business affairs but essentially waited upon hand and foot from dawn to dusk. It's a system with much to recommend it, especially when it takes care of unmarried mothers (who are barred from marrying men), who come into the family as "wives" – surrogate mothers – and whose children are automatically adopted. Ironically, despite these apparently female-controlled arrangements, it's male children that women-families want – and men who inherit land.

Homa Bay

Unless you're lucky enough to be travelling after the rains, the approach to the dreary little town of **HOMA BAY** from the landward side is almost bound to be a disappointment after the green, well-watered hills around Kisii. One of the greatest freshwater lakes in the world lies right in front of you, but around are only dusty plains of grass and sisal. Arriving by boat, impressions are slightly less forlorn, but whichever way you look at it, Homa Bay remains scruffy, charmless and barely worth a stay.

If you sacrifice a day in Homa Bay, you can at least rely on a handful of reasonable **B&Ls**. The *Masawa Hotel* is a pleasant old colonial-style place with a large, bird-filled garden and cheap rooms (①). It's also the best place to check out the local pulse, though a little difficult to find – head uphill by the right side of the market, then left at the top, past the police station, then take the first right, and it's at the top of that street on the right. Other tolerable lodgings include *Nyanza Lodge* (①), on the same street as *Barclays*, where the rooms are decent for the price but you'll have to hold your breath in the shared shower/toilets; and *New Brothers,* on the main road (①), equally basic but with mosquito nets in some rooms. The most "upmarket" place in town is the *Homa Bay Hotel* (PO Box 521; ☎0385/22070; *Msafiri Inns*, address p.49, but may soon change hands; B&B ⑦), where those who can't claim Kenyan residency pay through the nose for its tidy but ordinary rooms, irregularly supplied with water. In reality it rarely has many guests and if you stop for a drink or a meal you may well find nobody else enjoying the huge lakeside garden, where colonies of ibis and weaver birds populate the trees. Lake Victoria's elusive hippos occasionally venture through the fence to chomp on the lawns.

The most consistent spots for **food** are the *Kasongo Hotel*, behind the Migori *matatu* stage, which serves good beans, rice and other staples; and *Lucyali's Chicken Palace*, by *New Brothers* on the main road.

Got Asego

Hike up **Got Asego**, the impressive conical hill on the east side of town, and you get a much cheerier view of Homa Bay. The hill is the highest of dozens of volcanic plugs (cores of old volcanoes) across the plain; from its table-sized summit, you'll have a 360-degree panorama of lakeshore and surrounding plains. It is remarkable how little of the land is not used – Luo thatched huts are interspersed with tin-roofed homesteads, a patchwork of small plots and agave hedges. Take binoculars and you can see more: clumps of papyrus drifting across the lake and traffic along the road where it snakes east to Kendu Bay.

It takes about an hour to reach the top from the centre of town (actual ascent 20min), an easy climb but best tackled in the cool of dawn or late in the afternoon. Take the second left after the *Total* petrol station and turn right up the murram road after Homa Bay School. The hill itself is best approached up the northwest ridge, where there's a footpath. Beware of columns of ants.

Onward from Homa Bay

When you decide to flee, *matatus* leave from the stage near the ferry dock for Kendu Bay and Kisumu, and from the stage on the main road for Kisii and Migori (near the Tanzanian border). If you're heading east, the swiftest exit from Homa Bay is probably aboard a Migori *matatu*, which drops you at Rongo on the A1 highway, where you can soon find a Kisii-bound vehicle coming up from the south. Northbound, the road to Kendu Bay looks short on the map, but *matatus* take a good hour and a half to bump along its rough surface. The road is then paved from Kendu Bay to Kisumu.

Ruma National Park

Open daily; National Park fees apply (Category D), see p.61; warden: PO Box 420, Homa Bay; ☎0385/22007.

Ruma National Park (previously known as Lambwe Valley Nature Reserve) can be a little tricky to reach – the nearest *matatu* route skirts the reserve by 10km – but if you're independently mobile and self-sufficient the effort of getting there is usually repaid by animal-watching undisturbed by the presence of other visitors; you're virtually guaranteed the place to yourself.

The Lambwe Valley's 194 square kilometres of tsetse fly-ridden bush is one of the few places in Kenya where you can see **Jackson's hartebeest** and two opposite extremes of antelope: the enormous, horse-like **roan** and the miniature **oribi**. There are about seventy of the beautiful **Rothschild's giraffe** and they're not hard to see above the tall grass. You'll have more difficulty spotting **cheetah** and **leopard**.

Practicalities

To get there, head south out of Homa Bay along the main Rongo/Migori road, and turn off at the southern edge of the town onto the Mbita road leading southwest; from this (signposted) turning, a 34-kilometre drive along the rough murram brings you to the northeast gate, where another murram road to the left runs for 7km to a signpost for the reserve. Now you know you're on the right track: the Nyatoto Gate is 3km further on. You are likely to be greeted by surprised rangers: they get few visitors. There are no facilities of any kind, so although you can camp in the park with your own equipment, you'll need to bring food and water.

Work is in progress to make Ruma National Park more accessible to visitors, in order to safeguard its future, but for the present it isn't practical without your own transport. If you're dedicated, your best hope is to talk to the park warden in Homa Bay. You can find him through the manager of the *BP* petrol station and spare parts store.

Thimlich Ohinga

Thimlich Ohinga is an archeological site of potentially huge significance – "the greatest stone enclosures in East Africa", as the Kisumu Museum bumper stickers declare.

The site is the most striking example of an architecture whose remnants are scattered across South Nyanza. Similar to the drystone enclosures of Zimbabwe (of which Great Zimbabwe is the classic example), its main structure consists of a compound about 150m in diameter, inside which are five smaller enclosures – probably used as cattle pens – and at least six house pits, the sites of former dwellings. The walls range in height from 2.5m to 3.5m – higher than those of the seventeenth- and eighteenth-century stone ruins in the Inyanga Highlands in Zimbabwe. Outside the main compound wall on the southeast side, evidence of iron-working has been discovered.

Thimlich Ohinga in Luo means "thick bush with stone enclosures". It's estimated they were built around the fifteenth century by a people whose history has been forgotten. But successive generations of various communities have used stone enclosures and, in some places, modern Luo families have their homesteads inside such walls.

Thimlich Ohinga is an unusual and worthwhile site: in up-country Kenya it rates as the equal of Hyrax Hill (see p.207) and is quite absorbing compared to Chetambe's Fort (p.276), but, as usual, if your interest in ruins is limited at best, pass on.

Getting there

You really need your own transport to get to Thimlich. **From Kisii** (105km) or **Homa Bay** (60km), you follow the C20 Rongo–Homa Bay road as far as Rod Kopany, which is some 15km from Homa Bay and 19km from Rongo. From Rod Kopany the route runs southwest, through Mirogi and Ndhiwa to Miranga. After Miranga's shops there's a signpost showing the direction of Thimlich Ohinga; look out for following signs which should get you the whole way there.

If you're approaching **from Migori**, take the Isebania/Tanzania road, and after 4km turn off right, at the junction for Muhuru Bay, where there is a National Cereals and Produce Board depot. A couple of kilometres from the depot you reach another junction where you take a right and drive straight on through Suna and Macalder, looking out for the Thimlich signposts as you go. The journey is about 55km from the Cereals Board Depot.

Rusinga Island

Far more practical than Ruma National Park or Thimlich Ohinga is a trip to **Rusinga Island**. This can be accomplished by land, whatever your map may show, since the narrow channel has been bridged by a **causeway**. But the road from Homa Bay is rough – repeatedly closed in the rainy season – and *matatus* and buses are always packed, so it's recommended you make at least one journey by ferry. This doesn't take much longer and is a lot more fun.

Mbita, where the ferry docks on the mainland, is very unprepossessing indeed, but things improve once you get on to the island. The building of the causeway – partly over two dumper trucks which fell into the lake during the operation and couldn't be recovered – has had some unwanted side effects. Vervet monkeys now move onto the island to raid crops, and fish have become scarce on the Kisumu side of Rusinga because the causeway blocks the current, turning the water there into a stagnant pond. A bridge to replace the old chain ferry would have been the best solution to the island's access problem. As it is, the single bit of civil engineering represented by the causeway has ended Rusinga's slight isolation at what many local people feel is an unacceptable cost.

Mbita and around: practicalities

If you want to get back as far as Homa Bay on the same day, you'll need to be in **MBITA** by 3pm to catch the last transport. You can't continue to Mfangano (see p.250) the same day, though you could come to Mbita by road on a Tuesday or Thursday

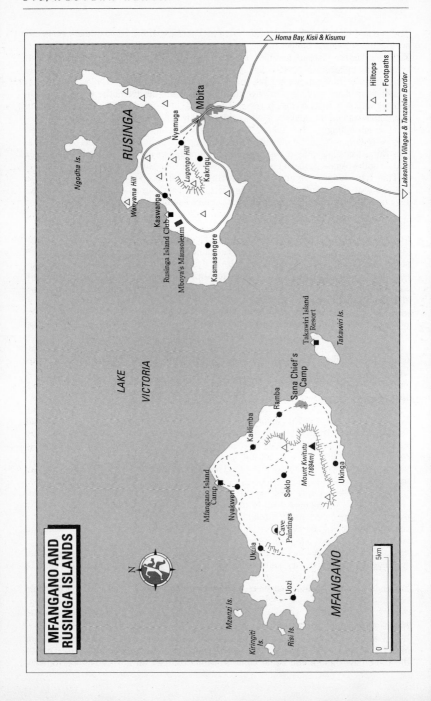

MFANGANO AND
RUSINGA ISLANDS

△ Homa Bay, Kisii & Kisumu

△ Hilltops
- - - Footpaths

▽ Lakeshore Villages & Tanzanian Border

RUSINGA

Ngodha Is.

Nyamuga
Mbita

Wanyama Hill

Lugongo Hill
Kakrigu

Kaswanga

Rusinga Island Club

Mboya's Mausoleum

Kasmasengere

LAKE
VICTORIA

Takawiri Island
Resort

Takawiri Is.

Sana Chief's
Camp

Ramba

Kakimba

Mfangano Island
Camp

Mount Kwitutu
(1694m)

Nyakweri

Soklo

Ukinga

Cave
Paintings

Ukula

Uozi

MFANGANO

N

Mzenzi Is.

Kiringiti
Is.

Risi Is.

0   5km

morning and take the *MV Alestes* ferry the next morning. If you have all the time in the world, spend a night or two in the middle of your cruise at Mbita. There's a flourishing birdlife in the vicinity and doubtless a lot more to be uncovered by adventurous travellers. **Sindo**, 10km south of Mbita, is reckoned a good place to go out in fishing boats, while from the top of **Gemba Hill**, just a few kilometres from the Mbita–Sindo road, there's a superb view across to Homa Bay and down towards Tanzania.

In Mbita itself, *Safari Lodge* is probably the best **B&L**. For **food**, try the *Calypso Bar* which serves good fish.

The island

RUSINGA is small and austerely pretty, high crags dominating the desolate, goat-grazed centre, and a single dirt road running around the circumference. Life here is difficult, drought commonplace, and high winds a frequent torment. The occasional heavy rain either washes away the soil or sinks into the porous rock, emerging lower down where it creates swamps. Ecologically, the island is in very dire straits: almost all its trees have been cut down for cooking fuel or to be converted into lucrative charcoal. These conditions make harvests highly unpredictable and most people do some fishing to make ends meet, either selling the catch on to refrigerated lorries or bartering directly for produce with traders from Kisii. And now the causeway has forced them to make longer fishing trips.

The island does have two significant claims to fame. It is rich in **fossils**, and was the site of Mary Leakey's discovery of a skull of *Proconsul africanus* (a primitive anthropoid ape), which can be seen in the National Museum. And it was the birthplace of **Tom Mboya** (see "Historical Framework" in *Contexts*), civil rights champion, trade unionist and charismatic young Luo politician who was gunned down in Nairobi in 1969, sparking off a crisis that led to over forty deaths in widespread rioting and demonstrations and was a turning point for the worse in Kenya's independent history.

Tom Mboya's mausoleum lies on family land at **Kasawanga** on the north side of the island, about 7km by the dirt road from Mbita, or roughly 5km directly across the island. You might possibly get a lift from Mbita to Kasawanga (in theory there are five *matatus* a day each way), but you need to be prepared to walk the whole way there and back if necessary (allow four hours and take some water). You're likely to find someone to show you the way but Rusinga is so small you're unlikely to get lost. Aim for the crags in the centre (if you're feeling energetic, you could climb the tallest to get a view of the whole island), skirt them to the right and then walk down to rejoin the road on the other side of the Tom Mboya Memorial Health Centre (which has some European staff). There's a little *hoteli* here with cold sodas. From here, it's less than 2km to Mboya's mausoleum, the white dome clearly visible just off the road. The mausoleum (open most days to visitors) contains various mementoes and gifts Mboya received during his life. The inscription on the grave reads:

> *THOMAS JOSEPH MBOYA*
> *August 15th 1930 – July 5th 1969*
> *Go and fight like this man*
> *Who fought for mankind's cause*
> *Who died because he fought*
> *Whose battles are still unwon!*

You don't have to know anything about the man to be impressed. In any other surroundings his memorial might seem relatively modest, but on this barren, windswept shore, it stands out like a beacon. Mboya's family live right next door and are happy to see foreign visitors, who rarely come here. His mother and father, both very old and proud, died in 1987.

Fifty metres past the Tom Mboya Secondary School, the path to the right takes you through *shambas* of millet and corn to a seasonally grassy lakeside called Hippo Bay.

Here you can watch nesting fish eagles as well as, usually, hippos. If you're lucky you may see the pretty and little-known spotted-necked otters that live around Lake Victoria and nowhere else in Kenya.

Also on this side of the island is the *Rusinga Island Club* (Radiocall Nairobi ☎2020), the sort of rustic-luxury retreat you would expect, with a high proportion of its clients taking a side trip from a Maasai Mara air safari (reservations: PO Box 24513, Nairobi, ☎02/447224 or 447228 or 447231, fax 02/447268; club closed during May and sometimes at Christmas). The main attraction here is sport fishing – Rusinga holds the record for the heaviest Nile perch ever landed – but with water-skiing, windsurfing and guided sightseeing on offer, and plans for tennis courts and a pool, there's plenty to divert fishing widows and widowers too. It's possible (and a joy) to stay overnight – the club sleeps ten in thatched cottages. Excursions, activities, meals and drinks are all included in the price ($230 per person).

Mfangano Island

The diesel ferry to **MFANGANO ISLAND** leaves Mbita dock late on Wednesday and Friday mornings, returning the next day. Said to have been inhabited for centuries, Mfangano is enigmatic. Out of range of the smallest fishing boats, and entirely without vehicles, the island is populated by a curious mixture of immigrants from all over Kenya, administered by a chief and three sub-chiefs with help from a trio of policemen. Monitor lizards swarm on the sandy shores and **hippos** are much in evidence out in the water.

Larger and more populous than Rusinga, with a similarly rugged landscape but better vegetation cover, Mfangano's greatest economic resource is still the lake itself. Traditional **fishing techniques** are unusual: the islanders fish with floating kerosene lamps hauled shorewards, or towards a boat, to draw in the schools to be netted. Of more immediate interest, however, are the island's **rock paintings**, certainly worth the trip if you're into such things, and a good excuse to get to know the island in any case.

Practicalities

Mfangano used to see few visitors of any kind and perhaps a handful of travellers each year. With the success of **Mfangano Island Camp**, a fishing lodge similar to Rusinga's, tourist numbers have increased slightly, but again most of the camp's visitors fly in from the Maasai Mara on a day trip (fishing and birdwatching in the morning; lunching and lounging in the afternoon; $360 per person, including return flight, trips and meals) and barely connect with the local people. The camp, a huddle of clay and thatch buildings laid out in the shape of a Luo homestead but fitted out in deluxe style, overlooks a private bay and sleeps twelve (FB $125 per person). If you're interested, reservations can be made through *Governor's Camps* (see p.48). There's a similar, though less expensive place on **Takawiri Island**, off Mfangano: the *Takawiri Island Resort*, which offers windsurfing and sailing, as well as fishing and birdwatching; like *Mfangano Island Camp*, it faces west, for unforgettable sunsets. Access, by light aircraft and/or chartered boat, is pricy ($180–220 per double room FB; reservations through *Lake Victoria Game Safaris*, PO Box 188, Kisumu; ☎035/43141 or 45088, fax 035/44644).

Although isolated, access to Mfangano for **independent travellers** is not really a problem. Large wooden boats with outboard motors run a *matatu* service, shuttling local people and their produce between Mbita and surrounding islands and peninsulas, supplementing *Kenya Railways*' limited service. The Mbita–Mfangano run departs Mbita daily at 9am from the beach on the west side of Mbita causeway. It's a ninety-minute crossing to **SENA** – the chief's camp (PO Mfangano Island Chief's Camp, Sena; Radiocall Nairobi ☎3756) and also the capital of Mfangano. Because there are no vehicles, Mfangano's people rely on a network of temporary **footpaths** which are constantly changing course. If you arrive at Sena by ferry, you can walk all over the island, though it's always easier if you have a guide – $2–3 per day is a fair fee. If you come by the smaller taxi-boat, Sena is the first of a half-dozen minor ports of call along the north coast. The last one, **UKULA** (pronounced "Wakola"), is closest to the rock paintings, and it makes sense to go there first, then work your way back, perhaps over a few days, to Sena.

Sena has a small *duka*, a post office and a government rest house. This **accommodation** is officially free, but you'll need permission from the chief or one of his senior men to use it, so some kind of fee will be called for. Finding places to stay elsewhere on the island is rarely a problem. People have camped wild in the past; at Ukula they've seen the odd traveller before and are more than happy to earn the cost of a B&L for putting you up overnight. You can even be selective, choosing to stay in a house on the lakeshore or up in the hills as the fancy takes you. Don't forget that Mfangano is desperately poor, without electricity or a piped water supply, and you should bring with you anything you think you might need.

Mfangano's rock paintings

From Ukula, an hour or two's walk into the interior (with a guide) brings you to a high, north-facing bluff, with startling views out across the island's north coast. Here, in a gently scooped cave, are the **rock paintings**: reddish spirals and whorls, some with rays, up to half a metre across, that could come from any Von Daniken paperback. People will tell you they're very old; nobody knows who painted them or why, or what they depict. But they exercise a fascination over the islanders, some of whom credit them with peculiar properties. It's said that if you go purposefully looking for the paintings, or ask too many questions about them, they'll elude you. But walk as if you didn't care and you'll suddenly come across them. On last check, some of the paintings had got wind of our approach and disappeared from view. Stories like these suggest the paintings were indeed put on the rock by an earlier and distinctive culture, of which people today have no recollection.

Kendu Bay

KENDU BAY's local fame comes from the curiosity of **Simbi Lake**, about 4km (45 minutes' walk) west of the village. If you arrive by ferry, head out of the village on the Homa Bay road and pass the left turn to Kisii. Two kilometres further on, over the river bridge, turn right down the path and walk for another fifteen minutes.

The lake, and the nearby Ondago Swamp, are the recently adopted feeding grounds of a couple of thousand **flamingoes**, refugees from Lake Nakuru, where dropping water levels and shrinking food supplies are squeezing the water bird population out. With a steady trickle of naturalists and tourists now coming to Kendu Bay to bird-watch, the villagers are, inevitably, keen for a slice of the action. Among the suggestions that have been made are that the Homa Bay County Council should fence off Simbi Lake, impose admission charges, and make provision for local traders to set up stalls. However, it remains to be seen whether the lake contains enough spirulina algae to support a large flock of flamingoes for more than a season or two.

Flamingoes or no flamingoes, the lake is unquestionably weird: several bright green but changeable acres of opaque water sunk twenty or thirty metres below the surrounding land and only a few kilometres from Lake Victoria itself. It has no apparent source and its origins are somewhat mysterious. It looks like a huge meteorite crater with a footpath around the rim.

The story goes that an old woman was refused fire one rainy night at the village that once occupied the site of the lake. A big beer party was going on and she was ignored.

Only one woman would allow her to warm herself and the old woman insisted she leave the village with her. The young woman tried to persuade her husband to come with them, fearing the old lady's revenge for her ill treatment, but in vain. So the two women left alone. And later that night there was a tremendous cloudburst and the rain came down so hard that the village was swamped to become Simbi Lake.*

The little lake's shores are almost devoid of vegetation. Nobody goes out on it in boats and it doesn't look as if they fish there either. It's usually described with the catch-all term "volcanic" and is apparently extraordinarily deep. According to one local belief, visitors should throw money in to avoid bad luck. Whatever the natural explanation, it seems plausible that the area was inhabited when the lake was formed, the disaster accounting for the legends. Similar, though smaller, lakes can be seen east of Kendu Bay along the new road to Kisumu.

If you're heading on to Homa Bay, you might like to see the **Oriang Pottery Centre** in the village of the same name, 2km past the Simbi Lake turning. It's a UNDEP-funded programme, relying on clay from the local river bed.

Practicalities and onward travel

Kendu Bay itself is much smaller than Homa Bay and has a good deal more intrinsic charm. Like Homa Bay, however, if has next to nothing to offer the casual visitor. The ferry dock (a pier partly made of concrete-filled barges) is about a kilometre from the one-street village. One notable building is the gorgeous Masjid Tawakal mosque. You can look around it – though there's not much to see – and climb on the roof.

There are a number of **B&Ls** in town (all ①): worth trying are the *New Biafra Hotel* on the Kisumu road and the even more basic but incredibly reasonable *Kasarani Lodgings*, on the main street in the village. The *New Wedero*, a *hoteli* on the Kisumu road near the Oyugis junction, serves unbeatable *mandaazi*.

The murram road up **to Oyugis** (on the main A1 highway between Kisii and Kisumu) is generally firm but it sometimes takes a beating in wet weather and becomes, on occasions, impassable. Normally, though, you'll have no difficulty getting a *matatu* up to Oyugis or west to Homa Bay. The obvious alternative escape route is the tarred **lakeshore road** from Kendu Bay to Katito, where it meets the A1 on to Kisumu. This is an excellent, fast highway – another from an Israeli company – which swings beautifully for some 40km, the first 20km close to the lake. There's a wealth of interest in the surrounding Luo countryside, most of it so recently a rural backwater, with scenes of fishing boats and compounds of square, mud-brick-built, thatched houses (a fairly recent change; traditionally they were round). Now that this route has become a lakeside drive, the handful of modern houses – two-storey "villas", complete with tiles and wrought iron – barely look out of place: they suggest a district that people are prepared to invest in.

Migori

MIGORI, down near the Tanzanian border, is an expanding town with a rough reputation. The main centre of activity seems to be the hospital, where the doctors are adept at treating arrow wounds inflicted during land skirmishes between Gusii, Maasai, Kipsigis and the new Kikuyu settlers. Market days are interesting for the variety of peoples and for traditional activities untainted by tourism. The Maasai people here are far less calculating and aloof than many of those further to the east whose lives have

---

* Further variations on the story (there are many) improve on the theme of drunkenness and debauchery to give a Sodom and Gomorrah ring to the tale. Other lakes in Kenya have similar tales of origin.

been invaded by cameras and minibuses, but you're likely to be the object of some curiosity. Among places to **stay**, the *Gilly Hotel* (PO Box 831; ☎191 Migori; ③) is the best in town, with a very good breakfast; *Gateway Lodge* is basic and cheap.

If you find yourself in Migori, just arrived from Tanzania, there are "direct" (though not non-stop) **buses to Nairobi** leaving at 6am and 7am or in the evening. While you are in this area, it's worth knowing that local police are aware of the requirement for a yellow fever vaccination certificate for travellers arriving from Tanzania. Whether or not you've crossed the border, the certificate may be demanded at roadblocks.

THE WESTERN HIGHLANDS

The highlands of the west rise all around Lake Victoria in a great bowl. There's superb walking country throughout, in the **Nandi Hills**, for example, or in the little-known **Mau Massif** east of Kericho. But the undoubted highlights are **Saiwa Swamp National Park** and the **Kakamega Forest**, recently accorded National Park status of its own. For serious, sensibly equipped hikers, **Mount Elgon** must also be a major temptation, sharing much of Mount Kenya's flora and fauna but none of its popularity. Also wonderful walking country are the high hills of the **Cheranganis**, though, like Elgon, they take some getting to. The highland towns are, on the whole, not arresting. **Kisii** is lively and worth a visit, but **Kericho** ("tea capital of Kenya"), **Eldoret** and **Kitale** are best thought of simply as bases for getting to the real attractions.

Kisii and around

Headquarters of the **Gusii** people, and district town of a region vying with Nyeri in having the fastest-growing population in the country, **KISII** is a fresh, verdant trading centre in the hills, prosperous and hard-working. For its small size, the town creates terrific noise and energy. It has more lodging houses per head than anywhere else in Kenya, and enjoys a profusion of excellent fruit and vegetables all year round, especially bananas and sugar cane. Lavishly fertile, the region gets rain all year, in remarkable contrast to the semi-arid lowlands of the lakeshore just a few kilometres away.

Kisii is also famous for its fine **soapstone**. Surprisingly, there's little of this to be seen in the town itself. The best locality for watching the carvers and making on-the-spot purchases is Tabaka, some way south (see p.255).

Accommodation

You'll find plenty of choices when you look for **somewhere to stay**, although prices have always been a little higher than elsewhere, with even ordinary lodgings towards the top of the ① bracket. You should be prepared for power fluctuations during heavy rain – have some candles handy. It's worth staying the night, though, as, once you've settled in, there are several rewarding local **excursions**:

Hotel Capital (PO Box 966; ☎0381/20944). Unremarkable, and overpriced for what you get, with a noisy bar. Rooms are notionally s/c, but water is not guaranteed. ②.

Highway Lodge (PO Box 910; ☎0381/21213). A very ordinary B&L, about the cheapest in town. Cleanish rooms, but depressing: you enter through a reeking courtyard behind a butcher's shop. ①.

Kiango Bar & Restaurant B&L (PO Box 973; ☎0381/21190). This is a dingy place geared to short-term guests (soap, towel and condom provided), but the balconies compensate, and there's a busy bar-restaurant. Buckets of water are heated for "s/c" rooms on request. ②.

Kisii Hotel, on the road out to Kisumu (PO Box 26; ☎0381/30134). There's a certain degree of comfort here, and safe parking if you have a car. By far the best of Kisii's four slightly more upmar-

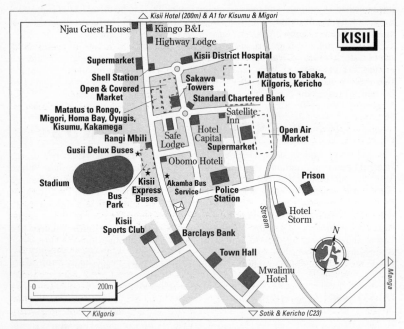

ket addresses, with a creaking colonial atmosphere, a popular bar and large, lovely, bird-filled garden. Most of the s/c rooms, however, are very basic – and it's often full. ②.

Mwalimu Hotel (PO Box 2427; ☎0381/20957). A modern hotel, ostensibly of a similar standard to the *Kisii Hotel*, but run-down and far from clean. There's an unsavoury atmosphere about the place; and at weekends, raucous and very male-oriented discos take over. ③.

Njau Guest House (PO Box 156; ☎0381/21375). With the same owner as *Safe Lodge*, this has quite OK s/c rooms, but don't count on the water. ①.

Safe Lodge (PO Box 156; ☎0381/20945). An engaging lodging house with a good reputation – if sometimes rather noisy (there's a popular bar downstairs). Rooms are small and have a dilapidated air, but overall the place is clean and welcoming. ②.

Sakawa Towers (PO Box 541; ☎0381/21218). A friendly, bright hotel in a block (until recently the tallest building in town) named after a Gusii medicine man and prophet. There are great views of Kisii from the roof. All the rooms have balconies but some are cramped and terrifically noisy. Good restaurant. ②–③.

Satellite Inn (PO Box 16; ☎0381/30181). A big, grubby boozer, inclined to overcharge. ①.

Hotel Storm (PO Box 973; ☎0381/30649). A new, slightly pretentious place at a discreet distance from the thick of things but with unremarkable rooms. ③.

Eating

Despite the noxious drain smells, the overflowing **market** is the first base for hungry travellers. The lodgings mostly have dining rooms or restaurants of their own, of which *Sakawa Towers*' is probably the most recommended. *Safe Lodge*'s restaurant used to be the best place to eat, but they closed it to concentrate on beer and *nyama choma*. Currently the nicest *hoteli* is the *Obomo*, which offers plain food, but good juices and a very pleasant atmosphere (closed Sun). Despite a dwindling menu, the *Kisii Hotel* on the north side of town is still considered the place where one dines out, especially at lunchtime, when the tables are spread out on the garden lawns.

Listings

Banks *Standard* and *Barclays* both Mon–Fri 9am–3pm, Sat 9–11am. Don't go near the *KCB*: they charge outrageous commission here.

Earth tremors Kisii lies on a fault line and minor earthquakes are not uncommon – only a slight worry if you're asleep at the top of *Sakawa Towers* hotel at the time.

Football Kisii stadium is the home ground of Shabana FC, now in the First Division.

Kisii Show Held in the first week of July.

Post office Mon–Fri 8am–5pm, Sat 9am–noon. Cardphone outside.

Rangi Mbili (PO Box 532; ☎0381/20318). A very helpful parts store/workshop if your car is in trouble. Helpful anyway, for that matter – they're eager to meet travellers.

Sports club Swimming pool, tennis, squash, darts, bar, bingo. Saturday discos. A friendly place with temporary membership available.

Tabaka

TABAKA is one of the most important centres in the world for **soapstone** (steatite) production. Strangely enough, it has never become widely known, and the expected sprouting of signposts and tourist shops is nowhere to be seen. Most of the carvings are bought up by buyers from the curio shops in Nairobi and elsewhere, and on arriving, you might think you've come to the wrong place, it's such a low-key industry.

Getting to Tabaka, it is best to get a **matatu** that goes direct, even if this means waiting around in Kisii. The alternative is hanging around just as long at the halfway point, or a very long walk. If you don't mind the latter, grab any *matatu* heading towards Migori and get out at **Nyachenge**, from where the murram road to Tabaka heads off to the southeast. To get to the soapstone carvers and quarries, continue 5km on the murram road, passing the turn for the Tabaka Mission Hospital on your right; then

---

SOME GUSII HISTORY

The Bantu-speaking **Gusii** (after whom the town is named) were only awakened to the brutal realities of British conquest in 1905, when they rebelled – pitching themselves with spears against a machine gun. It was "not so much a battle as a massacre", one of the participants recalled, leaving "several hundred dead and wounded spearsmen heaped up outside the square of bayonets". In 1908, after the District Commissioner was speared in a personal attack, the same thing happened again, only this time the Gusii were trying to escape, not attacking. Crops were burned, whole villages razed to the ground. Churchill telegraphed from the Colonial Office: "Surely it cannot be necessary to go on killing these defenceless people on such an enormous scale."

The Gusii were totally demoralized. In a few brief years, the fabric of their communities had been torn apart, hut taxes imposed, and cattle confiscated to be returned only in exchange for labour. And then came World War I. Kisii was the site of the first Anglo-German engagements in East Africa, and thousands of men were recruited into the hated Carrier Corps by trickery or press gang.

It seems extraordinary that the exceptionally friendly people of Kisii are the grandchildren of the conscripts. The powerful, millennial religious movements which burst among them during the colonial period under the name **Mumboism** may partly account for the very strong ties of community they've maintained against all odds. Prophets and medicine men have always been important here, and even in today's superficially Christianized society, the Gusii have solidly kept their cultural identity. **Witchcraft and sorcery** still play important roles in village life. The practice of **trepanning**, for example, which involves tapping a small hole in the skull to relieve headache or mental illness, seems to be as old as the Gusii themselves: it has recently received the ironic laureate of medical journal credibility and the attentions of a German film crew. "Brain operations" are still performed, clandestinely but apparently quite successfully.

head downhill from the T-junction. The last *matatus* from Tabaka back to Kisii leave at 5pm.

If you're **driving** to Tabaka from Kisii, head out of town to the north and, after 1km, turn left – south – onto the A1 Migori/Isebania road and proceed 17km to a sign indicating (left) the Tabaka Mission Hospital and Kisii Soapstone Carvers Co-operative Society. From here it's a further 5–6km.

The soapstone quarries and carvers

There are two main **quarries** – one on the left, another further down on the right – but there must be vast reserves of stone under the ground all over the district, which provides almost the entire world supply of soapstone. It emerges in a variety of colours and densities: white is easiest to work, shades of orange and pink harder, and rosy-red the hardest and heaviest. A number of families have become full-time carvers, but for most people it's simply a spare-time occupation after agriculture, a way of making a few shillings. You'll even see children walking home from school carving little animals from chips of stone. The professional carvers often specialize: one in inlaid chessboards, another in chess pieces, others in traditional animals (hippos, elephants, lions, fish) and boxes (square, round, duck, tortoise), vases and cups, ashtrays, candlesticks, snake-boxes, napkin rings, egg cups, mugs and more recent designs – human figures, soapstone "Makonde" and various fruit.

Recommended teams of carvers are run by Gabriel Mogendi and his father Alexander; Aloyce Abuya and his wife Queen; and the Obonyo family. They, among others, will happily show you around, sell you their work, and perhaps give you pieces of stone to try carving yourself: it's great therapy. The stone is dampened to bring up the colour and make it easier to work, then waxed to retain the lustre.

Manga Ridge

This dramatic escarpment **cliff** is two or three hours' walk north of Kisii, wonderful in the early morning – or the late afternoon, as long as you can arrange a ride back again.

Leaving Kisii on the Kericho road, turn left into Manga Road at the bottom of the hill, 500m after *Barclays*, and follow the road as it sweeps you towards and then alongside the ridge. After about 5km you can cut down one of the tracks across the lush valley to your left and continue straight up the escarpment (several hundred metres high). Beware of snakes lurking among the rocks and grass on the upward scramble. Alternatively, you can continue along the road for a further 5km to come up behind the ridge; from here it's a ten-minute hike up to the edge, where a path follows the cliff for a kilometre or two. Magnificent views out over Kisii and down to Lake Victoria are your reward. It's possible to get *matatus* to Manga from Kisii, but make it clear you want to get off at the ridge.

If you set off early enough, there should be time to walk the whole way around to **Oyugis** (see p.244), through the villages of Manga, Marani and Rioma, a total distance of about 40km. Down at Oyugis you arrive in the town past the pelican breeding site on the right. From Oyugis it's a quick *matatu* hop back to Kisii. A fine walk, this also makes for exuberant **cycling**, through the heart of Gusii-land, as the road loops and swerves in a landscape changing magically with every ridge and valley. Up here you'll find dusty lanes, avenues of cypress trees, grassy verges, old women smoking pipes, and self-contained, reserved, country hamlets, just a few kilometres from the mêlée of Kisii.

Onwards from Kisii

Kisii is something of a route focus, with Kericho and Kisumu each a couple of hours away, and a minor but increasingly popular route to **Maasai Mara** setting out from here. Beware that beyond **Kilgoris**, the road to the Mara is difficult, even with 4WD, and the section down the Oloololo Escarpment can be impossible after rain. Heading for the east end of the reserve, the fastest route is via Sotik and the new road to Bomet and Amala River (see p.321).

Heading south, **Tanzania** is accessible by services to the **border crossing**, variously known as Serira, Siria, Isebania or Nyabikaye.

If you're trying to leave Kisii by *matatu*, it's worth trying to pick them up, when they're nearly ready to go, at the *Shell* station for points north, south and west, and near the *Mwalimu Hotel* for Kericho and points east; even if a *matatu* doesn't pass, someone else may offer you a lift.

Sotik

From Kisii to Kericho, the road first snakes up through banana gardens, fields of corn and sugar cane and patches of tea. **Keroka**, the largest town along the way, is an urgent and chaotic community, strung out along the highway.

At **SOTIK**, just off the road to the south, you've reached a high plateau and the start of the rolling swathe of **tea bushes** that stretches for hundreds of square kilometres up towards the crest of the Mau Escarpment. Sotik is quite a pretty little centre – despite the rutted side streets, you'd almost say well-kept – with its shrubs and borders. The village has a post office, a branch of *Barclays*, petrol, and the usual cluster of shops, bars and eateries. There's a choice of dirt-cheap ① category lodgings you might conceivably stay in: the *Sotik Restaurant B&L* (PO Box 615; ☎0360/32097) with its popular downstairs video bar, the *Bidii Hotel* next door, or *Roger's Villa* (PO Box 126; ☎0360/32313).

On the approach to Kericho itself, the small *shambas* virtually cease, especially on the eastern side of the road where the land shelves to the Kimugu Valley.

Kericho and the tea country

KERICHO, named after the early English tea planter John Kerich, is Kenya's **tea capital**, a fact that – with much hype from the tourism machine embellished by the presence of the *Tea Hotel* – is not likely to escape you. Its equable climate and famously reliable, year-round afternoon rain showers make it the most important tea-growing area in Africa. While many of the European estates have been divided and reallocated to small farmers since Independence, the area is still dominated by giant tea plantations. Compact and orderly, Kericho itself seems as neat as the serried rows of bushes that surround it. The central square has shady trees and flowering bushes – a bandstand would make it complete – and even the *matatu* park has lawns around it. It's a gentle, hassle-free place to wander, the people mild-mannered. Clipped, clean and functional, there's little of the shambolic appearance of most up-country towns. And, in many ways, it's an oddity. With so many people earning some sort of salary on the tea plantations or in connection with them, and so few acres under food or market crops, the patterns of small-town life are changed here. Most workers live out on the estates, their families often left behind in the home villages. Kericho is above all an administrative and shopping centre, and a relay point for the needs of the estates: the produce market is small and trading limited. Everything seems to close at 5pm.

In town, there's a substantial Asian population. Many of the streets have a strikingly oriental feel – single-storey *dukas* fronted by colonnaded walkways where the plantation "memsahibs" of forty or fifty years ago presumably did their shopping. This curious, composite picture is completed by the grey stone **Holy Trinity Church**, with its small assembly of deceased planters in a miniature cemetery. Straight out of the English shires and entwined with creepers, it tries so hard to be Norman that it hurts to report it was built only in 1952.

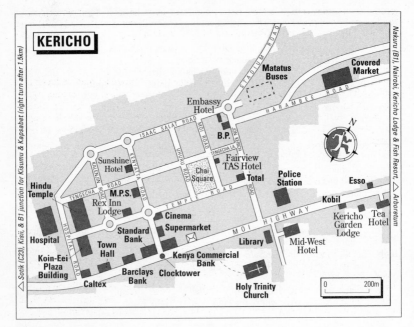

Accommodation

Kericho has a decent number of **places to stay** and you should find something to suit. A couple of the best options are out along the Nairobi road, Moi Highway.

Embassy Hotel, Isaac Salat Rd (PO Box 1505). Ordinary and basic accommodation, near the transport park – marginally the best of the rock-bottom places but don't eat here. ①.

Fairview TAS Hotel, Moi Rd. Basic and none-too-clean lodgings below a noisy but characterful bar. ①.

Kericho Garden Lodge, Moi Highway (PO Box 164). The s/c rooms here are scruffy but some look out over the pleasant gardens, and there's secure parking. Unappetizing food, half-awake service and an unattractive atmosphere in the restaurant/bar/television room. B&B. ②.

Kericho Lodge & Fish Resort, off Moi Highway (PO Box 25; ☎ 0381/20035). To get there, take the signposted turning opposite Agip, 700m northeast of the town centre, and follow this track for about 500m. A fairly new set-up, alpine chalet in style and atmosphere, perched directly above the Kimugu River, with a good bar and restaurant on site. Simple but very comfortable twin rooms with independent hot water, plus space to pitch a couple of tents. Wonderfully situated for river walks in the lush, tree-filled valley. ③.

Mid West Hotel (PO Box 1175; ☎0381/20611, fax 0381/20615). A large, soulless European-style place and popular conference venue. Nothing special to recommend it, but usually a safe bet if you must have a proper hotel room. There's a new health club with a gym, sauna, steam room, snooker, darts, etc: daily fee about Ksh250. ④.

Rex Inn Lodge, Temple Rd. Bog-standard lodging. ①.

Tea Hotel, Moi Highway (PO Box 75; ☎0361/30004 or 30005, fax 0361/20576; reservations made through *Msafiri*, address p.49). Built, along with the nearby church, in 1952, the *Tea Hotel* formerly belonged to the giant tea corporation Brooke Bond. Now that they've sold it and the plantation tours have been cut out (the photographs of the workers and their housing were tarnishing the corporate image), its *raison d'être* is slightly questionable. It still attracts a few tour groups, though, as well as a steady trickle of travelling businessmen. The small pool and grassy, well-watered gardens are appealing enough, but the rooms themselves vary greatly: you should aim at getting a bungalow with bath and shower or one of the upstairs rooms in the separate block. Despite its abundant failings and a steady decline in recent years, it can't help being charming and peaceful. ⑤.

Around Kericho

Mostly it's **tea country**. Kenya is the world's third largest producer after India and Sri Lanka, and the biggest exporter to Britain. The estates were first set up after World War I with tea bushes imported from India and China. Big business as it is, though, and despite the relative prosperity of Kericho, you can't help feeling that the local population would be better served if this fertile land were given over instead to intensive cultivation of food.

The estates are not too anxious for visitors (enquire with *Brooke Bond* if you like: PO Box 20; ☎0381/20482 or 20146), and the *Tea Hotel* no longer provides a guided **tour**. You could try applying in writing to Kenya Tea Packers (KETEPA), PO Box 413, Kericho. But your best bet might be to try to fix something up through chatting to estate workers in town. The factories operate every day except Monday, the day after the pickers' day off.

Tea production is not complicated but it is very labour-intensive. Picking continues throughout the year: you'll see the pickers moving through the bushes in their brilliant yellow and green (KETEPA) plastic smocks, nipping off the top two leaves and bud of each bush (nothing more is taken) and tossing them into baskets. Working fast, a picker can collect up to seventy kilos in a day, though half that is a more typical figure; the piece-rate is set at less than three shillings per kilo picked. After withering, mashing, a couple of hours' fermentation and a final drying in hot air, the tea leaves are ready for packing and export. The whole process can take as little as 24 hours.

Kimugu Valley and Chagaik Dam

Down in the **Kimugu Valley**, behind the *Tea Hotel* and *Kericho Lodge & Fish Resort*, you can get some idea of what the land was like before the settlers arrived. The valley is a deep, tangled channel of sprawling trees and undergrowth, with shafts of sunlight picking out clouds of butterflies. The cold brown waters of the Kimugu flow down from Chagaik Dam and allegedly harbour **trout**. See "Listings" for information on fishing.

To get to **Chagaik Dam** and the graceful **arboretum** nearby, you'll need a lift in the Nairobi direction, past the KETEPA buildings to the turn marked "Chagaik", about 8km east of town. From there, turn right, then immediately left: it's a five-minute walk to the arboretum – "Founded by Tom Grumbley, Tea Planter 1946–75". Acres of beautiful trees from all over the tropical and subtropical world lead steeply down through well-tended lawns to a lily-covered lake. There are magnificent stands of bamboo on the banks. Entry to this haven of landscaped tranquillity is unrestricted and you can picnic or rest up as long as you like, though there are gardeners around who will probably insist you don't camp.

Across the lake, thick **jungle** drops to the water's edge. Mysterious splashes and rustles, prolific bird and insect life, and at least one troop of colobus monkeys, are a surprising testament to the tenacity of wildlife in an environment hemmed in on all sides by the alien ranks of the tea bushes.

Listings

Banks *Barclays, Standard* and the *KCB* (all Mon–Fri 9am–3pm, Sat 9–11am) are on Moi Highway at the Kisumu end of town.

Fishing All the gear used to be available to rent from the *Tea Hotel*. These days the quaint world of flies and casting seems rather remote. Try the *Fish Resort*.

Hotelis for food The *Sunshine Hotel*, Kenyatta Rd, is popular, as is the Indian restaurant on Isaac Salat Rd.

Library By the *Mid West Hotel*. Not bad at all, though they go for quantity rather than diversity, with about ten copies of each title.

Market Much better at weekends than weekdays, when there's a variety of fruit and vegetables, snacks and spices, at lower-than-expected prices.

Post office Mon–Fri 8am–5pm, Sat 9am–noon.

Swimming pool Clean but chilly, at the *Tea Hotel*.

Taxis A bit of a problem in Kericho: there are very few apart from *matatus*. After dark it's hard to get out much if you don't have your own vehicle or aren't prepared to walk.

Onward travel

Kericho has hassle-free travel options in every direction: **southwest** to Kisii, **east** over the Mau Escarpment to Nakuru (route covered on pp.214–216 in Chapter 3), or **northwest** to Kisumu on Lake Victoria and Kapsabet in the Nandi Hills. Heading **south to Maasai Mara** is more problematic, though the first part of the route, from Litein (30km or so from Kericho) to Bomet, follows a fine new road through splendid farming country (see p.321). If you're going **east**, Nairobi and Nakuru buses generally originate in Kisii and don't depart from Kericho until about midday: you should have time for a leisurely morning.

The Nandi Hills

The journey **from Kericho to Kapsabet** is one of the most varied and spectacular in the west, through country often far wilder than you'd expect: bleak mountainous scrublands and jungle-packed ravines. Midway, you cross the Kano Plains and usually have to change transport at **Chemelil**, a major crossroads on the flat sugar lands. Beyond, the road zigzags into high tea country again, the homeland of the **Nandi**, the fiercest early opponents of the British, and the haunt of a zoological mystery known as the **Nandi bear** (see box opposite).

Kapsabet

KAPSABET is the only town of any size before Eldoret but, even here, unless you arrive at the end of the day, there's little point in stopping. There's a branch of *Barclays* (next to the site earmarked for a new municipal library) and three **lodgings**, all okay and all well inside the ① bracket. *Kapsabet Hotel* (PO Box 449; ☎03231/2176) is a fairly quiet place but a popular boozer, clean if scruffy and boasting a restaurant that serves mountainous portions of chips. *Keben Hotel* contains three "lodges" on its three floors, *Tanzania, Kenya* and *Uganda*, with rooms named after towns accordingly. Its noisy bar, restaurant, and discos at weekends and holidays make it Kapsabet's main nightspot. Lastly, the Somali-run *Bogol Inn* serves typically tasty and cheap food in its restaurant. Amenities match the very low rates.

Eldoret

Although more bustling with trade than Kericho, and somewhat healthier and pleasanter than Nakuru, **ELDORET** has, in all honesty, hardly anything to do or see that couldn't be done or seen in dozens of other highland centres. Life here is pleasantly humdrum, at least on the outside: ordinary occupations and careers are actively

THE NANDI AND THE NANDI BEAR

At the end of the nineteenth century, the **Nandi** (one of the Kalenjin-speaking peoples) were probably in the strongest position in their history. Their warriors had drummed up a reputation for such ferocity and daring that much of western Kenya lived in fear of them. Even the Maasai – at a low point in their own fortunes – suffered repeated losses of livestock to Nandi spearsmen, whose prestige accumulated with every herd of cattle driven back to their stockades. The Nandi even crossed the Rift Valley to raid Subukia and the Laikipia Plateau. They were intensely protective of their own territory, relentlessly xenophobic and fearful of any adulteration of their way of life. Foreigners of any kind were welcome only with express permission.

With the killing of a British traveller, Peter West, who tried to cross their country in 1895, the Nandi opened a decade of guerrilla warfare against the British. Above all, they repeatedly frustrated attempts to lay the railway line and keep communications open with Uganda. They dismantled the "iron snake", transformed the copper telegraph wires into jewellery, and took whatever livestock and provisions they could find. Despite increased security, the establishment of forts, and some efforts to reach agreements with Nandi elders, the raiding went on, often costing the lives of African soldiers and policemen under the British. In retaliation, **punitive expeditions** shot more than a thousand Nandi warriors (about one young man in ten), captured tens of thousands of head of livestock, and torched scores of villages. The war was ended by the killing of Koitalel, the *Orkoiyot* or spiritual head of the Nandi who, having agreed to a temporary truce, was then murdered at a meeting with the British. As expected, resistance collapsed (his people had believed Koitalel to be unassailable); the Nandi were hounded into a reserve and their lands opened to settlers.

Traditionally keepers of livestock, the Nandi have turned to agriculture with little enthusiasm and focus instead on their district's milk production: the highest in Kenya. *Shambas*, however, are widespread enough to make your chances of seeing a **Nandi bear** – the source of scores of Yeti-type rumours – remote. Variously said to resemble a bear, a big wild dog or a very large ape, the Nandi bear is believed to have been exterminated in most areas. But in the less accessible regions, on the way up to Kapsabet, many locals believe it still exists. They call it *Chemoset*. Exactly what it is is another matter, but it doesn't seem to inspire quite the terror you might expect; the occasional savagely mutilated sheep and cattle reported in the press are probably attributable to leopards. A giant anthropoid ape, perhaps a gorilla, seems the most likely candidate for the *Chemoset* and the proximity of the Kakamega Forest may account for the stories. This is a surviving tract of the rain forest that once stretched in a continuous belt across equatorial Africa and is still home to many western and central African species of wildlife (though not, as far as is known, giant apes). The *Chemoset* possibly survived up until this century in isolated valleys, even if it is extinct today. Whatever the truth, if you camp out in the Nandi Hills, you won't need to be told twice to zip your fly sheet.

pursued; the **Uasin Gishu Plateau** all around is reliably fertile cereal, vegetable and stock-raising country; wattle plantations provide the tannin for the town's leather industry; the Raymond textile factory – one of the country's biggest – provides employment; and a centre of higher education, Moi University, has proved a shot in the arm for local schools. Eldoret's prosperity is shown clearly enough by the windows of the *Eldoret Jewellers* on the main road. In short, this is Kenya's "Middletown"; not very prepossessing perhaps, but with its own momentum for development and, you can be reasonably sure, hardly a tour bus in sight.

The other face of Eldoret is serious **ethnic strife**. In recent years, thousands of refugees from local fighting have flooded the town and its sprawling, poor suburbs. Eldoret – "the town where everyone thinks he is president", according to one disenchanted local – has repeatedly been the focus of conflict between the district's Kalenjin-speakers (who are seen to be – and increasingly are – aligned with Moi and the KANU party) and Kikuyu- and Luo-speaking immigrants (who tend to favour a change of government). None of which is likely to impinge on a casual visit.

A little history

Eldoret was a backwoods post office on *Farm 64*, later chosen in 1912 as an administrative centre because the farm's soil was poor and the deeds were never taken up by the owner. The name started as Eldare (a river), was then Nandi-ized to Eldaret, and finally misprinted in the *Official Gazette* as Eldoret. Pronunciation is fluid.

Before the town existed, the area was settled by **Afrikaners**; they gave it much of the dour worthiness that seems to have characterized its first half-century and which is perceptible even today, though most of the Boers trekked on after Independence. Modern inhabitants are mainly Kalenjin (Elgeyo and Nandi) but there's also a long-established and respected Asian community (*Juma Hajee's* supermarket, now an arcade, was the oldest business in the town); in addition there are Somali-speakers, the remnants of a European community, and immigrants from the rest of Kenya.

Eldoret's status as capital of the Kalenjin homelands probably has a great deal to with its choice as the location for Kenya's newest international **airport**, as yet only half built. The original projected cost of Eldoret airport ran to over $83.3m but the Kenyan government has been forced to scale down the project under tough proposals from the International Monetary Fund and the World Bank. Sparks flew when Kenya recently requested a $50m loan for repairs to the Nairobi–Mombasa road – international donors jettisoned the request, arguing that if Kenya could afford a new international airport in an up-country town (not to mention a new presidential jet), it could afford to cover the cost of routine repairs to its principal highway as a matter of priority.

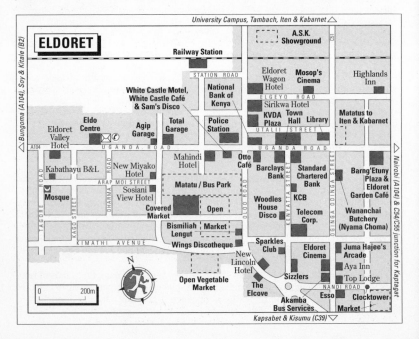

Practicalities

There's no real reason to stay in Eldoret very long, although you might find it a useful stop-over. The town's affluence is reflected by a wide variety of places to stay, eat and drink – and enough nightlife to see you through an evening or two.

Accommodation

Eldoret has no shortage of **accommodation**. Cheap places tend to be grubby or clearly intended for "short-term guests". You may have to explain to the management the innocent way you intend to spend the night. There are also one or two quaint old haunts from way back. As in the old days, you may still be able to **camp** in the yard of the *Wagon Hotel*. The Reformed Church Centre, too, should agree to a tent in the field.

CHEAPER HOTELS AND LODGINGS

Aya Inn, Oginga Odinga St. A spotless new place with a rowdy but good-natured and fun bar attached. Reasonable rates for small s/c rooms with one double bed. ①.

Eldoret Valley Hotel, Uganda Rd (PO Box 734; ☎0321/31488). For peace and quiet, this is clean and scrupulous, but rather gloomy and somewhat lacking in character. An excellent Somali-style menu compensates. ②.

Kabathayu Hotel & Lodging, Arap Moi St (PO Box 832; ☎0321/22160). A simple, clean B&L over a very male-dominated bar: not one for lone women. Good views from the roof terrace and good food to be had nearby – a Somali area. No twin rooms, only doubles. ②.

Mahindi Hotel, Uganda Rd (PO Box 1694; ☎0321/31520). A large, friendly, fairly bright place that allows two to share a single room, though also one of the less restful abodes in town. Decent bar. ②.

New Miyako Hotel, Moi St (PO Box 1073; ☎0321/22594). Not great, and noisy till midnight, but an oft-used stand-by with s/c rooms. ②.

Reformed Church of East Africa Conference and Training Centre, 2km out of town on the Kapsabet road (PO Box 746; ☎0321/32935). Be securely accommodated and cheaply fed, with a minimum of stimulation. ①.

Sosiani View Hotel, Moi St. Right by the transport park, so good for early-morning starts. ②.

Top Lodge, corner of Nandi and Oginga Odinga roads (PO Box 703; ☎ 0321/22148). They are not used to doing so but will give you a clean room for the whole night. ①.

MORE EXPENSIVE HOTELS

Eldoret Wagon Hotel, Elgeyo Rd (PO Box 2408; ☎0321/32271). Sunny, and with quiet, comfortable rooms, this gets quite lively at weekends. ④.

Highlands Inn, Elgeyo Rd (PO Box 2189; ☎0321/22092). Spacious, presentable and normally quiet, with safe parking. Outside there's a small kids' playground and an alfresco bar/restaurant serving *nyama choma* and other standards. ③.

New Lincoln Hotel, Oloo Rd (PO Box 551; ☎0321/22093). With original fixtures and fittings, and a creaking charm that seems to augur imminent collapse, this is Eldoret's most interesting hotel. Far from quiet (close as it is to Eldoret's transport park and top-volume nightclubs), it's still something of an oasis, with lovebirds chirruping in the courtyard, a pleasant bar and decent food (give the coffee a miss, though). ③.

Sirikwa Hotel, Elgeyo Rd (PO Box 3361; ☎0321/63433, fax 0321/61018; reservations through *Magret International*, Phoenix House, 3rd floor, Kenyatta Ave, PO Box 67440, Nairobi; ☎02/224273, fax 02/223245). The town's "premier" hotel, this is a monolithic and faintly pompous pile with redeeming features (see "Listings" below). ⑥.

White Castle Motel, Uganda Rd (PO Box 566; ☎0321/33095 or 33732). Unpromising first impressions – a bland modern building on a noisy road – but the rooms are far better than average. Good value for sharers. ③.

Eating, drinking and nightlife

Eldoret has plenty of good places to grab a bite, with a clutch of established snackeries, several places to dine at greater length, and one or two evening haunts.

Bismiliah Lengut, Oloo Rd. A large, bright eating place near the market.

Eldoret Valley Hotel, Uganda Rd. Good, Somali food and other fare.

Garden Café, Barng'Etuny Plaza, Uganda Rd (☎0321/61156). New venue on the ground floor of this commercial and shopping centre, for food, drink, parties and special events.

New Wagon Hotel (☎0321/32271), Elgeyo Rd. Good four-course dinners.

Otto Café, Uganda Rd. Popular *hoteli* with a long and well-priced menu and excellent *mandaazi*.

Paul's Fresh Bread Bakery, corner of Kimathi Ave and Nandi Rd. Just what's needed on a chilly July morning.

Sam's Disco, Uganda Rd, under the *White Castle Motel*. Middle-of-the-road nightspot with a mixed clientele.

Sirikwa Hotel (☎0321/31655), Elgeyo Rd. Good barbecue buffet lunches at weekends for about $4 – worth it if you've just spent three days in the Kakamega Forest or up Mount Elgon.

Sizzlers, Kenyatta St. A popular American-style joint, offering speedy, high-quality burgers plus ice cream and other desserts.

Sparkles Club, Kenyatta St. A loud and enjoyable nightclub, packed out at weekends.

White Castle Café, Uganda Rd. Fry-ups a speciality.

Wings Opera House, Oloo Rd. Very firmly established nightspot.

Woodles House Disco, Kenyatta St. Where Eldoret's elegant ones hang out: lively and sweaty.

Listings

Banks *Barclays* and *Standard Chartered*, both Mon–Fri 9am–3pm, Sat 9–11am.

Books There's a semi-permanent second-hand and exchange stall on Kenyatta Rd; a library with a good African history section; and a new supermarket at the *Eldo Centre* that stocks a fair range of paperbacks.

Car rental Try *McNaughtons* (PO Box 717; ☎0321/22464) on Kisumu Rd. Apart from a hefty deposit, their rates for 4WD are reasonable – and much cheaper than renting in Kitale if you're headed for Mount Elgon.

Eldoret Show Held in the first week of March.

Post office Mon–Fri 8am–5pm, Sat 9am–noon. Cardphone outside.

Supermarket The supermarket at the *Eldo Centre* is the best in the country outside Nairobi.

Swimming pool The *Sirikwa Hotel* has a pool (non-residents Ksh75) in its large, dull, grassy gardens. At weekends it's overrun with Kenyans in holiday mood.

Onwards from Eldoret

Moving on is probably your main concern. Heading directly **towards the Ugandan border**, there's little to delay your progress to Malaba, two or three hours away. Bungoma and Webuye, en route, are covered on pp.275–277. **Eastbound** on the busy A104 road from Eldoret to Nakuru, uphill and then down again, the sombre scenery is pretty with moors and conifers, but the road itself is a fast one.

For **Kakamega Forest** (see p.277) there's a daily, late-morning *matatu* to Kakamega via the road leading past the *Forest Rest House*; ask for a ticket to Isecheno. Alternatively, you can take any bus or *matatu* going to Kisumu via Kapasabet, and get off at the D267 turning about 20km after Kapasabet (signposted Kisieni 12km), from where it's a walk of about three hours to the *Rest House*.

If you arrived in Eldoret early enough in the day, there are two worthwhile **bases outside town** to head to for a night or longer.

Kaptagat and the Tambach Escarpment

Naiberi River Campsite, near **Kaptagat** (PO Box 142, Eldoret; Kaptagat ☎26 or Eldoret ☎0321/31069), is 20km from Eldoret on the well-surfaced C54/C55 road, en route to the Kerio Valley. There's camping by the Naiberi River, a pair of s/c chalets and several *bandas* (③). They also have a restaurant with *hoteli*-style basics at reasonable prices and more expensive Indian specialities. Getting here by public transport is a problem: if you arrive in Eldoret during the week, call the owner on the Eldoret number and transport will be provided. The nearby *Kaptagat Hotel* used to be a good place, too, but it's pretty run-down these days.

If you intend to cross the Rift Valley to Lake Baringo, you'll find a fair number of *matatus* bound for Kabarnet, using the new **Tambach Escarpment** route. This is a spectacular journey: from the high pastures and wheat fields of the plateau, the valley suddenly yawns out beneath, some 1500m below. However, the route down to the fluorspar mine at Kimwarer, which passes through Kaptagat and used to be the main way across the valley, no longer sees much traffic. Still worth the effort if you have time, or a solid vehicle of your own, it's an incredible hairpin descent that seems to go on forever. Kerio Valley route details continue on p.225.

Soy

In the other direction (west) out of Eldoret, there's transport towards Kitale by bus, minibus or Peugeot at most times of the day, but the **Soy Country Club**, a third of the way there, is nice enough to break your journey for (PO Box 2, Soy; Soy ☎6; ③). Once a very pukka country retreat, this is a peaceful place to stay, with single-storey wings laid out in classic colonial style, complete with wood-tiled roofs, brick chimneys and a formal garden. It's run-down but the rooms are comfortable enough, and there's a swimming pool (small and rather stagnant; non-residents Ksh30), restaurant and bar. You can camp here cheaply, too. Guests are very rare except at weekends. **SOY** itself is nothing at all – you'll hardly notice it – so if you want to camp at the *Country Club*, bring supplies.

In the Soy area, look out for the famous herd of **Rothschild's giraffe**, now very rare. Most often seen as specks in the distance – barely distinguishable from dead trees – on the dry plain near the junction between the B2 (to Soy) and the A104 (from Eldoret), they occasionally appear near the road. They stand their ground and, for giraffe close-ups, the only place you'll do better is at the Langata Sanctuary near Nairobi, where a number of the Soy animals have been relocated in recent years. Be warned, however, that it's definitely not a good idea to be seen taking photographs near the military barracks to the south of Soy.

Kitale and northward

KITALE is smaller than Eldoret, and not much more exciting, but it has more going for it from a traveller's point of view, primarily because it is the base for visits to **Mount Elgon** and the superb, very underrated, hiking country around Kenya's second giant volcanic cone. It is also an obvious base for the **Cherangani Hills**; the most straightforward departure point for trips into the **northern deserts**; and the only town with a regular bus service to **Lake Turkana**. There's a **national park** nearby – the little-known but easily accessible **Saiwa Swamp**, where for once the tables are turned on drivers: you can explore on foot only. And the town itself boasts a good **regional museum**.

It has to be said that Kitale itself is an unprepossessing place for a rest stop: the majority of travellers spend just one night here on the way to Lake Turkana. It's well planted with trees, though, and warm – despite its highland location, warm enough to hint at the desert that begins not far to the north. However, unless you're on a tight schedule, the museum and Saiwa Swamp add up to a good reason to delay a day. Nor is the road to Turkana so daunting as to make getting a ride there a problem: the buses go early, but there are usually other vehicles heading off north until early afternoon.

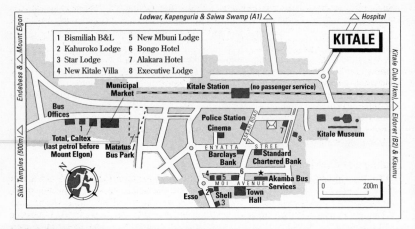

1 Bismiliah B&L	5 New Mbuni Lodge	**KITALE**
2 Kahuroko Lodge	6 Bongo Hotel	
3 Star Lodge	7 Alakara Hotel	
4 New Kitale Villa	8 Executive Lodge	

Some history

Originally Quitale, a relay station on the old slave route between Uganda and Bagamoyo in Tanzania, the modern town was founded only in 1920, as the capital of Trans-Nzoia District. When the first settlers arrived (mostly after World War I), this vale of rich grasslands between Mount Elgon and the Cherangani Hills was apparently almost uninhabited. But just a few years earlier it had been a Maasai grazing area, and a group who refer to themselves as "Maasai" still live on the eastern slopes of Elgon.

With the arrival of the railway in 1925, the town and the region around it began to flourish, with a fantastic array of fruit, cereals, vegetables and livestock, and all the attendant settler paraphernalia of agricultural and flower shows, church fêtes and gymkhanas. This heady era lasted barely forty years, but the region's **agriculture** is still famous: almost anything, including such exotic fruit as apples and pears, can be grown here. The Kitale Show happens each year at the end of October or beginning of November.

Accommodation, eating and drinking

If you're heading north out of town anyway, you may want to stay at *Barnley's House* (see p.268). If you don't have your own vehicle, allow at least an hour to get there. In Kitale itself there are a number of **cheap lodgings**, the most economical up at the grubby north end of town, past the market. The less ornate of the two **Sikh temples** up here also takes travellers; remember to leave a donation.

Hotels and lodgings

Alakara Hotel, Kenyatta St (PO Box 1984; ☎0325/20395). Probably the best lodging in town, a large, clean, bright place with an efficient air, surprisingly good beds and 24-hour hot water. ③.

Bismiliah B&L, in the row of shops between the market and the bus offices. Adequate and dirt cheap. ①.

Bongo Hotel, Moi Ave (PO Box 530; ☎0325/20593). Decent, properly furnished s/c rooms, but since the rise of the *Alakara* no longer the first choice. ③.

Executive Lodge, Kenyatta St. Off-puttingly dark but one of the town's better B&Ls, secure with excellent rooms, hot showers down the hall and a TV room. ③.

Kahuroko Lodge, Moi Ave, behind the Shell garage (PO Box 2290; ☎0325/31066). Basic lodgings fronted by a bar-restaurant. ①.

Kitale Club, on the road out towards Eldoret (PO Box 30; ☎0325/20030). The site of the old slave quarters (the circle of stones in the car park is said to have surrounded a ring to which slaves were chained at night), accommodation and atmosphere at this old colonial club have in the past received diverse reports: visitors have found it variously "hostile", "a bit of a rip-off" and "relaxing, but not cheap". But the management are doing their best to move with the times and a swish new accommodation block has been built. If you're just passing by, politeness can earn you a look at their airmail *Daily Telegraphs* and permission to buy a beer. There's a golf course, pleasant swimming pool, laundry service and acceptable meals available. ⑤.

New Kitale Villa, Moi Ave (PO Box 1856). Clean but basic; women on their own might prefer to look elsewhere. ①.

New Mbuni Lodge, Moi Ave (PO Box 951). Cheap and noisy, with a bar upstairs. ①.

Star Lodge, along the road south of Moi Ave. Comes highly recommended: well worth checking out considering its low prices. ②.

Eating and drinking

Currently the best **food** in Kitale is to be found at the *Alakara Hotel*, which also has a pleasant bar. As elsewhere, many restaurants are closed on Sundays. On other days, the *Bongo Bar and Restaurant* is worth patronizing. Meals at the *Kitale Club* are thoroughly dependable, and its restaurants are normally open to non-residents. Wherever you eat, do it early. Many places close after dark (the *Alakara* and *Bongo* stay open later).

Once it's dark, the places to head for a drink and lively conversation are, again, the *Alakara*, the *Bongo* and, most feverish of all, the *Mombalero*, opposite the *Bongo*.

Kitale Museum

Open daily 9am–6pm; Ksh200; curator: PO Box 1219; ☎0325/20670.

Given its location, **Kitale Museum** (or the Museum of Western Kenya) is remarkably successful. Originally the "Stoneham Museum", a collection opened to the public by a Lieutenant Colonel on his Cherangani farm in 1927, it was transferred here in 1972. Most of the early exhibits are now on the right as you enter. For the most part, Stoneham's curious collections are just that: collected curiosities in striking contrast to the recent Kenyan additions with more educational motives. The directly exhortatory display at the back of the main hall makes "An Appeal to All Kenyans" on issues of soil conservation, crop rotation and land terracing.

The **ethnographic displays** on Pokot, Elkony (Elgon), Maasai, Marakwet, Turkana and Luo are interesting, though perhaps more so if you've seen the stuff in real life and now have a chance to return and see it again. Among the artefacts are Kamba carvings – skin-covered animals and smooth polished abstracts; a goat bell made from a tortoise shell; Pokot bowls used for collecting blood from cattle; and intricate belts and beadwork from Turkana. The motley wildlife collection on the walls and downstairs is perhaps best ignored, but the entomology is more interesting – a very fine collection of butterflies and bugs collected in the region in recent years, sadly mostly as yet unlabelled.

Outside, there's a **snake pit** and the inevitable **tortoise pen**, with its hinged and leopard tortoise inmates. Unless it's the mating season, though, it's as boring for you as it must be for them. The re-creations of Nandi and Luyia homesteads make an interesting point of comparison with the realities of present-day villages.

Next to the main building, the octagonal **Museum Hall** has some bold murals of Turkana, Maasai, Nandi and Luo domestic life, commissioned by the National Museum and painted by Maggie Kukler. There's occasionally live music or a disco here. The museum also has a craft shop, laboratories and a surprising **nature trail**, which transports you, in a few steps, from suburban Kitale to a chattering, dripping, rain forest where the trees are numbered (the curator apparently has a key of Latin names) and the birds abundant: look out for Ross' turaco, a large, deep purple species with a square red crest, commoner here than in other forests. The trail follows a stream with a path and footbridges, but the forest itself is natural and some of the trees stately. The picnic sites, near the end of the trail which leads back to the main road, are the best places for a picnic in Kitale.

Onwards from Kitale

Looking **to the west**: if you're interested in exploring **Mount Elgon**, it's very much a case of following your nose (full details start on p.270). If you're using public transport, the closest you can get is Endebess or Kimilili, both reached quickly enough by *matatu*; you should arrive early in the day if you want to make significant progress up the mountain before dark. **Southwards**, Kakamega and Kisumu are, with luck, no more than two or three hours away down the A1, a very busy road.

But most people setting off from Kitale are **heading north** (route details in Chapter 7). The rough road north from Kitale to Lodwar and Ferguson's Gulf on Lake Turkana is frequently hard on the wheels and may even on occasion be impassable after heavy rain. But if the weather's been good, there are several buses and *matatus* a day (Nissans are best; remember to take water), and enough traffic to make hitching a practical option. If you're driving yourself, note that there is nowhere to get fuel between Kapenguria and Lodwar. With a tent, it may be more fun to spend the night before at **Saiwa Swamp National Park** rather than in Kitale itself. And you could further delay your progress north by stopping over at the *Marich Pass Field Studies Centre*.

Sirikwa Safaris – Barnley's House

You could also stop off for a day – or quite happily for a week – at **Sirikwa Safaris Guesthouse and Campsite** (bookings through *Barnley's House*, PO Box 332, Kitale; no telephone), precisely 23.6km north of Kitale, on a tree-covered hill to the right and sign-boarded with a green-topped frame (if you still can't find it, try asking for *Bwana Tim's*). There are superb gardens to camp in (hot water and barbecue facilities), furnished tents and a fine old house with rooms if you're lazy (③–④; big breakfasts and excellent meals to order). Staff will undertake your washing – most days. There's exceptional birdwatching in this **Cherangani** foothills area and skilled guides to show you the avifauna if you've caught the bug.

Saiwa Swamp National Park

Open daily; National Park fees apply (Category D), see p.61; car park; entry on foot; warden PO Box 753, Chemeron; Chanira ☎22.

Specially created for the protection of the **sitatunga**, a rare and vulnerable semi-aquatic antelope, **SAIWA SWAMP NATIONAL PARK** is the country's smallest park. Despite its accessibility – no distance from *Barnley's House* – it is rarely visited, which is a pity: the requirement that you walk around the two square kilometres of jungle and swamp, plus the virtual guarantee of seeing the antelope as well as various monkeys and birds, make it an exciting and interesting goal for a day. If you're staying at *Barnley's*, think about hiring a guide there for the trip – not at all expensive, and really worthwhile.

Game watching

The **sitatunga** (pronounced "statunga") is an unusual antelope with strange splayed and elongated hooves. You probably won't see these because the animal lives most of its life partly submerged in water and weed. It's hard to see quite how the hooves help it "to move freely on the surface of boggy swamps": the theory makes sense, but the design needs more work. Otherwise, the sitatunga is reddish-brown and moth-eaten, with very large, mobile ears and, on the males, horns.

Sitatunga can be found in scattered locations throughout western and central Africa, but only at Saiwa Swamp have they grown really used to humans. They can be watched from the **observation platforms** which have been built in the trees at the side of the swamp – one on the east side, three on the west. The best times are early morning and late afternoon, and the furthest platform is less than a kilometre from the campsite. These lookouts are unmaintained, Tarzan-esque structures enabling you to spy down on the life among the reeds. The park also shelters plenty of **bushbuck**, easily distinguished from the sitatunga by their terrified, crashing escape through the undergrowth as you approach. The sitatunga evidently have steadier nerves, as they pick their way through the morass of water weed regardless of human attention.

A delightful, simple to follow, **early-morning walk** takes you across the rickety duckboards over the swamp and down a jungle path on the eastern shore. Here you're almost bound to see the park's four species of **monkey**: colobus, vervet, blue, and the distinctively white-bearded de Brazza monkey.

Saiwa Swamp is also a great draw for ornithologists, with a number of untypical Kenyan **bird species**, including several turacos (though the great blue is apparently no longer among them), many kingfishers, and the splendid black-and-white casqued hornbill. Most conspicuous of all are the **crowned cranes**, whose lurching flight is almost as risible as their ghastly honking call.

Practicalities

The park – known locally as *Swam'* – lies to the right of the main Kitale–Lodwar road, near the village of **Kipsain** (also known as Kipsoen). *Matatus* and the *Akamba* bus to Kapenguria (7am only) call at the village, which is some 18km from Kitale and off the main road. From here, if you fail to get a lift, it's a five-kilometre walk to the park gates. For the camping fee and park fees (once you've been spotted by a ranger), you'll find three good sites grouped together, but nothing at all in the way of facilities, apart from a clean, piped water supply at the staff village, plenty of firewood, and a small *duka*, open sporadically. You will need to make a fire, as the swamp mist makes it very chilly up here at night.

Kapenguria, Ortum and the Marich Pass

KAPENGURIA – off the highway north, but somewhere you might find yourself if you're in the district – seems to have no lodgings, nor much else except a role of minor notoriety in colonial history (see the background on Kenyatta's trial in *Contexts*, p.509). If you turn off the main road to visit, you'll find an immaculately tarred main street leading incongruously up through the hovels of "old Kapenguria" to the smarter new town on higher ground, with its hospital, large police station, huge red octagonal Catholic church (stained-glass windows and a spire), and the West Pokot District headquarters. If you're hungry, the *Talik Hotel* is a worthy target. For **accommodation**, there's a couple of B&Ls down in **Makutano** – the service town for the western Cherangani Hills, at the Kapenguria intersection.

Much more interesting, however, is **ORTUM**, beautifully positioned beneath the heights of the Cheranganis, close to the **Marich Pass**, and a good locale to start hiking in the hills. There are at least two cheap **B&Ls** here (*Karumaindo Inn* and *Somtowo Hotel*). People are pleasantly disinterested in your presence. Of a large number of *hotelis*, the winner is *Rafikis' Hotel*, which serves tasty meals and manages cold sodas despite the absence of electricity. You can do a short **hike to a waterfall**, three hours' walk up from Ortum. Cross the main road beyond the post office, down by the *Karumaindo Inn*, and the first dirt track takes you straight there. On Sundays, a constant stream of vehicles heads from Ortum to the weekly market at Chesegon, on the other side of the Cheranganis, assuring transport into the Kerio Valley if you want it (see p.225).

A good base to make for in this district is the **Marich Pass Field Studies Centre** (c/o PO Box 2454, Eldoret; ☎0321/31541), a residential set-up beautifully sited on the banks of the Moruny River, just north of the small shopping centre of **Marich**, at the junction of the B4 and A1: follow the signpost off the Lodwar road, 2km north of the A1/B4 junction at Marich; the Centre is 1km to the right, keeping right. At the moment there are inexpensive double *bandas* and a secure campsite, and various improvements and additions – electricity, bar-restaurant, swimming pool – are under way or newly installed. The food is basic but impressively plentiful and drinking water comes pure from the well. The centre is surrounded by dense bush, quivering with bird and animal life, and there are guides to help you on excursions if you have the energy. **Mount Sekerr** (Mtelo) is the peak that looms to the northwest – it's a three-day hike to the top (3354m) and back.

Mount Elgon

The Maasai's **Ol Doinyo Ilgoon** (Breast Mountain) is hidden in clouds most of the time and its precise outline hard to discern. Like Mount Kenya, **MOUNT ELGON** is an extinct volcano, and around its jagged and much eroded crater rim, the flat-topped peaks crop up like stumpy fingers of an upturned hand. The two mountains are comparable in bulk, but Elgon is lower (below the snowline) and less precipitous – an encouragement, perhaps, if the thought of tackling the "loneliest park in Kenya" was putting you off. Up near the peaks there's invigorating walking country and the smoothing effects of erosion make hiking relatively easy. The highest peak, **Wagagai** (4321m), is across the caldera in Uganda, but the most evocatively shaped peaks (Sudek, 4176m; Lower Elgon, 4301m; Koitoboss, 4187m; and Endebess Bluff, 2563m) belong to Kenya. The mountain has good rock-climbing if you're properly equipped; the best is on the cliffs of Lower Elgon, Sudek and the nearby pinnacles. Actually up in

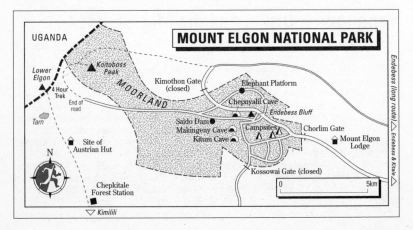

the caldera (again, technically in Uganda), the **warm springs** by the Suam River make a tempting bath.

Part of the east side of the mountain is enclosed within the confines of **Mount Elgon National Park**. Outside this zone, however, you're as free to hike and camp as anywhere in Kenya, subject always to the mountain's potentially restricting location on what the authorities have often considered a sensitive border (see box on p.273).

Wildlife

Vegetation here is similar to Mount Kenya's, and very impressive, with bamboo and podocarpus forests giving way to open moorland inhabited by the strange statues of giant groundsel and lobelia. **Wildlife** isn't easily seen until you get onto the moors but elephant and buffalo do roam the woods. The best place to see **elephant** used to be the Elephant Platform – herds would congregate here to feed on the acacias – but poaching has made them reclusive. Large numbers of elephant were wiped out by Ugandan poachers in the turbulent 1980s. While the Kenya Wildlife Service is confident that poaching is now under control, and estimates that the elephant population now exceeds 400, it remains to be seen how long they will remain under effective protection. The lions have long gone and, though there are still leopards, you're not likely to see one. The primates are more conspicuous: blue monkeys (found only in western Kenya) and shaggy colobus crash through the forested areas, troops of olive baboons patrol the scrub, and along the Kimothon River there's a scattering of rare de Brazza's monkeys.

The Elkony Caves

Elgon's most captivating attraction is the honeycomb of caves on the lower slopes, inside the national park boundaries. Some of these were long inhabited by one of the loosely related Kalenjin groups, the **Elkony** (whose name, in corrupted form, was

---

KITUM CAVE AND THE EBOLA VIRUS

Kitum Cave earned a certain notoriety when it featured as the opening and closing location of *The Hot Zone*, a "true-life thriller" about Ebola written in 1994 by an American journalist, Richard Preston. **Ebola** is a virus so deadly it is scientifically classed as a Level 4 pathogen (HIV is only Level 2). Mercifully, it's rare; the only serious outbreaks in the last twenty years occurred in Zaire and Sudan in 1976, and then again in April 1995 in Zaire. In the more recent plague, around 250 people in the Zairean town of Kikwit died after contracting the virus. The manner of death by Ebola is so gruesome that hysterical global media coverage surrounded the outbreak – effectively, the virus liquefies the vital organs of the living victim, and death occurs within days. Scientists have yet to gather any solid data about the origins and means of transmission of the virus, or the identity of its natural host. The link to Kitum Cave is a tenuous, probably meaningless one. Isolated incidences of Ebola infection are reported every few years, and, in two such cases (described in gut-churning detail by Richard Preston in his book), the victims had visited Kitum Cave shortly before they became ill. In an attempt to discover whether the cave harbours the virus in some form, the US Army's Infectious Diseases Unit, in conjunction with the Kenya Medical Research Unit, mounted a research operation in Kitum Cave in 1988. The team made *Mount Elgon Lodge* their base, donned spaceman-type anti-virus bio-safety suits, and set about making a comprehensive examination of the cave, testing thousands of resident insects, birds, hyraxes, bats, monkeys, baboons, and samples of guano and dung, for Ebola. They found absolutely nothing. Preston's book, going all out for sensationalism, hangs a question mark over the conclusiveness of these findings, but those who know the Elgon area well unanimously write the theory off as irresponsible trouble-stirring.

given to the mountain), and used both as living quarters and as stock pens at night. There is evidence that the caves may have had a ritual function as well – **Chepnyalil Cave** contains a structure that might have served as an altar or shrine, and its walls are painted with a red and white frieze of cattle. The Elkony were officially evicted from the caves by the colonial government, who insisted that they live in the open "where they could be counted for tax", but caves with ceilings as high as two-storey buildings were still occupied by extended families within living memory.

Some of the caves are so large and labyrinthine that deep exploration is only possible with navigational aids and breathing apparatus. It is rumoured that there is a route that leads far into the mountain and emerges in Uganda, a secret passage known only to coffee smugglers. The largest and most spectacular cave is **Makingeny**, marked by a cascade falling over the entrance.

At least a few of the caves were thought to have been man-made, and an early report refers to "thousands of chisel and axe marks on the walls". It's now more generally believed, however, that generations of elephants were responsible: **Kitum Cave** achieved television fame as the salt fix of local elephants, which used to walk into the caves at night to gouge the salty rock from the walls with their tusks. The elephants, though no longer free to migrate back and forth between Elgon and the Cheranganis as they once did, are still occasional troglodytes. There have been cases of them falling into crevasses or dying under rock falls caused by their over-eager salt-mining.

Planning a trip

In most respects, you should treat a trip up Mount Elgon much as you would one to Mount Kenya (see p.164). However, **altitude** is less of a problem on Elgon and, given several days to climb it, few people will be badly affected by the ascent, except perhaps near the summits. Access to the mountain can be a little difficult – certainly it's not as straightforward as Mount Kenya – and for this reason it is one of the least-visited national parks in Kenya. The rangers, eager to receive more visitors, are optimistic that the opening of the airport at Eldoret should do much to encourage people to come. Having your own transport is a definite advantage, both for reaching the mountain and for getting to the hiking trails once you're there. Within the park zone, the only areas that hikers are permitted to explore without a vehicle are the eastern section near Chorlim Gate, the caves, and Endebess Bluff; you're advised to take a ranger as a chaperone/guide. To reach the trail to Koitoboss Peak and explore the rest of the park you must have a vehicle. Be warned, however, that the tracks can be muddy (even in the dry season), rocky and steep – tough going even with four-wheel-drive, impassable without. You might think about **renting a 4WD** in Kisumu or Eldoret for a few days (try *McNaughtons*; see "Listings", p.264). In Kitale car rental is often impossible to arrange – and very expensive. The *Golf Hotel* in Kakamega (part of the same *Msafiri Inns* group as *Mount Elgon Lodge*) may be able to help with transport.

Timing and guides

Elgon is best from December to March and rather less good in June and July, with the heaviest rains falling during the April–May and August–September periods. This is a lonely mountain, and while there are no specific permanent restrictions on hiking outside the park boundaries (which enclose less than a quarter of the Kenyan slopes), it's probably better not to go up alone. You aren't likely to see anyone else for a day or two, and if something were to happen to you on the heights you can forget about rescue. Men can find **guide-porters** easily enough in villages around the base: just ask around, and expect to pay up to $6 per day. As usual, women travelling alone will be at a disadvantage when it comes to such one-to-one arrangements.

Maps

If you plan more than a look into the park by vehicle, it's useful to have the *Mount Elgon Map & Guide* by Andrew Wielochowski, obtainable in Nairobi or in the UK from *Executive Wilderness Programmes*, Haulfryn, Cilycwm, Llandovery SA20 0SP (☎01550/ 721319, fax 01550/720053; £6 including postage within the UK). Survey of Kenya maps are also available, and the 1:125,000 map can be obtained without clearance, though border sensitivity means some other sheets may be restricted at times (see p.127).

Equipment

Take a **compass** and supplies for at least two to three days of self-sufficiency. Suggestions on clothing and equipment can be found in the Mount Kenya section (p.164). A **tent** will enable you to stay up in the peaks area. If you have a vehicle, preferably 4WD, you can adjust these requirements. The park rangers are often willing to accompany drivers for a fee.

The routes

There are three **routes** up the Kenyan side of Elgon: one directly into the park and two hikes around either side, both passing through fine scenery and neither very severe. You should try, if at all possible, to **camp** at one of the sites in the lower half of the park – they're highly recommended as some of the most beautiful in the country – and visit the caves.

  Mount Elgon Lodge (PO Box 7, Endebess; Endebess ☎11Y6; reservations through *Msafiri Inns*, address p.49; B&B ⑤, FB ⑥), is located on the track leading to Chorlim Gate, but its status is marginal. It has been run at a loss for many years and isn't certain to be open. It's an atmospheric retreat, however, despite the emptiness: the reception rooms have lovingly polished wood-block floors and quintessentially English garden views, and the bedrooms are comfortable enough. You can choose between one of the original rooms, up a creaking flight of stairs, or a modern room in the block overlooking the lawns. **Camping** in the grounds is an accepted, and very acceptable, alternative to taking a room.

Direct to the park

Open daily; National Park fees apply (Category D), see p.61; warden PO Box 753, Kitale; ☎0325/20329.

The only way into the park, if you're driving, is through **Chorlim Gate**, the main entrance to the **National Park**, which lies some 10km beyond Endebess. Kimothon

---

TEMPORARY DIFFICULTIES: SOME NOTES OF CAUTION

Elgon's location occasionally makes it a sensitive area. If you plan to go down into the crater and visit the Suam warm springs, remember that they are in Uganda: stories of rebel soldiers have long been rife.

  In the 1980s, Elgon was the scene of a number of violent confrontations between elephant poachers and armed park rangers. The last serious outbreak was in 1988 and resulted in several deaths. For some time, Kenyan officials were turning back non-4WD vehicles, even outside the park, and preventing hikers on foot from climbing.

  The most recent threat to Elgon's status as a hiking attraction is the ethnic strife that has swept the communities of its eastern slopes since the democracy movement gained momentum. The people of Kimilili and Endebess towns have seen arson, sporadic violence and furious bouts of intimidation directed against non-Kalenjin by gangs of youths of uncertain identity. Access up the walking routes may be refused at one point or another, or you may be advised to abandon your attempt. Talk to local people and take a guide, or guides.

and Kossowai Gates have been closed and unstaffed for some time. To reach Chorlim Gate, stock up on petrol at Kitale, and head northwest towards Endebess. The tarmac road breaks up outside Kitale proper and drivers have swerving cyclists and pedestrians to contend with, as well as potholes. There is a brown Kenya Wildlife Service signpost marking the left-hand turning to the National Park, 500m after the Kenya Seed Company and ADC compounds. From here a murram road heads straight to *Mount Elgon Lodge* and Chorlim Gate. If you miss the turning, there's another left turn signposted at Endebess, leading to the same murram road. *Matatus* frequently make the trip from Kitale to Endebess, but getting up to the gate is a problem without a car and you may have to walk it. Hoping to find a spare seat in a tourist vehicle isn't really an option: with barely a handful of visitors per month you might be in for a long wait.

Once **inside the Park**, the fine (signposted) campsites a few kilometres from the gate are a good target. If you're exceptionally lucky, a night vigil at **Kitum Cave** may be repaid by a visit from the elephants; the bats and the forest are compensation if you're not. You'll need permission from the rangers and a good torch. For **Koitoboss Peak** (4187m), follow the drivable track into the moorlands to the trailhead outside the park (allow 3–4hr to cover the 30km; a ranger should accompany you in your vehicle). From here it's a three-hour hike to the pass at the southern base of the peak, where there are flat (but cold and windy) places where you can camp. You can then make the one-hour scramble to the top, or take a two- to three-hour diversion to the Suam Springs in the crater.

Kimilili and the Western Trail

The **second route** is the most popular with **hikers** (but note caveats: see box above). It begins in **KIMILILI**, a village on the way to Bungoma from Kitale (heading south from Kitale towards Webuye, turn right off the A1 after about 30km), from where it's a long but invigorating trek up to the moorlands (lifts are scarce). In Kimilili, *Jasho Lodging* is recommended for **rooms**, the *Wanyika Hotel* for **meals**. Kimilili is a lively place on a Thursday, when the **market** attracts rural dwellers from a wide radius. You may be allowed to **pitch a tent** at Kimilili Catholic Secondary School, just outside the town.

The next day, by allowing yourself a good eight to ten hours to cover the 40-odd kilometres, you should be able to reach the Elgon Hut (or Austrian Hut); the hut is disused but it is usually possible to camp near here. The first step **up the mountain** is to take a ride by *matatu*, starting as early as possible in the day, from Kimilili to **Kapsakwony**, 7km away (top up with water here if you forgot in Kimilili). At the fork above the village, bear left, then after 2km turn right at the "Forest Station 25km" signpost. You may get a lift from here, past the Forest Reserve Gate (small fee) to the last village, **Kaberua**, 2.5km further up (see the sign there, "Chepkitale Forest Stn 21km"), but from Kaberua on, you'll almost certainly have to walk. Eight kilometres above Kaberua, the trail gets noticeably worse as it plunges into the cathedral gloom of bamboo forest. An hour of this and you break into open stands of moss-enveloped giant podocarpus trees ("podos") with spiralling trunks. The trail rolls upwards, you crest a hill, and the entire southern Elgon Ridge system is spread out before you.

The **Chepkitale forest station** has plenty of abandoned buildings for shelter but uncertain water supplies, so it is worth struggling on the last two hours (7km) to the **Elgon Hut**. There's a stream near the hut but little firewood, so remember to collect some on the way. A rough jeep track continues past the hut, but you're unlikely to meet anyone up here.

The **trail** from the hut is well marked with occasional cairns and white blazes: a brisk three to four hours the following morning should see you to **Lower Elgon Tarn**, a good place to camp, from where it's another hour to the top of Lower Elgon itself, the highest peak on the Kenya side. Starting out from the hut, a two-hour hike will bring you up to the ridge that leads up to the peak of Lower Elgon. (Just beyond this, there is

ELIJA MASINDE'S DINI: THE CULT OF THE ANCESTORS

In the 1940s and 1950s, there was a resurgence of **Bukusu resistance** and nationalism in the Dini ya Msambwa (Cult of the Ancestors) movement, spearheaded by the charismatic prophet-rebel, **Elija Masinde**. The heart of the movement was in the Elgon foothills between Kimilili and the Ugandan border. It called for the eviction of all *wazungu* and the transfer of their property to Africans. As the *Dini* spread, there were violent confrontations with colonial forces and a number of deaths. Masinde was sent into internal exile but, by now a folk hero, his followers kept the sparks of resistance alive throughout the more organized uprising of *Mau Mau* in the Central Highlands, until Independence was finally obtained. The movement collapsed in the early years of *Uhuru*, when Masinde was allowed home to Kimilili and his continued denouncements of all authority and claims to divine inspiration began to lose their coherence. He could recently still be seen on the streets of Kimilili – a rather terrifying figure shouting at the wind.

a high valley which has the southeast caldera rim, seen from the rear, as its head.) There are duiker antelope to be seen bouncing away through the scrub everywhere. Next, you climb a false summit, then dip down, parallelling the series of tabular peaks on your right which form the southern crater lip. From the **tarn**, the trail swerves cruelly up through a gap in the rock wall to put you on the summit of Lower Elgon.

Alternatively, you could make the five-hour trek from the hut to **Koitoboss Peak** and the **Suam warm springs**. To get down to the springs, instead of following the ridge at the two-hour mark, leave the trail and cut across the valley, following the rim to Koitoboss Peak, inside the National Park. Down in the crater, to the left, are the springs. Depending on your life support system, you can either turn back to the hut for a second night there or continue around the crater rim to drop down off the mountain on the northeast side, traversing the upper part of the National Park and, ideally, allowing a night camped on the mountain. Note that if you're found in the Park, or if you exit through Chorlim Gate, you may have some explaining to do and you'll have to pay Park fees at least.

Kimothon route

There's a **third route**, on the north side of the park, which obviates some of the lengthy foot-slogging of the trail from Kimilili, but, like the Kimilili route, it may be closed. It starts in Endebess and leads west about 12km up to the village of **Masara** and thence to **Kimothon Forest Station**. It's recommended that you stay the night here and continue the next day on the well-marked trail to Koitoboss and the Elgon hut. Downhill from here, you can follow the Kimilili trail (about 40km, as described above) in reverse. Once you reach Kapsakwony there are *matatus* for the last 7km to Kimilili; it's a ten-hour knee-wobbler of a hike if you want to walk the whole way.

The Uganda road: Webuye, Bungoma and Malaba

This is perhaps the least interesting part of western Kenya to look at: largely monotonous undulating grasslands and sugar fields, dotted here and there with gigantic granite boulders. But it is still the route by which the majority of Africa overland travellers come into the country, and the most obvious one for those planning to head **out to Uganda**; despite the lack of attractions, it sees a fair number of travellers passing through.

If you're making your way to the south from this district down towards Kakamega and Kisumu, the busy A1 will take you through some fine stands of forest and tropical woodland, heralding the pristine zone of Kakamega Forest (see opposite) to the southeast.

Webuye and around

WEBUYE certainly offers very little to attract visitors. It's the site of the giant Panafrican Paper Mills (visitors' enquiries: PO Box 535, Webuye), which dominate the countryside around – with their strong, strange odour as much as anything else. The explanation for the factory's siting is **Webuye Falls**, gushing through rock clefts behind and above the mills, about 5km from the main road. Formerly known as Broderick Falls, Webuye is a nice spot for a picnic, as long as you have a car for access, but the falls are hardly spectacular. To reach them, turn off the main road at the factory and climb northwards between housing developments and mills, passing a school. From there, the plant (the largest paper factory in Africa), belching smoke across the hot plains, is a powerful statement about change in Kenya.

Webuye has the usual assortment of banks, shops and petrol stations, and if you find yourself in need of a **room**, there are two reasonably comfortable options: the *Webuye Motel* (Webuye ☎41328; ③), on the southeast side of town, and the *Park Villa Hotel* (PO Box 1000, Webuye; Webuye ☎41290; ③), a well-kept roadside stop with busy bars and a small pool.

Chetambe's Fort

A few kilometres away, on top of the steep scarp that rears up beyond the Kitale road, lies a different kind of monument, the remains of **Chetambe's Fort**. This was the site, in 1895, of a last-ditch stand by the Bukusu group of the Luyia tribe against the motley line-up of a British punitive expedition, which had enrolled Ugandan, Sudanese, Maasai and even other Luyia troops. A predictable – Hotchkiss gun – massacre took place, with negligible losses on the attackers' side. How they managed to storm the scarp in the first place, however, is a mystery: presumably the Bukusu were all inside their walled fort at the top.

With Kenya's historical sites being so few, it's worth the effort to scramble up the steep slope if you're interested. Not surprisingly, perhaps, the "Fort" itself is quite unimpressive: all that remains these days is an overgrown, semicircular ditch, perhaps 100m from end to end. A more convincing reason for going there is to talk to some of the people who live nearby – this is really the only way to weave together the differing threads of history. You can be shown the site by people who live around it: the compound is just another field now, but one informal guide explained how he used to find bones here when he was young, and women would come here to weep in the evenings. There were even animal sacrifices to the dead warriors. Some "awful machine" had killed them.

If you have your own transport, a roundabout alternative to the slog up the cliffs is to continue following the road which leads past Webuye Falls. The *Nabyole Lodge* up here is quite a good **B&L**, with cold drinks and a restaurant. They'll direct you on to Chetambe's, about 8km further on reasonable murram.

Bungoma and into Uganda

The main road to Uganda continues west. The smooth tarmac and dull scenery encourage fast driving, with light vehicles shuddering in the slipstream of thundering lorries. Number-plate spotters will be able to tick off vehicles from all over eastern and central Africa on this one well-pounded stretch.

Sizeable as it is, **BUNGOMA** manages to be unremittingly dull. Unless you're drawn by the siren calls of the *Bungoma Tourist Hotel*'s unexpected "sugar-belt style" comforts (PO Box 972; ③), there's scarcely any reason to visit the town, as it isn't on the main road. If you do find yourself here, *Grandma's Hotel* (PO Box 225), just 200m south of the A104 Bungoma junction, before you get into the town, is less of a drain on the resources and provides clean, quiet rooms. If you miss this, or find it full, *Hotel Simba B&L* (PO Box 663), has cheap double beds and seems better than the other competition in town. Apart from suggesting that you eat at the *New Yemeni Hotel*, a superior *hoteli*, Bungoma's interest can't be further improved.

Malaba: the Ugandan border

MALABA lies at the end of both the road and the railway line. Conditions in **Uganda** are changing so rapidly that anything like up-to-date advice and news from the border is next to impossible to provide. However, while there are usually endless lines of lorries waiting on both sides of the border, pedestrians are crossing without difficulty. See "Kenya's Neighbouring States" in *Basics* (p.70) for recent travel information about Uganda.

Arriving in Kenya on a Wednesday, Saturday, or Sunday, you might feel like collapsing onto the train to Nairobi (departs Wed 4pm, Sat & Sun 11.05pm, arriving about 16hr later) for a good night's sleep and some old-fashioned customer service – such as a man ringing a bell for meal times. Otherwise, there's no shortage of unappetizing **B&Ls** along the kilometre of lorry-choked road which is Malaba. And if you're glad to be in Kenya at last, don't make the mistake of relaxing your security routines: many people are robbed soon after arriving.

Kakamega and Kakamega Forest

KAKAMEGA is the headquarters of the **Luyia**, a loosely defined group of peoples whose only clear common denominator is a **Bantu language**, spoken in more than a score of vernaculars, that distinguishes them from the Luo to the south and the Kalenjin to the east. Numerically, the Luyia (Abaluyia/Luhya) are Kenya's second largest ethnic group, and most are settled farmers.

The town itself was founded as a buying station on the ox trail known as Sclater's Road, which reached here from the coast in 1896. Historically, its only fame came in the 1930s, when gold was discovered nearby and more than a thousand prospectors came to the region. Very few fortunes were made. Today, it's a lively town, but with little to detain casual visitors.

Conversely, the nearby **Kakamega Forest** is one of western Kenya's star attractions; if you have any interest at all in the natural world, it's worth going far out of your way to see. Fortunately, it's fairly easy to get to from Kisumu or, if you've been in the Mount Elgon region, from Webuye along a very scenic stretch of the A1.

Kakamega town – practicalities

If you arrive late in the day, you may want to **stay in town** rather than arrive in the forest after dark. There are several decent lodgings and one or two pleasant places to eat.

Accommodation

Bendera Hotel & Restaurant (PO Box 423, ☎0331/20777). Unexpectedly good B&L – clean and welcoming, with decent-sized s/c rooms. Happily the ear-splitting country and western music from the downstairs bar-restaurant doesn't really filter upstairs. ②.

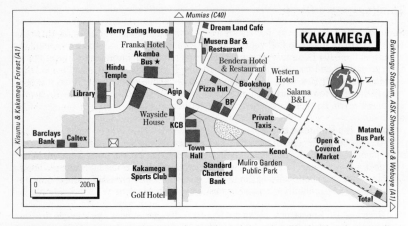

Franka Hotel. Plenty of clean s/c rooms, some with good views, but this place has the oppressive atmosphere of a wide-boys' hangout and is probably not a good choice for lone women. ②.
Golf Hotel (PO Box 118; ☎0331/30150, fax 0331/30155; *Msafiri Inns*, address p.49 but may soon change hands). A relatively luxurious hotel – one of the best in the west – with its pretensions comically clipped by the vultures hopping over the lawns. All residents become temporary members of the adjacent Sports Club (golf, squash courts, etc) and there's a pool. ⑤.
Salama Board and Lodging. Very basic but one of the cheapest in town, with rooms off a courtyard at the back of a fly-blown eating place. ①.
Wayside House (PO Box 900; ☎0331/20128). Sparse rooms and filthy shared washing facilities. The bar is good, with a jukebox well stocked with west Kenyan sounds, but eat elsewhere. ②.

Eating and drinking

In addition to the hotel restaurants, there's a highly recommended **eating house** in the shape of the *Dream Land Café* ("The Pride of the Town"), which offers plentiful, tasty food – great curries – in clean, pleasant surroundings, with outstanding service. They also do a nice line in special occasion cakes for anniversaries, birthdays, and the like (given one or two days' notice). Alternatively there's good basic food at the *Merry Eating House* (don't be put off by its dingy exterior) and the *Total Service Station* cafeteria, and a long list of Kenyan standards at the *Western hoteli*. The bright little place that calls itself *Pizza Hut* only actually has one variety of pizza on the menu – and you have to order it in advance to avoid a long wait – but offers plenty of other choices. For a **drinking place** with character, you can do no better than the very mellow *Musera Bar and Restaurant*.

Listings

Books There's a good bookshop with a few foreign paperbacks down at the back of town. The library is open Mon–Thurs 9am–6pm, Fri 9am–4pm, Sat 9am–1pm; it should have some background on the Kakamega Forest.
Disco The weekend discos at the Teachers' Social Club, near the *Bendera*, are events to remember. And check out the *Wayside* for local jukebox sounds.
Kakamega Show End of November for three days.
Market There's a very lively one next to the bus station. Among the local produce on offer you'll find natural remedies and medicines made from forest plants. Main market days are Wed and Sat.
Mount Elgon trips If you're thinking about a trip, contact the deputy manager at the *Golf Hotel* who can provide very helpful information, and possibly arrange for cars to take people up to *Mount Elgon Lodge* and down again.
Swimming pool A small one at the *Golf Hotel*.

The Kakamega Forest

Some four hundred years ago, the tract of rain forest now called **KAKAMEGA FOREST** would have been at the eastern end of a broad expanse of forest stretching west, clear across the continent, virtually unbroken as far as the Atlantic. Today, it's a tiny patch of relict equatorial jungle, famous among zoologists and botanists around the world as an example of how an isolated environment can survive cut off from its larger body. The Kakamega Forest is a haven of shadowy gloom for hundreds of species of birds, snakes and butterflies, as well as monkeys and other mammals, many of which are found nowhere else in East Africa because similar habitats no longer exist.

The protection of the forest is being extended, though there are no plans at present for it to become a national park and entry is free for the time being, although all visitors are invited to make a donation towards the conservation of the forest (see below). With no coherent conservation plan in action, the long-term future of the forest isn't looking bright. Pressure from the local people who need grazing for their livestock, land to cultivate, and firewood, amounts to a significant threat. Much of the wardens' time is spent patrolling the forest or observing it from lookout points on nearby hilltops. The way things stand, the survival of this unique habitat depends to a considerable degree on the continued support and concern of visitors to the region.

The forest is fragmented, interspersed with open fields of grassland, cultivated stream margins and small settlements. **Two main areas** can be visited; the first, which has been accessible for many years, is the central **Kakamega Forest Reserve**, lying to the southeast of Kakamega town and somewhat off the beaten track. It is to a part of one of the densest stands in this area that most visitors come, to the **Forest Rest House** in the glade at its edge. The second section, the recently opened-up **Kakamega Forest National Reserve**, is northeast of the town and very easy to get to.

The central district: Kakamega Forest Reserve

There are several ways of **getting to the Rest House** – beware that maps of Kenya invariably locate the forest incorrectly. If you're using **public transport**, the best way to get there is to take one of the *matatus* that ply once daily in each direction between Kakamega and Eldoret, via the village of Shinyalu and the small town of Kapsabet. Either *matatu* can leave you right by the *Rest House* trail, marked by a green Forest Department signpost – ask to be dropped at **Isecheno**. From here, the *Rest House* is ten minutes' walk away. The *matatu* leaves Kakamega around 7.30–8am and passes Isecheno on its way to Eldoret around 8.30–9.15am; the midday run from Eldoret passes by at about 2pm.

If you don't manage to catch this direct service, there are other routes that involve some footwork. *Matatus* run fairly frequently **from Kakamega** as far as **Shinyalu**, from where it's a lovely two-hour walk to Isecheno, along the road heading left – there's a small chance you might be able to hitch a lift with a passing vehicle or bicycle (baggage permitting). Shinyalu often has a cattle auction and a major market on Saturdays, when it's worth pausing an hour to soak up the atmosphere of cowboys and corrals in the jungle. It's perfectly possible, of course, to hire a private **taxi** for the trip from Kakamega to the *Rest House* (Ksh600–800) but beware that both taxi drivers and *matatu* touts sometimes overcharge tourists for the run to the forest. **From Eldoret**, any bus or *matatu* heading towards Kisumu via Kapsabet, Chavakali and Maragoli will pass the turning for Isecheno at **Chepsonoi**, signposted "Kisieni 12km D267". From the junction it takes about three hours to walk through the gorgeous forest scenery to the *Rest House*.

If you're **driving up from Kisumu**, you turn up the A1 highway onto the southerly earth road to Shinyalu at a place called **Khayega**, some 10km before Kakamega. The junction is marked by signposts for the Arap Moi Girls' School and the Office of the

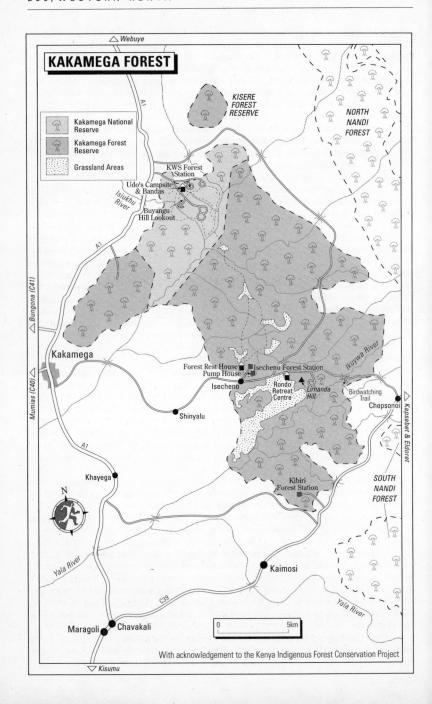

KAKAMEGA FOREST

Kakamega National Reserve

Kakamega Forest Reserve

Grassland Areas

△ Webuye

KISERE FOREST RESERVE

NORTH NANDI FOREST

KWS Forest Station

Udo's Campsite & Bandas

Isiukhu River

Buyangu Hill Lookout

Kakamega

Bungona (C41) △

Mumias (C40) △

Forest Rest House
Pump House
Isecheno

Isecheno Forest Station

Rondo Retreat Centre

Lirhanda Hill

Ikuywa River

Birdwatching Trail

Chepsonoi

Kapsabet & Eldoret △

Shinyalu

A1

Khayega

N

Kibiri Forest Station

SOUTH NANDI FOREST

Yala River

Kaimosi

C39

Yala River

Maragoli Chavakali

0   5km

With acknowledgement to the Kenya Indigenous Forest Conservation Project

▽ Kisumu

President. It's 13km to the *Rest House* from here: take the right branch after 7km at **Shinyalu** (heading in the direction of Isecheno); then, after a further 5km, go left at the Forest Department signpost. From here, it's less than a kilometre up the trail to the *Rest House*. Driving **from Kakamega**, the turning onto the northerly earth road to Shinyalu is on the southern edge of town (heading towards Kisumu, turn left off the main road).

ACCOMMODATION

The **Forest Rest House** is a delight. Someone writing in the visitor's book calls it a "budget *Treetops*", a description that scarcely does it justice. Ringed by forest, the *Rest House* has just four first-floor double rooms, with a long verandah facing onto the wall of tropical greenery a few metres away. Water supplies are somewhat erratic: when the pump is working, each room has a functioning bathroom and toilet, otherwise you have to fetch water from the pumphouse. There's no electricity and the closest reliable *dukas* are about 3km away on the road to Shinyalu, so it's best to bring your own supplies. For simple staples – bread, chai, mineral water, beer and sodas – there's a small dedicated *duka*/canteen on the way to the pumphouse, which is open daily. Here hot meals are cooked to order (given a few hours' notice); the food is generous, reliable and very fresh, and a much better bet than struggling to build your own cooking fire in the campsite or underneath the *Rest House* itself (during the rainy season it can rain for days on end).

To be sure of a room – especially at weekends – you can **reserve in advance** (write to: The Forester, PO Box 88, Kakamega, Western Province; rates are very economical, at Ksh120 per person). Alternatively you can **camp** at the site next to the *Rest House*, but don't leave tents unattended. In dire straits, other arrangements can probably be made locally: Kakamega Forest is becoming popular.

An alternative to the *Rest House* is the **Rondo Retreat Centre**, a fine old 1928 sawmiller's house (location for much of the filming of Harry Hook's *The Kitchen Toto*) about 4km east of the *Rest House* turning (reservations through PO Box 2153 Kakamega; ☎0331/30268, fax 20145, no phone at the centre; ⑨). This is a comfortable, much more upmarket base: very fresh and elegant, it's furnished like an English country house, with just enough clutter to make it feel homely, and wonderful bright four-poster bedrooms. Crowned cranes strut about on the cool lawns. The dining room is open to non-residents when the hotel is not fully booked, but the Christian management do not serve alcohol. Arrangements can be made to collect guests from Kakamega town.

SEEING THE FOREST

On arriving in the forest, visitors are greeted by an official guide (a member of KABICOTOA, the Kakamega Biodiversity Tour Operators Association). You will be given a brief introduction to the region and asked for a modest contribution to the conservation effort (a minimum of Ksh100 per person). You are free to explore the forest under your own steam, or to take a **guide**. There is no fixed fee for a guided walk so it's up to you to decide how much to offer on top of the standard donation. The guides are very knowledgeable – some are nothing short of encyclopedic and will rattle off the Latin name of any plant or creature you care to enquire about – and their walks are tremendously enjoyable. Expect a three-hour wander along the labyrinthine jungle paths, with birds, monkeys, chameleons and other animals pointed out to you, most of which you would miss on your own. Your guide may be carrying John Williams' *Field Guide*, too (see "Books" in *Contexts*), making the whole pastime of birdwatching even more satisfying. A pair of **binoculars** is more or less indispensable.

Among the most common **birds** are the noisy and gregarious black-and-white-casqued hornbill and the very striking, deep violet Ross' turaco. You may also see familiar-looking African grey parrots and, circling above the canopy on the lookout for unwary monkeys, the huge crowned hawk eagle. But Kakamega's avian stars are the **great blue turacos**, glossy, turkey-sized birds looking like dowagers in evening gowns. They're easily located by their raucous calls; a favourite spot at dusk is the grove of very tall trees down by the pumphouse. They arrive each evening to crash and lurch among the branches as they select roosting sites.

The forest draws mammal-watchers as well, particularly for the **monkeys**: troops are often seen at dusk, foraging through the trees directly opposite the *Rest House* verandah. Apart from the ubiquitous colobus, you can see blue monkeys and the much slimmer black-cheeked white-nosed monkey (most easily recognized by its red tail). They're often seen milling around with the hornbills. You may also see pairs of giant forest squirrels capering in the treetops: the deep booming call you sometimes hear in the morning is theirs.

At night, armed with a powerful torch, you might catch a glimpse of bushbabies or a potto, a slow-moving, lemur-like animal whose name aptly conveys appearance and demeanour. The forest is also home to several species of fruit bat, of which the hammer-headed fruit bat (*Hypsignathus monstrosus*) is the largest in Africa, with a wingspan of a metre and an enormous head. Other nocturnal Kakamega specialities are the otter shrew, which lives in some of the forest streams, the tree pangolin (a kind of arboreal scaly anteater) and the flying squirrel.

The forest's **reptile life** is legendary, but few people seem to actually see any **snakes**. You're much more likely to come across **chameleons**. Reptiles spend a good deal of time motionless, especially when frightened, and to see any in the dense foliage you have to be well tuned in. Visible or not, however, snakes are abundant and you certainly shouldn't walk in the forest in bare feet or sandals: the gaboon viper, growing to a metre or more in length, and fatter than your arm, is a dangerous denizen of the forest floor. To avoid an encounter, simply walk heavily: they're highly sensitive to vibration and will flee at your seismic approach.

If you have time for more than one daylight walk, you could ask a guide to show you the way to **Lirhanda Hill**, via a trail rich in medicinal plants. You will be shown which leaves, berries and saps the forest dwellers chew, swallow or anoint themselves with to treat various ailments. Lirhanda Hill itself is a lookout point, offering fine views over the whole expanse of forest, with the sombre bulk of Mount Elgon glowering in the distance. Cutting into the hillside near the top is a gold-mining shaft, long disused and now home to a large colony of bats. With a powerful torch and a steely nerve you can grope your way along the tunnel to meet them at close quarters.

Kakamega Forest National Reserve

Some 20km north of Kakamega town, there are two turnings off to the right: one is signposted to the Kakamega Forest National Reserve; the other, 50m further on, is signposted "Kenya Wildlife Service Kisere Nature Reserve 6km" and "Kambiri 7km D267". It's the first track you want. The Kakamega Forest National Reserve forest station is 2–3km along the way and you can pick up a guide to help you orientate yourself if you wish (though they have far less wildlife knowledge than the team at the *Forest Rest House*).

For visitors with their own vehicles, it's easier to get around this part of Kakamega Forest than the central zone. The forest proper is, in fact, a fair walk from the base of *Udo's Bandas and Campsite*, named after the ornithologist Udo Savalli. Here there are seven thatched rondavels, sleeping five each, and a stream for fresh water, but no food (book through the Kenya Wildlife Service District Warden, PO Box 879, Kakamega, ☎0331/20425). As in the central district, all visitors, whether staying or just there for the day, are asked to make a contribution to the forest conservation programme. A number of drivable – and walkable – tracks through the coolness of the forest begin just beyond the forest station. The main trail is well signposted and there are numerous branches and "exit" trails that allow for a relatively quick return when you've had enough of the deep forest. It's not a place you're likely to get lost, despite its remoteness.

The significant difference between the reserve here and the forest further south is the age of the growth in the reserve: many of the **trees** are colossal (indeed some have plaques inviting you to guess the girth: answers round the back). The climate is generally drier and there's a greater diversity of habitat, including areas of scrub, young forest and ancient forest. It's an impressive area and, as in the southern forest, there's a huge variety of birdlife and many monkeys.

An easy excursion from the forest station is to the **Isiukhu Falls**, a rather feeble waterfall 1.5km away along a rocky path. **Buyangu Hill viewpoint**, some four kilometres' drive or walk from the forest station, is much more worthwhile – a precipice with a spectacular vista east across the forest to the Nandi Escarpment.

The **Kisere Forest Reserve** (as signposted at the turn-off) is a separate area, a small outlying part of the main reserve and home to de Brazza's monkeys among others, with some superb examples of the prized timber tree, the Elgon olive.

Onwards from Kakamega

The obvious routes out of the area lie along the A1 to Kitale or Kisumu. The road **down to Kisumu** is a real roller-coaster, though in good condition, with a final eight-kilometre descent over the picturesque, boulder-strewn Nyando Escarpment, which brings Lake Victoria into view. In clear weather it allows fantastic panoramas across the sugar fields of the Kano plains towards the massif of the Mau and the Kisii hills. Look out for the florid **church** on the left, the headquarters of a local denomination that models itself on the Coptic church, founded in Egypt in the early years of Christianity.

Alternatively, there's a beautiful road **east to Kapsabet** in the Nandi Hills, starting at the bustling rural centre of Maragoli/Chavakali (also spelled Chyvakali and Kyavakali), along the Kisumu road. Note that Maragoli is the "shopping centre" on the A1, while Chavakali, effectively part of the same community, is a kilometre or so off to the east.

Lastly, if you have time and inclination for a diversion far off any beaten track, you could visit the small town of **Mumias**, the sugar belt's biggest processing centre and also one of western Kenya's Muslim strongholds. The road from Kakamega is paved and there's regular transport.

Mumias

MUMIAS was originally *Mumia's*, one of the more important up-country centres, capital of the Luyia-speaking mini-state of **Wanga**, and well established by the middle of the nineteenth century at the head of an important caravan route to the coast. **King Mumia**, who came to power in 1880, was the last King of Wanga. He inherited an army of 10,000 soldiers, half of whom were dispossessed Maasai from the Uasin Gishu Plateau known as the Kwavi. It was this army that was largely responsible for the smashing of Bukusu resistance at Chetambe's Fort fifteen years later (see p.276).

Even at the beginning of Mumia's reign, Europeans were beginning to arrive in the wake of Arab and Swahili slave-traders, who in turn had been settling in since the 1850s with the full accord of the Wanga royal family. The first was Joseph Thomson in 1883, and by 1894 there was a permanent British sub-commissioner or collector of taxes posted here. Mumia had always welcomed strangers, and he allowed the slavers to continue their work on other groups of the Luyia (notably the Bukusu), but he was unprepared for the swift usurpation of his authority by the British, whom he'd assumed were also there to trade. He was appointed "Paramount Chief" of a gradually diminishing state and then, as an old man, was retired without his real knowledge. He died in 1949, aged 100, and with him expired Kenya's first (and only) indigenous, up-country state, almost without notice.

The town's present **mosque** was built in King Mumia's honour and its Koran school is just one of about 25 around the town. Mumias has long been a centre of Islam, famous for its coastal ways, but today women in *buibuis* – the long, black coverall of the coast – are rarely seen. According to the chairman of the Mumias Koran Schools Committee, Islam is losing ground to Catholicism because of sectarian quarrelling between Muslim leaders and because, while mission and government education have an equal standing, the *madrassas* must take second place after school hours. If you're interested, Mumias Mission has published a slim pamphlet outlining their side of the story, and the Catholic church is quite an impressive old building.

The Butere–Kisumu train

Leaving Mumias, a paved road leads directly to Kisumu but, if you have time to spare you might like to hop on the daily **train from Butere**, 12km down the road, instead. This branch line was intended to reach Mumias but never did. The daily train service (no longer steam-hauled since 1988, but nearly as slow and one class only) remains a boon to rural dwellers with more time than money. It leaves Kisumu at 8.45am, arrives in Butere about noon, and returns in the afternoon, taking more than three hours to cover barely 60km.

travel details

Kisumu is the west's transport centre. Buses and *matatus* run from there to most major centres in this chapter within half a day.

BUSES

From Kisumu to:

Nairobi numerous daily runs on *Akamba* etc (5–8hr) via **Kericho** (2hr) and **Nakuru** (4–5hr); **Eldoret** several daily runs via **Kapsabet**; **Kakamega** daily *Akamba* bus at 5.30am (2hr); **Mombasa** at least 2 daily via Nairobi (14hr).

From Kisii to:

Nairobi at least 6 daily (7–9hr) via Kericho; **Mombasa** several daily; **Migori** 2 daily (2pm, 4pm) via Homa Bay; **Kisumu** numerous daily runs.

From Kericho to:

Nairobi many runs daily; **Kisumu** several daily; **Kisii** several daily.

From Eldoret to:

Nairobi frequent daily runs (7–8hr), eg *Akamba*, *Eldoret Express*, via **Nakuru**; **Kitale** (through buses from Nairobi) eg *Akamba* 4pm; **Kisumu** several daily runs.

From Kitale to:

Nairobi several services daily and overnight (8–11hr) via **Eldoret** and **Nakuru**; **Kapenguria** daily at 7am; **Lodwar** several daily (5hr) continuing to **Ferguson's Gulf** (7hr) – Nissans are best (4hr to Lodwar).

From Bungoma to:

Nairobi several daily (9–10hr); **Kisumu** several daily (2–5hr); **Kitale** *Mawingo* country bus at 5am & 11am (3hr) via **Kimilili**.

From Kakamega to:

Nairobi several runs daily (7–9hr) via **Kisumu**.

TRAINS

Reservations can be made with *Kenya Railways* in Kisumu on ☎035/42211.

From Kisumu to:

Nairobi d. 6pm (via Nakuru, 2.40am), a. 12–13hr later, daily (first-class sleeper Ksh1500, second-class sleeper Ksh1140); **Butere** d. 8.45am, a. noon daily.

From Eldoret to:

Nairobi via Nakuru and Naivasha, d. 9pm Wed, a. 8.15am Thurs; d. 3.55am Sat & Sun, a. 2.25pm (first-class sleeper Ksh2340, second-class sleeper Ksh1840); **Malaba**, for Jinja and Kampala, d. 4.10am Wed, a. 8.15am; d. 9.45pm Sat & Sun, a. 1.40am Sun & Mon.

From Malaba to:

Nairobi d. 4pm Wed (via Eldoret 9pm and Nakuru 3.30am), a. 8.15am Thurs; d. 11.05pm Sat & Sun (via Eldoret 3.55am and Nakuru 10.25am) a. 2.25 pm Sun & Mon.

From Kitale: passenger services suspended.

MATATUS

With nearly half the population of Kenya living in this region, *matatus* are widespread and most minor roads have services. Many also run on bus routes at approximately the same fare, but to even less predictable schedules. As usual, Peugeots move faster than minibuses, which are faster than vans. Average journey times:

From **Kisumu** to: Kisii 2hr; Kakamega 1hr; Kitale 3hr; Kericho 1hr 30min; Kendu Bay 1hr 30min; Nairobi 5–6 hr.

From **Kisii** to: Rongo 30min; Migori 1hr 30min; Homa Bay 1hr.

From **Eldoret** to: Soy 20min; Kitale 1hr; Malaba 2hr 30min; Nairobi 4–6hr.

From **Homa Bay** to: Rongo 30min; Kendu Bay 1hr 30min; Mbita 2hr.

PLANES

From Kisumu to:

Nairobi scheduled daily services (morning and evening on Tues, Wed, Fri & Sun; morning only on Mon, Thurs & Sat) on *Kenya Airways* (1hr). **Mombasa** 12 flights a week, continuing from Nairobi (total flight time 2hr 30min–3hr).

Economy-class **fares**: Nairobi $47; Mombasa $136.

FERRIES

Kenyan lakeshore services see box on p.241.

Weekly service between **Kisumu** and **Mwanza** (Tanzania) on Fri (first-class Ksh1050, second-class Ksh850, third-class Ksh600). Twice-weekly service to **Port Bell** (Uganda).

CHAPTER FIVE

THE MOMBASA ROAD AND MAJOR GAME PARKS

T his chapter can't really be said to deal with a region. It covers the well-travelled **route from Nairobi to Mombasa** and a number of detours off it, along with five of the country's **major game parks**, all within reasonably easy reach of the capital.

The **Mombasa Highway** is Kenya's most important thoroughfare, but the scenic interest is marginal for much of the journey and the temptation is to head straight for the coast, stopping only at the **Amboseli** or **Tsavo game parks**. If you have time enough, however, and the inclination to get off the main road, there are some reward-ing diversions: east into **Akamba country** and the towns of **Machakos** and **Kitui**, or south towards the base of **Kilimanjaro** (the mass of the mountain lies across the border in Tanzania) and the **Taita Hills**. Despite the trail of safari vans towards the parks and coast, these are side roads that are not greatly explored.

The **game parks** in this chapter are, together with the coast, the most visited parts of Kenya – and the archetypal image. This is not to take anything away from their appeal. If you travel around Kenya, it would be absurd not to visit at least one of the parks, for the experience is genuinely fabulous. In the 25,000 square kilometres (10,000 square miles) covered by the five parks, animals, not humans, hold sway. Their seasonal movements, most spectacularly in **Maasai Mara**'s wildebeest migration, are the dominant plots in the drama going on all around. It's not difficult to see the wildlife but it does require patience and an element of luck that makes it exciting – and addictive.

Summaries of the game parks' individual attractions are given in the introduction on p.299. **To visit**, most people will either already be on a safari, or will book one once in Kenya – either from the coast or while in Nairobi. The increasingly popular alternative is to **rent a vehicle**, a sensible if quite expensive option if you want to have more than a few days of wildlife viewing. With a limited budget, a no-frills camping safari is still about the only practical way: there are more details on the ins and outs in *Basics*, p.26, and plenty of operators listed at the end of the Nairobi and Mombasa sections. It remains possible, though by no means easy, to explore the parks by **hitching around**

ACCOMMODATION PRICE CODES

Rates for a standard double or twin room. For a full explanation of these price codes, see p.46.

① Under Ksh300	(under approx. £3.30/$5)	⑤ Ksh2000–4000	(£22/$33–£44/$67)
② Ksh300–500	(£3.30/$5–£5.50/£8)	⑥ Ksh4000–6000	(£44/$67–£67/$100)
③ Ksh500–1000	(£5.50/$8–£11/$17)	⑦ Ksh6000–8000	(£67/$100–£89/$133)
④ Ksh1000–2000	(£11/$17–£22/$33)	⑧ Ksh8000–10,000	(£89/$133–£111/$167)
	⑨ Over Ksh10,000	(over £111/$167)	

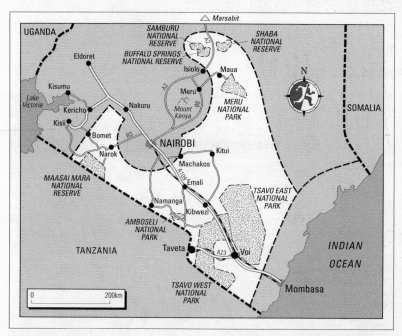

with whoever you meet and **camping** at designated sites. More specific details are included in the sections on each park and a summary of parks' access is included in "travel details" at the end of the chapter.

BETWEEN NAIROBI AND THE COAST

If you take one of the **express buses** for your journey down from Nairobi to Mombasa, you might well end up believing that there's nothing worth stopping for along the way. If, on the other hand, you take the **night train**, you won't see anything anyway.

With a little touch of imagination and, ideally, the luxury of a hired vehicle of some kind (which will enable you to drive into and out of Tsavo National Parks – see p.302 – at will), this stretch of the country has a great deal to offer. And any detour into the less well-known parts of **Kamba territory** or down to **Taveta** and the foothills of **Kilimanjaro** should prove a worthwhile antidote to the more purple-rinse excesses of safari-land.

Machakos and Kitui – "Ukambani"

One very good way to start a trip heading towards the coast, if you're in no particular hurry, is to take an excursion right into the heart of **Ukambani**, the land of the Akamba people (adjective and language: Kamba). There are buses, *matatus* and Peugeot taxis leaving from Nairobi's Country Bus Station (aka "Machakos Airport") for

Machakos all the time, although what used to be a journey of a little under half an hour is more likely to take an hour and a half, thanks to vastly increased traffic along the two-lane Mombasa road. In addition, there's also at least one company that runs a daily Nairobi–Mombasa service by way of the town.

Machakos

The IBEA'S first up-country post, established in 1889, **MACHAKOS** is ten years older than Nairobi and, in comparison, a striking indication of the capital's rapid growth.

THE AKAMBA

The largely dry stretch of central Kenya from Nairobi to Tsavo park and north as far as Meru has been the traditional homeland of the **Akamba people** for at least the last five centuries. They moved here from the regions to the south in a series of vague migrations, in search, according to legend, of the life-saving **baobab tree** whose fruit staved off the worst famines.

With a diverse economy in better years, including mixed farming and herding as well as hunting and gathering, the Akamba slowly coalesced into a distinct tribe with one Bantu language. As they settled in the hilly parts, the population increased. But drier areas at lower altitudes couldn't sustain the expansion, so **trade** for food with the Kikuyu peoples in the fatter highlands region became a solution to the vagaries of their generally implacable environment.

In return for farm produce, the Akamba **bartered** their own manufactured goods: medicinal charms, extra-strong beer, honey, iron tools, arrowheads and a lethal and much sought-after hunting poison. In the eighteenth and nineteenth centuries, as the Swahili on the coast strengthened their ties inland, **ivory** became the most important commodity in the trade network. With it, the Akamba obtained goods from overseas to exchange for food stocks with the highlands tribes.

Long the **intermediaries** between coast and up-country, acting as guides to Swahili and Arab caravans, leading their own expeditions and settling in small numbers in many parts of what is now Kenya, the Akamba were naturally enlisted by early European arrivals in East Africa. Their broad cultural base and lack of provincialism made them confident travellers and employees, and willing **soldiers and porters**. Even today, the Kenyan army has a disproportionately high Akamba contingent, while many others work as policemen and private *askaris*.

In the early years of **colonialism**, the Akamba were involved in occasional bloody incidents, but these seem to have been more often the result of misunderstandings than anything concerted. The most famous of these blew up after an ignorant official at Machakos cut down a sacred *ithembo* tree to use as a flagpole. On the whole, the Akamba's old trade links helped to ease their relations with the British. Living – and dying – with British soldiers during **World War I** gave them insights into the ways of the Europeans who now ruled them. Together with the Luo and Kikuyu, the Akamba suffered tens of thousands of casualties in white men's wars.

Akamba **resistance to colonialism** was widespread but mostly non-violent. As early as 1911, however, a movement of total European rejection had emerged. Led by a widow named Siotune wa Kathake, it channelled opposition to colonialism into frenetic dancing, during which teenage girls became "possessed" by an anti-European spirit and preached radical messages of non-compliance with the government. Later, in the 1930s, the Ukamba Members Association (one of whose leaders was **Muindi Mbingu**) was formed in order to pre-empt efforts to settle Europeans in Ukambani and reduce Akamba cattle herds by compulsory purchase. Five thousand Akamba marched in peaceful protest to Kariakor market in Nairobi – a show of collective political will that succeeded in getting their cattle returned.

"Machakos" is really a corruption of Masaku's, after the headquarters of an Akamba chief of the time. The name is still seen all over town.

Distinctly friendly, and overwhelmingly Kamba, the town has a backdrop of green hills and a tree-shaded, relaxed atmosphere to its old buildings that is quickly endearing. The surrounding Mua Hills have lent their name to a brand of jam from the orchards which thrive on their slopes. The weaving of **sisal baskets** is a more visible industry, though, and a major occupation for many women, either full-time or behind the vegetable stand. Machakos effervesces and it's a great place to stay for a day or two, especially on Monday and Friday, market days, and above all if you are into buying some *vyondo* (baskets). Look for (though you can scarcely miss) the truly splendid and quite venerable **mosque**.

Practicalities

The town is rarely visited by tourists but **accommodation and meals** are easy. Machakos has the usual range of eating places. Three of the best are the highly recommended *Ivory Restaurant* – chips with everything, but it's all tasty and well served; the enjoyable *Kenny's Boiling Pot,* with its balcony overlooking the street; and the *T.Tot Hotel*, popular with expats and serving good samosas, *chai* and passion juice. As for **hotels**, the *Masaku Motel* (PO Box 274; ☎0145/21745; singles only), *T.Ten* and *Lalla Salama* by the mosque (PO Box 66; ☎0145/21198) are utterly basic B&Ls (all ①), the last with rooms ranging from rank to airy and comfortable (ask to see a selection). Otherwise try:

Garden Hotel, ex-*Machakos Inn*, ten minutes from the town centre (PO Box 223; ☎0145/20037, fax 0145/21515). Something of an aberration, a totally plush, muzak-piped, "international class" hotel with air-conditioned rooms, a health club, sauna, steam bath – and a pool planned for the future. Compared to its Nairobi counterparts, a bargain too. Resident Tanzanian band *Everest Kings* – formerly *Mavalo Kings* – are another bonus, almost reason enough to visit Machakos in themselves. ⑤.

Ikuni Hotel, ex-*Safari Hotel* (PO Box 1069; ☎0145/21080). A large place with a wide range of rooms, mostly grotty, but its busy restaurant makes up for it a little. Ask for a net. ③.

Kafoca Club (Kenya Armed Forces Old Comrades Association; PO Box 595; ☎0145/21933). Despite the uninspiring name, this businessmen's hangout is well run, and fairly wholesome, with a bar and TV-video lounge and a good restaurant which does filling fried platters. ②.

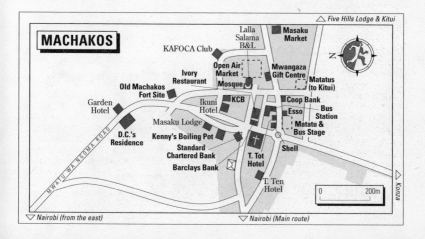

Crafts

For **vyondo**, visit the **market**. The finished articles are much cheaper without the strap (buy lengths of sisal braid and fit your own), and there are reductions if you buy several: the choice of colours is second to none. If you like the genre, it's worth buying several and posting home a parcel. In connection, the Machakos branch of the women's Maendeleo ya Wanawake Organization can be contacted at PO Box 904; ☎0145/21600.

The *Mwangaza Gift Centre* deserves a look, too: they have some splendid wood and goat-skin **drums** – the kind of thing often seen used as tables in hotel lobbies – but volume restrictions may prevent you from sending the large ones home, even if their price (under Ksh1200), and sometimes their timbre, make them irresistible. Less desirable are the East African clothes-moths they frequently harbour – which later hatch in suitably heated living rooms – and the possibility of catching anthrax from them. Be warned that customs officers tend to impound such items on arrival.

On to Kitui

Buses and *matatus* ply this route: the road passes through some attractive scenery, particularly as you wind down the hill out of Machakos, where high cliffs and chunky, maize-covered hills rise everywhere. **Wamunyu**, en route, was the birthplace of the modern **Kamba carving** industry, evidence of which seems to be absent from Machakos. Akamba men who served in World War I were introduced to the techniques of wood sculpture by the Makonde ebony carvers on the Tanganyikan coast. Today, the vast majority of carvings in Kenya are produced by Akamba artists, often in workshops far from Ukambani. It's a disappointment that the serried ranks of identical antelopes and rhinos don't do justice to the tradition, even if it is a short one.

Kitui town

KITUI is an impoverished area and, from time to time, is badly hit by drought, with attendant malnutrition and occasional outbreaks of cholera. Despite its proximity to Nairobi, this region at the very edge of the highlands is one of Kenya's least developed. The town is small and hasn't any outstanding features of interest, but there's a sizeable Swahili population, descendants of the traders and travellers who crisscrossed

Ukambani in the nineteenth century. The town's mango trees were planted then, and the abundance of lodging houses is a reminder of the trading tradition.

Kitui was the home village of **Kivoi**, the most celebrated Akamba trader. He commanded a large following which included slaves, and it was he who met the German missionary **Ludwig Krapf** in Mombasa and guided him up to Kitui in 1849, where the European was the first to set eyes on Mount Kenya.

Practicalities

There's nowhere to **stay** in Kitui above the ① category. The *Riverside Motel* on the way into town is arguably the best, with a restaurant serving especially good chicken and fish. A row of cheap **eateries** backs on to the Swahili quarter. One good find on the north side of town is *Ramrook's Place* – clean, friendly and reasonable, as is *Parkside Hotel* around the corner from the *KCB* bank. *Travellers Café*, facing the Mwanzi Lodging, is good for snacks and is popular with NGO staff.

Akamba, the main **bus service**, has departures to Nairobi three times daily and a night bus which calls at around 7pm on its way to Mombasa. *Mbuni* has some cheap fares (twice a day to Mombasa). Getting up to Embu (p.180) can be a problem; public transport is scarce on this route, but short *matatu* hops, or hitching, are possible. The road to Embu via Kangonde is newly tarred, both scenically dreary.

The Mombasa highway

It's ironic that in a country overflowing with scenic beauty, the most important **highway** passes through so much monotonous landscape – not for nothing is one particularly desolate stretch called the Taru Desert. But the appearance of the bush does depend on the time of year. After heavy rains, the plains may be bursting with colour: during May and June they can be carpeted in white and blue convolvulus flowers. If you travel down by bus, it's best to sit on the right of the vehicle, which gives you the best of the scenery and from which vantage you may, in clear conditions, see **Kilimanjaro**: either on the stretch between the small town of Sultan Hamud and the service station oasis of *Hunter's Lodge*, or to the south of Tsavo train station.

Whichever time of year you travel down it, there are reasons to stop and detour along the Nairobi–Mombasa highway, at least if you have the luxury of your own transport and pace. But if you do drive this route yourself, **be careful**. It's fast, narrow in places, broken up and always dangerous: road-users frequently encounter each other with deadly impact. Also be sure to drive with a full fuel tank. **Petrol stations** appear fairly regularly at the settlements between Nairobi and Voi – although you're advised to fill up wherever possible – but supplies thereafter are not guaranteed until Mariakani, 120km further on and just 32km inland from Mombasa.

This section does not cover the Amboseli or Tsavo National Parks – see p.302 and p.310.

Night stops along the highway

There are at least two possible **overnight stops**, perhaps most useful if you're coming from Mombasa and don't fancy arriving back in Nairobi late at night:

Small World Country Club, 37km from Nairobi, before Athi River (PO Box 78 Athi River; ☎0150/22006). A motel-restaurant with basic self-contained *bandas*, secure parking, basic snacks, and a bar with a disco at weekends. Painfully slow service. ③.

Hunter's Lodge, 160km from Nairobi at Kikumbu (PO Box 77 Makindu, ☎2021 Radiocall Nairobi; reservations through *Empress Fashion*, Eagle House, Kimathi St, PO Box 40683 Nairobi, ☎02/220592). Named after the J. A. Hunter of rhino-potting notoriety, this promises a lot as a place to

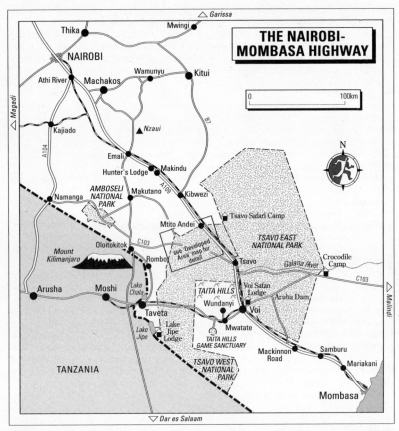

△ Garissa

Thika
Mwingi

NAIROBI
Wamunyu
Kitui
Athi River Machakos
△ Magadi

THE NAIROBI-
MOMBASA HIGHWAY

0   100km

Kajiado
▲ Nzaui
B7

Emali
Makindu
Hunter's Lodge
A104
A109
Kibwezi
N

AMBOSELI
NATIONAL
PARK
Makutano
Namanga
Tsavo Safari Camp

Mtito Andei
TSAVO EAST
NATIONAL PARK

Oloitokitok
C103
see 'Developed
Area' map for
detail
Crocodile
Camp
Mount
Kilimanjaro
Rombo
Tsavo
Galana River
C103
△ Malindi

Arusha
Moshi
Lake
Chala
TAITA HILLS
Voi Safari
Lodge
Aruba Dam
Taveta
Wundanyi
Voi
Lake
Jipe
Lake
Jipe
Lodge
Mwatate
TAITA HILLS
GAME SANCTUARY
Mackinnon
Road
Samburu

TANZANIA
TSAVO WEST
NATIONAL
PARK
Mariakani

Mombasa

▽ Dar es Salaam

stay, with its acacia-backed garden on the banks of the dammed Kiboko (Hippo) River, a tranquil haven for storks and apes over on the other side. However, the "old rooms" are nothing special for the money, and the food varies between quite ordinary and baronial; the "new rooms" have verandahs overlooking the pool, which more or less makes up for everything. Ask nicely and they'll probably allow you to camp. It's also a good place to hitch lifts. ④.

For accommodation in Athi River itself, see p.311. Further away from Nairobi, you might try a number of cheap B&Ls in the one-horse towns of **Sultan Hamid** and **Nunguni**, lodging with truckers and lost-looking Maasai.

Around Emali: Kibiki and Nzaui

At **Emali**, half an hour before *Hunter's Lodge*, a road heads off south for Amboseli. **Kibiki**, the small centre just 1km down the Amboseli road from the junction, is the regular Friday venue for a major **cattle market** which attracts hundreds of Maasai herders, as well as Akamba people and Kenya Meat Commission buyers. It's an animated scene and worth a pause if you coincide.

A north turn from Emali leads up into the Machakos Hills with the dramatic **peak of Nzaui**. Enthusiastic reports have been received from hikers who have climbed this steep pinnacle. Without transport, you'll need a *matatu* ride from the Emali crossroads to Matiliku, some 15km from the main road. Nzaui rears up ahead. With luck, you'll find some schoolchildren to guide you up – it's a popular local trip. From the top of the 500-metre precipices on the south face there are sweeping views across the Kamba and Maasai plains to Mount Kilimanjaro. If you have a vehicle, there's also a lazy way up Nzaui from the north, approached from the village of Nziu, further along the same road.

Makindu

Back on the main highway, twenty minutes east of *Hunter's Lodge*, you pass the ostentatious Sikh temple at **Makindu**, sometimes strung with what look like Christmas lights, and prettily unmistakable. They give a warm welcome here to travellers who want to stay, on the usual understanding.

Thirteen kilometres further is the **Makindu Handicrafts Co-operative**, which has blossomed in recent years to provide work for almost fifty active members. Fifteen percent of the take goes to run the place and buy wood; the remainder is divided equally among the carvers. You can watch and photograph members at work, though it has to be said many of their carvings are fairly obnoxious, with "Maasai maidens" and similar panderings more and more prominent. Still, they know their market and the set-up obviously suits the co-op members. There are some nice pieces among the tour-bus fodder, but for a more personal souvenir, the rejects heaped up outside the shop are better value and have more character than the polished creations inside.

Kibwezi: soursops and honey

KIBWEZI is a small Akamba trading centre off the main road at the B7 Kitui junction. There are one or two B&Ls. The best and cleanest rooms, at the *Riverside Lodge*, come with mosquito coils, towel, soap and kerosene lamp (there's still no electricity in town), all for a rock-bottom price. The *Riverside* runs the *New Face Hoteli*, which offers good food and fantastic murals. Kibwezi also boasts a small **market** where you can often buy spiky green **soursops**, one of those fruits you either love or loathe.

Along this stretch of the main highway you'll probably also see **honey** sellers. When it's good, the honey is delicious, but try it before buying. The art of beekeeping is a Kamba speciality but local custom varies – the honey is best when the bees haven't been smoked out, as this taints it. Bottom price is about Ksh120 for a wine-bottle full. In and around **Kinyambu**, 16km from Kibwezi, you'll see thirty or so grass and brick huts, distinguishable from human dwellings by their lack of windows. Each hut contains up to ten hives, owned and tended by a number of local women's co-operatives, together called "The Kibwezi Honey Project".

Mtito Andei to Tsavo

A big sprawl of service stations and snackeries rises out of the dry country at the start of **Tsavo National Park**; it marks **MTITO ANDEI** (which means "Vulture Forest"), a town surrounded by stands of baobab trees. The *Tsavo Inn* here (PO Box 20; ☎0147/30217) is a pleasant retreat, with a tempting pool, and fortunately, *Rough Guide* readers get residents' rates – just show your copy. **Rooms** in the bungalow rows are neat, almost over-disinfected, with their lino floors (nets, but no AC or fans; HB ⑤ residents, ⑥ non-residents). Don't miss the fascinating 1963 *Michelin* map in the lobby (there was no tarmac at all to Mombasa in those days). **Camping**, unfortunately, is out of the question, but you can walk from here to camp at the Tsavo West Gate (see p.302). If you want a cheap lodging in town, try the *Okay Safari Lodge* (PO Box 34; ☎0147/30120; ①); clean and basic but loud, it's okay for a cold beer or three. They also have a sister hotel, the *Okay Hillside Lodge* (☎0147/30463; ②), a few kilometres before town, which is marginally more expensive but has self-contained rooms. A vehicle breakdown, if you're unfortunate enough to suffer one, is best taken to the Akamba mechanic next to the *Esso* station. The *Esso* station itself has a pleasant shaded cafeteria. A few words of Kamba here work wonders (good evening – *watindata*, response – *nehsa*; thank you – *muvea*).

Between Mtito Andei and Voi, the only place to get anything to **eat** is at **Manyani**, 2km past Manyani gate for Tsavo East National Park. It has a number of very basic *dukas* and *hotelis* serving *githeri* and *ugali* to weary travellers. There's no guarantee of fuel here or at the almost derelict *Maneaters' Motel*, by the gulch of the Tsavo River (*tsavo* is Kamba for "slaughter") – you should be extremely wary of the baboons here as someone who was foolish enough to feed them died recently after he was savagely mauled. The motel is in the vicinity of the famous **man-eating lions** that played havoc with the building of the railway in 1898. The two lions seem to have been preternaturally lucky, since they eluded Colonel Patterson's various weapons for nearly a year and ate 28 Indian labourers in that time. The Field Museum in Chicago has the two stuffed man-eaters on display. Lions you won't see any more and need not fear, but along this section of the road through Tsavo park you may well come across **elephants**. Always a brick-red colour from the soil, they used to be one of the commonest animals on the road but increased traffic and the gradual erosion of their habitat (by herders, agriculture and the elephants themselves) means you'd be very lucky to see them. There's a **campsite** here, on the north side of the Tsavo River to the left, 200m from the road. It's 500m from the Tsavo Gate into the national park, on the river bank but, although there's an *askari*, there are no facilities of any kind. However, it's free (and no park fees apply) and you should be able to get water, or arrange to have it provided, from the rangers at the gate.

Voi – and onwards

The only sizeable town on the road is **VOI**, a place you'd probably only want to stay in if you were heading into Tsavo East park or the Taita Hills and Taveta. If you have time to kill, check out the **sisal factory**: you can watch the whole simple process from the crushing of the sisal spikes, through drying and combing, to the final twisting into rope. The town's market days are Tuesday and Friday.

If you're staying, Voi possesses several excellent **lodgings** (if you're hoping for a lift into Tsavo East, it may be worth checking out *Lion Hill Safari Camp* outside the gate – see p.307).

Jambo Guest House, next to the market square and bus park (PO Box 193; ☎0147/2059). Can be noisy, but cheap enough considering it offers s/c rooms. ②.

Maendeleo B & L, about 1km from the bus station on the way out to the highway for Nairobi (400m from the *Caltex* station at the junction). Very cheap, basic and clean. ①.

Sagalla View Lodge, 500m from the bus station on the way out to the highway for Nairobi, off the road a little on the left (PO Box 123; ☎0147/30053). The most congenial place, with accommodation beyond the B&L level and breezy upstairs rooms, all s/c. ④.

Vuria Lodging, 600m from the bus station (PO Box 29; ☎0147/2269). With fans, mosquito nets and real toilets, and a bar downstairs, this is also recommended. ①.

Voi transport details

Moving on, the **train** to Mombasa pulls into Voi at about 3am, the one to Nairobi at midnight. Trains to Taveta, with connections through to **Tanzania**, leave only on Wednesday and Saturday at 5am. **Buses** come in all day, in the morning bound for Nairobi, and in the afternoon headed for the coast. There are two country buses to Taveta each day (9.30am & 3pm), one of which continues past Lake Chala to Oloitokitok, 30km from Amboseli. Wundanyi in the Taita Hills has at least one bus service along the steep route, departing Voi at 11.30am daily, and frequent *matatus*. For Taveta and the Taita Hills, see below and p.297. Since January 1996, the "Kilimanjaro Link" has been resumed, from Voi to Moshi in Tanzania, departing Saturdays only at 5am.

The Taru Desert

After Voi, the road veers across the relentless **Taru Desert**, a plateau of "wait-a-bit" thorn and occasional baobabs. Before you get away from the Voi area completely, there is one possible overnight halt: unfortunately, *Westermann's Safari Camp*, which used to be called *Rockside*, just north of **Maungu** and 10km of sandy track from the road (PO Box 5 Voi; ☎0147/2140; HB ⑤), is not very appealing, with tiny, dark chalets, no power and little atmosphere. Its guests are almost exclusively German package tourists.

After Maungu, the next place with food (but not much, and no petrol) is **Mackinnon Road**, distinguished by its Sayyid Baghali Shah Pir Padree Mosque, right by the railway track. Past **Samburu** ("butterfly" in Maa; again no fuel supplies) the country is peopled mostly by members of the large **Mijikenda** ethnic group, though their distinctive, droopy, thatched cottages are often replaced nowadays by more formal square ones, increasingly also whitewashed and tin-roofed in the coastal manner. The **Duruma** Mijikenda of this district herd cattle and grow a little sisal – there's little else they can do in such a dry region. The small centres of **Maji ya Chumvi** ("salt water"), **Mariakani** ("place of the *mariaka"*, the Kamba arrows used in nineteenth-century wars against the Maasai), and Mazeras bring you closer into the coastal domain.

Mazeras is a largely Duruma village and here **the coast** really takes over. The landscape has a quite different cast with its mango trees, lush cultivation of bananas and cassava, and (encouragement for weary travellers) the sublime sight of endless stands of **coconut palms**. For details about Mazeras and the route along the ridge to the north of Mazeras, see p.374. Ahead, the main road plunges with a certain abandon down the steep scarp to the Indian Ocean.

The Taita Hills

A good option, if you have your own car and a spare day or two – or if efforts to hitch into Tsavo proved fruitless – is to head off **west from Voi to Taveta**, a very accessible but largely unvisited region. Apart from being a route into Tanzania, the **Taveta road** has some interesting possibilities to the north and south, while for much of the time the magnificent mass of Kilimanjaro looms on the horizon.

Taita Hills Game Sanctuary

The only place attracting much tourist traffic in this district is the **Taita Hills Game Sanctuary** (entry $12), run by the *Hilton* chain with two of their hotels, *Salt Lick* and

---

THRUSH UNDER THREAT

Keen ornithologists head for the Taita Hills in search of *Turdus helleri*, the **Taita olive thrush**. This robin-like bird, the size of a European thrush, has a close relative in the ordinary olive thrush of the highlands: olive brown on top, red-breasted and red-billed. The Taita *Turdus* is distinguished by its much darker head and the fact that it appears to live only in the Taita Hills above 1600m – which gives it all of four square kilometres (1000 acres) of potential habitat. As it depends on virgin forest for its survival, the Taita olive thrush is a very rare bird indeed, and may even be extinct. Two or three were seen at Mbololo in 1953, and eight in the Ngangao Forest in 1965. It may also survive on Mount Ngangai. It has a bold, liquid warbling song. Good luck with the binoculars.

Taita Hills lodges, acting as bait (both addressed simply PO Bura; ☎44 Mwatate; both ⑨; reservations through *Hilton*, address p.49). The twelve-tent *Hilton Safari Camp* (⑨) is a permanent satellite in the bush, with no electricity but a good atmosphere, for those with more time. Children under 5 aren't welcome at either *Salt Lick Lodge* or *Hilton Safari Camp*. The setting of the lodges can't compete with Tsavo or even Amboseli, though you can do early-morning **balloon safaris** here (around $300 for 90min).

The private, 110-square kilometre reserve is not actually in the Taita Hills, but south of them in a hillocky, bosky landscape, 15km west of **Mwatate** on the south side of the road. Many of the visitors here are on fleeting air safaris from coast-hotel holidays. If you're managing without your own transport, there is virtually no chance of getting a lift into the sanctuary itself, though you could walk the half-kilometre from the road to the first hotel, *Taita Hills Lodge*, just outside the reserve, if you felt like indulging in a *Hilton* meal. Having used the lodge facilities (which include a large pool and water-hole game-viewing terraces), you're entitled to free entry to the sanctuary.

The sanctuary is well managed and, for most of the year, full of wildlife. Its small size means the rangers always have a good idea of where the animals are hiding out and it's not uncommon to see two dozen species of mammals – among them large numbers of lions, elephants and grazers – in a morning game drive (included in the rates if you're lodging there).

During the drier parts of the year, when the animals are not dispersed, *Salt Lick Lodge* on the southern side of the sanctuary provides water hole game-viewing to rival the "tree hotels" of the Central Highlands. But it's for its bizarre **architecture** that *Salt Lick* is most famous: from a distance it looks like a clump of mushrooms sprouting from the swamp. Each of its rooms is a kind of turret on stilts, all of them linked by mock-suspension bridges – there's even a drawbridge at the lobby. This camp ensemble is supposedly in keeping with the area's **World War I** battle history – most of the important Anglo-German engagements in East Africa were fought on these plains.

Wundanyi

To get a glimpse of the less ephemeral **history** of this region, go up into the **Taita Hills**. *Matatus*, and one or two buses a day from Voi, pitch through the fertile chasms on a switchback road to the little district capital of **WUNDANYI**. After the sultry, dry plains, you're transported into another world. The hills are amazingly precipitous and beautiful, striped with cliffs, waterfalls and dense cultivation, and highly populated. Near the peaks are patches of thick forest. There's notable prosperity up here, and a strong sense of community. Most of the people speak the Taita language, a member of the coastal Bantu family related to Swahili and Mijikenda.

Practicalities

For **accommodation**, try the calm and clean *Wundanyi Lodge* by the market, with hot water in the mornings. There's a choice of good **places to eat** in town: the *New Wundanyi Motel* is particularly recommended for tasty meals, a lively atmosphere – especially emanating from the bar – and music from an expensive-looking sound system; whilst *Tsavo Hill Café*, overlooking the market, has great service and wicked pizza. The big **market days** in Wundanyi are Tuesday and Friday.

Taita traditions

The Taita are welcoming, and Wundanyi an attractive and enjoyable centre. The conifer trees and a genuine babbling brook running past the football field reinforce the feeling of departure from the thornbush and scrub below. This sense of suspended reality is accentuated by the **cave of skulls** outside the town, one of many ancestor shrines in the hills. Ask someone to show you the way: it's halfway to the now-defunct *Mwasungia Scenery Guest House*, hidden in a banana grove just below the road. In the niche rest the skulls of 32 Taita ancestors, exhumed from their graves. Traditionally, the cave was an advice centre where life's perplexities were resolved by consultation with the dead. Christianity has eroded some of the reverence that the Taita once had for these shrines, but the niches are left undisturbed nonetheless.

Taveta and Lakes Chala and Jipe

West of the Taita Hills turning, the **road to Taveta** soon jumps off the tarmac and you follow the railway branch line through the southern arm of Tsavo West, mostly in a cloud of brilliant red dust. A number of maps mark a *Murka Lodge* along here, but it has been closed for years and Taveta is the first, and only, place worth stopping at. You're almost certain to see some game on these plains, especially in the rainy season (and especially if you take the train).

Taveta

Somewhat off the beaten track, **TAVETA** is situated in the rural corridor between the Tanzanian border and Tsavo West National Park. Electricity has recently arrived, the *KCB* bank near the border post is now fully operational (Mon–Fri 8.30am–1pm, Sat 8.30–11am), and the town is gradually joining metropolitan Kenya. Taveta has a mixed population of Taveta, Taita, Maasai, Akamba, Kikuyu and Luo, with strong hints of coastal influence. And with the recent improvement in East African relations amid talks of resurrecting the East African Union, and the reopening of the railway in Tanzania, things look set to change still further. Trains run to Voi on Tuesday, Wednesday, Friday and Saturday at 2.30pm, and to Moshi in Tanzania on Saturday around 8.30am. If you're leaving Kenya at Taveta, note that there is a longer walk than you might expect to the Tanzanian side of the frontier – allow at least an hour.

The main **accommodation** options are at the end of the main street, which runs to the right (north) on the other side of the railway level crossing as you enter the town. The fairly new *Lake Challa Safari Lodge* (PO Box 16; ☎0149/2212; ⑥) is the best bet for a comfortable night, but unfortunately it's vastly overpriced; there's a good restaurant and bar, and the chance to organize local excursions. In the cheap lodgings bracket, the not-very-salubrious *Green View Guest House* is next door; opposite, but cleaner and brighter, is *Kuwoka Lodging House* (PO Box 51; ☎0149/228), which features magnificent, gaudy murals in its front restaurant.

The best places to **eat** in town, however, are the *Taveta Hotel*, between the *Chala Hotel* and the bus station, and a couple of restaurants near the bank: the *Taveta Border*

Hotel (good samosas and chips) and a nameless *hoteli*, known as *Better Food For More People*, which is what it says on the wall outside: they do a fine chicken stew here. The local banana stew is also popular, though you might balk at eating eight bananas in one sitting – even if they are smothered with gravy.

To **explore** the Taveta region without wheels of your own you'll have to rely on infrequent *matatus* (better on market days, Wed & Sat) and the occasional private vehicle.

Lake Chala

Transport isn't such a problem to **Lake Chala**; you could, if necessary, walk most of the twenty-kilometre round trip, and there's a bus a day at least to Oloitokitok. A four-square-kilometre crater lake north of Taveta, Chala has one shore in Kenya and the other in Tanzania. It's right by the road to Amboseli, exactly 8km from the junction outside Taveta and just a ten-minute walk up the slope. Hidden in its crater, however, it is easily missed.

The lake is a deep and unbelievably transparent blue. It once had a population of harmless dwarf crocodiles (imported from Madagascar by Ewart Grogan; see opposite), but they are rare now and it's inhabited today only by mythical monsters and paddled over by a few fishermen in dugouts. You can **camp** in a number of places on the rim and scramble easily down to the water, which is bilharzia-free, for a very pleasant swim. When Kilimanjaro is visible behind it, it's an exceptionally lovely scene and well worth the slight effort of getting there; you need to take supplies if you're going to stay the night. Keep an eye open for the luminous, pink snake that a number of readers have independently reported seeing inside the crater wall, on the path down to the water's edge. Although allegedly harmless, its attitude is convincingly aggressive. You may also see monitor lizards, large skinks (another lizard) and baboons.

Lake Jipe

Equally interesting, and totally different, is **Lake Jipe**. It's fed by Kilimanjaro's snow-melt at its northern end as well as by streams flowing to the south from the Pare Mountains, across the border in Tanzania. The Kenyan shore is flat and thickly carpeted in reed beds. Several villages at the northern end make a living from fishing, while Jipe's southeastern shore lies inside Tsavo West National Park.

There are a number of paths down to the lakeshore from the Taveta–Voi road and finding the right one can be a problem if you're **driving**. Ask the way before leaving Taveta. The easiest route is to turn right roughly 10km east of the town where a rusty and almost illegible circular sign reads "Jipe Sisal Estate". Some 25km down this track, you reach an obscure gate for the park – Jipe Gate – close to the lakeshore.

The only **public transport** to the lake ties in with market days in Taveta, Wednesday and Saturday. This, the *Black Rhino* bus, leaves Taveta at 6am and 3pm and returns from Jipe at 7.30am and 4.30pm. Get a place on board an hour before. Another market-day alternative is to run into the *Lake Jipe Lodge* minibus buying produce in town. They are generally very helpful and will usually offer a lift down to the park gate and campsite. These vehicles apart, transport is rare indeed and your only option, and by no means an unpleasant one, is to walk. The flat land **between the Voi road and Lake Jipe** is heavily planted under sisal, cotton fields and even coconuts. There are also wide areas of low bush. It is an unusual part of Kenya, rustling with bird and animal life. The *Macmillan* map, "Tsavo East and West National Parks", is a useful aid in the area.

On the lakeshore

At **Mukwajoni**, the village 2km before the park gate, you'll find only the most basic provisions (apart from fish), so bring supplies from Taveta. You should be able to drink

THE WILDLIFE OF EAST AND SOUTHERN AFRICA

A ROUGH GUIDE

This field guide provides a quick reference to help you identify the larger mammals likely to be encountered in East and Southern Africa. It includes most species that are found throughout these regions, as well as a limited number whose range is more restricted. Straightforward photos show easily identified markings and features. The notes give you clear pointers about the kinds of **habitat** in which you are most likely to see each mammal; its daily rhythm (usually either **nocturnal or diurnal**); the kind of **social groups** it usually forms; and general **tips about sighting** it on safari, its rarity and its relations with humans.

 HABITAT   DIURNAL/NOCTURNAL ☒ SOCIAL LIFE ☑ SIGHTING TIPS

FOR MORE DETAILED INFORMATION ON KENYA'S WILDLIFE TURN TO CONTEXTS

Baboon *Papio cynocephalus*

■ open country with trees and cliffs; adaptable, but always near water

■ diurnal

■ troops led by a dominant male

☑ common; several subspecies, including Yellow and Olive in East Africa and Chacma in Southern Africa; easily becomes used to humans, frequently a nuisance and occasionally dangerous

Eastern Black and White Colobus
Colobus guereza

■ rainforest and well-watered savannah; almost entirely arboreal

■ diurnal

■ small troops

☑ troops maintain a limited home territory, so easily located, but can be hard to see at a great height; not found in Southern Africa

Patas Monkey *Erythrocebus patas*

■ savannah and forest margins; tolerates some aridity; terrestrial except for sleeping and lookouts

■ diurnal

■ small troops

☑ widespread but infrequently seen; can run at high speed and stand on hind feet supported by tail; not found in Southern Africa

Vervet Monkey *Cercopithecus aethiops*

■ most habitats except rainforest and arid lands; arboreal and terrestrial

■ diurnal

■ troops

☑ widespread and common; occasionally a nuisance where used to humans

PRIMATES

**White-throated or Sykes'
Monkey/Samango**
Cercopithecus mitis/albogularis
◼ forests; arboreal and occasionally
terrestrial
◼ diurnal
◼ families or small troops
☑ widespread; shyer and less easily
habituated to humans than the Vervet

Aardvark *Orycteropus afer*
◼ open or wooded termite country; softer
soil preferred
◼ nocturnal
◼ solitary
☑ rarely seen animal, the size of a small pig;
old burrows are common and often used
by warthogs

Spring Hare *Pedetes capensis*
◼ savannah; softer soil areas preferred
◼ nocturnal
◼ burrows, usually with a pair and their
young; often linked into a network,
almost like a colony
☑ fairly widespread rabbit-sized rodent;
impressive and unmistakable kangaroo-
like leaper

Crested Porcupine
Hystrix africae-australis
◼ adaptable to a wide range of habitats
◼ nocturnal and sometimes active at dusk
◼ family groups
☑ large rodent (up to 90cm in length),
rarely seen, but common away from
croplands, where it's hunted as a pest

PRIMATES – AARDVARK – RODENTS

Bat-eared Fox *Otocyon megalotis*
- ◨ open country
- ◨ mainly nocturnal; diurnal activity increases in cooler months
- ◨ monogamous pairs
- ☑ distribution coincides with termites, their favoured diet; they spend many hours foraging using sensitive hearing to pinpoint their underground prey

Black-backed Jackal *Canis mesomelas*
- ◨ broad range from moist mountain regions to desert, but drier areas preferred
- ◨ normally nocturnal, but diurnal in the safety of game reserves
- ◨ mostly monogamous pairs; sometimes family groups
- ☑ common; a bold scavenger, the size of a small dog, that steals even from lions; black saddle distinguishes it from the shyer Side-striped Jackal

Hunting Dog or Wild Dog
Lycaon pictus
- ◨ open savannah in the vicinity of grazing herds
- ◨ diurnal
- ◨ nomadic packs
- ☑ extremely rare and rarely seen, but widely noted when in the area; the size of a large dog, with distinctively rounded ears

Honey Badger or Ratel
Mellivora capensis
- ◨ very broad range of habitats
- ◨ mainly nocturnal
- ◨ usually solitary, but also found in pairs
- ☑ widespread, omnivorous, badger-sized animal; nowhere common; extremely aggressive

African Civet *Civettictis civetta*
- ☒ prefers woodland and dense vegetation
- ☒ mainly nocturnal
- ☒ solitary
- ☑ omnivorous, medium-dog-sized, short-legged prowler; not to be confused with the smaller genet

Common Genet *Genetta genetta*
- ☒ light bush country, even arid areas; partly arboreal
- ☒ nocturnal, but becomes active at dusk
- ☒ solitary
- ☑ quite common, slender, cat-sized omnivore, often seen at game lodges, where it easily becomes habituated to humans

Banded Mongoose *Mungos mungo*
- ☒ thick bush and dry forest
- ☒ diurnal
- ☒ lives in burrow colonies of up to thirty animals
- ☑ widespread and quite common, the size of a small cat; often seen in a group, hurriedly foraging through the undergrowth

Spotted Hyena *Crocuta crocuta*
- ☒ tolerates a wide variety of habitat, with the exception of dense forest
- ☒ nocturnal but also active at dusk; also diurnal in many parks
- ☒ highly social, usually living in extended family groups
- ☑ the size of a large dog with a distinctive loping gait, quite common in parks; carnivorous scavenger and cooperative hunter; dangerous

WEASEL RELATIVES – SPOTTED HYENA

CATS

Caracal *Caracal caracal*
- ☒ open bush and plains; occasionally arboreal
- ☒ mostly nocturnal
- ☒ solitary
- ☑ lynx-like wild cat; rather uncommon and rarely seen

Cheetah *Acionyx jubatus*
- ☒ savannah, in the vicinity of plains grazers
- ☒ diurnal
- ☒ solitary or temporary nuclear family groups
- ☑ widespread but low population; much slighter build than the leopard, and distinguished from it by a small head, square snout and dark "tear mark" running from eye to jowl

Leopard *Panthera pardus*
- ☒ highly adaptable; frequently arboreal
- ☒ nocturnal; also cooler daylight hours
- ☒ solitary
- ☑ the size of a very large dog; not uncommon, but shy and infrequently seen; rests in thick undergrowth or up trees; very dangerous

Lion *Panthera leo*
- ☒ all habitats except desert and thick forest
- ☒ nocturnal and diurnal
- ☒ prides of three to forty; more usually six to twelve
- ☑ commonly seen resting in shade; dangerous

Serval *Felis serval*

■ reed beds or tall grassland near water

■ normally nocturnal but more diurnal than most cats

■ usually solitary

☑ some resemblance to, but far smaller than, the cheetah; most likely to be seen on roadsides or water margins at dawn or dusk

Rock Hyrax or Dassie *Procavia capensis*

■ rocky areas, from mountains to isolated outcrops

■ diurnal

■ colonies consisting of a territorial male with as many as thirty related females

☑ rabbit-sized; very common; often seen sunning themselves in the early morning on rocks

African Elephant *Loxodonta africana*

■ wide range of habitats, wherever there are trees and water

■ nocturnal and diurnal; sleeps as little as four hours a day

■ almost human in its complexity; cows and offspring in herds headed by a matriarch; bulls solitary or in bachelor herds

☑ look out for fresh dung (football-sized) and recently damaged trees; frequently seen at waterholes from late afternoon

CATS – HYRAX – ELEPHANT

Black Rhinoceros *Diceros bicornis*
- ◩ usually thick bush, altitudes up to 3500m
- ◪ active day and night, resting between periods of activity
- ◩ solitary
- ☑ extremely rare and in critical danger of extinction; largely confined to parks where most individuals are known to rangers; distinctive hooked lip for browsing; small head usually held high; bad eyesight; very dangerous

White Rhinoceros *Ceratotherium simum*
- ◩ savannah
- ◪ active day and night, resting between periods of activity
- ◩ mother/s and calves, or small, same-sex herds of immature animals; old males solitary
- ☑ rare, restricted to parks; distinctive wide mouth (hence "white" from Afrikaans *wijd*) for grazing; large head usually lowered; docile

Burchell's Zebra *Equus burchelli*
- ◩ savannah, with or without trees, up to 4500m
- ◪ active day and night, resting intermittently
- ◩ harems of several mares and foals led by a dominant stallion are usually grouped together, in herds of up to several thousand
- ☑ widespread and common inside and outside the parks; regional subspecies include *granti* (Grant's, East Africa) and *chapmani* (Chapman's, Southern Africa, right)

Grevy's Zebra *Equus grevyi*
- ◩ arid regions
- ◪ largely diurnal
- ◩ mares with foals and stallions generally keep to separate troops; stallions sometimes solitary and territorial
- ☑ easily distinguished from smaller Burchell's Zebra by narrow stripes and very large ears; rare and localized but easily seen; not found in Southern Africa

RHINOCEROSES · ZEBRAS

Warthog *Phacochoerus aethiopicus*

■ savannah, up to an altitude of over 2000m

■ diurnal

■ family groups, usually of a female and her litter

☑ common; boars are distinguishable from sows by their prominent face "warts"

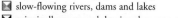

Hippopotamus *Hippopotamus amphibius*

■ slow-flowing rivers, dams and lakes

■ principally nocturnal, leaving the water to graze

■ bulls are solitary, but other animals live in family groups headed by a matriarch

☑ usually seen by day in water, with top of head and ears breaking the surface; frequently aggressive and very dangerous when threatened or when retreat to water is blocked

Giraffe *Giraffa camelopardalis*

■ wooded savannah and thorn country

■ diurnal

■ loose, non-territorial, leaderless herds

☑ common; many subspecies, of which Maasai (*G. c. tippelskirchi*, right), Reticulated (*G. c. reticulata*, bottom l.) and Rothschild's (*G. c. rothschildi*, bottom r.) are East African; markings of Southern African subspecies are intermediate between *tippelskirchi* and *rothschildi*

African or Cape Buffalo *Syncerus caffer*

◨ wide range of habitats, always near water, up to altitudes of 4000m

◨ nocturnal and diurnal, but inactive during the heat of the day

◨ gregarious, with cows and calves in huge herds; young bulls often form small bachelor herds; old bulls are usually solitary

☑ very common; scent much more acute than other senses; very dangerous, old bulls especially so

Hartebeest *Alcelaphus buselaphus*

◨ wide range of grassy habitats

◨ diurnal

◨ females and calves in small, wandering herds; territorial males solitary

☑ hard to confuse with any other antelope except the topi/tsessebe; many varieties, distinguishable by horn shape, including Coke's, Lichtenstein's, Jackson's (right), and Red or Cape; common, but much displaced by cattle grazing

Blue or White-bearded Wildebeest
Connochaetes taurinus

◨ grasslands

◨ diurnal, occasionally also nocturnal

◨ intensely gregarious; wide variety of associations within mega-herds which may number over 100,000 animals

☑ unmistakable, nomadic grazer; long tail, mane and beard

Topi or Tsessebe *Damaliscus lunatus*

◨ grasslands, showing a marked preference for moist savannah, near water

◨ diurnal

◨ females and young form herds with an old male

☑ widespread, very fast runners; male often stands sentry on an abandoned termite hill, actually marking the territory against rivals, rather than defending against predators

BUFFALO – HARTEBEEST RELATIVES

Gerenuk *Litocranius walleri*

- ■ arid thorn country and semi-desert
- ■ diurnal
- ■ solitary or in small, territorial harems
- ☑ not uncommon; unmistakable giraffe-like neck; often browses standing upright on hind legs; the female is hornless; not found in Southern Africa

Grant's Gazelle *Gazella granti*

- ■ wide grassy plains with good visibility, sometimes far from water
- ■ diurnal
- ■ small, territorial harems
- ☑ larger than the similar Thomson's Gazelle, distinguished from it by the white rump patch which extends onto the back; the female has smaller horns than the male; not found in Southern Africa

Springbok *Antidorcas marsupalis*

- ■ arid plains
- ■ seasonally variable, but usually cooler times of day
- ■ highly gregarious, sometimes in thousands; various herding combinations of males, females and young
- ☑ medium-sized, delicately built gazelle; dark line through eye to mouth and lyre-shaped horns in both sexes; found only in Botswana, Namibia and South Africa

Thomson's Gazelle *Gazella thomsoni*

- ■ flat, short-grass savannah, near water
- ■ diurnal
- ■ gregarious, in a wide variety of social structures, often massing in the hundreds with other grazing species
- ☑ smaller than the similar Grant's Gazelle, distinguished from it by the black band on flank; the female has tiny horns; not found in Southern Africa

GAZELLES

Impala *Aepyceros melampus*

▣ open savannah near light woodland cover

▣ diurnal

▣ large herds of females overlap with several male territories; males highly territorial during the rut when they separate out breeding harems of up to twenty females

☑ common, medium-sized, no close relatives; distinctive high leaps when fleeing; the only antelope with a black tuft above the hooves; males have long, lyre-shaped horns

Red Lechwe *Kobus leche*

▣ floodplains and areas close to swampland

▣ nocturnal and diurnal

▣ herds of up to thirty females move through temporary ram territories; occasionally thousand-strong gatherings

☑ semi-aquatic antelope with distinctive angular rump; rams have large forward-pointing horns; not found in East Africa

Common Reedbuck *Redunca arundinum*

▣ reedbeds and tall grass near water

▣ nocturnal and diurnal

▣ monogamous pairs or family groups in territory defended by the male

☑ medium-sized antelope, with a plant diet unpalatable to other herbivores; only males have horns

Common or Defassa Waterbuck
Kobus ellipsiprymnus

▣ open woodland and savannah, near water

▣ nocturnal and diurnal

▣ territorial herds of females and young, led by dominant male, or territorial males visited by wandering female herds

☑ common, rather tame, large antelope; plant diet unpalatable to other herbivores; shaggy coat; only males have horns

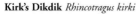
Kirk's Dikdik *Rhincotragus kirki*

■ scrub and thornbush, often far from water

◪ nocturnal and diurnal, with several sleeping periods

■ pairs for life, often accompanied by current and previous young

☑ tiny, hare-sized antelope, named after its alarm cry; only males have horns; not found in Southern Africa except Namibia

Common Duiker *Sylvicapra grimmia*

■ adaptable; prefers scrub and bush

◪ nocturnal and diurnal

■ most commonly solitary; sometimes in pairs; occasionally monogamous

☑ widespread and common small antelope with a rounded back; seen close to cover; rams have short straight horns

Sitatunga *Tragelaphus spekei*

■ swamps

◪ nocturnal and sometimes diurnal

■ territorial and mostly solitary or in pairs

☑ very localized and not likely to be mistaken for anything else; usually seen half submerged; females have no horns

Nyala *Tragelaphus angasi*

■ dense woodland near water

◪ primarily nocturnal with some diurnal activity

■ flexible and non-territorial; the basic unit is a female and two offspring

☑ in size midway between the Kudu and Bushbuck, and easily mistaken for the latter; orange legs distinguish it; only males have horns; not found in East Africa

DWARF ANTELOPES – BUSHBUCK ANTELOPES

Bushbuck *Tragelaphus scriptus*

■ thick bush and woodland close to water

■ principally nocturnal, but also active during the day when cool

■ solitary, but casually sociable; sometimes grazes in small groups

☑ medium-sized antelope with white stripes and spots; often seen in thickets, or heard crashing through them; not to be confused with the far larger Nyala; the male has shortish straight horns

Eland *Taurotragus oryx*

■ highly adaptable; semi-desert to mountains, but prefers scrubby plains

■ nocturnal and diurnal

■ non-territorial herds of up to sixty with temporary gatherings of as many as a thousand

☑ common but shy; the largest and most powerful African antelope; both sexes have straight horns with a slight spiral

Greater Kudu *Tragelaphus strepsiceros*

■ semi-arid, hilly or undulating bush country; tolerant of drought

■ diurnal when secure; otherwise nocturnal

■ territorial; males usually solitary; females in small troops with young

☑ impressively big antelope (up to 1.5m at shoulder) with very long, spiral horns in the male; very localized; shy of humans and not often seen

Lesser Kudu *Tragelaphus imberbis*

■ semi-arid, hilly or undulating bush country; tolerant of drought

■ diurnal when secure; otherwise nocturnal

■ territorial; males usually solitary; females in small troops with young

☑ smaller than the Greater Kudu; only the male has horns; extremely shy and usually seen only as it disappears; not found in Southern Africa

Gemsbok *Oryx gazella gazella*

- ☒ open grasslands; also waterless wastelands; tolerant of prolonged drought
- ☒ nocturnal and diurnal
- ☒ highly hierarchical mixed herds of up to fifteen, led by a dominant bull
- ☑ large antelope with unmistakable horns in both sexes; subspecies *gazella* is one of several similar forms, sometimes considered separate species; not found in East Africa

Fringe-eared Oryx *Oryx gazella callotis*

- ☒ open grasslands; also waterless wastelands; tolerant of prolonged drought
- ☒ nocturnal and diurnal
- ☒ highly hierarchical mixed herds of up to fifteen, led by a dominant bull
- ☑ the *callotis* subspecies is one of two found in Kenya, the other, found in the northeast, being *Oryx g. beisa* (the Beisa Oryx); not found in Southern Africa

Roan Antelope *Hippotragus equinus*

- ☒ tall grassland near water
- ☒ nocturnal and diurnal; peak afternoon feeding
- ☒ small herds led by a dominant bull; herds of immature males; sometimes pairs in season
- ☑ large antelope, distinguished from the Sable by lighter, greyish colour, shorter horns (both sexes) and narrow, tufted ears

Sable Antelope *Hippotragus niger*

- ☒ open woodland with medium to tall grassland near water
- ☒ nocturnal and diurnal
- ☒ territorial; bulls divide into sub-territories, through which cows and young roam; herds of immature males; sometimes pairs in season
- ☑ large antelope; upper body dark brown to black; mask-like markings on the face; both sexes have huge curved horns

ORYXES · ROAN ANTELOPE · SABLE ANTELOPE

Grysbok *Raphicerus melanotis*
- ☒ thicket adjacent to open grassland
- ☒ nocturnal
- ☒ rams territorial; loose pairings
- ✔ small, rarely seen antelope; two subspecies, Cape (*R. m. melanotis*, South Africa, right) and Sharpe's (*R. m. sharpei*, East Africa); distinguished from more slender Steenbok by light underparts; rams have short horns

Oribi *Ourebia ourebi*
- ☒ open grassland
- ☒ diurnal
- ☒ territorial harems consisting of male and one to four females
- ✔ localized small antelope, but not hard to see where common; only males have horns; the Oribi is distinguished from the smaller Grysbok and Steenbok by a black tail and dark skin patch below the eye

Steenbok *Raphicerus campestris*
- ☒ dry savannah
- ☒ nocturnal and diurnal
- ☒ solitary or (less often) in pairs
- ✔ widespread small antelope, particularly in Southern Africa, but shy; only males have horns

Klipspringer *Oreotragus oreotragus*
- ☒ rocky country; cliffs and kopjes
- ☒ diurnal
- ☒ territorial ram with mate or small family group; often restricted to small long-term territories
- ✔ small antelope; horns normally only on male; extremely agile on rocky terrain; unusually high hooves, giving the impression of walking on tiptoe

and eat at *Lake Jipe Safari Lodge* if you don't mind some expense. The **lodge** is reasonably good value compared with others (☎2016 Radiocall Nairobi; reservations at Shariff House, Kimathi St, PO Box 31097 Nairobi; ☎02/227623; ⑧), and can arrange tours to Grogan's Castle (see below).

There are simple national parks' **bandas** near the park gate as well as showers, toilets and a **campsite**. Tent or no tent, the *bandas* are recommended, as they offer shade, a place to keep food cool, and protection from some unbelievably vicious mosquitoes. Despite the attentions of these, this is a peaceful and rewarding spot, and a paradise for ornithologists. A **boat** is available to take you out on the lake for a couple of hours. If you can persuade the ranger the outboard motor is working, you'll see hippos and crocodiles, and of course you could cruise all the way around the lake.

The usual camping or *banda* fees are payable on arrival, as, normally, are Tsavo West's daily fees: you may not choose to go through the Jipe Gate entrance, but all of the southeastern shore of the lake is technically within the park's boundaries.

When exploring the bush around the lakeshore and campsite early in the morning, beware of **hippos**. You should keep a sharp eye out, especially between the park gate and the village. A feasible target for a couple of hours' walk would be the two hills, Vilima Viwili, just outside the park boundary and about 2km east of the track.

Grogan's Castle

If you have transport, **Grogan's Castle**, a white mansion on an isolated hill rising from the plain back near the main road, deserves a little detour. This extraordinary residence was built in the 1930s by Ewart Grogan, one of the most influential early colonists. His reputation was founded on a walk from the Cape to Cairo which he undertook in 1898, on a notorious public flogging he carried out on three of his servants (nearly killing one of them), and on his wealth: his gilt-edged reputation was such that Grogan was able to dictate terms to the governor before he even arrived in Kenya. At the peak of his prosperity, he owned over a quarter of a million hectares of land.

The "castle" was evidently built as a kind of hacienda for the **sisal estates**. It is totally run-down these days – the only residents of the house are a large colony of rats – but it can be visited if you tip the *askari*. It's an enigmatic building, much of it stuck together with aircraft aluminium and tin roofs. There are two enormous circular living rooms with spectacular 360-degree views out towards Kilimanjaro and Lake Jipe. The huge bedrooms have mosquito-screened bed niches. On one of the landings an ostentatious cash cupboard is suitably positioned, presumably for the casual display of wealth to passing guests. It will probably end up one day as a casino or a nightclub. Judging by the comments in the visitors' book, there's no lack of interested buyers.

THE PARKS

In these animal-rich national parks, the first realization of where you are – among real, uncaptured wildlife – is truly arresting. Which parks to visit can seem at first a pin-in-the-map decision: any of them can provide a store of amazing sight and sound impressions.

Amboseli and **Tsavo** are the two most accessible, with ever-busy game lodges, well-worn trails, large numbers of tourists in the high seasons, and large, if brutally diminished, herds of elephant. Amboseli is perhaps least recommended of the popular parks, despite its position at the foot of Kilimanjaro: it is just too small and too well trodden, and it's still recovering from heavy flooding in 1993. Tsavo, in contrast, is huge enough to escape company completely, except at **Mzima Springs**, for which it's worth being part of the crowd if necessary.

Maasai Mara has the most fabled reputation, with horizons of wildlife on every side. Somewhat isolated in the west, it requires a specific, usually there-and-back, visit, but it's well worth the effort (and perhaps the cost), especially during the yearly **wildebeest migration** that takes place sometime between July and November. The Mara is also *the* place to see lions – lots of them – and one of the best places to see naturally constituted elephant herds.

Samburu and **Meru**, on the north side of Mount Kenya, have different varieties of animals, such as northern species or races of giraffe, zebra, antelope and ostrich. Samburu – dry, thorny and split by the Ewaso Nyiro River – is increasingly popular and noted for its **crocodiles** and **leopards**, albeit baited ones. Meru, however, is perhaps the most beautiful Kenyan park – isolated, verdant and surprisingly unvisited.

Practical considerations

Conditions can change rapidly in the parks. The effects of **climate and poaching** have led to several temporary closures over recent years and impressions one season may be quite different the next.

It's important, if you want to get as much as possible out of your visit, to have detailed **maps** of the parks. These are often available in the park lodges or on the gates, but not always, and prices are higher than you'll pay in Nairobi. The best map for each park is mentioned in the brief details at the start of each park section.

The latest **entry fees** for non-residents are also given at the beginning of each park section: the most popular, Amboseli and Maasai Mara, are also the most expensive, followed in price by Tsavo East and West, then Meru, and then the Samburu, Buffalo Springs and Shaba reserves.

For some idea of their current **animal-viewing potential**, the order of enthusiasm in recent travellers' accounts places Samburu and Maasai Mara way out in front, Tsavo East third, followed some way behind by Tsavo West and Amboseli, with Meru last of all – though Meru's compensation is its wonderful quota of wilderness. If you're interested in **birds**, you'll find favourable places to watch with your binoculars in all the parks, but it's worth pointing out that Maasai Mara (mostly open plains) is not, on the whole, good for birds, while by contrast Samburu (with its riverine environment) can be exceptionally rewarding.

When to visit – and accommodation rates

The parks usually get two rainy seasons – brief in November or December, more earnest in April and May – but these can vary widely. In Maasai Mara, they merge together in one season from November to May. Meru also gets heavy rainfall, but it's more scattered. As a general rule, you will see more animals during the dry season when they are concentrated near water. After the rains break and fill the seasonal watering places, the game tends to disperse deep into the bush. Moreover, if your visit coincides with the rains, you may have to put up with some frustrating game drives, with mud and stranded vehicles. By way of compensation, if your plans include luxury accommodation, you'll save a fortune at lodges and tented camps in the low season (April 1–June 30 and, to a lesser extent, July 1–November 30). Most places reduce their tariffs by anything from a third to a half between April and June, with savings particularly spectacular for singles.

Driving – and damage to the environment

The parks in this chapter are open all year round (though note the recent abnormal conditions in Amboseli). If you're **driving** during the rains, remember that none of the park roads are paved and unless you'd be content to keep to the main graded tracks, you will need a four-wheel-drive vehicle to venture down the smaller ones: a night spent stuck in the mud in Maasai Mara (a likely enough occurrence if you only have two-wheel drive) isn't recommended, nor is trying to reverse down a boulder-strewn slope in Tsavo West. Some car-rental companies will insist you have 4WD in any case. If you're driving and can claim residence in Kenya, you can get a special one-year national parks' pass, which allows you multiple entry into all the KWS parks and reserves bar Maasai Mara and the Samburu complex. The passengers must also have a pass or pay the usual fees, though there is a couples' pass available. Details are given on pp.61–62 in *Basics*.

Be sensitive in the parks to the great damage to delicate ecosystems that can be done by **off-track driving**. Despite the lush, tropical growth after the rains, there's nothing tough about the very seasonal vegetation. Even apparently innocent diversions off the main track can scour fragile, root-connected grasslands for years, spreading dust, destroying the integrity of the lowest levels of vegetation, and hindering the life cycles and movements of insects and smaller animals, with consequent disruption to the lives of their predators. Thus a destructive chain reaction is triggered which is difficult to halt. It's a good rule never to create your own tracks, though in some areas it can be hard to judge whether you're following an agreed route, or the tracks of others who broke the rule . . . If you're with a safari group, agree not to encourage off-track driving for the sake of getting closer to the animals. And don't be afraid to ask the driver to keep to the main route: most are only doing what they perceive their clients want. Fortunately, the parks that have suffered most from off-track driving (Amboseli and Maasai Mara) provide information at the gates and try to enforce a code of good conduct.

Accommodation in the parks

If you're visiting independently, with or without a vehicle, it may well be worth bringing a **tent** (consider hiring one in Nairobi – see p.126). Without one, Maasai Mara and Samburu are very limiting if you are watching your budget as there is virtually no cheap *banda* accommodation at either. In any case, camping out adds to the adventure. If you're visiting the parks on a more comfortable basis and staying in **lodges** or **tented camps**, it would be wise to make **advance reservations**. Surprisingly, perhaps, such places are fairly few and there's heavy pressure on beds during the peak seasons. A booking gives you an advantage, and you can usually telephone or radio-call ahead if you're delayed or need to alter your plans. Obviously if you reserve rooms or tents at places in the same hotel group (see p.48), making changes to bookings is easier.

Animal watching

Game viewing soon loses its more self-conscious aspects. Our wildlife colour section will help you identify the larger mammals you're likely to encounter, and "Wildlife" in *Contexts* provides further background reading (see also "Books" in *Contexts*). **Rangers** can usually be hired for the day and, if you have room, someone with intimate local knowledge and a trained eye is a good companion: knowing some Swahili animal names is a help (see p.527). Most of the lodges and tented or luxury *banda* camps have their own 4WD vehicles and run regular "game drives". These can be very worthwhile because the drivers usually know the animals and the area. Expect to pay between $30 and $40 per person for scheduled departures and around $120 to $150 for exclusive use of the vehicle for two to three hours.

BABOONS: A WARNING

More serious than the occasional robbery in the parks is the continued, unstoppable damage done by those loutish hooligans, **baboons**. A locked vehicle might be safe; an unwatched tent certainly isn't. Insurance companies don't cover such contingencies.

The usual pattern is two (or sometimes three) game drives a day: at dawn, mid-morning and late afternoon (though if you keep this up for more than a day or two you'll be exhuasted – best to skip one). In the middle of the day, the parks are usually left to the animals; you'll be told it's because they are all hiding. A more likely reason is that the midday hours are a lousy time to take pictures. The animals are around, if sleepy, and if you can put up with the heat while most people are safely in the lodges, it can be a tranquil and satisfying time.

To see as much as possible, stop frequently to scan with **binoculars**, watch what the herds of antelope and other grazers are doing (a predator will usually be watched intently by them all), and talk to anyone you meet on your way. The best time of day is sunrise, when nocturnal animals are often still out and about and you might see that weird dictionary leader, the aardvark.

The Tsavo National Parks – East and West

Daily fees: each park $23 ($10 students, $8 children); $8 to camp ($12 in a "special camp-site"); warden of Tsavo West: PO Box 71 Mtito Andei (☎39 Mtito Andei); warden of Tsavo East: PO Box 14 Voi (☎0147/2211). Maps: Macmillan "Tsavo East & West National Parks Map" at 1cm:4.2km (1988); Survey of Kenya on separate sheets, Tsavo West SK78 and Tsavo East SK87, at 1cm:2.5km (1972).

Biggest by far of Kenyan national parks, and together one of the largest in the world, the combined areas of **Tsavo West** and **Tsavo East** sprawl across 21,000 square kilo-metres of dry bush country, an area the size of Wales or Massachusetts. Tsavo East is the larger portion, though all of it north of the Galana River has been closed to the general public for some years and is only now reopening. South of the river, the great triangle of flat wilderness with Aruba Dam in the middle has recently become popular with coastal safari departures, since you can be sure of seeing plenty of animals in a very open environment. However, the traditionally popular part of Tsavo is a mere 1000 square kilometres, the tall grass-and-woodland **"developed area"** of Tsavo West, located between the Tsavo River and the Mombasa highway. Here, the combination of good access, excellent facilities and magnificent landscapes attracts tourists in large numbers, while the well-watered, volcanic soils support wooded grasslands and a great quantity and diversity of animal life – though it's not always easily observed.

With their numbered junctions and clearly defined murram roads and tracks, the Tsavo parks are easy to get around, so long as you have a map. Don't forget the distances involved, however: if you set off somewhere, be sure you have time to get back to base by nightfall.

Tsavo West: access and accommodation

If you're looking for a visit outside a safari tour and don't have your own car, Tsavo West is probably the easiest of the big parks to explore. From Nairobi, take a bus or hitch to **Mtito Andei** (Tsavo West park headquarters and a service town for the lodges; see p.293). The gate here is one of the busiest park gates in the country and your chances of getting a ride are good. If you get stuck, the rangers are usually help-ful and will allow you either to camp just inside, or accommodate you in a spare *banda*. You *may* not be expected to pay park fees unless you get a lift.

The dearth of low-budget **accommodation** – a problem that affects all the main parks to some degree – is also less of an obstacle in Tsavo West. There are six or more **campsites** dotted around the park, but the two most often used are those marked on our map of the "developed area": one just inside Chyulu Gate, with shower and toilet, and conveniently close to *Kilaguni Lodge*; the other, again with basic showers and toilets, a twenty-minute drive from the Mtito Andei Gate near the park headquarters at Kamboyo Hill.

In addition, there are two well-equipped self-service **banda camps**, *Kitani Safari Camp* and *Ngulia Safari Camp*, located a few kilometres from the main lodges, where you can stay in reasonable comfort (both ⑤). Bring plenty of dried food. The *bandas* include a kitchen, a bathroom with hot water, mosquito nets – the works. *Ngulia SC* (PO Box 42 Mtito Andei; ☎2002 Radiocall Nairobi) even has its own water hole; at *Kitani* (PO Box 3 Voi), there are frequent sightings of buffalo and plains game. Both camps are delightful places to stay, and popular with Kenyans: you might even strike up a friendship and get a lift around the park for some animal-spotting. These places operate an irregular evening escort service for low-budget visitors who want to go to the lodges for dinner or a drink by the floodlit water holes (driving at night in the parks is not normally allowed). **Bookings** for *Ngulia* and *Kitani* safari camps can be made through *Let's Go Travel* (PO Box 60342 Nairobi; ☎02/340331).

If you want to spend a night or two in some luxury, you could do a lot worse than Tsavo West's four principal **game lodges and tented camps** (isolated *Lake Jipe Lodge* is covered on p.299).

Finch Hatton's Safari Lodge, about 65km from Mtito Andei Gate at the Loolturesh River, 15km from Post 38 (PO Box 71 Mtito Andei, ☎0302/22468, fax 0302/22473; reservations PO Box 24423 Nairobi, ☎02/604321, fax 02/604323). Named after the aristocrat who introduced royalty to the bush, *Finch Hatton's* must be the suavest and most accomplished of numerous luxury tented camps springing up around Kenya: fine bone china, cut crystal, Mozart, impeccable service and food. The camp is sited around the springs and pools of a source of the Loolturesh River, where crocodile and great pink-and-grey hippo splash. The 35 tents are, of course, totally luxurious – far better appointed than the average 5-star Nairobi hotel, with antique commodes, brass lamps and afghan rugs (rooms 1–7 are best). Not the best place for children as the site and the pools are unfenced. ⑨.

Kilaguni Lodge, about 30km (1–2hr) from Mtito Andei Gate (PO Box 2 Mtito Andei, ☎0302/22471, fax 0302/22470; reservations through *AT&H*, address on p.48). The oldest park lodge in Kenya (1962), and still one of the better ones, as much as anything for its prime site by a large (floodlit) water hole and its terrific wildlife ambience. There's a busy atmosphere and it's very often full – this is not a quiet place – but it keeps up impeccable service. Good-sized rooms (most facing the wildlife action, with stunning views towards the Chyulu Hills and Kilimanjaro), lush gardens, pool, petrol. Excellent value for the price; highly recommended. ⑦ low, ⑨ high.

Ngulia Safari Lodge, about 48km (1hr 30min–2hr) from Tsavo Gate (PO Box 42 Mtito Andei, ☎2002 Radiocall Nairobi; reservations through *AT&H*, address on p.48). Somewhat isolated in a quieter part of the park, *Ngulia* is open-plan and offers tremendous views, but has less immediate wildlife appeal than *Kilaguni*. Beds have mosquito nets. ⑦ low, ⑨ high.

Ziwani Tented Camp, on the park's western boundary by junction #44, about 40km south of the "developed area", but most easily reached from the Taveta–Taita Hills road (bookings through PO Box 42196 Nairobi, ☎02/331960, fax 02/331422; or PO Box 236 Ruiru, ☎0151/21024). On a glorious site by a small hippo and crocodile pool, beside a dam in the Sante River, with 16 full-size, permanent tents and excellent food. More informal and cheaper than its rival, *Finch Hatton's*. ⑥ low, ⑧ high.

Exploring the "developed area" of Tsavo West

While *Kilaguni* and *Ngulia* lodges are expensive places to stay, sooner or later, whatever you do, you're bound to turn up at one or the other. And rightly so: a visit is rewarding enough just for the pleasure of sitting on the terrace with a cold beer and watching the enthralling circus going on a few yards away at the **water holes**. (Neither *Finch Hatton's* nor *Ziwani* encourage day-trippers.)

Kilaguni Lodge: birds and beasts at the bar

Kilaguni has a policy, in the high seasons, of herding casual visitors into a separate "visitors' centre", with its own bar, restaurant and information desks. Try to infiltrate

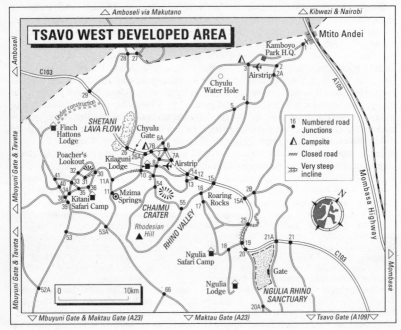

the main reception area anyway, because the lodge has considerable wildlife assets in and around the bar, which is open to the panorama of the savannah and Chyulu Hills along one side. Dazzling **birds** hop everywhere, **hyrax** scamper between the tables, and **agama lizards** skim along the walls (the miniature orange and blue dragons are the males). In the grass below the terrace lives a colony of **dwarf mongooses**, while pompous **marabou storks** pace slowly up and down awaiting jettisoned bread from the dining room. Out by the water hole, **baboon troops, antelope, buffalo, zebra, giraffe** and **elephant** provide constant spectacle, with the occasional kill adding tension. At dusk, hundreds of **swallows** swoop back and forth over the human drinkers to their nests in the roof; and later, the **bats** take over the airways while **genets, jackals** and **hyenas** come for the meat scattered under the floodlights.

You can be sure that half the people in the hotel won't be paying any attention at all to this scene, but the incongruity of the whole place is brought home when dinner is called and the other half switches its attention as well.

Ngulia Lodge: ornithological highlight

The autumn **bird enthusiasts** at *Ngulia Lodge* are far more earnest. The lodge is a stop-over on the annual southern migration of hundreds of thousands of European birds. It seems to be situated on a narrow migration "corridor", but the reasons for its attraction for the birds – apart from its isolated lights – aren't really known. Ornithologists gather in November and early December to band the birds that are trapped in mist nets, and their occasional recapture in places as far afield as Malawi, Iran and Germany slowly helps to build a picture of where the birds are moving to. Perhaps not altogether surprisingly, few are ever caught at *Ngulia* again.

Elephants, almost orange from the dust, are Tsavo's recurring image: they're drawn to *Ngulia* by the delicious top water hole which is a sump for the lodge's laundry. And **leopards** occasionally show up for a meal of meat tied to a tree by two nervous young men.

Mzima Springs

The biggest attraction in Tsavo West is **Mzima Springs**, 48km from Mtito Andei. This stream of crystal-clear water was made famous by Alan Root's film *Mzima: Portrait of a Spring*, which followed crocodiles and hippos in their underwater lives. Go very early to avoid the tour-bus atmosphere and you won't be disappointed. The luxuriant growth around the water reverberates noisily with birds and monkeys, and, with luck, some of the night's animal visitors may still be around.

There are **two large pools**, connected by a little rush of rapids and shaded by stands of date and raphia palms. The upper (or long) pool is the favoured **hippo** wallow, while the **crocodiles** have retreated to the broader expanse of water lower down. It's worth walking around this lower pool to the right where, if you're stealthy, you have a good chance of seeing them. Just make sure there's not one on the bank behind you. This word of caution applies equally to hippos, but they seem settled in their routine, content to snort and flounder at an irritating point just a little too far from the path for visitors' satisfaction. At the side of the top pool, a circular underwater **viewing chamber** has been built at the end of a short pier. Unless you are exceptionally lucky, all you'll see is the underside of the clumps of floating papyrus and a blue swirl of perpetually revolving fish.

Mzima's two **nature trails** (really tree trails) aren't of great interest unless you happen to be a botanist, but it is easy nevertheless to spend a couple of hours in the area. Try to sit for a while completely alone on the bank and you'll begin to piece together the ecological miracle of the place, as the animals and birds forget about your presence. This is where those khaki safari outfits are actually practical.

Mzima Springs has a direct pipeline to Mombasa, completed in 1966, and is the source of most of the city's **drinking water**. Two hundred and fifty million litres of water per day gush out here, filtered to aquarium transparency by the lava of the **Chyulu range** to the north. This dark, unexplored, forested ridge creates its own rainfall: the porous rock absorbs the water like a sponge and gravity squeezes it into Mzima.

Plans were mooted in 1952 to build a weir in order to raise the lower pool's level. This would have destroyed the river terrace, however, and by ruining the hippos' "nursery" would probably have caused them to stop breeding. The National Parks trustees stepped in and effectively stalled development, summoning independent engineers to devise a way of taking water from beneath the lava, *above* the spring. There are one or two signs of the pipeline in the area but most are unobtrusive. Mzima has been left whole.

Lava flows

The **lava** that purifies Mzima's water can be seen in black outcrops all around this part of Tsavo. The **Shetani lava flow** is a spectacular example. Only 200 years old (the Chyulu hills themselves are less than 500 years old), the eruption that spewed it out must have been a cataclysmic event for local people, and it is still the focus of stories about fire and evil spirits (*shetani* means "devil" in Swahili, deriving from the same Arabic linguistic root as "satan"). Legend has it that many people were buried by the hot lava flow, and their plaintive cries can be heard on certain nights. The local people appease the ghosts by leaving them offerings of food which, of course, are gone by daybreak. There are **caves** here that, despite one or two "warnings", are worthy of investigation (you'll need a torch). One of them even has a ladder and a trail of identification plaques by the bones of luckless animal victims who stumbled down.

Chaimu lava flow is fun to walk over, but also dodgy. The lava is brittle, honeycombed and unstable, and very few plants have taken hold yet. It is possible to climb up to the volcano's crater rim, but this can be surprisingly hard work on the scree and shouldn't be attempted in the heat of the day. And beware: when poking around Tsavo's caves and lava zones, you should be alert to the possibility of disturbing large **sleeping animals**. Remember, too, that Tsavo's lions have a reputation for ferocity. In the park, you should leave your vehicle at designated nature trails only, or where there's an obvious parking area. And beyond the national park boundaries you should stay on your guard – the animals aren't fenced in.

Seeking the animals

If you are eager to see particular species, *Kilaguni's* **information centre** (usually open during the high season) should have up-to-date locations of **lion prides** and **cheetahs**, and possibly **leopard sightings**, too. But **touring around** the rest of Tsavo West is, for the most part, a question of following your inclinations.

The "developed area" is the hilliest sector of any of the five parks covered in this chapter, and there's an unending succession of fantastic views across volcanic plains, dotted with volcanic cones and streaked with forest at the water margins. When the animals are abundant – and their numbers fluctuate tremendously with the seasons – every turn in the track seems to bring you face to face with zebra, giraffe, huge herds of buffalo, casual prides of lions, or methodical, strolling elephants. Among the more unusual animals to look for are the beautiful and shy **lesser kudu** antelope (always, it seems, running away).

In the 1960s, Tsavo had the biggest population of **black rhinos** in Africa – between 6000 and 9000 – and they were a common sight. By 1981, they had been poached to barely 100 individuals (the story is enlarged in the box overleaf). The situation today has improved a little, though most rhinos have been removed to the safety of the **Ngulia Rhino Sanctuary** (free, but the accompanying ranger expects a tip), where if you drive around for long enough you're almost bound to see one (you can always visit the holding pen in the middle of the sanctuary and inspect the latest arrivals). It's best to get there immediately after dawn.

The trip further on, that takes you around the foot of **Rhodesian Hill**, is recommended too, and **Poacher's Lookout**, near *Kitani*, is a very promising place for a quiet scan with binoculars.

Tsavo East National Park

Across the highway, the railway, and the apparent natural divide that separates Kenya's northern and southern environments, lies **Tsavo East**. Apart from some tumbled crags and scarps near Voi, this is an uninterrupted plain of flat bush, vast and empty, dotted with the crazed shapes of monstrous baobab trees. It is a forbiddingly enormous reserve and at times over the last couple of decades it has seemed an odd folly, especially since the whole of the northern sector – almost two-thirds of the park's area – was, until recently, closed to the public due to the long years of war against elephant and rhino poachers (see box overleaf). Since 1991, however, the situation has changed dramatically: the poaching has been stamped out; the elephants, if not the rhinos, are once again on the increase; and Tsavo East, just a few hours' drive from the charter arrivals hall at Mombasa airport, finds itself very much the centre of tourist attention, especially for budget camping safaris. The northern sector is still not routinely open to that kind of tourism, but now by choice rather than necessity: the warden is restricting access to up-market, low-profile camping and walking parties. Private visits to the northern sector, if you've made overnight arrangements in advance, should be fine.

There are also five **campsites** available: you have to go with a ranger, however, who you should pick up at Voi Gate, and pay around $12 per day.

Voi Gate campsite and Voi Safari Lodge

Tsavo East has five **gates** (including Mtito Andei and Manyani in the north, Buchuma at the southern end and remote Sala Gate in the east towards Malindi), but the only one used much, and the one you should aim for if hitching, is at **VOI**, about 4km from the town. If you have difficulty getting lifts into the park, check out the campsite and *bandas* 1km before the gate at *Lion Hill Safari Camp* (PO Box 298 Voi; ☎0147/2647). At the time of writing, the *bandas* were all but derelict, though there were rumours of new management for the near future.

At the gate itself, there's a small educational centre (though the insects in the glass cases look as if they flew in and perished there), and a short **nature trail**, plus a small **staff canteen** with the usual warm beers, sodas, bread and dusty vegetables.

There's a good national parks' **campsite** just 500m inside the gate where you can generally get permission to camp without a vehicle (it probably depends on how recently a lion was spotted there). The unfurnished wooden cottages give some shade; you can rent them if you want for the camping fee, and they'll give you additional security and protection against baboons. There are basic toilets, showers and running water. This is the most popular campsite in Tsavo East, and plays host to a fair number of organized tours. Apart from its convenience, close to the gate and Voi town, it provides considerable excitement in the shape of Eleanor, one of Daphne Sheldrick's **elephant orphans**, and her young, male consorts. The elephants, now fending for themselves and completely unafraid of humans, visit the small artificial water hole in front of the cottages every evening. They can, and regularly do, steal food and anything else that appears to be edible. Take care: there's an accident waiting to happen here.

The rangers at Voi Gate seem a helpful crowd, with sensible attitudes to lifts and hitching: you can go with them to **Voi Safari Lodge** on their 8pm staff bus (returns 3am). This lodge, a few kilometres away up the hill (Box 565 Voi; ☎0147/30019, fax 0147/30080; ⑦ low, ⑨ high; reservations through *AT&H*, address on p.48), is almost as busy as its Tsavo West counterparts, with a magnificent savannah-scape plunging to the horizon and almost guaranteed game viewing from the terrace.

Mtito Andei Gate and Tsavo Safari Camp

Tsavo East has another entrance at its own **Mtito Andei Gate**, 2km past Mtito Andei then 16km along a dirt track, but this is effectively only for access to the exclusive **Tsavo Safari Camp** for pre-booked visitors. This tented camp is located on the other side of the Athi River – accessible only by dinghies powered by pulley – and you can do escorted game-viewing trips once there. It's a remote and peaceful place, with enthralling **birdlife**, and even has a pool (closed mid-April to end June; ⑦ low, ⑨ high; reservations through *Kilimanjaro Safari Club*, address on p.49). There is no other way into the main body of Tsavo East until you get down to the **Manyani Gate** near Mudanda Rock (see below), and also no way to access the park north of the Galana River other than passing through Voi Gate and obtaining express permission from the Rangers' HQ near *Voi Safari Lodge*.

Aruba Lodge

Once an obvious focus in Tsavo East, *Aruba Lodge* is now closed indefinitely, while rumours of big-buck deals and new management abound (you may get news of any reopening from *Let's Go Travel* in Nairobi). It's a beautiful site, though, about 30km along the north bank of the seasonally meandering Voi River by Aruba Dam, and well worth getting to, for lunch or a picnic, if you have wheels. The dam lake gets visited by thousands of animals; nights can be noisy. You can pitch your tent here for a small fee ($8) – probably the nicest site in the whole park.

THE TSAVO POACHING WARS

Saving the elephants...
Tsavo East was for a long time the contentious focus for **conservation issues**. The question of how to manage the **elephants** – or whether to manage them at all – is still the paramount one, in theory. The policy for years has been to hunt the **ivory poachers** and allow the elephants to reach a natural balance by starving themselves to a population their habitat could sustain. But the cycles of overpopulation and drought were too long for anyone to know if this was working out or not. Elephants, which are intelligent animals with complex kinship patterns, soon migrate to the increased security of national parks, often assembling in huge herds out of protective instinct.

Such questions have been submerged for many years by the overbearing problem of poaching. In 1972, Tsavo's elephant population was over 17,000. Today it is barely 8000, and most of these survivors are still young animals, poorly adjusted to the sophisticated culture of their species. Taking account of only natural factors, orphaned infant calves are automatically doomed, while young elephants under ten years have only a fifty-fifty chance of surviving to maturity.

There was a lull in the poaching in the early 1980s, but by the end of the decade any complacency was brutally shattered by an unprecedented **slaughter of elephants** in their thousands – mostly mature animals with large tusks, but including many with little ivory to offer. The poachers were no longer marginalized Akamba killing an occasional elephant with an old gun or poisoned arrows but a new breed of ivory-hunters, equipped with automatic weapons, going in and wiping out a whole family group in a single attack.

In 1988, it emerged that the Somalian government (as it then was) was mounting a concerted assault on Tsavo's ivory – perhaps in collusion with Kenyan Somalis and park-rangers-turned-poachers – aiming to profit from the tenfold increase in the value of ivory on the world market over the previous three years. Somalia announced it would be exporting 8000 tusks of what it called "confiscated ivory", an incredible figure equivalent to Somalia's own entire elephant herd.

The Kenya Ministry of Tourism and Wildlife, concerned for the country's tourist image and allegedly covering up for some people on its own payroll, reacted in a curiously defensive way, admitting to poaching tallies far less than the reliable estimates available. President Moi was said to be furious. He personally ordered park rangers to shoot poachers on sight, then beefed up manpower and equipment in the Anti-Poaching Unit and deployed the paramilitary General Service Unit (or GSU, a force more commonly seen on the University campus) into the bush. Ethnic Somalis living near the boundaries of Tsavo East were summarily rounded up and trucked north to Wajir and Mandera, rekindling a bitter resentment which goes back a long way and has nothing to do with poaching.

As the news made the headlines in Kenya, some people started counting the casualties among the defending park staff, a number of whom were also killed. The spectacle unfolding – of a dirty war being fought on the plains among mutilated and unmovable elephant corpses, while the tourist minibuses followed each other in search of the perfect picture – was not a glamorous one.

The 1989 international agreement on a five-year **ivory trade moratorium** had a remarkable effect on the numbers of new elephant corpses being logged in Tsavo.

Tracking through the park

With minibus safaris increasingly taking in Tsavo East, the emptiness of the park is no longer as overwhelming as it was until recently, but its vast size means you will still have the uninterrupted pleasure of exploring the wilderness, much of the time, completely alone. It's easy to get away off the two or three beaten tracks, and you may find something special – a **serval** perhaps, or a **striped hyena**.

The Voi River's wooded margins often hide a profusion of wildlife: try the **Kanderi Swamp/Ndolo campsite** at junction 173 and the pretty lookout point at junction 174; keep the windows up when driving through the tall grass and undergrowth, not only

Equally dramatic was the unprecedented aggression with which the Kenyan parks authorities started carrying out their duties under the auspices of the bluntly pragmatic new Director of Wildlife and Conservation Management, Richard Leakey. Leakey obtained huge injections of cash and military equipment for the war: armed men caught in the parks without authority were liable to be shot on sight, which deterred even the most reckless poachers and raised another human rights cloud over the country. Before the 1989 ban, three elephants a day were being killed by poachers; in 1990 fifteen were lost; in 1991 and 1992, almost none. The problem, however, has not disappeared completely – in 1995 some 35 elephants were lost, though still well below pre-1989 levels.

But such apparent success is not simple. The difference between a flourishing population of elephants and one that has no future is hard to detect: the social structure of the herds in many districts has been badly distorted, with many elders wiped out and too many inexperienced younger elephants unable to fend for themselves or to act in a properly mature, elephantine way. And with pressure from some southern African countries to open up the ivory trade again, there is no guaranteed future for the elephant in Kenya.

...and the rhinos

The **black rhinos**, of course, are even further down this vicious path to near-annihilaton. Their estimated number in Kenya is about 500 – that is somewhere around a quarter of the total population of the species, which remains under a serious and shocking threat of total extinction. More than 95 percent of Kenya's rhino population (most of them in Tsavo) was destroyed in the 1970s. The poaching business suddenly and dramatically escalated when the hunters began buying automatic weapons to slaughter what are essentially quite vulnerable animals.

This escalation wasn't just the result of land pressure and human hardship in the countryside. More significant was a radical expansion of the market for **rhino horns** – not, as is popularly supposed, in China (where minute quantities of powdered rhino horn are used for tonics and aphrodisiacs), but in Yemen. Oil money made the rhino horn dagger handle – traditionally the prerogative of the rich – suddenly within reach of thousands of Yemeni men. Many tons of horns were smuggled out of Mombasa in dhows. *Run, Rhino, Run* by Esmond and Chryssee Bradley Martin (see "Books" in *Contexts*) follows this trail in extraordinary and depressing detail.

Yet the savage groundwork was laid long before. After World War II, the Makueni area southeast of Machakos was designated as an Akamba resettlement area. The colonial Kenya Game Department sent in one J. A. Hunter to clear it of unwelcoming rhinos: he lived up to his name, shooting 1088 black rhinos from 50,000 acres. The Akamba didn't take to the scheme and it fizzled out. Today, your chances of seeing black rhinos in the wild in Tsavo are slim. They still hang on in the wilderness sector north of the Galana, where the war between the poachers and the Wildlife Service has fizzled out.

At the brink of disaster, there are now concentrations of breeding black rhinos in a number of ranches and sanctuaries – notably at Ngulia in Tsavo West, Nakuru, Solio, and in Laikipia to the northwest of Mount Kenya – and saving the rhino has become a national cause.

for security against large animals, but as a defence against the tsetse flies that may mistake your vehicle for a large animal.

Mudanda Rock is particularly recommended at certain times of the year. Like a scaled-down version of Ayers Rock in Australia, it towers above a natural dam which, during the dry season, draws elephants in their hundreds.

As recently as 1990, you were likely to get unforgettable glimpses of the mountainous carcasses of elephants. Today, the most you'll see of the carnage are the bleached bones of a bad memory. The elephants of Tsavo, attuned to the potential dangers they face in the bush, have taken to spending much of their time near the lodges and park roads where, shot by cameras, they are relatively safe. Large herds are not uncommon, but, when you see them, you'll notice the scarcity of mature adults.

From Aruba, most people head up towards the **Galana River**'s brown gully. If you're visiting the northern sector of the park, it's possible to cross the Galana at junction 160, but beware the smoothness of the rock bed, which belies the fact that many unwitting drivers all too easily get stuck in the attempt (note that Suzuki 4WD jeeps are notoriously underpowered, which makes judging your line all the more important). There are several spots where you can park and scramble down to the sandy banks. Lugard Falls seem hardly worth the naming, but there are always dozens of **crocodiles** in the vicinity, extraordinarily hard to see until you get up close. The luxury-tented, Swiss-run *Galdessa Camp* (PO Box 38807 Nairobi, ☎02/890032, or book via *Let's Go Travel* in Nairobi; ⑨) by the Galana organizes foot and fishing safaris along the river, plus camel safaris ($60 half-day), but with the surrounding bush vegetation, there's little chance of seeing much wildlife at the camp itself – and its accommodation rates are well over the odds even for the upmarket bracket.

To the coast

Heading **coastwards** from the defunct *Aruba Lodge*, a track leads almost dead straight for 80km to the lonely Sala Gate on the banks of the Galana. *Crocodile Camp*, a pleasant tented camp, lies a couple of kilometres outside the gate but at the time of writing was closed for renovation (due to reopen late 1996; ☎0147/30124, fax 0147/30123; or PO Box 500 Malindi, ☎0123/20481). You can normally camp here quite cheaply, but be prepared to be directed across the airstrip and down to the river bank where camping is free – and without any facilities at all. Each of the thirty-odd crocs at the camp has its own name and many of them come to the bank to feed when called.

Beyond *Crocodile Camp*, you pass the *Galana Game Ranch*, a 6000-square kilometre private experiment in mixed cattle and game ranching and wildlife conservation. It's on the north side of the river, reached across a causeway, but has been closed to the public by the government, its future status unknown. Two or three hours' drive east (100km) is Malindi.

Amboseli National Park

Daily fees $27 ($10 students/children); $8 to camp ($15 in a "special campsite"); warden: PO Box 18 Namanga (☎2 Amboseli). Maps: Macmillan "Amboseli National Park Map" at 1cm:750m (1988), Survey of Kenya SK87 at 1cm:500m (1975).

AMBOSELI is a small and very touristy park. It has suffered badly from off-road driving and its climate makes it a bleak, shimmering plain most of the year. Scenically, however, it is totally redeemed by the stunning spectacle of **Kilimanjaro**, towering over it and (as in those clichéd safari photographs taken with telephoto lenses) appearing almost to fill the sky. Sunrise and sunset are the best times to see the mountain, especially during the rainy season when the air is much clearer. In the right light, the snowy massif, washed coral and orange, is devastatingly beautiful. Much of the time, like Mount Kenya, it's tantalizingly muffled behind thick cloud.

On the animal side, Amboseli, like Tsavo, is **elephant** country *par excellence*. You will see large herds, some with big tusks. Predators, apart from hyenas and jackals, are relatively scarce (lions almost absent) but good numbers of herbivores are present. In the dry season, most of the animals crowd into the impenetrable marshy areas and patches of acacia woodland where food plants are available. But during and shortly after the rains the picture is different, the animals more dispersed and the landscape greener.

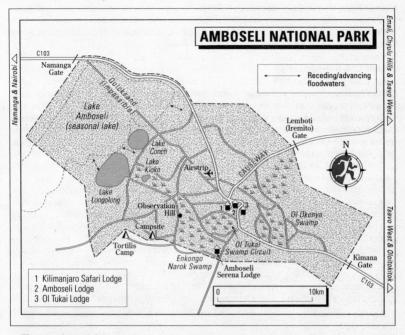

The **erosion** of the grasslands by circling minibuses did much to destroy the park's purpose in the 1980s, turning it into a vehicle-clogged dustbowl that appealed little to animals or tourists. A concerted programme of environmental conservation, road-building and ditch-making was initiated, and this, combined with the toughest approach of any park to off-road driving (including fines and ejections), improved the situation enormously. In 1992–93, however, heavy rains caused major floods, turning Amboseli into a swamp. The Kenya Wildlife Service responded with a $2-million reha-bilitation plan to rebuild park roads and culverts that had been destroyed; but with the possibility of further major floods in the years to come, the future of the park as a viable ecosystem and tourist asset seems far from assured.

The route from Nairobi

The road is excellent most of the way (about four hours' drive from Nairobi) and rollingly scenic as well. Without your own transport, either take a bus down to Namanga from Nairobi country bus station, or get as far as Athi River on a *KBS* bus #109 or 110 and hitch from there. As usual, the best chances are with Kenyan weekenders.

Athi River
ATHI RIVER isn't particularly interesting and pongs rather strongly due to the Kenya Meat Commission's giant butchery in the area, but if you get stuck hitching, the *Congress Club* (also known as *Studio 45*) is the local hot spot and offers good self-contained **rooms** (④); couples can share a single, which seems to be the norm around here. Run on similiar ethics is the astonishingly glam-kitsch *Moran Hotel* (☎0150/

22911; ⑤), with a nightly disco full of desperate businessmen and hookers, a fluorescent video-lounge, and clean and tidy little "cottages" out the back at a reasonable distance from all the noise. It also has a pool (Ksh100 for non-guests). Athi River has a colonnaded colonial post office and a *Standard Bank*.

Isinya and Kajiado

After a dull start through the Kapiti plains, the roadside interest increases after **ISINYA**. Here, there's a **Maasai Leatherworking and Handicrafts Centre**. It is touristy, but you can find some unusual work among the beaded key-rings and "marriage necklaces". Check out the handmade shoes and massive, heavy leather bags. If your stomach is strong, you can visit the tannery, and they're happy to see you in the workshops, too. Donations from a church in Folkestone, England, of all places, help Isinya's community.

Further south, in the gentle hills where Maasai country really begins, is the district capital **KAJIADO**, which lies on the Magadi railway line (see p.153). Set among sisal spikes and acacia, it's a friendly market town with a relaxed provincial feel, that provides an ideal stop-over after the hassle of Nairobi. Maasai in all their gear mix with other Kenyans in its busy streets and bars, and the daily **market**, part of which shelters in a modern breeze-block and corrugated iron building near the mosque, is fascinating. *Kajiado Inn* (②) opposite the railway station has the best **rooms** in town, plus a *nyama choma banda* and a bar-restaurant downstairs. Cheaper options (all ①) include the basic *Thayu B&L* on the main Nairobi–Namanga road, and the weird Maasai *1811 1971 Day and Night Club* which has scrubby rooms but bags of atmosphere; the cheapest rooms of all are to be found at the very basic but usually clean *Hotel Naramat*, next to *Small World Boutique*. For **cheap eats**, try *Impala Restaurant* opposite *KCB*. If you're after **nightlife**, there are a number of busy bars and day-and-night clubs: expect inquisitive stares but a friendly response.

Namanga

NAMANGA sits square on the border, only 130km from Arusha in Tanzania. The petrol station, from where the murram road leads off east towards Amboseli, is probably the best place to start if you're trying for a lift into the park. *Namanga River Hotel* is the grandest **accommodation** option (PO Box 4 Namanga, ☎67 Namanga; reservations ☎02/330773; ④): a colonial oddity composed of wooden cabins set amid pretty gardens, it was the halfway house on the old safari trail between Nairobi and Arusha. The place has a likeable, slightly cranky atmosphere – the era of baggy trousers and printed frocks seems just around the corner – and while it has seen better days, it's undeniably a good deal. Good snacks are served, and there are plans for a swimming pool; you can also happily camp in the garden (Ksh150 per person). Cheaper, s/c rooms are available at the *Namanga Safari Lodge* next door (PO Box 5 Namanga; ☎29 Namanga; ②), with its pleasantly kitsch garden and bar. Best of the three basic B&Ls is *Agip B&L* (①), behind the petrol station, which has a lively, unpredictable bar and a noisy disco.

On the main road from Nairobi are several large **tourist emporiums**, including one not far north of Namanga and the other in the town itself, at the big petrol station. Both are packed to overflowing with Maasai bead- and leather-work, as well as Makonde ebony carvings from southern Tanzania and, of course, Kamba animals and Kisii soapstone. They're not especially cheap but, depending on the volume of business, you can strike reasonable bargains and the choice is huge. The glass beads used in the beadwork are not African; they come from the Czech Republic, which exports them to Peru and the Native American reservations as well as East Africa. And don't be misled by the expensive black and white marriage necklaces, which are not traditional Maasai ware. As with any art, styles change and innovations are emulated. Among all the trinketry

AMBOSELI'S HISTORY

The park has been getting smaller and smaller ever since it was created. It began as part of the Southern Maasai Reserve at the turn of the century. Tourism arrived in the 1940s and Amboseli Reserve was formed as a wildlife sanctuary. Unlike Nairobi and Tsavo National Parks, created at the same time and sparsely inhabited, Amboseli's **swamps** were used by the Maasai to water their herds and they saw no reason not to continue sharing the area with the wildlife and – if necessary – with the tourists. In 1961, the Maasai District Council at Kajiado was given control of the area. But the combined destructive capacities of cattle and tourists began to tell in the 1960s; a rising water table in the following decade brought poisonous alkali to the surface and decimated huge tracts of acacia woodland. Kenyatta declared the 400-square-kilometre zone around the swamps (the present-day Amboseli) a **national park**, a status that utterly excluded the Maasai and their cattle. Infuriated, they all but exterminated the park's magnificent long-horned **black rhinos** over the next few years, seizing on Amboseli's tourist emblem with a vengeance. Not until a piped water supply was set up for the cattle did the Maasai finally give up the portion of land within Amboseli's boundaries. They still, however, periodically pursue lion (which, of course, kill their cattle) well into the park.

are genuine used articles which tend to attract high prices. For these, you might do better by making offers to people you meet on the road. Bartering clothes or food often works to the benefit of both parties.

Park accommodation

From Namanga, a long, corrugated road – comfortable only at cowboyish high speed – takes you to the park gate. At present, only one road connects the gate with Ol Tukai park centre; a second, which cut right across Lake Amboseli in drier years, is still marked on many maps and indeed is signposted in the park, but is totally impassable. Arriving, as most people do, around midday, Amboseli seems a parched, unattractive place, with Kilimanjaro disappointingly hazed into oblivion. And heading straight for Ol Tukai, with its group of lodges, *bandas*, a filling station, fences and barriers, doesn't improve first impressions by an awful lot.

Lodges and bandas

Reserve judgment on the place, however, until the late afternoon or early the next morning and hunt out your **accommodation**. Without spending lavishly – and the lodge rooms are often fully booked in the high season, anyway – the options are limited.

OL TUKAI AREA

"Drivers' bandas". If you haven't got a vehicle and get dropped off at Ol Tukai, the only cheap possibility would be an unofficial bed in the staff area. Tour drivers pay low, B&L-type rates, but you'll have to pay a little more or chat up the right people. You can certainly eat cheaply in the drivers' canteen, and make friends in their bar – a more enlivening experience than the luxury lodges – and you may even be able to arrange a reasonably priced game drive.

Amboseli Lodge (☎2061 Radiocall Nairobi; reservations through *Kilimanjaro Safari Club*, address on p.49). The main package destination, but it falls far short of the standards you'd expect from a "luxury" safari lodge. Service is sloppy, even rude, the food is dire and the bar expensive – although the chalet *bandas* are quite cute. Pool and showers available to casual visitors. ⑨.

Kilimanjaro Safari Lodge, within walking distance of *Amboseli Lodge*. Same management as *Amboseli Lodge*, and suffers from similar problems. Rates are the same at both, but all accommodation at *KSL* is in individual cottages. Pool and showers available to casual visitors. Micro-light flights over the parks can be booked here, at around $80 for 15min. ⑨.

MAASAI VOICES

The following excerpts are from interviews with **Muriankha**, at Olgirra Cultural Boma near Tsavo West National Park; **Olurei**, a Maasai elder from a group ranch near Oloitokitok; **Metoe ole Loombaa**, a group ranch member near Amboseli National Park; and **Ntoros ole Baari**, a Maasai elder from the Loita Hills. The interviews, which have been edited but not changed in style or tone from the original translations, were conducted by Ruth McCoy in January 1993. They have subsequently appeared in *Nomansland* by George Monbiot (see "Books" in *Contexts*).

At the moment, Amboseli is going through a spell of unprecedented wetness. For years on end "Lake Amboseli" – filled in with optimistic blue on so many maps – had never been more than a soggy mud flat and a pointless excursion. In 1993 it flooded almost the entire park and Amboseli seemed on the point of transforming itself into a wetlands zone. If it completely dries out again, at least the **Olokenya Swamp**, a permanent water source in the southeast, will always be worth a slow exploration. It makes a good start to the trip at dawn, if you're heading south out of the park through the Kimana Gate.

TOURISTS

What is tourism doing to Maasai culture?
Ntoros ole Baari: It is doing a lot of damage; much of Maasai culture is now being tailored to suit the interests of tourists, much of it is fake. Tourists bring a lot of changes to Maasai society, many of which are negative and difficult to cope with. Tourism does provide some financial benefits and cannot be dismissed completely, but we must aim to have culture-friendly tourism.

What do the Maasai feel about being photographed?
Ntoros ole Baari: We don't like it but are forced to accept it as a kind of business. We hate the idea of someone capturing our image for nothing, and sometimes we aren't even prepared for it. People may use our photographs in questionable ways, putting them to uses to which we haven't consented.

WILDLIFE

Would you prefer it if there were no wild animals on your land?
Olurei: Isn't it true that they have their place – the Amboseli National Park? If too many of them come out here and eat our grass, that's bad, but the pastoralists like having some animals around, depending on which ones and the numbers of them. The ones that compete for food with our cattle are the wildebeest and zebra. They bring many other problems; especially when the wildebeest are calving. If their afterbirth enters drinking water or falls on the grass, it can kill cattle through malignant catarrh. Nothing can cure it. It can be devastating. Likewise, when the antelopes give birth, the goats get a sickness of the nose and mouth. This can be very severe as well. And the lions cause us a lot of trouble. From July to September they harass our animals a lot as all the other wildlife has gone into the park.

What do you say to the conservationists who are trying to increase the numbers of wild animals in Maasai-land?
Olurei: It would be really good to have the elephants and rhinos back – there have been very few in recent years. The elephants break down trees, adding to the grass and they dig water holes far from the river where the livestock can water; so they're friends of the herders. And rhinos keep back the thorn bush. But wildebeest and zebra, we don't need any more of them.

The authorities have argued that the Maasai have had to leave Amboseli because they were causing too much damage . . .
Metoe ole Loombaa: No. The Maasai have coexisted with wildlife for a long time and have never caused any damage. We don't eat wildlife, so we never hunt. The manure our

cattle were leaving in the park was making the vegetation grow. Now it's completely destroyed and the animals are following us to our ranch to follow our livestock. The park was better off when we were there – you could find rhinos and lions there. But now all the animals have moved out. Poaching was less when we were there.

THE GOVERNMENT AND PARK AUTHORITIES

What problems have the wildlife around Tsavo West National Park caused you?
Muriankha: They've caused a lot of damage. The lions have killed people and are taking livestock. You can see my leg: this was bitten off below the knee by a lion. The weapon we had to protect ourselves was a spear. Now the government doesn't allow us to use it to protect ourselves from wild animals. Sometimes elephants come through here, and although they have not killed anyone, they have done all the damage to our village imaginable. We're helpless; we don't get any assistance. We have to walk a long way to report incidents to the game rangers, and they sometimes come when the animal has already gone.

Has the creation of the Amboseli National Park been a good thing or a bad thing for the Maasai?
Olurei: It's a very bad mistake. The park is where all the animals are in the dry season because of the swamps and the river. But then in the rains, all the animals are out and eat our grass, and only go back into the park in the dry season. The wild animals have a grazing reserve but we don't. I have asked the government to let us in and just recently some conservation people have come and talked to us, but it's the first time they have listened to us. When one of my friends tried to graze in the park, he was grabbed, jailed and fined heavily. They forget the park was made out of our land.

Has the Kenya Wildlife Service done anything in Amboseli to mitigate the effects?
Metoe ole Loombaa: There is no policy of allowing us into the park in times of need. It's all a matter of negotiation, depending on the warden of the day.

Will revenue-sharing and tourist money compensate you?
Metoe ole Loombaa: No, it is not enough compensation as we've lost property and human life. Revenue-sharing can't compare. We're not being helped to earn anything from tourism. KWS isn't assisting us. The problems we are facing cannot be valued against money.

Do you agree with conservationists who say that wildlife and livestock compete in the Mara?
Ntoros ole Baari: The land could easily accommodate both the livestock and wildlife. There are as many wild animals on the Maasai lands as in the reserve. Livestock and wildlife are complementary; wildlife follows the pastoralists' cows wherever they go for their security, as the cows keep the grass down.

What has happened to the Maasai kept out of the Mara?
Ntoros ole Baari: The Maasai are forced to overgraze as so much of their land has been reduced by conservation. By keeping the Maasai out of the reserve, conservationists are in fact contributing to the threat to the environment.

Who in your opinion benefits from the Tsavo West National Park?
Muriankha: It's the government that benefits, as it is a source of permanent income for it during the dry and wet seasons. Those who own the tourist companies and hotels also benefit; the people who live on the land surrounding the park don't benefit and that's what we've been trying to tell the government: we too should benefit from wildlife because we are losing a lot from it, and our livestock is just as crucial to us as wildlife is to the government.

Ol Tukai Lodge (reservations through *Block Hotels*, address p.48). Once a cheap self-service *banda* site, this reopened as a fully fledged lodge shortly before this book went to press, amidst bitter controversy among the Maasai inhabitants of Kajiado district (receipts from the old *banda* went partially to them), and growing fears of the ecological damage of yet more tourists. ⑦ low, ⑨ high.

SOUTHERN PARK AREA

Amboseli Serena Lodge (☎0302/22622, fax 0302/22430; reservations through *Serena*, address on p.50). If you're looking to unload money, this lodge, a 20-minute drive from the Ol Tukai tourist sanctuary, is an interesting and tranquil place to do it. They have made great efforts to hide the building behind a jungle of tropical plants and creepers, and this has encouraged a kind of intimate, pseudo-bush feeling accentuated by touches like a stream running through the dining room. Located by the Enkongo Narok swamps, there's plenty of wildlife activity here, too. Unfortunately, they don't encourage casual visits, and the pool is for hotel residents only. Three-hour game drives cost $35 per person. ⑦ low, ⑨ high.

Tortilis Camp (bookings via *Let's Go Travel* in Nairobi, see p.122). Further west, and just outside the park boundary at Kitirua, this newish luxury camp has 15 "tents" (under wicker roofs) with all the usual mod cons. Set atop a low hill, it gives stunning views of Kilimanjaro and northern Tanzania as far as Mount Meru. The pool at sunset is quite something, and there's a feeling of intimacy with the wildlife. The camp is managed as a conservation project, which includes paying a proportion of your fee to the local Maasai; it recently won an award from *British Airways* for promoting sustainable tourism. ⑨.

Camping

Real budget accommodation can only be had outside the park boundary at a **campsite** on Maasai land (Ksh600 per person), south of *Amboseli Serena Lodge*. Apart from warm sodas, a couple of toilets are the only facilities, and even water supplies are unreliable. It's a fine, wooded site, though no longer overrun with wildlife since it was partially fenced. The main problem, if you're with a camping safari, is midday heat: persuade your driver to ferry you over to the Ol Tukai lodges for swims and cold drinks, then do a game drive on the late afternoon return.

Exploring the park

Small enough to cover easily in two or three game drives in a single day, most of Amboseli is open country with good visibility. Because of this, you escape the nagging feeling you may get in other parks, that you may be in the wrong place and *that's* why you're not seeing any animals – here, you can look everywhere.

A good first stop is **Observation Hill**. Early in the morning, with Kilimanjaro a pervasive sky-filler to the south, the swamps of **Enkongo Narok**, replenished underground from the mountain top, are looped out in a brilliant emerald sash beneath. You can get out and walk around up here.

There's always a concentration of animals along the swamps and the drivable tracks which closely follow their fringes. The swamps are permanent enough to keep **hippo** here all year and there are hundreds of **elephant** and **buffalo**, plus, predictably, a raucous profusion of **birdlife**. Lake Kioko at the northern end is a special oasis.

Lions are counted in ones and twos at the moment but **cheetahs** are seen fairly frequently in the woods a little further south and there must be thousands of giraffe among the acacias. Look out, too, for the beautifully formed, rapier-horned **fringe-eared oryx** antelopes.

The open plains are scoured by **zebra** and haphazard, solitary **wildebeest**. The two species are often seen together – a good deal from the zebras' point of view because in a surprise attack the predator usually ends up with the less fleet-footed wildebeest. There are tail-flicking gazelle out here, too: the open country provides good protection against lion or cheetah ambushes.

Oloitokitok and points onwards

Once in the park, you shouldn't have too much difficulty lining up lifts onwards. If you're **driving**, there are several routes east out of Amboseli. One heads through Iremito (Lemboti) Gate towards the **Chyulu Hills**, then winds south to Tsavo West along the spine of the lava ridge – definitely a 4WD route unless you're feeling reckless. The Chyulus are favourite caving country with long, safe explorations possible. The Cave Exploration Group of East Africa found Leviathan Cave here, the longest and deepest lava tube in the world. Before reaching the Chyulus, this route forks back at **Makutano** (a tiny Maasai trading centre with absolutely nothing), where a reasonable murram road shoots off north to Emali on the Mombasa highway.

The second main road (the C103) leaves Amboseli in the southeast through Kimana Gate. As a result of concerns about security, you still have to travel in convoy with an official vehicle to Tsavo West. The latest schedule is thrice-daily departures in each direction at 8.30am, 10.30am and 2.30pm from Ol Tukai (Amboseli) and Mtito Andei Gate (Tsavo West) via Chyulu Gate; the trip takes two to four hours. Be prompt: it's a long way between the two parks if you miss the convoy.

Branching off the C103 between the parks, you can climb south to the Maasai country town of **OLOITOKITOK** with Kilimanjaro's jagged satellite peak Mawenzi dead ahead. Oloitokitok (pronounced "Loytoktok") should be nothing to get excited about – just an interesting, bustling little town by the Amboseli–Tsavo circuit. But it is ignored by 99 percent of the tourist minibuses, and it's in a fabulous position, closer to Kilimanjaro than anywhere else in Kenya and high above the plains. It is a recommended place to settle into if you're interested in finding out more about the **Maasai**, as this is their easternmost major centre. Oloitokitok is also a border crossing for the Tanzanian town of Moshi a couple of hours away, nestled behind the mountain. And it's close to Kilimanjaro's Kibo Peak, 25 illegal kilometres as the crow flies. It's possible to find a porter/guide to take you to the top, but don't get caught in Kilimanjaro National Park, fees unpaid. The Tanzanians take the offence extremely seriously.

On the big market days (Tues & Sat), many Maasai are in Oloitokitok centre and there's a fair amount of *matatu* traffic between here and Taveta and the nearby villages. At other times, you will have to take potluck with **transport**, though there's at least one daily country bus to Nairobi, passing through Taveta and Voi. Oloitokitok has a post office and *KCB* bank, as well as a few **B&Ls**. *Mwalimu Lodge* in the lower part of town is a serious watering hole, but there are a couple of quieter places up the hill near the market, both of which are reasonable.

Maasai Mara National Reserve

Daily fees Ksh1500, private vehicle Ksh500, camping Ksh480 per person; warden PO Box 60 Narok. Reserve gates open at 6.30am and close at 7pm daily. Driving inside the reserve is prohibited after 7pm except by special arrangement. Speed limit of 50kph at all times. Maps: Macmillan "Maasai Mara National Reserve Map" at 1cm:1.25km (1988); Survey of Kenya SK86 at 1cm:1km (1975).

For a long list of reasons, **MAASAI MARA** is the best animal reserve in Kenya. The panorama sometimes resembles one of those wild animal wall charts, where groups of unlikely looking animal companions are forced into the artist's frame. You can see a dozen different species – or more – at one time: gazelle, zebra, giraffe, buffalo, topi, kongoni, wildebeest, eland, elephant, hyena, jackal, ostrich, and a pride of lions waiting for a chance.

The reserve is a great wedge of undulating **grassland** nearly 2000m above sea level, watered by one of Kenya's bigger rivers, the Mara. It is in the remote, sparsely inhab-

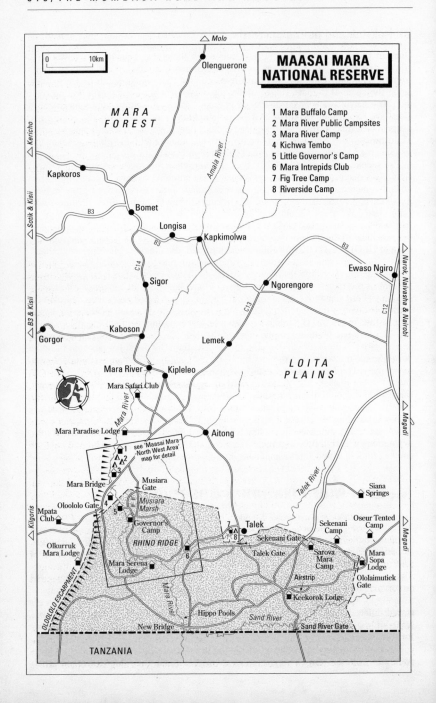

MAASAI MARA NATIONAL RESERVE

1 Mara Buffalo Camp
2 Mara River Public Campsites
3 Mara River Camp
4 Kichwa Tembo
5 Little Governor's Camp
6 Mara Intrepids Club
7 Fig Tree Camp
8 Riverside Camp

△ Molo

0   10km

△ Kericho

MARA FOREST

Olenguerone

Amala River

△ Sotik & Kisii

Kapkoros

B3

Bomet

Longisa

Kapkimolwa

B3

△ Narok, Naivasha & Nairobi

C14

Sigor

Ngorengore

Ewaso Ngiro

△ B3 & Kisii

Kaboson

C13

C12

Gorgor

Lemek

LOITA PLAINS

Mara River

Kipleleo

N

Mara Safari Club

Mara River

Mara Paradise Lodge

Aitong

see 'Maasai Mara -North West Area' map for detail

Talek River

Siana Springs

1
2
3

Mara Bridge

Musiara Gate

Musiara Marsh

7
8

Talek

Sekenani Camp

Oseur Tented Camp

△ Magadi

△ Kilgoris

Mpata Club

Oloololo Gate

4

5

Governor's Camp

Sekenani Gate

Sarova Mara Camp

Mara Sopa Lodge

Olkurruk Mara Lodge

RHINO RIDGE

6

Talek Gate

Ololaimutiek Gate

Mara Serena Lodge

Mara River

Airstrip

Keekorok Lodge

OLOOLOLO ESCARPMENT

Hippo Pools

Sand River

New Bridge

Sand River Gate

TANZANIA

ited southwest part of the country, snugged up against the border and, indeed, an extension of the even bigger **Serengeti plains** in Tanzania. This is a land of short grasses, where the wind plays with the thick, green mantle after the rains and, nine months later, whips up dust devils from the baked surface.

But Maasai Mara's climate is beneficently predictable, with ample rain, and the new grass supports an annual **migration** of millions of wildebeest from the dry plains of Tanzania. To travel through the reserve in September or October, while the wildebeest are in possession, is a staggering experience, like being caught up in the momentum of a phenomenal historic event. Whether you're watching this or a pride of lions hunting, a herd of elephants grazing in the marsh, or hyenas squabbling with vultures over the carcass of a buffalo, you are conscious all the time of being in a realm apart. There are few places on earth where animals hold such dazzling sway – it's as if you had found yourself in the New York of the natural world.

Getting to the Mara from Nairobi and Narok

Part of the reason for the Mara's fantastic spell is its isolation: a trip here is an expedition, and you might as well plan it as such. The vast majority of visitors come on pre-booked safari packages.

If you're organizing it yourself, access is most straightforward, and most expensive (currently $87 one-way, $150 return), by the scheduled twice-daily **air service** from Nairobi (see "Travel Details", p.156). By **road**, however, rewards are greater, including the long **drive** across the Rift Valley from Nairobi, sweeping across dry, stupendous vistas of range lands – the heart of the Maasai country. Cattle are the economic mainstay, but extensive wheat fields are pushing south. While the land often looks empty, if you stop for five minutes, chances are that someone will appear – to request something or to offer a photo pose, or just to pass the time of day.

Beware: if you're driving from Nairobi (B3) or Naivasha (C88 then B3) you'll have to be prepared to cover more than half the distance on a barely tolerable surface. The C88 and the eastern section of the B3 have been improved but the remainder of the road, from 40km before Narok all the way to the Mara via Ewaso Ngiro and the C12 or the C13, is in a totally disgraceful state. Minibuses and 4WD vehicles manage to bump their way along it but more and more visitors are being advised to fly into the reserve. Narok County Council is responsible for maintaining the Mara's access roads (the Kenya Wildlife Service having washed its hands of this) but appears to be making little effort to fulfil its responsibilities, secure in the knowledge that tourists will always want to come to the Mara, whatever the state of the roads. In January 1996, the Kenya Tourist Guides Association, anxious for immediate action, agreed to stump up Ksh300,000 towards the grading of the road. If improvements are not made soon, flying will be the only practicable option for all but the hardiest of travellers, effectively making the Mara the preserve of the wealthy elite.

If you do decide to drive to the Mara, give yourself plenty of time – a good six to seven hours from Nairobi or Naivasha to the eastern end of the reserve, or all day with an early start to the western end. And if you intend to do more than a tank's worth of driving, remember to stock up with cans of **petrol** at the last town you pass through. Although you may be able to buy petrol at one of the lodges (at a price), don't depend on it. Many only keep enough fuel for their own vehicles; others only keep diesel.

Narok

NAROK is the funnel through which almost all road transport enters the Maasai Mara. It is the last place to get fuel, a cold drink or almost anything for over 100km before you enter the reserve. First impressions aren't encouraging. *Africana*, on the left as you enter from the east, is a tourist trap of the first order, charging exorbitant prices for curios, food and drinks. In the same vein, over the road, a brassy atmosphere pervades the *Kobil Montorosi Service Station* (and *Motorists' Snack Bar*) which, being the first filling station on the way into town, waylays most of the minibuses with its big-game cut-outs, reticulated sunshades and cluster of souvenir shops selling very expensive Maasai paraphernalia (the same stuff is half the price in Nairobi). When buying petrol, watch the pump counter and check the bill. If you're **hitching** this is probably the best point to wait and ask. If the direct approach doesn't appeal (there'll be plenty of refusals), try the bridge over the Engare Narok River on the other side of town. If you're driving, and want a quieter refuge, go right through Narok to the *Total* station on the far side of town, which also tends to have cheaper petrol.

If you have to **spend the night** in Narok, there are a number of lodgings near the action on the main road. Marginally the best are the *Transit Hotel* (③), the *Osupuko* – safe parking, good food, rather grubby rooms but s/c (②) – and *Wanja's Bar & Restaurant* (PO Box 71 Narok; ☎0305/2161; ②). *Hillside Cave (Day and Night Club)*, on the main road, does good chicken and *kienjeji*. *Barclays Bank* (Mon–Fri 9am–3pm, Sat 9–11am) and the **post office** are both on the main road. If you want cheap **beer** in the Mara, stock up now (you'll have to truck back the empties to reclaim the deposit).

Alternative routes to Narok: over the Mau Escarpment

From Lake Naivasha (at the end of the lake road tarmac by the South Lake police station), and **from Nakuru via Njoro**, steep roads twist up over the **Mau Escarpment**. If you're starting out **from further west** you can also get to Narok by the gradually improving Molo–Olenguerone road (see p.215). But this latter route also allows the option of a more direct approach to the west end of the reserve (see opposite).

The **Mau range**, not as high but just as massive as the Aberdares, is little known and rarely visited. In the thin, clear air, Maasai and Nandi graze their cattle on luxuriant pastures, and large domains of thick, dark forest are still the home to Okiek (Dorobo) hunter-gatherers – though many are mixing the hunt with farming and have moved to the edge of the forest tracts and the margins of Kenya's mainstream economy. It is enrapturing country and highly recommended for **hiking** if you have the time. As a preliminary to Maasai Mara, the Mau is a compelling alternative to the long rolling switchback of the main Nairobi–Narok road, but you shouldn't attempt the climb – or the descent – in a saloon car, especially if it's raining. By **matatu**, the Nakuru–Narok route is a little easier than the other two; the village of East Mau, near the peaks, is your first destination.

There's little **accommodation** in the Mau range: **Enangiperi**, for example, roughly the halfway point, has one, very basic "lodging" (more a bed in a barn) and you may find yourself asking, or being invited, to **stay with people**. This can arouse suspicions in the local authorities, who are very unused to travellers in these parts and are sensitive to the arrival of strangers because of ongoing friction between local people and immigrant farmers and landlords from other parts of Kenya. This shouldn't put you off visiting the region – it is wonderful countryside.

Into the reserve from Narok

Once through Narok, you have to make a choice of route after about 20km. You could branch left for the potholed **C12** road, which makes its way south towards the Sekenani Gate and the eastern section of the reserve, where *Keekorok Lodge* and the reserve headquarters are the main human focuses. Or turn right, along the even more rugged **C13** road, for the western end of the reserve, the Mara River, and most of the other lodges and camps. This route can be tough and uncomfortable during or after rains, and isn't to be contemplated without a 4WD vehicle. In the wet, you're looking at 5–6 hours' driving and sliding from Narok to the Musiara or Oloololo gates.

Other routes to the Mara

You can also arrive in Maasai Mara **from Kisii** in the west (see p.253) and **Kericho** in the north (see p.257); with a little difficulty from **Lake Magadi** in the east (see p.152); and with no trouble at all from *Lobo Lodge* in Tanzania's **Serengeti National Park**.

Take a good look at a good map before setting off: if you're heading for the lodges and tented camps along the Mara River or camping in that **northwest** area of the Mara, you might well find that an approach via Kericho (even if you're starting out from Nairobi) is the fastest and, especially in wet weather, certainly the smoothest.

Into the reserve from the north and west: Bomet, Kilgoris

From Kericho, due north of the reserve, leaving the the C23 Kericho–Kisii road at **Litein**, the route goes via the fast new tarmac highway to Bomet (40km). There's a fair number of *matatus* making this run but nothing much at **BOMET** when you get there: just three streets running round the back of the *Esso* station (pricy fuel), some basic lodgings (*Kwa-Sisi Lodge, Safe Lodge*), a few meagre *hotelis* and *dukas*, a *KCB* bank (Mon–Fri 9am–3pm, Sat 9–11am) and a post office. From Bomet, the B3 (for Narok) heads southeast; the tarmac goes just beyond the Amala River (which becomes the Mara River). *Matatus* run along this route. If you're driving, you can follow the B3 for about 40km, then turn right onto the C13 for the western side of the reserve, or continue for another 40km to the turning onto the C12 for the eastern side. It's also possible to head straight for the western side of the Mara from Bomet by turning right off the B3 onto the (unpaved) C14 for Sigor and Kaboson, but this route, though shorter, is rougher, and difficult to navigate. The turning, which is unmarked, is about 5km south of Bomet. At Kaboson the C14 continues northwest towards Kilgoris and Kisii; you need to turn off left in order to cross the Mara River and join the C13.

From Kisii and South Nyanza, you have two options if you're driving: either heading south to **Kilgoris** and Lolgorien and thence over the Oloololo Escarpment to the gate of the same name at the far west of the reserve (note if you're on public transport that there are few *matatus* south of the tarmac which ends at Kilgoris); or going via the new Sotik–Bomet road and then south or southeast to the centre or east of the reserve.

Into the reserve from the southeast: Magadi and the Ngurumans

From Lake Magadi, you can get as far as the Ewaso Ngiro river by lorry (arranged at Magadi police station – see p.152), but west of the river is remote, 4WD country. It's a favourite way into the Maasai Mara with well-equipped private safaris, but a tough climb in any vehicle up the game-rich **Nguruman Escarpment** to Morijo, and thence a further 60km or so through the **Loita Hills** to the Ololaimutiek Gate.

Into the reserve from Tanzania

On this last route, you're bound to be in a private vehicle; there's a twelve-kilometre gap between the Tanzanian formalities and the Kenya Police post at the Sand River Gate, where they'll sign you in and tell you where to go to complete formalities when you reach Nairobi. If you need to change money, *Keekorok Lodge*, 10km away, will do so for you, but sometimes imposes a small maximum of $20 or so unless you're going to stay.

If you're driving out of Kenya to Tanzania in your own vehicle (not a hired car), you should, if possible, check the formalities at Nyayo House in Nairobi, or a provincial headquarters like Nakuru or Kisumu. As there are no facilities at Sand River, the police there seem to like photocopies of everything to be left with them, including your log book.

Camping on a budget

Travellers on a budget aren't well catered for in Maasai Mara – the reserve has acquired something of an exclusive reputation on which its remoteness can capitalize. If you can't afford the more expensive lodges and luxury tented camps, there are very few alternatives to **do-it-yourself camping**. It's not possible to camp inside the reserve itself, but the Mara extends far beyond the limits of the reserve, and game is usually in plentiful supply north of the boundaries, where most of the campsites are found.

You should remember, however, to be particularly wary of snatch-and-run **baboon** raids at the Mara campsites – baboons are prone to grab anything inviting-looking, whether edible or not, and dash off with it to examine it later. Apparently they have a particular fondness for toothpaste but your camera bag is just as likely a target, if left within reach.

Camping at the gates

Driving in yourself on a small budget, you might prefer to camp at the informal **camp-sites at the main gates** – clockwise, from west to east: Oloololo, Musiara, Talek (see below), Sekenani, Ololaimutiek and Sand River – which charge around Ksh400 per person per night.

Musiara is one of the most popular campsites. You can camp by a little stream and, while you're safe enough here, you're almost guaranteed to hear at close quarters the spine-tingling grunting roars of the Musiara lion prides. The rangers are quite happy to have campers and, if you have your own vehicle, will often be prepared to accompany you after dark for a meal at *Governor's Camp*. The **Oloololo campsite** has wonderful views of the escarpment and is also very welcoming. **Sand River campsite** (which acquired an unsavoury reputation after the murder here of Julie Ward) is perhaps the best, with toilets and fresh water from a stream, and it's nicely located in a spot where animals come to drink at night.

At the others, there are virtually no facilities, though drinking water may be available, and you can expect some good-natured pestering by the rangers, who will try to extract a few bob by taking you on game drives in your vehicle – sometimes with success, other times not.

Talek Gate campsites

There's a large number of **"campsites"** (with nothing laid on) in the vicinity of Talek Gate, along the north bank of the Talek River, east of the gate, outside the reserve. Several are the more-or-less permanent territories of camping safari operators – fetch up when a group is in and you may be able to avail yourself of facilities, water and drinks, for a small charge. *Riverside Campsite* is a public site with basic facilities five minutes' walk west of Talek Gate and the bridge. Nearby, the small centre of **Talek** has a few *hotelis* and *dukas*.

Wild camping

There are further sites along various other rivers outside the reserve. The best of these **wild campsites**, with no facilities (and nothing to keep the animals out but the strong smell of humans), are three sites on the **east bank of the Mara River**, just outside the reserve. These can be booked through the warden in Narok (see the Maasai Mara introduction), but in practice you can turn up and camp without making prior arrangements. These Mara River camping places are hard to locate but better than most of the Talek River's, with deep shade from the trees and fewer flies.

There's another recognized camping site just downstream of *Mara River Camp* on the river bank, reached by turning sharp left before entering the *Camp*. There are some lively hippos here and the site has the advantage of being close to the road and

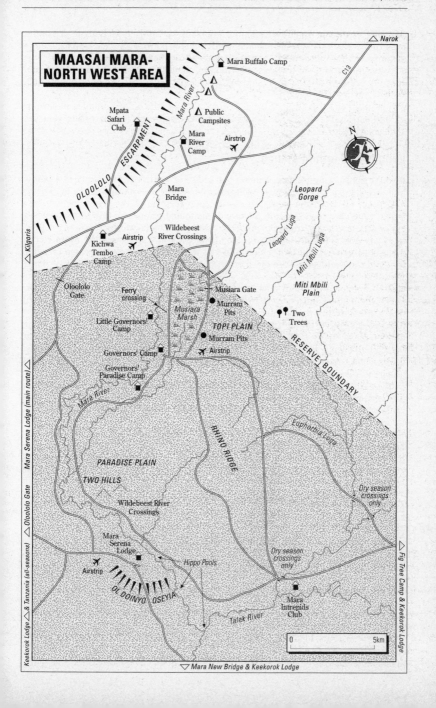

MAASAI MARA-
NORTH WEST AREA

△ Narok

Mara Buffalo Camp

△
△

△ Public
Campsites

OLOOLOLO ESCARPMENT

Mara River

C13

Mpata
Safari
Club

Mara
River
Camp

Airstrip

Leopard
Gorge

N

Mara
Bridge

Leopard Luga

Miti Mbili Luga

Kilgoris △

Kichwa
Tembo
Camp

Airstrip

Wildebeest
River Crossings

Miti Mbili
Plain

Olololo
Gate

Ferry
crossing

Musiara Gate

Two
Trees

Little Governors'
Camp

Musiara
Marsh

Murram
Pits

TOPI PLAIN

RESERVE BOUNDARY

Governors' Camp

Murram Pits

Airstrip

Governors'
Paradise Camp

Euphorbia Luga

Mara River

Mara Serena Lodge (main route) △   △ Olololo Gate

RHINO RIDGE

PARADISE PLAIN

TWO HILLS

Dry season
crossings
only

Wildebeest River
Crossings

Keekorok Lodge △△ & Tanzania (all-seasons) △

Mara
Serena
Lodge

Hippo Pools

Dry season
crossings
only

Fig Tree Camp & Keekorok Lodge ▷

Airstrip

OL DOINYO OSEYIA

Mara
Intrepids
Club

Talek River

0   5km

▽ Mara New Bridge & Keekorok Lodge

near the *Camp*. You would be asking for trouble if you left your tent unguarded: either from robbery or wreckage by baboons (and probably both). Either pack up each morning or leave someone behind – perhaps a ranger if you can agree about his fee.

You can also camp at a spectacular vantage point near *Olkurruk Mara Lodge*, high above the reserve an hour's drive from the Oloolo Gate. This is a good site if you're arriving late from the west.

Note that you can, with tact, usually camp in the vicinity of lodges and tented camps located outside the reserve boundaries. A low-key approach (and stressing your self-sufficiency) helps.

Lodges and tented camps

If you're considering treating yourself to a **lodge or tented camp**, either in a Maasai Mara package or independently, it is worth choosing where you stay carefully. The six lodges are all about the same price (with the exception of the very expensive new *Mpata Club*), but there are now about a dozen tented camps and they vary considerably in style and price, from expensive to extremely expensive (approaching $400 per night for two). Pressure on the thousand-odd beds in and around the Mara can be intense, so booking ahead is essential if you want to be sure of your camp or lodge. **Reservations addresses** are given either below or in the "Hotel Reservations" box in *Basics* (see p.48).

One common **additional cost**, worked into the full-board price by the most luxurious of the tented camps, covers two or three **game drives** per day in the camp vehicles. The camps that operate like this generally have exclusive pretensions and most of their guests arrive by air (transfers from the nearest airstrip also included). This doesn't mean they're not also attractive places to burn money. Competition, and demanding clients, keep standards high in every price range. There's nothing intrinsically cheaper about sleeping under canvas: private bathrooms, hot showers and some remarkably **good food** in the middle of the wilds naturally hoist prices sky-high.

If you're **driving in yourself**, however, it makes most sense to go to a tented camp with optional game drives. If you have poor luck with animals in your own vehicle, you can always go out on an organized game drive. These are the camps that tend to be favoured by Kenya residents.

Lodges

Keekorok Lodge (☎0305/2525–6, fax 0305/2412; reservations through *Block*). A perennially busy hotel in the bush, *Keekorok* is situated in a rather open location. The longest-running accommodation in the reserve, though quite modern, it has good facilities, including a pool, but rooms vary in size and style. It's a good hour closer to Nairobi by road than *Mara Serena*, its main competitor, and good during the rainy season for access to the plains. There's a pleasant walkway round the back to

---

VICARIOUS PLEASURES

As usual, if you're not staying in luxury accommodation, a taste of the high life can be had if you drop into a lodge for a drink or something to eat (generally expensive: establish the price first, and don't forget to leave a tip). Some of the lodges and camps, *Keekorok* especially, get heavily invaded during the high seasons, and casual visitors have been known to abuse the lodges' hospitality, so these lodges may turn away non-residents. Changing into decent clothes probably won't help – staff know exactly who's who – but discretion and some words of Swahili might. Swimming pools are usually out of bounds. The only shops are lobby gift boutiques. If you're lucky you might find a lodge willing to sell you some fuel, though at high prices. If you don't see pumps or anticipate a refusal, go direct to the oiliest part of the staff compound and ask.

a bar overlooking a small lake, where there are hippos and monkeys. Balloon flights are available daily at 6am. As well as daytime game drives, guests can experience drives at dusk or after dark – a new venture – when you're likely to see leopards, lions, jackals and porcupines. ⑦ low, ⑨ high.

Mara Paradise Lodge (reservations through *Paradise Safari Hotels Management*, PO Box 41789 Nairobi, ☎ 02/229262). Opened in 1991, this is upstream on the Mara, between *Mara Buffalo* and *Mara Safari Club*, well outside the reserve. Good game viewing in the vicinity, but the hippos seen from the bar don't quite compensate for few elephants, or predators (cattle are widely grazed here). Rooms are adequate, but small. No pool. ⑥ low, ⑦ high.

Mara Serena Lodge (☎0305/2252, 2059 or 2137; reservations through *Serena*). Although the largest hotel in the park, this has, perhaps, fewer tour groups and is a touch less streamlined than *Keekorok*. It's located in a quieter area of the reserve and its architecture is more integrated into the surroundings. The design of the lodge is based on a re-creation of two Maasai *enkangs* with smallish but appealing cave-like rooms, up on a ridge with excellent views. Balloons again, and a pool. ⑦ low, ⑨ high.

Mara Sopa Lodge (☎0305/2196–7; reservations through *Kenya Holidays*, PO Box 72630 Nairobi, ☎02/336088 or 336724, fax 02/223843). By Ololaimutiek Gate, outside the boundary. Beautiful, large *banda*-style rooms with huge bathrooms. Pool. Maintains a low profile in its remote corner – and high prices. Good location for the wildebeest migration. ⑦ low, ⑨ high.

Mpata Club (☎/fax 0305/2538; reservations through *Mpata Investments Inc*, 20th Floor, Anniversary Towers, PO Box 58402, Nairobi, ☎02/217017, fax 02/217016). Up on the Oloololo Escarpment, about 25km from the Mara River Bridge, north of *Olkurruk Mara Lodge*. Twenty stone-built *bandas*, including twelve suites, designed by the architects of the *Safari Park* in Nairobi. Each *banda* has, among other comforts, a private verandah and a jacuzzi from which to watch the sunset. The restaurant serves French cuisine and there's a twenty-metre pool. ⑨.

Olkurruk Mara Lodge (☎0305/2493–4, fax 0305/2495; reservations through *AT&H*). One of the smallest lodges (small enough to be really friendly), with extraordinary views over the western half of the reserve. Very isolated on Oloololo escarpment and, if you're coming by road, not for the faint-hearted – it's a good hour up from the Mara Bridge and the two western gates, which also means that game trips down to the reserve proper are once-a-day-only or all-day affairs. Thatched, luxury *bandas*, each divided into two twin rooms (room numbers 1 and 4 have the finest outlooks). No pool – as yet. ⑦ low, ⑨ high.

Luxury tented camps: game drives included

Governors' Camp (☎/fax 0305/2273; reservations through *Governors' Camp*, see p.48). Located in the woods on a bend in the river on the site of an old hunting camp and close to the fantastic gameviewing of the Musiara marsh (but note, the Musiara area gets very soggy during the rains) *Governors'* has retained its exclusive "bush" atmosphere, with no expense spared. The big canvas tents have solid bathrooms at the back; elephants trundle through at night; guards keep watch for more dangerous visitors and escort guests between their tents and the (excellent) restaurant. Nice staff and recommended. No pool – but few guests seem to miss it. Very high ⑨ rates.

Little Governors' Camp (☎/fax 0305/2040; same reservations details as main camp). Reached by a two-kilometre drive and then a dinghy across the Mara, this is the annexe from which the *Governors'* balloons fly. Hidden in the trees by its own water hole, with wonderful birdwatching, it's the smallest and most intimate set-up in the reserve, always fully booked in advance of the main camp. It has just 27 beds, 3 of them double. No pool. Very high ⑨ rates.

There's also an annual encampment called **Governors' Paradise Camp** – which is set up between *Governors'* and *Little Governors'* in May or June after the rains and charges the same rates – and an entirely private mobile set-up (**Governors' Private Camp**) which will happily go wherever you please, for a price.

Mara Intrepids Club (☎0305/2168; reservations through *Prestige Hotels*). Parked on a bluff overlooking the Talek River in the heart of the reserve, with a swimming pool. "Tented suites" conveys the scene – they run a tight ship here, very much geared to German and Italian visitors. Baited leopards come daily. No longer the most expensive bed and board in the Mara, but still a stylish way to dispose of your savings. ⑧ low, ⑨ high.

Mara Safari Club (☎0305/2172, fax 0305/2105; reservations through *Lonrho*). Very modish tented camp, co-managed with *Mount Kenya Safari Club*. Spaced out in a garden high up on a calm loop of the Mara River are forty "tents", all the last word in luxury, with four-poster beds, huge bathrooms, and verandahs with private views of the river. Hippos wallow and yawn in the chocolatey water below the camp, while monkeys rampage through the trees on the opposite bank. The site, which is outside the reserve, includes a heated swimming pool – at nearly 2000m not such a bad idea. Balloon flights and visits to Maasai villages are available. Even the low-season discounts don't reduce prices below a dramatically high ⑨ rate.

Mid-range tented camps

The following tented camps ("mid-range" is purely a relative description: nearly all are luxurious) offer optional game drives and airstrip transfers *above* their basic, full-board rates. A "package" including three game drives a day adds about $40–50 per person per day to the bill.

Fig Tree Camp (☎0305/2163; reservations through Mada Hotels, 1st Floor, Kimathi House, Kimathi St, PO Box 40683 Nairobi, ☎02/221439 or 218321, fax 02/332170). Close to the Talek Gate and just outside the boundary. This is not the most inspiring set-up but as no part of the reserve is more than 40km distant from it, it is well situated for an extended stay. There are solid-built rooms as well as tents, and a small pool. Balloon flights, microlight flights and horseback safaris are available. The friendly, on-site balloon team can always advise on the whereabouts of local wildlife. ⑦ low, ⑨ high.

Kichwa Tembo (☎0305/2465, fax 0305/2501; reservations through *Conservation Corporation*). A very highly thought-of *Abercrombie & Kent* operation and rival to nearby *Governors' Camp* with many loyal repeat guests. Deep in the trees at the foot of the Oloololo Escarpment with excellent food and a pleasant pool. Famous for its black-tie dinners. Meryl Streep and Robert Redford stayed here while filming *Out of Africa*. Due to the liveliness of the local fauna, *Kichwa Tembo* (which means "elephant's head") is fenced in. ⑦ low, ⑨ high.

Mara Buffalo Camp. In the northwest, outside the reserve, on the Mara River. Not one to visit for a casual drink or meal, as all their guests are packaged by *African Safari Club* in Europe and Canada, and they no longer take reservations in Kenya. A pretty camp, with *banda*-roofed tents ranged along the banks of the Mara, in a good game area – often noisy at night with rowdy hyenas.

Mara River Camp (☎0305/2187; reservations through *Savannah Camps and Lodges*). Just outside the reserve 3–4km north of the Mara Bridge. With more rustic facilities than most tented camps – plain but wholesome food, water heated over log fires – *Mara River Camp* is highly rated by enthusiastic naturalists and serious photographers and film-makers, but it isn't the one to choose for a honeymoon. Wandering hippos and elephants rule out the possibility of manicured gardens or a pool. ⑦ low, ⑨ high.

Oseur Tented Camp (reservations through PO Box 8114 Nairobi). A relatively new camp on a hillside outside the eastern side of the reserve, with tents arranged in groups, *manyatta*-style, each group with its own kitchen, bar and dining tent. A huge campfire is the focal point in the evenings. Pool due to be built. ⑦ low, ⑨ high.

Sarova Mara Camp (☎0305/2386 or 2194, fax 0305/2371; reservations through *Sarova*). The most accessible of all the Mara camps and lodges, on the main C12 entrance road, just inside the Sekenani Gate. Disappointing at the time of inspection – average food, dank and unwelcoming tents, gloomy public areas and neglected pool – but much-needed renovation is under way. The gardens are jungly and pleasant, with lily ponds full of fish and families of mongoose populating the shrubberies. ⑦ low, ⑨ high.

Sekenani Camp (☎0305/2454, fax 0305/2458; reservations through Campus Towers, 3rd Floor, University Way, PO Box 61542 Nairobi, ☎02/333285, fax 02/228875). On the reserve boundary, 6km southeast of Sekenani Gate. Select and highly recommended, this is the smallest camp in the Mara (ten large, very private tents, with *baths* as well as showers), and one of the newest, with a very personal approach – though the management and cuisine are both perhaps a little too *nouvelle* for the bush. No pool. ⑦ low, ⑨ high.

Siana Springs Tented Camp (☎0305/2553, fax 0305/2429; reservations through *Conservation Corporation*). On the site of the former *Cottar's Camp* (an old Kenya residents' favourite), and co-managed with *Kichwa Tembo* – same prices, similar high standards. This complete refit (a lovely pool and sultan-esque tents with every conceivable comfort) is a determined effort to reproduce an old-style mood and manners. The main advantages here – apart from the convenient location, off the main Narok entry road – are the long-established site outside the reserve, shaded by mature trees, and a good programme of walking trips in the vicinity, accompanied by a first-rate naturalist. ⑦ low, ⑨ high.

Around the reserve

Wherever you go there are **animals**. This is the one part of Kenya where the concentrations of game that existed in the last century can still be seen. The most interesting areas, scenically and zoologically, are **westwards**, signalled by the long ridge of the Oloololo Escarpment. If you only have a day or two, you should spend most of your time here, near the **Mara River**.

Unfortunately it sometimes seems that wherever there are animals there are **people** – in minibuses, in land cruisers, in hired Suzukis. This popularity is highly seasonal – it can be overbearing around Christmas – but it needn't spoil your visit. If you aren't driving yourself, encourage your tour driver to explore new areas and perhaps stress you'd rather experience the reserve in its totality than tick off animal species (provided, of course, that you would).

The reserve is crisscrossed with **tracks** but the level plains tend to encourage off-track driving. So far this hasn't had the damaging effect it has in Amboseli – the Mara's ecosystem is less fragile and there's more of it – but there are signs that a balance won't be maintained much longer: look at the stretch along the edge of the forest to the north of *Governors' Camp*. Fast **roads**, with improved, hard-core surfaces and uncrossable banks and ditches alongside, have been laid in various parts of the reserve, especially the east, and there is now an exceptionally fast route from Talek Gate to Sekenani Gate, inside the reserve. During the rains, however, and for some weeks after, the western parts of the reserve can be very wet. The bolder tracks on our maps should be passable all year round, but the smaller tracks, especially in the northwest, are often waterlogged. Here too, the crossings over the tributaries of the Talek are often impassable: if you're trying to cross the reserve at this time of year, the downstream one, close to *Mara Intrepids Club*, is the one to aim for, as the camp's Land Rovers may be able to tow you across if the water is high – an experience in a Suzuki that's slightly more exciting than most people want. It's worth noting that the **only permanent east–west route** across the Mara is the long haul via Mara New Bridge on the southern boundary.

One final point: you only have to pay fees if you go into the reserve. The wildlife roam over a vast area that extends well beyond the reserve boundaries, so if you're based outside the reserve proper, you can make economies by not entering at all. If you do want to go into the reserve, however, do so via a gate, rather than skirting the gates to avoid payment. High though the fees may seem, the alternative – spending the day watching for rangers – doesn't mix well with intensive animal viewing and simply isn't worth it (plus you'd be depriving the Maasai economy, and the reserve, of vital funds).

Visiting Maasai villages

One diversion which you are likely to be offered, especially if you are travelling on an organized safari, is a visit to a **Maasai** *enkang*, usually called, incorrectly, a *manyatta* (see boxes, p.314 and p.328). Forget about the authenticity of tribal life: this is the real world. Many children are sick, many of the young men have fled to the fleshpots, and everyone wants your money. Unprepared and uncomfortable, most visitors find the experience a deeply depressing rip-off – about $20 each in a group. If you can forget any TV-documentary illusions – and actually sit down and talk to people – the experience can be transformed and full of laughter, as it will be if you have your own children with you (see, for comparison, the accounts of similar meetings with Njemps, Samburu and Elmolo people – p.224, p.467 and p.472).

Lions

Big, brunette **lions** are the best-known denizens of the reserve and there are usually several prides living around the **Musiara Swamps**, which are dry much of the year. It is sometimes possible to watch them hunt, as they take very little notice of vehicles. We accompanied one gang of adolescent lions and lionesses for a whole afternoon, just outside the boundary. After scanning a big herd of cattle across the plain for some time, they made several attempts at some impala, chased a lone hippo into the Mara River, pounced on a warthog with a broken leg but failed to catch it, and finally surrounded an elderly buffalo in the marsh and settled down to wait for darkness. The next morning, the kill was cold and they were burrowing in the old bull's carcass like bloated maggots.

Cheetahs

While lions seem to be lounging under every other bush, finding a **cheetah** is much harder (they can often be seen on the murram mounds alongside the new Talek–Sekenani road, eyes piercing the horizon for prey). These are solitary cats – slender,

THE MAASAI AND THE MARA

After deep reflection on my people and culture, I have painfully come to accept that the Maasai must change to protect themselves, if not their culture. They must adapt to the realities of the modern world for the sake of their own survival. It is better to meet an enemy out in the open and to be prepared for him than for him to come upon you at home unawares.

Tepilit Ole Saitoti, *Maasai* (Elm Tree Books).

When the first European hunting safaris made the Mara world famous in the early years of this century, they were ransacking a region recently deserted by the **Maasai** (see also "Maasai Voices", p314). Smallpox had ravaged their communities and rinderpest had torn through their herds. The wild animals had the country virtually to themselves. Traditionally, Maasai hunted only lion and, in times of famine, eland and buffalo, the "wild cattle". Only the **Dorobo** ("people without cattle" in Maa) hunted for a living. The Maasai had always lived in some harmony with the wildlife.

By 1961, the white hunters had succeeded in bringing the lion population down to nine and, to a chorus of alarm, the Maasai Mara Game Reserve was created, to be administered by the Maasai District Council at Narok exclusively as a game sanctuary – and a tourist attraction. By then, improved medicine and veterinary facilities had eased the old hardships of the Maasai way of life. They were expanding again, and land had become the biggest issue.

Of all Kenya's peoples, the Maasai have received the most attention. Often strikingly tall and slender, dressed in brilliant red cloth, beads and metal jewellery, the young men with long, ochred hairstyles, they have a reputation for ferocity, pampered by an arch superiority complex. Traditionally, they lived off milk and blood (extracted, by a close shot with a stumpy arrow, from the jugular veins of their live **cattle**), and they loved their herds more than anything else, rarely slaughtering a beast. They maintained rotating armies of spartan warriors – the *moran* – who killed lions as a test of manhood. And they opposed all interference and invasion with swift, implacable violence. Their scorn of foreigners was absolute: they called the Europeans, who came swaddled in clothing, *iloridaa enjekat* or "those who confine their farts". They also derided African peoples who cultivated for digging the earth – the Maasai even left their dead unburied – while those who kept cattle were given grudging respect so long as they conceded that all the world's cattle were a gift from God to the Maasai, whose incessant **cattle-raiding** was thus righteous reclamation of stolen property.

Some of this noble savagery was undoubtedly exaggerated by slave- and ivory-traders, anxious to protect their routes from the Europeans. That said, the Maasai have on the whole been stubbornly conservative, with a disinclination to change their traditional ways which has tended to mark them out as the whipping boys of Kenyan development. At the same time, something close to a cult of the Maasai has been around ever since Thomson

unobtrusive and somewhat shy. When they move, their speed and agility are marvellous. If you are lucky enough to witness a kill (cynicism about such voyeurism is quickly dispelled when you find yourself on the spot), it is likely to take place in a cloud of dust, a kilometre from where the chase began. But cheetahs are vulnerable to too much harassment. Traditionally, they hunt at dawn and dusk (at the same times as tourists are hunting for photographs), but there is evidence that they are turning to a midday hunting pattern when the humans are shaded in the lodges – not a good time of day for the cheetah, which expends terrific energy in each chase and may have to give up if it goes on for more than thirty or forty seconds.

Leopards

Leopards are rarely seen by visitors, though there are plenty of them. You can give yourself a serious case of risen hair when you come across their footprints down on the

walked *Through Maasailand* in 1883. In the early years of the colony, Delamere's obsession with the people and all things Maasai spawned a new term, "Maasai-itis", and with it a motley crop of romantic notions about their ancestors alluding to ancient Romans, Egyptians and even the lost tribes of Israel.

These days, the **tourist industry** has given the Maasai a major spot in its repertoire. Maasai dancing is *the* entertainment, while necklaces, gourds, spears, shields, *rungus* (knobkerries), busts (carved by Akamba carvers) and even life-sized wooden *morani* (to be shipped home in a packing case) are the stock-in-trade of the curio and souvenir shops.

For the Maasai themselves, the rewards are fairly scant. **Cattle** are still at the heart of their society; there are dozens of names for different colours and patterns, and each animal among their three million is individually cherished. But they are assailed on all sides: by uplands farmers expanding from the north; by eviction from the tourist/conservation areas within the reserve boundaries to the south; and by a climate of opposition to the old lifestyle from all around. Sporadically urged to grow crops, go to school, build permanent houses, and generally settle down and stop being a nuisance, they face an additional dilemma in squaring these edicts with the fickle demands of the tourist industry for traditional authenticity. Few make much of a living selling souvenirs, but enterprising *morani* can do well by just posing for photos, and even better if they hawk themselves in Nairobi or down on the coast.

Many men persevere with the status of **warriorhood**, though modern Kenya makes few concessions to it. Arrested for hunting lions, and prevented from building *manyattas* for the *eunoto* transition in which they pass into elderhood, the *morani* have kept most of the superficial marks of the warrior without being able to live the life. The ensemble of a cloth tied over one shoulder, together with spear, sword, club and braided hair, is still widely seen; and after circumcision, in their early days as warriors, you can meet young men out in the bush, hunting for birds to add to their elaborate, taxidermic headdresses.

But there is considerable local frustration. When the pasture is poor, the *morani* have little compunction about driving their herds into the reserve to compete with the wildlife. All but a few of the Mara's black rhinos have been slaughtered for their horns in the last two decades. And there have even been isolated attacks on tourist vehicles.

Land is the great issue today. The Maasai have still not fully come to terms with the idea of individual *ownership* of it. "Range schemes" – plans for growing wheat or rearing cattle – are common now in Maasai-land, but they are just as likely to benefit newcomers from other parts of Kenya as the local Maasai. The lifestyle is changing: education, MPs and elections, new laws and new projects, jobs and cash, all impinge. The ubiquitous *ugali* is rapidly replacing the diet of curdled milk and cow's blood that now seems almost mythical. Many Maasai have taken work in the hotels and lodges while others end up as security guards in Nairobi. For the majority, who continue to live semi-nomadic lives among a welter of constraints, the future holds little promise.

sandbanks at the edge of the Mara River outside the reserve boundary. But they are largely nocturnal and prefer to remain well out of sight. You would have to crane your neck at a lot of trees to have much chance of seeing one. Their deep, grating roar at night – a grunt, repeated – is a sound which, once heard, you carry around with you.

Rhinos and other heavyweights

If you have a ranger with you, he's certain to know the current news about the **black rhinos** – every calf born is a victory – though finding them is often surprisingly difficult. Check out Rhino Ridge, where a handful of the reserve's surviving *faru* are sometimes obligingly positioned. There are also now a couple of **white rhinos** in the reserve, brought up from South Africa and closely guarded. They seem to be doing well.

Maasai Mara's other heavyweights are about in abundance. The Mara River surges with **hippo**, while big families of **elephant** traipse along the forest margins and spread out into the Musiara marshes when the herbage is thick and juicy. The park is home to an estimated thousand or so elephants, with another five hundred living in the districts beyond its boundaries. **Buffalo** are seen all over and can be menacing when they surround a small Jeep in a thundering herd of several hundred tons. It is the solitary old bulls that you need to watch out for – their reputation (and that of old rhinos) is not exaggerated. Tourists' vehicles get stoved in quite often, so always back off.

Lesser grunters and grazers

Among all these outstanding characters, the herds of humble grazers fade quickly into the background. It's easy to become blasé when one of the much-hyped "big five" (elephant, rhino, buffalo, lion, leopard) isn't eyeballing you at arm's length – but those are the hunter's trophies, not the photographer's. **Warthog** families like rows of dismantled Russian dolls, **zebra** and **gazelle**, odd-looking **hartebeest** and slick, purple-flanked **topi** are all scattered with abandon across the scene.

The topi are peculiarly characteristic of Maasai Mara, and there are always one or two in every herd standing sentry on a tussock or an old termite mound. Topi and **giraffe** – whose dream-like, slow-motion canter is one of the reserve's most beautiful and underrated sights – are often good pointers for predators in the vicinity. And the reserve has rare herds of **roan antelope** – swaggering, horse-sized animals with sweeping, curved horns, that you'll see elsewhere only at the Shimba Hills National Park near Mombasa or Ruma National Park near Kisii.

The wildebeest migration

It is the annual **wildebeest migration**, however, that plants Maasai Mara in the imagination. With a lemming-like instinct, finally gelled into mass movement, the herds gather in their hundreds of thousands on the withering plains of Serengeti to begin the long, streaming journey northward following the scent of moisture and green grass in the Mara. They arrive in July and August, pouring over the Sand River and into the eastern side of the reserve around *Keekorok*, gradually munching their way westwards in a milling, unsettled mass and turning south again in October. Never the most graceful of animals, wildebeest play up to their appearance with frolicsome, unpredictable behaviour, bucking like wild horses, springing like jack-in-the-boxes, or suddenly sprinting off through the herd for no apparent reason.

The **Mara River** is the biggest obstacle they come up against. Heavy rains falling up on the Mau range where the river rises can produce a sudden brown flood which claims thousands of animals as they try to cross. Like huge sheep (they are, in fact, most closely related to goats), the brainless masses swarm desperately to the banks and plunge in. Many are fatally injured on rocks and fallen branches; others are skewered by flailing legs and horns. With every surge, more bodies bob to the surface and float downstream. Heaps of bloated carcasses line the banks; injured and dying animals struggle mournfully in the mud; vultures and marabou storks squat in glazed, post-prandial stupor.

The migration's full, cacophonous impact is awesomely melodramatic – both on the plains where the multitudes graze and cavort, and at the deadly river crossings. This superabundance of meat accounts for the Mara's big lion population. Through it all, the **spotted hyenas** scamper and loiter like psychopathic sheep dogs. Half a million wildebeest **calves** are born in January and February before the migration; two out of three perish without returning to the Serengeti.

Balloon and microlight flights

From the ground, the migration of the wildebeest is a compelling phenomenon, bewildering and strangely disturbing, as you witness individual struggles and events – in particular if you have a chance to watch near one of the river crossings. From the air, in a **hot-air balloon**, it resembles an ant's nest. At around $360 per person for the sixty- to ninety-minute flight plus breakfast (cooked on the burners) with *vin mousseux*, **balloon "safaris"** are the ultimate in bush chic. Just watching the inflation and lift-off at dawn is a spectacular sight, especially at *Little Governors' Camp*, deep in the woods. And if irrepressible urges overtake you, this is probably the best place to get standing room in the basket – the balloon drifts serenely at around tree height above the Mara Triangle to the west of the river. Balloon trips are now being run by several of the larger camps and lodges, including *Serena* and *Fig Tree*. From *Keekorok*, the prevailing winds tend to carry the montgolfiers westwards and higher: fine for a grand view, but less satisfactory for animal watching. In order to avoid frightening the animals unduly, however, there is now a minimum height below which the balloons are not permitted to fly.

You don't have to be staying at the lodge they fly from: they'll come and pick you up at 5.30am. Operators include:

Balloon Safaris Ltd, for flights from *Keekorok Lodge*; reservations through PO Box 43747 Nairobi (☎ 02/502850, fax 02/501424);

Mara Balloon Safaris Ltd, for flights from *Little Governors' Camp*; reservations through *Governors' Camps*, International House, Mama Ngina St, PO Box 48217 Nairobi (☎02/331871, fax 02/726427);

Adventures Aloft, for flights from *Fig Tree Camp*; reservations through *Mada Hotels*, 1st Floor, Kimathi House, Kimathi St, PO Box 40683 Nairobi (☎02/221439 or 218321, fax 02/332170).

The latest way to enjoy the Mara from the air is to book a flight in a **microlight**. The greatest advantage of microlighting over hot-air ballooning is that you are free to take a trip at any time of day – not just at the crack of dawn. While buzzing about in a microlight can't hope to match the romance of ballooning, it's certainly an exciting airborne experience, and prices compare very reasonably – around $60 for 20 minutes, or $90 for 30 minutes (details of flights from *Fig Tree Camp* from *Adventures Aloft*, see above).

The Samburu/Buffalo Springs/Shaba National Reserves

Daily fees: each reserve $15 (students and children $5); $8–10 to camp. District warden Samburu PO Box 53 Maralal, ☎0368/2053 or 2412. Map – Survey of Kenya, Samburu and Buffalo Springs SK85 at 1cm:500m (1974).

Up in the north of the country, in the hot, arid lowlands beneath Mount Kenya, **Samburu National Reserve** was set up only twenty years ago, a tract of country around the richest stretch of the Ewaso Nyiro (Uaso Ngiro) River. In this region, the permanent water and the forest shade on the banks draw plentiful wildlife in the dry season and maintain many of the less peripatetic species year-round. While the wildlife spectacle doesn't always match that of the southern parks, the peace and scenic beauty of Samburu is unquestionable and, in the kind of mood swing which only an equatorial region can produce, the contrast with the fertile farming country of the highlands just a few kilometres to the south couldn't be more striking. In the background, the sharp hill of **Koitogor** rises in the middle of Samburu Reserve, making a useful reference point. And on the horizon, 30km to the north, looms the gaunt red block of **Ol Olokwe** mountain. Head up into the scratchy bush in the south of Buffalo Springs Reserve and the whole region is spread out before you.

Of the popular game parks, Samburu is usually reckoned the most remote and inaccessible. This has more to do with its location than with present practicalities. On the fringes of what is still called the "NFD" (Northern Frontier District), the combined Samburu/Buffalo Springs/Shaba National Reserves were closed for many years after their creation, because of the war against Somali irredentists that flared over northern Kenya in the 1960s and early 1970s.

Practicalities

In practical terms, **access** isn't difficult. If you're circling Mount Kenya, Samburu Reserve is close at hand, a couple of hours north of Nanyuki (see p.175). Buses and *matatus* run down onto the hazy plain as far as Isiolo (p.475), as does the tarmac, and, if you don't have wheels, this is normally as far as you can go without hitching, although there are one or two *matatus* which daily venture across the jolting dirt track to Archer's Post. But waiting at the Isiolo police barrier usually gets you a lift into the reserve itself in a few hours. If you're driving independently, Isiolo is a straightforward

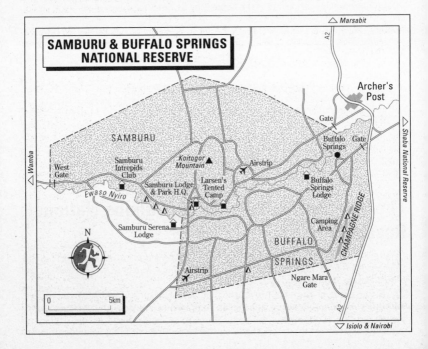

target. You'll probably be required to wait at the police checkpoint for a convoy to form for the short continuation to the reserve.

Note that the **daily fees** chargeable in each reserve apply even if you're only in transit to the other: if you enter, you pay.

Lodges and tented camps

There are six lodges/camps in the reserves. They mostly offer very good low-season rates (April to July, except Easter) at between 50 percent and 60 percent of high-season rates for doubles and dropping right down to 30 percent for singles.

Buffalo Springs Lodge (PO Box 71 Isiolo, ☎0165/2259; reservations through *AT&H*, address p.48). On the south side of the river, in the reserve of the same name. Pleasant, relaxed atmosphere and the most economical lodge accommodation available, with quite good rooms and some much cheaper *bandas*. Good game- and croc-viewing across the swamp from the bar: they bait a crocodile for the cameras, just as other lodges bait leopards. At peak periods, *Buffalo Springs* is also the one to head for as a casual visitor, if you're looking for a swim in the pool (Ksh200), a shower, a few drinks or a meal: the other lodges are likely to give you short shrift. You can also cash travellers' cheques here, but at a bad rate. ⑥ low, ⑧ high.

Larsens Tented Camp (reservations through *Block*, address p.48). East of *Samburu Lodge*, this is very upmarket and highly recommended, with game drives as part of the deal and excellent food. It doesn't take children under 7. ⑦ low, ⑨ high.

Samburu Intrepids Club (reservations through *Prestige Hotels*, address p.49). Upstream of the other lodges and camps on the north bank. Impressive, small and very luxurious development, all on stilts. Good value in this context. ⑥ low, ⑨ high.

Samburu Lodge (☎2051 Radiocall Nairobi; reservations through *Block*, address p.48). On the northern bank, beautifully located on a broad bend of the river as it passes near the Samburu Reserve headquarters, this is the oldest lodge in the reserves – with rooms of various standards and a pool – and it could do with the odd lick of paint here and there. Despite a frenetically busy atmosphere around the riverside terraces and crocodile-viewing bars, this glorious setting is hard to fault. Excellent food. Good mechanics and fuel available. ⑥ low, ⑨ high.

Samburu Serena Lodge (☎3900 Radiocall Nairobi; reservations through *Serena*, address p.50). On the south bank, just outside Buffalo Springs Reserve. Well managed, with a good pool and great food. ⑦ low, ⑨ high.

LEOPARDS AT SAMBURU

Samburu's **leopards** are a regular sight – at least from the terraces at *Samburu* and *Samburu Serena* lodges, both of which have taken to baiting the trees on the opposite banks with haunches of meat. Between drinks and dinner, guests get a floodlit view of the stealthy predator reduced to a giant pussycat. The stampede for cameras doesn't encourage the leopards to stay long, so efforts are made to attach the meat firmly to the tree. It's all pathetically contrived (and you can forget worthwhile pictures or videos at that distance without expensive equipment), but only with luck or dogged persistence will you see a wild leopard other than in such circumstances, and it's hard to blame the hotels for making the most of the local attractions. You should beware, at *Samburu Lodge*, of occasional excursions by the leopards across the river to the human zoo. Several recent sightings on the lodge grounds have been reported early in the evening; hence the signs warning "Do not stray beyond the lit path".

Recent research has shown how little is really known about these cats. For the most part, they live off any small animals that come their way. The popular notion that they consume many baboons is apparently wrong: baboon troops will turn on an attacking leopard instantly and, unless surprised, usually manage to fend it off. Less organized monkeys of all kinds, however, are often caught, and in Samburu (for those leopards not on the lodge gravy train), the favourite hunting grounds are the stands of forest and clumps of strange, branching doum palms by the river – these sometimes shake with monkeys. Black-faced vervet and blue monkeys are the commonest inhabitants.

Sarova Shaba Lodge (reservations through *Sarova*, address p.50). Downstream on Ewaso Nyiro River in the otherwise empty Shaba Reserve. Immaculate and very attractively landscaped, with a superb swimming pool (Ksh345 for visitors) and streams running through public areas (though the thick vegetation obscures views of big animals). Mosquito-netted rooms with fans. High standards of food and service. Petrol available. ⑦ low, ⑧ high.

Campsites

There are **campsites** in Buffalo Springs Reserve, not far from the first gate, Ngere Mara, but this Champagne Ridge camping area has a nasty reputation for robberies. If you do stay here, you're strongly advised to take up the offer of night guards which the rangers will probably make – or insist upon. The camp is near the main road and visits by intruders are common. As usual, you also face the hassle of having to pack your tent each day before setting off on the animal trail. If you don't have a vehicle, being dropped off at Champagne Ridge could prove painful if nobody turned up to give you a ride out again. Still, it's a pretty area among the acacias, and it abounds with giraffe and other animals.

Three other sites, without anything much in the way of facilities, lie just to the west of the Ewaso Nyiro Bridge, barely a kilometre from the lodge and park HQ. There are a further four "special campsites" – three strung out along the north bank of the river in Samburu Reserve, with the last one by the Maji ya Chumvi Stream in Buffalo Springs Reserve – which are reportedly equipped with showers and toilets. These need to be reserved in advance (try the warden), and prices are vague and perhaps negotiable.

Initially, the best move for the wheel-less is to get to the area of *Samburu Lodge* and **camp near the park headquarters**: not a wonderful site, with no toilets or running water (and the lodge may even make you pay for that commodity), but convenient and legal, if somewhat unhygienic. You can walk to the lodge's riverside bars and restaurant (though if after 6.30pm, get an escort: there are animals everywhere), sometimes flop in the pool (depending on circumstances and numbers: it's occasionally restricted to guests), gloat over the crocodiles in the river below, and peer darkly through binoculars at the regular but brief evening cabaret of leopards retrieving bait from a tree on the far bank. If your finances stretch, you can shell out $30 or so for a two-hour morning or evening game run in one of the lodge's land cruisers, or around $115 for the whole vehicle. Most people camping here without their own vehicles seem to manage to find the occasional ride around the reserve, if only because the opportunities exist to meet travellers with their own transport over a drink.

Note that the baboons at the campsite here are beyond being an amusement. Leave your tent and its contents only under guard. The fact that baboons sometimes fall shrill victims to crocs at the water's edge seems less distressing after a day or two spent in the area.

Exploring the reserves

The terrain makes off-track driving difficult in most parts, which may account for the lack of shyness of many animals. Except during and immediately after the rains, scrubby bush country takes up most of the reserve district, but there are some large acacia thickets, especially in the eastern part of Buffalo Springs. Here, **the springs** themselves are a welcome target; there are pools of clear if weedy water, one of which has been sanitized with concrete for the benefit of swimmers and (most of the time) the exclusion of crocodiles: it's always a good idea to check before diving in. *Buffalo Springs Lodge*, a few kilometres away, is low-key and always welcoming for a drink. There's a fine jungly marsh reaching nearly to the terrace, where you'll often see animals.

If Samburu's **wildlife** is occasionally disappointing, it may be fairer to say that the dry country ecosystems are prone to large variations in animal populations as they move in search of water and pasture. Some visitors have tremendous luck and it can provide consistently excellent animal-watching. The best areas, recently, are along the south side of the river in Buffalo Springs Reserve, close to *Samburu Lodge*. Poaching has wiped out the rhino here, but lions are often seen, again, most often in Buffalo Springs.

Meanwhile, the locally burgeoning **elephant herds** have ruined some sections of the riverine forest. The range of rarer, and localized, races and species compensates, though. Among these, the **reticulated giraffe** with its beautiful jigsaw marking; **Grevy's zebra**, the large, finely striped species that has a bushy mane and outsize ears; **Somali ostrich**, which has blue rather than pink legs; and **gerenuk** ("camel head" in Somali), the antelope species that stands on its hind legs to reach the foliage which it feeds upon, are all common and conspicuous. Samburu's **birdlife** is diverse, and prolific if you look for it.

Shaba

Across the rutted surface of the Marsabit road lies the **Shaba National Reserve** (more fees to pay), the third of the Samburu district reserves. Unfortunately, if *Sarova*'s grandiose lodge is not within your budget, you'll have to leave the park by nightfall, as the only alternative accommodation near the main gate – the *Shaba Tented Camp* – has recently closed down and the reserve is otherwise still blissfully undeveloped. But for animals, it's rated the equal of its two neighbours and its **springs** mean that it is better watered. If you can put up with the intense heat, the scenery provides spectacular compensation and the animal-watching is good – with lots of elephants, plains game, jackals and a few lions. This was the area where Joy Adamson experimented with the release of hand-reared **leopards**. So, if you're mobile and have a day to spare, Shaba is highly recommended and it's certainly much less visited than Samburu or Buffalo Springs.

Meru National Park

Daily fee $20 (students $10, chidren $5); $8 to camp ($10 in a "special" campsite); warden PO Box 434 Meru, ☎0164/0613. Map – Survey of Kenya SK65 at 1cm:1km (1978).

You don't see **Meru National Park** on many safari itineraries. Of the main parks covered in this chapter, it is least visited, most obviously untrampled, unspoiled and pristine. Abundantly traversed by **streams** flowing into the Tana River on its southern boundary, and luxuriantly rained upon, the rolling **jungle** of tall grass, riverine forest and swamp is lent a hypnotic, other-worldly quality by wonderful stands of prehistoric-looking **doum palms**; and with the high cover they provide, you can never be certain of what's going to be around the next corner.*

True, the animals aren't always as much in evidence here as they can be in some other Kenyan wildlife parks, but the even more noticeable absence of minibuses and land cruisers in Meru more than compensates. After visiting some of the less bushy parks, where the animals can be spotted from miles away, Meru's intimate, unusual

---

*What you should no longer fear round the next corner are the gangs of armed Somalian poachers who, in 1988 and 1989, virtually ruled the park. During their bloody tenure, two French tourists were shot dead when they unwittingly drove into a poachers' hideout. Such was the international outcry that followed their murder, and that of George Adamson in the adjoining Kora National Park a few months later, that the Kenya government made a huge and successful effort to rout them.

336/THE MOMBASA ROAD AND MAJOR GAME PARKS

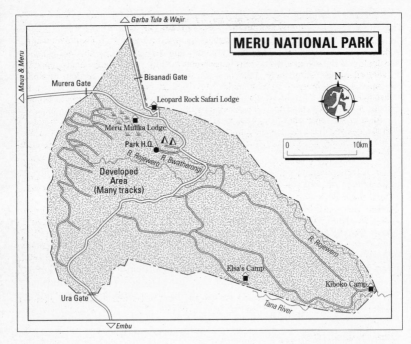

landscape is quickly entrancing. Most of the time you really are alone in this surreal wilderness.

Meru is the area where the Adamsons released their most famous lioness **Elsa** back into the wild, and where their later series of experiments with orphaned cheetahs was cut short by the murder of Joy Adamson. Until 1988, the biggest wildlife attraction in the park was its precariously-surviving herd of **white rhino** – huge, instantly appealing animals that had the full-time attention of a team of rangers employed to protect them.

Getting there and accommodation

Getting to Meru National Park without your own vehicle isn't easy. From Meru town (see p.178), the last fuel and supplies (there's no fuel in the park) are in **Maua**, one hour's drive into the **Nyambeni Hills** on a pretty, paved road, with steep tea terraces and plantations of *miraa*. Maua, or rather about 3km up the hill before it at the junction, is where you'll have to wait for a lift if you are determined to try and reach the park by **hitching**. There's a hotel at the junction, where you might be lucky with a lift, but you could stand for days without getting one. Maua itself has the *Maua Hotel* and *Silent Lodge* – both cheap and pleasant enough. *Matatus* run as far as Kiangu – a third of the way between Maua and the park gate – several times a day.

Murera Gate is about 30km from Maua, down a red murram road – the condition of which is sometimes diabolical – with magnificent scenery over your shoulder as you go: the Nyambenis towering above exotic *shambas* of bananas, sugar and corn; and the sky, as often as not, a gaudy cloud-mural of gathering storms. Gradually, as you

---

THE RHINOS' TALE

Until November 1, 1988, you could always guarantee a close encounter with **white rhinos** – close enough to see how they got the name, from the Afrikaans *weit* (meaning wide), a reference to their lugubrious grass-cropping mouths. Morning and evening, the five docile beasts were gently prodded out to graze around the park headquarters and campsites, then brought back at midday to the dust-wallow of their pen to snooze through the heat. The thousands of pounds' worth of horn that they carried on their noses ensured they could never be left unguarded.

All of this simply wasn't enough to keep them alive. Full details have never emerged of what happened, but a gang of about thirty poachers, armed with automatic rifles, stormed the rhinos' night-time paddock, killing all five, injuring several rangers and escaping with the booty of hacked-off horns.

Meru's location is dangerous; given evidence that Somalian poachers were mainly responsible for the carnage that tore through the eastern parks in the late 1980s, it seems doubtful whether the park will be chosen for any future attempts to resettle the white rhino in Kenya. Several of the staff at Meru lost their jobs.

The white rhino has been extinct in Kenya since prehistoric times and the nucleus of the group at Meru came from Umfolozi Game Reserve in South Africa. There are still some white rhinos in private sanctuaries, the best-known of which is Solio Ranch (p.191). Unlike black rhinos, they are remarkably good-natured animals. The head keeper of the Meru herd used to encourage visitors to pet them and even sit on them when they were lying down.

---

descend, the scene gives way to the lank grass, termite cathedrals and the scattered trees and streams that characterize the park's savannah.

Meru Mulika Lodge

If there's time left in the day, follow the signs to *Meru Mulika Lodge*, where you can soak in the pool (small fee if you're not staying) or stretch out on the terrace in front of the verdant **Mulika Swamp** and watch elephants, oryxes, ostriches and others. The place seems paradisiacal. However, the lodge itself – formerly a delightful, unpretentious hide-away – has become simply down-at-heel. With virtually no custom for several years now – and none at all from the big package operators – it's ticking towards dereliction, with poor food and service, cracked tiles and ripped mosquito nets. They have no fuel supplies here and guests are often asked to sell them any surplus petrol they may have . . . If you're determined to brave it out and extract what comfort you can (it always was, and still is, one of the cheapest game lodges in the country; PO Box 273 Maua, ☎0164/20000; ⑤ low, ⑦ high), you can reserve through *Msafiri Inns* (address on p.49) – although it's very likely that the lodge will have been sold, or even closed, by the time you read this.

Budget accommodation

The real **budget accommodation** is further into the park, near the headquarters. Down here, on a stretch of open ground running down to a wooded stream, are several plain campsites, a handful of cottages/*bandas* (④) and toilet and shower blocks. Firewood is plentiful. A third option might be *Leopard Rock Safari Lodge*, which may have reopened by the time you read this (information through PO Box 45456 Nairobi, ☎02/742926; or through *Let's Go Travel*, address p.122). Before its latest closure, this was an excellent-value *banda* establishment with everything you might need: electricity, warm showers, mosquito nets and fully equipped bush kitchens including fridges. Behind the site, the Leopard Rock is occasionally visited by lions, not leopards, while in front a foliage-entangled stream contains crocodiles.

Exploring the park

Meru's many tracks are mostly sandy and firm; the junctions have useful signposts (useful as long as you have the *Survey of Kenya* map); and the whole park is uncontaminated by tourism. You're no longer required to take a ranger with you on your explorations unless you want to go southeast of the main track around the "developed area". The tracks to "Elsa's Camp" and "Kiboko Camp" are in bad shape: you're advised not to go down to the Tana River and some tracks are physically blocked off.

There are still plenty of enticing areas to investigate. The **Rojewero River**, the park's largest stream, is an interesting watercourse for exploring: densely overgrown banks flash with birds and monkeys and dark waters ripple with turtles. Large and very visible herds of **elephant, buffalo** and **reticulated giraffe** are common, as are, in the more open areas, **gerenuk, Grevy's zebra** and **ostrich**. Predators seem scarce, though they may simply be hidden in the long grass – the smaller grazers must have a nerve-wracking time of it here. Large numbers of **leopards** captured in the stock-raising lands of Laikipia have been released in the park in recent years, but as usual you have little chance of seeing them.

Onwards to the Tana River

Kora National Park and the three national reserves south and east of Meru – **Bisanadi, North Kitui** and **Rahole** – are all in the Land Rover expedition category, a total of 4500 square kilometres of scrub and semi-desert, and the Tana's dense forest where they fringe the river. With the right vehicle and preparations, it would be possible, in theory, to follow the Tana down to Garissa (p.493). **Mbalambala**, about halfway there, is a highly rated place for seeing hippo and crocodile.

Regrettably, with the current bad security of the area, such a trip would be ill advised and, unless you were to flout roadblocks and official advice, probably impossible; permission to visit the park and reserves needs to be obtained from KWS's HQ in Langata by Nairobi National Park. Furthermore, the track along the river was washed out several years ago and has still to be replaced.

Kora was the home of George Adamson (of *Born Free* fame), murdered by poachers or illegal cattle-herders in August 1989 when he drove through their barricade. The reserve was promptly upgraded to National Park status, but Adamson's grave was subsequently desecrated.

travel details

BETWEEN NAIROBI AND THE COAST

Road and rail details for the main Nairobi–Mombasa route are given in Chapters 1 and 6. For **Voi**, see p.294. **From Machakos,** *Akamba Bus* and several other companies make frequent runs to Nairobi. In the other direction, the last bus leaves Nairobi at 4pm and goes through to Kitui. **From Kitui,** most buses leave for Nairobi in the morning. Transport to Embu and the Garissa road is difficult. **Mombasa-bound,** there are buses daily through Machakos and at least one come through Kitui. To **Taveta,** there are country buses on most days from Nairobi through Emali and Oloitokitok and others through **Voi**.

SUMMARY OF PARKS ACCESS

The following notes summarize the easiest access to each park if you are not driving. For further details on flights to Tsavo West, Amboseli, Maasai Mara and Samburu, see Nairobi "travel details" (p.155). Remember to buy maps for any parks you'll be visiting before setting out from Nairobi.

Tsavo West National Park: Mtito Andei Gate

Mtito Andei town is reached from Nairobi or Mombasa by bus, *matatu*, hitching or train. The gate, five minutes' walk from the town centre, is worth hitching from. Weekly flights (Fri) from Nairobi Wilson Airport to *Finch Hatton's*, returning Sun.

Tsavo East National Park: Voi Gate

Voi town is easily reached from Nairobi or Mombasa by bus, *matatu*, hitching or train. The gate is a one-hour walk from the town centre and worth hitching.

Amboseli National Park: Namanga

To Namanga town, daily bus services from the Nairobi country bus station, fairly frequent *matatus* and hitching also possible. From the town to Namanga Gate there are occasional *matatus*, or you can hitch. Flights from Nairobi Wilson airport land in the centre of the park.

Maasi Mara National Reserve: Narok

Several country buses daily, some *matatus*, but hitching very slow and lifts into the park rare. Sekenani Gate in the eastern part of the reserve offers the easiest access. Flights from Nairobi Wilson airport call at the Mara airstrips as required.

Samburu-Buffalo Springs-Shaba National Reserves: Isiolo

No lack of transport to Isiolo, and lifts into the reserve from Isiolo are quite possible, even likely. Flights into Samburu from Nairobi Wilson airport.

Meru National Park: Meru or Maua

Public transport to Meru town is straightforward, but lifts from town into the park are unlikely.

CHAPTER SIX

THE COAST

Nearly everyone arrives on the coast at **Mombasa**, a much more enjoyable place to spend time than Nairobi. Kenya's second city, this is a tropical centre *par excellence*: steamy, lazy, at times unbelievably dilapidated, but genial. To the north and south there are superb **beaches** and a number of pockets of tourist development – the resort strip to the immediate north of the city is the busiest – but the coast is not yet highly developed in the Florida or Spanish *costa* sense. For many visitors (and this is one area where inexpensive package tourism has really taken off) the resort areas represent little more than sun, sea, sand and, even in the post-AIDS era, sex. You can, of course, have a wonderful time on the beaches doing nothing very much, but there's much more to this part of Kenya than some travel brochures might have you believe – and plenty to do if total lassitude drives you nuts after a few days.

Most obviously, the beaches are the launch pad for one of the most beautiful **coral reefs** in the world, rated in the top three by experienced divers, along with Australia's Barrier Reef and the Red Sea. With breathing apparatus you can do some spectacular dives, including night dives and wreck dives, but with even the most limited equipment – a snorkel and mask (or "goggles"), easily obtained almost anywhere – you can still enter what really is another world, either taking a boat or swimming out to discover sections of reef for yourself. The three most spectacular zones, enclosed in **marine national parks**, are far to the south off Wasini Island, the area between Watamu and Malindi, and in the extreme north, off Kiwaiyu Island.

The string of **islands** that runs up the coast – the main ones being Wasini, Funzi, Chale, Mombasa itself, Lamu, Manda, Pate, Kiwaiyu – are all worth visiting. Apart from their beach and ocean attractions, most of them have some archeological interest, which is also a constant theme on the mainland: the whole coast is littered with the **ruins** of forts, mosques, tombs and even whole towns. Some of these – including **Fort Jesus**, **Lamu** and the ruined town of **Gedi** – are already on the tourist circuit, but there are dozens that have hardly been cleared or investigated and they make for compelling exploration. Fort Jesus Museum in Mombasa has a map of locations.

Nature and wildlife
The hundreds of kilometres of sandy beach that fringe the low-lying coastal strip are backed by dunes and coconut palms, traversed by scores of streams and rivers. Flowing off the plateaus through tumbling jungle, these waterways meander across a

---

ACCOMMODATION PRICE CODES

Rates for a standard double or twin room. For a full explanation of these price codes, see p.46

① Under Ksh300	(under approx. £3.30/$5)	⑤ Ksh2000–4000	(£22/$33–£44/$67)
② Ksh300–500	(£3.30/$5–£5.50/$8)	⑥ Ksh4000–6000	(£44/$67–£67/$100)
③ Ksh500–1000	(£5.50/$8–£11/$17)	⑦ Ksh6000–8000	(£67/$100–£89/$133)
④ Ksh1000–2000	(£11/$17–£22/$33)	⑧ Ksh8000–10,000	(£89/$133–£111/$167)
	⑨ Over Ksh10,000	(over £111/$167)	

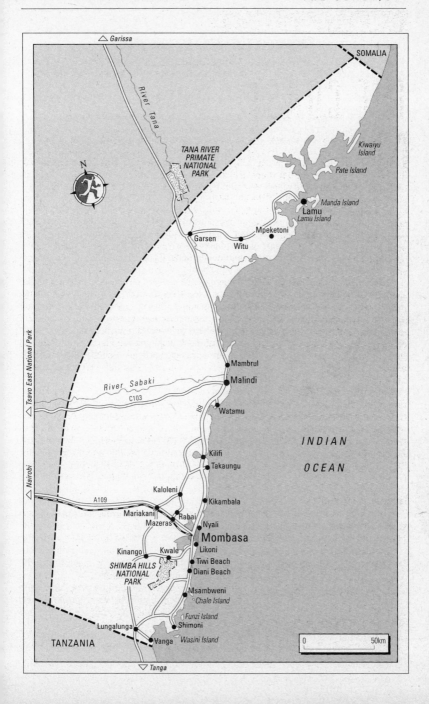

ISLAM AND RAMADAN

Islam has been a major influence on the coast and the annual month of fasting – *Ramadan* (see p.59 for dates) – is widely observed. Visiting the coast during **Ramadan** might leave a slightly strange impression of a region where everyone is on night shift perhaps, but in practical terms it usually makes little difference. If you're travelling on a budget, it can sometimes be difficult to track down a cheap room during the day, if only because everything appears to be closed, but you can usually find a lax restaurant serving food, and you'll do most of your eating after dark in any case. During *Id ul Fitr*, at the end of Ramadan, and *Maulidi al Nebi*, the holiday for the prophet's birthday, lodgings often fill up early.

narrow, fertile plain to the sea. In sheltered creeks, forests of **mangrove** trees cover vast areas and create a distinctive ecological zone of tidal mud flats.

Wildlife on the coast is in keeping with the region's lush, intimate feel. The big game of up-country Kenya is more or less absent (though Shimba Hills National Park near Mombasa is an exception), but smaller creatures are abundant. Monkeys are especially common, with troops of baboons regularly seen by the road and Vervet and Sykes' monkeys frequently at home in hotel gardens. Birdlife is prolific – if you suspect you may harbour even a mild interest you should make a point of bringing binoculars. On the reptile front, snakes – brilliant disguise artists – are rarely seen, but lizards skitter everywhere, including upside down on the ceiling at night, and bug-eyed chameleons waver across the road, sometimes making it to the other side. So do giant millipedes, up to thirty centimetres long, harmless scavengers of rotten fruit and known as Mombasa Expresses after the well-known slow train. Insects, including some fierce mosquitoes, are here in full force. But most, including the glorious butterflies of the Jadini and Arabuko-Sokoke forests, are attractive participants in the coast's gaudy show.

Transport to the coast

For getting to the coast, the **train journey** between Nairobi and Mombasa is one of the highlights of Kenyan travel: even if you usually drive, you should try to make at least one journey between capital and coast with *Kenya Railways* (see the section on trains in *Basics* on p38). Although it has faltered since a disastrous accident in 1993, the institution of leisured rail travel is still well preserved here. With just one service a day in each direction, at 7pm, the carriages (some of them ancient British-built ones) are spotless and the service usually impeccable. Couples can only share a first-class compartment, as the four-berth second-class compartments are single-sex. The following morning, the sun comes up as the train nears Mombasa, winding down the steep scarp from arid semi-desert to jungly coast. Arriving in Nairobi, you can breakfast across the Athi plains, passing Nairobi National Park with the chance to see some game.

Buses from Nairobi to Mombasa offer a big saving on the train and go by day as well as night, but most of the road is dull and the experience not as much fun as the train. For coverage of the route, see Chapter 5.

You can also **fly** to Mombasa, Malindi or Lamu from Nairobi. Flying to Lamu from Nairobi makes sense if you have the cash (about Ksh6700; see Nairobi "Travel Details") and not much time, as you avoid retracing your steps between Lamu and Mombasa, but it's not an interesting flight. If you'd like to fly for the fun of it, the Malindi–Lamu hop (see "Travel Details" at the end of this chapter) costs only Ksh3900 and gives stunning views over jungle and reef. For details on flying into Mombasa's Moi International Airport, see p.346.

Coast practicalities

There are four main **resort** areas – three to the north and one to the south. The suburban district north of Mombasa, consisting of **Nyali**, **Bamburi**, **Mtwapa** and almost merging into **Kikambala**, is the first, often known as "North Coast"; further north comes **Watamu**, about two hours from Mombasa; and lastly **Malindi**, twenty minutes beyond Watamu. Along the "South Coast", south of Mombasa, **Diani Beach**, forty minutes' drive from the city, is the principal focus. Apart from the odd small development, the rest of the coast is virtually untouched.

The coast is the part of Kenya most affected by the **seasons**. April, May and June are much less busy, and much cheaper, than the rest of the year. While the beaches tend to be damp and the weather muggy and overcast, you can make large savings on package holidays or, if you're travelling independently, reduce your hotel costs by as much as fifty percent.

As an alternative to hotels, you can stay in **self-catering villas, apartments and cottages**. There are various options along the beaches north of Mombasa, at Malindi and at Tiwi and Diani beaches, and it's a very sound financial proposition for families or groups. *Kenya Villas*, PO Box 57046, Westminster House, Kenyatta Ave, Nairobi (☎02/338072), act as agents for many holiday home-owners. Large houses, to sleep eight for example, can be had for under Ksh3000 a night.

One word of warning: tempting as it can be, **sleeping out**, except on the most deserted of beaches, is very unwise. Although the reputation of some areas for daylight theft and more grievous assaults is unfairly exaggerated, to sleep out anywhere near Mombasa or Malindi is asking for trouble – you'll have to find a room or pitch up at one of the handful of recognized campsites.

MOMBASA AND AROUND

Arriving in **Mombasa** by plane or train in the morning, there's ample time, if the heat doesn't fell you, to head straight out to the beaches. But you should consider spending a day or two in Mombasa itself, tuning in to the coast, catching the cadences of "Kiswahili *safi*" (pure Swahili) and looking around Kenya's most historic city. If you have time, there are two worthwhile trips you can make inland to areas that are much less known: **Shimba Hills National Reserve** to the southwest and, well off the beaten path to the northwest, the **Mijikenda country** between Mazeras and Kaloleni. If you would rather take this latter detour before reaching the coast proper – and it's a pleasant introduction to the region – buses from Nairobi will drop you at **Mazeras** (see p.374), a simple hitchhike or bus ride away from Mombasa.

Mombasa

Kenya's second city can come as a revelation. There's a depth of history here, and a sense of community which Nairobi lacks. Sleazy, hot – you're always thirsty – and

CULTURE SHOCK

If you've not been to Africa before, flying into Mombasa and merely driving through the suburbs to your hotel throws you into the place more quickly than arriving in Nairobi's cosmopolitan embrace. Some level of culture shock – from the poverty, the noise and the up-frontness of everything, all melting in the heat – is perhaps to be expected. But for most people it's not a shock that lasts long.

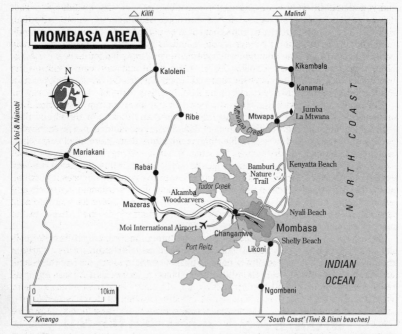

physically tropical in a way that could hardly be more different from Nairobi, **MOMBASA** is the slightly indolent hub of the coast – a faded, flaking, even occasionally charming city that still feels, despite its gentle sprawl, like a small town that was once great.

Mombasa is actually an island, connected to the mainland by two causeways to the west, and by a bridge to the north, but still linked only by ferry to the south. The city is intricate and its streets wriggle deceptively. At its most appealing heart is the **Old Town**, a lattice of lanes, mosques and cramped, elderly houses sloping gently down to the once-busy dhow harbour. **Fort Jesus**, an impressive reminder of Mombasa's complicated, bloody past, still overlooks the Old Town from where it once guarded the harbour entrance. It is now a national monument and museum.

Clustered all around you, within easy walking distance, is the whole expanse of downtown, twentieth-century Mombasa, with its wide streets and a refreshing lack of high-rise buildings. While you won't doubt it's a chaotic city – there's only one remaining set of working traffic lights, and every once in a while you'll question how a million people can manage without a predictable water supply or a functioning city council – the atmosphere, even in the commercial centre of one of Africa's busiest ports, is invariably relaxed and congenial. Rush hours, urgency and paranoia seem to be Nairobi's problems (as everyone here will tell you), not Mombasa's. And the gaping, marginal slums that one expects to find outside African cities hardly exist here. True, Likoni and especially Changamwe, on the mainland, are burgeoning suburbs that the municipality has more or less abandoned, but the brutalizing conditions of the Mathare Valley and Kibera shantytowns in Nairobi are absent.

Despite the palms, the sunshine and the happy languor, all is not bliss and perfection: **street crime**, though it hardly approaches Nairobi's level, is a serious problem, and you should be wary of displaying your valuables or accepting invitations to walk down dark alleys. But, as a general rule, Mombasa is a far less neurotic city than Nairobi. There's nowhere in the centre that could be considered a no-go area. One indication of this is that the city stays awake much later. Climatic considerations may partly explain it, but, at an hour when central Nairobi is empty but for taxis and *askaris*, Mombasans are to be seen strolling in the warm night, old men conversing on the benches in Digo Road, and many shops are still open. The small-town freedoms remain healthy here and it all adds up to a city that is richly satisfying and rewarding to stay in.

Ethnically, Mombasa is perhaps even more diverse than Nairobi. Asian and Arab influence is particularly pervasive, with fifty mosques and dozens of Hindu and Sikh temples lending a strongly oriental flavour. Still, the largest contingent speaks Swahili as a first language and it is the **Swahili civilization** that, more than any other, accounts for Mombasa's distinctive character. You'll see women wearing head-to-foot *bui-buis* or brilliant *kanga* outfits, men decked out in *kanzu* gowns and hip-slung *kikoi* wraps. The smaller community of settlers and European expatriates figures less prominently here than in Nairobi, but it continues to wield disproportionate economic and social clout. For up-country settlers, Mombasa and the coast have long represented "sea level and sanity" – a holiday break from the grind of making a living in the highlands.

As a tourist town, Mombasa doesn't go out of its way. Indeed, one of its best qualities is its utter lack of pretension. It is principally a port: **Kilindini**, with a harbour recently dredged by the Americans, takes up most of the western side of the island. Increasingly, too, Mombasa is an industrial city, boasting one of East Africa's major oil refineries (on your right as you arrive by train). In short, Mombasa is not a resort. Visiting sailors are as important to its tourist economy as bona fide tourists, and (a grievous shortcoming) the island has no real beaches. Even the biggest hotels in town are relatively modest. The vast majority of the obvious tourists that you'll see around the place are here only for the purpose of a shopping trip from their north- or south-coast beach hotels. You may not be able to resist the lure of the beaches for too long, but Mombasa deserves a little of your time unless you are in a big hurry; there are few places in the country with such a strong sense of identity.

Arrival and information

Arriving on the night **train** from Nairobi is the best way: it loops down the steep scarp to the ocean as you wake up to the rustle of starched waiters and the clatter of shiny teapots. When you walk out of the station into the glare of the morning sun, **Haile Selassie Road** is directly ahead, leading in one straight kilometre to the city's main north–south thoroughfare, **Digo Road**. The **Old Town** begins on the far side of Digo Road. To the left of Haile Selassie are markets and bus stations; to the right, a concentration of hotels; then, parallel to it, **Moi Avenue** – the tourist strip. If you pick a taxi out of the swarm awaiting the train's arrival, Ksh100 is about the going rate to be taken to any town-centre hotel, no more than a five-minute ride.

Arrival by road

Arriving by **bus or car from Nairobi**, first impressions can be dismal. You come over the Makupa Causeway with the railway, then diverge from it on the island to head 4km straight down **Jomo Kenyatta Avenue**. Shabby is the adjective that comes irresistibly to mind as you bump down this erstwhile showcase avenue: a scene of broken windows, crumbling facades and out-of-date hoardings smothers the street from its inception, via the triumphalist Independence Roundabout (almost in ruins), to its final disintegration in the diesel-laden environment of the Mwembe Tayari bus parks. If you

COASTAL CULTURE: THE SWAHILI

The coast is where East Africa meets the classical world. Partly through the intermediary of **Islam**, with its direct and simple tenets, foreign ideas have shaped the society, language, literature and architecture. More than the pragmatic Portuguese, whose interests seem to have been entirely mercenary, immigrants and traders from Arabia and Asia – once or twice even China – have been a subtle and gradual influence on the coast. They would arrive each year in March or April on the northeast **monsoon**, the dry *kaskazi* wind, and return in September on the southerly monsoon or *kusi*.

Some, by choice or mishap, would be left behind. Through intermarriage from the earliest times (even before Islam appeared on the scene in the seventh century), a distinct ancient civilization called **Swahili** emerged. Swahili, which is thought to derive from the same Arabic root as *sahel*, meaning edge or coast, is also a language, known to its speakers as **ki-Swahili**. It is one of the more mainstream of the Bantu languages, which are spoken throughout much of Africa south of the equator. Like all old languages used by trading peoples, Swahili contains strong clues about whom they mixed with. Despite popular misconception, Swahili isn't based on Arabic any more than English is derived from Latin, but it is full of words derived from Arabic and peppered with others of Indian, Portuguese and English origin.

The Swahili are not a "tribe" in any definable sense. Who they are should emerge throughout this chapter. No less than, say, Americans, they are the result of the mixed heritage reflected in their language. Questions of family background and status in the community have traditionally loomed large: families that trace their roots – not always very plausibly – to foreign shores in the distant past tend to claim superior social status. Nor, predictably, was skin colour ignored. Essentially Muslim, the Swahili interpretation of the religion varies from place to place and according to circumstance: rigidity of form is an alien concept in Swahili culture. Essentially coastal, not all Swahili trade, nor do they all fish – some Swahili groups even avoid eating fish. Coconuts, mixed farming, cattle and goats are all vitally important.

THE TOWNS

Like the language, it was long thought that the **towns** of the coast began as implants, that is, as Arab, or even Persian, trading forts. It is now known that most were already in existence before any of the great post-Islamic wars and migrations took place in the Middle

---

get out at Mwembe Tayari, walk on down Kenyatta to Digo Road and your mood should lift a little.

Arriving **by road from Dar-es-Salaam**, you first reach the swarming suburb of Likoni, where you take the ferry to Mombasa island (5-min crossing, every 10–15min; passengers free, cars Ksh25). Be **warned**: in recent years there have been increasingly frequent incidents of muggings and sneak-theft around the ferry, usually at dusk. Keep an eye on your vehicle windows while waiting in line and, if you walk onto the ferry while someone else drives the vehicle aboard, leave your valuables inside: there's evidence to suggest that one or two gangs are targeting people just as the ferry is about to depart, giving them the advantage over passengers who risk being stranded.

Note, if you're driving into Mombasa, that there's rarely any problem **parking**. There are lots of parking bays, some with meters (charges nominal), around the intersection of Digo Road and Moi Avenue. Don't, of course, leave anything valuable unattended in the car.

Arrival by air

By air, you arrive some 10km from the city centre at **Moi International Airport** on the mainland near Port Reitz. Try to change into cool clothes before arrival – essential

East. Mombasa, Malindi, Lamu and a host of lesser-known settlements are essentially ancient African towns that have always tolerated and even encouraged peaceful immigration from overseas. The Swahili style has always been to welcome the new and the sophisticated.

With few exceptions, however, any attempt to compromise the independence of these towns was met with violent resistance. The Portuguese were the least successful. When they arrived at the end of the fifteenth century, cultural memories of the Moorish occupation of their own country were still fresh. Accommodation to Islam, or to dark-skinned strangers, was not on their agenda and, despite a long acquaintance with the coast, they never established an enduring colonial presence, as they did in Goa on the south Indian coast, further along the same trading route.

THE SLAVE INHERITANCE

Slavery on the coast was originally less a black and white moral issue than is commonly assumed. In the past, it was not unusual for people in need to "lend" a member of the family to others in exchange for goods or services. The **Mijikenda peoples** (see p.375 for more background), for example, maintained close links with the coastal towns, trading their produce, providing armed forces when the towns were under threat, and being supplied in return with overseas trade goods, especially cloth and tools. As traders, the Swahili sometimes accumulated surpluses of grain on the coast at times of severe drought inland. In exchange for food supplies, Mijikenda children would be taken to the towns by their relatives and fostered with Swahili families with whom they had links – to become, in effect, slaves. Later, the children intermarried, or paid off the debt and returned, though a small number were probably sold overseas. But when slavery itself became a major aspect of commerce, and the available foreign goods irresistible (cloth, firearms and liquor from Holland, France, England and America), then any trace of trust in the old arrangement vanished. The weak and defenceless were captured and sold to slavers from the coast, often to end up on Dutch or French plantations around the Indian Ocean or in Arabian households. And, with the domination of the **Sultan of Oman** on the coast in the early nineteenth century, and the large-scale emigration of Arabs to East Africa, slaves from the far interior were increasingly set to work on their truly colonial coastal farms and plantations. When the British formally freed the slaves in 1907, they became part of Swahili society.

if you're being picked up from the airport and going straight on safari – as there's really nowhere to do it at the airport. Although the shabby building routinely swarms with the newly arrived and the soon-to-depart, the staff stay admirably cool and formalities are carried out with a minimum of fuss: passport checks take seconds. The luggage carousels seem to work more often than not and reports of items going missing are rare. As at Nairobi, before being allowed on your way, or to meet your holiday representative, you'll usually be gently quizzed about video camcorders, radios, electrical equipment and so on, and also about gifts for people in Kenya. Acknowledge the former and they may be recorded in your passport; admit to the latter and you'll have to pay duty, up to a hundred percent of the value. There are **bank booths** for exchanging money just outside the customs area. Note that if you're flying directly on to Nairobi, you'll be clearing customs in Mombasa. And if you're going straight on safari, you won't touch Mombasa island at all. Vehicles pass through the back of Changamwe, a poor suburb, on their way out to the highway.

There is no airline bus service **from the airport into town**: *KBS* **buses** run hourly to Mwembe Tayari, the main bus station. **Taxis**, the best of which are the London-style cabs, have their rates posted and the hassle is generally not severe. The fixed price to the centre of Mombasa is Ksh550, sometimes bargainable to under Ksh400, depending

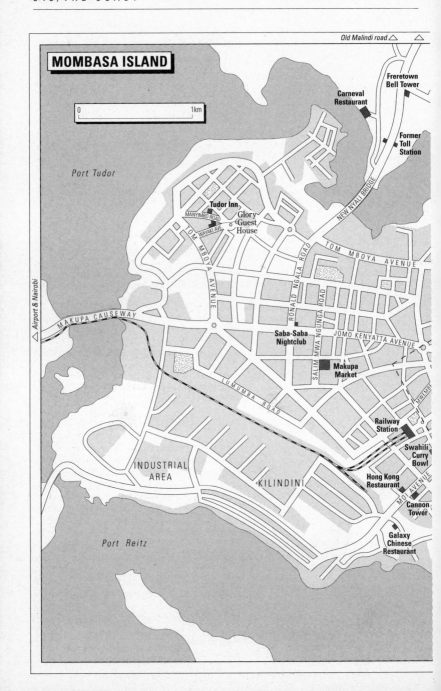

Old Malindi road

MOMBASA ISLAND

0   1km

Freretown
Bell Tower

Carneval
Restaurant

Former
Toll
Station

Port Tudor

Tudor Inn
MANYIMBO ROAD
WAYAKI AVE
Glory
Guest
House

NEW NYALI BRIDGE

TOM MBOYA AVENUE

RONALD NGALA ROAD

Airport & Nairobi

MAKUPA CAUSEWAY

TOM MBOYA AVENUE

JOMO KENYATTA AVENUE

Saba-Saba
Nightclub

SALIM MWA NGUNGA ROAD

Makupa
Market

LUMUMBA ROAD

MWEMBE

Railway
Station

Swahili
Curry
Bowl

INDUSTRIAL
AREA

KILINDINI

Hong Kong
Restaurant

MOI AVENUE

Cannon
Tower

Port Reitz

Galaxy
Chinese
Restaurant

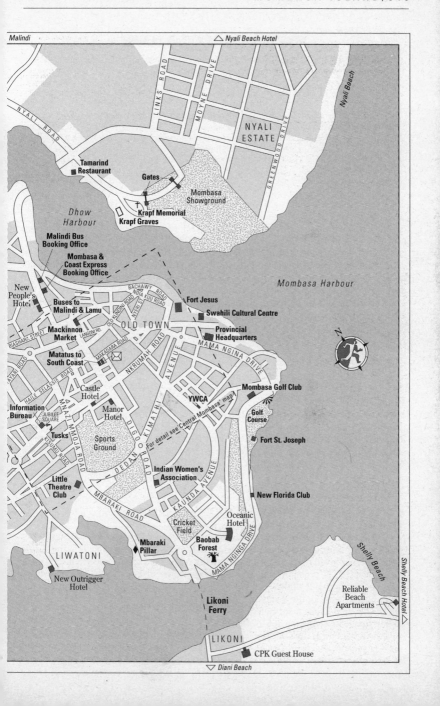

Malindi
△ Nyali Beach Hotel

NYALI ROAD

LINKS ROAD
MOYNE DRIVE
GREENWOOD DRIVE

NYALI ESTATE

Nyali Beach

Tamarind Restaurant

Gates
Mombasa Showground

Krapf Memorial
Krapf Graves

Dhow Harbour

Malindi Bus Booking Office

Mombasa & Coast Express Booking Office

Mombasa Harbour

New People's Hotel

BACHAWY ROAD
NDIA KUU ROAD
INTERSECT

Buses to Malindi & Lamu

OLD TOWN

Fort Jesus

Swahili Cultural Centre

Mackinnon Market

OLD KILINDINI ROAD
LANGONI RD

BIASHARA STREET

Matatus to South Coast

MAKADARA ROAD

NKRUMAH ROAD

JAMHURI AVENUE

Provincial Headquarters

MAMA NGINA DRIVE

Castle Hotel

HAILE SELASSIE ROAD

NYALI ROAD

Information Bureau
JUBILEE SQUARE

Manor Hotel

KIMATHI ROAD

YWCA

Mombasa Golf Club

Golf Course

Tusks

DEDAN ROAD

For detail see Central Mombasa' map

Fort St. Joseph

Sports Ground

Little Theatre Club

MBARAKI ROAD

Indian Women's Association

KAUNDA AVENUE

New Florida Club

Mbaraki Pillar

Cricket Field

Baobab Forest

Oceanic Hotel

MAMA NGINGA DRIVE

LIWATONI

New Outrigger Hotel

Shelly Beach

Shelly Beach Hotel ▷

Likoni Ferry

Reliable Beach Apartments

LIKONI

CPK Guest House

▽ Diani Beach

on the day's business. Fares are also fixed for hotels on the south coast (Diani Beach), the north coast, and as far afield as Malindi (about ten times the fare to Mombasa centre). You'll make a small saving but pay in lack of comfort by taking an unlicensed cab. You can call *Airport Taxi Services* on ☎011/433211.

You can also arrange to have a rented **car** waiting for you at the airport. Most rental companies that have offices or outlets in Mombasa will do this for you, though you will usually need to go to their office in town to complete the paperwork and pay the deposit.

If you can handle it, the hour-long four-kilometre **walk** to the road into town (where you'll quickly pick up buses and *matatus*) is not unpleasant, and along the road, on the left, is an enormous Kamba woodcarvers' "village", where the art of woodcarving has been reduced to not much more than a human conveyor belt. It isn't a place you're likely to bother visiting unless you are out here anyway and there are no special reductions should you want to buy; it's just a good education in a lowly sector of the tourist industry and, that said, quite entertaining.

Tourist information

Mombasa's **Tourist Information Office** is on Moi Avenue, near the tusks (PO Box 99596; ☎011/225428; Mon–Fri 8am–noon & 2–5pm, Sat 8am–noon). The service here has improved out of all recognition and they can advise on a wide range of transport and accommodation matters, although they have little to offer in material terms. One item they usually have is the *Kenya Coast Tourist Guide*, a monthly magazine of adverts and advertorial which is always worth a look, also available direct from the publisher, *Friedrich Kenya*, in Jubilee Insurance Plaza.

Accommodation

None of the well-known resort hotels is located on Mombasa island and tour operators almost never offer city hotels. A city-centre landmark, currently closed, is the *Castle Hotel*: whether it will rise again from behind the corrugated iron is uncertain. The most upmarket place is probably the *New Outrigger*, some distance away from the town centre on the port side of the island. Hardly any further from the centre, if you're driving or using taxis, is the recommended *Nyali Beach Hotel*, on the mainland to the north. This, and subsequent hotels along the north-coast beaches, are covered in the section that follows this (pp.366–374).

At the other end of the scale, the city has a fair scattering of cheap lodgings, but none that really stands out as the obvious focus for budget travellers. There's a YWCA – good for long stays for men as well as women – but no youth hostel and no campsite. Note that **water supplies** in Mombasa are notoriously erratic (you'll see the water carriers with their hand carts all over the city) and many cheap places feature the tell-tale buckets and plastic basins in bathrooms that indicate water often has to be carried up.

Basic lodgings

You might reasonably expect to find a concentration of cheap lodgings in the Old Town. Curiously enough, this isn't the case, though most of them cluster in the streets just to the west.

Hotel Balgis, Digo Rd, across from the junction with Old Kilindini Rd (PO Box 1506; no telephone). Similar to the nearby *Mvita* and equally dirt-cheap, but lacks a bar downstairs. Most rooms have no fans and some are without windows. Not a comfortable place for women alone. ①.

Bhallo's Hostel and Restaurant, Nkrumah Rd (PO Box 88825; ☎011/313833). Humble sort of lodgings for the price. Basic rooms with fans, decent communal showers and toilets, and dependable water. ②.

Cosy Guest House, Haile Selassie Rd (PO Box 83011; ☎011/313064). A regular first base for many budget travellers – conveniently close to the railway station – but increasingly under fire for crumbling facilities and unwholesome management. Some mosquito nets. Try to get a first- or second-floor room to overcome the low water pressure. ②.

Excellent Hotel, Haile Selassie Rd (PO Box 90228; ☎011/451926). S/c rooms with nets and fans. A good first base if you're arriving on the train. ③.

Glory Guest House, Waiyaki Rd, Tudor (PO Box 85527; ☎011/494470). Simple, clean, safe lodging in an untouristy part of town. Part of a "budget" chain that advertises widely, but not to be confused with the branch on Kwa Shibu Rd (see below). ②.

Hydro Hotel, corner of Digo and Langoni roads (PO Box 85360; ☎011/223784). Usefully located, friendly old stand-by, but very limited and no longer the place it once was. ②.

Kivulini B&L, corner of Digo Rd and Haile Selassie Ave (PO Box 8219i2; no telephone). Clean, but cramped and basic, with no running water, so overpriced. Top-floor rooms (no fans) are much to be preferred to the rooms with fans on the first floor, off the spookily narrow corridor. No nets. ②.

Likia Guest House, off Chembe Rd, behind Moi Ave (PO Box 85345; ☎011/223460). Down this unprepossessing back alley is a cheap, friendly little place. Fairly hygienic, with clean sheets and fans in most rooms. No mosquito screens or nets and the water problems are a pain. ②.

Leejim Hotel, Duruma Rd (PO Box 80094; ☎011/222868). A sizeable place, with reasonable facilities and very friendly, though somewhat lacking in atmosphere. ③.

Mvita B&L, corner of Hospital St and Turkana St, near Digo Rd (PO Box 85215; ☎011/220361). Grubby, bug-ridden and noisy, to say the least, but at the same time disarmingly friendly, with a great bar downstairs if you want to make friends. Surprisingly breezy location and some rooms have fans. ①–②.

New Palm Tree Hotel Boarding & Lodging, Nkrumah Rd (PO Box 90013; ☎011/311756). Beginning to fall apart, but, with its sunny first-floor courtyard and spacious rooms, it's a pleasant old joint. Cheap. ③.

New People's Hotel, Abdul Nassir Rd (PO Box 85342; ☎011/312831). Big undistinguished block – supposed to have been a mosque as far as its Saudi financiers were concerned – that is the established place to stay if you're taking a bus up to Malindi or Lamu in the morning, as they leave from right outside. Noisy and packed out with refugees most of the time, so hard to get a room. Singles tend to be cube-like but some rooms are s/c. There's a cheap restaurant downstairs. ①.

Taj Hotel, Digo Road (PO Box 82021; ☎011/223198). Better kept than most, and some rooms are s/c, but still a little expensive at this level. On the other hand, they have some four-bed dorm rooms for the price of a double – which makes them almost as cheap as the *Hydro*. ②.

YWCA, corner of Kaunda and Kiambu avenues (PO Box 90214; ☎011/312846). Pleasant ambience and open to men as well as women. Funds generated assist local women's projects. For long stays, on HB basis during the week and FB at weekends, they charge Ksh6420 per person per month, including laundry. At little more than £2 ($3) per day, this is quite a bargain.

Mid-range hotels

Head to any of these for basic hotel services, with breakfast included and self-contained rooms, some with air conditioning. You might care to check your AC unit before choos-

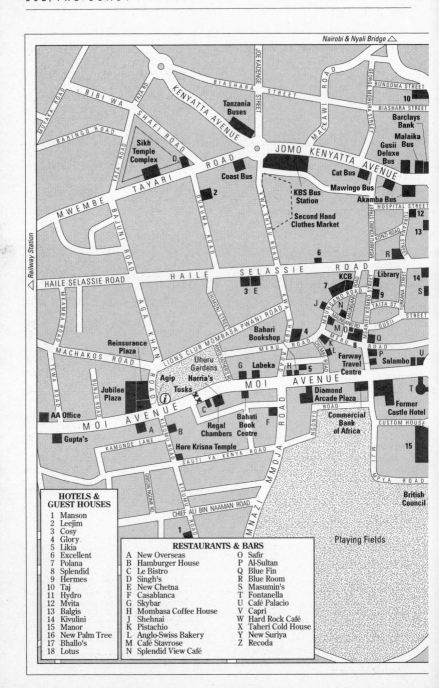

Nairobi & Nyali Bridge △

△ Railway Station

**HOTELS &
GUEST HOUSES**

1   Manson
2   Leejim
3   Cosy
4   Glory
5   Likia
6   Excellent
7   Polana
8   Splendid
9   Hermes
10 Taj
11 Hydro
12 Mvita
13 Balgis
14 Kivulini
15 Manor
16 New Palm Tree
17 Bhallo's
18 Lotus

RESTAURANTS & BARS

A   New Overseas
B   Hamburger House
C   Le Bistro
D   Singh's
E   New Chetna
F   Casablanca
G   Skybar
H   Mombasa Coffee House
J   Shehnai
K   Pistachio
L   Anglo-Swiss Bakery
M   Café Stavrose
N   Splendid View Café

O   Safir
P   Al-Sultan
Q   Blue Fin
R   Blue Room
S   Masumin's
T   Fontanella
U   Café Palacio
V   Capri
W   Hard Rock Café
X   Taheri Cold House
Y   New Suriya
Z   Recoda

Playing Fields

British
Council

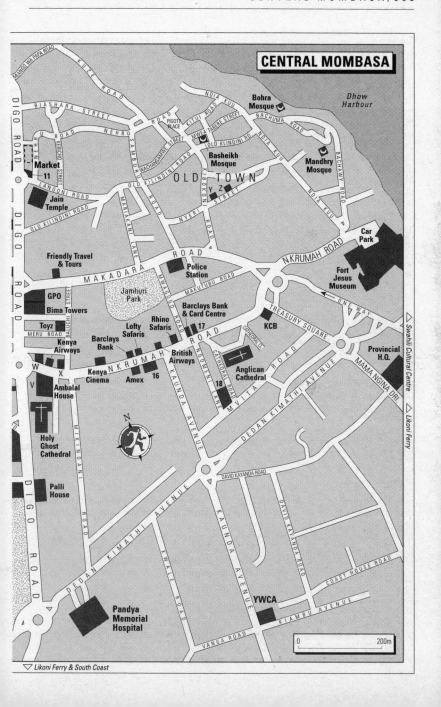

ing the room. Some generate so much water that your windowsill can become a verita-ble bird bath, attracting all the pigeons in Mombasa.

Glory Guest House, Kwa Shibu Rd (PO Box 85527; ☎011/313204). An unappealing proposition, with an unsavoury reputation for brusque treatment of guests and endless comings and goings. A variety of s/c and non-s/c rooms, some with AC and even fridge and TV, some with fans and nets. Somewhat disconcertingly, guests are advised to bring an extra padlock for their rooms. ③.

Hotel Hermes, Msanifu Kombo St (PO Box 98419; ☎011/313599). Not a great choice and becom-ing run-down and boozy. Large rooms with AC, though cracks can hinder its effectiveness. ③.

Hotel Splendid, Msanifu Kombo St (PO Box 90482; ☎011/220967, fax 011/312769). A clean, effi-ciently run establishement (with elevator) right in the thick of things, popular for its fourth-floor roof garden bar/restaurant. Number 42 is the best of several of the larger-than-average rooms, with balconies and fans. Avoid the small, windowless, interior rooms. AC, and nets can be provided. ③.

Upmarket hotels

Remember that the resort hotels are out of town. In this higher price bracket, you will generally find comfortable, old-fashioned hotels with self-contained rooms, fans or air conditioning. Compared with Nairobi, they tend to be good value.

Lotus Hotel, corner of Mvita and Cathedral roads (PO Box 90193; ☎011/313207, fax 011/220673). Overflowing with greenery, with plain but very neat and clean rooms, and located on a quiet corner not far from Fort Jesus, the *Lotus* is the best bet in Mombasa and often full. Every room has AC and a phone. ④.

Manor Hotel, Nyerere Ave (PO Box 84851; ☎011/21821). Stylish atmosphere and all the mod cons you could desire. ④.

Manson Hotel, Kisumu Rd (PO Box 83565; ☎011/222356, fax 011/222420). A recent opening, with large, clean rooms and good balconies. TV lounge and bar-restaurant on the ground floor. Good value. ④.

New Outrigger Hotel, Ras Liwatoni, on the southwest side of Mombasa island (PO Box 82345; ☎011/220822, fax 011/315831). The closest Mombasa has to a resort hotel (Belgian management; one or two European tour operators use it), with perfectly adequate AC rooms and a pleasant atmos-phere, overlooking the creek. A little far to walk for city centre shopping or strolling. Pool and a small beach (but swimming in Kilindini creek isn't recommended). Residents get 25 per cent discount. ⑤ low, ⑥ high.

Oceanic Hotel, Mbuyuni Rd, ten minutes' walk from the Likoni ferry (PO Box 90371; ☎011/311193, fax 011/228480). Overpriced for the tired, semi-functioning, clunkingly 1960s hulk that it is. Hopeless staff, zero atmosphere, small pool. On a positive note, all rooms have a fine sea view, and the adjoining *Terrazza* Italian restaurant is quite reasonable. ④.

Polana Hotel, Maungano Rd (PO Box 41; ☎011/229171, fax 011/229181). New hotel in the centre of the city, offering spacious, clean, comfortable accommodation – at a price. Great views from the upper floors. ⑤.

Mombasa's history

Mombasa is one of East Africa's oldest settlements and, so long as you aren't anticipat-ing spectacular historical sites, it's a fascinating place to wander. The island has had a town on it, located somewhere between the present Old Town and Nyali Bridge, for at least 700 years, and there are enough documentary snippets from earlier times to guess that some kind of settlement has existed here for at least 2000 years. Mombasa's own optimistic claim (frequently repeated in the tourist literature) to be 2500 years old comes from Roman and Egyptian adventure stories.

Early tales

Precisely what was going on before the Portuguese arrived is still barely discernible. An armchair traveller, Al-Idrisi, wrote the following in the early twelfth century about a place called *Manfasa* that was in roughly the right location: "This is a small place and a dependency of the Zanj [coastal people]. Its inhabitants work in the iron mines and hunt tigers. They have red-coloured dogs which fight every kind of wild beast and even lions." This sounds most unlikely, but then the history of Mombasa is a series of unlikely episodes. **Ibn Battuta**, the roving fourteenth-century Moroccan, spent a relatively quiet night here in 1332 and declared the people of the town "devout, chaste and virtuous . . . their mosques . . . strongly constructed of wood . . . the greater part of their diet . . . bananas and fish". But another Arab writer of a hundred years later found a less ordered society:

> *Monkeys have become the rulers of Mombasa since about 800 AH [1400 AD]. They even come and take the food from the dishes, attack men in their own homes and take away what they can find. The master of the house chases the thieving monkey and does not cease cajoling him until the animal, having eaten the food, gives back the dish or vessel. When the monkeys enter a house and find a woman they hold congress with her. The monkeys divide into bands each with its own chief and march behind him in an orderly manner. The people have much to put up with.*

Vasco da Gama and other Portuguese visitors

Mombasa had considerably worse depredations to put up with after **Vasco da Gama's** expedition, full of mercenary zeal, dropped anchor on Easter Saturday 1498. After courtesy gifts had been exchanged, relations suddenly soured and the fleet was prevented from entering the port. A few days later, richer by only one sheep and "large quantities of oranges, lemons and sugar cane", da Gama went off to try his primitive diplomacy at Malindi, and found his first and lasting ally on the coast.

Mombasa was visited again in 1505 by a fourteen-strong fleet. This time, the king of Mombasa had enlisted 1500 archers from the mainland and stored arsenals of stone missiles on the rooftops in preparation for the expected **invasion** through the town's narrow alleys. The attack, pitching firearms against spears, poisoned arrows and stones, was decisive and brutal. The town was squeezed on all sides and the king's palace (of which no trace remains) was seized. The king and most of the survivors slipped out of town into the palm groves which then covered the island, but 1513 Mombasans had been killed – as against five Portuguese.

The king attempted to save Mombasa by offering to become a vassal of Portugal, but the request was turned down, the Portuguese unwilling to lose the chance to **loot** the abandoned town, picking over the bodies in the courtyards and breaking down the strongroom doors until the ships at anchor were almost overladen. Then, as a parting shot, they fired the town. The narrow streets and the cattle stalls between the thatched houses produced a conflagration that must have razed Mombasa to the ground.

In 1528, the Portuguese returned once again to wreck and plunder the new city that had grown on the ashes of the old. In the 1580s, it happened twice more; on the last occasion, in 1589, there was a frenzied **massacre** at the hands of the Portuguese and – coincidentally – a marauding tribe of nomads from the interior called the Zimba (about whom little is known except their cannibalistic notoriety). The Zimba's unholy alliance with the Europeans came to a treacherous end at Malindi shortly afterwards, when the Portuguese, together with the townsfolk and 3000 Segeju archers, wiped them out.

Remarkably, only two years after this last catastrophe, Mombasa launched a major land expedition of its own against its old enemy, Malindi. It had finally met a decisive match. The party was ambushed on the way by Malindi's Segeju allies, who themselves stormed and took Mombasa, later handing over the town (in which they had little interest) to the Portuguese at Malindi. The Malindi corps transferred to Mombasa, the Malindi sheikh was grandly installed as sultan of the whole region, and the Portuguese set to work on **Fort Jesus**, dedicated in 1593.

Fort Jesus

Once completed, the fort became the focus of everything that mattered in Mombasa, changing hands a total of nine times between the early seventeenth century and 1875.

The first takeover happened in 1631, in a **popular revolt** that resulted in the killing of every last Portuguese. But the Sultan, lacking support from any of the other towns under Portuguese domination, eventually had to desert the fort and the Portuguese, waiting in Zanzibar, reoccupied it. For the rest of the seventeenth century they continued to hold Mombasa, at first consolidating their control of the Indian Ocean trade.

Meanwhile, however, the **Omani Arabs** were becoming increasingly powerful. And as Dutch, English and French ships started to appear on the horizon, time was clearly running out for the Portuguese trading monopoly. Efforts to bring settlers to their East African possessions failed, and they retreated more and more behind the massive walls of Fort Jesus. Portugal's East African "empire" was under siege, and in 1696–98 Fort Jesus itself was isolated and besieged into submission by the Omanis who, with support from Pate and Lamu, had already taken the rest of the town. After 33 months almost all the defenders – the Portuguese corps and some 1500 Swahili loyalists – had died of starvation or plague.

Under Arab rule

Rapid disenchantment with the new Arab rulers spilled over in 1728 into a mutiny among the fort's African soldiers. The Portuguese were invited back – for a year. Then the fort was again besieged and this time the Portuguese gave up quickly. They were allowed their freedom, and a number are said to have married and stayed in the town. But Portuguese power on the coast was shattered for ever.

The new Omani rulers were the **Mazrui** family. Soon after the return of some kind of normality in Mombasa, they declared themselves independent of Oman, a direct challenge to the **Busaidi** family who had just seized power in the Arabian homeland. Civil war in Oman prevented the Busaidis from doing much about their wayward overseas agents: with the **Nabahani** family in Pate no longer paying much allegiance either, control of what were fast reverting to independent states was increasingly difficult. As usual, though, the lack of unity on the coast prevented any lasting independence.

Intrigue in the Lamu archipelago led to the Battle of Shela (p.423) and Lamu's unwittingly disastrous invitation to the **Sultan of Oman, Seyyid Said**, to occupy its own fort. From here, and by now with British backing, the Busaidis went on to attack Mazrui Mombasa repeatedly in the 1820s.

There was a hiccup in 1824 when a British officer, **Captain Owen**, fired with enthusiasm for defeating the slave trade, extended British protection to Mombasa on his own account, despite official British support for the slave-trading Busaidis. Owen's "Protectorate" was a diplomatic embarrassment and – no surprise – did not last long. The Busaidi government was only installed when the Swahili "twelve tribes" of Mombasa, the traditional inhabitants of the immediate hinterland, fell into a dispute over the Mazrui succession and called in Seyyid Said, the Busaidi leader. In 1840, he moved his capital from Oman to Zanzibar and, with Mombasa firmly garrisoned, most of the coast was soon in his domain.

Surviving members of the Mazrui family went to Takaungu near Malindi and Gazi, south of Mombasa. British influence was sharpened after their guns quelled the mutiny in 1875 of al-Akida, "an ambitious, unbalanced and not over-clever" commandant of the Fort. Once British hegemony was established, they leased the **coastal strip** from the Sultan of Zanzibar and Fort Jesus became Mombasa's prison, which it remained until 1958.

Fort Jesus

Open daily 8.30am–6.30pm; Ksh200; warden: PO Box 82412, ☎011/312839.

Today **Fort Jesus** is a quietly studious museum-monument, surprisingly spacious and tree-shaded inside its giant walls, and retaining most of its original (over the centuries much repaired) character. The curious angular construction was the design of an Italian architect and ensures that assailants trying to scale the walls would always be under crossfire from one of the bastions. It is a classic European fortress of its age.

The best time to visit is probably first thing in the morning; the guidebook on sale is an interesting store of information. Look out especially for the restored **Omani House**, in the far right corner as you enter the fort. Avoiding head contact with the lintel, climb up to the flat roof for a wonderful view over Mombasa. Interesting in their own way, too, are the uncomfortable-looking, wall-mounted **latrines**, which would presumably have been closed in with mats. It is immediately obvious that Fort Jesus was not so much a building as a small, resolutely fortified town in its own right. The ruins of a church, storerooms, and possibly even shops are up at this end and, to judge by some accounts, the main courtyard was at times a warren of simple dwellings. Captain Owen described it in 1824 as being: ". . . a mass of indiscriminate ruins, huts and hovels, many of them built wherever space could be found but generally formed from parts of the ruins, matted over for roofs."

Most of the archeological interest is at the seaward end of the fort, where you'll find the **Hall of the Mazrui** with its beautiful stone benches and eighteenth-century inscription – and a sad quantity of twentieth-century graffiti as well. A nearby room has been dedicated entirely to the display of a huge plaster panel of older **graffiti**, scribbled and etched onto the wall by bored Portuguese sentries. Their subjects are fascinating: ships, figures in armour (including caricatures of the captain of the fort wielding his baton), fish, a chameleon and various motifs. Illiteracy precluded much writing but, oddly enough, there's nothing obscene either (perhaps it has been erased?). The small **café** up here has been serving first-class lime juice for years (if you want something to eat, the museum restaurant, behind the ticket office, has a lunch dish each day and various snacks).

Fort Jesus Museum

The **museum**, on the eastern side of the fort where the main soldiers' barracks block used to be, is small, but it manages to convey a good idea of the age and breadth of Swahili civilization. Most of the displays are of pottery, indigenous or imported, some from as far afield as China and some of it over 1000 years old. A number of private collections have contributed pieces and there's probably still a wealth of material in private hands. Look out for the big carved door taken from the Mazrui house in Gazi (p.390) and also the extraordinary whale vertebra used as a stool. The museum has a good exhibit on the long-term project to recover as much as possible from the wreck of the *Santo Antonio de Tanna*, which sank in 1697 while trying to break the prolonged siege of the fort. Some 7000 objects have already been brought to the surface, but the bulk of the ship itself remains nine fathoms deep in the harbour.

Around town

From Fort Jesus, the **Old Town** is an easy objective. First impressions – of a quarter entirely devoted to gift and **curio shops** – are none too encouraging. But this turns out to be purely the result of Fort Jesus' adjacent car park and tourist appeal, and the shops don't extend far into the Old Town. They are especially ostentatious down at the end of Ndia Kuu Road, where several emporiums are overwhelmingly luxuriant in their displays and multilingual enticements. One or two of them provide free coffee, which alone is nice. Many of them sell a lot of worthless junk and some deal in shells, including shell lamp stands, ornaments and the like, a trade which operates on the fringes of the law in Kenya. Further west, away from the fort, the stores are smaller, and correspondingly cheaper and less pretentious. For more about buying crafts, see "Shopping" on p.359.

Mosques and other architecture

The Old Town is not in fact that old. Most buildings date from the nineteenth century, and though there may be foundations and even walls that go back many centuries, you'll get a clearer guide to the age of the town from its twenty-odd **mosques**.

The **Mandhry Mosque** on Bachawy Road, founded in 1570, is officially the oldest; rarely open to visitors, it has a striking minaret. The **Basheikh Mosque** on Old Kilindini Road, recently repainted in fresh cream and white, is also acknowledged to be very old – "about 1300", they'll tell you, though this may be exaggerated. Entering the mosques – as long as they aren't locked – is usually all right for men who arrive properly covered and barefoot. Sometimes you may be expected to wash hands and feet as well. Women, however modestly dressed, will as often as not be politely refused.

Much of the other **architecture** in the Old Town is profoundly influenced by the Indian-style Zanzibari tastes of the Busaidi occupiers of the nineteenth century. This is particularly noticeable in the elegant fretwork balconies and shutters still maintained on a few houses, notably on Ndia Kuu. For older relics, you'll have to poke around more conscientiously. There are a number of quite ancient tombs along the seafront, especially towards the northern end of the Old Town, some of which have pillars; this is the part of Mombasa considered to be "medieval", or in other words pre-Portuguese.

Returning south along the twisting **seafront road** ("seafront", although the harbour can only be glimpsed), you come to the gigantic mosque of the Bohra Muslims: "Burhani Masjid for Dawoodi Bohra Community", says the sign. In the unassuming setting of the Old Town, it is an imposingly massive edifice.

The dhow harbour

The **dhow harbour** is wildly overrated. There are usually a few boats in port but you can no longer expect to see dozens, let alone hundreds, of dhows, even at the end of the northeast monsoon in April, traditionally the peak time for arrivals. Seasonal variations are less important now that the big *jahazis* have engines. Nor are you likely to have the opportunity to go aboard one of these exotic vessels – a tourist tradition, with coffee and souvenirs, that has died out as port officials have become more officious (for "Port Cruises" on the other side of the island, see "Listings"). Instead, try to imagine how it must once have looked, chat to the many policemen standing around and don't, whatever you do, raise your camera. Attempting to travel by dhow from Mombasa is, regrettably, an equally discouraging story. Lamu holds more promise (see "Travel Details").

The Jain temple

Heading up towards Digo Road, you might enjoy stopping by at the **Jain temple**, whose entrance is in Langoni Road. Take your shoes off. This sublime creation – intricate icing sugar outside, scrupulously clean and scented interior, decorated in dozens of pastel shades – was only built in 1963. Jainism is a Hindu religion closely related to Buddhism and commonest in Gujurat (home of the majority of Kenyan Asians), which prohibits the eating of any kind of animal – in its extreme form, even root vegetables are taboo – and aspires to release adherants from the physical universe and its eternal cycle of death and rebirth. The temple interior is ornamentally and substantially magnificent: the painted figurines of deities in their niches are each provided with a drain so they can be easily showered down, while around the ceiling, exquisitely stylized pictures portray scenes from a human life, including a familiar snake temptation in a garden.

The Swahili Cultural Centre

The name is promising, but at present the **Swahili Cultural Centre** offers nothing likely to impress the casual visitor. Located on the quiet east side of Mombasa island, off Mama Ngina Drive, the Centre is part of a United Nation Development Programme project on the coast, created to alleviate youth unemployment and foster traditional skills. Crafts courses operate in joinery and woodcarving, textile manufacture and embroidery, with associated classes in Swahili design and business management running alongside. It's possible to visit, informally, at any time during the week, though you should go in the morning or late afternoon if you want to find any students there. Let the Centre know in advance if you're coming with a large group (free entry; PO Box 82412; ☎011/227643). The variety of buildings that make up the Centre are set among trees on ancient coral cliffs above Mombasa Harbour, and could become a popular attraction if there was a bit more to do. Meanwhile, embroidery (including some very fine *kofia* skull caps) and a limited selection of carvings are available for sale, at more or less fixed prices.

Walks around Mombasa

For the most part, the rest of Mombasa's pleasures derive from just being here. Strolling, with plenty of cold-drink stops, is a time-honoured Mombasan diversion. You will probably want to see that immortal double pair of **elephant tusks** on Moi Avenue. To get to them, you have to run the gauntlet of curio booths that have almost hidden the cool hideaway of Uhuru Gardens on the right, with its Africa-shaped fountain. And when you get there, you may regret your determination to view the tusks close up: they are revealed as grubby aluminium.

More rewarding, if you have the time and inclination for **a long walk**, is the circuit that takes off around the breezy, seaward side of the island down **Mama Ngina Drive**: a fine morning's or afternoon's walk, with lots of places to sit and watch the waves pounding the coral cliffs through the break in the reef. On the clifftop, protruding from the far side of the golf course (Mombasa Golf Club; KGU affiliates Ksh450, others Ksh900), are the stumpy, insignificant remains of Fort St Joseph, built in 1826 to defend Mazrui Mombasa against the attacks of the Busaidi Omanis. Come down this clifftop promenade at weekends or in the early evening and you'll find half of Mombasa doing the same – there are food stalls in several places. At the end of Mama Ngina is an extensive and surprising forest of enormous **baobab trees**, frequently associated with ancient settlements on the coast.

Finally, just to the west of the Likoni ferry roundabout is a huge pillar tomb, the **Mbaraki Pillar**. Supposedly the burial place of a seventeenth-century mainland sheikh, chief of one of the "twelve tribes", its eight-metre height is impressive enough, but it is nevertheless dwarfed by the towers of the nearby molasses refinery.

Beaches and swimming

Mombasa island has no proper beaches of its own. The nearest are **Shelly Beach**, covered in more detail on p.380 (*matatu* or bus from Kenyatta Ave to the Likoni Ferry, then turn left and walk/hitch 2–3km), and **Nyali Beach**, covered on pp.366–368 (*matatu* or bus from Abdul Nassir Rd to Nyali Bridge, then turn right and go 4km). Shelly Beach is relatively uninteresting and narrow, with the reef close to the shore, but fairly peaceful. Nyali is pretty good, crowded at weekends and holidays, and the reef here is much further out. There are several public points of access to Nyali beach, but the easiest is right by the entrance to the *Nyali Beach Hotel*. Most of the time, hotels do not mind if you use their own beaches, bars and restaurants. If it's simply a swim you're after, your best bet in town is probably the **pool** at the *New Outrigger Hotel* (p.354) or the one at the Indian Women's Association, Nyerere Ave, halfway to the Likoni Ferry (during school terms Mon–Fri 5–7.30pm; school holidays Mon–Fri 9am–noon & 2–6.30pm).

Shopping

Mombasa is a good city for **shopping**, with a generally wide choice, and fewer hassles as you window-shop than in Nairobi. Once you know where to go for crafts, the busi-

BARGAINING

The usual rules apply when **bargaining** – don't start the ball rolling if you're not in the mood and never offer a price you're not prepared to pay. If you want quite a few items, it's worth browsing for a well-stocked stall and then, as you reach one near-agreement after another with the stallholder, add a new item to your collection. This way you should be able to buy well-finished *vyondo* (sisal baskets) in the range of Ksh200–300, small soapstone items for Ksh50–100, and bracelets and necklaces for a similar price. It's impossible to estimate what you'll pay for carvings as the price depends as much on the workmanship as on the size of the piece. If you expressly *don't* want to purchase ebony (the wood is increasingly rare), you'll run into some amusing conversational one-way streets with stallholders who are a dab hand at "proving" their lumps of dyed acacia wood are ebony.

ness of buying souvenirs improves markedly. For cloth, Mombasa is blessed with Biashara Street.

The main tourist street, as you'll soon discover, is the stretch of Moi Avenue between the Tusks and Digo Road. A number of the retail businesses here are housed in quite old premises, going back to the turn of the century (look out for *Kitui General Stores*, which is housed in Old Tusk Lodge, a fine example of an old trading house). However, it's hard to take in the architecture when the pavement is lined with souvenir stalls. Sisal baskets, soapstone, beadwork and fake ebony carvings make up eighty percent of the wares. Those at the Digo Road end of Moi Avenue tend to be the most aggressive at touting their wares, and getting past without stopping is not easy, while, if you do halt, making cool decisions can be fraught. The stalls along Digo Road to the south of the Moi Avenue roundabout are barely any less hassle. Since the demise of the nearby *Istanbul*, the line of stalls on **Chembe Road** seem to be in something of a backwater, and are more fun to deal with.

If you're **buying crafts** in Mombasa, whatever else you do, first go and have a look at *Harria's Gift Shop* on Moi Avenue, near the Tusks. They consistently offer good deals and you may even be able to get things here more cheaply than on the street. *Labeka*, also on Moi Avenue, is another good store for browsing, with sensible prices and a pleasant, hassle-free environment.

Markets

For a return to earth, visit Mombasa's municipal market, **Mackinnon Market**, which has a splendid abundance of tropical fruit, including such exotics as jackfruit (too big for most people at around 10 kilos) and soursops (a taste you'll either love or hate). Behind the market is a row of stores devoted to spices, coffee and tea – good for bulk turmeric or what-have-you – and several good sweet shops.

Apart from the Mackinnon and the big street market off Mwembe Tayari, there's **Makupa market** in the heart of Majengo, the island's low-income housing district. A colourful, multipurpose market with a busy, rural atmosphere, it's well worth a visit. Go 1500m up Jomo Kenyatta Avenue, then turn left at Salim Mwa Ngunga Road.

Cloth and hardware

Mombasa is also a cheap place to buy the **fabrics** the coast is famous for. Check out the latest *kanga* designs in **Biashara Street**, where they are usually available before anywhere else in Kenya. Some of the home-produced patterns are so good – unusual combinations of brilliant fast colours are used to startling effect – they are beginning to make an impact abroad. It is worth checking prices in several shops before buying, and perhaps going with company so you can bargain for several lots at once: they are always sold in pairs. In the high season, Biashara Street swarms with other tourists looking for "the real Mombasa", so you'll need all your haggling skills; it's actually quite difficult to budge prices more than a token Ksh40–50 for the sake of politeness, as business is just too good.

Beyond Kwavi Road, Biashara Street shifts from textiles to a less gaudy section of **household goods**, such as winnowing trays, coconut graters, palm bags, mats, spoons and furniture. It's more mundane, but just as interesting to browse.

Eating, drinking and nightlife

The city is full of places to eat and drink, and street food is generally better here than in Nairobi: try the spicy little kebabs (sometimes chicken, and called "chicken tikka" anyway); young coconuts bursting with juice and lined with soft jelly; and cuplets of thick ginger coffee. There are several nightclubs, too, though you might not guess as much during the day. Always check bills carefully as mistakes are increasingly common.

Restaurants

Mombasa is well supplied with good, **cheap restaurants**. Especially if you're newly arrived from up-country, they are one of the city's chief delights, as a discernible cuisine involving coconut, fish, chicken, rice and beans, incorporating spicy Asian flavours, begins to make an impression on your palate.

SWAHILI FOOD

Banadir Café, Kibokoni Rd, Old Town. Basic but satisfying Swahili food – and very cheap.

New Suriya Restaurant, Nyeri Rd, Old Town. Very similar to the *Recoda* up the street and worth knowing about if the *Recoda* is full.

Recoda, Nyeri St, Old Town. Mombasa's best restaurant for Swahili food and one of its oldest (opened 1942, partly to record old Mombasa – hence the name and the photos on the walls). Open evenings only, it's a good excuse to throw off any misgivings and plunge into the Old Town after dark. Sitting at pavement tables, choose from a limited but very cheap list of fish, creamed beans, cassava, plantain, *mahamri* and *mushkaki* with salad. If you're not prepared to pick your portion, they'll bring you a never-ending selection. Go early, as by 8pm they're running out of favourites. Ksh200 sees most people incapacitated, though you can eat pretty well for half that. Closed Ramadan.

Swahili Curry Bowl, Tangana Rd, off Moi Ave, close to the railway station. Like *Recoda*, 100 percent authentic Swahili cooking. Here the menu's more extensive but prices are still low – a great spot for a meal before the train trip back to Nairobi.

FAST FOOD, HOTELIS AND UP-COUNTRY COOKING

Bhallo's, Nkrumah Rd. A popular greasy spoon, with *mkate mayai* and chicken tikka cooking on the pavement outside.

Blue Fin, Meru Rd. Fish and chips and other dollar-a-meal fry-ups. Open daily.

Blue Room, Haile Selassie Rd. Self-service *bhajias*, chips, samosas, sausages and good juices. Lots of tables, fans and a cool courtyard. Heavily patronized by locals and deservedly popular for its spotless surfaces and competitive prices on serve-your-own food – you can eat a lot here for Ksh150.

Café Palacio, corner of Digo Rd and Moi Ave. A gleaming, fairly new and more up-market version of the *Blue Room*, with tasty fast food, mostly burgers, fried chicken, pizza and kebabs.

Fontanella Restaurant, corner of Moi Ave and Nyerere Ave (courtyard off the street). A good lunchtime hideaway and rendezvous, but slightly expensive for ordinary café-restaurant fare (check your change). And eating here in the evening becomes hazardous when the figs on the trees overhead ripen and the air is full of fruit bats and their waste products.

Masumin's, Digo Rd, opposite Bima House. Dingy but cheap and worth patronizing for all-in breakfasts (under Ksh100), and for curries and pilau dishes costing even less. Open Tues–Sun 7.30am–6pm.

Splendid Hotel, Moi Ave. The rooftop *nyama choma* is fun, and the rooftop itself delightfully airy, but ordering from the general menu can be unpredictable, and is often slow.

Tudor Inn, Manyimbo Rd, Tudor. No tourists here – one of the most pleasant and economical places in Mombasa, with attentive management. Grills, chicken and chips, *ugali*.

INDIAN COOKING

Al-Sultan, Meru Rd. Mughlai cooking and air conditioning.

New Chetna, Haile Selassie Ave, under the *Cosy Guest House*. Traditional – and hot – Indian food at low prices.

Safir, Maungano Rd, behind the *Splendid Hotel*. Indian and Swahili food in a small dining room or at one or two pavement tables. Curries, biriani and pilau for lunch; chicken tikka and tandooris for dinner. Good eating for under Ksh200.

Shehnai Restaurant, Fatemi House, Maungano St (☎011/312492). Mughlai specialities with a good reputation, owned by a former head of the Mombasa and Coast Tourist Association. Closed Mon.

Singh's, Mwembe Tayari. A bit of a walk from the centre of town, but very tasty Punjabi curries when you get there.

Splendid View Restaurant (tucked behind the *Splendid Hotel*, with a view of it). Try the *Faluda* for an extraordinary gastronomic experience.

Café Stavrose, Maungano Rd. A small place that's been serving Indian snacks, tikka dishes and kebabs for years. Lunches from around Ksh150–200.

FOREIGN CUISINES

Le Bistro, Moi Ave. Very reasonable charcoal-grilled offerings every evening after 5pm. Count on less than Ksh1000 for two.

Capri Restaurant/Hunter's Bar, Ambalal House, Nkrumah Rd (☎011/311156). One of the best eating houses in Mombasa, arguably the best on the island, with steaks and seafood to the fore. Around Ksh1000 a head. Closed Sun.

Galaxy Chinese Restaurant, Achbishop Makarios Rd, off the far end of Moi Ave. Good Chinese – they also have branches on Diani Beach and Bamburi Beach.

Hamburger House, Kisumu Rd, just past the tusks off Moi Ave. Well above average, with an extensive menu.

Hard Rock Café, Nkrumah Rd. Always buzzing and not bad at all – if you want their kind of musical background and fancy pizzas, seafood and steaks chosen from hide-behind laminated menus. Around Ksh150–Ksh400, with large cocktails about Ksh200. Daily 7am–2am.

New Overseas Restaurant, Moi Ave. Excellent-value Cantonese cooking: the owners lurk in the background overseeing all operations.

SEAFOOD

Carneval, out of Mombasa, over Nyali Bridge; turn left on the mainland, following the signposts (☎011/474041). Big, fancy, Italian-owned restaurant complex in a prime setting overlooking Tudor Creek. Seafood, African, occasional wild game and Japanese – though not much evidence of *sushi* or *sashimi*. Popular and often busy, and they provide free transport from North Coast hotels.

Tamarind, out of Mombasa over Nyali Bridge; go right at the traffic lights by Frere-town Bell Tower, then follow the signs (☎011/471747). In a stupendous position, with Mombasa spread out panoramically across the creek, the *Tamarind* is one of the best eating houses in Kenya. Go for the seafood platter – excellent value, in this kind of place, at about Ksh2000 for two. Open daily for lunch and dinner, last orders 10.30pm.

Snacks and juice bars

For **snacking**, and the **drinks** you'll probably want to consume ceaselessly, there are corner cafés, hole-in-the-wall juice bars, and confectionery shops all over town.

Anglo-Swiss Bakery, Chembe Rd. The best bakery in Mombasa, and the place to buy something to eat with your coffee at the *Kenya Coffee Board*.

Mombasa Coffee House, Moi Ave. The Kenya Coffee Board's elderly establishment does a good pineapple pie and the management resent coffee drinkers smuggling in cakes from the *Anglo-Swiss Bakery*.

Pistachio, Chembe Rd. Hard to beat this snack bar for the quality of its ice cream and various kinds of coffee, but it isn't cheap. Breakfast is good value however, and they also do lunch dishes. Mon–Sat 7.30am–10pm, Sun noon–10pm.

Taheri Cold House, Nkrumah Rd. Excellent juices and delicious, filling dishes of *chana bateta*. Closed weekends.

Pan shops

Highly characteristic of Mombasa are the Indian **pan shops**, often doubling as tobacconists and corner shops. You have to try *pan* at least once. It's essentially a mildly narcotic dessert, chewed and sucked but not swallowed, consisting of your choice of sweet spices, chopped nuts and vegetable matter, syrup, and white lime, from a display of dishes, all wrapped in a hot-sweet, dark green betel leaf. Pop the triangular parcel in your mouth and munch – it tastes as exotic and unlikely as it sounds – then spit out the pith when you're finished.

Bars

Casablanca, Mnazi Moja Rd, just off Moi Ave. On the site of the once notorious *Rainbow Club*, this draws a big mixed crowd to a lively terrace, and the prostitutes gather here in force. They can be a pain – or a laugh – depending on your mood. Cold beers, some food, rooms by the hour, or even for the whole night.

Hard Rock, Nkrumah Ave. See "Restaurants". This is the island's fanciest bar, selective in its choice of customers because of the relatively high prices, yet still in danger of becoming a pick-up joint.

Lotus Hotel, corner of Mvita and Cathedral roads. One of the nicest places in town for a civilized beer.

New Palm Tree, Nkrumah Ave. A calm and cool, if somewhat dull, bar, where you can drink at about the lowest prices in the town centre.

Skybar & Restaurant, Moi Ave. Lots of action – gay as well as straight – if you want company, and a perfectly acceptable, though undeniably lively, place to sit and have a drink.

Nightlife

The major tourist hotels are situated outside town and, consequently, so are the flashiest **discos**, as most of them are attached to hotels: consistently the best is *Bora Bora*, which you'll find at the beginning of Bamburi Beach, a little to the north of the city (see p.371). This, unfortunately, leaves Mombasa itself depleted of high-tech action, and few bands find it worthwhile to play on the island when the resorts pay more. Most of Mombasa's older-style nightclubs at the more disreputable, dock end of Moi Avenue have passed away. The recommendations given below are established and enjoyable.

If you don't want to join the throngs in the clubs but don't feel inclined to stay in your room either, **walking after dark** is generally safe in the Old Town and along the main thoroughfares. Around the Old Town, you'll still come across one or two coffee-sellers selling their thick black *kahawa* from traditional high-spouted jugs. Like the men who used to sell glasses of water, their trade has almost died out. At the corner of Langoni and Old Kilindini roads, there's a very good *halwa* shop, normally open late: a hundred grams of fragrantly perfumed almond *halwa* is a fine accompaniment to coffee.

New Florida Nightclub & Casino, Mama Ngina Drive, overlooking the ocean (☎011/313127). Attempts a slick scene, with a choreographed floor show and lots of glitter. While in the essentials it doesn't seem to differ noticeably from its Nairobi namesake – thumping disco, grinding hookers – it does benefit from the terrace by the sea, a pleasant little gaming room (free entry; open from 6pm) and keg beer. A two-kilometre walk from the centre, so it's preferable to take a taxi here, or at least back. Men Ksh200, women Ksh100.

Saba-Saba, corner of Jomo Kenyatta Ave and Ronald Ngala Rd (☎011/493877). Often has live music, even in the day, and always provides a sweaty, local atmosphere.

Salambo, Moi Ave (☎011/220180). Less pretentious and more down-to-earth than its nearby rival, *Toyz*. Mostly a reggae and drinking club, with a dance floor, DJs, food and the occasional live band. Less than Ksh100.

Toyz, Baluchi St, behind the post office (☎011/313931). Mombasa's hottest real club with professional DJs and a good mix of sounds: you'll hear everything from technothrash to reggae. Live music on Sunday afternoons. Air-conditioned. About Ksh150.

Arranging onward travel and safaris

Although it doesn't touch Nairobi for variety, you can do most travel-related business in Mombasa; and, with direct charter flights from Europe, Mombasa is increasingly a **safari hub** in its own right, typically for short safaris to Tsavo East and West aimed at coast-based tourists. For advice about **buses to Lamu**, see the Malindi section, p.408; information on **sea travel** to Lamu is in "Travel Details" on p.448. For **railway** bookings, the ticket office at the station is open daily 8am–noon and 2–6.30pm (☎011/312221).

Airlines and agents

Air Kenya Aviation, Ambalal House, Nkrumah Rd (☎011/229777 or 229106).

British Airways, Nkrumah Rd (☎011/312427 or 224206; open Mon–Fri 8am–noon & 2–5pm, Sat 8.30am–noon). Can confirm *Caledonian Airlines* charter flights.

Coast Aviation, Freight Terminal, Moi International Airport (PO Box 93996; ☎/fax 011/433494). Charter flights and sightseeing.

Eagle Aviation, c/o *Rhino Safaris*, Ambalal House, Mikindani Rd (☎011/316055, fax 011/316054).

Kenya Airways, Moi Ave (☎011/221251).

Prestige Air Services, Ambalal House, Nkrumah Rd (☎011/221443, fax 011/228157).

Uganda Airlines, Flitestar Travel, Mji Mpya Rd (☎011/228751, fax 011/313347).

Car rental

Car rental tends to be a little cheaper in Mombasa than in Nairobi. You'll find the majority of outlets on Moi Avenue and Nkrumah Road. Mini-mokes are sometimes also available (for coast cruising but nothing more adventurous) and are the cheapest option. The following are all safari operators or agents as well.

Avis, Moi Ave (PO Box 84868; ☎011/223048).

Galu Safaris, Ambalal House, Mikindani Rd (PO Box 99456; ☎011/229520, fax 011/314226).

Glory Car Hire, Trans-Ocean House, Moi Ave (PO Box 85527; ☎011/221159).

Gupta's, Moi Ave, opposite the Jubilee Insurance Building (PO Box 83451; ☎011/311182, fax 011/311302).

Hertz/UTC, Moi Ave (PO Box 84782; ☎011/316333, fax 011/314549).

Safaris, travel agents and ground handlers

There are a number of safari possibilities from Mombasa apart from an overnight at the Shimba Hills National Reserve (see p.376). Expect to pay $70–100 for a one-day safari (5am pick-up from your hotel) to Tsavo East, including lunch at *Voi Safari Lodge*. Air safaris, even to the Mara, are also quite feasible, though much more expensive (from around $400 for two days). If you're going to Lamu, don't bother with inclusive arrangements: just take a flight there and sort out accommodation when you arrive.

Abercrombie & Kent, 3rd floor, Palli House, Nyerere Rd (PO Box 90747; ☎011/316549, fax 011/314734).

Farways Safaricentre, Msanifu Kombo St (PO Box 87815; ☎011/223307, fax 011/227239).

Friendly Travel & Tours, Makadara Rd (PO Box 87016; ☎011/312493).

Marineland Touring Co, 2nd Floor, Makena House, Nkrumah Rd (PO Box 88950; ☎011/224894, fax 011/316056).

Lofty Safaris, 1st Floor, Hassanali Building, Nkrumah Rd (PO Box 81933; ☎011/220241, fax 314397).
Pollman's Tours and Safaris, corner of Taveta Rd and Shimanzi Rd (PO Box 84198; ☎011/316732, fax 011/314502).
Rhino Safaris (Hayes & Jarvis), Nkrumah Ave and Ambalal House, Mikindani Rd (PO Box 83050; ☎011/311141l, fax 011/315743).
Somak Holidays, Somak House, Nyerere Ave (PO Box 90738; ☎011/313871, fax 315514).
UST, 7th Floor, Ambalal House, Nkrumah Rd (PO Box 90030; ☎011/314541, fax 011/316576).

Listings

American Express c/o *Express Travel Services*, Nkrumah Rd (PO Box 90631; ☎011/223307, fax 011/314408).

Banks For speed and efficiency in foreign exchange (four minutes), use the *Commercial Bank of Africa*, Moi Ave (Mon–Fri 8.30am–2.30pm; ☎011/224711, fax 011/315274). You may lose a few shillings from rates minutely less favourable than the others, but the well-oiled machinery is worth the price. *Barclays'* bureau de change on Moi Ave is open Mon–Sat 8.30am–12.30pm & 2–4.30pm. There's a less busy, more helpful branch of *Barclays* on Digo Rd, opposite Mackinnon Market. The main branch on Nkrumah Rd is open Mon–Fri 9am–3pm and on the first and fourth Sats of the month 9–11am.

Bookshops Mombasa has few compared with Nairobi, so don't rely on finding maps here. *Bahati Book Centre*, on Moi Ave, *Bahari Bookshop*, also on Moi Ave, and *Between the Lines,* behind the Jubilee Insurance Buidling, are the best.

British Council Biashara Bank Building, Nyerere Ave (PO Box 90590; ☎011/223076; Mon 1.30–5.30pm, Tues–Fri 10am–6pm, Sat 9.30am–12.45pm). Has a small air-conditioned library with recent editions of British papers and temporary membership available at Ksh30 per day.

Cinemas The *Kenya*, Nkrumah Rd, is the most promising. Otherwise, try the *Lotus* on Makadara Rd. Both often show American films.

Contraception The Family Planning Clinic, where you can get cheap condoms and supplies of oral contraceptives, is in Mali House, Kenyatta Ave, off Digo Rd (☎011/316937).

Groceries *Valu-Plus* is currently one of the best supermarkets in Mombasa (Mon–Sat 9am–6pm, Sun 9am–1pm).

CONSULATES IN MOMBASA

The following diplomatic representatives are mostly honorary appointments.

Austria, Mr T Gaal, 3rd Floor, Palli House, Nyerere Ave (PO Box 84045; ☎011/313386; residence ☎011/485550).

Belgium, Mr F Van Burkom, c/o Mitchell Cotts & Co Building (PO Box 90141; ☎011/220231; residence ☎011/471315).

Denmark and Finland, Mr J Nielsen, c/o *Comarco*, Liwatoni Rd (PO Box 99543; ☎011/316776; residence ☎011/471616).

France, Mrs Z Blevins (PO Box 86103; ☎011/314935; residence ☎011/485944).

Germany, Mr G Matthiessen (PO Box 86779; ☎011/314732).

Greece, Mr P Ch Lagoussis, Dar-es-Salaam Rd (PO Box 99211; ☎011/224482; residence ☎011/485637).

India, Bank of India Building, Nkrumah Rd (PO Box 90614; ☎011/224433; residence ☎011/311819).

Italy, Jubilee Insurance Plaze, Moi Ave (PO Box 80443; ☎011/314705; residence ☎011/472091).

Netherlands, Mr L Van de Lande (PO Box 80301; ☎011/311043, fax 011/315005; residence ☎011/471250).

Norway, Mrs A Sondhi, c/o *Reef Hotel*, Nyali (PO Box 82234; ☎011/471771).

Sweden, Mr I Hellman (PO Box 87336; ☎011/316172; residence ☎011/473468).

Switzerland, Mr E Habermachr, Ambalal House, Nkrumah Rd (PO Box 85722; ☎011/316684; residence ☎011/485314).

Tanzania, Mr Juma A Ali, Consul General, 3rd Floor, Palli House, Nyerere Ave (PO Box 1422; ☎011/228596).

UK, Captain R G C Diamond (PO Box 80424; ☎011/312817; residence ☎011/316502).

Hospitals A recommended hospital (if you need to be in one) is the Pandya Memorial Hospital on Dedan Kimathi Ave (☎011/314140). It's hygienic and efficient.

Immigration You can get visitor's pass extensions at the Provincial Headquarters on Mama Ngina Drive (☎011/311745); and it shouldn't cost you anything, unlike in Nairobi, but leave enough time, as you always have to wait.

Library, Msanifu Kombo St. Open Mon–Thurs 9.30am–6pm, Fri 9.30am–4pm, Sat 8.15am–12.15pm.

Luggage storage Apart from hotels, the only place to leave bags is the railway station, and their rates seem excessive.

Maps The Survey of Kenya town plan *Mombasa Island and Environs* is useful but it predates the new Nyali Bridge and many recent street name changes. The street-plan book *Mombasa A to Z* (Kenway) is helpful if you're living in Mombasa. If you want to get Survey of Kenya maps of the coast, it's the same story as in Nairobi (see p.127), but authorization is unlikely to be given to tourists. The relevant addresses are the Provincial Surveyor's office, 12th Floor, Bima House, Digo Rd (Mon–Fri 9am–12.30pm & 2–4pm), where you can go to look at what they have, and the DC's office, Room 19, Provincial Headquarters, Mama Ngina Drive, which is the stultifying department you must visit if you think it's worth trying to get "the letter of authorization". If you fail, as you probably will, return to Bima House and see if there's anything they can do to help.

Pharmacies The staff at *Diamond Arcade Pharmacy*, Diamond Arcade, Moi Ave (☎011/316351; Mon–Fri 8am–6pm, Sat 9am–2pm), are pleasant and helpful. There's no longer any 24-hour cover in Mombasa: hospital dispensaries can supply necessary drugs and medicaments out of hours.

Port cruises The *MV Mvita*, one of the Likoni ferries, has been rigged up as a "pleasure craft" and in the high season, when interest is sufficient, trundles around Kilindini Creek for a couple of hours (departures at 10am, 2pm and 6.30pm; about $10) to give you ample viewpoints of the Container Terminal, the General Cargo Berths, the Bulk Handling Facilities and other attractions. Enquiries at the Likoni Ferry Office (☎011/226220). It hardly compensates for not being allowed to look around the dhow harbour on the other side.

Post office and telephones The post office for free poste restante and main services is the General Post Office (GPO) in Digo Rd (Mon–Fri 8am–6pm, Sat 8am–noon). There are cardphones here and a staffed, 24-hour telephone service.

Theatre The Little Theatre Club (PO Box 81143; ☎011/312101) on Mnazi Moja Rd is the occasional venue for the *Shangari Players*, who put on works by African playwrights. *LTC Players* occasionally put on African productions, but on the whole they're an outlet for amateur dramatics in the expat/settler community. Seats are about $1 for non-members.

Tide tables Can be very useful, especially in the Lamu archipelago where ferry departures are dependent upon them; available in bookshops.

Vaccinations The Public Health Department in Msanifu Kombo St gives yellow fever and cholera jabs Wed morning and Fri afternoon and typhoid Wed afternoon. For women only: yellow fever and cholera Tues afternoon, typhoid Mon morning.

Worship The Catholic Holy Ghost Cathdral is on Nyerere Ave. The Anglican Memorial Cathedral is off Nkrumah Rd, down on the right near Fort Jesus.

North of Mombasa

It's easy to get **out of Mombasa** for the day to explore the nearby North Coast. If it's busier, brasher, and generally less pastoral than the South Coast (see p.378), there are also more targets for a day trip up here, with correspondingly less appeal if you simply want to stretch out on the beach. The resorts start just ten minutes' drive from the city centre. Alternatively, if you're on foot, there is ample transport from the Abdul Nassir Road bus and *matatu* area near the *New People's Hotel*. Or simply walk over to the other side of Nyali Bridge and flag down transport near the old toll station. You won't wait long.

Nyali and Nyali Beach

Nyali, the comfortable suburb of Mombasa closest to the town, has a few minor items of interest of its own – apart from three of the North Coast's main hotels. It was the site of

Johan Ludwig Krapf's first missionary toe-hold on the east coast, four years before Livingstone arrived in Africa. Krapf reached Nyali with his wife and baby daughter in May 1844. His wife died of malaria on July 13; their baby the next day. The pathetic graves – still carefully tended by parishoners of St Peter's Church, Nyali – are to be found at the end of the road leading past the *Tamarind Restaurant* (see p.362). Nearby, on a small knoll, is the stone **Krapf Memorial**.

There's another reminder of the early history of Mombasa in the site of the **Freretown Bell**, at the Nyali Road junction. The bell was erected by the Society of Freed Slaves in the 1880s to warn the people of Freretown (named after Sir Bartle Frere, who founded the freed slave community here) of any impending attack by Arab slavers. The district still has inhabitants who trace the roots of their freed-slave ancestors back to Malawi and Zambia. For years the old bell hung silently under its small stone arch: then, in 1994 it was removed for safekeeping to a nearby Lutheran church, where it is in use, and replaced by a plastic replica – which has now been spirited away.

Behind Nyali Beach and the hotels, you can't miss **Mamba Village** on Links Road. Nothing to do with poisonous snakes, this is the biggest crocodile (*mamba*) farm in Kenya, with hefty entry fees to the "crocodile trail" and film show (daily 8.30am–6.30pm; visitors Ksh400, residents Ksh150). A series of semi-natural pools, created in a disused quarry, houses many hundreds of crocodiles at all stages of growth (and a special freaks sideshow of congenitally deformed croc-lets – not a pleasant sight). The overall effect – with "croco-burgers" in the snack bar and unlimited saurian souvenirs – is tacky in the extreme, and the crocodile trail sits uneasily with the skin-farming half of the "village", which is not on show. You might come expecting some sign of respect from the owners, or even some affection for these extraordinary ancient reptiles. Not a bit of it.

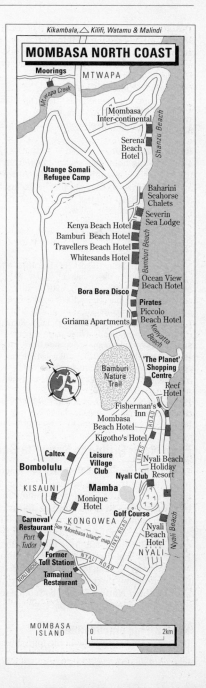

MOMBASA NORTH COAST

Kikambala, △ Kilifi, Watamu & Malindi

Moorings
MTWAPA
Mtwapa Creek

Mombasa Inter-continental
Serena Beach Hotel
Shanzu Beach

Utange Somali Refugee Camp

Baharini Seahorse Chalets
Severin Sea Lodge

Kenya Beach Hotel
Bamburi Beach Hotel
Travellers Beach Hotel
Whitesands Hotel
Bamburi Beach

Ocean View Beach Hotel

Bora Bora Disco
Pirates
Piccolo Beach Hotel

Giriama Apartments
Kenyatta Beach

N

Bamburi Nature Trail

'The Planet' Shopping Centre

Reef Hotel

Fisherman's Inn
Mombasa Beach Hotel
Kigotho's Hotel

Caltex
Bombolulu
Leisure Village Club

Nyali Beach Holiday Resort

Nyali Club

KISAUNI
Mamba
Monique Hotel

Golf Course

Carneval Restaurant
KONGOWEA
See "Mombasa Island" map
Nyali Beach Hotel

Port Tudor
LINKS ROAD
Nyali Beach

Former Toll Station
NYALI ROAD
NYALI

Nyali Bridge
Tamarind Restaurant

MOMBASA ISLAND

0   2km

Across the road from *Mamba Village* is **Nyali Golf and Country Club** (PO Box 985678; ☎011/472632), a stuffy sort of place that doesn't go out of its way to welcome non-members. They maintain a dress code for men (shirts with collars, socks on feet) in return for which they offer an ordinary swimming pool, squash, tennis (all about Ksh150 a session for non-members) and, of course, golf (Ksh1000 a round for non-members or Ksh200 if playing with a Nyali Club member). A restaurant of the reliable *Minar* group has opened next door, specializing in Mughlai cuisine (☎011/472136).

The main **public access to the beach** at Nyali is right by the entrance to *Nyali Beach Hotel*. It gets pretty busy at weekends.

Accommodation

The following hotel listings are given from south to north. Note that we've omitted the trio of hotels just south of *Mombasa Beach Hotel* – namely *Bahari Beach*, *Silver Beach* and *Silver Star* – as they are for the exclusive use of *African Safari Club* clients.

Nyali Beach Hotel (PO Box 90581; ☎011/471567, fax 011/471987; reservations through *Block*, see p.48). Pleasant, bustling and well maintained, this is one of the coast's oldest and most reputable hotels – establishment in feel but not in any way exclusive. There are two good pools (one huge and rectangular for lengths) and extensive gardens – a delight for naturalists. Some ramps for wheelchair users; limited children's facilities; PADI diving school. Standard rooms are very comfortable. B&B ⑤ low, ⑧ high.

Nyali Beach Holiday Resort (PO Box 1874; ☎011/226521). Reasonable apartment complex – self-catering or eating in the restaurant. ③ low, ④ high.

Mombasa Beach Hotel (PO Box 90414; ☎011/471861, fax 011/472970; reservations through *AT&H*, see p.48). Despite the clumsy 1960s architecture, there's a good atmosphere here – largely the result of its long-established, shady, clifftop location and pleasant, helpful staff. B&B ⑤ low, ⑦ high.

Kigotho's Hotel (Fawlty Towers), Links Road. Nicknamed Fawlty Towers (the owner is a big fan of the TV sitcom), this is a little oasis of personal attention in a sea of big hotels. Pool, cheap bar, and apartment-style rooms in separate blocks in the garden. ④ low, ⑤ high.

Reef Hotel (PO Box 82234; ☎011/471771, fax 011/471349; reservations through PO Box 61048 Nairobi, ☎02/214322). Large, brash, somewhat anonymous and expensive. Pretentious, too: guests must dress for dinner. Unexceptional beach and grounds, but plenty of activities. B&B ⑤ low, ⑦ high.

Fishermen's Inn (PO Box 99087; ☎011/472214, fax 011/222930). Formerly the *Nyali Inn*, not by the beach and not an obvious choice but very reasonably priced for the neighbourhood. No nets, but the AC rooms are decent, there's a pool and the Sunday curry buffet is famous. ⑤.

From Nyali Bridge to Kenyatta Beach

Beyond the Freretown Bell and the junction for Nyali – always jostling with people trying to get transport to their shifts at the hotels – the main coast road ploughs through an area of burgeoning suburban growth. Ignored by the resort developers because it's too far from the sea, the primitive living conditions and milling activity here can come as a shock if you're fresh off the plane. Utange Camp (a Somali "intellectuals" refugee camp, full of writers, performers, musicians and their families) is not far away and its inhabitants have imposed an additional burden on the district. This is the Kenya coast that doesn't appear in the brochures. The *KBS* bus #31 comes along this way, as far as Mtwapa town on the other side of Mtwapa Creek. Before you get back to the shore again, there are two very worthwhile objectives to be visited – **Bombolulu** and **Bamburi Nature Trail** – both of them recommended outings whether you're travelling independently or on a package.

Nyali Bridge practicalities

If you're not going to stay in the tourist haunts on the seafront, check out the following hotels.

Monique Hotel, 1.5km north of Nyali Bridge, just after the Agip station, then signposted 200m to the right (PO Box 97263; ☎011/474231). Good-value, clean, well-ventilated local hotel, with large single beds (intended for two). ③.

Leisure Village Club, 1.6km north of Nyali Bridge, signposted left. Huge disco/bar with attached rooms "for those who need a rest" – but as well run as any such place and always lively and popular. Basic s/c rooms with fans but no nets. ③.

Bombolulu

Workshops Mon–Fri 8am–12.45pm & 2–5pm (free); Showroom Mon–Sat 8am–6pm (free); Cultural Centre Mon–Sat 8am–5pm (visitors Ksh200, residents Ksh50); PO Box 83988, Mombasa (☎011/471704, fax 011/473570).

Just off the main road 3km north of Nyali Bridge (KBS bus #31 from Abdul Nassir Road in Mombasa, beyond the Malindi buses area), **Bombolulu** is a crafts training school and manufacturing centre that employs over 250 disabled people, mostly polio victims, from Coast Province. The **jewellery workshop** is the programme's biggest money-spinner, with hundreds of original designs in metal and local materials (old coins, seeds) now being exported to the USA and Europe – you'll come across them in charity gift catalogues. A more recent development is the opening of a **cultural centre**, incorporating traditional architecture from several of Kenya's peoples, around a central restaurant and dance floor, where daily dance and acrobatics performances take place at lunchtime.

Bamburi Nature Trail

Open daily 9am–5pm; feeding time 4pm; visitors Ksh300, residents Ksh50; PO Box 81995, Mombasa (☎011/485729).

Five kilometres beyond Bombolulu, the **Bamburi Nature Trail** is the result of an unusual attempt to rehabilitate a giant quarry. The Bamburi Cement Factory (whose giant kilns are visible from miles around) has been scouring the land for limestone here since 1954, at the rate of 35 hectares each year. In 1971, they began a concentrated programme of tree-planting in an effort to rescue the disfigured landscape. Later, as the project gained momentum, fish-breeding was established, and large numbers of animals and birds introduced, including several **hippos**. There are plenty of **crocodiles** in a setting devoid of *Mamba Village's* landscaped excesses and quite a comprehensive collection of snakes, including some dangerously unprotected poisonous ones. You'll have the opportunity to get close to a number of other, harmless, creatures, including pelicans, crowned cranes, various antelopes and some splendid giant tortoises.

The paths wind through dense groves of casuarina, a tree known for its ability to withstand a harsh environment, across ground which is mostly below sea level, permanently moist with salty water percolating through the coral limestone bedrock. The fish-farming side of the operation experiments with different types of **tilapia**, a freshwater fish highly tolerant of brackish conditions, many tons of which now reach shops and restaurants every year. The Bamburi Trail is a serious bid to put the small-is-beautiful principle into conservation practice: a modest contribution in a land of vast wildlife parks, but a terrific success. *KBS* bus #31 (see "Bombolulu", above) will drop you at the nature trail bus stop; don't catch a Bamburi bus – you want Bamburi Cement Factory.

Kenyatta, Bamburi and Shanzu beaches

These three contiguous stretches of beach are the heart of the "North Coast". If you're out for the day, there should, in most cases, be little difficulty in visiting a hotel and using its beachfront. (The beach itself is entirely public; it's the access to it which has been progressively restricted by the hotel developers.) Drift into a hotel in "smart-casual" attire and avail yourself of the facilities. If your presence is questioned, you may pay up to Ksh200 per day visitor's fee so, alternatively, be comfortable and pay upfront (the money is often recoupable against drinks or food). Either way, *Whitesands* and *Serena Beach* are perhaps the nicest hotels along this stretch.

One beach that is unquestionably public and, unfortunately, not very interesting, is **Kenyatta Municipal Beach**. It is, however, the site of a waterslide set-up, *Pirates*, with a bar and restaurant, which has become quite an attraction on Friday and Saturday nights. The slides are a required outing for kids, in any case. They're as good as you'll find anywhere, certainly in Africa, consisting of one long, steep and fast one, with a big jump, and one curling and gentle. It's open daily and twenty slides cost Ksh200, or you can wear yourself out with an all-day (or evening) pass for Ksh300.

Accommodation

Between Bamburi Quarry and Mtwapa Creek, nearly twenty **beach hotels** throng the six-kilometre shoreline. Most of those that can be booked in the usual way (or in which package tourists may find themselves staying) are marked on our map of the beaches, but seven along Shanzu Beach, run by the Swiss *African Safari Club* company as resorts exclusively for their clients, have been omitted. The following hotel listings are arranged from south to north.

If you're travelling on a tight budget, you'll find there's nowhere cheap to stay in the vicinity and – unless you're returning to Mombasa – you should forge on to the other side of Mtwapa Creek for some cheap hotels, or continue to the altogether more appealing beach and budget accommodation at Kikambala (see p.373).

Giriama Apartment Hotel (PO Box 86693; ☎011/485090, fax 011/485964). Large apartment complex, which also offers hotel rooms to the rear of the plot. Spacious, but not fancy. B&B ⑤ low, ⑥ high.

Piccolo Beach Hotel (PO Box 82671; ☎011/485236, fax 011/485463). Very small, unpretentious and inexpensive, with a narrow plot (no gardens to lounge in) and a small pool. The best rooms have bath and balcony and are a good size. Very ordinary food. B&B ⑤ low, ⑥ high.

Ocean View Beach Hotel (PO Box 81127; ☎011/485601, fax 011/314199). Co-owned with the *Oceanic* in Mombasa town – a bit of a warning. Really quite down-market with little space, or shade, in the garden. Fairly suitable for children (the pool has a springboard and slide) and a very informal (perhaps too informal) atmosphere. B&B ⑤ low, ⑥ high.

Whitesands Hotel (PO Box 90173; ☎011/485926, fax 011/485652; reservations through *Sarova*, see p.50). A very impressive, very self-confident operation. Enormous public areas, with several large pools and busy restaurants. Similar to *Nyali Beach Hotel* in its attention to detail, but on a grander scale (346 rooms). HB ⑦ low, ⑧ high.

Bamburi Beach Hotel (PO Box 83966; ☎011/485611, fax 011/485900). Barely adequate, mid-sized resort hotel with reasonable facilities and a nice pool. Crowded. HB ⑤ low, ⑥ high.

Travellers Beach Hotel (PO Box 87649; ☎011/485121, fax 011/485678). Big, fun, package-tour set-up with lots of shops and activities. You can swim into the lobby then slide out again, but you can't go on the beach at high tide, when it's submerged. Dull gardens, and somewhat tenement-like rooms, though spacious and well appointed. HB ⑥ low, ⑦ high.

Kenya Beach Hotel (PO Box 95748; ☎011/485821, fax 011/485574). A former *African Safari Club* establishment and still popular with Swiss and German tourists. Well-established hotel (over 20 years old) but simple and smaller than most with little in the way of watersports. HB ⑤ low, ⑦ high.

Severin Sea Lodge (PO Box 82169; ☎011/485001, fax 011/485212). Large, well-run and highly expensive resort hotel, with excellent sports and watersports but no beach at high tide. HB ⑦ low, ⑨ high.

Baharini Seahorse Chalets (PO Box 90371; ☎011/485633). An oasis in tourist-land, this is an excellent, inexpensive, locally managed apartment complex – most apartments have cooking facilities and hot water and all are well maintained. If you're coming by public transport, it's one stop past the *Fontana* restaurant, then about 700m down the access road. ④ low, ⑤ high.

Serena Beach Hotel (PO Box 90352; ☎011/485721, fax 011/485453; reservations through *Serena*, address p.50). Beautifully put-together in "high-Swahili" style, and very stylishly maintained, this is the most attractive proposition on this stretch of coast, even if the rooms are on the small side. Most watersports are free to guests, and they even take proper care of children. Great food. B&B ⑦ low, ⑨ high.

Mombasa Inter-continental (PO Box 83492; ☎011/485811, fax 011/485437; for reservations see p.49). Not many concessions to (or concerns with) local taste here: bland air-conditioned comfort in robust, international style, based around monolithic accommodation blocks. Happens to be by the sea, but you wouldn't know it. However, it's one of the few places you can do parascending on the coast (Ksh1500). B&B ⑦ low, ⑨ high.

Other practicalities

There are three main tourist **shopping centres** along the hotel stretch, each with adequate, if expensive, supermarkets and pharmacies. The first is a development called *The Planet*, on the corner of Links Road and the main highway. *Ocean View Shopping Plaza*, next to the hotel of the same name, has a branch of the efficient *Commercial Bank of Africa* (Mon–Fri 9.30am–2.30pm) and the best **disco** on the coast, *Bora Bora*. And the shops just north of *Whitesands* include a *KCB* **bank** (Mon–Fri 9am–1pm & 3–5pm, Sat 9–11am) and a small **post and telephone office** (Mon–Fri 8am–12.30pm & 2–5pm).

Mtwapa Creek and north

Mtwapa Creek marks the edge of Greater Mombasa, and tropical suburbia – with its scattered villas, supermarkets, clubs and restaurants (and poverty) – is more or less left behind. From here on, the road heads more determinedly, with fewer distractions, up to Kilifi, Watamu and Malindi. Note: if you're **continuing north**, beyond Kikambala, skip to p.395.

Mtwapa

There are one or two fairly rudimentary places to stay in and around **Mtwapa town** itself, including, just north of the creek on the right, the *Peemcea Hotel*, a great barn of a beer hall with a few cheap and basic rooms (PO Box 86743; ☎011/485083; ①), and some 3km further on the left, as Mtwapa fades away, the co-owned and slightly more up-market *Brisbane Hotel* (☎011/4856587; ②). But the main reasons to pause in Mtwapa are **boats** and **big fish**: the creek is fast becoming a focus for yachties and game fishermen. The floating *Moorings Restaurant*, in a fine, breezy location on the north side of the creek, accessible down a track immediately left after the bridge, has a seafood and vegetarian menu (☎011/487014; main courses Ksh200–300) and reasonably priced drinks, and is a good place for talk and tales – and to hook up with others, either in person or via the notice board. *James Adcock Fishing Ltd* (PO Box 95693; ☎/fax 011/485527) is based here, and there are always a dozen or more yachts and game-fishing boats moored around. *The Workshop*, just up the creekside behind *Moorings*, is a recently opened club (Wed, Fri & Sat; Ksh100 on Sat, otherwise usually free) that switches on when *Moorings* switches off, around 11pm; at the last check, it looked set to become a lively place.

Jumba la Mtwana

A totally different site worth pausing for (and worth a day out of town in its own right) is **JUMBA LA MTWANA** (open daily; Ksh200). This national monument, one of three between Mombasa and Malindi, is the ruined centre of a wealthy fourteenth- or fifteenth-century Swahili community. The sign for the 3km access road is about 1km past Mtwapa Creek bridge: if you're travelling by public transport and are dropped off at the junction, you have a good chance of getting a lift.

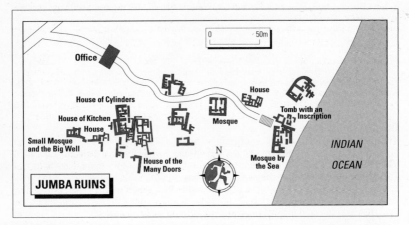

Jumba la mtwana means "mansion of the slave", but it has been deserted for some 500 years and probably had a different name in the past. It's a small site in an enchanting setting among baobabs and lawns above the beach. This seems a strange place for a town, right on an open shore, with no harbour, and it's possible the inhabitants were pushed here by raiding parties from inland groups, and relied on Mtwapa Creek as a safe anchorage for the overseas traders who visited yearly. Jumba is fortunate in having good water. But why it was deserted, and by whom, remains a mystery.

Compared with Gedi, further north (see p.401), Jumba's layout is simple. Though it lacks the eerie splendour of that much larger town, it must once have been a sizeable settlement; there were three mosques within the site and a fourth just outside. Most of the population would have lived in mud-and-thatch houses, which have long since disintegrated. In Swahili culture, building in stone (in fact, coral "rag" of different densities) has traditionally been the preserve of certain privileged people, principally the long-settled inhabitants of a town; newcomers would almost always build in less durable materials appropriate to their shorter-term stake in the community. It is also believed that building in stone required legal sanction, as it was the material used for mosques.

The best of Jumba's mosques is the **Mosque by the Sea** (a helpful little guidebook is sometimes available at the ticket office – much of this account has been culled from it), which shows evidence of there having been a separate room for women, something which is only nowadays becoming acceptable again in modern mosques. The cistern where worshippers washed is still intact, with coral foot-scrapers set nearby and a jumble of tombs behind the north wall facing Mecca. One of these has a Koranic inscription carved in coral on a panel facing the sea and must have been the grave of an important person:

> *Every soul shall taste death. You will simply be paid your wages in full on the Day of Resurrection. He who is removed from the fire and made to enter heaven, it is he who has won the victory. The earthly life is only delusion.*

The **people of Jumba** seem to have been very religious and hygienic – virtues that are closely associated in Islam. Cisterns and water jars, or at least the remains of them, are found everywhere among the ruined houses, and in most cases there are coral blocks nearby which would have been used to squat on while washing. Latrines are all stone-lined with long-drops. Of course, it is possible that the poorer people of Jumba lived in squalor in their mud huts, yet even the **House of Many Doors**, which seems to have been a fifteenth-century "boarding and lodging", provided guests with private washing and toilet facilities.

Look out for the two **smaller mosques**, each with its well-preserved, carved coral *mihrab* (the arched niche that indicates the direction of Mecca), and for the strange chinks in several walls (in the House of the Cylinders and the Small Mosque), the purpose of which is unknown.

Jumba Beach is a good place to while away an afternoon – in fact late afternoon, when the atmosphere hangs among the ruins like cobwebs, is probably the best time to come. Strange but attractive screw pines grow, aerial-rooted like mangroves, in the sand. You can **camp** here as well; there are toilets and showers by the ticket office.

Kikambala

For a day trip out of Mombasa without your own transport, **KIKAMBALA**, a few kilometres further up the coast, is about as far as you'd want to come. Note that the topography here is very flat: the sea goes out for nearly a kilometre and it's largely impractical for bathing except at high tide, so if you're just coming for the day, consult a tide table before setting off. The only official **campsite** in the area is here, at the *Kanamai Conference and Holiday Centre*, or *"Kanamai Youth Hostel"*. The first low-budget beach spot north of Mombasa, it makes a good stop-over, and if you plan to stay more than a night you're not utterly marooned: there's usually someone with a vehicle at the site who'll be going to the *dukas* on the main road most mornings and, once or twice a week, if you help with petrol, into Mombasa.

Much of the coastal strip here is still thickly forested and the beach itself is a glorious white expanse, though it's 2–3km from the highway. From *Kanamai*, a half-hour stroll north along the sandy lane through the emerald woods brings you to the *Whispering Palms Hotel*, where you can join in all the usual holiday pursuits. You could also splurge on a day pass at the all-inclusive *Club Sun 'n' Sand* (10am–5pm Ksh1400; 5pm–midnight Ksh1800), which is another half-hour's walk further north. Unless you happen to be staying at them, the other Kikambala addresses are not worth a special visit. Vehicles normally approach the beach properties from the northern access road, and the following places are listed in that order. Only *Kanamai* is quicker to reach from the southern access road. See the "Mombasa Area" map on p.344.

ACCOMMODATION

The Kikambala hotels are virtually the last on the coast north of Mombasa until you reach Kilifi. One downside of being this far out of town, if you haven't got a car, is that taxis into Mombasa cost over Ksh1200 each way.

Sea Top Lodging, 1.7km from the main road (PO Box 226, Kikambala; ☎0125/32184). Substantial *nyama choma* bar and nightspot, with decent s/c rooms for weary clients. Fans, but no nets. ①–②.

NK Villa Palm Garden Hotel, 1.8km from the main road (PO Box 115, Kikambala; ☎0125/32011, fax 0125/32471). Quite an attractive, shady establishment, but plays on its sleazy reputation with low-budget German package tourists. Studio apartments with kitchen and living room. Modest pool. ④.

Club Sun 'n' Sand, 2.1km from the main road (PO Box 2, Kikambala; ☎0125/32008, fax 0125/32123). One of the oldest hotels on the Kenya coast, originally built in 1932 and recently reopened as an all-inclusive club – it's among the biggest in the country, with nearly 300 bright, functional rooms, furnished with some style. Three large pools, with diving boards, an extended "river" and slides. Lots of activities, including a kids' club. Efficient, pleasant staff make this one of the most popular and regularly recommended club-hotels on the coast. There are several small shops and *dukas* near the gate if the club atmosphere begins to get claustrophobic. ⑦ low, ⑧ high.

Palm Tree Cottages, 2.6km from the main road (PO Box 82448; ☎0125/26436). Four-bed houses with room for two more in each. Not especially good value and a very uninspiring plot. Four-bed cottages with space for two more beds: Ksh2000.

Le Soleil Beach Club, 3.2km from the main road (PO Box 84737, Mombasa; ☎0125/32343, fax 0125/32164). More like a tropical office block than a hotel, this is tacky and unimaginative, but nonetheless busy, with a cosmopolitan variety of budget package tourists. All-inclusive, and daily visits are not possible – no great loss. ⑦.

Continental Beach Cottages, 3.6km from the main road (PO Box 124, Kikambala; ☎0125/32077, fax 0125/32190). Not a great deal of atmosphere, but tranquil enough, with a reasonable, slightly green pool, all set amid lots of tall, established coconut trees. The relatively expensive cottages have TV, AC and nets. Choice of self-catering or eating in the restaurant. Self-catering cottages for two with one double bed: Ksh2300 low, Ksh2600 high.

Whispering Palms Hotel, 3.9km from the main road (PO Box 5, Kikambala; ☎0125/32620, fax 0125/32029). Peaceful, isolated hideaway for a mix of package tourists from Britain and Europe, but old-fashioned and in need of an overhaul. Well-shaded grounds of, at times, quite noisy palm trees. Slightly cheaper than its equivalents closer to Mombasa. HB ⑤ low, ⑥ high.

Kanamai Holiday Centre, 5.5km from the north junction of the main road, 3km from the south junction (PO Box 46, Kikambala; ☎0125/32046). Big, sprawling – but pretty – place under the coconuts, run by the National Christian Council of Kenya. The options are beds in dormitories (very basic, B&L level; ①), double room accommodation (roomy and well furnished, with good fans; ③), or camping pretty much wherever you like (Ksh100 per person). *Kanamai* offers basic meals in the dining room (Ksh80–200) and has a shop with a few provisions, but there's no bar and, for a stay of several days, you should bring supplies.

Inland from Mombasa: Mijikenda country

If you're coming from Nairobi, **MAZERAS** marks the end of the long vistas of scrub; it's perched right on the edge of the steep scarp, amid bananas and coconuts. If you're travelling by road, it isn't a bad idea to break your journey here and savour the new atmosphere; city buses run between Mazeras and Mombasa, about thirty minutes away. The *hotelis* serve good, flavourful, coastal *chai* and, for the travel-weary, Mazeras has some delightful **botanical gardens** – bamboo, ponds and green lawns for a snooze in the shade – just a couple of hundred metres back towards Mombasa. Across the road and up the hill a little way is a **mission** and its century-old church, signs of an evangelical presence in the hills behind Mombasa that goes back, remarkably, nearly 150 years.

For historians of Methodism and the Church Missionary Society or (more likely) connoisseurs of palm wine, the **road to Kaloleni**, 22km north of Mazeras (see the map on p.344), is a required sidetrack. It is a beautiful trip in its own right: wonderfully scenic, looping through lush vales with a wide panorama down to the coast on the right and millions of **coconut trees** all around. There's at least one bus every hour from Mombasa, which makes this an easy day trip away from the coast, especially appealing in the high season if your sense of adventure has become numbed by the influx of tropical paradise-seekers.

Rabai

RABAI, capital of the **Wa-Rabai** Mijikenda and site of the first mission to be established in East Africa, is the first village you come to. The German pastor, the Reverend **John Ludwig Krapf**, came here in 1846 after losing his family at Nyali (see p.367), and left his mark on the community when, 33 years later, a very imposing **church**, now blue and white, was erected to preach down at the wayward coconut palms. The centre of the village and the church, surrounded by school rooms and sports fields, lie half a kilometre off the main road on the right. The first church to have been built is now used as a school room, as is the cottage of Johann Rebmann, Krapf's proselytizing partner. Between them, the two missionaries managed to explore a great deal of what is now Kenya without the demonstrations of firepower so many of their successors thought necessary. Krapf worked out the grammar of Swahili and produced a translation of the Bible. Krapf's own house has recently been renovated and is now a private

THE MIJIKENDA PEOPLES

The principal people of the coastal hinterland region are the **Mijikenda** ("Nine Tribes"), a loose grouping whose Bantu languages are to a large extent mutually intelligible, and closely related to Swahili. They are believed to have arrived in their present homelands in the sixteenth or seventeenth century from a quasi-historical state called Shungwaya, which had undergone a period of intense civil chaos. This centre was probably located somewhere in the Lamu hinterland or in the southwest corner of present-day Somalia. According to oral tradition, the people who left it were the Giriama, the Digo, the Rabai, the Ribe, the Duruma, the Chonyi, the Jibana, the Kauma and the Kambe (not to be confused with the Kamba of the interior).

All these "tribes" now live in the coastal hinterland, with the **Giriama** and **Digo** the largest and best-known groups. They share a degree of common cultural heritage. Each tribe has a traditional **kaya** central settlement, a fortified village in the forest, usually built on raised ground some kilometres from the coast, but sometimes right by the shore. Some Mijikenda peoples built only one *kaya*; others spawned secondary *kayas* or even whole clusters of *kayas*. The *kayas* still exist, although they are now sacred glades rather than fortified villages. In theory, they each contain a *fingo* – a charm said to derive from the ancestral home of Shungwaya – but these have nearly all been destroyed or, like the grave posts made from the *brachylinum* tree called *kigango* (*vigango* in the plural) that were also formerly a feature of each *kaya*, stolen for private collections of "primitive art" or loft-converters' ideas of interesting *objets d'art*.

Today, most *kayas* are run-down, but they are still remembered and visited by one or two elders. While their sacred aspect has ceased to have much relevance for most Mijikenda, their true significance comes out under pressure: when a German hotel developer took a fancy to Chale island (the whole of which is a gazetted *kaya*), he had to "buy" two Digo medicine men to appease the spirits – not best pleased with having their groves smothered in concrete. Nor is their human value the only reason to care about the *kayas*: along with belief in their sacred qualities comes a local conservation tradition. In these forest tracts of between five hectares and three square kilometres nothing has ever been cultivated or disturbed. They represent a biological storehouse of immense diversity, unique along the East African coast. A WWF-backed botanical research programme is underway to map out the *kaya* ecosystems and to encourage the elders to reassert their authority over each one. More than twenty *kayas* have so far been gazetted in Kwale district, south of Mombasa, and the process has now started in the Kilifi area. There may be more than fifty altogether, though some could be so small they will disappear under the hoe or the caterpillar tractor before anyone remembers them. It may be possible to visit a *kaya* (write to the project headquarters if you are genuinely interested – PO Box 86, Ukunda; ☎0127/2518; E-mail cfcu1@tt.gn.aopc.org) but they are by no means tourist attractions. The possibility that one or two of the old sacred groves might be opened to tourists to generate income still seems some way off. *The Kaya Complex* (Thomas Spear, Kenya Literature Bureau) provides interesting reading.

Like so many other Kenyan peoples, the Mijikenda had age-set systems that helped cut across the divisive groupings of clan and subclan to bind communities together. Much of this tradition has been lost during this century; the installation of a new ruling elders' age-set, for example, required the killing and castration of a stranger.

Economically, the Mijikenda were, and still are, diverse. They were cultivators, herders (especially the Duruma and, at one time, the Giriama), long-distance traders with the interior, makers of palm wine (a Digo speciality now diffused all over Mijikenda-land), hunters and fishermen. They have local market cycles – four-day weeks in the case of the Giriama (days one and two for labour, day three for preparation, and day four, called *chipolata*, for market). They have successfully maintained their cultural identity, warring with the British in 1914 over the imposition of taxes and the demand for porters for World War I, and preserving a vigorous conservative tradition of adherence to their old beliefs in spirits and the power of their ancestors. Many Mijikenda, however, have found conversion to Islam a helpful religious switch in their dealings with coastal merchants and businessmen. This conversion seems to be the latest development in the growth of Swahili society.

home. For all its significance, though, and despite the presence of the Krapf Memorial Secondary School, Rabai "centre" has, in all truth, hardly anything to offer.

Ribe

RIBE (the **Wa-Ribe** village) is more substantial than Rabai but harder to get to. Seven kilometres from Rabai, an unmarked track snakes up to the right from a deep valley floor: the village is one and a half kilometres along it. Buses stop by the track. If you're driving, continue to a sign (on the right) for a lead mine. Ribe is the second village along the track, about 4km from the main road. It consists of a few small shops and a shady bar-restaurant with a courtyard and rooms (②).

Fifteen minutes' walk away, through the *shambas* and dense undergrowth, is a tiny **cemetery**, regularly cleared of weeds and creepers, near the site of Ribe's Methodist mission, itself crumbled to its foundations and now completely overgrown. It isn't hard to find, and it's worth visiting if only to take a look at the pathetic graves of those few missionaries who struggled all the way here before succumbing in what must have been nearly impossible conditions. They were often very young: the Reverend Butterworth, whose carpentry skills ensured him a welcome arrival, died aged 23, just two months after getting there; they used his new tools to make the coffin. It isn't surprising that the cemetery faces out to sea: towards Mombasa, supplies, the mail and new settlers.

Kaloleni

The paved road comes to its end at **KALOLENI**. On the way, you pass through dense coconut groves where many of the trees have been initialled to avoid ownership disputes. The tapping of **palm wine** (*tembo*), banned by the government, is still widely practised here, with the **Giriama** section of the Mijikenda leading the field. They call palm wine "the mother of the coconut", since tapping the trees for juice hinders formation of the nuts.

Tapping is done by cutting off the flower stem, binding it tightly and allowing the sap that would have produced new coconuts to collect in a container – usually a baobab pod – tied to the end. Here it ferments rapidly and has to be regularly collected. Variations in the local demand for *tembo*, which is most often drunk at community gatherings like weddings and funerals, and in the coastal market for *copra* (the dried coconut flesh used in soap and oil manufacture), tend to influence the owners of trees in their decision whether to tap or to grow *copra*. You will often see trees with the step-notches that enable the tappers to reach the top sometimes ending several metres below the crown, indicating that a tree has been left a number of years to develop coconuts.

Palm wine is locally available up and down the coast. In Kaloleni a beer bottle-full costs just a few shillings. It is best when cold, but rarely is, and you drink it (discreetly) through a reed straw with a coconut-fibre filter.

The best place to **stay** in Kaloleni is the clean and friendly *Kaloleni Central Restaurant* (PO Box 34 Kaloleni; Kaloleni ☎64; ②) in the town centre, opposite the main bus stop.

Shimba Hills National Park

Entry $20, students $10, children $5; warden PO Box 16030, Kwale, ☎0127/4159. Map – Survey of Kenya SK93 at 2.5cm:1km (1980), or Sapra Safari's "The Kenya Coast".
Probably Kenya's most underrated wildlife refuge, **SHIMBA HILLS** is less than an hour from Mombasa and, at 500m above sea level, a real refresher after the humidity

down below. The hilly park of scattered jungle and grassland is comparatively little visited, which is all to the good: it has a quite wonderful game-viewing lodge and one of the best situated camping and *banda* sites anywhere.

Kwale and access to the park

The most straightforward option for visiting Shimba is a **safari from Mombasa** (tickets from most coast hotels and travel agents – about $60–90 for a day trip, $120 for an overnight at *Shimba Lodge*). These prices include park entrance fees but not game drives or nature walks.

Otherwise, unless you're driving your own vehicle (note that Kwale doesn't always have petrol), there are fairly frequent country buses and hourly *KBS Stagecoach* #34 buses to **Kwale** from Mombasa's Likoni ferry bus park. The park's **main gate** is some 5km beyond Kwale along an elephant-dunged murram road. Here, you can try for **a lift** around the park. Since your best bet is with Mombasans, Sundays and public holidays are the easiest times. If you have no luck, you can always **catch the next bus** going on to **Kinango**. There are often elephants on this stretch of the road, which actually passes through a corner of the park. If you come up to Kwale on the bus, the last one back to Mombasa is the *Stagecoach* at 8pm. In case of need, there are two B&Ls in town. *Kwale Guest House* (①) is the better one.

A third alternative is to enquire about **a lift with the park vehicle**, which usually goes to Kidongo Gate on the southeast side of the park to collect gate money on Sunday and Wednesday afternoons. You should be able to get a ride, though people will want *chai*. Ask at the warden's house and offices just outside Kwale.

Shimba Lodge

Shimba is a tree hotel, a kind of coastal *Treetops*, though actually superior in all respects to the original. Check-in is from 3pm and vehicles park at the lodge gate, from where you're escorted – by armed ranger – to the lodge. It's all intensely atmospheric, as the building, apparently constructed entirely of pitch-dark timber, piles up through the trees and creepers, with aerial plantlife, birds, butterflies and humans all sharing the deep forest glade. The staff are instructed to speak in whispers, and remind guests to do so (children under 7 are not admitted). From nearly all the rooms, on three floors, and from several bars and observation platforms, you have views across a small, still lake to thick forest. The best feature is the **tree-level walkway**, which runs for 100m or so from one end of the lodge to a platform high above the ground near a small clearing. Hear you can watch elephants, warthogs, forest antelope and monkeys galore. After dark, spotlights illuminate bushbabies, hundreds of bats and a whirling hailstorm of jungle insects. It's a memorable evening – and the food is good.

The early-evening "sundowner" **nature walk** (4.30pm; Ksh460) is always enjoyable. The next morning there's the option of a proper **game drive** in the park (6am; Ksh730), with the opportunity to see the sable antelope for which Shimba is famous.

Half-board rates are ⑤ in low season, ⑥ high (suites with private facilities ⑦ all year; reservations through *Block*, see p.48). For solo travellers it's worth knowing the per-person rate is exactly half the twin, which makes it good value. At these prices, the standard rooms at *Shimba*, with shared showers and toilets, are adequate but basic. And exciting – when there are bushbabies on the branch outside and the possibility of a leopard, you don't spare too much thought for luxuries. If you're driving yourself and give advance notice, you can arrive early at the lodge and have lunch (Ksh600).

Around the park

Predators are rare in Shimba Hills but you may well see elephant, buffalo and the park's four Maasai **giraffe**. The giraffe, two males and two females, have so far failed to produce offspring – nobody knows why. Shimba is best known for its herds of **sable antelope**, magnificent-looking animals as big as a horse, with great, sweeping horns. The park is their only habitat in Kenya. (The similar but even bigger roan antelopes, which were relocated from Western Kenya, died out, it's thought, through lack of necessary minerals.) You are almost certain to see groups of chestnut-coloured sable females but the territorial, jet-black males are more solitary and harder to find. If you have a guide he'll know where to look, but they're most commonly seen in the area overlooking the ocean, between the campsite and Giriama Point.

Camping in Shimba Hills

What Shimba Hills may lack in wildlife it more than makes up for with enchanting views in every direction, especially seawards. Haze tends to blot out Mombasa itself but the fringe of Diani Beach is usually visible. The **camping and banda site** (Ⓓ) is located at one of the best vantage points in the park, about 3km from the main gate. The *bandas* here are adequate (though the bedding, lamps, shower, nearby toilet, and kitchen tents can't be relied on), but the setting is sublime: a thickly forested bluff hundreds of metres above the coconut-crowded coastal plain. It is well worth spending the night up here just for the sunrise. If you do, you'll probably have the place to yourself.

Mwaluganje Elephant Sanctuary

To the northwest of Shimba Lodge and the area where the "sundowner walks" normally take place, just outside the national park, lies the newly founded **Mwaluganje Elephant Sanctuary**. This a joint venture of the local Digo and Duruma people, the Kenya Wildlife Service and a natural history charity called the Eden Wildlife Trust. The sanctuary consists of hardwood and cycad forest and riverine vegetation and harbours a surprising wealth of wildlife. You are "guaranteed" to see elephants here and, in time, it is hoped that threatened species can be relocated here from other parts of Kenya. For the present, there are virtually no facilities, but Land Rovers make the day trip here from Diani Beach on request. *Diani Advice* (see p.389) can provide details.

THE SOUTH COAST

A continuous strip of beach runs between Likoni and Msambweni, backed by palms and broken once or twice by small rivers. Along the whole coast south from Mombasa to the Tanzanian border there's just one highly developed resort area, **Diani Beach**. South of Diani, the coast is little known and, in most tour operators' minds at least, nobody stops again until they reach **Shimoni**. This is great news if you have the time to go searching out untrodden beaches by car, bicycle or motorbike (all available to rent), or using the good local public transport.

Most of the people who live along the coastal strip here are **Digo** and their neat rectangular houses, made of dried mud and coral on a framework of wood, are a distinctive part of the lush roadside scene. Although they belong to the Mijikenda group of peoples, the Digo are unusual in being matrilineal: they traditionally traced descent through the female line, so that a man would, on his death, pass his property on to his sister's sons rather than his own. It is an unusual system with interesting implications for the state of the family and the position of women. However, the joint assault of Islamic and Western values over the last century has shifted the emphasis back towards the male line, and in many ways women in modern Digo society have less freedom and autonomy than they had at the turn of the century.

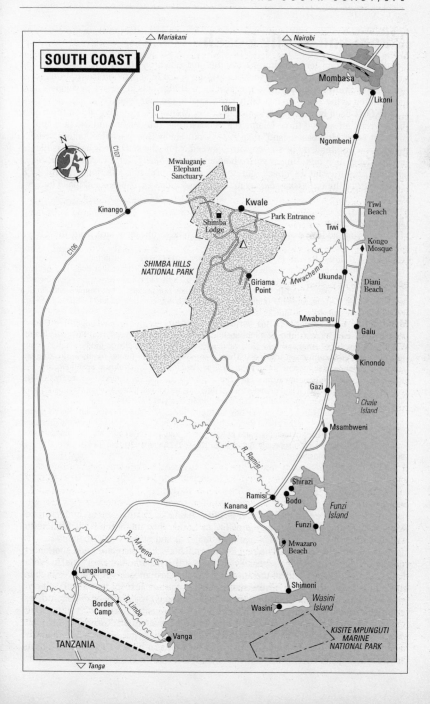

Likoni and Shelly Beach

Mombasa's Likoni ferry (*matatus* from the post office on Digo Road) makes all the difference: compared with the North Coast, the sense of separation from Mombasa is immediate. More pragmatically, the lack of a bridge has deterred developers and contributed to the South Coast's fairly late arrival in the tour brochures.

LIKONI itself is a busy creekside suburb of Mombasa, straggling down the south-bound road for a good three kilometres. A coast road runs off around the headland to the east (see "Mombasa Island" map, p.348), but Shelly Beach – named after its shells – is narrow and tends to be strewn with seaweed, while the sea here is only feasible for swimming at high tide. Unless you're booked into the *Shelly Beach Club* or the *Reliable Apartments*, or want to check out the slightly improbable offerings at the *CPK Guesthouse* or the *Children's Holiday Resort*, hop on a bus – any bus – and make for Tiwi or Diani.

Accommodation

The following addresses are all Mombasa PO boxes: distances are from the Likoni junction.

Childrens' Holiday Resort (3.5km; PO Box 96048; ☎011/451417). An indefinable low-budget bungalow establishment from another age, the *Resort* is a non-profit trust that goes way back. A peaceful, flat sandy site under the palms, it's run by a friendly old couple who will decide the rate according to your means and their convenience. Families are preferred but couples and singles aren't excluded. Self-catering only (utensils provided), with outside showers and toilets and nets on request. Twin rooms from as little as Ksh300.

CPK Guest House (300m; PO Box 96170; ☎011/451619). Even on a low budget, the Church Province of Kenya's coastal retreat might seem an odd choice. But it's well run, the better rooms are fine (showers and fans) and very good value and, while it's not exactly on the beach, it is handy for Mombasa and south coast transport. There's an attractive patio dining room overlooking the road, and a couple of shops and the very good *Island Paradise Bar & Restaurant* next door. ③.

Reliable Beach Apartments (2.5km; PO Box 82630; ☎011/451595, reservations ☎011/491954). Good-sized apartments on a plot of unsurpassed ugliness, with no facilities whatsoever, apart from a small pool. Two-bedroom apartments (up to 6 people) from about Ksh1800.

Shelly Beach Club Hotel (2.8km; PO Box 96030; ☎011/451001, fax 011/451349). By no means the most beautiful hotel on the coast, the *Shelly Beach Club* has always provoked widely divergent views: some rooms were undeniably basic but the place had a comfortable, slightly old-fashioned atmosphere that appealed, especially to families. Its 1996 conversion to an all-inclusive club has seen some modifications. ⑦.

Tiwi Beach

South of Likoni, the first real magnet is **TIWI BEACH**. Popular among budget travellers more for the old hippy hangout of **Twiga Lodge** than the beach itself, Tiwi nevertheless rates as genuine tropical paradise material and attracts lots of Anglo-Kenyan families down from Nairobi. The reef lies just offshore, and there are good snorkelling opportunities at high tide, especially at the northern end. And everyone uses the beach. Beach hustlers and all the attendant hassles have mostly yet to arrive, as there are no big hotels, nor even tarmac roads down to the sea (except for one stretch on a new development at the southern end): this is cottage territory, with nearly a dozen plots vying with each other for business.

There are two roads down to the beach from the main South Coast highway. The first, signposted "Tiwi Beach", is reached after a bit of a hill, some 17km from the Likoni ferry; the second, about 1.5km further south, has a bigger clump of signboards. If you're using the second road, you're stongly advised to heed the notice about not walking: although there have been no incidents for some time, many *panga*-point robberies of *Twiga*-bound back-packers have taken place on the lonely track through the cashews. Wait for a ride. This shouldn't be a huge problem as there's a fairly frequent taxi service (bargain hard: it should be no more than Ksh300).

In the dry season you can walk to the end of Tiwi Beach and wade across the Mwachema River to Diani Beach and the strange Kongo Mosque, right next to the *Indian Ocean Beach Club*. But check locally that it's safe: there have been one or two incidents of robbery down here and a pair of policemen have been stationed on duty in the bushes.

Accommodation

The seasons on Tiwi, as regards prices and availability, are slightly different from other parts of the coast in that they reflect the school holidays of their regular clients. At Christmas, Easter, and in July and August, it's hard to get in anywhere: advance booking is a good idea. Note that a large new development is under construction at the southern end of the beach. It opened briefly as *Falcon Bay Lodge* and may open again during the lifetime of this edition as *Travellers' Tiwi Beach Hotel*. If the impact of the developers' road-building activities extends to their hotel-management skills, Tiwi Beach may be in for a rude shock. The following listings are arranged from north to south. Note that although cottage prices are seasonal, the high-season supplement is small, say fifteen percent. Price codes refer to the cost for two people sharing a one-bedroom cottage; there are always big savings for groups in larger cottages.

Sand Island Beach Cottages (PO Box 96006, Mombasa; ☎0127/51233, fax 0127/51201). Very attractive site, with the island exposed, just yards across the water, nearly all the time, and safe swimming possible at all tides (there's a coral garden nearby). The products of a working farm are available, and lashings of old Kenya atmosphere. Prices for the fully equipped rustic cabins, all sea-facing, start at Ksh1200 low, Ksh1300 high for a small double,

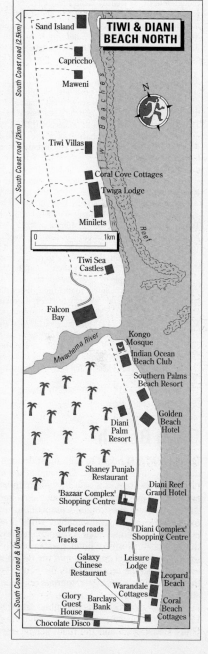

though four or six sharing is obviously cheaper per person. There are two even more basic two-bed *bandas* – "campettes" – in the ① and ② categories.

Capricho Beach Cottages (PO Box 96093, Mombasa; ☎0127/51231, fax 0127/51010; office hours 8–11am & 4–5pm). Where *Sand Island* has the advantage in its beach and flakey ambience, *Capricho* concentrates on its flashier amenities – well-designed vault-roofed cottages with plenty of cool space, and a pool (and no dogs – *Sand Island* love dogs). Closed in May. Much the same prices as *Sand Island*, basically ④.

Maweni Beach Cottages (PO Box 96024, ☎0127/51008, fax 0127/51225). Variety of relatively simple cottages in various positions. Slightly cheaper than either of its northerly neighbours but good value. The site is conscientiously managed and guarded, and there's a pretty little cove – though *Sand Island*'s and *Capricho*'s beaches are just a short stroll away. ③ low, ④ high.

Tiwi Villas (PO Box 86775, Mombasa; ☎0127/51265). Overpriced, cramped and dark cottages with no self-catering facilities apart from fridges (use their restaurant at Ksh200 a meal, or go else-where). Small pool but no beach. The inactive management appears to signal its decline. ③ low, ④ high.

Coral Cove Cottages (PO Box 96292, Mombasa; ☎0127/51061, fax 0127/57062). Pleasant, roomy cottages with fine new bathrooms and an attractive, palm-shaded beach, all bathed in a laid-back atmosphere provided by low-key but helpful management, who also run dhow trips to Kinonzini island next to Funzi ($75 all in). Twice a week *Coral Cove* makes transport available to Diani for shopping – otherwise the only food on site is eggs. Recommended. ④.

Twiga Lodge (PO Box 80820, Mombasa; ☎0127/51267). Basic hostel and campsite, which used to be the one place on the South Coast where overlanders and budget travellers were made to feel completely at home. For several years, however, it has been beset by security problems and inade-quate management; unless you have to park a large vehicle, or are bent on camping, it's now just the place you end up if you don't know about the alternatives. Another drawback: its beach is not as good as those a couple of kilometres to the north – it's hard to swim here at any tide. Apart from a variety of cell- or barrack-like rooms (no self-catering facilities), you can camp (Ksh120) or sleep in your vehicle. There's an adequately stocked provisions store and the bar-restaurant does reason-able food and sometimes gets lively in the evenings. Overpriced at ④.

Minilets (PO Box 96242, Mombasa; ☎0127/51059). One of the most southerly of the Tiwi proper-ties (*Twiga Lodge* is right next door). The neat chalets here are prettily scattered down a sloping old coral garden hillside, with a swimming pool at the bottom. Conscientiously managed, *Minilets* is busier than some of the more "private" properties at the north end of the beach, and its lively bar makes it a little less peaceful, but it's also cheaper. And Tiwi's only dive centre is located here. ③–④.

Tiwi Sea Castles (PO Box 96599, Mombasa; ☎0127/51220, fax 012751222). Comfortable, Dutch-run cottages – one of the most luxurious developments on Tiwi. ⑤.

Diani Beach

DIANI BEACH ought to fulfil most dreams about the archetypal palm-fringed beach; it could be simply fantastic. The sand is soft and brilliantly white; the sea is crystal-clear turquoise; the reef is a safe thirty-minute swim, or ten-minute boat ride away; while, arching out overhead, the coconut palms keep up a perpetual slow sway as the breeze rustles through the fronds. Competition for space, however, has begun seriously to mar Diani's paradisiacal qualities, while droves of hustlers and vendors – the "beach boys" – had become such a threatening presence a few years back (see box, p.387), that the vast majority of hotel guests virtually never ventured across the boundary from their guarded hotel gardens onto the public sands. Now several pairs of "tourist police" are posted to the area full-time, the beach boys have become more astute and formed themselves into cartels, and tourists do, once again, dig sandcastles and walk along the strand.

Whether driving or using public transport, you'll first arrive on the outskirts of Ukunda, just a few years ago a village on the highway, now a scruffily burgeoning South Coast town and the main service centre for the resort hotels. If you're using public transport, you're likely to need to change here for a *matatu* down to the beach road. Don't walk: the three-kilometre link road has a bad reputation – hard to tell how well-founded – for muggings.

Accommodation

Running three hundred metres behind the beach, the Diani Beach road feels like Kenya's number one strip in the high season. Fortunately, thick jungle separates the road from the beach, though more of the **Jadini Forest** disappears every year as one new plot after another is cleared. The **tourist hotels** that fill the plots are expensive by Kenyan standards and, if you've been travelling on a budget, the prices will come as a shock. If you're coming from abroad they seem more reasonably priced, and you'll find standards generally high. Most offer low-season reductions, but during the high season you'll be lucky to find a twin room with half-board for less than $140.

Budget accommodation along the beach is sparse and none of the hotels will entertain campers in their gardens. Although some of them offer tempting low-season rates, few of them drop to budget levels. The distances in the following listings are from the Ukunda junction on the Diani Beach road, by *Barclays Bank*.

Camping and cheap rooms

Dan Trench's used to be the only place to stay that could be described as "low-budget". Now there's some competition, the facilities at Dan's have improved a little.

Dan's Camping (1.4km south of the junction; c/o PO Box 867, Ukunda; ☎/fax 0127/2507). A kind of coastal *Ma Roche's*, this is the former home of Dan Trench, the son of the family who once owned much of the land down here – indomitable survivor of the development around him, until he died in 1990. The garden, for years a clutter of luxuriant foliage and deteriorating whitewashed *bandas*, has been cleared up and previously lamentable security tightened. It's all still very basic, but quite adequate if you're used to B&Ls, though it

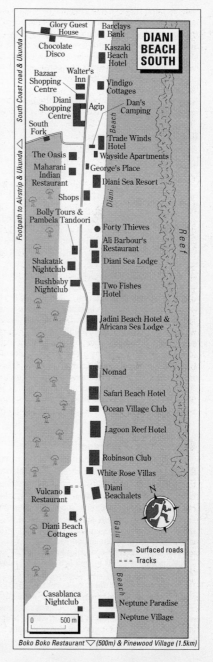

lacks the atmosphere it had when the old man was alive. A bicycle fruit-seller still arrives unfailingly every morning from his orchard farm in the bush, with bananas, papayas, mangoes, mandarins and exceptional grapefruit. Camping Ksh200. ②–③.

South Fork (1.4km south, then 800m from the road; PO Box 231, Ukunda, ☎0127/3053). Low-budget accommodation and campsite, set back in the bush and fields, opened in 1995. Several large, s/c studio rooms and a number of smaller non-s/c rooms, plus a cheap restaurant. Pleasant people, and well worth a look, though it's a good fifteen-minute walk to the beach at *Trade Winds*. Camping Ksh150. ③–④.

Glory Guest House, 500m west of the beach road junction on the way to Ukunda. Secure and more than adequate unit in this mini-chain of hotels, with a pool. ③ low, ④ high.

Cottages and apartments

As in the Tiwi beach cottage listings, price codes refer to the cost for two people sharing a one-bedroom cottage. There are always big savings for groups in larger cottages.

Coral Beach Cottages (300m north; PO Box 168, Ukunda, ☎0127/2206). A collection of cottages whose owners evidently live overseas, and which are rented out in their absence. On a parched, run-down site, this isn't an obvious first choice. ③ low, ④ high.

Warandale Cottages (600m north; PO Box 11, Ukunda, ☎0127/2186, fax 0127/2187). A tangle of different-sized houses and a small pool, all nestled under luxuriant vegetation, this is an exceptionally nice set-up – the staff clean and cook – and gets a lot of repeat bookings. Good for kids. *Mlima* (5 beds) is the best house. Two-bed cottages ③–④ low, ⑤ high, but cheaper in a bigger group.

Vindigo Cottages (700m south; PO Box 77 Ukunda; ☎0127/2192). Rustic charm – mosquito-screened windows, fans, electricity, running water in the showers and high-level toilets. Nothing fancy but very private – and, again, staff come with the rental. Slightly overpriced, especially for two beds. ④.

Wayside Beach Apartments (1.4km south; PO Box 83451, Mombasa; ☎0127/2440). Stylish two-to six-bed apartments in a horshoe-shaped building around a good pool, set between the main road and *Trade Winds*. Sauna and jacuzzi. ⑤.

White Rose Villas (6.4km; PO Box 80, Ukunda; ☎0127/2236). Six very spacious self-catering, sea-front cottages, sleeping four to six, with high makuti roofs, on a two-hectare plot. One "villa" has AC, others have fans. There's a decent pool and the whole place feels pleasantly laid-back. ⑤.

Diani Beachalets (6.5km south; PO Box 26, Ukunda; ☎0127/2180). Peaceful refuge with a variety of abodes, from simple two-bed *bandas* with fridge, electric light, communal showers and cooking area to reasonable, self-contained cottages. The beach is narrow, but pretty well deserted. Accommodation only. Two-bed huts ②; better-appointed cottages ② low, ③ high.

Diani Beach Cottages (6.8km south; PO Box 14; ☎/fax 0127/3471). Pleasant, modest set-up, with a relatively good pool, but overpriced. B&B ⑤.

Hotels north of the junction

Generally, the more interesting abodes worthy of major expenditure are to the south of the Ukunda junction – an area which also retains some flicker of pre-hotel times. To the north, the scene is brasher and more despoiled.

Leopard Beach Hotel (800m; PO Box 34, Ukunda; ☎0127/2111, fax ☎0127/2113). Similar to *Leisure Lodge*, but with a much better staff atmosphere. ⑤ low, ⑧ high.

Leisure Lodge & Club (1.2km; PO Box 84383; ☎0127/2011, fax 0127/2046). One of the earlier Diani hotels, this is beginning to look its age (1971). Club rooms are luxurious; standard rooms offer functional accommodation with nets and optional AC, yet it's always full of German package tourists. Redeemed by a striking location on low cliffs hollowed by bat-filled caves. The fine, tree-shaded private beach is tucked beneath. PADI diving school. No sea-swimming at low tide. ⑦ low, ⑨ high.

Diani Reef Grand Hotel (1.6km; PO Box 35, Ukunda; ☎0127/2723, fax 0127/2196). With over 300 centrally air-conditioned rooms (no fans, no nets), this is one of the largest hotels on the coast, with an international accent – fussy public areas, seven restaurants and numerous bars. Uninspiring regular and deluxe rooms in different wings, with not much to distinguish them but the quantity of gold chrome. Very overrated. On a positive note, it's ramped throughout. There's also a dive school. HB from ⑦ low, ⑨ high.

Golden Beach Hotel (2.7km; PO Box 31, Ukunda; ☎0127/2625, fax 0127/3188; reservations through *AT&H*, address on p.48). Almost unbelievably ugly concrete monolith. Irritating Muzak in reception. After that it's downhill all the way. Give it a miss. B&B ⑤ low, ⑦ high.

Southern Palms Beach Resort (2.9km; PO Box 363, Ukunda; ☎0127/3721, Mombasa fax 011/ 3381). Opened in 1992, this is a spacious and well-appointed package hotel, with a fabulous pool that kids adore. Unaccountably unhelpful management. HB ⑤ low, ⑥ high.

Indian Ocean Beach Club (3.6km; PO Box 73, Ukunda; ☎0127/3730, fax 0127/3557; reservations through *Block*, address p.48). Also opened in 1992, this is one of the best hotels on the coast. State-of-the-art rooms, wonderful architecture and attentive management, with most watersports free and swimming possible at all tides. Fine groves of baobabs in the gardens. Very grown-up, not ideal for kids, but a great place for a honeymoon. Stunningly expensive – B&B ⑧ low, ⑨ high.

Hotels south of the junction

Apart from the most popular hotels covered in the following listings, there are several others, and more look set to appear for years to come – to the depreciation, at least in aesthetic terms, of the whole area. Rough tarmac now continues another 4km beyond the end (6.5km south) of the good road, as far as the *Pinewood* on Galu Beach. Distances given are south from the junction.

Kaskazi Beach Hotel (300m; PO Box 135, Ukunda; ☎0127/3170, fax 0127/2233). Cool hotel, in camp Swahili manner – all white-tiled floors, tinkling fountains and soaring *makuti* roofs. All rooms with balcony, AC and fan. Recommended. There's a sad little ruined mosque in the garden. HB ⑥ low, ⑨ high.

Trade Winds (1.4km; PO Box 8, Ukunda; ☎0127/2016, fax 0127/2010; reservations through *AT&H*, address p.48). Unpretentious, happy-go-lucky sort of place – the oldest at Diani – right down on the shore, with a coconut lawn in front of the bar. Adequate rooms and an old-fashioned pool (ie rectangular, good for lengths). It's no longer quite the local pub as far as Diani veterans are concerned, but still fondly regarded. ⑤ low, ⑦ high.

Diani Sea Resort (2km; PO Box 37, Ukunda; ☎0127/3081, fax 0127/3439). Initial tawdry impressions – garish murals, fountains, rather formal gardens – aren't improved by the TV-equipped rooms, which could be anywhere. But very nice staff almost compensate, and the guests, mostly German, seem to have a good time. Great pool; game-fishing centre (Ksh3000/hr). HB ⑥.

Diani Sea Lodge (3.5km; ☎0127/2114). A slightly downmarket version of the jointly owned *Resort*, above (the same *Welcome Inns* group owns *Lawfords* and *Blue Marlin* in Malindi), consisting of small holiday bungalows with good-sized double beds and frame-fitted nets. Not special, and few rooms even have a sea view. HB ⑤.

Two Fishes (3.8km; PO Box 23, Ukunda; ☎0127/2101, fax 0127/2041). One of the older Diani hotels and a great favourite with German visitors, with mature gardens, a relaxed holiday atmosphere and a wonderful pool, with a simulated river. Dive club; mountain bike rental (Ksh1000/day). HB ⑥ low, ⑦ high.

Jadini Beach Hotel (4.2km; PO Box 90690, Mombasa; ☎0127/2622, fax 0127/2269; reservations through *Alliance*, address p.48). A long-established, traditional resort hotel with high standards and good atmosphere. Busy and cosmopolitan, but the public areas are in danger of getting tired in parts. Good for kids. St Stephens Chapel; petrol station with regular prices. One of three *Alliance* hotels on Diani; guests can use facilities at the *Africana Sea Lodge* and the *Safari Beach Hotel*. HB ⑥ low, ⑧ high.

Africana Sea Lodge (4.2km; PO Box 90690, Mombasa; ☎0127/2624, fax 0127/2145; reservations through *Alliance*, address p.48). See the *Jadini*, above. The *Africana* is sold as a fun hotel for couples, with accommodation in comfortable but unembellished *bandas*. It's also the cheapest of the group. HB ⑤ low, ⑧ high.

Nomad (4.8km; PO Box 1, Ukunda; ☎0127/2155, fax 0127/2391). Cheapest of the Diani hotels, this was formerly quite a basic place, even low-budget. It's still not luxurious, but the *bandas* (non-AC) are perched nicely between the palms, directly behind the beach, and there's a good seafood restaurant. Comparable with the *Driftwood* in Malindi and *Ocean Sports* in Watamu (though no pool); game fishing; dive school. Closed in May. B&B ④ low, ⑤ high.

Safari Beach Hotel (5.1km; PO Box 90690, Mombasa; ☎0127/2726, fax 0127/2357; reservations through *Alliance*, address p.48). The latest and best of the *Alliance* hotels, with good sports and watersports facilities, excellent food and a daily children's programme with full-time staff. Rooms are in large, two-storey *bandas*, up a gentle, wooded hillside, all ramped. Recommended, but request a room down the hill. HB ⑤ low, ⑨ high.

Ocean Village Club (5.3km; PO Box 88, Ukunda; ☎0127/2188, fax 0127/2035). Modestly conceived, well-presented club-style hotel, with a lot of French guests. Dual emphasis on cool, dark interiors (wonderfully quiet AC) and riotous tropical gardens with magnificent trees. HB ⑥.

Lagoon Reef Hotel (5.5km; PO Box 83058, Mombasa; ☎0127/2627, fax 0127/2216). Not the cream of Diani's crop, this is a reasonable holiday hotel, in fine gardens, with rather below-average food. The beautiful pool is a saving grace, ideal for small children with its sloping "beach" end. HB ⑤ low, ⑦ high.

Robinson Club Baobab (5.9km; PO Box 32, Ukunda; ☎0127/2026, fax 0127/2032). Part of the German international *Robinson* chain, located at the rocky end of Diani Beach proper. Very organized, a tropical holiday camp. You can stay independently – people do – but it would be very inconvenient if you didn't speak, or at least read, fluent German. All-inclusive ⑧.

Neptune Paradise (8.5km, on Galu Beach; PO Box 696, Ukunda; ☎0127/3061, fax 0127/3019). Jointly owned with *Neptune Village* (below) and you pay extra here for larger rooms with pink cane furniture. Otherwise this is no more imaginative. The plot has been extended seawards with the aid of Kikuyu grass lawn to the point where there is no beach left at high tide. B&B ⑥ low, ⑦ high.

Neptune Village (8.5km; PO Box 517, Ukunda; ☎0127/2350, fax 0127/2354). Smallish rooms and an uninteresting long, narrow plot (like the *Paradise*) that requires lengthy, shadeless walks. Moderately priced but not recommended. B&B ⑤ low, ⑥ high

Pinewood Village (10.5km; PO Box 90521, Mombasa; ☎0127/3720, fax 0127/3131). An extremely stylish recent condominium development at Galu, a nearly deserted stretch of beach far to the south of the main Diani strip. Extremely well thought-out four- or six-bed, staffed houses, with direct dial phones, free sporting facilities and laundry, and (unusually) water from their own wells. They aim to avoid nasty hidden extras. Self-cater or use the restaurant. HB ⑤ low, ⑥ high.

Daytime activities

Enjoying yourself on Diani isn't difficult. You can rent snorkelling gear (about Ksh150) from just about anywhere, and float out across the lagoon to the **reef**. Remember how fiercely the sun is likely to burn and wear a T-shirt unless you're very brown. You need to be a confident swimmer: there are no strong currents nor any real danger, but the reef is 600 to 1000 metres away and swimming back on the ebb tide can be tiring. Alternatively, a trip to the reef at low tide on one of the outrigger **canoes** is highly recommended. The crews know all the good (or at least the more reasonable) spots for snorkelling and it shouldn't cost you more than Ksh500 for an hour or two. One of the best areas is directly opposite *Robinson Baobab*, about 300m out towards the reef, where there is a cluster of coral heads. Many hotels have **dive centres**, where you can do everything from a basic beginner lesson plus assisted dive ($100) to a full course giving you an internationally recognized qualification ($400). You can nearly always take a free dip in the pool wearing diving equipment, to test your affinity: most people find breathing underwater curiously addictive. The sheltered lagoon behind the reef is also ideal for **windsurfing** (Ksh400/hr).

When you tire of the beach and the sea, or of just lying under the palm trees, you could **rent a bicycle** and go off exploring – from about Ksh600/day (bargain hard) – or a **motorbike** from about Ksh3000/day (see "Listings", p.389). Mini-mokes work out at about $80 a day all in. Watamu, Malindi or Wasini are easy enough targets for a day out. There's also a new nine-hole **golf course** on the north side of the junction.

Kongo Mosque

For a short excursion with a goal, you could aim for the **Kongo Mosque** at the far north end of the beach, at the mouth of the Mwachema River. It's most easily reached through the grounds of the *Indian Ocean Beach Club* – which gives you the opportunity to visit one of Diani's best-looking hotels. Beyond the boundary fence and inevita-

BEACH BOYS AND THE TOURIST POLICE

If you're staying in a hotel, spending some peaceful time on the beach can appear virtually impossible. Frustration can set in as the days slip by and you still haven't really been for a swim, or a wander by the shore, because of the hordes of **hustlers** plying their wares, or their camel rides, or their boat trips, or just themselves. Always acknowledge them: ignoring their greetings really is considered very rude. The least painful solution is quickly to strike up a friendship of sorts with one beach boy, to buy at least something, or to go on a boat trip. Once you have a friend, and have done some business, you have some rights, and you'll find you can then stroll on the beach with far fewer hassles from the others. It's not so easy for single women, but the principle for most situations still applies: don't fight it. There is no need, incidentally, to feel physically threatened on the beach. Every hotel has its *askaris* (security guards) posted along the boundary between the plot and the beach, and they usually stay alert to the slightest sign of trouble – which is rare indeed. There is now a tourist police service, though it may be in danger of collapsing through underfunding, while the vendors and beach boys defend their patches against each other with more vigour than before, increasingly aware of how easy it is to kill the goose that lays the golden egg by harassing tourists off the beach entirely. One piece of practical advice: if you're bargaining, don't complicate matters by trying to swap clothes for crafts. You'll still be expected to pay some cash, and will end up feeling more ripped off than ever.

ble *askari*, the Kongo Mosque is surrounded by venerable baobabs. Also known as Diani Persian Mosque, the building is enigmatic, and disconcerting, with its five heavy wooden doors. There's an electric atmosphere here, the barrel-vaulted mosque brooding like a huge tomb under the trees. It is too complete to be considered a ruin, and it has recently been fenced in by local Islamic leaders who have encouraged the community to start using it again. Although a sign suggests otherwise, you will, suitably attired and accompanied, be allowed to have a look around. Named after the Kongo Forest, the mosque is thought to be fifteenth-century and the one remaining building – maybe the only stone one – of a Wa-shirazi settlement here (see p.391). The river mouth was the first safe anchorage south of Mombasa.

Jadini Forest

For a walk, or a jog (fitness mania overcomes a fair number of visitors), it's more interesting to head south along Diani road. Here there are more hotels, of course, but also, approaching the end of the paving, some wonderful patches of jungle comprising the dwindling **Jadini Forest**. There's the almost obligatory snake park, but if you'd like to search for some animals in the wild rather than support this venture, then any of the tracks leading off to the right will take you straight into magnificent stands of hardwood trees, alive with birds and butterflies, and rocking with colobus and vervet monkeys. Snakes, it's true, you're unlikely to come across. You will be told the forest is the haunt of leopards. Come down here at night and you will see eyes in the dark, probably those of bushbabies: it's hard to believe that even leopards would put up with so violent a destruction of their habitat.

Eating, drinking and nightlife

Most of the hotels have snack menus, salad bars and all the rest: if you're on a budget, choose carefully and avoid the dubious temptation of Ksh200 fruit-juice cocktails, and you can still depart satisfied. The following listings, in north-to-south order (distances from the junction), include some of the best, and some of the best-value, places to eat and drink apart from the hotels.

Restaurants

Galaxy (300m north; ☎0127/2529). Chinese restaurant with main dishes from Ksh300.

Gallos, Diani Shopping Centre (1km south; ☎0127/3150). Inventive menu with Mexican flavours (main courses around Ksh500) and cheaper options like pizza and pasta. Seems to appeal to the jaded palates of hotel managers. Closed Tues.

The Oasis (2km south). Monstrous Italian construction, originally intended to be a casino, now operating as a totally over-the-top restaurant – half-acre swimming pool, *boriti* poles painted pink, elderly crooner on white piano accompanied by drum machine. Excruciating. Nice espresso.

Maharani (2.5km south; ☎0127/2439). An expensive restaurant, with Tandoori specialities. Not the most generous, but exceedingly tasty. Closed Wed.

Ali Barbour (3km south; ☎0127/2033). Bizarrely built inside a deep coral cave: you enter at ground level and descend. Even if you have no intention of disposing of around Ksh3000 for two (with wine) on the lavish French and seafood menu, it's worth dropping in just to have a look. Good food, well presented. Dinner only; closed Sun.

Nomad's Restaurant (4.8km south; ☎0127/2155). Reliable seafood menu. Friday night is "locals' night" and Sunday lunch is a curry buffet – a real family affair, with a regular jazz band. Good value.

Vulcano (6.7km south). Italian, and said to be very good. However, so off-putting is the combination of packs of guard dogs, ice-cold air conditioning, empty pink and white dining room and extra-terrestrial prices that you may not want to stay to find out.

Boko Boko (9.3km; ☎0127/2344). Seychellois restaurant (slightly spicy, creole cooking) set in a lush garden. Large *makuti*-cone hall with a few tables. Recommended, and surprisingly reasonable, with main dishes from under Ksh400.

Cheap eating and bars

Paradise Restaurant (500m north). African food and cheap drinks.

Shaney Punjab (1.4km north). A fairly down-to-earth Indian restaurant, spelled in various ways, serving African, Indian, tourist and continental food with main curries from about Ksh250.

Walter's Inn (800m south). Big and breezy roadside "pub" – the main local for Diani residents – with keg Tusker and country music under a soaring *makuti* roof.

Sensimilla Café, Diani Shopping Centre (1km south). Mysteriously named snack bar, merely popular for coffee and ice cream.

Forty Thieves Beach Bar & Restaurant (3km south). Ali Barbour's budget beachside hangout is a good place for a daytime drink – a bit of a local watering hole – and perfect in the evening when their beach front is floodlit. Discos on Wed, Fri and Sat; live band and curry buffet on Sun.

Pambela Tandoori, opposite *Diani Sea Lodge* (3.5km south). Down-to-earth place, always popular in the high season.

Mr T Roof Garden Bar & Restaurant (9.2km). A little overpriced for the standard menu of tourist and African food (main dishes around Ksh200–300) but it's the breeze and the company that attract the clientele.

Nightlife

To get around **Diani Beach at night**, without your own vehicle, you'll have to rely on getting rides or walking. Hitching up and down the Diani road is generally safe and not too difficult; and, while hotels issue warnings about walking on the beach at night (and there are *askaris* in number to underline them), under a full moon it's a pleasure that's hard to resist. In a group, minus your valuables, and not passing long stretches of bush, you're most unlikely to have any problems.

   Giriama dancing is one often touted entertainment – probably not something to go out of your way to find, but fun if you happen upon it: a couple of professional troupes work the hotels, performing acrobatically to the accompaniment of superb drumming. And there are two or three **taarab bands**, too (see p.563), who sometimes play in hotel dining rooms on special occasions or public holidays. Such entertainment is very seasonal and you won't find much going on when the crowds aren't in occupation. Diani nightlife mostly used to revolve around the hotels' fairly sterile **discos** and the casino at *Leisure Lodge*. There are now four or five discos along the road, each with its own idiosyncrasies. None of them even start to warm up before 11pm. Drinks are priced at hotel rates, or even a little less, but you'll find they don't sell large beers.

Tropicana, behind Agip petrol station. The oldest disco on Diani, open-air, with *makuti* roofs and a basic cement dance floor. Theme nights. Ksh100–150.

Shakatak (3.5km south). Wooden dance floor and air conditioning, but a bit of a dive. Tends to play the heaviest mix on the strip. Ksh100. Closed Mon.

Bushbaby (3.8km south). Open-air club opposite the *Two Fishes*, which attracts hotel staff as well as intrepid hotel guests in search of local colour (or the equivalent in German). Slightly sleazy, but fun for a bop and they do serve tasty kebabs. Free for guests at *Two Fishes* (who own it). Ksh50.

Casablanca (8.5km south). Recent addition, well air-conditioned and rather civilized, with a very good, wooden dance floor. Good sound system, too, which pumps out dance and disco. Free or Ksh50–100.

Listings

Finding food for self-catering and getting ordinary **business** done in Diani is straightforward enough, and there's an increasingly heavy scattering of shops along the strip (though as yet no post office; you have go to Ukunda). The main shopping areas on the north side are the *Bazaar Complex* (1.6km north of the junction) and the *Diani Complex* (1.4km). On the south side, the commerce kicks off with *The Bazaar Shopping Centre* (800m south) followed by the *Agip* petrol station and *Diani Shopping Centre* (1km), where the vervet monkeys scamper across the designer *makuti*. There are more shops and businesses outside *Diani Sea Resort* and opposite *Diani Sea Lodge*.

Bakery Good little Danish deli with fresh crusty bread behind Agip petrol station

Banks *KCB Bank*, Diani Complex (Mon–Fri 9am–3pm, Sat 9am–11am); *Barclays* (same hours); and the very efficient *Commercial Bank of Africa* (Mon–Fri 8.30am–2pm).

Bicycle and motorbike rental *Southern Palms Bike Rental*, opposite the hotel, rents ordinary road bikes for Ksh90/hr, Ksh400/day. *Edward Bike Rental*, Bazaar Complex, rents mountain bikes Ksh500–1000/day, depending on season, and Yamaha 600s for Ksh3500/day, including helmet.

Book exchange At Diani Shopping Centre, north end: trade a paperback (and pay Ksh40).

Car rental *Glory Car Hire*, Diani Shopping Centre (☎0127/3076); *Gupta's Car Hire* (Mon–Sat 9.30am–12.30pm & 2.30–6pm, Sun 10am–1pm); *Roadsters Rent-a-Car* (☎0127/3184; Mon–Fri 9am–5.30pm, Sat 9am–1pm).

Doctors Dr Rekhi, Diani Shopping Centre, recommended (☎0127/24356, emergency ☎0127/2207; Mon–Fri 9.30am–6pm, Sat 9.30am–1pm); Dr Philip Varghese, outside *Diani Sea Resort* (☎0127/2588; Mon–Fri 9am–12.30pm & 2.30–6pm, Sat 9am–1pm); Dr Lalit D Kotak, opposite *Diani Sea Lodge* (Mon–Fri 8.30am–2.30pm, Sat 8.30am–12.30pm).

Fresh produce Nameless fruit and veg stall at the south end of Diani Shopping Centre. Remember the ambulant fish and fruit sellers can often give really good deals to supplement what you buy in the shops, especially if you're around for a few days.

Notice boards *Onjiko's*, behind Agip petrol station, has a reasonable board for buying and selling.

Supermarkets *Muthaiga Mini Market*, Diani Shopping Centre (expensive; Mon–Sat 9am–6.30pm, Sun 10.30am–1pm); *Onjiko's*, behind Agip petrol station (much cheaper but limited range); *Shan-e-Punjab*, Diani Complex (Mon–Sat 9am–7.30pm, Sun 10am–7.30pm), which has the best range of wines and spirits on the South Coast; and *Quinnsworth*, 300m north of the junction (Mon–Sat 8.30am–7pm, Sun 8.30am–2pm). Note that *Galu Kinondo* supermarket, at the south end of the beach, is only a very basic provision store.

Telephone and fax *Phone Home* office, Bazaar Complex (competitive); *International Call Centre*, Bazaar Shopping Centre (daily 8.30am–8pm), charges Ksh290/min to Europe, Ksh 390/min to the USA; incoming faxes on 0127/3568.

Travel Agents *Diani Advice*, Diani Shopping Centre (PO Box 644, Ukunda; ☎/fax 0127/2548), are independent and good for travel bookings and general travel agent business.

Ukunda

You can walk, hitch, take a bus or taxi into **Ukunda** on the main highway – though note that the link road up to the highway is getting notorious for muggings: perhaps the new tourist police will change that. Ukunda is Diani's fast-growing town, with a post office (Mon–Fri 8am–12.30pm & 2–5pm), various *dukas* and the locally notorious *Diani Farmers' Club* – a raucous disco and bar, 500m south of the Diani Beach junction. Ukunda has a life of its own, not entirely dependent on Diani tourism, and if your holiday isn't otherwise adventurous, it's worth a visit to see something of Kenya a little less unreal than the strip. If you need accommodation in Ukunda, there are several possibilities (all ① or ②).

There's a pleasant walk to Ukunda through the bush past the airstrip, down the two-kilometre track that begins directly opposite *Trade Winds'* entrance. This takes you past a truly gigantic baobab tree (girth 22 metres) which has been given presidential protection "for the enjoyment of the people of Kenya and their children". Check the safety of this path with hotel staff before going, or take a companion.

Southwards to Shimoni

The Diani Beach road returns to gravel south of the *Pinewood*, although it continues in a drivable condition, through the little village of Kinondo, right down to Chale Point and, 300m offshore, **Chale island**. Chale, until recently an uninhabited beauty, has sadly been acquired by a German developer, with the help of two local MPs, despite its being a gazetted Mijikenda *kaya* (see p.375) and not the property of anyone. The resulting, ill-conceived *Chale Paradise Island* (⑨) has totally disrupted local relations and wiped out acres of natural vegetation. If the ancestors are to be allowed their say, its days are numbered: yet the new owners claim the development has been sensitive, that only a third of the island has been built upon and that the other half is a "nature reserve". If you want to see for yourself, you can't avoid bumping into adverts and hoardings for the place all over the South Coast.

Gazi

Down the main coastal highway south of Ukunda, **GAZI** is next, a sleepy little village just off the road. It was once headquarters of the Mazrui leader **Sheikh Mbaruk ("Baruku") bin Rashid**, who acquired a reputation for torturing prisoners after half-suffocating them in the fumes of burning chillies. The story was perhaps intended to discredit him, as he was the principal figure behind the Mazrui Rebellion in 1895, an uprising against British authority that saw Mbaruk flying a German flag at his house and supplying his men with arms donated by the Germans. The British had to send for troops from India; even so, fighting continued for nine months before an Omani puppet regime was re-established and the rebels crushed. Mbaruk died in exile in German Tanganyika.

His mansion is now a primary school, which you can look around out of school hours. More than 150 years old, it was obviously a very grand place – the heavy ceiling timbers show that it once had an upper storey – but it is now sadly neglected. Fort Jesus Museum has plundered its fine front door and unfortunately left an ugly scar. To know where to stop for Gazi, you'll have to ask, as there isn't a sign on the highway. The village itself is on a deep, mangrove-filled bay and has no beach to speak of. "Gazi Beach", about 2km south of the village, is more promising.

Msambweni

Continuing down the road, **MSAMBWENI** is a sizeable village with a famous leprosarium. The road to the beach (there's often a police checkpoint at the junction) goes through the village, following the coast for several kilometres before turning back to the highway. The beach is lovely – low cliffs and less uniformity than Diani – and there are no beach hassles down here, but the tide goes out for miles, with lots of rock pools.

ACCOMMODATION

Several plots at Msambweni have been developed, but in a low-key fashion, with only a few cottages and one or two quasi-exclusive clubs. You really need a car for these, unless you're content to stay in one place the whole time. There are few taxis and the main road is a half-hour walk away.

Beachcomber Club (PO Box 54, Msambweni; ☎0127/52074, fax 0127/3112; reservations through *Diani Advice*, see p.389). Small, reasonably priced hotel. HB ⑤ low, ⑥ high.

Club Green Oasis (PO Box 80, Msambweni; ☎0127/52205, fax 0127/52099). The biggest establishment in Msambweni, recently reopened. ⑥ low, ⑦ high.

Club Salima (PO Box 9, Msambweni; Msambweni ☎32). A hard place to leave (only the prices could possibly shift you). The architect-owner has done some original and beguiling work here on half a dozen staffed, beachfront cottages, with curved passages and atria melding with lush vegetation. Beautiful pool beneath a baobab. No restaurant. Very expensive for a couple (⑦ low, ⑧ high); more reasonable if two or three couples share a four- or six-person house.

Seascapes (PO Box 77, Msambweni; reservations in Nairobi on ☎02/334280, fax 02/224952). A newer, more uniform development of six-bed villas, set on the cliffs. ③ low, ④ high.

Funzi island

If instead of returning to the main road from Msambweni, you follow the coastline (either on the rough track or the beach), you will eventually reach **Funzi island**, separated from the mainland by a narrow channel that you can walk across at low tide. You can easily camp on the island if equipped for a fair amount of self-sufficiency. Funzi village is at the southern end, about 6km from the mainland, and there are beaches and sections of reef scattered close to the forested shore on both sides of the island. The exclusive *Funzi Island Club* – a tented camp in a grove of mango trees (PO Box 1108, Ukunda; ☎0127/2044, fax 0127/2346; all-inclusive ⑨; closed May & June) – is a place to dream about.

Shirazi (Kifunzi)

The coast highway meanwhile passes through verdant regions of parkland, with borassus, doum and coconut palms (borassus are the ones with a bulge in the trunk) interspersed with swampy dells, before the landscape is firmly established as rolling fields of sugar cane, culminating in **Ramisi**, the coast's main sugar-producing area until the closure of its factory recently.

On the shore, just before you reach Ramisi, is the tiny and very old settlement of **SHIRAZI**, also known as Kifunzi (which means "little Funzi"). Any of the tracks through the sugar fields on the left of the road will take you to the hamlet – a scattering of houses in the jungle and a small harbour among mangroves. The people of Shirazi call themselves **Wa-shirazi** and are the descendants of a once-important group of the Swahili-speaking people. During the fifteenth and sixteenth centuries, they ruled the coast from Tiwi to Tanga (Tanzania) from their eight settlements on the shore. Around 1620, these towns were captured by the Wa-vumba, another Swahili group. The Washirazi, now scattered in pockets along the coast, speak a distinctive dialect of Swahili. Historians used to think they originally emigrated from Shiraz, in Persia, but it now seems likely that very few of them have Persian ancestry and that the name was adopted for political reasons. Shirazi/Kifunzi, which may be one of the original eight villages, is an important Wa-shirazi centre.

Shirazi, like many villages on the coast, is a backwater in every sense. The people cut a small quantity of *boriti* (mangrove poles) – much less than they used to; they fish and they grow some produce in their garden plots, which are continually being raided by monkeys. But the setting is memorably exotic and worth the three-kilometre walk from the main road. They don't have sodas at Shirazi, but they do have coconuts and tranquillity.

The people who run *Funzi Island Fishing Club* have a camp on the shore at **Bodo**, just to the southwest of Shirazi. Bodo is a small cargo port, where you can sometimes pick up a ride to Pemba, Tanzania, a seven-hour voyage. See "Travel Details", p.448.

There are some unspectacular ruins of walls and a disused well amid tangled foliage just a hundred metres or so to the south of the village. On the north side is the more interesting hulk of a Friday mosque, its mihrab still standing. Elders here describe how earlier inhabitants were routed by the Maasai and fled to the Comoros Islands. They remember when the mosque was still intact, though by the turn of the century it had already been abandoned.

Shimoni

There are several buses and *matatus* each day from Mombasa to **SHIMONI**. The turn-off is indicated by a small cluster of tourist signs – you might expect more to be sprouting up all the time, but there has so far been virtually no development down here. A few years back, when Reagan's America enjoyed cosy relations with Kenya, the United States had its eye on getting a naval base on Wasini. This would be a far worse calamity for this remarkable area than the reach of another tentacle of tourism, but thankfully, for the moment, it seems to be on the back burner. For the present, Shimoni and the rocky sliver of Wasini island, just offshore, remain both idyllic and fascinating – a rare combination.

The caves of Shimoni
While you are in Shimoni, you should visit the **caves** after which it was named (*shimo* in Swahili). Shimoni's caves have achieved fame in Kenya, if not much further afield, through singer Roger Whittaker's melodramatic warblings. Whether they were actually used for storing slaves prior to shipment, or whether (as the alternative version has it) they were a secret refuge from Maasai and other raiders, are questions you can ponder as you pick your way around the piles of bat droppings and stinging creepers (beware!) on the floor. The path to the caves winds into the jungle from a point directly opposite the jetty. Stamp on the ground and you'll notice it's hollow in places. These are coral caves and you descend a ladder through a jagged hole in the ground to reach them. Once down, shafts of sunlight pierce through holes in the forest floor to illuminate the stalactites and dangling lianas quite beautifully. Caving expeditions have found that the cave system extends some 20km underground.

With more time, there are some ruined buildings in Shimoni that might be worth a look (the Imperial British East African Company used to have its headquarters here), including a large two-storey house in the heart of the village near the fish auction house. The auctions themselves are also interesting – there's one every morning – though exciting exhibits like marlin and shark are rarely on the slab.

Accommodation
Although Shimoni is small, the demand for **accommodation** by big-spending game-fishermen has brought two hotels. The Pemba Channel (the Tanzanian island of Pemba lies 50km offshore) is considered one of the world's very best stretches of sea for hunting big fish: it is impressive to think that marlin weighing a quarter of a ton and tiger sharks of close on half a ton race through these waters.

If you're looking for budget accommodation, the only option is the KWS *Camp Eden Bandas*, quite attractive in themselves if you want to experience a real night in the forest. Since Wasini island is an alluring ten-minute boat ride away, there's no other reason to spend the night on the mainland unless you have the transport to get to Mwazaro Beach, down a turning halfway along the rough road between the highway and Shimoni village.

Shimoni Reef Lodge, 500m to the left (east) from village centre (PO Box 82234, Mombasa; Shimoni ☎9, fax 011/471349). Part of the *Reef* group of hotels, open all year, and aimed less at sport fishermen than at divers. Excellent accommodation, rather average food. Huge residents' discounts. ⑦ low, ⑨ high.

Camp Eden Bandas, 500m to the right (west) from the village centre (reservations through KWS, PO Box 55, Ukunda). Wonderful for naturalists, a group of tented *bandas* run by the Kenya Wildlife Service. Basic facilities, no electricity, bring your own nets. Accommodation only ④.

Pemba Channel Fishing Club, 800m to the right from village centre (PO Box 86952, Mombasa; ☎011/3132749, fax 011/316875). Essentially for serious anglers, this usually closes for three months at the end of the fishing season in March or April, reopening on August 1. They now have a swimming pool and also welcomes non-fishing guests – though if the whole gory business turns you right off, you won't presumably rush to make a booking. Boat charter, with all the gear for up to four people, is $450 for a nine-hour day (at $50 or Ksh3000/hr, pretty standard on the coast). FB ⑧; singles half-price.

Mwazaro Beach, 7.5km from the main road junction (PO Box 14 Shimoni; no telephone). "Where God makes holidays" is how the German owner describes his newly opened and very low-key development on the east coast of the Shimoni peninsula, exactly halfway between the highway and Shimoni. Simple *bandas*, with good fitted nets; no electricity or private facilities; Zanzibari cooking; creek and sea trips. Camping Ksh100. FB only, ⑤.

Wasini island and offshore

WASINI is easily reached. Between July and April, when *Wasini Island Restaurant* (PO Box 281, Ukunda; ☎0127/2331) is open, there's a boat to speed lunchers across the channel for about Ksh200 a load, and this is the going rate for other motorboat operators. Local people use *jahazi*, sailing boat "*matatus*" which – notwithstanding the resentment of the diesel men – you should be able to use, too (Ksh40 each way). This is certainly more fun but you'll need to haggle determinedly. If you've got a reservation at the restaurant you can often arrange a free transfer in advance.

Only five kilometres long and one across, Wasini is delightfully adrift from the mainstream of coastal life. There are no cars, nor any need of them: you can walk all the way around the island in a couple of hours on the narrow footpaths through the bush. With something of Lamu's cast about it, the island is completely undeveloped, and **Wasini village**, an old Wa-vumba settlement, is built in and around its own ruins. It is a fascinating place to wander and there's even a small pillar tomb which still has its complement of inset Chinese porcelain. The **beach** in front of the village is littered with shells, but don't assume anything: a lot of them have been collected from the reef and dumped here, and people will try to sell them to you, so it wouldn't be wise to treat them as legitimate beachcombings. Nevertheless, the wealth of interesting items on the shores of Wasini – not just shells but shards of pottery, pieces of glass, scrap metal – add up to a beachcomber's paradise you could explore for hours.

Behind the village is a bizarre village green, an area of long-dead **coral gardens** now raised out of the sea but still periodically flooded at spring tides. It is covered in a short swathe of "sea grass" – a tasty vegetable called simply *mboga pwani* (sea vegetable). Walking through the coral grottoes with birds and butterflies in the air leaves a surreal impression of snorkelling on dry land. Exploring the rest of the island is highly recommended: look out for the monkeys in the mangroves and the parrots in the palms.

Accommodation in Wasini is very limited (more by the island's total reliance on rainwater than by anything else), but there are usually houses for rent for under Ksh200 per day in either the ancient village of Wasini itself or the newer settlement at the other end of the island, **Mkwiro**. There's also a **banda and camping site** known as *Mpunguti Lodge* (PO Box 19, Shimoni; FB ③). It's very simple – no electricity, no running water and no nets (but there are very few mosquitoes). The owner has quite an impressive collection of old pottery and ceramics: he's trying to persuade the Fort Jesus people to help him set up a museum. There's magnificent Swahili cooking and, if you want to ring the changes, guests get a substantial discount at the *Wasini Island Restaurant*. **Camping** at *Mpunguti Lodge* costs only Ksh100, but try to bring food (including fruit) and as much drinking water as possible with you, particularly out of season.

Kisite-Mpunguti Marine National Park

Open daily; $5 (pay rangers who accompany boats or on shore – organized trips include the fee); warden: PO Box 55, Ukunda; Shimoni ☎3.

Wasini has ideal conditions for **snorkelling**, with limpid water all around. The couple who run the *Wasini Island Restaurant*, a few minutes to the west of the village, run full-day trips in a large dhow to the reefs around Kisite island, part of **Kisite-Mpunguti Marine National Park**, which usually has some of the best snorkelling in Kenya. The trip is not cheap but the price includes a wonderful and seemingly endless **seafood lunch** on your hungry return. The *Wasini Island* office at *Jadini Beach Hotel* on Diani Beach can tell you morning departure times from Shimoni jetty, but there's usually a 6–7am pick-up from North or South Coast hotels (prices vary according to distance, in addition to the flat rate of Ksh3000). Equipment and field guides are available on board, but you'd benefit from your own mask and snorkel. Similar trips, on a more informal, *ad hoc* basis are run from *Mpunguti Lodge*, and you can sometimes borrow masks and snorkels from the marine park warden.

The boats normally go out of the Wasini channel to the east, then turn south to pass the islets of **Mpunguti Ya Chini** and **Mpunguti Ya Juu** ("little " and "great") on the port side. Kisite islet, a coral-encircled rock about 100m long, 5km to the southwest, is the routine destination. The best parts of the Kisite anchoring area seem to be towards the outer edge of the main "coral garden". There are fish and sea animals in abundance, including angel fish, octopuses, and some spectacularly large (60cm) sea cucumbers. At certain times of the year, however, the water is less clear, and it looks as if repeated anchorings have destroyed much of the coral in at least one small area, where the shallow sea bed is littered with broken ends and grey debris. Ask the crew if you'd like to try to find a better area: **Mako Koke Reef**, the other main part of the park, is about 4km to the west.

Vanga

Kenya's **southernmost town**, VANGA, is also the largest of the coastal settlements to have been left alone by the tourist industry. Getting here involves travelling down one of the country's most beautiful, and usually deserted, roads, from the Shimoni junction to Lungalunga, on the Tanzanian border. The seventeen-kilometre murram road to Vanga begins, curiously, midway through the Kenyan border post at Lungalunga (a couple of lodgings there but nothing of interest). It skims the Tanzanian border through *shambas* and, as it nears the sea, tunnels through tall forest in deep shade. Vanga itself is in the **mangroves**, approached through the swamp down a causeway which is regularly flooded by spring tides.

Vanga is a largish village with a main street, a number of stores and *hotelis* (the first on the right, the *First and Last*, is the main one), where men come in the evening to chew *miraa* and reflect on the community's isolation. "We have no employment" is a common complaint; the fishing co-operative is the only local provider of a cash income but it isn't always able to buy the entire catch and members are not supposed to sell to anyone else. Many people sell garden produce in Mombasa, which explains the *matatu* departures through the night to ensure early arrival at the markets.

Most people are unlikely to come to Vanga as there isn't anywhere to stay in the town or anything much to do. The big old house on the seafront is a nineteenth-century British customs house, cared for, in theory, by the National Museums of Kenya, in practice falling down. For the less fastidious, dugout canoes can be rented very cheaply for wobbly punting trips through the mangroves. Vanga is a sure antidote to a surfeit of Diani and Malindi: locals are more than willing to accommodate visitors and you may be plied with excellent palm wine.

If you're intent on staying in the area, there is one organized possibility between Lungalunga and Vanga: *Border Camp*, 7km from the Lungalunga customs post (PO Box 167, Lungalunga; no telephone). This is a jungle homestead run by a German-Meru couple, with ambitious reforestation and conservation plans. You can camp here (Ksh200), or sleep in the "treehouse" or one of the new banda rooms (③). The owners are committed to their plans and knowledgeable about the area, which includes nearby lakes and a good variety of flora and fauna, which they are happy to guide you around.

THE NORTH COAST: KILIFI TO MALINDI

From Mtwapa Creek up to **Malindi**, the landscape is a diverse collage: from rolling baobab country and sisal plantations as you near **Kilifi** to groves of cashew trees after it; thick, jungly forest and swamp around Mida Creek; then a more compact, populated zone of *shambas* and thicket as you approach Malindi. **Kilifi and Takaungu creeks** are stunning – the clash of blue water and green cliffs almost unnatural.

There is wide scope for **beach hunting** along this part of the coast. Malindi and, to some extent, Watamu have been developed, but Kilifi functions largely as a Giriama market-centre and district capital, while Takaungu seems virtually unknown, a throwback to pre-colonial days. There's also superb **snorkelling** at **Watamu and Malindi Marine National Parks**. And the ruined town of **Gedi**, deep in the jungle near Watamu, is one of the most impressive archeological sites in East Africa.

Kilifi and environs

Between Kikambala and Kilifi lies a major **sisal-growing** area, focusing around the small town of **Vipingo** (one or two *dukas* and *hotelis*, but not much else). Across thousands of acres, plumb-straight rows of fleshy-leafed, cactus-like sisal plants stretch in every direction, the surviving **baobab trees** standing out bizarrely (see box below). Towards Kilifi, the road bucks through a hilly area and the baobabs grow more profusely amid the scrub.

If you want **to stay** cheaply on this relatively undeveloped coastline, **Jauss Farm**, on the shore (PO Box 19, Vipingo; ☎0125/32218), is a good target. If you're travelling by public transport, ask the bus or *matatu* driver to drop you 1.6km north of Vipingo, where you'll see a gravel track off to the right and a small rash of signboards, including one to "Timeless Camping". The site is 3.4km from here down a shady avenue, turning right after 1.4km at the junction signposted "Fourways Beach Cottages" and "Howden", and forking left where a sign points right to "Jervis House". *Jauss Farm* has various accommodation options, ranging from camping (a safe but not very attractive site) to cheap *bandas* and rooms in one of several bungalows. A nice touch is the avoidance of cash transactions (until you leave), so that everything you eat and drink goes on your account, with a ten-percent service charge (no tipping). Accommodation is all in the ① category, with inexpensive meals (Ksh150–200), snacks and drinks. There's a pleasant cove right below the farm and diving and horse riding can be arranged. Significantly, the reef is much closer to the shore in this area than further south – a plus point for snorkellers.

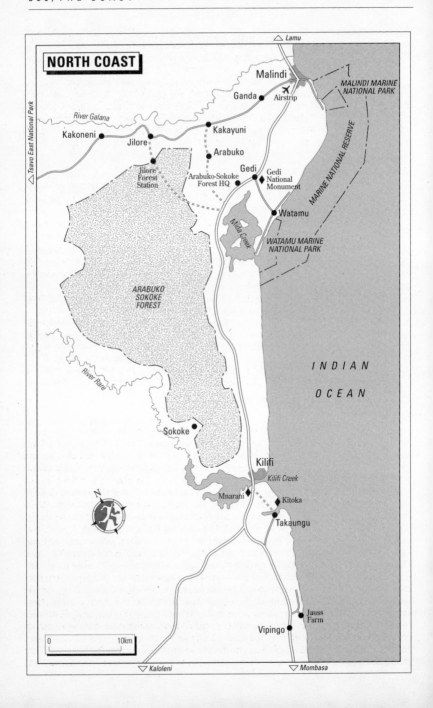

NORTH COAST

Lamu

Malindi

MALINDI MARINE
NATIONAL PARK

Ganda   Airstrip

River Galana

Kakoneni   Kakayuni

Jilore

Arabuko

Jilore
Forest
Station

Arabuko-Sokoke
Forest HQ

Gedi   Gedi
National
Monument

MARINE NATIONAL RESERVE

Watamu

Mida Creek

WATAMU MARINE
NATIONAL PARK

ARABUKO
SOKOKE
FOREST

INDIAN

OCEAN

River Rare

Sokoke

Kilifi

Kilifi Creek

Mnarani   Kitoka

Takaungu

N

Jauss
Farm

Vipingo

0   10km

Tsavo East National Park

Kaloleni   Mombasa

BAOBAB STORIES

The **baobab**'s strange appearance has a number of explanations in mythology. The most common one relates how the first baobab planted by God was an ordinary-looking tree, but it refused to stay in one place and wandered round the countryside. As a punishment, God planted it back again – upside down – and immobilized it. Baobabs may live well over 2000 years, making them among the longest-living organisms. During a severe drought, their large green pods can be cracked open and the nuts made into a kind of flour. The resulting "hungry bread" is part of the common culture of the region.

Takaungu

Ten kilometres before you reach Kilifi, there's a turn-off to the right to **TAKAUNGU**. Although there are two *matatus* most days from Mombasa to Takaungu, the chances of a lift are relatively slim if you get dropped off at the turning. But it is not a long walk (5km) and it gives you time to shed the highway and "the coast" from your mind. Takaungu is enchanting – a quiet, composed village of whitewashed Swahili houses situated on a high bluff above **Takaungu Creek**. There are three mosques and one or two small shops and *hotelis,* but no formal lodgings; if you want to stay and you speak a little Swahili, people will put you up for a very reasonable price. Food supplies are variable; women will prepare food if you ask, and especially if you supply the ingredients. There's no produce market, but a small fish market by the creek – be there when the catch arrives to get the tasty ones. Takaungu is a place that repays time spent getting to know it: if you just want to kick back and rest up, pass it by and head on to Lamu.

There's a small seaside **beach**, 1km east, through the secondary school. **Takaungu Creek** is startlingly beautiful, the colour of blue Curaçao, and absolutely transparent. The small swimming beach on the stream is covered at high tide, but you can still dive from the rocks. Upstream, the creek disappears between flanks of dense jungle. When you're ready to move on, the tiny, council-operated rowing boat provides a slow and almost free service across the creek to the Kilifi side; from there, it's a five-kilometre (ninety-minute) walk through the sisal fields to Kilifi bridge.

Kilifi and the creek

Kenya's coastline was submerged in the recent geological past, resulting in the creation of the islands and drowned river valleys – the creeks – of today. **KILIFI**, a small but animated place, is on such a creek. When the Portuguese knew it, Kilifi's centre was on the south side of the creek and called **Mnarani**. Together with Kitoka on the north side of Takaungu Creek, and a settlement on the site of the present town of Kilifi, these three constituted the "state" of Kilifi. Mnarani's few **ruins** sit under the trees high above Kilifi Creek, to the west of the old road that led down to the ferry before the bridge was built. Turn left at the former toll station before you get to the bridge, and the ruins are 1500m down here, though there's no sign to show you the way: you'll see the flight of steps leading up from near the old ferry landing (there's a Ksh200 fee, if there's anyone to collect it). There's not a lot to see at the site apart from a very tall pillar tomb supported by iron props, a couple of mosques and a precipitous well that plummets right down to creek level. The site is archeologically famous mainly for the large number of inscriptions found on its masonry, all in a difficult, and so far untranslated, form of monumental Arabic. Truthfully, however, for the non-buff, Mnarani's most memorable aspect is its superlative position overlooking the creek, from where you used to be able to watch the to-ing and fro-ing of the ferry.

With the building of the **bridge**, Kilifi's economy has been dealt a hard blow. All the creek-side trade made possible by the ferry's endless delays and breakdowns has

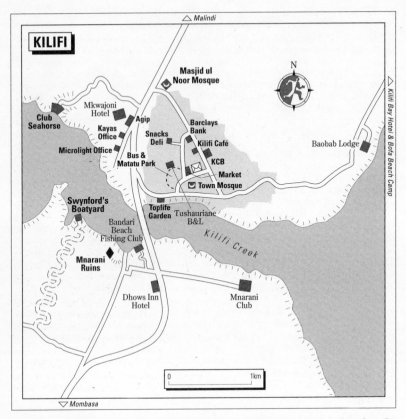

△ Malindi

KILIFI

N

△ Kilifi Bay Hotel & Bofa Beach Camp

Masjid ul Noor Mosque

Mkwajoni Hotel

Club Seahorse

Agip

Kayas Office

Microlight Office

Bus & Matatu Park

Snacks Deli

Barclays Bank

Kilifi Café

KCB

Market

Town Mosque

Baobab Lodge

Swynford's Boatyard

Toplife Garden

Tushauriane B&L

Bandari Beach Fishing Club

Kilifi Creek

Mnarani Ruins

Dhows Inn Hotel

Mnarani Club

0 _____ 1km

▽ Mombasa

ceased; many bars and *hotelis*, and half the town's lodgings, have closed; as has the rather good serpentarium that used to entertain travellers with tame, wrap-around pythons.

Kilifi town

Kilifi is draped along the north side of the creek to the east of the bridge. If you're driving you'll probably pass it by: even most public transport travellers only see it from the inside of a bus while more fares are being picked up. But staying the night is not an unpleasant prospect, and while there's not a lot of choice it's certainly a better plan than arriving late in Malindi.

There's little of **sightseeing interest** in Kilifi: its two main **mosques** – one a stumpy shed in the town centre, the other a new and attractively minareted blue, green and white temple, the Masjid ul Noor, at the north junction – more or less sum it up. You can get a rather wonderful view of the whole area, though – town, creek and beach – by taking an escorted **microlight flight**. The office of *Microlight Kenya* is near the *Mkwajoni Hotel* (PO Box 824; ☎/fax 0125/22000). Flights last about half an hour and cost $60, and they go from the small airstrip reached up the beach road.

If you have time on your hands, you could also enquire about a visit to the **cashew factory** a short distance up the highway (PO Box 49; ☎0125/2411), which is said to be interesting. The nuts are expensive because there are so few of them on the small trees: each one hangs, in an unlikely fashion, from a juicy, pear-shaped, yellow-and-orange fruit – refreshing to suck but inedible. The nut shells are processed to extract an oil used for making preservatives, for waterproofing and even for brake linings.

PRACTICALITIES

Accommodation is rather thin on the ground. If you want to stay in Kilifi town, one of the few lodgings is the tall *Tushauriane B&L*, directly behind the bus station, which has basic, dingy rooms with mosquito nets but no fans (PO Box 259; ☎0125/22486; ①). Just outside town, behind the *Agip* service station off the highway, is the more upscale *Mkwajoni Motel* (PO Box 172; ☎0125/22472; ②), which offers good clean rooms with mosquito nets (no fans), a very pleasant open-air bar and restaurant, and the attractive added prospect of manic discos on Wednesdays, Fridays and Saturdays. If you don't mind being a little out of town, there are reasonable rooms at *Dhows Inn*, right by the road on the south side of the creek (PO Box 431; ☎/fax 0125/22028). This is a popular local boozer with good beer prices, which also attracts the more adventurous of the packaged guests from the *Mnarani Club* (*African Safari Club*, closed at time of writing and rumoured to have been sold to a big hotel group). *Dhows Inn* has a penchant for Country music, especially Kenny Rogers – as do a number of other places in Kilifi. The final overnight option in the vicinity of the town is close by *Dhows Inn*, above the creek: *Bandari Beach Fishing Club* is a small new, German-run guest house (PO Box 508, Kilifi; ☎/fax 0125/22151) that hosts parties of game fishermen on an informal basis; if they have a room, they'll probably put you up (④). It's 300m off the road between *Dhows Inn* and the Mnarani ruins (parking is very difficult: get out and ask) .

As for **eating in town**, the **Oloitipitip Market** has a wide range of fruit and vegetables. A good stand-by for snacks and fry-ups is the long established *Kilifi Café*, while the newer *Snacks Deli* does fresh juices and tasty bites in fresh, clean surroundings. Otherwise, there are various basic **dukas** and the odd **hoteli** along the road that leads out of town back to the highway.

Other practicalities can also be dealt with along this street, which has Kilifi's main **pharmacy** and a *KCB* **bank**. *Barclays* (Mon–Fri 9am–3pm, Sat 9–11am) is on the corner of the road that goes back to the bus station and the "centre" of town. The **post and telephone office** (Mon–Fri 8am–12.30pm & 2–5pm) is down near the market.

Kilifi Creek

Kilifi's seaside-settler/yachtie community tends to hover around the informal bar-restaurant at **Swynford's Boatyard**, which is *the* place for making contacts if you have any ideas of Indian Ocean crewing in mind. There's no public transport to this place: if you don't have your own car you'll have to walk, unless you can get a lift. It's a little further up the south side of the creek from the old ferry landing, accessible via a dirt road from the old main road, 1km inland, then right 2km down a steep track to the waterfront. *Swynford's* is a friendly place, with fine views of the creek and the dramatic new bridge. They turn out fresh and simple seafood dishes, including fish and chips (Ksh140) and weekend lunch buffets (Ksh300), and there's a notice board for yachties and fishermen to exchange news and trade kit. Opposite, on the sheltered north side of the creek, the *Seahorse Hotel*, a twenty-minute walk landward of the main road, used to be the yachting fraternity's focus. It still is in a small way, although the fact that it is an exclusively *African Safari Club* compound for mostly Swiss, German and French clients, doesn't encourage the Kilifi crowd to come here for a drink in the evenings.

Kilifi Beach

The real **beaches** around Kilifi are mostly accessible only through private property, and the best are up on the open coast to the northeast of the town. Along this ten-

---

THE GIRIAMA AND THE KILIFI KAYAS PROJECT

In recent decades, as the **Giriama** section of the Mijikenda (see p.375) have expanded, Kilifi has become one of their most important towns. Giriama women are quickly noticed by everyone for their unusual **dress**. Traditionally a kind of kilt of grass or leaves, it is now made of *kanga* cloth with hips and buttocks accentuated by a bustle of coir fibre stuffed underneath. Older women still occasionally go topless but younger women usually cover up, at least in town. The Mijikenda peoples, and the Giriama especially, are known as great sorcerers and practitioners of witchcraft, and Kilifi is still the frequent scene of accusations that sometimes reach the press. Kilifi is also now the site of an office of the coastal project working to conserve the Mijikenda's sacred groves, or *kayas*. The main work at present is to identify and gazette the *kayas* of the district, but, in time, it's hoped that tourist visits will be feasible. If you're interested in finding out more about the project, which has WWF backing, call at the office near the *Mkwajoni Hotel* , or contact them in advance (PO Box 596, Kilifi; ☎0125/22140; email cfcu2@tt.gn.apc.org).

kilometre tarred road, however, there are several fairly recent developments, the following being the most notable among them.

Baobab Lodge (2km from Kilifi; reservations through *Empress Fashion*; Eagle House, Kimathi St, Nairobi; PO Box 40683, Nairobi; ☎02/220592). Attractively sited amid densely planted gardens, in a pleasant position on a bluff above the shore. Good swimming pool (with lots of shade), but little beach to speak of and no sea-swimming at low tide. The rooms, though, are spacious and well furnished, with AC and fans. Altogether a good find in this corner of the coast. Closed May and June. HB ⑤.

Kilifi Bay Hotel Village (5km from Kilifi; PO Box 156; ☎0125/22264). Italian-run, and over-the-top in design, though the rooms are smaller and less attractive than at the *Baobab Lodge*. A pretentious, rather overpriced place with a boring beach. Closed May and June. HB ⑤.

Bofa Beach Camp (8km from Kilifi; PO Box 660; ☎0125/22561). Camping and *banda* site at the end of the hard-surfaced beach road. The small cottages are roomy and cool, but not smart, and the restaurant has drinks and can rustle up food. Having opened, shadeless, in 1992, the site is now beautifully cool and overgrown. This could still become a backpacker's focus, but access from Kilifi is the problem: get here by taxi, hitching, or a long walk. Camping Ksh150. B&B ④.

Out of Kilifi: the Arabuko-Sokoke Forest

Cashew trees line both sides of the road north of Kilifi, but they soon give way to tracts of jungle where monkeys scatter across the road and hornbills plunge into the cover of the trees as you approach. This is the **Arabuko-Sokoke Forest**, the largest patch of indigenous coastal forest left in East Africa. At one time it would have covered most of the coastal hinterland behind the shoreline settlements. If you have a car or a few days for some walking, there are some 400 square kilometres to explore. Much of it has been penetrated and cut, as the sawmills you'll come across testify, but several good-sized areas of untouched hardwood forest and stands of rubber trees remain. Although this isn't the Amazon, a degree of preparation is wise if you plan on venturing far down any of the tracks leading off the main road. Survey of Kenya maps would be useful (the "Kenya Coast" tourist map at the very least), though new tracks are constantly being cut and old ones allowed to grow over. A **compass** is also helpful. For details on driving or cycling through the forest from Malindi, see p.418.

The easiest point of entry is the Kenya Wildlife Service's **Arabuko-Sokoke Forest Headquarters**, 1500m south of Watamu junction, where there's also a basic campsite. They don't get hundreds of visitors here and will be delighted to take you on a guided bird walk. Early in the morning is best and fixing it up the day before is a good idea. There are no official fees but a tip of a couple of dollars would be suitable. A kilometre south on the Mombasa road there's a nature trail and, 2km south of that, where the dirt road to Jilore starts, a reserve for the region's unique *Brachystegia* woodland.

The forest is home to a glorious variety of butterflies and several unusual species of birds and mammals. The six **birds** to look out for are the Sokoke scops owl, Sokoke pipit, Amanu sunbird, Clark's weaver, East Coast akalat and Spotted ground thrush, all found only here. A tiny, shy antelope, the 35-centimetre-high **Zanzibar duiker**, also inhabits the forest, usually living in pairs. But like the extraordinary **golden-rumped elephant shrew** (see p.403), you're more likely to see these rare animals around Gedi, where the thump and smell of tourists no longer disturbs them as much. The exceedingly rare Sokoke bush-tailed mongoose is unlikely to put in an appearance – there have been no sightings since the mid-1980s.

Gedi ruins and Kipepeo Butterfly Farm

Ruins open daily 7am–6pm; Ksh200; warden: ☎0122/32065; signposted from near Gedi village by the turning for Watamu on the Mombasa–Malindi road.

The Arabuko-Sokoke Forest may partly explain the enigma of **GEDI**. This large, thirteenth- to seventeenth-century Swahili town was apparently unknown to the Portuguese, despite the fact that, for nearly one hundred years, they maintained a strong presence only 15km away in Malindi, at a time when Gedi is judged to have been at the peak of its prosperity. It is not mentioned (at least by the name of Gedi) in any Arabic or Swahili writings either, and, bafflingly, it has to be assumed that, set back from the sea and deep in the forest, it was never noticed.

The **ruins** are confusing, eerie, and, in the late afternoon, hauntingly beautiful. Even if you are resolutely uninterested in seeing any of the other sites on the coast, don't miss this one. Forest has invaded the town over the three centuries since it was deserted, and baobabs and magnificent buttress-rooted trees tower over the dimly lit

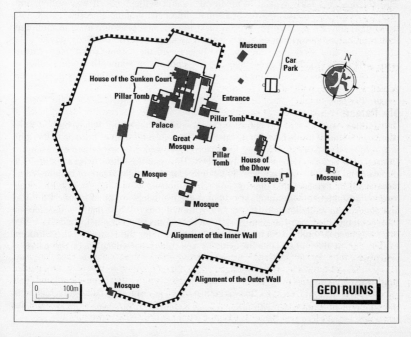

walls and arches. Gedi has a sinister reputation and local people have always been uneasy about it; it has collected an unhealthy share of ghost stories and tales of inexplicable happenings since 1948, when it was opened as a national park and tourists started to visit it. Some of this cultural memory may derive from the supposed occupation of the ruins in the eighteenth century by the **Galla**, a tribe of irrepressible expansionists whose violent and unsettled lifestyle was long a major threat to the coastal communities. The Galla, it's believed, were the original cause of Gedi's desertion by its inhabitants.

The longer you stay here, the further you seem from an answer to Gedi's anomalies. The display in the small **museum** shows that the town must have been actively trading with overseas merchants, yet it is 5km from the sea and 2km from Mida Creek; the coastline has probably moved inland over the centuries, so it might have been further away still. Then, at times of supposed Galla aggression, sailing into Mida Creek would have been like entering a lobster pot. The reasons for Gedi's location remain thoroughly obscure and its absence from historical records grows more inexplicable the more you think about it.

Gedi tingles spines easily, even today, particularly if you are on your own. James Kirkman, the archeologist who first worked at the site, remembers: "when I first started to work at Gedi I had the feeling that something or somebody was looking out from behind the walls, neither hostile nor friendly but waiting for what he knew was going to happen." Kirkman's booklet, usually available at the entrance gate, has a lot of interesting details as well as a plan of the site, which we've reproduced here. Its directions, however, tend to lead you in circles; it's better just to follow your nose.

The site

The town seems fairly typical of medieval Swahili settlements. It was walled, and originally covered about a quarter of a square kilometre – some 45 acres. The majority of its estimated 2500 citizens, or at least inhabitants, probably lived in mud and thatch huts, long overwhelmed and dissolved by jungle, on the southern, poorer side of town, the side away from Mecca. The palace and the "Stone Town" were in the north. When the site was reoccupied at the end of the sixteenth century, after a hiatus of fifty or so years, a new inner wall was built, enclosing just this prestigious zone.

The Palace

The **Palace**, with its striking entrance porch, sunken courts and honeycomb of little rooms, is the most impressive single building. The concentration of **houses** to its right is where most of Gedi's interesting finds were made and they are named accordingly: House of the Scissors, House of the Ivory Box, House of the Dhow (with a picture of a dhow on the wall). If you have already been to Lamu, the tight layout of buildings and streets will be familiar, although in Gedi all the houses were single-storey. As usual, sanitary arrangements are much in evidence. Gedi's toilets are all of identical design, and superior to many long-drops you find in Kenya today. While many of the houses have been modified over the centuries, these bathrooms seem original, almost as if the town was purpose-built, like a housing estate. Look out for the **House of the Sunken Court**, one of the most elaborate, with its self-conscious emulation of the palace's courtyards.

The Great Mosque

Gedi's **Great Mosque**, one of seven on the site, was its Friday mosque, the mosque of the whole town. Compared with other ruined mosques on the coast, this one is very large and had a *minbar*, or pulpit, of three steps in stone, rather than the usual wood construction. Perhaps an inkling of the kind of people who worshipped here – and they were both men and women – and their form of Islam, comes from the carving of a broad-bladed **spearhead** above the arch of the mosque's northeast doorway. Whoever they were, they were clearly not the "colonial Arabs" long believed by European classical scholars to have been the people of Gedi: it's hard to believe that Arabs would have made use of the spear symbol of East African pastoralists.

Tombs

Nearby is a good example of a **pillar tomb**. These are found all along the coast and are associated with men of importance – chiefs, sheikhs and senior community elders. The fact that this kind of grave is utterly alien to the rest of the Islamic world is further indication that coastal Islam was distinctly African for a long time. Such tombs aren't constructed any more, though there's a nineteenth-century one in Malindi. It looks as if the more recent waves of Arab immigration to the coast have tended to discourage what must have seemed to them an eccentric, even barbaric, style. The **Dated Tomb** next door gives an idea of Gedi's age. Its epitaph reads 802 AH – or AD 1399.

Gedi wildlife

It is easy to spend hours here and rewarding to walk down some of the well-swept paths through the thick jungle away from the main ruins. In the undergrowth, you catch spooky glimpses of other buildings still unexcavated. And with patience you'll see a **golden-rumped elephant shrew**. The size of a small cat, this bizarre animal resembles a giant mouse with an elongated nose, running on stilts. In one of those mystifyingly evolved animal relationships, it consorts with a small bird, the **red-capped robin chat**, which warns it of danger and picks up insects disturbed by the shrew's snufflings. Your best chance of seeing a shrew is to look for its fluttering companion among the tangle of branches: the shrew will be close by. Gedi also has monkeys, bushbabies, tiny duiker antelope and, according to local belief, a huge, mournful, sheep-like animal that follows you like a shadow down the paths.

Watch out, incidentally, for the *siafu* **ants** that have colonized many of the ruins. They form thick brown columns massing from one hole to another and sometimes gather in enormous clumps. Be careful where you put your feet when stepping over walls. And try not to stand on the walls themselves: they are fragile, and the freedom to walk around Kenya's ruins without restriction isn't likely to continue if they suffer as a result.

Kipepeo Butterfly Farm

Open daily 8am–5pm; Ksh50; PO Box 57 Kilifi, ☎0125/22078.

Close by the entrance to Gedi ruins is sited Kenya's first working butterfly farm, **Kipepeo**. Based on the overseas market for exotic butterflies – for preserved collections and walk-through butterfly "farms" – Kipepeo ("butterfly" in Swahili) supplies local farmers in the Arabuko-Sokoke Forest with newly hatched larvae which they rear through the caterpillar stages to pupation, selling the pupae back to the project for cash. The farmers are also responsible for delivering live butterflies for the flight houses. There are three main houses: one, with large growing food plants, for females to lay eggs; one, full of shelves and potted food plants in net cages, for hatching larvae; and one for males to flap around while visitors wander among them. It's a worthwhile, positive place to visit, with some interesting information about the butterflies and the Arabuko-Sokoke Forest in general.

Watamu

After Gedi, **WATAMU** seems fairly superficial. It consists simply of a small agglomeration of hotels, a strip of beachfront private homes, a compact coconut village of *hotelis* and curio stands, and the **beach**. Although one or two of the hotels are very pleasant, the beach, and the coral offshore, are really the only justification for visiting Watamu. Fortunately, they are justification enough: this is an exceptional shoreline, with three stunning **bays** – Watamu Bay, the Blue Lagoon and Turtle Bay – separated by raised coral cliffs and dotted with tiny, sculpted coral islets. Out in the **Watamu Marine National Park** the submerged crags of living coral gardens are – despite all the visits in glass-bottom boats – as vivid and magically perfect as they must have been for millennia. And despite the high profile of tourism here, there's an easier-going atmosphere than at, say, Diani or Malindi, with fewer security problems than at Malindi and the coastline north and south of Mombasa. Watamu is a good place to go **diving** – or to learn the skill, with at least three diving schools offering one-off dives or approved courses at very reasonable rates. It's worth knowing, however, that from June to August seaweed is often swept onto the beach and the sea can be murky, while in July it's often too rough to snorkel anyway.

The road from Gedi and the junction runs dead straight for six kilometres, passes Watamu's **post and telephone office** (Mon–Fri 8am–12.30pm & 2–5pm), then hits the Watamu beach road, up and down which *matatus* scud all the time. Turn left and there's a **supermarket** and, straight on, a superb little **reptile park**, *Bio-Ken*, 2km from the junction (daily 9am–noon & 2–5pm; Ksh200). Turn right again for **Watamu village**, *Watamu Beach Hotel*, and a number of smaller hotels.

A right turn at the beach road junction brings you to four main resort hotels – *Blue Bay Village, Ocean Sports, Hemingways* and *Turtle Bay* – twenty or thirty private homes and, at the end of the narrow bar along which the road runs, the marine park ticket office. And that's Watamu.

Watamu village

Watamu village is a weird mixture of unhurried fishing community and frenzied Germanophile souvenir centre. The traditional rubs elbows with the pseudo-hip; Samburu and Maasai *morani* in full ochred splendour stand around waiting for photographers (and potential female customers); the Jamia Mosque has a notice which reads "All Muslims are Well Come for Prayers. No Trespass. By Management."

The centre of the village is a small **square** at the end of the tarmac road, with a couple of shops and a *Barclays* bank (Mon–Fri 9am–3pm, bureau de change until 4.30pm). The square's main purpose seems to be to allow the curio-stand owners to size up the latest punters as they arrive (Geman and Swiss tourists on their way to the *Watamu Beach Hotel* pass this way). But the pressure to buy is relatively subdued and after a couple of visits down here your face, and dress, become known and you can go about your business with a nod and a smile. Not that there's anything much to be done: there are several bars and **restaurants** on the road into the village (*Watamu Paradise, Dante* and *Happy Night Club* are usually good), but in the village itself, apart from the dubious attractions of the *Video Café* and the *Ujamaa Bar & Restaurant* (pick-up joints posing as a *hoteli* and a pub), there's really only a handful of tourist bric-a-brac stores (the best is *Harmony Curios*) to keep you away from the beach.

Bicycle rental is offered by a number of outlets, especially in high season when it gets quite competitive (around Ksh300–600 per day, depending on season and number of days). Bikes are a great way of getting to know Watamu, with the Gedi ruins and anywhere on the beach road easily reachable in half an hour or so.

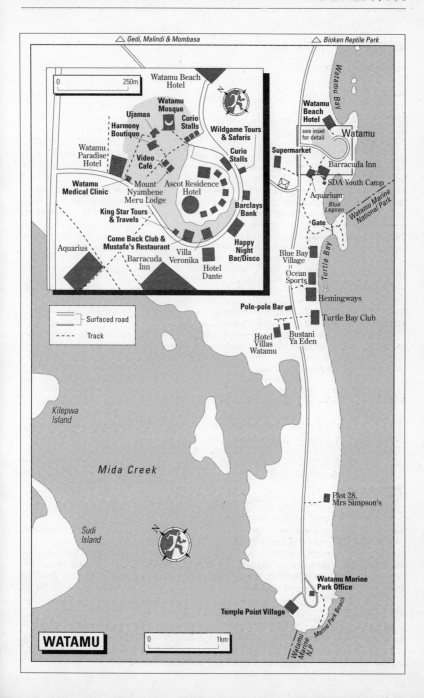

△ Gedi, Malindi & Mombasa

△ Bioken Reptile Park

0 ___ 250m

Watamu Beach Hotel

Watamu Mosque

Ujamaa

Curio Stalls

Harmony Boutique

Wildgame Tours & Safaris

Watamu Paradise Hotel

Video Café

Curio Stalls

Watamu Medical Clinic

Mount Nyambene Meru Lodge

Ascot Residence Hotel

King Star Tours & Travels

Barclays Bank

Aquarius

Come Back Club & Mustafa's Restaurant

Villa Veronika

Happy Night Bar/Disco

Barracuda Inn

Hotel Dante

Watamu Beach Hotel

see inset for detail

Watamu

Supermarket

Barracuda Inn

SDA Youth Camp

Aquarium

Blue Lagoon

Watamu Bay

Watamu Marine National Park

Gate

Blue Bay Village

Ocean Sports

Turtle Bay

Pole-pole Bar

Hemingways

Turtle Bay Club

Hotel Villas Watamu

Bustani Ya Eden

Kilepwa Island

Mida Creek

Sudi Island

Plot 28, Mrs Simpson's

Watamu Marine Park Office

Temple Point Village

Watamu Marine N.P.

Marine Park Beach

──── Surfaced road

- - - - Track

WATAMU

0 ___ 1km

Should you need any **medical treatment** in Watamu, the Watamu Medical Clinic (Mon–Thurs & Sun 8am–6pm & 8–11pm, Fri 8am–1pm; ☎0122/32241) is on the main road down into the village.

Village accommodation

There's a wide variety of **accommodation** in the few establishments in the village itself – everything from a humble and uninviting B&L to a pleasant holiday hotel. Bear in mind that out of season some establishments either close or just tick over, remaining open with a skeleton staff.

Ascot Residence Hotel (PO Box 14; ☎0122/32326). Seems to occupy most of the middle of what you feel should be Watamu village. Presentable, well-designed rooms with fans and patios. It can become a fairly lively place in high season, when there's not a lot of privacy. There's a good-sized pool. B&B ④.

Come Back Club Typical boozer, with some food and basic accommodation. Fans and nets. B&B ③.

Hotel Dante (PO Box 183; ☎0122/32243). If you're counting the pennies, this might be the one to go for, though it doesn't have the *Veronika*'s shady garden – or breakfasts. Don't let anyone tell you they have a pool: they do, but it's empty. Smallish s/c rooms with fan. ③.

Mt Nyambene Meru Lodge (no PO Box; no telephone). You'd have to be doing some kind of bizarre research to want to stay in this gloomy flophouse in a dark corner of the village. Rooms are all a single flat rate, averagely clean (though it's hard to tell in the twilight) and dirt cheap. ①.

Villa Veronika Mwikali (PO Box 57; ☎0122/32083). More or less a B&L, run by a Mkamba-Austrian couple, with fairly ordinary, rather pricey s/c rooms with fans and nets. Little touches, however, like the potted plants and table cloths, and the overall shady, intimate, almost Mediterranean feel of the place help to make it a favourite with most people who stay here. ③.

Watamu Beach Hotel (PO Box 1; ☎0122/32620; *African Safari Club*-owned so no private guests). Shame you can only book this on an *ASC* package as it has probably the best sea view of any hotel in Kenya. Casual visitors are welcome to sit and gaze at the sheltered bay, the coral outcrops, the fishermen – and join in on all sports, unlimited lunch and drinks. The catch is the entry charge of Ksh1500 for adults and Ksh750 for 2- to 12-year-olds. You won't be allowed past the gate without paying.

Watamu Paradise Restaurant and Cottages (PO Box 249; ☎0122/32062, fax 0122/32436). In the high season this gets top marks from many visitors. Not bad value at all, but there are several grades of room: some resemble a B&L, smartened up with whitewash and fancy *kanga* bed covers, and the small pool doesn't exactly sparkle. Fans and nets. ④.

Beach hotels and other accommodation

Several of these establishments focus on watersports, with diving and game fishing on offer. The big fishing competition in the first or second week of March can make accommodation scarce. But in May and June the hotels usually have excellent low-season rates, sometimes available only in packages of seven nights. The following listings are arranged from north to south.

Barracuda Inn (PO Box 402; ☎0122/32331, fax 0122/32330; no credit cards). Unusual hotel on the shore of the Blue Lagoon, well worth considering for an excellent-value getaway break (though note that the second-floor open-air dining terrace is inaccessible to wheelchairs). The beach outlook is only matched by the *Watamu Beach* and here the scene is more intimate. Ground-floor rooms are more spacious – all have telephones and AC. Closed in May. HB ⑤.

SDA Youth Camp (PO Box 80; no telephone). A very pleasant place if you're on a really low budget: three simple rooms in the main building with a basic but well-equipped kitchen and adequate water and toilet facilities, plus lots of camping space if you want it, all set in the dunes under coconuts and casuarinas with a view of the Blue Lagoon you could die for. Seldom full, but rarely unoccupied. ①.

Aquarius (PO Box 96; ☎0122/32069, fax 0122/32211). Very pleasant hotel, closed in the off-season. Italian-owned, with mostly Italian guests, but good value if you just turn up. Rooms have AC plus floor fans. ⑥.

Blue Bay Village (PO Box 162; ☎0122/32626, fax 0122/32422). Well-established, again mostly Italian-patronized holiday complex, with beautiful, palmy gardens and a good pool. If you're going to stay, don't compromise – only the deluxe rooms are worth the money. FB only, ⑧.

Ocean Sports (PO Box 100; ☎0122/32008, fax 0122/32266). Extremely likeable, if slightly macho place, of whitewash and hairy legs, whose reputation ("Open Shorts") has sailed before it for years. During holiday times it swarms with young Anglo-Kenyans doing very much their own thing, but it's right on the beach and has a welcoming atmosphere that owes nothing to tour brochures. Decent-sized rooms with fans and AC and good food, with a famous seafood lunch buffet on Sun and a Chinese dinner on Wed (Ksh500). Good value for HB, snorkelling trips included in the price – ⑥.

Hemingways (PO Box 267; ☎0122/32624, fax 0122/32256; Nairobi bookings with *Bookings Ltd*, New Stanley Building, ☎02/225255). Sharing a plot with *Ocean Sports*, the former *Seafarers* has expanded greatly from its early game-fishing days. From October to April, landing sharks and marlin is still high on the agenda, but this is a really top-class hotel where you won't feel out of place if fishing isn't your bag. Tends to be full of Brits. Rooms in the new wing are wonderful, with huge beds, direct-line telephones, fans and AC. A very appealing set-up and great for families, though becoming very expensive. Closed May and June. B&B ⑤ low, ⑨ high.

Turtle Bay Club (PO Box 457, Malindi; ☎0122/32003, fax 0122/32268; reservations through PO Box 22309, Nairobi; ☎02/221143, fax 02/217261). Expertly run, all-inclusive holiday club, full of happy holiday makers. Lots to do, lots to eat, plenty to drink, and no complaints from anyone it seems, except perhaps Watamu villagers, who won't see much out of it. You can have a one-day sample of club life for Ksh1500. From ⑦ low, ⑧ high.

Bustani ya Eden (PO Box 276; ☎0122/32262). Plain, comfortable chalet-style rooms attached to a locally renowned (not to say notorious) bar-restaurant, with reasonably priced seafood and African dishes. A night club licence means the music often goes on till very late. No beach. B&B ④.

Hotel Villas Watamu (PO Box 150; ☎0122/32298, fax 0122/32487). Some 400m from the road, a Mediterranean-style villa development (not a *makuti* roof in sight) with a dramatic line in verandahs and a huge pool. Timeshare looks like the plan, but meanwhile the overnight rates, for spacious AC accommodation, are very reasonable. No beach. B&B ⑤.

Plot 28 – Mrs Simpson's (PO Box 33; ☎0122/32023). Barbara Simpson has been hosting word-of-mouth guests at her house near the shore for years. To decide if you'll like it, it's still best to talk with someone who's recently stayed before getting a *matatu* down here and walking the final 500m down the track. This is not a hotel: where you sleep and what you eat are up to your hostess and the fixed daily payment covers bed and full-board. Barbara's company and life's worth of African experience are a delight, and her car and small boat are at your disposal – if available. The beach here is deserted. FB ④.

Club Temple Point (PO Box 296; ☎0122/32057, fax 0122/32289). Casual Italian holiday complex, with dull, shadeless gardens and a murky pool. Curiously sited, too – it's on Mida Creek and there is no beach. Closed April–June. ⑦ low, ⑨ high.

Watamu Marine National Park and other excursions

The **Watamu Marine National Park** (daily dawn to dusk; $5) stretches along the coast from the Blue Lagoon to Mida Creek. Its **total exclusion zone** for fishermen has not been greeted with rhapsody all round. On the other hand, tourists come in larger numbers every year and Watamu evidently hasn't gone far wrong in identifying their needs. For **visits to the park**, *Ocean Sports* and *Hemingways* both provide free glass-bottom boat snorkelling trips to guests (park fees extra). Otherwise, expect to pay about Ksh1000–2000 per boat plus the park entrance fee. Down at the end of the Watamu road, a track leads 500m or so from the marine park ticket office to a pretty little beach, with some sunshades and small boats, by the entrance to Mida Creek. It's all a lot lower-key than Malindi.

If you've never taken a swim before in a shoal of coral fish, the spectacle before your eyes can be breathtakingly stupendous: every conceivable combination of colour and shape – and a few inconceivable ones – is represented. It seems impossible that fish should take such forms: the ostentatious dazzle of some of them, especially the absurd parrot fish, can be simply hilarious. The most common destination is the "**coral gardens**", a kilometre or two offshore, where the boat drifts, suspended in five or six metres of scintillatingly clear water. Here, over a group of giant coral heads, where fish naturally congregate and where offerings of bread have obviously further encouraged them, you enter the unusual park.

If you can **dive to the sea floor**, you'll get an intense experience of sharing the undersea world with the fish and the coral. Watch out for the small, harmless octopuses that stay motionless until disturbed and then jet themselves across the sea bed. Above, the boat's hull creates a deep shadow which, associated with food from the passengers, attracts thousands of fish. As you return to the surface, they move out of the way in mysterious unison, each one avoiding all the others in a kind of natural light show of fantastic beauty. If such adventures aren't your forte, the glass bottoms of the boats provide an alternative view – but it's often a rather obscure and narrow one.

Grouper and dolphin spotting – and Sudi Island

At the entrance to Mida Creek is a famous group of caves. Known as the **"Big Three Caves"**, these are the meeting place of a school of **giant groupers**, or rock cod, that once numbered only three but are now many more. Up to two metres long and weighing over 300 kilos, these are placid, stationary monsters – thankfully for anyone intrepid enough to dive down three or four metres for a closer look. The site is a good kilometre offshore and there are some moderate currents: boat trips nomally only take place at the turn of neap high tides, when visibility, depth and currents give the optimum conditions. You need a permit from the park warden to visit the Big Three Caves: this is usually given freely.

Less predictable sea excursions are also arranged in quest of **dolphins**. These are fairly frequently seen offshore, but it's become accepted practice to pay only a nominal charge for the trip if you're unsuccessful. Check it out before committing yourself.

A new excursion, offered by most hotels, is to **Sudi island** in Mida Creek, where a boardwalk takes you right through the mangrove swamps.

Diving and diving schools

From September to April, the **diving** possibilities are extensive at Watamu and you don't need to go far; most of the best dives sites are within thirty minutes of the beach. There are three dive centres, and if you're an experienced diver the best plan is probably to visit all of them and make your own assessment of their competence and suitability. If you're an absolute beginner, go for *Aqua Ventures*.

The sort of **money** involved, if you're a qualified diver, is Ksh1400 for a dive on the reef, including tanks and weights, plus about Ksh500 for renting mask, fins, suit and regulator. There are reductions if you book a series of dives, and small supplements for night- and wreck-dives. If you haven't dived for a while, you should be asked to do a check-out dive (free, or sometimes Ksh500) or a one-day refresher (Ksh3500). Lastly, if you're a beginner, you can do either a one-day, one-dive course (Ksh5000), or opt for the proper PADI course of four dives over five days – leading to certification and your log book – for around Ksh22,000 inclusive.

Aqua Ventures (Steve Curtis), at *Ocean Sports* (PO Box 275; ☎0122/32008). Slightly cheaper and a BSAC school.

Scuba Diving Kenya (Lorenz Reidl), next to Blue Bay Village (PO Box 160; ☎0122/32099).

Turtle Bay Beach Club (PO Box 457 Malindi; ☎0122/32003, fax 0122/32268). Charming people.

Malindi and around

When Vasco da Gama's fleet arrived at **MALINDI** in 1498, it met an unexpectedly warm welcome. The king of Malindi had presumably heard of Mombasa's attempts to sabotage the fleet a few days earlier and, no friend of Mombasa himself, he was swift to ally himself with the powerful – and dangerous – Portuguese. Until they finally subdued Mombasa nearly one hundred years later, Malindi was centre of operations for the Portuguese on the East African coast. Once Fort Jesus was built, Malindi's ruling family was invited to transfer their power base there, which they did, and for many years Malindi was virtually a ghost town as its aristocrats lived it up in Mombasa under Portuguese protection.

Malindi's reputation for hospitality to strangers has stuck, and so has the suggestion of sell-out. As a steadily growing, rock-solid development area for the cultivation of, principally, Deutschmarks and lire, the town is slipping towards cultural anonymity: it can't seem to make up its mind whether it is Mombasa or Lamu. While retaining a Swahili atmosphere, which Mombasa has partly lost in urban development, it utterly lacks Lamu's self-contained tranquillity. Here is one town in Kenya that would go into precipitate decline were the crutch of tourism removed.

Consequently, whether you enjoy Malindi or not depends, at least in part, on how highly you rate the unsophisticated parts of Kenya, and whether you appreciate a fully fledged resort town for its facilities or loathe it for its tackiness. And of course it depends on when you're here. During the summer holiday season (Malindi's best month, sea- and weather-wise, is August), as well as in December and January, the town can be a bit nightmarish. In a busy high season (and there have been some disappointing ones in recent years) everything African about it seems to recede behind the swarms of window-shopping tourists and Suzuki jeeps. Even so, Malindi at its worst is still relatively placid compared with, say, the Mediterranean, and off-season (reduced here to the long rains only – April to June) can seem positively subdued, as if exhausted. At this time of year, when it is often damp and grey, with piles of seaweed washed ashore, Malindi has the air of a Bournemouth, Bognor or a Jersey Shore resort: the faded muddle of an ageing seaside town – garnished with tropical plants. It was opened as a settlers' coastal escape in the 1930s, which in Kenyan terms is a very long time ago, and the last of the sun-wrinkled generation of a bygone era can still be seen walking on Lamu road.

Fortunately, Malindi has some important saving graces in this mixed bag of characteristics. Number one is the **coral reef**. The combined Malindi/Watamu Marine National Parks and Reserve enclose some of the best stretches on the coast. Kisite-Mpunguti, on the south coast, and Kiunga, further north, are reckoned by some connoisseurs to be even better, but the Malindi fish have seen many more strange faces in masks and have become so used to humans that they swarm in front of you like a kaleidoscopic snowstorm. Malindi is a **game-fishing** centre with regular competitions. And it's also a bit of a **surfing** resort, too: good-sized rollers steam into the bay through the long break in the reef during July and August, whipped up by the southerly monsoon winds.

Despite the heavy reliance on tourism, Malindi remains a thriving and ancient town. An interesting old Swahili quarter, one or two "ruins", a busy market, shops, *hotelis* and plenty of lodgings all compensate for the tourist boutiques, beauty salons and real estate agencies. The fact that Malindi has a broad range of places to stay within walking distance of the beach – and a broad range of places to eat and spend money within walking distance of the hotels – gives it a clear advantage over Watamu, Diani or the places north of Mombasa.

Arrival and accommodation

As far as practicalities go, Malindi is uncomplicated. The main **bus station** and *matatu* area (for points north and Lamu) is in the town centre, between the market and the messy, noisy high street where the cheapest of the B&Ls are found. The main focus of town is from here up to the misleadingly named Uhuru Gardens (a dusty patch of shade) and then north along the commercial Harambee Road. Malindi **airport** is

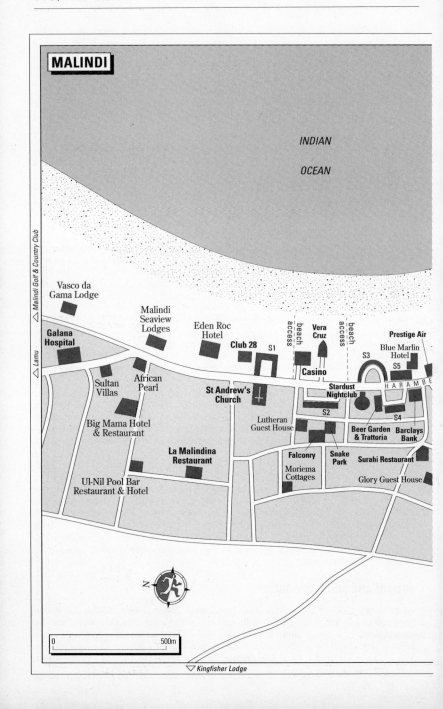

MALINDI

INDIAN

OCEAN

Malindi Golf & Country Club

Lamu

Vasco da
Gama Lodge

Malindi
Seaview
Lodges

Eden Roc
Hotel

Club 28

S1

beach access

Vera
Cruz

beach access

Prestige Air

Galana
Hospital

Casino

S3

Blue Marlin
Hotel

S5

Sultan
Villas

African
Pearl

St Andrew's
Church

Stardust
Nightclub

HARAMBE

Big Mama Hotel
& Restaurant

Lutheran
Guest House

S2

S4

Beer Garden
& Trattoria

Barclays
Bank

La Malindina
Restaurant

Falconry

Moriema
Cottages

Snake
Park

Surahi Restaurant

Ul-Nil Pool Bar
Restaurant & Hotel

Glory Guest House

N

0   500m

Kingfisher Lodge

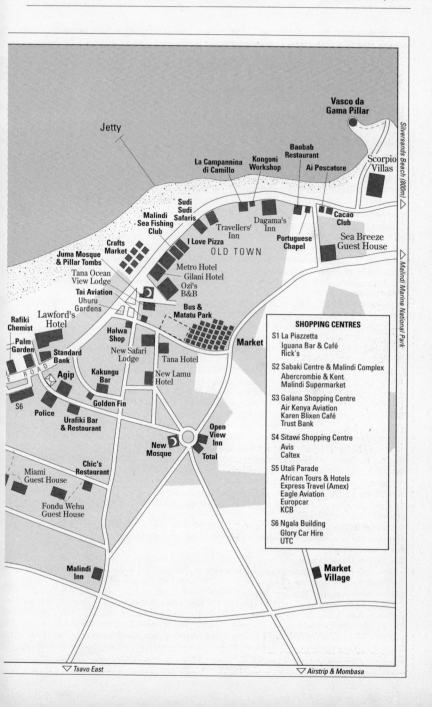

Jetty

Vasco da
Gama Pillar

Scorpio
Villas

Baobab
Restaurant

Kongoni
Workshop

La Campannina
di Camillo

Ai Pescatore

Sudi
Sudi
Safaris

Dagama's
Inn

Cacao
Club

Malindi
Sea Fishing
Club

Travellers'
Inn

Portuguese
Chapel

Sea Breeze
Guest House

Crafts
Market

I Love Pizza

OLD TOWN

Juma Mosque
& Pillar Tombs

Metro Hotel
Gilani Hotel

Tana Ocean
View Lodge

Ozi's
B&B

Tai Aviation

Uhuru
Gardens

Bus &
Matatu Park

Rafiki
Chemist

Lawford's
Hotel

Halwa
Shop

Market

Palm
Garden

New Safari
Lodge

Standard
Bank

ROAD

Tana Hotel

Agip

Kakungu
Bar

New Lamu
Hotel

S6

Golden Fin

Police

Urafiki Bar
& Restaurant

Open
View
Inn

New
Mosque

Total

Chic's
Restaurant

Miami
Guest House

Fondu Wehu
Guest House

Malindi
Inn

Market
Village

Silversands Beach (800m)

Malindi Marine National Park

SHOPPING CENTRES

S1 La Piazzetta
   Iguana Bar & Café
   Rick's

S2 Sabaki Centre & Malindi Complex
   Abercrombie & Kent
   Malindi Supermarket

S3 Galana Shopping Centre
   Air Kenya Aviation
   Karen Blixen Café
   Trust Bank

S4 Sitawi Shopping Centre
   Avis
   Caltex

S5 Utali Parade
   African Tours & Hotels
   Express Travel (Amex)
   Eagle Aviation
   Europcar
   KCB

S6 Ngala Building
   Glory Car Hire
   UTC

▽ Tsavo East

▽ Airstrip & Mombasa

barely 3km from the town centre and you can walk into Malindi in forty minutes. Taxis charge from Ksh500. There is no tourist office in Malindi.

As for **accommodation**, there's plenty of it: several dozen hotels, villa complexes and "clubs" provide for the crowds of high-season visitors, though over Christmas room availability may be restricted. The cheap town lodgings, too, tend to fill up in high season, and also during Maulidi and at the end of Ramadan. Establishments catering essentially for tourists generally vary their prices seasonally, by up to fifty percent, though as usual the cheapest places keep the same low prices all year round.

Budget rooms and camping

There are lots of cheap choices among the town lodgings, with some good traveller-oriented guest houses as well as standard B&Ls, and one or two more unusual offerings. The Youth Hostel, still much referred to in travel guides and tourist information, has been well and truly defunct since the early 1990s. If you want to stay for some time, consider one of the bungalows at the *Lutheran Guest House*. Lastly, beware that solo travellers walking between town and the *Silversands Campsite* have been the victims of muggings several times in recent years.

Dagama's Inn (PO Box 5073; ☎0123/30295). Not bad if you can get one of the two front rooms with fans (both doubles), but somewhat overpriced. ③.

Fondo Wehu Guest House (PO Box 5367; ☎0123/30017). Extremely good-value, charming guest house run by an English-Giriama family. Good rooms with nets and fans, or sleep in the roof dorm under the *makuti*, with nets and a breeze. Healthy breakfasts, free laundry. Very laid-back and always popular. B&B ②.

Gilani Hotel (PO Box 380; ☎0123/20307). Entirely overhauled and refreshed, but still insufficiently to justify the prices. The four rooms at the front, with balconies, are the best and only reasons to stay here. Nets and fans ③, AC ④.

Glory Guest House (PO Box 994; ☎0123/30309). A surprisingly gloomy block at the back of town, which doesn't look as if it can last much longer without business. Rooms with fans and nets, or AC. ③.

Lutheran Guest House (PO Box 409; ☎0123/21098). Set in a large garden, this has double rooms only (clean and mosquito-netted, with fans): singles may have to share if they're full. There are also two fully equipped bungalows, each for four people. There's a no-alcohol policy. Rooms ③, bungalows Ksh3500 per week or Ksh10,000 per month, including utilities.

Metro Hotel (PO Box 352; ☎0123/20902). No fans, no nets, no good reason to stay here unless you're flat broke. Beers are as cheap as they come. A basic sleaze-house and dirt cheap. ①.

Miami Guest House (PO Box 998; ☎0123/31029). Spacious and very clean and airy – a posh kind of B&L, with several s/c and non-s/c rooms. Use of kitchen if required. ③.

New Lamu Hotel (PO Box 333; ☎0123/20864). Basic, reasonably well-kept lodgings above a busy Swahili restaurant. "Backside" rooms are quieter and a few shillings more than the ones near the neighbouring beer hall. Nets, but no fans. No single rooms. Extremely cheap. ①.

New Safari Lodge (PO Box 259; no telephone). Cheap and noisy, but okay if you're just looking for a place to drop your gear and crash – mosquito coils provided. Energetic ground-floor restaurant with tasty food. ①.

Ozi's Bed & Breakfast (PO Box 60; ☎0123/20218). Very secure, this is one of the best in the town centre. The rooms vary quite widely but most are good value. Limited free laundry. Restaurant. Non-s/c ③.

Sea Breeze Guest House (PO Box 5333; ☎0123/20718). A well-kept house, with plenty of rooms – some with balconies – that does less business than it should. The house has its own water. All doubles and triples have fans. Good value – and great views from the roof. ②.

Silversands Campsite, 2km from the town centre (PO Box 422; ☎0123/20412). If you're prepared to forego a little comfort in order to camp on the beach then this is the only place – Ksh90 per person. Various *bandas* are also on offer, ranging from cramped and basic tents with roofs ("green"; ①), to adequate huts with mosquito nets ("white"; ②), to quite attractive, small s/c chalets ("mzuri"; ②), sometimes discounted for long stays. There's a callbox and a snack and cold drinks store on the site, which is guarded and supervised. Old-fashioned bikes are available for Ksh200 per day. Many people pay a small fee (Ksh100) to spend the day in the neighbouring *Driftwood Club*.

Tana Hotel (PO Box 577; ☎0123/20234). Formerly the *New Kenya*, this is much improved, and more expensive than its previous incarnation. While still quite basic, it's clean and well-kept, with nets as well as fans. In addition to ordinary rooms there are three rather dark s/c rooms around a quiet courtyard at the back. Good, busy restaurant with plenty of choice. ③.

Tana Ocean View Guest House (PO Box 766; ☎0123/31447). Connected with the Tana River Bus company, this plain hotel is light, airy, spacious and very clean, with fans and nets in all rooms. Good rooftop views of town. The main possible drawback is its close proximity to a noisy mosque. No s/c singles. B&B ②–③.

Traveller's Inn (PO Box 589; no telephone). Quite an established haunt of travellers on a very low budget. All on the ground floor, with a communal back patio for breakfast. Fans in all rooms, but no nets. No alcohol allowed. Rooms 1 and 4 at the front are the best. Cheap. ②.

Hotels in the town centre and north

The three most established hotels (*Blue Marlin*, *Eden Roc* and *Lawford's*) are on the main beach, with newer establishments scattered to the north, and behind the town centre to the west. All have pools. Distances are from the Uhuru Gardens in the town centre.

Blue Marlin (700m; PO Box 20; ☎0123/20441, fax 0123/20459). Much rebuilt, this is where Ernest Hemingway once contemplated game fishing but stayed in the bar instead. It has, appropriately, some Spanish touches, but furnishings and decor are utterly unspecial. Guests can use facilities at the jointly owned *Lawford's*. HB ⑤.

Eden Roc Hotel (1.5km; PO Box 350; ☎0123/20480, fax 0123/20333). Smartest hotel of the big three, and offering the best value, but frankly in need of a complete refit – which it may well get if rumours of an extremely well-connected new Kenyan owner prove true. Friendly, but somewhat disorganized management. Convenient for town but a very long walk from its own beach. HB ⑤.

Moriema Cottages (1.5km; PO Box 235; ☎0123/30816). Worth considering if you want to self-cater for a short time – each cottage has gas rings, sink and fridge – but it seems expensive. Cottages come equipped with fans and nets – and furnished with mildewed carpets. B&B ⑤.

Kibokoni Riding Centre (4km; PO Box 857; ☎0123/21273, fax 0123/21030). As you head north out of town along the beach road, the scene becomes one of extreme ostentation. Out of the bush rise vast *makuti* roofs, Malindi's limpet-like status symbols. The last cluster is *Kibokoni*, an ideal retreat for horsey honeymooners, offering excellent rooms with remarkably robust beds constructed from solid tree trunks. ⑥.

Kingfisher Lodge (4km; PO Box 29; ☎0123/20123, fax 0123/30621). Located inland, this is an unusual and pretty, family-run lodge with a pool, consisting of just four very spacious double rooms with wonderful bathrooms. Good for couples or families with very young children (there's nothing out here for older kids). Transport to the beach and town is included in the tariff and remote-area safaris can be arranged. Highly recommended for a honeymoon, or a pretension-free splurge. Renowned cuisine. Closes in low season. Top of the range ⑨.

Lawford's Hotel Beach Club (300m; PO Box 20; ☎0123/20440, fax 0123/20459). Very uninspiring all-inclusive hotel (minimum stay three days), co-owned with the *Blue Marlin*. If you want to stay in Malindi town centre, however, the location is ideal. "Standard" rooms are mediocre: the "superior" ones are much nicer than the superficial surcharge would suggest. Dive centre. All-inclusive ⑥.

Vasco da Gama Lodge (2.1km; PO Box 639; ☎0123/21027, fax 0123/31442). A good-value, small place, with big grounds and above-average rooms (fans and king-size, netted four-poster beds). Closed April–Aug. HB ⑥.

Hotels south of the town

This is where the greatest development has taken place in the last few years, with one resort hotel after another reaching almost down to Casuarina Point. Some of the more noteworthy bases follow, listed from north to south (with approximate distances from Uhuru Gardens in the town centre).

Scorpio Villas (1km; PO Box 368; ☎0123/20194). An exceptionally well-conceived "village", dense with tropical vegetation. Each villa has a kitchen and dedicated staff and is divided into large rooms, each with its own bathroom and private patio. Eat "at home" or in the restaurant. Great for families and very cosmopolitan. Excellent value. HB ⑤ low, ⑥ high.

Driftwood Club (2.2km; PO Box 63; ☎0123/20155, fax 0123/30712; reservations through *Bunson Travel Service*, address p.122). Trading on its good food and established reputation among the Anglo-Kenyan community, this is an informal set-up, similar to *Ocean Sports* in Watamu. Prices are non-seasonal, but vary depending on the cooling system, the bathroom arrangements, and which part of the beach the room faces. Squash court, game fishing, diving. B&B ④–⑨; the two beautiful four-bed cottages sharing a private pool cost Ksh10,800.

Coconut Village (2.4km; PO Box 868; ☎0123/20928). Quite an attractive place without much character. Most guests are Italian. They tend to play Euro Rock rather loudly round the pool, which – as most rooms surround it – proves noisy. Not very private. ⑤ low, ⑦ high.

African Dream Village (2.7km; PO Box 939; ☎0123/20442, fax 0123/20119). *Makuti* and tropical gardens – an Italian-slanted holiday resort with a wide range of watersports available. ⑤ low, ⑦ high.

New Kivulini Bay (7.1km; PO Box 5662; ☎0123/20898, fax 0123/31396). A picturesque enough complex, in the ornate Italian style so predominant in Malindi, but situated on an uncomfortably barren and craggy headland with no beach. It looks like it's just about able to pay its way to maintain appearances. ⑥ low, ⑦ high.

The Town

Other than the beach and the sea, **strolling around town** is the occupation of most of Malindi's temporary residents, and not without its idiosyncratic rewards. The old part of Malindi is a half-hour diversion: interesting enough, even though there's nothing specific to see and few of the buildings date from before the second half of the nineteenth century. But the juxtaposition of the earnest and ordinary business of the old town with the near-hysterical *mzungu*-mania only a couple of minutes' walk away on Lamu road produces a bizarre, schizophrenic atmosphere that epitomizes Malindi.

The town has an amazingly salacious reputation which is not entirely home-grown: some European tour operators have in the past been quite inventive in their every-comfort-provided marketing strategies. In the immediate aftermath of the first AIDS-awareness crisis in the late 1980s, there was a massive slump in German tourism to Malindi, so perhaps the era of the sex safari is really over. The Italians now dominate absolutely, and have increased in numbers to the extent that one supermarket even sells Italian canned dog food.

Monuments

Archeologically, Malindi's offerings are scant. The two **pillar tombs** in front of the Friday mosque on the waterfront are fine upstanding examples of the genre, though the shorter one is only nineteenth-century. This being Malindi, its appearance is usually described as "circumcized". Islamic scholars on the coast tend to dispute the automatic phallic label applied by foreigners.

Malindi's other monuments are Portuguese. **Vasco da Gama Pillar** (1499), down on the point of the same name, makes a good target for a stroll. The **Portuguese Chapel** is a tiny whitewashed cube of a church, whose foundations were laid in the sixteenth century on the site of a Portuguese burial. The most recent Portuguese bequest is the 1959 **Vasco da Gama Monument** on the seaward side of Uhuru Gardens – a subject of neglect that would be shameful were it not so ugly in itself. It either needs renovating and its missing plaques replaced, or demolishing.

Wildlife attractions

If you're drawn to wildlife, you could visit one of Malindi's **snake parks** – the best is certainly the one at Casuarina Point (daily 9am–5pm; feeding time Wed & Fri 4pm; Ksh300). There's also the rather sad **falconry** (daily 9am–5.30pm; Ksh200), though it's tempting to recommend avoiding this place entirely.

Be sure to avoid the great **camel ride** racket on the beach. Several of the swaggering beasts are often stationed on the sands (if they're not in Watamu) and, if you allow yourself to be talked into a ride, it's amazing how swiftly the price can go up and the duration diminish. It all depends how desperate you are to get on one. In any case, pay nothing until you're aboard – or preferably down again.

For a much more interesting natural history experience, visit the Arabuko-Sokoke Forest visitor centre, near Gedi, and take a guided walk with the resident ornithologist (details on p.400).

Crafts and shopping

There are two main outdoor areas to head for when you're in the buying mood. Most obvious is the **crafts market** on the seashore below the old town. Naturally if you stray down here you'll be pounced upon, and leaving without buying anything isn't easy. On the other hand, you can also leave with all sorts of little free gifts if you strike the right bargain. The other area is the **woodcarving co-operative**, in the market in the town centre – a good place for photos. Note there's no bargaining at all in their shop, but you can discuss prices direct with the carvers.

Alternatively, for more expensive crafts and the possibility of browsing unhurriedly, try one of the **upmarket shops** along Harambee Road, just to the north of Uhuru Gardens. Prices are naturally very high, but visits are useful for checking comparative values and gauging top prices. At *Rasani's Arcade*, for example, they have lots of top-quality crafts and *objets d'art,* including old Lamu silver and jewellery as well as more familiar items available on the street. *Kongoni Workshop*, on the seafront (Mon–Sat 9.30am–1pm & 3.30–7pm), offers fixed-price bead- and leatherwork and very nice *vyondo* baskets.

Snorkelling and watersports

Not unexpectedly, **snorkelling** ("goggling") and other **watersports** are Malindi's touristic *raison d'être*. Windsurfing, water-skiing, diving and deep-sea game fishing are all cheaper here than at the resorts around Mombasa. Malindi Bay is the main wave-surfing stretch and surfboards are available from all the tourist hotels in town. Unfortunately, all watery activities are marred somewhat by the Sabaki River's annual outpouring of thousands of tons of prime red topsoil from the up-country plateaus. The cloudy water prevents the growth of coral as far south as Vasco da Gama Point and, ironically, Malindi Bay and the tour-group hotels dotted along it face out across dun-coloured sands to a muddy-brown seascape for much of the year. Murky as it is, this water is not unpleasant to swim in.

Beach **access** is not a big problem, though the easiest place – and closest to the road – is on the south side of town at Silversands beach. The beach at the town centre and to the north is a good five to ten minutes' walk from the road. There are one or two public access points (see our map) and the hotels are usually willing to allow access for a small fee. *Eden Roc*, for example, charges Ksh120 per day, which allows you use of their pools and a sunbed.

Malindi Marine National Park

Daily dawn to dusk; US$5; warden: PO Box 109; ☎0123/20845.

Trips out to the **marine park** can be arranged with the boat trip salesmen who make their rounds of *Silversands Campsite* (and elsewhere) most mornings. Alternatively, make your own way down to the **park office** and very pretty beach at Casuarina Point, 5km from town, where you can choose your boat, captain and all. You should find a little room for discussion but won't be able to knock down prices much below the current going rate of about Ksh600–700 (excluding park fees) for two hours, especially at peak seasons. Note that your outing may be curtailed if you bargain too ruthlessly. Try to check out the condition of masks and snorkels, and insist on a set for each member of the party. Flippers aren't likely to be up to much (assuming they fit you). The six square kilometres of the **national park** take in the loveliest areas of coral garden, a couple of kilometres offshore, and the trip – usually in a glass-bottomed boat – is worth every shilling you finally agree on.

With your own or rented gear, of course, you could swim to the reef outside the boundaries of the marine park. All the beachfront hotels from Vasco da Gama Point south as far as *White Elephant Sea Lodge* (3.6km from the town centre) are to the north of the marine park, but the reef is anything from 300m to 800m offshore.

If you have the qualifications, you can **dive**. The *Driftwood* and *Lawford's* both have dive centres: the one at *Driftwood* is a school. For general information about diving, see the Watamu account (p.407).

Eating, drinking and nightlife

You're presented with two basic options for **eating** in Malindi. The first is ordinary *hoteli* fare supplemented by a scattering of Indian-style juice and samosa bars; the second is a much higher price bracket that includes the big hotels and a small number of more lavish restaurants. If you're buying your own food, you'll find **Malindi Market** is celebrated for fruit and vegetables – second, on the coast, only to Mombasa's.

Basic eateries and bars

Bawaly and Sons Halwa Shop, town centre near Uhuru Gardens. Highly deserving of a mention, a long-established spot to try several varieties of the gooey jelly (of which "Turkish Delight" is a dull relation). Tiny cups of spiced *kahawa* come free.

Beer Garden, Harambee Rd. Come here for the keg beer and snacks, and to start the evening.

Chic's Restaurant. Popular beer garden at the back of town.

Golden Fin Restaurant, back of the town centre. Clean new place with cheap sodas and fried and African food.

New Lamu Hotel. Good Swahili food in the downstairs restaurant.

New Safari Lodge. A busy *hoteli* on the ground floor, with a wide choice, at least in the daytime.

Oasis Gelateria, south side of Malindi, on the beach before *Silversands*. With Italian money flooding into Malindi, a certain scepticism seems in order. But this big new snack bar is simply very good – though more perhaps for the metropolitan touches like cheap soda water on tap, inexpensive homemade bread, delicious omelettes and espresso – than for the forty flavours of rather watery ice cream. Sadly, it's part of a huge and hideous time-share complex which has occupied what remained of Silversands public beach. Open daily 9am–1pm.

Open View, by Total roundabout on the outskirts of town. Good local food.

Ozi's Restaurant. Reliable and inexpensive curries and *dahls* at the guest house of the same name.

Palm Garden. A convenient rendezvous that's primarily a bar, serving inexpensive – and usually very good – curries and seafood. To avoid the prostitutes and rather hustly scene on the front patio, eat in the garden at the back. Always a good place to hit on a Friday, often with live music (small entrance charge then).

Sea Fishing Club (PO Box 364; ☎0123/30550). A regular rendezvous for fishermen and boating people, with a daily membership of Ksh50 and mid-price beer.

Urafiki Bar & Restaurant. A cheap down-to-earth *hoteli* with the dual bonuses of cold beer and loud music.

Upmarket restaurants

Ai Pescatori, near the Portuguese Chapel on the seafront (☎0123/31198). Mostly pizzas, cooked in a woodfired oven. From about Ksh300.

Baobab, next to the Portuguese Chapel on the seafront. Expensive seafood (Ksh500–700), curries and African dishes (Ksh200), but well worth patronizing for cheap, cold beer.

Campannina di Camillo (☎0123/30251). High-class, slightly quirky, Italian restaurant. Closed in low season.

Driftwood Club (☎0123/20155). Always a good place to eat, but the Ksh500 Sunday curry buffet is worth planning your day around.

I Love Pizza, on the seafront (☎0123/20672). Quite flashy with a good atmosphere, and the pizzas are really not bad – from around Ksh200. They push their seafood, though, which is also good. Recommended.

Kingfisher Lodge 4km inland (☎0123/20123). Very good food, generally a set menu, and a great place to cool off in the evening as it's a little higher up. Essential to book ahead.

Surahi Restaurant (☎0123/20911). A fancy Indian restaurant (rated one of Malindi's best) with a limited range of fairly expensive dishes and an uncluttered, cool dining room. Worth a try but not unmissable.

Trattoria (☎0123/21121). A very good Italian, no longer related to the one in Nairobi. Service tends to be agonizingly slow.

Vera Cruz, north on Harambee Rd, fronting onto the beach. Galleon-shaped theme restaurant, pool and pub, executed with panache. Waiters are dressed as sailors and the whole experience is supposed to remind you of the good old days when the only "tourists" were Portuguese arms traders.

Nightlife

After dark, through the high season, Malindi throbs with action and you may even find live music. The biggest and best **club** is the air-conditioned *Stardust*. *Club 28* (originally exclusively for under-28s, for some reason) is also not bad, though a lot smaller. **Hotel discos**, a speciality of the south side of Malindi, tend to happen in a different hotel each night through the week: *Coconut Village* on a Monday, the *Driftwood Club* on Saturday, and *African Dream Village* on Sunday, for example. When you're weary of bopping, the *Casino Malindi* has free entry (daily from noon), no dress code and powerful air conditioning. Play if you want, or just watch the grim-looking Italian bosses tending their novice Giriama croupiers.

Local dives in town include the *Kakungu Bar*, which hosts bands once in a while, especially on public holidays; and the *Malindi Inn*, a little way out of town on the road to Tsavo East. Malindi has five working bands: listen out for the *Travellers Band* and the *Black Warriors*. Try *Mgadini* and *Come Back*, both on the way out of town on the left, before you reach the airport. Out here too, you'll find the *Market Village* club, inside the Malindi Showground, where international stars of Afican music sometimes perform. The entrance price for all these places is nominal – except, of course, when they are hosting someone like Samba Mapangala. Drinks are also cheap and you can usually feast on a half-kilo of *nyama choma*. It's always more fun to go with a Malindi local – though you should have no worries at all about taking a taxi and going on your own.

Listings

American Express Mon–Sat 8am–12.30pm & 2–5pm.

Banks *Trust Bank* (Mon–Fri 9am–4.30pm, Sat 9–11.30am), *Barclays* bureau de change (Mon–Fri 9am–4.30pm, Sat 9–11am), *KCB* and *Standard Bank* (both Mon–Fri 9am–3pm, Sat 9–11am). The *Standard* is much the most efficient. Rates, when you take commission and charges into consideration, are much the same. The Casino also changes money at any time, but at less favourable rates.

Bicycle rental Available everywhere. *Silversands Campsite* are old hands and their bikes cost around Ksh200 per day or Ksh1200 per week. Other places may have better bikes, but prices are higher – *Sudi Sudi* charges Ksh60 an hour, Ksh400 a day, for example.

Car rental *Glory Car Hire*, Ngala Building, across from the post office (PO Box 994; ☎/fax 0123/20065), maintains a high profile on the coast and you can leave the vehicle in Nairobi or Mombasa for a supplement. Prices start at Ksh2200 per day plus Ksh14 per kilometre, including insurance. Alternatively, there's *Avis*, at Sitawi Shopping Centre (PO Box 197; ☎0123/20513), and *Payless*, at La Piazzetta centre. Or try *Galu* or *Hertz/UTC* (see "Travel agents", below).

Flights *Prestige Air Services* (☎0123/20861), *Eagle Aviation* (☎0123/21258, fax 0123/21099) and *Air Kenya Aviation* (☎0123/30808) connect Malindi with Nairobi, Mombasa and Lamu. You can book seats on all of them at any of the three offices, or at any travel agency, and the price should be the same. You may be quoted dollars but you can pay in Kenya shillings, which can work out cheaper as they may be persuaded to split their commission with you. It's also worth checking if *Tai Airlines* are still operating (office in the town centre – see our map): they've been undercutting the other airlines on the Malindi–Lamu run and come recommended.

Game fishing The Malindi Festival takes place in October and the Billfish Tournament in January, but, if you're into it, you can go hunting big fish from September to April. In 1995 a marlin was hooked that weighed 1250kg (1.25 tonnes). It will cost you $300 and upwards a day for the boat and the gear. The *Driftwood* is probably the best place to get details. The Malindi Sea Fishing Club (PO Box 364; ☎0123/30550; daily membership fee Ksh50), next to *I Love Pizza*, can also put you in touch with fishing operators.

Horse riding Try the *Kibokoni Riding Centre* north of town (see p.413). You'll pay around Ksh500 an hour, including a guide, for short bush rides in the vicinity. Beginners can go on a leading rein.

Hospitals There are three in Malindi, but the Galana Hospital is the best.

Immigration A decrepit-looking office on the waterfront road by the Jumaa Mosque.

Post and telephone office The post office is open Mon–Fri 8am–5pm, Sat 9am–noon, and has a good poste-restante service. The telephone office is open Mon–Fri 7am–12.30pm & 2–6pm. They sell phone cards for the cardphone, which is cheaper to use than placing a call through the operator. There's also a fax machine.

Supermarkets There are several small places in the shopping arcades up Harambee Road in the town centre. But the widest and cheapest range is undoubtedly at the *Jolly Market Supermarket and Greengrocers*, which is part of the *Oasis* complex on Silversands beach. Here, you'll find Italian wine from under Ksh200 a bottle, and dairy produce.

Travel agents A good scattering along Lamu road and the seafront all offer similar services, including train bookings: try *Galu Safari Ltd*, Malindi Complex (☎0123/20493, fax 0123/30032); *UTC* (☎0123/20069); or the very pleasant and helpful *Sudi Sudi Safaris* (owned by *Prince Travel* in Nairobi; ☎0123/20596, fax 0123/30175).

Out of Malindi: the Arabuko-Sokoke Forest and Hell's Kitchen

The best way to get around town and its environs is **by bicycle** (several places rent bikes – see "Listings"). If you've been relying on public transport – or organized tour buses – cycling can give you a tremendous lift, enabling you to go virtually anywhere. The flat countryside around Malindi is ideal and Gedi (an hour and a half) or Watamu (two hours) are easy objectives, with the guarantee that you'll be blown either there or back by the wind, depending on the time of year.

You might be tempted to head north to what one piece of tourist literature describes as "the Arabian Nights town of **Mambrui**". True, there's a pretty mosque and the unusual spectacle of cows on the beach, but the very ruinous pillar tomb certainly isn't worth the dust-blown journey and the village itself could hardly be less exciting. Better to head for one of the following.

The northern Arabuko-Sokoke Forest

For immersion in raw nature, drive, or pedal for an hour, along the road out of Malindi towards Tsavo East and, as you near the banks of the Sabaki (or Galana) River, you'll enter the **Arabuko-Sokoke Forest**. To make the most of the day, try setting out early by *matatu*, with your bike on the roof rack. There are several *matatus* daily, and one country bus service, but departure times are unpredictable. Take lots of water. Beware: the sandy tracks on some sections of the routes described below can be very hard going. A car, motorbike or mountain bike is the best solution; an ordinary rented bike may need to be pushed for up to two hours – a punishing slog.

The places to aim for are **Kakayuni** (12km inland from Malindi) and **Jilore** (20km). Kakayuni is the larger of the two and offers a forest road of 10km or so, leading via the small centre of **Arabuko** back to the main Kilifi–Malindi highway. Mostly, however, this path goes through marginal forest lands; continuing to Jilore is more promising. Jilore is a tiny centre, with a scattered collection of huts and one nominal *duka*. The village's position, though, on a ridge overlooking a bend in the Sabaki/Galana River, contrasts impressively with the deep forest into which you now plunge.

The turning for Jilore Forest Station is to the left, just before you reach Jilore village, and the station about 3km down the track. At the first crossroads after the forest station's three huts, turn left: a good trail leads for 16km in a southerly direction to the Kilifi–Malindi highway. If you're doing this trip by car, the track is drivable, and it's also clear enough for walkers to follow without getting lost. The track is seldom used by motorists and you're not likely to see other people. Around its halfway mark, the soil changes from red murram to a light grey, soft coral sand, signalling the transition back to the coast proper. If you've been pootling along gently on a rented cycle from Malindi, this is pretty well the end of the relaxing bit, where you'll have to start getting off to push. Your eventual emergence onto the main highway, five or six kilometres south of Gedi, is sudden. Here, you could wait for a short time for a *matatu* straight back to Malindi or, if the day is still young and your energy not completely sapped, turn inland again a couple of kilometres north up the road, where the other track (described above) leads to Arabuko and Kakayuni.

For a short, and much less strenuous, visit to the forest – and more about its natural history – see p.400.

The Marafa Depression: Hell's Kitchen

Northwest of Malindi, the **Marafa Depression** is the remains of a large sandstone ridge, now reduced by wind, rain and floodwater to a series of gorges, where steep gullies and narrow arêtes alternately eat into or jut from the main ridge wall. The colours of the exposed sandstone range from off-white through pale pinks and oranges to deep crimson, all capped by the rich tawny topsoil. It's particularly dramatic at sunset.

"Hell's Kitchen" is the common nickname for this pretty spectacle, though the locals call it *Nyari* – "the place broken by itself" – and tell numerous moralizing **stories** about its dark origins. The village that once stood here was favoured by God with the news of a forthcoming miracle, delivered to the inhabitants by an angel. They were commanded to move on, and all did so, except one old woman who refused to believe such nonsense. The village (and the old lady) disappeared soon after, leaving *Nyari*. Whether that was the miracle is not reported, but it's interesting to note how the story varies according to the teller – in Islamic circles "God talked through an angel", while among traditionalists, "the gods informed a wise woman".

To get there, fork right at the end of Marafa village, and the canyon is about 500m along on the left, invisible until you're right at its edge. At the lip of the gorge the first signs of commercialism – a small car park and a couple of seasonal souvenir stands – don't detract much from the site. It's easy to descend the steep path to the bottom and you can count on spending an hour or two exploring the natural architecture of what looks like an early *Star Trek* set. There's a scattering of *dukas* and *hotelis* among Marafa village's whitewashed, thatched houses, but no lodgings.

With a vehicle, you might sensibly combine the Arabuko-Sokoke Forest with a visit to the Marafa Depression by crossing the Galana/Sabaki River – if the bridge across the river at Jilore (marked on some maps) actually existed. In its absence, take the road out of Malindi heading north (which involves a left turn on the other side of the Sabaki bridge) and from there go via **Marikebuni** and **Magarini**. You're looking at a round trip of about 80km, one which – given the vagaries of **public transport** – only drivers can manage in a day. The daily **bus** to Marafa leaves Malindi in the morning, returning to the coast the same day. Buses to **Mbaini** (leaving Malindi in the morning) and **Dikatchal** (in the afternoon) also pass through Marafa.

AROUND THE TANA DELTA

If you have your own 4WD vehicle, the trip north to Lamu can be stretched over several days, with time to explore the fascinating region around the **Tana Delta**: on the west side, the Pokomo village of **Ngao** and other villages on the river itself; on the east, a dune-shrouded coast and **Kipini**, with the Swahili ruins of **Ungwana**, **Shaka** and **Mwana** all within twelve kilometres. If you're genuinely interested in nosing around this region for a few days, it's suggested you try to see the warden of the museum at Fort Jesus for further information. You can also take a **safari** in the delta with *Tana Delta Ltd* (PO Box 24988, Nairobi; ☎02/882826, fax 02/882939; about $200 a day), who run *Tana Delta Camp*, a tented camp in the dunes near the ocean (⑨; closed low season, minimum stay three nights), and whose eleven-metre converted dhow, *African Queen*, is used to give people a look at a very unvisited part of the country (pick-up from Malindi; ☎0123/20819). We'd be very interested to hear accounts of trips in the Tana Delta for the next edition.

Onwards to Lamu

The **flight to Lamu** ($65 from Malindi) is an experience not to be missed and the usual mode of transport for visitors these days. But the **bus journey** is an adventure in its own right and repays you with more than just a cheaper ticket. On a number of occasions in the early 1990s, it repaid all the occupants of the bus, including its armed escort, with summary eviction from their seats while a gang of bandits made a careful collection of all belongings. Once they stole all the passengers' clothes, too. Security has been stepped up but the banditry has gone on too long for the majority of people, and only the most intrepid or penniless tourists use the two existing services. The old companies on the route – *Tana River Bus, Malindi Bus* and *Garissa Express* – pulled it from their schedules before they lost all their buses. The plucky *Faza Bus* and *TSS Bus* now both operate a daily service from Mombasa via Malindi to Lamu. The price on *Faza Bus* is Ksh300 from Malindi (Ksh350 from Mombasa), while *TSS Bus* charges Ksh350 (Ksh400 from Mombasa).

Installed by a window (ideally on the left, to avoid the sun), you can fully appreciate the flat, gentle, dull landscape, sometimes brown and arid but more usually grey-green and swampy, which opens out as Malindi's low hills are left behind. When the scenery palls totally, the trip is enlivened by the other passengers, by stops at fly-blown Garsen and little Witu for *chai* and a bite to eat, and by occasional flashes of colour: the sky-blue cloaks of **Orma** herders or the red, black and white of shawled **Somali** women. Wonderful **birdlife** and **wild animals** are evident, too: giraffe and antelope, notably waterbuck; even the odd elephant if you look hard enough. And impeccable sources attest to having recently seen **lions** between Garsen and Mokowe.

The road is intermittently hard-surfaced from Malindi to Garsen. The Chinese-built New Garsen Causeway now spans the Tana outside Garsen with a bridge and provides a flood-proof highway. In the past, bus services were often disrupted during the rains, either because buses were stuck in mud or because the river was too high for the primitive, hand-hauled car ferry to operate. In that case they used to ferry people across the Tana by dugout canoe and, *inshallah*, there'd be another bus waiting on the other side. For more on Garsen, see p.494.

THE LAMU ARCHIPELAGO

A cluster of hot, low-lying desert islands tucked into the coast near the Somalian border, **Lamu** and its neighbours have a special appeal that many find irresistible.

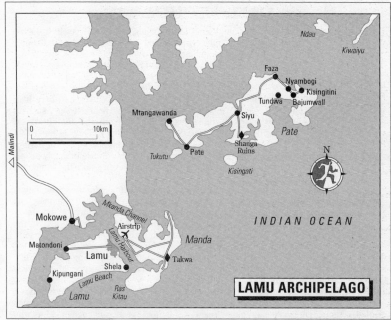

While each town or village has its own distinct character, together they epitomize a separate spectrum of Swahili culture. For although the whole coast is – broadly – "Swahili", there's a world of difference between these islands and the coconut beaches of Mombasa and Malindi.

To a great extent the islands are anachronisms. Electricity arrived here less than thirty years ago; there are still no motor vehicles; life moves at the pace of a donkey or a dhow. Yet there have been considerable internal changes over the centuries and Lamu itself is now changing faster than ever. Because of its special position in the Islamic world, Saudi Arabian direct aid has poured into the island: the hospital, schools and religious centres are all supported by it. At the same time, there have been efforts to open up Lamu beyond its present tourist market, which so far has encompassed only low-budget travellers and short-stay air safaris. Rich foreign sponsors are eagerly sought and several lodging houses have been set up with what is bluntly called "white girl money". Islanders are ambivalent about the future. A string of hotels along the beach, a bridge to the mainland – all seems possible, and all would contribute to the destruction of Lamu's timeless character. Some up-country officials working here might not disapprove: with only two bars, the town is not a popular posting.

But the damage that would be done goes further than spoiling the tranquillity. The Lamu archipelago is one of the most important sources for knowledge about pre-colonial Africa. **Archeological sites** indicate that towns have existed on these islands for at least 1200 years. The dunes behind Lamu beach, for example, are said to conceal the remains of long-deserted settlements. And somewhere close by on the mainland, archeologists expect one day to uncover the ruins of Shungwaya, the town which so many coastal peoples claim as their ancestral home. The whole region is an academic's delight, a source of endless confusion and controversy, and a place where there is still real continuity between history and modern life.

LAMU IN HISTORY

The undeniably **Arab** flavour of Lamu is not nearly as old as the town itself. It derives from the later nineteenth century when the **Omanis**, and to some extent the **Hadhramis** from what is now Yemen, held political and cultural sway in the town. The first British representatives in Lamu found themselves among pale-skinned slave-owning Arab rulers. The cultural and racial stereotypes that were subsequently propagated have never completely disappeared.

Lamu was established on its present site by the fourteenth century but there have been people living on the island for very much longer than that. The fresh water supplies beneath Shela made the island very attractive to **refugees from the mainland** and people have been escaping here for 2000 years or more – most recently in the 1960s, when Somali secessionists and cattle-raiders caused havoc. It was also one of the earliest places on the coast to attract settlers from the Persian Gulf; there were probably people from Arabia and southwest Asia living and intermarrying here even before the foundation of Islam.

In 1505, Lamu was visited by a heavily armed **Portuguese** man-of-war and the king of the town quickly agreed to pay the first of many cash tributes as protection money. The alternative was the sacking of the town. For the next 180 years Lamu was nominally under Portuguese rule, though the Portuguese favoured Pate as a place to live. In the 1580s, the **Turkish** fleet of Amir Ali Bey temporarily threatened Portuguese dominance, but superior firepower and relentless savagery kept them out and Lamu, with little in the way of an arsenal, had no choice but to bend with the wind – losing a king now and then to the Portuguese executioners – until the Omanis arrived on the scene with fast ships and a serious bid for lasting control.

By the end of the seventeenth century, Lamu's Portuguese predators were vanquished and for nearly a century and a half it had a revitalizing breathing space. This was its **Golden Age**. Lamu became a republic ruled over by the *Yumbe*, a council of elders who deliberated in the palace (now a ruined plot in the centre of town), with only the loosest control imposed by their Omani overlords. This was the period when most of the big houses were built and when Lamu's classic architectural style found its greatest expression. Arts and crafts flourished and business along the waterfront made the town a

At least for the present, the islands survive. **Lamu island** itself, most people's single destination, still has plenty to recommend it, despite a serious fire in 1993 and the inevitable sprouting of TV satellite dishes; **Manda**, directly opposite, is little visited except for the lifeline it provides with the outside world, the local airstrip; **Pate island** (see p.440), accessible by a scheduled motorboat service, makes a fascinating excursion if you have a week or more in the area; and **Kiwaiyu** (see p.445), not quite within the archipelago but exotic and alluring enough to be worth the effort if you have time, is a wisp of a beach island 9km long and less than 1km across, lying to the northeast of the other islands. Those who visit Kiwaiyu normally arrive by private plane, but you can easily reach it by grouping together to charter a dhow in Lamu.

Lamu island

Perhaps best left until the end of your stay in Kenya, **LAMU** may otherwise precipitate a change in your plans as you're gently lulled into a slow rhythm in which days and weeks can pass by unheeded and other objectives can easily be forgotten. For many people, Lamu's deliciously lazy atmosphere is the best worst-kept secret on the coast. Eyes, ears, tongue and nose get a comprehensive work-out here, so that actually *doing* anything is sometimes a problem – like walking through treacle. Hours can be blissfully spent on a roof or a verandah just watching the town go by, its mood swinging

magnet throughout the Indian Ocean. Huge ocean-going dhows rested half the year in the harbour, taking on ivory, rhino horn, mangrove poles and cereals. There was time to compose long poems and argue about language, the Koran and local politics. Lamu became the northern coast's **literary and scholastic focus**, a distinction inherited from Pate. Women achieved a higher status than in the past, though ironically the best known Lamu woman of the time, the poet **Mwana Kupona**, is famous for her "Advice on the Wifely Duty" given to her daughter. The house where she lived for a while is up behind the fort.

For a brief time Lamu's star was in the ascendant in all fields. There was even a famous victory at the **Battle of Shela** in 1812. A combined Pate-Mazrui* force landed at Shela with the simple plan of capturing Lamu – not known for its resolve in battle – and finishing the construction of **the fort** which the Nabahanis from Pate had begun a few years earlier. To everyone's surprise, particularly the Lamu defenders, the tide had gone out and the invaders were massacred as they tried to push their boats off the beach. Appalled at the overkill and expecting a swift response from the Mazruis in Mombasa, Lamu sent to Oman itself for **Busaidi** protection and threw away independence forever. Had the eventual outcome of this panicky request been foreseen, the Lamu *Yumbe* might have reconsidered. Seyyid Said, Sultan of Oman, was more than happy to send a garrison to complete and occupy Lamu's fort – and from this toehold in Africa, he went on to smash the Mazrui traitors in Mombasa, taking the entire coast and moving his own Sultanate to Zanzibar.

A stepping stone in the plans of the mighty, Lamu gradually sank into economic collapse towards the end of the nineteenth century as Zanzibar and Mombasa grew in importance. In a sense, it has been stagnating ever since. The building of the Uganda railway from Mombasa, and the banning of slavery, did nothing to improve matters for Lamu in purely economic terms, and it seems that decline has kept up with the shrinking population. However, the new **resettlement programme** on the mainland at Lake Kenyatta (Mpeketoni) is already spinning off new faces to Lamu, and a revived commercialism from up-country has taken root around the market square.

* The Mazrui were the Omani family who had set themselves up independently in Mombasa, incurring the wrath of the Busaidi rulers back in Oman.

effortlessly from one of the day's five prayer calls to the next, from tide to tide, and from dawn to dusk.

If this doesn't hit the right note for you, you may actually rather hate Lamu. Hot, dirty and boring are adjectives that have been applied by perfectly sane, pleasant people, and you can certainly improve your chances of liking the place by not coming here at the tail end of the dry season, when the town's gutters are blocked with dried refuse, the gardens in the houses wilt under the sun and the heat is sapping.

Lamu is something of a **myth** factory. Conventionally labelled "an old Arab trading town", it is actually one of the last viable remnants of the **Swahili civilization** that was the dominant cultural force all along the coast until the arrival of the British. In the late 1960s and early 1970s, Lamu's unique blend of beaches, gentle Islamic ambience, funky old town, and host population well used to strangers, was a recipe which took over where Marrakesh left off. It acquired a reputation as Kenya's Kathmandu: the end of the (African) hippie trail and a stop-over on the way to India. Shaggy foreigners were only allowed to visit on condition they stayed in lodgings and didn't camp on the beach.

Not many people want to camp out these days. The proliferation of good, reasonably priced lodgings in the heart of the town encourages an ethos more interactive than hippie-escapist. Every other traveller you've met along the way seems to end up here, in an ever recycling community. Happily, travellers and locals cross paths enough to avoid any tedium – though for women travelling without men, this can itself become tedious (see p.435). Having said that, there can hardly be another town in the world as

---

IMPORTANT ADVICE

If you're staying in Lamu a few days only, it's a very good idea to go straight to the appropriate airline office on arrival to **reconfirm** your return seat. There's no guarantee otherwise that your booking will still be there when you come to fly.

Something else to beware of: the **police** in Lamu sometimes organize raids on the guest houses, not just looking for *bangi*, as you might reasonably expect, but to check people's passports. If you're coming to the end of your permitted stay in Kenya, don't outstay it in Lamu: it can prove expensive.

---

utterly unthreatening as Lamu. Leave your room at midnight for a breath of air and you can stroll past the lantern-lit shopfronts on hushed Harambee Avenue, shopkeepers dozing in front, or gingerly tread up the darkest of alleys, where you need fear absolutely nothing. This is an exhilarating experience.

Arrival and orientation

The **bus trip** ends at **Mokowe** on the mainland, where a chugging *mtaboti* (motorboat bus; Ksh20) takes you out around the creek for the thirty-minute ride to the town.

If you **drive** to Lamu yourself, you'll have to leave your vehicle in the car park where it will, by all accounts, be safe: tipping the *askari* beforehand may improve security further. Don't be misled by boys who try to sell you a *mtaboti* charter. Wait instead for the next bus to arrive and take the public *mtaboti* with everyone else.

Flying in, planes land on Manda island, across the harbour directly opposite the town; the short boat trip from here (Ksh50) gives a wonderful, spreading panorama of Lamu's nineteenth-century waterfront.

Whichever way you arrive, you'll inevitably be met by a **guide** or three, offering "the best room in Lamu". Much as you might prefer to wander unguided, soaking it all in, and tracking down a room yourself, you probably won't escape; unless you've already made a booking, your first hour or so is likely to be full of milling confusion as you're led from one suggested lodging to another through a baffling maze of streets. It's best not to fight this little hustler's ritual: carrying bags gives you away as newly arrived and nobody's going to lead you up an alley and rob you – the town is really too small for that. The guides, who have recently formed the *Lamu Tour Guides Association*, and who carry small white laminated ID cards, work on commissions from various hotels and guest houses, though some landlords resent the thirty-percent commission they have to pay on the first night's rent and refuse to be involved. If you don't like the guide's choice, ask him to take you to yours: you shouldn't have to pay anything and if you think there's any doubt in his mind, make it clear. Once you've settled on a room – and the landlord has perhaps paid the hustler his tip – you'll be left in peace. It's when he offers to continue to be your guide that you need to decide if you want him around, and discuss openly how much you're prepared to pay for his help if you do. If there are specific things, people or places you want to visit, you should seriously consider it: Ksh200–300 per day would be a very acceptable wage.

When discovering Lamu for yourself, you shouldn't get lost too easily if you remember that **Harambee Avenue** – the Usita wa Mui or Njia Kuu – runs parallel to and fifty metres behind the waterfront, and that streets leading into town all climb slightly uphill; but getting lost is rather wonderful anyway. In the listings that follow, the terms Mkomani and Langoni are quite often used. These are the two main parts of Lamu town – Mkomani the northern end and Langoni the southern.

Accommodation in Lamu town

The better **lodgings** in Lamu town are generally those on the waterfront or those with a height advantage: places on Harambee Avenue tend to be suffocatingly hot. Best known is *Petley's Inn* (PO Box 4; ☎0121/3107) but having almost the only bar in town has grossly inflated its reputation (for the lowdown on beer, see the box on p.433). *Petley's* accommodation is not great value and, if you happen to be booked in here on a short package from Nairobi or Mombasa, you should still look for lodging elsewhere, even paying the modest extra from your own pocket.

If you want real luxury, *Peponi Hotel*, out on Shela beach, is much more expensive than anything in town and altogether a different prospect. There's also a small number of relatively pricey lodgings and private houses in **Shela** – which is gradually becoming an alternative base to Lamu town, with its own atmosphere. Shela acccommodation is covered on p.436.

Room availability and prices

In December, January, July and August, and particularly during Maulidi (see the box on p.432), **room availability** can be tight. It's a good idea to book ahead if you can. We've given PO Box and telephone numbers where available; one or two box numbers crop up rather often, indicating common ownership, and several places don't have phones. Out of season, you may find some places closed.

Prices vary dramatically. You can pay up to three times as much in some lodgings in the high-season months as in April or May, the cheapest period. And another trend in recent years has been the "gentrification" of a number of erstwhile hippie hangouts – with attendant price increases that outstrip those in the rest of the country. If you like the place, aim to agree a rate for the duration of your stay and pay daily. You may find, at peak times, that some lodge owners insist their prices are fixed – simply a rather unfair bargaining position when rooms are scarce.

Budget guest houses

These are the lodgings where you really have the opportunity to hone your bargaining skills – there can be huge seasonal variations. How many people you are, how long you intend to stay and when you will actually pay are all useful chips and, unless the town is heaving with travellers, you shouldn't have any problem getting some kind of discount. Everyone who stays in Lamu has their **favourite lodging houses**, determined as much by the owners and staff as by the state of the rooms. The listings given below are fairly comprehensive and include personal favourites and establishments that travellers have regularly recommended. All abbreviations are explained on p.46. Note that "no touts" means you won't be guided here by a hustler – because the establishment in question does not pay commission.

Alipenda (PO Box 115; ☎33119; bookings only; no touts). Some distance from the town centre, but an exceptional house, with a good kitchen and five rooms, three of which (three windows, two windows and one window) are s/c and huge, with fans. Room only, ③.

WATER IN LAMU

Before you settle in, try to ascertain the quality of the lodging's **water supply**. You'll soon appreciate the critical problem here: a handful of lodgings seem to have overcome it and advertise 24-hour water as a feature. Lamu is one place where it's quite common to catch hepatitis – an unpleasant and lasting souvenir usually associated with drinking infected water. You should check where the water comes from. If the house or lodging has a long-drop toilet and an open drinking-water cistern in the same bathroom, move on. It only takes one cockroach falling in the water to contaminate it.

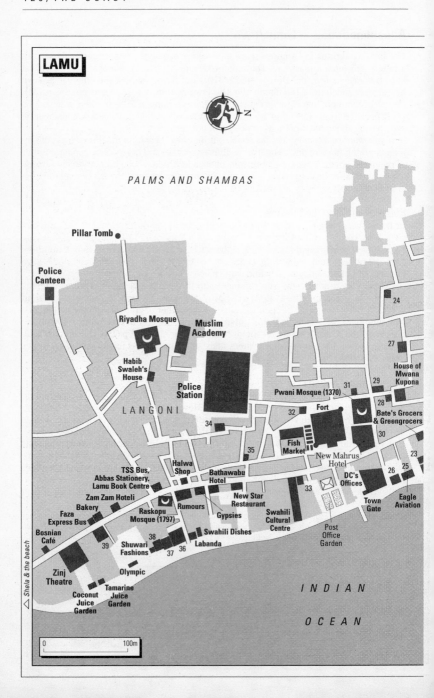

LAMU

PALMS AND SHAMBAS

Pillar Tomb

Police Canteen

Riyadha Mosque

Muslim Academy

Habib Swaleh's House

Police Station

LANGONI

24

27

House of Mwana Kupona

Pwani Mosque (1370)

31

29

28

Fort

Bate's Grocers & Greengrocers

32

30

34

35

Fish Market

New Mahrus Hotel

23

Halwa Shop

Bathawabu Hotel

TSS Bus, Abbas Stationery, Lamu Book Centre

New Star Restaurant

33

DC's Offices

26   25

Town Gate

Eagle Aviation

Zam Zam Hoteli

Bakery

Rumours

Gypsies

Swahili Cultural Centre

Post Office Garden

Faza Express Bus

Raskopu Mosque (1797)

Swahili Dishes

Bosnian Café

Labanda

39

Shuwari Fashions

38

37   36

Zinj Theatre

Olympic

Coconut Juice Garden

Tamarine Juice Garden

INDIAN

OCEAN

◁ Shela & the beach

0   100m

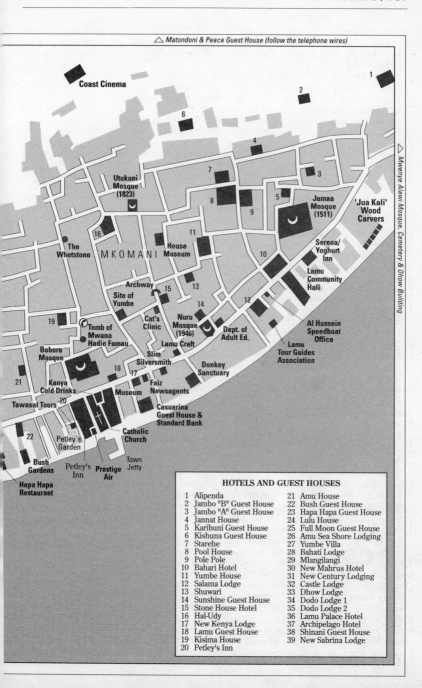

△ Matondoni & Peace Guest House (follow the telephone wires)

Coast Cinema

Utukuni
Mosque
(1823)

The
Whetstone   MKOMANI   House
Museum

Archway
Site of   15
Yumbe   13
Cat's   14
Tomb of   Clinic   Nuru
Mwana   Mosque
Hadie Famau   (1946)   Dept. of
Lamu Craft   Adult Ed.
Slim
Bohora   Silversmith
Mosque   Donkey
18   17   Sanctuary
Kenya   Faiz
Cold Drinks   Museum   Newsagents
Tawasal Tours   20
Casuarina
Guest House &
Petley's   Standard Bank
Garden   Catholic
Bush   Church
Gardens   Petley's   Town
Inn   Prestige   Jetty
Hapa Hapa   Air
Restaurant

Jumaa
Mosque
(1511)   'Jua Kali'
Wood
Carvers

Serena/
Yoghurt
Inn

Lamu
Community
Hall

Al Hussein
Speedboat
Office

Lamu
Tour Guides
Association

△ Mwenye Alawi Mosque, Cemetery & Dhow Building

HOTELS AND GUEST HOUSES

1 Alipenda	21 Amu House
2 Jambo "B" Guest House	22 Bush Guest House
3 Jambo "A" Guest House	23 Hapa Hapa Guest House
4 Jannat House	24 Lulu House
5 Karibuni Guest House	25 Full Moon Guest House
6 Kishuna Guest House	26 Amu Sea Shore Lodging
7 Starehe	27 Yumbe Villa
8 Pool House	28 Bahati Lodge
9 Pole Pole	29 Mlangilangi
10 Bahari Hotel	30 New Mahrus Hotel
11 Yumbe House	31 New Century Lodging
12 Salama Lodge	32 Castle Lodge
13 Shuwari	33 Dhow Lodge
14 Sunshine Guest House	34 Dodo Lodge 1
15 Stone House Hotel	35 Dodo Lodge 2
16 Hal-Udy	36 Lamu Palace Hotel
17 New Kenya Lodge	37 Archipelago Hotel
18 Lamu Guest House	38 Shinani Guest House
19 Kisima House	39 New Sabrina Lodge
20 Petley's Inn	

Casuarina Rest House (PO Box 10; ☎0121/33123). The old police station, with a whole variety of rooms from very basic to quite comfortable, in an admirably dreamlike welter of staircases and floors. S/c and non-s/c rooms, most with fans. Excellent waterfront roof terrace. Room only, ②–③.

Dodo Lodge (PO Box 210; ☎0121/33324). One s/c room only, on the top floor of the owner's house, but very good value with a great view. The other *Dodo* house, nearby, has a number of rooms, is well run and has a good atmosphere. Both ② low, ③ high.

Full Moon Guest House (PO Box 115; no telephone; no touts). Two large breezy rooms at the front and the town's prime location with a wonderful verandah above the harbour. Nets, but no fans and nothing fancy. If you're on a tight budget, this is the first lodging to try on arrival. ①.

Hapa Hapa Guest House (PO Box 213; ☎0121/33226). Above the popular eatery of the same name. Two big rooms at the front and two less appealing ones at the back. Solid walls, but no fans (and no ceilings) – rooms are open to the *makuti* roof, which keeps a breeze blowing while reducing security and privacy. It was badly damaged in the big fire of 1993 and hadn't been fully repaired when last checked. Non-s/c; front rooms ③, back rooms ②.

Lamu Guest House (PO Box 240; ☎0121/33338 bookings only). A well-maintained, old Indian family home in the heart of things, with high ceilings, nets and fans in the downstairs rooms. Omar Sharif stayed here – or filmed here. Inevitably somewhat hot and stuffy given its location, but good value. ②–③.

Lulu House (PO Box 142; ☎/fax 0121/33539). A pleasant, if somewhat soulless, purpose-built lodging house, with ten rooms. Breakfast on the roof. S/c and non-s/c. ② low, ③ high.

Peace Guest House (PO Box 160; ☎0121/33020). A good ten- or fifteen-minute walk from the town centre, out in the sand and palm trees, the *Peace* is the only place to camp in Lamu – if you really want to. Most people use the dorms or double rooms (s/c, with fans). A travellers' hideaway, perhaps for those less enamoured of wailing mosques and narrow alleys. Ksh100 or less to camp; a bit more for a dorm; rooms ②.

Pole Pole (PO Box 242; no phone). Getting a bit run-down, but still pleasant, with a bird's-eye view from the roof – the highest in Lamu. Given some upkeep, could re-emerge as one of the favourites. S/c and non-s/c rooms with nets and fans. B&B ②–③.

Shinari Guest House (PO Box 155; ☎0121/33207). Above *Lamu Bakers*, a very basic, scruffy lodging. Rooms 4 and 5 are the only ones you'd really want. ①–②.

Sunrise Guest House (PO Box 20; ☎0121/33175). Uninspiring location but in high season they please their guests greatly. First-floor rooms are muggy; upstairs rooms catch the breeze. Nets provided. ①.

Sunshine Guest House (PO Box 224; ☎0121/33078). A pleasant place with a good terrace and competitive rates. Use of kitchen possible. S/c rooms with nets and fans. ②–③.

Lodgings and hotels

Some of these are gems and in most cases worth the extra outlay if you can afford it. Breakfast is always included.

Amu House (PO Box 230; ☎/fax 0121/33420). Restored, American-owned stone house with additional rooms on top, built in the same style. Extremely attractive and welcoming. Good value. ④.

Archipelago Hotel (PO Box 12; ☎0121/33247, fax 0121/33111). Rather unfriendly reception, and the s/c rooms aren't that great. The position, right on the waterfront, is a plus though. Don't take a back room. ③ low, ④ high.

Bahari Hotel (PO Box 298; ☎0121/33172, fax 0121/33231). A big lodging on several floors paying token tribute to local styles. Basic but spacious s/c rooms, with four-poster beds, nets, fans and fridges. Always a crowd of travellers. Haggle hard for a good deal. ③–④.

Hal-Udy (PO Box 25; ☎0121/33001). Four good s/c rooms and a roof terrace, hidden away at the back of town. Owned by the Mahrus family. ③ low, ④ high.

Lamu Palace Hotel (PO Box 83; ☎0121/33272, fax 0121/33104). The biggest thing to hit Lamu's waterfront in years, an Arabian Nights construction incorporating the old *Equator* restaurant and a bar. Two floors with a total of 23 s/c rooms, but only four face the sea (no balconies). An unexceptional tourist-class hotel. No nets, no fans: all rooms have AC. B&B ④ low, ⑥ high.

New Mahrus Hotel (PO Box 25; ☎0121/33001, fax 0121/33001). Rambling old place in a good location, though not on the waterfront, and one of the least Lamu-esque hotels. Wide variety of rooms and rates. The top floor is "first-class" and nothing special (rooms 1 and 2, overlooking the fort, are the best), the second floor is second-class and just ordinary B&L standard. Certainly good value in the low season. First-class rooms ③ low, ④ high.

Petley's Inn (PO Box 4; ☎0121/33107, fax 0121/33378). Tends to be hot, as the rooms are ranged above the alley. Fans and nets, but no AC. There's a small, not very clean, roof-level swimming pool. The rooftop bar is a lively evening hangout. Overpriced rooms, but they do take credit cards. ④.

Stone House (PO Box 193; ☎0121/33149, fax 0121/33544). A much modified old house, furnished in a mixture of Swahili and up-country styles. Rooms have phones. ⑤.

Yumbe House (PO Box 81, Lamu; ☎0121/33101, fax 0121/33300). A lovely conversion, professionally managed, and a positive alternative to *Petley's* if you want some real comfort and style, with guaranteed 24-hour water. Every room has a fridge, but the top room is definitely the best. *Yumbe Villa* is an annexe a few minutes' walk away. ④–⑤.

House rentals

The following are essentially **private houses**, occupied part of the year by their owners (often *wazungu* Lamu-philes) and for the rest of the year rented out in part or in whole. There's always a kitchen, usually a houseman (though for his services you'll pay an extra negotiated rate), and varying quantities and standards of furnishings.

Another possibility is to ask around to find an **empty house** whose caretaker would be willing to let you stay – unofficially – for a reasonable fee. This can work out cheaper than any other arrangement, but bear in mind that the caretaker is sticking his neck out. Finding a private house can seem an impossibility at first, but persist in putting your requirements about and you shouldn't have to wait more than a few days.

Jannat House (PO Box 195; ☎0121/33414). Owned by a Swedish family: a few rooms are available (with fans and nets but non-s/c) when they aren't there. ③.

Mlangilangi (PO Box 260; no phone). A large old Swahili house, often used by American student groups. Not fancy, and could do with a fair bit of renovation. An entire six-bed apartment for under Ksh1000. Room only.

Pool House (PO Box 48; phone via the museum). An interesting creation and it does have a swimming pool – though it often lacks the vital ingredient. Less traditional, more an accretion of rooms and architectural ideas. ③ low, ④ high.

Starehe (PO Box 10; ☎0121/33123). A lovely house, German-owned, with a shady garden. ③ low, ④ high.

Lamu town

Perhaps surprisingly for so laid-back a corner of Kenya, there's no shortage of things to do in Lamu. The **town** itself is unendingly fascinating to stroll through, with few monuments but hundreds of ancient houses, arresting street scenes and cool corners to sit and rest. And the **museum** outshines all others in Kenya bar the National Museum in Nairobi.

Initially confusing, Lamu is not the random clutter of houses and alleys it appears. Very few towns in Africa have kept their original **town plan** so intact (Timbuctoo in West Africa is another) and Lamu's history is sufficiently documented, and its architecture well enough preserved, to give you a good idea of how the town developed. The main division is between the **waterfront** buildings and the town behind, separated by **Usita wa Mui**, now Harambee Avenue. Until around 1830, this was the waterfront, but the pile of accumulated rubbish in the harbour had become large enough by the time the fort was finished to consider reclaiming it; gradually, those who could afford to, built on it. The **fort** lost its pre-eminent position and Lamu, from the sea, took on a different aspect, which included Indian styles such as arches, verandahs and shuttered windows.

Behind the waterfront, the **old town** retained a second division between **Mkomani** district, to the north of the fort, and **Langoni** to the south. These locations are important as they distinguish the town's long-established quarter (Mkomani) from the still-expanding district (Langoni) where, traditionally, newcomers have built their houses of mud and thatch rather than stone or modern materials. This north–south division is found in most Swahili towns and reflects the importance of Mecca, which is due north.

Lamu is divided further into over forty *mitaa* or **"wards"**, corresponding to blocks. The names of these suggest a great deal about how the town once looked: they're all listed in *Lamu Town A Guide* by James Allen, excellent if you can find it. Kinooni ward ("whetstone corner") boasts to this day a heavy block of stone on the corner for sharpening swords, reputedly imported from Oman. And Utakuni ward ("main market") still has a row of shops, even though most of this north side of town is now purely residential.

It is difficult to construct a guided tour of Lamu – serendipity comes to everyone here, and in any event, you're better off exploring in snatches, wandering around whenever you have a spare hour or two – but the following ideas are worth pursuing whenever you lack the energy for the beach.

Stone architecture

Lamu's **stone houses** are unique, perfect examples of architecture appropriate to its setting. The basic design is an open, topless box enclosing a large courtyard, around which are set inward-facing rooms on two or three floors. These rooms are thus long and narrow, their ceilings supported by close-set timbers or mangrove poles (*boriti*). Most had exquisite carved doors at one time, though in all but a few dozen homes these have been sold off to pay for upkeep. Many also had *zidaka*, plaster-work niches in the walls to give an illusion of extended space, which are now just as rare. Toilet arrangements are ingenious, with fish kept in the large water cisterns to eat the mosquito larvae. On the top floor, a *makuti* roof shades one side. In parts of Lamu these old houses are built so close together you could step across the street from one roof to another.

The private space inside Lamu's houses is inseparable and barely distinguishable from the public space outside: the noises of the town – mosques, donkeys, cats (Lamu is a veritable cat's Calcutta*)– percolate into the interiors, encouraged by the constant flow of air created by the narrow coolness of the dark streets and the heat which accumulates on upper surfaces exposed to the sun.

In the least spoiled part of Lamu, the regional museum has restored an eighteenth-century house to an approximation of its original appearance – the **House Museum** (daily 8am–6pm; Ksh200; curator: PO Box 48, Lamu, ☎0121/33073). Unfortunately, the house is very small and the guided tour included in the entrance fee is embarrassingly brief. Since the house consists only of a small courtyard, two sleeping galleries, two toilets and an upstairs kitchen and roof, this is very poor value. Indeed, there are plenty of private houses, and even a number of guest houses, with superior architectural interest. There's talk of a combined Ksh200 ticket for Lamu Museum and the House Museum to encourage visits, though that wouldn't make the House Museum any more worthwhile.

The Fort

Specific buildings and monuments to seek out in Lamu are few. The **Fort** (daily 8am–6pm; Ksh200), which dates from 1821, seems oddly stranded in its modern-day position, deprived of its role as defender of the waterfront. At least you need no longer

---

* In response there's now a "cat clinic" in Mkomani.

worry about accidentally getting it in your camera viewfinder, as was the case until a few years ago, when it served as a prison. It has recently become a national monument and is now open as a museum. The "temporary exhibition" first installed in 1993, however, is still there, unrefreshed. It's an enthusiastic display of information about the environment and evolution, incorporating local sea life in tanks, but it looks more like an elaborate school project than anything you would expect to find in a public building.

It's fun to walk round the ramparts of the fort, getting bird's-eye views of the town. Look out for the very interesting set of colour photos of archeological sites in the Lamu archipelago. The town's library is here, too; see "Listings" on p.439.

Lamu Museum

The one place you should definitely count on devoting an hour or so to is **Lamu Museum** (daily 8am–6pm; Ksh200; curator: PO Box 48, Lamu, ☎0121/3307). Of Kenya's regional museums, Lamu's is the only one that lives up to its name. There's no need to fill spare rooms here with game trophies and trivia; the region's history provides more than enough material.

As you enter, there's a large aerial photo of the town for a fascinating bird's-eye insight. Elsewhere, exhibitions of **Swahili culture** – architecture, boats and boat-building, domestic life and life cycle – are displayed. There are also rooms devoted to the non-Swahili peoples of the mainland: farmers like the **Pokomo**, **Orma** cattle herdsmen and **Boni** hunters. Two magnificent ceremonial **siwa horns**, one in ivory from Pate, the other from Lamu itself in brass, are the prize exhibits – probably the oldest surviving musical instruments in black Africa. The Pate *siwa*, slightly more ancient, dates from the mid-seventeenth century. Wooden imitations are on sale all around town.

Mosques

When you start checking out some of Lamu's 23 **mosques**, you'll find that any tone of rigid conformity you might expect is lacking. Most are simple, spacious buildings, as much refuge-cum-men's club as place of prayer. There's no special reason to enter

---

TRADITION AND MORALITY IN LAMU

A number of **old photographs** on display in the museum give the lie to pat pronouncements about "unchanging Lamu". The women's cover-all **buibui**, for example, turns out to be a fashion innovation introduced comparatively recently from southern Arabia. It wasn't worn in Lamu much before the 1930s when, ironically, a degree of emancipation encouraged women of all classes to adopt the high-status styles of **purdah**. In earlier times, high-born women would appear in public entirely hidden inside a tent-like canopy called a *shiraa*, which had to be supported by slaves; the abolition of slavery at the beginning of this century marked the demise of this odd fashion.

Outsiders have tended to get the wrong end of the stick about Swahili seclusion. While women are undoubtedly heavily restricted in their public lives, in private they have considerable freedom. The notion of **romantic love** runs deep in Swahili culture. Love affairs, divorces and remarriage are the norm, and the *buibui* is perhaps as useful to women in disguising their liaisons as it is to their husbands in preventing them. Which gives a slightly different timbre to the attentions shown by Lamu men to unattached *wazungu* women. Frustration isn't always the reason.

All this comes into focus a little when walking the backstreets. You may even bump into some of Lamu's **transvestite** community – cross-dressing men whose community is accepted and long-established and derives from Oman. In fact, the more you explore, the more you realize that the town's conventional image is like the walls of its houses – a severe facade concealing an unrestrained interior.

them: their doors are always open and there's little to see. Male visitors, covered up and suitably humble, are normally allowed inside; women are generally excluded. But you might enquire about the **Mwenye Alawi Mosque** at the north end of town. This used to be Lamu's one exclusively female mosque but it may have been taken over by the men, leaving the women to pray at home.

The oldest-known mosque is the **Pwani Mosque**, by the fort, parts of which date back to the fourteenth century. At one time, it would have been the place of worship on a Friday for the whole of Mkomani quarter. Lamu's present Friday mosque is the **Jumaa Mosque**, the big one in Pangahari ward ("sword-sharpening place"), near the *Yoghurt Inn*.

However, the star of Lamu's mosques, as well as being one of the youngest, is the sumptuous **Riyadha Mosque** down in Langoni, well to the back of town. It was built at the turn of the century and has brought about a radical shift in Lamu's style of Islam, and indeed in the status of Lamu in the Islamic world. It was founded by a descendant of the prophet, or sharif, called **Habib Swaleh**, who came from the Hadramaut (Yemen) to settle in Lamu in the mid-nineteenth century. (His house is close by the mosque, acknowledged with a plaque, but still a more or less empty wattle-and-daub structure, containing a caretaker's bed and a few old papers.) Habib Swaleh and his group introduced a new freedom to the five-times-daily prayers with singing, tambourines and spontaneous readings from the Koran. They attracted a large following, particularly from the slave and ex-slave community, but gradually from all social spheres, even the aristocratic families with long Lamu pedigrees. Some of the other mosques adopted the style but the Riyadha, apart from being Lamu's largest, is still the one most closely associated with this kind of inspirational worship. Non-Muslim men who visit while worship is in session are likely to be invited in and encouraged to sit cross-legged with the rest of the assembly. Any sense of stale ritual is far removed: the atmosphere is light and the music infectious. More than one *mzungu* has converted to Islam here. The Riyadha is also famous as the spiritual home of Lamu's annual **Maulidi** celebration (see box below).

Next to the Riyadha is the big, square **Muslim Academy** – like the Riyadha itself, and so much else in Lamu, heavily under Saudi patronage. Men and women are both allowed to have a look around but there's very little to see. More interesting is the chance to talk to some of the foreign students.

Other sights

After the fort, the only other national monument in Lamu (though you may not believe it when you see it) is the fluted **pillar tomb** behind Riyadha Mosque. This may date from as far back as the fourteenth century and the occasional visit by a tourist might persuade the families in the neighbourhood that it's worth preserving; it can only be a matter of time before it leans too far and collapses on a passing *mtoto*. In the middle of town by a betel plot is another tomb, that of **Mwana Hadie Famau**, a local woman of

---

MAULIDI IN LAMU

Lamu's annual **Maulidi**, a week-long celebration of Muhammad's birth, sees the entire town involved in processions and dances, and draws in pilgrims from all over East Africa and the Indian Ocean. For faithful participants, the Lamu Maulidi is so laden with *baraka* (blessings) that some say two trips to Lamu are worth one to Mecca in the eyes of God. If you can possibly arrange it, this occasion is the time to be in Lamu; but unless you make bookings, you'll need to arrive at least a week in advance to have any hope of getting a room. Starting dates for the next three years are roughly 18 July 1997, 8 July 1998 and 27 June 1999.

the fifteenth or sixteenth century. This has been walled up and lost the porcelain-embedded pillars which would have stood at each corner.

Up along the waterfront you won't miss the **donkey sanctuary**. Lamu district has over 3000 donkeys and the International Donkey Protection Trust, a Devon-based charity, has put energy and resources into setting up and maintaining this rest home for old and lame beasts that would otherwise perish of exhaustion or end up in a stew. It's not a tourist attraction, but it does rely heavily on donations from visitors and the staff are welcoming (visits daily 9am–12.30pm). If you call in, don't forget to shut the gate behind you.

Heading north out of town, through *Tundani* ward ("fruit-picking place") and *Weyoni* ward ("donkey racetrack"), you reach the **cemetery**, goal of many religious processions and an interesting short walk. Past suburbs, you come out by the slaughterhouse and rubbish dumps, populated by marabou storks. In the inlet behind them, several large **dhows** and smaller boats are moored. Many are rotting, but one or two are quite new, even unfitted. Tradition notwithstanding, Lamu, rather than Matondoni (see p.436), seems to be the island's main boat-building centre. If you have dreams of owning a dhow (they make great houseboats), a representative price for a forty-foot hull is £4000 ($6000). The price depends entirely on the time the *fundis* take to build it – two years isn't unusual.

Eating

There are enough **restaurants** and passable *hotelis* in Lamu to enable you to eat out twice a day for a week before going back to your first port of call. And not only are there lots of them, but they serve a wonderful range of food. Nowhere else in Kenya is there such a concentration of eating places with an overwhelmingly budget-traveller clientele. Unfortunately, the rock-bottom prices of only a few years ago are rising fast and some places are already expensive by Kenyan standards. It's still possible to eat for as little as Ksh30, but you can easily pay twenty times as much in some of the waterfront eating houses. Again, prices really rocket in the peak seasons.

A fine balance has been achieved between what is demanded and what can be supplied: yoghurt, fruit salad, pancakes, muesli, milkshakes and puréed fruit juices have become Lamu specialities. Superb lobster and crab dishes, oysters, swordfish and delicious shark are also on many menus – it's a nice change to find a fishing town where you can actually eat seafood relatively cheaply. A number of ordinary **hotelis** serving the up-country staples – beans, curries, pilau, steak, chicken, chips, eggs, even *ugali* and *karanga* – crowd along Harambee Avenue, particularly down in Langoni. Meat is notoriously stringy: several of the tourist-oriented places receive regular supplies from Malindi by plane.

Lamu eating can be too much of a good thing and it's easy to slip into the habit of always eating out. But if you find it too expensive and have a camp stove or charcoal-burning *jiko* at your disposal (note that several lodgings have kitchens you can use), a whole new world starts to open up. Try, for example, **cooking** fish in coconut: any restaurant will show you how to grate out the flesh and strain off the cream from the

---

DRINKING

In the old days, when *Petley's* restricted its roof to guests, and casual drinkers in the downstairs bar were sneered at, they often used to "run out" of **beer**; in which scenario, people would buy it direct from the *Kenya Breweries* depot, or go to the police canteen. Nowadays, although you can always get a drink, only *Petley's* or the *Lamu Palace* have alcohol licences. At other places, you can sometimes order "ice-cold tea".

coconut to use it as a basis for sauces, using a conical coconut basket; but get to the **fish market** early to pick up the best buys. Tamarind is another good complement to fish. The **fruit and vegetable market** in front of the fort – run for the most part by up-country women – has everything else you'll need. Lamu has wonderful fruit and is famous for its enormous, aromatic **mangoes**, but you should also try the unusually sweet and juicy **grapefruit**.

Hotelis and cheap eating

Bathawabu Hotel, Harambee Ave, Langoni. Dead cheap, busy local *hoteli*.

Bosnian Café. Cheap hole-in-the-wall *hoteli* for juice and snacks. Seems out of the way, but it's only yards from the *Coconut* and the *Tamarnine*, and has easily the cheapest juices in town.

Halwa shop, Harambee Ave, Langoni. Lamu's main outlet for the sticky confection, just Ksh120 per kilo; nameless and unidentified except for its blue door, but once you've been you'll never forget the hot kitchen and the huge copper vat.

New Star, Harambee Ave, Langoni. Unchanged in fifteen years, with an extravagantly supercilious head waiter. One of few restaurants catering even-handedly to travellers and locals, and one of the cheapest in town. Especially good for breakfast before an early-morning walk to the beach. Daily 5.30am–10.30pm.

Swahili Dishes, at the south end of the waterfront. A very cheap little *hoteli* and travellers' restaurant with good and bad days. Pilau is only Ksh40 and *karanga* just Ksh25.

Zam Zam Hotel, Harambee Ave, Langoni. Cheap *hoteli* with rarely a *mzungu* to be seen.

Cafés and tourist restaurants

Bush Gardens, on the waterfront, competing for the same business as *Hapa Hapa*. A seafood and kebab place with a popular following and a charming proprietor. The food, when it comes, is first-rate and not as costly as you might expect. Worth patronizing for the garlic bread alone.

Coconut Juice Garden, on the waterfront in the south of Langoni. Best juices on Lamu; you can order any combination you want – orgasmic coconut and banana; wonderful passion and pawpaw; and a pint of avocado, with extra ice cream, is lunch in itself.

Hapa Hapa, on the waterfront. Popular, very central rendezvous with an ambitious menu, though slightly less busy and more down-to-earth than *Bush Gardens*.

Kenya Cold Drinks, Harambee Ave, town centre. Very reliable snack and breakfast bar, with a limited menu of main seafood dishes.

La Banda, at the southern end of the waterfront. Unpredictable and sometimes positively basic, but usually busy and often good. Prices aren't high – Ksh250 for an excellent "Monster Crab" with rice.

Lamu Palace Restaurant, at the southern end of the waterfront. This impressive restaurant (or rather the *makuti*-roofed part at the back) used to be the *Equator*, the town's fanciest establishment. It's still quite reliable and often does realistically priced all-you-can eat seafood buffets as well as the more expensive crab and lobster staples. However, it can feel rather uncomfortable spending all this money just yards away from the impoverished waterfront.

Mazingira Café, Lamu Fort. A good place to sit and watch the square, the "Environment" café does mostly drinks (all Ksh25–50) and snacks, but also good breakfasts for under Ksh100. Closed Sun.

Olympic, at the southern end of the waterfront. Popular for juices and snacks, assuming it opens again (closed mid-1996).

Petley's Inn. The rooftop restaurant does genuinely good food at prices that are not grossly inflated. If only they wouldn't play the same few tapes night after night.

Rumours at Baraka, Harambee Ave, Langoni. Pretentious it may be, but it's not easy to resist real espresso and wonderful cakes and pastries, unless you're really counting the pennies. Expensive. Open 9.30am–1.30pm & 4.30–9pm.

Tamarine Juice Garden, waterfront, Langoni. Competition for the larger *Coconut Juice Garden* next door. Possibly a few shillings cheaper, but almost as good.

Serena Vegetarian Restaurant at Yoghurt Inn. The *Yoghurt Inn* was once a Lamu institution renowned for breakfasts to set you up for the day. Now under new management, the vegetarian options include the likes of stuffed aubergine and cheese pudding. They also serve seafood, and still make yoghurt.

Around the island: beaches and beyond

The one place everyone goes on Lamu is, of course, the **beach**, which more than repays the slight effort of getting there. The walk is enlivened by the village of Shela en route, one of three villages on Lamu. Alternatively, you can go to the beach the easy way, by dhow (Ksh50). Fewer people see the **interior** of Lamu island itself, which is a pity, as it's a pretty, if rather inhospitable, reminder of how remarkable it is that a town exists here at all. Much of it is patched into *shambas* with the herds of cattle, coconut palms, mango and citrus trees that still provide the bulk of Lamu's wealth. The two villages you might head for are Matondoni and Kipungani.

Dhow trips with a beach barbecue are the stock-in-trade of the waterfront hustlers, and as such hard to avoid even if you wanted to; always fun, they also give you the chance to see the ruins of Takwa on Manda island (see p.437).

Shela Beach

A usually deserted twelve-kilometre sickle of white sand, splashed by bath-warm sea and backed by empty **sand dunes**, Lamu's **beach** is the real thing; you half expect Robinson Crusoe to come striding out of the heat haze. Unprotected by a reef, the sea here has some motion to it for once: it is one of the few places on the coast where, at certain times of the year, you can body-surf (August is probably best). Beyond *Peponi Hotel*, it's also a beach where formerly, on your private square kilometre, you could sometimes dispense with a swimming costume. Not any more. Many more local people now use the beach (it can be busy on Sundays); there were two rapes a few years ago; and there is now a two-man Kenya Navy security post in the dunes. Women may still find that wanderers along the beach can be a nuisance. Stay in shouting distance of other sunbathers and preferably go to the beach in company.

Beware of the **sun**, a more likely assailant. There's absolutely no cover and you'll find that the cooling breeze is too strong for erecting a sunshade. You'll need to take a drink or a bag of grapefruit and some skin protection. Coconut oil, sold in town, is used by some to avoid drying out, but you need a deep tan to begin with, otherwise it fries your skin. Ordinary sunscreen cream is available in town, too. Lastly, and perhaps obviously, bear in mind that if you walk for miles along the beach in the early morning, you'll have to do it back again in the heat of the day.

Getting to the beach, you can either walk the pleasant shoreline from Lamu's harbour down to Shela (about 40min) and then head as far down the sands as you like, or you can take a motorboat or dhow to *Peponi* (usually Ksh50). The third option you might be tempted to try – striking out across the *shambas* behind town and heading direct for the middle of the beach, is actually a time-consuming and exhausting short cut that involves wading through deep sand. If you walk along the shore, on arrival at Shela you can collapse into the *Stop Over* or the *Bahari Restaurant* for a cold drink or a bite to eat, or head straight for the cold beers at *Peponi*.

Shela

SHELA, once a thriving settlement, is now in limbo, midway between rural decline and tourist boom. Its people, who trace their ancestry back to Manda island and speak a dialect of Swahili quite distinct from Lamu town's, are gradually leaving the village, many of them going to Malindi; a number of fine old houses have been bought by foreigners and converted into ravishing holiday homes, decked in bougainvillea and empty most of the year (some can be rented, if you ask around, and one or two are now guest houses). Shela's only sight is the strange, much-photographed **Friday mosque**, built in 1829, which stands out for its rocket-shaped minaret, unusual in East Africa. If you're suitably dressed and bare-footed, ask politely to go up to the top.

After the mosque, the focus is the **Peponi Hotel** (PO Box 24; ☎0121/33154, fax 0121/33029), where everyone stops in for a cold drink. It is fabulously situated, offers windsurfing and a PADI diving school, and, if you can afford it (B&B ⑨; closed May and June), you won't want for much – though to feel right, you need to be on honeymoon at least (best rooms are the high numbers, from 21 upwards). And while it's an utterly hedonistic place to lounge away a few days, you won't have the thrill of staying among the mosques and street life of Lamu town itself.

The gaggle of beach boys playing football at low tide, or loafing around the hotel terrace sizing up the latest speedboat tourist arrivals from Manda airstrip, are part of the limited **gay scene**. The atmosphere of an embryonic Key West is beginning to pervade Lamu, and *Peponi* ("Heaven"), its only international-class hotel, is the natural venue.

ACCOMMODATION

If you seriously want to spend all your time on the beach, **staying** in Shela seems the obvious solution, and there are several quite stylish possibilities. The huge white hotel-like structure on the front, just before *Peponi*, looks as if it was expected to cope with large numbers. It opened briefly as a restaurant and now stands unfinished, abandoned by its owners. "Their financial sphere declined", explained a local. Yours will, too, if you stay around here for long, as, unlike Lamu town, there's nowhere in the cheap price categories. Equally restrictive, there are virtually no restaurants aside from those in the hotels.

If you're looking to rent a house, there are a dozen or more private houses available from time to time. Ask for *Bustani*, *Jasmin House* (good for kids as it has a large garden), *White Rock*, *Kismani* or *Nyumba ya Giovanna* (Giovanna's House).

Bahari Guest House (PO Box 59; ☎0121/33091). You pay for the location here, which, above the sea-lapped restaurant of the same name, is immaculate. The rooms, brand-new in 1996, are simple but nicely done and will just about give good value if the place is kept up well. ④ low, ⑤ high.

Island Hotel (PO Box 179; ☎0121/33290; closed May to mid-June). Spacious, attractively furnished rooms and restful atmosphere. Rustic luxury just about sums it up, and the penthouse is especially appealing – almost open-air, like sleeping on the roof but in privacy and comfort. Fans in all rooms and nets on frames. Good, reasonably priced rooftop restaurant – the *Barracuda* – but no alcohol licence. Non-seasonal rates, but excellent single-room and residents' discounts. ⑦.

Kijani House (PO Box 266; ☎0121/33235, fax 0121/33237; closed May and June). Pretty and comfortable French-owned hotel, but not as luxurious as you might imagine from their glossy brochure – and their high prices. The superior rooms are excellent (5 is the best), but the standard ones are overpriced. Small pool. Non-seasonal rates. ⑧.

Shela Pwani Guest House (PO Box 59; ☎0121/33540). Stylish, roomy house, co-owned with the *Bahari*, overlooking *Peponi*. Several rooms here offer various options, but all, by Shela standards, are a good deal. The top rooms are brilliant. B&B ④ low, ⑤ high.

Matondoni and Kipungani

MATONDONI is the most talked-about destination on Lamu apart from Shela and the beach. It's a fine walk if you start early, with a hot return made more bearable by the prospect of a cold drink at the end – the soft sand track isn't fun in blazing sunshine. A sane, enjoyable alternative is to go **by donkey**: fix up a beast through your guest house reception; or you can take one of the sand dhows on its trip from Lamu jetty to Matondoni, get some lunch and walk back along the line of the telephone wires. In truth, Matondoni itself is not wildly exciting and its fame as the district's principal dhow-building centre seems misplaced.

If you really want to look **around the whole island**, proceed from Matondoni to **KIPUNGANI**, a half-hour walk from the end of the beach. This is the halfway mark on the round-the-island walk; the whole trip takes eight or nine hours. It is useful to know the state of the tides for the stretch from Matondoni to Kipungani, as you can take a direct route through the mangroves at low tide. Kipungani has an upmarket **hotel** in

---

SWAHILI PROVERBS AND SAYINGS

The Swahili are renowned for the imagery, rhythm and complexity of their proverbs. *Kangas* always have some kind of adage printed on one side and these are often traditional Swahili saws. The first of these few – an admonishment to be patient – is the one you will most often hear.

Haraka, haraka: haina baraka – Haste, haste: there's no blessing in it.

Nyumba njema si mlango – A good house isn't (judged by) its door [ie, don't judge by appearances].

Mahaba ni haba, akili ni mali – Love counts for little, intelligence is wealth.

Faida yako ni hasara yangu – Your gain is my loss.

Haba na haba kujaza kibaba – Little by little fills the jug.

Kuku anakula sawa na mdomo wake – A chicken eats according to her beak [interpretations invited].

Mungu alitolandika, haliwezi kufutika – What God has written cannot be erased.

Heri shuka isiyo kitushi, kama shali njema ya mauwa – Better an honest loincloth than a fancy cloak (of shame).

Mke ni nguo, mgomba kupalilia – A wife means clothes (like) a banana plant means weeding.

---

the shape of *Kipungani Sea Breezes* (PO Box 232; ☎0121/33191; ⑨), a delightful *makuti* complex for just ten couples, with bar and restaurant. It's expensive, but with justification as the food is superb and the welcome and service everything you could ask for. Excursions, windsurfing and snorkelling trips are all on offer.

Dhow trips

Lamu hustlers must be the least disagreeable in the world. That said, where the hotel guides left off after you settled in, the dhow-ride men take up the challenge. You'll be persistently hassled until you agree to go on a trip and then, as if the word's gone out, you'll be left alone. The truth is that your face quickly becomes familiar to anyone whose livelihood depends upon *wazungu*.

In fact the **dhow trips** are usually a lot of fun and, all things considered, very good value. The simplicity of Swahili sailing is delightful, using a single lateen sail that can be set in virtually any position and never seems to obstruct the view of passengers. Slopping past the **mangroves**, with their primeval-looking tangle of roots now at eye level, hearing any number of squeaks and splashes from the small animals and birds that live among them, is quite a serene pleasure.

Basically, the **price** you pay will depend on where you want to go, for how long, and how much hard work it's going to be for the crew. Agree on the price beforehand (a full day with lunch for less than Ksh300 is really rather unlikely, but, on the other hand, if you're in the area out of season, you might get a couple of hours for Ksh100) then gather as large a group as is practicable and pay up afterwards. Try also to agree on who's supplying food and drink apart from any fish you might catch (funny, but the guests rarely catch fish; it's the crew who keep hauling them up).

A couple of pertinent **practical points**: cameras of the more expensive kind are easily damaged on dhow trips; wrap them up well in a plastic bag. And take the clothes and drinks you'd need for a 24-hour spell in the Sahara – you'll burn up and dry out otherwise. Dhow crews think it's all very amusing.

DHOW DESTINATIONS

There are limitless possibilities for dhow trips, though only a short "menu" is usually offered. One variation which is not especially recommended is a dhow trip to

Matondoni: these tend to end up being over-organized when you get there. The cheapest trip is a slow sail across Lamu harbour and up Takwa "river", fishing as you go, followed by a barbecue on the beach at **Manda island**, then back to town. This might commence with some squelching around in the mud under the mangroves digging for huge bait-worms. If the trip is timed properly against the tides, you can include a visit to **Takwa ruins**, or, for rather more money, you can stay the night on the beach behind the ruins and come back the next day. This is usually done around full moon. Few sailors are prepared to venture out into the ocean, so Takwa has to be approached from the landward side up the creek, and this can only be done at high tide – and if misjudged can mean a long wait at Takwa before you can set off again.

A further variation has you sailing south down Lamu harbour, past the headland at Shela and out towards the ocean for some snorkelling over the reefs on the southwest corner of Manda around **Kinyika rock**. Snorkel and mask are normally provided but bringing your own is obviously much better.

Listings

Banks The *Standard Chartered Bank* has low commission and is now the only bank in Lamu. Open Mon–Fri 9am–3pm, Sat 9–11am. Note that you can't get credit-card cash advances.

Betel One of Lamu's traditional exports, betel is the green vine you see trailing out of all the empty plots in town. The sweet-hot tasting leaves are wrapped around other ingredients, including white lime and betel nut, which stains the teeth red, to make *pan*.

Books Try the museum for a selection of new and souvenir books, and the *Lamu Book Centre*, Harambee Ave south (Mon–Fri 8am–12.30pm, 2–5pm & 7–9pm, Sat 8am–12.30pm), for the best second-hand choice.

Buses Buy bus tickets as early as possible. The *Faza Express Bus* office is open daily 8.30am–12.30pm, 2.30–4.30pm & 7–8.30pm; *TSS* is open daily 8am–12.30pm & 2–9pm.

Cinemas The *Zinj Theatre* in Langoni and the open-air *Coast Cinema* have regular sceenings.

Clothes and tailors A number of shops along Harambee Ave will run up clothes very cheaply in a day or so. The easiest way to end up with something that fits is to provide a model garment. *Shuwari Fashions*, on the waterfront in Langoni, is recommended. *Ziwadi Lamu*, in Langoni, is a good place to buy *kangas* and *kikois*.

Crafts and souvenirs Woodcarving shops are mostly found along Harambee Ave in Mkomani. Model dhows, chests, furniture and *siwa* horns are all attractive but bulky. Beautifully hand-carved safari chairs are also a hassle to carry but worth the effort for the prices. Some of the shops selling jewellery and trinkets have some genuinely old and interesting pieces. Look out for tiny lime caskets in silver, earlobe plugs in buffalo horn or silver, and old coins. A recommended silversmith is *Slim Silversmith* on at the northern end of Harambee Ave. They'll make jewellery for you; bargain hard. There are also jewellery pieces at *Gypsies* at the southern end of Harambee Ave (Mon–Sat 9am–1pm & 3.30–7.30pm).

Dhows to Mombasa See "Travel Details" on p.448.

Discos There's usually a disco every Friday at the *Civil Servants' Club* on the hill just south of town and every Saturday at the police canteen (ask at the police station).

Fax Several guest houses now have fax machines. The going rate for a page to Europe or America is about Ksh400.

Film From *Faiz*; see "Newspapers and magazines", below.

Food shopping If you want to buy fresh fish or shellfish to cook yourself, get to the fish market very early. By 9am all the interesting ones have been sold. The *halwa* shop and the bakery – lovely bread – are both on Harambee Ave in Langoni. *Bates* grocers and greengrocers on Harambee Ave just north of the Fort has slightly odd opening hours: 8.45am–12.45pm, 5–7.45pm & 8.45–11pm.

Health Be more than ordinarily careful about the water you drink. Malaria can also be a problem: if you get a fever go straight to the hospital. For your teeth, you can buy toothbrush sticks (*msuake*) from the market.

Henna painting A number of women around town offer this attractive dye-painting for hands and feet. The best have portfolios of designs from which you can choose. Expect to pay several hundred shillings for both hands or both feet. If done properly, your hands or feet will be bound in cloth for twelve hours and the design should stay for up to six months.

Hospital The new hospital (☎0121/33012) is one of the best in Kenya (it certainly attracts patients from a huge part of northeast Kenya), but treatment is often woefully inadequate. There are several private clinics – ask around.

Immigration In the District Commissioner's (DC's) offices on the waterfront.

Library The museum library has been moved to the top floor of the fort (Mon–Fri 8.30–12.30pm & 2–5.30pm). You can obtain a weekly pass for Ksh50.

Newspapers and magazines Tide tables, film and film processing too (Ksh500 to develop and print 36 exposures), all from *Faiz*, at the northern end of Harambee Ave.

Photocopying *Lamu Book Centre* (see "Books" above).

Planes Having a ticket is not the same as holding a confirmed seat reservation. Seats back to Malindi or though to Mombasa should be booked – or, if already booked, reconfirmed – as early as possible (as should Nairobi, though because it's a bigger plane this is not so critical); see "Travel Details" at the end of the chapter for prices. If you're in Lamu for only a day or two, reconfirm your flight back as soon as you arrive. Cancelling plane tickets you've already got from Mombasa, Malindi or Nairobi is a big pain, as refunds are usually only available from the issuing agent. *Prestige* is under the casuarinas next to the church; *Air Kenya Aviation* (for Nairobi) is at *Gypsies*, Harambee Ave, Langoni (daily 8am–12.30pm & 1.30–6pm); *Eagle Aviation* is in a run-down office under the *Full Moon Guest House*. *Tawasal*, down Petley's alley (see "Travel agents"), can book all of them.

Police The days of hassle are long gone. Don't fail to stand still, however, if you're on the waterfront whenever the national flag is lowered, or you'll find yourself "in discussion" with them. Lamu is also a favourite place to trap *wazungu* who have failed to extend their visitor's permit (see "Immigration").

Post and telephone office Open Mon–Fri 8am–5pm, Sat 8–11.30am. Poste restante available. The international cardphone is handy – when they have phone cards for sale.

Safe deposit At the bank.

Speedboat charter Not exactly in keeping with the spirit of Lamu's lifestyle, but it certainly gets you from A to B effectively. It also drinks diesel fuel at an unbelievable rate, which makes it expensive. *Al Hussein*, which comfortably seats four, plus captain and "small captain", can be chartered through PO Box 156 (☎0121/33509 or 33255). A day trip to Kiwaiyu, for example, will cost you from Ksh10,000 to Ksh20,000, depending on where you want to stop en route.

Spices and herbs There's a good little shop just north of *Lamu Book Centre*.

Swahili lessons Lamu is a good place to learn but as yet nothing is organized. Get in touch with the Department of Adult Education on Harambee Ave, and see if they can help.

Travel agents *Lamu Archipelago Tours* at the hotel of the same name (PO Box 12; ☎0121/33368, fax 0121/33500); *Tawasal Tours* (PO Box 248; ☎/fax 0121/33513), in the alley next to *Petley's Inn*, is a highly recommended general agent, established since 1991.

Windsurfing At *Peponi* in Shela. About Ksh500 per hour, Ksh1500 for a half-day.

Manda island

Practically within shouting distance of Lamu town, **Manda** is almost uninhabited and, apart from being the site of the main airstrip on the islands, and the location of the old ruined town of Takwa – favourite destination of the dhow trip operators – it is not much visited. Water supplies are tenuous and elephants often trudge across the narrow Mkanda Channel from the mainland, destroying any crops. Significant archeologically for the ruins of Takwa and Manda, the north side of the island is also the location of the very exclusive *Blue Safari Club* (PO Box 3205; Radiocall Nairobi ☎3791; bookings through PO Box 41759, Nairobi; ☎02/338838, fax 02/218939; ⑨), a more or less private establishment catering for heads of state and similar clients. The former hotel at Ras Kitau, facing Lamu island, is abandoned.

The island is crisscrossed with paths through the jungle, should you be taken by the urge to spend a day there. But go soon. **Rumours** have been flying around the archipelago as fast as in the days of the old sheikhdoms that either an **American naval facility**, or a **new seaport** for northeast Kenya, or a **gas terminal** for the finds around

Garissa, is going to be built on Manda. The hoteliers and farmers were given notice to leave a few years back and the dredgers started clearing the channels. For the moment it's all quietened down again. **Motorboats** frequently make the crossing from Lamu town to the Manda **airstrip jetty** – where they sell "duty-free mangoes" in the "departure lounge" – and there's nothing to stop you using them if you want to visit the island.

Takwa ruins

Open daily 8am–6pm; Ksh200.

Whether you make a flying visit to **Takwa** or sleep out on the beach behind it (there are some shelters), the site is well worth seeing. A flourishing town in the sixteenth and seventeenth centuries and deserted, as usual, for no one knows what reason, Takwa is in many respects reminiscent of Gedi. As at other sites, toilets and bathrooms figure prominently in the architecture. In Islam, cleanliness is so close to godliness as to almost signify it – the Takwans must have been a devout community. The doors of all the houses face north towards Mecca, as does the main street with the **mosque** at the end of it. The mosque is interesting for the pillar at one end which suggests it was built on a tomb site (that of a founder of the town perhaps?), and for the simple lines of its mihrab, so different from the ornate curlicues of later designs. Another impressive **pillar tomb** stands alone, just outside the town walls, its date translating to about 1683. It has a very ancient significance and still occasionally attracts pilgrims from Shela (some of whom claim descent from Takwa), who come to pray for rain.

Takwa has been thoroughly cleared but, in order to preserve it for the future, hardly excavated at all. What has been found, however, suggests an industrious, healthy, well-balanced community. They lived in an easily defensible position with a wall all around the town, the ocean on one side behind the dunes and mangroves on the other. Despite this, they appear to have left in a panic and, as usual, there's ample room for conjecture about why. In this sense, most of Kenya's ruined towns are very different from those of the classical world, although influenced by them. Part of their great appeal lies in the open debate that still continues about who, precisely, their builders and citizens were, and why they so often left in such evident haste. And there's always the fascinating possibility that old Swahili manuscripts will turn up to explain it all.

Pate island

Only two hours by ferryboat from Lamu, totally unaffected by tourism, and rarely visited, **Pate island** has some of the most impressive ruins anywhere on the coast and a clutch of old Swahili settlements which, at different times, have been as important as Lamu or more so. There are few places on the coast as memorable.

Pate is mostly low-lying and almost surrounded by mangrove swamps; no two maps of it ever agree (ours on p.421 shows only the permanent dry land, not the ever-changing mangrove forests that surround it in the shallow sea), so getting on and off the island requires deft awareness of the tides. This apparent remoteness coupled with a lack of information deters travellers but, in truth, Pate is not a difficult destination, and, in purely physical terms, it's an easier island to walk around than Lamu, with none of the exhausting soft sand.

A *matatu* **motorboat** (one of three plying the route) leaves daily, about one hour before high tide, from the municipal jetty at Lamu. On reaching the **Mkanda Channel**, you pass the ferry making the return trip; the Mkanda is navigable only at high tide, and even then it can be a close call when the boat is overloaded, as it usually is. The boat then calls at a deserted spot called **Mtangawanda** (the dock for Pate town, which

HISTORY OF PATE

According to its own **history**, the *Pate Chronicle*, the town was founded in the early years of Islam with the arrival of Arabian immigrants. This statelet is supposed to have lasted until the thirteenth century, when another group of dispossessed Arab rulers – the **Nabahani** – arrived to inject new blood into Pate. The story may have been embellished by time but archeological evidence does support the existence of a flourishing port on the present site of Pate as early as the ninth century; probably by the fifteenth century the town exerted a considerable influence on most of the quasi-autonomous settlements along the coast, including Lamu. As usual, the claims of the royal line to be of overseas extraction were by now more political than biological in nature.

The first **Portuguese** visitors were friendly, trading with the Pateans for the multicoloured silk cloth for which the town had become famous, and they also introduced gunpowder, which enabled wells to be easily excavated, a fact which must have played a part in Pate's rising fortunes. During the sixteenth century, a number of Portuguese merchants settled and married in the town. But as Portugal tightened its grip and imposed taxes, relations quickly deteriorated. There were repeated uprisings and reprisals until, by the mid-seventeenth century, the Portuguese had withdrawn to the security of Fort Jesus in Mombasa. Even today, though, several families in Pate are said to be *Wareno* (from the Portuguese *reino*: kingdom), meaning of Portuguese or part-Portuguese descent.

During the late seventeenth and eighteenth centuries, having thrown out the old rulers and avoided domination by new invaders like the Omani Arabs, Pate underwent a **cultural rebirth** and experienced a flood of creative activity similar to Lamu's. The two towns had a lively relationship, and were frequently in a state of war. At some time during the Portuguese period, Pate's harbour had started to silt up and the town began to use Lamu's, which must have caused great difficulties. In addition, Pate was ruled by a Nabahani king who considered Lamu part of his realm. The disastrous Battle of Shela of 1812 (see p.423) marked the end of Lamu's political allegiance to Pate and the end of Pate as a city-state.

takes about two hours from Lamu), followed by **Faza** at the northern end of the island, which is up to four hours away from Lamu.

The obvious plan, having walked to Pate town from Mtangawanda dock, is to walk from there, through **Siyu** to Faza, returning to Lamu by ferry from there. You could also do this in reverse, of course, but there is a major drawback in that the boat might not pick you up at Mtangawanda on its return if, as often happens, it's full. The walk itself can be done in a day if the tides force an early start, but you may well find yourself wanting to stay longer and breaking for at least a night in Siyu.

Practicalities

The daily motorboat leaves Lamu in time to catch a high tide in the Mkanda Channel about an hour later. **Tide tables** could be useful here, and don't be dissuaded by hustlers who insist the service doesn't operate and offer their dhow instead. Keep asking – it sometimes seems there's a conspiracy of silence on this one. You can, of course, choose to take a dhow to Pate, and even up to Kiwaiyu. If you have the time, and some companions, it's a fine trip, for which you should allow a good four to five days in all. Alternatively, if you have less time but can afford to spend a lot more, you might look into taking a speedboat (see "Listings", p.439) which would enable you to reach Pate town direct, from the south, at high tide, in less than half an hour. But you'd have to wait until the next high tide to get out of Pate creek, unless the speedboat went round to Mtangawanda or Siyu, leaving you to walk. There are many possible permutations.

Accommodation on Pate island is rarely a problem but, with no proper lodgings, a **tent** is a useful back-up. Normally, you'll be invited to stay by someone almost as soon as you arrive in a village. It is wise to take **water** with you (five litres if possible) as Pate's supplies are unpredictable and it's often very briny. As for **food**, most islanders live on home-produced food and staples brought from Lamu and, although there are a few small shops on the island, it's a good idea to have some emergency provisions. These make useful gifts as well. **Mosquitoes** are a serious menace on Pate. The shops sell mosquito coils but, during the day, you may be glad to have some repellent.

If you plan on spending several days on Pate, and you're interested in the archeology of the region, you should ask for **advice and contact names** from Lamu Museum and Lamu Fort, and don't forget to have a good look at the photo display at the latter.

Pate town

From the dock at Mtangawanda, a narrow **footpath** leads to Pate through thick bush; ask for the *ndia ya Pate*, the "path to Pate". Once on the trail it's easy to follow. You cross a broad, tidal "desert", pockmarked with fiddler crab holes, then climb a slight rise to drop through thicker bush, and arrive after an hour on the edge of town.

Small as it is, you would hardly describe **PATE** as a village. After Lamu it comes as a series of surprises. The town plan is pretty much the same – a maze of narrow streets and high-walled houses – but here the streets are made of earth, and the houses are built of coral and dried mud, unplastered and somehow forbidding. The overall layout is confusing, with little slope, as in Lamu, to help direction. Pateans do, in fact, refer to the "upper" and "lower" parts of town – Kitokwe and Mitaaguu respectively. The lower part is down near the town dock, which is only briefly underwater at high tide. This part of town is said to be richer and more welcoming. There's a house which sometimes lets out rooms in this quarter: ask for the *nyumba ya Abala Hassan* (Abala Hassan's house).

If you arrive from Mtangawanda in the "upper" part of town – reputedly poorer and less friendly – you're likely to be struck immediately by the *Wa-pate* – the **people**, and notably the women. Brilliant, determined ladies, with short, bushy hair and rows of gold earrings, stare out directly, unhidden by *buibuis*. Some wear nineteenth-century American gold dollars or half-dollars, though these reminders of the great Yankee trading expeditions of the last century have become so valuable that many have been sold. Big **earlobe plugs** made of silver, gold or buffalo horn can also be seen, as well as nose-rings. If you speak any Swahili, you're likely to find the dialect here unrecognizable. *Wazungu* are rare, and, after Lamu's studied repose, Pate is arrestingly upfront in its dealings with foreigners.

Unless you can stay at the house mentioned above, you may find yourself in the sticky position of bargaining with a family for **bed and board**, an unusual situation with not much room for manoeuvre. It's not unusual to be somewhat peremptorily offered a room, brought a dish of food and left to your own devices. At night, the town resounds with the chimes of dozens of big old **wall clocks**, further reminders of American trade here in the last century; which, juxtaposed with the muezzins' calls to prayer, sound thoroughly bizarre.

Pate town **today** is a shadow of its former self, reduced to the status of sub-location: its only link with government an assistant chief, its sole provision a primary school. But at least its inhabitants are said to remain the richest on the island, thanks to their cash crop, **tobacco**, possibly introduced by the Portuguese and certainly grown here longer than anywhere else on the coast.

The Nabahani ruins

More layers are peeled off Pate's enigmatic exterior when you start to explore the ruins of the **Nabahani** town just outside the modern one. The acres of walls, roofless buildings, tombs, mosques and unidentifiable structures are fascinating, the more so perhaps because this isn't an "archeological site" in the commonly expected mould. Tobacco farmers work in the stony fields between the walls.

Boys will guide you around the ruins for a small payment. Most impressive are the **Mosque with Two Mihrabs** (one for men and one for women?), a nearby house that still has a facing of beautiful *zidaka* (niches) on one wall, and the remains of a sizeable mansion. This last building, you'll be told, is a **Portuguese house**. Certainly, the worn-down stumps of bottle glass projecting from the top of one of its walls do lend it a curiously European flavour, and in the plaster on another wall are scratched two very obvious galleons. Its ceiling slots are square for timbers rather than round for *boriti*, as elsewhere in the ruins.

Shards of pottery and household objects lie in the rubble everywhere but many of the interiors of the buildings are so clogged with tangled roots and vegetation that getting in is almost impossible. It is worth persevering, however: the sense of personal discovery is exciting and immensely satisfying if you can ignore the mosquitoes that silently home in on bare legs when you walk through the weeds.

Many of the walls and buildings have already been demolished to obtain lime for tobacco cultivation. Without weighty financial backing, it's hard to see how the National Museums of Kenya (NMK) could ever preserve the remains of old Pate as well as compensate the farmers. Gradually, tragically, it is all returning to the soil. In the meantime, see it – and photograph it – while you still can.

Siyu

The **path from Pate to Siyu** is a slightly tricky eight kilometres. Having set off in the right direction, the first half-hour is fairly straightforward; if in doubt, bear right. You come to a crossroads (easily missed unless you look backwards) and turn right. This narrow red dirt path soon broadens into a track known as the *barabara ya gari* (the "motor highway" – there was once a car); it takes you to a normally dry tidal inlet where you veer left a little before continuing straight on through thick bush for another hour to reach Siyu.

Wherever the bush on either side is high enough you may come across gigantic **spider's webs** strung across the path. The matching spiders are brightly coloured, non-hairy, and merely waiting for insects, but they are nevertheless intimidating enough to remind you of where you are. Fortunately they have the sense to build their webs well out of reach.

Siyu town

SIYU is less documented than Pate. Even less accessible by sea, the town was a flourishing and unsuspected centre of Islamic scholarship from the seventeenth to the nineteenth century and apparently something of a **sanctuary** for Muslim intellectuals and craftsmen. While Lamu, Pate and other trading towns were engaged in political rivalry and physical skirmishing, Siyu never had its heart in commerce or maritime activities, and never attracted much Portuguese attention. Instead, there was enormous devotion to **Koran-copying**, **book-making**, **text illumination**, and cottage industries like the **woodcarving** and **leatherwork** for which it's still famous locally. Siyu **sandals** are said to be absolutely the best, though plastic flip-flops have forced almost all the makers out of business. Siyu **carved doors** are among the most beautiful of all Swahili doors, with distinctive guilloche patterns and inlays of ground shell.

The sources of wealth and stability for Siyu's florescence are a little mysterious, but the town's agricultural base obviously supported it well and it was probably the largest settlement on the island in the early nineteenth century, with up to 30,000 inhabitants. In 1873, the British vice consul in Zanzibar could still describe it as "the pulse of the whole district".

These days you wouldn't know it. Less than 4000 people live here, and signs of the old brilliance are hard to find. Siyu lost its independence and presumably much of its artistic flair when the sultan of Zanzibar's Omani troops first occupied the fort in 1847 – though it was twenty years before the Omanis were able to hold it for more than a brief spell. Built in the early nineteenth century (no one knows for sure by whom), **Siyu Fort** is the town's most striking building and indeed, in purely monumental terms, the most imposing building on the whole island. Substantially renovated, it is one of the few surviving traces of the glory days. It's freely accessible, though watch out for dangers like the well and the unstable walls. Around the outskirts of Siyu on the south side are a number of quite impressive **tombs**. The big domed tomb with porcelain niches dates from 1853.

Most of Siyu's houses today conform to the "open-box" plan typical of the Kenyan coast: yellowish mud with a ridged *makuti* roof, open at each end. These houses stand, each on its own, with no real streets to connect them, so, although it's larger than Pate, Siyu feels far more like a village. The cultural isolation of these communities from each other, a separateness which continues to this day, is easily appreciated after arriving in Siyu from Pate. There are still few *buibuis* here but there's much less jewellery in evidence and the atmosphere is altogether less severe.

For **accommodation**, it helps if you've had a word with Museums people in Lamu. The death in 1995 of Bakari Maalim, an employee of the NMK who used to guide visitors to some of the sites, has left Siyu bereft of a natural host. At the time of writing it was still unclear who might replace him.

Shanga ruins

You'll need the help of Bakari Maalim's successor – or another qualified guide – if you hope to visit the ruins of **SHANGA**, a large Swahili town at least 1000 years old, which would be almost impossible to find unaided. Expect to pay around a couple of hundred shillings for a guide. Shanga is on the south coast of the island, about an hour's walk from Siyu. You have to fight your way, literally, through the undergrowth when you arrive at the site. The most impressive sight is the white pillar tomb, eminently phallic, which you come to first. The very large Friday Mosque nearby and a second mosque nearer the sea are only the most obvious of innumerable other remains in every direction.

In 1980, Shanga was largely cleared, and partly excavated, by a team from the NMK, with Cambridge University archeologists and Operation Drake participating. More recently, London University excavated the site. What they found is a walled site of thirteen acres, with five access gates and a cemetery outside the walls containing 340 stone tombs. There was even a sea wall. Inside the town, 130 houses were surveyed, together with what looks to have been a palace similar in some respects to the one at Gedi. Shanga is believed to have been occupied from the ninth to the fourteenth century and, like Gedi, no very convincing reasons have been found for why it should have been abandoned, nor why it was never mentioned by travellers and traders of the time.

Limited work has been done here to restore some of the plaster in a set of wall niches and on the fluted pillar tomb, but on the whole the clearing and excavating only seems to have encouraged the jungle. Getting from one ruin to the next isn't easy. Dangerously camouflaged **wells** and **snakes**, both common, add further to the Shanga experience. If you walk on down to the sea – and assuming you have a certain capacity for hardship in paradise – there's said to be a beautiful **beach** and some ideal camping spots.

Faza

Siyu to **FAZA** is a shorter walk than from Pate to Siyu and more interesting, through waist-high grass, fertile *shambas* and sections of bush. It takes about two hours, but you'll need guidance, at least as far as the airstrip inherited from an early 1980s oil-prospecting venture. From there it's straightforward. An hour or so out of Siyu, you reach the first *shambas*. There are usually people on the path; if you catch up with someone from behind, announce your presence before trying to pass. Strangers are rare and you could give someone – especially an old person – quite a fright.

On a coast of islands, it's not surprising that Faza itself is almost an island, surrounded by tidal flats and mangroves. A secondary school, health centre, police station (with nothing to do) and even a post office and telephone exchange have made Faza the most important settlement on Pate island. There's even a Land Rover ambulance, donated by Saudi Arabia, the only vehicle on the island. Every few years a lodging house opens, but the lack of visitors forces them to close sooner or later. There's a very unprepossessing council guest house which is available in theory. **Private accommodation**, though, is easy to find. Fishing is the commonest occupation, with much of the catch going to a cold room at Kisingitini, from where it's shipped to Mombasa. Faza suffered a serious fire in 1990, which razed many houses to the ground and caused devastation. Today, you would hardly know.

As a contemporary Kenyan rural centre, Faza makes an interesting place to walk around and you're almost certain to have plenty of time to fill before the boat leaves. One part of the village is devoted exclusively to cattle stalls, but goats run everywhere, ruining the efforts of the primary school headmaster to prevent soil erosion on the badly rutted and sloping football field. A fine evening stroll takes you across the mud on a new concrete causeway to the thickets on the "mainland", where the island's expanding secondary school is located. From Faza you could, if you wanted, walk on to the **other villages** on the island, all fairly modern and bunched together within forty minutes of Faza: Kisingitini, Bajumwali, Tundwa (Chundwa), and the closest, Nyambogi.

Faza's history and archeology

Archeologically Faza has less to offer than its neighbours. Of Swahili towns, it was one of the most defiant to any attempts to usurp its independence; it was razed by the Pate army after a dispute over water rights in the fifteenth century, and again by the Portuguese in 1586 after collaborating with the Turkish fleet of Amir Ali Bey. On this occasion the entire population was massacred and the head of Faza's king was taken to Goa in a barrel of salt to be paraded triumphantly in the streets. Faza's unfortunate history may partly account for its relative lack of ruins, but one success is commemorated in the **tomb** of Seyyid Hamed bin Ahmed al-Busaidy (also known as Amir Hamad), commander in chief of the sultan of Zanzibar's forces, who met his death in 1844 under a hail of arrows. He was on an expedition against Siyu and Pate, and retreating to the relative safety of Faza when he was ambushed by a party of Siyu bowmen. His grave (*kaburi*), with a long epitaph, lies just outside Faza.

There are several ruined mosques around Faza, including the very crumbled Kunjanja Mosque. The ruins of the eighteenth-century **Mbwarashally Mosque** (also known as the Shala Fatani Mosque) merit a visit, however. Now theoretically protected by the National Museums of Kenya, the mosque – barring its *mihrab* – is just a pile of rubble; the *mihrab*, however, turns out to incorporate exquisite and unusual heart motifs, including the *shahada* (the Islamic creed) inscribed within an inverted heart shape.

Kiwaiyu

From Faza you're within striking distance of the desert island retreat of **Kiwaiyu**, about an hour by *mtaboti*, if you can find one. It is likely, however, that a group dhow charter in Lamu would be a cheaper way to visit Kiwaiyu. For around Ksh2000–3000 a day, you can charter a small dhow for four or five days, including breakfast and dinner, snorkelling and fishing gear, and plenty of fresh water. Split this price among five or six people and it becomes very cheap. The best advice is to form an enthusiastic group around the lodgings in Lamu, then start negotiations, as soon as possible, directly with whoever is going to be running the show. Too often, arrangements are made with dhow hustlers that owners and crew can't or won't honour.

You can expect to spend 24 to 36 hours on the journey in each direction, depending on wind, tides and the skill of the crew – though with the wind behind you it's possible to get up to Kiwaiyu in under eight hours. The snorkelling around the **Kiunga Marine National Reserve** is nice enough, though not as consistently good as Malindi/Watamu, but the experience of sailing, the nights under stars, and the acquaintance of the Swahili crew are altogether highly recommended.

On Kiwaiyu, **budget travellers** stay at the reasonable *Kasim's* camping and *banda* site, near the beach on the inshore coast of the island just a few hundred metres north of **Kiwaiyu village**. *Kasim's* consists of several palm-mat *bandas*, plus a couple of unusual tree houses (③; camping Ksh100). Most people just drag one of the cane beds down onto the beach and sleep under the stars. The village has limited provisions in a couple of shops, but most people eat what is prepared each day and served in the little "dining room".

There's not a lot to do, and not much that anyone wants to do. Five minutes south of *Kasim's* is the village, a quiet, rural place but friendly enough. A further ten minutes south, you come to the "Italian cold store" – a stalled shellfish export project with attached accommodation, which looks like a long-term investment that's being ignored. Ten minutes' walk further still, you reach a house on the high southern tip of the island. This is a fishing camp (the plane you may have seen parked near the village belongs to the owner) but it's strictly private and does not provide accommodation to walk-in visitors. From here, the superb, ocean-facing beach, with the reef close offshore, is just a scramble down the sandy hillside. There are one or two first-class **snorkelling** spots off this southern tip of the island, with huge coral heads and a multitude of fish. Ask for precise directions as it's possible to spend hours looking and still miss them. You'll need good footwear to survive the dead coral reef.

Luxury lodges

There are two **luxury lodges** at Kiwaiyu. The one on the island itself is *Munira Safari Camp*, about 2km north of Kiwaiyu village, a group of *bandas* planted around on the crest of the island to catch the breeze (PO Box 40088, Nairobi; ☎02/512213; ⑧). "Mike's *bandas*", as the establishment is also known, is very laid-back in a civilized kind of way, with plentiful birdlife in the vicinity. It's a favourite with Anglo-Kenyans and those who find even *Peponi* too busy. Transfers are Ksh9000 by speedboat from *Peponi*, or free from *Kiwaiyu Safari Village*, the other lodge, on the mainland a little further north. This is a hedonist's delight, combining the privileges of its remote location (peace, security) with exceptional food and perfectly conceived architecture – nineteen individual palm-leaf and wood cottages, nearly all of them right by the water's edge (PO Box 55343, Nairobi; ☎02/503030, fax 02/50349; best rooms 1–15; ⑨).

The flight to the *Safari Village* airstrip from Lamu operates more or less on demand, at the cost of $50 a seat, and there are also fairly regular flights from Nairobi. There's a Ksh1000 Land Rover transfer to the lodge.

Kenya's northeastern corner

There is nothing to keep you from visiting the **far northeastern coastal region** by land if you're determined – nothing, that is, apart from roaming Somali guerillas, armed to the teeth. Make careful enquiries before you set off: at the time of writing (July 1996), firm advice to the contrary was being proffered.

If things have quietened down, you could *matatu*-hop from the jetty at Mokowe to **Hindi**, then leave the Malindi to Mombasa route and head for the Somalian border at **Dar-es-Salaam/Shakani**. On the way, you pass the sweetly named **Mundane Hills**, but back on the coast things should improve. There are plenty of Swahili ruins, including the **walled city of Ishakani**, recently partly cleared by the National Museums of Kenya, and a reportedly pretty coastal road leading back south to the headland opposite Kiwaiyu. In the dry season it's certainly worth slogging up here with a Suzuki. If you go, let us know.

WARNING

Tourists on coastal bus services, especially Mombasa to Malindi, have been targeted by thieves using drugged food and drink to render their victims unconscious. Beware!

---

travel details

BUSES

From Mombasa (corner of Mwembe Tayari and Jomo Kenyatta Ave) **to Nairobi and the west**: *Akamba Bus* (☎011/316770), *Goldline* (☎011/220027), and the safe and recommended *Coast Bus* (☎011/220916) each operate at least one day (6–7hr) and one night (8hr) service. The night journey can be cold: take warm clothes. *Akamba* connects with its services to western Kenya. *Mawingo* and *Kisii Express* have daily services to destinations in the west.

From Mombasa to Dar-es-Salaam: Various companies (including *Cat, Tawfiq*) run several services daily; 14–16hr, via Tanga (7hr).

From Mombasa (Abdul Nassir Rd) **to Malindi**: Frequent, on the hour; 90min.

From Mombasa (Abdul Nassir Rd) **to Garissa**: Early departure daily on *Mbuni* (☎011/225441), *Tana River* (☎011/225053) or *Garissa Bus Service*. Buses can be picked up in Malindi, or later in Garsen.

From Mombasa (Abdul Nassir Rd) **to Lamu, via Malindi**: *TSS* daily; *Faza Express Bus* daily; 6–8hr.

From Lamu to Garsen, Malindi and Mombasa: *TSS* and *Faza Express* daily.

MATATUS

Frequent services between various points on the **main coast road** (Malindi–Vanga). Limited services north of Malindi.

TRAINS

For booking details, see Mombasa "Listings".

From Mombasa to:

Nairobi daily at 7pm (arr. 8.30am);

Moshi (Tanzania, via Voi) Fri at 7pm, changing in Voi to connect with the 5.05am Sat service to Moshi (night in Voi);

Kampala (Uganda, via Nairobi) Tues at 10am (arr. Wed 9am).

HITCHING

From Mombasa to Malindi and **Likoni to Diani Beach**: Straightforward enough.

From Mombasa to Nairobi: Take a bus to Mazeras and hitch from there.

From Malindi to Lamu: Difficult and not worthwhile.

PLANES

Prestige Air Services, Air Kenya Aviation, Eagle Aviation, Tai Aviation and *Kenya Airways* are the main carriers. If you're flying from Lamu to Nairobi, it's worth knowing that a saving can be made by flying via Malindi and connecting with *Kenya Airways*, rather than going direct.

From Mombasa to:

Nairobi: 6–10 times daily on *Kenya Airways* (1hr–1hr 15min according to aircraft; $85).

Lamu: at least twice daily (60min; $85) **via Malindi** (30min; $65) and back to Mombasa.

Zanzibar: 6 times weekly on *Kenya Airways* and *Air Tanzania* (1hr; $54 plus $20 departure tax) .

From Malindi to:

Nairobi: 1–3 flights a day non-stop on *Kenya Airways* (1hr 10min; $85).

From Lamu to:

Nairobi: *Air Kenya Aviation*, daily at 3.45pm (2hr; $112).

Kiwaiyu: daily on demand (20min; $95).

SEA TRAVEL

From Mombasa to:

Lamu Catamaran ferry service MV *Sepideh* operated by *Zanzibar Sea Ferries* (many agents on the Kenya coast) .

Tanzania (Pemba, Zanzibar, Dar-es-Salaam) Catamaran ferry service MV *Sepideh*; also cargo vessels MV *Maendeleo* and MV *Mapinduzi*, which you can trace by asking at the port (sleep out on the tarpaulin)

Europe Difficult: ask around the ships' captains at Kilindini. The *Mediterranean Shipping Company*'s monthly service through the Suez canal to Livorno and the UK is available if you have the money (see p.12).

Bodo (small village near Shirazi) to:

Pemba, Tanzania frequent cargo dhow (7hr; Ksh500); exit stamp needs to be arranged at Mombasa or Lungalunga before embarkation.

Indian Ocean voyages

Check the Mombasa Yacht Club or, more likely, *Moorings* at Mtwapa Creek or *Swynford's Boatyard* in Kilifi for crewing possibilities. There are no passenger services to Asia.

Dhows from Mombasa to Lamu

Dhows from Mombasa to Lamu or beyond are difficult to find these days. Passengers are sometimes taken but there are no hard and fast rules for getting passage. The stumbling block — at least the first one — is that dhows have no passenger insurance, so any passage is effectively illegal and a proportion of the fee you negotiate will be needed for official "*chai*".

Dhows from Lamu to Mombasa

Relatively straightforward, once you've found an agreeable captain and assuming it's the right time of year (Dec–March). There's a protocol: first you should go to the District Commissioner's secretary's office (first floor on the right, opposite the town jetty) for a form absolving the captain and the government of all responsibility in the case of mishap. Then take one copy to him, which he'll present to Customs, on the first floor across the courtyard, when he files his crew and passenger manifest. They'll tell you it's a 36-hour trip to Mombasa but count on some doldrums and allow up to three or even four days. Bring fruit and anything else you anticipate needing to break the monotony of unvarying fish and *ugali* meals. You should get a passage for less than Ksh1000.

CHAPTER SEVEN

THE NORTH

There is one half of Kenya about which the other half knows nothing and seems to care even less.

Negley Farson, *Last Chance in Africa*

K enya is rarely thought of in terms of desert, but **the North** – over half the country in area – is exclusively arid land, burned out for more than ten months of the year. The old Northern Frontier District (still called NFD by many) remains one of the most exciting and adventurous parts of Africa for independent travel: a vast tract of territory, crisscrossed by ancient migration routes, and still tramped by the nomadic Samburu, Rendille, Gabbra, Turkana, and Somali herders.

The target for most travellers is the wonderful jade splash of **Lake Turkana**, very remote in feel and highly unpredictable in nature (when British sailors first ventured out on it, they reckoned it could turn "rougher than the North Sea"). To get to Turkana, you have the option of organized camping safaris, as well as buses and lorries up from the hub of highlands Kenya. Elsewhere in the north travelling can be harder going, usually by gut-shaking lorries, with heat and dust constant, the water often briny and useless for washing. But the **desert towns** have their own rewards, not least in the bewilderment of arriving and finding places so little known yet so important to an enormous compass of countryside and population.

Because of the layout of the **roads and tracks** that radiate north from the central highlands, you'll need to make a decision about which "spokes" to cover: there are few east–west routes. Don't be over-ambitious. Bus services are patchy at best, whilst lorries and hitching can work out, but are exhausting. If you're driving, water and mechanical know-how should be your priorities since you'll need to be almost self-sufficient.

A **seasonal** factor in the Islamic eastern parts of the region is **Ramadan** (see p.59): during the month of fasting you'll find many *hotelis* closed during the day – which, with the efforts of daytime travel, can be hard to handle. And, of course, there are the annual **rains**. Though the landscape is parched for most of the year, when the rains do come (usually around May) they can have dramatic effect, bringing torrents of water along the ravines, tearing away fords and bridges, and sweeping over the plains to leave an ooze of mud and new shoots. In these conditions, you can easily be stranded – even along the paved road up to Lodwar. However, if your plans are flexible, it's an exciting time to explore. Several of the Turkana camping trip operators run their vehicles throughout the year, adding mud and river crossings to the usual challenges. Driving

---

ACCOMMODATION PRICE CODES

Rates for a standard double or twin room. For a full explanation of these price codes, see p.46.

① Under Ksh300	(under approx. £3.30/$5)	⑤ Ksh2000–4000	(£22/$33–£44/$67)
② Ksh300–500	(£3.30/$5–£5.50/$8)	⑥ Ksh4000–6000	(£44/$67–£67/$100)
③ Ksh500–1000	(£5.50/$8–£11/$17)	⑦ Ksh6000–8000	(£67/$100–£89/$133)
④ Ksh1000–2000	(£11/$17–£22/$33)	⑧ Ksh8000–10,000	(£89/$133–£111/$167)
	⑨ Over Ksh10,000	(over £111/$167)	

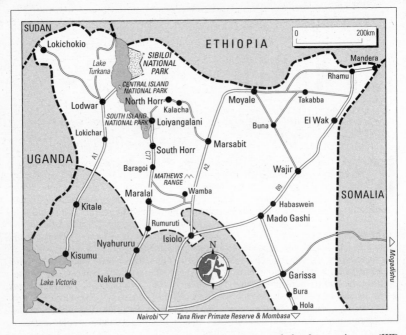

your own vehicle during the rainy season is not recommended unless you've got 4WD and experience.

TURKANA

Straddled at its northern end by the Ethiopian border, **Lake Turkana** stretches south for 250km through Kenya's arid lands, bisecting the rocky deserts like a turquoise sickle. It is hemmed in by sandy wastes and by black and brown volcanic ranges, and the lake scene changes constantly. The water, a glassy, milky blue one minute, can become slate-grey and choppy or a glaring emerald green, sometimes even jade, the next. It feels remote and hallucinatory – an unexpected departure from the natural order of things.

The lake was discovered for the rest of the world as late as 1888 by the Austrians **Teleki** and **von Hohnel**, who named it "Rudolf" after their archduke and patron. Later, it became eulogized as the "Jade Sea" in John Hillaby's book about his camel trek. The name "Turkana" only came into being during the wholesale Kenyanization of place names in the 1970s. By then, it had also been dubbed the "Cradle of Mankind", the site of revelatory fossil discoveries in the field of human evolution. And it was becoming something of a spiritual mecca for atavists, an excuse for a week of riotous assembly in a safari lorry or a dignified weekend in a *Cessna* and a lakeshore lodge.

But to depict Lake Turkana as "Kenya's latest touristic discovery" as one or two glossies would have you believe is, thankfully, a monstrous piece of hype: there are two lodges, one on each shore, catering for perhaps two dozen people between them at any one time. Otherwise there are one or two windy campsites and that's it. As yet, the only

A NOTE ON SECURITY AND ROADBLOCKS

For fear of rebellion among the Somali population, because of occasional highway robberies, and as a result of the arrival of large numbers of refugees from war-torn Sudan and Somalia, the military presence in the north is pervasive: roadblocks, vehicle searches and armed escorts are part of everyday life and you should be sure your passport is in order for the duration of your trip up north. Yet the incidents that Kenyans fear are rare and usually attributed to "bandits" without political motives. In any case don't be deterred by misconceptions from "down-country" Kenya (as the highlands and populated districts of southern Kenya are called up north). The sheer lack of traffic probably makes travelling up here safer. And foreign travellers are certainly a welcome sight in a region which is frustrated to be eddying in the margins of Kenya's mainstream. If you're thinking of heading out **beyond Isiolo** to the far northeast, however, take careful advice: this is one region where the rest of the country's traditional fear and ignorance is no longer just prejudice. It may be closed to casual travellers. See the boxes on p.474 and p.487 for more detail.

asphalt – that certain sign of imminent change – is the crooked finger that reaches north from **Kitale** to **Lodwar** and on to **Kalokol** on the western shore.

Ecology and climate

Lake Turkana is the biggest permanent desert lake in the world, with a shoreline longer than the whole of Kenya's sea coast. Yet today it has been reduced to a mere sliver of its former expanse. Like some gigantic sump, with rivers flowing in but no outlet available, a staggering average of three metres' depth of water **evaporates** from its surface each year (nearly a centimetre a day). As a result, it is alkaline, though not inimical to water life (or human life – drinking it, should you have no other source, should pose no major problems). Recent years of drought, and fairly major irrigation projects in southern Ethiopia, have seen the inflow drying up, so that the water level is at the lowest point in living (or passed down) memory. Less than 10,000 years ago the lake was 150 metres deeper and spread south as far as Baringo; this mammoth inland sea fed the headwaters of the Nile, which accounts for the presence of **Nile perch** – though not for why they grow to such enormous weights (sometimes over 100kg). It is also home to the biggest surviving world population of **Nile crocodiles** – between 10,000 and 22,000 – and is one of the few places where you can still see great stacks of them basking on sand banks. There is a profusion of **birdlife**, including European migrants seen most spectacularly on their way home between March and May. And **hippos**, widely hunted and starved from many of their former lakeshore haunts through lack of grazing, still manage to hang on in fairly large numbers, though you won't see many unless you go out of your way.

Climatically, Turkana is devastatingly hot and dry for ten months of the year, and unpleasantly muggy during the rains. It is notorious for its strong easterly **winds** which, while not incessant, puff and gust energetically most of the time and occasionally become demonic. The winds, more than hippos or crocodiles, are the cause of most accidental deaths of local people on the lake.

The **people** you are most likely to meet are **Turkana** on the western and southern shores of the lake, **Elmolo** around Loiyangalani in the southeast, and **Samburu** on the way up to Loiyangalani. The Turkana (see box on p.454) and Samburu (p.467) are pastoral people with great reverence for their cattle, while the Elmolo (p.472) are traditionally property-less hunters and fishers.

Getting there

There are **three road routes** to Turkana: one to the western shore from Kitale and two to the east shore from Maralal and Marsabit (the latter very remote). There is no

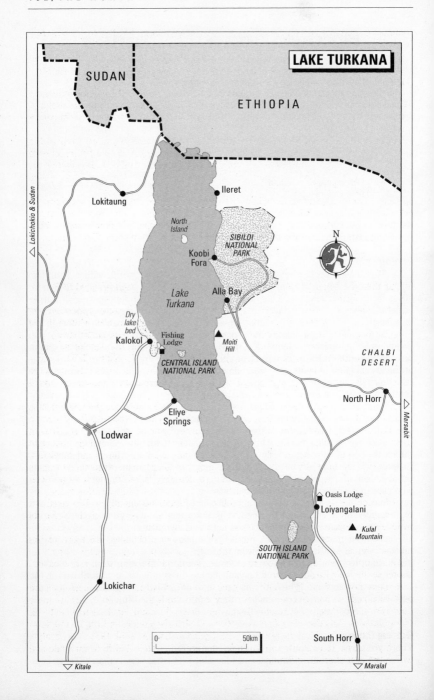

LAKE TURKANA

SUDAN

ETHIOPIA

◁ Lokichokio & Sudan

Lokitaung

Ileret

North
Island

SIBILOI
NATIONAL
PARK

Koobi
Fora

Lake
Turkana

Alla Bay

Dry
lake
bed

Kalokol

Fishing
Lodge

Moiti
Hill

CHALBI
DESERT

CENTRAL ISLAND
NATIONAL PARK

North Horr

▷ Marsabit

Eliye
Springs

Lodwar

Oasis Lodge

Loiyangalani

Kulal
Mountain

SOUTH ISLAND
NATIONAL PARK

Lokichar

0   50km

South Horr

▽ Kitale

▽ Maralal

route connecting the east and west shores: the volcanic **Suguta Valley** forms a blazing hot barrier.

The **western approach from Kitale** is the one used by most independent travellers without their own vehicles. A **bus** runs up to Lodwar every other day, and there are a number of crammed Nissan **matatus** every morning.

On the east, the **Maralal–Loiyangalani route** is the one used by nearly all of the Turkana **camping safari** lorries. If you can afford $400–500 or so for a week-long trip, it has definite advantages: magnificent scenery and that sense of adventure that comes only from travel into a desert.

The third route, **from Marsabit via North Horr**, is feasible if you are prepared to wait around for a lift in Marsabit. But it's not much used and you should be prepared to give up the idea after a day or two if nothing is going westwards. One or two of the camping safari firms use this route for their longer trips, and may give you a lift (some route details are given on p.483).

A last option is **flying**. In principle, there are fairly frequent flights from Nairobi's Wilson Airport. **Air safaris** (around $500 for 3–4 days) destroy much of the sense of the lake's isolation, and they don't give enough time to explore, but the flight itself – low down between the Aberdares and Mount Kenya – is sublime. See "Travel Details", p.497.

North to Lodwar and the western lakeshore

There is now only one **bus** (*Igana Bus*) to Lodwar from Kitale, leaving every other day at around 8am. Otherwise there are a number of Nissan *matatus*, also leaving in the morning, and one or two pick-up *matatus* at around 6am or 7am. Alternatively you might try **hitching** – there are plenty enough trucks and jeeps bound for the aid centre at Lokichokio, north of Lodwar, and stopping a vehicle is not too difficult. The prices for all these options vary widely, and you should bargain hard. It's worth taking some water for this trip: everyone who does it has a different story to tell of punctures, break-downs and inexplicable delays.

The best part of the **five- to eight-hour journey** is the beginning (for more details about this district see pp.268–270), as you pass **Saiwa Swamp National Park** then go through the green valleys of **Trans-Nzoia** towards **Kapenguria**, site of the trial of Kenyatta and five colleagues in 1953. This inaccessible town was deliberately chosen to hinder the work of the defence lawyers – "a maze of rascalities", one of them called it. All six defendants were found guilty of belonging to Mau Mau and sentenced to seven years in jail with hard labour. Beyond Kapenguria (or rather the turn-off for it at Makutano, since the highway itself bypasses the town by two or three kilometres), the road scales a neck of the Cherangani Hills, then plunges headily along their northern slopes, following a tributary of the Turkwel River before slipping through the defiles of the **Marich Pass** and down on to the southern Turkana plains.

The last petrol station and bank before Lodwar are at Makutano. From **the plains** on, it's hard to extract much of scenic interest, though the regular stops to pick up increasingly wild-looking passengers maintain gently heightening expectations about the far north you're heading into.

If you're driving there is a possible detour to the **Turkwel Gorge** (signposted on the left). This route drops several hundred metres into the heat – a steep, rough, winding road with plunging precipices and spectacular views all round. At the small centre of **Kongolai** you meet the sizeable **Suam River** (which rises on Mount Elgon and flows into the Turkwel) which represented the Ugandan border until 1970. The bridge, which you cross to continue to the Turkwel Gorge, is dominated by a dramatic and towering tooth-like rock outcrop.

The main A1 Lodwar road simply extends through the thorny wilderness between the **Nasalot** and **South Turkana** national reserves, neither of them distinctive.

Lodwar

For most Kenyans, mention of **LODWAR** conjures up remote and outlandish images of the badlands, an aberrant place where anything could befall you. And the Turkana District capital is, to put it mildly, a wild town: unformed, loud, and somehow incongru-

THE TURKANA

Until very recently, **the Turkana**, the main people of the **western shore of the lake**, had very little contact with the outside world, or even with the Republic of Kenya. You'll still see older people in more remote parts wearing very few clothes or, in some cases, animal skins; and some of the head-loads carried by Turkana women seem little short of miraculous. Linguistically, the Turkana are related to the Maa-speaking Samburu and Maasai. Indeed, along the northwest shore of the lake, the people are probably an old mixture of Turkana and Samburu, although, like the Luo (also distantly related by language), the Turkana did not traditionally practise circumcision. They moved east from their old homeland on the borders of Sudan and Uganda in the seventeenth century. The desolate region between the lake and the Ugandan border which they now occupy is barely habitable land, and their daily struggle for existence has profoundly influenced the shape of their society and, inevitably, helped create the funnel into modern Kenya which Lodwar, with its new road, has become.

The Turkana are more individualistic than most Kenyan peoples and they show a disregard for the ties of clan and family that must have emerged through repeated famines and wars. Although essentially **pastoralists**, always on the move to the next spot of grazing, they do grow crops when they can get seed and when the rains are sufficient. Often the rains fail, notably during the prolonged drought of the early 1980s, which took a terrible toll of children. The situation has eased since then but life is still very much a matter of day-to-day survival, aided here and there by hand-outs from the UN and other agencies. With characteristic pragmatism, the Turkana have scorned the taboo against fish so prevalent among herders, and **fishing** is a viable option that is increasingly popular.

Turkana **bellicosity** is infamous in Kenya (Turkana migrants to the towns of the south are frequently employed as *askaris* – security guards). Relations with their neighbours, especially the Merille to the north of the lake and the Pokot to the southwest, have often been openly aggressive. British forces were engaged in the gradual conquest of the Turkana – the usual killings, livestock raids and property destruction – and they succeeded, at some cost, in eventually disarming them of their guns in the 1920s. But the Merille, meanwhile, were obtaining arms from Abyssinia's imperial government, and they took savage advantage of the Turkana's defenceless position. When war was declared by Italian-held Abyssinia in 1940, the British rearmed the Turkana, who swiftly exacted their revenge on the Merille. They were later disarmed again.

Violence is no longer in the air down at **Ferguson's Gulf** – though you might see older Turkana men with scars on their arms and chests to indicate who they've killed: females on the left upper arm and chest, males on the right. Further north, however, the Turkana are themsevles victims: Toposa raiders from Sudan are thought to have killed thousands of Turkana in recent years.

But while the killing is largely a thing of the past, Turkana directness is unmistakable in all their dealings with *wazungu*. They are, for example, resolute and stubborn bargainers (even if you're not interested in buying), while offers of relatively large sums for photos often leave them stone cold – not necessarily from any mystical fear of the camera, but because of a shrewd estimation of what the market will stand, and hence, presumably, of their own reputation. Unlike the Maa-speaking warriors, the Turkana rarely pose for a living, although the exceptions are increasing in number.

ous in this searing wilderness. During the 1980s it became Kenya's desert boom town, the lake's fishing, the possibility of oil discoveries and the new road from Kitale all encouraging inward migration. This expansion has now all but fizzled out and the harsher realities of economics – too many people, too little money – have made themselves visible: children plead for "shilling" wherever you go, and the "guides" and hustlers are more persistent than elsewhere.

While **Turkana people** predominate, **Luo** and **Luyia** have also arrived in search of opportunities. As the exhaustion of farming country in the south drives people further and further afield in the quest for land and work, Lodwar and the area around it is becoming increasingly attractive to pioneers and cowboys of all sorts. The distinct and lasting impression is of a town with a high population of men. Newspapers arrive with the bus or first *matatu* each afternoon, eight hours after the rest of the country have received theirs. All around the shady trees in the centre of town, men sit reading them, discussing the daily stories, trying to reduce the **isolation** felt here. When news of the August 1982 "coup" came through, the police in Lodwar immediately freed all the prisoners and relaxed with beer for the rest of the day. It's that sort of town.

The Turkana have been able to go south more easily with the new road, though elders who don't speak English or Swahili tend to get pushed around and ripped off. Coming north, there has been a lot of overpriced fruit and vegetables from Kitale (shrivelled apples and oranges in the grocery stores) and all the little signs of affluence – radios, bicycles, stereos, factory furniture – that still draw in the people from the boondocks. And then there's us: the tourists. Hand-me-down trinkets are suddenly worth a day's wages – or a week's, with the right customer – and wrist knives are worth making again, even if they'll probably never be used in earnest. To be frank, Lodwar has become rather sad. Whispers about **oil** in the north have long since ceased; most of the NGOs pulled out as the famine receded in the late 1980s, taking their money with them, and the only dream that is left to chase lies in the pockets of the tourists.

Practicalities

Lodwar is an incredibly hot, dusty town most of the year, but for a day or two you may find the rough, frontier atmosphere exhilarating, especially after the faintly parochial airs of the highlands. There are **banks** (*KCB* changes travellers' cheques), a **post office** (open Mon–Fri) and a number of **places to stay**. Most presentable of the ones in town is the *Turkwel Lodge* (PO Box 14; ☎0393/21201; B&B ②, cottages ③), a fairly clean place, with the very definite luxury of fans in each room, a good restaurant and a rowdy bar, with a disco on Friday and Saturday (free before 9pm). This is where officials and aid workers stay. A sign in the rooms says: "We hope your stay with us will be quite nice"; it's certainly quite noisy, with Lingala tunes thumping out until the early hours. Considerably cheaper and less salubrious are the *Lucky Star Hotel*, around the corner, and the *Mombasa Hotel*, opposite the Kitale *matatu* stand, both ①. The latter, astonishingly, has working fans in the rooms, ice-cold sodas and beer, and fresh *miraa* at Ksh120 a kilo; the downside is its dirty, almost squalid, rooms. You might also try the *Naoyapong Guest House* (①) – near the slaughter house, but odourless.

Some 3km out of town (1km south and 2km to the right) is the *Nawoitorong Guest House and Conference Centre* (PO Box 192; B&B ①; camping Ksh100). This is a co-operative which aims to rehabilitate and care for widows, single mothers and drought victims. Perched on a slight hill, and shaded by acacias, *Nawoitorong* has a lot to recommend it, especially if you're staying more than just a night. They bake their own bread, and have recently constructed a *manyatta* to serve as a cultural centre, supported by the National Museum. There's a pool nearby at the *Lodwar Club* which guests can use (Ksh50 for non-residents); the club itself, no longer members only, now offers rooms with ceiling fans (②).

For **food**, there are a few reasonable *hotelis* in town. *Hotel Salama* is good all round; the *Africana* has good chapatis (and many tourists); *Mombasa Hotel* has hot, spicy food; *Lucky Star* serves pilau; *Lala Salama* does the best fish; and *Delicious Café* is the only place to eat *irio*. All are fast and cheap. There's even a 24 hour *chai na mandaazi* stop.

Apart from just hanging around and taking in the scene, though, there's not a lot to do here and you'll probably want to move down to the lakeside after a night. If you have the time and some spare energy, you can **hike up one of the hills** behind the town. Lodwar's canopy of acacias makes it surprisingly invisible below, but the view stretches for miles. The town's **California Market** (behind *Barclays Bank*) is worth checking out, too, particularly if you're into weaving or want to buy baskets – there's always a crowd of women making them. You might also visit the *Turkana Handicraft Shop*, run by a women's basket-making co-operative, 300m from the first Kitale round-about. Also worth investigating is the *Diocesan Crafts Shop*, which has a big selection of baskets, trays and mats marketed by the Catholic mission.

Note, when **heading back to Kitale** by *matatu*, you will have to book your seat – and almost certainly pay for it – the evening before. You leave at midnight, connecting nicely with buses returning to Nairobi.

Kalokol

Ferguson's Gulf is the most reliable place to head for on the lakeshore, though not quite as scenically stunning as Eliye Springs (see below). The village you want initially is called **KALOKOL** (formerly known as Lokwar Kangole). Most days there will be several vehicles and *matatus* making the trip there: ask around or wait by the ford across the (seasonal) Turkwel River outside Lodwar. During the one- to two-hour journey to Kalokol, look out for the **standing stones of Namotunga**, about 15km before Kalokol on the right. Like a miniature Stonehenge, the metre-high pillars are a spiritual focus and the scene, usually in December, of a major gathering of Turkana clans.

There is little point in visiting Kalokol for its own sake. It has a surprising amount of hassle for such a small place (600 or so inhabitants) – a result, perhaps, of the receding lake which has taken with it much of Kalokol's *raison d'être*. If you do stay, Kalokol has a pair of **lodgings**, both very basic. *Skyways* (PO Box 49; ①) is currently renovating its rooms, serves good meals and has the edge over the larger *Kalokol Tours Lodge & Hotel* (PO Box 3; ☎18; Kalokol ①). The latter is overrun by wannabe guides, though it does have space to pitch your tent (Ksh50) and also offers **camel**

A FISHY STORY

In the late 1970s, **Kalokol** acquired a big Norwegian-aided fish-filleting and freezing plant and many Turkana came to the co-operative there looking for a livelihood. Altogether, as many as 20,000 Turkana homed in on the lake's fishing opportunities in the early 1980s. Many were persuaded to give up their herds, but thousands of animals were driven down to the lakeshore while their owners looked for work, bringing ecological disaster to the area around Kalokol and Lodwar. Firewood gathering and over-grazing were the main causes, coupled with the prolonged drought that afflicted much of sub-Saharan Africa at that time. The project was a failure almost from the beginning. The plant's electricity requirements could not possibly be met with the local supply; it ran its cold rooms for just two days. Then the trawler sank. And as these major setbacks were contemplated, the diversion for irrigation of water from the Omo River in Ethiopia began to decrease the lake's supply, leaving the Norwegian jetty high and dry several kilometres from the shore. The project now has to cope with severe under-employment as the lake's fish stocks have plummeted, too.

safaris (the catch being that you have to buy the camel, only to resell it later at half the price). As to **guides**, you will certainly be offered their services in Kalokol, if not already in Lodwar, but beware, they can be expensive and unpleasant stories circulate regarding theft.

While **food** supplies have improved a little with the opening of a few *dukas*, Kalokol doesn't have a lot in this line and it's not a bad idea to bring some fruit, at least, with you from Kitale or Lodwar. Water supplies, too, have become rather erratic and iodine or purifying tablets are essential.

The village is especially good for buying **Turkana crafts** and souvenirs: wonderful (and far too big) baskets, sharp wrist knives and finger knives, rich-smelling, oiled head stools, ostrich shell necklaces, and a whole array of snuff and tobacco horns made of cowhorn (traditionally) or pieces of plastic piping.

If you are ready to leave Kalokol for Kitale, transport of one sort or another usually leaves at midnight, and a number of *matatus* leave throughout the day for Lodwar.

Ferguson's Gulf

To visit the lake, you might want to pay something to one of the children in the village as a guide, though it's easy to find your own way there (just follow the track east). Ferguson's Gulf has been dry since 1988 and the lakeshore itself is now a wild eight-kilometre walk from Kalokol.

Simply being by the lake fills the time here, with the constantly mutating background of the western shore across the bay, as well as the closer prospect of Turkana fishermen, hundreds of species of birds, and the occasional glimpse of crocodile or hippo on the water surface. From a distance, the activity at the water's edge seems silent since the wind whips the sound away westwards, lending the whole scene a bizarre, dream-like quality. Down on the shore you can talk with the children who follow you everywhere and often speak good English. If you make friends, you can be taken looking for snakes (be careful), to see *changaa* brewing (always by women) or, if you're lucky, to a wedding dance. Ordinary teenagers' and children's dances happen several times a week, but are best when there's a full moon: the boys tie cans of stones to their ankles and pretend to ignore the girls' flirting.

The lodge and Longech

It's about 6km through scrub and palm groves from Kalokol to the *Lake Turkana Fishing Lodge* (PO Box 509 Kitale; ☎2142 Radiocall Nairobi; reservations through *Ivory Safaris*, see "Travel Details"). At the time of writing it was closed for renovation, but should reopen in early 1997. Ferguson's Gulf itself has no more than a narrow, knee-deep channel of water, easily forded (ignore the children screaming "Crocodile! Crocodile!" and trying to get you in their boats – unless you want a short boat trip and a new friend). The receding lake, however, has left a number of water-filled craters which attract pelican, flamingo, cormorant and a variety of waders.

The lodge is perched at the end of a sandy spit, offering shade, shelter from the fanheater wind and a beautiful view across the lake (the waters of which are no longer very close). It caters mostly to weekend visitors who arrive by air, and midweek it's often empty. Its **campsite** has moved down to the lakeshore and the price (Ksh500) includes use of the lodge bar and water supply, though with the amount of hassle you can expect from local kids this isn't likely to appeal for very long. In low season, you might negotiate a cheap, midweek stay in the lodge. Alternatively, people may give you bed space in **LONGECH**, the village that stretches a couple of kilometres down the former shoreline, for a few dozen shillings, or for an exchange: "What have you?". Fresh or dried fish is usually available but the only other food is the lodge's expensive set menu.

Swimming

Swimming is generally fine and pleasantly warm and while the crocodiles are often big, they seldom attack (there are few, in any case, near Ferguson's Gulf). They are not rated as man-eaters, since they haven't been widely hunted. This is apparently because their skins aren't up to standard due to the alkaline water. Hippos are certainly much more to be feared, as are the lake's peculiarities of climate.

The tales surrounding the two human skulls that lay (and may still lie) in the sand below the lodge are varied, but they are probably the result of drowning accidents on the remote eastern coastline. One of them was certainly far from ancient. They're a very effective reminder of the precariousness of life here.

Game fishing

When you're tired of wandering around Longech, being mobbed by toddlers, watching the fishermen paddling out on their waterlogged rafts, and the pied kingfishers hover and plunge over the shallows, there are a few active things to do. If you're feeling rich and macho, you can rent **fishing** rods and the lodge's boat and, with luck, land several hundred pounds of Nile perch: the game fishing is rated as some of the most exciting and rewarding in the world. By all accounts, though, the perch don't play properly and almost line up to be landed. Fishermen rate the tiger fish as more of a fighter. The lodge will cook your catch for you (or some of it) and you can add your mark to the fishermen's tales on the walls of the bar.

Central Island National Park

A trip to **Central Island National Park** is highly recommended. This is one of two island national parks in the lake (the other is the less accessible South Island). Central Island is a unique triple volcano poking gauntly out of the water; the island covers just five square kilometres, most of which is taken up by two crater lakes (a third has dried up) hidden behind its rocky shores. One of the lakes is the only known habitat of an ancient species of tilapia, a reminder of the time when Lake Turkana was connected to the Nile. The island is the nesting ground for big colonies of water birds but, like some African Galapagos, it really belongs to the reptiles. Crocodiles breed here in the largest concentration in Africa, and at the right time of year (usually April–May) you can witness the newly hatched croclets breaking out of the nests and sprinting with loud squeaks down to the crater lake where they'll pass their first season. The vegetation is scant, but some of the sheltered lees are over-grown with thick grass and bushes for a short period each year, and the nests are dug beneath this foliage.

Boat trips from the lodge (90min–2hr each way) cost the better part of $120 for a nine-passenger vessel and $55 for a boat that takes up to four only. Alternatively, *Kalokol Tours Lodge & Hotel* (see p.456) can arrange a trip for around Ksh2000 (up to four people) but expect to pay extra for "guiding fees" and transport from and back to Kalokol. The only other option is to walk south, down the lakeshore in front of Longech, and try to hire a fishing boat for the trip. It's worth knowing that the park game warden, who accompanies the lodge's boat trips, will normally want to intervene at this point and generally makes it impossible for you to make the trip privately – in fact the most recent reports suggest the villagers aren't interested. A national parks' entry fee of $15 each ($5 students/children) is liable to be demanded which, in view of the activities of some of the national parks staff in the area, leaves a very bitter taste. If you find a boat the best plan is to go immediately rather than make arrangements in advance. Do be sure, however, that it is thoroughly lake-worthy and that the crew know what they are doing: vicious squalls can blow up fast and it's at least 10km to the island; taking your own compass might be a good idea.

Boats across the lake

Also worth enquiring about, both in Lodwar and Kalokol, is the Fisheries Commission **boat to Loiyangalani**, on the eastern side of the lake, which leaves at the end of each month to collect taxes and fees. The trip takes upwards of eight hours and, should you be given a lift, you are likely to pay through the nose for the privilege. You may also be able to **rent a boat** with a helmsman at Ferguson's Gulf or Eliye Springs (see below) for the same trip, but unless you offer a more than substantial sum (something over Ksh10,000) the fishermen may not consider the risk as being worthwhile. Check the state of the boat before you go. Similarly, there's an outside chance of convincing someone to take you over to **Sibiloi National Park** (see p.473), some 48km due east.

Eliye Springs

ELIYE SPRINGS, 66km from Lodwar, used to be *the* place for travellers on the lakeshore and still attracts the occasional overland truck and self-sufficient 4WD weekenders. **Getting there** and back is the main problem. Failing a lift in Lodwar (where you might wait for days), you might **rent a vehicle** (4WD advisable) with driver at around Ksh1500 for the round trip. However, if you'll be staying overnight or longer at Eliye Springs, don't count on the vehicle coming back to pick you up, as our researchers found out to their cost.

Alternatively, you could **walk** from Ferguson's Gulf or Kalokol: just follow the coast for 55 or so sweltering kilometres, and take plenty of water if you don't fancy the lake's. There may be a Dutch-run **campsite** about halfway, apparently with working fans in its *bandas* – believe it when you see it (and if so, let us know about it). There are crocodiles for much of the way, which makes a night walk ill advised. The other possible route from Kalokol is a little shorter (45–50km); it cuts across the desert inland and is really only feasible overnight, preferably by moonlight. A guide will cost around Ksh1200, and it's one hell of an adventure – bring plenty of water. The only other possibility is to **rent a boat** to or from Ferguson's Gulf for up to Ksh500 per hour; the boat seats four, and the trip takes four to six hours.

Eliye Springs itself easily compensates for the hassles of the journey – a paradisiac place with rustling doum palms watered by hot springs, gorgeous views, and nothing to do except lounge about and swat flies. The *bandas* (③; camping Ksh200), although run-down, are adequate and have comfortable beds. There is also a pool fed by the springs (though swimming in the lake here is safe) and a bar; meals can be prepared if ordered in advance. Plans are afoot to upgrade the *bandas* out of budget range. Also under construction is *Nataba Lodge*, 5km north of Eliye Springs.

Onwards from Lodwar: Lokichokio

It's possible, but by no means easy, to explore the region of Turkana **north of Ferguson's Gulf and Lodwar**. A road, partly paved, turns left across the Turkwel River outside town and goes up to **Lokitaung**, branching left after about 60km for **Lokichokio** (Lokichoggio, often called just **Loki**) and the Sudanese border. Travel here is strictly in convoy but even this does not guarantee safety: 1996 saw an upsurge in shootings and armed banditry on this road, with several fatalities, one as close as 7km to Lodwar. If you do get stopped by bandits, give in to their demands. Clearly, travel here is not advisable, though, if you must, *matatus* leave Lodwar early in the morning and foreign relief vehicles may also consider giving you a lift. Alternatively, you might try approaching *Trackmark Aviation* at Wilson Airport in Nairobi, who operate daily NGO flights to Lokichokio. Loki itself is the major UN aid centre for southern Sudanese fleeing the civil war in Sudan, with hundreds of personnel, a busy supply airfield and numerous bars for tired and frustrated relief workers. There's no accommodation for travellers, so you have to arrange matters with the aid workers. The refugee centre itself is at **Kakuma**, 108km south of Loki on the Lodwar road.

Maralal, the Mathews and East Turkana

This is the exciting route to Lake Turkana. Anyone who has been up to **Loiyangalani** will talk your ear off telling you about the adventures they had on the way. It is one of the most exhilarating and remote journeys you can make.

From Nairobi, the distance is a good deal shorter than to the west coast, but even full tilt on the rough roads it's a two-day **drive**. Saloon cars can make it as often as not, though vicious bedrock greets many a sump, and the car-rental companies aren't enthusiastic, but to be sure of arriving you'll need 4WD (a long-wheel-base Suzuki jeep is ideal). Even then, if you go during the rainy season, you could be held up for 24 hours or more at several points.

The obvious solution is a **camping safari**, though, as with any group travel, this has its limitations. Still, a week isn't long enough for irritations to detract from the experience and most people thoroughly enjoy these trips, coming back loaded with amazing souvenirs and photographs, and stories of weird and wonderful encounters. A major drawback is the brevity of organized trips and the fact that they therefore run to a rough timetable. The oldest, and many think the best, outfit is *Safari Camp Services'* **Turkana Bus**, which runs every other Saturday throughout the year. They have loads of experience – and with the ancient Bedford lorries they use, they need it. The Turkana Bus has participants sitting outwards, which is preferable to a back-to-front-facing seating arrangement. Look out for this when making bookings. *Gametrackers* also use Bedfords; their fortnightly round trips (departing Fridays) via the Chalbi Desert are unique and highly recommended. Other companies are *Special Camping Safaris*, whose trip is longer than most (ten days) and excellent value, and *Bushbuck Adventures*, who run an outstanding eighteen-day "Northern Frontier Expedition". Addresses of **safari operators** are given in the Nairobi chapter on p.118. You can also reserve in advance from abroad or through local agents in your own country – see "Basics", for examples of tour operators.

If your budget is tight but you have time and a flexible attitude, and don't want a spoon-fed adventure, the maximum exposure to Turkana and the north comes from travelling completely independently. This may require some patience, especially at **Maralal**, the terminus for most **public transport**, where you'll have to line up a lift (though some *matatus* continue to **Baragoi**).

The routes to Maralal

Three roads lead to Maralal, the Samburu district town at the end of the first stage of the trip north.

Nyahururu to Maralal: C77

The easiest route, the **C77**, rolls up from Nyahururu via Rumuruti. Each morning at least one **bus** and sometimes a *matatu* or three leave Nyahururu. The C77 bounds over the ranching and cereal country of **Laikipia**, settled after World War I by British soldiers, but once a Maasai stronghold. Most of the settlers have left, and it's a bleak, somewhat forlorn region.

Rumuruti (onomatopoeic Maa for "mosquito") is hardly noticeable any more; it merely marks the end of the paved road. The road to Rumuruti was built in the early 1980s for a minister who lives there and needed to be able to get to and from Nairobi without using a tractor. Maralal was connected with electricity at the same time, because, say the cynics, it would have been too obvious if the lines had only gone to his house. There's some very good game country in the vicinity, and for **night stops** in Rumuruti you might check out the *Tumaini Country Restaurant* which has rooms and claims: "We are famous for making people happy". Equally inviting is the dilapidated *Laikipia Club* with its improbable efforts to preserve the old values.

The road follows the **Ewaso Narok River** for some way beyond Rumuruti, passing the turn-off (after 27km) for the luxurious *Colcheccio Lodge* sited on its banks (information from *Let's Go* in Nairobi, see p.122; ⑨; closed April–June), before climbing, broad and stony, towards Maralal's plateau. On the way, the two other routes join it.

Lake Baringo to Maralal: D370

The second route is the lonely but well-constructed **murram road from the Rift Valley**, which in its earlier stages has breathtaking views back over Lake Baringo and some fascinating Pokot villages on the way. It's only a D road, but don't be discouraged from driving it. There are no buses, though, and you'd be lucky to find a *matatu*. For the best chances of **hitching** success, ask at *Lake Baringo Club* or wait at the Kampi ya Samaki junction (see p.223).

Isiolo to Maralal: A2 and C79/C78

The maddeningly corrugated **A2** comes up from **Isiolo** past Archer's Post, then heads off left as the **C79** past the turn for Wamba, where it becomes the **C78**. Despite a continuation of the A2's washboard surface, the C79/78 has everything to recommend it scenically, including some magnificent desert buttes and sweeping views over the valley of the Ewaso Ngiro River, which flows on through Samburu. 1992 to 1994 saw a few isolated incidents of **banditry** but these appear to have ceased. The garishly decorated Babie Coach runs this route (Isiolo–Maralal), leaving either town every other day, usually packed full of Samburu warriors. *Matatus* run daily in both directions. Your best chances of **hitching a ride** are at the Samburu lodges inside the reserve, or at the Isiolo police barrier.

Maralal

Some of the Laikipia settlers would have dearly liked to set themselves up around the cool, conifer-draped highlands of **MARALAL**. But even before British administrators made this the district capital, Maralal had been a spiritual focus for the **Samburu people** and, despite some dithering, the colonial administrators didn't accede to the settlers' demands.

Maralal is a peculiar town, spread with exaggerated spaciousness around a depression in the hills. Samburu people crowd its dusty streets, with a brilliant collage of skins, blankets, beads, brass, and iron, and a special smell, too – of sour milk, fat, and cattle. The main hotel is called *Buffalo Hotel*. The place sets itself up for Wild West comparisons and even the climate is appropriate – unbelievably dusty, almost always windy, and, at 2220m, sharp enough at night for log fires and braziers. All it needs is wolves – and even there hyenas fill the role.

Of course, the regular arrival of safari lorries means that Maralal has plenty of persistent souvenir salesmen. Yet despite this (or perhaps because of it – very few *wazungu* stay more than a few hours), it's a good place to get to know the Samburu and especially worthwhile on Christian holidays. Many Samburu around the town have become Catholics and even the colourful procession on Palm Sunday – mostly women in their thousands, waving branches and leaves – is riveting.

A notable resident of Maralal until recently was the travel writer and Arabist, **Wilfred Thesiger**, who had made the town his adoptive home and had adopted a

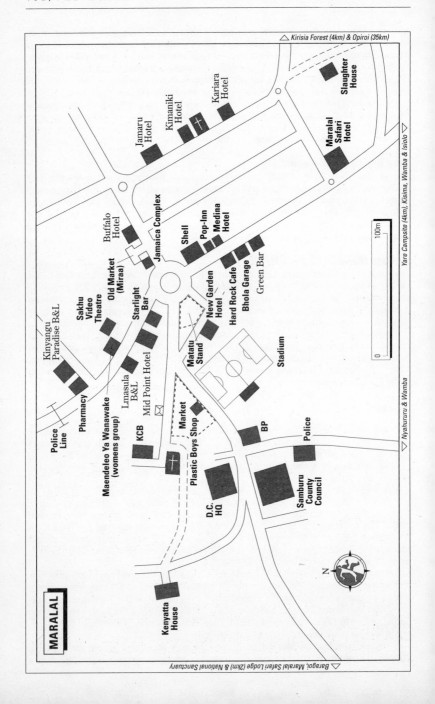

MARALAL

△ *Kirisia Forest (4km) & Opiroi (35km)*

Slaughter House

Kariara Hotel

Kimaniki Hotel

Jamaru Hotel

Maralal Safari Hotel

▷ *Yare Campsite (4km), Kisima, Wamba & Isiolo*

Buffalo Hotel

Jamaica Complex

Shell

Pop-Inn

Medina Hotel

Old Market (Miraa)

Hard Rock Cafe

Bhola Garage

Green Bar

Kinyangu Paradise B&L

Sakhu Video Theatre

Starlight Bar

New Garden Hotel

Pharmacy

Lmasula B&L

Mid Point Hotel

Matatu Stand

Stadium

Police Line

Maendeleo Ya Wanawake (womens group)

KCB

Market

Plastic Boys Shop

BP

Police

▷ *Nyahururu & Wamba*

D.C. HQ

Samburu County Council

100m

0

N

Kenyatta House

△ *Baragoi, Maralal Safari Lodge (2km) & National Sanctuary*

number of orphaned boys. Thesiger made his name with his accounts of the Shiite Arabs of the southern Iraqi marshes and the Bedu of the Arabian peninsula, and followed up these achievements with several books on Kenya, notably *My Kenya Days*. Among the Samburu he found equally congenial companions for his old age, and was well respected throughout the district for his services to them.

If you forget to visit the liberally signposted **Kenyatta House**, don't fret. The fact that Kenyatta was detained here in 1961 before his final release doesn't really improve the interest of this unexceptional and empty bungalow. It seems a pity it's a national monument and not some family's home.

Guides and crafts

On arriving in Maralal, you will invariably attract a litany of remarkably persistent and annoying "guides" offering evening excursions to see **traditional dancing** in nearby *manyattas*, or else visits to local **Samburu witch doctors and blacksmiths** and a nearby **Turkana village**. Bear in mind that many wily con artists are at work in town, so use your judgement before accepting, making it absolutely clear how much you are prepared to pay, and bring plenty of chewing tobacco and *miraa* for the old men. The reason behind this unwelcome attention is the town's high unemployment, caused by a massive influx of previously nomadic herders following the drought of 1982–85 and the subsequent explosion in poaching, which led many Turkana and Samburu to lose their livestock.

A recent attempt to tame the guides by organizing them into disciplined groups is the **Plastic Boys' Co-operative Self Help Group**, so named after the street children who used to make dolls and trinkets using plastic bags and cartons. They have now progressed, under the guidance of the Kenya Wildlife Service and various NGOs, to carving and selling woodcrafts, spears and other touristic items. Their shop is in the market, and they should be able to sort you out with some of the more reliable guides, should you need one. For more "authentic" souvenirs, the women's group *Maendeleo Ya Wanawake* has a shop selling distinctly used calabashes, headrests and dolls. They can also point you in the right direction should you want Samburu beadwork.

Maralal National Sanctuary and Safari Lodge

Maralal Safari Lodge (PO Box 70; ☎0368/2060), signposted two or three kilometres out of town on the Lake Turkana road, is comfortable and under-subscribed – and very attractive with its huge wooden chalet-style rooms (⑦ low, ⑧ high; Kenya residents half-price and frequent special offers). Your patronage is welcome in the bar and restaurant, and you can sit on the terrace to watch the animals from the surrounding **Maralal National Sanctuary** and Yamo Forest (zebra, baboon, impala, eland, warthog, buffalo and hyena) filing up the hill to the concrete water hole a few metres away.

Accommodation

Setting aside the excellent lodge in the Maralal National Sanctuary, Maralal has a number of **cheap lodgings**, the more acceptable of which are listed here; the mid-range *Yare Safari Club* also has **camping facilities**.

Buffalo Hotel (PO Box 28; ☎0368/2028). The main travellers' haunt, decent but more expensive than usual and not for light sleepers – its infamous back bar closes when the last punter hits the floor. ③.

Green Bar (PO Box 7). Friendly with a decent restaurant. Singles only. ①.

Jamaru Hotel (PO Box 245; ☎0368/2215). Maralal's largest and newest, rather spartan but with a good, busy restaurant. ③.

Kariara Hotel (PO Box 68). The cheapest and best in town, this is also Maralal's only two-storey hotel. It has basic but clean rooms, festooned with bougainvillea, all with mosquito nets but bring your own padlock. Get a room on top – on a good morning you can see Mount Kenya. ①.

Kimaniki Hotel (PO Box 117; ☎0368/2444). Rooms behind a noisy bar-disco to suit night owls. ①.

Kinyangu Paradise B&L (PO Box 193; ☎0368/2297). Another local joint, its bar is open till midnight and is frequented by Samburu and Turkana tribesmen. ①.

Mid Point Hotel (PO Box 93; ☎0368/2254). Formerly the *Lokudishu*, acceptable if not overly clean. Singles only. ①.

Yare Safari Club and Campsite (PO Box 281; ☎/fax 0368/2295; reservations PO Box 63006, Nairobi, ☎02/725610, fax 02/213445). Just over 4km down the Isiolo road, beyond Wilfred Thesiger's old home, *Yare* offers beautiful thatched *bandas*, a good restaurant and well-stocked bar, and "traditional" Samburu dancing in the evenings. Camel safaris can be arranged. Singles are overpriced but the campsite is fine and you can hire a tent too (Ksh400). ④.

Eating, drinking and entertainment

Maralal boasts a surprising number of good **restaurants** as well as the usual run of cheap and filling eating houses. The popular Somali-run *Pop-Inn Hotel* is easily the best, with a great atmosphere, solid breakfasts, pilau and *dengo* (a delicately spiced stew of root vegetables and small beans). Also recommended is the anomalous *Hard Rock Café* which specializes in beefburgers, chips and espresso coffee. *Maralal Safari Hotel* serves *githeri* to Samburu warriors with lolloping reggae in the background. *Jamaica Complex Hotel* is big on *nyama choma*, whilst the *New Garden Hotel*, by the *matatu* stand, has huge portions of Swahili food (*mchele* stew a speciality) at criminally low prices.

A night spent in Maralal's numerous **bars** can be exhilarating, infuriating, dangerous or just plain daft. *Buffalo Hotel* is the most popular: a heady place with skulking expats, wheedling con merchants and a host of bizarre local nuts. Round the back is its late-night video bar with footage of reggae and soukous bands to drown in – unless they're showing *Delta Force* or *King Solomon's Mines* yet again. There's a real **cinema** opposite *Starlight Bar* which usually gets in some genuine celluloid on Saturdays. The bar itself is a straightforward drinking den full of broken stools and fallen pride. Predictably enough, *Jamaica Complex* resounds to baseline slow jam and rootsy reggae, while *Kimaniki* hosts the dancey *Club 24* from Friday to Sunday.

MARALAL INTERNATIONAL CAMEL DERBY

The Maralal International Camel Derby provides a strange, and by all accounts hugely enjoyable, weekend out at the end of October. Anyone may enter, or just spectate, as dozens of competitors from East Africa, Europe, Japan and the Arab Emirates battle it out over amateur and professional stages. The event is based at the *Yare* site, and entry costs $30 per person plus $125 for the hire of a camel (with handler) over the whole event. For more details, contact *Yare Safari Club* (see "Accommodation") or GKCER Secretariat, PO Box 47874, Nairobi (☎02/544770, fax 02/545645).

Other practicalities and moving on

If you're **continuing north**, note that Maralal is the last place where you can **change money** – at the smart new *KCB* bank (open Mon–Fri, plus Sat morning), at *Yare Safari Club*, or at the *Maralal Safari Lodge* (where they don't have much cash); where there's a **post office** (Mon–Fri 8am–1pm & 2–5pm); and where you can be reasonably sure of getting **petrol** if you're driving. And if **beer** is important to you (and it can assume great importance up in the desert), then stock up on that, too, before following the route described next.

If you don't have your own vehicle, you may find a source of **rides onward** at the campsite or the lodge, but you're more likely to catch vehicles by staying in town and spreading the word at the petrol stations. Let it be known you are willing to travel in the back of a lorry; many people will assume you're not. Supply lorries do go up to Loiyangalani and your chances of – eventually – scoring a lift are good. Land Rover *matatus* leave for Baragoi around noon, and for Nyahururu and Isiolo at 10am or 11am. Nakuru is served daily by *Nyayo Bus*, and Nairobi by *Goldline Bus* which leaves nightly at 2am.

Wamba and the Mathews Range (the Lenkiyio Hills)

In terms of the vastness of the north, the **Mathews Range** is virtually on Maralal's doorstep. The range, most of which is a forest reserve, is impressively wild hill country, with Mathew Peak (*Ol Doinyo Lenkiyio*) rising to 2375m. Lower down, the mountains are heavily cloaked in forest and thick bush; unusual vegetation includes "living fossil" cycad plants, giant cedars and podocarpus; and among the animal life, you can look out for (but shouldn't expect to meet) small numbers of black rhinos – every one of them known and tracked, for its own safety, by forest guards and their Samburu staff – and really outstanding butterflies. This is first-rate walking and exploring country for hardy travellers, but you need to be fully self-sufficient, which includes having all your food requirements.

First target is **WAMBA**, a one-street town 5km off the C78/79 highway, roughly midway between Maralal and Isiolo. You can get the odd *matatu* here from Maralal, or use the *Babie Coach* which passes by the Wamba turning just after midday (heading out from Maralal one day, coming back from Isiolo the next). Wamba's main focus is its large, modern Catholic hospital outside town. *Saudia Lodge*, in town, is pretty well the only **B&L**, with clean, pleasant and very cheap rooms. There are a few *dukas*, though they have no fuel and little in the way of fresh food, only basic fruit or veg. You might try *Imani Bar & Restaurant* which serves the usual limited range of stews and a reasonable *githeri*.

The big mountain you can see outside town (9km to the peak as the crow flies) is **Warges**. Guides from Wamba will take you up there, though they'll stress how full of wild animals it is and how much their lives (not yours of course) are at risk. If you have a serious interest in witchcraft, one of Kenya's most respected **witch doctors** lives in the shadow of the mountain. Forget the guides – he is resolutely *not* a tourist attraction; instead, make discreet enquiries with the Kenya Wildlife Service rangers who regularly pass through Wamba, or else, if your Samburu is good enough, with one of the young *morani*, but make sure you are accompanied by someone who really knows the place.

Kitich Camp and campsite

The main route from Wamba, however, is towards the bush-luxury Kitich Camp and the nearby Kitich campsite. If you're four-wheel-driving, you basically set off towards Barsaloi (Parsaloi) along a rough road that commences just half a kilometre along the Wamba access road. From here you drive 15km, then turn right and do a further 17km to **Ngilai** (follow the yellow stones). Some 6km further, you fork left to ford the **Ngeng River**. With the mountains looming all around, this is the way into the heart of the Mathews: the campsite is a couple of kilometres up the track on the other side, and *Kitich Camp* some 4km further north. Note that there's no fuel along the way and normally none for sale at Kitich.

If you're on foot, find a guide in Wamba and set off cross-country, direct to Ngilai, crossing several *luggas*, and seeing almost nobody on the way. The distance is about 30km and an exhausting day's walk. Ngilai has a Lutheran mission (2km out of the centre to the north) and a single shop, which may put you up for the night if you can't make it the final 8km to the campsite before nightfall.

The **campsite** is pleasant and shady, with showers and toilet, and water available from the nearby pools. You pay at *Kitich Camp*, a three- to four-kilometre walk away; but if you have to walk up there, at least you can fix on the cold drinks at the bar as you slog up. Note that there is no food available at the campsite and, while you can go angling in the river, there's a limit to how much catfish a person can stand.

Kitich Camp itself seems a miracle of sensitive planning, nestled unobtrusively on the river bank beneath towering giant figs. Facilities are basic, yet it's extremely comfortable. Generator electricity is reserved for the freezer, and the ten double tents are equipped with kerosene lamps, bucket showers and long-drop toilets (PO Box 14869 Nairobi, ☎02/444288; or reserve through *Let's Go Travel*, address p.122; Ksh6200 per person). Transport from Samburu costs Ksh10,950 per vehicle, from Wamba, Ksh6120.

If you want to walk any distance, you're strongly advised to take a guide, either from the camp or from the campsite (where they'll seek you out if you're camping). There are some fine **excursions**, including short walks up the valley to wonderful, deep, rock pools where you can swim. The area around the Ngeng Valley is thick with wildlife. There are elephants everywhere, buffalos, hyenas, leopards and plenty of more innocuous game. You really have to watch yourself, especially if you go down near the river. It's a lot of fun, but take care .

North from Maralal: into Samburu-land

The first stretch of the road **north from Maralal** climbs higher into the **podocarpus forests** of the national sanctuary. Twenty kilometres from the lodge, a detour to the left takes you through the village of **Poror**, past a large wheat-farming project and, after 6km, to the dramatic scimitar edge of the **Losiolo Escarpment**. The Rift Valley is, by its nature, bordered from end to end by vertiginous escarpments and each one seems more impressive than the last. But Losiolo is not just an escarpment, it's a colossal amphitheatre dropping down to Suguta Valley, 2000m below. Try to get here very early in the morning – it is awesome. From Poror, the road north is increasingly rough and hot. Settlements are few but evenly scattered: the first is **Marti**, which has a few basic *chai* kiosks, one or two Somali-run *dukas*, a mission and a police station.

Baragoi

BARAGOI lies in the heart of the barren Elbarta plains, watered only occasionally by run-off from the Samburu Hills and Ndoto Mountains. The river which skirts the town is dry for much of the year, and in times of drought the pits which are dug into it by women fetching water can reach depths of over six metres (20ft). It's a blistering, dusty and unforgiving land, dotted here and there with sun-bleached bones and populated only by red-robed semi-nomadic herders armed with spears or bows and arrows to protect their cattle, goats and camels against rustlers.

First settled in the 1930s, Baragoi retains its original function as the region's major livestock market, yet things have changed a lot over the last few years. A construction boom has spawned dozens of one-storey cinder-block buildings in which half a dozen new hotels, numerous bars and restaurants have taken root. A clue to this sudden expansion lies in the name of one bar: *Bosnia Wines & Spirits*. Shortly after the UN resolved to send peace-keepers to former Yugoslavia, a 900-strong Kenyan battalion was despatched to help patrol a cease-fire line around the self-proclaimed (and now defunct) Serbian Republic of Krajina. News of the detachment spread quickly, particularly of the astronomical sums to be made serving in UNPROFOR (soldiers were paid up to $1200 a month, compared with the average Kenyan monthly wage of perhaps $75). Samburu warriors from around Baragoi and Lesriken, 25km east, were quick to enlist for the second and third missions to Bosnia, the last of which returned in 1994.

THE SAMBURU

The Samburu are historically close to the Maasai. Their languages are nearly the same (both Maa) and culturally they are virtually indistinguishable to an outsider. Both came from the region around northwest Turkana in the seventeenth century: the Samburu turned east, establishing themselves in the mountain pastures and spreading on to the plains; the Maasai continued south.

Improvements in health and in veterinary care over the last century have swelled the Samburu population and the size of their **herds**. Many in the driest areas of their range in the northeast have turned to **camel herding** as a better insurance against drought than cattle. Since livestock is the basis of relations between in-laws (through the giving of "bridewealth" from the husband to his wife's family), having camel herds has disrupted patterns of marriage and initiation into new generations because camel herds increase more slowly than cattle herds. And the reality on the ground is all about twice as confusing as it sounds on paper. Memories, recording every transaction over successive generations, are phenomenal (the Samburu have only just begun to acquire writing).

The Samburu **age-set system**, like many others in Africa, is a complicated arrangement to which a number of anthropologists have devoted lifetimes of investigation. Essentially it's a gerontocracy (rule by old men) and the elders are assured, by the system they manipulate, of having the first choice of young women to marry. The promiscuous and jingoistic – but, by Samburu reckoning, still juvenile – warriors are forced to wait, sometimes until their thirties, before initiation into elderhood, marriage and children brings them a measure of real respect. In turn, they perpetuate the system on their own sons, who have everything to gain by falling in line and much to lose if they withdraw their stake in the tradition, perhaps by going to Nairobi or the coast to look for work.

For **women** the situation is very different. They are married at fifteen or sixteen, immediately after their clitoridectomy and before they have much chance to rebel. But they may continue affairs with their *morani* boyfriends, the unmarried juniors of their new, much older husbands. They spend more of their lives married than their male peers, which accounts for how most men have more than one wife. This **polygamy** in itself seems to be an important motivating force for the whole generation system. For the warriors and their girlfriends, there's a special young people's language – a vocabulary of conspiratorial songs and idioms – which has to be modified with the initiation of every age-set, so that it's kept secret from the elders.

This highly intricate system is now beginning to collapse in many areas, with a widespread **disruption of pre-colonial ways**; even the circumcision initiation of boys to warriorhood is less of a mass ceremony. While herds are still the principal criterion of wealth, people in some areas are turning to agriculture: after the rains you can see planting holes at the roadside in certain places, with corn the main crop. There are enormous problems for such initiatives, especially when there's no aid or government support, but they do show that the standard stereotypes don't always fit. As for the *morani* warriors, opportunities for cattle-raiding and lion-killing have diminished with more efficient policing of their territories. For some, tourist hunting has taken over. You can even see *morani* in full rig striding past the hotels on the Indian Ocean beaches.

The rewards were indeed beyond belief for the veterans, and for men who in the past had been expected to kill a lion in order to prove their manhood, the ferocity of the fighting left them unfazed. What did shock them, however, were the atrocities they witnessed, committed against ordinary civilians and now the subject of war crimes tribunals.

The Bosnian experience has not been without its problems. For some, sudden wealth has led to alcoholism (hard spirits have become affordable), even cocaine abuse, and on arriving in Baragoi you'll be assailed by the usual band of desperate types and "guides" who missed out on their brothers' good fortunes. But it's a fascinating place nonetheless, and well worth a day or two of anyone's time.

Livestock and courting

Despite the UN money, life for the majority remains a hard and restless search for water and pasturage, often violently conflicting with other herders grazing the same territory. Down off Bosnia Street to the northwest of town is the **livestock market**. It's a gentle, unhurried affair where old men with gnarled hands and ostrich plumes in their hair play *ngiles* with stones and seeds on "boards" carved out of the bone-dry earth as they wait for business to arrive. Here, Samburu deal with Rendille and Turkana, some of whom may have spent up to seven days walking their livestock down from the lake. In turn the Samburu, and sometimes Turkana, trek eastward for five and a half days to reach Isiolo where, with luck, they resell their animals at a profit.

If the herder is of **courting** age (Samburu *moran*; Turkana *lmoli*), Isiolo is also where he buys the beads, necklaces and bangles with which to woo his bride. Once back home, he will not only present her with these gifts but mime and sing the attributes of the animals which will provide him and his family with their means of survival. For these semi-nomads, animals are the source of all wealth, and the young herder must represent them favourably to attract the attention and confidence of a bride. To this end, he selects a single castrated bull, camel or goat which he then mimics, indicating with his hands and gestures its size, colour, the shape of its horns, even its temperament. There's a comical side to all this, too, for even the poorest herder, whose beast may only be a goat with lopsided horns, must dance to attract a spouse and presumably does this by raising a few smiles with a self-deprecating parody of his goat. Dances are held almost nightly in the *manyattas* on the outskirts of town, wild and hugely enjoyable events at which you are bound to be made welcome. Cameras, of course, are generally not acceptable. Ask around at the market or else try one of the *manyattas* behind the primary school.

Practicalities

The best **accommodation** in town is the basic but clean *Morning Star Guest House* (PO Box 37; singles only, Ksh200 per person) with a decent restaurant and bar. *Bosnia Wines & Spirits*, also singles only, is spartan but clean and cheap (Ksh140 per person); the beds are narrow but have the benefit of nets. *Mount Ngiro B&L* distinguishes itself in having the only doubles in Baragoi; it's full-board only and comparatively expensive, though bargaining is possible (③).

The *Morning Star* has a pleasant courtyard and good, scalding *chai*, but by far the best **bar and restaurant** is *Zaire Hotel* on Nachola Road, a colourful and cheerful place, open till 11pm, with Baragoi's only really cold drinks, Zairiean music and the weird sight of Samburu and Turkana herders in full rig supping tea and nibbling scones. It may have rooms to let in future. For simple and filling staples like *githeri*, the *Flora Hotel* is cheap.

There are no official **moneychanging** facilities, but there is a **post office** (Mon–Fri only), an **Oxfam** office and a decent **car mechanic** (*Dalfer Welders*, opposite the post office). Emergency **petrol supplies** can be had, at a price, from *Mount Ngiro Supplies*. There's talk of a new Bosnia-financed petrol station at the head of, curiously enough, Bosnia Street.

Moving on from Baragoi

Baragoi marks the end of **northbound** public transport, which means you have to line up a lift with supply lorries, mission jeeps and the like. The police station on the north side of town is helpful. You might also find a *Turkana Bus* safari lorry to take you to Loiyangalani: a generous tip for the driver and cook(s) is in order. Going **south to Maralal** is easy if uncomfortable: two Land Rover *matatus* leave daily from outside the post office (7am & 9am).

South Horr and Kurungu Camp

Baragoi marks the end of the forbidding Elbarta plains, as the road now climbs into ravine and mountain country, fantastically green if there's been rain. Some 30km from Baragoi, a track to the left towards Nyero, signed by a red post box, leads to *Desert Rose Camel Safaris* (booking via *Safari Camp Services*, PO Box 44801, Barclays Plaza, Nairobi; ☎02/330130, fax 02/212160; $660 per group per day, plus $94 per person per day), who organize luxury camel treks of six days or more in the surrounding *luggas* and hills and up to Lake Turkana, with vehicle back-up and two nights at their lodge.

There's a positive jungle all year round at the oasis village of **SOUTH HORR**, wedged tightly between the Nyiru and Ol Doinyo Mara mountains. It's a somnolent contrast to Baragoi, with a few cheap *hotelis* and cold drinks at *Nhiro Serima Bar*, but only rarely beer. If you stay the night, you've a choice of half a dozen basic **B&Ls** (all ①). There is good, dirt-cheap **camping** at the *Forest Department Campsite*, located up a rough trail to the left of the road a kilometre before South Horr. Facilities consist of long-drops, an *askari*, and a river for drinking water, bathing and washing the dust out of your clothes. This site, a short walk from South Horr village where most vehicles stop, is a good base for meeting up with supply or mission vehicles in hopes of a lift north.

Well worth a visit in the village itself is SALTLICK (Semi-Arid Lands Training and Livestock Improvement Centres Kenya), which concerns itself with supporting the local pastoralist Samburu communities via honey-production projects and cash-crop experiments involving the Senegalese acacia gum tree. If anything, it's a mine of information on Samburu culture. For a more intimate experience, you might try asking about the **camel market** which is held on occasions a few kilometres south of the village at a roadside well.

Kurungu Camp

For a place to bump into motorized tourists, the delightful **Kurungu Camp**, a half-dozen kilometres past the village along the sandy, vegetation-festooned track, is preferable to Loiyangalani. This is a well-kept **campsite** operated by *Safari Camp Services*, surrounded by flowering bushes and shaded by distinguished old trees. The *bandas* are derelict and supplies of cold drinks can't be relied on, but there are bucket showers – get in the queue early on arrival. Camping out here (about Ksh50) is fabulous.

It is worth spending a couple of nights at Kurungu and exploring the **mountain forest** around you – it hides lots of wildlife, including elephants and buffaloes, and it bursts with birds and butterflies. You can be guided by Samburu *morani* up the lower slopes or, more ambitiously, on the stiff hike up to **Nyiru peak**, which has stunning views over Lake Turkana. If you entertain thoughts of any more daring expeditions in the region, you should know that **camel hire** should cost in the region of Ksh600–1000 per beast per day. Be careful if you're embarking on anything way off the beaten track. Many men who will sell themselves as **guides** have led surprisingly sheltered lives; they don't know the desert like the backs of their hands any more than you do. Real knowledge and experience are sought after and more expensive.

At Kurungu, you are also likely to have the (mixed) pleasure of **Samburu dancing**, especially if on an organized safari. For about Ksh100–200, you are allowed into the arena to take as many pictures of the dancers as you want, although they do not mask their displeasure. Scepticism is briefly swamped by the hour-long jamboree that follows. A troupe of *morani* go through an informal dance programme, flirtatiously threatening the audience with whoops and pounces. Young women and girls join in –

sometimes with the evident disapproval of older Samburu onlookers – to be proposi-tioned with whisks of the men's ochred hair-dos. Meanwhile, there's the constant offer-ing of necklaces, trinkets, spears, pouches and more photo poses, to be negotiated individually with those who are too old or too young to dance.

The *morani* dance and dance and no one feels the money was badly spent. But is it authentic? Does it mean anything? What do *they* think? It's extremely difficult to disen-tangle motives from relations, and better to forget about the fleeting illusion of "authen-ticity" on these occasions, accepting the dances for what they are: vivid, funny, dynamic entertainment.

Down to the lake

After South Horr, the track opens onto featureless plains of black lava with the massif of Kulal dominating the northern horizon. The lava is hard and jagged – a vicious test for tyres – and the track itself, pummelled to a fine dust, can become a quagmire after a rainstorm. The numerous stone circles and cairns around here are probably the remains of ancient settlements and burial sites.

The lake appears – just when you were beginning to wonder – as the road drops away in front: a stunning vista of shot blues and greens, with the black, castellate silhouette of South Island hanging as if suspended between lake and sky. Descending a little further, there are safe bays for swimming, and, an hour or so later, you reach Loiyangalani.

Loiyangalani and around

LOIYANGALANI – "the place of the trees" – is a vague agglomeration of grass huts, mud huts, tin shacks, a police station, a school, a pair of campsites, "the mission" and "the lodge". It's a small community far from metropolitan Kenya, without newspapers and often without beer (a real measure of its isolation!). The land around is mostly barren and stony, scattered with the carcasses of livestock, with palm trees and acacias clustered around the settlement's life source, a **spring** of fresh water.

The village came into being in the early 1960s with the *Oasis Lodge* and its airstrip, and the Italian mission to the **Elmolo** people, a small group who live by hunting and fishing on the southeastern lakeshore. Somali raiders ransacked both establishments in 1965, but since then the two institutions have been left alone. The mission is now starting to thrive and its net of influence has reached most of Loiyangalani's more permanent inhabitants, especially the children who come to the school.

For all its apparent drabness, the village isn't dull. When you've had enough of haggling through the campsite fence for artefacts and fantastic quartz, onyx, amethyst, and other semi-precious stones collected from Kulal – as well as the odd fossil – you can wander over to the springs and the school. You'll inevitably pick up a cluster of teenagers – Turkana, Elmolo, Samburu, Rendille – eager to practise their English. Swahili has never made much impact up here and English is the usual teaching medium. Education is perhaps the most positive of the major influences – including state interference and tourist money – bringing pressure to bear on local customs and traditions.

The **mission**, while changing the structure of traditional society (through conver-sions to Catholicism, which have been particularly effective among the Elmolo), is at the same time helping to make local people sufficiently independent to resist unwanted change and to make choices about their future, by helping to set up income-generating schemes such as the shops, some of the boats and a new service station. Some of the Italian missionaries are extremely open and informative and, although you can't be assured they'll have any time to meet you, the chance to talk to them about Loiyangalani may well arise if you're around for a few days. Guilt-ridden travellers, even the most atheist, who want to help bridge the north-south divide so starkly portrayed in the town, could probably do worse than shell out a few shillings' donation for the mission's projects.

Loiyangalani's **"beach"** is a grubby strip a couple of kilometres down the road. People do swim, but the dingy water is hardly enticing. Many of the loose stones on the shore also shelter scorpions (not serious) and carpet vipers (very serious), both of which seem to be absent from the campsite.

In the evenings, **dances** often take place around Loiyangalani: informal, energetic, pogoing performances for fun, always worth checking out. Track them down by the booming sound of collective larynxes. It's the girls who ask the boys to dance, and you're welcome to join in (no cameras or torches unless permission is expressly given and paid for).

Practicalities

The **lodge** (reservations through *Northern Kenya Lodges Ltd*, see "Travel Details", p.497; FB ⑨; closed mid-May to mid-July) tries to be exclusive, usually charging at least Ksh300 daily entrance fee to casual visitors to discourage them from drinking the entire stock of beer; the fee at least entitles you to swim in its two, jealously guarded pools. The accommodation, however, in wind-blown and rather basic "chalets", is certainly not worth the expense. More useful is the lodge's **car-rental service**, ideal for visiting Sibiloi National Park (see p.473), with daily fees at around Ksh17,500 for 200km. Fishing boats can be rented for Ksh1800 per hour, with fishing licences an additional Ksh400.

Loiyangalani also has some budget-oriented places to camp or stay. After a long spell of dereliction, *El Molo Lodge* should be reopening its concrete *bandas* at the end of 1996 (reservations through PO Box 34710 Nairobi, ☎02/723177; probably ③), and in the meantime offers cheap camping (Ksh200) and the use of its pool (Ksh200). The *bandas* at *Sunset Strip* have collapsed but the *Strip* offers pretty enough camping sites between the palms (same price as *El Molo*, if you can find anyone to pay it to), which give some shelter from the wind lashing down from the fortress bulk of Kulal. The site is marred only by the high wire perimeter fence – built to allow you to leave your gear with some confidence. There are no facilities to speak of. Alternatively, *Gametrackers* operate a paradisiac campsite with thatch *bandas*, 7km to the south of Loiyangalani. They only use it for two or three days each week, so you may be able to do a deal with the caretaker.

Loiyangalani has one B&L, plus one or two minimal *hotelis* and *dukas*. The misnamed *Cold Drink Hotel* (its fridge broke down in 1984; ①) has eighteen cleanish rooms at the back, each with a kerosene lamp and some interesting murals, but **food** is cheaper and drinks colder from the *Hilton Hotel* opposite and *South Island Hotel* a little further down. If there are beers in town, you'll find them at *El Molo Bar*.

South Island National Park

If you want to visit **South Island National Park** ($15, $5 students/children), you should ask about a trip at the lodge first, but spread the word and you may find a much cheaper means of getting there. It's a thirty-kilometre round trip, so the weather needs to be fair. By all accounts it's one of the weirdest places to stay a night, in the unlikely event of the warden allowing you to do so; its volcanic vents, rising some 1000 feet above sea level, give out a ghostly luminous glow that has long put off local fishermen from venturing there.

Mount Kulal

On dry land, you could make a stab at climbing **Mount Kulal**, if you have the energy. There are two summits, joined by a narrow and dicey ridge. The climb itself, once

THE ELMOLO

The people of Loiyangalani with the best claim to be the original inhabitants are the **Elmolo**, about which much has been written and little said. In Kenya, they're famous for being famous. Dubbed "the smallest tribe in the world" (in number, not size), they are the only hunter-gatherer community in the country who can be visited quite easily and who don't resent the intrusion.

The Elmolo call themselves *el-Des*; their usual name comes from the Samburu *loo molo onsikirri*, "the people who eat fish". They once inhabited South Island and, until recently, a small island in Elmolo Bay, but their main settlement now is a gathering of grass huts on the torrid shore 8km north of Loiyangalani. Most of the 450-strong community live here, partly by **fishing** and the occasional heroic crocodile or hippo hunt, partly by **cash receipts** from tourist visitors.

The Elmolo are enigmatic. At the time of Teleki's discovery of the lake, they spoke a **Cushitic** language, the family to which Somali and Rendille belong. Recent linguistic research on historical migrations points to their having arrived on the shores of Lake Turkana at a very early time – perhaps over 2000 years ago. They seem to have no tradition of livestock-herding, which might have been kept up if they had turned, like the Turkana, to fishing as a supplement. Today they speak **Samburu** and have started to intermarry with them. This, as well as the mission's influence, has been quite significant in raising their numbers (from less than 200 twenty years ago) and also in diluting their cultural identity: once strictly monogamous, polygamy isn't uncommon now; they send some children to the school in Loiyangalani as weekly boarders. And on the slope, right behind the village, a new Catholic church looms ominously.

All this signals the final curtain for a culture and history that has been largely ignored or refuted. The conventional wisdom about hunter-gatherers in Kenya is that they are often the descendants of pastoralists who lost their herds. But if the Elmolo are, as some say, pastoral Rendille who took to fishing in order to survive, then it's strange that they have never tried to replace their herds. For without herds, they could never hope to pay bridewealth for wives from their non-fishing neighbours in the traditional way. A better explanation, and one favoured by the Elmolo themselves, is that their people have always been fishermen and hunters, and, until very recently, pressures from other tribes, particularly the Turkana, had pushed them almost to the point of annihilation.

At the end of the twentieth century, the Elmolo fishing culture is beginning to rub off on other ethnic groups and even the Samburu have started to eat fish. As long as twenty years ago, Peter Matthiessen could write in *The Tree Where Man was Born*: "The Samburu and Turkana may linger for weeks at a time as guests of the Llo-molo, who have plenty of fish and cannot bear to eat with all these strangers hanging around looking so hungry. Other tribes, the Llo-molo say, know how to eat fish better than they know how to catch them . . . 'We have to feed them,' one Llo-molo says, 'so that they will feel strong enough to go away.' "

The Elmolo are charming, hospitable people, though how they survive in their chosen environment is almost beyond belief. Outwardly similar in dress and appearance to the other people of the area, they are slightly smaller, but the bowed legs which are supposed to be the characteristic result of their diet seem to be confined to the older people – you might have thought all that fish would give them strong bones.

you're on the right track, is straightforward enough, but talk to some gem-hunters who may guide you up. And note that, although Kulal seems to tower over Loiyangalani, two days is barely enough to walk to the base and back: you really will need transport unless you're very determined and suitably equipped. The views from the top are fabulous, with the lake on one side and the searing Chalbi Desert on the other, and bird-watchers have the added incentive of a rare species of **white-eye** peculiar to the mountain. Bring all the **water** you will need, as there are no supplies on the mountain.

Elmolo Bay

At **Elmolo Bay**, 8km north of Loiyangalani, lives the last viable community of **Elmolo people** (see box opposite). To visit them, you pay a fixed fee per person, depending on the size of your party (about Ksh300 at the last check), to the headman, to be given the freedom of the village, including the right to take photos and a trip to the island opposite the bay to look for crocodiles. During the week, the children are nearly all at school in Loiyangalani; they come home at the weekend, which is the best time to visit. Impromptu dances start, little hands are slipped engagingly into yours for a walk around the low, grass huts. Older people stare rather blankly from the entrances. The ground is a litter of fishbones, string, shreds of cloth. Someone sets up a stall of beadwork and gourds – apparently identical to what you could find up and down the Rift Valley. It's a novel, disturbing experience which contrives to be stage-managed and voyeuristic at the same time. Because of their friendliness, their small number and the increased interest shown in them, the Elmolo risk being taken advantage of by tourists. However, the usual tourist rules apply: ask before you take pictures and be generous with your time and your wallet.

Over on the island – which, because of Lake Turkana's lowering, you can now reach by a causeway – you should see **crocodiles** if you walk softly and approach the far shore cautiously. On the island's stern, rocky beaches, the remains of Elmolo fish picnics and old camps can be found everywhere; one find was a nearly fossilized hippo tusk from some long-ago feast. Today, a hippo hunt has to be organized discreetly (strictly speaking, hunting hippos is illegal) and usually takes place further north on the marshier shores below Moiti Hill. Hippos have gone from Loiyangalani.

Sibiloi National Park

Sibiloi National Park (daily fee $15, $5 students/children) provides a powerful temptation to go further north – even for jumping ship if you came up to Turkana by safari tour. The park is in theory accessible even by saloon, but you shouldn't risk it without careful enquiries. If you're looking for a lift at Loiyangalani, a steady trickle of sturdier vehicles does pass through, heading for the park, and you shouldn't have too much difficulty returning south again.

Discoveries in human prehistory

Sibiloi was created to protect the sites of numerous remarkable **hominid fossil** finds that have been made since 1968 by Richard Leakey's, and latterly Kamoya Kimeu's, team from the University of Nairobi. The park, more than 1600 square kilometres of rock desert and arid bush, is an exceptional source because many of the fossils are found on the surface, blown clean by the never-ending wind. The finds set back the dates of intelligent, co-operative, tool-making behaviour among hominids further and further all the time, but most of the species concerned are assumed to have died out. The crucial discoveries that will link humankind to our prehuman ancestors have yet to be made. One striking find made at Sibiloi in 1972 was "1470", the skull of a *Homo habilis* over two million years old, believed to be a direct ancestor of modern *Homo sapiens*. Sibiloi was declared a national park a year later. As more and more discoveries are made here (currently nearing 200), and in southern Ethiopia and at Olduvai in northern Tanzania, evolutionary theories are beginning to flesh out. The most important current site is in the north of the park at Koobi Fora.

The so-called **museum** at the "expedition" headquarters in Alia Bay, where some of the fossils (including part of a one-and-a-half-million-year-old elephant) are supposedly displayed *in situ*, isn't easily traced: all that was found recently were empty ranger buildings and unhelpful staff. There are no real facilities for visitors and, apart from water supplies, you need to be self-sufficient. In Nairobi, you might try contacting *Safari Camp Services* (see p.119) who organize occasional specialist tours to Sibiloi for visiting US paleontologists, archeologists and anthropologists, guided by experts in the field.

Animal life

At times, Sibiloi has a surprising wealth of **wildlife**. Indeed, until the 1930s, there were large numbers of elephant living here. Rainless years, ivory hunters, and especially the increase in the herds of livestock, contributed to their demise. But lion, cheetah, hyena, both kinds of zebra (the ordinary Grant's and the finer-striped, taller Grevy's), giraffe, ostrich, Grant's gazelle, topi, kudu and gerenuk all occur here, though there's no guarantee you'll see much. Because of the protection from hunters, hippos and crocodiles are numerous. The tree cover is minimal. The closest you're likely to come to finding trees is the petrified forest of stone trunks, reminders of the lush vegetation of the lakeshore in prehistoric times.

THE NORTHEAST

Northeastern Kenya has a single and limited travel circuit: up through **Isiolo** to **Marsabit Mountain and National Park**. It's well worth doing. But so is some of the rest of this vast wilderness region, even though Kenyans themselves will imply you are deluded to consider the idea.

Beyond, or east of Marsabit, the few towns – Moyale, Mandera, Wajir and Garissa – are considered remote administrative outposts, controlling land essentially peripheral to the onward thrust of development and change. Few travellers (and no tour groups) ever

THE NORTHEAST AND THE SOMALI CIVIL WAR – A WARNING

Northeastern Kenya has borne the full brunt of Somalia's desperate refugee crisis. Because the border with Somalia is largely an uncontrolled one, the war itself occasionally spills over too. Whatever the complicated situation on the ground, you can be sure of one thing: there are more people than before with guns, ammunition and little else. The whole of the region (which in practical terms means everywhere north of Lamu and east of the Isiolo–Moyale road, and sometimes including that road) is considered a high-risk zone. Since the flight of dictator Siad Barre from Somalia and that country's descent into near-anarchy, the Isiolo–Wajir–Mandera route has been periodically closed to travel: when it's open, you may be advised that travelling in the convoys of trucks or Land Rover *matatus* is unsafe and flying up your best option. It's impossible to be more than slightly helpful about this: areas and routes that are reckoned dangerous at any time may be the domain of a particular gang, or of several, or simply on a route used by armed exiles, and the degree of safety is dependent entirely on how many serious incidents have taken place over, say, the last year. Talk to everyone you meet and use your judgement – though also bear in mind that the region has never been declared a safe zone by the government, even since before independence, and that driving at night is not only the height of folly but illegal. For much of the time, serious incidents of banditry have been few and infrequent, and travelling in convoy has seemed quite safe. The latest "bad time" was 1992–94 but things seem to have eased since then, meaning that a serious incident occurs perhaps once a month. In the hope that the region returns to some kind of normality in the lifetime of this edition, relevant practical information is given in the account of the Northeast here (especially p.477) and in "Travel Details" at the end of the chapter. See also the box on p.487.

make it up here and the rewards if you venture out into these districts are hard to pin down. Savagely hot, rebarbative wastelands unfold for hours on end as you bus or truck your way along interminable dirt roads to towns that can at first seem devastatingly anticlimactic. But there is, as ever, fascination in the regional population: the Somalis, Rendille and Boran, who live by herding their camels and cattle, moving from well to well, crisscrossing the deserts on old migration routes. Being among them is a reward in itself. They tend to be stern and indifferent until you break the ice, and then the kindness and hospitality they show are astonishing. The dusty, fly-blown towns, too, take on distinctive characters as you get to know them; they owe little in atmosphere to down-country Kenya.

Travel throughout the northeast has a special quality. The normal stimuli of passing scenery, animals, people and events fleetingly witnessed is replaced with a massive open sky, a shimmering greenish-brown earth, and just occasionally a speck of movement – some camels, a pair of ostriches, a family moving on with their donkeys. It is a sparse, selective, absorbingly simple landscape. And not the least of its attractions is its restful absence of hassle and shove, and a solitude hardly found anywhere else.

But, except for the Marsabit run, this is travel almost entirely for its own sake. If you decide to go all the way to **Moyale** or **Mandera** (the two towns at the end of the route "spokes"), the greatest reward is in getting there. Retracing the journey in the opposite direction is a more dubious pleasure. However, Moyale also offers the possibility of a brief visit to **Ethiopia**. There are generally no special conditions attached to crossing for a few hours to wander around. Crossing the border at Mandera is, for the foreseeable future, a dangerous and pointless exercise, as the town on the other side has ceased to exist.

Isiolo

ISIOLO is the hub for travel to Marsabit, Moyale, Wajir and Mandera, and the northeast's most important town; there's no problem getting here from the Mount Kenya region and it's perfectly safe to do so.

Southernmost of the "Northern Frontier" towns, Isiolo is on the border between two different worlds – the fertile highlands and the desert. The terrific **Somali influence** here is something you'll notice everywhere you travel in the northeast. Isiolo is one of their most important towns in Kenya because it was here that many veteran Somali soldiers from World War I were settled. Recruited in Aden and Kismayu, they gave up their nomadic lifestyle to become livestock and retail traders.

But **the town** is really a cultural kaleidoscope, with Boran, Meru, Samburu and Turkana inhabitants as well as the Somalis. To someone newly arrived from Nanyuki or Meru, the upland towns seem ordinary in comparison. Women from the irrigated *shambas* around Isiolo sell cabbages, tomatoes and carrots in the busy market. Cattle owners, nomadic camel traders and merchants exchange greetings and the latest news from Nairobi and Moyale. In the livestock market, goats scamper through the alleys. Hawkers stroll along the road raising their Somali swords and strings of bangles to the minibuses heading up to Samburu National Reserve (see p.331). And, in the shade, energetic *miraa*-chewing and hanging around are the major occupations. *Miraa* has a long history in Somali culture, and the Nyambeni Hills, where most of the Kenyan crop is grown, are just 30km away.

Practicalities

Arriving here is particularly exotic at night. The 8.30pm bus from Nairobi doesn't get in till about 2am, and the town can be seen glittering out on the plain far below for an hour or more beforehand. During Ramadan, lanterns glow along the pavements for the *miraa* sellers and most of the shops are still open. You can find a B&L or crash on the

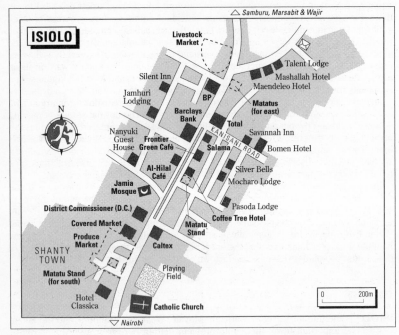

bus until dawn. For **changing money**, *Barclays'* extravagant Foreign Legion fortress is still the only bank in town (Mon–Fri 8.30am–1pm, Sat 8.30am–11am), and there's a **post office** (Mon–Fri 8am–1pm & 2–5pm).

Accommodation

Isiolo boasts one reasonable, mid-range **hotel**. Of the more humble **lodgings**, all are cheap, and several surprisingly good value.

Bomen Tourist Class Hotel (PO Box 67 Isiolo; ☎0165/2225 or 2389). Rated the best in town: clean, polite and they do good breakfasts, but the rooms are rather gloomy and don't have fans (which they should at these prices in this climate). Overpriced. ④.

Hotel Classica, on the south side of town, opposite the gargantuan Catholic church. A newish place with comfortable beds in s/c rooms, but already showing signs of old age. ②.

Jamhuri Lodging (PO Box 88; ☎0165/2065). Newly renovated, clean, courteous and mellow – currently the most popular cheap place. ①.

Mashallah Hotel (PO Box 378; ☎0165/2142). Clean, functional, Somali-run apartment block. Doubles and singles. S/c ②, non-s/c ①.

Mocharo Lodge (PO Box 106; ☎0165/2385). Good value, safe parking. Recommended. ②.

Nanyuki Guest House (PO Box 451; ☎0165/2168). Reasonable and cheap, with spartan rooms, nets, fresh cold milk, dry-cleaning facilities and safe parking. ①.

Pasoda Lodge (PO Box 62; ☎0165/2162). Quiet and clean, with inexpensive meals. All rooms s/c with nets. Safe parking. ②.

Silent Inn, near the *Jamhuri* (PO Box 12; ☎0165/2116). Usually lives up to its name, with the little luxury of morning hot water. A sign reads "Prostitution and Alcohol not Allowed". ①.

Silver Bells Hotel, between the *Bomen* and *Pasoda* (PO Box 247; ☎0165/2251). Clean, quiet and mid-priced, with a grubby cocktail bar which sells only beer and soda. ②.

Talent Lodge (PO Box 174; ☎0165/2262). Pleasant and very cheap but sometimes dirty. ①.

Eating and drinking

Somali *hotelis* provide excellent **food**, day and night. Now that you're in the northeast, you'll see pasta (usually spaghetti) appearing quite prominently on menus – one of the better Italian bequests to the Somalis.

Al-Hilal Café. Pretty good – especially noted for its samosas – and it has some ultra-cheap accommodation.

Bomen Hotel. The *nyama choma* at the patio bar is worthwhile for meat-eaters.

Coffee Tree Hotel. Down-to-earth eats.

Frontier Green Café. A brilliant, tree-filled garden-restaurant with disco (Wed, Fri and Sat), fluorescent spider's webs and UV tubes – in outlandish contrast with the rest of the town. Long popular for its good spiced *chai* for next to nothing a glass; the bar is open 24hr.

Salama Restaurant. The best in town – especially for an early breakfast or their very good spaghetti.

Talent Lodge. A worthwhile move on a hot afternoon for a cold beer on their rooftop terrace, though the broken bottles and legless chairs somewhat mar the atmosphere.

Crafts, salesmen and other distractions

Isiolo is one of the best places to buy **bracelets** of copper, brass and aluminium. Prices are generally around Ksh50 for the simple ones, up to Ksh100 for the heavier, more complicated designs. In the tourist low season, you may present the day's only opportunity for a sale, so prices can drop even further. Short "Somali swords" in red leather scabbards are also much in evidence. The "sharp boys" who mob you near the markets will invariably offer to guide you to one of the few blacksmiths in town to watch the fascinating process of twisting the wires for the bangles. Profits come from buying rough bangles, then polishing and selling them. If you go, you're generally expected to make a purchase and tip a few shillings to the boys.

While the bangle and knife salesmen throng as soon as you sit down for a *chai*, their approach is rarely aggressive (though see the note about tyre-slashing below). Women offer small, woven dolls.

If you're at a loose end in the evening, the *Comix Cinema*, up near the *Pasoda*, has a **video screen** with an endless mix of movies you'd forgotten about, plus more up-to-date war, ninja and kung-fu fare. And if you happen to be near Isiolo on or around October 10, the annual **Great Kenya Camel Endurance Race** sounds unmissable. Details from Nanyuki County Council, or see the placards along the road.

Moving on from Isiolo

Isiolo is a great town for passing the time. Memorable conversations are one of its strong points, although being reeled into slurred soliloquies with men drunk on *changaa* can get rather tiresome. However, when heading north or east, waiting in Isiolo is a predictable part of the trip.

With the lamentable collapse of bus services in the north and northeast (the few exceptions in this chapter are noted), your only options for travel to Marsabit, Moyale, Wajir or Mandera are either **self-drive**, which is ill advised for all but the most experienced driver (and you have to travel in convoy, except to Maralal, Archer's Post and Samburu and Shaba national reserves), or **hitching a ride** with a truck, also in convoy. If you're lucky, you might cadge a lift with one of the mission or aid vehicles, but even these rarely venture further than Kalacha or Wajir and are, in any case, often too wary to give lifts to strangers. Note if you're driving that Isiolo is the last **fuel** stop until Marsabit or Wajir, and beware also that tyre spikers were until recently at work at Isiolo police barrier: while you stamp about, change your wheel and arrange for your puncture to be repaired, an army of souvenir peddlars pitch their gear at you.

North to Marsabit and Moyale

For many years considered highly dangerous, this road is now relatively safe. The only major recent incident involved an attack on a lorry at night, of which the authorities washed their hands and said "told you so" – driving at night is officially illegal. *Matatus* go as far as Archer's Post, which is only helpful if you're visiting Samburu or Shaba national reserves (see p.331). Otherwise, try for trucks at the **police roadblock**, 3km north of Isiolo, where drivers sign their vehicles out of town. At the time of writing, a truck called *Moyale Express* covered the route once or twice a week. Alternatively, *Gametrackers'* Turkana Bus passes Isiolo every other Friday in the late afternoon – this may take you as far as Marsabit, probably for a fee. If you do get a lift, the journey to Marsabit takes seven to ten hours, with the next leg to Moyale anything from ten hours to two days, depending on the frequency of hold-ups, natural or otherwise. Drivers charge upwards of Ksh800.

Northeast to Wajir and Mandera

Land Rover *matatus*, departing from under the tree beside *Maendeleo Hotel*, only ply as far as Mado Gashi, 160km short of Wajir, though they may venture further if security in the region improves. You may find a further connection here, or you may not. Departure times are sporadic and often they do not depart at all. Otherwise, **hitching a lift** with an **armed convoy** (police ride shotgun) is the only option. Early morning is the time for this, again, at the **police checkpoint**, although *miraa* sales can add hours to journey times. You'd be wise to secure the lift, and the price, the night before. The journey to Wajir should take around nine hours unless the convoy leaves late, in which case a night in Mado Gashi, where the armed guard is changed, is likely. Wajir to Mandera should take nine hours, again assuming minimal hold-ups. Be warned, again, that this is the most dangerous leg of the trip and incidents are common. If you're still determined, it's a wild and often extremely uncomfortable journey but worth it for the subsequent feeling of elation at having survived the trip.

West to Maralal

Still considered by some to be a trifle dangerous (there were a few isolated incidents of banditry in the early 1990s), the Isiolo–Archer's Post–Maralal run is now served by the wacky *Babie Coach*, a converted Bedford lorry which runs between Isiolo and Maralal every two days, leaving either town at around 9am. The trip takes five to six hours, though you could stop off in Wamba (p.465) to explore the grandly mysterious Mathews Range. On the days that *Babie Coach* isn't running, you may find the odd *matatu* going to Maralal. If you're **driving**, bring enough fuel for the whole journey – there are no supplies at Wamba.

Back to Nairobi via the Central Highlands

If you're travelling by **bus**, *Akamba* has two daily services (☎0165/2122; via Nanyuki, Kiganjo, Nyeri and Karatina) departing at 7.30am and 8pm, arriving in Nairobi at 1pm and 2am respectively. Their office is in the *Maendeleo Hotel* building. The cheaper *Eastern Express*, opposite *Barclays Bank*, has one daily departure at 7.30am, which doesn't stop in Nyeri. For *matatus* you have to be at the market stage before sunrise – last departures at 6am are not unheard of.

To Marsabit – and North Horr

If the truck is travelling at a good speed, the trip from Isiolo isn't uncomfortable, despite corrugations that shake smaller vehicles to breaking point. Passing over the usually dry Ewaso Nyiro River, you hit the agglomeration of shiny-roofed shacks and rows of *dukas* which is **ARCHER'S POST**. This is as far north as you'll get by *matatu*, although lifts into Samburu and Shaba national reserves may be forthcoming from Kenya Wildlife Service personnel, who frequent a number of particularly good bars. There are some **rooms** here, too, should you fail. Note, however, that there is no **petrol** available, and the only alternative – should you have forgotten to fill up in Isiolo – is an expensive trip to either *Samburu Lodge* or *Sarova Shaba Lodge* in the reserves. Finally, advertising "hard and pertinent facts about the Samburu people", **Samburu Cultural Centre** (daily 10am–4pm; PO Box 548 Isiolo), half a kilometre from Archer's Post market along the Samburu National Reserve road, has a small **ethnographical museum** and *manyatta*, complete with ironmongery, woodwork and beadwork for sale, displays of dancing, and more.

North of Archer's Post, the road veers northwest and for half an hour the great mesa of **Ol Olokwe Mountain** spreads massively across the horizon in front of you. If you are travelling independently with a vehicle, it can be climbed.

For several hours beyond Ol Olokwe you roar across the flat **Kaisut Desert**. Laisamis isn't much of a break and the Losai National Reserve – which you have just crossed – isn't any different from the rest of the scenery. The **approach to Marsabit**, though, is unmistakable. The road begins to climb and suddenly you're on a hilly island in the desert, a region of volcanic craters, lush meadows and forest. The branches of the trees on the steep slopes are disguised by swathes of Spanish moss, looking at first glance like algae-covered rocks in shades of grey and green.

Marsabit town

MARSABIT is a surprise: it's hard to prepare yourself, after the flat dustlands, for this fascinating hill oasis, in the desert but not of it. Rising a thousand metres above the surrounding plains, it is permanently green, well watered by the clouds which form and disperse over it in a daily cycle. The high forest is usually mist-covered until late morning, the trees a characteristic tangle of foliage and lianas.

The town is capital of the largest administrative district in the country, as well as a major meat- and livestock-trading centre. It is small and intimate in feel; walking around, you're always bumping into familiar faces. The lively cultural mix in the main

---

PEOPLES OF THE NORTHEAST

Identities in Marsabit can be confusing. The **Boran** and the **Gabbra** are closely related in language and custom, both part of the **Galla peoples**, a migrating drift of pastoralists who arrived in northern Kenya several hundred years ago from the Horn of Africa. At the time, they caused havoc in the region, only to be themselves pressured by the ensuing expansion of **Muslim Somalis** from the east. Many Boran and Gabbra, especially those who have adopted a more sedentary life, are now Muslims and have taken on Somali styles in dress and culture. The **Rendille** look and act like Samburu, with whom they are frequently allied; they speak a language close to Somali but have non-Muslim religious beliefs. They normally herd camels rather than cattle and, to a great extent, they continue to roam the deserts, facing the prospect of settling down without any enthusiasm at all and visiting Marsabit only for vital needs or a brief holiday.

These days, however, distinctions other than superficial ones are increasingly hard to apply as more and more children are sent to school and down-country ideas percolate up the road. The concept of "tribe", which in many regions has never been very relevant, seems more useless than ever. Still, language and religious beliefs remain significant in deciding who does what and with whom. Gabbra and Boran, traditionally scathing about trade, have begun to change through their long association with groups of trading Somalis.

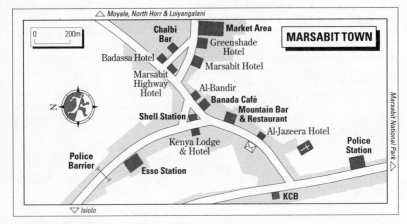

market area is the biggest buzz: transient **Gabbra** herdsmen and **Boran** with their prized short-horn cattle, women in the printed shawls and chiffon wraps of **Somali** costume rubbing elbows with ochred **Rendille** wearing skins, high stacks of beads and wire, and fantastic braided hairstyles. There are government workers here, too, from other parts of Kenya, and a scattering of **Ethiopian immigrants** and refugees. For some Marsabit background, try Mude Dae Mude's novel *The Hills are Falling*, widely available in Kenya and perhaps in Marsabit.

Accommodation

As *Kenya Lodge & Hotel* (PO Box 176; ☎0183/2221; ①) is such an outstanding **place to stay**, there seems little need to mention the others; but it's quite likely to be full, so you're recommended to make a beeline for it as soon as you arrive. It's a gem, clean, modern, cosy and fantastic value. The restaurant does superb Ethiopian food – basically *njera* (soured, unleavened bread) and *wat* (stew) – which makes a real change from *karanga* and *chapati*. Other places in town include the large but rather miserable *Marsabit Highway Hotel* (PO Box 110; ☎0183/2236; ②), with a bakery below (fresh bread every afternoon), and some self-contained rooms with double beds; the *Badassa Hotel*, an unexceptional B&L with a decent *hoteli* (①); the *Al-Jazeera*, which offers extremely cheap and peaceful accommodation and very safe parking (①); and the clean, Muslim-run *Al-Bandir Hotel* (①). A little further out, by the market, are two more cheap B&Ls, *Greenshade Hotel* and *Marsabit Hotel*. Whichever you choose, ask about **hot water** before moving in: night temperatures can drop very low (*Marsabit* means "place of cold") and lukewarm showers are no fun. Recent water problems have cut off piped water completely in the dry season, but new boreholes should solve this problem. Work is also under way on a new diesel-powered generator which should eradicate the frequent power cuts.

If you want **to camp**, head for the National Park's main gate (see below).

Other practicalities

For **changing money**, the *Kenya Commercial Bank* is open Monday to Friday 9am–1pm and Saturday morning 9–11am. There's also a **post office** (Mon–Fri 8am–1pm & 2–5pm), and several reasonable places to **eat and drink**. For Ethiopian food and a varied menu of Kenyan food, visit the *Al-Bandir Restaurant*; the *Al-Jazeera* serves decent meals, too. Or simply head for the market. There is very cheap food in a lively atmosphere at any time of day from the *hotelis*: hefty pancakes, *githeri, mandaazi* and *nyama* *choma*. The *hotelis* double as butchers so you can select your own slab for roasting from the carcasses hanging up. There's a well-stocked grocery next to the *Kenya Lodging*. If you're thirsty, the *Mountain Bar & Restaurant* (PO Box 20; ☎0183/1342) is the die-hard's drinking den, with an eclectic melange of characters and the occasional dispute over prostitutes; or try the *Chalbi Bar B&L*, opposite the *Marsabit Highway Hotel*.

Walks out of town

There are a number of trips you can make on foot from Marsabit in a few hours or less – particularly good restoratives if you haven't got your own vehicle and failed to get into the national park (see below). The easiest, with rewarding views, is the short walk up to the big wind-powered **generator** on a hill just west of the town. Turn left just before the police barrier and simply follow the path.

A longer excursion takes you up to the **VOK transmitter** behind the town, an excel-lent morning or afternoon hike through lush forest with magnificent panoramas of the whole district from the top. There are wells up here, too (see below). During the rainy season, everything is tremendously green and you walk over flowering meadows through clouds of butterflies.

From there, you should be able to see the closest sizeable crater, **Gof Redo**, about 5km north of the town in the fork of the roads to Moyale and North Horr. Follow either road from where they fork for about 3km, then turn left or right accordingly for a one-kilometre cross-country walk. The crater is quite a favoured hideout for greater kudu, and there's a population of cheetah around here too, not infrequently seen from a vehi-cle (but likely to flee if you're on foot). You can scramble down the crater wall. Gof Redo can't really be missed, but a friend from town would be reassuring.

Even easier is a walk to the **"singing wells"** at Ulanula (called Hulahula by some). These are less exotic than they sound, but they're still a good excuse to explore. Ulanula is a conical peak to the right of the Isiolo road, about 6km from town. Leaving Marsabit, you cross two bridges, then turn left and climb 200–300m up a narrow, tangled ravine. A concrete holding tank, visible from the road, gives the place away. Behind it are two natural wells, the first with a wooden trough in front, the second longer and apparently deeper, containing a fluctuating depth of brown, frog-filled water. A silent pumphouse stands by.

The **singing** is done not by the wells but by the Boran herders who use them. When the water is low, human chains are formed to get it out with luxuriantly leaking leather buckets: singing helps the work. At the driest times of the year you may be lucky and witness this but try to get here early. Animals are usually driven to the wells after dawn, and it's a brisk 75-minute walk from town. Go out there in the late afternoon, though, and you should get a lift back with one of the day's vehicles up from Isiolo.

Onward from Marsabit

One or two trucks do occasionally spend the night in Marsabit, to or from Moyale or Isiolo. Otherwise, the convoy to Moyale usually passes in the afternoon, and that towards Isiolo anytime between 5pm and 11pm. The best place to wait is at the **police checkpoint**, 300m from the Esso garage on the Isiolo road. Ask around the petrol stations if you are trying to hitch a lift to Loiyangalani; your first target is North Horr. If you are **driving**, supplies of petrol are usually available.

Marsabit National Park

Daily fees: $15, students/children $5; map – Survey of Kenya Marsabit National Reserve SK 84 at 1cm:1km.

Having made the long journey to Marsabit, you will certainly want to get into the **park**. The forest is wild and dense, its two crater lakes idyllically beautiful. Except during the

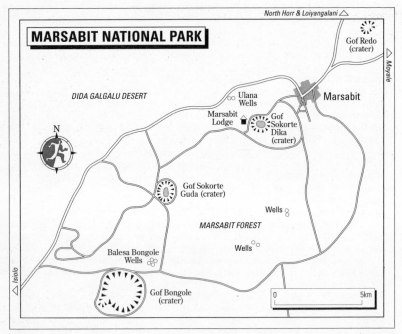

long rains (March–June), there is a good chance you'll see some of the long-tusked Marsabit **elephants**, relatives of the famous Ahmed – a big tusker to whom Kenyatta gave "presidential protection", with elephant guards tracking him day and night (now replicated in fibreglass in the National Museum in Nairobi). Marsabit's new king is Mohammed, his tusks estimated at a cool 45kg each side. The park is also renowned for its **greater kudu** antelope and there's a very wide range of other wildlife. Between the nearly impenetrable forests of the peaks and the stony scrub desert at the base of the mountain, however, you'll need a little luck for sightings. This is a rewarding park but one where you have to look hard.

Practicalities

The park's **main gate** is at the edge of town, past the bank and the District Commissioner's office. It is not often visited and you may be in for a long wait if you want a lift around its forest tracks. On the other hand, the inverse law of hitching will probably come into play when a vehicle does arrive. In addition, government officers and soldiers garrisoned in town drive up to the **lodge** (see below) fairly frequently; this short trip, with the view over the first lake – Gof Sokorte Dika – and its forested rim, is a lot better than nothing.

If you venture to **drive in the park** without 4WD, make sure you can get back out. Some of the tracks in the forest are steep and tend to be muddy. *Marsabit Lodge* has a pair of land cruisers which you can take out, with driver – three hours for around Ksh1200. You can sometimes fix up similar deals with locals in town: ask around.

There's a **campsite** near the main gate (100m down the hairpin to the left of the ranger's house) which is free in theory, although the rangers may request a small fee, especially if you wish to use their water/shower. There are toilets at the campsite, and wonderfully shaded places overrun with baboons swinging on the lianas. The lodge will usually let campers use their facilities (Ksh120) – take over a chalet for an hour or two to wash in more comfort.

There are several other places to camp in the park. Gof Sokorte Guda (Lake Paradise), a stunning, dark pool a kilometre across for much of the year, has wonderful sites on its crater rim, where a night would be chilly and thrillingly spent – lion, leopard and the rare and shaggy striped hyena are all seen and heard from time to time. This *Lake Paradise Special Campsite* costs $10 per person (plus park entry fee), but does not include the Ksh500 or so "guiding fee" for the obligatory accompanying ranger.

Marsabit Lodge (PO Box 45, ☎0183/2044 Marsabit; reservations through *Msafiri Inns*, address on p.49; ⑤ low, ⑦ high), about 3km from the gate, is a little run-down, and both facilities and service are basic, but the exquisite beauty of its location and outstanding views from all its rooms renders these mundane complaints irrelevant. Elephants are common visitors in late afternoon, attracted by the water, lush vegetation and the salt lick right by the bar – they are all descendants or relatives of Ahmed, who died the year the lodge opened, and have been protected since October 1991 by a crack anti-poaching unit. If you'd like to stay, the staff might come and get you from the gate, but they often walk between the lodge and town, and you should be able to accompany them. It's a wonderful walk through the forest, with clouds of butterflies and the occasional mouth-drying encounter with buffalo or elephant.

Marsabit's fauna

Your animal count in the park will very much depend on the season of your visit. Good rains can encourage the grazers off the mountain and out into the temporarily lush desert, and the predators (always far fewer) will follow. **Elephants** especially are tremendous wanderers, sometimes strolling into town, causing pandemonium. More problematically, the people of Marsabit have been encouraged to cultivate around the base of the mountain, at the same time creating a barrier to the elephants' free movement and unintentionally providing them with free lunches.

The **birdlife** in the park is amazing: almost 400 species have been recorded, including 52 different birds of prey. Very rare **lammergeiers** (bearded vultures) are thought to nest on the sheer cliffs of Gof Bongole, the largest crater, which has a drivable track around its ten-kilometre rim. Marsabit is also something of a **snake** sanctuary, with some very large cobras – this isn't a place to go barefoot or in sandals.

To Kalacha and North Horr

Reaching North Horr from Marsabit is getting easier all the time, though continuing the logical next step down to Lake Turkana and Loiyangalani is still somewhat difficult. There is a more or less regular passenger lorry which leaves Marsabit "often", as well as mission, Education Department, commercial and oil industry vehicles.

En route, **MAIKONA** is a friendly Gabbra settlement on the fringes of the **Chalbi Desert**, with a thriving daily market for goats and cattle (the camels which become ubiquitous from here on tend to be traded at Isiolo). *Kamkunji Hotel* may have one or two rooms. Some 5km north is a small, seemingly miraculous oasis pond of blue water with a sweet green grass fringe. It's the last fresh water until **KALACHA**. Kalacha is a regular night stop for some of the longer Turkana expeditions (*Gametrackers* stay here). It's the neatest village in all Africa, with its "streets" defined by rows of carefully placed stones, and litter, if there were any, is quickly blown away by the furnace wind. There are two very basic *dukas*, a bar that sells very hot beer, and the humble but friendly *Bismillahi Hotel* which has rooms. But the real treat is the remarkably good mission-run **campsite** – dusty and barren yet with decent showers and even a rather inventive swimming pool/water tank, that subsequently feeds an irrigation system. The water, pumped up by a windmill, is sporadically chlorinated. Local Gabbra cluster to sell their wares and to pick up what useful items they can.

From Kalacha to North Horr, the track streaks out over blinding white salt pans and shifting quicksands, ducks behind straggly oasis clusters of half-dead palm trees, and finally loses itself in a vast orange expanse rimmed only by the floating hulks of very distant mountains. The exact path of the road varies annually, and in April is often impassable when the rains bring with them a circus of flamingoes. **NORTH HORR**, when you finally reach it, is a welcome haven, with a handful of *dukas*, the Somali *Al-Rachid Hotel*, opposite the mosque, for traditional fare, rooms at the *Mandera Central Hotel*, and even a red phone box that works. From here on down to Loiyangalani, the terrain becomes even tougher as the road painfully climbs the volcanic foothills of Mount Kulal, but the view from the top, looking down over the lake far away, can be spellbinding.

To Moyale and beyond

From Marsabit, the **journey to Moyale** takes between five and nine hours depending on the vehicle (see box, p.486). For the first three of these you descend from the mountain's greenery past spectacular craters – Gof Choba is the whopper on the left – to the forbidding black moonscape of the **Dida Galgalu Desert**. Dida Galgalu means "plains of darkness" according to one Boran story. Another account derives it from Galgalu, a woman buried here after she died of thirst trying to cross it. The road arrows north for endless miles, then cuts east across watercourses and through bushier country beneath high crags on the Ethiopian frontier. En route, you pass a new refugee centre at Lugga Walde (or Walda), 80km before Moyale (a UN and American IRC charity camp), and the turning to the small village of **Sololo** on the Ethiopian border, arrestingly sited between soaring peaks, which can be climbed for stunning views over the northern plains and Ethiopian highlands. Sololo has a mission, which may let you camp in their grounds, and a single lodging/brothel (the *Treetop*).

There are some magnificent, spiring **termite mounds** along the northern part of the route, a sight that is quintessentially African, yet one which can be quickly taken for granted, like leafless trees in a northern winter. And, as the distances roll away, the 250km from Marsabit to Moyale is resolved as just a few bends, a couple of scenery changes. Over spaces that would take days to cover on foot you can see where you have been and where you are going – the pastoralists' conservatism reflected in the landscape.

The road bends north again and winds up through the settlements of Burji farmers – Boran who have given up the nomadic herding life – past their beautifully sculpted houses and sparse fields, to Moyale.

Moyale

Straddling the Ethiopian border, **MOYALE** makes Marsabit look like a metropolis. Though the town is growing rapidly, and was recently supplied with electricity, the centre is small enough to walk around in fifteen minutes. You'll find several sandy streets, a pretty mosque, a few *dukas*, a bar, a camel-tethering ground, two petrol stations (one of which occasionally belies its defunct appearance), a big police station, a fairly large market area, a new *KCB* bank and an incredibly slow post office – five weeks to Europe. Moyale is not much to write home about in fact, and there's not a lot to do except wander around, perhaps try some camel milk (very rich and creamy) and pass the time of day with everyone else, with or without the aid of *miraa*. Note that there have been a number of shootings recently involving "Ethiopian bandits", with the local population as victims. It's a regular enough occurrence, it seems, judging by the practised haste of the shopkeepers in sealing up their businesses on hearing even distant gunfire.

The most interesting aspect of Moyale is its **architecture** – at least, the good number of traditionally built houses which are still standing (the rest were bombed and shelled during World War II, after which the good citizens of Moyale clubbed together for "less fortunate people", contributing £80 to the colony's "Food for Britain Fund"). The Boran build in several styles, including circular mud and thatch huts, but in town the houses are rectangular, of mud and dung on a wood frame, with a flat or slightly tilted roof projecting a metre or two to form a porch, supported by sturdy posts and tree trunks. The roof is up to half a metre thick, a fantastic accretion of dried mud, sticks, scrap, and vegetation. Chickens and goats get up there, improving the roof's fertility, and every time it rains another layer of insulating herbage springs up. As a result, the houses are cool while the outside temperature hovers above 30°C for most of the year (July and August are cooler).

Practicalities

Accommodation is very limited and all firmly in the ① category. The most established B&L is *Barissah Hotel*, which shares frontage with the bar. The *Barissah* has a dozen dark cubes around an earth compound, and, while it's hardly clean, it is friendly enough. The **restaurant** has *karanga* and *chapatis* every evening, 24-hour *malayas*, and a permanent supply of warm tea. You need to bring a padlock; "showers" (a basin of water) have to be ordered.

A second lodging, where family and guests share the same roof, is *Bismillahi B&L*, across the way from the *Barissah* behind the *Esso* pumps. It's slightly more expensive, and facilities here don't match the *Barissah*'s, but the food is good. *Silent Lodge*, just outside town near the police barrier, has clean, three-bedded rooms and is perhaps the most promising place. There are other B&Ls on the main street, past the mosque.

The water in Moyale can be briny at times and it's worth bringing a few litres of drinking water up from Marsabit. You can obtain **clean water** in Moyale from the Ministry of Water.

Into Ethiopia

The most interesting prospect in Moyale is to cross the valley into **Ethiopia** (see box overleaf) and spend a few hours, or even a night, there. For Kenyans and Ethiopians, the border is an open one. For foreigners there are just a few formalities, and crossing is easy considering the restrictions on tourists' movements in Ethiopia until just recently. Recent reports suggest that border controls here – and even an interest in whether or not you have a camera – have virtually ceased. Doubtless it depends much on the latest directives from Nairobi and Addis, and on relations between the two governments, which have generally been good. You can increase your chances by ensuring your Kenyan visa (if you have one) is a multiple-entry type, thus allowing you back in again. Naturally, an Ethiopian visa wouldn't hinder your progress either, though the embassy in Nairobi is not likely to concede that entry through Moyale would be permitted (by the rule book, tourists go into Ethiopia only by air through Addis Ababa). Kenya has built a big new border-crossing post at Moyale, presumably anticipating increased trade and communications.

A FEW HOURS IN SOUTHERN ETHIOPIA

First you visit the Kenyan police sentry box down the hill, where you may be told that, strictly speaking, your intentions are unlawful and if their senior officer got to hear of it . . . The usual arrangement applies, so have some small notes with you. From here the road up the hill to Ethiopia is wide and invitingly tarred, though used almost exclusively by pedestrians and livestock. At the Ethiopian post they will ask you if you have an entry visa and, if you have, your passage should be straightforward. Otherwise, explain you're just visiting briefly and go to see the customs and immigration officials at the office on the right as you go up the hill. After they've made one of two phone calls you should be allowed in. On no account go on up the hill if you haven't seen the immigration officer. You may well be given permission to stay the night, but note that customs searches are thorough. Probably the best plan is to take a room in Kenya and leave your gear there.

Ethiopian Moyale is larger than its Kenyan counterpart and noticeably more prosperous – a result, it seems, of the paved road to Addis, some piped water, and a long-established electricity supply. There are several bars, a hotel that wouldn't look out of place in a small town in Greece, lots of simple stores, and plenty of eating places. The market buzzes colourfully with camels and goats, piles of spices, flour and vegetables. Otherwise life here seems much the same as over the border, but easier. As a back-door view of Ethiopia, however, it may be no more representative than the other side of town is of Kenya.

But never mind that; there are some new tastes to try. A good place to **eat** *njera* and *wat*, the Ethiopian equivalent of *karanga na chapati*, is the *Negussie Hotel* (up the hill, take the first left past the wooden slogan "bridge", then the first right). *Njera* is soft, unleavened millet bread, with an uncanny resemblance to a dish cloth, sometimes delicious, other times not. *Wat* is a spicy stew that can be made of any kind of meat or vegetables. The *Negussie* also has a bar serving Ethiopian beer or white wine from *Awash Wineries*, not for sensitive palates but cheap enough. You can pay for everything in Kenya shillings; Ethiopian currency is the *birr*.

If you are **staying the night**, head for the state-chain *Bekele Molla Hotel*, about 2km from the border. The bar here appears to be the focus of night-time action for hundreds of kilometres and the rooms are clean and nominally self-contained. *Zibib*, on sale in the bar, is Ethiopian *ouzo* and easily drunk. If your bill seems predated, that's because the Amharic calendar is eight years behind the Gregorian one.

English will serve you much better than Swahili, which is spoken by very few people. The people in this part of Ethiopia are mainly **Boran** and **Konso**, not Amhara, but an Amharic word worth remembering is thank you – *amaser-genalehu*.

Onward travel from Moyale

Unless you were lucky enough to have a visa and be given clearance to travel overland to Addis Ababa, you'll probably be thinking about **returning to Marsabit and Isiolo** on the next truck or, if your thirst for adventure is still not quenched, getting to **Wajir** and **Mandera**. You can also find occasional food-aid transport trucks heading straight down to **Mombasa via Garissa**.

In Moyale, the police are very helpful and will let you know if any GKs (government vehicles) are going your way. Only GK vehicles can travel when they like. Others have to go in escorted convoy. One quite likely possibility is hitching a ride to Buna (about halfway to Wajir), where there is a mission, and then finding another vehicle to Wajir.

The track from Moyale to Wajir is infrequently used and often impossible after rain, while the one along the border to Mandera was virtually abandoned until recently, and strictly speaking it is illegal to travel on it. Your only hope would be to hitch a lift with the daily, early-morning armed convoy.

Moyale to Wajir

Until 1994, this route was covered by the now-defunct *Mandera Express*. Latest reports indicate that the eight- to twelve-hour journey is travelled only rarely, usually by convoy. Should you manage a lift, the route passes through the pretty, northern borderlands (much woodland, lots of wildlife) towards Takabba, cutting back south before it reaches that village and passing through **Buna**; from there, Wajir is monotonously and uneventfully reached in a few hours. There are police checks at every little settlement along the way.

Moyale to Mandera

This route tells the same story, with the once six-times-monthly *Mandera Quick Service* bus suspended indefinitely. This is a region well beyond the reach of the Kenyan Armed Forces and travel here is ill-advised (for want of any concrete information rather than specific reports of attacks). Should you somehow find a vehicle, it takes two days to cover the severe track, with a night stop in the small centre of **Takabba**. Vehicles that use the track along the border, rather than via Takabba (mostly lorries), are driving illegally, and your comfort tends to be ignored: it gets cold in the back at night and there are no food supplies of any kind between Moyale and **Rhamu**. Your personal security is in the lap of the gods.

From Isiolo to Wajir

Undoubtedly the hottest, wildest, most remote route in the country, Kenya seems all but left behind when you set off from Isiolo for Wajir and Mandera. The journey unfolds predictably enough, with the truck running full tilt for hours on end in a cloud of dust across a sizzling pancake of sand, gravel and meagre scrub. The road stretches, empty in both directions, to indiscernible melting points on the horizon.

Mado Gashi and Habaswein

Land Rover *matatus* are currently most unlikely to venture farther than **MADO GASHI**, and even this may be one step too far – most end up 80km short at **Garba Tula**, leaving you to hitch a lift with the convoys from Isiolo. By truck, a late departure usually means a night stop at Mado Gashi, a witheringly unappealing Somali and "Somali-ized" Boran village which is a crossroads for coast, northeast, and Central Highlands traffic. The Boran, like the Samburu more recently, for long bore the brunt of Somali atrocities, but they recently got wise and purchased automatic weapons en

---

BEYOND ISIOLO – A WARNING

The Isiolo–Wajir–Mandera route has been closed at times recently and is heavily patrolled and garrisoned by the army (see also the box on p.474). Isiolo is the furthest extent of "normal" traffic and, by the time you get there, you're likely to know whether you're allowed to proceed at all. At the latest reckoning (1996), the entire section from Mado Gashi to Mandera was reckoned unsafe, partly from fears caused by attacks on buses and tourists around Lamu and Garissa. It is impossible to state categorically whether these fears are justified until an incident occurs – keep your ear to the ground and ask everyone you meet about the latest news. When the previous edition of this guide was published, Isiolo to Mado Gashi was reckoned the most dangerous part, but is now considered safe; things could easily change again. If you're serious about visiting this region, you might consider taking a *miraa* plane from Nairobi Wilson airport – there are several daily departures to Wajir, Mandera and back again.

masse – an uneasy stand-off between Boran and bandits now holds. The people here aren't exactly unfriendly but the long stares, more than at most places, can be a little intimidating.

While there are numerous **lodgings**, the village has no electricity or running water, so they're spartan and generally dirty; marginally preferable is *Mount Kenya Lodge* at the Isiolo end of town. If you're exceptionally lucky, Mado Gashi's **"cinema"** will be showing something: one of the *chai* shops has a generator and a projector, and a small killing is made whenever the owner gets some reels. The impact of such entertainment on a community like this has to be seen to be believed.

The only settlement of any size between here and Wajir is **HABASWEIN**. This is located right on the edge of the Lorian "swamp", the seasonal flood plain where the Ewaso Nyiro River sheds the rain that falls on the north and east sides of Mount Kenya.

Wajir

First impressions of **WAJIR** are of its size, a fair amount of construction going on, a "Centre for the Disabled", whitewashed, blue, and yellow buildings, and a feeling of Araby in the air which genuinely reflects the town's considerable Arab population. The

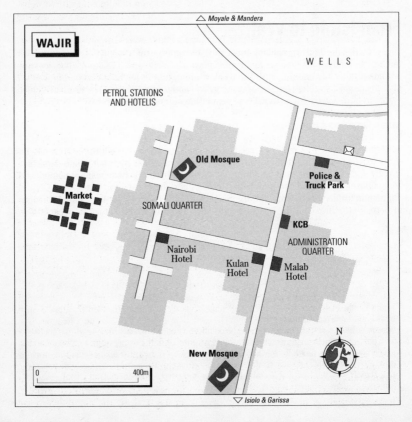

place has a real gravity of its own, electricity and running water, and the "legionary" castellated fortress for which it's famous.

Some background

Like most major settlements in the northeast, Wajir's significance comes largely from its **wells**. More than a hundred of them are scattered across seventy square kilometres of desert, providing the basis of a livelihood for the **Somali** people of the region through their milk camels. At the last count, the region supported some 2.3 million camels as well as 2.8 million cattle; unsurprisingly, the wells have always been bitterly fought over and jealously protected. Conflict between Somali clans and clan sections over water rights is probably as old as the clans themselves. Feuds are never forgotten: vengeance and blood money are traditional elements in the struggle for survival in this inimical environment.

In 1984, tensions were running higher than usual and parliamentary balance had gone awry with some sections feeling unrepresented by the town's two Somali MPs. Amid accusations of atrocities between rival clans, the regional administration announced an amnesty for those Somalis who surrendered their guns. Wajir's notoriety stems from this point, when thousands of men and boys of the Degodia clan were rounded up and interned by the authorities in a fenced military airstrip at Wagala, west of the town, for refusing to comply. Hundreds subsequently died of exposure or dehydration or were killed trying to escape. A local tragedy of catastrophic proportions, the **massacre** left many families without their menfolk.

Visiting Wajir today, the trauma is still obvious, though rarely spoken of to strangers. The provincial officials held to blame for the massacre were transferred and there have been some attempts to bring improvements to the town's services. But the problem remains one of communication – between the different Somali clans, between Somali and non-Somali, and between Wajir and metropolitan, down-country Kenya. Despite all this, there's a measure of tolerance on both sides at the personal level that is often little short of remarkable.

The Town

The main pastime in Wajir seems to be chewing *miraa*, but you'll probably soon get tired of that (or at least your jaws will). There are one or two **bars** with cheap AFCO (armed forces) beer on the eastern, administrative, side of town: try the *Soweto* for mixed Somali/Administration company.

The **market area** on the west side of town is fascinating and well worth wandering around. Quite different from any market you'll have seen before in Kenya, it's a maze of Somali *herio* (grass and stick huts) and wooden shelters. There's a wide assortment of locally made domestic odds and ends including beautiful and simple pottery incense burners for scenting clothing. Fruit and vegetables are in short supply and fairly uninteresting: you'll usually find oranges and sometimes slashes of brilliant red watermelon, though often on the main street between the *Nairobi* and the *Kulan* hotels rather than in the market itself. On the next street up you'll find **tailors** sitting under the trees at their treadle machines in a scene duplicated in thousands of towns across Africa. There is a **craftsmen's quarter** of metal workers and other artisans around the big new mosque on the way out to Isiolo.

If you'd like to visit some **wells**, the closest are just a little north of town past a flurry of street activity, the administrative departments and the post office. Obviously the activity around the wells depends on the condition of the pasture in the region, and for much of the year the big herds of camels are out in the desert on clan grazing grounds. But when they are here at the wells the scene is memorable. While out wandering, you may also come across some newcomers to the town, a herd of **reticulated giraffes**. These, pestered out of their browsing grounds in the bush by the disruption to the region brought about by the Somali civil war, have taken to the streets of Wajir for security. They are completely tolerated, not to say ignored.

Lastly, and equally bizarrely, there's a **squash club** in town, now called the Gamia (Camel) Club, though originally christened the Royal Wajir Yacht Club. It was named thus to bring a bit of a smile to the faces of the British officials posted here in the 1940s and 1950s. Wajir, otherwise, isn't exactly a bundle of laughs.

Practicalities

Finding **somewhere to stay** in the town is no problem (all ①–②). You'll probably end up in the *Nairobi Hotel*, desperate for shade, a cold drink or ten, food, a shower and sleep: it has it all. There are a number of other lodgings: the *Kulan* is good value with decent, rather basic food; and the *Malab*, right by the bus stop, is reportedly excellent, with fans as well as mosquito nets.

The **food** is generally pretty good in Wajir, with many places offering pasta, pilau rice (*mchele*) and the distinctive, delicious, spiced black tea of the northeast called *strungi*.

Because of Wajir's very high **water table** (only 10m below the surface), mosquitoes are a terrible menace here, and you should come adequately prepared with your favourite repellent. For the same geological reason, long-drop toilets are not in use, but there's not much you can do to prepare yourself for the horror of the *kimbo* tins. Avoid drinking the water if you can.

There's a **bank** (*KCB*, open Mon–Fri 8.30am–1pm & Sat 9–11am), a **post office** (Mon–Fri 8am–1pm & 2–5pm, Sat 8am–1pm) and part-time **petrol station**.

The best place to wait for **trucks** to Mandera is outside the police station. **Flights** from Wajir airfield (used by the US and UN in 1993–94 to transport relief supplies to Somalia) to Mandera and Nairobi are operated by *Blue Bird Aviation*. Flights to Nairobi (daily) are also run by *Suez Air*.

Onwards to Mandera

While it's not a journey for sybarites or weak bladders (vehicles roll non-stop for hours), the final desperate kick from Wajir up to Mandera takes you as far from Nairobi as you can get, which for many people is not an altogether unattractive proposition.

El Wak and Rhamu

About halfway from Wajir to Mandera is **EL WAK** (The Wells of God) and a scramble of people eager to buy whatever *miraa* the bus travellers have for sale. There used to be a camel corps here, but the police today seem to have abandoned the dromedary as a way of getting around. Should you end up spending the night here – and, travelling by bus and lorry, it is amazing how many unscheduled night stops you'll make in the northeast – the bed and board on offer at the only **lodging** is pretty insalubrious.

Another possible overnighter is **RHAMU** (confusingly, often pronounced "Lamu"). Renowned for its mosquitoes, it is right on the Ethiopian border by the seasonal Daua River. There's a National Christian Council of Kenya centre here where you can stay and a garrison of numbingly bored soldiers to talk to.

From Rhamu, the **paved road**, which has been an on-and-off affair since El Wak, is continuous to Mandera but in a very sorry state indeed. The road is straight and largely empty, with the barren fastnesses of Ethiopia rising up remotely on the left, but it's one of the most dangerous in Kenya as it crosses, unperplexed, a series of steep north–south ridges with a broadside lack of regard for gradient. Shattered hulks of vehicles litter the slopes, having stalled and rolled backwards. If you are in the back of a heavily laden lorry, it is worth at least finding a suitable position for leaping off. Some of the slopes have been circumvented by zigzags and the latest news is that the worst of them are being levelled. There's ample compensation for an unpredictable journey in the startling quantities of wildlife that's often to be seen along this way, including ostriches, warthogs, giraffes and gazelles.

If your vehicle makes the Wajir–Mandera connection by way of the Somalian border route, you veer to the right after El Wak and make straight for Mandera via the village of **Arabia**.

Mandera

More than a thousand kilometres from Nairobi and only half that to Mogadishu (capital of Somalia), **MANDERA** nestles at the tip of a much disputed salient of Kenyan territory wedged uncomfortably between Ethiopia and Somalia. The town, more even than Wajir, has only the most tenuous lifeline to Nairobi – and this thanks mainly to one or two daredevil light aircraft operators who fly in daily shipments of *miraa*. The same planes collect and deliver mail, messages (Mandera has telephones but only just) and government workers.

Because of the difficulties of land communication with Nairobi, the town formerly relied heavily and uneasily on food supplies from Somalia. As at Moyale, the **border** here was always virtually an open one for local people. Since the destruction of Bula Hawa – the town on the Somali side of the border – supplies are less easy to come by and the trade in Kenyan *miraa* for food (rice, sugar, pasta, milk powder and flour), supplied as foreign aid to Somalia and sold into Kenya, has vastly declined, while the needs of Mandera's swollen population have dramatically increased.

The town itself lacks the established atmosphere of Wajir and makes its southerly neighbour look positively urbane. The Girls' Secondary School, for example, is the only one in the entire district (25,000 square kilometres) and it has just 22 students. The heart of Mandera consists of a cluster of Somali *bula* (hamlets) interspersed with administrative buildings.

At the time of writing, however, Mandera is effectively a giant **refugee camp**, over-run by victims of the war in Somalia. Some 55,000 people (more than Mandera's own population) cram into a huge area of *herio* huts and shelters spread across the waste-

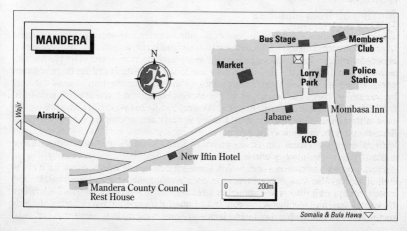

land between the airstrip and the centre of the town. Their presence makes Mandera tense and the army is much in evidence.

Practicalities

Mandera has critical water problems outside of the rainiest months of the year, December and April – to perverse effect in early 1996, when drought forced many residents and herders to flee into Ethiopia in search of water and pasture, leaving the Somali refugees behind them. All the town's water is supplied by the Daua River. If you can choose a time to visit the town, however, come in August for the annual Agricultural Society of Kenya (ASK) show, when Mandera gets a rare chance to blow its own trumpet.

A Mandera branch of the *Kenya Commercial Bank* has opened (Mon–Fri 8.30am–1pm, Sat 8.30–11am), but so far it doesn't seem to have set off the sweeping changes in the region you might expect. (Whether changing money or not, though, the air conditioning makes it a fine place to hang out.) They're as helpful as possible, but they have to radio Nairobi for the day's rates and the transaction can take hours (which can be spent watching the *miraa* barons come and go with their colossal wads).

There are few **lodgings** and their continued existence is permanently threatened by the instability of the town. The only decent ones are the *Jabane*, which is close to the middle of things, offers fans, showers and towels, and does the best food; and the *Mombasa Inn*, next door, which is a little more basic and not as comfortable. The *Mandera County Council Resthouse* is a third option, a surprise with its neat, self-contained rooms, fans and clean water (take note). It's hard to resist after the journey, though you'll score better on conversation and local immersion down at the cheaper places: the *Resthouse* is just a bit far from the town centre. The *New Iftin* and the *Mombasa Inn* both have restaurants – scruffy, rapid-turnover joints swirling with old chits and face-stuffing patrons.

Mandera's **market** is the town's focus and, like Wajir's, a bustling maze of huts and shelters – liveliest around 9 or 10am after the *miraa* arrives – with small stores and *hotelis* all around. For a **beer**, try the *Members' Club*, the only licence holder in town and open after 4pm, which occasionally comes up with a few crates. To post letters from this far corner of Kenya, you can use the **post office** (Mon–Fri 7.30am–12.30pm & 2.30–4.30pm, Sat 7.30am–12.30pm), but post takes at least four days just to reach Nairobi and at bad times it might sit there for weeks. To send something faster, go down to the airstrip in the morning and hand it to the pilot when the plane comes in.

Moving on from Mandera

Getting on the **plane** to return to Nairobi is quite an entertainment: amid the confusion of activity centring on the pilot and the *miraa* big shots, the potential passengers vie for seats – or rather places, since some of the seats have been removed. The big bales of *miraa* are off-loaded, sped into town in a Land Rover and exchanged for huge volumes of banknotes, which are then brought back to the pilot for the purchase of the next consignment. The scene is fraught with confusion but if there's a seat you'll be offered it by the Somali charterer, not the pilot. The price falls between $70 and $120 for the two- to three-hour flight, which usually stops at Wajir before clipping past the peaks of Mount Kenya to Nairobi's Wilson Airport.

Apart from the **plane** out (a daily service that's often increased to two or three flights, and sometimes a whole flock, before public holidays, especially during Ramadan when lots of *miraa* is chewed), there used to be two **bus** services back to the hub of Kenyan life. These, however, have been discontinued due to bandit raids; if the situation improves, the buses should return. As it is, if you want to travel anywhere from Mandera without flying, **trucks** (more often than not in convoy) are your only option. Try around the big tree by the police station.

Garissa

GARISSA, North Eastern Province's capital, is the least interesting of the desert towns, relatively close to Nairobi and Mombasa, and visibly influenced by both. Still, it comes across as a friendly, unhustly place and it has its ethnic interest: a large Somali contingent who live more harmoniously with their non-Somali neighbours, many of whom are coastal Muslims. Garissa was, until recently, the lowest bridging point across the **Tana River**. While the Tana is not mighty, the view of the loop of brownish-red water where it flows under the new bridge just outside town is quite impressive, especially after rain: a sullen reminder of Kenya's water and erosion problems, when you suddenly realize this is the biggest river you've seen in the country. However, a severe drought in the area since 1995 has severely hit livestock; wily local businessmen have cashed in by selling grass cut from the river banks to the desperate herders.

Garissa hovers uncertainly between coast, up-country and desert. It was recently in the news several times as the site of various serpentine encounters – a large python was found in the District Commissioner's office and a cobra in a school toilet. They were probably fleeing the heat: this is Kenya's hottest town and often unflaggingly humid as well. During the day the thermometer rarely leaves the 32–37°C zone.

You'll probably want to take the first transport out of Garissa, but if you have some time to kill, stroll down to the **Tana bridge** in the late afternoon and watch Kenya's precious topsoil flowing to the ocean. You can sometimes see hippos from here and even crocodiles (Garissa District has a high incidence of death by *mamba*), and there are signs warning you about the banks where they lurk.

Practicalities

The best **lodging** is the *New Safari Hotel* (PO Box 56), a clean B&L with running water, mosquito nets (bring your own door padlock), and a good restaurant doing *mkate mayai* each evening. The *Green Garissa Hotel* is very basic, without running water, while the cut-price beer and gloomy, self-contained rooms at the *Garissa Guest House* (PO Box 55; ☎0131/2019) aren't worth the longish walk. *Kenya Hotel and Lodging* has a busy restaurant but its rooms are unappetizing. Just over the Tana bridge on the right is a row of *hotelis* and **bars** that come alive in the evenings. (Be careful about taking photographs by the bridge: the local police don't approve.)

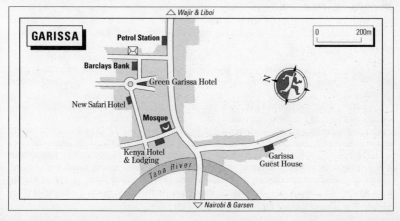

The town has a **bank** (Mon–Fri 8.30am–noon, Sat 8.30–11am), a pretty good **market** and **petrol stations**.

Getting out of Garissa

See the boxes on p.474 and p.487 about transport difficulties and security in the region. As ever, the situation is fluid and you are advised to thoroughly check out your plans before travelling further. At the time of writing, the *Garissa Express* to **Wajir** had been suspended but seemed likely to be reinstated; before suspension it set off north on Tuesday, Thursday and Saturday, arriving in Wajir the same day and **Mandera** the following evening. There is a service to **Liboi** via Dadaab, but it's pointless going there (the Somali border is closed) and, at the time of writing, the region was in the throes of a cholera epidemic. **Nairobi** has several daily connections with Garissa. Buses arrive at and depart from a spot opposite the *KBS* terminus in Eastleigh. All the Nairobi-bound buses (6–7hr) from Garissa depart at 6.30am in an armed convoy.

To **Mombasa** and **Malindi**, *Garissa Express*, *Mbuni*, and *Tana River* buses share the route, with 6am departures from the *Kobil* station, or from outside the *New Safari Hotel*; *Garissa Express* runs a daily 12.30pm service as well. Catch an early bus, though, and you can connect at **Garsen** with a Lamu-bound vehicle on the coastal route. If you're in Garissa on Monday, Wednesday or Friday you can also catch *Garissa Express* to the resettlement zone of **Mpeketoni** near Witu (departs 1pm), which is a forty-kilometre *matatu* hop from Mokowe and the hedonistic pull of Lamu.

Down the Tana to Garsen

The route down to the coast runs through Orma and Pokomo country – low-lying, flat, and densely bush-covered. The Orma **cattle herders** of this region are invariably swathed in distinctive, brilliant, deep blue cloth, a much-favoured colour which was being imported along the coast over a thousand years ago. Don't expect much of the Tana's remaining pockets of **riverine forest** to grace the scene, however, much less the river itself, as for most of the way the newly gravelled road isn't close. The bus calls at **BURA**, a desolate resettlement area, with the oddly sited *Bura Country Club* – a sure target for motorists or others moving under their own steam (*bandas* or camping). Next comes **HOLA**, site of an infamous massacre during the dying days of the colonial period. Not far from the river and consisting more or less entirely of grass huts, with an animated main street, it's a nice place to spend a day or two. **Arawale National Reserve** lies on the opposite bank of the river and has a sizeable population of the seriously threatened Hunter's hartebeest or *hirola*; you can (like everyone else) get a free ride across the Tana in a Pokomo dugout. Try the *Safari Hotel* in town for a clean, quiet, friendly stay and good cakes. And there's evening entertainment, too: the *Riverway Cinema* shows American and Indian films on a tiny screen under the stars.

For Lamu, leave the bus at **GARSEN** and pick up the *TSS* or *Faza Express* the following day. Garsen isn't anyone's favourite place – and has no electricity and no bank – but there are **lodgings** and no shortage of *hotelis*. Try the *3-in-1 Lodging and Restaurant*, which lacks some basic amenities but is reasonably clean, with a passable restaurant. Or, if the restaurant has gone further downhill, check out the *Happy Family Restaurant & Hotel*, right by where the buses stop, which happily subverts its name with bright murals of gun-toting bandits on its walls. Wherever you stay it won't cost you much; there's nowhere outside the ① category. In season, incidentally, Garsen's **mangoes** are reckoned to be some of the best and cheapest in Kenya.

Tana River Primate National Park

No charges at present.

Getting to the **Tana River Primate National Park** – main refuge of two of Kenya's rarest and most beautiful monkeys – doesn't look easy without your own vehicle. In fact, with only a small degree of perseverance, you can find your way to the river and the research headquarters (make prior enquiries with the Kenya Wildlife Service in Nairobi if possible). **Mnazini** is the easiest place to head for if you're without wheels: the 6am bus from Garissa makes the side trip down to the village itself (so long as the area isn't flooded); the midday bus will drop you only as far as the junction, a six-kilometre walk. If the district is flooded, you'll almost certainly find yourself being carried by poled canoe from just down the Mnazini track all the way to the village itself: it takes about an hour.

Mnazini is a fine, coastal-style village beneath mango trees. There are no lodgings but *hotelis* will take you in for the night once you've cleared it with the sub-chief and the headman. One of the **village shops** also has most of what you're likely to need for a few days' stay in the reserve. Beyond Mnazini, there's nothing in the way of food but occasional fruit and garden vegetables.

Nobody in the area knows Tana River Primate National Park by that name. Locals all refer to **Mchelelo**, the site of the primate research headquarters. The twelve-kilometre walk to get there involves two river crossings over the Tana's meanders, and there's no way you'd find the route through the **bush and gallery forest** unguided. Pokomo **guides** are happy to help and not hustling.

Depending on water levels, you may find you can wade across. If you need a boat, it shouldn't normally cost anything. You enter the forest at Kitere and walking thereafter becomes much more pleasant in the cool shade.

Reserve practicalities

Mchelelo campsite is small, secluded, and ravishingly pretty, with a shower and long drop. It's the site of a National Museums of Kenya research camp and the primatologists here are not used to visitors. If you don't have a letter from the NMK (and preferably an introduction and advance warning sent ahead) you may not be able to stay here. In that case they are likely to direct you on to the park headquarters at **Makere**.

If you're **driving**, the Baomo or Mchelelo tracks to the river are the ones to use, though the latter doesn't seem to be signposted from the road. It's also possible to approach the reserve from **Wenje** village, to the north. The track to Baomo is indicated on the road, but *Baomo Lodge* itself, while it still appears on some maps, is abandoned.

If you're lucky, you'll be made reasonably welcome at Makere, or at least allowed to camp. It has to be reiterated, however, that they don't have organized facilities for visitors – and you may even be given a section of fully armed rangers on the anti-poaching force to accompany you, in military fashion, as you walk the paths looking for monkeys and watching the area's superb birdlife. One or two young guides from Makere village will also help to locate the primates, as will the KWS rangers.

Wildlife

The reserve's protected inhabitants include **Tana River red colobus** and **Tana River crested mangabey** monkeys, both extremely rare and vulnerable unless the tourists turn up to keep the reserve functioning – something that has not happened for many years. In the meantime, continued encroachment on the forest threatens both species of monkey; the colobus very rarely leaves the trees.

Your chances of seeing groups of both monkeys are really good. The forest areas are fairly restricted, even within the reserve, and it's not difficult to find them in a day or

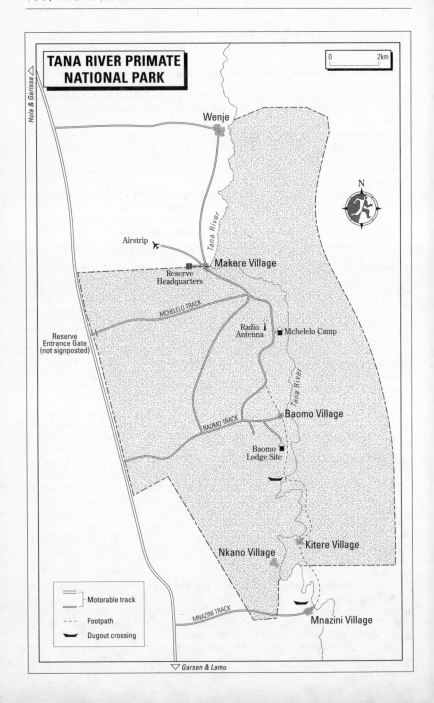

TANA RIVER PRIMATE
NATIONAL PARK

0   2km

Hola & Garissa

N

Wenje

Tana River

Airstrip

Makere Village

Reserve
Headquarters

MCHELELO TRACK

Radio
Antenna

Mchelelo Camp

Reserve
Entrance Gate
(not signposted)

Tana River

BAOMO TRACK

Baomo Village

Baomo
Lodge Site

Kitere Village

Nkano Village

Motorable track

Footpath

Dugout crossing

MNAZINI TRACK

Mnazini Village

▽ Garsen & Lamu

two. Other wildlife in the area includes blue monkeys, baboons, various squirrels and even lions, giraffe and buffalo; on the east side of the park you can see elephants, and there are some 300 of the rare Hunter's hartebeest, too. At one time it was possible to make raft and boat trips on the sluggish river, dodging large numbers of hippos and crocodiles, but such adventures haven't operated as commercial safaris for several years (see the Tana Delta box, p.420, for some details about something like this further downstream). You're likely to find local people willing to take you.

travel details

Because of their importance, particulars about **road transport** are given throughout the chapter. On the main axes – Kitale–Lodwar, Nyahururu–Loiyangalani, Isiolo–Moyale and Nairobi–Garissa – you will rarely be stuck for a ride too long. Least frequented is the route up to Loiyangalani and this, together with Isiolo–Moyale and Isiolo–Wajir–Mandera, has no bus service. For the northeast, see the box on p.474.

Buses: a summary

This indicates the minimum service you can expect in the north. The reverse service applies on each route with the same frequency. Arrival times are not guaranteed.

From Kitale to Lodwar: every 2 days.

From Nyahururu to Maralal: 1 daily arriving same day.

From Isiolo to Maralal: every 2 days, arriving same day.

From Garissa to Nairobi: 3 daily.

From Garissa to Mombasa and Malindi: daily.

Because of the security position, the following routes are currently suspended or discontinued:

From Isiolo to Marsabit
From Isiolo to Wajir
From Moyale to Mandera
From Moyale to Wajir
From Garissa to Wajir

Planes

Charter flights to Mandera Hitching a lift on the daily charter to Mandera is harder than getting a lift back again because *miraa* is a more profitable cargo than passengers.

Flights to Lake Turkana are usually part of inclusive weekend packages at around $500 per person. Contact: *Ivory Safaris Tours*, Esso Plaza, Muthaiga Road, Nairobi (PO Box 74609 Nairobi; ☎02/760546), or *Northern Kenya Lodges Ltd*, Nairobi (PO Box 14829; ☎02/332717).

Air Kenya Aviation also offers an occasional flight-only service to any or all of the **Turkana airfields** (Lodwar, Kalokol and Loiyangalani). Air hops **across the lake** are possible but depend on the number and departure or arrival points of passengers paying the full fare from Nairobi.

THE
CONTEXTS

THE HISTORICAL FRAMEWORK

The picture of Kenya's past that the first Europeans formed – a multitude of primitive peoples with no appreciable history – has been brushed aside in this century. Techniques have been found for tracing past events and migrations by combining oral traditions and comparing languages. Nevertheless, Kenya's precolonial past is still the subject of endless conjecture and, up-country, it's difficult for the traveller to keep much sense of it – especially since the physical record in ancient architecture is virtually nonexistent. On the coast, settlement ruins, old documents and the Islamic tradition help considerably to retain the feeling of a long past. What follows, up to the colonial period, is a simplified and much condensed overview, intended to pull together the historical accounts of individual peoples that are given throughout the guide. More emphasis here is given to the firmer history of the last hundred years or so.

THE CRADLE OF MANKIND

Kenya could be the place where human beings first evolved. The oldest remains belonging indisputably to **ancestral hominids** have been found on the shores of Lake Turkana. But it's hard to say whether this is conclusive proof: older finds made elsewhere could suddenly turn the theory upside down.

The east African **Rift Valley**, however, is ideal territory for the search for human origins: volcanic eruptions have repeatedly showered thick layers of ash and cinders over fossil beds, building up strata that can be reliably used to compare ages. The **Leakey** family have been instrumental in much of the work that has been done. Olduvai Gorge, in Tanzania, was the first major site to disclose evidence of human prehistory, and Louis Leakey and his wife, Mary, worked there from the 1930s. Their son, Richard, went on to explore the Turkana region and found even older fossils, putting Kenya in the spotlight of scientific attention. A suggestion in support of the "cradle of mankind" idea is that the Rift Valley's very formation – a major event on the earth's crust, which began some twenty million years ago – may have been the environmental spark that catalysed human evolution.

At any rate, while current research pushes the dates back further and further, it hasn't answered the biggest question: if this is the cradle, who were the parents? The search for an **evolutionary line** linking humans directly with more primitive primates is still the number one priority. Theories change so fast that books published in the 1960s and early 1970s contain ideas that today have been completely overturned. The **"ape-men"** australopithecines are no longer regarded as ancestors of *Homo sapiens* and it is now known that our own ancestors shared evolutionary time with them in east Africa. The fossil skull 1470 (its catalogue number), discovered by **Bernard Ngeneo** in 1972 and now in the National Museum in Nairobi, is evidence of this. Between two and three million years old, it's an example of *Homo habilis*, "handy man", a direct human ancestor.

Until Ngeneo's discovery, it was thought that while the massive, plant-munching *Australopithecus boisei* did eventually die out, its slighter, higher-brow neighbour *A. africanus* survived, adapting and evolving into the *Homo* line. Now it's believed all three species lived on the savannah and forest margins at the same time. A recent flood of discoveries of *Homo* fossils shows that the evolutionary line that eventually led to human beings was already established as long as five million years ago. Most spectacular in recent years has been the discovery of the nearly complete 1.5-million-year-old skeleton of a twelve-year-old boy of the species *Homo erectus*, our immediate ancestor. It was *erectus* ("upright" man – though in fact the australopithecines probably spent most of their time upright, too) who developed **speech**, discovered how to make **fire** and improved enormously on the **tool-making** efforts of *Homo habilis*. **Olorgasailie** and **Kariandusi** are two "hand axe" sites, probably belonging to *Homo erectus*, which have been used within the last five hundred thousand years. And it was *erectus* who, if the "cradle" theory is right, spread the humanoid gene pool to Asia, Europe and the rest of Africa, where, over the next few hundred thousand years, *Homo sapiens* emerged on the scene.

EARLY INHABITANTS

Real history begins with the **hunter-gatherers**. Numbering probably fewer than a hundred thousand, living in small units of several families, and either staying in one place for generations or moving through the country according to the dictates of the seasons, these earliest human inhabitants may have been related to the ancestors of present-day Pygmy and Bushman peoples, and probably spoke "click" languages similar to those spoken by the Bushmen today (Khoi and San). Remnant hunter-gatherer groups still live in remote parts of Kenya – the **Boni** on the mainland north of Lamu, the **Sanye** along the Tana River and the **Okiek** and **Dorobo** in parts of the highlands – but their languages have mostly been adopted from neighbouring peoples. The hunting and gathering way of life is one that has persisted in the cultural memories of most Kenyan peoples, and some of the groups who still practise it may have veered away from farming or herding societies in times of hardship.

The earliest distinct migration to Kenya was of **Cushitic**-speaking people from the Ethiopian Highlands. Occasional hunters and gatherers themselves, they were also livestock herders and farmers; over the centuries, they filled the areas that were too dry for a purely subsistence way of life. They also absorbed many of the previous inhabitants through intermarriage. Having herds and cultivating land brought up questions of ownership, inheritance

and water rights, and an elaboration of social institutions and customs to deal with them. The Cushites left evidence of their settlements in burial cairns and living sites at places like **Hyrax Hill**, near Nakuru. Stone cairns and hollow depressions in the ground are found all over the Kenya Highlands and in the Rift Valley, especially out in the dry areas towards Lake Turkana. The same people may have built the **irrigation works** still used today along the Elgeyo Escarpment, west of Lake Baringo. They had a strong material culture, using stone, particularly obsidian, to produce beautiful arrowheads, knives and axes, and they made a whole range of pottery utensils.

The **Somali** and **Rendille** of the northeast are the main groups still speaking Cushitic languages, though their arrival in Kenya was more recent. Today, only the Boni still speak a language related to the Southern Cushitic of the first farmers and herders, although the Boni themselves are hunter-gatherers. For the most part, the earliest Cushites were absorbed by peoples who came later and they adopted new languages and customs. The changes were not all one-sided, however: **circumcision** and **clitoridectomy**, practised by the early Cushites, became important cultural rituals for many of the peoples who succeeded and absorbed them.

For present-day Kenya, the most important arrivals began to reach the country in the first few centuries AD. From the northwest and the headwaters of the Nile came the **Nilotic**-speaking ancestors of the **Kalenjin**; from the west and the south came speakers of **Bantu** languages, forebears of today's **Kikuyu**, **Gusii**, **Akamba** and **Mijikenda**, among others. (Bantu, a word coined by twentieth-century linguists, derives from the common stem for "person" – *ntu* – and the plural prefix *ba*. The word is not found in any of the six hundred contemporary Bantu languages, spread across the continent, but it may have been the one used for "people" in the original proto-language before it diversified.)

The new arrivals brought not just themselves and their languages, but also new technologies, including iron-working. **Iron** had enabled the Bantu to spread from the Nigeria/Cameroon area across central Africa, clearing the virgin forests and hoeing the ground for their crops. Eastwards, they encountered new

Asian food crops – bananas, yams and rice – which had arrived in east Africa by way of the Indonesian colonization of Madagascar. This new diversity of foods helped people to settle permanently in chosen regions. The Kalenjin consolidated in the Western Highlands. The Bantu were particularly successful and, as their broad economic base took hold across the southern half of Kenya, their languages quickly spread. Herding, hunting, fishing and gathering were important supplements to the agricultural mainstay, while trade conducted with their exclusively pastoral or hunter-gatherer neighbours, especially in iron tools, carried their influence further.

By about 1000 AD, Kenya's Stone Age technology had been largely replaced by an Iron Age one, and as human domination of the country increased, the beginnings of real specialization in agriculture and herding set in among the peoples.

Down on **the coast**, Bantu immigrants mixed, over several hundred years, with the longer-established Cushitic-speaking inhabitants and with a continuous trickle of settlers from Arabia and the Persian Gulf. With the advent of Islam, this melange gradually gave rise to a distinct culture and civilization – **Swahili** – speaking a Bantu language laced with foreign vocabulary. The Swahili were Kenya's link with the rest of the world, trading animal skins, ivory, agricultural produce and slaves for cloth, metals, ceramics, grain, ghee and sugar, with ships from the Middle East, India and even China. The Swahili were the first Kenyans to acquire firearms. They were also the first to write their language (in the Arabic script) and the first to develop complex, stratified communities based on town and countryside. Swahili history is covered in more depth in Chapter Six.

LATER ARRIVALS

New **American crops** – corn, cassava and tobacco – spread through Kenya after the Portuguese arrived at the beginning of the sixteenth century. They undoubtedly increased the country's population capacity, while enabling a greater degree of permanent settlement and providing new trade goods.

At about this time, a pastoral **Nilotic**-speaking people, distantly related to the earlier Kalenjin arrivals, began a migration from the northwest. These were the first **Luo**-speakers who, some generations earlier, had left their homeland (around Wau in southern Sudan) for reasons that were probably largely economic. In the alternately flooded and parched flatlands around the Nile, unusual conditions could be catastrophic. The Luo ancestors were always on the move, herding, planting, hunting or fishing. Politically, they had a fairly complex organization, as, for months on end, while the Nile flooded, communities would be stranded in concentration along the low ridges. Several good years might be followed by drought, and population pressure then forced less dominant groups to go off in search of water and pasture. The overall trend was southwards. Groups of migrants picked up other, non-Luo-speakers on the way, gradually assimilating them through intermarriage and language change, always drawing attention with the impressive regalia and social standing of their *ruoth* – the Luo kings.

On the shores of Lake Victoria, where they finally settled, sleeping sickness is thought to have wiped out many of the Luo herds. But they were pragmatic, resourceful people, whose background of mixed farming and herding during the era of migration supported them. They turned to agriculture and, increasingly, to fishing.

Towards the end of the seventeenth century, another Nilotic, pastoral people, the **Turkana**, appeared in Kenya. Linguistically closer to the Maasai Nilotes, they seem to have shared the Luo resilience to economic hardship and they, too, have (recently) turned to fishing. Also like the Luo, and almost unique among Kenyan peoples, they have never practised circumcision.

The Maa-speakers – **Maasai** and **Samburu** – were the last group to arrive in Kenya, and their rise and fall had far-reaching effects on neighbouring peoples. Moving southwards from the beginning of the seventeenth century, their nomadic pastoral lifestyle enabled them to expand swiftly and, in a few generations, they were transformed from an obscure group into a dominant force in the region. Culturally, they borrowed extensively from their neighbours, especially the **Kalenjin**. Kalenjin words and cultural values were adopted, including circumcision, the age-set system and some ancient (originally probably Cushitic) taboos against eating fish and certain wild animals. It is likely that much of the "traditional" Maasai appearance also owes something to these contacts. The Maasai migration was no slow spread. Their cattle were periodically herded south and other peoples were raided en route to enlarge the herds; by 1800, they were widely established in the Rift Valley and on the plains, everywhere between Lake Turkana and Kilimanjaro. In response to Maasai dominance, many of the Bantu peoples adopted their styles and customs. Initiation by genital mutilation, probably already practised by most Bantu-speakers, was imbued with a new significance – especially for the Kikuyu – by intermarriage and close, if not always peaceable, relations with the Maasai.

Severe **droughts** in the nineteenth century pushed the Maasai further and further afield in search of new pastures, bringing them into conflict, and trade, with other peoples. Drought, disease and rinderpest epidemics (which killed off their cattle) were also responsible for a series of civil wars between different Maasai sections in the second half of the nineteenth century.

These **Maasai civil wars** disrupted the **trading networks** which had been set up between the coast and the interior, mainly by Swahili, Mijikenda, Akamba and Kikuyu. Dutch, English and French goods were finding their way up-country, and American interests were already being served nearly two centuries ago, as white calico cloth (still called *amerikani* today) became a major item of profit. From western Kenya and Uganda, **slaves** were being exported in exchange for foreign commerce in the last throes of the slave trade's existence. Largely in response to slavery and widespread fighting, the first **missionaries** installed themselves up-country (the earliest went inland from Mombasa in 1846). Throughout this period, the Maasai disrupted movements through their territories and attacked Swahili slavers, Bantu traders and explorer-missionaries alike. The Maasai *morani* were specifically trained for raiding – a kind of guerrilla warfare – but, while their reputation lived on, they were bitterly divided among themselves and not organized on anything like a tribal scale.

By the time Europe had partitioned the map of Africa, the Maasai, who could have been the imperialists' most intractable enemies, were unable to retaliate effectively. The Kalenjin-speaking **Nandi** of the Western Highlands, who had begun to take the Maasai's place as Kenya's most feared adversaries, put up the stiffest resistance. They were organized to the extent of having a single spiritual leader, the *orkoiyot*, who ruled what was in effect a theocracy. Their war of attrition against the British delayed advances for a number of years. But the Nandi did not have the territorial advantage that would have helped the Maasai, and the murder of their *orkoiyot*, **Koitalel**, by the British, destroyed their military organization.

THE INVASION: 1885–1902

All Kenya's peoples resisted colonial domination to some degree. In the first twenty years of British attempts to rule, tens of thousands were killed in ugly massacres and manhunts, and many more were made homeless. Administrators – whose memoirs (see "Books", p.542) are the most revealing background for that period – all differed in their ideas of the ultimate purpose of their work and the best means of imposing British authority.

British interests in east Africa at the close of the last century had sprung from the European power struggle and the "scramble for Africa". The 1885 Berlin Conference chopped the continent into arbitrary spheres of influence. Germany was awarded what was to become Tanganyika; Britain got Kenya and Uganda. In 1886, formal agreements were drawn up and Kilimanjaro was ceded to Victoria's grandson, the Kaiser, giving each monarch a snowcapped equatorial mountain.

But rivalry wasn't far beneath the red tape and Germany clearly had Uganda earmarked. Sir William Mackinnon, who for a decade had been pressing for a licence to start trading, was now given permission to start commercial operations with his Imperial British east Africa Company (IBEAC) in 1888. The company officers – mostly young and totally inexperienced English clerks – established a series of trading forts at fifty-mile intervals in a line connected by a rough ox-track leading from Mombasa into Uganda. Machakos, Murang'a and Mumias all began as IBEAC stations. **Uganda** was the focus of interest, since Kenya – decimated by drought, locusts, rinderpest and civil war – seemed largely a deserted wasteland. And

Uganda was strategically important for **control of the Nile** – which had long been a British preoccupation. Conspiring foreign powers were mentioned darkly in the House of Lords. Britain's claim was in danger of lapsing if Uganda could not be properly garrisoned and supplied. It was also a centre for the **slave trade** that Britain, in need not of slaves but of new markets, was committed to wiping out. And in the back of many minds was the kind of sentiment expressed by the London *Times* in 1873:

There seems no reason not to believe that one of the finest parts of the world's surface is going to waste under the shroud of malaria which surrounds it, and under the barbarous anarchy with which it is cursed. The idea dawns upon some of us that some better destiny is yet in store for a region so blessed by nature, and the development of Africa is a step yet to come in the development of the world.

In the end, the practicability of developing "some better destiny" for Uganda proved out of reach.

With the bankruptcy of the IBEAC and its failure to establish any kind of administration, the British government formally stepped into the breach in 1885 and declared a **protectorate** over Uganda and Kenya. Having acquired the region in a haphazard lottery, the government was now forced to do something with it. A useful gesture was required: Her Majesty's government decided to build a **railway**. This classic, valedictory piece of Victorian engineering took six years to complete and cost the lives of hundreds of Indian labourers. Financially, it was a commitment which grew out of all proportion to the likely returns and continued to grow long after the last rail was laid. But its completion transformed the future of east Africa. From now on, the supply lines were secure and the interior only a month's journey from Europe by ship and rail. Suddenly the prospects for developing the cool, fertile Kenya highlands looked much more attractive than the distant unknowns of Uganda and its powerful kingdoms.

More immediately, the railway physically divided the **Maasai** at a time when they were already disunified and moving into alliances with the British. Their grazing lands, together with the regions of the **Kalenjin** and **Kikuyu** on the lower slopes of the highlands, were to become the heartland of white settlerdom.

THE KENYA COLONY

While the government, typically, dragged its feet, the story circulated that Kenya might be a land of opportunity: a new New Zealand, or even a Jewish homeland. A party of Zionists was in fact escorted around Kenya but declined the offer. It was Sir Charles Eliot, the Protectorate's second governor, who was the main mover behind the settlement scheme. While there was an undercurrent of consideration for "the rights of natives" which shouldn't be forgotten, the growing clamour of voices claiming the support of British taxpayers – who had met the bill for the railway – outweighed any altruism. Eliot's extravagant reports on the potential of BEA (British east Africa) were published and, willy-nilly, government policy was directed towards getting the settlers in and making the railway pay. Landless aristocrats, middle-class adventurers, big-game hunters, ex-servicemen and Afrikaners (the farming land was also advertised in South Africa) began to trickle up the line. Using ox-wagons to get to the tracts of bush they had leased, they started their farms from scratch. Lord Delamere, governor himself for a time, was their biggest champion. In the years leading up to World War I, the trickle of settlers became a flood and by 1916 the area "alienated" to Europeans had risen to 15,000 square kilometres of the best land. Imported livestock was hybridized with hardy, local breeds; coffee, tea, sisal and pineapples were introduced and thrived; European crops flourished in superabundance and cereals soon covered thousands of hectares.

Nearly half the land worth farming was now in the hands of settlers, but it had rapidly become clear that it was far from empty of local inhabitants. Colonial invasion had occurred at a low point in the fortunes of Kenya's peoples and, unprepared for the scale of the incursion, they were swiftly pushed aside into "native reserves" or became "squatters" without rights. As populations recovered, serious land shortages set in. The British appointment of "chiefs" – whose main task was to collect a tax on every hut – had the effect of diverting grievances against colonial policy on to these early collaborators and laying the foundations of a class structure in Kenyan society. Without a money economy, employment was the only means available to pay taxes and, effectively, a system of forced labour had been created. The whole apparatus quickly became entrenched in a series of **land and labour laws**. A poll tax was added to the hut tax; all African men were compelled to register to facilitate labour recruitment; squatters on alienated land were required to pay rent, through labour; and cash cropping on African plots was discouraged or banned (coffee licences, for example, were restricted to white farmers). The highlands were strictly reserved for white settlement, while land not owned by Europeans became Crown Land, its African occupants "tenants at will" of the Crown and liable to summary eviction.

Asians, too, were excluded from the highlands. While the leader of Kenya's Indians, **A M Jeevanjee**, had called for the transformation of Kenya into the "America of the Hindu", the proposal never came near consideration by the British. Barred from farming on any scale – except in the far west, where they developed sugar cane as an important crop – Indians concentrated on the middle ground, setting up general stores (*dukas*) across the country, investing in small industries and handling services.

WORLD WAR I

World War I, although there were comparatively few battles in Kenya itself, had a number of profound effects. Some 200,000 African porters and soldiers were conscripted and sent to Tanganyika (German east Africa), where one in four of them died. Those who returned were deeply influenced by the experience. They had seen European tribes at war with each other, they had experienced European fallibility, and witnessed the kind of organization used to overcome it.

General von Lettow Vorbeck, the German commander, waged a dogged campaign against British forces despite the fact that his own were vastly outnumbered, with the aim of engaging as much manpower as possible and taking the heat off German forces in Europe. He earned a respectable place in the history books as a result.

Nevertheless, the Germans lost the war – and Tanganyika – to the British, and the Crown's commitments in east Africa were suddenly multiplied.

Sir Edward Northey, governor of Kenya at the time of armistice, pushed his **Soldier Settlement Scheme** through without difficulty. Its aim, to double the settler population in Kenya to nine thousand and increase revenue, seemed promising enough to a government sapped by war. But the Soldier Settlement Scheme was bitterly resented by Africans, particularly those who had fought beside the soldiers and were now excluded from their gains.

EARLY NATIONALISM AND REACTION

Political associations sprang up among those with a mission education and ex-servicemen: the Kikuyu Association, the Young Kikuyu Association and the Young Kavirondo Association. **Harry Thuku,** secretary of the Young Kikuyu Association, realized its potential and re-formed it as the east Africa Association in order to recruit on a nationwide basis. The hated registration law by which every African was obliged to carry a pass – the *kipande* – was a prime grievance, but tax reduction, introduction of land title deeds and wage increases were demanded as well. Alliances were built up with embittered Indian associations and 1921 saw a year of **protests** and rallies. These culminated in Thuku's detention, **violent suppression** and the shooting by police of 25 demonstrators at a mass rally calling for Thuku's release. He remained in detention for eleven years.

The Indian constituency eventually secured two nominated seats (not elected) on the Legislative Council. Africans, meanwhile, remained voiceless, landless, disenfranchised and segregated by the colour bar.

As the settlers became established, they began to contribute appreciably to the income of **the colony** (which Kenya had officially become in 1920). Most of them seem to have believed that they were in at the beginning of a long and glorious pageant of white dominion. Indeed, settler self-government, along Canadian or South African lines, was a declared aim. African demands were hardly heeded by the authorities, but the Colonial

Office was in a difficult position over the **Indians**, who were already British subjects and whose demands for equal rights they had trouble in refuting. Tentative proposals to give them voting rights, allow unrestricted immigration from India and abolish segregation caused alarm and indignation among the settlers. Their **Convention of Associations**, already arguing the case for white home rule, formed a "Vigilance Committee", which worked out detailed military plans for rebellion, including the kidnapping of the governor and the deportation of the Indians. Sensing a crisis, the Colonial Office drew up a white paper and a grudging settlement was reached that allowed five Indians and one Arab to be elected to the Legislative Council (the colony's local government), as opposed to eleven Europeans.

The primacy of African "interests", admirably reiterated yet again in the Devonshire Declaration, was still denied any real expression, least of all by Africans themselves. A system of de facto **apartheid** was being practised. It was in this climate in the 1920s and 1930s that, floating above their economic troubles, the settlers had their heyday – the **Happy Valley life** so appallingly and fascinatingly depicted in *White Mischief* and other books.

EDUCATION, KENYATTA AND THE KIKUYU

The opportunities available to Africans came almost entirely through **mission schools** at first. Again, there was conflict between government and settlers on the question of **education**. The Colonial Office was committed, on paper at least, to the general development of the country for all its inhabitants, while the white farmers were on the whole adamant that raising educational standards could only lead to trouble. A crude form of Swahili had become the language of communication between Africans and Europeans. But the teaching of English was a controversial issue that hardliners foresaw eventually rebounding on government and settlers alike. In frustration, self-help **Kikuyu independent schools** were set up in the 1930s, primarily in order to teach their own children English.

Whether barring access to English education would ultimately have made any difference is debatable, but by the late 1930s there were already enough educated Africans to pose the

beginnings of a serious challenge to white supremacy. One of these was **Jomo Kenyatta**.*

After Thuku's imprisonment and the subsequent bloodshed at Nairobi in 1921, the east African Association was dissolved. It was succeeded by the **Kikuyu Central Association (KCA)**, which Kenyatta joined in 1928. The KCA was the spearhead of **nationalism** and lobbied hard for a return of alienated land, the lowering of taxes and for elected African representatives on the Legislative Council. It also protested against missionary efforts to outlaw "**female circumcision**", on the grounds that the church was attempting to undermine Kikuyu culture. This last conflict led to a leadership crisis in the KCA and for a number of years threatened to swamp other issues. But Kenyatta spent most of the period between 1931 and 1946 in Britain, campaigning for the KCA, studying anthropology under Malinowski at the London School of Economics and writing his homage to the Kikuyu people, *Facing Mount Kenya*.

Kenya survived the 1929 stock market crash and the resulting world **trade slump** as the colonial government became increasingly committed to the struggling settlers it was now bailing out. Exports fell catastrophically; coffee-planting by non-whites was still prohibited and the tax burden continued to be placed squarely on Africans. Faced with this crisis, even some of the settlers began to accept that large-scale changes were in order. Just as awareness was growing that the economy could not survive indefinitely unless Africans were given more of a chance to participate in it, Kenya was thrown into World War II.

WORLD WAR II – AND MAU MAU

Perhaps not surprisingly, soldiers were easily recruited into the **King's African Rifles** when Italian-held Ethiopia (then Abyssinia) declared

---

*Kenyatta, born in the late 1890s, went to a mission school and was baptized a Christian. He was also circumcised, and initiated into Kikuyu adulthood. His name was adopted from the shop he ran in Nairobi, *Kenyatta Stores*, which in turn was named after the traditional beaded belt (*kenyatta*) he always wore.

war on Kenya. Volunteers wanted money, education and a chance to see the world; conscripts, filling the quotas assigned to their chiefs, faced a life at home or on the reserve that was no better. Propaganda immediately succeeded in casting Hitler's image as the embodiment of all racist evil. Some Africans thought the war, once won, would improve their position in Kenya. They were partly right. Military campaigns in Ethiopia and Burma owed much of their success to African troops and during the war their efforts were glowingly praised by Allied commanders.

On the soldiers' return, a new awareness, more profound than that felt by the returning porters and *askaris* of World War I, had crept up on them. The white tribes of Europe had fought the war on the issue of self-determination; the message wasn't lost on Africans. Yet still, in almost every other sphere of life, they were demeaned and humiliated. The KCA had been banned at the outbreak of war, allegedly for supporting the Italian fascists, and African political life was subdued. Real change, for 99 percent of the population, was still a dream.

Kenya's food-exporting economy had done well out of the war and it was clear the colony could make a major contribution to Britain's recovery. The post-war Labour government encouraged economic expansion without going far to include Africans among the beneficiaries of the investment. Industrialization gathered momentum and there was a rapid growth of towns. There was also further promotion of **white immigration** – a new influx of European settlers arrived soon after the war – and greater power was given to the settlers on the Legislative and Executive Councils. Population growth and intense **pressure on land** in the rural areas were leading to severe disruptions of traditional community life as people were shunted into the reserves or else left their villages to search for work in the towns. On the political front, militant **trade unionism**, dominated by ex-servicemen, gradually usurped the positions of those African leaders who had been prepared to work with the government.

POSTWAR AFRICAN POLITICS

A single African member, Eliud Mathu, was appointed to the Legislative Council in 1944. More significant, however, was the formation of the **Kenya African Union** (**KAU**), a consultative group of leaders and spokesmen set up with the governor's approval to liaise with Mathu. The KAU's first president was Harry Thuku, but it was **Kenyatta's return** from England in 1946, to an unexpectedly tumultuous hero's welcome, that signalled a real departure for African political rights and the birth of a new current of nationalism. KAU was transformed into an active political party – and ran straight into conflict with itself. The **radicals** within the party wanted sweeping changes in land ownership, equal voting rights and abolition of the pass law. The **moderates** were for negotiation, educational improvement, multiracial progress and a gradual shift of power. Nor were the moderates convinced that their own best interests lay in confronting the British head on: they had all achieved considerable ambitions within the settler economy. Kenyatta was ambitious himself but the Europeans mistrusted his intentions and rumour-mongered about his communist connections, his visit to Russia during his time abroad and his personal life.

Despite Kenyatta's efforts to steer a middle course, KAU became increasingly radical and Kikuyu-dominated. While he angled to give the party a multi-tribal profile to appease the settlers, he also managed to sacrifice some moderates in the leadership for the sake of party unity. But there were defections as well. Several radicals, including **Dedan Kimathi**, joined an underground movement and took **oaths** of allegiance against the British. Betrayal of the movement was punished by execution and collaborators with the government faced the same threat. Oathing groups emerged secretly all around the Central Highlands and, by 1952, a central committee was organized to coordinate activities.

THE MAU MAU REBELLION

The question of how much the KAU leadership was involved in what came to be known as **Mau Mau** (from *muma*, a traditional Kikuyu oath) is one that reappeared time after time in the years leading to and after Independence. Certainly Mau Mau attracted large numbers of young men from the rural periphery of towns like Nyeri, Fort Hall and Nairobi, and they used Kenyatta's name in their propaganda. Many members had taken part in strikes in the late 1940s: they were mobilized into violent action by the shortage of land on the reserves and the contrast with the new-found success of the settlers. There was a burning desire to oust the Europeans from the "White Highlands". The Mau Mau oath-takers called themselves the **Land and Freedom Army**. **Ex-soldiers** who had fought for the British, many of whom had learned guerrilla warfare in Burma, were crucial to their military effort.

Kenyatta played a delicate political game, condemning strikes and even oath-taking but ready to seize on any chance to exploit the situation. In 1952, incensed by simmering African nationalism and random outbursts of violence on white farms, the settlers pressured the government into declaring a **state of emergency**. Mau Mau was banned and all African nationalist organizations were proscribed. Kenyatta and other KAU leaders were arrested, convicted of founding and managing Mau Mau – on the flimsiest evidence – and sent into internal exile. For the next four years, while **"The Emergency"** blazed and African political life was brought, once again, to a virtual standstill, the full weight of British military muscle was brought to bear against the revolt, barely forty years since the era of "punitive expeditions".

Thousands of **British troops** were sent to Kenya. To them, every African was a potential terrorist, every homestead a Mau Mau hideout. As the troops moved in, the hard-core guerrillas fled into the forest and lived off the jungle for months on end, launching surprise attacks at night. They relied on considerable support from the Kikuyu homesteads for supplies, intelligence reports and stolen weapons. Under emergency powers, a policy of "villagization" was enforced and tens of thousands of Kikuyu were relocated to "secure villages" or detained in barbed-wire concentration camps. At one point, one-third of the entire male Kikuyu population was being held in detention.

The **end of the revolt** came with the British capture and execution of Dedan Kimathi, the Land and Freedom Army's commander-in-chief. Helicopters and defoliant were brought in to flush out the last pockets of resistance, but in any case morale was low. The Western press made much of Mau Mau atrocities, though a total of just 32 European civilians and about 50

troops were killed in the struggle. For Africans, the figure was around 13,000 men, women and children, mainly Kikuyu. Many of these, uncommitted to Mau Mau, yet living in key locations as far as the British were concerned, were caught, sometimes literally, in the crossfire.

The authorities described Mau Mau as a tribal uprising, a meaningless explosion of tension. Paranoid settlers perceived an external communist threat in the revolt. Some observers went so far as to call it a Kikuyu civil war between those established on the reserves and others – the guerrillas – newly displaced from European farms. And while Akamba, Maasai, Luo, Meru and Embu did join the Land and Freedom Army, its membership was overwhelmingly Kikuyu-speaking. As a focus for nationalism, the revolt served as a political barometer: the tension between the loyalists and the rebels and their sympathizers was the fulcrum on which Kenyan politics was to swing in the years leading up to and after Independence. Jomo Kenyatta was in many ways lucky to have been forced to sit out the period in detention.

INDEPENDENCE – *UHURU*

With the emergency over, the KAU leaders still at liberty set about exploiting the European fear of a repeat episode. Anything that now delayed the fulfilment of African nationalist aspirations could be seen as fuel for another revolt. There was no longer any question of a Rhodesia-style, white-dominated Independence. Settlers, mindful of the **preparations for independence** taking place in other African countries, began rallying to the cry of multiracialism in a vain attempt to secure what looked like a very shaky future.

At the 1960 Lancaster House Conference in London, African representatives won a convincing victory by pushing through measures to give them majorities in the Legislative Council and the Council of Ministers. Members, all nominated by the colonial authorities, included **Tom Mboya**, the prominent and charismatic Luo trade unionist, and the radical politician **Oginga Odinga** (another Luo), as well as **Daniel Arap Moi** and the Mijikenda leader **Ronald Ngala**. A new constitution was drawn up and eventual access to the White Highlands was accepted. The declaration promised that "Kenya was to be an African country": the path to Independence was guaranteed. **Macmillan** was saying as much in his "Wind of Change" speech given to the South African parliament at the time the Lancaster House Conference was meeting.

The settlers perceived a "calamitous betrayal", with universal franchise and African-dominated independence expected within ten years. (In fact, it happened earlier than anticipated.) Minority tribal associations, meanwhile, foresaw troubles ahead if the **Kikuyu-Luo elite** achieved independence for Kenya at the cost of the smaller constituencies. In 1960, the Kenya African National Union (**KANU**) was formed. Soon after, a second, more moderate party, the Kenya African Democratic Union (**KADU**), was created, with Britain's help, to federate the minority, largely rural-based, political associations in a broad defensive alliance against Kikuyu-Luo domination. One of KADU's leading members was Daniel Arap Moi.

Elections were held in 1961 and KANU emerged with nineteen seats against KADU's eleven. But KANU refused to form a government until Kenyatta was released. Settlers began to leave the country, selling their farms and evacuating before the predicted collapse of European privilege – or even holocaust – that some feared if the "leader unto darkness and death" were set free.

A temporary coalition government was formed, composed of KADU, European and Asian members. Kenyatta was duly released and, six months later, a member resigned his seat, making room for him on the Legislative Council. In 1962, Kenyatta became Minister for Constitutional Affairs and Economic Planning – a wide portfolio – in a new coalition government formed out of the KADU alliance and KANU. Despite a second London conference to try to reach an agreement about the federal constitution demanded by KADU, the question was left in the air. Independence elections the following year (though the Somalis of the northeast, who had no wish to be in Kenya, boycotted them) seemed to answer the constitutional question. KANU emerged with an even greater lead and a mandate for a non-federal structure. On June 1 – Madaraka Day – Kenyatta became Kenya's first prime minister. And on December 12, 1963, control of foreign affairs was handed over and Kenya became formally **independent**.

THE KENYATTA YEARS – HARAMBEE

It was barely sixty years since the pioneer settlers had arrived. Many of them – those who hadn't panicked and sold out – were now determined to stay and risk the future under an **African government**. Despite his unjust seven years in detention, Kenyatta turned out to have more consideration for their interests than could have been foreseen. He held successful meetings with settlers in his home village; his bearded, genial image and conciliatory speeches assuring them of their rights and security quickly earned him the respected title *Mzee* (Elder) and wide international support. Many Europeans retained important positions in administration and the judiciary.

Milton Obote and Julius Nyerere, leaders of newly independent Uganda and Tanzania, held talks with Kenyatta on setting up an **east African Community** to share railways, aviation, postal services and telecommunications, and customs and excise. This was formally inaugurated in 1967. There was a mood of optimism: it looked very much as if Kenya had succeeded against all the odds.

But there were urgent issues to contend with. **Land reform** and the rehabilitation of freedom fighters and detainees were the most pressing. Large tracts of European land were bought up and a programme to provide small plots to landless peasants was rapidly instigated. Political questions loomed large as well. On December 12, 1964, Kenya became a republic, its head of state no longer the Queen, but rather President Kenyatta. KADU was dissolved "in the interests of national unity", its leaders absorbed into the ruling KANU party. There was, it seemed, no longer any need for an opposition: everyone was on the same side and Kenya was henceforth a de facto one-party state. For the sake of "national security", British troops were kept on, initially to quell a revolt of ethnic Somalis in the northeast and an army mutiny in Nairobi. A defence treaty has kept a British force at Nanyuki ever since.

There was heavy emphasis on cooperation and unity. The spirit of *harambee* (pulling together) was endorsed by Kenyatta at all his public appearances. *Harambee* meetings became a unique national institution, fundraising events at which – in a not untraditional way – donations were made by local notables and politicians towards self-help health-care and educational programmes. During the 1960s and 1970s, hundreds of *harambee* schools were built and equipped in this way. But the ostentatious gifts, and particularly the guaranteed press coverage the next day with donors listed in order of value, sometimes reduced the *harambee* vision of community development to an exercise in patronage and competitive status-seeking.

On the **economic front**, the first decade of Independence saw remarkable changes and rapid growth. Although only a quarter of the country gets enough rainfall to make it agriculturally reliable, the settlers' fairly broad-based crop-exporting economy was a powerful springboard for development; one, moreover, that wasn't difficult to transfer to predominantly African control. While many large landholdings were sold *en bloc* to African investors, smaller farmers did begin to contribute significantly to export earnings through coffee, tea, pyrethrum and fruit.

Industrialization proceeded at a slower pace. Kenya's mineral resources are very limited and the country relies heavily on oil imports. **Foreign investment** wasn't especially beneficial, as investors were given wide freedoms to import equipment and technical skills and to re-export much of the profit.

Growth, rather than a radical redistribution of wealth, was the government's main concern. Although by 1970 more than two-thirds of the European mixed farming lands were occupied by some 50,000 Africans, and the overall standard of living had improved considerably, income disparities were greater than ever. And 16,000 square kilometres of ranch lands and plantations remained largely in foreign hands.

From the outset, it was clear that the fruits of Independence were not going to be shared fairly. Kikuyu-Luo domination – but particularly Kikuyu – was irksome and strongly resented by other groups. It was perhaps inevitable that the people who had lost most and suffered most under British rule should expect to receive the most benefits from Independence. However, many Kikuyu had also been able to take advantage, as far as it was possible, of the settler economy by earning wages, setting up businesses and sending their children to school.

The resettlement programme was abandoned in 1966, its objectives "largely attained". But many peasants, having been squatters on European farms, were now "illegal squatters" on private African land. Thousands migrated to the towns where unemployment was already a serious problem. Kenya was becoming a class-divided society.

POLITICAL OPPOSITION ... AND REACTION

It was in this climate that KANU's leadership split. **Oginga Odinga**, the party vice-president, resigned in 1966 to form the socialist **Kenya People's Union (KPU)** and 29 MPs joined him. The ex-guerrilla Bildad Kaggia became deputy head of the KPU and a vocal agitator for poorer Kikuyu. Kenyatta and Mboya closed ranks in KANU and prepared for political conflict. KPU was anti-capitalist and claimed to speak on behalf of the masses, who it maintained had been betrayed by *Uhuru*. On foreign affairs it was firmly non-aligned. Denouncing the opposition, KANU – led in this respect by Tom Mboya – stressed the need for close ties with the West, for commercial enterprise and foreign investment, and for economic conditions that would attract foreign aid. Ideologically, KANU talked of "African socialism". KPU's stand was claimed to be divisive: the country should be pulling together to fight the triple evils of poverty, ignorance and disease. KPU was barely tolerated for three years, its members harassed and detained by the security forces, its activities obstructed by new legislation and constitutional amendments.

In KANU, Odinga was succeeded (briefly) in the post of vice-president by Joseph Murumbi and then, with behind-the-scenes encouragement from the British government's Foreign & Commonwealth Office in London (which wanted to avoid a radical in the job), by Daniel Arap Moi.

Odinga had strong, grassroots support in the Luo and Gusii districts of western Kenya. But **Tom Mboya**'s supporters came from an even broader base, including many poor Kikuyu. By the end of the 1960s, speculation was mounting about whether he would be able to take over the presidency on Kenyatta's death. As the *Mzee's* right-hand man he was widely tipped to succeed – a possibility that alarmed

Kenyatta's Kikuyu supporters. The republic's second political **assassination*** decided the matter: Mboya was gunned down by a Kikuyu assassin in central Nairobi on July 5, 1969. No high-level complicity in the murder was ever brought to light, but Mboya's death was a devastating blow to Kenya's fragile stability, setting off shock waves along both class and tribal divisions. There was widespread fighting and rioting between Kikuyu and Luo, fuelled by years of rivalry and growing feelings of Luo exclusion from government. During a visit by Kenyatta to Kisumu – where he attended a public meeting at which Odinga and his supporters were present – hostility against his entourage was so great that police opened fire, killing at least ten demonstrators.

The KPU was immediately banned and Odinga detained without trial. Although the constitution continued to guarantee the right to form opposition parties, non-KANU nominations to parliament were, in practice, forbidden. There was a resurgence of oath-taking among Kikuyu, Meru and Embu, pledging to maintain the Kikuyu hold on power. The Kikuyu contingent in the army was strengthened and a new force of shock troops, the General Service Unit (GSU), was recruited under Kikuyu officers: independent of police and army, it was to act as an internal security force. In the early 1970s, Kikuyu control – of the government, the administration, business interests and land – gripped tighter and tighter.

Internationally, however, Kenya was seen as one of the safest African investments – a model of stability and democracy only too happy to allow the multinational corporations access to its resources and markets. The development of the tourist industry helped give the country a bright and positive profile. And, in comparison with most other African countries, some still fighting for independence and others beset by civil war or paralysed by drought, Kenya's future looked healthy enough.

But in achieving record economic growth, foreign interests often seemed to crush indigenous ones. An elite of rich profiteers – nicknamed the **Wabenzi** after the Mercedes Benz they favoured – extracted enormous private gains out of transactions with foreign companies. Nepotism was blatant and Kenyatta himself was rumoured to be one of the richest men in the world. For the mass of Kenyan people, life was hardly any better than before Independence. Graduates poured out of the secondary schools with few prospects of using their qualifications; population increase was (and remains) the highest in the world; and, most damaging of all, land distribution was still grossly unfair in a society where land was the basic means of making a living for nearly all.

In 1975, in the first ever explicit public attack on the Kikuyu monopoly of power, the radical populist MP **J M Kariuki** warned that Kenya could become a country of "ten millionaires and ten million beggars". He was arrested for his pains, then, some weeks later, was found murdered in the Ngong Hills. Reaction was stunned and a massive turnout at his funeral was followed by angry **student demonstrations**. Kariuki's appeal had derived from unimpeachable honesty and forthrightness and a stubborn perseverance in addressing the issues of economic and social justice. He riled his opponents by his sincerity and his refusal to espouse any easily shot-down ideology. Although a Kikuyu himself, from a non-ruling northern clan, a former Mau Mau detainee and at one time a close associate of Kenyatta, he was unquestionably a threat to the Kikuyu power base. A parliamentary report on his death had two prominent names deleted at Kenyatta's demand. "Kariuki's death", wrote the then outspoken *Weekly Review*, "instils in the minds of the public the fear of dissidence, the fear to criticize, the fear to stand out and take an unconventional public stance." Kenyatta and the Kikuyu clique meant business. In the following years, a number of other MPs were detained. The burning issue of landlessness was no longer one many people were prepared to shout about.

As criticism at home was suffocated, foreign criticism of the direction Kenya was taking began to grow. Early in 1975, a series of bomb explosions in Nairobi – attributed to a "poor people's" liberation group – drew attention to the country: the foreign press carried reports of entrenched **corruption** from the president and his family down. Kariuki's murder and, later, a parliamentary row over ivory smuggling in which Kenyatta was heavily impli-

---

*The first was that of Pia Gama Pinto, an outspoken Goan communist politician who was killed in 1965.

cated, refocused attention on Kenya. But the government was far from inviting serious condemnation from the West. Kenya was seen, despite its formal non-alignment, as a staunchly anti-communist ally of Britain and America, and a recipient of massive grants and loans (for which, in return, foreign investors were allowed to reap handsome profits). And, as was rightly pointed out, there was no clear successor to the president nor any effective opposition worth cultivating.

Kenyatta had retreated into dictatorial seclusion, propped up by close Kikuyu cronies, among them Chief Koinange and Charles Njonjo, who ten years later was to cause a political storm. As parliament, and even the cabinet, took an increasingly passive role in decision-making, the pronouncements from the *Mzee*'s "court" began to be accompanied by vague suggestions of threats to his government from unspecified foreign powers. By 1977, the **east African Community** had ceased to function. Its structure had always favoured Kenya as the strongest member, and it was wracked by mistrust between Kenya and Tanzania, then further torn by Idi Amin's 1971 coup in Uganda. Kenya finally seized the lion's share of community assets, mostly ships and rolling stock in the territory at the time. Hostility towards socialist policies in Tanzania, delayed elections, further detentions and growing allegations of corruption formed the sullen backdrop to **Kenyatta's death**, in bed, on August 28, 1978.

KENYA IN THE 1980s – NYAYO

The passing of the *Mzee* took Kenya by surprise. There was a nationwide outpouring of grief and shock. Mourners filed past the coffin for days. For many, however, there was also a profound sense of relief and anticipation. An era was over and the future might better reflect the ideas of twenty years earlier.

Fears about the succession proved unfounded as vice-president **Daniel Arap Moi** smoothly assumed power with the help of Mwai Kibaki and Charles Njonjo. He quickly gathered popular support with moves against corruption in the civil service (where the mass of Kenyans felt it most), his stand against tribal nepotism (he himself comes from a minority group, the Kalenjin), and the release of all

Kenyatta's political prisoners. The press, too, traditionally circumspect and conservative, relaxed a little. Moi assured Kenya and the world that, while he would not be making radical departures from Kenyatta's policies, the more blatant iniquities of the old guard's paternalistic system would be ironed out.

But the honeymoon was short. Odinga and other ex-KPU MPs were prevented from standing in the general elections of 1979. **Student protests**, focusing on the anniversary of Kariuki's murder, began again; the closing of the university became an annual event. On the international scene, the whole Indian Ocean region became strategically important with the fall of the Shah of Iran and the Soviet invasion of Afghanistan. Kenya developed significantly closer ties with the **United States**, extending military facilities to American vessels in exchange for gifts of grain after a failure of the harvest in 1983. Ironically, the country's own surplus had been exported the previous year.

In the first year or two of his presidency, Moi's **Nyayo** (footsteps) philosophy of "peace, love and unity" in the wake of Kenyatta found wide appeal, and his apparent honesty and outspoken attacks against tribalism impressed many, making him friends abroad. But the failure to make any adjustments in economic policy in favour of the rural and urban poor soon resulted in strong, if muted, criticism at home.

THE COUP ATTEMPT

Two major events rocked the government in the 1980s. On Sunday August 1, 1982 – three months after constitutional amendments were pushed through by Njonjo to make Kenya officially a one-party state (to prevent Oginga Odinga registering a new political party, the Kenya Socialist Alliance) – sections of the Kenya Air Force attempted a **military coup**. Kenyans woke to the sound of continuous Bob Marley on the radio, a repeated coup broadcast and, in Nairobi at least, sporadic gunfire. There was widespread confusion for several hours. The People's Redemption Council, who had taken the radio station, were unknown: there had been no lead-up. Most of the army was on military exercise in the north, and at first the Air Force rebels were in control. During the course of the day, hundreds of shops, especially in Nairobi, were looted, mostly by civilians. Asians, particularly, suffered huge losses: Asian women were raped and many Asian homes ransacked.

By the end of the day, the "coup" had disintegrated into a free-for-all. But as it became clear that there was no prearranged support among other armed forces, the army and the GSU consolidated against the KAF, shooting hundreds of men, raping and killing women and patrolling the streets on the lookout for rebels. Dozens of students were killed. The government announced 159 deaths, but witnesses claim to have seen more bodies on a single street.

In the immediate aftermath of the coup attempt, thousands of airmen were arrested and the service itself was disbanded. The university, believed to be a "breeding ground for subversion", was dissolved. Fourteen airmen were sentenced to death though only two, who had fled to asylum in Tanzania, were eventually executed when handed back to Kenya. There had been considerable Luo involvement in the attempt to seize power and Oginga Odinga was once again placed under house arrest.

THE NJONJO AFFAIR AND AFTER

Foreign investors held their breath and tourist bookings slumped, but postmortems of the uprising faded as the country was distracted by a new political drama – the "**Njonjo affair**". In May 1983, Moi announced to parliament that he had evidence that a foreign power was grooming a senior colleague to take over as president. The charges were unspecific but the Attorney General **Charles Njonjo**'s name was mentioned and he rapidly fell from grace. A member of the Kikuyu elite who had shored up Kenyatta, Njonjo was a skilled politician with a wide circle of influence outside Kenya. His name was often linked with South Africa and Israel and, during the judicial inquiry into his activities, it was alleged that he had embezzled KANU money, and that he was privy to the coup attempt and also to another in the Seychelles. More crucially, there was intense rivalry between Njonjo and **Mwai Kibaki**, the sober and respected vice-president, over the question of succession.

The case, which filled the papers for over a year, was brought to a close with the purge from KANU of Njonjo's associates. He himself was ordered to pay back misappropriated

funds, but was eventually granted a pardon by the president on Independence Day 1984, with the understanding that his political life was terminated.

Whatever lay behind it – most likely Njonjo's designs on the presidency – the Njonjo affair succeeded in easing away the volatility engendered by the coup attempt. Odinga and a number of other political detainees were released. More broadly, provincial administration was increasingly "de-tribalized", with officials working away from their home areas. And, on another front, a complete restructuring of the educational curriculum put new emphasis on technical and vocational studies. For university candidates, a new quasi-military National Youth Service programme was launched, with students engaged in public works across the country. **Student unrest** continued, however. Twelve students were killed in February 1985 when the GSU broke up a meeting on the campus, ostensibly about canteen food, but considered subversive by the authorities. On the other side of the political fence, KANU "youth wingers" began taking the law into their own hands, forming vigilante groups to attack criminal suspects and those suspected of "causing disunity".

KENYA TODAY

Economically, Kenya has come a long way since Independence. But, with the population today standing at more than three times what it was thirty years ago (8 million then; around 30 million today), the rate of improvement in standards of living is levelling off, and by some indexes has actually declined since 1980. Politically, there's less room for doubt. Kenya's enduringly positive overseas reputation of the 1970s and 1980s has gone very sour since 1991, while the steady decline suffered since Independence in democratic practice, the rule of law and human rights, appears to have bottomed out with the multi-party elections of 1992.

THE ECONOMY: AGRICULTURE AND TOURISM 1985–93

Imports continue to outstrip exports, but servicing the national debt costs Kenya a far smaller proportion of export earnings than many poor countries have to surrender. **Development** is, however, deeply dependent on foreign aid grants and loans (when they are not suspended for non-compliance with IMF and World Bank conditions): few African countries receive as much. And behind the fairly optimistic figures for economic growth there are persistent spectres: a fresh half-million school leavers each year competing for barely 100,000 new jobs in the swelling towns; an unwieldy, obstructive bureaucracy; minimum wage rises that trail behind inflation; and agricultural cooperatives and marketing boards in the rural areas that are notoriously corrupt and inefficient.

Natural factors, too, have been important in trimming development. The savage **drought** of 1984 and poor rains in 1992 resulted in near-famine conditions in many parts of the north and east. While the bad years tend to be balanced by bumper harvests in the good years, there's a continuing chronic shortage of **storage facilities** and little guarantee that similar disasters won't recur.

Kenya is still heavily reliant on the fortunes of **coffee** and **tea** on the world markets, and also has to import three-quarters of its energy requirements.

In the **tourist industry** – now the biggest earner of foreign exchange – foreign tour operators were unnerved by the attention given to Kenya's **AIDS** problem. Highlighted by the British Army's ban on some coastal resorts for soldiers on leave, and the rumour that the virus could be spread by mosquitoes, the scare caused bookings, particularly from Germany, to plummet.

Further adverse publicity damaged the industry in Britain as the case of **Julie Ward**, whose murder in the Maasai Mara was at first clumsily covered up, unfolded for month after month. The inquest that was finally held delivered a verdict of murder; Scotland Yard detectives were called in, but on Moi's orders their report was never made public; and the perpetrators are still unknown.

Bad news continued to come from the parks, with serious **elephant poaching** polluting Kenya's glossy safari image. While the ivory scandals which smeared Kenyatta's family have not been repeated under Moi's presidency – and indeed Moi is known to take poaching very seriously, issuing orders to shoot poachers on sight – internal corruption was partly responsible for the scale of the slaughter that far exceeded anything during Kenyatta's rule. In 1989, Kenya announced a major **offensive on ivory smuggling** and succeeded in persuading most importing countries, including the USA, Britain, Hong Kong and (remarkably) Japan, to place a blanket ban on any further consignments. The Wildlife Service, under the new directorship of **Richard Leakey**, has taken stern control of the situation and, largely through force of arms – hunting down poachers – and greatly increased revenue from entrance fees, has stemmed a holocaust that, for a few months, looked close to burning itself out as the elephants in some areas were poached to near-extinction.

THE POLITICAL CLIMATE 1987–89

In 1987, an **Amnesty International** report condemned Kenya's human rights record. An American congressional delegation was "stunned" by the mistreatment of political detainees and the fears expressed by Kenyans – as well as by its own abrupt treatment at the hands of the Kenyan Special Branch. While the USA does not want to jeopardize its strategic geopolitical relationship with Kenya, there has been a dramatic chill in relations between Washington and Nairobi, largely as a result of the outspokenness on human rights of the American ambassador **Smith Hempstone**.

Until the end of the 1980s, Moi appeared firmly in control and it was never clear why opposition of any kind was dealt with so harshly. Despite efforts to throttle all dissent, the ground swell of resentment continued to grow, and, for a while, during the period of heaviest repression, attitudes were polarized less along tribal lines than in the past. An opposition group, **Mwakenya** (a Swahili acronym for Union of Nationalists to Liberate Kenya), one of several shadowy organizations mounting anti-government campaigns, attracted attention through its pamphlets, calling for the replacement of the Moi government, a return to democracy and an end to corruption and Western influence. While such groups barely identified themselves and didn't appear to pose any united threat to the government, hundreds of people were arrested in the late 1980s. Their defence lawyers tended, in turn, to get arrested themselves. As reported by Amnesty, a number of detainees died in custody and prisoners were routinely tortured and kept in waterlogged cells beneath Nyayo House in Nairobi.

The development of an underground **opposition** in Kenya wasn't surprising. For years public meetings of more than five people were subject to police approval. Dissent, even within the sole party, KANU, was crushed, and further illiberal measures were adopted by the government, including the change from secret balloting at elections to a public be-seen-and-counted **queue-voting** system, in which voters lined up behind the candidate of their choice. The government also passed a law empowering it to dismiss judges. As the independence of the judiciary was eroded, so the power of the party was consolidated. As a result of this rigging and intimidation, at the 1988 presidential and parliamentary elections (one presidential candidate, one party), a number of independent-minded politicians, including **Charles Rubia** and **Kenneth Matiba**, lost their seats.

Measures intended ostensibly to ensure ethnic balance in the **cabinet** have actually meant a lack of security of tenure for most ministers, whom the president frequently shifts around or dismisses if their power base begins to assume threatening proportions. Under these circumstances, the effectiveness of ministries is greatly reduced. The infiltration of **Kalenjin** people into high civil service posts has also thwarted ministers. The cabinet never meets as a body, and ministers have to make private representations to one or two Kalenjin mandarins in the civil service in order to speak to the president.

As power became increasingly concentrated in fewer and fewer hands – and whose hands became a topic for rumour – only the **church** and a few powerfully connected politicians dared to question the government. President Moi, a regular churchgoer, has always sought to avoid head-on collisions with senior clergy – though the suspicious death of one clergyman in a head-on collision on the A104 (see next section) was partly instrumental in pushing the government into conceding to the demands for a multi-party system.

THE PATH TO MULTI-PARTY DEMOCRACY

It was the grisly murder in February 1990 of **Robert Ouko**, the Luo foreign minister, at his farm near Kisumu, that sparked off the first explosion of **civil unrest** in a rolling crisis that has beset the government ever since. Ouko, a stout Moi supporter who enjoyed excellent personal relations with governments in both Britain and the USA, was widely viewed as a potential successor to the presidency, and was backed by Britain for the vice-presidency in 1988.

A week of **rioting** shook the country, although it was most violent in Kisumu, Ouko's home town. It is widely believed that his murder was the work of government agents exceeding their briefs (and a parallel has been drawn with the murder of J M Kariuki in 1975). His popularity with the foreign press and the suave and articulate contrast he made with the president – combined with his threat to expose corruption – were the likely motivating factors.

Although the riots of February dismayed the government, July 1990 saw Central Highlands towns in **violent tumult** as public opposition to the government mounted in the wake of demands for a multi-party system by three heavyweight public figures. The former cabinet minister **Kenneth Matiba**, **Raila Odinga** (son of the veteran politician Oginga Odinga) and the ex-mayor of Nairobi, **Charles Rubia**, all declared themselves for a multi-party system and denounced the violent mass evictions that had recently taken place in the Nairobi slum of **Muoroto**: they were subsequently detained without charge and not released for over a year. Several human rights and pro-democracy lawyers were also arrested, while one who escaped arrest, **Gibson Kamau Kuria**, was given refuge in the US embassy. A Nairobi **pro-democracy rally** (banned by the government) degenerated into attacks on buildings and security forces. There were dozens of deaths in street battles with armed police. President Moi blamed "hooligans and drug addicts" for the explosion.

Ouko's murder and the July riots were followed by the gravely embarrassing death in a road accident of the outspoken **Bishop Alexander Muge** on his return from a visit to western Kenya. Muge's car collided head-on with a lorry which veered on to the wrong side of the road. The Archbishop, who had spoken out forcefully against the Muoroto evictions, had been warned against his visit to Luo-land in the most menacing terms by the Minister for Labour, who subsequently resigned from the cabinet.

In this hostile, nervous climate, the government came down hard on **journalists**, virtually stifling local newspapers and accusing the foreign press, and particularly the **BBC** in Nairobi, of mischief-making. The corporation was just the latest in a notorious line-up of divergent – and diversionary – "enemies" of Kenya, including the Ku Klux Klan and Colonel Gaddafi.

Whatever its political climate, there is no doubt that Kenya is one of the best places in Africa in which to work as a foreign correspondent. The large community of journalists, duty-bound to seek out the dirt, put Kenya, more than most African countries, under intense international scrutiny. But, even without the flocks of reporters picking over its problems, Kenya was beginning to look tragically isolated – under siege to events and opinion, at home and abroad.

Relations with the international community were at an all-time low by 1991. Against all the prevailing trends in Africa, Moi's stubborn

ETHNIC VIOLENCE

Between 2000 and 3000 people have been killed in **violence between different language groups** in the Rift Valley and western Kenya since late 1991. At least 200,000 people have been displaced, nearly all of them non-Kalenjin – a kind of ethnic cleansing.

For years, any reference to multi-party politics by KANU leaders was accompanied by dire warnings of the bloody consequences for tribal harmony of such a system. Once the government was forced into a corner on the issue by foreign aid donors, the prophecy was quickly realized. Ethnic allegiance swamped the new political order before it had even consolidated, so that the opposition parties were unable to formulate policies and election strategies that were free of ethnic considerations. Every move involved calculations of ethnic voting. FORD-Kenya tried the hardest to be ethnic-free, but KANU still seemed to be pulling the strings.

The **Kikuyu**, **Luo** and **Luyia** have been emigrating from their densely populated parts of Kenya for decades, buying marginal farmlands in the **Rift Valley** and other normally unproductive areas, trying to apply their farming techniques among the local Kalenjin speakers and benefiting from local aid and subsistence initiatives. In most towns, at least until recently, it has been Kikuyu traders who ran many of the shops and small businesses.

Victims of early attacks in various parts of Rift Valley Province described organized gangs of youths terrorizing non-Kalenjin homesteads and villages while local police arrived too late to do anything or appeared to stand by. As KANU politicians warned that the Kalenjin should watch their backs for attacks by "outsiders", so their predictions were soon coming true. The KANU "policy", if such it was, began to work, as Kikuyu vigilante groups began to retaliate and, in turn, provided spurious justification for Kalenjin fears. In elec-

tioneering terms, however, it proved totally counterproductive, as the government lost more votes from disgust with their inaction than it gained from forcing opposition voters out of marginal KANU constituencies. Probably the aim was simply to demonstrate to the world at large, through the media, that multi-partyism in Africa leads to tribal violence. In this – to the Moi government's lasting shame, and despite all the evidence of its fabrication – it succeeded.

Although FORD had feared that an early election date would defeat it in its disorganized infancy, as the delays on setting the date continued through 1992 against the background of ethnic violence (while Moi declared he was waiting for everything to be "all right in the country"), it began to look like the government agenda was to allow tribal divides to set in firmly in advance of the election. Accusations of *majimboism* – the creation of ethnic blocks – began to fly.

The violence was not so much the "clashes" or "fighting" (certainly not "tribal war") of newspaper headlines, as unprovoked attacks, muggings and vandalism. The perpetrators, who carried spears, *pangas*, bows and arrows and clubs – but rarely guns – looted property, stole livestock, burned houses, and beat up or killed anyone who got in their way. Their message was, "Get off our land", and thousands moved to refugee camps outside Eldoret and other big towns. Now the people of the affected communities, while often cynical about government pronouncements, have been drawn willy-nilly into conflict with each other.

An official report by the commission on ethnic violence laid blame for the provocation at the door of the KANU party and particularly Nicholas Biwott. The report was rejected by the (then) still exclusively KANU parliament. Shortly after came the violent arrest of commission member Dr John Makanga (a colleague of Wangari Maathai) in front of the IMF team at the *Hilton Hotel*.

resistance to adopting a multi-party system riled his overseas backers. It seemed he was unaware of the end of the Cold War and the hard reassessment of the distribution of aid taking place among the rich countries.

1991 saw the steady build-up of an opposition lobby so powerful it could not be dismantled and jailed, member by member. For the first time in over a decade, the threat to the government looked substantial and enduring. The much-respected veteran of the political scene, **Oginga Odinga** – effectively Kenya's elder statesman – set up the **Forum for the Restoration of Democracy (FORD)** in association with his radical son Raila Odinga and a committed group of lawyers, chief among whom was the influential chairman of the Law Society, **Paul Muite**. FORD quickly attracted government opponents from all quarters and was soon established as a mass movement for change, far removed from the ideology-laden opposition movements of the previous decade, such as Mwakenya. **Kenneth Matiba** and **Charles Rubia**, recently released from prison, both joined FORD. Dissatisfied with KANU, and sensing a sea change in Kenyan politics, the long-time government critic, **Martin Shikuku**, also joined, having defected from the ruling party.

The response to FORD, at home and overseas, was mixed. President Moi, in typically conciliatory mood, referred to the movement as "rats" that would be "crushed", and blamed the energetic Nairobi diplomatic corps – and in particular the American ambassador – for supporting anti-government forces. But foreign support was not unanimous: the British High Commission kept their heads down and the UK Foreign Office quietly – but unconstructively – opined that multi-party democracy might bring about tribal clashes.

By the end of 1991, however, Kenya's immediate future was increasingly being mapped out beyond the confines of Nairobi's civil service departments. John Troon, the ex-Scotland Yard man hired by Moi to investigate Ouko's murder, revealed that the greatest suspicion fell on Moi's closest advisor, the energy minister **Nicholas Biwott**, and his internal security chief, **Hezekiah Oyugi**. Biwott and Oyugi were both sacked and then arrested (they were later released "for lack of evidence", but not reinstated).

In the wake of this damaging news, the **Paris group** of donor nations agreed, with rare unanimity, to suspend balance-of-payment support to Kenya for at least six months, pending economic and political reforms. Moi got the message. Within days he announced there would be multi-party elections for the next parliament and a free vote for the presidency. The constitutional amendment that had legalized the one-party state in 1982 was repealed and the stage was set for the registration of opposition parties and the first, legal, mass rallies.

THE 1992 ELECTIONS

There were convulsions in KANU. Many, if not all, ministers faced losing their seats in a free election. Among those who quickly resigned was former vice-president **Mwai Kibaki**, who formed the **Democratic Party** (DP) which soon found support among the Kikuyu and in the east and northeast.

FORD found the transformation from opposition lobby group to **political party** very hard to manage. As a party it was promiscuous in the welcome it extended to every ex-KANU minister who made the leap. Within weeks, the contest for the leadership of FORD and the nomination for a presidential candidate was in full swing.

Less than six months old, the FORD party began to disintegrate. There had always been a division between the established opposition, fronted by Oginga Odinga and led by Paul Muite and his lawyers' circle, and the newer opposition of displaced KANU people and establishment and business figures out of favour with the ruling party. Three months before the election, FORD split into FORD-Kenya (FORD-K; presidential candidate Odinga) and FORD-Asili (FORD-A; candidate Matiba).

In parts of Kikuyu-land, **FORD-K** earned the nickname FORD-Kihii (*kihii* means an uncircumcised boy), an ethnic jibe against FORD-Kenya's Luo supporters. With the split, the ethnic divisions of multi-party politics were revealed. It became impossible to enter the political arena without constant reference to the language groups of the politicians and their supporters. Of all the parties, FORD-K were the most ardent in their rejection of tribally based politics. With a Luo, Odinga, as presidential candidate and a Kikuyu, Muite, as his running mate, the country's two largest ethnic groups were well represented. FORD-K was intellectually the strongest party, too, with a radical programme, but pragmatic economic policies, drawn up by an impressive group of economists, including expat businesspeople.

FORD-A was the big, centrist, Kikuyu party, with major support from business, its leader Matiba a serious threat to KANU. During Matiba's year of incarceration he had suffered two strokes and been refused permission to travel abroad for treatment. There was well-founded fear in KANU about his personal animosity toward the ruling party.

The **Democratic Party**, despite support from a range of backgrounds, never looked like a serious contender to win the presidency or a majority in parliament as its opposition credentials were suspect (leader Mwai Kibaki having only recently resigned from KANU).

There were efforts until the last minute to forge tactical alliances in order to oust Moi and KANU. But, in the climate of mutual suspicion and risk-assessment, none materialized. KANU, meanwhile, having started 1992 in disarray, was looking stronger again by the end of the year. By printing billions of shillings, the government was able to buy patronage for KANU on a massive scale. Encouraged by the largesse, there were a number of significant returns to the KANU fold as the divisions among the opposition became clearer and a KANU victory less unthinkable. Many had no deep-seated opposition to KANU, just an opportunistic fear of being on the losing side.

At the last minute, the election date was switched from December 7th to **December 29th**, the worst possible date for a good voter turnout. It was sure to favour the rural rather than the urban, the unemployed rather than those in work (who had registered to vote at their places of work rather than in their home villages, where many would be over Christmas), and, on balance, KANU over the opposition.

And so it turned out. Voting was low and, when the boxes were finally counted after several days, KANU had 100 seats out of the total of 188. Seventeen of these were returned "unopposed" as the opposition candidates had been physically prevented from presenting their nomination papers. There was, undoubtedly, widespread ballot-stuffing and fraud, but, with only 200 local and foreign election monitors to check 7000 ballot boxes, little to prevent it.

The first session of Kenya's new multi-party parliament was suspended for two months, a slap in the face for opposition MPs whose disgust with the outcome of the election had at first led to a call to boycott their seats. The two months gave KANU a chance to buy back a number of MPs into the party (as a result there were a number of by-elections in western Kenya, usually accompanied by violence) and to try to come up with some sort of strategy for dealing with the vastly superior intellectual and rhetorical strengths of the opposition.

KANU had lost all but one of its cabinet ministers to opposition candidates and, with a total lack of people of ministerial calibre on the government back benches, Moi was put in the

WINNING THE ELECTIONS, KANU-STYLE

The government had dealt itself a good hand before the elections were announced. Kenya's first-past-the-post electoral system and KANU's popularity in underpopulated districts (leading to huge overrepresentation for the areas of KANU support) were both very helpful. As, too, was the overwhelming (if more or less obligatory) support for KANU from the media, particularly the radio. But the party in power had some aces up its sleeve that were only revealed weeks before polling day.

To begin with there was the **voter registration scandal**. Since the last election, in 1988, between three and four million young people had turned 18. Few of them had received national identity cards, a prerequisite of voter registration, and there were unexplained delays in issuing the cards in time for the elections, at least in many non-KANU-voting areas. Then, parliament quietly passed a law that almost guaranteed Moi's continued presidency whatever the outcome of the general elections. To win the presidency, the candidate had to have at least 25 percent of the vote in five out of the eight provinces. Barring unexpected, huge reversals, only one man would achieve that.

Another new law came into force shortly before the election specifying the president had to form a government entirely from his own party (an anti-coalition law). Having split the opposition, this was nice timing.

extraordinary position of having to offer defeated cabinet ministers their posts back as nominated MPs (the Kenyan parliament has 200 seats – 188 elected seats and 12 nominated seats, the latter in the president's gift). KANU has almost no MPs from the Kikuyu or Luo communities.

POLITICS SINCE THE 1992 ELECTIONS

Despite the bad taste left by the elections, the international community was little better impressed with the divided opposition parties, who, acting together, could easily have defeated KANU. The **IMF** and **World Bank** decided that there had, in the end, been much support for the incumbents and, after a false start – with a row in which Moi called their economic demands "suicidal and dictatorial" – agreement was reached with foreign donors to pick up the aid programme, two years after it had ceased. In November 1993 donor nations finally agreed around US$500 million in new aid, although this did little to refill the badly depleted coffers pilfered since the end of the 1980s. The aid was contingent on stringent conditions, foremost among them a dramatic raft of privatizations of nationalized industries, including post and tele-communications, the railways and the national produce and cereals board. Privatization was demanded partly out of obedience to economic theory, partly in an effort to reduce the cash available for political patronage.

In the FORD-K party, the activities of its elderly leader alarmed some of the membership. Oginga Odinga's agreement in 1993 with Moi to seek a partnership with the government to improve the economy and infrastructure in western Kenya rather than going all-out to topple KANU, was judged a sell-out, and when it was further revealed that Odinga had received at least Ksh2 million from the director of the scandal-ridden financial institution **Goldenberg International**, the party was torn apart. As a result, the hard-line younger FORD-K activists, including Oginga's son Raila Odinga, quit the party and formed the Mwangaza Trust (Ray of Light), which was banned early in 1996 "for engaging in politics". Oginga Odinga died in January 1994, his departure hailed by KANU as a sad day for Kenya. State TV and President Moi paid him moving tributes and KANU offered to help meet funeral and other expenses.

Meanwhile, FORD-A has steadily declined in confidence and credibility while its aging leader, Kenneth Matiba, makes increasingly wild accusations and anti-government pronouncements. In 1996, he made a bluntly racist attack on Kenyan Asians, whom he accused of plundering the country for their own ends. Apologists suggested he was playing the wily politician, garnering support from society's poorest, often employed by Asian bosses. The Asian community were mostly too surprised to be angry: Matiba's own business interests depend heavily on the Kenyan Asian market. All but two of the remaining FORD-A MPs represent solidly Kikuyu areas and there seems no chance of the party's fortunes improving.

In May 1995 came a decisive moment for recent Kenyan politics. Ex-KWS boss **Richard Leakey** joined lawyer Paul Muite to form a new political party, **Safina** ("The Ark"). Moi's reaction was typically direct: "What do I say to Leakey? I say no, no and no to any white man who wants to lead Kenya". The party was denied the right to register and, at a meeting in Nakuru, Leakey and party leaders were beaten up.

With a general election bound to take place by the end of 1997, senior figures in the three main parties (Martin Shikuku of FORD-A, DP leader Mwai Kibaki, and Kijana Wamalwa of FORD-K) finally agreed, in January 1996, to work together as an **alliance**, which would put forward a single presidential candidate. Leakey coordinated the alliance and raised funds. But Kenneth Matiba's ambitions for the presidency, not to mention those of Martin Shikuku, should the alliance not work out, look like leaving the opposition in no better a state of united readiness than in 1992.

ECONOMY AND SOCIETY SINCE THE 1992 ELECTIONS

The latest release of aid to Kenya – US$730 million announced in March 1996 in Paris – seems no longer to be conditional upon anything. With a sober and apparently committed Minister of Finance, **Musalia Mudavadi**, putting through some of the IMF's and World Bank's requirements, the two agencies are anxious to avoid a confrontation with the KANU government, the more so because there seems no likelihood of an opposition win at the next election.

RICHARD LEAKEY AND THE KENYA WILDLIFE SERVICE

Although now internationally renowned as a wildlife conservationist, **Richard Leakey** rose to prominence as a **paleontogist** from the shadows of his eminent parents Mary and Louis Leakey. They had made the first really significant finds in the history of early human evolution, at Olduvai Gorge in Tanzania, but Richard went on to make even more remarkable discoveries at Koobi Fora near Lake Turkana. He published several books and eventually became head of the National Museums of Kenya in Nairobi.

In 1989, facing an international outcry over the poaching of elephants and the serious impact that was already having on the tourist industry, President Moi hired Leakey to take charge of the **Kenya Wildlife Service**. Leakey's first move was a characteristically bold one: he invited the world's press to watch Moi ignite Kenya's US$3 million stockpile of confiscated ivory – producing the most memorable photo opportunity of the Moi presidency. With Moi's solid support, Leakey created anti-poaching units, briefed to shoot to kill any poachers apprehended in the parks, and transformed the KWS from a demoralized sector of the civil service into what one senior member of staff called "the most radical institution in Africa". The World Bank and other donors were so impressed they granted over US$140 million in grants. The poaching stopped; the elephants and rhinos were saved from the brink of extinction; and Kenya's international image was partially restored.

But Leakey's success went too far for some local politicians, particularly in Maasailand. His confrontational approach to the balance of human and animal needs in the parks – all humans out – infuriated many. And he was incorruptible: the KWS had dried up completely as a source of patronage.

In June 1993 on a routine flight at the controls of his Cessna plane, Leakey crashed, losing both legs in the accident. Within months he was walking on artificial feet, anxious to get back to work. But there had been a mood change in his employers. The minister of tourism, Noah Katana Ngala, announced that a secret probe had found evidence of corruption and serious mismanagement at the KWS. No more bitter irony could be imagined. In January 1994, Leakey called a press conference and publicly announced his **resignation**.

Leakey's departure wasn't just the result of refusing to countenance graft. The KWS had become a ruthless organization to work for, in which failure to come up to Leakey's standards could mean lack of prospects and poor financial rewards. However, it was the intense campaign of vilification by certain Maasai politicians that was the crucial factor in engineering his downfall.

Leakey's replacement is David Western, a milder, less charismatic figure who has been able to find a modus operandi that seems to be producing results acceptable both to local people and to conservationists. His park fee reforms have been widely praised.

Leakey, meanwhile, has entered politics. In May 1995 he joined a group of opposition intellectuals and applied to register a new party, **Safina**, announcing that Kenya needed a solution to its manifold failures. "If KANU and Mr Moi will do something about the deterioration of public life, corruption and mismanagement, I'd be happy to fight alongside them. If they won't, I want somebody else to do it." The party's application was turned down and there is no immediate prospect of its being accepted. Leakey was denounced by Moi, accused of being a racist colonial, bent on destabilizing Kenya with foreign backers. There is no doubt that Leakey commands support and respect overseas, earned by his thick-skinned energy rather than diplomatic skills. But, unfortunately for Moi, Leakey is a Kenyan, born and bred, and only the most shameless hypocrisy is likely to remove this thorn from KANU's side.

Particularly galling for the agencies, however, was Moi's purchase of a a new jet with public money, while seeking an international loan to the same value for the upkeep of the vital Nairobi–Mombasa highway, and the fact that KANU officials ignored requests to put on hold or reduce in expense the new **international aiport at Eldoret** – widely seen as proof positive of Moi's regionalism. Another unusual Eldoret development is a new ammunition factory, but there's an interesting chink in the Kalenjin armour with which Moi is shielding himself in the town – the Nandi. Many Nandi don't accept the Kalenjin label foisted on them, and increasing numbers in Eldoret – their main home – are refusing to have any truck with KANU.

Meanwhile, the **press**, especially the new magazines that burst on to the scene immediately after the unbanning of the opposition, are less free than before. A number of production facilities have been wrecked by police under KANU orders.

As for the **universities**, there is an anti-intellectualism at the highest levels of government that seriously jeopardizes the viability of higher education. Many colleges are frequently closed for extended periods following student unrest, and university lecturers went on an extended strike in 1994.

On the coast, the fundamentalist **Islamic Party of Kenya** – still banned – is something of a wild card. Khalid Salim Ahmed **Balala**, the IPK leader, spent much of the run-up to, and aftermath of, the election in detention, charged with "imagining" the death of President Moi.

Socially, Kenya is going through a bitter period, with **ethnicity** dangerously to the fore. Questions of prior **rights over land** are being brought up, even when there is little history of dispute, in order to raise the political temperature and increase KANU's leverage. Ethnic violence (see box, p.517) continues sporadically in the Rift Valley and the government seems powerless or even unwilling to stop it. In the worst-affected communities, it has led to a resurgence of Kikuyu **oathing** (see p.508), a particularly powerful form of secret social sanction, binding the oathers together and almost guaranteeing revenge attacks on members of opposing ethnic groups.

The current ethnic rifts are mirrored by long-existing economic disparities that need to be addressed. The supporters of KANU (mostly Kalenjin, Maasai, Samburu, people of the northeast, and some small coastal ethnic groups) include most of Kenya's most marginalized communities, who have benefited most from the KANU government's limited hand-outs and subsistence support. Because of their poor – often pastoral – economies, they tend to lag behind in educational opportunities. In contrast, the opposition – ethnically dominated heavily by the Kikuyu and Luo – is based in the most economically developed regions and communities, where ambitions constantly outstrip the limited rewards that Kenya can offer to educated and business-minded people.

Perhaps Kenya will hold together because the country is a political patchwork – the KANU-supporting marginal districts separated from each other by fertile opposition regions of high-population density. But the possibility that an east African regional power base is being constructed in Eldoret is the disturbing conclusion that may have to be drawn from the revelations about its airport and bullet factory.

Kenya now finds itself in a disastrous predicament, and any sense of stability is illusory. More than ever before, resolving the linked problems of landlessness, unemployment and poverty – the root causes of conflict

WANGARI MAATHAI AND THE GREEN BELT MOVEMENT

One of the government's most outspoken and consistently credible critics is the former chairwoman of the National Council of Women of Kenya, Professor **Wangari Maathai**. A founding member of FORD, she was also the instigator, in 1977, of the **Green Belt Movement**, Kenya's remarkable grassroots environmental lobby. The Green Belt Movement has planted some 12 million tree saplings around the country and is responsible for a transformation in environmental awareness, especially among the rural poor, and particularly among the women who have done most of the planting.

In March 1992, Maathai, on hunger strike in Uhuru Park with the wives and mothers of political prisoners, demanding their release, was clubbed unconscious by police. She recovered and campaigned on behalf of FORD-Kenya, making a bid just a few weeks before the elections to unite the Odinga and Matiba factions before they split, and later becoming involved in the commission of inquiry over ethnic violence in the Rift Valley.

Articulate and trenchant, Maathai has clashed directly with President Moi over his plans for a high-rise development in Uhuru Park. She has often accused the government of corruption and the misappropriation of aid funds. After her colleague John Makanga was violently arrested in February 1993, and she received death threats, Maathai went into hiding. She came out to receive the 1993 Edinburgh Medal, awarded for an outstanding contribution to humanity through science.

Wangari Maathai claims to have no political ambitions, but her charisma, her fame and her impeccably nationalist and internationalist views must make her a leading candidate for Kenya's – and Africa's – first woman president or prime minister.

– must remain the priority. It would be refreshing if the KANU government were to initiate pragmatic reforms to its practices, by actively prosecuting the embezzlers of Kenya's precious public funds, and by putting humanity plainly at the top of its agenda, signalling a genuine concern for the country's people. The brute realities of the international economic order make these tasks difficult for the best-intentioned governments. But, after more than three decades in power, it would appear the KANU government is incapable of addressing these issues independently. The best that can be hoped for is that it avoids completely alienating the opposition parties and the international community. Without their involvement, Kenya's future, on current form, is not bright.

WILDLIFE

Despite the tremendous losses this century, Kenya teems with wildlife. In one place or another, not just inside the protective boundaries of the forty-odd parks and reserves, it is possible to see almost all of the country's big animals. Even outside the parks, if you travel fairly widely, you're almost certain to note various gazelles and antelopes, zebra and giraffe – even hippo, buffalo, crocodile and elephant. Monkeys and baboons can be seen almost anywhere and are a regular menace.

If this impression of abundant wild animals slightly alarms you, rest assured that, outside the park boundaries, any danger is minimal. The big cats are hardly ever seen, and man-eating lions and enraged elephants are no more a realistic cause for concern than the few remaining rhinos, which live entirely within the parks; buffalos, though plentiful, are only really dangerous when solitary. For lonely hikes – on Mount Kenya, Mount Elgon and the Aberdares, for example – hiring a guide is sometimes a good idea. Statistically, however, your chances of being attacked by a wild animal in Kenya are very small.

The country's **birdlife** is even more noticeable than its mammals, and astonishingly diverse, attracting ornithologists from all over the world and converting many others as well. Superb starlings, iridescent relatives of our own subtler species, are everywhere, but there are over a thousand species in all, ranging from the thumb-sized red-cheeked cordon bleu to the ostrich.

This introduction to Kenya's habitats, mammals, birds, reptiles and amphibians supplements our full-colour guide to "The Wildlife of East and Southern Africa" in the centre of this book, which will prove useful in identifying the main species of mammals likely to be seen on safari. For more detailed coverage, a good full-length field guide is very valuable – some recommended **books** are listed on p.540.

FOREST AND WOODLAND HABITATS

Several forest types are present in Kenya, including montane, coastal and lowland dry forests.

HIGHLAND FORESTS

The highlands support rich montane forests, which give way to agricultural lands as one approaches Nairobi. The characteristic landscape in the highlands is patches of evergreen forest separated by vast meadows of grasses – often wire grass and Kikuyu grass.

The highland forest is quite limited in extent in Kenya; it is typically found above 1500 metres, and also on isolated massifs. It bears some resemblance to lowland forest, but contains different tree species and does not normally grow as tall and dense. Typical trees of this forest include **camphor**, **Juniperus procera** (the "cedar" tree of east Africa) and **podocarpus**. The better-developed forests are found on the wetter, western slopes of the massifs. Above the forest line, stands of giant bamboo are found at altitudes of over 2500 metres. Along the lower, drier edge of the highlands, trees grow less high and are dotted in fields of tall grass; various species of olive tree are commonly found here.

The **main highland forest areas** are to be found on Mount Kenya, Mount Elgon, the Mau escarpment, the Aberdares and Mount Marsabit. **Mount Kenya** displays a mountain summit plant community (known as **Afro-Alpine**), which bears a strong similarity to that found on other high east African mountains (there's more on Mount Kenya's high-altitude flora on p.170). The highest part of the montane forest belt, at altitudes over 2900 metres, is characterized by a giant form of St John's wort. Above this, giant heather and *Proteus* trees form a heather belt, whilst at even higher altitudes, open marshy moorland is found, dominated by tussock grasses, giant groundsel and giant lobelia. Higher still, the tree groundsel comes into its own (this has an upper limit of 4460 metres).

Several species of **near-endemic birds** are associated with the highland forest habitat. These are Jackson's francolin (a game bird of high-altitude forest undergrowth), the dazzling golden-winged sunbird (golden-yellow wings and long, yellow tail streamers) and Hartlaub's turaco. Other typical birds of these forests and streams include African black duck, mountain buzzard, bar-tailed trogon, white-starred robin, mountain warbler and mountain wagtail.

THE KAKAMEGA FOREST

West of the Rift Valley, the 240 square kilometres of Kakamega forest, and a few adjacent outliers, are examples of the Guineo-Congolian **equatorial forest**, which is more typically a feature of central and west Africa and is now very restricted within Kenya. For this reason, many bird and plant species not encountered elsewhere in Kenya are found here – it's a memorable experience to be in the forest at first light when the shafts of morning sun spear their way through the tallest boughs of the semi-evergreen trees.

LOWLAND AND COASTAL FOREST AND WOODLANDS

Very few areas of **lowland rain forest** are left in Kenya, mainly restricted to the coastal strip, and the banks of the lower Athi and Tana rivers. The soils of these forests quickly lose their fertility when cleared for agriculture, and many of the areas that remain are degraded.

Lowland woodland areas are found inland of the coastal forest strip and away from the rivers. Woodlands are defined as more open forest areas with the ground flora dominated by grasses and the forest canopy covering as little as twenty percent of the area. Trees in such woodlands may average only four to five metres high.

The rain forests, all threatened by human incursions, include **Witu forest** near Lamu, the **Mida-Gedi forest**, the **Sabaki river forest** near Malindi, forest fragments in the **Shimba Hills** and the **Ramisi river forest** on the southern coast.

The most important area of natural forest is the **Arabuko-Sokoke forest**, which lies slightly inland along the western side of the main coast road, south of Malindi and north of Kilifi. Arabuko-Sokoke is unique in that it comprises a largely unbroken block of 420 square kilometres of coastal forest, consisting of *Brachystegia* woodland (containing a huge variety of birdlife), dense *Cynometra* forest, and zones of mixed lowland rain forest that are very rich in plants, mammals and insects.

Large areas of the coastal plain are covered in moist, tree-scattered grasslands. On the beach itself, tall **coconut palms** and the rather weedy-looking **casuarina** (known as whistling pine) dominate the high tide line.

GRASSLAND

Grassland with scattered trees (wooded savannah) covers vast areas in Kenya, both in the **Lake Victoria basin** (which includes the Mara), and **south and east of Mount Kenya** at elevations of 1000 to 1800 metres. This type of ecosystem prevails because of regular fires. Many of the trees that persist are broad-leaved, deciduous trees, protected from fire damage by their corky bark. In areas with a similar altitude, but with more erratic rainfall, a thin scattering of tall, flat-topped acacia trees, along with shorter acacias, occurs amongst the grassland, producing the archetypal imagery of the east African landscape.

DESERT AND SEMI-DESERT

Typical desert and semi-desert flora comprises **thornbush and thicket**. Thirty kilometres inland from the Indian Ocean, beyond the fringes of the Arabuko-Sokoke forest and others, is the eastern edge of the **Nyika wilderness**, which stretches west to the edge of the highlands. Nyika is characterized by an often impenetrably thick growth of stunted, thorny trees, which are grey for most of the year, but become green during the rainy season. Scaly-barked species such as acacia and euphorbia species occur in this plant community.

Desert grass-bush and the drier **desert scrub** communities cover nearly seventy percent of the land area of Kenya, mainly in the east, north and northeast. These areas are at low altitude (below 600 metres) and have unreliable rainfall, suffering long droughts, a lack of regular flowing water and strong wind exposure. Vegetation is sparse and scrubby, with bushes and occasional, widely scattered tall trees, mainly baobab, *mwangi* and *mgunga* (acacia) trees. Much of the ground free of bushes is covered by dispersed bunches of grass and other low shrubs. However, much of the soil surface here is bare.

The true desert habitat is drier still and plant life is very limited in some areas. Many of the trees and bushes (if present at all) are dwarf. Large areas are bare, stony desert with a thin and patchy growth of desert grasses and perhaps a few bushes along dry river margins or dry water courses.

WET HABITATS

The Kenyan coast is dominated by two major habitat types, sandy beach and mangrove forest. There are also some offshore rocky islands and coral reefs along the coast, which provide refuge for birds, but there are no breeding sites of pelagic seabirds (birds of the open ocean) in the country. Many species of shore birds (waders) are found in tidal creeks and estuaries, for example at Mida Creek, on the Sabaki estuary, and also on the Lamu archipelago. One unique wader species, the **crab plover** – a pied wader which runs to catch crabs for food – overwinters at Mida Creek.

LAKES

The savannah of the **Great Rift Valley** is dotted with bird-rich lakes, ranging from the two freshwater lakes – Naivasha and Baringo – to intensely saline ones like Magadi and Bogoria. The Rift Valley acts as a magnet to passage and wintering birds.

The vast expanse of **Lake Victoria** is an example of an oligotrophic lake – fed mainly by rainwater falling on to the lake's surface, rather than being fed by rivers and streams. As a result, it has a relatively low nutrient concentration. A feature of the lake is its papyrus beds and marshlands which harbour birds not found elsewhere in Kenya.

RIVERS

There are very few permanent riverine habitats in Kenya, because the country is so dry, but those river systems which exist are extremely attractive to birds and mammals. The best examples of such rivers are the **Tana** and **Athi-Galana-Sabaki** systems.

MANGROVE FOREST

Marine mangrove swamps are found in many parts of the coast. The largest tracts, and the areas from which most mangrove poles (*boriti*) are cut for the building trade, are in the Lamu archipelago, but all the coastal creeks are more or less bordered by mangroves (*mkoko* in Swahili). There are also areas of saline grassland on the landward side of some of the mangrove thickets. Although fun to travel through by boat, mangrove forests are not noted for their faunal diversity. One unusual animal you're bound to see is the **mudskipper**, a fish on the evolutionary road to becoming an amphibian.

MAMMALS

Kenya has over a hundred species of large native mammals. The majority of species are vegetarian grazers, browsers and foragers at the lower end of the food chain – animals such as monkeys, rodents and antelopes. The big predators are fewer in species and tend to be the dominant topic of conversation at game lodges. Everyone remembers seeing lions for the first time or cheetahs. To see a leopard is often a personal goal, and a highlight. Once you get the bug, you'll be looking out for a lone striped hyena, rather than the common and gregarious spotted version, or for a serval cat rather than a cheetah. But don't ignore the less glamorous animals. There can be just as much

SWAHILI ANIMAL NAMES

Bweha	Jackal	*Nigri*	Warthog
Bweha masigio	Bat-eared fox	*Nsya*	Duiker
Choroa	Oryx	*Nungu*	Porcupine
Chui	Leopard	*Nyamera*	Topi
Dondoo	Steinbok, grysbok	*Nyani*	Baboon
Duma	Cheetah	*Nyati*	Buffalo
Faru	Rhinoceros	*Nyegere*	Ratel
Fisi	Hyena	*Nyoka*	Snake
Fisi maji	Otter	*Nyumbu*	Wildebeest
Fungo	Civet	*Paa*	Suni antelope
Kalasinga	De Brazza's monkey	*Paka*	Cat
Kamandegere	Springhare	*Pala hala*	Sable antelope
Kanu	Genet	*Pimbi*	Rock hyrax
Kiboko	Hippopotamus	*Pofu*	Eland
Kima	Monkey	*Punda*	Horse, ass
Komba	Bushbaby	*Punda milia*	Zebra
Kongoni	Hartebeest	*Sange*	Elephant shrew
Korongo	Roan antelope	*Sibamangu*	Caracal
Kuru	Waterbuck	*Simba*	Lion
Mamba	Crocodile	*Sunguru*	Hare, rabbit
Mbega	Colobus monkey	*Swala granti*	Grant's gazelle
Mbwa mwitu	Hunting dog	*Swala pala*	Impala
Mdudu	Insect, bug	*Swala tomi*	Thomson's gazelle
Mondo	Serval	*Swala twiga*	Gerenuk
Muhanga	Aardvark	*Tandala*	Kudu
Ndege	Bird (also means plane)	*Taya*	Oribi
Ndovu	Elephant	*Tohe*	Reedbuck
Nguchiro	Mongoose	*Tumbili*	Vervet monkey
Nguruwe	Pig, hog	*Twiga*	Giraffe

satisfaction in spotting a shy, uncommon antelope, or in spotting rarely observed behaviour, as in ticking off one of the more obvious predatory status symbols.

The **cross-references** given below lead to pages in our colour guide to "The Wildlife of East and Southern Africa" in the centre of this book.

PRIMATES

There are twelve species of primates in Kenya, excluding *Homo sapiens*. They range from the pint-sized, slow-motion, lemur-like potto, found in Kakamega forest, to the baboon. Kenya no longer has any great apes (the family to which the gorilla and the chimpanzee belong), although they probably only became extinct in the western forests, of which Kakamega is a relic, in the last five hundred years, during which time the region was widely settled by humans. The legend of the Nandi Bear (see p.261) is probably connected with those passed-down memories. A new **chimpanzee sanctuary** has recently been established at Sweetwaters in Laikipia, "stocked" with chimps from Jane Goodall's famous Gombe Stream reserve in Tanzania. Today, the primate you are certain to see almost anywhere in Kenya, given a few trees, is the **vervet** (p.2), a small, lightweight monkey that has no difficulty adjusting to the presence of humans and, if possible, their food. The vervet is one of the guenons – typical African monkeys, with distinctive facial markings and hairstyles, all wonderfully adapted to a life on the prowl for fruits, leaves, insects and just about anything else small and tasty. Almost as common in certain areas, notably on the coast, is **Sykes' monkey** (p.3). At Diani Beach, a number of Sykes' troops have become notoriously accustomed to stealing food from hotel dining tables, and large males will even raid bedrooms. Up-country populations of Sykes' (or blue) monkey appear to be more timid.

Black and White Colobus

It is up-country where you are most likely to see the beautiful, leaf-eating **black and white colobus monkeys** (p.2) – although they can also be spotted in the Diani forest. They are usually found high in the tree canopy; look out for the pure white young. The related Tana River red colobus is only found in the remote Tana River Park, which also shelters the dwindling population of Tana River crested mangabeys, a partly ground-dwelling monkey with a characteristic Mohican-style crest of hair. Other rare or more localized monkeys include: the red-tailed guenon of the far west; the stocky but distinguished looking De Brazza's monkey, with its white goatee, found almost exclusively in Saiwa Swamp National Park; and the **Patas monkey** (p.2), a moustachioed plains runner of the dry northwest and Laikipia.

If you stay in a game lodge, you are quite likely to see **bushbabies** at night, as they frequently visit dining rooms and verandahs. There's a large, cat-sized species (the greater galago) and a small bushbaby not much bigger than a kitten (the lesser galago). Both are engaging animals, with sensitive, inquisitive fingers and large eyes and ears to aid them in their hunt for insects and other small animals.

On safari you'll have plenty of opportunities to watch **baboon troops** (p.2) up close. Large males can be somewhat intimidating in size and manner, disconcertingly so towards women. Troops average forty to fifty individuals, who spend their lives, like all monkeys, in clear, but mutable social relationships. Rank and precedence, physical strength and kin ties all determine an individual's position in this mini-society led by a dominant male. The days are dominated by the need to forage and hunt for food (baboons will consume almost anything, from a fig tree's entire crop to a baby antelope found in the grass). Grooming is a fundamental part of the social glue during times of relaxation. When baboons and other monkeys perform this massage-like activity on each other, the specks which they pop into their mouths are sometimes parasites – notably ticks – and sometimes flakes of skin.

RODENTS – AND HYRAXES

Rodents aren't likely to make a strong impression on safari, unless you're lucky enough to do some night game drives – or preferably walks. In that case you may see the bristling back end of a **crested porcupine** (p.3) or the frenzied leaps of a **spring hare** (p.3), dazzled by headlights or a torch. In rural areas off the beaten track you may occasionally see hunters taking home **giant rats** or **cane rats** – shy, vegetarian animals, which make good eating. Kenya has several species of **squirrel**, the most spectacular of which are the giant forest squirrel, with its splendid bush of a tail, and the nocturnal flying squirrel – which actually glides, rather than flies, from tree to tree, on membranes between its outstretched limbs. Both these squirrels are most likely to be seen in Kakamega forest. Very widespread, however, are the two species of **ground squirrel** – striped and unstriped – which are often seen, dashing along the track in front of the vehicle, in Tsavo National Park and the Samburu reserves.

Rock hyraxes (p.7), which you are certain to see at Hell's Gate National Park and on Mount Kenya, look like they should be rodents. In fact the rock hyrax and closely related tree hyrax are technically ungulates (hoofed mammals) and form a classificatory level entirely their own. Their closest living relatives are elephants, with which they share distant common ancestry. Present-day hyraxes are pygmies compared with some of their prehistoric ancestors, which were as big as a bear in some cases. Rock hyraxes live in busy, vocal colonies of twenty or thirty females and young, plus a male. In a few places they are extremely tame and wait to be fed by passing hikers. Usually, however, they are timid in the extreme – not surprising in view of the wide range of predators that will take them.

CARNIVORES

Kenya's carnivores are some of the most exciting and easily recognizable animals you'll see. Although often portrayed as fearsome hunters, pulling down plains game after a chase, many species do a fair bit of scavenging and all are content to eat smaller fry when conditions dictate or the opportunity arises.

Of the large cats, **lions** (p.6) are the easiest species to find. Lazy, gregarious and physically large – up to 1.8 metres in length, not counting the tail, and up to a metre high at the shoulder – they rarely make much effort to hide or to move away, except on occasions when a large number of tourist vehicles intrude. They can be seen in nearly all the parks and reserves, and their presence is generally the main consideration in determining whether you're allowed out of your vehicle or not. Popular parks where lions are normally absent are Hell's Gate and Lake Bogoria (you can hike in both); parks which are inhabited by lions, but in which you can generally hike, include the Aberdares and Mount Kenya. "Man-eating" lions appear from time to time but seem to be one-off feline misfits. Normally, lions hunt cooperatively, preferring to kill very young, old or sick animals, and making a kill roughly once in every two attacks. When they don't kill their own prey, they will steal the kills of cheetahs or hyenas.

Leopards (p.6) may be the most feared animals in Kenya. Intensely secretive, alert and wary, they live all across the country except in the most treeless zones. Their unmistakable call, likened to a big saw being pulled back and forth, is unforgettable. Although often diurnal in the parks, they are strictly nocturnal wherever human pressures impinge, and some-

times survive on the outskirts of towns and villages, carefully preying on different domestic animals to avoid a routine. They tolerate nearby human habitation and rarely kill people unprovoked. Accidents do occur, however, and disturbed individuals occasionally take to human-hunting – or are forced to become "man-eaters" through infirmity. For the most part, leopards live off any small animals that come their way, pouncing from an ambush and dragging the prey up into a tree where it may be consumed over several days. Monkeys, especially the relatively less organized species such as colobus and vervet, are frequent prey. Baboons, unless very unlucky, are usually able to mob a leopard to defend the troop. The spots on a leopard vary from individual to individual, but they always appear in the form of rosettes. Melanistic (black) leopards are known as panthers or black panthers, and seem to be more common in some areas (Mount Kenya and the Aberdares, for example) than others.

In the flesh, the **cheetah** (p.6) is so different from the leopard, it's hard to see how there could ever be any confusion. Cheetahs are lightly built, finely spotted, with small heads and very long legs. Unlike leopards, which are highly arboreal, cheetahs never climb trees. Cheetahs live alone, or sometimes briefly form a pair during mating. Hunting is normally a solitary activity, down to eyesight and an incredible burst of speed that can take the animal up to 100kph (70mph) for a few seconds. Cheetahs can be seen in any of the large, up-country parks, though Nairobi National Park is as easy a place to find them as any.

Other large, Kenyan cats include the beautiful part-spotted, part-striped **serval** (p.7), found in most of the parks, though somewhat uncommon; and the aggressive, tuft-eared **caracal** (p.6), a kind of lynx, which is seen even less often than the serval, favouring drier zones like Tsavo East and the Samburu complex.

The biggest carnivore after the lion is the **spotted hyena** (p.5); it is also, apart from the lion, the meat-eater you will most often see. Although considered a scavenger *par excellence*, the spotted hyena is a formidable hunter, most often found where antelopes and zebras are present. Exceptionally efficient consumers, with immensely strong teeth and jaws, spotted hyenas eat virtually every part of their prey, including bones and hide and, where habituated to humans, often steal shoes, unwashed pans and refuse from tents and villages. Although they can be seen by day, they are most often active at night – when they issue their unnerving, whooping cries. Clans of twenty or so animals are dominated by females, which are larger than the males and compete which each other for rank. Curiously, female hyenas' genitalia are hard to distinguish from males', leading to a popular misconception that they are hermaphroditic. Not surprisingly, in view of all their attributes, the hyena is a key figure in local mythology and folkore.

In comparison with the spotted hyena, you are not very likely to see a **striped hyena**. A usually solitary animal, it's slighter and much rarer than its spotted relative, though occasionally glimpsed very early in the morning.

The commonest members of the dog family in Kenya are the **jackals**. The black-backed or silver-backed jackal (p.4) and the similar side-striped jackal, can be seen just about anywhere, both species usually in pairs. The golden jackal is most likely to be seen in the Mara. **Bat-eared foxes** (p.4) are also not uncommon, and unmistakable in appearance. However, the unusual and rather magnificent **hunting dog** (p.4) is probably now extinct in Kenya, having been present in reasonable numbers just twenty years ago. Canine distemper has played as big a role in their decline as human predation and habitat disruption.

Among smaller predators, the unusual **honey badger** or **ratel** (p.4) is related to the European badger and has a reputation for defending itself extremely fiercely. Primarily an omnivorous forager, it will tear open bees'

Lioness

nests (to which it is led by a small bird, the honey guide), its thick, loose hide rendering it impervious to their stings. **Genets** (p.5) are reminiscent of slender, elongated cats (they were once domesticated around the Mediterranean, but cats proved better mouse-hunters). In fact they are viverrids, related to mongooses. and are frequently seen after dark around national park lodges, where they live a semi-domesticated existence.

Most species of **mongoose** (p.5) are also tolerant of humans and, even when disturbed out in the bush, can usually be observed for some time before disappearing. Their snake-fighting reputation is greatly overplayed: in practice they are mostly social foragers, fanning out through the bush like beaters on a shoot, rooting for anything edible – mostly invertebrates, eggs, lizards and frogs.

The **civet** (p.5) is a stocky animal, resembling a large, terrestrial genet. It was formerly kept in captivity for its musk (once a part of the raw material for perfume), which is secreted from glands near the tail. Civets aren't often seen, but they are predictable creatures that can be seen wending their way along the same paths at the same time night after night.

ELEPHANTS

Elephants (p.7) are found throughout Kenya. Almost all the big plains and mountain parks have their populations. These are the most engaging of animals to watch, perhaps because their interactions, behaviour patterns and personality have so many human parallels. Like people, they lead complex, interdependent social lives, growing from helpless infancy, through self-conscious adolescence, to adulthood. Babies are born with other cows in close attendance, after a 22-month gestation. The calves suckle for two to three years, from the mother's two breasts between her front legs.

Elephants' basic family units are composed of a group of related females, tightly protecting their babies and young and led by a venerable matriarch. It's the matriarch that's most likely to bluff a charge – though occasionally she may get carried away and tusk a vehicle or person. Bush mythology has it that elephants become embarrassed and ashamed after killing a human, covering the body with sticks and grass. They certainly pay much attention to the disposal of their own dead relatives, often dispersing the bones and spending time near the remains. Old animals die in their seventies or eighties, when their last set of teeth wears out and they can no longer feed.

Seen in the flesh, elephants seem even bigger than you would imagine – you'll need little persuasion from those flapping, warning ears to back off if you're too close – but they are at the same time surprisingly graceful, silent animals on their padded, carefully placed feet. In a matter of moments, a large herd can merge into the trees and disappear, their presence betrayed only by the noisy cracking of branches as they strip trees and uproot saplings.

Managing the elephant population (see the "Poaching Wars" box on p.308) leads to arcane ecological puzzles in which new factors keep emerging; current wisdom suggests that elephants are in a way "architects" of their environment. Overpopulation is usually the result of old migration routes being cut off, forcing the animals into unnatural reserves – like the Mara – where their massive appetites can appear to be destructive. Adults may consume up to 170kg of plant material daily – that works out at well over a hundred tons of foliage through the Mara's collective elephant gut every day. However, this foliage destruction by crowded herds also puts new life into the soil. Acacia seeds sprout much better after being eaten and dunged by elephants than if they simply fall to the ground. Dung beetles gratefully tackle the football-sized elephant droppings, break them into pellets and pull them into their burrows where the seeds germinate. Elephants also dig up dried-out water holes with their tusks (they're either right- or left-tusked, in the same way as humans favour one hand or the other), providing moisture for other animals.

RHINOS

There are two species of **rhinoceros** (p.8) found in Africa – the hook-lipped or black rhino, and the much heavier wide-lipped or white rhino. Both are on the brink of extinction in the wild. The shape of their lips is far more significant than any alleged colour difference, as it indicates their respective diets (browsing for the black rhino, grazing for the white) and favoured habitats (thick bush and open grassland respectively).

Rhinos give birth to a single calf, after a gestation period of fifteen to eighteen months, and then the baby is not weaned until it is at least a year, sometimes two years, old. Their population growth rate is slow compared with most animals – another factor contributing to their predicament.

White rhinos have been extinct for several hundred years in Kenya, but reintroduced animals (principally from South Africa) have always done well – when allowed the chance to do so out of the telescopic sights of poachers.

The smaller black rhinos were, until the mid-1970s, a fairly common sight in most of the parks. In the 1960s, Amboseli, for example, had hundreds of magnificent black rhinos, some with graceful, long upper horns over a metre in length. The facts behind their rapid and depressing decimation are given in some detail on p.308, while the story of one particular group of white rhinos is recounted on p.337.

Today, there are fewer than 500 black rhinos in Kenya, and just a few dozen white rhinos. You can see black rhinos in Maasai Mara, Lake Nakuru, Nairobi, Aberdares and Mount Kenya national parks and Ngulia Rhino Sanctuary in Tsavo West. White rhinos can be seen in Maasai Mara and Lake Nakuru. Small numbers of both species can also be encountered at private ranches in northern Kenya, especially in Laikipia, north of Mount Kenya. Such is the threat to their survival, the exact location of rhino groups is not always made widely known.

HIPPOS

Hippopotami (p.9) are highly adaptable, and found throughout Kenya wherever rivers or freshwater lakes are deep enough for them to submerge in and have a surrounding of suitable grazing grass. By day they need to spend most of their time in water to protect their thin, hairless skin from dehydration.

Hippos can be found everywhere from the humid estuary of the Tana River to the chilly mountain district of Nyahururu, including the briny Lake Nakuru in the central Rift Valley and Lake Turkana in the semi-desert of the northwest. After dark, hippos leave the water to spend the whole night grazing, often walking up to 10km in one session. In the Maasai Mara, they wander across the savannah; at Lake

Naivasha they plod through farms and gardens; and everywhere they are rightly feared.

Hippos are reckoned to be responsible for more human deaths in Africa than any other animal. These occur mostly on the water, when boats accidentally steer into hippo pods, but they can be aggressive on dry land, too, charging and slashing with their fearsomely long incisors. They can run at 30kph if necessary and have a small turning circle. Although uncertain on land (hence their aggression when cornered), they are supremely adapted to long periods in water. Their nostrils, eyes and ears are in exactly the right places and their clumsy feet become supple paddles – as can be seen from the underwater observatory at Mzima Springs in Tsavo West National Park, for example.

ZEBRAS

Zebras (p.8) are closely related to horses and, together with wild asses, form the equid family. Of the three species of zebra, two live in Kenya. Burchell's has thick stripes and small ears and is found in suitable habitats in most parts of the country, while Grevy's is a large animal with very fine stripes and big, saucer-like ears, restricted to Tsavo East and the northern parks and reserves.

Burchell's zebras found in Kenya are mostly the *granti* subspecies and often called Grant's zebras. In the far north, they have a tendency to have a very short mane, or even to lack a mane.

Burchell's Zebra

In Tsavo West and other parts of southern Kenya, they tend to exhibit the "shadow striping" typical of the species in southern Africa (fawn stripes between the black ones). In Amboseli and the Mara, Burchell's zebras gather in migrating herds up to several thousand strong, along with wildebeest and other grazers. In contrast, Grevy's zebras live in small territorial herds.

PIGS

The commonest wild pig in Kenya is the **warthog** (p.9), regularly sighted throughout Kenya up to altitudes of over 2000m. Quick of movement and nervous, warthogs are notoriously hard to photograph as they're generally on the run through the bush, often with the young in single file, tails erect. They shelter in holes in the ground, usually old aardvark burrows. They live in family groups, usually of a mother and her litter of two to four piglets, or occasionally two or three females and their young. Boars join the group only to mate. Boars are distinguishable from sows by their prominent face warts, which are thought to be defensive pads protecting their heads during often violent fights. Although a favourite prey animal of large cats – and humans – the warthog's survival doesn't appear to be threatened, although its rooting and wallowing behaviour brings it into conflict with farmers.

Two other much rarer pigs, both nocturnal, live in Kenya: the huge, dark-coloured **giant forest hog**, a bristly, big-tusked pig which lives in the highlands and is most likely to be seen from a tree hotel on Mount Kenya or in the Aberdares; and the **red river hog** or **bush pig** which is very rarely seen, though not uncommon in dense forest, close to agriculture and river margins.

GIRAFFES

The tallest mammals on earth, **giraffes** (p.9) are common and unmistakable. Their daylight hours are spent browsing on the leaves of trees too high for other species; acacias and combretums are favourites. At night they lie down and ruminate. Non-territorial, they gather in loose leaderless herds. Bulls test their strength while in bachelor herds. When a female comes into oestrus, which can happen at any time of year, the dominant male mates with her. She will give birth after a gestation of approximately

Maasai Giraffe

fourteen months. Over half of all young, however, fall prey to lions or hyenas in their early years.

Kenya has three types of giraffe, differentiated from each other by their pattern and the configuration of their short horns. Most often seen is the **Maasai giraffe**, with two horns and a very broken pattern of dark blotches on a buff or fawn background. This is the giraffe you'll see in Maasai Mara, Amboseli and Tsavo West. Roughly north of the Nairobi–Mombasa road (a natural dividing line) lives the dramatically patterned **reticulated giraffe**, which normally has three or five horns and boldly defined chestnut patches on a very pale background. The more solidly built **Rothschild's giraffe**, which has a pattern more like crazy paving (also with well-defined blotches) and usually two horns, is found only in parts of western Kenya (and over the border in Uganda). There's disagreement among zoologists over whether any of the giraffe's subspecies should be accorded the status of separate species – particularly concerning the reticulated giraffe – but they all interbreed.

HOLLOW-HORNED RUMINANTS

This category of mammals includes buffalo and all the antelopes – exemplified by the 28 two-toed cud-chewers illustrated on pp.10–16 of our colour wildlife guide. The **buffalo** itself (p.10) is a very common and much-photographed safari animal, closely related to the domestic milk-and meat-producing cow. Buffalos live in herds of 100 to 300 and rarely make much effort to move when vehicles approach. Indeed, they aren't troubled by close contact with humans,

and you don't have to read the papers in Kenya long before finding an example of buffalos trampling crops or goring a farmer.

The rather ungainly **hartebeest** family (p.10) includes one of the rarest antelopes in Kenya, Hunter's hartebeest of the lower Tana river. The Coke's hartebeest or kongoni, however, is found widely in southern Kenya, and **topi** (p.10) are practically emblematic of the Maasai Mara, their main habitat. The white-bearded **wildebeest** (p.10) is also particularly associated with the Mara. Their spectacular annual migration through the reserve is described on p.330.

Of the **gazelles**, the most obvious are **Thomson's** and **Grant's** (both p.11), easily seen at the roadside in many parts of southern Kenya. The range of Grant's gazelle extends further north to encompass the northern parks (Samburu, Meru) where "Thommies" are absent. The **gerenuk** (p.11) is an unusual browsing gazelle able to nibble from bushes standing on its hind legs (its name is Somali for "giraffe-necked"). Although considered an arid land specialist, its range encompasses most of Kenya east of the Rift Valley. The **impala** (p.12), although not a gazelle, is closely related and very common throughout much of Kenya.

The **reedbuck** and **waterbuck** (p.12) are related to each other, both spending much time in or near water. The common or Bohor reedbuck has a patchy distribution in southern Kenya, whereas the waterbuck is common in many central and southern areas.

Some of the smallest antelopes in the world are quite easily seen in Kenya. **Kirk's dikdik** (p.13) is a common miniature antelope found all over the country, measuring no more than 40cm in height, which usually pairs for life. The **suni**, which is uncommon, but can be encountered almost anywhere in forest cover, is even smaller (32cm). Other small Kenyan antelopes – all fairly widespread but nowhere common – include the surprisingly aggressive **steenbok** (p.16) which, despite a height of only 50cm, defends itself furiously against attackers; the **oribi** (p.16), with its rather charming foreplay (when the female is in oestrus, the male pushes his head under her hindquarters and pushes her along on her forelegs like a wheelbarrow race); and the **klipspringer** (p.16), which has hooves wonderfully adapted for scaling near-vertical cliffs.

Greater Kudu

The duikers (from the Dutch for "diver", referring to their plunging into the bush) are larger – the **common duiker** (p.13) is around 60cm high – though they appear smaller because of their hunched posture. The common duiker is found throughout the country in many habitats, but most duikers are more choosy and prefer plenty of dense cover and thicket. These include the tiny Zanzibar duiker, whose range in Kenya is restricted to the Arabuko-Sokoke forest, the widespread red duiker and blue duiker, and the more localized black-fronted duiker (Mount Kenya and Mount Elgon) and yellow-backed duiker (Mau forest).

Kenya's big antelopes are the *Tragelaphinae* – twisted-horn bushbuck types – and the *Hippotraginae* – horse-like antelopes. The **bushbuck** itself (p.14) is notoriously shy – a loud crashing through the undergrowth and a flash of a chestnut rump are all most people witness. The **bongo** is a particularly impressive member of this group, now confined to the highlands of Mount Kenya, the Aberdares (where it's sometimes seen at tree hotels), and possibly the Cheranganis and Mau escarpment. The **sitatunga** (p.13) is a smaller relative, semi-aquatic by nature, found in Kenya only in remote corners of the Lake Victoria shoreline and at the very accessible Saiwa Swamp National Park, where they are easy to see. Also easily seen, almost anywhere in the country, is the huge, cow-like **eland** (p.14), with its distinctive dewlap. The two species of kudu are not uncom-mon where they exist at all, but they are very localized. Both are browsers. You're most likely to see **greater kudu** (p.14) at Lake Bogoria or Marsabit and **lesser kudu** (p.14) in Tsavo West or East, but neither species in the Mara.

The horse-like antelopes include the very fine **fringe-eared oryx** (p.15), which is found almost everywhere except the Mara; the massive **roan antelope** (p.15), restricted to the Mara and the Lambwe valley in western Kenya (after an abortive relocation attempt to Shimba Hills, southwest of Mombasa); and the hand-some **sable antelope** (p.15) which lives, and thrives, only in the Shimba Hills.

OTHER MAMMALS

Of Kenya's other mammals, you're not likely to see more than a glimpse. Rarest of all is the **dugong**, the marine mermaid-prototype, of which there are believed to be seven or eight individuals remaining, drifting in the shallows around the Lamu archipelago.

The insectivorous **elephant shrews** are worth looking out for, simply because they are so weird. Your best chance of a sighting is of the golden-rumped elephant shrew, at Gedi on the coast (see p.403).

The **aardvark** (p.3) is one of Africa's – indeed the world's – strangest mammals, a solitary termite-eater weighing up to 70kg. Its name, Afrikaans for "earth pig", is an apt description, as it holes up during the day in large burrows – excavated with remarkable speed and energy – and emerges at night to visit termite mounds within a radius of up to 5km, to dig for its main diet. It is most likely to be common in bush country well scattered with tall termite spires.

Pangolins are equally unusual – nocturnal, scale-covered mammals, resembling armadillos and feeding on ants and termites. Under attack,

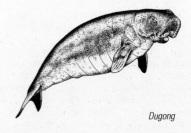
Dugong

they roll themselves into a ball. The ground pangolin, the only species found in Kenya (most pangolins are arboreal), lives mainly in savannah districts.

Kenya's many **bats** will usually be a mere flicker over a water hole at twilight, or sometimes a flash across the headlights at night. The only bats you can normally observe in any meaningful way are fruit bats hanging from their roosting sites by day. The hammer-headed fruit bat, sometimes seen in Kakamega forest, has a huge head and a wing span of over a metre.

BIRDS

Kenya boasts the second-highest country bird list – after Zaire – in Africa, at over 1070 species (this compares with no more than 300 for Britain and around 600 for North America). Nearly eighty percent of Kenya's birds are thought to breed in the country, with the remainder breeding during the northern summer in the Palaearctic region (Europe, north Africa and Asia north of the Himalayas) but wintering in tropical Africa. Many of these are familiar British summer visitors, such as swallows, nightingales and whitethroats, which have to negotiate or skirt the inhospitable Sahara on their migration. In winter, the migrant terns and waders can seem to dominate Kenya's shorelines, and the Palaearctic swallows and warblers may comprise a large proportion of the birds in bushland habitats.

If you're a novice birder, Kenya is an excellent place to start **birdwatching**. No amount of wildlife documentaries can do justice to the thrill of glimpsing your first colourful bee-eaters overhead (twelve species have been recorded in Kenya, three or four of which you might expect to encounter), watching rollers and shrikes swoop from perches to hunt insects, or seeing groups of vultures wheeling and dipping in the skies overhead as they prepare to arrive at a kill. The wide variety and accessibility of habitats makes birdwatching in Kenya highly rewarding. The keenest independent birdwatchers might expect to encounter over 600 species in a four-week period, whereas some of the organized birdwatching tour groups, living and breathing birds for a three-week period, might record over 700 species in that time; one tour group holds the African record of 797 species in 25 days. However, even for those just dipping into the

hobby or with limited time and choice of itineraries, Kenya offers some wonderful surprises.

Interesting bird records from the country can be submitted to Don Turner, east Africa Natural History Society Ornithological Sub-Committee, PO Box 48019, Nairobi.

DISTRIBUTION

Only a few species of birds are found throughout Kenya. Three which will become familiar to sharp-eyed visitors are the **laughing dove**, the **African drongo** (an all-black crow-like bird with a forked tail) and the **grey-headed sparrow**. Most other species have well-defined distributions dependent on habitat type, itself a reflection of altitude and rainfall patterns.

Part of Kenya's bird diversity can be explained by the large numbers of species reaching the edge of their known ranges inside its borders. These include birds originating in the Horn of Africa but having their western or southwestern limits in Kenya (for example, the Somali bee-eater), species widespread in southern Africa which reach their northern limits here (such as the rufous-bellied heron), coastal species which are confined to the east (for example, the mangrove kingfisher), species from west African equatorial forests whose ranges just overlap the forest patches in west Kenya (for example, the grey parrot), and species occurring along the southern edge of the Sahel which reach the extreme southeast of their range in Kenya (for example, the Abyssinian roller).

Many Kenyan birds display two more or less separate populations, one on the coast, the other in the highlands. This is determined by habitat: the coastal areas tend to have much less rain than the highlands, and are much hotter with a more severe dry season. In some species, such as the widespread speckled mousebird, two distinct races are evolving.

ENDEMIC AND NEAR-ENDEMIC SPECIES

Of over a thousand species of bird found in Kenya, there are only six **endemic species** (that is, species found only in Kenya). Although these species are unlikely to be encountered by the novice and can be difficult to identify, their existence serves to emphasize Kenya's remarkable birdlife. They comprise two species of cisticola (small, skulking species, found in dense vegetation), a species of lark found only in the Marsabit and Isiolo areas, Sharpe's pipit (found in high grasslands in western and central Kenya), Clarke's weaver (found only in and around the Arabuko-Sokoke forest), and Hinde's pied babbler (found in the vicinity of Kianyaga near Embu).

Many birdwatchers are attracted to Kenya by the large number of **near-endemic species**, confined to northeast Africa, for which Kenya offers a reasonably accessible chance of a sighting. These include Heuglin's bustard, the Somali bee-eater (a very pale, open-country bee-eater found in the north and often noted at Samburu), Hartlaub's turaco (a green species of turaco, only found in highland forests in east Africa), and the small Sokoke Scops owl found most easily around the Arabuko-Sokoke forest.

LARGE WALKING BIRDS

Several species of large, terrestrial (or partly terrestrial) birds are regularly seen on safari. Their size and common form of locomotion (though the secretary bird and marabou stork can both fly perfectly well, and the ground hornbill is not flightless) makes them the birds most frequently spotted by non-ornithologists.

The locally common, distinctive **ostrich** is found in dry, open plains and semi-desert. The world's biggest bird, at up to 2.5m high, it is virtually absent from the coastal strip, but can be readily seen in Nairobi National Park and most others.

The **secretary bird** is a large, long-tailed, long-legged bird, grey-white in colour with a

Marabou Stork

scraggy crest (the quills of which gave it its name), black on the wings and black "stockings". A bird of dry, open bush and wooded country, often seen in pairs, it is most commonly noticed stalking prey items which it has disturbed from grassland. Prey includes beetles, grasshoppers, reptiles and rodents, sometimes up to the size of a hare. Secretary birds are scarce in west Kenya and at the coast, but can be seen easily in Nairobi National Park.

The **marabou** is a large, ugly stork, up to 1.2m in height, with a bald head and a dangling, pink throat pouch. Most specimens look as if they're in an advanced state of decomposition. The marabou flies with its head and neck retracted (unlike other storks) and is often seen in dry areas, including towns, where it feeds on small animals, carrion and refuse.

Another reasonably common walking bird is the **ground hornbill**. This impressive creature lives in open country and is the largest hornbill by far, black with red face and wattles, bearing a distinct resemblance to a turkey. It's not uncommon to come across pairs, or sometimes groups, of ground hornbills, especially in the Mara, trailing through the scrub on the lookout for small animals. They nest among rocks or in tree stumps. (The other hornbills are covered below.)

Secretary Bird

FLAMINGOS AND IBISES

Many visitors to Kenya are astounded by their first sight of **flamingos** – a sea of pink on a soda-encrusted lake, which, together with the salt-rich smell of the lake and the stench of the birds' guano, powerfully evokes east Africa. Two species are found in Kenya, the greater flamingo and the lesser flamingo. Both are birds of the Rift Valley lakes and adjacent areas, and both are colonial nesters.

Much the commoner of the two is the **lesser flamingo**, smaller, pinker and with a darker bill than its greater relative. The Rift Valley population of lesser flamingos, with over a million birds gathering at one time at Lakes Bogoria and Nakuru, is one of only three populations in Africa. This species is nomadic, moving in relation to fluctuating food supplies, water levels and alkalinity. Flocks can leave or arrive at an area in a very short period of time – an estimated 400,000 birds have been recorded leaving Lake Bogoria over a seven-day period. Lesser flamingos feed by filtering suspended aquatic food, mainly blue-green algae that occurs in huge concentrations on the shallow, soda lakes of the Rift.

Greater flamingos may occur in their thousands but are considerably fewer in number than the lessers. They are bottom feeders, filtering small invertebrates as well as algae. Although greaters tend to be less frequently nomadic than their relatives, they are more likely to move away from the Rift Valley lakes to smaller water bodies and even the coast.

The most widely distributed **ibis** species (stork-like birds with downcurved bills) is the **sacred ibis**, which occurs near water and human settlements. It has a white body with black head and neck, and black tips to the wings. Also frequently encountered is the **Hadada ibis**, a bird of wooded streams, cultivated areas and parks in southern Kenya. It is brown with a green-bronze sheen to the wings, and calls noisily in flight.

WATER BIRDS

Most large water bodies, apart from the extremely saline lakes, support several species of **ducks and geese**, many of which breed in Europe, but overwinter in Africa.

Several species of **herons, storks and egrets** occur in areas with water, or can be observed overflying on migration. The commonest large heron is the black-headed heron, which can sometimes be found far from water. Mainly grey with a black head and legs, the black heron can be seen "umbrella-fishing" along coastal creeks and marsh shores: it cloaks its head with its wings whilst fishing, which is thought to cut down surface reflection from the water, allowing the bird to see its prey more easily.

The **hamerkop** is a brown, heron-like bird with a sturdy bill and mane of brown feathers, which gives it a top-heavy, slightly prehistoric appearance in flight, like a miniature pterodactyl. Hamerkops are widespread near water and build large, conspicuous nests that are often taken over by other animals, including owls, geese, ducks, monitor lizards or snakes.

GUINEAFOWL

Four species of these large, grey game birds are found in Kenya. The **vulturine guineafowl** is a bird of very arid areas, recognized by the long tapered feathers hanging from the base of the neck over a royal blue chest. The well-known **helmeted guineafowl**, a bird of moister areas, has a bony yellow skull protrusion (hence its name). The crested and the Kenya crested guineafowl are both birds of thickets.

BIRDS OF PREY

Kenya abounds with birds of prey – kites, vultures, eagles, harriers, hawks and falcons. Altogether, over 75 species have been recorded in the country, several of which are difficult to miss.

Six species of **vulture** range over the plains and bushlands of Kenya and are often seen soaring in search of a carcass. All the species can occur together, and birds may travel vast distances to feed. The main differences are in feeding behaviour: the lappet-faced vulture, for example, pulls open carcasses; the African white-backed feeds mainly on internal organs; the hooded vulture mainly picks from bones.

Two other birds of prey that are firmly associated with east Africa are the **bateleur**, an eagle that is readily identified by its silver wings, black body, chestnut red tail, stumpy body shape and wedge-shaped tail; and the **fish eagle**, whose haunting calls render a sense of emptiness and space to many a wildlife television documentary. Fish eagles are generally found in pairs near water, often along lake shores.

CRANES AND BUSTARDS

Kenya's national bird, the **crowned crane**, is found in the south and west of the country. It is a distinctive, elegant bird, the head crowned with an array of yellow plumes. Crowned cranes are often seen feeding on cultivated fields or in marshy areas.

Some nine species of **bustard** occur in the plains and grasslands of Kenya. These large, open-country species are long-legged and long-necked and are very well camouflaged among the browns and yellows of their African backdrop. The heaviest flying bird in the world, the Kori bustard, is commonest in the Rift Valley highlands. Bustards are affected by intensive, small-scale agricultural and human presence, and several species have undergone a decline in Kenya.

Crowned Crane

PARROTS AND LOVEBIRDS

Eight species of *Psittacidae* have been recorded in Kenya, three of which are introduced. The parrot species that you're most likely to see is the **brown parrot**, which occurs in wooded areas in the west of the country. Lovebirds are small, green, hole-nesting birds (like small parrots) and are readily seen in the acacias around Lake Naivasha, where a feral breeding population of **yellow-collared lovebirds** has become established. This species has been introduced to Kenya from Tanzania, and hybridizes with the introduced and very similar **Fischer's lovebird**.

GO-AWAY BIRDS AND TURACOS

These distinctive, related families are found only in Africa. Medium-sized and with long tails, most **go-away birds** and **turacos** have short rounded wings. They are not excellent fliers, but are very agile in their movements along branches and through vegetation. Many species are colourful and display a crest. The largest, the magnificent **great blue turaco** (blue above, and green and brown below) is found only in the western forests in Kenya – notably at Kakamega, where it is one of the largest species in the forest. Other turacos are generally green or violet in colour, and all are confined to thickly wooded and forest areas. Open-country species, such as the widely distributed and common **white-bellied go-away bird** (go-aways are named after their call), are white or grey in colour.

MOUSEBIRDS

Three species of mousebird are found in Kenya. Their name derives from their rapid scampering through thick tangles of branches using unusually adapted claws. They can be identified by their slight crests and their long, tapering tails. Generally grey or brown in colour, they're noisy and feed actively in quite open vegetation. The **speckled mousebird** is a very common species throughout southern Kenya, often found in small groups at forest margins and in suburban gardens.

ROLLERS, SHRIKES AND KINGFISHERS

A family of very colourful and noticeable birds of the African bush, **rollers** perch on exposed bushes and telegraph wires and hawk flying insects. They take their name from their impressive courtship flights – a fast dive with a rolling and rocking motion, accompanied by raucous calls. Many have a sky-blue underbody and sandy-coloured back; long tail streamers are a distinctive feature of several Kenyan species. The **lilac-breasted roller** is a common and conspicuous species.

Shrikes are found throughout Kenya. Fierce hunters with sharply hooked bills, they habitually sit on prominent perches, and take insects, reptiles and small birds.

Kingfishers are some of Kenya's most colourful and noticeable birds, with eleven species found here. They range in size from the tiny **pygmy kingfisher**, which feeds on insects and is generally found near water, to the **giant kingfisher**, a shy fish-eating species of wooded streams in the west of the country.

Several kingfishers eat insects rather than fish and they can often be seen perched high in trees or on open posts in the bush where they wait to pounce on passing prey. A common and widespread insectivorous species is the **chestnut-bellied kingfisher**.

HORNBILLS

Named for their long, heavy bills, surmounted by a casque or bony helmet, hornbills generally have black and white plumage. Their flight consists of a series of alternate flaps and glides. When in flight, hornbills may be heard before they are seen, the beaten wings making a "whooshing" noise as air rushes through the flight feathers. Many species have bare areas of skin on the face and throat and around the eyes, with the bill and the casque often brightly coloured, their colours changing with the age of the bird. Thirteen species have been recorded in Kenya, most of them omnivorous, but tending largely to eat fruit. Several species are common open-country birds; **silvery-cheeked hornbills** are sometimes seen in Nairobi. Hornbills have interesting breeding habits: the male generally incarcerates the female in a hollow tree, leaving a hole through which he feeds her while she incubates the eggs and rears the young. (The unusual ground hornbill is covered under "Large walking birds", above.)

WOODPECKERS

The abundance of trees within such a variety of habitats in Kenya means that many species of woodpecker (up to fourteen) are present. One species you're almost certain to encounter is the sparrow-sized **cardinal woodpecker**.

SUNBIRDS

Sunbirds are bright, buzzy, active birds, feeding on nectar from flowering plants, and distributed throughout Kenya, wherever there are flowers, flowering trees and bushes. Over 35 species have been recorded in the country, with many confined to discrete types of habitat. Common species in the Nairobi area are **variable** and **scarlet-chested sunbirds**. Males are brightly coloured and usually identifiable, but many of the drabber females require very careful observation to identify them.

STARLINGS

The glorious orange and blue starlings which are a common feature of bushland habitats – usually seen feeding on the ground – belong to one of three species. The **superb starling** is the most widespread of these, found everywhere from remote national parks to gardens in Nairobi. It can be identified by the white band above its orange breast. Similar starlings are the larger **golden-breasted**, often seen in Tsavo National Park, and **Hildebrand's** (also orange-breasted), which is commonest around Machakos but can be encountered all over southern Kenya.

WEAVERS AND WHYDAHS

These small birds are some of the commonest and most widespread of all Kenyan birds. Most male **weavers** have some yellow in the plumage, whereas the females are rather dull and sparrow-like. In fact, many species appear superficially very similar; distinctions are based on their range and preferred type of habitat. Weavers nest in colonies and weave their nests into elongated shapes, which can be used to help in the identification of the species. Many nests are situated close to water or human habitation and sometimes hang suspended. The **golden palm weaver** is the species you'll commonly see on the coast, often in hotel gardens.

Whydahs are also known as widow birds. The **paradise whydah** has extremely ornate tail feathers, with the central pair of tail feathers flattened and twisted into the vertical. Male paradise whydahs are mainly black in colour, and perform a strange bouncing display flight to attract females.

REPTILES AND AMPHIBIANS

There is only one species of crocodile in Kenya – the big **Nile crocodile** which, left to grow, can reach six metres or more in length and is considered a cunning and dangerous animal. You'll see them in the Mara river, in the Tana, at Mzima Springs in Tsavo West, in great numbers in Lake Turkana and, if you take the trouble to look, in many other rivers and large bodies of water.

Kenya has many species of **snakes**, some of them quite common, but your chances of seeing a wild specimen here are more remote than in Australia or the USA, or even certain parts of Europe. In Kenya, as all over Africa, snakes are both revered and reviled and, while they frequently have symbolic significance for local people, that is quite often forgotten in the rush to hack them to bits with a *panga* upon their discovery. All in all, snakes have a very hard time surviving in Kenya: their turnover is high and their speed of exit from the scene when humans show up is remarkable. If they fascinate you, wear boots and go softly. If you hate them, be sure to tread firmly and they will flee on detecting your bad vibrations.

Common **non-poisonous species** of snakes include the rock python (a constrictor, growing up to five metres or more in length), the egg-eating snake and the sand boa. Common **poisonous species** include the green and black mambas (fast, agile, arboreal snakes), the boomslang, the spitting cobra and the dangerous puff adder, which is probably responsible for more bites than any other, on account of its sluggish disposition.

Tortoises are quite frequently encountered on park roads in the morning or late afternoon. Some, like the leopard tortoise, can be quite large, up to 50cm in length, while the hinged tortoise (which not only retreats inside its shell but shuts the door, too) is much smaller – up to 30cm. In rocky areas, look out for the unusual pancake tortoise, a flexible-shelled species that can put on quite a turn of speed but, when cornered in its fissure in the rocks, will inflate to wedge itself inextricably, to avoid capture. Terrapins or turtles of several species are common in ponds and slow-flowing streams. On the coast, sea turtles breed and it's not unusual to see them from boats during snorkelling trips.

Lizards are common everywhere, harmless and often colourful. The commonest are **rock agamas**, the males often seen in courting "plumage", with brilliant orange heads and blue bodies, ducking and bobbing at each other. They live in loose colonies often near human habitation; one hotel may have hundreds, its neighbours none. The biggest lizards, **Nile monitors**, grow to nearly two metres in length and are often seen near water. From a distance, as they race off, they look like speeding baby crocodiles. The other common monitor, the smaller savannah monitor, is less handsomely marked.

A large, docile lizard you may come across is the **plated lizard**. This intelligent, mild-

Jackson's Chameleon

mannered reptile is often found around coastal hotels, looking for scraps from the kitchen or pool terrace. At night on the coast, the translucent little aliens on the ceiling are **geckoes**, catching moths and other insects, and worth encouraging. By day, their minuscule relatives, the day geckoes (velvet grey and yellow), patrol coastal walls. In the highlands you may come across prehistoric-looking three-horned **Jackson's chameleons** creeping through the foliage – and there are several other species, living in most parts of the country, which you are most likely to see squashed flat on the road.

In the **amphibian** world, night-time is usually the right time. Unless you make an effort to track down the perpetrators of the frog chorus down by the lodge water pump, you will probably only come across the odd toad, sitting under a footpath light, waiting for insects to drop on to the ground. There are, however, dozens of species of frogs and tree frogs, ranging from the common squeaker to the red and black rubber frog.

BOOKS

Having a **field guide**, especially to the hundreds of species of birds that will pass your way, makes a huge difference to travelling on safari. The Collins field guides are not published in the US, but American readers can safely assume they'll be available in Kenya.

COLLINS FIELD GUIDES

Michael Blundell, *Wild Flowers of east Africa* (HarperCollins). Botanical companion in the series.

Jean Dorst and Pierre Dandelot, *Larger Mammals of Africa* (HarperCollins). Readable and accessible with lively illustrations, though it tends to favour classifying many races as separate species.

T Haltenorth and H Diller, *Mammals of Africa* (HarperCollins). A rival for Dorst and Dandelot, which tends to find fewer species in the variety of mammals out there. With its superabundance of detail, this might look like first choice, but the somewhat stylized paintings are less meaningful than Dorst and Dandelot's when you're thumping through the bush, and much of the text is superfluous for all but the professional zoologist.

D Hoskings and M Withers, *Handguide to east African Mammals* (HarperCollins).

Ber van Perlo, *Birds of Eastern Africa* (HarperCollins). An essential pocket guide, providing clear colour illustrations and distribution maps for every species known to occur in east Africa, though little by way of descriptive text. Overall, an improvement on Williams's now outdated and less user-friendly bird guide (see below).

John Williams, *Birds of East and central Africa* (HarperCollins). The standard spotter's tome, but getting past its sell-by date.

John Williams, *Field Guide to the Butterflies of Africa* (HarperCollins). Exotic and useful – if you can get hold of a copy (it's currently out of print).

John Williams, *National Parks of east Africa* (HarperCollins). Covers parks, reserves, mammals and birds, but there's too much space devoted to long lists of fauna, and the practical details for the parks are too dated to be of any use.

OTHER FIELD GUIDES

Ray Moore, *Where to Watch Birds in Kenya* (Transafrica Press, available in Kenya and sometimes in the UK). Invaluable tips and background for the devoted birder.

Dave Richards, *Photographic Guide to the Birds of east Africa* (New Holland). Over three hundred colour photos.

Nigel Wheatley, *Where to Watch Birds in Africa* (Helm). Tight structure and plenty of useful detail make this a must-have for serious birders in Africa; 25 pages on Kenya.

Zimmerman, Turner and Pearson, *A Field Guide to the Birds of Kenya and Northern Tanzania* (Helm). Comprehensive coverage in hardback.

Richard Trillo and Tony Stones
With thanks to Tony Pinchuck for extra mammal input

BOOKS

There is a substantial volume of reading matter on Kenya, though much of the European output has been fairly light-weight and the more scholarly works tend to be indigestible. For pre-departure reading, the growing body of Kenyan literature provides a good foretaste. Some of the following titles may be most easily available in Kenya (for imports in the UK, try the Africa Book Centre, 38 King St, London WC2E 8JT; ☎0171 240 6649, fax 0171 497 0309; E-mail africabooks@dial.pipex.com). British and American publishers are given in the order UK/US – and note that UP means University Press. It's worth visiting libraries and second-hand bookshops to find those titles which are out of print (o/p), although, increasingly, anything good will be republished before long. In the UK, the interlibrary loan system can find you most books, given time. Or try one of the advertisers at the back of the book or the addresses on pp.34–35.

TRAVEL AND GENERAL ACCOUNTS

Bartle Bull, *Safari: A Chronicle of Adventure* (UK & US: Penguin). A great, macho slab of a book, jammed with photos. It's grotesque but utterly compelling – even if the cruelty and foolish waste of the hunting era, so recently past, is emotionally wearing.

Negley Farson, *Behind God's Back* (Zenith o/p/Harcourt Brace Jovanovich o/p). An American journalist's account of his long overland journey across Africa on the eve of World War II. A lively book if you can stomach the alarming

shifts between criticism of the colonial world and participation in its worst prejudices.

Dick Hedges, *Tilda's Angel* (UK only: Book Guild). If you want to know all about the man behind *Safari Camp Services* and the *Turkana Bus*, this is for you. Good on what makes Anglo-Kenyans tick.

John Hillaby, *Journey to the Jade Sea* (UK only: Constable). An obvious one to read before a trip to Lake Turkana. Hillaby's account of his walk in the early 1960s is dated and not always informative – an adventure, as he writes, "for the hell of it", with sprinklings of tall stories and descriptions of loony incompetence.

David Lamb, *The Africans* (Mandarin o/p/Random House). There's really no contest between Lamb, a *Los Angeles Times* hack, and Marnham (see below) for a contemporary view of the continent. *The Africans* has been something of a best seller, but Lamb's fly-in, fly-out technique is a muddled, statistical rant, couched in Cold War rhetoric; even when ostensibly uncovering a pearl of wisdom, he can be unpleasantly offensive.

Patrick Marnham, *Fantastic Invasion: Dispatches from Africa* (Penguin o/p/Viking Penguin o/p). Although written in the 1970s, nothing since has matched this withering and devastatingly sharp collection, which includes several essays on Kenya. Tunnels beneath the mountain of dross written about Africa.

Peter Matthiessen, *The Tree Where Man Was Born* (Harvill/NAL-Dutton). Wanderings and musings of the Zen-thinking polymath in Kenya and northern Tanzania. Enthralling for its detail on nature, society, culture and prehistory, and beautifully written, this is a gentle, appetizing introduction to the land and its people.

George Monbiot, *No Man's Land* (UK only: Picador). A journey through Kenya and Tanzania, providing a shocking exposé of Maasai dispossession and a major criticism of the wildlife conservation movement. Some of the interviews on p.314 were used in the book.

Dervla Murphy, *The Ukimwi Road* (Flamingo/Overlook). Murphy's bike ride from Kenya to Zimbabwe becomes – for her – a trip through lands lost to AIDS and neo-colonialism.

Shiva Naipaul, *North of South* (Penguin/Viking Penguin o/p). A fine but caustic account of the late Naipaul's travels in Kenya,

Tanganyika and Zambia. Always readable and sometimes hilarious, the insights make up for the occasionally angst-ridden social commentary and some passages that widely miss the mark.

Craig Packer, *Into Africa* (UK & US: University of Chicago Press). A professor of ecology, evolution and behaviour, Packer puts it all to good use in day-by-day reflections during an eight-week field trip.

Wilfred Thesiger, *My Kenya Days* (UK only: HarperCollins). The account of thirty-odd years in northern Kenya by a very strange man indeed – an old Etonian noble savage with no interest in modern Africa, wedded to his own ego and a reactionary, glamour-laden view of his tribal companions.

Daisy Waugh, *A Small Town in Africa* (UK only: Mandarin). A year in the life of Isiolo.

Evelyn Waugh, *A Tourist in Africa* (Methuen/Greenwood Press). First published in 1960, Waugh's diary of a short trip to Kenya, Tanganyika and Rhodesia is determinedly arrogant and uninformed, but funny, too – and brief enough to consume at a single sitting.

TRAVEL BIBLIOGRAPHIES

Oona Strathern, ed, *Traveller's Literary Companion: Africa* (In Print Publishing/Passport Books o/p). Brief selections of literature from or about virtually every African country, including a good raft of Kenyan pieces.

Louis Taussig, *Resource Guide to Travel in Sub-Saharan Africa: Vol 1 East and West Africa* (Zell/Bowker-Saur). The definitive guide to the guides and much more. Extraordinarily detailed country-by-country coverage of every published source of interest to travellers or expatriates, as well as bookstores, libraries, mapping institutes, children's resources and conservation societies, to list just a few. Libraries will obtain it for you.

EXPLORERS' ACCOUNTS

The following explorers' books deal largely with Kenya and make for interesting pre-departure reading.

Rev. J L Krapf, *Travel and Missionary Labors in Africa* (1860; Frank Cass/Johnson Reprint o/p).

C H Stigand, *The Land of Zinj* (1912; US only: Bibilo Distribution Centre o/p).

Joseph Thomson, *Through Maasailand: To the central African Lakes and Back* (1885, 2 vols; Frank Cass/available in the US through International Specialized Book Services).

COLONIAL WRITERS

Not surprisingly perhaps, settler society produced few notable authors. Karen Blixen was the literary prima donna.

KAREN BLIXEN

Isak Dinesen (Karen Blixen), *Out of Africa* (Penguin/Random House). This has become something of a cult book, particularly in the wake of the movie. First published in 1937, it describes Dinesen's life (Blixen was a pseudonym) on her Ngong Hills coffee farm between the wars. Read today, it seems to hover uncertainly between contemporary literature and historical document. It's an intense read – lyrical, introspective, sometimes obnoxiously and intricately racist, but worth pursuing and never superficial, unlike the film. Dinesen's own *Letters from Africa* (Picador o/p/University of Chicago Press) gives posthumous insights.

Judith Thurman, *The Life of Isak Dinesen* (Penguin/St Martin's Press). A biography that sets the record straighter and was the source of much of the material for the *Out of Africa* film.

Peter Beard, *Kamante's Tales from Out of Africa* (Chronicle Books/Harcourt Brace Jovanovich o/p). Fascinating photos of Blixen and friends, as well as an unnecessarily condescending handwritten text by the grandsons of Kamante (her houseboy in Kenya), transcribing the memories of one of the principal characters in *Out of Africa*.

OTHER WORKS OF THE COLONIAL ERA

Beryl Markham, *West with the Night* (Penguin/Northpoint o/p). Markham made the first east–west solo flight across the Atlantic. This is her first and last book about her life in the interwar Kenya colony, drawing together adventures, landscapes and contemporary figures. Not great literature, but highly evocative.

Errol Trzebinski, *The Lives of Beryl Markham* (Mandarin/Norton). In which, among much else, it is suggested that Markham did not, and could not, have written *West with the Night*. A movie must be on the way.

Elspeth Huxley, *The Flame Trees of Thika* (UK & US: Penguin); *The Mottled Lizard* (Penguin o/p/Penguin). Bland entertainment based on her own childhood, from a prolific author who has also written numerous works on colonial history and society, including *White Man's Country* (o/p), a biography of the settlers' doyen, Lord Delamere, and *Out in the Midday Sun: My Kenya* (Penguin o/p/Viking Penguin o/p), both as readable (if also predictable) as any. Her most recent book is *Nine Faces of Kenya* (Harvill/Viking Penguin o/p), a dewy-eyed anthology of east African ephemera. More interesting is the collection of her mother's letters, *Nellie's Story* (Weidenfeld & Nicolson o/p/Morrow o/p), which includes some compelling coverage of the Mau Mau years from the pen of a likably eccentric settler.

Richard Meinertzhagen, *Kenya Diary (1902–1906)* (UK only: Eland Books o/p). The haunting day-to-day narrative of a young British officer in the protectorate. Meinertzhagen's brutal descriptions of "punitive expeditions" are chillingly matter-of-fact and make the endless tally of his wildlife slaughter pale inoffensively in comparison. As a reminder of the savagery that accompanied the British intrusion, and a stark insight into the complex mind of one of its perpetrators, this is disturbing, highly recommended reading. Good photos, too.

Harry Hook, *The Kitchen Toto* (Faber & Faber o/p/Faber Inc o/p). By way of an antidote to a surfeit of settlers' yarns, this screenplay tells the story of Mwangi, a Kikuyu houseboy caught up in the early stages of the Mau Mau rebellion. Writer-director Hook's **movie** is as keen as a country *panga* and draws masterful performances from a largely unknown cast.

KENYA IN MODERN WESTERN FICTION

Kenya has been the setting for the work of a number of recent writers, most noticeably three women.

Justin Cartwright, *Maasai Dreaming* (Picador/Random House). A compelling novel juxtaposing a film-maker's vision of Maasailand with the barbarities of the Holocaust, linked by the tapes of a Jewish anthropologist.

Martha Gellhorn, *The Weather in Africa* (Eland/Hippocrene). Three absorbing novellas, each dealing with aspects of the Europe–Africa relationship, set on the slopes of Kilimanjaro, in the "white highlands" of Kenya and on the tourist coast north of Mombasa. Highly recommended.

Jeremy Gavron, *Moon* (UK only: Viking). Vivid short novel about a white boy growing up on a farm during The Emergency.

David Lambkin, *The Hanging Tree* (Viking/Counterpoint). A human-nature-through-the-ages saga which makes a good yarn – in fact, several yarns – though the style is pretentious.

Paul Meyer, *Herdsboy* (US only: Northwest Publishing). American tourist "finds herself captive of a native tribe". A pacey first novel, set in Samburuland, that overcomes that jacket description.

Maria Thomas, *Come to Africa and Save Your Marriage* (Serpent's Tail o/p/Soho Press). Most of these tales are set in Kenya or Tanzania. Thomas's characters are solid, but the stories leave a wearying aftertaste as if there were nothing positive to be had from the expatriate experience. Her first novel, *Antonia Saw the Oryx First* (same publishers), is painfully detailed – a good antidote to *Out of Africa*.

HISTORY AND PEOPLES

There's a good range of background reading on Kenyan history and a large number of anthropological works on different peoples. Few of the latter are mentioned here. In the UK, the best source for specialist ethnographic titles is probably the School of Oriental and African Studies Library in London (see p.34).

KENYA IN AFRICAN HISTORY

Roland Oliver and J D Fage, *A Short History of Africa* (Penguin/Viking). Dated, but still the standard paperback introduction.

Basil Davidson, *Let Freedom Come: Africa in Modern History* (Penguin o/p/Little, Brown o/p). Lucidly argued and very readable summary of nineteenth- and twentieth-century events.

Alan Moorehead, *The White Nile* (Penguin/Random House o/p). Moving closer to Kenya, this is a riveting account of the search for the source and European rivalries for control in the region.

Christopher Hibbert, *Africa Explored: Europeans in the Dark Continent 1769–1889*

(UK only: Penguin o/p). Entertaining read, devoted in large part to the "discovery" of East and central Africa.

KENYA IN GENERAL

William R Ochieng, *A History of Kenya* (Macmillan, Kenya). Somewhat pedestrian but the best general overview from prehistory to 1980, with useful maps and photos to show the way. *A Modern History of Kenya 1895–1980* (UK only: Evans) covers the twentieth century in eight chapters – solid enough up to the middle of Kenyatta's reign.

William R Ochieng, ed, *Themes in Kenyan History* (James Currey/Ohio UP o/p). A new collection of writings by historians and other academics, all teaching in Kenyan universities.

Jeffrey A Fadiman, *When We Began There Were Witchmen* (US only: University of California Press). Recounts the story of the Meru people from their mythical origins in Shungwaya in northeastern Kenya to the decimation of Meru culture by a tiny handful of missionaries and colonial administrators.

Fedders and Salvadori, *People and Cultures of Kenya* (UK only: Transafrica and Rex Collings o/p). A useful tribe-by-tribe introduction. Cynthia Salvadori's *Through Open Doors: A View of Asian Cultures in Kenya* (Kenway Publications o/p) combines a stack of lively and readable erudition with fascinating marginal notes and sketches – superlative.

Terry Hirst, *The Struggle for Nairobi* (Mazingira Institute, Kenya). Sort of large-format "Nairobi for Beginners" that manages to make town planning (or the lack of it) fascinating, bringing together a mass of otherwise hard-to-get information about the city's growth.

Kenya's People (series of ten pamphlets, Evans, Kenya). Simple and reliable background on ten of Kenya's peoples. Aimed at Kenyan secondary schools, they're pitched just right for culturally uninitiated visitors.

Jomo Kenyatta, *Facing Mount Kenya* (Heinemann o/p/Random House). A traditional, functionalist, anthropological monograph, but written by a member of the society in question – in this case, the Kikuyu – under the supervision of Bronislaw Malinowski at the London School of Economics, shortly before World War II. One of the few scholarly works ever written on traditional Kikuyu culture, this is as interesting for the insights it offers on its author as for its quite readable content. Interesting Kikuyu glossary.

Bethwell A Ogot, *Historical Dictionary of Kenya* (US only: Scarecrow Press, Metuchen, New Jersey o/p). From a reliable series that covers nearly every African country, this is an A to Z of Kenya's history to 1979, written by one of the country's leading historians. Includes an extensive bibliography.

Thomas Spear and Richard Waller, eds, *Being Maasai* (James Currey/Ohio UP). Articles about Maasai identity – a subtle and interesting field, and vital reading for anyone concerned with the ethnic politics of modern Kenya.

COASTAL HISTORY

G S P Freeman-Grenville, *The east African Coast* (UK only: Oxford UP o/p). If you're heading for the coast, this is fascinating – a series of accounts from the first century to the nineteenth – vivid and often extraordinary.

Sarah Mirza and Margaret Strobel, *Three Swahili Women* (UK & US: Indiana UP). Three histories of ritual, three women's lives. Born between 1890 and 1920 into different social backgrounds, these biographies document enormous changes from the most important of neglected viewpoints.

James de Vere Allen, *Swahili Origins: Swahili Culture and the Shungwaya Phenomenon* (James Currey/Ohio UP). The life work of a challenging and readable scholar, bound to raise a fascinating field of study to new prominence.

PROTECTORATE AND COLONIAL KENYA

Errol Trzebinski, *The Kenya Pioneers* (Heinemann o/p/Norton o/p). Despite academic pretensions, this is something of a paean to the early settlers.

Charles Miller, *The Lunatic Express* (Westlands Sundries, Kenya). The story of that railway. Miller narrates the drama of one of the great feats of Victorian engineering – as bizarre and as madly magnificent as any Wild West epic – adding weight with a broad historical background of east Africa from the year dot. The same author's *The Battle for the Bundu* (UK only: Macmillan o/p) follows a little-known corner of World War I, as fought out on the plains of Tsavo between British Kenya and German Tanganyika – immensely readable.

James Fox, *White Mischief* (Penguin/Random House o/p). Investigative romp through the events surrounding the notorious unsolved murder of Lord Errol, one of Kenya's most aristocratic settlers, at Karen in 1941. Well told and highly revealing of British Kenyan society of the time. Michael Radford's 1987 **film version** is equally enjoyable, and a good deal more stimulating than the *Out of Africa* movie.

THE MAU MAU REBELLION

Bruce Berman, *Control and Crisis in Modern Kenya* (James Currey/Ohio UP). A study of the growth of state control, from the 1890s through to interwar crisis and postwar disintegration.

Tabitha Kanogo, *Squatters and the Roots of Mau Mau 1905–63* (James Currey/Ohio UP). Delves into the early years of the "White Highlands" to show how resistance, and the conditions for revolt, were built into the relations between the settler land-grabbers and the peasant farmers and herders ("squatters") they usurped. Strong on the role of women in the Mau Mau movement.

David Throup, *Economic and Social Origins of Mau Mau* (James Currey/Ohio UP). An examination of the story from the end of World War II, covering the colonial mentality and differences in efficiency between peasant cash-cropping and more wasteful plantation agriculture.

Frank Furedi, *The Mau Mau War in Perspective* (James Currey/Ohio UP). Furedi analyses, using new archival sources, the continued struggle for land redistribution once the struggle for Independence had been won.

R G Edgerton, *Mau Mau: An African Crucible* (I B Tauris/Free Press). An account of the revolt based on guerrillas' testimonies. Includes explorations of the role of women and class formation in modern Kenya.

J M Kariuki, *Mau Mau Detainee: The Account by a Kenya African of His Experience in Detention Camps* (Oxford UP o/p/Books on Demand, University of Michigan o/p). A remarkably forbearing account of life and death in the detention camps. Kariuki's vision for the future of Kenya and his loyalty to Kenyatta have a special irony after his assassination in 1975. Recommended.

Donald L Barnett and Karari Njama, *Mau Mau from Within: Autobiography and Analysis of Kenya's Peasant Revolt* (Monthly Review Press o/p). An account based on personal recollections.

AFTER INDEPENDENCE

Anthony Howarth, *Kenyatta: A Photographic Biography* (east African Publishing House, Nairobi, o/p). A roughly hewn biography composed of an amalgam of black and white photographs, news clippings and quotations. It doesn't pretend to be exhaustive, but manages to capture the spirit of the leader and the struggle for Independence.

Kenneth King, *Jua Kali Kenya* (James Currey/Ohio UP). First serious study of Kenya's important informal sector – the self-employed fixers and manufacturers who work under the "hot sun" (the *jua kali*). Great photos.

Jeremy Murray Brown, *Kenyatta* (US only: E P Dutton o/p), and **David Goldsworthy** *Tom Mboya: The Man Who Kenya Wanted to Forget* (UK & US: Holmes & Meier), are the two big biographies: both weighty and deeply researched.

Oginga Odinga, *Not Yet Uhuru* (UK only: Heinemann o/p). The classic critique of Kenya's direction at the time it was written.

B A Ogot and William Ochieng, eds, *Decolonization and Independence in Africa 1940–93* (UK & US: James Currey). Set to become a standard new work on these years, this asks how much Kenya's – and other countries' – difficulties are linked to the colonial past and the process of growing away from it.

Tom Mboya, *The Challenge of Nationhood* (UK & US: Heinemann). The vision of Kenya's best-loved statesman – and a Luo – assassinated in 1969 for looking like a clear successor to Kenyatta.

Ngugi wa Thiong'o, *Detained – A Writer's Prison Diary* (UK & US: Heinemann). A retrospective of Kenya's history up to 1978, woven into the daily routine of political detention during Kenyatta's last year. Ngugi discourses widely and, while his reflections are occasionally pedantic or obscure and sometimes written with almost religious fervour, he hits home often. His *Barrel of a Pen: Resistance to Repression in Neo-Colonial Kenya* (New Beacon/Africa World) hones some of his points sharply. (See also the box on p.548).

Guy Arnold, *Modern Kenya* (UK only: Longman o/p). A digestible look at Kenyan politics, economy and society. A concise, if guarded, survey, but meatier than it might appear.

Anonymous, *In Dependent Kenya* (UK only: Zed Books). Published in 1982, a book that pulls no punches, fully and bitterly condemning the status quo and Kenya's paralysis in the neo-colonial web. Remorseless, trenchant and to the point; read it for instruction, but don't take it with you.

Jean Davison, *Voices from Mutira: Change in the Lives of Rural Gikuyu Women 1910–1995* (UK & US: Lynne Rienner). Rich, unselfconsciously moving and particularly interesting for the attitudes it documents on brideprice and genital mutilation.

WorldFocus Kenya (Heinemann). Children's introduction to the country – one of a series for the seven-plus age group – written with style and intelligence, and incorporating good photos and case studies of real people.

ARTS

Most works dealing with the arts cover the whole continent.

Susan Denyer, *African Traditional Architecture* (Africana/Holmes & Meier). Useful and interesting, with hundreds of photos (most of them old) and detailed line drawings.

Frank Willett, *African Art* (Thames & Hudson/Thames & Hudson o/p). An accessible volume; good value, with a generous illustrations–text ratio.

Geoffrey Williams, *African Designs from Traditional Sources* (UK & US: Dover). A designer's and enthusiast's sourcebook, from the copyright-free publishers.

Roy Braverman, *Islam and Tribal Art* (Cambridge UP/Cambridge UP o/p). A useful paperback text for the dedicated.

Jane Barbour and Simiyu Wandibba, *Kenyan Pots and Potters* (Oxford UP/Oxford UP o/p). This comprehensive description of pot-making communities includes techniques, training, marketing and sociological perspectives.

KENYAN FICTION IN ENGLISH

Although a number of authors have written in the older languages of Kenya, English still predominates as the medium for artistic expression, a situation which creates dilemmas for writers struggling both to reach a readership at home and to find viable channels for publication.

Ngugi wa Thiong'o, *Decolonising the Mind: The Politics of Language in African Literature* (James Currey/Heinemann). Ngugi has long been closely associated with attempts to move Kenyan literature and African literature in general towards expression in the readers' mother tongues (see box on p.548).

PROSE COLLECTIONS

African Short Stories, edited by Chinua Achebe and C L Innes (UK & US: Heinemann). A collection which treats its material geographically, including Kenyan stories from **Jomo Kenyatta**, **Grace Ogot**, **Ngugi** and a spooky offering (*The Spider's Web*) from **Leonard Kibera**, brother of Sam Kahiga.

Unwinding Threads: Writing by Women in Africa, edited by Charlotte H Bruner (UK & US: Heinemann). Also geographical, with succinct introductions to each region. east Africa features Kenyan writers **Charity Waciuma** and the excellent **Grace Ogot**, whose *The Rain Came* is a bewitching mystery myth, combining traditional Luo tales with her own fiction in a perplexingly "Western" form. There's a new Heinemann collection edited by Bruner, entitled *African Women's Writing*.

Two Centuries of African English, edited by Lalage Bown (UK & US: Heinemann o/p). Includes non-fiction extracts from the work of **J M Kariuki** (*Mau Mau Detainee* – see opposite), **Ali Mazrui** on intellectuals and revolution, **Githende Mockerie** and **R Mugo Gatheru** recounting their childhoods, and **Tom Mboya** on Julius Nyerere, first president of Tanzania.

NOVELS AND SHORT STORIES

Meja Mwangi, *Going Down River Road; Carcase for Hounds; Kill Me Quick* (all in Heinemann's African Writers series). Mwangi is lighter and more accessible than Ngugi, his fiction infused with the absurdities of urban (Nairobi) slum life. *Going Down River Road* is the best known: convincing scenes, chaotic action and sharp dialogue (though it's never clear whether the English/American street cool is meant to be real, or an effort to render the

NGUGI WA THIONG'O

The dominant figure of modern Kenyan literature currently lives in exile in Britain: although most of his books in English are not banned in Kenya, his political sympathies are.

Ngugi's work is art serving the revolution – didactic, brusque, graphic and unsentimental. His novels, especially the later ones, are unforgiving: the touch of humour that would leaven the polemic rarely comes to the rescue. Powerful themes – exploitation, betrayal, cultural oppression, the imposition of Christianity, loss of and search for identity – drive the stories along urgently. Characters deal with real events and the changes of their time, struggling to come to terms with the influences at work on their lives.

Ngugi's style is heady, idealistic and undaunted, never teasing or capricious. Disillusioned with English ("Whom do I write for?"), his first work in Kikuyu, in collaboration with Ngugi wa Mirii, was the play *Ngahiika Ndeenda* (I will Marry When I Want), and its public performance by illiterate peasants at the Kamiriithu Cultural Centre in Limuru got him detained for a year. He'd found his mark. Ngugi's work in the Kikuyu language is now banned, or rarely available, in Kenya.

Most of Ngugi's writings in English are published in the Heinemann paperback African Writers series. Try *Secret Lives* for short stories, *Weep Not Child* for a brief but glowing early novel, or, for the mature Ngugi, *Petals of Blood* – a richly satisfying detective story that is at the same time a saga of wretchedness and struggle (see p.553 for an excerpt). Others include *The River Between*, on the old Kikuyu society and the coming of the Europeans; *A Grain of Wheat*, about the eve of Independence; *Devil on the Cross* (written in detention on scraps of toilet paper); and *Matigari* (The Patriots). *Matigari*, first published in Kikuyu by Heinemann in 1986, had a remarkable effect in the Central Highlands. Rumours circulated that a man, Matigari, was spreading militant propaganda against the government. The police even tried to track him down, before realizing their mistake and confiscating all copies of the book.

Ngugi has written two other plays, *The Black Hermit* and *The Trial of Dedan Kimathi* (with Micere Mugo). Academic works include *Moving the Centre* (James Currey/Heinemann Inc), a collection of essays (see also p.546). His contribution to Kenyan literature – and liberation literature – is enormous; delving in is rewarding, if not always easy.

Swahili-Kikuyu "Sheng" slang of the slums). Great *in situ* reading. Mwangi's latest, short-listed for the Commonwealth Writers' Prize, is *Striving for the Wind*, set in a rural rather than urban location.

Thomas Akare, *The Slums* (UK & US: Heinemann). A bleaker read than Mwangi, but also more humane. Without quotation marks, the dialogue melds seamlessly into the narrative; no doubts about the authentic rhythms of Kenyan English here. But much is assumed to be understood and there's much that won't be, unless you're sitting under a 25-watt light bulb in a River Road Boarding & Lodging.

Sam Kahiga, *Flight to Juba – Short Stories* (Longman, Kenya); *The Girl from Abroad* (UK & US: Heinemann o/p). Vital, exasperating, obnoxious and plain crazy – a writer to love to hate (see excerpted story, p.558).

Ali Mazrui, *The Trial of Christopher Okigbo* (UK & US: Heinemann). A clever "novel of ideas" from the US-based political scientist, who always succeeds in infuriating both critics of Kenya and its supporters. His latest book,

Cultural Forces in World Politics (James Currey/Heinemann) is a survey of cultural and political ideas which also addresses the issues surrounding Salman Rushdie's *Satanic Verses*.

Marjorie Oludhe Macgoye, *Victoria* and *Murder in Majengo* (UK only: Macmillan). Two novels – available in one volume – putting a Luo woman's view on life in Kenya from one of the country's few published women writers.

Bramwell Lusweti, *The Way to the Town Hall* (Macmillan, Kenya). Enjoyable satire aimed at small-town politicians and businessmen. A Swahili dictionary (to translate the characters' names!) is a help.

David Mulwa, *Master and Servant* (UK only: Longman o/p). Growing up in colonial Kenya: a funny and affecting string of episodes.

Mude Dae Mude, *The Hills are Falling* (Kenya Literature Bureau, Nairobi). Life from Marsabit to Nairobi.

Kenneth Watene, *Sunset on the Manyatta* (east African Publishing House, Nairobi). A Maasai man in Germany.

KENYAN POETRY

The oldest form of written poetry in Kenya is from the coast. Inland, poetry in the sense of written verse is a recent form. But oral folk literature was often relayed in the context of music, rhythm and dance.

SWAHILI POETRY

Swahili poetry reads beautifully even if you don't understand the words. Written for at least 300 years, and sung for a good deal longer, it's one of Kenya's most enduring art forms. An *Anthology of Swahili Poetry* has been compiled and rather woodenly translated by **Ali A Jahadmy** (Heinemann o/p). Some of Swahili's best-known classical compositions from the Lamu archipelago are included, with pertinent background.

There's a more enjoyable anthology of romantic and erotic verse, *A Choice of Flowers*, with **Jan Knappert**'s idiosyncratic translations and interpretations (UK & US: Heinemann o/p), and the same linguist's *Four Centuries of Swahili Verse* (UK & US: Darf), which expounds and creatively interprets at much greater length. A translation of an exquisite poem from the latter is included on p.557.

KENYAN POETRY IN ENGLISH

Poems of Black Africa, edited by Wole Soyinka (Heinemann/Heinemann o/p). A hefty and catholic selection. From Kenya, it includes the work of **Abangira**, **Jared Angira**, **Jonathan Kariara** and **Amin Kassam**.

Heinemann Book of African Poetry (UK & US: Heinemann). A new volume, which includes the work of Kenyan poet Marjorie Oludhe Macgoye.

MOUNTAIN AND HIKING GUIDES

The following should prove detailed enough for most purposes. See also the Mount Kenya "Guidebooks and Maps" section on p.168.

David Else, *Trekking in East Africa* (UK & US: Lonely Planet). Well-produced guide to hiking in the region, including detailed sections on Mount Kenya, the Aberdares and Mount Elgon.

Guide Book to Mount Kenya and Kilimanjaro (Mountain Club of Kenya, Nairobi). For fully equipped alpinism, this is indispensable.

Mountains of Kenya (Mountain Club of Kenya, Nairobi). A detailed and practical guide, comprehensively updated since its earlier incarnation and well worth buying if you plan to do any Kenyan hiking.

Andrew Wielochowski, *East Africa International Mountain Guide* (West Col Productions o/p). Fairly up-to-date for Mount Kenya and other more obscure ascents.

COFFEE-TABLE BOOKS

John Schmid, *The Kenya Magic* (UK only: Beachwood Publications o/p). A light introduction to the country and the best by far of the general coffee-table offerings, including some perceptive commentary to accompany the travelogue. The photos, on 35mm format, are superb and refreshingly simple.

Mohamed Amin, *Cradle of Mankind* (Camerapix/Overlook Press). Stunning photographs but a balefully inadequate text. Covers the Lake Turkana region.

Anne Arthus-Bertrand and Anne Spoerry, photos by Yann Arthus-Bertrand, *Kenya from the Air* (Thames and Hudson/Vendome). Superb images of the country from the eagle's viewpoint.

Tepilit Ole Saitoti and Carol Beckwith, *Maasai* (Elm Tree o/p/Abrams). The Maasai coffee-table book; some photos are too much to take at reading distance. Exquisite but largely staged portraits of a vanishing culture (and even Beckwith's camera can't disguise the tourist souvenirs in the background). Variably interesting, chauvinistic text, which plays the cult value of the Maasai for all it's worth.

David Keith Jones, *Shepherds of the Desert* (UK only: Hamish Hamilton). Brilliant photos (many in black and white), with a text more lucid and less superficial than most glossies; this book concerns itself only with northern Kenya.

Brian Jackman and Jonathan Scott, *The Marsh Lions* (Elm Tree o/p/Godine o/p). Beautifully produced and painstakingly researched study of the lions and other animals around the Musiara Marsh in Maasai Mara. To come across a lion you *recognize* in an animal book (she with the missing tail-tip) is different, anyway.

Mitsuaki Iwago, *Serengeti* (Thames and Hudson/Chronicle). Stunning scenes and portraits from Serengeti (the Tanzanian continuation of the Maasai Mara) from a master photographer. Simply the best volume of wildlife photography ever assembled, this makes most glossies look feeble. If you're trying to persuade someone to visit east Africa – or if any aesthetic argument were needed to preserve the parks and animals – this is the book to use.

WRITING FROM KENYA

Very little Kenyan literature appeared in print before World War II. But while east Africa has tended to lag behind the rest of the continent in modern forms – the novel, short stories, drama and modern poetry – there's a rich tradition of oral literature and a specifically coastal Swahili verse culture that put African stories into writing as long as three hundred years ago.

THE ORAL TRADITION IN PRINT

*With the exception of the coast, precolonial Kenyan literature was entirely oral, and stories were passed – and modified – from generation to generation. These **folk tales**, commonly told by the leaders of the community to the children, were very often "trickster" tales about animals. While they frequently contained a moral, their main purpose was to entertain.*

THE HARE'S PRACTICAL JOKE

A long, long time ago, there were two people who were very good friends. One was Mr. Hare and the other Mr. Hyena. They used to visit each other and on each of these visits, the Hare used to carry in his bag some honey and sweetened meat. He used to put his little finger in the bag and give his friend to lick. Said the Hare: "Brother, I have something very, very sweet in my bag here. Take it and see for yourself." The Hyena liked it very much.

"Hi, Hi, Brother Hare, give me some more, more I say. It is very, very . . ."

"No, no, this is a sweetness that you must have a little at a time."

And the same thing happened day after day for many days. One day, the Hare came on as usual and said:

"Brother Hyena, may I give you something very, very sweet, sweeter than sweetness itself?"

"Yes, my good friend, I'd love some very, very much." And the Hare gave his sweetened finger to the Hyena to lick.

"Oh, Hare, my very good friend do give me more."

"No, no, old man, you cannot eat much of this sweetness. It is a sweetness that must be eaten sparingly."

"But brother, where do you get much much sweetness?"

"I get it from those mountains you see above our heads," pointing at the white clouds. "Once you eat this sweetness you should never pass piss or shit because then the sweetness gets lost."

"Then what do people do so that they do not pass out piss or shit after they have eaten this sweetness?"

"Ah, Mr. Hyena, that is very simple, they have their bottoms sewn up and if you want, I can do the sewing up for you."

"Yes, yes, do sew it up for me." And the Hare sewed the Hyena's bottom.

They took three bags each and the Hare led the way to the sweetness that never passes. Now the Hyena ate the honey, the honeycombs and the dead bees. Then the Hare said: "Now that we have filled our stomachs and our bags let us go home." Now when they were on the way, the Hyena went down to the stream to drink some water. And when he drank he just dropped down like a stump of a tree. He stayed and stayed and stayed there; his eyes popping out like sweet potatoes. He stayed there for so many days, until he thought he was going to die.

One day he saw the Eagle coming down to drink some water – said he:

"Good Brother Eagle, help me."

"Hi, brother, how shall I help you?"

"Come round behind me at my bottom end. You will see a string going right through it, prick it and pull carefully because I feel pain. I was sewn up by the Hare and he did a very bad thing."

Now as soon as the Eagle touched this string a flood of piss and shit rushed out and covered the Eagle and the piss was like a mountain with the Eagle as the core.

One day there was a heavy rain which washed away the piss and shit, slowly by slowly until the Eagle emerged with a scratch on the neck. He flew away swearing revenge on the Hyena. For many days he and the Hyena played hide and seek until one day the Hyena, being the foolish person, forgot that he was the sworn enemy of the Eagle. The Eagle being clever did not want a physical contact with the

Hyena. He knew very well that the Hyena was stronger than him. Now he started to show the Hyena the choice pieces of meat that he carried in his bag and every day he gave a little to the Hyena saying: "Brother, I carry this kind of meat, have a bite" and the Hyena said: "Brother Eagle, these delicacies, this choice meat you give me, where does it come from?"

"Now, Brother Hyena, these delicacies, the choice meats are very, very many. If you like, I can take you where they come from. But," continued the Eagle, "it is impossible to get that meat alone. You must come too. Now go and collect all your people. Let them bring bags, tins and drums. Then we shall bring as much meat as will last for three years."

The Hyena was very happy and he ran to collect all his people. Panting: "Do you see all that meat above? My friend brings it to me every day. Now this friend has told me to collect all my people so that we can go and fetch this meat. Let each one of you bring tins, bags or drums and I, with your permission, will ask the Eagle to mention the day on which we can go."

Said all Hyenas: "Hi, we also would like to eat the white choice meat."

All the Hyenas of that country had gathered together and when they saw the Eagle coming towards them they said: "Now, Brother Eagle, let us go to get this meat. Tell us when we can go".

The Eagle said, "We shall go on the third day from today. Be ready."

On that day the Hyena gathered and the Eagle arranged them in a line according to age, the smallest one being put at the back. The Eagle was right in front. He said to the Hyena behind him: "Now, Brother, hold tight to the feathers of my tail," and the Hyena held tight. "Everybody hold each other's tail," he shouted and then he flew up, up, up, and heading to the choice meats in the sky. Now when they had gone very high, the Eagle asked:

"Are you all clear off the ground?"

"No, no, some are still touching the ground." He flew, flew and flew.

"Can you see the earth?"

"Yes, yes, we can see it." The Eagle was waiting to hear that all the Hyenas could no longer see the earth.

"Can you see the earth?"

"We see it dimly now." The Eagle flew and flew.

"Do you still see the earth?"

"We see only black, black darkness, we cannot tell where the earth is."

The Eagle knew then that the distance from the earth was very, very great. Then he said to the Hyena behind him:

"Hi, hi, my friend, a scratch, a scratch on my back wing," and the Hyena behind let go the tail feathers of the Eagle. Suddenly the whole line of Hyenas went tumbling down. Kuru Kuru Kuru like the sound of thunder. Some Hyenas crushed their limbs, their bones and died instantly. Some died before they reached the earth. Only the last Hyena was left, but she acquired a limp in the leg which she carries to this day.

Reprinted from Kikuyu Folktales, *edited and translated by Rose Gecau. By permission of Kenya Literature Bureau.*

HARE AND HORNBILL

Hare and Hornbill were great friends. One day Hare said: "My friend, we have looked for girls all over this land, and there are none that are good enough for you and me. Let us go up to Skyland, perhaps we will find some suitable ones."

Hornbill replied: "I know it is getting a bit late for us to get married, but you know my problem, you know I have this terrible thing!"

"You mean your chronic diarrhoea? But that is nothing to worry about." Hare produced a cork of the right size and blocked up Hornbill's anus.

The two friends made preparations for the journey, and after saying good-bye to their families, Hare got on Hornbill's back and they flew up through the clouds into Skyland. There was a big marriage dance. Hare and Hornbill put on their dancing costumes and went straight into the arena. Hornbill danced gracefully, touching the ground lightly and moving his wings up and down to the rhythm of the drums. His neck swayed this way and that way, and his eyes sparkled with love. Hare danced as best he could, but he could not follow the rhythm of the dance, and sang out of tune; moreover, his big ears looked funny. Beautiful girls fought to dance before Hornbill, but none came anywhere near Hare; and when he approached the girls they ran away from him.

That night Hornbill slept with a very pretty girl. Hare slept cold.

The next day Hornbill won two girls; Hare again slept cold. The next night when Hornbill was asleep, resting beside his fourth lover, Hare tip-toed into the house and unhooked the cork. Three days' accumulation of diarrhoea spewed out and flooded the entire house. The stench rose like smoke and the dancers fled from the arena, and Hornbill woke up, and in great shame flew down through the clouds, leaving Hare behind.

There was much commotion as the Skylanders tried to find out what had happened. Hare denied all knowledge of the cause of the trouble.

"But where is your handsome friend?" they asked.

"I am also looking for him," said Hare, adding, "I must find him otherwise it will be a bit difficult to return to earth."

When they failed to find Hornbill the Skylanders decided to get rid of Hare by lowering him down to earth on a rope of plaited grass. The girls cut many heaps of grass. They made the rope and tied one end around Hare's waist and continued to plait the other end as Hare was lowered downwards. The Skylanders gave Hare a drum and told him, "As soon as you reach the earth beat this drum very hard so that the girls may stop plaiting the rope." Hare thanked the Skylanders, said good-bye and began his homeward journey.

Hare descended slowly through the clouds, but on seeing the faint tips of the highest mountain he hit the drum very hard. The skylanders stopped plaiting and dropped the rope. Hare came hurtling down like a falling stone. But just before hitting the ground he cried to the smallest black ants, "Collect me! Collect me! Collect . . ."

Hare hit the ground and broke up into many many very small pieces. The smallest black ants collected the pieces and put them together again, and Hare became alive. But today when Hare is running you hear his chest making crackling sounds, because the bones of his chest were not put together properly.

Reprinted from Hare and Hornbill, *a collection of folk tales edited and translated by Okot p'Bitek. By permission of Heinemann Educational Books.*

PETALS OF BLOOD

Ngugi wa Thiong'o *is Kenya's best-known writer and one of the country's most consistently outspoken critics. The following extract from the satirical* Petals of Blood *has been taken from the middle of the book. The people of Ilmorog, a village in the Rift Valley, are beginning to appreciate the power and influence of the New Kenya.*

CHANGES COME TO ILMOROG

Munira folded the newspaper and went to Wanja's place to break the news. He felt for her and Nyakinyua. He did not expect favours. He just wanted to take her the news. And to find out more about it. She was not at her Theng'eta premises. Abdulla told him that she had gone to Nyakinyua's hut. Munira walked there and found other people. News of the threatened sale must have reached them too. They had come to commiserate with her and others similarly affected, to weep with one another. They looked baffled: how could a bank sell their land? A bank was not a government: from whence then, its powers? Or maybe it was the government, an invisible government, some others suggested. They turned to Munira. But he could not answer their question. He only talked about a piece of paper, they had surrendered to the bank. But he could not answer, put to sleep, the bitter scepticism in their voices and looks. What kind of monster was this bank that was a power unto itself, that could uproot lives of a thousand years?

He went back and tried to drink Theng'eta, but it did not have the taste. He remembered that recently he had seen Wambui carting stones to earn bread for the day and he wondered what would happen to the old woman. She was too old to sell her labour and sweat in a market.

"The old woman? Nyakinyua?" Munira echoed Karega's question, slowly. "She died! She is dead!" he added quickly, almost aggressively, waking up from his memories.

Karega's face seemed to move.

Nyakinyua, the old woman, tried to fight back. She tramped from hut to hut calling upon the peasants of Ilmorog to get together and fight it out. They looked at her and they shook their heads: whom would they fight now? The

Government? The Banks? KCO? The Party Nderi? Yes who would they really fight? But she tried to convince them that all these were one and that she would fight them. Her land would never be settled by strangers. There was something grand, and defiant, in the woman's action – she with her failing health and flesh trying to organise the dispossessed of Ilmorog into a protest. But there was pathos in the exercise. Those whose land had not yet been taken looked nervously aloof and distant. One or two even made disparaging remarks about an old woman not quite right in the head. Others genuinely not seeing the point of a march to Ruwaini or to the big City restrained her. She could not walk all the way, they told her. But she said: "I'll go alone . . . my man fought the white man. He paid for it with his blood . . . I'll struggle against these black oppressors . . . alone . . . alone . . ."

What would happen to her, Munira wondered.

He need not have worried about her. Nyakinyua died peacefully in her sleep a few days after the news of the bank threat. Rumour went that she had told Wanja about the impending journey: she had said that she could not even think of being buried in somebody else's land: for what would her man say to her when she met him on the other side? People waited for the bank to come and sell her land. But on the day of the sale Wanja redeemed the land and became the heroine of the new and the old Ilmorog.

Later Munira was to know.

But at that time only Abdulla really knew the cost: Wanja had offered to sell him her rights to their jointly owned New Building. He did not have the money and it was he who suggested that they sell the whole building to a third person and divide the income between them.

So Wanja was back to her beginnings.

And Mzigo was the new proud owner of the business premises in Ilmorog.

Wanja was not quite the same after her recent loss. For a time, she continued the proud proprietor of the old Theng'eta place. Her place still remained the meat-roasting centre. Dance steps in the hall could still raise dust to the roof, especially when people were moving to their favourite tunes:

How beautiful you are, my love!
How soft your round eyes are, my honey!
What a pleasant thing you are,
Lying here
Shaded by this cedar bush!
But oh, darling,
What poison you carry between your legs!

But Wanja's heart was not in it. She started building a huge wooden bungalow at the lower end of her shamba, some distance from the shanty town that was growing up around Abdulla's shop, the lodgings and the meat-roasting centre, almost as a natural growth complement to the more elegant new Ilmorog. People said that she was wise to invest in a building the money remaining after redeeming her grandmother's shamba: but what was it for? She already had a hut further up the shamba, hidden from the noise and inquisitive eyes of the New Ilmorog by a thick natural hedge. She went about her work without taking anybody into her confidence. But it was obvious that it was built in the style of a living house with several spacious rooms. Later she moved in: she planted flower gardens all around and had electric lights fixed there. It was beautiful: it was a brave effort so soon after her double loss, people said.

One night the band struck up a song they had composed on their first arrival. As they played, the tune and the words seemed to grow fresher and fresher and the audience clapped and whistled and shouted encouragement. The band added innovations and their voices seemed possessed of a wicked carefree devil.

This shamba girl
Was my darling
Told me she loved my sight.
I broke bank vaults for her,
I went to jail for her,
But when I came back
I found her a lady,
Kept by a wealthy roundbelly daddy,
And she told me,
This shamba-lady girl told me,
No, Gosh!
Sikujui
Serikali imebadilishwa
Coup d'état!

They stopped to thunderous handclaps and feet pounding on the floor. Wanja suddenly stood up and asked them to play it again. She started dancing to it, alone, in the arena. People were surprised. They watched the gyrations of her body, speaking pleasure and pain, memories and hopes, loss and gain, unfulfilled longing and desire. The band, responding to the many beating hearts, played with sad maddening intensity as if it were reaching out to her loneliness and solitary struggle. She danced slowly and deliberately toward Munira and he was remembering that time he had seen her dancing to a juke-box at Safari Bar in Kamiritho. As suddenly as she had started, she stopped. She walked to the stage at the bandstand. The "house" was hushed. The customers knew that something big was in the air.

"I am sorry, dear customers, to have to announce the end of the old Ilmorog Bar and meat-roasting centres, and the end of Ilmorog Bar's own Sunshine Band. Chiri County Council says we have to close."

She would not say more. And now they watched her as she walked across the dusty floor toward where Munira was sitting. She stopped, whirled back, and screamed at the band. "Play! Play! Play on. Everybody dance — Daaance!" And she sat down beside Munira.

"Munira, wouldn't you like to come and see my new place tomorrow night?"

Munira could hardly contain himself. So at long last. So the years of waiting were over. It was just like the old days before Karega and the roads and the changes had come to disturb the steamy peaceful rhythm in Ilmorog, when he was the teacher.

The next day he could not teach. He could not talk. He could hardly sit or stand still in one place. And when the time came, he walked to her place with tremulous hands and beating heart. He had not been inside the new house and he felt it an honour that she had chosen him out of all those faces.

He knocked at the door. She was in. She stood in the middle of the room lit by a blue light. For a second he thought himself in the wrong place with the wrong person.

She had on a miniskirt which revealed just about everything, and he felt his manhood rise of itself. On her lips was smudgy red lipstick: her eyebrows were pencilled and painted a luminous blue. What was the game, he wondered? He thought of one of the many advertisements he had earlier collected: Be a platinum blonde: be a whole new you in 100% imported hand-made human hair. Wanja was a really new her.

"You look surprised, Mwalimu. I thought you always wanted me," she said, with a false seductive blur in her voice. Then in a slightly changed voice, more natural, which he could recognise, she added: "That's why you had him dismissed, not so? Look now. They have even taken away my right, well, our right to brew. The County Council says our licence was sold away with the New Building. They also say our present premises are in any case unhygienic! There's going to be a tourist centre and such places might drive visitors away. Do you know the new owner of our Theng'eta breweries? Do you know the owner of the New Ilmorog Utamaduni Centre? Never mind!" She had, once again, changed her voice: "But come: what are you waiting for?" She walked backwards: he followed her and they went into another room — with a double bed and a reddish light. He was hypnotised. He was angry with himself for being tongue-tied and yet he was propelled toward her by the engine-power of his risen body and the drums in the heart. Yet below it all, deep inside, he felt a sensation of shame and disgust at his helplessness.

She removed everything, systematically, piece by piece, and then jumped into bed.

"Come, come, my darling!" she cooed from inside the sheets.

He was about to jump into bed beside her and clasp her to himself, when she suddenly turned cold and chilly, and her voice was menacing.

"No, Mwalimu. No free things in Kenya. A hundred shillings on the table if you want high-class treatment."

He thought she was joking, but as he was about to touch her she added more coldly:

"This is New Kenya. You want it, you pay for it, for the bed and the light and my time and the drink that I shall later give you and the breakfast tomorrow. And all for a hundred shillings. For you. Because of old times. For others it will be more expensive."

He was taken aback, felt the wound of this unexpected humiliation. But now he could not retreat. Her thighs called out to him.

He took out a hundred shillings and handed it to her. He watched her count it and put the money under the mattress. Now panic seized him. His thing had shrivelled. He stood there and tried to fix his mind on the old Wanja, on the one who had danced pain and ecstasy, on the one who had once cried under watchful moonbeams stealing into a hut. She watched him, coldly, with menace, and then suddenly she broke out in her put-on, blurred, seductive voice.

"Come, darling. I'll keep you warm. You are tonight a guest at *Sunshine Lodge*."

There was something pathetic, sad, painful in the tone. But Munira's thing obeyed her voice. Slowly he removed his clothes and joined her in bed. Even as the fire and thirst and hunger in his body were being quenched, the pathetic strain in her voice lingered in the air, in him, in the room everywhere.

It was New Kenya. It was New Ilmorog. Nothing was free. But for a long time, for years to come, he was not to forget the shock and the humiliation of the hour. It was almost like that first time, long ago, when he was only a boy.

Indeed, changes did come to Ilmorog, changes that drove the old one away and ushered a new era in our lives. And nobody could tell, really tell, how it had happened, except that it had happened. With a year or so of the new Ilmorog shopping centre being completed, wheatfields and ranches had sprung up all around the plains: the herdsmen had died or had been driven further afield into the drier parts, but a few had become workers on the wheatfields and ranches on the earth upon which they once roamed freely. The new owners, master-servants of bank power, money and cunning came over at weekends and drove in Landrovers or Range Rovers, depending on the current car fashion, around the farms whose running they had otherwise entrusted to paid managers. The peasants of Ilmorog had also changed. Some had somehow survived the onslaught. They could employ one or two hands on their small farms. Most of the others had joined the army of workers who had added to the growing population of the New Ilmorog. But which New Ilmorog?

There were several Ilmorogs. One was the residential area of the farm managers, County Council officials, public service officers, the managers of Barclays, Standard and African Economic Banks, and other servants of state and money power. This was called Cape Town. The other – called New Jerusalem – was a shanty town of migrant and floating workers, the unemployed, the prostitutes and small traders in tin and scrap metal. Between the New Jerusalem and Cape Town, not far from where Mwathi had once lived guarding the secrets of iron works and native medicine, was All Saints church, now led by Rev. Jerrod Brown. Also somewhere between the two areas was Wanja's *Sunshine Lodge*, almost as famous as the church.

The shopping and business centre was dominated by two features. Just outside it was a tourist cultural (Utamaduni) village owned by Nderi wa Riera and a West German concern, appropriately called Ilmorog African Diamond Cultural and Educational Tours. Many tourists came for a cultural fiesta. A few hippies also came to look for the Theng'eta Breweries which, starting on the premises owned by Mzingo, had now grown into a huge factory employing six hundred workers with a number of research scientists and chemical engineers. The factory also owned an estate in the plains where they experimented with different types of Theng'eta plants and wheat. They brewed a variety of Theng'eta drinks: from the pure gin for export to cheap but potent drinks for workers and the unemployed. They put some in small plastic bags in different measures of one, two and five shillings' worth so that these bagfuls of poison could easily be carried in people's pockets. Most of the containers, whether plastic or glass bottles, carried the famous ad, now popularised in most parts of the country through their sales vans, newspapers and handbills: POTENCY – Theng'a Theng'a with Theng'eta. P=3T.

The breweries were owned by an Anglo-American international combine but of course with African directors and even shareholders. Three of the four leading local personalities were Mzigo, Chui and Kimeria.

Long live New Ilmorog! Long live Partnership in Trade and Progress!

Reprinted from Petals of Blood. *By permission of Heinemann Educational Books.*

SWAHILI POETRY

Swahili poetry is Kenya's oldest written literature, recorded in Arabic script since the seventeenth century and in the Roman alphabet since the turn of this century. The oldest poems are praise and wedding songs from the oral tradition and narrative epics relating the early years of Islam. There's a wide variety of forms, but the rhythms and rhymes are not too unfamiliar to Western ears. Swahili, with its infinite capacity for allusion and imagery, has produced some beautiful verse. **Shaaban Robert**, who died in 1962, is probably the greatest twentieth-century Swahili poet. This lament for his wife was written in the *shairi* metre of sixteen syllables to the line.

AMINA

Amina unmejitenga, kufa umetangulia,

Kama ua umefunga, baada ya kuchanua,
Nukuombea mwanga, peponi kukubaliwa.

Mapenzi tuliyofunga, hapana wa kufungua.

. . . .

Nilitaka unyanyuke, kwa kukuombea dua,
Sikupenda ushindike, maradhi kukuchukua,

Ila kwa rehema yake, Mungu amekuchagua.
Mapenzi tuliyofunga, hapana wa kufungua.

. . . .

Majonzi hayaneneki, kila nikikumbukia,
Nawaza kile na hiki, naona kama ruia,

Mauti siyasadiki kuwa, mwisho wa dunia.

Mapenzi tuliyofunga, hapana wa kufungua.

. . . .

Nasadiki haziozi, roho hazitapotea,
Twafuata wokozi, kwa mauti kutujia,

Nawe wangu mpenzi, Peponi utaingia.

Mapenzi tuliyofunga, hapana wa kufungua.

. . . .

Jambo moja nakumbuka, sahihi ninalijua,
Kuwa sasa umefika, ta'bu isikosumbua,

Kwayo nimefurahika, nyuma nilikobakia.

Mapenzi tuliyofunga, hapana wa kufungua.

. . . .

Ninamaliza kutunga, kwa kukuombea dua,
Vumbi tena likiunga, roho likirudishiwa,
Mauti yakijitenga, mapenzi yatarejea.

Mapenzi tuliyofunga, hapana wa kufungua.

Amina, you have withdrawn yourself, you led the way in dying,

Like a flower you have closed, after having opened first,
I pray for you, my light, that you may be welcomed in paradise.

The love we made between us, no one ever will undo it.

I had hoped that you would rise again, and I prayed for you,
I did not want you to be defeated, and be carried away by the disease,

But by His mercy, God has chosen you.
The love we made between us, no one ever will undo it.

My grief is indescribable, every moment I remember,
I keep thinking this and yonder I see things as if I were dreaming,

I did not believe in death first, that it was the end of the world, this life.

The love we made between us, no one ever will undo it.

I believe that souls don't perish, they cannot be lost forever,
We pursue salvation's pathway, when death's angel comes to meet us,

And you, my beloved partner, you will enter heaven's gateway.

The love we made between us, no one ever will undo it.

Just one thing I do remember, one I know for sure and truly,
That you have now reached the place where no suffering can plague you,

Therefore do I still feel gladdened, here where I am left behind.

The love we made between us, no one ever will undo it.

I have finished my composing, while for you I pray,
When dust is rejoined together, when the soul returns into it,
While the power of death retires, then our love will be returning.

The love we made between us, no one ever will undo it.

Translated by Jan Knappert, 1979. Reprinted from *Four Centuries of Swahili Verse*, by permission of the translator.

SHORT STORY – SAM KAHIGA

Short stories are immensely popular in Kenya and you'll find stacks of well-thumbed, short romantic novels at any second-hand bookstall. **Sam Kahiga***'s energetic, exasperatingly racy style, sprinkled with a combination of British and American idioms, is strange at first, but his stories are revealing about the values of modern, urban Kenya.*

A HIGH VOLTAGE AFFAIR

At school I was afflicted by that chronic laziness that is often the lot of young students who think they are especially clever and can pass any exam through sheer genius. After getting my "O" levels with nine points and no sweat at all, I went to Strathmore College for "A" levels. I remember my goal then – to be a nuclear physicist. And if that was too advanced for the Third World then I'd compromise gracefully, step down, and just be a bloody good research scientist. The Third World could do with some of those.

Well my "A" levels were a disaster. What could I blame it on? Girls, booze or drugs? I blame it on the lot – plus the sort of risky confidence that comes after you've been top of the class too many times. Of my days in Strathmore I remember the movies and the parties rather than what happened in the labs. Except for jokingly trying to invent a drug that could give one a trip I hardly applied myself. And when the final results came out I realised that I was on a bad trip that just wouldn't end up in the university. It was bad, shocking, in fact.

Guys whose IQs were nowhere near as high as mine got called up to the university. As for me I was bad news in academic circles. Trying to save face I applied feverishly to foreign universities. My daddy could afford to send me to one. But no foreign university seemed interested. I kept trying until my daddy casually let me know that if I was intending to go abroad I would have to get the dough myself. That's what is known as fatherly affection.

Let me explain his attitude, for I understood it perfectly. My daddy (his friends and enemies call him GM) was no kid-spoiler. Although he could afford to send me round the world seven times he wasn't going to help because I had

proved I was a failure. If I had failed at home I would not succeed abroad. I realised for his acid comments that he knew about the kind of life I had led at Strathmore – girls, booze, drugs. Could he then seriously think of sending me to America, that modern Babylon and hippy headquarters.

"Go on your own," said GM. He had turned a blind eye to my mischief until I let him down and failed to make it to the university. And GM is not the kind of man you let down and get away with it. He himself had never failed. Where he couldn't work his way out smoothly he bulldozed. If the front door was closed he tried the back door. That was the way he made his millions in the construction business.

Sons of poor men were going to university, so why not GM's first-born? He felt betrayed. What was it that he had not done for me? My pocket money had been two hundred and fifty bob a month. And he had told me to buy any book that I wanted. So why had I not gone to university?

GM had never even been to high school because he had been born too many years before the fruit of independence ripened. When independence came he was just a mason grade three. We lived at Shauri Moyo. GM grabbed his share of the fruit and we moved off to Lavington where I had my own motor-cycle and a couple of rooms to myself which were a mess of wires, novels and beat music that made my mother ill. The smell of my strange "cigarettes" made her ill too, but mothers are like that. You have to be patient with them.

I agree that GM spoilt me. But all the money and stuff he showered on me was on the understanding that I would live up to his expectations, which I did until those hazy "A" levels. In fact I did more. For instance at seventeen I was the maintenance man around the place, the little genie who knew what was wrong with the TV, the fridge or even his car. GM couldn't even change his own spark plugs. He trusted me to tune and service his car and considered me the last word in wiring. Now you can begin to understand about the two hundred and fifty bob pocket money. I spent most of it on cocaine.

After I had failed GM didn't want to see me around. He is a very unforgiving man. He had dug up my Strathmore background and it had shocked him so much that he didn't want to even touch his car.

What finally broke up our relationship was when the disciplinarian daddy in him came to the surface and he thought he could teach me a physical lesson just because my room smelt of something strange. He sniffed and realised that it was grass.

The rest is embarrassing. Let's just say that there was yet another side of me that he hadn't known. I had a panther's reflexes that had come from picking up all that one needs to know about judo and karate. I didn't hurt him at all but he stared at me from the floor with great surprise. Through his gaping mouth I saw a little film of blood on his small white teeth — nothing serious.

After that there was nothing else to do except pack. The mansion at Lavington was a bit too small for both of us.

Somehow I feel that this background is important before I tell the story that follows. When I went to the Power Institute to train as a technician for the Power Company I went on my own ticket. The exams accompanying the interview were tough and gruelling to most of the boys but I sailed through, although I was half-starving. They accepted me at the Power Institute on my own merit, not a millionaire's influential word. It is important that this is understood.

Every young boy carries in his heart the soft-focus image of a woman he could love, serve and die for. I'm still not sure whether she eventually turns up, this ever youthful, totally compliant dream girl whom you want to set on a pedestal and worship. She is mutable, changing with your fancy and experience, but something remains constant about her, whether you are twelve or forty.

This constancy I guess is the subservience to your ego. She will love you no matter what happens, no matter who else is there. She loves you when you are vomiting into the toilet bowl and sticks by your side as you piss into a dark alley. She will be petite and cuddlesome when you are in a gentle mood and you want her to be like that. She will have an Afro hairdo if that's what you want. She's a virgin, nobody ever touched her before. Sometimes her breasts are small, sometimes her breasts are large. Sometimes she's innocent, sometimes she's master of the Kama Sutra, a deep well of erotic knowledge.

The first time she came to me in the flesh (or was it her more mundane twin sister?) was at the Power Institute at the beginning of the second year. My thoughts were hardly on love but on electro-magnetic forces, watts, ohms and coulombs. Instead of breasts I was thinking of turbines and transformers and the only kick I ever got during those sober, sombre months was the flow of electrons through me whenever I was fool enough to step on a live wire. In short, I was immersed in electricity, my biggest love since childhood. I hadn't seen anybody for a year — nobody mattered. For companions I had watts, coils and ohm's law. If I needed a drink, coke was enough, thanks. The hostel supplied the grub. There wasn't much else I felt I needed.

Then during Easter we had a dance at the hostel and this chick came along with one of the boys. I remember I was pretty lonesome hanging around the stuffy room with my coke and yet expecting nothing from all the bull-shit. To make things worse it was raining badly outside and I couldn't walk back to the hostel even if I had wanted to.

What is dancing? I asked myself. Some hangover from some primitive era. Some sort of savage convolution totally outside the realm of scientific discipline. I wanted to go home but the damn rain was falling. When I looked out of the window the world was suddenly lit up by the taut gnarled roots of a devilish lightning flash. "Jupiter's thunder-bolt." "God's footstep." To scientists: atmospheric electric phenomena. I wanted to go to bed.

She was very pretty but couldn't have been with a worse man. Mbote was rude, coarse and argumentative. He was a slum child and he was proud of the fact. No efforts at all to be a gentleman. The girl he was with was a lady from the toe up to the rich mass of black hair. And if I wasn't wrong she was trying to catch my eye.

I put my ginger ale on the ledge of a window (tired of cokes by now). I singled her out from the rest of the clumsy humanity, forgave her for imperfections and danced with her to a slow number.

"What's your label?" I asked.

"I beg your pardon?"

"The name. What's your name?"

"Esther."

"Esther what?"

"Mbacia."

Esther Mbacia. I was a bit annoyed with her for looking like my dream girl while going around with a guy like Mbote. My dream girls are supposed to be my own. They shouldn't be wandering around among crude wolves. They might get eaten. I wouldn't have been surprised if she ended up in Mbote's cubicle.

"You didn't tell me your name, but I know you," she said. "You are GM's son, aren't you?"

"So?" I asked coldly.

"I used to see you when you were in Strathmore. I was then in Kenya High. You know, when you had that motor-cycle." I couldn't help grinning.

"Your girl-friend was my classmate, Edith." Edith, a grass addict.

"Mbacia," I said. "Is your father the Mbacia? Mbacia Enterprises?"

"Happens to be," she said.

"Oh."

"Oh, what?"

"Nothing."

We laughed together. And then I saw the livid angry eyes of Mbote staring at me over the rim of his glass of alcoholic poison. He was mixing everything, the only way he could get drunk cheaply. He had drunk changaa ever since he was a small boy in Majengo slums, so beer to him was mere water.

"Your boyfriend looks angry and dangerous," I said.

"He's not my boyfriend," said Mbacia's daughter.

There might have been a fight that night had I been just any other boy. But my reputation was good. They knew my reflexes. Mbote was a dreaded street fighter who bullied almost everybody else but he knew I could paralyse him by just touching a nerve. Neatly, with no glasses being broken. He didn't want that. I didn't want to be unfair so I gave her a date and went to bed.

So that's how the tragic triangle started. Poor slum boy grabs a rich girl, wants to make her happy in his own rude way. Rich boy comes along with polished karate and his father's millions behind him and poor boy has no chance. The fact that I was broke most of the time didn't worry her one bit. In fact it seemed to add to my attraction. GM's son, but always broke. How funny!

I liked serious movies but also liked seeing Chinese movies to improve on my karate. She liked ice-cream, chewing gum and I'm not quite sure what else. I liked her. A girl doesn't have to have a line of interest to be liked. I still don't know her line of interest. She doesn't share my passion for turbines and transformers but so what? So nothing. She was high voltage. There were electrostatic forces in her breasts. When she smiled at me the electrons flowed. She was my cathode and I was her anode.

She was Mbote's heartbreak. Poor slum boy, son of a Majengo prostitute, he had never had any love in his life. He thought he had found it in Esther. Esther thought she had found it in me. The eternal triangle.

He came to me one night when I was reading and knocked on the door of my cubicle. He was totally drunk. I threw him out. I threw him out because he called me a hybrid.

"Just because you are a hybrid and she's a hybrid you feel you must cross-breed. To keep the millions in one family."

"Get the hell out," I said. But I had to remove him physically.

What I think shattered him was my bringing Esther to the end of term dance. At first he was vulgar and insulting, though not talking to us directly. I heard the words "hybrid" and "cross-breeding" and tried to take no notice. Then I saw that he was staring at us silently, no longer speaking. The jilted lover: why not just find a girl? Why let this thing play on his complexes? I wished I could give him the girl but I was already in love with her. Or maybe there was this vacuum in my soul that she very conveniently filled. Sometimes it's difficult to distinguish love from the flight from loneliness.

The following morning was Sunday and that was when the nightmare began. Most of the boys had already gone home and the hostel was almost deserted.

With a towel around my loins I went into the shower room. Mbote who was waiting for that move came and locked the door with a key. Standing outside the door he told me a lot of things. How he had loved and how I had ruined his chances.

"What's the point of locking the door?"

"I want to kill you."

The shower was running, the warm water caressing my skin. He was going to kill me. He must be joking. And yet I knew how reckless he was, the kind of strange practical jokes he used to play on people. Better watch out.

"Look Mbote, Esther is mine," I said, wearily.

"You snatched her. You rich people think you can snatch everything. You think you are smart. You'll pay for it."

"How?"

"I want to make you dance. You like dancing I'll make you dance."

"Look, open the door and stop being stupid. What are you up to?"

"When you come out of there you won't be alive."

"Why?"

"The shower room is wired. I'm just about to give you a thousand volts." I got the idea. I broke into a sweat. I stared at the wet floor of my death cell. The water would conduct the electricity from wherever the terminals were.

"Open the door and don't be stupid," I cried and that was the last thing I said before the current shot up through my bare feet and shot me up to the ceiling. I screamed, then hit the floor unconscious.

Hospital. The first week was a blank. The next one I began to recognise people – chaps from the Power Institute, GM, Esther.

The third week I was fine and that was when they told me that Mbote had electro-cuted himself when I was in a coma. The cops had come for him and rather than face the law he had taped electric wires to his head. He had turned on the switch, died instantly and made headlines for the first and last time.

I try to look on it all to see why and how it happened but I'm still not strong enough to sort out little psychological details. Or perhaps my mind just refuses to work. I saw a picture of Mbote's mother in the papers and she was wailing, saying he was a good boy. I take my own refuge behind public opinion for that's all I can do. Public opinion has it that Mbote was crazy to try and electrocute GM's son. He was quite right to electrocute himself, though. But he shouldn't go round trying to electrocute heirs to millions. (GM wants to know if I need bodyguards.)

It all depresses me. When my heart is really low I call up Esther on the phone.

"Doctor says I need lots of therapy, girl, and only you can give it to me. So come over quick."

She always does. I told you she's high voltage – if you see what I mean. Maybe she really *is* hybrid.

Reprinted from the collection Flight to Juba *by permission of Longman Kenya.*

MUSIC

Although its music is less well known abroad than that of a number of other African countries, Kenya's home-grown musical vitality is there if you listen. And Nairobi's audiences and recording facilities have long been a draw for musicians from all over east and central Africa, bringing to the city a pan-African, musical flavour.

THE MUSICAL BACKGROUND

Kenya's oldest musical tradition is **ngoma**, still the central term used to describe all the facets of a musical performance, including the accompanying dances. *Ngoma* in most Bantu languages of Kenya refers to a specific kind of **drum** and a related dance, but more broadly the term refers to drums in general and a genre of music using drums as its main instruments.

Although an inter-ethnic *ngoma* called *beni* (band) emerged on the coast around the turn of the century and spread inland (you can still witness this anachronistic, marching-band form on special occasions in Lamu), *ngoma* music today is essentially ethnic, related to a specific language group and using the respective vernacular and local dance rhythms. *Ngoma* also provides most of the music used during the life-cycle festivities (birth, initiation and circumcision, marriage and death), whether in the town or the country. You can buy *ngoma* music on singles. Look out for recordings by Luyia **sukuti** groups: the *sukuti* is the central drum of these ensembles.

From the early 1950s on, with society rapidly changing, the coming of recording and broadcasting, and the introduction of new instruments, especially the **guitar**, an acoustic guitar-based music developed as accompaniment to songs sung in **Swahili**. A basis for Swahili-language popular music had already been laid by the *beni* groups flourishing in east African towns during the first half of the century. *Beni* songs, as well as the new guitar songs, featured the strong and critical social commentary so beloved of Kenyans. The songs are usually in the form of a short story and may comment on an actual political or social topic, or perhaps recount a personal experience of the musician. Romantic songs are almost non-existent, even in songs dealing with men and women.

The guitar styles themselves developed out of different instrumental techniques and musical perceptions, but they were influenced by the records available at the time, mainly from other parts of Africa. Kenyan musicians of the period cite **Jean Bosco Mwenda** and **Losta Abelo**, both from Katanga (today, Shaba Province, Zaire), and **George Sibanda**, from Bulawayo in Zimbabwe, as important inspirations. From this period, the notables of Kenya's acoustic guitar styles are **John Mwale**, **George Mukabi** (directly out of the Luyia *sukuti* tradition) and **Isaya Mwinamo**.

The 1960s saw the introduction of **electric guitars** as well as larger groups (of three to four guitars). **Kwela** and **twist** were the rage, coming from, or via, southern Africa. These were the days of the **Equator Sound Band** (Equator being the main record label), featuring the songs of **Daudi Kabaka**, **Fadhili William**, **Nashil Pichen** and **Peter Tsotsi**.

MODERN KENYAN STYLES

It isn't very meaningful to speak of **Kenyan pop** as a genre. There are really a number of styles that borrow freely and influence each other in a cross-fertilization that gives the music its unifying Kenyan flavour. What is fundamental, though, is the prominent role of guitars and guitar solos. The Earthworks compilations *Guitar Paradise of east Africa* and *Kenya Dance Mania*, along with Rounder Records' *The Nairobi Beat*, provide ample evidence of that, with an excellent cross-section of Kenyan pop spanning the last twenty years. Another ingredient in the Kenyan mix is the *cavacha* rhythm popularized in the mid-1970s by Zairean groups such as **Zaiko Langa Langa** and **Orchestra Shama Shama**. This pacy percussion, usually on the snare or high-hat, quickly took hold in Kenya and continues to underlie a great sweep of Kenyan music from the **Kalambya Sisters** to **Les Wanyika**.

Many Kenyan musicians direct their efforts towards their own linguistic groups and perform most of their songs in one of Kenya's indigenous languages. Alongside this regional/ethnic orientation – often bluntly referred to as "tribal" in Kenya itself – are two other local pop music varieties: one consisting of songs with lyrics in **Swahili** or **Lingala** (from Zaire), aimed at a national and largely urban audience, and the other propelled by foreign tourism and Kenyans with a taste for international pop.

REGIONAL AND ETHNIC PERFORMERS: BENGA BANDS

The regional/ethnic pop groups play a style generally known as *benga*, and this, perhaps more than anything else, is characteristic Kenyan music. Although the word and what it represents originated with the Luo people of western Kenya, *benga*'s transition to a popular style has been so pervasive that practically all the local bands, Luo or otherwise, play variants of it. As a pop style, *benga* dates back to the 1950s when musicians began adapting traditional dance rhythms and the string sounds of the *nyatiti* and *orutu* to the acoustic guitar and later to electric instruments. During its heyday much of the early *benga* was exported to west

and southern Africa where it was very popular. Throughout the 1970s and into the 1980s, *benga* music dominated Kenya's recording industry and, although the whole industry is in serious decline, it remains an important force.

Luo

By any measure, the most famous Luo *benga* group is **Shirati Jazz** led by **D O (Daniel Owino) Misiani**. Born in Shirati, Tanzania, just south of the Kenyan border, he has been playing *benga* since the mid-1960s. His style is characterized by soft, flowing and melodic two-part vocal harmonies, a very active, pulsating bass line that derives at least in part from traditional *nyatiti* and drum rhythms, and stacks of invigorating guitar work, the lead alternating with the vocal.

Misiani may be a "*benga* wizard", but *benga* is not his exclusive property and, contrary to the impression you might receive in London or New York record shops, there are many other important *benga* artists. Pioneering Luo names include **Colella Mazee** and **Ochieng Nelly** – either together or separately in various incarnations of **Victoria Jazz** and the **Victoria Kings** – as well as **George Ramogi** and his **Continental Luo Sweet Band**. All are still active in Kenya, although Misiani's Shirati is one of the few full-time Luo groups. Other current Luo groups are **Migori Super Stars**, **Omore Kings**, **Ambira Boys Band**, **Sega-Sega**, and **Sega Matata Band**. The Ambira Boys and Sega groups have done very well as storytellers of the trials and tribulations of modern life, and they have set off a trend that has spread to other language groups.

TARABU MUSIC

Tarabu, the main popular music of the coastal **Swahili** people, deserves special mention. It has a long tradition in the festive life of the Swahili and is also the general music of entertainment of the coastal communities. But the music has strong Arabic-Islamic overtones in instrumentation, especially in the haunting vocals. Earlier *tarabu* (*taarab*, *tarab*) groups used the full Arabic orchestra, including the lute-like *oud* and violins. Today the main instruments are mandolin or guitar and either an Indian harmonium or a small electronic organ/piano, plus a variety of local, Arabic or Indian drums. Indian movies, with their strong musical component, are very popular among the coastal people and under their influence many features of Indian music have entered *tarabu*. From as early as the 1940s *tarabu* has been sung not only in Swahili but also in Urdu/Hindi. Many of the lead singers and bandleaders of *tarabu* groups are women, almost unique in Kenyan traditional music. The focus of *tarabu* is intricately rhythmic poetry and, in this, **Juma Balo** is one of its masters. Leading female voices are **Malika** and **Zuhura**, while mixed-sex vocals are the feature of the **Black Star** and **Lucky Star Musical Clubs**, originally from Tanzania.

One Luo name which doesn't fit neatly into any of these stylistic categories is **Ochieng Kabaselleh** and his **Luna Kidi Band**. There are some typical examples of his music (as it was in 1985) on the Earthworks compilations. His songs are mostly in Luo, but sometimes with a liberal seasoning of Swahili and English. Likewise, the melodies and harmonies are from the Luo *benga* realm, but the rhythm, guitar work and horns suggest influences from the Zairean/Swahili-dominated sound. Kabaselleh, who languished in prison for several years (for "subversion"), is back in the music world with a flood of new releases.

Luyia

The Luyia highlands to the north of Luo-land are home to many of Kenya's most famous guitarists and vocalists. **Daudi Kabaka**, despite his renowned early career, struggles today with only the occasional hotel gig and few recording opportunities. The humorous social commentary of **Sukuma bin Ongaro** has made him a giant of the current scene, although mainly among his fellow Luyia-speakers. **Shem Tube**, however, is an artist who straddles both past and present in his music, though it's his musical past which has given him a popular following in the UK and Europe.

In 1989, GlobeStyle Records released *Abana Ba Nasery* (The Nursery Boys), a compilation of songs by Tube and his group in the **omutibu** style. With two acoustic guitars (playing high and low), and rhythm played on a Fanta bottle, the *Abana Ba Nasery* collection offers a glimpse of a musical era of the 1960s and early 1970s that has largely vanished. Coming together as a trio in the early 1960s, Abana Ba Nasery were innovators, blazing a path for Kenyan pop to follow. While using traditional Luyia rhythms and melody lines, their two-guitar line-up and three-part vocal harmonies (and the Fanta bottle) were a hint of things to come. Abana's style from the 1960s contains the major elements of today's contemporary pop sound in Kenya: the central position of the solo guitar in Kenya's electric groups is anticipated in Shem Tube's solos of 25 years ago. Justo Osala's guitar parts in the lower ranges are like the rhythm and bass parts in today's electric bands. Even Enos Okola's Fanta rhythms are a precursor of the modern drum kit.

While Abana's first CD release created tremendous interest – a rootsy but very accessible African sound – the compatibility of their music with strands of European folk tradition is clear in their second CD release, recorded by GlobeStyle in London, *Nursery Boys Go Ahead!* Guest artists included members of the Oyster Band and Mustaphas as well as Ron Kavana and Tomás Lynch. Although it's all-acoustic, several songs on this collaborative effort are true rockers. Which is not out of character with the group on their home turf. Although they've never earned enough money to buy their own electric guitars and amps, Abana Ba Nasery have had a string of local hits as an electric band under the stage names **Mwilonje Jazz** and **Super Bunyore Band** (listen, for example, to Super Bunyore's *Bibi Joys* on the *Nairobi Beat* compilation). If the Nursery Boys have their way, it won't be long before audiences outside Kenya get a taste of their electric music, too.

Kikuyu

As Kenya's largest ethnic group, the **Kikuyu**-speaking people of Central Province and Nairobi are a major market force in Kenya's music industry. Perhaps because of this large "built-in" audience, few Kikuyu musicians have tried to cross over into the national Swahili-or English-language markets. On the international scene, Kikuyu-language music is conspicuously absent but for the few songs that have made it on to some of the compilation CDs. Kikuyu melodies are quite distinct from those of the Luo and Luyia of western Kenya, and their pop manifestations also differ significantly in harmonies and rhythm guitar parts. In contrast to Luo and Luyia pop, women vocalists play major roles as lead and backing singers for Kikuyu groups. Many of the top groups have women's auxiliaries – duos and trios invariably called the something-or-other sisters. While Kikuyu pop music has a traditional melodic structure, there is a good deal of stylistic variety and innovation. Most often, Kikuyu pop takes the form of the *benga/cavacha* style, but popular alternatives are also based on country & western, reggae and Zairean soukous.

The king of Kikuyu pop is **Joseph Kamaru**, who has been making hit records since the release of *Celina* in 1967, performed, on one guitar and maracas, with his sister Catherine

Muthoni. Since then he has carved a small empire – which included his Njun'wa Stars band and the Kamarulets dancers, two music shops and a recording studio. He sees himself as a teacher, expressing the traditional values of his culture, as well as contemporary social commentary, in song. One recent number, *Mahoya ma Bururi* (Prayers for the Country), that gently criticized the government, resulted in his shop being raided and the banning of the song from the airwaves. Kamaru takes pride in his lyrics for going beyond trivial matters:

> My songs are not like other people's . . .
> "I love you, I love you", they keep on singing . . . No, no, no! My songs are not that way. I can compose a love song but very deep, a grown-up loving.

Following *Mahoya ma Bururi* in 1990, Kamaru's popularity continued to soar. Thus his announcement in 1993 that he had been "born again" came as a bombshell for his fans. Much to their disappointment, Kamaru abandoned the pop music scene to devote his efforts to evangelistic activities and gospel music promotion.

Kamaru may not write songs for teenage lovers but someone who does, and who has become famous in the process, is hit-maker **Daniel "DK" (Councillor) Kamau**. Kamau released his first three records in 1967 while still at school and continued with a highly successful career through the 1970s. He is regarded as having brought Kikuyu music into the *benga* mainstream, but it was not until 1990 that he returned to the stage with a new **Lulus Band**. In Kenya's rapidly changing political climate, the councillor found a responsive chord in his fans and the population at large with his Top Ten hit, *FORD Fever*. DK has continued to address political and human rights issues: in partnership with singer-composer Albert Gacheru, his 1993 cassette, *Clashes – Mbara ya Molo na Narok*, denounces the ethnic violence in the highlands of western Kenya.

Kamba

Linguistically close relations of the Kikuyu, the **Kambas'** pop music is firmly entrenched in the *benga/cavacha* camp. Although distinctive melodies distinguish Kamba pop from other styles of *benga*, there are other special Kamba features. One is the delicate, flowing, calliope-like rhythm guitar that underlies many Kamba arrangements. Its gentle presence is discernible in many of the recordings of the three most famous Kamba groups: the **Kalambya Boys & Kalambya Sisters**, **Peter Mwambi and His Kyanganga Boys** and **Les Kilimambogo Brothers Band**, led, until 1987, by the late **Kakai Kilonzo**.

These groups have dominated Kamba music since the mid-1970s. Mwambi, although he can get into some great guitar solos, has a following that comes largely from within the Kamba community: his musically simple, "pound 'em-out", pulsing-bass drum style may not have enough musical variation to keep non-Kamba speakers interested.

The Kalambya Sisters are a different story. Backed by **Onesmus Musyioki**'s Kalambya Boys Band, the Sisters are famous, even notorious, throughout Kenya and they even had a minor hit in Europe with *Katelina*. This relates the comic plight of a young woman, Katelina, who likes to drink the home brew *uki*, but gets pregnant with annual regularity in the process. The soft, high-pitched, feline voices of the Sisters whine engagingly in unison over the delightfully sweet guitar work of Musyioki and the Boys.

To reach a larger audience, a number of local language artists have turned to Swahili, which is widely spoken throughout east and central Africa. Kakai Kilonzo and Les Kilimambogo Brothers Band were always identified as a "Kamba" band, but once Kakai started recording in Swahili, the group enjoyed widespread popularity in Kenya. With socially relevant lyrics, a good dose of calliope guitar and a solid dance-beat backing, Les Kilimambogo were national favourites until Kakai's death in 1987.

These days, a new generation of musicians, relative newcomers to the Kamba hall of fame, is drawing most of the limelight away from the old guard. The **Katitu Boys Band** and the **Kimangu Band** both started the 1990s with a series of briskly selling cassettes.

THE BIG NAME BANDS

The big name bands in Kenya can usually muster sufficiently large audiences for shows in sprawling, ethnically diverse towns like Nairobi, Nakuru or Mombasa. Unlike the groups with a particular ethnic leaning, the national performers can appeal to a broad cross-section of the population with music which tends to be either a local variant of the **Zairean** sound, or **Swahili music**, a Kenyan–Tanzanian hybrid sound, unique to Kenya.

In both Zairean and Swahili popular music, **rumba** has always been a major ingredient. Songs typically open with a slow-to-medium rumba which ambles through the verses, backed by a light percussion of gentle congas, snare and high-hat. Then, three or four minutes into the song, there's a transition – or, more often, a hiatus. It's goodbye to verses and rolling rumba as the song shifts into high gear. A much faster rhythm, highlighting the instrumental parts, especially solo guitar and brass, takes over with a vengeance.

There are some significant points of divergence in Swahili and Zairean styles. The tempo of Swahili music is generally slower, even in the fast section. Swahili music over the last twenty years has been particularly faithful to this two-part structure although, today, both Swahili and Zairean musicians often dispense with the slow rumba portion altogether. While the Zaireans are famous for their vocals and their intricate harmonies, Swahili groups are renowned for their demon guitarists and crisp, clear guitar interplay.

While Swahili music is usually associated with Swahili lyrics, it isn't distinguished by the language. In fact, one of the greatest Swahili hits of all time, *Charonyi Ni Wasi*, is not in Swahili but in the closely related Taita language. Similarly, Nairobi's Zairean scene has become less Zairean as it has moved from the near-exclusive use of Lingala twenty years ago to a preponderance of Swahili lyrics. Nearly all the songs on the recent *Feet on Fire* CD from the immensely popular **Orchestra Virunga** are in Swahili, helping to guarantee popularity with a mass audience. As for Lingala songs, while few Kenyans understand the lyrics, their mysterious incomprehensibility and a veneer of Gallic sophistication gives them a certain sex appeal.

Most of the Swahili and Zairean music produced in Kenya came from giants like *PolyGram* and CBS (now Tamasha and Music World) or was released by independent labels run by Kenyans of British or Asian descent. When European and American interest in African music began to emerge in the early

1980s, it was these companies with their international connections that put out the first, tantalizing sounds from Nairobi. Although they were also involved in the vernacular language scene, the early Kenyan recordings released in London were drawn from the big names and featured artists such as **Super Mazembe**, **Orchestra Makassy**, **Orchestra Virunga**, **Lessa Lassan**, **Issa Juma** and **Lovy Longomba**. Of these, all but the Tanzanian-born Issa Juma come from Zaire – there's not a Kenyan among them. (It was not until several years later, after Shirati Jazz had done their first British tour, that Kenya achieved an international reputation for its indigenous *benga* dance music.)

THE ZAIRE CONNECTION

Zaireans (or Congolese as they were previously known) have been making musical waves in Kenya since the late 1950s. It was the Congolese **OS Africa Band** that opened Nairobi's famous *Starlight Club* back in 1964. But it wasn't until the mid-1970s, after the passing of the American soul craze, that music from Zaire began to dominate the city nightclubs. One of the first musicians to settle in Kenya during this period was **Baba Gaston**. The rotund Gaston had already been in the business for twenty years when he arrived in Nairobi with his group **Baba National** in 1975. A prolific musician and father (he has twelve children), he stole the scene until his retirement as a performer and recording artist in 1989.

In the mid-1970s, at about the same time Baba Gaston was just getting settled in Nairobi, the Zairean group **Boma Liwanza** was already on the scene at the *Starlight Club* and the popular **Bana Ngenge** were about to leave Nairobi for a year in Tanzania. **Super Mazembe** had just completed their migration from Zaire to Kenya by way of Zambia and Tanzania. And soon to follow were **Samba Mapangala and Les Kinois**, though they stopped along the way in Uganda for a couple of years – and had a near-fatal encounter with the army – before moving to Nairobi in 1977. With the break-up of **Les Kinois** in 1980, some members moved to Mazembe while Samba began putting together his first version of **Orchestra Virunga**. The famous "Malako" recordings included several members of Bana Ngenge, including vocalist **Fataki Lokassa** and the late **Lawi Somana** who went on to lead Tabu Ley's Afrisa.

Meanwhile, despite their rising popularity in 1982–83, Super Mazembe began to fragment. The group's versatile lead singers **Lovy Longomba** and **Kasongo wa Kanema** (of *Kasongo* and *Shauri Yako* fame) quit the band – Kasongo to team up with Virunga and Lovy to front his own group **Super Lovy** and later **Bana Likasi** and **Orchestre Afriso Ngoma**.

By 1984, Samba Mapangala's line-up had experienced a number of changes in personnel but was still going strong. It wasn't long, however, before Virunga also ran into the Kenya Immigration Department. With extensions to their work permits refused, Virunga were soon out of money and falling apart.

Out of Virunga's misfortune came **Ibeba System**. It was led by ex-Virunga guitarist **Sammy Mansita** and other Virunga/Kinois alumni including **Siama Matuzungidi** on guitar, **Johnny-Ko Walengo** on bass, and vocalists **Kasongo wa Kanema** and **Coco Zigo Mike**. Lovy Longomba also did a spell with Ibeba System before setting off to Dar es Salaam to join Afriso Ngoma. When Ibeba first took over from Virunga at the *Starlight*, the group was a virtual clone of the Virunga sound. Over several years performing at the *JKA Resort Club* they became one of Nairobi's most accomplished club acts with a good mix of their own soukous and covers of African pop.

The ultimate Zairean cross-over band in Nairobi, and darlings of Kenya's young elite, were **Vundumuna**. The group formed in 1984 with guitarist **Tabu Frantal** of Boma Liwanza and Shika Shika, Ugandan vocalist **Sammy Kasule**, and bassist **Nsilu wa Bansilu** of Bana Ngenge and Virunga. Vundumuna quickly gained institutional status at the *Carnivore*, packing in the crowds with their Wednesday and Saturday night performances. With the best equipment in the city, they presented a clean, high-tech sound fusing Zairean soukous, *benga* rhythms, and elements of Western jazz. Their flawless horn arrangements blended beautifully with leader **Botango Bedjil**'s keyboards and Frantal's guitar. After three LPs and riding a crest of popularity, the future was looking bright until, once again, the Immigration Department struck.

The group played its farewell concert at the *Carnivore* in late 1986 and, since then, they have worked abroad in places as far afield as Japan and Oman. In between jobs, they return to Kenya – several band members have Kenyan wives and children – and they have been allowed to play short stints as guest performers.

By the 1990s, Nairobi's status as an island of opportunity for Zairean musicians had fallen flat. With harder economic times, a declining record industry, fewer live music venues, and restrictive work rules for foreign musicians, Nairobi has become a departure point for greener pastures.

When Virunga returned to *Garden Square* in Nairobi in early 1988 they had no trouble recapturing the abundant enthusiasm they left behind after their untimely departure from the music scene three years before. With a captivating stage show, they played dazzling renditions of all their familiar hits. New compositions like *Safari* and *Miaka Kumi ya Enzi ya Nyayo* (Ten Years of the Nyayo Era) joined the list of favourites. Sadly, in 1993, Samba gave up on the local nightclub scene and disbanded the group. He still performs for special events in Kenya, tours abroad and makes records. Although the musicians continue to change, nothing has altered Samba Mapangala's formula for brilliant music – a catchy, not over-complex melody, faultless vocal harmonies, innovative, interlocking guitar lines and superbly crafted horns floating over light, high-tensile percussion.

SWAHILI BANDS: THE TANZANIAN INFLUENCE

Songs with Swahili lyrics are part of the common currency of east African musical culture. Kenya's own brand of Swahili pop music has its origin in the Tanzanian pop styles of the 1970s but, since that time, the Kenyan variety has followed a separate evolutionary path from the Tanzanian mainstream.

In addition to the stylistic features it has in common with the Zairean sound (light, high-hat-and-conga percussion and a delicate two-three-guitar interweave), the Kenyan Swahili sound is instrumentally sparse, allowing the bass to fill in gaps, often in syncopated rhythms. Trumpets and saxes are common in recorded arrangements but usually omitted in club performances because of the extra expense.

One of the first groups to migrate to Kenya was **Arusha Jazz**, the predecessor of what became the legendary **Simba Wanyika Original** (*simba wanyika* means "lion of the savannah"). Founded by **Wilson Peter Kinyonga** and his brothers **George** and **William**, the group began performing in Mombasa in 1971. The following year, they started recording for Phonogram (*PolyGram*) making a name for themselves with single releases such as *Eliza Wang* (My Eliza), *Jose Twende Zaire* (Jose, Let's Go to Zaire) and *Mama Suzie*. In 1975, the three brothers, along with Tanzanian recruit **Omar Shabani** on rhythm and Kenyan **Tom Malanga** on bass, shifted their base to Nairobi and released their first album, *Jiburudisheni na Simba Wanyika* (Chill Out with Simba Wanyika). Over their twenty-year history in Nairobi (to 1995), the group were favourites of the city's club scene and made scores of recordings.

Despite George Kinyonga's death in 1992, the band continued to perform, but after the death of Wilson Kinyonga, in 1995, Simba Wanyika rapidly collapsed. The Kinyonga brothers had been its essential ingredient, maintaining a consistent style throughout their career, despite several major changes in personnel. However, one of their most widely circulated recordings outside Kenya aims for a rather different sound from their typical *PolyGram* sound. In *Simba Wanyika Original (Kenya Vol. 1)*, the group borrowed from the *benga* formula and quickened the pace considerably, though the vocal and instrumental parts are indeed the "original" Simba Wanyika of great guitars, creamy sax and simple, listener-friendly vocals. The mood, at least in Europe, before the band's demise, is best represented by the 1992 CD release *Pepea* (Kameleon, Holland). For purists interested in Simba Wanyika's *PolyGram* sound, the albums *Haleluya* and *Mapenzi Ni Damu*, recorded before and after *Kenya Vol. 1*, are more representative of what might be heard in Nairobi.

The Wanyika name is famous in east Africa not only for Simba Wanyika, but for several other related bands that emerged from the Wanyika line. The first big split occurred in 1978 when the core of supporting musicians around the Kinyonga brothers left Simba Wanyika to form **Les Wanyika**. Among those who made the move were rhythm guitarist **"Professor" Omari Shabani**, bass player Tom Malanga, drummer **Rashid Juma**, and vocalist **Issa Juma** who had only joined Simba Wanyika the month before. The group added another crucial member in Tanzanian lead guitar player **John Ngereza** who had been playing in Kenya with the Zairean group **Bwambe Bwambe**. After six months' practice, Les Wanyika began performing at *Garden Square* and soon found fame across Kenya with their massive hit *Sina Makosa* (It's Not My Fault), which was quickly followed by singles such as *Paulina*, *Pamela*, and *Kajituliza Kasuku*.

Under Ngereza's leadership, Les Wanyika have remained one of Nairobi's top bands. While cut from the same mould as the Simbas, Les Wanyika have distinguished themselves with imaginative compositions and arrangements, a typically lean, clean sound and the delicious blend of Professor Omari's rhythm-guitar mastery with Tom Malanga's bass. The sparse percussion majors on the high-hat and a muted, pulsing kick drum. This lean instrumentation provides the backing for vocalist and lead guitar player John Ngereza who alternates between the two roles. During vocal choruses, there's solid vocal backing in multi-part harmonies from **Mohamed Tika** and other Swahili session vocalists. The finest example of their work is on the *Dunia Kigeu-geu* compilation, released in Kenya in 1985.

Some of Les Wanyika's recent recordings have attempted to cash in on the popularity of disco music in Kenya. The remake of their greatest hits into two disco medleys (on *Les Les Non-Stop '90*) was locally quite successful and carried over into their next album, *Kabibi* – an unlikely twist to the usual cross-over dilemma facing African musicians in Europe, under pressure to Westernize their sound to find a larger audience, often with dismal results. In Les Wanyika's case, it's the local market that has pushed the group towards international disco cross-over anonymity. They have more than enough raw talent to get a solid international following, but if they ever make it abroad, it will be for their classic Wanyika sound and not synthesized disco effects.

An important figure in the Wanyika story is Tanzania-born **Issa Juma** who quickly established a name for himself in Kenya as a premier vocalist in the early days of Les Wanyika.

Mention his name today and many Kenyans will immediately think of *Sigalame*, a character from his 1983 single of the same name and now a part of Kenyan vocabulary. *Sigalame* is Issa Juma's most famous song, not because of the music, which is generic *cavacha*, but because of its entertaining lyrics. Sigalame is a mysterious character who has disappeared from family and friends but is rumoured to be living in Bungoma doing "business".

Although the Wanyika bands have been dominant in Swahili music, it is not their exclusive domain. Foremost among other Tanzanians and Kenyans performing in the Swahili style are the **Maroon Commandos**. Still members of the Kenya Army, the Commandos are one of the oldest performing groups in the country. They first came together in 1970, although they had a serious setback with deaths of several band members in a road accident in 1972. In the mid-1970s, the group was mainly a "covers band" playing the current hits of Zaire. But by 1977 they had come out as a strong force in the Swahili style with the Taita-language song *Charonyi Ni Wasi*. Within their genre, the Commandos do not limit themselves to any sort of rigid formula. Like many of the Swahili groups, they use trumpets and sax liberally but they're also quite experimental and have at various times added a keyboard, as in *Usiniambie Unanenda* (1981) and innovative guitar effects, as in *Viely* (1985). The lead song on *Kenya Dance Mania*, *Mwakaribishwa Na Maroon*, displays them at their most creative, mingling Swahili and *benga* styles.

TOURIST AND INTERNATIONAL POP

Tourist pop bands typically have highly competent musicians, relatively good equipment and, overall, a fairly polished sound. In live performances, they play a schizophrenic mixture of old Congolese rumba tunes as warm-ups, popular international covers, a few Zairean favourites of the day, greatest hits from Kenya's past, and then some original material that leans heavily towards the American/Europop sound but with lyrics relating to local topics.

The most successful Kenyan group in this realm is the excruciatingly named **Them Mushrooms**, closely followed by **Safari Sound**. These two, as well as most of the groups in this category, either come from the coast or have experience on the coastal tourist

circuit. Them Mushrooms have no less than six albums to their credit and Safari Sound has the honour of having Kenya's best-selling album ever in *The Best of African Songs*. Both groups have released versions of the classic tourist hit *Jambo Bwana (Hakuna Matata)*, a tremendous singalong Swahili pop song that goes down a storm in the package hotel discos even if its lyrics sound desperately ironic these days. For a twist-style precursor, listen to *Jane Umrongo* on *Before Benga Vol. 2*. Another regular tourist ditty is *Malaika* – actually a beautiful old composition about ill-starred love first sung by Fadhili William – that's rarely given the soulful treatment it deserves (see "Swahili pop lyrics" box, p.571).

Other groups that have made a name for themselves in the international music scene are **Mombasa Roots**, **The Forest People**, **African Vibration**, **The Pressmen** and **Tausi Five**.

KENYA DISCOGRAPHY

○ = CD

○ **Abana Ba Nasery**, *Abana Ba Nasery: Classic Acoustic Recordings from Western Kenya* (GlobeStyle, UK). As it says, "classic acoustic" guitar and Fanta bottle in the *omutibo* style.

○ **Abana Ba Nasery**, *Nursery Boys Go Ahead! The Guitar and Bottle Kings of Kenya* (GlobeStyle, UK). More *omutibo* in more recent recordings with some interesting guest collaborations.

○ **Kapere Jazz Band & Others**, *Luo Roots – Musical Currents from Western Kenya* (GlobeStyle, UK). The traditional music of the Luo people today, suggesting the foundations of *benga*.

○ **Fundi Konde**, *Retrospective Volume 1* (RetroAfric, UK). Classic tunes of 1947 to 1956 from one of Kenya's most popular guitarists of the late colonial period.

○ **Orchestra Makassy**, on *Belle Epoque* by Mose Se "Fan Fan" (RetroAfric, UK). If you want a taste of the Orchestra Makassy sound (east African versions), four Makassy tunes are featured on this CD retrospective. Orchestra Makassy's vinyl LP, *Agwaya* (Virgin, UK), is absolutely perfect, however, and difficult to find.

○ **Samba Mapangala & Orchestra Virunga**, *Virunga Volcano* (Earthworks, UK). A perfect album of beautifully crafted songs that sound as fresh and enticing today as they did when first released in the early 1980s. Includes their most famous number, *Malako*.

○ **Orchestra Virunga**, *Feet on Fire* (Stern's, UK). First-rate Mapangala in his last recordings with Orchestra Virunga as an ongoing band.

○ **D O Misiani & Shirati Band**, *Benga Blast!* (Earthworks/Stern's, UK). Old Shirati but a nice collection.

○ **D O Misiani & Shirati Jazz**, *Piny Ose Mer/The World Upside Down* (GlobeStyle, UK). More recent Shirati recorded in Kenya.

○ **George Ramogi and CK Dumbe Dumbe Jazz Band**, *1994 USA Tour – Safari ya Ligingo* (Dumbe Dumbe Records, Kenya). Ramogi is regarded as one of the founding fathers of the Luo *benga* style. This CD was recorded on a 1994 US tour and, although not a very polished production, it's certainly authentic *benga*.

○ **Simba Wanyika**, *Pepea* (Kameleon, Netherlands). Recorded in Holland, this superb 1992 release is probably the best representation of the SWO sound before the sad demise of the band. The label is a pun on the Kinyonga brothers' name, which means "chameleon" in Swahili. Highly recommended.

Various "Wanyika", *Dunia Kigeu-geu* (Polydor cassette, Kenya). Four of Les Wanyika's best, with solid tunes from Simba Wanyika and Orchestra Jobiso.

○ **Various Artists**, *Before Benga Vol. 1, Kenya Dry* and *Before Benga Vol. 2, The Nairobi Sound* (Original Music, US). Both CDs provide an excellent cross-section of acoustic and electric guitar music from the 1950s into the 1970s. These are styles which have largely disappeared in Kenya.

○ **Various Artists**, *Guitar Paradise of east Africa* (Earthworks/Stern's, UK). This CD and its companion, *Kenya Dance Mania*, provide an excellent introduction to Kenya's various styles – some wonderful intros – although not always the best or most representative materials of the artists in question.

○ **Various Artists**, *The Nairobi Beat (Kenyan Pop Music Today)* (Rounder, US). Personal favourites of producer Doug Paterson, compiled from mid-1980s releases, with an emphasis on regional styles. Listen out for the "feline ecstasy" of the Kalambya Sisters whining out the saga of *Kopulo Onesi*, and the ever-enduring Maroon Commandos with their great Swahili rumba sound in *Amua Nikuachie Kazi*.

○ **Various Artists**, *Top Hits of Kenya* (GEFRACO, France). Features a number of favourite tourists' Kenyan pop tunes. An international pop sound with African themes and the odd African melody/rhythm, but not really representative of what Kenyans listen to. If you've participated in a fun-filled Kenyan adventure, this collection will bring back fond memories. Highlights include Them Mushrooms doing *Jambo Bwana* and the lovely Fadhili William version of his own *Malaika*.

○ **Various Artists**, *The Most Beautiful Songs of Africa* (ARC Music, UK). Despite the pretentious title and a worn-out-stereotype cover image, this is a decent collection of Kenyan and Tanzanian music from the 1970s and 1980s, including two of Super Mazembe's best songs – *Kasongo* and *Shauri Yako* – some *taarab* music, and one of Miriam Makeba's best versions of *Malaika*.

○ **Various Artists**, *Kenyan and east African Music: The Rough Guide* (World Music Network, UK). Compiled to accompany this guide (see the order form at the back of this book).

○ **Victoria Kings**, *Victoria Kings* (GlobeStyle, UK). A different perspective on *benga* (in other words, not Shirati Jazz) from one of the other great Luo groups from western Kenya. Features two of *benga*'s most renowned artists, Ochieng Nelly and Colella Mazee, playing some of their energy-packed hits of the late 1970s and early 1980s.

TARABU DISCOGRAPHY

○ **Maulidi Musical Party**, *Mombasa Wedding Special* (GlobeStyle, UK). One of Kenya's leading *tarabu* groups in a 1989 recording by the GlobeStyle "expedition".

○ **Various Artists**, *Songs the Swahili Sing* (Original Music, US). This collection of scratchy oldies is a good introduction to the coastal region's *tarab* sounds.

○ **Zein Musical Party**, *Mtindo wa Mombasa: The Style of Mombasa* (GlobeStyle, UK). Some great tunes from this often over-

SWAHILI POP LYRICS

Jambo Bwana
by Teddy Kalanda Harrison

Jambo, jambo Bwana	Greetings, greetings Bwana
Habarai gani?	How are you doing?
Nzuri sana	Very well
Wageni mwakaribishwa	Visitors, you are all welcomed
Kenya yetu	In our Kenya
Hakuna matata	There are no problems
Kenya ni nchi nzuri	Kenya's a beautiful country
Hakuna matata	There are no problems
Nchi ya kupendeza	A pleasing country
Hakuna matata	There are no problems
Nchi ya maajabu	A country of wonders
Hakuna matata	There are no problems
Nchi yenye amani	A country of peace
Hakuna matata	There are no problems

Malaika
Authorship disputed, first popularized by Fadhili William

Malaika, nakupenda malaika	Angel, I love you angel
Malaika, nakupenda malaika	Angel, I love you angel
Nami nifanyeje, kijana mwenzio	What else could I do? A young woman like you
Nashindwa na mali sina wee	If I weren't struggling for money
Ningekuoa malaika	I would marry you angel
Nashindwa na mali sina wee	If I weren't struggling for money
Ningekuoa malaika	I would marry you angel
Pesa zasumbuwa roho yangu	Money is the source of my heartache
Pesa zasumbuwa roho yangu	Money is the source of my heartache
Nami nifanyeje, kijana mwenzio	And me? What shall I, your boyfriend, do?
Nashindwa na mali sina wee	If I weren't struggling for money
Ningekuoa malaika	I would marry you angel
Nashindwa na mali sina wee	If I weren't struggling for money
Ningekuoa malaika	I would marry you angel
Kidege, hukuwaza kidege	Little bird, I'm always dreaming of you, little bird
Kidege, hukuwaza kidege	Little bird, I'm always dreaming of you, little bird
Nami nifanyeje, kijana mwenzio	And me? What shall I, your boyfriend, do?
Nashindwa na mali sina wee	If I weren't struggling for money
Ningekuoa malaika	I would marry you angel
Nashindwa na mali sina wee	If I weren't struggling for money
Ningekuoa malaika	I would marry you angel

looked master of the *oud*. A personal favourite is the *tour de force* on *Wanawake wa Kiamu* (Ladies of Lamu) — just *oud*, *dumbak* and vocals.

○ **Zuhura and Party**, *Jino la Pembe* (GlobeStyle, UK). A compendium of Mombasa singing star Zuhura Swaleh's most popular chakacha numbers, most notably *Parare* and

the title tune. Recorded on her European tour with the Maulidi Musical Party, this is one of the best introductions to *taarab*.

Adapted from contributions by Doug Paterson and Werner Graebner to the Rough Guide to World Music

A BEGINNER'S GUIDE TO SWAHILI

Surprisingly, perhaps, Swahili is one of the easiest languages to learn. It's pronounced exactly as it's written, with the stress nearly always on the penultimate syllable. And it's satisfyingly regular, so even with limited knowledge you can make yourself understood and construct simple sentences.

In Kenya, you'd rarely be stuck without Swahili, but it makes a huge difference to your perceptions if you try to speak it. People are delighted if you make the effort (though they'll also tend to assume you understand more than you do). Don't forget that for many Kenyans Swahili is another foreign language they get by in, like English. For travels further afield in east Africa, and especially in Tanzania, some knowledge of Swahili is a very useful backup.

The language has spread widely from its coastal origins to become the lingua franca of east Africa and it has tended to lose its richness and complexity as a result. Up-country, it is often spoken as a second language with a minimum of grammar. On the coast, you'll hear it spoken with tremendous panache: oratorial skills and punning (to which it lends itself with great facility) are much appreciated. Swahili is a Bantu language (in fact one of the more mainstream of the family), but it has incorporated thousands of foreign words, the majority of them Arabic. Far more of this Arabic inheritance and borrowing is preserved on the coast. The "standard" dialect is derived from Zanzibar Swahili, which the early missionaries learned and first transcribed into the Roman alphabet. **Written Swahili** is still not uniform and you'll come across slight variations in spelling, particularly on menus.

PRONUNCIATION

Once you get the hang of voicing every syllable, **pronunciation** is easy. Each vowel is syllabic. Odd-looking combinations of consonants are often pronounced as one syllable, too. *Mzee*, for example, is pronounced "mz-ay-ay" (rhyming with "hey!") and *shauri* (troubles, problem) is pronounced "sha-oor-i". Nothing is silent.

You'll often come across an "**m**" where it looks out of place: this letter can precede any other. It's almost always pronounced as one syllable with the letter(s) that follow it: eg *mnyama* – animal; *mbwa* – dog; *mboga* – vegetables. Just add a bit of an "m" sound at the beginning; "mmmb-oga". Don't say "erm-bwa" or "mer-boga"– you'll be misunderstood. The letter "n" can precede a number of others and gives a nasal quality.

For memorizing, it often helps to ignore the first letter or syllable. Thousands of nouns, for example, start with "ki" (singular) and "vy" (plural), and they're all in the same noun class.

A as in **A**rthur
B as in **b**ed
C doesn't exist on its own
CH as in **ch**urch, but often sounds like a "t", a "dj", or a "ky"
D as in **d**onkey
DJ as in py**j**amas
DH like a cross between **dh**ow and **th**ou
E between the "e" in **E**dward and "ai" in **ai**ling
F as in **f**an
G as in **g**ood
GH at the back of the throat, like a growl; nearly an "r"
H as in **h**armless, sometimes contracted from KH as in lo**ch**
I like the "e" in **e**vil
J as in **j**ug
K as in **k**iosk, sometimes like soft "t" or "ch"
KH a "k" but breathier
L as in **l**ullaby, but often pronounced "r"
M as in **M**artian
MN one syllable, eg *mnazi* (coconut), "mna-zi"
N as in **n**onsense
NG as in wro**ng**, but sometimes pronounced with no "g" sound at all
O as in **o**range, never as in "open" or "do"
P as in **p**enguin
Q doesn't exist (except in early Romanized texts; now "k")
R as in **r**apid, or rolled as in the French *rapide*
S as in **S**amson
T as in **t**iny
TH as in **th**anks, never like the "th" in them
U as in l**u**te
V as in **v**ictory
W as in **w**obble
X doesn't exist
Y as in **y**ou
Z as in **z**ero

ELEMENTARY GRAMMAR

Noun classes put people off Swahili. They are something like the genders in French or Latin in that you alter each adjective according to the class of noun. In Swahili you add a prefix to the word. Each class covers certain areas of meaning and usually has a prefix letter associated with most of its nouns. For example, words beginning "ki" or "ch" (singular), and "vi" or "vy" (plural) are in the general class of "things", notably smallish things (eg *kitoto* – small child, infant). Words beginning "m" in the singular and "wa" in the plural are people (eg *mtu/watu* – person/people; *mtalii/watalii* – tourist/s). Words beginning "m" (singular) and "mi" (plural) are often trees and plants (eg *mti, miti* – tree/s), or have connections with life.

Most abstract nouns begin with "u" (eg *uhuru* – freedom, *utoto* – childhood). There are seven or eight classes (and plurals for each), but this gives you some idea.

Prefixes get added to adjectives, so you get *kiti kizuri* – a good chair; *mtu mzuri* – a good person; *miti mizuri* – lovely trees. Really correct Swahili, with everything agreeing, isn't much spoken except on the coast, and you can get away with murder. But once you've grasped the essential building blocks – the root meanings, the prefixes, suffixes and infixes of one or two letters which turn them into words – it becomes a very creative language to learn.

VERBS

There are a few exceptions and irregularities, but the **verb system** is basically straightforward and makes conversational Swahili a realistic goal even for convinced non-linguists.

to want	*ku-taka*
to come	*kuja*, irregular; the infinitive "ku" part stays with the root
to go	*kwenda*, ie ku-enda but, again, usually keeps the "ku" part
to eat	*ku-la*
to drink	*ku-nywa*
to sleep	*ku-lala*
to be tired	*ku-choka*
to stay	*ku-kaa*
to say, speak	*ku-sema*
to see, to meet	*ku-ona, ku-onana*
to look	*ku-tazama*
to hear	*ku-sikia*
to buy	*ku-nunua*
to know	*ku-jua*
to think	*ku-fikiri*
to like/love	*ku-penda*
to be able (can)	*ku-weza*
to give	*ku-pa*
to bring	*ku-leta*
to be/become	*ku-wa*
to come from	*ku-toka*
to have	*ku-wa na* (lit. "to be with")

PRONOUNS

me, I	*mimi, ni*	she/he	*a*	you (pl.)	*ninyi, m*
you	*wewe, u*	us, we	*sisi, tu*	them, they	*wao, wa*
him/her	*yeye*				

TENSES

present tense	*-na-*	future tense	*-ta-*
past tense	*-li-*	just past, or still going on	*-me-*

EXAMPLES OF PRONOUNS, VERBS AND TENSES

she wanted	*a-li-taka*	have they gone?	*wa-me-kwenda?*
I'm tired	*ni-me-choka*	she said...	*a-li-sema...*
we will sleep	*tu-ta-lala*	can I...?	*ni-na-weza...?*
did you hear?	*u-li-sikia?*	I will bring	*ni-ta-leta*
they like...	*wa-na-penda...*	we are staying (at/in)...	*tu-na-kaa...*
are you (pl.) going?	*m-na-enda?*	I know	*ni-na-jua*
has he come?	*a-me-kuja?*		

For the present tense of "to have", you can say *mimi nina gari* (I am with a car/I have a car) or just *nina gari, una gari, ana gari*, etc.

WORDS AND PHRASES

The words and phrases listed here are all in common usage but Swahili (like English) is far from being a homogeneous language, so don't be surprised if you sometimes get some funny looks. And, for lack of space for explanation, there are a number of apparent inconsistencies; just ignore them unless you intend to learn the language seriously. These phrases should make you understood at least.

USEFUL GREETINGS

Jambo or *Hujambo*	Hello, good day, how are you? (multi-purpose greeting, means "Problems?")	*Kwaheri/ni*	Goodbye to one/many
		Asante/ni	Thank you to one/many
		sana	very (a common emphasis)
Jambo or *Sijambo*	(the response) No problems	*Bwana*	Mister, the equivalent of *Monsieur* in French
Habari?	How are things? (literally "News?")	*Mama*	like the French *Madame* or *Mademoiselle*, for adult women
Nzuri	Fine, good, terrible		
Hodi!	Hello? Anyone in? (said on knocking or entering)	*kjana*	youth, teenager (pl. *vijana*)
		mtoto	child, kid (pl. *watoto*)
Karibu	Come in, enter, welcome (also said on offering something)	*Jina lako nani?*	What's your name?/What
		Unaitwaje?	are you called?

BASICS

My name is/I am called...	*Jina langu/Nina itwa...*	I don't know where (is)?	*Sijui*
Where are you from?	*Unatoka wapi?*		*wapi?*
		here	*hapa*
Where are you staying?	*Unakaa wapi?*	when?	*lini?*
		now	*sasa*
I am from...	*Ninatoka...*	soon	*sasa hivi*
I am staying (at/in)...	*Ninakaa...*	why?	*kwa nini?*
		because...	*kwa sababu. . .*
See you!	*Tutaonana!* (lit. "We shall meet")	who?	*nani?*
		what?	*nini?*
yes	*ndiyo* (lit. "it is so")	which?	*gani?*
no	*hapana* (a general negative); *la* (Arabic – heard mostly on the coast)	true	*kweli*
		and/with	*na*
		or	*au*
I don't understand	*Sifahamu/Sielewi*	(it) is/(they) are	*ni* (a useful little connector when you can't think of an alternative, eg *njia ni nzuri* – the road is good)
I don't speak Swahili, but...	*Sisemi kiswahili, lakini...*		
How do you say... in Swahili?	*Unasemaje kwa kiswahili...?*	isn't it?	*siyo?* (equivalent of French *n'est-ce pas?*)
Could you repeat that?	*Sema tena* (lit. "speak again")	I'm British/American/ German/ French/ Italian	*Mimi Mwingereza/ Mwamerika/Mdachi/ Mfaransa/Mwitalia.*
Speak slowly	*Sema pole pole*		

DAILY NEEDS

Where can I stay?	*Naweza kukaa wapi?*	washing water	*maji ya kuosha*
Can I stay here?	*Naweza kukaa hapa?*	hot/cold water	*maji moto/baridi*
room/s	*chumba/vyumba*	I'm hungry	*Nina njaa*
bed/s	*kitanda/vitanda*	I'm thirsty	*Nina kiu*
chair/s	*kiti/viti*	Is there any...?	*Iko...?* or *Kuna...?*
table/s	*meza*	Yes there is...	*Iko...,* or *Kuna...*
toilet, bathroom	*choo, bafu*	No there isn't any	*Haiko...,* or *Hakuna...*

DAILY NEEDS

How much?	*Ngapi?*	Reduce the price, come down a little!	*Punguza kidogo!*
money	*pesa*	shop	*duka*
What price...?	*Bei gani...?*	bank	*benki*
How much is...?	*Pesa ngapi...?*	post office	*posta*
I want...	*Nataka...*	café, restaurant	*hoteli*
I don't want...	*Sitaki...*	telephone	*simu*
Give me/Bring me (can I have?)	*Nipe/Niletee*	cigarettes	*sigara*
again/more	*tena*	I'm ill	*Mimi mgonjwa*
enough	*tosha/basi*	doctor	*daktari*
expensive	*ghali sana*	hospital	*hospitali*
cheap (also "easy")	*rahisi*	police	*polisi*
fifty cents	*sumni*	tip, bribe	*"chai"*

TRAVEL AND DIRECTIONS

bus/es	*bas, basi/mabasi*	Stop!	*Simama!*
car/s, vehicle/s	*gari/magari*	Where are you going?	*Unaenda wapi?*
taxi	*teksi*	To where?	*Mpaka wapi?*
bicycle	*baiskeli*	From where?	*Kutoka wapi?*
train	*treni*	How many kilometres?	*Kilometa ngapi?*
plane	*ndege*	I'm going to...	*Nenda...*
boat/ship	*chombo/meli*	Move along, squeeze up a little	*Songa!/Songa kidogo!*
petrol	*petroli*	Let's go, carry on	*Twende, endelea*
road, path	*njia/ndia*	straight ahead	*moja kwa moja*
highway	*barabara*	right	*kulia*
on foot/walking	*kwa miguu*	left	*kushoto*
When does it leave?	*Inaondoka lini?*	up	*juu*
When will we arrive?	*Tutafika lini?*	down	*chini*
slowly	*pole pole*	I want to get off here	*Nataka kushuka hapa*
fast, quickly	*haraka*	The car has broken down	*Gari imevunjika*
Wait!/Hang on a moment!	*Ngoja!/Ngoja kidogo!*		

TIME, CALENDAR AND NUMBERS

What time is it?	*Saa ngapi?*	this month	*mwezi huu*	9	*tisa*
four o'clock	*saa nne*	(lit. "moon")		10	*kumi*
quarter past	*na robo*	Monday	*jumatatu*	11	*kumi na moja*
half past	*na nusu*	Tuesday	*jumanne*	12	*kumi na mbili*
quarter to	*kasa robo*	Wednesday	*jumatano*	20	*ishirini*
minutes	*dakika*	Thursday	*alhamisi*	21	*ishirini na moja*
early	*mapema*	Friday	*ijumaa*	30	*thelathini*
yesterday	*jana*	Saturday	*jumamosi*	40	*arobaini*
today	*leo*	Sunday	*jumapili*	50	*hamsini*
tomorrow	*kesho*	1	*moja*	60	*sitini*
daytime	*mchana*	2	*mbili*	70	*sabini*
night time	*usiku*	3	*tatu*	80	*themanini*
dawn	*alfajiri*	4	*nne*	90	*tisini*
morning	*asubuhi*	5	*tano*	100	*mia moja*
last/this/next week	*wiki iliopita/hii/ ijayo*	6	*sita*	121	*mia moja na ishi- rini na moja*
this year	*mwaka huu*	7	*saba*	1000	*elfu*
		8	*nane*		

SIGNS

Danger	*Hatari!*	Fierce dog!	*Mbwa mkali!*
Warning	*Angalia!/Onyo!*	No entry!	*Hakuna njia!*

WORDS WORTH KNOWING

good	*-zuri* (with a prefix at the front)	problems, hassles	*wasiwasi, matata*
		No problem	*Hakuna wasiwasi/Hakuna matata*
bad	*-baya* (ditto)		
big	*-kubwa*	friend	*rafiki*
small	*-dogo*	sorry, pardon	*samahani*
a lot of	*-ingi*	It's nothing	*Si kitu*
other/another	*-ingine*	Excuse me (let me through)	*Hebu*
not bad	*si mbaya*		
OK, right, fine	*sawa*	What's up?	*Namna gani?*
fine, cool	*safi*	If God wills it	*Inshallah* (heard often on the coast)
completely	*kabisa*		
just, only	*tu (kitanda kimoja tu* – just one bed)	please	*Tafadhali* (rare up-country and not heard much on the coast either)
thing/s	*kitu/vitu*		

And two phrases you're more likely to hear than to ever say:

Take a picture of me!	*Piga picha mimi!*	Help the poor!	*Saidia maskini!*

BOOKS AND COURSES

There are a number of published teach-yourself **courses** around. *Swahili Grammar* by E O Ashton (Longman) is very turgid and unchanged since 1947. *Teach Yourself Swahili* by D V Perrrot (Teach Yourself Books) has had a redesign but isn't a lot better. For the analytical approach, the best book is probably *Simplified Swahili* by Peter M Wilson (Longman). *Kiswahili kwa Kitendo* ("Swahili by Action"; Harper & Row) is the best bet if you find ordinary grammars indigestible, although it is expensive. The course by Joan Maw, *Twende!* (Oxford University Press), is good. On the phrasebook front, the new one from Berlitz is currently the best. As for dictionaries, the *Swahili Dictionary* from Teach Yourself Books suffers amazing gaps (it's the kind of dictionary that would lead you to ask the waiter for "some puree of oranges and sugar" when you wanted marmalade) but it's cheap and about all there is.

OTHER LANGUAGES

The following brief lists are intended only for introductions and as a springboard for communication. If you'll be spending time in a particular linguistic region, you may be surprised at how difficult it is to track down usable primers

and phrasebooks for these languages. Very little material exists for non-native speakers of African languages, though you can make some progress if you're prepared to struggle (with a dictionary) with short novels or the Bible and the like. Try the sources on p.34 for further ideas. However, even the library of the School of African and Oriental Studies is rather bereft of user-friendly material.

LUO (LAKE VICTORIA)

How do you do?	Iriyo nade?	3	Adek	8	Aboro
Response:	Ariyo maber!	4	Angwen	9	Ochiko
Thank you	Erokamano	5	Abich	10	Apar
1	Achiel	6	Auchiely		
2	Ariyo	7	Abiriyo		

MAA (MAASAI)

Greetings to a man:	Lo murrani! Supa!	3	Okuni
Response:	Ipa!	4	Oonguan
Greetings to a woman:	Na kitok! Takuenya!	5	Imiet
Response:	Iko!	6	Ile
Thank you (very much!)	Ashe (naleng!)	7	Oopishana
Goodbye!	Sere!	8	Isiet
1	Obo	9	Ooudo
2	Aare	10	Tomon

KIKUYU (CENTRAL HIGHLANDS)

How are things?	Kweruo atia?	1	Imwe
Fine!	Ni kwega!	2	Igiri
How are you?	Waigua atia?	3	Ithatu
Are you well? (pl.)	Wi mwega/Muri ega?	4	Inya
Response: ("Nothing wrong")	Asha, ndi mwega	5	Ithano
		6	Ithathatu
Goodbye (when you're leaving)	Tigwo na wega	7	Mugwanja
		8	Inyanya
Goodbye (when you're staying)	Thii na wega	9	Kenda
		10	Ikumi

GLOSSARY

These words are all in common usage. Remember, however, that plural forms often have different beginnings.

AFCO Armed Forces Catering Ordnance

ASK Agricultural Society of Kenya

ASKARI policeman, security guard

BANDA any kind of hut, usually round and thatched

BARABARA main road

BOMA a fort or defensive stockade, sometimes meaning village

BORITI mangrove poles, used on the coast for building and exported to the Gulf states for the same purpose

BUIBUI the black cover-all cloak and scarf of Swahili women

BWANA Mister, a common term of address

CHAI not just tea, but also the common term for a tip, or more often a small bribe or persuasion

CHOO toilet (pronounced *cho*)

DUKA shop, store

DUKA LA DAWA chemist

FORD Forum for the Restoration of Democracy

FUNDI mechanic, craftsman, expert

GARI car

GK Government of Kenya

HARAMBEE "pull together" – the ideology of peaceable community development espoused by Kenyatta. *Harambee* meetings are local fund-raising gatherings – for schools, clinics, etc – but they've come in for some criticism in recent years as politicians vie to contribute the most money.

HOTELI small restaurant, *chai* shop, café

JUA KALI "hot sun" – open-air car repairer's yard or small workshop

KANGA printed cotton sheet used as a wrap, often incorporating a motto

KANISA church

KANU Kenya African National Union, Kenya's ruling political party

KBC Kenya Broadcasting Corporation

KIKOI brightly coloured woven cloth

LUGGA dry river valley (usually in the north)

MAENDELEO progress, development

MAGENDO corruption, bribery, abuse of power

MAJIMBOISM the creation of ethnic blocks in formerly heterogeneous regions – a kind of "ethnic cleansing"

MAKONDE beautifully worked Tanzanian wood carving, typically in ebony and representing entwined spirit families – much copied in the tourist markets

MAKUTI palm-leaf roof common on the coast

MALAIKA angel

MALAYA prostitute

MAMA common term of address for married women

MANAMBA *matatu* tout, "turnboy"

MANYATTA temporary cattle camp (Maasai)

MASKINI the poor, beggars (*Saidia maskini!* – "Help the poor!")

MATATU pick-up taxi, usually full to overflowing

MKENYA Kenyan citizen (pl. *wakenya*)

MORAN man in the warrior age group of Maasai or Samburu (pl. *morani*)

MSIKITI mosque

MTALI tourist (pl. *watali*)

MUNGU God

MURRAM red or black clay soil, usually referring to a road

MWANANCHI person, peasant, worker (pl. *wananchi*, the people)

MZEE old man: "*the* Mzee" is Kenyatta

MZUNGU white person (pl. *wazungu*)

NCCK National Christian Council of Kenya

NGOMA dancing, drumming, party, celebration

NJIA road, path

NYAYO "footsteps" – the follow-in-his-footsteps philosophy of post-Kenyatta Kenya propounded by President Moi

PANGA multi-purpose short machete carried everywhere in the countryside

SAFARI journey of any kind

SHAMBA small farm, plot

UHURU freedom, independence

UKIMWI AIDS

ULAYA Europe

INDEX

Amsterdam	1-85828-086-9	£7.99	US$13.95	CAN$16.99
Andalucia	1-85828-094-X	8.99	14.95	18.99
Australia	1-85828-141-5	12.99	19.95	25.99
Bali	1-85828-134-2	8.99	14.95	19.99
Barcelona	1-85828-106-7	8.99	13.95	17.99
Berlin	1-85828-129-6	8.99	14.95	19.99
Brazil	1-85828-102-4	9.99	15.95	19.99
Britain	1-85828-208-X	12.99	19.95	25.99
Brittany & Normandy	1-85828-126-1	8.99	14.95	19.99
Bulgaria	1-85828-183-0	9.99	16.95	22.99
California	1-85828-181-4	10.99	16.95	22.99
Canada	1-85828-130-X	10.99	14.95	19.99
Corsica	1-85828-089-3	8.99	14.95	18.99
Costa Rica	1-85828-136-9	9.99	15.95	21.99
Crete	1-85828-132-6	8.99	14.95	18.99
Cyprus	1-85828-182-2	9.99	16.95	22.99
Czech & Slovak Republics	1-85828-121-0	9.99	16.95	22.99
Egypt	1-85828-075-3	10.99	17.95	21.99
Europe	1-85828-159-8	14.99	19.95	25.99
England	1-85828-160-1	10.99	17.95	23.99
First Time Europe	1-85828-210-1	7.99	9.95	12.99
Florida	1-85828-184-4	10.99	16.95	22.99
France	1-85828-124-5	10.99	16.95	21.99
Germany	1-85828-128-8	11.99	17.95	23.99
Goa	1-85828-156-3	8.99	14.95	19.99
Greece	1-85828-131-8	9.99	16.95	20.99
Greek Islands	1-85828-163-6	8.99	14.95	19.99
Guatemala	1-85828-189-X	10.99	16.95	22.99
Hawaii: Big Island	1-85828-158-X	8.99	12.95	16.99
Hawaii	1-85828-206-3	10.99	16.95	22.99
Holland, Belgium & Luxembourg	1-85828-087-7	9.99	15.95	20.99
Hong Kong	1-85828-187-3	8.99	14.95	19.99
Hungary	1-85828-123-7	8.99	14.95	19.99
India	1-85828-104-0	13.99	22.95	28.99
Ireland	1-85828-179-2	10.99	17.95	23.99
Italy	1-85828-167-9	12.99	19.95	25.99
Kenya	1-85828-192-X	11.99	18.95	24.99
London	1-85828-117-2	8.99	12.95	16.99
Mallorca & Menorca	1-85828-165-2	8.99	14.95	19.99
Malaysia, Singapore & Brunei	1-85828-103-2	9.99	16.95	20.99
Mexico	1-85828-044-3	10.99	16.95	22.99
Morocco	1-85828-040-0	9.99	16.95	21.99
Moscow	1-85828-118-0	8.99	14.95	19.99
Nepal	1-85828-190-3	10.99	17.95	23.99
New York	1-85828-171-7	9.99	15.95	21.99

Pacific Northwest	1-85828-092-3	9.99	14.95	19.99
Paris	1-85828-125-3	7.99	13.95	16.99
Poland	1-85828-168-7	10.99	17.95	23.99
Portugal	1-85828-180-6	9.99	16.95	22.99
Prague	1-85828-122-9	8.99	14.95	19.99
Provence	1-85828-127-X	9.99	16.95	22.99
Pyrenees	1-85828-093-1	8.99	15.95	19.99
Rhodes & the Dodecanese	1-85828-120-2	8.99	14.95	19.99
Romania	1-85828-097-4	9.99	15.95	21.99
San Francisco	1-85828-185-7	8.99	14.95	19.99
Scandinavia	1-85828-039-7	10.99	16.99	21.99
Scotland	1-85828-166-0	9.99	16.95	22.99
Sicily	1-85828-178-4	9.99	16.95	22.99
Singapore	1-85828-135-0	8.99	14.95	19.99
Spain	1-85828-081-8	9.99	16.95	20.99
St Petersburg	1-85828-133-4	8.99	14.95	19.99
Thailand	1-85828-140-7	10.99	17.95	24.99
Tunisia	1-85828-139-3	10.99	17.95	24.99
Turkey	1-85828-088-5	9.99	16.95	20.99
Tuscany & Umbria	1-85828-091-5	8.99	15.95	19.99
USA	1-85828-161-X	14.99	19.95	25.99
Venice	1-85828-170-9	8.99	14.95	19.99
Wales	1-85828-096-6	8.99	14.95	18.99
West Africa	1-85828-101-6	15.99	24.95	34.99
More Women Travel	1-85828-098-2	9.99	14.95	19.99
Zimbabwe & Botswana	1-85828-041-9	10.99	16.95	21.99
Phrasebooks				
Czech	1-85828-148-2	3.50	5.00	7.00
French	1-85828-144-X	3.50	5.00	7.00
German	1-85828-146-6	3.50	5.00	7.00
Greek	1-85828-145-8	3.50	5.00	7.00
Italian	1-85828-143-1	3.50	5.00	7.00
Mexican	1-85828-176-8	3.50	5.00	7.00
Portuguese	1-85828-175-X	3.50	5.00	7.00
Polish	1-85828-174-1	3.50	5.00	7.00
Spanish	1-85828-147-4	3.50	5.00	7.00
Thai	1-85828-177-6	3.50	5.00	7.00
Turkish	1-85828-173-3	3.50	5.00	7.00
Vietnamese	1-85828-172-5	3.50	5.00	7.00
Reference				
Classical Music	1-85828-113-X	12.99	19.95	25.99
Internet	1-85828-198-9	5.00	8.00	10.00
Jazz	1-85828-137-7	16.99	24.95	34.99
Rock	1-85828-201-2	17.99	26.95	35.00
World Music	1-85828-017-6	16.99	22.95	29.99

FIG TREE CAMP
MASAI MARA

Fig Tree is one of the traditional camps of the Masai Mara. Beautifully located on the banks of Talek River, Fig Tree offers a choice of both Tents and Cabins. Game Walks, Horse Safaris and Night Game Drivers are part of the many activities available.

ADVENTURES ALOFT
MASAI MARA, KENYA

Adventures Aloft Balloon Safaris Fly daily from Fig Tree Camp and from Siana Springs in the Masai Mara. Flights over the Masai Mara are celebrated with a champagne breakfast on the Mara plains. Free transfers from surrounding lodges and camp sites can be arranged.

MADA HOTELS CENTRAL RESERVATIONS: 1ST FLOOR, KIMATHI HOUSE, KIMATHI STREET P.O. BOX 40683, NAIROBI KENYA TEL: (254-2) 221439/228321 FAX:(254-2) 332170

Oakwood Hotel
Kimathi Street   Nairobi

A lovely little hotel in the heart of the city. The hotel is tastefully furnished with an old world charm. All rooms are en suite with T.V. and in house movies.

THE BAOBAB LODGE
KILIFI

The Baobab Lodge is a sea front hotel in Kilifi, 50kms North of Mombasa. The lodge has 30 residential units, all spacious with air conditioning. The hotel is ideal for those wanting to enjoy a peaceful atmosphere. Activities available include, Tennis, Archery, Mopeds, Glass bottom boat and a "Booze Cruise" Pontoon boat.

CAMPING
AND
LUXURY

KENIA TOURS
AND SAFARIS

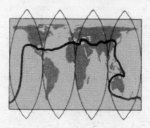